PSYCHOLOGY

PSYCHOLOGY

SECOND EDITION

Henry L. Roediger III
Purdue University

J. Philippe Rushton
The University of Western Ontario

Elizabeth Deutsch Capaldi
Purdue University

Scott G. Paris
The University of Michigan

LITTLE, BROWN AND COMPANY
Boston   Toronto

We dedicate this book to the people close to us:

Mary Schiller
Andrea, John, and Stephen Rushton
Frederick and Nettie Deutsch
Janice, Jeffrey, Kristin, and Julie Paris

Library of Congress Cataloging-in-Publication Data
Psychology.
  Bibliography: p.
  Includes indexes.
  1. Psychology. I. Roediger, Henry L.
BF121.P7915 1986   150   86-18611
ISBN 0-316-75388-2

Library of Congress Catalog Card No. 86-18611

ISBN 0-316-75388-2

ISE ISBN 0-316-75394-7

9 8 7 6 5 4 3 2 1

DON

Published simultaneously in Canada
by Little, Brown & Company (Canada) Limited

Printed in the United States of America

CREDITS AND ACKNOWLEDGMENTS

COVER: Oskar Schlemmer, *Groupe Concentrique*, 1925, 97.5 x 62 cm. © The Oskar Schlemmer Family Estate, Dadenweiler, West Germany, 1986. Photograph by Staatsgalerie, Stuttgart.

Photograph Credits

Chapter 1 page 8 (top): Culver Pictures; (bottom): Bruce Hoertel/Gamma/Liaison. page 9: The Bettman Archives. page 11: from *Physical Control of the Mind: Toward a Psychocivilized Society* by Jose M. R. Delgado. page 12: Alan Carey/Phototake. page 13: Mary Evans Picture Library. Sigmund Freud Copyrights. page 18: John Marmaras/Woodfin Camp & Associates. page 21: UPI/Bettmann Newsphotos. page 25: © Van Bucher 1982/Photo Researchers, Inc.

Chapter 2 page 39: © Lennart Nilsson from *Behold Man* (Boston: Little, Brown and Company, 1974)/photos courtesy of Bonnier Fakta Bokforlag, Stockholm. page 45: Ira Wyman/Sygma. page 48: © Lennart Nilsson from *Behold Man* (Boston: Little, Brown and Company, 1974)/photos courtesy of Bonnier Fakta Bokforlag, Stockholm. page 54 (left): Martin M. Rotker/Taurus Photos; (right): Lennart Nilsson/Bonnier Fakta Forlag. page 55: from J. A. Horel, "The brain and behavior in phylogenetic perspective," in Dewsbury and Rethlingshafer (eds.), *Comparative Psychology: A Modern Survey* (New York: McGraw-Hill, 1973), used by permission of McGraw-Hill Book Company/photo courtesy of Dr. J. A. Horel. page 59: Courtesy of Dr. Michael E. Phelps and Dr. John C. Mazziotta, UCLA School of Medicine. page 65: Philip Daly. page 67: from Sackeim et al., "Emotions are expressed more intensely on the left side of the face," *Science* 202:434–6, Fig. 1.27 (October 1978)/photos courtesy of

Dr. H. A. Sackeim. page 68: Courtesy of Dr. Michael Phelps and Dr. John C. Mazziotta, UCLA School of Medicine. SCIENCE Vol. 228 May 1985, pp. 779–809. page 69: Courtesy of Dr. Michael Phelps and Dr. John C. Mazziotta, UCLA School of Medicine. SCIENCE Vol. 228 May 1985, pp. 779–809. page 76: Courtesy, Jorge J. Yunis, M.D. page 77: (right) © Elizabeth Crews. page 77: (left) Courtesy of Elizabeth Capaldi.

Chapter 3 page 84: R. C. James. page 98 (Figure 3–11): © Lennart Nilsson from *Behold Man* (Boston: Little, Brown and Company, 1974)/photos courtesy of Bonnier Fakta Bokforlag, Stockholm. page 95 (top): Culver Pictures; (bottom): Alfred Pasieka/Taurus Photos. page 97: Fritz Goro, LIFE Magazine, © 1944 Time Inc. page 106: © Bob Nelson/The Picture Group. page 110: John Blanding/The Boston Globe. page 113: James Holland/Stock, Boston. page 118: Bohdan Hrynewych/Southern Light. page 121: Dana Fineman © DISCOVER Magazine 3/83 Time Inc.

Chapter 4 page 125: Philip Jon Bailey/Stock, Boston. page 128: Courtesy Kaiser Porcelain Limited. page 130: David Marr, *Vision* (New York: W. H. Freeman and Company, 1982). page 134 (top right): © Gerald H. Fisher, University of Newcastle upon Tyne, U.K.; (bottom right): Courtesy of Illusion, Park Ridge, Illinois. page 141 (Figure 4–20): © M. C. Escher

continued on page A47

Preface

EXCITING NEW THEORIES AND RESEARCH CONTINUE TO SHAPE AND refine psychology's domain. As teachers and researchers, our primary goal in writing *Psychology* is to communicate both the fundamental principles and the changing viewpoints within our discipline. We want our readers—your students—to explore not only the remarkable classic achievements of psychological research but also the discipline's frontiers, the areas in which theories outnumber facts and where new discoveries are likely to emerge. By doing so, we hope to instill in readers the enthusiasm and personal commitment we share for psychology. The notable success of *Psychology*'s first edition gives us the opportunity to continue the work and keep pace with psychology's changing developments. More important, we have added features and material in this second edition that make the book more accessible to a broader range of students.

We received reactions and reviews of the first edition from many instructors, students, and specialists. Their advice was critical to deciding how to revise and improve the book. With their help, and the help of several colleagues, the second edition was carefully drafted and revised several times. We indicate some of the major changes in the second edition in the following summary of the book's organization and features.

GENERAL ORGANIZATION

The text contains 18 chapters, which are divided among seven parts. The flow of topics follows the traditional organization for most introductory courses. We recognize that no single ordering of the field will satisfy everyone, so we have designed the parts and the chapters to be used flexibly, to suit a one-semester or two-semester course, or to fit particular curriculum needs. Perhaps the biggest change in the second edition's contents is an added chapter on adolescence and adulthood; but every chapter has been thoroughly revised.

In Part I we introduce the field of psychology by discussing the diversity of psychologists' interests and the research methods that psychologists use. In the first edition, we structured most of the discussion of research methods around a single experiment so that students could see the process of experimentation in detail. We expanded this presentation and used a new model experiment, based on the state-dependent retrieval phenomenon in memory. We also expanded the section on research issues, a popular feature in the first edition. (For instructors who enrich discussion of research methodology with statistical underpinnings, we have included an appendix at the end of the book introducing statistical reasoning.) Part I also contains a chapter on the biological bases of behavior, material that is fundamental to many concerns within the field of psychology. Important new developments in psychobiology occur almost daily. Our goal was to weave in new material (e.g. dopamine circuits) without disrupting the coherence and flow of the chapter. The organization of the chapter is much stronger overall. The discussion of brain parts, for example, has been linked together by the theme of evolutionary development.

Part II comprises chapters dealing with the individual's experience of the world—sensation, perception, and the varieties of conscious experience. Again, each chapter was thoroughly revised. Chapter 5, "Consciousness and Attention," for example, contains much more information on dreams and dreaming, as well as new research into the uses of hypnosis.

Part III now includes three chapters: "Conditioning and Learning," "Remembering and Forgetting," and "Thought and Language." The last chapter includes new sections on problem solving, cognitive skills, and decision making. This information is interesting and extremely useful to students.

Part IV contains two chapters on development and a full chapter on intelligence and intelligence testing. The first chapter on development, "Infancy and Childhood," is organized topically, covering the physiological, cognitive, and social milestones until puberty. This material is better organized, more complete, and more accessible to students compared with the first edition coverage. As we have mentioned, the second chapter on development, "Adolescence and Adulthood," is completely new to this edition, reflecting the broad shift in developmental research over recent years to encompass the entire life span. The coverage is particularly up-to-date in the area of adult development, a topic we expanded to satisfy the requests of many users. A special section of the chapter surveys some of the challenges facing adolescents and young adults today, topics many students will find particularly interesting.

Part V includes chapters on motivation and emotion—areas in which current research is especially active, requiring substantial changes from the first edition. Noteworthy additions to Chapter 12 include a section on work motivation. In Chapter 13, we have added cognitive theories of emotion and strategies for dealing with stress.

Part VI is devoted to personality, personality assessment, abnormal personality, and psychotherapies. One of the special features of this part is the new comprehensive approach to DSM III classification in Chapter 15. We have also added a new section on cognitive therapies to our discussion of psychotherapies in Chapter 16 and, in the same chapter, cover recent research comparing the relative effectiveness of psychotherapy and drug therapy in relieving mental disorders.

Part VII, concluding the book, covers social influences on behavior. Chapter 17 deals with the social psychological approach to behavior; the final chapter discusses many social issues to which psychologists apply their expertise. Throughout these chapters we have strengthened our focus on applied psychological research. Chapter 17, for example, contains a section on industrial and organizational psychology, a topic often ignored in introductory textbooks. We have also strengthened the focus on applied psychological research in other contexts. Wherever possible, we relate psychological theory to familiar settings—the classroom, the voting booth, or the offerings on TV.

We have expanded the illustration program for the second edition. Full-color graphs and tables appear in every chapter. There are also beautiful color reproductions of fine art at the front of each part and color photographs scattered throughout the book. As a result, the "look" of *Psychology* in the second edition is completely different from the first edition.

CHAPTER ORGANIZATION

Each chapter is organized by a set of five or six main headings, or themes. We maintain uniformity among chapters so that students can profit from familiar, coherent structure. In addition to the main topics, each chapter after the first contains three special features set off from the text: Research Frontier, Controversy, and Applying Psychology. This unique combination of features draws upon the fundamental principles discussed in each chapter.

RESEARCH FRONTIER. This is a new feature of the second edition. In this section we take a frontier area of psychology and explore it in greater detail than would be possible in normal text coverage. For example, in Chapter 3, we discuss the role of endorphins in modulating pain and stress; in Chapter 12, we discuss recent research on obesity and dieting; and in Chapter 14 we discuss new research indicating that personality traits may be inherited to some extent. We hope Research Frontiers will illustrate for students the dynamic character of psychology as a developing science.

CONTROVERSY. One of the compelling aspects of contemporary psychology is its intellectual ferment. Many issues are unsettled; many controversies exist. In this boxed section we take one such controversy, present its opposing viewpoints, and, if possible, draw tentative conclusions. For example, in Chapter 14 we consider whether people have general personality traits or if behavior is situationally specific; in Chapter 11 we consider whether I.Q. scores are predicted by family size and birth order; and in Chapter 10 we ask why males excel in math. We received many favorable comments concerning the Controversy feature in the first edition, and we have tried to maintain its strength in the second edition. Many of the controversies included are new to the second edition.

APPLYING PSYCHOLOGY. We have linked psychological knowledge to concrete examples and daily experiences throughout the text in order to clarify abstract issues. In addition, each chapter offers a section discussing one particular application of psychology at great length. For example, in Chapter 2 we discuss the applications of Positron Emission Tomography (PET scans); in Chapter 5 we consider sleep disorders and their remedies; and in Chapter 15 we consider the psychological and legal implications of criminal defenses based on pleas of insanity.

OTHER FEATURES. Immediately following this preface is a guide that contains tips on how to study, and how students can use this book most wisely. (Chapter 7 includes a new discussion of the PQ4R method of studying textbooks—Preview, Question, Read, Reflect, Recite, and Review.) Each chapter begins with an outline and an opening narrative that helps students focus their attention on key topics and concepts. Throughout the text, important terms are boldfaced as they are defined, and these definitions are collected in an extensive glossary. Each chapter ends with a numbered chapter summary, as well as a list of suggested readings. In addition to these learning aids, we offer a study guide, described below.

ANCILLARY MATERIALS

We have expanded the complete package of learning and teaching aids for *Psychology.* The *Study Guide,* prepared by Barbara and David Basden of California State University at Fresno, offers a unique selection of activities and features suitable for students of all abilities. For each chapter in the textbook, the *Study Guide* provides learning objectives, a completion outline, sample multiple-choice items, and short essay questions and their answers. The guide also includes, ''Psychology and Everyday Life''—brief articles tying psychological research to familiar problems—and ''Activities,'' designed to broaden the student's understanding of the psychological principles. The *Test Bank,* prepared by David G. Payne of the State University of New York at Binghamton in collaboration with the authors, provides some 2600 multiple-choice items. Each item is keyed to a learning objective, referenced to the textbook, and identified as either fact or comprehension type.

The test-generation program offers all 2600 test items on floppy disk for the microcomputer or on tape for the mainframe. With this program, instructors can generate printed tests for their own curriculum needs.

The *Instructor's Manual,* prepared by Hiram E. Fitzgerald and Cathleen McGreal of Michigan State University, provides chapter overviews, suggestions for lectures and class demonstrations, a guide to audiovisual resources, and a special section describing available classroom software for the introductory course. The transparency/slide package, prepared by David Miller of The University of Connecticut, includes over 100 classroom visual aids, many of which are not found in the textbook. They are available for those adopting the textbook either as 8½ × 11 inch acetate transparencies for overhead projection or as 35mm slides. We will also provide our adopters with the popular *Psychology Updates,* which contain brief articles by each of the authors focusing on new developments and research on topics covered in the text. *Updates* are published semiannually.

ACKNOWLEDGMENTS

Writing an introductory psychology text is a collaborative task. Although only four names appear on the cover of the book as authors, many more people helped in important ways. We wish to thank our colleagues who were instrumental in helping us develop the first edition of this book: Paul R. Abramson, University of California, Los Angeles; Bem P. Allen, Western Illinois University; Ruth L. Ault, Davidson College; Bruce L. Baker, University of California, Los Angeles; Barbara H. Basden, California State University–Fresno; Thomas J. Bouchard, Jr., University of Minnesota; James F. Calhoun, University of Georgia; David E. Campbell, Humboldt State University; Garvin Chastain, Boise State University; Margaret S. Clark, Carnegie-Mellon University; Helen J. Crawford, The University of Wyoming; Helen B. Daly, State University of New York–Oswego; Robert DaPrato, Solano Community College; Stephen F. Davis, Emporia State University; Anthony J. DeCasper, The University of North Carolina at Greensboro; Douglas R. Denney, University of Kansas; John W. Donahoe, University of Massachusetts–Amherst; James L. Dupree, Humboldt State University; Rand B. Evans, Texas A & M University; David R. Evans, The University of Western Ontario; Russell H. Fazio, Indiana University; Hiram E. Fitzgerald, Michigan State University; Barry Fish, Eastern Michigan University; Donald J. Foss, The University of Texas at Austin; James Geiwitz; M. M. Gittis, Youngstown State University; Michael J. Goldstein, University of California, Los Angeles; Richard L. Gottwald, Indiana University at South Bend; Richard A. Griggs, University of Florida; Ronald Growney, The University of Connecticut; Judith Harackiewicz, Columbia University; Peter C. Holland, Duke University; Karen L. Hollis, Mt. Holyoke College; Carroll E. Izard, University of Delaware; John Jonides, The University of Michigan; Robert A. Karlin, Rutgers University; Saul M. Kassin, Williams College; Katherine W. Klein, North Carolina State University; Lynn T. Koslowski, University of Toronto; Kenneth R. Livingston, Vassar College; Katherine Loveland, Rice University; Duane R. Martin, The University of Texas at Arlington; Antonio A. Nuñez, Michigan State University; Steven Penrod, University of Wisconsin; Ronald H. Peters, Iowa State University; James R. Pomerantz, State University of New York at Buffalo; George V. Rebec, Indiana University; Freda Rebelsky, Boston University; Michael E. Rashotte, The Florida State University; Mary Anne Sedney, Providence College; E. Eugene Schultz, The University of North Carolina at Asheville; Richard Schweickert, Purdue University; Jack Sherman, University of California, Los Angeles; Steven M. Smith, Texas A & M University; Judith M. Stern, Rutgers University; Robert J. Sternberg, Yale University; Joseph P. Stokes, The University of Illinois at Chicago Circle; Michael Tanenhaus, Wayne State University; Dennis C. Turk, Yale University; Joseph B. Thompson, Washington and Lee University; Gerald S. Wasserman, Purdue University; Michael J. Watkins, Rice University; Catherine C. Whitehouse, Western Maryland College; Arthur Wingfield, Brandeis University; Diane S. Woodruff, Temple University; and Paul T. P. Wong, Trent University.

To those instructors and specialists in various fields who provided invaluable advice on drafts of chapters or the whole manuscript for this second edition, we extend our deep appreciation:

Barbara Basden, *California State University–Fresno*
Horace O. Black, *Golden West College*
Brian H. Bland, *The University of Calgary*
Pam Blewitt, *Villanova University*
J. Jay Braun, *Arizona State University*
Celia Brownell, *University of Pittsburgh*
John P. Capitanio, *University of Massachusetts–Boston*
Thomas H. Carr, *Michigan State University*
David Chiszar, *University of Colorado at Boulder*
Helen Crawford, *The University of Wyoming*
Frank Curcio, *Boston University*
Robert Dale, *Southeast Louisiana University*
Joseph F. DeBold, *Tufts University*
William O. Dwyer, *Memphis State University*
Sandy Rappaport Fiske, *Onondoga Community College*
Paul W. Fox, *University of Minnesota*
Robert A. Frank, *University of Cincinnati*
Philip E. Freedman, *The University of Illinois at Chicago*
Sherryl Goodman, *Emory University*
Carol Grams, *Orange Coast College*
Lynn R. Kahle, *University of Oregon*
Saul Kassin, *Williams College*
Paul Kelly, *Toronto General Hospital*
Barry J. Krikstone, *University of Waterloo*
Stephen B. Klein, *Fort Hays State University*
Terry Maul, *San Bernardino Valley College*
Denis Mitchell, *University of Southern California*
Neil M. Montgomery, *Keene State University*
James C. Morrison, *Youngstown State University*
James S. Nairne, *The University of Texas at Arlington*
Gayle Olson, *University of New Orleans*
Matthew Olson, *Hamline University*
Patricia Owen, *St. Mary's University*
Joseph de Rivera, *Clark University*
Richard J. Sanders, *The University of North Carolina at Wilmington*
Beth A. Shapiro, *Emory University*
Eliot Smith, *Purdue University*
Steven M. Smith, *Texas A & M University*
Richard M. Sorrentino, *The University of Western Ontario*
John A. Stern, *Washington University*
Shelley E. Taylor, *University of California, Los Angeles*
Philip E. Tetlock, *University of California, Berkeley*
Gerald S. Wasserman, *Purdue University*
Robert C. Webb, *Suffolk University*
Kathleen M. White, *Boston University*
Randolph H. Whitworth, *The University of Texas at El Paso*
D. Louis Wood, *University of Arkansas at Little Rock*
Robert S. Wyer Jr., *The University of Illinois at Urbana, Champaign*

We would especially like to thank colleagues who helped us prepare our manuscript. John Capaldi of Purdue University played an important role in the early stages of the project. Jim Pomerantz, of the State University of New York at Buffalo, provided excellent drafts of Chapters 3 and 4. Eliot Smith of Purdue University provided a similar service for Chapter 17 in the second edition. Evelyn Oka of Michigan State University provided many useful ideas and references for Chapter 11, and David Saarnio of the University of Michigan helped in the revision of Chapter 8. David G. Payne helped with the glossary, and Mary Susan Weldon and Bradford H. Challis lent assistance in other ways.

Mary Schiller first interested us in embarking on this project and has provided helpful advice along the way. A number of people at Little, Brown deserve thanks. We are most grateful to Molly Faulkner for her aid in launching the first edition. Mylan Jaixen has diligently and skillfully helped shepherd the second edition through to completion, for which we are most appreciative. Garret White, editor-in-chief, generously provided his support and encouragement at all stages. Victoria Keirnan has served as a remarkably efficient production editor, expertly guiding us through this difficult phase. We appreciate her diligence, intelligence, and help, as well as that of copyeditor Barbara Flanagan, designer Catherine Dorin, photo researchers Sharon Donahue and Karen Coye, and editorial assistants Anne Starr, Bonnie Wood, Bruce Nichols, and Barbara Anderson, who skillfully edited the Study Guide.

Finally, we owe special thanks to Greg Tobin, our developmental editor, for his work on both the first and second editions. His enthusiasm, dedication, and continual push for excellence have been an inspiration to all four of us. His guidance in preparing the second edition has been outstanding. His many suggestions have greatly improved the book and his imprint is on virtually every page.

SOME ADVICE TO STUDENTS

Our goal in writing this book is to provide you with a broad, informative look at contemporary psychology. We are eager for you to use the book successfully, so here we pass along some advice you might find useful.

BECOME FAMILIAR WITH THE ORGANIZATION OF THE TEXT. Being aware of the overall organization of the book will help guide you through it. After an introductory chapter describing the nature of psychology, the next seven chapters describe fundamental processes that occur within the person—biological bases of behavior, sensation, perception, consciousness of the world, learning, memory, and thinking. The next ten chapters of the book describe people in more complete terms—their development, their intelligence and intellectual capacity, their motivations and emotional states, and their personalities. We also include chapters on abnormal behavior and therapy. In the last two chapters, we describe social forces that affect individual behavior. Thus, in rough terms, the organization of the book moves from within the person, to a consideration of the person as a whole, and finally to a discussion of outside social forces that act upon the individual.

BECOME FAMILIAR WITH THE FEATURES OF THE TEXT. Each chapter has a similar organization with features designed to highlight different aspects of the material. There are usually five or six main topic headings. In addition, each chapter after the first contains three special features entitled Research Frontier, Controversy, and Applying Psychology. In Research Frontier you will become acquainted with a topic on the cutting edge of psychological research. In Controversy you will encounter issues that require further research and debate among psychologists. These two features show that psychology is not a fixed system of thought. Although past research has provided a foundation of knowledge, many issues are actively investigated and many ideas hotly contested. Finally, in Applying Psychology, you will see how psychological research encompasses many important, practical aspects of daily experience. In fact, most psychological questions arise from such experience.

LOOK OVER EACH CHAPTER BEFORE YOU BEGIN READING. Start by studying the chapter outline on the opening page of each chapter. Then skim through the chapter, looking at each heading and reading a bit here and there. You might also read the chapter summary, which lists the chapter's main points.

FORCE YOURSELF TO THINK AS YOU READ. Many students try to read too quickly. It is much more effective to ready slowly and to think constructively as you read. When you come to a heading, ask yourself what topics are likely to follow. Note the logical connection between what you have just read and what you are about to read. At the end of the section look away from the book and try to summarize in your own words the central points. (If you cannot recall them at this point you will have difficulty later on.) Reread sections when your self-test shows that you did not comprehend the material the first time around.

MAKE AN OUTLINE OF THE MATERIAL. One way to read constructively is to outline the material in your own words, or at least to take notes on the important points. Another way is to underline critical passages with a marker for further study later.

REREAD AND RELEARN MATERIAL. Read a chapter once and then read other chapters or material from other courses before reading the chapter again. Reward yourself for studying, too. Set a reasonable goal for studying for a day, so that once you meet that goal, you can go to the movies, or whatever.

BEGIN STUDYING FOR EXAMS WELL IN ADVANCE. Feeling prepared will help relieve the test anxiety so many students experience. To prepare for exams you should test yourself by using the Study Guide available with the text.

Finally, if you have comments on the book, please write to us. We would enjoy hearing from you.

Henry L. Roediger III
J. Philippe Rushton
Elizabeth Deutsch Capaldi
Scott G. Paris

THE AUTHORS

Henry L. Roediger III is Professor of Psychology at Purdue University. He received his B.A. from Washington & Lee University in 1969 and his Ph.D. from Yale University in 1973. He has taught at Purdue and at the University of Toronto. Dr. Roediger's primary research has been in cognitive psychology, particularly in the processes involved in human learning and memory. He has contributed over 40 journal articles and reviews to psychology journals. He is Editor of the *Journal of Experimental Psychology: Learning, Memory, and Cognition*. He is also co-author of *Experimental Psychology: Understanding Psychological Research* (with B. H. Kantowitz) and *Methods in Experimental Psychology* (with B. H. Kantowitz and D. G. Elmes). Professor Roediger has taught the introductory course in psychology at Purdue for many years, as well as courses in cognitive psychology, memory, and research methodology. He is a Fellow of Division 3 (Experimental) of the American Psychological Association and a member of the Governing Board of the Psychonomics Society.

John Philippe Rushton is Professor of Psychology at The University of Western Ontario. He received his B.Sc. in 1970 and his Ph.D. in 1973 from the University of London. After a postdoc at Oxford University, he taught in Canada at York University and the University of Toronto before joining Western. Professor Rushton's research encompasses developmental, personality, and social psychology, in which he has contributed over 70 articles and book chapters on altruism, social learning theory, the effects of the mass media, the structure of personality, and more recently, sociobiology. His previous books include *Altruism, Socialization, and Society; Altruism and Helping Behavior* (with R. M. Sorrentino); and *Scientific Excellence* (with D. N. Jackson). Dr. Rushton is a Fellow of the American, British, and Canadian Psychological Associations, has served as a consultant to Government Commissions on the effects of the mass media, and is on the editorial board of *Developmental Psychology* and *Scientometrics*.

Elizabeth Deutsch Capaldi is Professor of Psychology and Head of the Department of Psychological Sciences at Purdue University. She received her B.A. from the University of Rochester in 1965 and her Ph.D. from the University of Texas at Austin in 1969 and has served on the Purdue faculty since that time. Professor Capaldi's primary research has focused on animal learning and motivation. She has contributed over thirty-five journal articles and reviews to psychology journals. In addition to her research, Professor Capaldi has taught the introductory course in psychology at Purdue, research methods, and both graduate and undergraduate courses in learning and motivation. In 1981 and in 1982, Professor Capaldi was awarded the School of Humanities and Social Science teaching award for the Department of Psychological Sciences.

Scott G. Paris is Professor of Psychology and Education at The University of Michigan, where he serves as Director of the Center for Research on Learning and Schooling. Since receiving his B.A. from the University of Michigan in 1968 and his Ph.D. from Indiana University in 1972, Professor Paris has taught at Purdue University (1973–1979) and Michigan. He has also been a visiting scholar at Stanford University, UCLA, the University of Auckland (New Zealand), and the Flinders University and the University of Newcastle (Australia). His research in developmental psychology has focused primarily on memory and problem-solving skills in children, while his research on education has investigated children's learning and reading. He has written more than 50 articles and book chapters, is a co-author of *Developmental Psychology Today* (5th ed.) and co-editor of *Learning and Motivation in the Classroom* (with G. Olson and H. Stevenson). He is a member of the editorial boards of *Child Development*, the *Journal of Educational Psychology*, *Developmental Review*, and *Reading Research Quarterly*.

Brief Contents

Contents

PART FIVE

MOTIVATION AND EMOTION

12

13

PART SIX

PERSONALITY AND ABNORMAL PSYCHOLOGY

14

PERSONALITY   494

15

ABNORMALITY AND DEVIANCE   530

PSYCHOLOGY

Painting opposite: "Simultaneous colors" by Sonia Delaunay-Terk, 1913. Kunsthalle, Bielefeld.

PART ONE
Foundations

1

The Nature of Psychology

From the most ancient subject we shall produce the newest science.

Hermann Ebbinghaus

SPEND A FEW MINUTES LEAFING THROUGH THIS BOOK AND YOU WILL quickly discover the enormous range of psychologists' interests and accomplishments. They ask questions about every aspect of human behavior. Your random survey may turn up examples such as these:

□ Does the brain produce a substance to blunt pain? Recent research indicates that the brain produces *endorphins* (substances chemically similar to morphine) that block pain by clogging the neural pathways to prevent transmission of pain signals. Further, animals and people can learn to produce endorphins automatically when a threatening situation arises (Chapter 3).

□ Do people show a general decline in all their abilities in old age, or do only some capabilities deteriorate? Do some qualities of life actually improve in old age? Most people subscribe to a number of myths about how aging affects us. To check your own beliefs, take the quiz on page 382 in Chapter 10.

□ How does our perceptual system sometimes lead us to inaccurate impressions of the world, such as when we experience visual illusions? Consider the two ''illusory figures'' shown in Figure 1–1. On the left, the light red ring is not physically present; neither is the yellow rectangle on the right. In both cases they are created by the perceptual system as it struggles to process the image on the page (Chapter 4).

FIGURE 1–1
Illusory Figures

The circle on the left and the rectangles on the right are not present but are constructed by the perceptual system from ambiguous cues. To demonstrate this, cover the corners of the rectangle and note that it disappears.

Source: Rock, 1984.

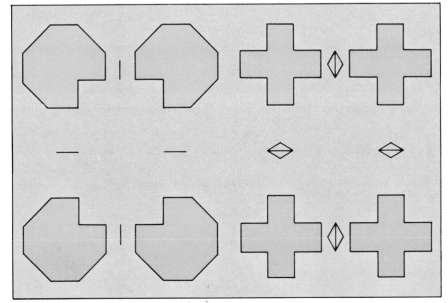

☐ Do people inherit some aspects of their mental abilities and personalities from their parents, just as they do their eye color, height, and weight? Research indicates that the answer is yes. Although learning plays a large role in the development of intelligence and personality, a genetic component exists, too (Chapters 13, 14).

☐ Are different parts of the brain specialized to serve different functions, such as control of seeing, hearing, talking, and walking? The answer is yes, and in Chapter 2 we describe the functions of various structures in the brain.

☐ Do some people have photographic memories? Trying to imagine things we want to remember usually helps memory, but some people claim to store an exact replica of their experience in the "mind's eye" (Chapter 7).

Each of these six questions illustrates psychological research into the nature of human behavior. Psychologists study every facet of the behavior of humans and other animals. These range from biochemical aspects such as the effects of hormones on behavior to global issues such as the nature of leadership in groups and the causes of aggression in society. But, given this diversity of interests, what unifying theme puts these areas of inquiry under the heading of *psychology*?

DEFINING PSYCHOLOGY

If a psychologist in 1910 had been asked to define the field, the answer may have been something like "the study of mind and mental processes." Early psychologists concentrated on studying mental life (conscious experience) largely by having people describe their perceptions and feelings. Later psychologists, called *behaviorists*, rejected this approach and argued that only actual behavior merited study since it alone could be observed and measured directly. Thus a psychologist in 1940 might have defined psychology as "the study of behavior." In the 1950s and 1960s psychologists returned to the problems of mental experience that the behaviorists had rejected—topics such as perception, remembering, and dreaming—but they adopted objective methods to study these inherently private events.

Psychology is defined now as the *study of mind (or mental processes) and behavior*, but even in studying mental processes psychologists observe behavior. They then try to draw inferences about the mental processes that must have occurred to produce the behavior. The examples above and the difficulty in defining the field provide an inkling of psychology's broad scope. We turn now to a brief survey of the history of psychology for an understanding of how the field developed.

EARLY SCHOOLS OF PSYCHOLOGY

The quotation leading the chapter was written by Hermann Ebbinghaus (1850–1909), one of psychology's pioneers. Psychology is indeed an ancient subject because people have always been interested in how their minds worked and what forces shaped their actions. However, systematic study of these problems is really only about one hundred years old.

Another often-quoted remark by Ebbinghaus is that psychology has a long past, but a short history. Many topics that interest psychologists have puzzled philosophers for thousands of years. Here is one such question: How much of human behavior reflects inherited factors and how much has been shaped by experience? Another question: Does a person's knowledge derive entirely from experience, or is it partly innate? A third puzzler: How are events perceived and remembered?

Although such issues have been pondered for centuries, psychology did not become an independent discipline until the late 1800s, when experimental methods were developed to study mind and behavior. This work was initiated by natural scientists, mostly physicists and physiologists, who eventually began to think of themselves as psychologists. At first psychology was usually considered a part of university philosophy departments, but eventually it became a separate discipline.

A scientific psychology developed slowly, in part because some of its basic premises conflicted with religious beliefs. For centuries, theologians taught that the human mind (or spirit or soul) had free will and was not governed by natural laws or principles. A scientific psychology did not begin until some German scientists questioned this notion. Hermann von Helmholtz (1821–1894) was one of the earliest to begin what could be called psychology experiments. Trained as a physicist, Helmholtz became interested in perception and the nervous system. According to tradition, in the 1840s he and three other radical young physicists signed a blood oath stating that all forces in the human organism were physical and chemical. Helmholtz went on to pioneer experiments in a number of important fields, including the first measurements of the speed of a nervous impulse.

Another German was an early contributor to psychology. Gustav Fechner (1801–1887) was interested in how physical stimulation, such as a bright light, translated into psychological experience. For example, does increasing the intensity of a light heighten its perceived brightness? How much brighter must a light of a certain intensity become before people can notice the difference? In attacking these and similar problems, Fechner helped found the field called *psychophysics*, which will be discussed in Chapter 3. Fechner's major work, *Elements of Psychophysics*, was published in 1860.

Structuralism: The Elements of Mental Life

Helmholtz, Fechner, and others helped spread the belief that psychological processes could be studied by objective methods. But modern psychology is often formally dated from 1879 when the first psychology laboratory was established in Leipzig, Germany, by Wilhelm Wundt (1832–1920). Wundt was probably the first person to call himself a psychologist, and his influence on the field was tremendous.

Wundt wrote prolifically; it is estimated that he published 50,000 pages. He is not known primarily for his brilliance or creativity but for his ability to systematize ideas. "Wundt's genius was the kind Thomas Edison described—1 percent inspiration and 99 percent perspiration" (Miller, 1962, p. 24). His ideas became influential in the United States when one of his students, an Englishman named Edward Titchener (1867–1927), emigrated

Wilhelm Wundt is credited with founding the first psychology laboratory in 1879 and founding the school of structuralism. (Photo courtesy of the Archives of the History of American Psychology.)

to America to set up a laboratory at Cornell University. Titchener was one of the earliest American psychologists.

Wundt developed the first systematic approach to psychology, called **structuralism.** Proponents of structuralism believed that psychology should be concerned with the elementary processes of conscious experience. They saw three primary questions: (1) What are the elements of experience? (2) How are they combined? and (3) What causes the elements to combine? Structuralists identified three major components of conscious experience: sensations, images, and affections. *Sensations* include sights, sounds, smells, tastes, and feelings. *Images* represented experiences not actually present—memories—and *affections* were emotional reactions such as love, joy, and jealousy. These elements were believed to be combined into our normal conscious experience by associations. An experience such as sitting in a lecture hall looking at a professor was thought to be composed of many independent components welded together by associations.

Making these assumptions, the structural psychologists wanted to break down complex experiences into elementary components—sensations, images, and affections—by a technique known as **analytic introspection.** To all naive observers (that is, all but structural psychologists) conscious experience seems to be all one piece, or stream—the stream of consciousness. But introspectionists were taught to overcome this view and to record the discrete, conscious contents of an experience. To be introspective about a beautiful flower, the reporter should describe the sensations of experiencing that flower: size, shape, texture, color, brightness, and so on, as well as the images and affections it evoked.

Analytic introspection was difficult. Many outside the structural camp found it sterile and boring. It also proved unreliable because introspectionists in different laboratories were unable to agree on the elementary parts of the same experience. Nonetheless, Titchener and his students believed that the structural program described how psychology should be studied and argued against newer trends in psychology that pushed structuralists from the forefront of the field after about 1920. These movements included functionalism, behaviorism, and Gestalt psychology, which were in part reactions to the structural views.

Functionalism: The Uses of Mind

Unlike structuralism, which developed in Germany and was transported to the United States, *functionalism* grew up in the United States. However, a strong influence was Charles Darwin's theory of evolution through natural selection, which swept through intellectual circles in both Europe and North America in the late 1800s. Darwin's theory fundamentally changed the conception of humans' place in the order of nature. For psychologists, Darwin's theory raised fascinating questions: Do mental processes of humans have an evolutionary history? Are our capabilities, such as learning from experience, similar to those of other animals? What is the adaptive significance of various human abilities? These questions helped give rise to functionalism.

Functionalism is not a systematic position like structuralism. Rather, it is a more general set of ideas with similar themes, particularly the issue of the usefulness or adaptive significance of mental processes. "In examining mental processes, [functionalism] asked the questions of the practical man:

John Dewey, the father of functionalism, also made great contributions to education and philosophy. (Photo courtesy of the Archives of the History of American Psychology.)

'What are they for?' 'What difference do they make?' 'How do they work?' '' (Heidbreder, 1933, p. 202). This is about as close to a definition of functionalism as can be found.

Functionalism is usually associated with John Dewey (1859–1952) and the two universities where he taught, the University of Chicago and Columbia University. Whereas structuralists asked questions about the contents of the mind, functionalists were interested in the uses (functions) of mental processes. They studied these through either subjective or objective measures and believed that psychologists could usefully study animals as well as humans. In addition, functionalists favored studying problems of practical significance and studying mental activity and behavior in its natural context. Functionalists pointed out that psychological processes were continuous, ongoing events that could not usefully be stopped and dissected as the structuralists proposed.

Another great American psychologist who is sometimes considered a functionalist was William James (1842–1910). (Actually, James wrote before functionalism developed.) His landmark two-volume work, *The Principles of Psychology* (1890), is still widely read today. Like the functionalists, James had little use for the German psychology of the time, finding it mostly sterile and boring. James was eclectic and included in his textbook whatever he found of interest. He cared most about mental activity and conceived of mental processes as active. The *stream of consciousness* about which he wrote was continually changing, active, and selective. Thus much of James's writing, along with the fact that he too was greatly influenced by Darwin, shows a kindred spirit to the functionalists' beliefs.

The ideas of Dewey and James led to several healthy trends previously discouraged by structuralism. Functionalism broadened the subject matter of psychology to include a variety of types of people (children, the mentally ill) and species (chimpanzees, dogs) that could not be studied through analytic introspection. Another new trend was to apply research to practical problems. The functionalists were the first in the United States to develop intelligence tests for classifying children, an endeavor discussed in Chapter 11.

Behaviorism: Excluding Mind from Psychology

The behaviorist revolution can be dated from 1913 when Watson published a paper called "Psychology as the Behaviorist Views It." He attacked structural psychology's emphasis on introspection, consciousness, and mental contents. He argued that psychology should rid itself of these concepts because they were not appropriate for scientific explanation. Psychology should also give up the old introspective methods that did not even create results that could be reproduced from one laboratory to the next. Instead, Watson argued, psychologists should study what all reasonable people could agree on: behavior. Watson wrote:

> I believe we can write a psychology, define it as [the science of behavior], and never go back on our definition: never use the terms consciousness, mental states, introspectively verifiable, imagery, and the like. It can be done in terms of habit formation, habit integration, and the like. Furthermore, I believe it is really worthwhile to make the attempt now. (1913, pp. 166–167)

William James, the first famous American psychologist, taught at Harvard. (Photo courtesy of the Archives of the History of American Psychology.)

John B. Watson, the father of behaviorism, eventually left academics to pursue a successful career in advertising.

B. F. Skinner is the most famous modern champion of behaviorism. His novel, *Walden Two* (1948), portrayed a society built on behaviorist ideas and principles.

Behaviorism attracted many younger psychologists; for them, it justified discarding a lot of the murky nonsense they felt had preoccupied psychology for too long. The behaviorists were intent on establishing psychology as a natural science. Its subject was to be observable, or overt, behavior. They saw no need to become embroiled in complicated arguments about the nature of consciousness and images or the number of sensations in an experience. These terms, and others used by structuralists and functionalists, were attacked for being vague and useless as scientific descriptions. Behaviorists did not deny the existence of mind and consciousness, as critics sometimes assert; rather, they asserted, these terms were not useful scientific concepts.

Behaviorists argued that the proper goal of psychology was to describe, explain, predict, and control behavior. Their emphasis was on how experience molds behavior, so they had a natural interest in the process of learning. Ivan Pavlov (1849–1936), a Russian physiologist, made a number of observations about learning through experiments with dogs, and his work showed the power of the behavioristic approach. Behaviorists tended to study learning in animals other than humans because it was easier to deal with simpler systems and because greater control could be maintained over their environments. (More will be said about Pavlov's experiments in Chapter 6.)

Behaviorism also attracted a large number of critics, both from within the discipline and from other fields. Today most of these people debate the ideas of B. F. Skinner (b. 1904), who is often called a radical behaviorist for his insistence on the correctness of the behavioral approach and his rejection of other approaches that explain behavior through internal mechanisms. It is important to remember that many psychologists who consider themselves behaviorists do not agree with some of Skinner's ideas. Many different behaviorist positions exist today. The basic ideas of the movement have also permeated contemporary psychology; they have been accepted by many, but certainly not all, of today's psychologists. Almost all psychologists would agree that the study of behavior is central to psychology, but only a few would reject all use of mental or physiological constructs as explanations in psychology, as some behaviorists have. Early behaviorists excluded many topics from psychology—perception, emotion, cognition—that are of central concern today.

Gestalt Psychology: Perception of the Whole

Functionalism and behaviorism developed in the United States partly in reaction to structuralism. About the same time, another protest against structuralism was being organized on its home ground, in Germany. The *Gestalt psychology* movement was a reaction against the structural idea of perception as the sum of many independent sensations. Gestalt psychologists argued that people perceived the world in unitary wholes, or *Gestalts* (from the German *gestalten,* which roughly translates as "whole," or "pattern").

Max Wertheimer (1880–1943) and the other Gestalt psychologists produced many demonstrations of this unity of perceptual processes. One of

Max Wertheimer created clever perceptual demonstrations that supported the Gestalt view of perception.

the earliest involved *apparent motion*. Wertheimer discovered that when two lights were spaced a slight distance apart in the dark and then lit successively at certain intervals, a curious perceptual phenomenon occurred. Rather than observing *two* lights being lit alternately, a person saw only *one* light that appeared to move back and forth. Since the light was perceived as moving through a region devoid of actual sensations, the phenomenon contradicted the structuralist position that all perception derived from independent sensations. More familiar to us are the illusions of movement produced by television and the movies, created by showing still pictures very rapidly. Human perceptual systems integrate these many scenes into continuous motion.

Gestalt psychology originally began as a protest against structuralism, but soon its proponents were arguing with behaviorists. The Gestaltists objected to behaviorists' analysis of complex phenomena in terms of elementary behaviors, just as they had objected to structuralists' theory of elementary sensations. Behaviorists, for their part, found the concepts of Gestalt psychology every bit as vague and fuzzy as those of structuralism and functionalism. Other factors alienated the respective schools: Gestalt psychologists relied on reports of conscious experience as their data, and they were often content to produce a demonstration of a phenomenon rather than study it carefully through behavioral methods. The influence of the Gestalt ideas remains strong in some areas of psychology, particularly in the study of perception, memory, and thinking, although behavioral methods are used to study these processes today.

Psychoanalysis: The Unconscious Mind

Sigmund Freud (1856–1939), a physician in Vienna who treated mental problems, invented the therapeutic method known as *psychoanalysis.* From the many patients he saw, Freud developed the idea that most mental problems were caused by conflicts and emotions of which his patients were unaware. He believed that psychological problems in adults could be traced to traumatic episodes in early childhood. Memories of those events would cause anxiety if allowed into consciousness, Freud thought, so they were blocked from consciousness, or *repressed,* and preserved in the unconscious. However, in his view, many of the bizarre symptoms of mental illness were outlets for these repressed memories of the early traumatic experiences. The task of the psychoanalyst, therefore, was to help bring these memories into consciousness through free association techniques and the interpretation of dreams, which Freud argued were the "royal road to the unconscious." The patient would then be able to deal rationally with the repressed memories in order to relieve the psychological disturbance.

Freud's theory is creative, complicated, and controversial. His analysis helped initiate the systematic study of personality development, abnormal behavior, and therapies for mental problems. It has also been roundly criticized by many psychologists (particularly behaviorists) as vague and generally untestable. Freud did, however, call attention to a number of interesting phenomena, such as dreams, slips of the tongue, and memory lapses, that have received careful scientific study more recently. Today other types of psychoanalytic theory have expanded on the traditional Freudian version.

TABLE 1–1
Summary of Five Primary Schools of Psychology

School	Subject Matter	Research Goals	Research Methods
Structuralism	Conscious experience	To break down conscious experience into its basic components: sensations, images, affections	Analytic introspection
Functionalism	The function of mental processes and how they help people adapt	To study mental processes in their natural contexts; to discover what effects they have	Both objective measures and informal observation and introspection
Behaviorism	Behavior: how it is changed under different conditions, with an emphasis on learning	Description, explanation, prediction, and control of behavior	Objective measures of behavior; formal experiments
Gestalt Psychology	Subjective experience, with an emphasis on perception, memory, and thinking	To understand the phenomena of conscious experience in holistic terms (not to analyze experience into arbitrary categories)	Subjective reports; some behavioral measures; demonstrations
Psychoanalysis	Abnormal human behavior	To understand normal and abnormal personality through study of abnormal cases	Lengthy dialogues with patients to uncover unconscious fears and memories; free association; dream interpretation

CURRENT APPROACHES TO PSYCHOLOGY

From 1890 to perhaps 1950 psychologists viewed the main organizational structure of their discipline in terms of the five schools just described. They tended to identify themselves as structuralists, functionalists, behaviorists, Gestaltists, or psychoanalysts. Today psychologists rarely do so. Instead, psychologists are usually classified by their specific topics of study, such as developmental psychology or clinical psychology. Yet the various schools of psychology continue to influence the major approaches taken to psychological phenomena. An "approach" is difficult to define precisely, but it has to do with the subject matter studied and the kinds of research techniques and theory used. Five main approaches are the biological, behavioral, cognitive, psychoanalytic, and humanistic. These categories overlap somewhat and should not necessarily be considered as competitors. Rather, they represent different points of view and complementary methods of understanding behavior and mental life.

The Biological Approach

As implied by the name, psychologists employing the biological approach look to biology as a model. One version of the biological approach, called **psychobiology**, studies the mechanisms of the brain and nervous sytem that control behavior. Psychologists who use this method are variously described

FIGURE 1–2
Inhibition of Aggression

In the top picture, a matador taunts the bull into charging. The bull has been previously implanted with electrodes in an area of his brain that controls aggression. As the bull approaches in full charge, a researcher activates an electric current to that part of his brain, which immediately stops the bull in his tracks. Stimulating certain parts of the brain electrically can initiate or inhibit aggressive responses.

as neuroscientists, neuropsychologists, psychobiologists, or physiological psychologists. A typical psychobiological research procedure is to alter some aspect of the nervous system surgically or chemically to determine how the change affects behavior. Such research is usually done with animals other than humans, although automobile accidents, gunshot wounds, or other tragedies sometimes create natural opportunities for experiment.

The human brain is extraordinarily complex, with billions of nerve cells and an almost infinite number of connections among them. Thus, any attempt to relate neural structures and changes to behavior is profoundly complicated. However, psychobiologists have made many fascinating discoveries. One is that certain areas in the brain seem to produce strong emotions, such an intense pleasure or fear and rage, when electrically stimulated. Aggressive behaviors can also be modified by stimulation (see Figure 1–2). Psychologists' knowledge of the brain and how it controls behavior advances steadily, but we are still far from having anything like a complete theory.

Another biological approach is *ethology,* the study of the behavior of animals in natural (as opposed to laboratory) settings. Inspired by Darwin's theory of evolutionary change through natural selection, ethologists examine the adaptive significance of various behavior patterns. Ethologists have identified a number of behaviors in insects, birds, fish, and other animals that appear to be species specific. For example, social insects such as bees and ants have rigid caste systems in which individual members' roles and functions are genetically programmed (Wilson, 1971).

A recent outgrowth of ethology is the field of *sociobiology,* the study of the biological bases of social behavior. As in ethology, the emphasis is often on the inherited social tendencies of lower animals. However, some lively controversies have flared recently as sociobiologists have extended some of their ideas to account for human behavior. We will consider their arguments in Chapters 12 and 18.

The Behavioral Approach

The behavioral approach, as its name suggests, is a legacy of the behaviorist school. Psychologists adopting it believe that behavior can be studied in its own right, without worrying about the brain mechanisms and the physiology that underlie the behavior. Typically, they try to manipulate aspects of the environment systematically and observe the effects of changes on behavior. Objects and events in the environment are often referred to as *stimuli* and changes in behavior as *responses,* and the behavioral approach is sometimes referred to as a *stimulus-response* (or *S-R) approach.*

The behavioral method emphasizes carefully controlled experiments, so research is usually conducted in laboratory settings rather than in natural environments. However, recently there has been much cross-fertilization between the behavioral and ethological approaches, as in the study of biological factors influencing learning (e.g., Seligman & Hager, 1972). The reluctance to explain behavior in terms of unobservable (internal) events has been relaxed by most modern practitioners of the behavioral approach, who are therefore sometimes called *neobehaviorists.* The behavioral approach is an important influence in clinical psychology, where practitioners attempt

Principles derived from the behavioral approach are often used in working with children who have behavior problems.

to apply principles derived from laboratory experiments to overcome maladaptive behavior in humans, such as treatment of temper tantrums in children or of phobias (irrational fears).

The Cognitive Approach

Practitioners of *cognitive psychology* pursue an interest in how people perceive, attend, remember, think, and use language. In short, cognitive psychologists study how people process information. Unlike behaviorists, cognitive psychologists focus on discussions of internal psychological processes rather than avoid them. As you read these words, a cognitive psychologist would argue, you perform a series of mental operations. You analyze the blobs of ink and understand them as concepts. Cognitive psychologists are interested in the internal changes that accompany a complex task such as reading. What mental operations are involved?

When cognitive psychologists explain a skill such as remembering, they usually refer to hypothetical psychological processes rather than physiological processes. For example, experiences may be assumed to create *memory traces* in the brain, even if the exact nature and location of the neural changes are unknown. Most cognitive psychologists would argue that brain processes are as yet insufficiently understood to permit the description of such complicated mental operations as reading in purely physiological terms; however, they welcome insights from neuropsychology.

Cognitive psychologists use behavioral methods to study mental structures and processes, and on the rare occasions when they employ introspection they do so only in conjunction with behavioral measures. Thus they scrutinize mental processes by observing their behavioral effects. This technique has been referred to as *neomentalism* to distinguish it from the old introspective mentalism of the structuralists (Paivio, 1975). For example, both structural psychologists and modern cognitive psychologists employed the term *mental image,* a psychological construct. But while the structural psychologists simply described their mental images introspectively, modern cognitive psychologists have devised a number of ingenious tasks to measure and study the effects of images on behavior, such as the speed of answering questions about images (Kosslyn, 1980).

The Psychoanalytic Approach

The psychoanalytic (sometimes called the psychodynamic) approach results from Freud's theorizing, described on page 9. Psychoanalysts are interested in the motivational dynamics of behavior. Freud, you recall, believed that his patients were often unaware or unconscious of their motivations and that most of their problems could be traced to early childhood conflicts. Psychoanalytic explanations of behavior are popular among many of today's therapists, and the full range of psychoanalytic theory and treatment is discussed in Chapters 14, 15, and 16. Note, however, that much of Freud's theorizing remains controversial and even many psychoanalysts prefer a different viewpoint.

Freud was trained as a medical doctor and saw humans as biological organisms with the same strong physiological needs as other animals. He called these *instinctual drives* and emphasized how personality development was affected by meeting the requirements of these drives. The general term for these biological needs is the *id,* and Freud especially emphasized sexual drives as a dominating force. The id attempts to fill biological needs blindly. Babies are dominated by the forces represented in the id, for their sole goal is to satisfy these basic physical needs. However, society does not long permit instant gratification of biological needs. The *ego* is the rational part of the mind that develops to keep the person in contact with reality. The ego mediates between the blind, instinctual cravings of the id and the reality imposed by the external world, which limits satisfaction of these cravings. The rules of society that are imposed by parents and others are internalized by the child as the *superego,* or conscience. The ego balances between the desires of the id and the constraints placed on it by the superego and the external world. Mental problems are caused by unsuccessful resolution of this conflict.

We will have much more to say about Freudian theorizing later in the book. For now we should point out that psychologists today who subscribe to a pure form of Freud's theory are about as rare as pure Watsonian behaviorists. Freudian theory has developed and been modified over the years by many other psychoanalysts, who have emphasized other mechanisms besides the internal ("intrapsychic") descriptions offered by Freud. For example, the *neo-Freudians,* such as Erich Fromm and Karen Horney, stress the role of social influences on the individual, a feature that had been relatively neglected by Freud. The psychoanalytic approach to psychology has been the most successful in permeating and influencing other fields. Although people in Freud's time were often scandalized by his writings on how biological needs, particularly sexual needs, determined personality development, his ideas have strongly influenced modern anthropology, philosophy, literature, and art.

Sigmund Freud, the father of psychoanalysis, is shown sitting in his office in Vienna.

The Humanistic Approach

The humanistic approach differs from the approaches just discussed. *Humanistic psychology* is difficult to define precisely, but it stresses the inherent goodness and worth of the individual and the individual's potential for growth and fulfillment. Humanistic psychologists argue that psychology should be concerned with subjective, conscious experience, primarily with feelings. It should explain the phenomena that humans experience. Thus it is sometimes referred to as a *phenomenological approach.* Its proponents tend to emphasize the uniqueness of the individual and the responsibility of individuals for their actions. Whereas other observers tend to see behavior as determined by external and internal factors, humanists emphasize free will.

The humanistic approach is in some ways a revolt against the mechanistic approaches, such as behaviorism. Subjective experience, not behavior, is of primary interest. Many humanistic psychologists believe, in fact, that a scientific approach is unsuitable to the study of human beings. They hold that psychology should help people reach their maximum potential, a view reflected in consciousness-expanding programs. The psychoanalytic approach is not favored by humanists, either. Freudians search for the causes of psychological problems in long-forgotten (or repressed) childhood experiences, whereas humanistic approaches emphasize that a person should deal with problems as they are currently experienced.

The humanistic movement has adherents with diverse beliefs. To the extent that it rejects scientific values, many psychologists hold humanism in disfavor. On the other hand, some leading proponents of the humanistic viewpoint emphasize the value of a more rigorous approach in examining the concepts of humanistic psychology (Rychlak, 1977).

Levels of Explanation

Because psychologists take varying approaches to their subject matter, they often try to explain the same phenomenon in different ways. The different types of explanations can be arranged in a hierarchy, as in Figure 1–3. The

---

TABLE 1–2
Summary of Five Approaches to the Study of Psychology

Approach	Goal
Biological	To discover and describe biological structures and processes that underlie behavior
Behavioral	To study behavior, usually in controlled laboratory settings, and to examine how environmental conditions determine behavior
Cognitive	To discover and study the mental processes that underlie knowledge and behavior
Psychoanalytic	To determine the unconscious motivations of behavior and to bring these motivations into conscious awareness
Humanistic	To examine the phenomena of experience and to help people maximize their potential for psychological growth

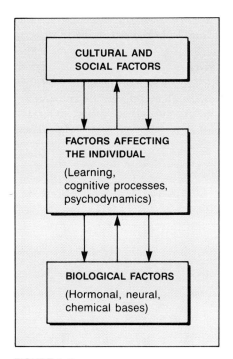

FIGURE 1–3
Hierarchical Arrangement of Explanations of Behavior

Researchers consider various levels in explaining many psychological phenomena. This figure can be applied to the range of factors causing obesity that are described in the text. Higher-level or molar factors are at the top, with lower-level or molecular factors at the bottom. The arrows indicate that factors at the different levels interact.

elements of the hierarchy range from social and cultural forces that might be emphasized by anthropologists and sociologists to the cognitive processes of the individual to biochemical and genetic determinants of behavior.

To illustrate the idea of levels of explanation we will take the problem of obesity. Many people in Western societies are overweight, some grossly so. Why? What causes obesity?

The whole range of explanatory levels can be invoked to explain this problem. First, consider *genetic* factors: weight is determined in part by inheritance. Second, consider *physiology:* there may be something wrong with parts of the brain that regulate eating so that the impulses signaling satiety ("I've had enough") are shut off; or metabolic factors that control fat deposits may have gone awry. Third, *learning* may play a role: many people are taught as children to consume everything on their plates and thus eat whether or not they are hungry. This leads, fourth, to *cognitive* factors: some psychologists propose that fat people are more sensitive to external cues about food than they are to internal, physiological cues (Schachter, 1971). They tend to eat when food is available (external cues) and do not pay attention to physiological cues telling them they have had enough. Fifth, some researchers propose that *psychodynamic* variables are important: people may eat to relieve stress or to avoid the stress of interpersonal relations, especially sexual situations, since fat people are less likely to attract partners. Sixth, *social* and *cultural* factors encourage people to be overweight: Westerners live in cultures in which food is plentiful, and advertisers make eating seem like a national obsession.

So researchers can explain obesity in many ways. Genetic, biochemical, and other physiological factors are important, as are learning, cognitive, and psychoanalytic aspects. Social and cultural factors too must be taken into account. The list of reasons could be extended. Which "correctly" explains the problem? Most psychologists would argue that no single true level of explanation exists. Instead, most complicated psychological phenomena can be understood only by considering various factors operating at different levels.

When explanations are arranged in a hierarchy, as in Figure 1–3, biological and chemical factors are on the lowest level; cognitive, learning, and psychoanalytic factors enter just above; and social and cultural factors occupy the higher levels. The lowest level refers to *molecular* events; the higher levels are called *molar* factors. The different levels are not independent but usually affect one another. If food is plentiful, for example, it may be eaten to relieve stress, with biochemical consequences.

Some scientists argue that the only appropriate type of explanation in psychology is to reduce all of the higher factors to their biological underpinnings. This molecular approach to explaining psychological phenomena is called **reductionism.** Most psychologists reject reductionism in favor of multiple levels of explanation, for the reasons we have already discussed.

Another example helps illustrate this point. Cognitive psychologists, who attempt to describe the structure and processes of the mind, defend an abstract level of explanation by employing a computer analogy. Suppose a Martian landed on Earth and wanted to know how a computer works. Computers, of course, require complicated electronic circuitry and programs that control their operation. Should the Martian first study electronic circuitry or programming to understand the computer? The answer depends on the type of knowledge desired, whether at a molecular level (circuitry) or at a molar level (programming). Cognitive psychologists defend their molar explanations of behavior in terms of abstract cognitive processes by saying that they are interested in the "program" that governs human behavior. By this analogy, psychobiologists deal with the internal circuitry of the mind. Ideally, the two approaches complement one another. Discoveries about aspects of the "program" can aid the study of neural function, and vice versa.

PROFESSIONAL ROLES IN PSYCHOLOGY

We have briefly described the history of psychology and some of the approaches psychologists take to their work. But what do psychologists actually do? You are probably most familiar with the image of a psychologist as a professional who works with people to solve their problems. This is certainly a major focus of clinical and counseling psychologists, but the range of psychologists' activities is much greater than this. Psychologists may teach and carry out research in colleges and universities. They may also be hired in industry to do research or to tackle practical problems. The American Psychological Association (APA) counts some 60,000 members (as of 1985). To see the wide variety of issues that interest psychologists, read through the names of the 42 divisions of the APA shown in Table 1–3. The five approaches to the study of psychology that we have just discussed can be used by people in many different divisions or subfields. The approaches do not map perfectly onto different subfields; however, certain approaches are more common in some subfields than others. Some of the primary categories of specialization are surveyed in the following paragraphs.

Experimental psychology covers fields in which practitioners rely almost exclusively on experiments to study behavior and mental life. It typically includes the study of biological bases of behavior (psychobiology), animal learning and behavior, and cognitive processes (perception, memory, language, thinking). Obviously, the psychobiological, behavioral, and cognitive approaches described earlier are used in the study of experimental psychology. The topics covered in experimental psychology are sometimes referred to as the basic areas in psychology (perception, learning, etc.), although some psychologists might dispute this claim. The term "experimental psychology" is old and somewhat inaccurate: psychologists interested in many topics other than those we have listed have also adopted experimental methods.

Social psychologists are interested in how social factors affect behavior. How does your friend's behavior affect yours in some situation? Social psychologists are also concerned with group processes, such as how leaders emerge. They are interested in questions such as how people perceive others, why they conform and obey, and how television affects behavior. In all of these cases the individual's behavior is affected by the influence of others. These topics are discussed in Chapters 17 and 18.

Personality psychologists are concerned with individual differences among people, and why people in the same situation will often behave differently. They often try to classify people in order to predict their behavior,

TABLE 1–3
The 42 Divisions of the American Psychological Association

Division Number*	Division Name	Division Membership
1	Division of General Psychology	5,052
2	Division on the Teaching of Psychology	1,933
3	Division of Experimental Psychology	1,472
5	Division on Evaluation and Measurement	1,226
6	Division of Physiological and Comparative Psychology	794
7	Division on Developmental Psychology	1,254
8	The Society of Personality and Social Psychology	3,233
9	The Society for the Psychological Study of Social Issues	2,832
10	Division of Psychology and the Arts	437
12	Division of Clinical Psychology	5,418
13	Division of Consulting Psychology	937
14	The Society for Industrial and Organizational Psychology, Inc.	2,499
15	Division of Educational Psychology	2,093
16	Division of School Psychology	2,261
17	Division of Counseling Psychology	2,588
18	Division of Psychologists in Public Service	980
19	Division of Military Psychology	621
20	Division of Adult Development and Aging	1,049
21	Division of Applied Experimental and Engineering Psychologists	583
22	Division of Rehabilitation Psychology	974
23	Division of Consumer Psychology	422
24	Division of Theoretical and Philosophical Psychology	519
25	Division for the Experimental Analysis of Behavior	1,317
26	Division of the History of Psychology	622
27	Division of Community Psychology	1,653
28	Division of Psychopharmacology	1,043
29	Division of Psychotherapy	4,684
30	Division of Psychological Hypnosis	1,352
31	Division of State Psychological Association Affairs	559
32	Division of Humanistic Psychology	788
33	Division on Mental Retardation	836
34	Division of Population and Environmental Psychology	466
35	Division of the Psychology of Women	2,203
36	Psychologists Interested in Religious Issues	1,193
37	Division of Child, Youth, and Family Services	1,465
38	Division of Health Psychology	2,507
39	Division of Psychoanalysis	1,949
40	Division of Clinical Neuropsychology	1,785
41	The Psychology and Law Society	1,018
42	Division of Psychologists in Independent Practice	5,020
43	Division of Family Psychology	998
44	The Society for the Psychological Study of Lesbian and Gay Issues	458
	Total	71,093†

*There are no divisions 4 and 11.

†An APA member may be affiliated with one or more divisions. There are about 60,000 total members.

and they ask, "Will one type of person behave one way in the situation, while another type will behave in a different way?" Personality psychologists have developed a number of tests to measure such differences, as we will see in Chapter 14.

Developmental psychologists study the physical and psychological changes that accompany growth and aging. They are concerned with the effects of maturation and experience across the life span from birth to adulthood to old age. These psychologists may study people at particular ages, such as infancy or adolescence, or they may be interested in how specific skills change with development. People who study developmental psychology may use any of the general approaches or methods used in other branches of psychology, as we will discover in Chapters 9 and 10.

The major specialty within psychology involves practitioners who perform therapy to relieve psychological distress. They are called *clinical* and *counseling psychologists.* In fact, slightly over half the members of the American Psychological Association engage in therapy. Clinical psychologists may work in mental hospitals, mental health clinics, universities, other institutions, or private practice. They diagnose and treat behavior problems that range from ordinary anxiety to bizarre disorders. These issues are discussed in Chapters 15 and 16.

People often confuse clinical psychologists with psychiatrists. Typically psychologists have a Ph.D. or, sometimes, a Psy.D. (doctor of psychology), whereas psychiatrists are required to be doctors of medicine (M.D.'s). Psychiatrists can prescribe drugs, while clinical psychologists cannot. Clinical psychologists often work in conjunction with psychiatrists. Students interested in pursuing a career in clinical psychology should be aware that at least four to six years of postgraduate training are usually required. Counseling psychologists also employ psychological methods of therapy; however, they often work with less severe behavior problems than those faced by clinical psychologists.

The fields of *organizational* and *industrial psychology* are concerned with psychological factors in industry. These may include developing an organizational hierarchy, creating tests to match people with appropriate jobs, and improving morale and working conditions. *Engineering psychologists* try to develop equipment and systems that can be used more effectively. They take the human factor into account and thus are also called *human factors psychologists.* An increasing number of industries hire psychologists to devise more efficient interactions between people and machines and to promote motivation and job satisfaction. Others work in advertising, consumer behavior, or marketing research.

Educational psychologists study factors involved in learning, teaching, and schooling. Some work directly with students and educators in school settings. Others conduct research or provide teacher training in universities and colleges. Many educational psychologists have practical goals of improving effective teaching practices and student achievement. *School psychologists* are usually employed in primary and secondary schools; they give tests to help classify students (intelligence and personality tests) and to point them in the direction of suitable jobs (vocational aptitude tests). They also are trained to evaluate and deal with learning and emotional problems as well as to counsel students.

As factories become increasingly automated, psychologists are needed to design equipment so that is can be easily used by the human operators.

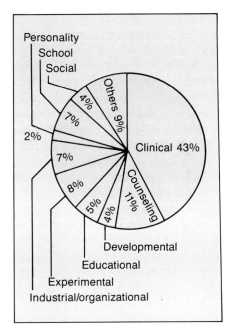

FIGURE 1–4
How Psychologists Divide Their Field

The chart shows the percentages of members of the American Psychological Association specializing in different areas of psychology.

Source: Based on data from Stapp & Fulcher, 1981, Table 2.

As is evident from Table 1–3, this chapter thus far has touched on only a few of the specialties within psychology. As psychology broadens to make contact with other fields, it spawns more subdisciplines. For example, some people now call themselves *environmental psychologists* because they study how noise pollution, air pollution, and crowding affect people's behavior. Figure 1–4 shows the breakdown of specialties among members of the American Psychological Association.

RESEARCH METHODS IN PSYCHOLOGY

Psychologists are curious about many different phenomena; they want to know how people's minds work and why they behave the way they do. But how do psychologists study these topics? What methods produce reliable information? In this section we will describe the main techniques psychologists use to study behavior.

Descriptive Research Techniques

Investigating any phenomenon first requires precise description of its features. Only after this preliminary stage can scientists develop theories to explain the phenomenon. Psychologists use several techniques to describe behavior, including naturalistic observation, case studies, interviews, surveys, and psychological tests.

NATURALISTIC OBSERVATION. Interest in many phenomena is sparked by simple observation. A researcher witnesses an event and wonders why it happened. Consider an occasional observation made by clinical psychologists working with chronic alcoholics. When intoxicated, the alcoholics would sometimes do something—such as hide a large sum of money—and then, when sober later, be completely unable to remember its location. This forgetting is hardly surprising because alcohol is one of many drugs that damages memory. The interesting observation made by the clinical psychologists was that when the alcoholics "fell off the wagon" the next time, they were able to remember their previous actions, in this case remembering the location of the money and retrieving it! This observation suggests an interesting idea: perhaps if people are intoxicated when they learn something, they later recall it better if they are drunk rather than sober. However, when using only an informal observation, we have no way of knowing if this hypothesis about the behavior is true. More advanced research methods—particularly experiments—are needed to answer this critical question.

As the name implies, *naturalistic observation* is the study of a phenomenon (such as an alcoholic's memory) in its natural context, outside a laboratory. The example of alcoholic amnesia represents the most casual form of observation. Typically, naturalistic observation is carried out much more systematically, so that researchers can measure frequency, time of occurrence, and other features of the phenomenon. This is often true in work by ethologists watching the ongoing behavior of a group of animals in the wild. Ethologists sample an animal's behavior at certain times and record its characteristics as carefully as possible.

One danger in observation is that if the objects of study know they are being observed, their behavior may change. This tendency seems especially true of humans. If a psychologist is interested in the factors that determine whether or not people will offer assistance during an emergency, the people under observation will probably be more helpful if they are aware that a psychologist is monitoring them. When a researcher's obvious presence affects the behavior observed, the observations are said to be *reactive* because they are partly a reaction to the presence of the observer. Researchers engaged in naturalistic observation strive for **nonreactive** or *unobtrusive* techniques to study behavior. For example, when studying animals in the wild, researchers may build blinds to hide themselves from the animals or let the novelty of their presence wear off before they begin recording data.

Naturalistic observation is often useful in the first stage of research and helps provide insight into the factors important in understanding a phenomenon. In studies of humans, such research is often complemented by case studies, interviews, and surveys.

CASE STUDIES. A *case study* is the intensive investigation of one particular instance of some phenomenon. By scrutinizing one case in detail, a researcher hopes to discover general principles concerning the phenomenon. Freud based his psychoanalytic theory on intensive case studies of his patients. In the example of an alcoholic who hides money while in a drunken stupor and can find it later only when in the same state, researchers might examine several case studies of such behavior. Do the alcoholics all behave similarly? Are the circumstances alike when they do so? To answer these questions, researchers must interview each alcoholic, record as precisely as possible the occurrence and the surrounding situation, and then note the outcome. The general aim would be to find principles that govern memory lapses and recoveries in alcoholics.

Information from case studies is not as useful as one would hope. First, since the event has already occurred, the researcher cannot vary the situation to see what effect different conditions might have. Second, people's memories might not be accurate; they might be unaware of the reasons for their forgetting, or they might even try to hide the reasons. This is especially true in cases where the subject was in an unusual state, such as being intoxicated. Obviously, one cannot place too much faith in reports made by someone who was drunk at the time events occurred. Third, even if useful information were obtained, how could a researcher know that the events true of one particular memory lapse would generalize to others? One danger of case studies is that they might mislead investigators into believing that principles derived from a single case apply to all cases. Do the principles Freud derived from observing a few neurotic Viennese patients apply to the personalities of all people? For all these reasons, psychologists do not view the case study method as a technique for producing conclusive results. As with naturalistic observation, case studies are mainly useful as sources of ideas that should then be better researched. However, case studies may be the only research tool available for studying the effects of unique events, such as brain damage, tornadoes, floods, and other natural disasters.

INTERVIEWS. Researchers can gather a great deal of information about people's behaviors, attitudes, and circumstances through personal question-

Biased polls predicted that Dewey would defeat Truman in the 1948 presidential election. When the vote was still close late on election night, some newspapers even went to press proclaiming Dewey's victory. Here Truman holds up one paper's blooper headline the day after the victory.

and-answer *interviews.* A researcher might interview alcoholics about their memories, their self-perceptions, or their family lives. In addition to recording a person's spoken answers, the interviewer might also note such nonverbal gestures as fidgeting and eye contact. The interview method is often used as part of the case study approach. The case study and interview approaches typically require extensive observation of a relatively limited number of subjects.

SURVEYS. The method of taking *surveys* is familiar to all of us from news reports. Surveys are used to measure our opinions of different politicians, the popularity of television shows, the degree of consumer confidence in the economy, and many other collective opinions. By sampling opinions of a small proportion of the population, a researcher can find information that will generalize to the population as a whole. The critical factor in survey research is obtaining the sample in an unbiased manner so that generalizations about the population will be accurate. A famous blunder in survey research was the prediction of the 1948 presidential election from a poll taken by *Literary Digest* magazine. The *Literary Digest* polled its readers and concluded that Thomas Dewey would beat Harry Truman in a landslide. The voting was quite close, and some newspapers even went to press with headlines proclaiming Dewey's victory. However, when the final vote was tallied, Truman won. *Literary Digest* had erred by assuming that its readership represented an accurate sample of American voters. However, the *Digest*'s readership was upper middle class and generally Republican, unlike the population as a whole.

Today survey researchers employ sophisticated techniques to ensure that the sample chosen is representative of the population at large. But any time researchers generalize to a population from a sample, there is some chance of error. Fortunately, the chances of error in a survey can be estimated and are often reported. You have probably heard statements such as "Our survey shows Reagan leading Mondale by 47% to 40% with 13% undecided. However, there is a 5% margin of error associated with these numbers." This means that the percentage of people favoring Reagan may vary from 42% to 52% and for Mondale from 35% to 45%. These numbers show that there is some small chance that the "true" preference would have Mondale leading Reagan at the time of the poll. Note, however, that this is unlikely.

Surveys are used to describe many psychological phenomena. For example, surveys can answer questions such as: What percentage of young adults visit a psychologist or other mental health worker? What percentage of new mothers breastfeed their children? What percentage of college students have engaged in premarital sex? What percentage of people over age 65 have been victims of a crime in the last 12 months? One potential drawback in survey research is in the lack of honesty and forthrightness on the part of the respondents. Questions about sensitive behaviors, such as sex and crime, may lead people to refuse to answer or to provide socially desirable, not necessarily true, answers.

PSYCHOLOGICAL TESTS. Psychologists have developed numerous paper-and-pencil *psychological tests* to measure and describe people's capabilities, characteristics, and interests. Chief among these are tests to measure mental abilities (intelligence tests) and personality characteristics. (These are reviewed in Chapters 11 and 14.) Other tests are designed to measure various forms of psychopathology, vocational interests, and creativity. You are probably most familiar with the Scholastic Aptitude Test (SAT), which many universities require. Individuals' scores on psychological tests provide useful information for describing and classifying people and for predicting their behavior.

A researcher's choice of naturalistic observation, case studies, psychological tests, interviews, or survey research depends on the situation and the goals of the research. Although such techniques yield much useful information, descriptive research is usually considered a first step. Rarely does detailed description permit a researcher to predict the behavior or explain why it occurs. To answer these questions other techniques are needed.

Correlational Research

One way to investigate a phenomenon is to study a number of cases, note the characteristics of each case, and see if the characteristics are related. To take a simple observation, weight and height tend to go together. Taller people usually weigh more than shorter people. Height and weight generally vary together, or are co-related. This type of observation is referred to as correlational; the relationship between two sets of measures is a *correlation.* In a correlational analysis a researcher wants to determine if two measures, or variables, are related. A *variable* is some characteristic that can be measured or manipulated. Height and weight are variables.

The *correlation coefficient,* a term we will use many times in this book, is a statistical measure of the relation between two variables. It can range from +1.00 through zero to −1.00. A positive correlation occurs when two variables change together in the same direction. For example, height and weight do tend to be positively correlated, with taller people being heavier, so the correlation coefficient for height and weight will be greater than zero. A correlation that is near zero indicates that the two variables are not related. For example, weight and intelligence are probably not correlated. If measures of weight and intelligence were taken from a large group of people, there would probably be no systematic relation between the two measures. The correlation coefficient would be near zero. A negative relation means that as one variable increases, the other decreases. There is a negative correlation between how overweight people are and how long they live. The more people exceed their optimal weight, the shorter their life expectancy. These concepts about correlation are discussed more fully in the Appendix, which is an introduction to the use of statistics in psychology.

Let us consider some further examples of correlations to show both their usefulness and their drawbacks. First, the average number of cigarettes smoked per day is positively correlated with the probability of getting lung cancer later. That is, the more cigarettes one smokes, the more likely one is to get lung cancer. An example of more interest to psychologists is the positive correlation between watching violent television programs and measures of aggression (such as the tendency for schoolchildren to get into fights or for adults to commit crimes). The correlation is far from perfect in both cases. That is, some people smoke heavily but never get lung cancer, and others watch much violence on television and yet never get in fights or commit crimes. Still, the correlation permits us to make predictions: all else being equal, we can predict that a person who smokes heavily will be more likely to develop lung cancer than another person who does not smoke. Similarly, a child who watches much violence on television is more likely to get into fights with friends. Correlations are most useful for making predictions about behaviors, although the stronger the correlation (the nearer to $+1$ or to -1), the better is the prediction.

The natural conclusion to reach in these cases is that smoking causes lung cancer and that watching violent television causes aggression. However, based simply on the fact of a correlation, both of these conclusions are unwarranted. Always remember that *correlation does not indicate causation*. Using only the facts given so far, one cannot conclude that smoking causes lung cancer or that watching violent television causes aggression. For example, perhaps children who are already aggressive for other reasons simply prefer to watch violent television. Thus, some other factor might cause both the children's aggressiveness and the desire to watch violent television programs. The danger inherent in correlational research is that one can arrive at misleading conclusions by not taking other factors into account. Further research is necessary to pin down a causal relationship.

Let us take an actual example from research by Sandra Scarr (1985), a developmental psychologist. She was interested in determining whether or not child-rearing techniques used by parents were related to later skills and behavior of the children, such as their intelligence, their ability to communicate, and their social adjustment. Scarr developed several measures of how mothers discipline their children, both from interviews and from observing the mothers interacting with their children in a teaching situation. Positive discipline behaviors included reasoning with children and explaining material verbally; negative behaviors included such things as physical punishment. Scarr found several positive correlations between good disciplinary techniques of the mother and the child's later IQ, communication skills, and social adjustment. Mothers who reasoned with their children had brighter, more communicative, and better-adjusted children.

The straightforward conclusion would seem to be that the good techniques of the mother caused the positive outcomes in the child's scores. However, Scarr performed another analysis that undermined this conclusion. She measured the mothers' IQs and correlated those with the effective discipline techniques of the mothers and the positive outcomes for the children. She discovered that mothers' intelligence correlated positively with their likelihood to use good teaching strategies and also with their likelihood of having children with higher IQs, better communication skills, and good social adjustment. Indeed, when the mothers' IQs were removed statistically, the teaching strategies used by the mothers were no longer related to the intelligence, communication skills, and social adjustment of the children! Apparently, more intelligent mothers simply employ good teaching strategies and have children with better skills, but no evidence could be found that the good teaching strategies *caused* the better skills in the children. (See Figure 1–5.) Of course, this is only one study, and so the conclusion that parents' disciplinary techniques have no effect on children's behaviors is clearly premature. However, this study does point out the dangers of simply using a positive correlation as evidence of a cause-and-effect relation.

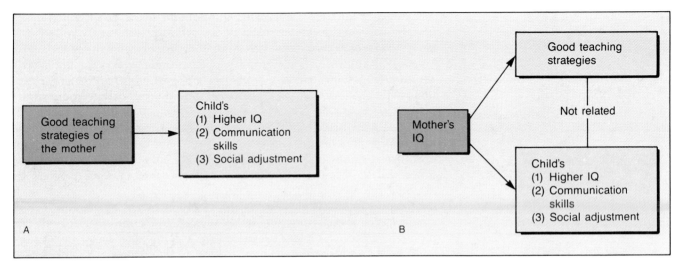

FIGURE 1–5
Correlation and Causation

Scarr (1985) found that good teaching strategies employed by mothers correlated later with their children's intelligence, communication skills, and social adjustment. A natural conclusion, shown in part A, is that the strategies used by the mothers caused the children's behaviors. However, an alternative interpretation—and the one supported by Scarr's data—is shown in B. Mothers' intelligence is correlated with the teaching strategies they use and with development of skills in their children. When mothers' IQs are taken into account, no relation exists between teaching strategies and children's skills. Researchers should not assume that correlation means causation because other factors may be the true cause of the correlation.

In summary, correlational analyses provide information about relationships between variables, but they typically cannot tell conclusively about the reasons for the relation because some factor other than the one under question may be responsible. The technical term for this problem is *confounding.* When a researcher cannot be sure which of two factors or variables caused some result, the two are said to be confounded. In the above example, the correlation between mothers' discipline strategies and children's intellectual and social skills could either be caused by (1) the teaching strategies or (2) some other factor, such as the mothers' intelligence. The potential for confounding is inherent in correlational research. Statistical procedures that take other factors into account when the correlation coefficient is computed can sometimes minimize the danger. However, experimental research is generally preferred to correlational research because the potential for confounding is greatly reduced.

Experimental Research

In correlational research the researcher observes relations between variables that occur naturally. In *experimental research,* the investigator creates a situation that allows for controlled observation. The essence of the experimen-

TABLE 1–4
Basic Research Procedures and Their Purposes

Procedures	Purpose	Questions to Answer
Observation	Description	What happens? How often? How much?
Correlation	Prediction	How do factors relate?
Experiment	Explanation Determine causation	Why? How?

tal method is to vary some aspect of a situation, control all others, and then observe the effects of the variation on the behavior of interest.

The simplest case of experimental research involves an experimental condition and a control condition. The experimental condition contains the variable of interest. The control condition does not but is included for comparison. The two conditions are arranged to be as similar as possible except for the one critical factor of interest. Imagine that there are two characteristics of the control condition that are important, and call them *A* and *B*. A researcher is interested in the effects of some critical variable, *C*, on behavior. Thus in the experimental condition there are three important factors, *A*, *B*, and *C*. In comparing the effects of the experimental and control conditions, the researcher can see what effect the critical factor *C* has on the dependent measure. The two other factors have been held constant in the two conditions, so the conditions differ only in the factor of interest.

An important part of experimental logic is ***random assignment*** of the research participants to the experimental and control conditions to ensure that there is no confounded variable. In random assignment, subjects have an equal chance of being placed in each condition, so bias can be avoided. Suppose men were assigned to the experimental condition and women to the control condition, and a difference was found between the two conditions. The researcher would not know whether to attribute the difference to the variable of interest (*C*) or the subjects' sex, or both. The variable of sex would be confounded with the experimental variable.

To make these matters more concrete, let us follow up an observation described earlier with an actual experiment. Recall the incidents reported by clinical psychologists about amnesia in alcoholics and how their forgetting could be reversed when they later became intoxicated again. Is this a general phenomenon or an observation true of only one or two striking cases? This question is difficult to answer by methods of casual observation, but it is

These researchers are testing a human subject to see how well she can perceive and remember different information presented simultaneously at a rapid rate to the two ears. The aim is to gain an understanding of how people attend to information and remember it. Research based on this technique is discussed in Chapter 5.

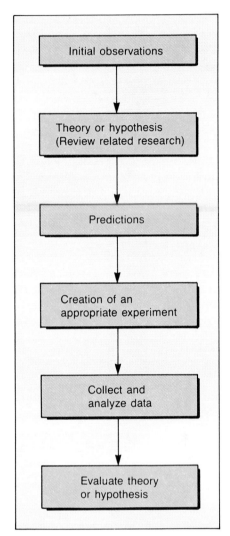

FIGURE 1–6
Stages in the Research Process

Research often proceeds from some initial observations that arouse curiosity to more systematic experimental inquiry.

made to order for experimental methods. We will follow through the stages occurring in typical experimental research with this example. An overview of the stages is presented in Figure 1–6.

INITIAL OBSERVATIONS. Research is often inspired by casual observations. The researcher might read about alcoholics' remembering better while intoxicated than while sober and wonder why it happens. Research can also be sparked by other experiments, from conversations in which ideas emerge, or from any other source. The genius of formulating a research problem from a casual observation is in taking commonplace examples and attempting to see behind them to what general principle or causal factor underlies them.

GENERATING A HYPOTHESIS. From the initial casual observations that spark research, one must generate a theory or hypothesis that can be translated into an experiment. A **theory** is a *set of statements proposing concepts and relationships among them in order to explain a phenomenon or a body of data.* The term *theory* is used when the statements are explicit and fairly formal. Famous scientific theories include Newton's laws of motion, Einstein's theory of relativity, and Darwin's theory of evolution by natural selection. We will meet many psychological theories in this book.

A **hypothesis** is usually a less formal conjecture that is put forward to explain some facts and to predict others. The hypothesis may be developed from a more formal theory, or it may simply be a hunch. Experiments are created to test hypotheses. A scientific hypothesis is useful only if it can be subjected to an **empirical test** that bears on its truth or falsity. (*Empirical* refers to knowledge based on observation.)

With regard to the alcoholic's memory problem described above, we may hypothesize that it represents a case of **state-dependent retrieval:** information is sometimes recalled better when a person's pharmacological (drug) state at the time of testing matches the original learning state than when the learning and test states mismatch. The informal observations agree with this idea, but more systematic research must be conducted to confirm it. Casual observation about the world often produces wrong answers. For example, the earth is not flat, although it appears so, and the sun does not revolve around the earth as the moon does. However, for centuries both of these ideas were believed because of people's direct observation. Systematic research can uncover people's erroneous beliefs and modify them.

PREDICTIONS. The next step in the scientific process is to obtain predictions from the theory or hypothesis under test. As just mentioned, a theory or hypothesis is useful in science only if it can be subjected to experimental test. Often creativity is required to derive predictions from a theory because predictions may not be obvious and may require a chain of reasoning. However, in the case of the state-dependent retrieval hypothesis, the prediction is mercifully straightforward: if people learn information when they are either sober or intoxicated and are then tested either in the same state or the opposite state, they should perform better when tested in the same state.

CREATION OF THE EXPERIMENT. Even when one has a simple hypothesis to test with concrete predictions, the creation and design of an appropriate experiment are not always straightforward. Any idea can be tested in many specific ways. Consider the questions that must be solved in designing an experiment to test the idea that state-dependent retrieval exists. How much alcohol does one give the intoxicated subjects? What kind of subjects should be chosen for the experiment? What kind of material should they learn? How long should the delay be between study and test? What kind of test should be given? This list could be extended almost indefinitely, but the critical point is that the creation of any experiment involves many choices that may affect its outcome.

Rather than considering hypothetical cases, let us examine an experiment conducted by Eric Eich and his colleagues (1975). With the permission of appropriate government agencies, they tested the state-dependent memory effects of marijuana. We can use their experiment for our purposes because the results with alcohol would be almost exactly the same (Eich, 1980). Subjects in the Eich experiment served in four different conditions depending on their "state" (drugged or sober) at the time of learning and testing of the material. To induce the drugged state, people smoked a marijuana cigarette 20 minutes before they learned the material or were tested on it. In the nondrugged state, they smoked a cigarette that tasted like marijuana but from which the active ingredient had been removed. (In experiments using drugs it is important to include such a *placebo* condition because the expectations aroused when people know they are taking drugs often help determine the effects of those drugs. Thus, in the *placebo control condition,* people expect that they are taking drugs, but they are not.) To ensure that the drug was having an effect, the experimenters checked both objective measures, such as heart rate (the drug increases it) and subjective reports obtained from rating scales (asking, for example, "How 'high' do you feel?"). Marijuana had a large effect on both measures relative to the placebo condition.

The volunteers who served in the experiment were tested in the four conditions as shown in Figure 1–7. They studied lists of words in either the placebo or the drugged condition and then were tested in either the placebo or the drugged state four hours later. The learning material consisted of 48 words from different categories (for example, furniture, professions, etc.). Thus subjects might have heard "Professions: doctor, lawyer, professor, dentist," and so on. Two types of tests were given. First, people were given a blank sheet of paper and simply asked to recall as many words as possible in any order (a *free recall test*). Another group of people was given a *cued recall test,* in which the experimenter provided specific category names (e.g., Professions) and then asked the subjects to recall words from the list belonging to the category.

COLLECT AND ANALYZE THE DATA. The next step in the research process is to test the subjects, collect the data, and perform statistical analyses on the data. In the Eich experiment, 15 subjects were tested in each of the four conditions. The researchers calculated the average number of words recalled in each condition (given on the right side of Table 1–5). Considering free recall first, performance was best if people were sober both when they studied the material and were tested on it (11.5 words recalled out of a possible 48). If the subjects learned the material when sober but were tested when under the influence of marijuana (the placebo–drug condition), they did not

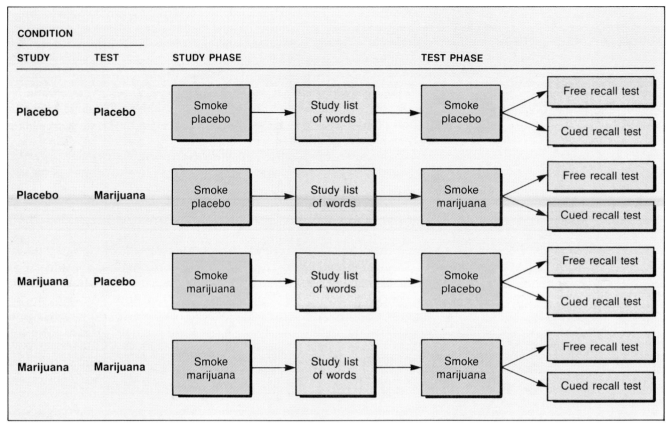

FIGURE 1–7
Experimental Design in the State-Dependent Retrieval Experiment

recollect as many words (9.9 words recalled). Thus, as other studies also show, marijuana impedes retrieval of information. The subjects did even worse if they studied the material under marijuana and then were tested sober (the drug–placebo condition)—6.7 words recalled. This indicates the usual impairment of learning and memory by drugs when people are removed from the drug.

A critical condition for the state-dependent retrieval hypothesis is the last one, where people studied information in the drugged state and then

TABLE 1–5
Results of the Eich et al. (1975) Experiment on State-Dependent Retrieval

Condition		Average Number of Words Recalled	
Study	Test	Free Recall	Cued Recall
Placebo	Placebo	11.5	24.0
Placebo	Drug	9.9	23.7
Drug	Placebo	6.7	22.6
Drug	Drug	10.5	22.3

When a person's "state" during the test matches the one in which the information was learned, free recall is improved. When strong retrieval cues are provided, however, the state-dependency effect is overcome.

were tested in the same state four hours later. Would these people recall the material better than those who learned while under the drug but were tested sober? As you can see in the drug–drug condition in Table 1–5, the answer is yes. When people acquired material in a drugged state, they recalled more words when placed back in the drugged state (10.5) than when tested sober (6.7). However, you should note that even when people are returned to the drugged state in the drug–drug condition, they do not recall as well as when both study and test were in the placebo condition (when people were sober). This difference between the placebo–placebo and the drug–drug conditions is even larger in other experiments. Thus, depressive drugs such as marijuana may affect how well information is stored, as well as affecting memory retrieval.

EVALUATE THE HYPOTHESIS. The free recall results confirm the hypothesis that state-dependent retrieval exists because people remembered the material better when the test state matched the study state than when the states mismatched. But the story is not that simple. Look now at the cued recall results shown at the far right of Table 1–5. This is the case in which people were given category names as retrieval cues to help them recall the list items. In general, the cues did help because the scores in cued recall were higher than in free recall. But a most interesting thing happens here: the state-dependency effect goes away! Recall in all four conditions was about the same. How can this be explained? Eich (1980) suggests that a person's state—drugged or not drugged—serves as a retrieval cue. If you learn something with the cue present, you will retrieve it better when the cue is present in the situation. However, if other powerful external retrieval cues are provided, such as category names, then people will rely on these, which will overpower the more subtle ''state'' cues. When such powerful external cues are absent, as on the free recall test, then the subtle physiological cues will come into play. Therefore, state-dependent retrieval may occur only when people do not have other strong cues to aid their memories.

An important point is that the type of test chosen could have determined the outcome of the experiment. If Eich and his colleagues had chosen to use only a free recall test, they would have concluded that state-dependent retrieval is a fact. If they had chosen to use only a cued recall test, then they would have concluded that state-dependent retrieval did not exist. Obviously, using both types of tests provides the most accurate picture of the situation. But as pointed out above, experimenters must make many choices when they create an experiment, and these choices may have unknown effects in determining the outcome. A single experiment rarely settles any issue; rather, many investigations using varying methods are needed to provide a more complete understanding.

Eich (1980) examined many studies of the state-dependent retrieval phenomenon. He discovered that only about half the studies showed a reliable state-dependent effect, with performance better in the drug–drug state than in the drug–placebo state. However, when he separated the experiments into groups on the basis of the type of test given, he discovered that almost all experiments that used a free recall test found the state-dependent retrieval phenomenon, whereas very few experiments that used cued recall tests found any effect. This kind of scientific detective work is critical in unraveling what seem to be conflicting results between experiments. Until

Eich's (1980) review, many writers had concluded that state-dependent retrieval was not a real phenomenon because only about half the studies obtained it. As Eich's incisive work shows, state-dependent retrieval is, in fact, a very reliable phenomenon, but it occurs only under certain conditions.

Systematic experimental research, such as that described here, takes us much further than do casual observations of alcoholics' memories. In an uncontrolled clinical situation, many other factors vary, and one cannot know which ones are critical in producing the phenomenon. Experimental methods are needed to establish cause-and-effect relations. Experiments employ a number of different variables, considered in the next section.

TYPES OF VARIABLES. Variables, you will recall, are characteristics of a situation that can be manipulated or measured. But there are several different types of variables in an experimental situation. *Independent variables* are those the researcher manipulates during the experiment to discover their effects on behavior. In the state-dependent retrieval experiment, the independent variable was the state of the person during the study and testing of the material (drug–placebo, drug–drug, etc.). *Dependent variables* are those the experimenter measures as part of the experiment. They are so named because what they show typically *depends on* the level of the independent variable. The dependent variables in the memory experiment were the number of words recalled by people under free recall and cued recall conditions. A *control variable* is some aspect of the situation that could be manipulated, or allowed to vary, but is kept constant by the experimenter. In the memory experiment, the type and amount of material, the type of subjects, and the situation in which the experiment was conducted were all control variables. By controlling variables except the independent variable, the experimenter can be reasonably certain that the observed effect is due to the independent variable rather than to some confounded variable. Once again, this control is a reason that experiments are the preferred method of psychological research. Other factors are held constant and cannot vary with the independent variables of interest (except by accident) to confound the outcome of the research. In naturalistic observation or correlational research, such confoundings usually cannot be ruled out.

Independent variables, then, are those that are manipulated; dependent variables are those that are measured; and control variables are those that are held constant. The experiment concerning the effects of marijuana on learning and memory involved two independent variables and two dependent variables. The independent variables were the state of the people when they learned information at study and at test. The two states at study (drug, placebo) and two states at test (the same) combine to give four separate conditions. The two dependent variables were the number of words recalled in free and cued recall. Technically, this type of experiment is called a *multifactor experiment* because there is more than one independent variable involved. Often experiments can be extended to include more variables than even two or three. Such multifactor experiments are useful because they can potentially provide more information than single-factor experiments. In a single-factor experiment, subjects might have been given the drug either at study or at test, but not both. Multifactor experiments are more efficient and can show whether the effect of some particular variable generalizes across other variables.

RESEARCH ISSUES

Several general issues about experimental research will appear repeatedly in this book. We briefly discuss five of them in this final section.

Use of Nonhuman Animals in Research

A good part of the research on some topics in psychology is conducted with animals other than humans. Students sometimes find this surprising and disheartening. Isn't the goal of psychology to understand the behavior of humans? While most psychologists might answer "yes," others are interested in the psychology of animals in its own right. The study of animal behavior poses some fascinating problems. How do homing pigeons find their way? Why is it so hard to poison rats? How do wolves and other animals establish social hierarchies? But psychologists can also study the behavior of so-called lower animals with hopes of finding principles that will generalize to the behavior of humans. Many types of research, such as those requiring brain surgery, cannot be done with humans for ethical or practical reasons.

The difficulty in applying research done with one species to another species, including humans, is that of *generality of results.* How do investigators know that principles derived from one species will generalize to another? They do not, for sure, but researchers generally assume that principles derived from animal research can be used as a hypothesis for human behavior, and they abandon this assumption only when forced to by contrary evidence. The issue of generality of animal research findings to humans is not, of course, unique to psychology. If some substance such as saccharin is shown to cause cancer in laboratory mice, should the government ban the item from supermarket shelves?

Internal and External Validity

The *internal validity* of a piece of research refers to whether or not the conclusion drawn about the cause-and-effect relation between variables is sound. If a researcher concludes that the independent variable did affect the dependent variable, can the conclusion stand? The main reason for doubting the internal validity of research is that some other variable might have been confounded with the independent variable of interest.

In general, case studies and correlational studies lack internal validity because of the potential problem of confounded variables. Experimental methods foster greater internal validity because they hold constant these other variables (which then become control variables) to make a more precise determination of the effects of the independent variable.

External validity refers to generalizability, which we touched on in the discussion of animal research. Over what range of conditions does a research conclusion remain valid? Does it generalize to other populations?

(Rats to humans? Males to females? Caucasians to Orientals?) Does it apply to different measures of behavior? Does it apply to different ways of varying the independent variable? A researcher could deprive an animal of food for different numbers of hours or keep it at various percentages of normal body weight (95 percent, 90 percent, 85 percent, etc.). Would these two ways of varying hunger—hours of deprivation and percentage of body weight—affect behavior identically? Would findings of one study generalize to the other method? All these are questions of external validity.

The external validity of a piece of research can be determined only by more research to see if the conclusions do generalize. Researchers often wonder whether their findings will generalize to other situations or settings. This concern leads to the next issue, that of laboratory and field research.

Laboratory and Field Research

Much experimental research in psychology is done in the laboratory. There, researchers have control over the situation and can improve the internal validity of their investigations. The researcher hopes to bring the important aspects of some interesting natural behavior into the laboratory for more careful study.

In the example of the effects of alcohol on memory, researchers tried to create a laboratory situation to examine the state-dependent retrieval phenomenon observed in alcoholics by clinical psychologists. But if the phenomenon had not been confirmed in the laboratory, would this mean that it did not exist or that the artificial laboratory conditions failed to capture the critical variables?

Some psychologists argue that psychological research has too often been beset by this difficulty. They contend that psychologists have often overemphasized experimental control so that a great deal of time and effort is spent studying artificial laboratory situations that have little to do with

Developmental psychologists often study children's behavior in the home with the mother present. The home environment can elicit more natural reactions from the child. Here, the psychologist's interest centers on which features in the pictures the child attends to.

naturally occurring phenomena. In other words, laboratory situations may have little external validity.

One way to try to maximize both internal and external validity is to do controlled research in the field, i.e., in natural settings. Through such "field research" investigators attempt to introduce a measure of control into the situation of interest and then vary some aspects to see how they affect behavior. Interesting findings may be obtained, but there are also pitfalls. Ethical problems may arise in experimenting with people who have not given their permission to be studied. In addition, the control that can be applied to natural situations usually is limited, so that confounding from uncontrolled variables can create a lack of internal validity.

Despite the problems connected with field research, more researchers are using the technique to increase the external validity of findings. However, laboratory research is also important. It has served other sciences well, and there seems little reason that the same cannot be true in psychology. For example, physicists have discovered a great deal about interesting properties of matter from studying how it behaves in a vacuum, yet no natural vacuums exist on our planet. When a laboratory analogue of some phenomenon is created, it is often desirable to mimic aspects of the naturally occurring situation as closely as possible. But the main reason for laboratory research is to test causal hypotheses about the relation between variables rather than to establish the generality (external validity) of this relation (Berkowitz & Donnerstein, 1982).

Basic and Applied Research

A distinction is often made between basic and applied research. *Applied research* aims at solving some practical problem. *Basic research* is done with no particular application to solving a practical problem in mind, but to discover basic facts about some phenomenon. The distinction is not an exclusive one, and there can be varying degrees on the basic–applied dimension. Students can readily appreciate the reasons for applied research since it is easy to understand why people want to solve practical problems. But scientists often have trouble convincing people that basic research deserves as much, or more, attention and support. People ask why scientists should spend their time working on problems whose solutions seem likely to provide no immediate practical benefit. The first answer, of course, is the desire to satisfy intellectual curiosity. But the more subtle reason is that basic research often allows more practical benefits in the long run than applied research. Basic research is concerned with understanding the general principles that govern some phenomenon; a great number of practical applications may flow from this knowledge. While applied research may answer some specific question, it may not provide the general knowledge to solve other problems. However, even applied research can sometimes open up new areas and provide basic understanding of phenomena (Garner, 1972). For example, interest in the problem of how air traffic controllers simultaneously monitor information from different sources led psychologists to do basic research on divided attention, a topic discussed in Chapter 5.

Psychologists who work in some areas, such as experimental psychology, tend to concentrate on basic research, while clinical, industrial, and school psychologists usually do applied research. Probably too much has been made of the distinction between basic and applied research. Good basic research will often pay dividends in application. Good applied research may help highlight basic principles of behavior.

Ethics in Research

Psychologists investigating some topics often come up against thorny ethical questions. For example, subjects in the experiment of Eich et al. (1975) were drugged as part of the experiment. Is this justified? The participants gave their consent to be in the study, were young and healthy, and were kept in the lab until the effects of marijuana wore off. Thus, potential harm was minimized.

The American Psychological Association (1981) has published a manual providing guidance on issues of research ethics. The Eich et al. (1975) experiment was done within the APA's current ethical standards. The guidelines encourage researchers to treat participants in the research in a considerate manner. Extremely stressful procedures are forbidden, and people are given the right to leave the situation if they feel uncomfortable. Any stress induced must be quite brief and mild and must be offset by gains in knowledge that should come from the research.

Psychologists usually take elaborate safeguards to ensure that their research is conducted within accepted ethical standards. After an experiment there is typically a debriefing session during which subjects are told the purposes of the research and what has been learned. They should emerge from the experience with knowledge about how psychological research is conducted and about the particular topic under study.

In most colleges and universities a committee ensures that research accords with ethical standards. Since many students reading this book will be asked to participate in research as part of a course requirement or for extra credit, you should be assured that any such research has been approved by an ethical standards committee.

Ethical standards have also been established for research with animals, and university and government committees approve and oversee experiments with animals. In general, these standards specify that animals must be housed in clean environments and suffer no unnecessary pain or discomfort during experimental procedures. Of course, many experimental interventions are carried out with animals that would not be possible with humans, both in psychological research and in many other types (biological, veterinary, medical). In recent years animal rights groups have protested many types of animal research and have uncovered some flagrant abuses. However, most research is conducted within the ethical standards established for the care and maintenance of laboratory animals. Work with animals carries great benefits both for humans and for the treatment of animals in veterinary settings. Neal Miller (1985) has described many of the benefits to humans that have grown out of basic research with animals. These include rehabilitation of neuromuscular disorders; discovery and testing of drugs for the treatment of anxiety, psychoses, and Parkinson's disease; knowledge about drug addiction; and many aspects of psychotherapy and behavioral medicine, to mention but a few. The ethical issues of experimenting on animals are difficult ones, but most psychologists believe that such research is permissible for its possible benefits, so long as it is conducted within the ethical guidelines that have been established.

SUMMARY

1. Psychology is the study of mental processes and behavior. Psychologists study mental processes indirectly by studying behavior.

2. Scientific psychology had its beginnings in the mid-1800s. The structural school of psychology was concerned with the study of conscious experience through analytic introspection. The functionalist school was concerned with the adaptive significance of mental processes. Behaviorists believed that psychology should be the science of behavior. Gestaltists argued for the study of the phenomena of conscious experience, mostly through verbal reports. They emphasized that perceptual events should not be divided into arbitrary sensations, as they accused the structuralists of doing. The psychoanalytic approach was concerned with discovering unconscious motivations.

3. Five current approaches to psychological phenomena are the biological, behavioral, cognitive, psychoanalytic, and humanistic. Most psychologists agree that the study of mind and behavior demands a scientific approach.

4. Numerous subfields or areas of special interest have developed within psychology. Most important are experimental, social, personality, developmental, clinical, counseling, organizational, industrial, educational, and school psychology.

5. Explanations for psychological phenomena are offered on various levels, ranging from biochemical to social. Most complex phenomena must be analyzed in terms of factors operating at different levels, from molecular (neural or hormonal factors) to molar (for example, social or cultural factors).

6. Methods for psychological research differ and include descriptive techniques (naturalistic observation, case studies, surveys and interviews), correlational analyses, and laboratory experimentation.

7. Naturalistic observation involves the study of a behavior under naturally occurring conditions. A case study is the intensive investigation of a single incident or event. Surveys and interviews usually involve less information from each person than a case study, but many more people are observed. The conclusions that can be drawn from these types of research are usually limited, but the methods can identify ideas for more systematic research.

8. Correlational research involves relating measures of two dimensions or variables to see how they go together. If the two measures vary together, researchers cannot conclude that one variable caused the other because there is always the possibility that some other variable may have produced the observed result, a situation called a confounding of variables.

9. Experimental research is generally preferred to other types because the danger of confounding can be minimized and firmer conclusions can be drawn. The variable that is manipulated is the independent variable; the variable that is observed and measured is the dependent variable; and the variables that are held constant are the control variables.

10. Internal validity refers to the soundness of research conclusions: Is the researcher correct in attributing the change in the dependent variable to the independent variable? External validity refers to generalizability of research findings: Do they apply to other subjects, other settings, and other manipulations and measures? Laboratory research typically has high internal validity, whereas field research usually has greater external validity.

SUGGESTED READINGS

American Psychological Association. (1978). *A career in psychology*. Washington, D.C.: American Psychological Association.

> A great deal of information is provided in this booklet on the different fields and careers within psychology. There is also discussion of what types of training are necessary to become a psychologist. You may obtain a free copy by writing to the American Psychological Association, 1200 Seventeenth Street N.W., Washington, D.C. 20036.

Elmes, D. G., Kantowitz, B. H., & Roediger, H. L. (1985). *Research methods in psychology* (2nd ed.). St. Paul: West.

> An introduction to research methods in psychology with emphasis on experimental methods.

Heidbreder, E. (1933). *Seven psychologies.* New York: Appleton-Century-Crofts.

> A lucid account of seven schools of psychology, including structuralism, functionalism, behaviorism, Gestalt psychology, and psychoanalysis.

Hyman, R. (1964). *The nature of psychological inquiry.* Englewood Cliffs, N.J.: Prentice-Hall.

> An engaging introduction to scientific inquiry as applied to psychology.

Schultz, D. (1981). *A history of modern psychology* (3rd ed.). New York: Academic Press.

> A readable history of psychology is presented here. The book is relatively brief, yet it provides a good overview of the history of psychology.

2

Biological Bases of Behavior

To look into our hearts is not enough, one must look into the cerebral cortex.

T. S. Eliot

As YOUR EYES SCAN THIS PRINTED PAGE, A SMALL MIRACLE TAKES place within your skull, a process you naturally take for granted. The cells within your brain, which make up a dazzling, complex network of electrical currents, are relaying information at speeds of up to 200 miles per hour. Somehow these electrical transmissions act to guide your eyes across the page, help you to perceive the size and shapes of letters, and let you translate these splotches of ink into a meaningful message. Meanwhile, the same network of cells is performing another complicated task: regulating the heart, the lungs, and all the muscles in your body.

The human brain has given us the ability to create literature, art, and music, to build great cities, to travel to the moon, and to attempt to understand itself—one of our most difficult challenges. Understanding the human brain and how it directs our behavior is the task of psychobiologists who are members of the rapidly growing field of neuroscience. The advances in neuroscience over the last decade have been remarkable. Discoveries have been made relating disorders in brain chemistry to psychological disorders such as depression and schizophrenia. The brain has been found to produce its own morphine, and speculation is that this may explain phenomena ranging from a runner's high (the euphoria some runners report) to the pain-reducing effects of acupuncture. We now know that in some sense humans really have two brains, with the right side of the brain having quite different functions from the left side. And we have exciting new ways to measure the level of activity of various parts of the brain, making it possible to relate specific behaviors to specific brain areas. In this chapter we will discuss the biological bases of behavior, beginning by describing what is known about the human brain and concluding with a discussion of evolution and genetics.

NEURONS AND TRANSMISSION OF INFORMATION

To understand the brain it is necessary to understand its basic element, the *neuron,* or nerve cell, and the network of connections linking neuron to neuron. To perform any function—to breathe, to sing, to write the great American novel—we must rely on the communication of information from neuron to neuron. Estimates of the number of neurons in the nervous system vary widely; the brain contains perhaps 100 billion neurons. One gram of brain tissue can contain 200 million neurons, and on average each of these neurons comes into contact with several thousand others. One major difference between neurons and other cells in the body, is that after a certain point shortly after birth no new neurons are produced. New connections among neurons are formed throughout life, however, and particular behaviors are the result of the development of particular connections. The number of possible connections among neurons in one human brain is estimated to be greater than the total number of atomic particles in the universe. Indeed, there really is no limit to the variety of possible connections (Thompson, 1985).

Structure and Function of Neurons

FIGURE 2–1
Neurons

A. *A sensory neuron.* The dendrites of sensory neurons receive information about the outside environment, and the axons of these cells pass this information on to other neurons. B. *A motor neuron.* The dendrites of motor neurons receive signals from neurons in the brain and spinal cord, and the axons of these cells activate the muscles, organs, and glands of the body. Also shown is the myelin sheath covering the axon. C. *Interneurons.* This is a highly simplified drawing of the network of neurons in the brain. Most interneurons connect with thousands of other neurons. The dendrites of interneurons receive information from other neurons, and the axons of these neurons send information to other neurons.

Neurons are made up of a cell body, dendrites, and an axon. The *cell body* of the neuron contains the nucleus and cytoplasm; it is where much of the metabolic work of the neuron takes place. The *dendrites* comprise a network of tiny fibers that reach out from the cell body, like the branches of a tree (*dendron* is Greek for "tree"). The *axon* is a long, slender tube that also extends from the cell body (see Figure 2–1). What we refer to as *nerves* are actually collections of axons in close proximity.

Communication of information among the billions of neurons is carried out by the dendrites, cell body, and axon. The dendrites and cell body receive signals from other neurons; the axon, in turn, sends the signals on to other cells. Conduction within the cell is one-way: from dendrite to axon. The neuron (cell body, dendrites, and axon) is enclosed by a *cell membrane,* which actively protects the cell, excluding some substances and admitting others. The membrane is complex: some of its regions contain specialized molecules that detect substances outside the cell and inform the inside of their presence; other regions do the reverse, detecting substances inside the

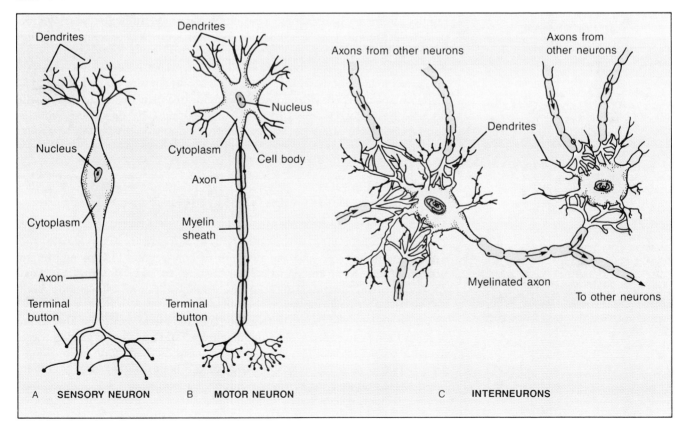

A   SENSORY NEURON   B   MOTOR NEURON   C   INTERNEURONS

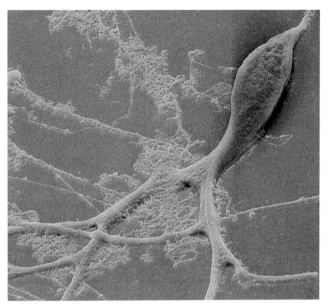

FIGURE 2–2
Photographs of Neurons

On the left is a photograph of an actual neuron. On the right is a partial cross section of the spinal cord showing the cell bodies, dendrites, and axons of neurons in the spinal cord.

cell and informing the outside. The membrane, as we will see, is the key to communication between neurons.

Neurons come in many different shapes and sizes. Scientists usually classify them into three types: sensory neurons, motor neurons, and interneurons (see Figures 2–1 and 2–2). *Sensory neurons* receive and convey information about the environment. Their dendrites pick up signals directly from specialized *receptor cells* that respond to light, pressure, and other external stimuli. The retinas of each eye, for example, are made up of thousands of receptor cells. Sensory neurons pass information about the environment on to other neurons, and this process enables us to see, hear, touch, smell, and taste. (We have much more to say about how the human senses work in Chapter 3.) Whereas information is conveyed to the brain via sensory neurons, *motor neurons* carry signals from the brain and spinal cord to the muscles, organs, and glands of the body. The third and by far most common type of neuron in the human brain is the *interneuron,* which connects one neuron with another.

Neurons are not the only type of cell in the brain. Among the other important types are the various *glial cells.* (*Glia* is Greek for "glue." Early researchers thought of glial cells as "gluing" the nervous system together.) Some glial cells may help to supply neurons with nutrients and to remove waste. Other glial cells eliminate neurons that have died of injury or disease; traveling around, they push against and ultimately engulf portions of dead neurons with which they come in contact. An important function of certain specialized glial cells is to provide the *myelin sheath,* a segmented tube of glial cells that insulates the axons of many neurons.

Conduction of Information Within the Neuron

As far as we know, neurons in such diverse animals as earthworms, jellyfish, ants, and humans all conduct information in the same way. Indeed,

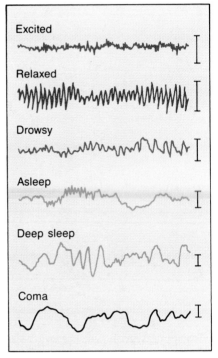

FIGURE 2–3
Electroencephalogram (EEG)

These EEG recordings illustrate the differences in the pattern of overall electrical activity in the brain. When a person is excited, there are rapid changes in electrical activity. A person in a coma, by contrast, shows very slow, erratic changes in electrical activity.

Source: Penfield & Jasper, 1954.

much of what we know about conduction of information within the neuron has come from studies of the axon of the giant squid.

The process of neuronal conduction is based on principles of electricity and chemistry. Like an ordinary household battery, the inactive neuron is polarized. Its inside has an electrical charge, or potential, relative to the outside of the cell, and neuronal conduction takes place when the cell depolarizes, or undergoes a decrease in its potential. Scientists can measure brain activity by "tapping into" the neuron's circuitry, with a device called the *electroencephalogram,* or *EEG.* The EEG measures the electrical activity of thousands of neurons in the brain's outer layer, or cortex, as they discharge together. Activity of different parts of the brain can then be compared by examining differences in EEG patterns (see Figure 2–3). Methods have even been developed to measure the electrical activity of single neurons in reaction to different stimuli.

Conduction of information within the neuron takes place in two stages, called the resting potential and the action potential. As we will see, the key to conduction is in the neuron's semipermeable membrane, which encases the axon, dendrite, and cell body.

RESTING POTENTIAL. An inactive neuron's electrical potential is called its *resting potential.* In voltage, the resting potential is equal to about -70 mv (millivolts). In other words, the inside of the cell contains a negative charge and the outside a positive one, just as the two poles of a battery contain opposite charges.

The cell's membrane protects this delicate balance by regulating the concentration of chemical substances both inside and outside the cell (see Figure 2–4). Inside the cell, the membrane maintains a high concentration of negatively charged proteins. These proteins are much too large to pass through the membrane's surface. Other **ions** (chemical substances), can pass through the membrane, but only potassium ions (K+) can pass fairly easily. The membrane blocks many of the sodium ions (Na+) from entering the cell. As a result of these different concentrations of ions and proteins, electro-

FIGURE 2–4
Ion Concentration Inside and Outside a Neuron

The drawing shows the relative concentration of some of the most important ions inside and outside the axon of a resting (nonconducting) neuron. Fluid inside the axon has a relatively high concentration of positively charged potassium ions (K+) and proteins with a negative charge and a low concentration of sodium ions (Na+) and chloride ions (Cl−). Sodium is actively pumped out of the cell, and potassium is pumped into the cell. Because of the unequal distribution of ions, the inside of the axon is negatively charged compared to the outside.

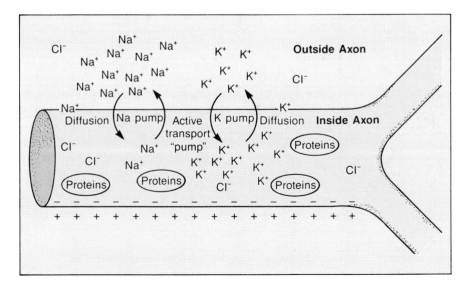

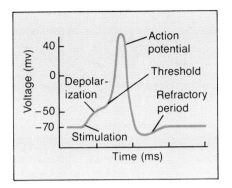

FIGURE 2–5
Action Potential

Electrical stimulation of the membrane causes it to become more permeable to sodium (Na+) ions. As a result the membrane's potential declines. At about −50 mV, its threshold, the membrane becomes completely permeable to sodium, and its charge momentarily reverses from negative to positive. A massive flow of sodium into the cell occurs, causing the membrane potential to shoot up to +50 mV. This sudden reversal in potential is called the *action potential.*

Source: Kolb & Whishaw, 1985.

static pressure builds between the inside and the outside. The negatively charged ions and proteins inside the cell attract the positive ions outside, and the cell is poised for action.

However, on the basis of the distribution of ions, the resting potential should be −75 mV and actually it is −70 mV. This is because sodium is much more heavily concentrated outside the cell than inside, even though it should be drawn into the inside by the negative charge inside the cell. The reason for this is a set of mechanisms called the ***sodium-potassium pump,*** which actively forces sodium ions outside the cell while drawing potassium ions into the cell.

ACTION POTENTIAL. Any change in the membrane's permeability disturbs the delicate balance of the resting potential. If the membrane is stimulated with an electrical pulse, the membrane's negative potential slowly decreases, a process called depolarization. When the potential reaches about −50 mV, the membrane suddenly becomes permeable to sodium. The movement of sodium across the membrane causes the membrane's potential to move all the way to +50 mV (see Figure 2–5). At about the time the membrane potential reaches +50 mV, the membrane closes itself off to the sodium. The membrane then restores the original resting potential of −70 mV. This entire process takes about 1 millisecond. The voltage at which the membrane shifts its potential (roughly −50 mV) is called the ***threshold of excitation.*** The sudden reversal in membrane potential from negative to positive is called the ***action potential.*** When an action potential occurs in one region of the membrane, it causes adjacent portions of the membrane also to change permeability, so the action potential moves down the length of the axon. The conduction of an action potential through the neuron is referred to as the cell's ***firing.***

The basic mechanism of neuronal conduction is the key to the success of certain drugs. Some commonly used local anesthetics, for example, block pain signals by changing the properties of the neuronal membrane, thereby suppressing the generation of action potentials. These "roadblocks" keep pain signals from reaching their destination (Iversen & Iversen, 1981).

One small point in Figure 2–5 may seem confusing. When the cell returns to resting potential after firing, its charge is still above threshold. Why doesn't the cell fire again in response? There is a brief period following an action potential when the neuron is resistant to firing. For one or so milliseconds after an action potential, the cell is in what is termed a *refractory period.*

ALL-OR-NONE LAW. Once elicited, an action potential continues down the length of the axon to its end, like a spark igniting a fuse—the spark travels down the fuse without diminishing. Neurons fire according to the ***all-or-none law:*** an action potential is triggered or it is not, but once triggered, the nerve impulse continues unimpeded. In addition, all action potentials are equal in intensity, regardless of the intensity of the eliciting stimulus. This makes sense when you consider that an action potential is determined by membrane permeability; therefore, the intensity of an action potential is a property of the cell, not of the stimulus.

If all action potentials are of equal intensity, then how do we distinguish intense stimuli, such as bright lights, from less intense stimuli? More intense stimuli trigger an increase in the *rate* of firing of action potentials.

FIGURE 2–6
The Myelin Sheath and Node of Ranvier

This axon is surrounded by a myelin sheath composed of glial cells. It is broken at intervals of about 1 mm by short, unmyelinated sections called nodes of Ranvier. The myelin insulates the axon by blocking the movement of ions, so action potentials jump electrically from one unmyelinated section to the next. This type of conduction occurs at a much faster rate than conduction on axons without a myelin sheath.

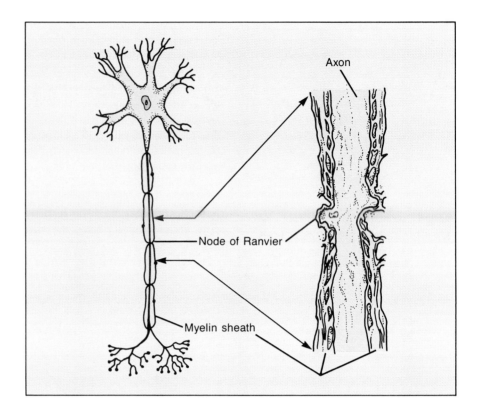

The relation of stimulus intensity to rate of nerve impulses is expressed in *Adrian's rate law* (Adrian also authored the all-or-none law). Simply stated, the law holds that there are more action potentials occurring in the time one looks at an intense stimulus than when one looks at a weak stimulus.

MYELINATED NERVE IMPULSE. In unmyelinated axons, conduction of an action potential occurs continuously, spreading from each point on the axon to the next. In myelinated axons, the myelin covers the cell membrane between the nodes. This insulation makes the action potential pass by electrical conduction to the bare portions between segments of myelin sheath. These bare portions are termed *nodes of Ranvier* (see Figure 2–6). The nerve impulses on myelinated axons travel much more quickly than those on unmyelinated axons because electrical transmission used in the myelinated segments is much faster than the action potential used in the nodes. If development of the myelin sheath is disrupted in some way, such as by gross malnutrition during the early period of myelination of the brain, conduction of neural impulses will be slowed. The defective myelination produced by early malnutrition may be associated with mental retardation (Davison & Dobbing, 1966).

REFLEXES. Around the turn of the century, Charles Scott Sherrington (1906) conducted behavioral research in which he studied reflexes in dogs. A *reflex* is an automatic response to a stimulus. If a dog's foot is pinched, the dog will flex (raise) the pinched leg, a simple reflex. Sherrington found that this movement was controlled by the spinal cord because it occurred after he cut the connection between the brain and the spinal cord.

In experimentation on this reflex Sherrington noted a delay between his pinching the dog's foot and the flexion response. During the delay, an impulse traveled up the axon from a skin receptor to the spinal cord (sensory neuron) and then another impulse traveled from the spinal cord to a muscle in the leg (motor neuron). Sherrington measured the total time it took from stimulation to response and found that this time was significantly longer than the known time it would take for an impulse to travel along the axons. Therefore he concluded that conduction must be slower at the junction of one neuron and another than it is along the axon. Whereas some people in the 1800s thought neurons were physically connected, Sherrington inferred that there must be spaces between neurons. He called these spaces *synapses.* Later research proved Sherrington to be right. We describe the process of *synaptic transmission* in the next section.

Synaptic Transmission

Axons branch at their ends. At the end of each branch is a tiny swelling, or button, called a *terminal button* (see Figure 2–7). The place where the buttons of one neuron adjoin the dendrites of another neuron is called a *synapse.* The small gap between the buttons and the dendrites of a neighboring cell at the synapse is called the *synaptic cleft.* Because transmission of information runs in one direction from the axon of the first neuron to the dendrites of the next, the membrane of the transmitting cell's button is called *presynaptic,* and the membrane of the receiving cell's dendrite is called *postsynaptic.*

When an action potential moves down the axon of a cell and arrives at a button, the neuron releases a minute amount of a chemical into the syn-

**FIGURE 2–7
Terminal Button**

The figure shows the activation of receptor sites by a transmitter substance from the terminal button.

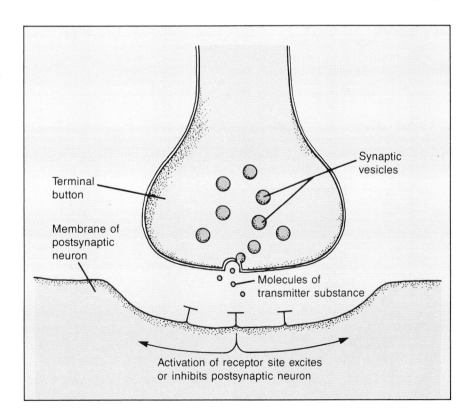

Synaptic
vesicles

Terminal
button

Membrane of
postsynaptic
neuron

Molecules of
transmitter substance

Activation of receptor site excites
or inhibits postsynaptic neuron

aptic cleft. This chemical is a *transmitter substance,* or **neurotransmitter.** Different neurons produce different transmitters: there are many different kinds of transmitter substances in the nervous system.

The terminal button contains a store of transmitters, usually within small, membrane-enclosed, spherical bodies called **synaptic vesicles.** Shortly after the arrival of an action potential at a button, the contents of several hundred synaptic vesicles are let go. The vesicles come into contact briefly with the presynaptic membrane and discharge their contents into the synaptic cleft.

The postsynaptic membrane of the receiving cell contains specialized *receptor sites* that interact with arriving neurotransmitters. The transmitter substance diffusing across the synaptic cleft meets its appropriate receptor site, initiating the receiving cell's response. The surface of the postsynaptic cell contains many transmitter-receptor sites because it receives input from many cells that use different transmitters. The transmitter acts on these specialized receptor sites to initiate changes in the permeability of the receiving cell's membrane. Depending on which transmitter substance and type of receptor site are involved, this alteration in membrane permeability can either excite (+) or inhibit (−) action potentials by the receiving cell. A neuron in the brain can share synapses with thousands of other neurons; thus, the combination of all of the incoming signals received determines whether or not the receiving neuron will fire.

If the transmitter substances were to remain in the synaptic cleft, continued communication among cells would be impossible. After entering the cleft, the transmitter substance is either deactivated or reabsorbed into the terminal button. Enzymes in the postsynaptic membrane *deactivate,* or destroy, a great number of transmitter substances. Most transmitters are reabsorbed by the terminal button, a process called **reuptake.** Many drugs affect these processes. The amphetamines and cocaine produce their effects by speeding up the release of a neurotransmitter called *dopamine* from the presynaptic membrane. The antidepressants (desipramine and imipramine) block the reuptake of norepinephrine. Most nerve gases and insecticides interfere with removal of another transmitter, *acetylcholine.* The effects of norepinephrine and acetylcholine are discussed in the next section.

Transmitter Substances

At present, there are several identified neurotransmitters: acetylcholine (ACh), norepinephrine (NE), epinephrine, serotonin (5-HT), dopamine (DA), histamine, and several amino acids including *GABA* and glutamate (see Table 2–1). In addition, many short peptides (a relatively short chain of amino acids connected together) have been located in the brain and are thought to be involved in neurotransmission. We will discuss the actions of three neurotransmitters (ACh, NE, and GABA) to give you an idea of the power of their effects (the actions of dopamine are discussed in "Research Frontier: The Effects of Dopamine" on page 47). Then we will discuss one class of brain peptides, the endorphins.

ACETYLCHOLINE (ACh). This neurotransmitter works primarily on motor nerves and causes skeletal muscles to contract. In general, ACh is an excit-

In order to be clearly classified as a neurotransmitter, the following criteria should be met (Kolb & Whishaw, 1985): the chemical is present in the terminal button; it is released when the neuron fires; placing the chemical on the organ acts like stimulating the nerve; there is an uptake mechanism in the area of the synaptic space to inactivate the neurotransmitter; and placing a substance in the synaptic space that blocks the action of the neurotransmitter blocks the effects of stimulating the neuron. We do not as yet have the ability to test all these properties, and so many chemicals are referred to as putative (supposed) neurotransmitters. The following chemicals are commonly agreed to be neurotransmitters.

TABLE 2–1
Chemicals Thought to Be Neurotransmitters

Acetylcholine: Found in many synapses of the central and peripheral nervous systems and the parasympathetic division. Excitatory at most central synapses and neuromuscular synapses; inhibitory at heart and some other autonomic nervous system synapses.

Serotonin: Produced in the central nervous system, involved in circuits that influence sleep and emotional arousal. Can be either excitatory or inhibitory.

Dopamine: Found in circuits involving voluntary movement, learning, memory, and emotional arousal, inhibitory.

Norepinephrine or chemically similar noradrenaline: Both a hormone and a transmitter. Found in circuits controlling arousal, wakefulness, eating, learning, and memory. Can be either excitatory or inhibitory.

Epinephrine or chemically similar adrenaline: Both a hormone and a transmitter. Either excitatory or inhibitory; actions include increased pulse and blood pressure.

Amino acids: Widely found in the brain.

GABA: The main inhibitory transmitter in the brain.

Glutamic acid: Possibly the chief excitatory transmitter in the brain.

Neuropeptides: Chains of amino acids found in the brain.

Enkephalins: Mostly inhibitory, as in pain relief, but excitatory in some locations.

Beta-endorphin: The most powerful pain reliever produced in the brain. Mostly inhibitory but excitatory in some locations; contained in the stress hormone ACTH.

Source: Adapted from Rosenzweig & Leiman, 1982.

Alzheimer's disease is characterized by emotional and behavioral abnormalities and intellectual deterioration, particularly marked memory loss. Recent evidence suggests that a reduction in the release of the neurotransmitter acetylcholine (ACh) may be a cause of Alzheimer's disease.

atory neurotransmitter; that is, it causes the receiving cell to fire. Botulinum toxin, which can be present in improperly prepared food, prevents release of ACh, resulting in paralysis and often death. Venom of the black widow spider, on the other hand, causes a large release of ACh, creating muscle spasms. The drug curare, used by South American Indians in poison darts, blocks certain receptors for ACh, including those that control the muscles for breathing. A person unable to breathe because of curare may remain fully conscious up to the point of death.

Recently ACh has been implicated in Alzheimer's disease, an affliction that destroys one's memory. Research has clearly shown that release of acetylcholine in a region of the brain called the hippocampus is critically important for memory formation. In the hippocampus and the cerebral cortex of Alzheimer's patients, strong evidence suggests that acetylcholine release has been severely restricted. If this hypothesis is correct, the next objective is to find a drug therapy that restores the level of ACh to these portions of the brain.

NOREPINEPHRINE (NE). NE has generally inhibitory effects on the brain and spinal cord, but it has an excitatory effect on heart muscle and smooth muscles of the blood vessels, intestine, and genitals. An excess of norepinephrine in the nervous system appears to produce a state of pleasure. As mentioned above, the antidepressant drugs imipramine and desipramine block reuptake in NE-containing neurons, suggesting that depression may be the result of a deficiency in norepinephrine (caused by the rapid reuptake of this chemical at the synapse). Consistent with this idea, the tranquilizer chlorpromazine blocks reuptake of NE, making the NE last longer.

GABA. GABA (for gamma-amino butyric acid) is one of the most common inhibitory transmitters in the body. It is found everywhere in the brain and spinal cord and is probably the transmitter in as many as one-third of the brain's synaptic terminals. Picrotoxin, a drug that blocks GABA receptors, causes convulsions because without GABA's inhibiting influence there can be no control of muscle movements. In Huntington's chorea, a serious hereditary disease, one symptom is involuntary muscle movements. Some researchers have suggested that Huntington's chorea results from degeneration of GABA cells in the brain that are concerned with motor control (Perry, Hansen, & Kloster, 1973). Valium, one of the most widely prescribed tranquilizers in our society, is believed to act in part by stimulating the inhibitory GABA receptors.

ENDORPHINS. Of the many short peptides thought to be involved in neurotransmission, at least two families act like opiates—that is, they suppress pain. In 1975 John Hughes and Hans Kosterlitz (Hughes et al., 1975) at the University of Aberdeen in Scotland isolated a substance in the brain with the same action as morphine and called it enkephalin ("in the head"). Since that time a number of enkephalins have been discovered, as well as other chemicals produced by the body known as brain opioids or endorphins (meaning morphine-within). There has been considerable speculation about the possible effects endorphins may have. For example, endorphins may cause the so-called runner's high, the euphoria and well-being some joggers experience. Enkephalin and endorphin release may also be stimulated by acupuncture, the Chinese art of placing sharp needles under the skin as a cure for many ailments. Researchers are actively collecting data to determine how endorphins function. We will return to this topic in Chapter 3.

Blood-Brain Barrier

Our discussion of neurons and neurotransmitters has emphasized the many ways in which drugs can affect the transmission of information between neurons. A unique relationship between blood supply and brain tissue called the *blood-brain barrier* helps determine how chemicals or other substances in the blood affect the brain. The term blood-brain barrier is somewhat misleading because a complete barrier does not exist. Instead, some molecules pass freely between the blood and the brain, while others do not pass at all. Generally (but not always) the larger the molecules, the more likely they are to be blocked. When you take a drug, it enters the bloodstream and then escapes into various body tissues via the capillaries, or small blood vessels, throughout your body. However, in the brain some drugs escape much less easily from the capillaries than they do in most other tissues. Some drugs cannot escape at all.

RESEARCH FRONTIER

The Effects of Dopamine

The study of chemical transmitter substances and circuits in the brain began only recently, but it has rapidly become the largest field of neuroscience. To get a sense of how fast research progresses in this field, we discuss the case of dopamine.

There are three known dopamine circuits in the brain, two of which have been shown to be important in behavior disorders. These systems are differentiated by where in the brain the cell bodies lie and where their axons lead. The best-understood dopamine circuit is the one that is deficient in Parkinson's disease. This system plays an important role in movement. In part of the lower brain is a structure called the *substantia nigra* (dark substance), where the cell bodies contain a dark pigment. Many cell bodies in this region contain dopamine. In Parkinson's disease, for an unknown reason, the neurons containing dopamine in the substantia nigra die, movement becomes difficult, and the hands demonstrate tremors and repetitive movements. Thus the effects of dopamine

in motor control are dramatic: as dopamine is depleted, the ability to move decreases. This dopamine system was discovered to be the cause of Parkinson's disease some years ago (Ehringer & Hornykiewicz, 1960). Administering L-Dopa, the substance from which dopamine is made in the brain, is a successful therapy for Parkinson's disease.

The role of the neurotransmitter dopamine in motor behavior has also been shown in animal studies. Electrical stimulation of the dopamine-containing cells in the substantia nigra on one side of the brain activates the motor system on that side, causing animals to run in circles (Arbuthnott & Ungerstedt, 1969). And recently it has been shown that the concentration of dopamine varies in different brain regions depending on what specific motor function is being performed (Freed & Yamamoto, 1985). Thus, measuring concentrations of dopamine may allow us to map which brain region is associated with specific motor functions.

A second dopamine system is thought to be involved in schizophrenia, a severe mental disorder often characterized by emotional turmoil, delusions, and hallucinations. Several tranquilizers (e.g., chlorpromazine, re-

serpine) that are helpful in treating the symptoms of schizophrenia interfere with synaptic transmission at the dopamine synapses. It is thought that schizophrenia may be related to overactivity in this dopamine system in the brain—i.e., there is too much dopamine. No relationship seems to exist between Parkinson's disease, caused by too little dopamine, and schizophrenia, perhaps related to too much dopamine, because the former is in one dopamine system and the latter is in a different dopamine system. However, drugs that increase or decrease dopamine do so in all circuits. When L-Dopa is administered to treat Parkinson's disease, it increases dopamine levels in all dopamine circuits; a side effect may sometimes be hallucinations and delusions, schizophrenia-like symptoms (Fahn & Calne, 1978). Likewise, antipsychotic drugs, which decrease dopamine levels, can have as a side effect Parkinson's disease-like symptoms.

As you can see, dopamine, as well as all of the neurotransmitters, is a tremendously powerful substance, and you can understand why the study of neurotransmitters and their effects is one of the most active areas of current research in the neurosciences.

The crippling disease multiple sclerosis (MS) further illustrates the importance of the blood-brain barrier. Scientists believe that multiple sclerosis occurs because myelin protein that is normally present in the brain's extracellular fluid enters the blood supply because the blood-brain barrier is not functioning properly. The presence of a foreign substance in the blood appears to mobilize the body's immune system, which in turn destroys the myelin in the myelin sheaths of axons in the nervous system. Without the myelin sheath, messages sent by these axons become scrambled, resulting in the loss of muscular control and sensory disorders typical of MS victims.

The roots entering the spinal cord as seen in this rear view are mostly incoming fibers from sense organs in the skin and muscles.

OUTLINE OF THE NERVOUS SYSTEM

The entire collection of neurons is called the *nervous system,* which has two main divisions: the central nervous system and the peripheral nervous system.

The Central Nervous System

The brain and spinal cord together make up the **central nervous system.** The spinal cord is a narrow tube that extends the length of the back, from the hips to the base of the skull, where it joins the brain. The brain is very soft and fairly heavy, typically weighing about 1400 grams, or a bit over three pounds. It floats in *cerebrospinal fluid,* which protects it from shock. Floating reduces its net weight to about 80 grams. The fluid also surrounds the spinal cord, and both the spinal cord and the brain are encased by bone— the vertebral column and skull, respectively (see Figure 2–8). The importance of the brain is demonstrated by the fact that 20 percent of the blood from the heart flows to the brain. A six-second interruption of that flow causes unconsciousness, and irreversible brain damage occurs within a few minutes.

The Peripheral Nervous System

All of the nervous system outside the skull and spine is called the **peripheral nervous system.** This system consists largely of sensory neurons, which carry information from sensory receptors to the central nervous system, and motor neurons, which carry information from the central nervous system to the organs and muscles. Sensory neurons are also referred to as *afferent* (carrying toward the central nervous system) and motor neurons are also referred to as *efferent* (carrying away from the central nervous system).

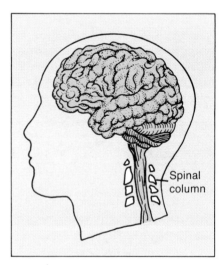

FIGURE 2–8
Relationship of the Spinal Cord and Brain to the Head and Neck

The brain and spinal cord together are called the central nervous system.

The peripheral nervous system has two divisions: the *somatic nervous system* and the *autonomic nervous system* (see Figure 2–9). In the somatic nervous system, efferent (motor) neurons activate *skeletal muscles,* such as those that move your arms and legs. Afferent (sensory) neurons in the somatic nervous system carry messages from the major receptor organs: eyes, ears, and so on. In the autonomic nervous system, in contrast, efferent neurons activate mainly *smooth muscles,* including those in the stomach, heart, blood vessels, gut, and gallbladder. Efferent neurons also regulate glands. Afferent neurons in the autonomic system carry information from the internal organs back to the central nervous system.

The autonomic nervous system itself has two divisions: *sympathetic* and *parasympathetic.* The sympathetic nervous system regulates the body's expenditure of energy; for instance, it increases blood flow to muscles, increases heart rate, and causes piloerection (erection of fur in animals, goose bumps in humans). When you are emotionally excited, your sympathetic nervous system dominates. Conversely, the parasympathetic division of the autonomic nervous system regulates processes that help the body consume and store energy. After you eat a meal your parasympathetic nervous system controls the various steps in digestion. With some exceptions, the parasympathetic and sympathetic nervous systems influence the same organs—the heart, blood vessels, and intestines—but they control opposite reactions, as schematized in Figure 2–10. Reactions associated with the para-

FIGURE 2–9
The Nervous System

This diagram outlines the relationship between the major parts of the nervous system.

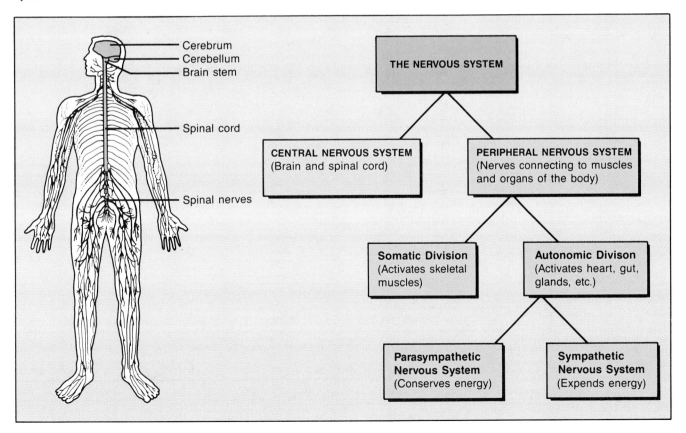

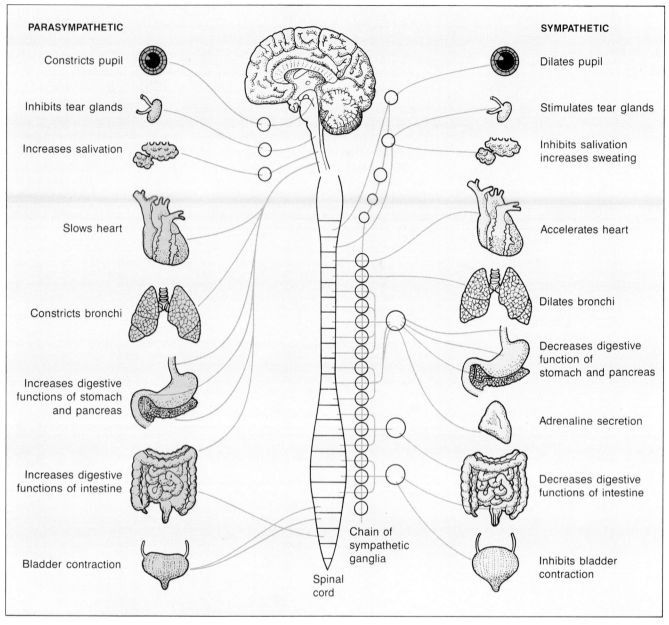

PARASYMPATHETIC

Constricts pupil

Inhibits tear glands

Increases salivation

Slows heart

Constricts bronchi

Increases digestive functions of stomach and pancreas

Increases digestive functions of intestine

Bladder contraction

SYMPATHETIC

Dilates pupil

Stimulates tear glands

Inhibits salivation increases sweating

Accelerates heart

Dilates bronchi

Decreases digestive function of stomach and pancreas

Adrenaline secretion

Decreases digestive functions of intestine

Inhibits bladder contraction

Chain of sympathetic ganglia

Spinal cord

FIGURE 2–10
The Autonomic Nervous System

The peripheral autonomic nervous system consists of the parasympathetic (left) and sympathetic (right) nervous systems. Parasympathetic nerves travel from the brain stem and bottom of the spinal cord directly to the organs; sympathetic nerves travel from the remainder of the spinal cord to sympathetic ganglia and then to the organs. Both sets of nerves control the same organs, but have opposite effects on those organs.

sympathetic nervous system include salivation, stomach contractions, and lowered heart action and breathing rate. The sympathetic nervous system, on the other hand, decreases salivation, relaxes stomach contractions, and increases heart action and breathing. The autonomic nervous system is of great importance in emotion and stress and will be discussed in more detail in Chapter 13.

Now that you have a basic overview of the nervous system and its divisions, we will begin discussing the various parts of the system. We will discuss the human brain beginning with the simplest and oldest structures (in evolutionary terms) and concluding with the cerebral hemispheres.

THE SPINAL CORD AND BRAIN STEM

In some very primitive animals, the nervous system consists only of a spinal cord. Sensory receptors on the body send inputs to part of the cord while axons from another part reach out to control muscles. In fully developed humans, all sensory information from behind the ears and below the neck enters the spinal cord, and all skeletal muscles except those of the head and throat are activated by motor neurons originating in the spinal cord. The central core of the spinal cord contains the cell bodies of the spinal cord neurons. These appear gray and are called *gray matter.* Surrounding the central core are bundles of axons, many of which are covered with a myelin sheath; they appear white and are called *white matter.*

Traditionally, the spinal cord has been thought to control simple reflexes, while more complicated functions have been attributed to the brain. Yet a dog whose spinal cord has been disconnected from its brain can scratch an irritating spot near its shoulder with its leg. Cats similarly operated on can walk, trot, or gallop (Trevarthen, 1980). The spinal cord of a human being is less independent. Humans can neither stand nor walk without the integration of information above the spinal cord. In humans the functions of the "lower" or simpler parts of the central nervous system are controlled or modulated by the higher systems. Nonetheless, the complexity of activity at the level of the spinal cord is surprising. Without any input from "higher influence," the spinal cord is capable of many reflex sequences. For example, genital stimulation can elicit sexual postures in cats and rats even after transection of the spinal cord from the brain (Beach, 1967; Hart, 1969). In humans a spinal reflex produces emission of semen.

Figure 2–11 contains a cross-sectional view of the human brain. The lowest part of the brain stem is the *medulla,* which is really the continuation of the spinal cord into the brain. It contains all the ascending and descending nerve fibers connecting the brain and spinal cord. The medulla controls heart rate, breathing, and some reflexes that help us maintain an upright posture. A sharp blow to the back of the head near the neck could kill by injuring the medulla. In front of the medulla is the *pons* (the Latin word for bridge). The name reflects the fact that the pons consists mostly of fibers crossing between the right and left. The pons holds many sensory neurons that receive input from hearing receptors and head position receptors in the ear as well as sensations from the head and face. The pons also contains motor neurons controlling facial movements. In the upper portion of the brain stem is a small structure called the *midbrain.* Structures in the midbrain coordinate whole-body movements with visual and auditory stimuli. Other structures in the midbrain contribute to the control of movement. Parkinson's disease is associated with degeneration of neurons in one part of the midbrain, as previously discussed in "Research Frontier: The Effects of Dopamine."

The medulla, pons, and midbrain developed early in the course of evolution. Their structure is highly similar in life forms from fish to humans, though there are some species variations in both structure and function. For example, in birds the midbrain is the location of visual and auditory systems. In humans and primates, these visual and auditory systems generally appear in a separate area called the *cortex.*

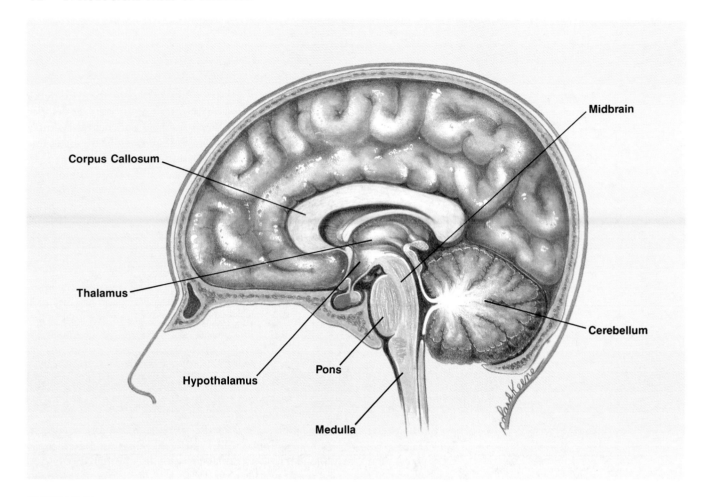

FIGURE 2–11
Brain Stem

This medial view through the center of the brain shows structures of the brain stem.

Source: Kolb & Whishaw, 1985, p. 14.

Off to the back of the brain on top of the medulla is a very old (in evolutionary terms) structure—the *cerebellum,* or "little brain" (see Figure 2–11). The cerebellum was probably the first brain structure in evolution to be specialized for sensory-motor coordination. Its neuron cell bodies form a surface covering myelinated white matter. The cerebellum coordinates information from the spinal cord and the neocortex to make movements smooth and precise. Damage to the cerebellum produces jerky patterns of movement. Damage to the cerebellum can also cause problems in maintaining equilibrium and posture.

In the center of the brain stem is a complex region with many groups of neuron cell bodies and short and long nerve fibers. This network of cells is called the *reticular formation* (*reticulum* is the Latin word for "network"). Because it is involved in activation or arousal of other parts of the brain, the reticular formation is now known as the *reticular activating system.* Severing parts of the reticular activating system can produce coma in animals, and its stimulation can awaken a sleeping animal. This system is generally believed to maintain general arousal and to control sleeping and waking.

The *thalamus* forms a bulge on the top of the brain stem and technically can be viewed as part of the brain stem (see Figure 2–11), but it is completely covered by other parts of the brain. The thalamus conveys information from sensory receptors on the periphery of the body to higher layers of the brain. All sensory information—for example, from the eyes, ears, and skin—passes through the thalamus, except smells, which take a different route. The thalamus also integrates information coming from other parts of the brain and sends it to the cerebellum and medulla. The thalamus can be thought of as a relay station.

The *hypothalamus* is a tiny structure lying beneath the thalamus (*hypo* is Greek for "under"), as shown in Figure 2–11. The hypothalamus has tremendous importance in emotion and motivation. Electrically stimulated, it can produce strong "pleasure" in animals. The hypothalamus regulates the internal state of the body, especially hunger, thirst, and temperature. Removal of one small part of the hypothalamus can cause rats to become grossly overweight, removal of a different small part drastically reduces weight, as will be discussed in more detail in Chapter 12. The hypothalamus also regulates the endocrine system, a chemical communication system within the body that we will discuss later in the chapter.

THE LIMBIC SYSTEM

Some groups of similar cell bodies in the thalamus, hypothalamus, and part of the brain above these structures combine to form a kind of border around the brain stem. These structures appeared during the evolution of the amphibians and reptiles and are referred to as the *limbic system* (*limbic* means "border" in Latin). Figure 2–12 shows the limbic system. Earlier the limbic structures were referred to as the "smell" brain. Indeed, in animals such as the crocodile, whose forebrain is largely limbic brain, the control of smelling, or olfaction, is a major function of the limbic system. In the course of evolution the neocortex developed, and much of the specific olfactory function of the limbic system was lost. Many other quite different functions of the limbic system have developed over the course of evolution. Parts of the limbic system seem to be involved in emotional behavior. The *amygdala* appears primarily to facilitate aggressive instincts. Destruction of cells (called *lesions*) in the amygdala tends to suppress attack and flight in wild animals (Carlson, 1986). The *septum* apparently restrains aggression. These effects vary by species, however. Septal lesions in rats induce highly aggressive behavior (Brady & Nauta, 1953), but mice flee rather than fight (Slotnick, McMullen, & Fleischer, 1974), and cats sometimes become more affectionate rather than more aggressive (Glendenning, 1972). In humans, portions of the limbic system have been removed in attempts to control aggression, a controversial procedure. Lesions of the amygdala have also been shown to affect social behavior, and damage to another part of the limbic system, the *hippocampus,* has been associated with memory problems.

A famous human example of the hippocampus's role in memory concerns H.M., a man who underwent surgery to correct a serious epileptic condition. The surgeon removed all of H.M.'s hippocampus and amygdala. The surgery successfully treated the epilepsy but resulted in serious side effects on H.M.'s memory. His memory of life before his surgery is fine, but he cannot store certain kinds of new memories. So if you met H.M. and talked to him for a while and then left and returned a few minutes later, he would have no memory of you. To help you imagine how this would be,

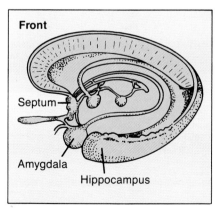

FIGURE 2–12
Limbic System

This diagram illustrates the major structures of the limbic system with the surrounding cerebrum dissected away.

Source: Thompson, 1985, p. 307.

here is a quote from H.M.: "Right now, I'm wondering, have I done or said anything amiss? You see, at this moment everything looks clear to me, but what happened just before? That's what worries me. It's like waking from a dream. Just don't remember." H.M. and the role of the hippocampus in memory are discussed further in Chapter 7.

CEREBRAL CORTEX

The *cerebral hemispheres* are the two large structures forming the top of the brain, one on the left, the other on the right. Their thin covering is the *cerebral cortex,* which forms the surface of the brain like the bark on a tree (*cortex* means "bark" in Latin). It appears gray and so is said to consist of gray matter—mostly cell bodies and short unmyelinated axons. The white matter—myelinated axons of the cell bodies—is on the inside; white matter plus various subcortical structures make up the *cerebrum.* (In the spinal cord, you will recall, the reverse is true: the gray matter is on the inside, the white matter on the outside.) The cerebral cortex is about one-quarter of an inch thick. Its deep wrinkles give it a big surface, thereby allowing the skull to contain a large number of neurons. A smooth brain of the same size would have considerably less surface.

As we mentioned, in the course of evolution the addition of the cerebellum to the back of the brain stem allowed coordination of movement; the development of the cerebellum plus the development of the cerebral hemispheres completes the mammalian brain. The human brain evolved from the mammalian brain with no basic change in design. However, the cerebral hemispheres and the cerebellum of humans are tremendously larger than in other mammals (see Figure 2–13). Humans have the largest cerebral cortex

On the left is a view of the brain from above, with the front of the brain at the top of the photograph.

A cross-section of the cerebellum is shown on the right.

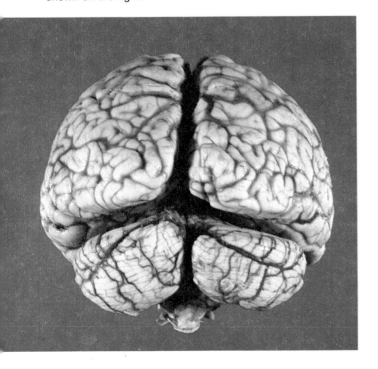

FIGURE 2–13
Comparison of Brain Sizes

This photograph of some representative brains of different animals shows how large the human brain is compared with those of other animals.

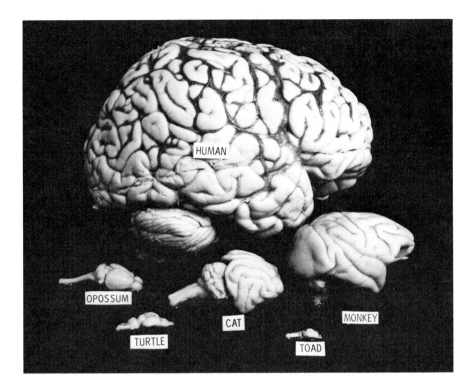

relative to total brain size. Other mammals such as the rat have a smaller, smooth cerebral cortex; reptiles and amphibians have less, and fish have none. It is accurate to say that the cerebral cortex is what makes humans what they are. It constitutes 80 percent of the human brain and is the source of our reasoning, imagining, consciousness, and language.

The surface of each hemisphere is divided into four sections, or lobes: *frontal, temporal, parietal,* and *occipital* (see Figure 2–14). Natural divisions called *fissures* occur on the surface of the cortex. The *central fissure* separates the frontal lobe from the parietal lobe; the *lateral fissure* constitutes the boundary of the temporal lobe; and the *longitudinal fissure* separates the right and left halves.

A major goal in the study of the cerebral cortex has been to determine whether and how the various parts of the cortex relate to behavior and experience. To answer these questions, scientists have, among other methods, observed the behavior of unfortunate victims of brain damage, performed surgery and other experiments on animals, and electrically stimulated areas of the brains of patients undergoing brain surgery (as a natural consequence of the surgical procedure) and observed the results.

Surprisingly, the last method, electrical stimulation, is not a new procedure. In fact, the first such experiments were carried out in 1874 by a Cincinnati surgeon named Dr. Robert Bartholow (Penfield & Rasmussen, 1968). He used as his unwitting subject his own house servant! In an account of this amazing procedure, Bartholow made a number of observations that have held up over time. The most important observation was that his "patient" apparently felt no pain from the crude procedure. Because electrical stimulation of the brain is painless, subjects in these experiments can report what they feel, an obvious boon to scientists.

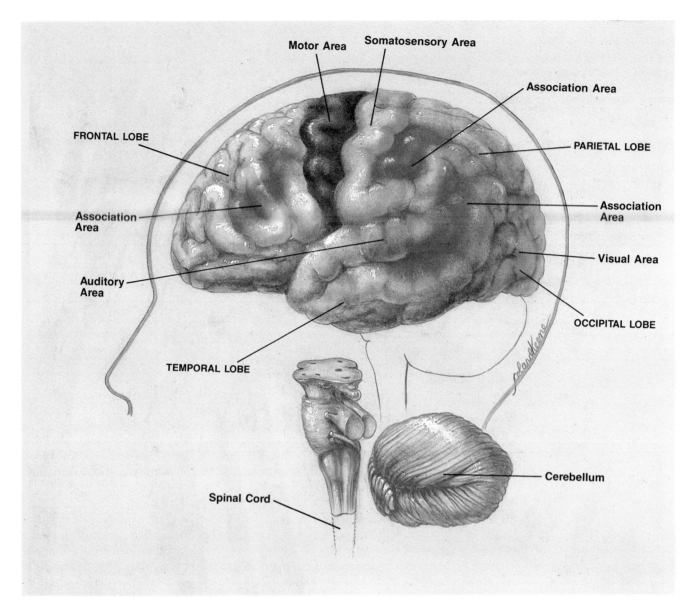

FIGURE 2–14
Map of the Left Side of the
Cerebral Cortex

These diagrams depict the locations of the major sections of the brain—the frontal, temporal, parietal, and occipital lobes—and show where the sensory, motor, and association areas lie within these lobes. The association areas are much larger than the sensory and motor areas.

Source: Netter, 1983.

A recent additional technique is positron emission tomography (PET), a visual technique in which the subject is given a radioactively labeled compound such as glucose that is metabolized by the brain. The most active area of the brain uses the most glucose, so by measuring the radioactivity of different brain areas researchers can see which area is most metabolically active during a particular activity and thus which brain area is specialized for which task. We will show you some results of this procedure later, and the possibilities of using this procedure in diagnosis of cerebral problems is discussed in "Applying Psychology: Positron Emission Tomography" on page 68.

By using all these methods, scientists have found that some areas of the cortex seem to be *sensory* in function; that is, they receive information from other parts of the body or the environment. Other areas appear to be largely *motor,* or involved in controlling bodily movements. Still others, termed *association areas,* are involved in understanding and producing language, thinking, and memory (see Figure 2–14). We will describe each of these areas individually, but bear in mind that all of them work together in a normal human being, so our separation is somewhat artificial.

The Sensory Cortex

Three different regions of the cortex have been identified as primary sensory areas: the somatosensory, the visual, and the auditory. The *somatosensory area* receives sensations of touch, pain, temperature, and positioning of the body. It runs across the middle of the cerebral cortex in the front of the parietal lobe (see Figure 2–14). Specific segments of the somatosensory cortex get information from particular parts of the body. So a person who suffers damage to a given area of the somatosensory cortex will also lose sensation in a corresponding section of the body. Also, electrical stimulation of the particular area of the somatosensory cortex will produce apparent sensations from the corresponding area of the body. These projection areas are indicated in Figure 2–15, which identifies only one side of the somatosensory cortex; the other side is its mirror image. The right hemisphere receives sensations from the left side of the body, the left hemisphere from the right side.

The *visual sensory area* is in the occipital lobe (see Figure 2–14). The area is sometimes known as the striate cortex because large layers of long axons give it a striped appearance. When this area is stimulated electrically, the subject reports seeing flashes of light.

Auditory areas are positioned in the temporal lobes. When stimulated here, subjects report hearing sounds.

FIGURE 2–15
Functions of the Sensory Cortex

This cross section of the human brain shows the localization of function within the sensory cortex. Only one side of the figure is labeled; the other side is a mirror image of the one shown. The right side of the cortex receives sensations from the left side of the body; the left side of the cortex receives sensations from the right side of the body. The amount of cortex devoted to a part of the body is related to how sensitive that area is. For example, a large amount of area is devoted to the lips and hands.

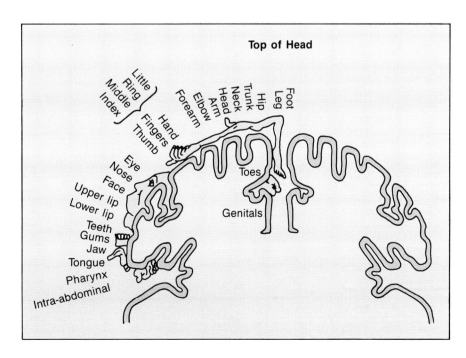

The Motor Cortex

The primary motor area of the cortex is located along a narrow strip immediately in front of the central fissure, that is, at the back of the frontal lobes (see Figure 2–14). Mild electrical stimulation of this general area produces body movements, and stimulation of particular areas causes movements of corresponding parts of the body. Figure 2–16 shows the areas of the brain that produce various reactions when stimulated. Below the head, movement of the right side of the body is associated with stimulation of the motor cortex in the left hemisphere, and movement of the left side with stimulation of the motor cortex in the right hemisphere. Damage to part of the motor area will usually result in inability to perform precise movements of the particular body part associated with that area, while damage to large parts of the motor area produces paralysis of the side of the body opposite to the motor area damaged.

Association Areas

Only a relatively small part of the cortex is devoted to the sensory and motor areas. The remaining areas of the cortex, located in all four lobes, are called association areas because early researchers hypothesized that associations between sensory input and motor output were made in these areas. How the association areas function is still unclear, but generally they seem to store and process information. For example, visual association areas (in the occipital and temporal lobes) somehow deal with information from the visual sensory area so that we can recognize objects. Humans have the greatest amount of association cortex, and the increase in association cortex is largely responsible for the increase in brain size when the human brain is compared with that of other primates.

FIGURE 2–16
Functions of the Motor Cortex

This cross section of the human brain indicates the localization of function within the motor cortex. Only one side of the figure is labeled; the other side is a mirror image of the one shown. The right side of the cortex governs movement on the left side of the body; the left side of the cortex governs movement on the right side of the body. The amount of area in the cortex devoted to a particular part of the body is related to the complexity of movement in that part of the body. Notice the amount of cortex devoted to the lips, jaw, and tongue, used in the complex activity of speech.

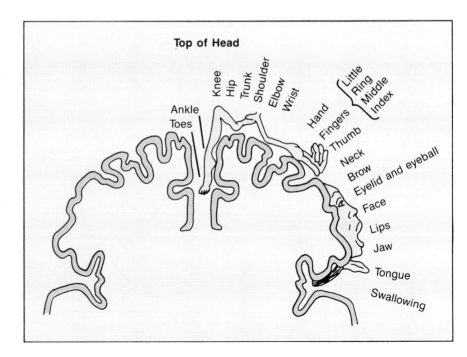

FIGURE 2–17
Cerebral Cortex Function as Shown by PET

PET scans 1 and 2 were taken, respectively, when a visual stimulus was presented, producing a response in the visual cortex, and when an auditory stimulus was presented, producing a response in the auditory cortex. A cognitive task (scan 3) produced frontal cortex activity, while a memory task (scan 4) caused activity in the hippocampus. Finally, a motor task (scan 5) involving the right hand caused increased activity in the left motor cortex.

Source: Phelps, M. E. & Mazziotta, J. C. (1985). Positron emission tomography: Human brain function and biochemistry. *Science, 228,* p. 804.

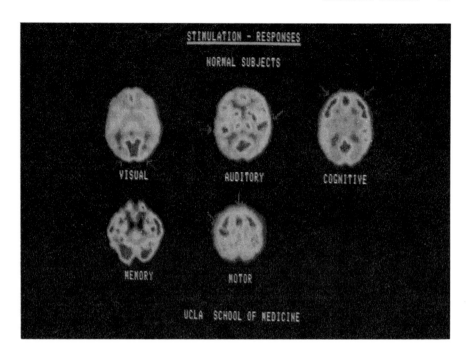

Damage to association areas causes disturbances in behavior that are quite complex and difficult to categorize, not clearly sensory or clearly motor. For example, injury in the frontal lobe seems to impair the ability to keep track of the order of events and may interfere with abstract reasoning. Fear, anxiety, and hostility apparently are also reduced, which is why frontal lobotomies were once performed on emotionally disturbed patients. Damage to the parietal association cortex can hamper recognition of objects by touch, even though sensory information still reaches the somatosensory cortex. Often patients with damage to the parietal association cortex have difficulty orienting themselves, distinguishing right from left, or using a map. Damage to the association areas in the temporal-occipital association cortex can result in problems in visually identifying complex forms, although visual input still reaches the primary visual sensory cortex. Figure 2–17 shows some of the localization of function we have been discussing as revealed by the PET technique.

Brain researchers do not know exactly how information is stored and processed in the cortex. Sometimes loss of brain cells produces loss of memory and disturbance of mental function. For example, severe cell loss due to either acute brain arteriosclerosis or to Alzheimer's disease is related to senility (Walker & Hertzog, 1975). However, in hydrocephalics (literally, "water-heads") there can be severe loss of brain tissue with little decline of function. In this disease a disturbance of cerebrospinal fluid leads to great swelling of the channels or reservoirs, called ventricles, within the brain. When the ventricle walls expand, the overlying brain tissue is damaged. One interpretation of such cases is that the cortex has considerable spare capacity. If damage to the brain occurs slowly, this spare capacity can take over brain functions. Also, the structures underlying the cortex may be capable of carrying out many of the functions ascribed to the cortex. In general, brain damage in the young has less severe effects than similar damage in adulthood. If injury is early enough (in infancy), there may be no effect on behaviors that have not developed at all at the time of the injury. Because hydrocephalus is a disease of the young, this is an instance of the general principle that brain function can be unimpaired if brain damage occurs very early in life. An account of the debate over the extent of localization of function in the brain is presented in "Controversy: Localization of Function."

CONTROVERSY

Localization of Function

Scientists have long debated the extent to which specific parts of the brain control specific functions.

As we will see later in the chapter, removal of a particular part of the left hemisphere (Broca's area) removes the ability to speak. This is an example of localization of function. A *strict* localization view is that each restricted area of the brain has a particular function, and damage to that area removes that and only that function. Experiments, however, have raised many questions regarding strict localization. Currently there are two major views competing with the idea of strict localization.

The *mass action hypothesis* is that the whole brain participates in every action. The deficit in brain function produced by destruction or removal of any brain part is proportional to the amount of brain removed. Many experiments have tested this, but they are not conclusive. Karl Lashley (1929) trained rats on a complex maze and then removed one part of the brain and then another. He could find no one part that stored knowledge of the maze. Rather, each rat was deficient proportional to the amount of cortex Lashley removed. He believed this supported the mass action hypothesis. However, other behaviors

such as speech are more localized. It appears that maze learning is too complex to be localized; the processes underlying this behavior are represented at many different sites (Gilinsky, 1984). That is, if maze performance depends on vision and smell and tactile sensations, then perhaps the whole cortex is involved in maze learning. Thus, for complicated learning tasks all parts of the cortex may contribute almost equally to performance. Generally today it is agreed that there is quite a bit of localization of function, particularly for simple behaviors. However, it is also true that damage to many different brain areas can interfere with the same behavior, especially complex behavior.

The *equipotentiality hypothesis* states that each portion of a given area of the brain is able to control the behavior normally controlled by the entire area. Experiments supporting the equipotentiality idea have shown that destruction of a particular area often produces a short-term deficit in performance followed by recovery. It seems as though a portion of the area can produce the behavior normally controlled by the whole area. Only complete destruction of an area produces long-lasting impairment. In another experiment by Karl Lashley (1929) rats were trained to discriminate between two or more visual stimuli. Lashley then removed various portions of their visual cortex. The rats could perform appropriately with as little as 2 percent of the critical area of

their visual cortex remaining. However, it is also true that destruction of the occipital area of the cortex interferes with performance on visual discrimination tasks more than does destruction of other parts of the cortex. Thus all parts of the cortex do not contribute equally to visual discrimination performance, although all parts of the occipital cortex may contribute. Lashley believed that the pattern of excitation responsible for behavior is duplicated over and over throughout an area responsible for a particular behavior, so that many neurons serve the same function. Others suggest that there are overlapping groups of neurons responsible for each function. The ones with most direct control do so unless they are destroyed or removed, in which case the next most dominant neurons take over and so on.

The concepts of localization of function, mass action, and equipotentiality underlie many discussions of cortical function. Most would agree that localization of function is not really incompatible with mass action unless a very strict localization view is adopted. Rather, researchers are concerned with what performance disruption is produced by particular lesions. And equipotentiality is most likely today to be seen as a matter of overlapping areas of similar function. Yet these issues are by no means settled and it is good to keep the general questions in mind when considering specific functions of particular brain areas.

HEMISPHERIC SPECIALIZATION

The two sides of the body are, generally speaking, symmetrical. You have two arms, two legs, two hands, and so forth, one on each side of your body. The brain also has two cerebral hemispheres, so it is natural to assume that each hemisphere is merely a carbon copy of the other. As we will see, this assumption is incorrect. The bilateral symmetry of the body and the brain is not perfect. Right-handed people usually have larger and stronger right arms than left arms, and they usually have slightly larger left hemispheres. (Recall that the left side of the motor cortex controls the right side of the body, and vice versa, so that the hemisphere that controls the preferred side of the body is more developed.)

A great amount of research over the past hundred years has indicated that the two halves of the brain are specialized to perform different functions. In 1869 a French physician, Paul Broca, reviewed evidence from a number of cases of brain damage and concluded that injury to a certain part of the left cerebral hemisphere caused a person's speech to become slow and labored but did not much affect the person's ability to understand speech (Boring, 1950). The area of the left brain that seems to control production of speech was named *Broca's area* (see Figure 2–18), and the difficulty in speaking after damage to this area is called *Broca's aphasia.* Broca discovered that when the same place was damaged in the right side of the brain, no speech impairment occurred.

About fifteen years later, Carl Wernicke reported another language disorder associated with a different area of the left hemisphere, now called *Wernicke's area* (see Figure 2–18). In *Wernicke's aphasia* speech is rapid and articulate but has little or no meaning. Examples of speech from Broca's and Wernicke's aphasia are presented in "Case Studies." A third speech disorder, conduction aphasia, is associated with damage to the conduction area between Broca's and Wernicke's areas, as shown in Figure 2–18. When this area is damaged, patients can understand speech and can also talk fluently,

FIGURE 2–18
Major Areas in the Brain Related to Speech

Damage to *Broca's area* causes slow, labored speech with no effect on speech understanding. Damage to *Wernicke's area* causes loss of understanding of speech and quick, articulate speech with no meaningful content. Damage to the *conduction area* between Broca's area and Wernicke's area produces a lack of relationship between speech comprehension and speech production. These language disorders are produced in most people by damage to the left hemisphere.

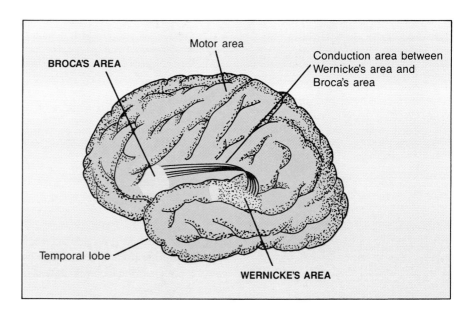

but the relation between the two abilities is impaired (Geshwind, 1972). Such patients can carry out instructions, but they cannot repeat them.

CASE STUDIES
Broca's Aphasia and Wernicke's Aphasia

The following examples of aphasic speech were collected by Howard Gardner and are reported in his book *The Shattered Mind: The Person After Brain Damage* (1975).

Broca's Aphasia. David Ford was a 39-year-old Coast Guard radio operator who suffered a stroke. Afterward he had lost the ability to use language, was confused, and had a weakness in his right arm and leg. The following interview occurred about three months after the stroke, when Ford was less confused, was alert, and scored in the normal range on nonverbal measures of intelligence.

> I asked Mr. Ford about his work before he entered the hospital.
> "I'm a sig . . . no . . . man . . . uh, well, . . . again." These words were emitted slowly, and with great effort. The sounds were not clearly articulated; each syllable was uttered harshly, explosively, in a throaty voice. With practice, it was possible to understand him, but at first I encountered considerable difficulty in this.
> "Let me help you," I interjected. "You were a signal . . ."
> "A sig-nal man . . . right," Ford completed my phrase triumphantly.
> "Were you in the Coast Guard?"
> "No, er, yes, yes . . . ship . . . Massachu . . . chusetts . . . Coastguard . . . years." He raised his hands twice, indicating the number "nineteen."
> "Oh, you were in the Coast Guard for nineteen years."
> "Oh . . . boy . . . right . . . right," he replied.
> "Why are you in the hospital, Mr. Ford?"
> Ford looked at me a bit strangely, as if to say, Isn't it patently obvious? He pointed to his paralyzed arm and said, "Arm no good," then to his mouth and said
> "Speech . . . can't say . . . talk, you see."
> "What happened to make you lose your speech?"
> "Head, fall, Jesus Christ, me no good, str, str . . . oh Jesus . . . stroke."
> "I see. Could you tell me, Mr. Ford, what you've been doing in the hospital?"
> "Yes, sure. Me go, er, uh, P.T. nine o'cot, speech . . . two times . . . read . . . wr . . . ripe, er, rike, er write . . . practice . . . get-ting better."
> "And have you been going home on weekends?"
> "Why, yes . . . Thursday, er, er, er, no, er, Friday . . . Bar-ba-ra . . . wife . . . and, oh, car . . . drive . . . purnpike . . . you know . . . rest and . . . tee-vee."
> "Are you able to understand everything on television?"
> "Oh, yes, yes . . . well . . . al-most." Ford grinned a bit.
> As can be seen, Mr. Ford's output in this brief exchange was extremely slow and effortful. Nearly every sound required a "fresh start," and many were imperfectly pronounced. (pp. 60–61)

Wernicke's Aphasia. A second patient, Philip Gorgan, was quite weak for a few days immediately after his admission to the hospital, but after that he had no difficulty carrying on a conversation with perfect grammar. However, his speech rarely made sense to his listeners.

"What brings you to the hospital?" I asked the seventy-two-year-old retired butcher four weeks after his admission to the hospital.

"Boy, I'm sweating, I'm awful nervous, you know, once in a while I get caught up, I can't mention the tarripoi, a month ago, quite a little, I've done a lot well, I impose a lot, while, on the other hand, you know what I mean, I have to run around, look it over, trebbin and all that sort of stuff."

I attempted several times to break in, but was unable to do so against this relentlessly steady and rapid outflow. Finally, I put up my hand, rested it on Gorgan's shoulder, and was able to gain a moment's reprieve.

"Thank you, Mr. Gorgan. I want to ask you a few—"

"Oh sure, go ahead, any old think you want. If I could I would. Oh, I'm taking the word the wrong way to say, all of the barbers here whenever they stop you it's going around and around, if you know what I mean, that is tying and tying for repucer, repuceration, well, we were trying the best that we could while another time it was with the beds over there the same thing . . ." (p. 68)

Source: Gardner, 1975. Reprinted by permission of Alfred A. Knopf, Inc.

In the vast majority of brain-damage victims, the language disorders result from injury to the left hemisphere, particularly for right-handed people. Currently accepted estimates (Craig, 1979) are that 99 percent of all right-handed people have speech abilities localized in the left hemisphere. (Thus, damage to the left hemisphere produces speech disorders, whereas right hemisphere damage does not.) This situation is more complicated for left-handers. For approximately half of all left-handed people, language functions appear to be localized in the right hemisphere, but the other half show either left-side or mixed localization.

The Split-Brain Patient

Until the middle of the twentieth century, the primary neurological generalization regarding higher mental processes was that speech was localized in the left cerebral hemisphere in right-handers. Actually, the majority of researchers believed that the left side of the brain was dominant not only for speech but also for processing all other information (Levy, 1980). The left hemisphere was called the dominant, or major, hemisphere and the right was called the minor hemisphere.

Recent studies have shown, however, that the right side of the brain is not as inferior as it once seemed. Interest in the right hemisphere was provoked in large part by the work of Roger Sperry and his colleagues (Sperry, 1970, 1974; Sperry, Gazzaniga, & Bogen, 1969), who performed experiments on *split-brain patients.* (For his contributions to this research, Sperry was awarded a Nobel Prize in 1981.) In these people the brain tissue that links the two hemispheres is cut as a medical treatment. The biggest connection between the hemispheres consists of the *corpus callosum,* a fiber bundle joining the areas of association cortex on each side of the brain. In certain cases of epilepsy, the corpus callosum can transmit a seizure from one side of the brain to the other. When the fibers are severed, the disorder may be controlled; the patient gets relief and can perform quite normally.

Split-brain patients offered researchers like Sperry a unique opportunity, yet the researchers had to resolve several thorny problems before pro-

FIGURE 2–19
How Information Travels from the Eye to the Brain

If a person is fixating straight ahead, information positioned on the right goes first to the left hemisphere and information on the left goes first to the right hemisphere. Stated another way, information from the right visual field is first represented in the left hemisphere, while information from the left visual field is first represented in the right hemisphere. In most right-handed people, the left hemisphere controls speech and writing, while the right hemisphere seems specialized for nonverbal, spatial cognition. The left hemisphere controls the right hand; the right hemisphere controls the left hand. The corpus callosum joins the two hemispheres and allows communication between them. When information is presented to the right (or left) visual field of the split-brain patient, its representation can be isolated in the left (or right) hemisphere.

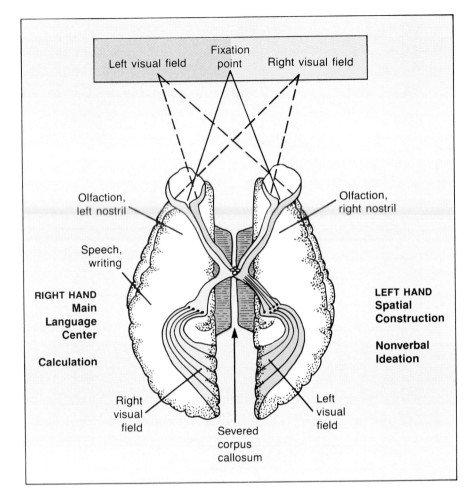

ceeding. Since verbal abilities are customarily controlled by one hemisphere, usually the left, an observer tends not to detect the operation of the right hemisphere when the split-brain patient describes experiences; in other words, the right hemisphere is "mute." However, in the laboratory, sensory information can be presented to the right hemisphere alone or to the left hemisphere alone. For example, a blindfolded split-brain patient can name a simple object felt by the right hand. This is because sensory information from the right hand goes to the left hemisphere, where language production is controlled. If the object is placed in the left hand, however, the patient cannot name the object because the right hemisphere is mute. But if the blindfold is removed, the patient can point to the recently touched object with the left hand. Such an experiment shows that the right hemisphere is capable of perceiving, remembering, and demonstrating its knowledge by initiating movement, although it is incapable of verbalizing these experiences.

Studying visual operations of each hemisphere is a little trickier. Because of the distribution of fibers in the optic system, information presented to each eye is projected almost equally to both hemispheres. For researchers

to ensure that information is presented to only one hemisphere, the split-brain patient must fixate on, or look at, a point. Then information projected to the right visual field goes only to the left hemisphere, and the right hemisphere "sees" objects on the left half of the visual field (see Figure 2–19).

Such experiments have shown that the right hemisphere has functions of its own that complement those of the left hemisphere. The right, for example, seems superior in accurately perceiving and remembering stimuli too complex to specify in words. Patients who have suffered damage to certain portions of the right hemisphere have great difficulty remembering a familiar face as seen in a snapshot (e.g., Yin, 1970). Work with split-brain patients has confirmed and extended these findings. In one experiment (Levy, Trevarthen, & Sperry, 1972) split-brain patients were presented with photographs combining the right half of one face with the left half of another (see Figure 2–20). The pictures were flashed briefly so that the two halves met

FIGURE 2–20
Photos Used to Test Split-Brain Patients

The composite photo on the left is presented to split-brain patients. When asked which of the above photos they have seen, the patients will pick the child if asked to respond verbally. This is the face presented to the right visual field and thus "seen" by the verbal left hemisphere. The respondents do not report anything unusual about the face; rather, they report seeing a whole face.

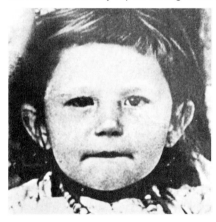

FIGURE 2–21
Drawings by a Split-Brain Patient

Drawings of the model were done by a split-brain patient with his right hand and with his left hand. He did a much better job with his left hand (controlled by the right hemisphere) than with his right hand, despite being right-handed.

Source: Bogen, 1969.

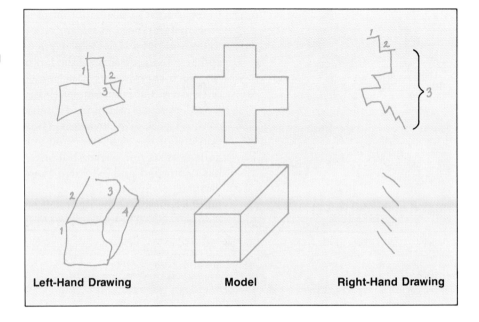

Left-Hand Drawing   Model   Right-Hand Drawing

FIGURE 2–22
Fitting the Arc to the Circle

In this experiment the split-brain subject has to match the part of a circle (arc) he feels with either his right or left hand behind the screen to the size of circle the arc would form if it were complete. The patients were accurate above the level of chance only when they were using their left hands, and therefore their right hemispheres.

Source: Nebes, 1974.

at the subject's point of fixation. When only half a picture was shown to one-half the visual field, the split-brain patient saw a whole picture—the brain completed it (Nebes, 1974). So with a composite, presumably each hemisphere "sees" a different whole picture. This appeared to be the case: when asked what they had seen, the patients always described the right-field face, i.e., the one seen by the left hemisphere. They did not report anything unusual about it but said they had seen a complete face. When asked to point to the picture they saw, they pointed to the left-field face, seen by the right hemisphere. This result seems to indicate that the right hemisphere is dominant for the perception of complex visual stimuli (Levy, 1980; Nebes, 1974).

The right hemisphere also appears to have a highly developed spatial and pattern sense. If each side of the brain receives a simple line drawing and the subject is asked to copy it, the left hand (controlled by the right hemisphere) will do a better job than the right hand (controlled by the left hemisphere), even in right-handed patients (see Figure 2–21).

The right hemisphere has shown superiority to the left in the ability to perceive the relationship between parts of a stimulus and the whole. In one experiment (Nebes, 1974), split-brain patients were presented with a part of a circle—an arc—in either their left or right hand, which they held behind a screen. They selected which of three different-sized circles the arc would form if it were complete (see Figure 2–22). The patients were accurate only when using their left hands and right hemispheres. The right hand, and thus the left hemisphere, generally performed no better than would be expected by chance.

Aside from visual and spatial abilities, the right hemisphere has some limited language abilities, as studies have shown that it can understand simple spoken or written language (Gazzaniga & Sperry, 1967). For example, subjects using their right hemisphere could correctly indicate whether they

FIGURE 2–23
Three Faces of Emotion

The original photograph is shown in the middle. It was divided in half and the left half with its mirror image is shown on the left. The right half and its mirror image is shown on the right. The expression of disgust is much clearer in the left-hand than the right-hand photograph. This suggests that emotions are expressed more intensely by the left side of the face, controlled by the right hemisphere.

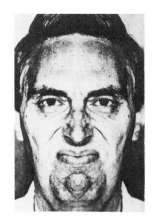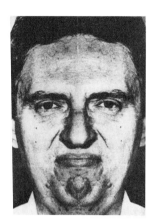

"saw" an object described by the experimenter, but they could not indicate whether the object had a name (Levy & Trevarthen, 1974).

Finally, some studies suggest that the right hemisphere could be important in the accurate interpretation of emotional stimuli and in communication of emotion (Tucker, 1981). In one study, photos of faces displaying emotion were divided, and the right and left halves were combined with their mirror images (see Figure 2–23). Researchers presented the combined photos to a panel of judges, who indicated that the left side of the face in right-handers expressed emotion more intensely than the right side of the face (Sackheim, Gur, & Saucy, 1978).

OTHER EVIDENCE FOR SPECIALIZATION

The research on specialization of the two hemispheres that we have reviewed so far was conducted primarily with split-brain patients. How can we be sure that findings from this small, special population generalize to normal adults?

Fortunately, the main findings of cerebral organization have been confirmed with other techniques on normal people. For example, Doreen Kimura (1961, 1964) presented information simultaneously to the two ears of people with no brain damage and asked the subjects to report what they heard. When presented with words, the subjects tended to recall the ones sent to the right ear slightly better than the ones sent to the left ear. However, when presented with competing melodies, the subjects could identify those played to the left ear slightly better than those played to the right. In general, Kimura and other researchers have found that there is a left-ear advantage for music and other noises. This makes sense in terms of other knowledge about cerebral organization. Neural connections are stronger from each ear to the cerebral hemisphere on the opposite side of the head. Thus information from the right ear is analyzed primarily by the left hemisphere, resulting in the right-ear advantage for speech. Information from the left ear is analyzed by the right hemisphere, leading to the left-ear advantage for nonspeech sounds. Results using positron emission

FIGURE 2–24
Right-Left Hemisphere Differences Shown by PET

As the bottom part of this photograph shows, verbal auditory stimuli primarily activate the left hemisphere, while music primarily activates the right hemisphere. Simultaneous music and language activates both hemispheres as shown in the upper right half of the photograph.

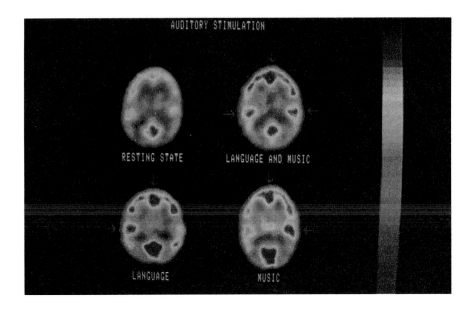

APPLYING PSYCHOLOGY

Positron Emission Tomography (PET)

A recently developed technique, positron emission tomography (PET), allows study of the brain in awake normal human subjects. PET is a visual technique in which the subject is given a radioactively labeled compound such as glucose that is metabolized by the brain. The idea is that the most active area of the brain will use the most glucose, so by measuring the radioactivity of different brain areas one can see which is metabolically active during a particular activity and thus which brain area is specialized for which function. Use of this technique has already given us a better understanding of brain organization and function, and the technique also seems to have great potential as a diagnostic tool for cerebral function. We will review just a few of the applications of PET.

Huntington's chorea is a genetic disorder that results in intellectual deterioration, psychiatric symptoms, and abnormal movement. The symptoms typically develop in people between the ages of 30 and 50. At present there is no way of determining whether a person will develop the disease before its symptoms appear. Since offspring of Huntington's victims have a 50% chance of inheriting the disease, it is especially important for scientists to identify carriers before their symptoms appear. PET studies of patients with Huntington's disease showed a reduction of glucose utilization in the portion of the brain most affected by the disease. In patients just beginning to manifest symptoms, glucose utilization in this portion of the brain was also severely reduced, even though X-rays showed no structural change. And in about half of the patients without symptoms, PET scans showed similar reductions in glucose utilization. One fifth of these people subsequently developed symptoms of Huntington's chorea (Kuhl, et al.,

1982). These findings offer the possibility that the PET technique may provide a way of identifying Huntington's chorea in patients before their symptoms appear.

PET may also help diagnose manic-depressive patients, people who suffer severe swings in mood. Studies using PET have shown changes throughout the brain in glucose utilization with the mood swings. In the depressive phase, glucose utilization is about 25% lower than normal (see Figure 2–25).

Some researchers think that various different cognitive tasks, which are reflected in differential glucose utilization in different parts of the brain (see Figure 2–25), can be used as a very sensitive measure of cerebral disorders. Much as a cardiologist uses an electrocardiogram to detect heart disease, in the future perhaps various cognitive tasks can be given to a patient and the information gained from PET techniques used to detect cerebral problems (Phelps & Mazziotta, 1985).

tomography also substantiate these findings (Phelps & Mazziotta, 1985) (see Figure 2–24).

Two interesting studies extend these observations on differences in brain organization. One showed that the lateralization of speech may not be confined to humans but may generalize to other species. Petersen et al. (1978) tested five Japanese macaques and five other monkeys of a different type for lateralization of speech sounds of the macaques. The animals were required to discriminate the sounds when they were presented to either the right or the left ear. The researchers found that the macaques showed a right-ear advantage when they discriminated sounds they used in communication, but a left-ear advantage (or no advantage) on sounds that were not relevant for communication. This is just the pattern shown by humans for speech and nonspeech sounds. The other monkeys generally showed no ear advantage on any of the sounds, which makes sense because they do not communicate with the same system of sounds as do the macaques. Other evidence also supports the idea of hemispheric asymmetries in animals, but its interpretation is more controversial (Springer & Deutsch, 1985).

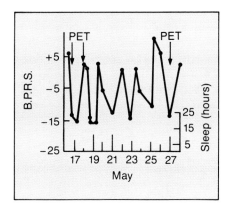

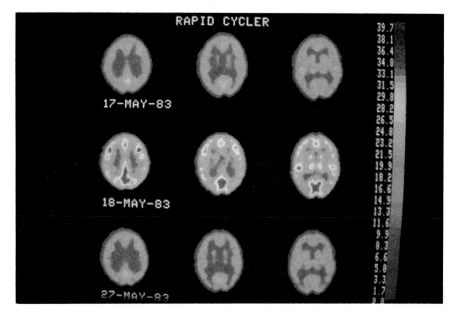

FIGURE 2–25
Manic-Depressive Cycle as Shown by PET

The graph shows the mood cycles of a rapidly cycling manic-depressive patient who cycles between mood states every 24–48 hours. The psychiatric rating scale indicates relative mania by positive values and relative depression by negative values. The PET results show how glucose utilization cycles in the same manner as the patient's mood. Each row has 3 cross-sectional PET images from high (left) to mid-level of the brain. The numerical scale at right is glucose utilization in units of μmoles/min/100gms of tissue.

Source: Phelps, M. E., & Mazziotta, J. C. (1985). Positron emission tomography: Human brain function and biochemistry. *Science, 228,* p. 802.

A second recent finding was obtained with human subjects. Gur et al. (1982) gave people verbal or visual tasks to perform and measured blood flow in the two hemispheres. Blood flow in both hemispheres was greater when people performed the tasks than when they rested, but the flow was greater in the left hemisphere when they performed a verbal task and greater in the right hemisphere when they performed a spatial task. Studies such as these indicate a firm basis for the belief that the hemispheres of the brain are differentially involved in processing varying sorts of information.

Recently, Kimura's (1983) research has focused on the issue of sex differences in cerebral organization. Are centers supporting language functions found in different places in the brains of men and women? Although answers to this question are still tentative and many similarities exist in lateralization of functions for men and women, some reliable differences also seem to appear. Kimura (1983) examined 216 patients with brain lesions in the left hemisphere. She found that speech disorders in women occurred more frequently from damage to the front part of the left hemisphere than from damage to the back part. Men, on the other hand, showed roughly similar patterns of disordered speech when brain damage was in the front or the back; if anything, the men showed somewhat more aphasia when the damage was in the back.

Other investigators have also concluded that sex differences exist in brain organization, one suggestion being that the asymmetry of function is greater in males than in females (McGlone, 1980). That is, right-handed males seem to have verbal operations more isolated in the left hemisphere, while right-handed females are more likely to show some language functioning in the right hemisphere as well as the left. Gur et al. (1982) also showed differences between males and females in the blood flow of the two hemispheres during processing of verbal and visual information.

THE ENDOCRINE SYSTEM

In addition to communication by neurons, signals are sent from one part of the body to another by means of the *endocrine system,* which consists of a set of glands. Endocrine glands (*endocrine* means "inside-secreting") secrete *hormones,* chemical messengers carried by the bloodstream to other body organs.

The major endocrine glands are shown in Figure 2–26. The endocrine system is linked to the nervous system by connections between the hypothalamus and the *pituitary gland,* which lies just below the hypothalamus. The hypothalamus controls the activity of the pituitary gland by the production and release of hormones that travel to the pituitary gland, which then synthesizes and releases pituitary hormones. Most of these hormones stimulate the production and release of other hormones in other endocrine glands. For this reason the pituitary gland is called the master gland.

The specificity of hormone action is accomplished by hormone receptor molecules. A given hormone receptor will be activated only by its particular hormone, and only cells that have receptor molecules for that hormone will react to that hormone.

Let us consider some examples of how the system works. The hypothalamus produces the hormone CRH (corticotropin-releasing factor). CRH

FIGURE 2–26
Locations of the Major Endocrine Glands

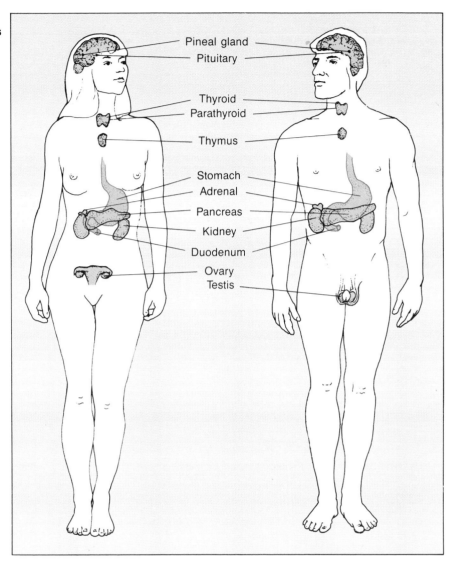

causes the pituitary gland to release ACTH (adrenocorticotropic hormone), which acts on the cortex of the adrenal gland, causing it to release a variety of hormones including the stress hormone cortisol. As another example, consider sex hormones. The hypothalamus produces GnRH (gonadotropin-releasing hormone), which acts on the pituitary gland to release two hormones, FSH (follicle-stimulating hormone) and LH (luteinizing hormone) into the bloodstream. In males LH acts on receptors on the testes to release testosterone (the male sex hormone) into the bloodstream. Testosterone in turn acts on many tissues to maintain male sexual characteristics. FSH causes the development and growth of sperm cells. In females, FSH and LH act on the ovaries to cause the release of the female sex hormones estrogen and progesterone. These hormones regulate the female cycle of ovulation and menstruation. In contrast, some pituitary hormones have direct effects. For example, growth hormone, as its name implies, released by the pituitary regulates growth: too much can produce a giant, too little a dwarf.

TABLE 2–2
Summary of the Major Hormones

Gland	Hormone	Controls
HYPOTHALAMUS	Releasing hormones	Secretion by the pituitary
	Oxytocin	(See pituitary)
	Antidiuretic hormone	(See pituitary)
PITUITARY	Growth hormone (somatotropin, GH, STH)*	Growth
	Thyroid-stimulating hormone (TSH, thyrotropin)	Thyroid gland
	Adrenocorticotropic hormone (ACTH, corticotropin)	Adrenal cortex
	Prolactin	Breasts (milk synthesis)
	Gonadotropic hormones: Follicle-stimulating hormone (FSH) Luteinizing hormone (LH)	Gonads (gamete production and sex hormone synthesis)
	Oxytocin	Milk secretion; uterine motility
	Antidiuretic hormone (ADH)	Water excretion
ADRENAL CORTEX	Cortisol	Response to stresses
	Androgens	Growth and, in women, sexual activity
	Aldosterone	Sodium and potassium excretion
ADRENAL MEDULLA	Epinephrine Norepinephrine	Cardiovascular function; response to stresses
THYROID	Thyroxine (T_4) Triiodothyronine (T_3) Calcitonin	Metabolism; growth Plasma calcium
PARATHYROIDS	Parathyroid hormone (parathormone, PTH, PH)	Plasma calcium and phosphate
GONADS Female: ovaries	Estrogens Progesterone	Reproductive system; growth and development
Male testes	Testosterone	Reproductive system; growth and development
PANCREAS	Insulin Glucagon Somatostatin	Plasma glucose
KIDNEYS	Renin Erythropoietin (ESF) 1,25-Dihydroxy vitamin D_3	Adrenal cortex; blood pressure Erythrocyte production Calcium balance
GASTROINTESTINAL TRACT	Gastrin Secretin Cholecystokinin Gastric inhibitory peptide Somatostatin	Gastrointestinal tract; liver; pancreas; gallbladder
THYMUS	Thymus hormone (thymosin)	Lymphocyte development
PINEAL	Melatonin	Sexual maturity (?)

*Names and abbreviations in parentheses are synonyms.
Source: Adapted from Thompson, 1985.

The *adrenal glands* lie just above the kidney (*adrenal* means "toward kidney" in Latin). Their central core, called the *adrenal medulla,* secretes the hormones *epinephrine* and *norepinephrine* in stressful situations (*epine-phros* means "on the kidney" in Greek, and *epinephrine* is synonymous with *adrenaline*). These hormones increase the liver's sugar output and accelerate the heart rate and the surge of blood to the skeletal muscles (as reflected in the phrase "your adrenaline is flowing" to indicate excitement). These changes reinforce the action of the sympathetic nervous system in excitement. Norepinephrine is also an excitatory neurotransmitter for organs controlled by the sympathetic nervous system (see pages 49–50). When the body reacts to stress, the activity of the sympathetic nervous system and the endocrine system overlap and reinforce one another. (The long-term effects of continued stress are considered in Chapter 13.)

The outer portion of the adrenal glands is called the *adrenal cortex.* It generates a large number of chemicals, including androgens, hormones that have actions similar to those of testosterone. Androgens are secreted by the adrenal glands of both men and women and are thought to be the determiners of sex drive in women. When the adrenal cortex overproduces male hormones in a woman, a malelike appearance may result. The sex glands, or gonads, also create sex hormones. The effects of sex hormones in producing sex differences in the brain, physical appearance, and behavior are discussed in Chapter 12. The major hormones and their effects are outlined in Table 2–2.

EVOLUTION, GENETICS, AND BEHAVIOR

Our discussion of the brain and the nervous system has included some information on evolution. Our evolutionary ancestry is part of our biological makeup. In this section we discuss the role of evolution and genetics and how scientists trace the effects of heredity on behavior. The theory of evolution is central to the biological sciences. As you probably know, the theory assumes that all existing species have evolved over millions of years. Our understanding of how evolution may have occurred is due to the work of Charles Darwin (1809–1882) and Gregor Mendel (1822–1884). Darwin developed the *theory of natural selection,* and Mendel provided the foundation for the science of *genetics.* Evolutionary theory and genetics were brought together in the 1930s with the development of the "modern synthetic theory of evolution."

Darwin published his theory in 1859 under the title *On the Origin of the Species by Means of Natural Selection, or the Preservation of Favoured Races in the Struggle for Life.* In every species, Darwin wrote, individuals differ, and these differences derive in part from heredity. If one individual proves more fertile or survives longer than another, its chances of leaving descendants become greater. This had been recognized for centuries. Darwin's originality lay in proposing that such selective survival could be a mechanism for changes in organisms. If an inherited trait influences the likelihood of surviving to maturity and reproducing, then the survivors' offspring and reproducers should possess slightly more of the trait than did the preceding generation. Thus, gradually, the characteristics of a population can change, and over a

From *Bloom County:* "Loose Tails," by Berke Breathed, Copyright © 1983 by The Washington Post Company. Reprinted by permission of Little, Brown and Company.

sufficiently long period the changes could become so great that in sum they would amount to a new species. The phrase "survival of the fittest" came to encapsulate the theory, although Darwin himself seems never to have used the term. For Darwin the concept of *fitness* simply referred to production of offspring that themselves successfully reproduce. Organisms that produce more viable offspring are the fitter. Darwin warned against the tendency to think of later stages in the evolutionary process as being higher or more advanced than earlier stages because organisms evolve to reproduce successfully in their local environment. If an amoeba is as well adapted to its environment as people are to theirs, who is to say which is the higher organism? Darwin did not even like to use the term *evolution* since in common language it suggested that organisms were evolving toward some goal state; he preferred the phrase "descent with modification" (Gould, 1977).

Gregor Mendel, an Augustinian monk, conducted his research on peas in a monastery garden. By crossing plants and observing their characteristics over many generations, Mendel concluded that some traits of the plants passed from parent to offspring and that they were not always visible in the offspring when they were visible in the parents or vice versa. Some attributes could be transmitted from "grandparent" to "grandchild" without being manifest in the physical appearance of the intervening generation. In 1909, the name *gene* was proposed for the fixed elements, or fundamental units, of heredity. Today we know that information in genes is coded as a sequence of complex molecular bases forming part of the large molecule deoxyribonucleic acid (DNA). Two terms have been used to distinguish the genetic and the visible characteristics of the organism. *Genotype* stands for the genetic composition of the individual, *phenotype* for the visible measurable characteristics, or traits.

The merger of the theories of natural selection and genetics can be summarized briefly as follows. Genetic variation occurs within species—individuals differ in what genes they possess. This process influences fitness, that is, the likelihood of having viable offspring. As a result, the sum of all genes, called the gene pool, changes over generations. Obviously organisms that do not reproduce do not add their genes to the pool of the next generation; individuals who bear more viable offspring contribute more of their genes. Changes in the gene pool are not mere fluctuations but are cumulative, thereby accounting for "descent with modification" over time, or evolution.

As we have seen, individual variation occurs within every species and some of that variation reflects differences in genes among individuals. However, a portion of the variation is also due to the environments in which individuals live or the experiences they have. The field of *behavior genetics* analyzes the contributions of genotype and environment to behavior.

Behavior Genetics

All the characteristics possessed by you or any animal are affected by genes and environment. Behavior geneticists ask how the environment and genes operate together to produce a particular characteristic. For example, drinking milk is harmless for most people; they have the enzyme lactase that is necessary to digest milk. If this enzyme is lacking, as it is in some populations, milk is a mild poison: the presence of milk sugar (lactose) produces a gastrointestinal disorder. The inability to digest milk is often termed hereditary, but of course the ability to digest milk is also hereditary. It is then appropriate to say that the difference among people in the ability to digest milk is produced by differences in their genes.

In general the strategy to determine if differences in genes relate to differences in behavior is simple: locate organisms of different genotypes, hold the environment constant, and see if behaviors differ. But since genes are not directly observable, determining genotypes may prove difficult. An observer cannot infer that organisms that look alike (have similar phenotypes) also have similar genotypes. With subjects other than humans, behavior geneticists employ two methods to find organisms differing in genotype: they use inbred strains of animals and they breed animals selectively.

Inbred strains of mice and other animals are produced by mating brothers and sisters, then mating brothers and sisters among their offspring, and so on. After at least 20 generations, virtual identity of genes results, i.e., members of a particular strain of mice each have the same genes. Many different inbred strains of mice have been developed. When two different strains are reared in the same environment, disparities in their behavior are related to variations in their genes. Inbred strains of mice differ, for example, in aggressive behavior (Southwick & Clark, 1968), sexual behavior (McGill, 1962), learning (Wahlsten, 1972), and emotionality (Thompson, 1953). Indeed, it is much easier to find strains of mice that diverge in behavior than strains that do not (Plomin, DeFries, and McClearn, 1980).

In *selective breeding,* phenotype rather than genotype determines the choice of animals. Recall that a phenotype is any observable trait. Behavior geneticists usually measure a behavioral trait and select animals for breeding on the basis of it. For example, an experimenter might record activity of animals in an open field. (In the laboratory, an open field is a large, walled-in area with sections marked on the floor.) Highly emotional animals are less active in the open field than less emotional ones. Males that score high in activity are mated with high-scoring females; low-scoring males are mated with low-scoring females. Activity of the offspring is measured, and again mating is based on comparable levels of activity. If activity has a genetic component, over generations the activity scores of the high and low lines should diverge. Results of a study in which investigators selected on the basis of activity scores in the open field are shown in Figure 2–27 (DeFries, Hegmann, & Halcomb, 1974). These investigators bred two high-scoring and two low-scoring lines and, to control possible environmental changes over generations, two randomly bred lines. Figure 2–27 shows the scores of one of each type of line. As you can see, the scores of the high and low lines diverged over the 20 generations—those of the high line increased, those of the low line decreased. The control line's scores did not change appreciably. These data indicate that differences in genes play a role in producing disparities in open-field activity.

Often whether or not a difference in genes is expressed in behavior depends on environmental variation. For example, in one study (Cooper & Zubek, 1958) rats were selectively bred for speed in learning a maze, producing a group of rapid learners and a group of slow learners. The two

FIGURE 2–27
Open-Field Activity Scores for Three Lines of Mice Bred over Twenty Generations

The top, solid color line shows the scores of animals bred for high activity; the middle, solid black line shows the control animals, which were randomly bred; and the dashed color line at the bottom shows the scores for mice bred for low activity. The divergence on the activity scores over generations suggests that there is a genetic component to open-field activity.

Source: DeFries, Hegmann & Halcomb, 1974.

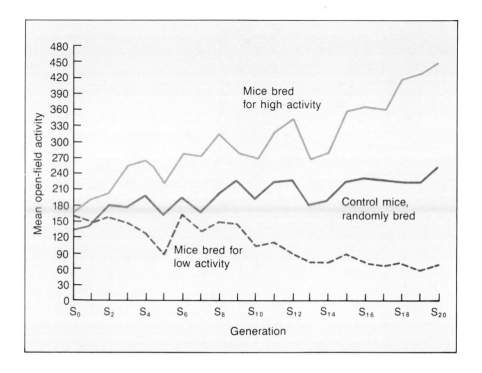

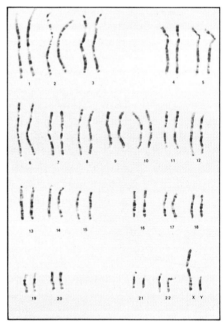

FIGURE 2–28
Male Chromosomes

Chromosomes come in pairs except for the sex chromosomes. These are shown on the lower right side of the photograph, one X and one Y chromosome.

groups differed significantly in performance, however, only if they were reared in a normal environment. When the environment was restricted, the two lines did about the same—poorly; the superiority of the rapid learners was not evident. When the environment was enriched, only a small difference favored the rapid learners; the slow learners' performance was much improved. This shows again that environmental and genetic influences combine to produce behavior.

To study the relationship between genes and behavior in humans the same strategy is used as in animal studies. Researchers find organisms whose genes differ, hold the environment constant, and measure behavior. In human beings this is more difficult than in animals. The two methods used are *twin studies* and *family studies.* Some background on human genetic makeup will precede our description of these methods.

Each of us receives half of our genes from each of our parents. Genes come in pairs (one from each parent), and they are contained in each cell of our bodies in molecules called *chromosomes.* Except for sex cells, every cell contains 46 chromosomes, 23 from the mother and 23 from the father (see Figure 2–28). Each sex cell (i.e., the sperm and the ovum) contains 23 of a possible 46 chromosomes (one-half of each pair of chromosomes found in the cells). Each sex cell can and does contain different chromosomes, but it always contains 23 of the total 46. At the time of conception the sperm from the father and the ovum from the mother unite to produce a new cell, called the *zygote,* the beginning of a new human being. Because each ovum has a random 23 of a possible 46 chromosomes from the mother and each sperm has a random 23 of a possible 46 chromosomes from the father, many different combinations of chromosomes will occur in different zygotes from the same parents. It is estimated that there are 20^{24} different combinations of genes possible from a single human pair, a number far greater than the total number of human beings who have ever existed (Stern, 1949). It is probable that no human beings except identical twins have ever been genetic duplicates. Thus there is genetic variation among children of the same parents. If you are not an identical twin, you are a unique genetic individual. There has never been a genotype nor probably will there ever be another genotype exactly like you.

At the same time, children of the same parents are more similar in heredity than are children of different parents. On the average, half of a person's genes are the same as those of a brother or sister. *Fraternal,* or *dizygotic, twins* develop from two different zygotes, so they are no more similar in heredity than other brothers and sisters. *Identical,* or *monozygotic, twins* develop from a single zygote, so they have identical genes. Comparing identical and fraternal twins is one way to measure genetic influences on human behavior.

TWIN STUDIES. If genes strongly influence a trait, identical twins should be more similar in that trait than fraternal twins; identical twins share identical genes while fraternal twins do not. To determine if there is a genetic basis for schizophrenia, for example, one strategy is to find schizophrenics who

Identical twins are genetically identical and so are always the same gender and always look alike (right photograph). Fraternal twins are no more alike genetically than other brothers and sisters and so can be the same or different genders and may or may not look alike (left photograph). The fraternal twins shown are Betty and David Deutsch visiting Santa Claus. Even though they are twins, Betty is taller than David because girls mature at a faster rate. However, David grew to 6'1", seven inches taller than his sister and played professional basketball for the New York Knickerbockers. (Betty is now Betty Capaldi, one of the authors of your book.)

are members of twin pairs and then to measure the percentage of co-twins who also have schizophrenia. The percentage is called the *concordance rate.* Kallman (1946) studied the incidence of schizophrenia and reported a concordance rate of .69 for identical co-twins and of .10 for fraternal co-twins. In later studies researchers have obtained similar results, although the exact rates depend on how broadly schizophrenia is defined and on whether or not mild cases are included (Fischer, Harvald, & Hauge, 1969; Gottesman & Shields, 1976). These data may implicate a genetic factor in schizophrenia. By themselves the figures do not establish a genetic factor because identical twins may be treated more alike by their parents than fraternal twins. Thus their greater similarity could result from their upbringing. However, the data are consistent with the hypothesis that a genetic influence underlies schizophrenia, and they are one type of information needed to conclude ultimately that schizophrenia has a genetic basis.

FAMILY STUDIES. Another method used to measure a genetic influence on behavior is to study families. Family members have similar genes. You share half your genes with your mother and half with your father. On average you also share half your genes with your brothers and sisters. However, most families also live together. So if families share a common trait it could be related to their common genes, to their common environment, or both.

One way to get around this problem is to study adopted children. Heston (1970) found subjects born to schizophrenic mothers who were permanently separated from them before they were one month old and were reared in foster or adoptive homes. Another group of children who also had been separated from their biological mothers before reaching one month of age and were reared in foster homes were used as controls. Their mothers had no record of psychiatric problems. As adults, the children of schizophrenic mothers showed significantly greater incidence of schizophrenia than the control subjects. These data, consistent with those from the twin studies, point to a possible genetic factor in schizophrenia.

In another type of family study, investigators measure a trait within a family over generations. The pattern of appearance of a trait in family members over generations can suggest specific hypotheses as to how genes are related to a trait. Not all genes are directly reflected in observable traits (phenotype is not the same as genotype). An example of this is a characteristic of genes termed *recessiveness. Recessive genes* will not be expressed in the phenotype unless both members of a pair of genes are the same. Blue eyes are produced by recessive genes. If one parent contributes genes for brown eyes and the other parent contributes genes for blue eyes, the child's eyes will be brown; the blue-eye gene is recessive, the brown-eye gene is dominant. Two brown-eyed parents could have a blue-eyed child if they both carried the recessive blue-eye genes and if these recessive genes were contributed to the child by both parents. Sickle cell anemia, a disease of the red blood cells that occurs almost entirely among blacks, is produced by a recessive gene. So if one suspects that a trait is carried by a recessive gene, one can see if the pattern of appearance of the trait follows the pattern expected for a recessive trait. Many forms of mental retardation are controlled by single recessive genes. A family pattern of epilepsy is shown in Figure 2–29. The parents of the two afflicted children are normal, but they have

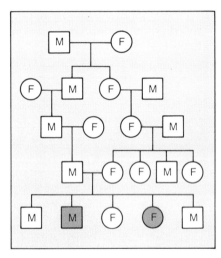

FIGURE 2–29
A Family History of the Occurrence of Epilepsy

Shown at the top are the great-great-grandparents, and below the following generations. A blue symbol indicates epilepsy; an open symbol indicates an unaffected individual. Females are represented by circles, males by squares. Parents are joined by a horizontal marriage line, with offspring listed below. Brothers and sisters are connected to a horizontal line that is joined by a perpendicular line to their parents' marriage line. As you can see, the disease occurred in two of five children from a marriage between people descended from the same ancestor. This suggests a recessive mode of inheritance.

the same great-great-grandparents. This is a strong indicator of recessive inheritance.

In later chapters, we shall present many more studies based on the methods we have outlined here. Human behavior genetics has been especially important in research on cognitive, social, and physical development (Chapter 9), intelligence (Chapter 11), personality (Chapter 14), and abnormal personality (Chapter 15). As we will see, the interactions of biological and environmental factors are central concerns of psychology.

SUMMARY

1. The basic unit of the nervous system is the neuron, which consists of a cell body, dendrites, and an axon. Neural conduction is an electrochemical process. Changes in the permeability of the cell membrane produce electrical changes that, if strong enough, create an action potential. An action potential travels down an axon causing terminal buttons to release neurotransmitters. These neurotransmitters cross the synaptic cleft to the dendrites and cell body of the next neuron.

2. Four of the neurotransmitters are acetylcholine (ACh), which elicits contraction of skeletal muscles in response to activity of motor nerves and may also be important for memory formation (it has been implicated in Alzheimer's disease); norepinephrine (NE), which has been implicated in mood; GABA, important in motor control (it has been implicated in Huntington's chorea); and dopamine, important in motor control (too little dopamine has been clearly shown to be the cause of Parkinson's disease) and possibly in schizophrenia.

3. The central nervous system consists of the brain and spinal cord. All neurons in the body outside the central nervous system are part of the peripheral nervous system, which includes the somatic and autonomic nervous systems. The autonomic nervous system consists of the parasympathetic system, important in reactions maintaining and restoring the body, and the sympathetic nervous system, important in emotional reactions.

4. The brain stem contains the medulla, pons, and midbrain, which are vital to the basic biological functions of sensing and moving. Also part of the brain stem, the cerebellum coordinates movements, and the reticular activating system is important in sleep and arousal. The thalamus transmits information from the body to the brain and within the brain.

5. The hypothalamus plays an important role in motivation (hunger, thirst, sex, temperature regulation) and regulates the endocrine system. The limbic system is important in emotion (amygdala, septum), and in memory (hippocampus).

6. The cerebral cortex is divided into four areas, or lobes: frontal, temporal, parietal, and occipital. Sensory areas of the cortex are located in the parietal, occipital, and temporal lobes; a motor area occupies the frontal lobes; and association areas are present in all lobes.

7. The endocrine system is a chemical communication system within the body. In general the hypothalamus stimulates the pituitary gland to secrete hormones, some of which have direct effects and some of which stimulate the production and release of hormones by other endocrine glands.

8. Studies of split-brain patients have indicated that to some extent humans have two brains, with each hemisphere of the brain being dominant for various functions (e.g., the left hemisphere is dominant for speech for most people).

9. According to the modern synthetic theory of evolution, individuals vary in their genes and this variation influences the likelihood of having viable offspring (fitness). As a result, the gene pool changes over generations, and with the passage of enough time these changes become so great as to produce distinct species, thereby accounting for evolution of different species.

10. In behavior genetics, organisms with different genes are compared to see if their behavior also differs. In animals this is done by using inbred strains of animals or by selective breeding. In humans, behavior genetic methods include comparing identical and fraternal twins and examining family histories of behavior patterns.

SUGGESTED READINGS

Carlson, N. R. (1986). *Physiology of behavior* (3rd ed.). Boston: Allyn and Bacon.

An excellent overview of methods and current knowledge in physiological psychology.

Gardner, H. (1974). *The shattered mind: The person after brain damage.* New York: Vintage Books/Random House.

This account details what happens to people whose brains are injured by disease or accidents and the lessons provided for the normal functioning of the brain.

Kolb, B., & Whishaw, I. Q. (1985). *Fundamentals of human neuropsychology* (2nd ed.). New York: Freeman.

An excellent coverage of human brain function, including many descriptions of motor and sensory disorders and other cerebral disorders.

Springer, S. P., & Deutsch, G. (1985). *Left brain, right brain* (rev. ed.). New York: Freeman.

An overview of the evidence for different functioning of the two central hemispheres; includes a chapter on "The Puzzle of the Left Hander."

Thompson, R. F. (1985). *The brain: An introduction to neuroscience.* New York: Freeman.

A more detailed exposition than was possible here of what is currently known about the human brain. No background in science is assumed.

PART TWO
Sensation, Perception, and Consciousness

3

Sensory Processes

The initial cause of any action always lies in external
sensory stimulation, because without this, thought is
impossible.

Ivan Sechenov

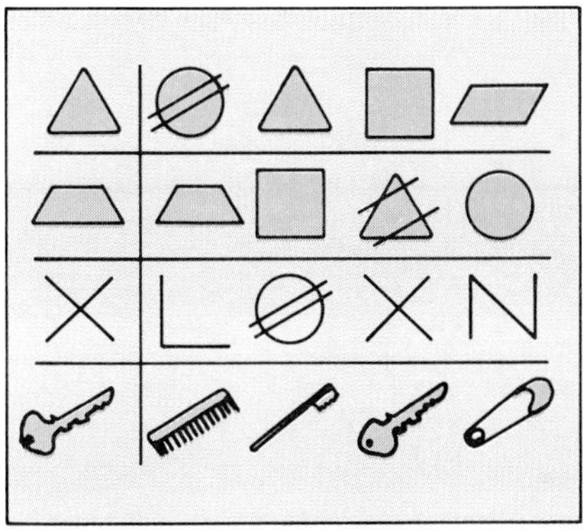

FIGURE 3–1
The Poisoned Soldier's Test

Part of the task assigned to a soldier who had suffered carbon monoxide poisoning involved matching the figures on the left side of this diagram to those on the right. The soldier was unable to perform the matching task.

Source: Benson & Greenberg, 1969, p. 84.

THE SCENE: A SENSORY PSYCHOLOGY LABORATORY. RESEARCHERS ARE performing a series of tests with a patient who is *cortically blind*. Although his eyes and optic nerves function perfectly, he cannot see because of damage to the visual cortex of his brain. When objects are placed in front of him and he is asked to name each one, he fails the test miserably; apparently, he cannot see anything. The researchers try a different test. They ask the patient to point to the objects. Incredibly, the patient now accurately points in the direction of the objects, performing far better than chance would account for. But he still denies seeing anything and is at a loss to explain how he is able to point to something he cannot see. This remarkable ability of cortically blind patients has been termed **blindsight.** Some researchers report that, over repeated tests, the accuracy of blindsight improves, although the patients never stop wondering how such ability is possible (Bridgeman and Staggs, 1982).

A similar type of visual impairment afflicted a soldier who suffered carbon monoxide poisoning (Benson and Greenberg, 1969). After awakening from a coma, the soldier appeared alert and talkative, but he had serious problems with visual perception. Although he could identify colors and tell which way an object was moving, he could not recognize faces and letters. He once identified his own face in the mirror as that of his doctor. When he was given a simple test, such as the sample item shown in Figure 3–1, he appeared to be guessing: he could not distinguish a circle from a square. The technical term of this soldier's malady is *visual form agnosia.*

Cases of blindsight and visual form agnosia are intriguing puzzles for researchers, who hope that some of these bizarre malfunctions will yield clues about how our sensory systems and neural pathways enable us to perceive the world accurately. In this chapter we will show how the sensory receptors—our eyes, ears, nose, and other organs—produce information that the brain can interpret into the full-blown experience called perception. In Chapter 4 we will examine how the mind perceives the world, and in Chapter 5 we will examine the next step—our conscious awareness of the world.

We will return later in this chapter to impairments of sensation and perception, but now we provide some basic information on the sensory systems. We begin with a pair of interesting demonstrations of how sensory input can (and cannot) lead to accurate perception and then review what we mean when we refer to the "senses."

FROM SENSATION TO PERCEPTION

The human sensory systems are remarkably sensitive and powerful. Like the heart, they work at their jobs constantly; as you read this page, more than 250 million light receptors in your eyes are relaying information about the lines and squiggles on this page to your brain, which sorts and interprets the information. The term *sensation* refers to this reception of stimulation from the environment. *Perception* describes the interpretation and understanding of that stimulation. Although sensation and perception are treated in separate chapters in this book, it is best to think of them not as two different processes but as two points along a continuum. From the instant a stimulus strikes one of the sensory receptors, the difficult but surprisingly rapid job of interpretation begins; there is really no sharp boundary between sensation and perception.

The different roles of sensation and perception are illustrated dramatically in Figure 3–2. At first glance, this photograph probably makes little sense. Stare at it for a few moments before reading on to see if you can figure it out.

The photo shows a dalmatian walking with its nose to the ground toward a tree in the upper left corner. What is the point of this demonstration? When you first looked at the photo, your sensory processes were presumably working as well as ever; your eyes were faithfully relaying information to the brain about which parts of the picture were black and which were white. This information was incoherent, however, because your perceptual processes were initially unable to organize the chaos of ink blotches. Perception usually operates so quickly that you are not aware of the inescapable delay before you understand what you are looking at. But with this image, the wait was noticeable. During the delay, your perceptual processes were interpreting the patterns of light and dark so that you could understand the scene.

FIGURE 3–2
A Hidden Object

The difficulty most people have interpreting this photo illustrates the distinction between sensation and perception. Your senses pick up the information in the photo, but the quality is so poor that perception of the object is quite laborious.

FIGURE 3–3
Another Hidden Animal

Examine the figure for 15 seconds and try to see an animal. If you cannot, turn to Figure 3–4 on page 86.

Source: Sekuler & Blake, 1985, p. 18.

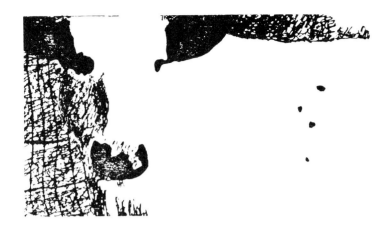

Let us take another example, one that is probably even harder. Look at the patterns in Figure 3–3 and try to discern another animal. Give yourself at least 15 seconds before turning to page 86 to see a clearer version in Figure 3–4. Again, you can see that sometimes perceptions are not achieved automatically—especially when the quality of the stimulus information is poor—but that perception takes effort, with clues being fit together to solve the puzzle. Another interesting point about these demonstrations is how long the memory for these patterns lasts. If you were to see Figures 3–2 and 3–3 months from now, you would probably recognize them immediately.

Classifying the Senses

Most people learn quite early about the five basic senses: vision, audition, taste, smell, and touch. Few learn that this five-way classification dates to the Greek philosopher Aristotle, and just as few know that in fact there are many more than five senses and that Aristotle's classification is largely arbitrary. For example, touch (or the *skin senses* as they are more properly called), tells much more than how things "feel"; it also registers temperature, vibration, pain, and many other properties. Similarly, much perceptual experience of the world results from the senses working in close coordination. Locating an object often depends on eyes, ears, and touch working simultaneously. You will, for example, find it harder to tell where a sound originates with your eyes closed than with them open. Last, people sense the position of their limbs (the *kinesthetic sense*) and state of balance with respect to gravity *(vestibular sense)* without drawing on the five classical senses.

All the senses have evolved to keep us aware of critical parts of our environment. Taste and touch may be termed the *near* senses because the stimulus to activate these systems must come into direct contact with the sense receptors. The near senses tell us about changes in our immediate environment, as when we touch something hot and quickly withdraw our hand or taste something bitter and spit it out. Seeing and hearing are *far* or *distance* senses because they can pick up information from remote sources. The distance senses inform us of changes away from our immediate vicinity. Hearing and particularly seeing provide important information to alert us to the approach of danger or food or friends. Smelling can be classified as a far

FIGURE 3–4
The Cow Revealed

The picture of a cow is more readily seen here than in Figure 3–3. What features make the perception of this picture much easier than seeing the cow in Figure 3–3?

Source: Sekuler & Blake, 1985, p. 20.

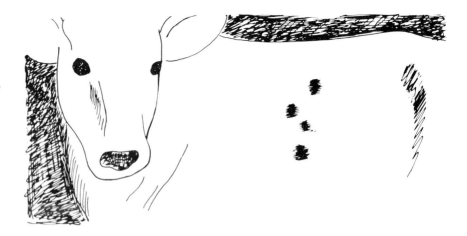

sense, but obviously it is in between the near and the far senses. Odors lose their intensity rapidly with distance, so smelling is much more effective for nearby objects.

VISION

Each sense has a characteristic sequence of events leading from the external world to interpretation of a stimulus. Figure 3–5 shows the characteristic pattern for vision, beginning when light is reflected from an object and continuing as it strikes the eye and is converted to the electrochemical signal carried by the nervous system to the various brain centers where the information is interpreted. A similar journey occurs for the energy directed at each sense, a process that constantly occurs throughout our lives, for we live in a welter of sensory stimulation.

The Physics of Light

The eyes are sensitive only to a particular region of the electromagnetic spectrum called light. Electromagnetic radiation can be thought of as traveling in waves, and different kinds of energy have different wavelengths. This is illustrated in Figure 3–6, where it is evident that the visible spectrum is only a small part of the total spectrum. Humans are blind to the regions in the infrared, ultraviolet, radio, TV, X-ray, and microwave portions of the spectrum. Other animals are not. Certain insects may look at a flower that appears solidly colored to us and discern patterns on the petals that are visible only in the ultraviolet range. It is difficult, and perhaps somewhat discomfiting, to reconcile such facts with the belief that the senses put us in direct contact with the physical world; we see only a limited portion of what is around us.

The two properties of light most important for the study of the psychology of vision are intensity and wavelength. The *intensity* of light affects the psychological experiences of *brightness* and *lightness* perception. (Brightness refers to intensity of a light source; lightness refers to reflected light from an object.) In general, the more intense a light source, the brighter a light will appear. When light illuminates an object, part of the

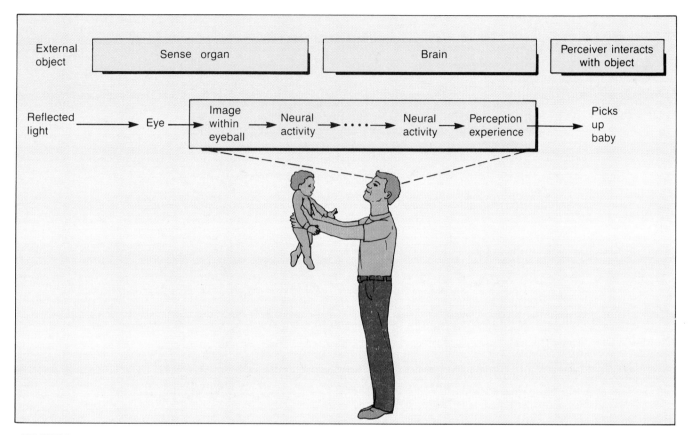

FIGURE 3-5
Chain of Events that Lead to Visual Perception

Each sense has a characteristic sequence of stimulation that gives rise to perception. In each case some specific energy from the environment strikes the sense organ, is converted (or transduced) into nervous impulses, and is interpreted by the brain.

light is absorbed and part reflected; the perceived lightness of an object depends on the proportion of light that is reflected. There is more to the perception of brightness and lightness, however, than intensity. A blacktop road will appear black whether it is seen in the evening, when there is relatively little light falling on it, or in broad daylight. In fact, a blacktop road in the noonday sun reflects more light to the eye than does a white shirt worn indoors in the evening. (You can verify that with any light meter, such as the kind built into many cameras.) Yet the road looks black and the shirt looks white.

The second important property of light is *wavelength*, which affects the light's perceived color, or *hue*. Wavelength is the distance between adjacent wave crests, and it is measured in *nanometers*, or billionths of a meter. As the wavelength of light increases through the visible spectrum, which ranges roughly from 400 to 750 nanometers, humans perceive the color of the light as changing from violet through blue, green, yellow, and orange to red at the longest wavelengths (see Figure 3-6). Color perception, however, involves factors other than the registration of wavelength. For example, many colors such as brown, pink, and even white are not in the spectrum. (Have you ever seen brown in a rainbow?) Such colors embody several different wavelengths, and the human visual system in effect mixes the wavelengths to produce perception of a nearly infinite variety of colors.

Ordinarily, light is the stimulus for visual sensations. But these sensations may come about in other ways. Pressure applied to the eye or a sharp

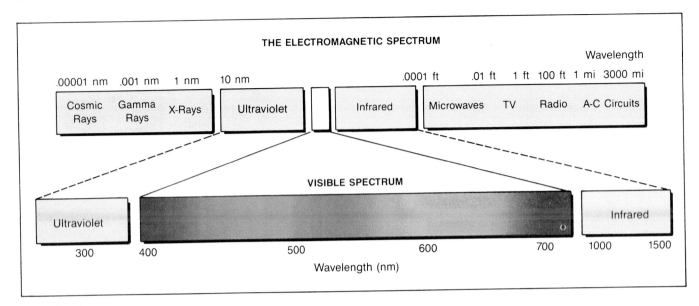

FIGURE 3–6
The Visible Spectrum

The range of the electromagnetic spectrum is portrayed at the top, from cosmic rays and gamma rays, with very small wavelengths, to long waves of radio and AC circuits. Human eyes are sensitive only to the visible spectrum (shown in color). Differing light wavelengths in the visible spectrum create perception of various colors.

FIGURE 3–7
Subjective Colors

After staring at the pattern for several moments, you should be able to see faint colors in the spaces between the black lines. You may need to jiggle the page slightly to get the effect. Such subjective colors appear in much "op art."

blow to the head can make you "see stars"; similarly, electrical stimulation of the brain (Dobelle, 1977) can produce visual sensations. A flickering white light appears to take on a variety of hues at different flicker rates. These hues are called *subjective colors* (see Figure 3–7). But before dealing with such unusual forms of vision, we examine the normal functioning of the visual system.

The Eye

The human eye is a marvelous device with intricate parts. A schematic view appears in Figure 3–8. A camera is in some ways structured like the eye, and we show a camera in Figure 3–8 for comparison.

The function of the eye is to focus a pattern of light entering the eye onto the back, light-sensitive surface, called the *retina,* much as a camera lens focuses an image on film. The image on the retina is inverted. Although the eye has no shutter and no film, it must, like the camera, bend, or refract, rays of light to achieve this focusing. The eye's frontmost surface, the *cornea,* performs most of this bending.

Let us follow a beam of light through the eye. After traversing the cornea and a body of fluid known as the aqueous humor, the light passes through the *pupil,* which is an opening in the iris. The *iris* is the pigmented structure that gives eyes their brown, blue, or green color. It is controlled by muscles that regulate the size of the pupil. The pupil typically opens wider in the dark, thus allowing more light into the eye, and narrows in bright light. Thus the pupil is analogous to the aperture, or f-stop, on an adjustable camera lens.

After shooting through the pupil, light enters the *lens,* where further refraction, or bending of rays, takes place. Unlike the camera's glass lens, the eye's lens is flexible. Its thickness is controlled by a set of muscles, called *ciliary muscles,* that stretch and release the lens, a process called *accommodation.* In this way, the focus of the eye can be finely tuned on objects at different distances.

FIGURE 3–8
The Eye and the Camera

Although it is incorrect to think of human visual perception as operating in exactly the same way as a camera takes photographs, there are some similarities between the two. In both cases an adjustable lens focuses sharp images on a photosensitive surface, the retina in the eye and film in the camera.

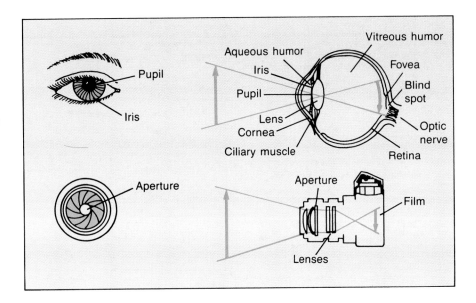

The aqueous and vitreous humors, shown in Figure 3–8, are thick, clear fluids that supply nutrients to the interior of the eye, eliminating the need for blood vessels that would interfere with vision. (There are some blood vessels inside the eye, however, which your doctor occasionally inspects with a flashlight.)

THE RETINA. The retina is a thin sheet of tissue lining the back of the eyeball. It gets its name from the Latin *rete* for "net," which it resembles. The retina contains about 127 million light-sensitive receptor cells, whose job is to convert light energy into the electrochemical language of the nervous system. These cells contain photopigments that react chemically to light. Their reactions ultimately cause neural signals (see Chapter 2) to be sent to the brain.

Approximately 7 million of the 127 million receptor cells in each eye are called *cones.* Cones are most numerous in a region of the retina called the *fovea.* The fovea is the area of sharpest vision; when you wish to look at an object closely, you move your eyes until the image of that object is centered on the fovea. Cones are largely responsible for perception of color. But they prove to be relatively insensitive light receptors; a large amount of light must fall on each cone for it to become activated. This helps explain why people perceive colors so poorly in the dark. For instance, can you identify the colors of other people's clothes in a darkened movie theater?

The remaining 120 million receptors in the eye are called *rods.* Rods are absent from the fovea, but they increase in density with distance from it. (At the far periphery, their density decreases.) Thus they are largely responsible for *peripheral vision,* or vision away from the fovea, the center of focus. Rods appear to play a relatively minor role in color vision. But they are extremely sensitive receptors, so they are responsible for night vision. This explains why it is easier to detect a faint star in the night sky if you look slightly away from it: you move the image of the star from the cone-filled fovea into the light sensitive, rod-filled portion of the retina.

FIGURE 3–9
Cross Section of the Human Retina

The retina is a complex network of cells for processing the information in light. At the bottom of the figure are the basic receptor cells, the rods and cones. Information from the rods and cones is transmitted to other levels of organization in the retina. During this higher-level collection of signals, information is compressed: signals from 127 million receptor cells in each retina must be recoded in order to be transmitted over the 1 million optic nerve fibers leading to the brain. Notice that before light is received by the rods and cones, it must pass through the cell bodies making up the higher levels of organization. This arrangement, which may have resulted from the eye evolving as an outgrowth of the brain, in fact causes little problem.

Source: Cornsweet, 1970.

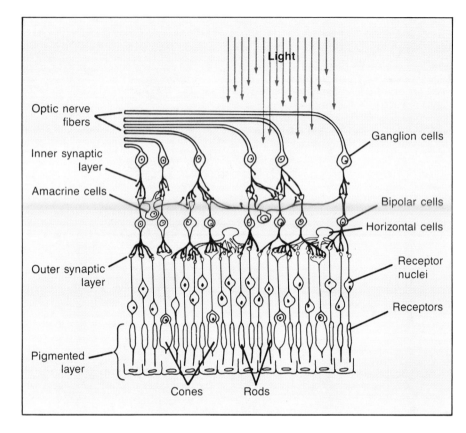

The retina contains other cells besides rods and cones. Neural signals from the receptors are passed along to the **bipolar cells** and from there to the **ganglion cells** (see Figure 3–9). These cells collect information from the receptors and compress it by eliminating unimportant or repetitious signals. (Note that there are other cell layers, too.) The retina is actually a complex signal-processing network that tells the brain about important, changing features of the visual field, such as the edges of surfaces or the onset of light. After all the cells of the retina have analyzed the visual field, signals are dispatched to the brain along the **optic nerve,** which is composed of the axons of the ganglion cells. The optic nerve of each eye is about as thick as a pencil and contains about 1 million nerve fibers. Since 127 million receptors must communicate with the brain through 1 million nerve fibers, the retina must compress a great deal of information.

The retina of each eye contains a single **blind spot** where the optic nerve exits the eye on its way toward the brain. Normally people are not aware of this hole in their field of vision (see Figure 3–10). They are also not aware that their retinal image is upside-down (see Figure 3–11). This inversion does not matter for vision, however, since the brain does not literally *see* the retina but only receives signals sent from it over the optic nerve.

THE BRAIN. After the neural signals have left the retina by way of the optic nerve, they proceed to a series of sites in the brain for further analysis (see Figure 3–12). Here the interpretive processes called *perception* occur. The first

FIGURE 3–10 ▶
How to Find Your Blind Spot

Hold the book close to you. Close your left eye and fixate on the X with your right eye. If the book is close enough, you will still be able to see the circle on the right. Move the book away from you slowly. The circle will disappear from view when it crosses the blind spot of your right retina at a distance of about 10 inches. It may be necessary to move the book back and forth a bit to find the blind spot.

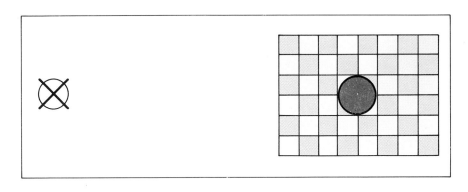

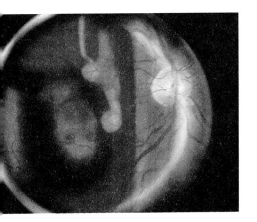

FIGURE 3–11 ▲
Picture of an Image on the Retina

By using a specially constructed camera, the photographer was actually able to capture the retina of a person's eye as the person viewed a woman talking on a telephone. Notice that the image is inverted. The yellow region at the right of the photo indicates the blind spot, where the optic nerve exits the eye.

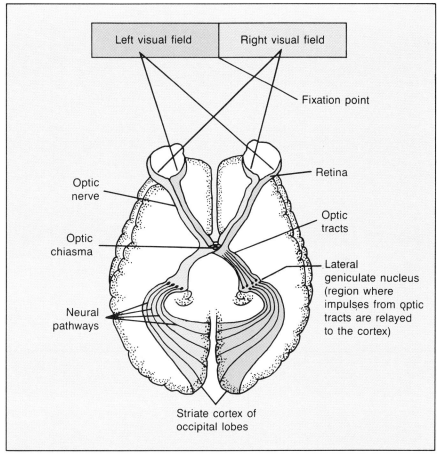

FIGURE 3–12 ▲
Neural Pathways for Visual Information

Light from the left visual field (to the left of where you fixate) strikes the right side of the retina, while light from the right visual field is received by the left side. The neural signals are carried to the optic chiasma, to the lateral geniculate nucleus, and then to the visual cortex. Notice that information from the right visual field goes to the left hemisphere of the brain, while that from the left visual field goes to the right hemisphere. Although information from the two eyes appears to meet at the optic chiasma, the neural tracts actually remain separated until they reach the lateral geniculate nucleus. Also see Figure 3–5.

stopping point for visual signals in the brain is the *lateral geniculate nucleus.* There are two such nuclei, one on each side of the brain, and each receives signals from both eyes. Thus, this is the first site where signals from the two eyes converge. Combining information from both eyes is essential for stereoscopic (3-D) depth perception. It is believed that the way in which color information is signaled to the brain may be dramatically altered at the lateral geniculate nucleus into a type of temporal (time-based) code (Kaufman, 1974). Different colors may be signaled by different rhythms of neural firing. This may explain why flickering white lights or moving black and white patterns may generate subjective colors: the flickering of the stimulus may be mimicking the neural time code for color (see Figure 3–7 again).

After leaving the lateral geniculate nucleus, most of the neural signals travel to the visual or *striate cortex* in the occipital lobe at the rear of the brain. What then happens to these signals has been the topic of a flurry of research over the past two decades that was begun by David H. Hubel and Torsten N. Wiesel (1968, 1979). Their investigations, for which they won a Nobel Prize in 1981, have been aided enormously by single-cell recording techniques in which a recording electrode monitors an individual cell of the cortex. Visual patterns are then focused on the retina of the test animal and the cell's response is observed. Many cortical cells have proved quite selective in that they respond only to particular stimuli, such as a line of a certain orientation that is moving in a specific direction. Some visual scientists believe that these cells, which have been dubbed *feature detectors,* are picking out the critical features of a visual stimulus that allow recognition of shapes (such as letters) and perhaps more complex forms (such as dogs). Although no cell has yet been found that actually responds only to a particular letter or only to a dog, some researchers believe that these highly specialized detector cells do exist (Lindsay & Norman, 1977).

Now that we have traced the visual image through the eyeball and retina and into the brain, we will return to the eye and study some of its features in more detail. First we will examine some common optical defects of the eye that can be corrected with glasses. Then we will explore the way in which the retina responds to light and perceives color.

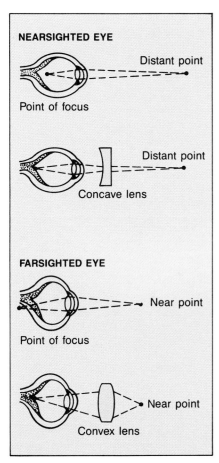

FIGURE 3–13
Nearsighted and Farsighted Eyes

For the nearsighted eye, distant points are focused in front of the retina. Concave lenses correct this problem by causing light rays to diverge. For the farsighted eye, the point of focus is behind the retina. Convex lenses correct this problem by causing light rays to converge.

NEARSIGHTEDNESS, FARSIGHTEDNESS, AND ASTIGMATISM. For us to perceive the world properly, visual images must be focused sharply on our retina. Many people need glasses to accomplish this because of structural problems in their eyes. Frequently the problem is the shape of the eyeball itself. If it is distorted so that the retina is too close or too far from the lens, the image on the retina will be blurred. If the image is focused in front of the retina, a person suffers from nearsightedness, or *myopia,* and has difficulty seeing objects at a distance. If the image is focused behind the retina, the diagnosis is farsightedness, or *hyperopia,* and the person finds it hard to see objects that are close (see Figure 3–13). *Presbyopia* is another condition of farsightedness that results from aging of the lens. With time, the interior portions of the lens rigidify, and the lens is less able to change shape to bring objects into focus. For this reason, as people age, their *near point—* the nearest distance at which they can see an object without blur—becomes more distant, as shown in Figure 3–14.

Another common problem is *astigmatism,* in which visual images are not focused to the same degree on different parts of the retina; for example,

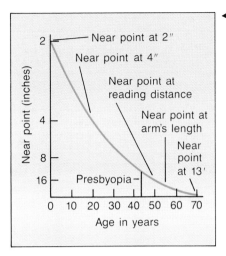

◄ **FIGURE 3–14**
The Near Point

The graph shows how the near point (the closest distance at which an object can be seen clearly) changes with age. For newborns, the near point is 2 inches and for college students it increases to 4 inches. With the onset of presbyopia in the fourth and fifth decades of life, the near point greatly increases. Most older people need some form of lenses to see nearby objects and to read. Note that the vertical axis on the graph plots inches from few (at the top) to many (at the bottom) on a logarithmic scale.

Source: Sekuler & Blake, 1985, p. 50.

the horizontal and vertical bars of a cross may not appear equally sharp. Astigmatism results from aberrations in the shape of the cornea, which should be spherical. (See Figure 3–15 to test yourself for astigmatism.)

Fortunately, all these problems are usually easy to correct with eyeglasses. Unfortunately, certain optical defects, such as presbyopia, worsen with age. Have you ever noticed an older person holding a newspaper at arm's length to read it? Often people with normal vision early in life will require glasses in their forties or fifties to correct presbyopia (see Figure 3–14 again).

Context Effects in Vision

The properties that we perceive in an object are determined not only by the object itself but by its context in space and time. For example, an object's apparent lightness and color are affected by the nature of the objects that surround it and by what has just preceded it in time. There are two general categories of context clues in vision, spatial context and temporal contrast.

SPATIAL CONTEXT. One well-known type of spatial context effect goes by the name of ***simultaneous contrast.*** A patch of gray will look darker if surrounded by a light border and lighter if surrounded by a dark border (see Figure 3–16). This effect results in part from the interaction of cells in the retina that tend to suppress one another's activity through a process called

FIGURE 3–15 ▲
Test for Astigmatism

Fixate on the center dot. Without moving your eyes, notice whether some of the black lines look noticeably lighter than others. If so, you may have astigmatism. If you wear corrective lenses (either eyeglasses or contact lenses), test yourself both with and without the lenses. (Most lenses correct for astigmatism if it is slight.) Astigmatism results when the cornea is not shaped in a perfect sphere. Almost all people's eyes have a small degree of astigmatism, but if the cornea is greatly misshapen vision will be blurred unless corrective lenses are worn.

Source: Sekuler & Blake, 1985, p. 51.

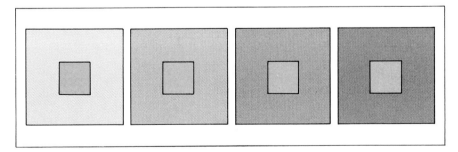

FIGURE 3–16 ▲
Simultaneous Contrast

The apparent lightness of objects depends on the lightness of surrounding objects. The center squares of the drawing are all the same shade of gray, but they appear to be different because of their contexts.

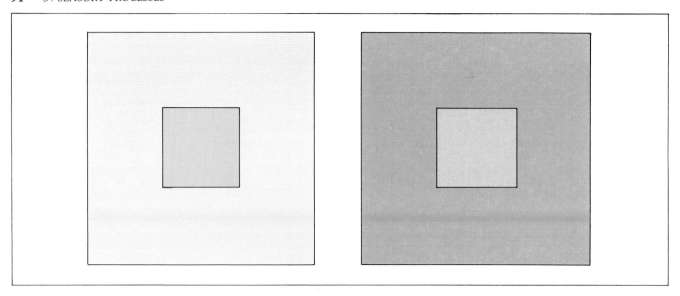

FIGURE 3–17
Color Contrast

The interior gray patches are physically identical, but the blue and yellow backgrounds make them appear different. The patch on the blue background looks faintly yellow, while the one on the yellow background appears tinged with blue.

lateral inhibition (Cornsweet, 1970). One cell, responding vigorously to a bright light, reduces the level of activity of adjacent cells. Since apparent brightness is determined by the level of neural activity, this reduced activity level of the adjacent cells is interpreted as indicating that these inhibited cells are not being exposed to bright light. For this reason, the gray patch in Figure 3–16 appears darker when surrounded by a bright border; the bright border inhibits firing of the interior cells, making the inside gray patch look darker than it really is. Simultaneous contrast also occurs with color (see Figure 3–17).

TEMPORAL CONTRAST. What people perceive at any moment is affected by what has come before. A familiar example is *dark adaptation.* When you first enter a dimly lit movie theater from broad daylight, it takes several minutes before you can see very well. By the same token, when you leave the theater and return to daylight, you may be temporarily blinded before *light adaptation* is complete.

FIGURE 3–18
Dark Adaptation Curve

The curve in the diagram shows the intensity of the dimmest light that a person can perceive after being placed in the dark. At first, only intense lights can be seen, but as time passes, progressively dimmer lights become perceptible. The curve contains a clear break after about the 8-minute point. The first 8 minutes indicate the rapid adaptation of the cones; the following 30 minutes show the slower (but more complete) adaptation of the rods.

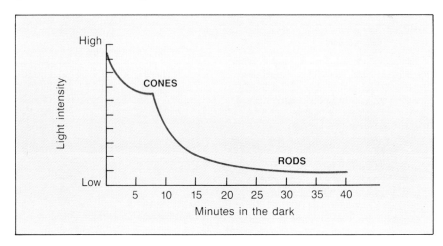

Dark adaptation results in part from changes in the chemical composition of the rods and cones caused by the presence and absence of light. The cones adapt to darkness much more rapidly than do the rods (see Figure 3–18). Even when they are fully adapted, however, the cones are not nearly as sensitive to light as the rods. As Figure 3–18 shows, adaptation is pretty much complete after about 30 minutes.

COLOR VISION

Although people could survive without being able to perceive color, the visual world would be much more drab and less informative in black and white. People with normal color vision can distinguish several million shades of color. Colors vary along three basic dimensions: hue, brightness, and saturation. Hue, which is nearly synonymous with the everyday meaning of color, is determined by the wavelength of light entering the eye, as discussed earlier (see Figure 3–6). A light with a wavelength of approximately 475 nanometers will appear to be pure blue and devoid of traces of green or violet. Wavelengths of 515 and 580 nanometers will be seen as pure green and pure yellow, respectively; those of 700 or more will look reddish. Brightness also has been discussed; recall that it corresponds to the intensity of the light.

Saturation is a new term that refers to the purity of the light's hue. This can be a difficult concept to grasp, so a thought-experiment may help clarify it. Suppose you had two pots of paint, one red and one white. If you were to begin mixing the two paints by adding white to red, the hue of the mixture would remain red, but its saturation would decline as the percentage of white increased. It would no longer be a true red but a desaturated red, or pink. As more and more white was added, the saturation would decline further, and the red component would become barely perceptible. Obviously, a similar result would occur if gray or black paint were added to the red. In sum, saturation is defined as the proportion of chromatic (colored) light to achromatic (noncolored) light.

The Spectrum Revisited

Sir Isaac Newton, discoverer of the laws of motion, was also the first to show (in 1704) that when white light is made to shine through a prism, all hues of the *visible spectrum*—the rainbow—are produced. Ordinary white light, of course, does not appear in the spectrum; it is the mixture of all of the wavelengths in the spectrum. Why is white light seen as white rather than as a dazzling array of all spectral hues?

To understand the answer to this question we must consider the *color circle* (see Figure 3–19). This circle is constructed by placing hues that appear similar to one another at adjacent locations. The order of these colors parallels the order of hues in the spectrum. But the circle has some additional interesting properties. First, the four unique hues of vision—red, yellow, green, and blue—are equally spaced. (The other hues are not unique because they can be described as combinations of unique hues; for example, violet is reddish-blue.)

By passing white light through a prism, Isaac Newton discovered that white light contains all the colors of the spectrum. Below is a picture showing white light shining through a prism.

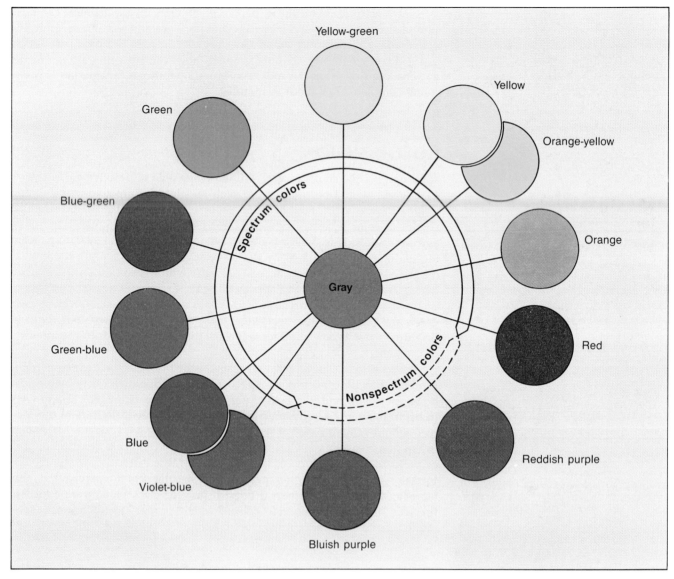

FIGURE 3–19
The Color Circle

This arrangement of colors places complementary colors on opposite sides of the circle. That is, if colors from opposite sides are mixed in proper proportions, they yield a neutral gray. The numbers indicate the wavelengths of the various colors. Notice that blue and yellow are not precisely complementary. Rather, the true complement to blue is orange-yellow and the true complement to yellow is violet-blue.

A second interesting property of the color circle is that colors that stand on opposite sides of the circle are **complementary colors.** If, for example, yellow and blue spotlights are projected on the same area of a screen, they will cancel one another to form a neutral gray. Similarly, if red and green lights are mixed, or any pair of lights drawn from opposite sides of the wheel are combined, gray results.

These facts of color mixture provide important clues as to how humans perceive color. But these same facts may seem to contradict what you already know. After all, don't yellow and blue paints combine to form green? Certainly. Yellow and blue *paints* mix to form green, but yellow and blue *lights* mix to form gray. What explains the apparent paradox is the difference between *additive* and *subtractive* color mixture. An additive color mixture occurs when different wavelengths of light stimulate the same part of the ret-

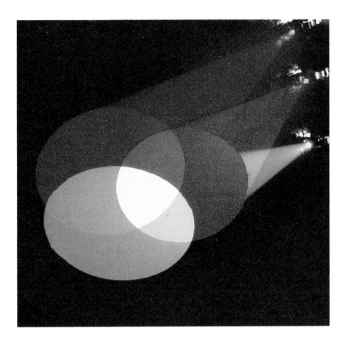

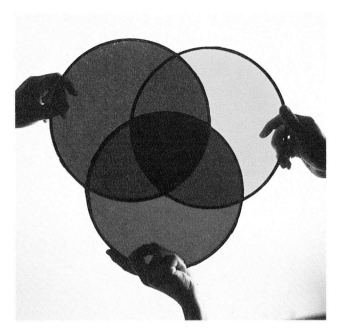

FIGURE 3–20
Additive and Subtractive Color Mixture

Additive color mixture (left) involves mixing of lights. Red and green lights combine to yield yellow, for example, and all three lights combine to form white. Mixing any two lights produces the complement of the third light, as shown. When the three lights are mixed in the proper proportion, any color of the spectrum can be produced by additive color mixture. Subtractive color mixture (right) takes place when pigments are mixed or (as here) when light is perceived through colored filters placed over one another. A yellow paint absorbs (subtracts) nonyellow wavelengths and reflects the yellow wavelength. Similarly, a blue paint absorbs nonblue wavelengths. When yellow and blue paints are mixed, the result is a pigment that reflects wavelengths between yellow and blue, which are green. In subtractive color mixture, complementary colors mix to produce black.

ina simultaneously. This would occur if blue and yellow lights were to shine in your eyes at the same time; you would see a neutral gray (see Figure 3–20).

Subtractive color mixture occurs when paint is mixed or when a child smears together colors from crayons on a sheet of paper. When light falls on a colored object, some wavelengths are absorbed and others are reflected. The wavelengths of the reflected lights determine the hue we perceive. Mixing different pigments such as paints causes different wavelengths to be absorbed, or subtracted, from the light. The remaining light is reflected to give the object its color (see Figure 3–20). Keep in mind that what is called an object's color is not inherent in the object but results from the interpretation that our visual systems draw from the object. (Recall the "subjective colors" in Figure 3–7.)

Trichromatic Theory

We explained earlier that the cones are responsible for color vision, but the exact mechanism producing color has been much debated. The longest-standing theory is known as the *Young-Helmholtz trichromatic theory.* It was first proposed by Thomas Young in 1802, before the existence of cones was known, and was modified fifty years later by Hermann von Helmholtz. The theory springs from the observation that all the colors of the spectrum can be derived from mixing only three wavelengths of light; hence the name *trichromatic.* These three wavelengths correspond to red, green, and blue, which therefore are called the three *primary colors.* (Note that yellow, according to this theory, is *not* a primary color.)

The modern version of this theory holds that there are three distinct types of cones in the retina. These three types, each containing a different photopigment, are maximally sensitive to three different wavelengths of

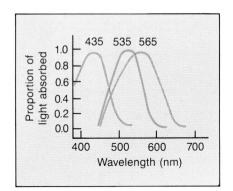

FIGURE 3–21
Responses of the Three Cone Systems

The graph shows the responses of the three cone systems to lights of varying wavelengths. One cone system is maximally sensitive to short-wavelength (435 nanometers) light, one to medium-wavelength (535 nm) light, and one to long-wavelength (565 nm) light. According to the trichromatic theory of color vision first articulated by Young and Helmholtz, the perception of all colors depends on the relative level of activity in the three cone systems.

light: 435, 535, and 565 nanometers (see Figure 3–21). We may loosely refer to these receptors as short-, medium-, and long-wavelength cones, but each type responds to a broad band of wavelengths, 'as the figure shows. A medium-wavelength cone, for example, responds most vigorously to light in the green region of the spectrum, but it responds also, with diminishing intensity, to wavelengths on either side of green. According to trichromatic theory, the perception of color is determined by the relative level of activity in the three cone systems. Any particular color produces some level of activity in all three cone systems, but the particular combination or ratio of activity levels uniquely pinpoints the color of light entering the eye.

The evidence supporting the trichromatic theory is fairly strong because researchers have had some success in isolating the three separate cone systems. But the theory is less than adequate in explaining other aspects of color vision, such as why complementary colors mix to form gray. A second and also widely supported theory of color vision, opponent-process theory, deals with this problem. Many visual scientists believe that both theories are largely correct and that the visual system in fact uses two kinds of mechanisms to perceive color.

Opponent-Process Theory

The opponent-process theory of color vision was originally proposed by Ewald Hering in 1878, but its modern champions are Leo Hurvich and Dorothea Jameson (1957, 1974). Hering believed there were six primary systems in color vision (rather than the three of the trichromatic theory): red, green, blue, yellow, black, and white. Hering proposed that the colors were grouped into three pairs: a red-green system, a blue-yellow system, and a black-white system. As you know, when the two members of any pair are mixed, they produce gray. According to *opponent-process theory*, the two members of each pair work in opposition to each other (thus the name *opponent-process*) by means of neural inhibition. So red inhibits green, blue inhibits yellow, and black inhibits white (and vice versa in each case). Only the red-green and blue-yellow systems are thought to affect the perception of hue, however; the black-white system contributes only to the perception of brightness and saturation.

Figure 3–22 shows the three opponent-process pairs receiving input from the three cone types proposed by the trichromatic theory. Opponent-process theory holds that if a stimulus excites both members of an opponent pair equally, the two will cancel one another and the net contribution of the pair will be zero. Thus when we look at white light—which contains all the wavelengths of the spectrum—the red-green system cancels itself, as does the blue-yellow system, so we perceive an achromatic (colorless) light. If a light contains more blue wavelengths than yellow, the blue inhibits the yellow; if a light contains equal amounts of blue and yellow, they cancel each other and we see gray. This explains why humans perceive no such shades as bluish-yellow or, for that matter, reddish-green.

Opponent-process theory accounts for a number of other phenomena of color vision, including colorblindness (see "Applying Psychology: Are You Colorblind?") Colorblind individuals are rarely blind to all colors; rather, they sometimes cannot detect pairs of colors, with the red-green pair the most frequently absent. Yellow-blue colorblindness is much rarer.

FIGURE 3–22
The Opponent-Process Theory of Color

The three types of cones that respond most strongly to the three different wavelengths of light (shown in A) are depicted in B and are labeled short, medium, and long (for the wavelengths to which they are most sensitive). Each of the three cones is believed to feed into each of the three opponent-process pairs (blue-yellow, red-green, and black-white), shown in C. Light at each wavelength either activates (solid lines) or inhibits (dashed lines) the opponent pair components as shown. The red-green and blue-yellow pairs mediate perception of color, while the black-white pair mediates the perception of brightness and saturation.

Source: Hurvich & Jameson, 1974, p. 91–92.

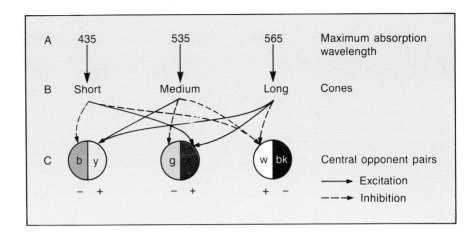

The opponent-process theory also explains color *afterimages* quite well. If you stare for a minute or so at a bright red patch and then turn your gaze to a blank white wall, a bright green patch will float before your eyes (see Figure 3–23). The explanation is that when you stare at the red patch for 60 seconds or more, you fatigue the red component of the red-green system. The green component is not being stimulated, however, so it does not tire. When you turn your eyes to the white surface, the light it reflects stimulates the red and green systems equally. But since the red system is fatigued, it cannot respond as vigorously as the fresh green system. The balance in the opponent pair has been disturbed, and the lopsided response in favor of the green system produces the faint green afterimage.

The trichromatic and the opponent-process theories of color vision do not rule one another out: probably two distinct mechanisms exist, a trichromatic system operating at the level of the cone receptors, and an opponent-process system working at later stages within the visual system (Hurvich, 1978).

FIGURE 3–23
Color Afterimages

Stare at the dot in the center of the flag for one minute. Afterward fixate quickly at the white area to the right. You should see a faint image of the traditional red, white, and blue U.S. flag. Notice that the colors in the original are the complements of red, white, and blue, namely green, black, and yellow.

APPLYING PSYCHOLOGY

Are You Colorblind?

Colorblindness is not always easy to detect: you may have been colorblind all your life and not know it. The chances that you suffer from color-blindness appear to be much slimmer if you are female. By estimates, 5 to 10 percent of males and less than 1 percent of females are at least partly colorblind. The disorder is inherited. It may stem from the absence of one of the three differently pigmented cone systems described by trichromatic theory or from malfunctions of the oppo-nent-process system.

People with normal color vision can match any color of light with a mixture of the three primary colors: red, green, and blue. (You may have noticed, if you stare closely at the screen, that color television sets produce only these three colors; but if you stand back at a normal viewing distance, you can see almost any color imagin-able, including black and white.)

These people are called *trichromats* since they can see all three primary colors. People who are partly color-blind are called *dichromats* because they use only two primary colors to match all the other colors. *Monochro-mats* are completely blind to color. They match any color of light with any other color as long as the two colors are equally bright.

Total colorblindness is rare, except among albinos. In albinism, which is also inherited, virtually all pigments, including those that should be in the cones, are absent from the body. Thus albinos lack all color vision, and their foveas (which contain only cones) are blind. Albinos learn to compensate somewhat by making jerky eye movements to keep images off the fovea.

Most colorblind people are dichro-mats. There are a few different types of dichromatic deficiency, but the most common involves a loss of red and green perception; blue and yellow re-main intact. The reverse situation oc-curs much less often.

Dichromats may not even notice their deficiency because they have

learned to name colors on the basis of their lightness. They have also learned the generally accepted color names for common objects, such as green for grass. Thus it may take a special type of test to detect their col-orblindness. One of the most popular is the *Ishihari test,* in which there are 16 patterns of dots. Four patterns are reproduced in Figure 3–24, which gives you some idea of what taking the test is like. To take the test, exam-ine each pattern carefully and note what number you see or whether you see no pattern at all. You can deter-mine whether you are colorblind by comparing your answers to those given beside the test. (This test may not be perfectly accurate because only four patterns are included and re-production of color in books is never completely faithful.)

The test has been designed to make it difficult to fake colorblindness. In patterns 1 and 2 in Figure 3–24, people with normal color vision see one number while people with a red-green color deficiency see a different number. In pattern 3, people with nor-mal color vision see a number, but

AUDITION

Who can say whether our hearing is worth more or less to us than our sight? All of us, to be sure, would prefer to have both. Audition, like vision, tells people about objects at a distance so that they may decide to approach or avoid them. More important, audition allows humans to enjoy the richest form of communication, spoken language. Before exploring how the ear and the brain deal with sound stimuli, we will consider the physical basis of sound and its psychological correlates.

The Physics of Sound

Sound ultimately derives from the vibration of surfaces in a medium, such as air. When an object vibrates, it sets air particles in motion, in particular into traveling pressure waves. One simple type of wave, a *sine wave* (see

FIGURE 3–24
Four Patterns Used in the Ishihara Colorblindness Test

When viewing pattern 1, people with normal color vision will see 29 and those with a red-green deficiency will see 70. Similarly, in pattern 2 normals will see 74; those with a red-green deficiency will see 21. Color-deficient people have a very hard time reading pattern 3, whereas people with normal color vision will see a 2. The case is reversed in pattern 4, where most normals see only a jumble of dots, but red-green deficient individuals usually see a 2.

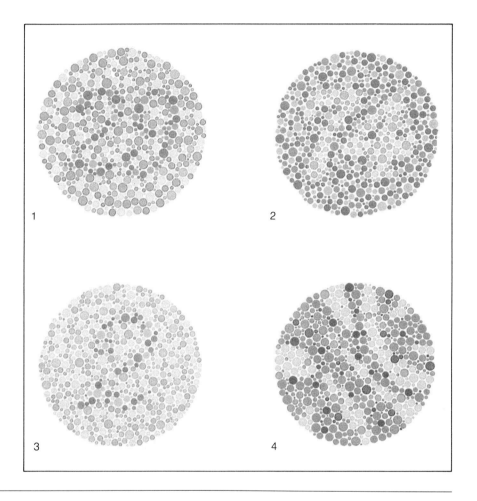

those with a deficiency see a random pattern. In pattern 4, people with normal color vision see only a random pattern, but those with a red-green deficiency usually see a number. This last works because colorblind people are typically more sensitive to differences in lightness, or intensity, than are trichromats. Since colorblind people cannot make reliable discriminations based on colors, they resort to doing so by lightness cues. Thus they can pick out numbers such as in pattern 4, which most people with normal color vision cannot see.

Figure 3–25), has two important properties: amplitude and frequency. *Amplitude* refers to the height and depth of the wave, which physically correspond to the difference between the maximum and minimum pressure level in the wave. Roughly speaking, the amplitude or intensity of a sound wave affects the *loudness* of a sound, just as the intensity of a light, in part, determines its brightness. Sound intensities are measured by a *decibel scale*, in which the intensity of a particular sound is expressed relative to a standard. The greater the sound on the decibel scale, the louder it is (see Figure 3–26).

The sound wave's second important property is its *frequency*, the number of complete cycles the wave undergoes in a given time. The frequency of a sound is analogous to the wavelength of a light; however, while a light's wavelength determines its perceived hue, the frequency of a sound determines its perceived *pitch*. Sound frequency is usually measured in *hertz* (Hz), or cycles per second. The lowest-pitched note on a piano has a

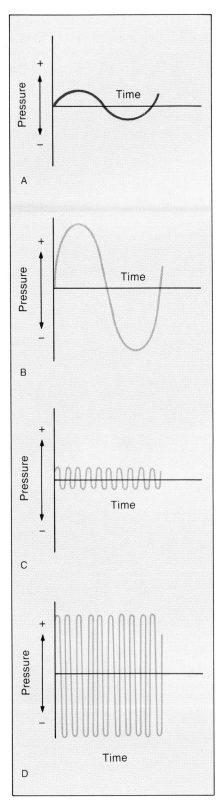

◀ **FIGURE 3–25**
Four Examples of Sound Waves

The physical characteristics of sound waves depicted here are amplitude—the height of the wave—and frequency—the number of times the wave goes through its cycle in a second. The amplitude of the wave largely determines perception of loudness, while the frequency gives rise to perception of pitch. The sound in A would be soft and have low pitch (low amplitude, low frequency), while that in D would be loud and high pitched since both its frequency and amplitude are great. What would the waves shown in B and C sound like?

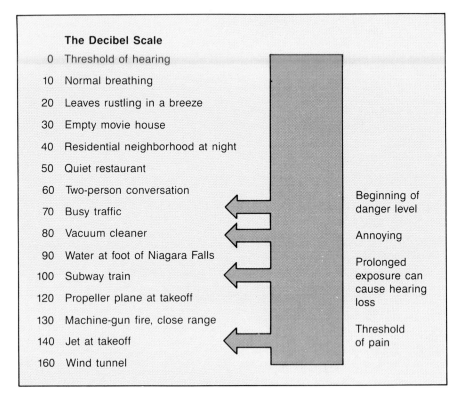

FIGURE 3–26 ▲
The Decibel Scale

The decibel scale measures the loudness of a sound in relation to a standard that is at the threshold of hearing (the softest sound that can be heard).

Source: Sekuler & Blake, 1985, p. 298.

frequency of 27.5 Hz; the highest stands at 4,180 Hz. (Every doubling of frequency corresponds to one octave.) The frequency range of human hearing under ideal conditions runs from about 20 to 20,000 Hz, although as people age, the upper limit of their hearing may fall below 10,000 Hz. Because the frequency of dog whistles is well above 20,000 Hz, they are inaudible to humans; vibrations below 20 Hz may be felt, but they are not heard as pitches. Figure 3–27 gives the range of sound frequencies that can be heard by various species.

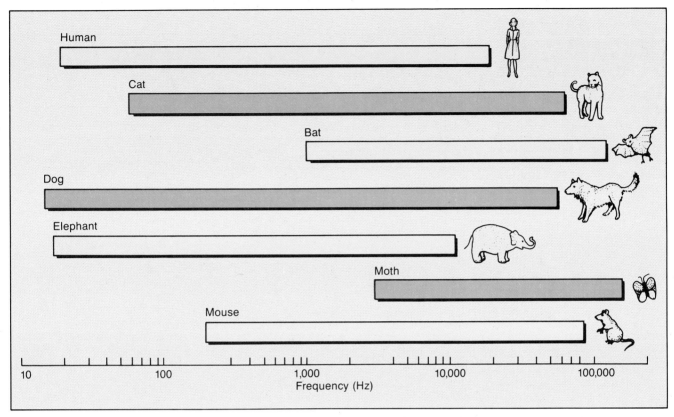

FIGURE 3–27
Differences in Hearing Among Species

Animals of different species are sensitive to sound waves of very different frequencies. For example, humans, dogs, and elephants are all sensitive to relatively low frequencies, but none of these species can hear sounds in the very high frequencies to which bats and moths are sensitive. Notice, however, that dogs and cats are sensitive to much higher pitched sounds than are humans.

Source: Sekuler & Blake, 1985, p. 338. Original data from Hefner & Hefner, 1983.

The Ear

The starting point for hearing is, of course, the ear. We will follow a sound wave from the moment it enters the ear to its ultimate transformation into a pattern of neural signals sent to the brain. Traditionally, the ear is described as being divided into three main parts, the *outer, middle,* and *inner ears* (see Figure 3–28). The outer ear contains the *pinna,* the odd-shaped flap that protrudes from the side of the head, and the *auditory canal.* The pinna collects and funnels sound waves into the auditory canal, where the waves strike the eardrum, or *tympanic membrane,* and set it vibrating.

The eardrum serves as the entrance to the middle ear. The back side of the eardrum is connected to a set of three interlinked bones called *ossicles* that are named, in order, the *malleus, incus,* and *stapes.* (Remember the sequence *M-I-S* and you can't miss.) When the eardrum is nudged into motion by sound, the ossicles act like a system of levers and amplify the intensity of the sound signal.

When the ossicles vibrate in response to sound, the foot of the last bone, the stapes, pounds against the final major structure of the ear, called the *cochlea.* The cochlea, which resides in the inner ear, is a snail-shaped structure of bone, hollow and filled with a salty fluid. The stapes actually pounds on an opening called the *oval window* in the otherwise rigid cochlea, setting up pressure waves in the fluid.

The inside of the cochlea is lined throughout with soft membranes, the most important of which is known as the *basilar membrane* (see Figure

FIGURE 3–28
Main Parts of the Human Ear

The pinna funnels sound through the auditory canal to the tympanic membrane (eardrum), which vibrates. The vibrations are carried and amplified by the three small bones of the middle ear to the cochlea of the inner ear. The pattern of vibration sets fluid in the cochlea in motion, and this motion activates hair cells that send nerve impulses to the brain via the auditory nerve. The semicircular canals of the inner ear are not involved in hearing, but they play a large role in the vestibular system, which is responsible for balance.

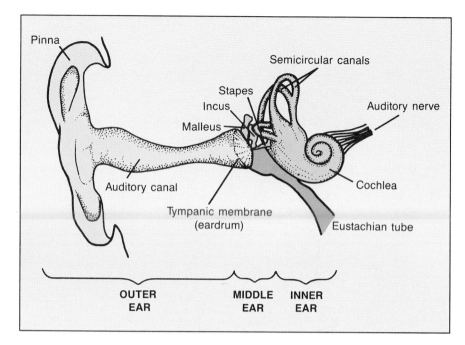

3–29). When pressure waves move through the fluid in the cochlea, they create bulges against the basilar membrane. The basilar membrane is lined with *hair cells,* and when a bulge humps its way down the membrane, the hairs are pressed into a neighboring membrane. The hair cells in turn convert this mechanical bending into neural impulses that are sent to the brain along the *auditory nerve* (Evans, 1982; Zwislocki, 1981).

Pitch and Loudness

Given this overview of the ear, how do the amplitudes and frequencies of sound waves become registered in the ear so that they can be signaled to the brain? When a sound enters the ear, it eventually leads to a neural response, or firing, in the hair cells. The greater the amplitude of the sound

FIGURE 3–29
A Look into the Ear

This is a simplified view of the middle ear and inner ear. Pressure at the stapes causes the oval window to pulsate, which starts pressure waves in the fluid surrounding the basilar membrane. The loudness and pitch of the sound are relayed to the brain by the frequency and pattern of hair cells firing on the basilar membrane. The hair cells on the basilar membrane are shown on the right.

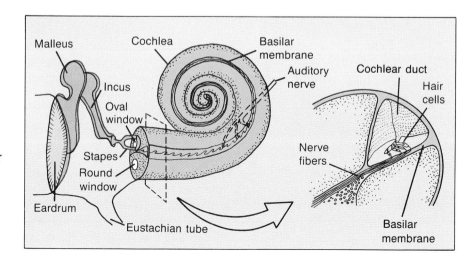

wave, the greater the number of hair cells that respond. Thus, the brain notes loudness of a sound in part by determining how many different cells are sending it signals. In addition, the rate at which neural firing occurs affects the loudness of a sound.

PLACE THEORY. The registration of frequency in the ear is more complex than that of amplitude. Our ideas about pitch perception derive largely from the theorizing of Helmholtz and more recently of Georg von Békésy, who won the Nobel Prize for his work in 1961. Békésy discovered that when sound creates a bulge that travels down the basilar membrane, the bulge reaches maximum size at some point and then shrinks. What is more, the place on the basilar membrane where this maximum bulge occurs differs for different frequencies. Thus, which hair cells along the basilar membrane are firing most vigorously gives the brain a clue as to the frequency of the sound entering the ear. This idea is called *place theory.*

FREQUENCY THEORY. A second theory of pitch perception is based on the observation that when a hair cell fires, its rhythm, or tempo, of firing is synchronized with the frequency of the sound entering the ear. For a tone of intermediate frequency (say, 262 Hz, or middle C on a piano), a given hair cell would respond at a steady rate of 262 firings per second. Thus, the frequency or rhythm of signals received by the brain would give it a clue as to the frequency of the sound entering the ear. This idea of how the ear signals pitch is called *frequency theory.* Of course, as the frequency of the sound increased, a single hair cell would be hard pressed to keep firing in synchrony with the sound wave. Most nerve cells in the body cannot fire more than 1,000 times a second, which implies that an individual hair cell could not stay apace of a sound with a frequency exceeding 1,000 Hz. But groups of hair cells could; when one cell in a group proved unable to fire, another would pop away. This version of frequency theory has the appropriate name *volley theory* (Wever & Bray, 1937), taken from the method of muskets firing during the Revolutionary War. Because of the time it took to reload their muskets, two ranks of men would fire alternately. While one rank fired, the other would reload, and vice versa, resulting in volleys of fire. The principle is the same with the firing of hair cells. When one is fatigued from a high rate of firing, a neighboring cell fires at the same rate. Thus, information about the frequency of the firing is continually supplied to the brain.

Which view of pitch perception is correct, place theory or frequency theory? Current thinking holds that both are, as with the coexistence of the trichomatic and opponent-process theories of color vision. For low-frequency sounds, frequency theory appears to be correct; for high-frequency sounds, place theory. For sounds of intermediate frequency (400 to 4,000 Hz), the ear may use both the frequency and the place mechanisms to signal pitch (Green, 1976).

Auditory Localization

Besides knowing the pitch and loudness of sounds entering our ears, it is useful to recognize the source of the sound. This ability is called *auditory localization.* People can usually localize sounds fairly well even with their eyes closed. The British physicist Lord Rayleigh first demonstrated this ability in the 1800s in an experiment in which he had a large circle drawn on a lawn and marked off in degrees. He stood blindfolded in the circle's center while his assistants moved around it, stopping at different spots and emitting sounds. Rayleigh proved to be accurate to within a few degrees in pointing to the source of each sound.

Why are people so sharp at localizing sounds in space even with their eyes closed? Basically, it is because humans have two ears, not one, and the sounds reaching them differ slightly. One difference is in the intensity of the sounds: if a sound occurs to the right side, the sound wave reaching the right ear will be slightly more intense than that reaching the left, since the latter will have to circle the head to reach the far ear. A second difference involves time of arrival. Sound travels through air at the relatively slow rate of about 1,100 feet per second. Thus a sound on the left will strike the left ear fractions of a second before it reaches the right ear. The human auditory system is remarkably good at detecting these minuscule time differences and using them to localize sound.

What happens when a sound comes from a source directly in front of us? Since its source is the same distance from each ear, there will be no difference in the amplitude or time of arrival at the two ears. Thus, we will hear the sound as coming from neither the left nor the right. But what about a sound coming from directly behind us? The sounds reaching our two ears will be identical in this case as well, so how can we tell if the sound is coming from the front or from behind (or, for that matter, from below or above)? The answer, which may be surprising, is that often we can't, at least under laboratory conditions. Outside the lab, we can simply turn our heads, thereby placing one ear nearer than the other to the sound source. (Have you ever noticed a dog tilting its head from side to side in response to an unknown sound? It is not trying to look at the problem from a different angle; it is getting a fix on the sound's origin.) When we listen to music through headphones, turning the head has no effect, of course; in this case, we often have great difficulty in localizing sounds, and sometimes they appear to originate from above or even within our heads.

THE OTHER SENSES

Although humans gather most of the information about their environment from their eyes and ears, life would be perilous without other senses. If people did not smell and taste, they could not recognize poisonous foods or gases; without touch, they might ignore wounds or freezing temperatures. For many animals, the sense of smell appears to be more important than seeing or hearing in warning of predators and recognizing prey, mates, and safe terrains. The sense of smell, for example, is far keener in dogs than in humans (Droscher, 1969), and a greater percentage of their sensory cortex is devoted to smell.

Smell

Dogs' keen sense of smell makes them ideal for sniffing out illegal drugs at border crossings.

Smells arise when molecules in the air dissolve in the *olfactory epithelium* high in the nasal passages. The dominant theory about the sense of smell is the *stereochemical theory* of odors, which holds that the receptors in the nose are configured to match the wide variety of shapes of molecules suspended in the air. Molecules entering the nose fit their appropriate receptors the way a key fits the lock it is designed to open (Schiff, 1980). As is true with vision, the olfactory system adapts quickly to unchanging stimulation. The adaptation of smell is more complete than that of vision, so people often become unaware of even powerful odors. Considering the variety of unpleasant smells we are sometimes forced to endure, that adaptation is often a blessing, as people living near a malfunctioning sewage plant can attest. But if gradually exposed to a poisonous gas such as automobile exhaust fumes, a person may adapt to the odor before recognizing it and become a statistic of accidental death.

Although the human nose is not as sensitive as that of other animals, it is nothing to be ashamed of. For example, people can detect ethyl mercaptan, which smells quite bad, even when it occurs in concentrations as weak as 1 part per 50 *billion* parts of air. For this reason mercaptan is put into natural gas (which has no smell) to warn users of gas leaks that could be dangerous (Engen, 1982). However, the sensitivity of the nose to smells varies tremendously from odor to odor.

The olfactory system may be quite sensitive in detecting smells, but people are much poorer at actually identifying or naming what the smell is (Sekuler & Blake, 1985). Of course, this ability also varies greatly depending on the odor and a person's familiarity with it. William Cain (1982) tested male and female college students on their abilities to identify 80 relatively common odors. The results are presented in Figure 3–30. The 80 odors that he tested are ranked from those accurately identified by the largest percentage of subjects (at the top) to those identified by the fewest subjects (at the

FIGURE 3–30
Naming of Odors

The figure shows the relative abilities of male and female college students to identify 80 common odors. The graph ranges from easily identified odors at the top to odors that were harder to name at the bottom. The bars show the differences between the sexes in naming odors, with white bars representing female superiority and black bars showing male superiority. In general, females identified odors more accurately than did males.

Source: Sekuler & Blake, 1985, p. 402. Data adapted from Cain, 1982.

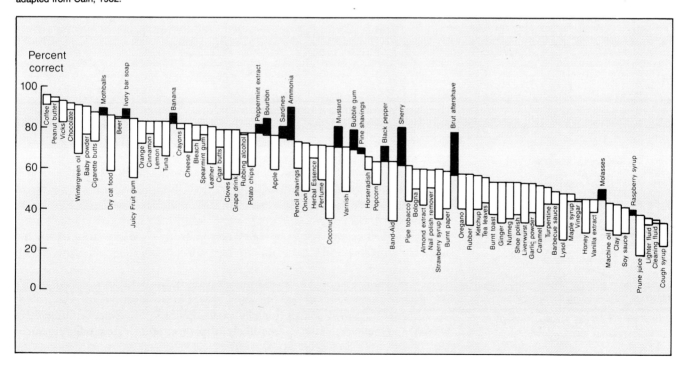

bottom). More than 90 percent of the subjects were able to identify correctly the odors of coffee, peanut butter, Vicks, and chocolate, but fewer than 40 percent were able to identify lighter fluid, cleaning fluid, and cough syrup.

The bars in Figure 3–30 represent gender differences in identifying odors, with black indicating male superiority and white indicating female superiority for the particular odor. The length of the bar represents the difference between the sexes in the percentage identifying the odor. Thus, for example, women are much better than men at identifying coconut, but only slightly better at identifying crayons. No difference exists between the sexes in identifying beer. The preponderance of white bars in the graph indicates that women were generally much better at the task than men, a result also obtained in other studies (described below). Of the 80 odors, men were better at naming only 15.

In many animal species, smell controls identification of mates, parents, and children and determines the selection of a mate. For example, in many species of birds, mothers feed their children only if they have a familiar scent. If the mother's young has been marked by a strange odor, the mother will reject it as an impostor. Females of many species, including some mammals, produce scents called pheromones from specialized glands. The pheromones attract potential mates and in many cases control mate selection. Males also produce distinctive scents. You have probably noticed that male dogs sniff one another when they meet and that they mark their territories by urinating at various locations. Should an intruding dog urinate within another dog's territory, the dog with original claim to the territory will rush over and spray the spot to reclaim it. One can often see the amusing spectacle (to humans) of dogs spraying and counterspraying repeatedly, each trying to leave his own scent last to claim the territory as his.

In many mammals, pheromones play a significant role in identification of the sexes, mate selection, and territoriality. Do pheromones play any role in human sexual behavior? Many cosmetic companies try to convince us that they do, manufacturing and advertising hundreds of scents in after-shave lotions and perfumes for the purpose of enhancing our sexual appeal. The role of pheromones, if any, in human sexual attraction is unclear, but humans do seem able to detect differences among people's smells reliably. Russell (1976) had college students bathe in clear water and wear a plain T-shirt and no deodorant for the next 24 hours. The shirts were then collected and placed in containers, and the subjects were asked to choose their own shirt from among three, two of which were selected randomly from other participants. One shirt had been worn by a member of the same sex as the subject and the other by a member of the opposite sex. Seventy-six percent of the subjects tested were able to select their shirts from among the three presented, which is considerably better than the chance rate of 33 percent. In addition, the subjects were able to choose with a better than chance percentage which of the other shirts had been worn by males and which by females. Similar studies have shown that subjects can determine the sex of a person by smelling the person's hands (Wallace, 1977) or breath (Doty et al., 1982). Females typically perform better on these tasks than males.

These studies show that humans are at least sensitive to sex-related scents and that smell can potentially play some role in attraction and mate selection. However, smell seems likely to play a minor role alongside such

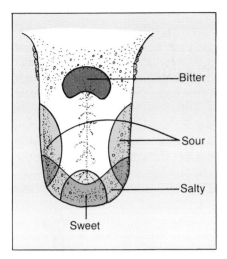

FIGURE 3–31
The Tongue's Sensitive Areas

Areas of the tongue are sensitive to
different tastes. You should sample
sweets with the front of your tongue.
Notice that there is some overlap among
the areas.

powerful cues as physical appearance and social influence. (Chapter 17 discusses social factors affecting friendship and attraction.)

Taste

Compared with vision and audition, taste is relatively poorly developed in humans. People often attribute the pleasure of eating good food to the sense of taste, but more often it is the smell that induces enjoyment. You have noticed, of course, that food resembles cardboard in flavor when a head cold congests your nasal passages. The tongue, which registers taste, is actually sensitive to a mere handful of properties, notably salty, sweet, sour, and bitter. These properties are detected by the 10,000 or so *taste buds* that line the tongue; taste buds live only a few days and then are replaced by new ones. Different taste buds are sensitive to different sensory properties, and they are not distributed uniformly on the tongue (see Figure 3–31). For example, the tip of the tongue is more responsive to sweetness, the base of the tongue to bitterness. However, most individual taste buds actually respond to more than one taste, so a substance's taste probably arises from the pattern of neural activity across many taste buds (Pfaffman, 1955). Of course, the tongue also senses the texture and temperatures of foods, which may add considerably to the enjoyment of eating.

Just as the nose adapts rapidly to odor, the tongue adapts quickly to flavors. The first salted peanut tastes much saltier than the second. Similarly, a drink such as orange juice usually tastes more sour if we imbibe it immediately after brushing our teeth (Schiff, 1980). This occurs because the drink contains both sweet and sour components, whereas toothpaste is sweetened. The tongue adapts to the toothpaste's sweetness and registers only the sourness of the juice.

The fact that taste, like the other senses, shows strong adaptation paves the way for some curious aftereffects and illusions of taste, which you can demonstrate yourself. Fill four glasses with distilled water and then strongly flavor three of them by mixing a teaspoonful of salt in one, lemon juice in a second, and sugar in a third. Sip the plain water to remind yourself what it tastes like and then choose one of the other glasses. Imbibe a mouthful of, say, the salt solution and swish it around for 30–40 seconds before spitting it out. Taste the plain water again, and you will notice that it tastes somewhat bitter and sour. After this effect wears off, try the experiment with the other solutions. If you adapt your taste buds to the sour lemon solution, the water will taste sweet. After you hold the sweet water in your mouth, the plain water will taste sour.

These taste aftereffects or illusions may remind you of similar color aftereffects in vision discussed earlier. However, the color afterimages are reciprocal (or complementary), whereas the taste aftereffects are not. Fatiguing the red system in vision produces a faint green afterimage, and vice versa. But the same reciprocity does not always hold in taste. Adapting the mouth to a salty taste makes plain water taste sour or bitter, but adapting it to a sour taste makes plain water taste sweet, not salty. This implies that, unlike vision, taste does not involve opponent-process mechanisms. A practical point is that the taste of one substance eaten during a meal can change dramatically depending on the other foods being eaten with it.

People show reliable taste preferences, which seem to change in consistent ways with age (Cowart, 1981). You will not be surprised to learn that almost all species, including humans, prefer sweet tastes to bitter ones. This is an important adaptation because sweet foods usually are high in energy value (calories) and bitter substances are often poisonous. However, natural aversions to bitter tastes can be overcome. People typically react negatively to their first tastes of beer, coffee, and quinine water, but on repeated exposure many people grow to like all three. Several studies have shown that children prefer stronger concentrations of sweet than do adults and that the "sweet tooth" of childhood does not usually survive into adulthood (Desor, Greene, and Maller, 1975). Changes in taste preference with age may reflect organic maturation or simply changing preferences with experience. Of course, many of our food preferences are learned from cultural experience. Children born into other cultures may grow up fancying ants, dogs, snails, and frogs as delicacies, but most people in our society would be repelled if given these items as food.

The Skin Senses

At least four types of sensation are usually lumped together as the sense of touch: pressure, pain, warmth, and cold. The skin contains various receptors that act together in ways that are still a bit mysterious, and it is not uniformly sensitive to all of these properties across its entire surface. When a small square of skin is touched with tiny needles that have been heated or chilled, some areas in the square sense only heat, some only cold, and some neither. Likewise, the skin is not uniformly sensitive to touch. If two pointed objects are pressed against the skin simultaneously, they often will be felt as one. The distance by which they must be separated to be experienced as two objects rather than one (a measurement called the *two-point threshold*) varies over the body as well; it is much greater on the back than on the fingertips, for instance.

The skin is more adept at sensing changes in stimulation than at registering unchanging stimuli. We adapt rapidly to the feel of our clothing after we dress, for example. The skin is particularly sensitive to the rate of stim-

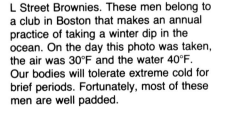

L Street Brownies. These men belong to a club in Boston that makes an annual practice of taking a winter dip in the ocean. On the day this photo was taken, the air was 30°F and the water 40°F. Our bodies will tolerate extreme cold for brief periods. Fortunately, most of these men are well padded.

ulation. For instance, a piece of cold metal feels much colder than an equally cold block of wood because metal conducts heat rapidly and so extracts warmth from the skin faster than does wood, a relatively poor conductor (Schiff, 1980).

To anyone who has plunged into chilly water from an ocean beach or a mountain lakeside, adaptation to temperature is a familiar experience. After a minute or two, the goose bumps vanish. You may want to try a temperature adaptation experiment originally suggested by John Locke in the seventeenth century that provides an odd experience. Fill three bowls with water, one hot, one cold, and one lukewarm. Dip your left hand into the hot bowl and your right hand into the cold one and keep them there for about a minute. Then thrust both hands into the bowl of lukewarm water. The lukewarm water will seem cool to your left hand and warm to your right. The experience seems strange since you are aware that both hands are in the same bowl. This aftereffect is similar to the ones described for color and taste.

Pain

Perception of pain is not well understood. We could not live without the capacity to experience pain because if we did not notice painful stimuli, we might well depart before the stimuli did. Some people feel no pain, that is, they lack sensitivity to it; while this might seem advantageous, they are in constant danger of serious yet undetected injury (Melzack, 1973). Pain does not always occur from damage to bodily tissues; amputees experience "phantom limb" pain in arms or legs long since severed. Psychiatric patients sometimes report severe pain for which no organic cause can be found (Veilleux & Melzack, 1976).

One explanation of pain is in terms of the *gate-control theory* of Melzack and Wall (1965). According to that theory, sensations of pain result from activation of certain nerve fibers that lead to specific centers of the brain responsible for pain perception. When these fibers are activated, say by an injury, the neural "gate" to the brain is opened for pain sensations. The theory also postulates another set of neural fibers that, when activated, reduce the effects of the pain fibers and "close the gate" on the pain sensations. The theory proposes that neural activity arising from other stimuli (e.g., those producing general excitement) may close the gate to pain signals. The important idea is that signals from the brain can be sent to other parts of the body to modify the incoming pain signals.

Gate-control theory may help explain some common phenomena of pain. For example, it has been reported that patients feel less pain when dentists working on them play music; the music may help close the gate for pain. Similarly, Melzack (1970) reports that amputees feel less phantom limb pain when the stump is massaged. The massaging may activate fibers that close the gate to pain.

The Chinese have long used *acupuncture* for controlling pain. The acupuncturist inserts needles into various parts of the body, depending on the pain's source. One theory of acupuncture's effectiveness is that the needles stimulate the fibers that block activation of the pain fibers. (Another theory accounting for this phenomenon is discussed in "Research Frontier: Pain, Stress, and Endorphins," page 112.) As researchers discover more about the

Pain, Stress, and Endorphins

The perception of pain involves many puzzles that have long been noted but never well understood. One is the enigma of phantom limb pain; another occurs in a crisis (such as in combat) when a person receives a bad injury but does not notice any pain until much later, after the crisis has passed. Pain often seems unrelated to the amount of tissue damage suffered (Wall, 1979), and great individual differences exist in pain perception. Beecher (1956) compared injuries suffered by soldiers in battle with similar injuries inflicted on civilians during surgery. Pain was greater for the civilians, who required narcotics more often than did the soldiers. Another curiosity is how a placebo—an ineffective and harmless substance—often reduces the pain of injury or headache when people are told that they are receiving a drug to block pain. Other puzzles of pain include the mechanisms of acupuncture and hypnotic suggestion in pain relief.

All these mysteries of the perception of pain have, over the years, been attributed to "psychological factors." But in the last ten years we have come closer to discovering physical causes. It is well known that certain drugs, such as morphine and heroin, block pain. As discussed in Chapter 2, researchers in the mid-1970s discovered that such drugs relieve pain by clogging the synapses between neurons so that the transmission of pain signals cannot be conducted from one neuron to the next. But this insight leads to another puzzle: why should the brain be affected by a substance like morphine? One possible answer is that the brain itself manufactures similar substances for control of pain. In other words, the body produces a form of its own morphine to block pain signals.

This startling idea proved true when researchers discovered a class of substances known as *enkephalins* (from the Greek meaning "in the head"; e.g., Terenius and Wahlström, 1975). The morphine-like factor was found in high concentrations in patients who suffered from a disease causing severe facial pain, suggesting that the body produced it to combat the pain. Enkephalins are actually peptides, short chains of amino acids linked together. Many varieties have been discovered, concentrated in the brain and the spinal cord. Currently the term *endorphins* (meaning "the morphine within") refers to an entire class of opioid peptides that are produced by the body to relieve pain.

Psychologists played only a small role in the discovery of the endorphins, but they are in the forefront of discovering how and when these substances are called into play to blunt pain. Here we will sample the interesting ideas suggested by psychologists in this area. Robert Bolles and Michael Fanselow (1980, 1982) have been concerned with the relation between pain and fear, suggesting that these are independent systems that serve different biological functions. Imagine yourself suddenly thrust into a life-threatening situation in which much pain is likely, such as a snake bite. Both fear and pain are aroused, but Bolles and Fanselow (1980; Fanselow, 1984) note that the pain must be suppressed so that you can escape the next bite rather than stop to tend to the pain. They argue that the release of endorphins suppresses the pain, thus enabling your response to the fear.

Experimental research with animals supports this idea. If an animal is returned to a situation in which it has been previously shocked and if cues

mechanisms responsible for pain, it may be possible to help those who suffer chronic agony from diseases such as cancer.

Your own experience may tell you that people don't adapt to pain as well as they do to other forms of stimulation. Actually, at the sensory level, the skin *does* adapt to pain reasonably well; it is the changes made at the site of the pain—such as moving an aching elbow—that keep the pain alive. By scratching an itch (a mild form of pain), the sufferer converts it into a low-level pain, which is apparently more tolerable. Pain seems also to be affected by the attention given to it (Schiff, 1980). For example, a football player may ignore a broken bone to stay in the game. Many methods of alleviating pain, including hypnosis and the Lamaze method of childbirth,

that were associated with the shock are repeated, the animal exhibits analgesia (reduction in pain) for the shock. The assumption is that the situation causes the animal to manufacture endorphins to reduce the anticipated pain (Fenselow, 1984).

Research has shown that many forms of physical "stress" that are repeatedly given to laboratory animals can produce pain relief. For example, after repeated shocks, animals will tolerate heat longer than will animals that did not have shock. In some (but not all) cases, endorphins appear to be the cause of the analgesia from shock stress (Lewis, Cannon, & Liebeskind, 1980; Watkins & Mayer, 1982). To test this, researchers give animals a substance called naloxone (or, in a slightly different form, naltrexone), which blocks the action of the endorphins and leaves the animals sensitive to pain. Interestingly, sometimes the pain relief from repeated stressful experiences is blocked by naloxone and sometimes it is not (Watkins & Mayer, 1982). The exact reasons for this are still under investigation, but one reasonable conclusion is that more than one mechanism underlies analgesia produced by stress. Whether or not an animal or person has control over the source of the

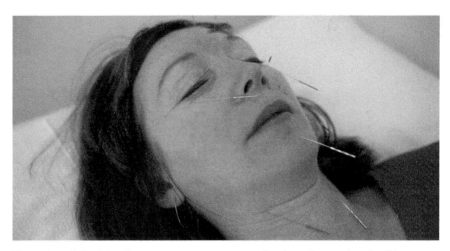

The pain relief arising from acupuncture seems to involve release of endorphins, because naloxone blocks the effectiveness of acupuncture.

stress also affects the production of endorphins. Rats given shocks they cannot control produce endorphins, whereas rats that can turn off the shock by pressing a lever do not produce endorphins (Maier et al., 1980; 1983).

The discovery of endorphins and the circumstances in which they are released may help explain some of the puzzles of pain. People's expectations may cause release of endorphins and thus account for pain relief from placebos, acupuncture, hypnosis, and the like. At least in the case of acupuncture, endorphins do seem to

play a role, for naloxone blocks the effectiveness of acupuncture. Our understanding of the role that endorphins play in pain control is in early stages, but it is clear that the discoveries discussed here are breakthroughs. Pain signals serve the useful biological function of calling attention to tissue damage, but in some cases pain persists long after it has served that function (as in the throbbing pain of a toothache or the terrible pain of terminal cancer patients). The discovery of endorphins gives rise to the hope that better ways of overcoming pain can be found.

may operate primarily by distracting the sufferer's attention from pain. (Along these lines, it may be simple distraction rather than closing of a neural gate that makes the dentist's music work.)

Kinesthesis and Equilibration

Aristotle's classical categorization of the five senses omitted consideration of two other important sources of sense information. One, *kinesthesis,* tells us the position of our limbs through sense organs in muscles, tendons, and joints; it allows us to react when a motion goes awry and we stumble or slip. As with our other sensory systems, we hardly even know that kinesthesis is functioning until it falters. When your foot "falls asleep" and you try to walk, the strange feeling signals the lack of kinesthetic feedback.

Equilibration is the technical term for keeping our balance; it involves information from the ***equilibratory senses*** in the middle ear meshing with kinesthetic feedback. One equilibratory sense organ is made up of three semicircular canals (see Figure 3–28) filled with fluid that moves as the head turns. When the fluid shifts in a certain way, it signals that motion. When the motion is extreme, as for a rider in the rear of a swaying bus or on a ship in rough water, we can feel dizzy and nauseated.

At the base of the semicircular canals are the ***vestibular sacs,*** also used for equilibration, in which movement of fluid signals motion and the tilt of the head. The equilibratory and kinesthetic senses work in tandem and usually do not call attention to themselves by malfunctioning. Motion sickness is an exception, as are illusions noticed by pilots when airplanes change speeds and bank in turns. In cases of poor visibility, pilots will guide their flights by instrument readings rather than trust the information they get from the "seat of their pants," or their equilibratory senses.

PSYCHOPHYSICS

So far we have discussed how the sensory systems operate but have not considered how psychologists measure sensory capabilities. For example, what is the intensity of the faintest tone that the human ear can detect, and how is it gauged? This area of study is called ***psychophysics*** because it is concerned with how changes in physical stimulation from the environment become translated into psychological experience.

Psychophysics is one of the oldest disciplines in scientific psychology; in fact, true laboratory experiments in psychology began with psychophysical research. Psychophysics addressed a central philosophical question: how is stimulation from the external world translated into the conscious experience of the perceiving human? If the intensity of a light is doubled, for example, does its perceived brightness also increase by a factor of two? As we will see, the answer is no. A central issue of psychophysics is the appropriate way to measure sensory capacities.

Thresholds

The earliest form of psychophysical measurement was a determination of sensory thresholds. An ***absolute threshold*** is defined as the weakest level of stimulus energy that the senses can detect. In the measurement of thresholds, people are given a number of trials and are asked each time whether or not they can detect the stimulus. If we were to measure the absolute threshold for a sound of a particular pitch, we might begin by giving trials in which the amplitude, or loudness, of the signal is so low that it is imperceptible to anyone. On successive trials the amplitude would be increased until the subject could hear the sound. This procedure would be repeated many times to ensure a reliable response. The absolute threshold would be defined as the loudness at which a person can detect a signal 50 percent of the time.

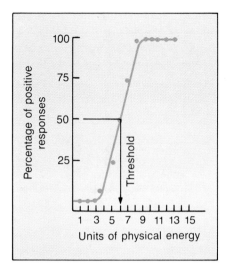

FIGURE 3–32
Psychophysical Function

A psychophysical function relates changes in units of physical energy to an observer's responses. In this case the observer's responses are the percentage of times he or she said "Yes" to indicate that he or she detected a signal. The absolute threshold is defined as the amount of stimulation that produces a positive response 50 percent of the time.

In measuring thresholds in this way, plotting the number of positive responses at every level of intensity, experimenters can create a psychophysical function (see Figure 3–32). The psychophysical function relates the changes in physical stimulation to their psychological correlates—in this case, to detection of the signal.

Table 3–1 lists some common values for the absolute thresholds of the different senses; bear in mind that values differ from person to person and even for the same person at different times, depending on motivation and alertness.

A second type of threshold is the *relative* or **difference threshold,** which is the minimum amount of stimulation necessary to tell two stimuli apart. A procedure often used in determining difference thresholds is to compare a series of *comparison stimuli* to a *standard stimulus.* Some of the comparison stimuli are almost exactly the same as the standard; others differ quite a bit. The difference threshold is the slightest variance from the standard stimulus that an observer can notice; this is also called the **just noticeable difference,** or *j.n.d.*

Psychophysicists have long known that for most sensory properties the j.n.d. is not a constant but depends on the magnitude of the standard stimulus. For example, people can much more easily tell the difference between a 1-pound standard weight and a 2-pound comparison weight than between a 31-pound standard and a 32-pound comparison weight, even though in both cases the difference is one pound. In general, the greater the magnitude of a standard stimulus, the greater the difference between the standard and comparison stimuli must be before it can be noticed; alternatively, the greater the standard stimulus, the greater the difference threshold, or j.n.d.

Although the difference threshold is not a constant for standard stimuli of different magnitudes, a German scientist named Ernst Weber proposed in 1834 that the j.n.d. is a constant proportion of the magnitude of a stimulus—that is, if 1 pound must be added to a 10-pound standard weight for a j.n.d., then for a 100-pound standard weight, 10 pounds would have to be added to produce a j.n.d. This idea is known as **Weber's law,** and it may

TABLE 3–1
Absolute Thresholds

Sense	Threshold
Vision	A candle flame seen at 30 miles on a dark, clear night
Audition	The tick of a watch under quiet conditions at 20 feet
Taste	One teaspoon of sugar in 2 gallons of water
Smell	One drop of perfume diffused into the entire volume of a 6-room apartment
Touch	The wing of a fly falling on one's cheek from a distance of 1 centimeter

The table shows how powerful the senses are, under ideal conditions, in detecting weak stimulation. Of course, the absolute threshold varies from person to person.

Source: Brown et al., 1962.

TABLE 3-2 Common Constant Values for the Weber Fraction	
Sense	Weber Fraction $(\Delta I/I)$
Vision (brightness, white light)	1/60
Kinesthesis (lifted weights)	1/50
Pain (thermally aroused on skin)	1/30
Audition (tone of middle pitch and moderate loudness)	1/10
Pressure (cutaneous pressure)	1/7
Smell (odor of India rubber)	1/4
Taste (table salt)	1/3

The Weber fraction is the proportional amount of increase in intensity needed to produce a just noticeable difference (j.n.d.). The smaller the fraction, the less change is necessary to produce a j.n.d. Thus, less than a 2 percent change in white light is needed to be detectable, while a 25 percent difference is needed in the smell of India rubber for it to be noticed.

Source: Schiffman, 1976.

be summarized as $\Delta I/I$ = Constant, where I is the intensity of the standard stimulus and ΔI is the difference in intensity that is just noticeable. Although Weber's law does not hold perfectly, it proves useful. It is accurate at intermediate levels of stimulation for such sensory properties as brightness, loudness, and pitch, but it breaks down at high and low levels of stimulation for the standard. Table 3–2 shows the values of the *Weber fraction* for a variety of common sensory properties.

Psychophysical Scaling

Recall once more that the intensity of a light and its perceived brightness are not the same. As the intensity of a light increases, at what rate does its brightness grow? The rate is certainly not linear—adding a single candle achieves a large effect in a dark room but a slight one in a well-lit room. Most sensory systems, in fact, are highly nonlinear; doubling the intensity of a tone does not come anywhere near to doubling its perceived loudness. This may help explain the high cost of stereo equipment that produces extremely loud sound. A moderately powerful amplifier, one that is rated at 60 watts, emits sound that is not perceived as much louder than one from an amplifier rated at only 30 watts. But amplifiers are priced by the watt and even slightly higher volume costs a good deal more.

Measuring the relationship between the physical intensity of a stimulus and its perceived intensity is called *psychophysical scaling.* One famous technique, devised by Gustav Fechner in 1860, assumes that each extra j.n.d. added to the intensity of a stimulus increases its perceived intensity by a constant amount.

To construct this type of scale for loudness, you could use any device that produces tones of known physical intensity, such as a stereo receiver. Adjust its volume control to the absolute threshold of hearing, so that you can just barely hear the sound. Mark a "0" at the relevant place on the dial. Next, turn the control until you can just detect an increase in volume. Do this carefully, and repeat the measurement several times to ensure accuracy. When you have located this setting on the volume control, place a second mark on the dial to indicate its location and label it "1." Repeat the process until the volume becomes unpleasantly loud. When you have finished, the dial will be covered with marks, which will constitute Fechner's scale for perceived loudness. If you were now to go back and record the physical intensity of the sound at each of your marks, your psychophysical scale would be complete.

An alternative way to construct a psychophysical scale for loudness is a procedure called *magnitude estimation.* Devised in 1956 by S. S. Stevens, it involves playing tones of varying intensity levels and asking listeners to supply a number indicating how loud each sounds. Suppose you begin with a tone of intermediate loudness and your subject responds with a magnitude estimate of 100. At this point you instruct that a tone twice as loud as the one just played should be designated 200, one only half as loud should be rated at 50, and so on. You would then present a long series of tones and record your subject's loudness estimates of each. When you were finished, you would compare the physical intensities of the tones you had pre-

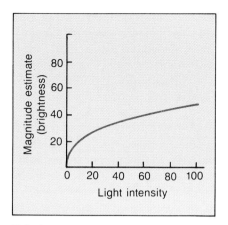

FIGURE 3–33
Stevens's Magnitude Estimation Method

The function for brightness was obtained using Stevens's magnitude estimation method. Notice that the function is curved, indicating that as light intensity is doubled, say from 40 to 80, brightness increases much more slowly, from roughly 35 to 43.

Source: Stevens, 1962.

sented with the magnitude estimates your subjects made. The result would be Stevens's psychophysical scale of loudness.

Both Fechner's and Stevens's scales may be shown in a graph that plots the perceived intensity of the stimulus against its physical intensity. The results are usually smooth and orderly and may be described quite well by mathematical equations. An example of the psychophysical function for brightness determined by Stevens's method of magnitude estimation appears in Figure 3–33. Notice that the psychophysical function is a curved rather than a straight line, which is typical of psychophysical functions. This indicates that the translation of physical energy to its psychophysical correlates is nonlinear; the doubling of the light intensity in Figure 3–33 comes nowhere near to doubling of the perceived brightness. Another example of this nonlinearity is found in people's estimates of the amount of light ordinary sunglasses filter out of the eyes. Most people assume that as much as 60 to 80 percent of the light gets through, but in truth only about 10 percent does.

Fechner's and Stevens's methods of calculating psychophysical functions produce slightly different results. The discrepancy between them is a source of controversy, but both methods produce curved psychophysical functions and both have had a great impact on psychophysics.

Signal Detection Theory

One final development to be discussed in the field of psychophysics is *signal detection theory*. This theory, imported to psychology from communication science, has redefined our understanding of thresholds. Recall that the absolute threshold is the weakest detectable intensity of a stimulus. The basic idea behind the threshold is that it constitutes a boundary between perceptibility and imperceptibility. Stimuli below the threshold evoke no response in the sensory system; those above the threshold result in conscious experience. This implies that sensation is an "all-or-none" matter and that either we perceive a stimulus or we do not.

There are two basic problems with this notion. First, sensory experience is not always all-or-none; instead, we are often unsure whether or not we are perceiving a weak stimulus, such as seeing a faint star in the night sky or hearing the telephone ringing while we are in the shower.

The second problem with the concept of a threshold involves a point of methodology. When a threshold is being measured, say in a hearing test, how do researchers know for sure that the subject really perceives a tone whenever the subject raises a hand in accordance with instruction? A subject who wanted to appear especially sensitive could simply keep his or her hand raised. Since sensation is so inherently private, how could anyone tell if the subject was lying?

Psychophysicists have tackled the problem by including "catch trials" in tests. On these trials, no stimulus is presented. If the subject reports perceiving a stimulus, it is clear that the subject is not responding accurately, deliberately or otherwise. Or is it? Virtually all subjects make such errors, which are called *false alarms*. Subjects are often unsure as to whether they perceive a stimulus or not and they guess, sometimes incorrectly.

Signal detection theory provides a formal, mathematical model of what subjects are doing when their thresholds are being measured (Green & Swets, 1966). This theory holds that the basic all-or-none idea behind thresholds is wrong. In its place, the theory's adherents propose that sensation is a graded or continuous experience. As the intensity of a stimulus increases from zero, it gradually becomes more perceptible; it does not spring full blown into consciousness.

Sensation is a graded experience because all sensory systems contain a steady background of randomly varying signals, called *noise*. This noise is due in part to random patterns of neural firing and might be likened to the static heard on any AM radio or the snow seen on television when the set is not tuned. This noise comes from many sources, one of them the sensory system itself. To demonstrate this phenomenon, place yourself in a light-proof environment, such as a closed closet at night. After you have adapted to the dark, look around. Of course, you won't be able to see anything. But is your sensory experience one of total blackness? No. It will be an intermediate level of gray. Why? Because the neurons in your visual system are firing spontaneously, even in the absence of physical stimulation. In other words, you are experiencing the noise in your own visual system. Likewise, if you entered a soundproof chamber you could hear not silence but auditory noise, supplemented by the sounds of your breathing and of blood rushing through your ears.

Radar operators must detect critical signals in noisy displays. Signal detection theory provides a model of this process.

According to signal detection theory, when you are presented with a physical stimulus, your sensory response to it simply adds to this ever-present background noise. It is the sum of the signal plus the noise that reaches your conscious awareness. When you are asked whether you perceive a stimulus in a threshold test, your problem is to decide whether you detect a genuine stimulus or only the noise. Often there is no way to tell, so you make your best guess. The theory says you make this guess by setting for yourself a *criterion*, or cutoff point. This criterion is an amount of perceived stimulus intensity above which you will say "Yes, I perceive a stimulus" and below which you will say "No, I don't." Sometimes on catch trials, where no stimulus is presented, the noise alone in your sensory channels will be sufficiently intense to exceed your criterion, and you will commit a false alarm error. By the same token, if a weak stimulus has been presented to you, but your personal noise level at the moment happens to be quite low, the sum of signal plus noise still might not be great enough to exceed your established criterion. You will therefore respond "No," even though a stimulus is present to be detected. This second type of error is simply called a *miss*.

Numerous trials are used in a signal detection experiment. On some a stimulus is presented, on others, none. By measuring the frequencies of your false alarms and misses as well as your correct responding, researchers can measure your actual sensitivity to the stimulus using the mathematics of the theory. In addition they can compute a second measure that indicates where you have set your criterion. These two measures are relatively independent of one another, and the measures quite ably tell truly sensitive observers from subjects who simply like to say "Yes, I perceived it." Signal detection theory has also proved useful in several other areas of psychology, such as the study of memory and decision making (Gescheider, 1985, chap. 5). In general, signal detection theory provides a useful conceptual tool for any situation in which yes/no decisions are made in an imperfect ("noisy") environment.

As one example of the uses of signal detection theory, consider the possible effects of treatments such as acupuncture or nitrous oxide ("laughing gas"), which are sometimes used as anesthetics in dentistry. Dentists report that these treatments block or reduce pain during drilling and extraction of teeth. But do they really affect the sensitivity of the teeth, or do they only affect the person's willingness to report the pain? The techniques of signal detection theory are made to order to answer such questions. In a controlled experiment Chapman, Gehrig, & Wilson (1975) tested the sensitivity of patients' teeth both while they were under treatment of acupuncture or nitrous oxide and when they were not. Sensitivity was measured by asking the patients to report whether or not their teeth were receiving electrical stimulation. As in all signal detection experiments, catch trials were included, and on these occasions no stimulations were given. The researchers found that both acupuncture and nitrous oxide reduced the actual sensitivity of the teeth and did not just shift the patient's criterion or the willingness to report pain. Signal detection theory is useful in all cases when researchers are concerned with deciding whether some treatment actually affects one's ability to detect stimuli or merely one's willingness to report them.

CONTROVERSY

Is There a "Sixth Sense"? Testing for ESP

At the beginning of the chapter we described the phenomenon of blindsight, in which some cortically blind patients can apparently perceive the location of objects that they cannot identify. They have no idea how they know the location of the objects, and their abilities leave them perplexed. Some people believe they have a similar power to know things that goes beyond normal means of perceiving. But whereas blindsight, puzzling though it is, can be interpreted in terms of what we know about the senses and the brain, these other claims about perception cannot. Some people believe they can read others' minds or see into the future, with no clues whatsoever from the senses.

We have all heard of people who seem to possess a "sixth sense," or **extrasensory perception (ESP).** The field devoted to the study of such extraordinary claims is called *parapsychology,* and it includes the subfields of psychokinesis and ESP. *Psychokinesis* refers to the supposed ability of the mind to move or otherwise control objects. ESP includes *clairvoyance,* the supposed awareness of objects or events that cannot be observed directly; *telepathy* (or mind reading), the transmission of thoughts; and *precognition,* the ability to see into the future.

Psychologists, philosophers, physicists, and magicians have debated repeatedly about whether these concepts of parapsychology should be regarded as established facts or mere

folly. As in many academic fields, parapsychology has its own devoted band of researchers, journals, research institutes, and critics. There is much evidence that believers can interpret in support of ESP; there are also many methodological problems in the research and some instances of fraud. Many of us are easily impressed by demonstrations of seemingly remarkable powers, such as shown by the Amazing Kreskin on television or the self-proclaimed psychic Uri Geller. However, before you accept such demonstrations as evidence for paranormal powers, stop and think about how convinced you are when you see a magician perform. Magicians also create illusions that seem impossible to the ordinary folk in the audience, but of course the magician makes no claims of paranormal powers. Rather, he or she tells us that we are being fooled by skillful application of the magicians' secrets of illusion. How then do we know, when viewing people who are alleged to have psychic powers, that they are not performing the same magic tricks but telling us a different story? In fact, it is now commonplace to have magicians join psychologists and other investigators when they seek evidence about claims of psychic powers. If the claimant is a fraud, the magicians are in the best position to know.

The inspiration for much work on parapsychology in the United States came from J. B. Rhine, who died in 1980. Rhine became interested in spiritual mediums, people who claim to be able to make contact with the dead and relate the thoughts of the dead to the living. Rhine's investigations led him to conclude that the me-

diums were using telepathy to read the minds of the people who were trying to communicate with deceased relatives. Thus, the medium would obtain information that seemed to come from a ghostly netherworld. Whether the medium was using telepathy or simply picking up normal sensory cues from the deceased person's relatives is a matter of debate.

Parapsychologists generally recognize that little useful scientific knowledge can be obtained from isolated cases. The chance of fakery is too high. So they undertake laboratory experiments. In a telepathy experiment, for example, one person might sit in one room and attempt to transmit messages to another person in another room. The sender might look at individual cards from a deck in which each card bears just one of five symbols. The receiver tries to determine which is being transmitted on each test. Since there are five symbols, the receiver who is merely guessing should be correct 20 percent of the time. But since some receivers will be luckier than others, one might get as few as 17 percent correct while another, also guessing, might get 25 percent. The existence of parapsychological powers then depends on whether there are people who can consistently perform the task better than chance, or the laws of probability, would predict. If so, and if it can be proved that the people achieved the feat without using any cues from their senses, such a result would constitute evidence for ESP.

There have been many claims of just such accomplishments over the years. Believers have found evidence for telepathy, clairvoyance, and pre-

Although parapsychologists were accepted as affiliates in the American Association for the Advancement of Science in 1969, their presence there remains hotly debated. The renowned magician James ("The Amazing") Randi argues that magicians, artists of deception, should be present to detect trickery in the performances of self-proclaimed psychics. To demonstrate his point, Randi recently revealed the results of a three-year "undercover operation," where, with Randi's help, the two young magicians pictured here disguised themselves as psychics to be observed by university scientists. After observing such feats as metal bending, distortion of photographic film, and movement of clock hands, the scientists declared the young men authentic psychics. But all of the tricks are easily explained by techniques such as distraction and illusion that magicians commonly use. Randi exposed the ruse at a Manhattan press conference, attacking the careless methods of psychic research.

cognition. Yet most psychologists remain skeptical for several reasons. One is that some experimental results have not been successfully repeated by experimenters in other laboratories. A second involves statistical issues: some tasks used in ESP research are quite complex, and determining what level of performance to expect by chance alone becomes tricky (Dia-conis, 1978). Third, there have been some clearcut cases of fraud in parapsychological investigations (Hansel, 1980). But parapsychology is not unique in this respect; a cancer researcher was caught painting black spots on the backs of white laboratory mice to fake the effects of a drug treatment. Fourth, some psychologists are skeptical of the paranormal simply because the claims conflict so sharply with what we know about the other senses. Where, for example, are telepathic waves received (or for that matter, transmitted) in the body? Through what physical medium do they pass? Fifth, if some people do possess powers of precognition, why aren't they busy warning of impending disasters like earthquakes? Why don't they get rich at Las Vegas or on Wall Street?

But many people still believe in parapsychology, and the debate continues. A recent development was the establishment of the Committee for the Scientific Investigation of Claims of the Paranormal, headquartered in Buffalo, New York. It is devoted to the scientific study of parapsychology as well as to other areas on the far fringes of science, including UFOs, the Bermuda Triangle, astrology, the Loch Ness monster, and "things that go bump in the night." The committee staff includes professionals from many fields, and members of the committee, including James Randi, have been able to duplicate the feats of Geller, who bends metal keys and spoons to demonstrate supposed psychokinetic powers. Since the committee used stage magic to do the same thing, its members concluded that Geller was a fraud (Hyman, 1977).

Parapsychology is a fascinating topic, but it should be approached with an open but skeptical mind. Two books about the scientific study of parapsychology are *Psi Search* by Bowles and Hynds (1978) and *Science and Parapsychology: A Critical Reevaluation* by Hansel (1980). The first is favorable to psychic research; the second is critical.

SUMMARY

1. Sensation refers to the reception of stimulation from the environment through the senses; perception refers to the interpretation and understanding of that stimulation. One view of how the senses work maintains that they always provide an accurate image of the environment. This simple view is discredited by several observations: the senses do not respond to certain types of stimulation, and conditions exist in which the senses seem to function well but perception of the world is poor.

2. Aristotle listed five categories of human sense experience: vision, audition, taste, touch, and smell. Scientists have identified at least two other sources of sense information: kinesthesis, or feedback about positions of the limbs, and vestibular information, about maintaining balance or equilibrium. In addition, the sense of touch can be broken down into more basic categories of pressure, pain, and heat and cold sensations.

3. The eyes are sensitive to a small band of the entire electromagnetic spectrum, the visible spectrum. The wavelength of light in the visible spectrum gives rise to perception of hue, while the intensity of light determines brightness perception. The eye functions somewhat like a camera, in that a sharp image is focused on a photosensitive surface. Light is bent or refracted by the cornea and lens of the eye to be focused on the retina. The fovea contains only the photoreceptors known as cones, which are responsible for color vision and determination of detail. Other photoreceptors, the rods, are concentrated outside the fovea; they are responsible for perception of black and white, for peripheral vision, and for night vision.

4. Perception of an object's properties depends on the context in which the object is placed. One illustration of this principle is the phenomenon of simultaneous contrast: if two gray squares of the same lightness are embedded in two other squares varying greatly in lightness, the interior squares will appear different. Part of this phenomenon is likely due to lateral inhibition, or the inhibiting effect that the firing of one neuron has on the firing of its neighbors.

5. The two main theories of color vision are the trichromatic and opponent-process theories. According to trichromatic theory, color perception is determined by the differing responses of three types of cones in the retina. According to opponent-process theory, three types of systems work in opposing pairs (red-green, blue-yellow, and black-white). The first two systems are responsible for perception of color. A modern synthesis of these theories suggests that each may be partly correct: the principles of trichromatic theory may operate at the level of receptors in the retina, whereas opponent processes may operate at later levels in the visual system.

6. Sound waves vary in frequency and amplitude. Frequency determines perception of pitch, and amplitude partly determines perception of loudness. The outer ear funnels sound waves to the small bones of the middle ear, which amplify and conduct the vibrations to the inner ear. The cochlea of the inner ear is filled with fluid that, depending on the sound, activates particular hair cells and initiates neural firing. The auditory nerve carries the impulses to the brain.

7. The basilar membrane in the cochlea contains hair cells. The intensity, or loudness, of sound is coded by the number of hair cells that are activated; pitch is coded by both the place of stimulation on the basilar membrane and the frequency of activation.

8. The stereochemical theory of smell holds that receptors in the nose are designed specifically to match the wide variety of molecular shapes in the air. The receptors for taste are the many taste buds that cover certain areas of the tongue. Separate taste receptors exist for sweet, salty, sour, and bitter. Preferences for tastes change with age. Adults prefer sweets less than do children.

9. Endorphins are substances produced by the brain that block pain sensations by clogging the postsynaptic membrane. They are produced when laboratory animals are given repeated experiences with a stressful event; animals in which such stress is produced tolerate pain more than animals that were not stressed, and show elevated levels of endorphins.

10. Psychophysics is the study of how changes in physical stimulation are translated into psychological experience. Two basic psychophysical measures are the absolute threshold and the difference threshold. The absolute threshold is the smallest amount of stimulation that can be detected by a sense receptor. The difference threshold is the smallest change in stimulation that can be detected. The difference threshold grows with increases in the standard of comparison; it is more difficult to notice the change of adding one candle to a well-lit room than to a dimly lit room.

11. Psychophysical scales relate physical energy such as light intensity to its perception, or brightness. Graphs of such scales are generally curved, indicating that perception does not change in a direct, linear fashion with changes in stimulation.

12. Some researchers have argued for a mysterious "sixth sense," that of extrasensory perception. Parapsychology is the study of telepathy, or mind reading; clairvoyance, or awareness of objects and events not directly observed; precognition, or awareness of future events; and psychokinesis, the ability to move objects mentally. Although some research has supported the notion of extrasensory perception, most psychologists remain skeptical for several reasons. These include difficulties in replicating the phenomena, the statistical problems in evaluating the results, and occasional cases of outright fraud.

SUGGESTED READINGS

Barlow, H. B., & Mollon, J. D. (Eds.) (1982). *The senses.* London: Cambridge University Press.
   A valuable text covering all the senses in detail. The chapters are written by leading experts in the field.

Gescheider, G. A. (1985). *Psychophysics: Method, theory, and application* (2nd ed.). Hillsdale, N.J.: Erlbaum.
   An excellent introduction to the field of psychophysics, this work includes discussions of the determination of thresholds, psychophysical scaling, and the theory of signal detection.

Goldstein, E. B. (1984). *Sensation and perception* (2nd ed.). Belmont, Calif.: Wadsworth.
   This is an up-to-date text that provides a survey of information about all the senses, with vision and hearing treated in the greatest detail.

Lindsay, P. H., & Norman, D. A. (1977). *Human information processing* (2nd ed.). New York: Academic Press.
   The first few chapters contain helpful information about vision and audition. Psychophysics is also included, and the appendix provides an extensive introduction to signal detection theory.

Sekuler, R., & Blake, R. (1985). *Perception.* New York: Knopf.
   An outstanding textbook on sensation and perception written by two leading researchers. As in most texts, vision is treated most thoroughly, but two excellent chapters are devoted to hearing and one chapter to smell and taste.

4

Perception

Of the real universe we know nothing, except that
there exist as many versions of it as there are
perceptive minds.

Gerald Bullitt

ORDINARILY PERCEPTION OF THE WORLD IS SO EFFORTLESS THAT WE rarely stop to marvel at what complicated processes must occur in order for us to discern things accurately. Consider the challenge of driving at night through a long tunnel. Entering from darkness, a driver is momentarily dazzled by bright lights. Once this sensation wears off, it is replaced by other confusions. Highway tunnels usually have double rows of fluorescent lights along each side. Although all the lights are equally spaced along the tunnel, the distant ones appear close together, and the nearby ones seem far apart. Lights up ahead seem to move slowly, but those on each side of the driver rush by. As though this were not enough, add the blinding glare of oncoming headlights and the distorted images of light reflecting from the polished hood of the car. Other elements contribute to the complex mix of sensations: the guard rail, the white line down the center of the road, and the tiles on the walls and ceilings. In a few seconds a driver must process and interpret a vast amount of sensory data in order to pass safely through the tunnel.

The example of driving at night through a tunnel illustrates how perception can be accurate, or *veridical*, even in complex situations. Of course, we do not perceive every stimulus with complete accuracy every time; eyes and ears can deceive. Some of us have seen a desert mirage or falsely heard our names called while we take a shower. The effects of misperceptions can be painful, as when we misjudge the position of the steps and fall down a flight of stairs, or even fatal, as when an airplane pilot misjudges the distance to the runway. Clearly, veridical perception has enormous survival value.

Errors of perception, including illusions, can be intriguing, as some of the demonstrations in this chapter will reveal. But researchers who study perception are more surprised by how veridical our perception normally is than by its occasional failures. Scientists and engineers are now moving rapidly toward building robots that can mimic human behavior by sensing objects in their environment, such as a machine part moving down a conveyor belt. In the process, these researchers are rapidly gaining an understanding of the problems perception entails and an appreciation of human perceptual abilities, which we often take for granted.

In Chapter 3, we distinguished sensation—the reception of stimulation from the environment through the senses—from perception—the interpretation of the sensory information relayed to the brain from the receptor organs—the eyes, ears, nose, mouth, and skin. To refresh your memory on the distinction between sensation and perception, look again at the dalmatian in Figure 3–2 on page 84. When you first scrutinized the photo, your visual system could not organize it into an image that made any sense. Only after a minute or so did its parts fall into place. During that frustrating delay your perceptual system was attempting to group the parts of the picture into meaningful configurations or patterns.

Flying a helicopter provides many challenges to the perceptual system. Even under conditions of good visibility, the pilot must interpret many rapidly changing visual cues, as well as monitor the dials in the cockpit.

In this chapter we will focus primarily on visual perception, although most of the principles we will discuss also apply to other perceptual systems. The chapter begins with two major problems in the study of perception. The first is *perceptual organization:* why does the world look as it does? Just as we asked in Chapter 3 why particular combinations of wavelengths of light produce the colors we experience, in this chapter we will ask why the particular sensory stimuli our receptors detect lead to our perceiving surrounding objects. The second, related problem involves explaining *pattern recognition,* or how we identify the shapes and patterns in the world from the raw sensations arising from our senses. How do we recognize a dog as a dog? The visual sensory system (that is, the retinas and the brain structures that receive information from the retinas) detects simple features in the visual field, such as line segments, corners, and angles. In like manner, the ear and auditory centers of the brain detect the frequencies and amplitudes of sound waves entering the ears. From these beginnings, our perceptual systems must create our structures and significant perceptions of the world, complete with barking dogs and talking humans. No robots yet exist that are capable of pattern recognition sufficient to, say, identify a dog in a photograph. Yet humans do so effortlessly. How?

Third, we will discuss our perception of the attributes of *depth, size, and shape* and how we can judge these qualities so accurately even in a rapidly changing environment. Fourth is the problem of perceptual *illusions,* which offer many important clues for understanding how veridical perception is achieved. Fifth and last, we will consider the *role of experience* in perception, including how we learn to adjust to new perceptual conditions, how we respond to perceptual deprivation, and a bit on how infants learn to perceive for the first time. This last topic is continued in Chapter 9.

✓PERCEPTUAL ORGANIZATION

When our eyes examine the world around us, the millions of rods and cones in each retina respond with electrical signals, as we learned in Chapter 3. But at a conscious level, we are aware only of the objects and surfaces of our environment. We are *not* aware of what the individual rods and cones are doing; if we were, we might see the world as a vast array of points varying in color and brightness rather than as a layout of natural objects in our environment. The structuring of elementary sensations such as points, lines, and edges into the objects we perceive is called *perceptual organization.* The Gestalt psychologists, including Max Wertheimer, Kurt Koffka, and Wolfgang Köhler, were most responsible for bringing this concept to the forefront of perceptual psychology in the first half of this century. They argued that a perception was more than, or at least different from, the sum of the sensations underlying it. Just as the nature of a molecule is determined not only by its component atoms but by their arrangement, the nature of a perceptual experience depends not merely on the sensations produced at the receptors but also on how those sensations are arranged into whole patterns, or Gestalts.

A Gestalt Demonstration

The following experiment illustrates one Gestalt concept (see Figure 4–1). Suppose a light is attached to the rim of a bicycle wheel and the wheel is

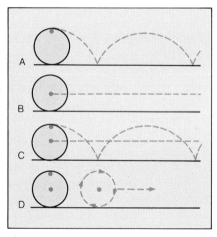

FIGURE 4–1
A Gestalt Demonstration

In part A, a single light is placed on the rim of a wheel as it rolls in the dark. The viewer sees the cycloid motion traced by the dotted lines. In B, the light is placed on the hub, and the observer sees horizontal motion. In C, both lights are turned on, but the dotted lines shown are not what an observer sees. Instead, D shows how most observers organize the stimuli: as one light circling around another as the whole configuration rolls. Thus the simultaneous perception of both lights is not simply the sum of the parts.

Source: Krech & Crutchfield, 1958.

rolled across a dark room. What does an observer see? Not the wheel, because the room is dark. Only the light is perceived; its path is called a *cycloid*. Next, suppose the light is moved to the wheel's hub. Now an observer sees only a point of light moving horizontally across the room. In neither case is anything resembling a rolling wheel perceived. Last, imagine that two lights are attached to the wheel, one on the rim and one at the hub. If the two perceptual experiences simply were added together, the observer now would see one light following a cycloid path and one following a straight line. That does not happen: the two lights are perceived as forming a unified, rolling wheel, and even the most persistent viewer cannot see the cycloid path of the light on the rim (Duncker, 1929; Johansson, 1975).

This demonstration exemplifies the Gestalt claim that perception of a whole pattern, or configuration of stimuli, differs from the simple sum of its perceived parts. Instead of the sum, observers perceive the pattern or relationships among the parts.

Grouping and Figure-Ground Principles

The Gestalt psychologists provided two sets of principles for describing how perceptions are organized into meaningful wholes (Kubovy & Pomerantz, 1981). The first set deals with *perceptual grouping* and the second with *figure-ground segregation*. Perceptual grouping illustrated in Figure 4–2, tells us how spatial patterns are organized into larger units. Part A in the figure shows a square grid with alternate rows of dots in different colors. You are

FIGURE 4–2
Perceptual Grouping Principles

Parts A and B show groupings by similarity: rows or columns of stimuli similar in brightness group together. Part C shows grouping by proximity: nearby stimuli tend to group in units. The dots group together as columns rather than rows. Part D demonstrates good continuation: stimuli that flow smoothly into one another are seen as forming a single group, so we see two intersecting lines ab and cd, not the other possible pairs (ad and cb; ac and bd). Finally, E shows a series of elements whose perception requires several different grouping principles.

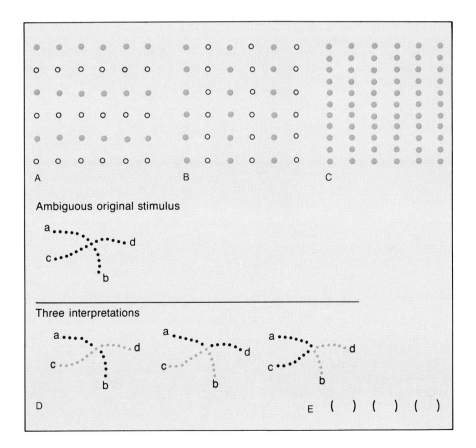

more likely to see these dots as being organized in rows, i.e., horizontal groups, than in columns, i.e., vertical groups. In part B, you are more likely to see the dots as organized in columns. These two panels demonstrate grouping by similarity: similar stimuli tend to be grouped into the same unit more readily than dissimilar stimuli. Part C demonstrates the comparable principle of grouping by proximity: stimuli that are close together are generally put in the same unit more frequently than stimuli that are farther apart. So you organize the dots into columns rather than rows. Part D demonstrates grouping by good continuation: stimuli that flow smoothly into one another are more likely to be seen as a single group than those that do not flow. Finally, part E demonstrates a combination of the grouping principles: how a viewer organizes a sequence of alternating left and right parentheses. You are most likely to see these elements as grouped in pairs as ( ) ( ) ( ) . Alternately you could see them as triplets, ( ) ( ) ( ) , or in isolated elements as ( ) ( ) ( ) , or in any of the other possible groups.

These Gestalt principles help provide a scientific understanding of everyday perception of the world. Imagine perceiving a moving car through a picket fence: although its image on the retina is cut into thin slices by the fence, you still see the car as a unitary object. This occurs in part because of similarity and good continuation: the slices of the car are similar in color and texture, and they flow smoothly into one another. Robots and other manufactured perceptual devices are often baffled by such images and would fail to see the car through the fence.

Similar grouping effects occur in auditory perception. When we listen to someone speak, we may have the impression that brief pauses clearly separate the words. When the sound waves of the speaker's voice are recorded and examined, however, this proves not to be the case. Although the sound stream in speech does contain pauses or silent intervals, they occur no more frequently between words than they do within words, so they are of little help in picking out the individual words of a sentence. When we listen to people speaking foreign languages, we often get the impression that they are talking too fast and running words together. They are running their words together, but the same is true of those who speak our own language. When we listen to English, our perceptual system groups the smeared sound elements together so that we hear distinct words.

The second Gestalt principle for perceptual organization is figure-ground segregation. A demonstration of the concept is shown in Figure 4–3. If you stare at the figure long enough, you will perceive it either as a single vase or as two faces looking at one another. It is difficult to detect both images simultaneously. When you see the vase, the areas that look like faces become the background rather than objects.

Figure 4–4 should clarify what makes the figure-ground problem tricky. When you first examine this figure, you may see a white triangle on a black square; the square seems to be a single, unbroken surface that continues behind the white triangle. With a little effort, however, you can make the white triangle disappear by perceiving the square as a black surface with a triangular hole. The inside of the triangle is now seen as part of the background. If you continue to examine this figure you may note other possible organizations. The point is that the visual system must decide which surfaces are part of the figure and which belong to the background. When peo-

FIGURE 4–3
Figure-Ground Reversal

This figure may be seen as a single vase or as two faces in silhouette looking directly at one another. It is difficult to see the faces and the vase simultaneously. If you have trouble seeing the faces, note that the deepest indentations in the vase represent noses.

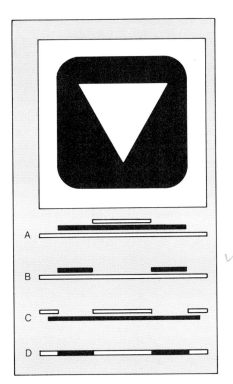

FIGURE 4–4
Ambiguous Figure-Ground Relation

The large figure at the top may be seen as a white triangle on top of a black square or as a black square with a triangular hole cut in it. These arrangements are presented in parts A and B below the figure, which show possible cross-sectional views. In the figure and ground arrangement in C, you would see the figure as a hole cut in a white page to reveal a black background underneath the page. The actual situation is represented in D—black ink and white paper in the same plane. Interestingly, the real situation on the printed page is probably the hardest to see because our visual system usually interprets figures as lying on top of the ground.

Source: Miller, 1962.

ple look at a black spot on a nearby white wall, they can decide easily whether they are seeing a spot on the wall or a hole in the wall. Robots with electronic eyes find this a more difficult task.

Although psychologists are well aware of the grouping and figure-ground problems in perception, they still do not completely understand how the perceptual system solves these problems. No one knows precisely how the system groups the various parts of the dalmatian in Figure 3–2 and separates the dog from its background. But even if this process were comprehended, how could the system recognize the figure as a dog rather than as a cat or a chair? What is it about the segregated set of blobs that makes them appear doglike? For that matter, what characteristics must *any* stimulus possess in order to be a dog?

PATTERN RECOGNITION

Humans recognize dogs immediately and without error every day, but few of us have a clue about *how* we do this. This feat of identification is called *pattern recognition,* which may be defined specifically as the process of classifying stimuli into meaningful object categories.

We can identify almost any object or event as a *pattern* or bundle of features. To define a dog, for example, we begin with a set of features: four legs, a hairy coat, a tail. Of course, this list so far describes a cat as well as a dog. So we add further features like round pupils (cats have vertical slits) and smooth tongues (cats' tongues are sandpapery). More features might distinguish a particular dog: a spot around the left eye, for example. Such features as antlers and flippers must be absent. Finally, we should allow some leeway for features that might be *missing* in a particular dog, such as a tail that has been bobbed. When we think about it this way, we see that the category "dog" is itself a complex, abstract concept. Most theories of human pattern recognition hold that our visual system uses features of these sorts in recognizing objects.

Theories of pattern recognition can be grouped into two classes, bottom-up and top-down. Both types assume that the perceptual system detects the kinds of features just mentioned. Consider the process of recognizing letters of the alphabet, which enables you to read this page. Letters can be represented by a short list of features such as horizontal, vertical, and diagonal line segments, simple curves, and perhaps intersections. For example, if you know that a letter contains just one vertical and one horizontal line, you know it must be either a *T* or an *L*. Letter recognition gets complicated since letters may be printed in so many different ways (see Figure 4–5), but all the variations can be described by distinct features.

Bottom-up Theories

Most theories of pattern recognition view the visual system as organized vertically, with the rods and cones at the very bottom and abstract categories or concepts such as "dog" and "chair" at the top, somewhere in the cortex of the brain. In Chapter 3, we described cells called *feature detectors* in the visual cortex that respond to simple features like lines and angles in different positions. These feature detectors would be located very near the bottom

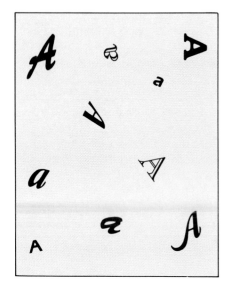

FIGURE 4–5
Pattern Recognition

Most people can easily recognize all of these patterns as the letter *A*, even though they vary greatly in shape, size, and orientation. A set of features can be defined for upper- and lowercase letters (A or a); people probably recognize letters by noting the critical features that distinguish letters from one another.

of the visual system according to the ***bottom-up theory,*** not far above the rods and cones from which they receive signals.

According to bottom-up theories, people recognize a visual pattern such as a letter of the alphabet by recording which feature detectors are activated when they look at the pattern. To be more precise, the line and angle detector cells feed into another set of cells, which may be called ***letter detectors.*** A letter detector for *L* would be excited by feature detectors that responded to horizontal and vertical lines, but it would be inhibited by detectors for diagonal lines, which are not contained in an *L.* Although bottom-up models of pattern recognition can become complicated in their details, they do a good job explaining certain errors of perception. For example, they predict that letters with similar features, such as *E* and *F,* will be confused more often than those with dissimilar features, such as *X* and *O,* a prediction that has been confirmed (Townsend, 1971).

Bottom-up processing is used in attempts to construct machines that can see. The approach is clearly an important one, with many practical applications. However, to date no entirely successful system has been developed, despite the great efforts of psychologists, engineers, and computer scientists. The most promising research currently is the work of David Marr, which is explained in his book *Vision* (1982).

In Marr's approach, perception works strictly from the bottom up, through a series of several steps. Figure 4–6A shows a plant as seen through a chain link fence. Perception of such a scene is first converted into a representation in terms of lines, as shown in Figure 4–6B. Marr refers to this step as a *primal sketch.* The lines in the primal (or first) sketch mark those places in the image where changes in brightness occur. The second and third stages in Marr's representation of the image add information from other sources, such as the slight differences in images presented to the two eyes in vision. These stages add depth and other features to the image. The final stage of Marr's scheme is construction of the three-dimensional (3-D) model, so named because height, width, and depth are all represented. The 3-D model is rather like the construction of an animal from pipe cleaners

FIGURE 4–6
The Construction of a Primal Sketch

Part A is a photograph of a plant behind a chain-link fence. B illustrates the first step in converting the image to a form in which lines reveal where sudden intensity changes exist in the original image.

Source: Marr, 1982, pp. 58, 72.

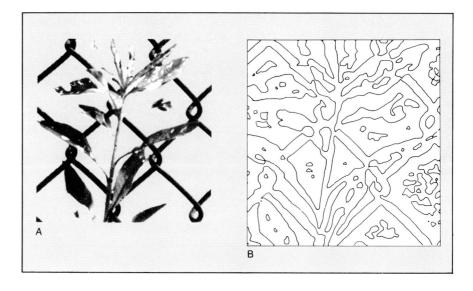

FIGURE 4–7
3–D Sketches

Notice how well these simple sketches for limbs, quadrupeds, bipeds, and birds capture differences both across and within the four categories.

Source: Marr, 1982, p. 319.

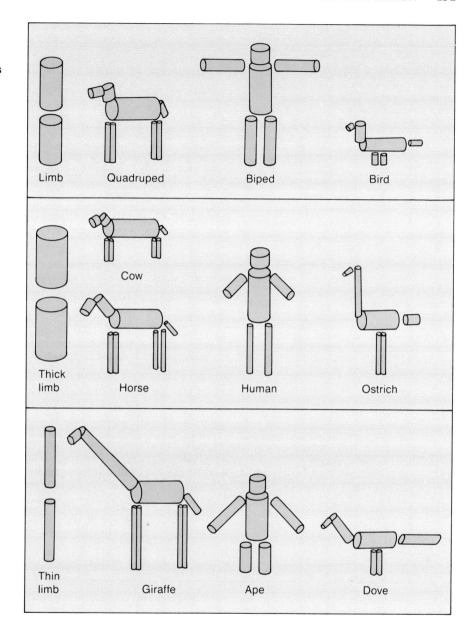

(see Figure 4–7). The essential information is provided through the cylinders that allow us to distinguish one animal from another.

Marr's theory is a bold attempt to provide an answer to the basic question of object recognition: how are distinguishing features represented? He tried to answer this question in a form that could be used by scientists to create mechanical devices that would see. Marr's model works automatically from the visual image, without the system knowing in advance what to expect. For this reason we mention it under bottom-up models. Although it is too early to know the final impact of Marr's model, psychologists and students of artificial intelligence currently hail it as a major breakthrough in understanding how vision should be conceptualized (Poggio, 1984; Winston, 1984). At the same time, however, most researchers acknowledge that other sources of information—the perceiver's past experience, expectations, and knowledge—also influence pattern recognition. This leads to top-down models, which assume that perception involves an active process of using past knowledge to help determine what objects are in the environment.

Top-down Theories

In bottom-up theories, pattern recognition begins down at the receptor organs and works up. In the *top-down* approach, recognition begins farther up in the brain and works its way down. Why would anyone propose this backward arrangement? Mainly because perception is so frequently a process of active exploration that is guided by higher-level psychological factors, such as what people expect to perceive. Consider again the act of reading. When you encounter the letter *Q* in English, you can almost be certain that the next letter will be a *u*. Therefore, it would be most effective to test actively for only those few features that define a *u*. If the first three letters of a four-letter word are *BOW*, what is the last letter likely to be? If it is an English word, the word is probably *BOWL* or *BOWS*. To decide which, we need only look to see whether the feature "horizontal line" or "curved line" is present at the bottom of the last figure. (Alternatively, we could check whether the last letter contains any curved lines.) It would be a waste of time for the brain to bother analyzing all the features in the letter when one or two suffice. Top-down theorists maintain that the brain constantly forms hypotheses about what pattern is present and then actively selects the features it wishes to check to confirm the hypotheses.

Top-down models help explain how pattern recognition works so rapidly by letting perceivers skip unnecessary steps. They also explain certain context effects in perception, such as the one depicted in Figure 4–8, where the same stimulus is recognized as either the letter *H* or the letter *A*, depending on its context. The context gives the perceptual system a hypothesis on which to work. If the stimulus fits the hypothesis well enough, the hypothesis is accepted and recognition is complete. Unlike their bottom-up counterparts, top-down models help explain other powerful effects of context in perception. For instance, a whole triangle can be recognized faster than any of its features, that is, faster than any of the three line segments that make it up (Pomerantz, 1981); a word can be recognized more accurately in a flash than any of its letters individually (Reicher, 1969); and an object can be recognized better in a natural scene than in isolation (Biederman, 1981). In all of these cases, a bottom-up model would lead us to expect the opposite.

Which approach is correct, the top-down or the bottom-up? Most theorists prefer an approach that combines the two, such as the model of word recognition illustrated in Figure 4–9 (Anderson, 1985; McClelland & Rumelhart, 1981). In this simplified model, excitatory and inhibitory signals flow both from the bottom (line detectors) upward through letter detectors to word detectors and also vice versa, from the top down. (In the figure, a line ending in an arrow represents an excitatory connection, and a line ending in a dot indicates an inhibitory connection.) In its bottom-up operation, notice that the horizontal line detector at the bottom left excites detectors for

FIGURE 4–8
A Context Effect

In this example, the same pattern is recognized as an *A* or an *H* depending on its context. The context of an object or pattern helps determine a viewer's recognition of it.

THE RAT SAT ON THE CHAIR

the letters *A*, *T*, *G*, and *S* but inhibits the detector for *N*, which contains no horizontal lines. In its top-down operation, notice that the various words inhibit detectors for features not contained in the words (as well as inhibiting one another), which effectively switches off detectors for features that are unlikely to appear. Thus, if you were reading a passage that started out "My car wouldn't start so I didn't make it to my class on _____," the detector for the word *time* would be activated by the sentence context, and detectors for features not contained in the word *time* would be inhibited. By working simultaneously from the top down and the bottom up, word recognition takes place extremely quickly when readers can predict upcoming words and letters from context. When this is not possible, as with highly technical material filled with unfamiliar words, top-down processing doesn't help and so reading must proceed solely from the bottom up at a much slower pace. And when a word appears that is totally out of place, top-down processes actually interfere with perception and make us do a double-take to read what is actually printed on the page.

FIGURE 4–9
Model of Reading

This diagram shows McClelland and Rumelhart's (1981) model for the recognition of printed words. The model incorporates both bottom-up signals, sent from the feature detectors at the bottom to the word detectors at the top, and top-down signals going in the opposite direction. These signals are both excitatory (connections ending in arrows) and inhibitory (ending in dots).

Source: McClelland & Rumelhart, 1981, p. 380.

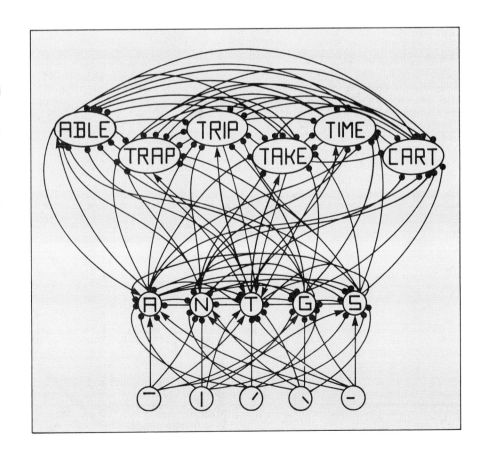

Ambiguous and Reversible Figures

Psychologists and artists have created a number of visual patterns that can be perceived in more than one way. Some of these are illustrated in Figure 4–10. Before reading the caption, look at the patterns. Does each seem to ''flip'' spontaneously into some new pattern after you examine it for several seconds? Many researchers believe that bottom-up processing alone cannot explain these changes; after all, the same visual features on the printed page produce both versions of each figure. Rather, these ambiguous figures show the operation of top-down processes at work, actively assembling visual features into different organizations.

Subjective Contours

Other phenomena that call for a top-down explanation are *subjective contours,* outlines of shapes that are seen even though no physical edges or lines are present. Figure 4–11 shows a pair of triangles whose edges seem

FIGURE 4–10
Ambiguous or Reversible Figures

In each case at least two scenes can arise from the same sensory pattern. Part A can be seen either as a beautiful young woman or as an unattractive old one. Is B a rabbit or a duck? C is the Necker Cube. Stare at an interior corner that you think is nearest to you, and you will suddenly discover that it has become the farthest corner. The cube spontaneously reverses in depth. (The "vase" in Figure 4–3 is another reversible figure.) D, viewed up close, reveals to most people a woman examining herself in the mirror; at a distance the same scene reveals a skull.

A

B

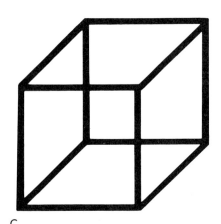

C

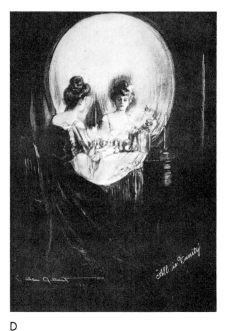

D

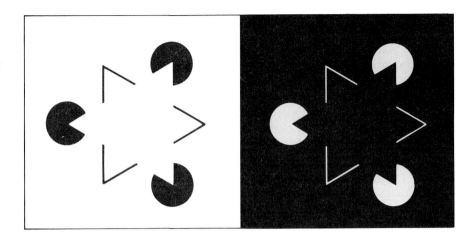

FIGURE 4–11
Subjective Contours

In the figure on the left, the viewer has a strong impression of a white triangle that is not really present in the figure. The triangle seems whiter than the background, although it is not. On the right, the same illusory triangle appears in black.

Source: Kanizsa, 1976.

real until you scrutinize them quite closely. Edge detectors working in the cortex from the bottom up should not detect the apparent lines; instead, the lines appear to be filled in by top-down processes that are led to expect edges to exist from the context that is physically present in the display. The same explanation holds for the similar figures on page 3 (Figure 1–1). Figure 4–12 shows a particularly noteworthy demonstration that mixes subjective contours with the reversible Necker Cube of Figure 4–10. The display can be seen as a Necker Cube either (a) floating above some red disks or (b) floating in a red space behind a white surface with holes in it (as though you were seeing the cube through a slice of Swiss cheese). Seeing these two possibilities takes some effort, but the effort is rewarded handsomely!

Subjective contours are only one of many types of visual images that are constructed from the top down in the brain, with little bottom-up help from the sensory receptors. Certainly when we dream, most of us "see" things that can be quite lifelike; drugs and sensory deprivation can lead to intense hallucinations in people who are wide awake. On a less extreme scale, quite a few people experience visual images in the "mind's eye," which they find pleasant and useful in planning and solving problems (see Chapter 8). But some psychologists are troubled by the idea of studying something so subjective as a person's private mental images. A controversy about the scientific status of visual imagery has boiled over; the current status of this debate is outlined in "Controversy: Are Mental Images Like Perceptions?" which begins on the next page.

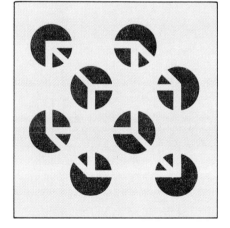

FIGURE 4–12
The Subjective Necker Cube

The Necker Cube can be seen here either as floating on top of the red disks, or, if figure and ground are reversed, as floating behind a light surface with holes in it. In the first case, subjective contours are seen, whereas in the second they are not.

Source: Bradley, Dumais, & Petry, 1976.

DEPTH, SIZE, AND SHAPE PERCEPTION

When we look at a dog, we not only recognize it but also gain information about its depth (or distance from us), its size, and its shape. Just as when we recognize patterns, however, identifying depth, size, and shape is more difficult than it seems at first. The size of the image that an object projects onto the retina (see Figures 3–8 and 3–13) depends on both the physical size of the object and its distance from the viewer. Problems such as depth perception have been studied for many years not only by psychologists but

Are Mental Images Like Perceptions?

Answer the following question accurately before reading further: How many windows are there in the room where you sleep? Most people can answer this question with little difficulty, and many report that they arrive at the answer by forming a picture or *mental image* of their bedroom in their "mind's eye" and scanning the image just as they would scan the room itself if they were standing in it. What is the status of such mental pictures? Are they mere figments of the imagination or are they real? If they are real, how similar is imagining to actually perceiving?

A debate about imagery has swirled for almost 100 years. As described in Chapter 1, the early psychologists who studied people's introspections about their experiences asked observers to rate the vividness and other qualities of their images. However, the behaviorists, in their relentless pursuit to rid psychology of the study of events that could not be directly observed in behavior, later argued that imagery should be abandoned as an object of scientific study. Even the introspectionists found that some people claimed to have frequent and vivid visual images while others claimed to

have no capacity to form images. Such unreliability in reporting images fueled the behaviorists' argument that studying imagery was like following a will-o'-the-wisp. In fact, the behaviorists succeeded in banishing the study of imagery from experimental psychology for almost 50 years, until the 1960s.

The debate about the existence of mental imagery has recently returned to psychology (Paivio, 1975; Pylyshyn, 1973). However, contemporary psychologists are not content simply to rely on introspection to study imagery but look to see if imagery can be studied, at least indirectly, by observing its effects on behavior. Of course, images cannot be studied directly because they are inherently private experiences. Psychologists study them by using a "what-if" approach. Such researchers say, in essence, "If images are real, what effects on behavior would be predicted?" Interestingly, many predictions have been borne out in careful experiments (Kosslyn & Pomerantz, 1977; Paivio, 1986).

One prediction is that if images are like perceptions, they may depend on the same brain mechanisms. If so, then it should be difficult to experience images and perceptions at the same time because the same neural circuitry could not be used for two different purposes at once. (Try imagining your mother's face both with your eyes closed and while watching TV.)

Studies by Segal (1971) have shown that when people are instructed to generate visual images in their minds (such as a flock of birds in flight), their ability to detect weak visual stimuli drops, but perception of auditory stimuli is relatively unaffected. Similarly, if asked to imagine an auditory event, such as an orchestra playing loudly, their perceptual sensitivity drops much more for auditory stimuli than for visual stimuli. These findings indicate that imagining and perceiving seem to rely on the same machinery in the brain. When one imagines sights or sounds, the ability to perceive actual stimuli in the same sense modality is diminished.

Another prediction is that, if visual images are similar to perceptions, then both should be scanned in a similar fashion. In one experiment, Stephen Kosslyn (1980; Kosslyn, Ball, & Reiser, 1978) showed college students a map of an imaginary island, like the one shown in Figure 4–13. The island contained a number of landmarks—a hut, a tree, a rock, a well, and so forth. Kosslyn asked the students to memorize the map and then he removed it from their sight. Next he asked students to form a mental image of the map and to focus their attention on a particular landmark, such as the well in the lower left-hand corner. Then the test began: subjects were asked to scan their mental image from that landmark to

also by painters, who attempt to create the illusion of depth on flat canvas. Let us see what has been learned from these studies.

Perception of Depth

Recall from Chapter 3 that the retina of each eye is a sheet of tissue lining the back of the eye's interior. It is essentially a two-dimensional surface, having height and width. But if the retina has only two dimensions, how

another landmark he named and to press a button as soon as their scan was complete. Kosslyn measured how quickly these scans were made. He found that his subjects were fastest in scanning to nearby locations; the more distant the feature, the longer the scan took. This is the result one would expect if subjects were actually scanning a mental image that had spatial properties like those that a physical image possesses. Again, this result suggests that perception of images is similar to actual visual perception.

These three illustrations are but a sample of the experiments that claim that images are like perceptions. We must note, however, that this evidence is largely circumstantial and in no way proves that mental images are comparable to perceptions. Some psychologists remain skeptical about images, pointing out that people who claim to experience images often can't use them effectively. For example, it is common for students answering an exam question to report that they can "see in their mind's eye" the page of their textbook where the answer lies, but they can't quite make out the words well enough to read them! For a demonstration, look now at the regular, geometric figure shown in Figure 4–14 and memorize it. Without looking back at the figure, decide from your mental image of it whether it contains any parallelograms within its contours. Most people find this question easy to answer when they examine the figure but hard when they examine their mental image. If mental images are as vivid and detailed as some people claim, why is this image so hard to scan for hidden parallelograms?

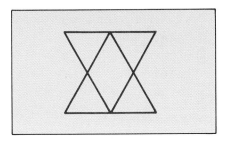

FIGURE 4–14
Image in the Mind's Eye

Study this figure long enough to memorize it. Then close your eyes, form a mental image of the figure, and see if you can spot any parallelograms hidden within your mental image. If you can't, look back at the figure again; three of them are to be found!

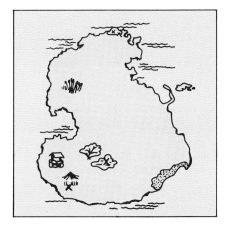

FIGURE 4–13
Image Scanning

In Kosslyn's image scanning experiments, subjects were asked to form a mental image of this map and then to mentally scan that image from one designated location to another. The amount of time it took them to complete the scan was proportional to the distance they had to cover from one object to the next. This result supports the idea that mental images have spatial properties similar to those of other, more tangible images.

Source: Kosslyn, Ball, & Reiser, 1978, p. 51.

Despite doubts by some psychologists, the study of visual imagery has returned to psychology and many workers currently pursue it. We will be describing more work in this area later in the book. Some researchers study imagery associated with dreaming (Chapter 5). Others have shown that imagery often greatly improves the ability to remember information (Chapter 7). Still others study the ways in which images can be manipulated and transformed as people think creatively (Chapter 8). Imagery seems to play a large role in mental life and uses the same cognitive mechanisms that are used in perceiving.

do people see the world in three dimensions (3-D)? What **depth cues** do we use to perceive depth?

BINOCULAR DISPARITY. One reason that people are capable of depth perception is that their eyes are a couple of inches apart, enabling them to see the world from two slightly different vantage points. Any image therefore differs a bit on the two retinas. This difference is called **binocular disparity.** You can demonstrate it for yourself by looking at this page while alternately blinking one eye at a time; the page will appear to shift its position. Normally, two images are fused in the brain into a single 3-D, or *stereoscopic, image.* The stereoscope (or 3-D viewer) works by presenting to the eyes photographs of a scene taken from two slightly different points, usually with a camera that has two lenses and exposes two segments of film simultaneously. This is analogous to stereophonic records or tapes, which are

FIGURE 4–15
Depth Perception
from Binocular Disparity

Part A shows two random dot patterns that, when presented separately to the two eyes, yield the perception of a square floating above the page, as shown in part C. Part B reveals how the stereoscopic pair was constructed with a square region of dots that is the same in both squares but is shifted to the left in the square on the right.

Source: Sekuler & Blake, 1985, p. 227.

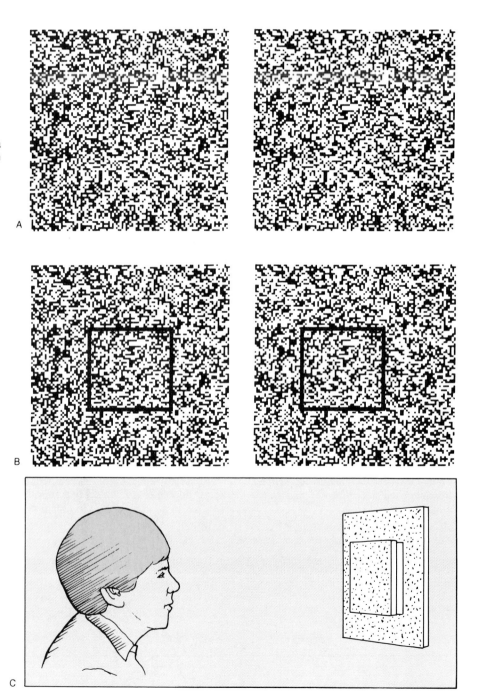

recorded with two microphones placed apart to simulate the separation between the ears.

The exact method the brain uses in fusing the images from the two eyes has been studied extensively by Bela Julesz (1971). One of Julesz's displays, called a random dot stereogram, is shown in Figure 4–15. The two texture patterns in part A are identical except for a small square area that has been shifted a bit to the left in the right-hand panel. (The two square areas in part B show this shift.) If the two images from part A are shown *separately* to the two eyes by a stereoscope—so that the left eye sees the left pattern and the right eye sees the right pattern—the observer with normal binocular vision actually sees the view depicted in part C, where the shifted square appears to float above the background. This result tells us that one way the visual system determines depth is by shifting the neural representation of images from each eye until they line up with each other. The closer the object is to the observer, the more shifting that is needed for alignment. To convince yourself of this point, blink your eyes one at a time while staring at a finger held only a few inches from your face and then as far as your arm can reach. Your finger will appear to jump around more when it is close to your eyes. Thus, to produce the single image in normal viewing, the brain must do more shifting for near than for far objects. It is not known exactly where in the brain this shifting and comparing takes place, but clearly it must be in the brain because information from the two eyes first comes together at the lateral geniculate nucleus (see Figure 3–12).

MONOCULAR DEPTH CUES. Even with one eye closed, people still see with reasonably good depth because of **monocular cues.** *Size* is one such cue, and its role in depth perception is illustrated in Figure 4–16. Which face does the ball appear closest to in depth? If the ball had been drawn to resemble clearly, say, a golf ball, the viewer would know its size and could use the information to decide which face the ball was closest to—probably the largest, leftmost face. If the ball were clearly a basketball, it would seem farther away from the viewer and therefore closer in depth to the second or third face because we know that a basketball is (very roughly) the same size as a

FIGURE 4–16
Monocular Depth Cues

Which face does the ball seem closest to in depth? It depends on what kind of ball you think it is. If you perceive it as small (a golf or ping-pong ball), it will seem nearer to you than if you see it as large (a basketball).

Source: Miller, 1962.

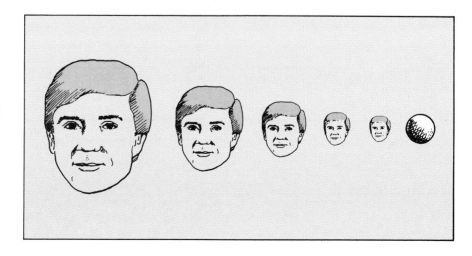

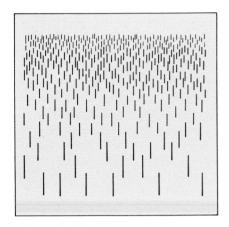

FIGURE 4–17
Texture Gradients

The texture gradients in this "landscape" are vertical lines that grow shorter and are more densely packed as they fade into the horizon, giving an impression of depth.

Source: Neisser, 1968.

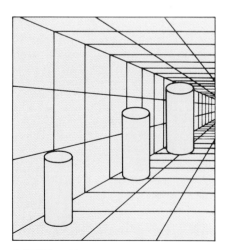

FIGURE 4–18
A Texture Gradient Size Illusion

Which of these cylinders is largest? All three are actually the same size, but the texture gradient makes them appear different.

Source: Gibson, 1950.

human head. Therefore, the ball should appear at the same distance as the face whose size it matches.

Another monocular cue involves *texture gradients*, or the density of the texture of the environment. Examples are shown in Figures 4–17 and 4–18. As the texture of the image becomes more finely grained, the observer sees the image receding. These figures include another cue to depth called **linear perspective.** Most people have been taught to draw scenes in depth by first laying down lines that approach a vanishing point on the horizon. Figure 4–18 shows an illusion of size that is based on changing the apparent distance of three cylinders through the use of texture gradients and linear perspective. The convergence of lines toward a vanishing point is evident in this figure.

Interposition, or overlap, provides another monocular depth cue, which is illustrated in Figure 4–19. When one object blocks out the view of another, the first one appears to be closer than the second.

One depth cue that operates only with moving stimuli is called **motion parallax.** When people move about, the images of nearby objects sweep across their field of vision faster than the images of faraway objects. This effect is easy to observe from an automobile. The pavement seems to fly by at great speed while trees on the horizon appear to move more slowly. Objects at still greater distance, such as the moon, appear not to move at all relative to the car.

Artists use various monocular cues to impart a sense of depth to their work. Can you identify the cues used by Georges Seurat in his masterpiece of Postimpressionist painting shown on page 81? Some artists have playfully combined various cues to create scenes such as the one shown in Figure 4–20. Can you determine how the artist created the impression that the water flows endlessly?

Size, Shape, and the Perceptual Constancies

The perception of size might appear to be simple, but it is not. In general, the larger an object, the larger will be the image it projects onto the retina (see Figures 3–8 and 3–13). If the brain could determine the size of the retinal image, it could use this information to determine the object's actual size. But the retinal size of an object depends on its distance from the viewer as well as its actual size: it is a simple fact of geometry that as an object moves away from a viewer, the size of its image on the retina shrinks.

A similar problem arises in the perception of shape. The shape of the retinal image of an object depends in part on the angle from which it is viewed. This is demonstrated in Figure 4–21, where the figure appears to be either an ellipse or a circle, depending on the viewing angle.

When we track a moving object, the size and shape of its retinal image change continuously; nevertheless, we normally see the object as remaining constant in both aspects. We do not believe cars shrink as they drive away from us. This phenomenon is known as **perceptual constancy.** *Size* and *shape constancy* are only two of a large number of constancies in perception. Another example is *lightness constancy.* Recall from Chapter 3 that a black road looks black whether it is viewed in broad daylight or in twilight, even though the amount of light it reflects differs. Such constancies are enormously valuable because they correct our perceptions and allow us to see

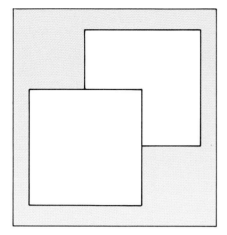

FIGURE 4–19 ▲
An Interposition Cue

This figure is seen as one square partly blocking the view of another. It is difficult to see this figure without perceiving this depth relationship.

FIGURE 4–20 ▲
Conflicting Perceptual Cues

In this 1961 lithograph, Waterfall, the Dutch artist M. C. Escher uses depth cues to make the water appear to flow up through channels that are level.

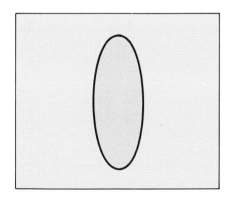

FIGURE 4–21 ▲
Shape Perception at a Slant

This shape is an ellipse as it is drawn on paper. But you can see it either as an ellipse or as a circle that is viewed from an angle.

the true shapes, sizes, and colors in the world rather than the momentary retinal images. Unfortunately, however, there are limits to the amount of correction the constancies can provide. When we look down from the top of a very tall building, the people below look ant-size, even though we know this is not true. This breakdown of the constancies occurs only in extreme situations such as this one, probably because our accuracy at perceiving depth dwindles at extremely great distances.

Psychologists have long puzzled over how the perceptual systems generally achieve constancy. Why don't people appear to shrink as they walk away? The constancies can be understood by first examining the distinction between proximal and distal stimuli. *Proximal* (nearby) *stimuli* are the physical energy patterns that strike the sensory receptors. The retinal image is a proximal stimulus, as is the sound pattern that strikes our eardrums. *Distal* (distant) *stimuli* are the objects at a distance that give rise to the proximal stimuli. The existence of the perceptual constancies demonstrates that perceptual experience is tied more closely to distal stimuli than to proximal stimuli. Thus, if you pick up this book and move it closer to you and then farther away, you will perceive the book's size and shape to remain the same; the distal stimulus, the book itself, does remain the same in size and shape, although the proximal stimulus, the retinal image of the book, fluctuates over a large range.

A powerful illusion based on shape constancy is illustrated in Figure 4–22. The two dark surfaces representing the tops of objects A and B appear to be quite different shapes. The top of A appears long and narrow, while

FIGURE 4–22
A Shape Constancy Illusion

The shaded parallelogram in part B is congruent with the one in A and with the dashed outline in C (that is, if you cut out the shaded area in A it would fit exactly on the shaded area in B). If you are skeptical, try tracing the outlines of these parallelograms on thin paper and placing them on top of one another.

Source: Shepard, 1981.

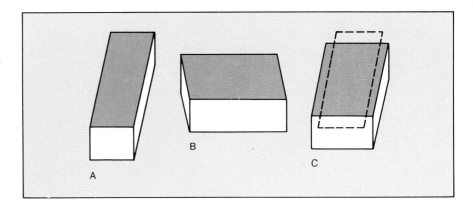

the top of B appears thicker and shorter. Yet the two darkened surfaces in A and B are actually congruent! That is, if you trace the outline of the top of A on a sheet of paper, it will fit exactly over the top of B when properly rotated. You will probably need to trace this to see for yourself; the illusion is so compelling that most people disbelieve that the two top surfaces can be congruent. (Most people falsely assume that the tops would actually fit as shown in C.)

This illusion demonstrates the essential idea of how constancies are achieved. The shapes in Figure 4–22 are viewed as three-dimensional despite the fact that they are shown on the page in only two dimensions. The visual system takes the available cues in the retinal image (the proximal stimulus) and uses these to construct the probable shape of the distal stimulus. In the case of A and B in Figure 4–22, you see the lines as rectangular blocks. Thus you tend to perceive all the surfaces as rectangular and as meeting at 90-degree angles. Yet if you look carefully, you will discover that the shaded surfaces are not rectangular because they contain no 90-degree angles. Thus the proximal stimuli are not rectangular either. Your perceptual system has constructed the most plausible scene from the proximal stimuli, thus creating the illusion. If you actually perceived proximal stimuli, the illusion would not occur because the proximal stimuli have the same shape. But since perception normally constructs a mental model of the distal stimuli, you perceive the two top surfaces as varying in shape. We consider *perceptual illusions* in more detail in the following section.

VISUAL ILLUSIONS

Visual illusions are fun to look at and experiment with, at least when they don't lead us into danger. Stage magicians often incorporate them into their acts to surprise and befuddle their audience. But to perceptual psychologists, illusions are more than mere amusements; they are potentially the key to understanding how normal perception operates (Coren & Girgus, 1978). As we noted earlier, our senses usually operate so fast and are so veridical that we sometimes take them for granted. When illusions occur, we become aware of the normally inconspicuous processes of sensation and perception. By examining them closely, we hope illusions will tell us how we perceive the world as accurately as we do.

Illusions That Originate in the Receptors

A number of visual illusions can be traced to processes occurring in the eye and retina long before neural signals reach the brain. One retinally based illusion is shown in Figure 4–23A. Called *Hering's grid,* the illusion created by the figure is due to lateral inhibition in the retina (which was also responsible for the simultaneous contrast effect shown in Figure 3–16). The faint gray spots you see at the intersections of the white bars, near the corners of the black squares, are purely illusory; if you stare at one of them, it disappears. The intersections are surrounded by more white space than surrounds the other white regions of the figure, as shown in Figure 4–23B. Because white regions inhibit neighboring neural cells from firing, the intersections are more inhibited than the other white regions and so appear darker. The spots disappear when you look at them because lateral inhibition is much weaker in the fovea than in the eye's periphery. Lateral inhibition normally serves the useful purposes of increasing the perception of contrast and sharpening fuzzy or blurred edges. Thus, the illusory spots actually result from a system that normally improves our vision.

Another illusion that originates within the eye involves pieces of tissue that become detached from the interior wall of the eye and float harmlessly

FIGURE 4–23
Hering's Grid

In A, illusory gray spots appear at each intersection except the one you are looking at. This illusion, unlike the ones shown in Figures 4–24 and 4–25, is caused by lateral inhibition, a form of interaction among neural cells in the retina. In B, lateral inhibition makes regions surrounded by lighter areas appear darker. Because the white regions at the intersections are surrounded by white on four sides, whereas the white regions away from the intersections are surrounded by white on only two sides, the regions in the intersections are more inhibited and appear darker.

Source: Sekuler & Blake, 1985, p. 75.

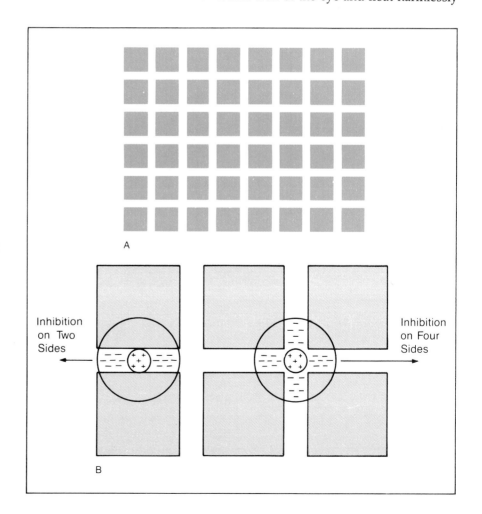

Inhibition on Two Sides

Inhibition on Four Sides

A

B

in the watery fluid of the vitreous humor, which fills the main chamber. Although these *floaters* (as they are called informally) are inside the eye, the shadows they cast on the retina look just like real objects. Floaters are common in people older than 30 and are most easily seen when examining a plain, blank surface such as a white wall or a clear blue sky.

Illusions That Originate in the Brain

Although some illusions originate in our sensory organs, an even greater number do not arise until sensory signals arrive in the brain for further processing. Because the organization of the brain is more complicated than that of the eye and ear, we do not know exactly *where* in the brain they originate, but this does not prevent us from learning *how* they operate.

McCOLLOUGH EFFECT. One striking example of such illusions is called the *McCollough effect,* named for the woman who discovered it in 1965 (McCollough, 1965). This effect is demonstrated in the three parts of Figure 4–24. First look at part C and confirm that it is entirely black and white and contains no colors. Now spend the next five minutes (it's worth the effort!) shifting your gaze back and forth between the colored parts A and B, spending about ten seconds on each before shifting to the other. Keep your gaze near the middle of each square, and don't alter your viewing distance or the tilt of your head during the five-minute period. When the time is up, look again at part C and you will now see colors, faint but unmistakable, where before you saw only black and white. Notice that in the sections of part C where the stripes are vertical, you see green, the color of the horizontal stripes during the five-minute adaptation; and where the stripes are horizontal in part C you perceive red, the color of the vertical stripes in part B. If you tilt your head (or the book) 45 degrees as you look at part C, these illusory colors will disappear; a 90-degree tilt will make the colors reverse!

What is the meaning of this dramatic illusion? On the surface, it resembles the conventional colored afterimages that we examined in Chapter 3. For example, adaptation to green produces an afterimage of red or pink, and vice versa. But the differences between colored afterimages and the McCollough effect are more important. First, the colors that are seen here depend completely on the orientation of the black and white stripes presented during the adaptation period. Second, this effect does not wear away in a matter of seconds like most colored afterimages. Look back at part C and verify that the illusory colors are still present. If you are like most people, this effect will last for hours or days if you completed the full five-minute adaptation.

What causes the McCollough effect? Recall that in Chapter 3, conventional colored aftereffects were explained in terms of separate components of the visual system that respond to red, green, yellow, blue, black, and white. The McCollough effect could be explained in a similar fashion except that the component affected would be cortical feature detectors that are sensitive not just to color (as cones are) but to combinations of color and orientation. In other words, the McCollough effect suggests the existence of "red-vertical edge detectors," "green-horizontal edge detectors," and so forth, a possibility that agrees well with recent findings of brain physiolo-

FIGURE 4–24
The McCollough Effect

Following the instructions explained in the text, stare alternately at A and B for about five minutes. Then look at part C and you will notice faint colors that change as you rotate the book clockwise and counterclockwise.

Source: Frisby, 1980, p. 70.

gists (Frisby, 1980). The lengthy persistence of the McCollough effect remains a puzzle. Conventional colored afterimages are explained by the fatiguing of cones during the adaptation period. These afterimages dissipate as quickly as the cones recover from fatigue. The fact that the McCollough effect lasts for days virtually eliminates fatigue as an explanation. But no good alternative explanation has yet been offered.

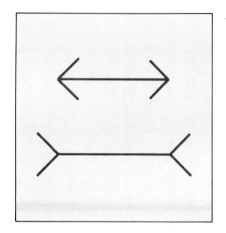

◀ **FIGURE 4–25**
The Müller-Lyer, or Arrow, Illusion

The line with the outgoing fins appears to be longer. See Figure 4–27.

SPATIAL ILLUSIONS. Other striking illusions that originate in the brain are *spatial illusions,* which involve distortion of geometric shapes, such as the length or straightness of line segments. In the *Müller-Lyer illusion,* shown in Figure 4–25, the two vertical lines appear to be unequal in length even though they are identical. (Measure them if you are doubtful.) Some other well-known spatial illusions are shown in Figure 4–26.

We know that the Müller-Lyer illusion does not arise in the retina from experiments in which relevant information is presented separately to the two eyes. The illusion persists, which must mean that it arises at some later point in the visual system where the signals from the two eyes are combined in the brain, probably in the visual cortex (Julesz, 1971).

Earlier in the chapter we presented two illusions that result from the operation of the perceptual constancies, which normally help keep perception stable (see Figures 4–18 and 4–22). What about spatial illusions such as the Müller-Lyer? Do they also result from a normally useful process gone awry? The British psychologist R. L. Gregory (1978) has answered yes: the illusion is due to the normal process of size constancy. He argues that the Müller-Lyer figure is seen in depth since its fins provide cues to linear perspective. In perspective, the fins represent right angles of a boxed shape. Figure 4–27 shows the component lines of the Müller-Lyer illusion in a 3-D scene. The line perceived as shorter corresponds to the vertical edge of the building that protrudes toward you and so is seen as nearer; the line that appears longer is the vertical edge of a room that recedes in depth behind the page and so appears farther away. If two lines have equally long retinal images, as do the two in this illusion, then the one that appears nearer must logically be shorter. If this confuses you, consider that you can block out the moon with a thumb held at arm's length. But you do not perceive your

FIGURE 4–26 ▼
Four Well-known Spatial Illusions

The illusions are named after their discoverers. A. In the Ponzo illusion, the upper horizontal line appears longer, but is not. B. In the Poggendorf illusion, the two lines do not look as though they would meet behind the figure, but in fact they are in line with each other. C. In the Hering illusion, the middle vertical lines appear to be bowed, but they are actually straight and parallel. D. In the Zöllner illusion, the vertical lines are also straight and parallel. Illusions show that human perceptions are fallible and are not just a copy of the images on the retinas. People construct perceptions from sensory information, and in the case of illusions they construct a scene that is not accurate.

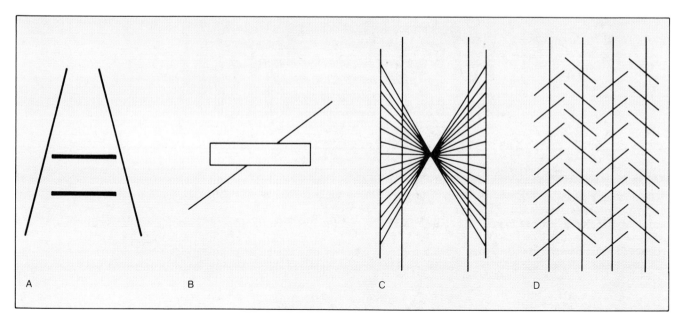

A   B   C   D

thumb as larger than the moon; rather, you see it as nearer than the moon and so as smaller. Gregory's account of the Müller-Lyer illusion, while not universally accepted, is representative of explanations offered for spatial illusions.

These explanations of spatial illusions are in accord with the idea that an observer determines the size of an object from inferences or intelligent guesses about how far away it is. But sometimes those guesses can be dead wrong. The young girl on the right in Figure 4–28 looks much larger than the man standing in the left corner. The illusion occurs because your visual system has made an intelligent, but false, guess that the room is rectangular. This would be reasonable because the angles in the room look like right angles and because most rooms are rectangular. But this room is trapezoidal, not rectangular; its geometry is shown in Figure 4–29. The man who appears smaller is actually much farther away than the girl who looks larger. By failing to notice this depth difference, the viewer sees an illusory size difference. This, of course, is a contrived demonstration. (If you were actually standing inside this room, would you still be fooled?) Nevertheless, it clearly shows how perception may be built on wrong guesses or assumptions.

FIGURE 4–27 ▲
R. L. Gregory's Explanation for the Müller-Lyer Illusion

The lines of the Müller-Lyer illusion are visible in these two scenes. The scene on the top seems to recede from the observer into the paper, so the center vertical line appears farther away than the corresponding line in the bottom figure, which seems to jut out from the page toward the observer. These differences in perceived distances lead to the variations in size "seen" by the observer.

Source: Gregory, 1978.

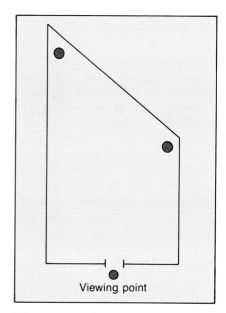

FIGURE 4–29 ▲
Actual Shape of the Room in Figure 4–28

The farther wall slopes away from the viewer to the left, but the walls and windows are arranged to provide the same retinal image as a normal rectangular room. Thus the viewer is misled into accepting the incorrect perceptual hypothesis that the room is rectangular and that the girl is larger than the man.

FIGURE 4–28 ▲
Illusory Size Differences

The girl on the right looks much larger than the man in the left corner. Impossible? No. We accept that the room is rectangular when actually it is not (see Figure 4–29). The man looks smaller because he is farther away from the viewing point.

APPLYING PSYCHOLOGY

Illusions in the Real World

Many of the illusions presented in this chapter appear only under laboratory conditions. But do people experience illusions outside the laboratory? Yes, although you may not have noticed them all or recognized them as illusions. To use an example from auditory perception, the pitch of the siren of an ambulance or fire engine appears to drop as the vehicle passes you and races off. This is known as the *Doppler effect.* The illusion is physical in origin and is not due to any error in your auditory system. When the vehicle was approaching you, the sound waves or air pressure differences created by the siren were affected by the vehicle's speed, so the frequency of the waves increased. As the vehicle moved away from you, the opposite situation prevailed: the frequency of the waves diminished, and the apparent pitch of the siren dropped.

A pencil appears to bend where it enters a glass of water, as shown in Figure 4–30. This illusion is also due to physical causes and not to an error in your visual system. Light rays bend when they pass from one medium to another. The water serves as a prism and shifts the optical image.

In contrast to the Doppler effect and the bent pencil in water, which are caused by physical phenomena, many illusions originate entirely within the perceiver. One of the most common of these is the *moon illusion.* You may have noticed that the moon looks much larger when it is near the horizon than when it is at its highest point

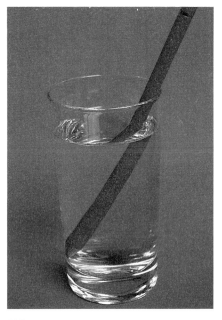

FIGURE 4–30
A Bent Pencil Illusion

The pencil appears to bend where it enters the water. The illusion arises from physical causes and not from errors in the perceptual system.

in the sky (its zenith). The effect is shown in Figure 4–31. The moon's projected image on the retina is the same size in both cases; if you photographed the moon at the horizon and at its zenith and measured its size on the developed pictures, it would be the same in the two.

The cause of the moon illusion has been hotly debated for centuries. In recent years, the most popular explanation has been that the moon appears to be farther away from the viewer when it is on the horizon. That is, the moon seems to appear to the eye as a disk attached to the dome-like surface of the sky. The sky's surface appears to be more distant at the horizon than it does overhead, as shown in Figure 4–32 (Kaufman &

Rock, 1962; Rock, 1984). Thus when the moon is on the horizon, it appears farther away. If the moon were always the same physical size, it should project a smaller image from the horizon than from the zenith because the horizon appears farther away. But the projected images of the moon are the same at the horizon and overhead. Our visual system thus interprets the moon as being *larger* at the horizon, in the same way as the cylinder in Figure 4–18 that appears most distant also appears largest.

Recently, however, C. F. Reed (1984) has offered a new explanation of the moon illusion. He points out that as objects traverse the sky from the horizon and cross over our heads, their size as projected on the retina usually grows steadily. For example, an approaching airplane may be only a speck on the horizon, but if it flies at a low altitude directly over us, its retinal size will become quite large. But the moon, being so far away from us (239,000 miles), does not produce an enlarged retinal image as it traverses the sky. Humans are accustomed to seeing such enlargement for moving objects, however, so we mistakenly interpret the moon as shrinking. We will have to await further experiments to see which of these two explanations is correct.

Another illusion involving the moon and motion perception is common. If we look at the moon through fast-moving clouds on a windy night, it may appear to be racing in the opposite direction from the clouds. This illusion, called *induced motion,* shows up in other everyday situations as well. If you are on a train and a train on the next track starts up, you may perceive your train to be moving. But if you look at the ground between the trains or at some other stationary frame of reference, you can tell immediately which one is moving. The illusion demonstrates that the visual system is much better at perceiving the motion of objects relative to one another than at perceiving the true motion of any one object.

At a waterfall, you may have experienced an effect called, not surprisingly, the **waterfall illusion.** If you stare directly for a minute or so at the plunging water and then shift your gaze to a rocky cliff nearby, the rocks will seem briefly to drift upward. A similar effect may occur if a car in which you are riding at high speed stops abruptly. You may feel for a moment as though the car were going backward. This effect seems to result from the fatiguing of feature detectors for motion in the visual system. The cause is similar to the effect of colored afterimages, explained in Chapter 3. The subject of motion perception surrounds another illusion: have you ever wondered why the red and white stripes on a barber pole seem to move upward when the pole is rotating horizontally? This illusion remains a puzzler, but it is due to the

FIGURE 4–31
The Moon Illusion

The moon appears larger when it is near the horizon than when it is high in the sky. This size difference has been simulated in this pair of pictures by enlarging the horizon photograph more than the zenith photograph. This alteration mimics the magnitude of the illusion when the real moon is viewed outdoors.

pole's shape: if the pole is made short and fat instead of tall and skinny, the stripes will seem to move sideways (Wallach, 1976). Stationary images may appear to move if they are flashed on and off at the proper rate. This effect, known as **apparent motion,** allows us to see movement in movie marquees and advertising signs. In fact, it is responsible for the illusion of motion we see in motion pictures and in television, which actually present to the screen only a rapid succession of still snapshots.

FIGURE 4–32
The "Flattened Dome" Explanation of the Moon Illusion

To an observer, the sky appears like a dome that has been flattened; it therefore looks farther away at the horizon than directly overhead. The moon looks to the eye like a bright disk attached to the surface of the sky. The horizon moon, while appearing farther away from the observer, projects exactly the same-size image to the eye as the zenith moon. Therefore, according to this explanation, the horizon moon looks larger.

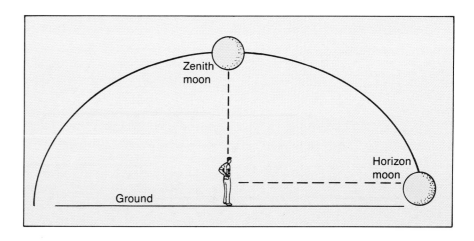

THE ROLE OF LEARNING IN PERCEPTION

We have seen that veridical perception is not achieved solely by passive, bottom-up processing of sensory data. In addition, we need help from top-down processes to take context into account and make educated hypotheses about what stimuli are present in the physical world beyond our senses. Does this need for intelligent guesswork mean that people need to *learn* to see?

This ancient question is at the root of a controversy over *nativism* and *empiricism.* The nativist argument is that some types of knowledge are innate: human beings are born with the ability to perceive stimuli, and learning plays only a small role in their development. The empiricist claim is that all knowledge comes from experience: without their senses, people would know nothing; their minds would be like blank slates.

In psychology, the argument is often referred to as the *nature versus nurture* debate. Is human behavior determined by inherited nature? Or is it nurtured and changed by experiences? It is not necessary that one position be completely correct and the other all wrong. Some types of perception, for example, may be greatly influenced by learning, while others may be built in from birth and not be affected much by experience. Current evidence favors this compromise position. One classical method of studying the role of learning in perception is to examine case studies of people who have regained their sight.

Restored Vision: Making the Blind See

The British philosopher John Locke (1632–1704) received a letter from his colleague William Molyneaux that posed this question:

> Suppose a man born blind, now adult, and taught by his touch to distinguish between a cube and a sphere of the same metal, nighly and of the same bigness, so as to tell, when he felt one and the other, which is the cube, which is the sphere. Suppose then the cube and the sphere placed on a table and the blind man made to see . . . could [he] by his sight, before he touched them . . . now distinguish and tell which is the globe, which the cube? (Locke, 1690/1950)

Molyneaux answered himself by saying "no." Locke, the good empiricist, agreed. Without the knowledge obtained through visual experience, Molyneaux's hypothetical person would be stumped.

The experiment that Molyneaux and Locke imagined has actually been performed many times. Many people born blind have acquired sight by surgery and have been examined by psychologists. A good number see little at first and fail to distinguish between even simple shapes (Von Senden, 1960). They are able to detect objects, fixate on them, and scan and follow them if they move, so perhaps these abilities are innate. But usually they cannot recognize objects by sight, even those that they could identify by touch, such as keys, fruit, and the faces of loved ones. They might identify a triangle, but only by counting its corners. Sometimes, after long training, they develop useful vision and become able to recognize objects on sight. But some of them, sad to say, give up and in effect revert to their earlier, sightless way of life, usually after a period of emotional disturbance.

The evidence from people with restored vision is probably not so important to the nativism/empiricism argument as it might seem. Although these cases appear to be critical experiments of nature's doing, several problems arise with their interpretation (Gregory, 1978, chap. 11). Until recently, many cases of restored vision have resulted from removing the lens of the eye. First, this surgery may not have been successful in removing all of the causes of the person's blindness. Second, it may take some time for a patient to recover fully from such an operation, and so some of these patients' immediate difficulties in perceiving may be due to a slow healing process. Finally, a few fortunate patients seem to see quite well very soon after the operation. Thus, the outcomes of cases of restored vision are so variable and can be due to so many factors other than lack of visual experience that it is probably best not to place too much weight on them. But several other lines of evidence are important in the debate about nature versus nurture in perception. We will examine three: the effects of visual deprivation, the effects of temporary sensory distortions, and the extent of perceptual capabilities in infants.

Visual Deprivation

Another way to find an answer to Molyneaux's question is to deprive young animals of perceptual experience and then to test their perceptual abilities after they have grown to adulthood. A typical experiment involves raising cats, monkeys, or chimpanzees with translucent goggles that allow light to pass through but destroy images. Such studies have shown that *visual deprivation* has little effect on simple perceptual tasks such as distinguishing differences in color, size, or brightness when animals are tested without the goggles. But after prolonged deprivation, more complex abilities requiring the recognition of patterns or the tracking of moving objects become seriously impaired (Riesen, 1960, 1965). This evidence supports the empiricist supposition that experience is essential in perceptual development, although experience must of course act on the inherited structure of the visual system.

This conclusion about the importance of experience is bolstered by neurophysiological recordings taken from animals kept in restricted environments. Kittens have been raised in pens that contain only horizontal and vertical stripes. Later they are tested to determine if they are sensitive to diagonal stripes, which they have never seen. In this circumstance, the kittens act as though they are blind to diagonal lines; it appears that they lack the neurons normally present in the visual cortex that are sensitive to diagonals (Mitchell, 1980). These feature-detecting cells atrophy, just as muscles do when they are not exercised.

Another type of visual deprivation that is a bit more subtle prevents an animal's active involvement with its environment. Held and Hein (1963) carried out research with pairs of kittens that were reared mostly in the dark and exposed to light only in a carefully controlled experimental situation.

FIGURE 4–33
Apparatus Used in Held and Hein's Deprivation Experiment

Both kittens were exposed to the same visual stimulation, but only one was actively moving about. The other kitten was carried passively. When visual stimulation was limited to this situation, only the active kitten was later able to perform visual tasks. The passive kitten seemed effectively blind.

Source: Held & Hein, 1963.

Two kittens were placed in baskets attached to opposite ends of a rod that could rotate around a central point, as shown in Figure 4–33. One basket contained holes for a kitten's legs so that the little creature could walk around the test chamber in a circle; the other basket had no leg holes. When the first kitten walked about, the second got a free ride. Both kittens were thus exposed to essentially identical visual stimulation.

When the pairs of kittens were tested later, only kittens that had been able to walk manifested normal perceptual capabilities; the others seemed functionally blind in many ways. The latter did not blink at objects thrust toward them, nor did they raise their paws defensively. Clearly, then, visual stimulation alone does not suffice for normal perceptual development. ***Proprioceptive feedback,*** the sensing of the limbs' positions from active movement, is also essential for development, and that is what the passive kittens lacked. That kind of feedback is also important for adaptation to visual distortions.

Effects of Visual Distortion on Perception

Another way to determine how experience shapes perception is to study how people adapt to lenses that produce visual distortion. The first experiment of this type was a heroic effort by George M. Stratton (1897). He blindfolded one eye and wore a lens system over the other that inverted the

Goggles can transform the visual world in systematic ways. These goggles are distorting prisms that move vision left or right, up or down. Research with such lenses helps psychologists understand how people adapt to severe distortion in sensory information.

visual image on the retina and reversed it from left to right. (Recall from Chapter 3 that the retinal image is normally inverted and reversed because of the lens of the eye; Stratton's lenses actually flipped the retinal image upright.) In one experiment Stratton wore the lenses continuously for eight days. At first he was totally disoriented and unable to walk without bumping into things. (Imagine having to look up to see the floor or to reach to the left to grasp an object that appears to be on your right.)

Over the eight days, Stratton learned to walk unimpeded and even to ride a bicycle and engage in sports. He concluded that if he were to wear the lenses indefinitely he would adapt completely, and his conclusion has been corroborated by more recent research (Welch, 1978). A subject who wore a similar lens system for 30 days was able to drive a car (Snyder & Pronko, 1952).

How does the world appear to these brave subjects? Is their visual system altered so that everything no longer appears topsy-turvy, or do they simply learn to reach up for objects that appear to be below them? Earlier in this century, the first view was widely accepted—that with prolonged experience the world would appear right-side-up again. However, recent research has refuted this belief (Harris, 1965). It is more correct to state that the proprioceptive sense is changed, as the second view claims; that is, the sense of touch is "educated" by experience with the distorted visual environment.

Perception in Infants

Another way to examine the role of learning in perception is to test the perceptual capabilities of human infants. If a newborn can perceive a stimulus in much the same way as an adult, we would have evidence that the perceptual ability involved is innate. If not, it would indicate either that the perceptual task has to be learned or simply that the infant's perceptual system has not matured physiologically to the level the task requires. Although experimentation to find the answers might seem simple, it takes considerable patience and ingenuity to determine what the world looks like to an infant. After all, infants can't tell researchers what they see, nor can researchers tell infants what to do. Even worse, infants often pay no attention to the stimuli poked at them; instead, they fall asleep or cry or look at their toes and fingers instead of the stimuli.

William James (1842–1910) asserted that to an infant, the world must be a "blooming, buzzing confusion" (James, 1890). James would probably be surprised if he could be told of the remarkable perceptual abilities that psy-

RESEARCH FRONTIER

Infant Recognition of the Mother's Voice

A traditional approach to the nature/nurture issue is the study of capabilities in newborn babies. The general assumption is that abilities that appear very early in life are likely to be determined by the baby's genetic endowment (nature) and that abilities that appear later in life are more likely due to learning or experience (nurture). This logic has been used in experiments with animals of many species in an attempt to unravel the aspects of behavior that are determined at birth and those that are shaped more by experience. Of course, for most behaviors, both nature and nurture play a role, but one can then ask about the relative contributions.

The research described here points up the difficulty in answering the nature/nurture issue conclusively through the logic outlined in the preceding paragraph. Recent work by Anthony DeCasper and his associates (DeCasper & Fifer, 1980; DeCasper & Prescott, 1984) has asked the interesting question of whether newborns can distinguish their mothers' voices from those of other women. Of course, as mentioned in the text, even

testing infants' perceptual capabilities requires ingenious and patient experimentation. How can we know what an infant perceives? How can the infant respond to indicate perception?

DeCasper and Fifer (1980) adapted a technique known as *high-amplitude sucking*, which has been found useful in much research with infants (Juscyzk, 1985). Whatever their other limitations, babies are great suckers, and psychologists have capitalized on this well-developed response to study perceptual abilities. The general idea is that if infants will modify their sucking patterns in response to external events, then they must be able to tell the events apart. DeCasper and Fifer tested infants that were only two to three days old by giving them an artificial nipple on which they could suck to hear sounds. One pattern of sucking let each baby hear its own mother's voice, while a different pattern of sucking produced another woman's voice. The critical question was whether or not a newborn could learn to suck to produce its own mother's voice. The exciting answer is yes, a finding that has been confirmed in later studies.

chologists now know infants possess. To be sure, they do not see the world as clearly as adults do, but this is largely due to physiological immaturity rather than lack of experience. For example, infants' eyes do not focus well on objects more than about a foot away, so they are quite nearsighted (Maurer, 1975). It probably takes about six months for infants' vision to approach adult levels (Marg et al., 1976), and recent evidence shows that eye movements of four-to-five-year-old children differ systematically from those of adults (Kowler & Martins, 1982). Nonetheless, young infants have greater perceptual abilities than researchers had expected prior to the experiments of the past 20 years. We will have much more to say about perceptual development in Chapter 9. Here we describe one exciting line of work in "Research Frontier: Infant Recognition of the Mother's Voice."

Babies prefer their mothers' voices to those of other women even when tested a few days after birth.

How are we to explain the fact that a newborn can already recognize its mother's voice? One possibility is that infants come into the world biologically prepared to distinguish their own parents from other people. That is, something in their genetic endowment permits their remarkable ability to distinguish their mothers' voices from those of other women only two to three days after birth. The logic outlined above for separating nature from nurture supports this interpretation because abilities that are shown soon after birth are assumed to have a genetically determined component. However, DeCasper rejects the notion that the baby's ability is inherited in favor of the idea that it arises from prenatal experience, or learning in the womb.

Several facts support the conclusion that the infants' ability is due to such prenatal nurturing (Gottlieb, 1985). First, sounds of low frequency, such as those of human speech, have been shown to penetrate the uterus and amniotic sac, where the infant cozily resides for nine months prior to birth. Second, the fetus has been shown to respond differentially to sounds in the external environment (Read and Miller, 1977). Thus, in all likelihood, the newborn's preference for its mother's voice is caused by the continuous presence of that voice throughout prenatal development. Interestingly, although newborns can distinguish among male voices, they will not suck differentially to hear their fathers' voices as they will their mothers' (DeCasper and Prescott, 1984).

The ability of an infant to distinguish and prefer its mother's voice illustrates the complexity of distinguishing contributions of genetics from those of experience on behavior. The usual assumption that abilities occurring very early in life are genetically determined seems unlikely in this case. However, the discovery of prenatal learning is fascinating in its own right. The exciting question—to which there is no firm answer yet—is whether the fetus is capable of learning more than simply to discriminate among sounds. If a mother repeatedly read aloud one story before the baby was born, would the baby later prefer that story to a different one read by the mother? Preliminary evidence indicates the answer may be yes, but further research is needed to establish this finding.

SUMMARY

1. Perception is the process of interpreting sensory information from the receptor organs to produce an organized image of the environment.

2. Veridical perception is accurate perception. Occasionally our perceptual system deceives us with illusions, but a major challenge to psychologists lies in explaining how perception works as veridically as it does.

3. The Gestalt psychologists argued that the perception of a stimulus is more than the sum of the sensations it produces. They developed principles of grouping and of figure-ground segregation to describe perceptual organization. Grouping links stimulus elements into units by the principles of proximity, similarity, and good continuation, among others. Figure-ground segregation shows that any region of a stimulus is perceived either as figure or ground, but not both.

4. Pattern recognition refers to the ability to classify the stimuli people perceive into familiar categories, such as dogs or grandmothers. Robots have not yet been developed to the point where they rival humans at performing this task. Bottom-up models of pattern recognition work passively to categorize a stimulus from the features it possesses. Top-down models include an active component that guides recognition through the use of context and expectations. Today's theorists prefer models that combine the top-down and bottom-up processes.

5. Depth perception is possible through the use of a large variety of depth cues, some of which depend on using both eyes. Depth, size, and shape perception all show the operation of the perceptual constancies, which tie perceptions closer to distal than to proximal stimuli.

6. Some illusions occur in the brain and may be due to inappropriate operation of the constancies. Other illusions occur in the receptor organs. Still other illusions are caused by physical effects in the environment and do not reflect any error in the sensory or perceptual systems. Although certain illusions are apparent only under laboratory conditions, many occur in everyday situations outside the lab. Most illusions provide useful clues about how normal perception operates, and many illusions are caused by processes that ordinarily improve perception.

7. Learning plays a definite role in perception, supplementing innate abilities. People who acquire vision after a lifetime of blindness often encounter difficulty perceiving for some time. Animals deprived of perceptual experience have similar problems.

8. People can adjust to drastic distortions in their sensory input, such as those created by goggles that invert or shift the retinal image. This adjustment takes time, however, and appears to involve more change in the proprioceptive system than in the visual system.

9. It is too simplistic to consider the nature versus nurture argument as an either/or matter. For most types of perception, both nature and nurture account for human abilities. For depth and color perception, innate factors appear to play a role, but for many other perceptual tasks, learning plays an important role. This is true for recognition of objects, adaptation to distorted vision, and various other complex forms of perception. Even though infants can recognize their mothers' voices, the ability probably arises through prenatal learning rather than through innate ability.

SUGGESTED READINGS

Coren, S., & Girgus, J. S. (1978). *Seeing is deceiving: The psychology of visual illusions.* Hillsdale, N.J.: Erlbaum.
   This interesting book surveys and discusses visual illusions and the principles of perception that underlie them.

Goldstein, E. B. (1984). *Sensation and perception* (2nd ed.). Belmont, Calif.: Wadsworth.
   An enjoyable and thorough treatment of all the human senses, including chapters on perceptual development, touch and pain perception, and visual disorders.

Gregory, R. L. (1978). *Eye and brain: The psychology of seeing* (3rd ed.). New York: McGraw-Hill.
   This popular introduction to the psychology of visual perception is a good starting point for supplementary information.

Kanizsa, G. (1979). *Organization in vision.* New York: Praeger.
   An intriguing and beautifully illustrated work by the Italian artist/psychologist who has created many noteworthy demonstrations of subjective contours.

Rock, I. (1984). *Perception.* New York: Scientific American Books.

A well-written, profusely illustrated introduction to perception by a major figure in the field.

Sekuler, R., & Blake, R. (1985). *Perception.* New York: Knopf.

An up-to-date and concisely written textbook on perception with an emphasis on vision.

5

Consciousness and Attention

Our brain is a democracy of ten thousand million nerve cells, yet it provides us with a unified experience.

Sir John Eccles

Is IT POSSIBLE TO KNOW SOMETHING WITHOUT BEING CONSCIOUSLY aware that you know it? Consider the plight of two women, both of whom live in Iowa, who have developed a disorder called *prosopagnosia*. In this condition people are unable to recognize faces, even of well-known people, because of damage in the occipital lobe of the brain (see Figure 2–14 on page 56). The women suffering from this malady cannot recognize the faces of close friends, relatives, or (for one of them) her own face in a mirror! Yet many of their other cognitive functions, such as language ability and perception of objects other than faces, are generally normal. The usual way of testing for prosopagnosia is simply to show patients a series of photographs and ask them to name the person in each. The faces include those of friends, relatives, celebrities, and strangers, too. Patients with prosopagnosia perform dismally on such tests, being unable to name people they have known for years. The difficulty is not in having forgotten the person, for hearing a familiar person's voice brings forth immediate identification. The deficit is specific to identifying faces.

The two women were tested by Daniel Tranel and Antonio Damasio (1985) for their ability to name faces from pictures. At the same time the researchers also recorded changes in the electrical conductivity of the skin, a procedure similar to that used in lie detector tests. They discovered that although the patients were unable to name close friends and relatives from their pictures, the electrodermal skin response showed a characteristic change when these pictures were shown. (The skin response did not change in response to photos of strangers.) Thus the physiological processes that signal recognition seemed to be intact, but the results of this physiological process could not be translated into conscious experience. Put another way, the women knew the faces subconsciously, but not consciously. This capability is quite similar to blindsight, discussed in Chapter 3.

The dual aspects of knowledge—knowing something at one level but not another—will be a recurring theme in this chapter. First we consider normal, waking consciousness and examine factors that control what people attend to in their environments and how "unconscious" factors sometimes influence attention. We then return to a topic from Chapter 2—hemispheric specialization—to explore the implications for two types of conscious experience. Later we consider altered states of consciousness: sleep and dreams, hypnosis, hallucinations, and drugs. Before we launch into our coverage of these fascinating topics, we should pause to get a better grip on a concept that has already been mentioned repeatedly: consciousness.

WHAT IS CONSCIOUSNESS?

An accurate definition of consciousness has eluded philosophers for centuries and stumped psychologists for the past hundred years, yet no generally agreed-upon answer is in sight (Natsoulas, 1983; Ornstein, 1977). The term is used in many different senses and, as the eminent psychologist George Miller (1962) has put it, "Consciousness is a word worn smooth by a million tongues." The behaviorists even tried to ban consciousness from the language of psychology, in part because of its slipperiness. However, the term will not go away because it refers to something immediately real for anyone reading this book. Here is a definition that will serve for our purposes: *Consciousness* is the current awareness of external or internal stimuli, that is, of objects in the environment and of bodily sensations, memories, daydreams, and thoughts. Now that we have defined consciousness, how do we describe it?

In Western civilization, a spatial metaphor, or image, has typically been used to characterize the conscious mind (Jaynes, 1976, pp. 54–56). People speak of or consider their minds as *containers* or *spaces* in which ideas and memories are stored (Lakoff and Johnson, 1980; Roediger, 1980b). They *hold* ideas in mind, or they have ideas in the *front* or *back* or at the *top* of their minds. Ideas may also lie in the mind's *dark corners* or *dim recesses.* Some people are said to have *broad* or *deep* or *open* minds, while others' minds are described as *narrow, shallow,* or *closed.* Consciousness, accordingly, can be thought of as the processes that occur in this mental arena—the spotlight of the mental space—and events of which people are currently aware stand in the spotlight of consciousness.

William James, using a rather different metaphor, described consciousness as a "stream" of awareness. He wrote, "Our normal waking consciousness, rational consciousness as we call it, is but one special type of consciousness, whilst all about it, parted from it by the filmiest of screens, there lie potential forms of consciousness entirely different" (1902).

Psychologists have found it useful to distinguish four mental states: conscious, preconscious, unconscious, and nonconscious. External and internal events on which the mental spotlight is focused are said to be *in* consciousness. Not many memories and thoughts are in consciousness at any one time, and they may be in either preconscious or unconscious states.

If memories can be called into consciousness fairly easily, they are described as being in a *preconscious* state. For example, as you read this you may not be thinking of the name of your psychology professor or the names of your best friends or of your brothers and sisters. Yet if you are asked for them, they are available in memory and immediately accessible to conscious experience (Tulving & Pearlstone, 1966).

Unconscious ideas and memories are those that cannot be brought to mind easily. Sigmund Freud popularized the idea that many important memories and thoughts reside in an unconscious state. Through his study of neurotic patients, Freud came to believe that the major factor in emotional problems was childhood trauma (see Chapter 14). Memories of painful experiences were *repressed,* or converted into an unconscious mental state, from which they could not easily be made conscious.

The concept of the unconscious remains controversial in modern psychology. Psychologists often try to study phenomena of the unobservable inner world of the mind indirectly by observing overt behavior, just as astrophysicists strive to demystify black holes in space by noting their effects on light and neighboring bodies. Since unconscious mental processes, like black holes, cannot be observed directly, how can psychologists measure repressed memories? If repression simply embodies any memories that are not easily called into consciousness, then repression undoubtedly occurs (Erdelyi & Goldberg, 1979). But if repression is taken to mean the unconscious suppression of a painful past, it becomes harder to study.

It is important to distinguish unconscious from *nonconscious* mental processes. We categorize a process as nonconscious when it cannot be hauled into consciousness and as unconscious if it *can* be brought into consciousness, but only with great difficulty. Many processes go on in our bodies of which we are not aware. For example, we are not directly conscious of the workings of the rods and cones of our eyes described in Chapter 3 or of the chemicals in the blood coursing through our arteries and veins or of the functioning of the kidneys, lungs, and heart, which the autonomic nervous system controls. We can become conscious of the effects of nonconscious processes—heavy breathing, a pounding heart—but we cannot normally become conscious of the processes themselves.

Now that we have briefly summarized the terms used to describe states of consciousness, we will look at the various ways psychologists investigate this slippery topic.

ATTENTION AND CONSCIOUSNESS

Normal consciousness is limited in its ability to keep things "in mind." People can focus on only so many things—sensations, memories, thoughts—at one time. When information overloads this capacity, when voices, sights, and thoughts overwhelm us, we need to concentrate on one source of information to the exclusion of others.

Attention can be defined as a focusing of perception that leads to a greater awareness of a limited number of stimuli. In terms of our earlier metaphor, stimuli to which people pay attention are in the spotlight of consciousness. How do people decide where to direct the spotlight of consciousness? As you stare at this page you could be paying attention to the voice of a radio disc jockey or to other noise in the background, to a tingling in your feet, or to the rumbling of a hungry stomach. You could be daydreaming, having sexual fantasies, remembering what happened to you last night, or planning what you will do tomorrow. As you well know, paying attention to what you are reading is often difficult. Competition among many stimuli impedes concentration on one type of information to the exclusion of others.

Selective Attention

How does someone select one message from the environment and ignore others? Psychologists became interested in the question of *selective attention* in the 1950s when they were asked to solve a problem involving the information overload with which air traffic controllers were burdened. To coordinate departures and arrivals and prevent midair collisions, the controllers had to receive reports from a number of pilots and tell each what to do, without help from today's electronic wizardry. Pilots' voices and messages often sounded alike, so controllers erred on occasion, with regrettable results. The psychologists' assignment was to determine how a controller could attend to one important message amid competition from other messages.

To study the problem, the psychologists devised a test called *speech shadowing* (Cherry, 1953). The subject wore headphones through which two different messages entered, one sent to each ear. The listener was instructed to repeat back as well as possible all the words that reached one ear and to try to ignore the words that entered the other ear. Imagine that the message to the right ear was about astronomy and the one to the left ear about baseball. You can get some idea of what this experiment was like by placing yourself between two radios (or a radio and a television set) tuned to different stations on which there is continuous chatter. Try to repeat back everything you hear from one source and to ignore the other. (See Figure 5–1.)

The result of your experiment should confirm what psychologists found in the 1950s. Even when the *accepted* message—the one on which the listener was to focus—was delivered at 150 words per minute, much faster than normal speech, its recipient could repeat it back with few errors and remembered it fairly effectively. The *rejected,* or ignored, message was remembered poorly. One experimenter reported that people he tested could not recognize the rejected message above a chance level even when it was repeated 35 times (Moray, 1959). In another study, information about a single sound was retained for a second or two, but then it was lost (Glucksberg & Cowan, 1970). Since the two messages usually are equally loud and otherwise physically similar, poor memory for the rejected message is purely psychological, reflecting lack of attention to the material. The psychologists working on the air controllers' problem helped solve it by discovering the characteristics that make messages easily distinguishable. Almost any physical differences be-

FIGURE 5–1
Speech Shadowing

In this experiment a person is presented with two messages simultaneously, one to each ear. The task is to repeat back one message and ignore the other one. This task is frequently used to study selective attention.

tween messages, such as those of loudness or pitch, aid selective attention (Cherry, 1953).

A considerably less crucial but much more common example of information overload shows up at noisy parties. You may be listening to someone speaking softly while loud conversations go on about you, and music adds to the din. You follow one voice and ignore the others by selective attention, an experience sometimes called the *cocktail party phenomenon.* Both auditory cues and visual ones—since you look at the face of your partner in the conversation—are employed. But what really happens in a scientific sense?

Models of Attention

Since the mid-1950s, psychologists have developed several different models to explain selective attention. We consider the most prominent examples here.

FILTER THEORY. The first important theory of how attention works was developed by Donald Broadbent (1957, 1958); it is called *filter theory.* Broadbent proposed that just as engineers can map the flow of electricity through a wiring system, psychologists can chart the passage of information through the mind. He postulated the existence of two general systems, the sensory and the perceptual, with different properties. The sensory system retains information only briefly after it reaches the sense organs. It can hold more than one sort of information at the same time, so it is said to have *parallel transmission.* The perceptual system is roughly equivalent to conscious attention. It selects one of the signals in the sensory system and decides what to pay attention to, according to the individual's current needs. Broadbent (1958) held that processing in the perceptual system was *serial*, with a person paying attention first to one thing and then another. He also assumed that if the perceptual system did not process information soon after it reached the sensory system, the information would be lost. Thus, he assumed that there was a *filter* between the sensory and perceptual systems that screened out data that were not selected by the perceptual system (see Figure 5–2). Hence, the theory was named after its crucial active component.

The basic problem of selective attention is to discover how it is possible to attend to one message in the face of other, competing messages that may be equally prominent perceptually. Broadbent's filter theory proposed that the competing messages are filtered out at the level of the senses, *before* the information is processed. Since the attended signal is selected early in processing for further attention, filter theory can be called an *early selection theory* of attention.

Filter theory has been used to help explain many everyday experiences. For instance, if you are listening intently to one conversation at a cocktail party, you are barely aware of the others, which seem to be "filtered out" before their meaning is processed. But if your name is mentioned nearby, you often hear it and switch your attention. If you are filtering out the other conversations at a sensory level, before you have determined the meaning of the signal, how can you catch your name in a competing conversation?

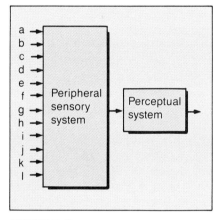

FIGURE 5–2
Broadbent's Filter Theory of Attention

All signals from the outside world are briefly held in a peripheral sensory system. Signals can be held in parallel in the sensory system; in other words, many signals can be registered simultaneously. One signal is selected for further processing by the perceptual system. Signals can be fully perceived only one at a time, or serially. How do people select one signal and ignore others? According to filter theory, ignored signals are "filtered out" at the level of the senses so that they do not interfere with selected signals. Since the selection occurs early in the sensory-perceptual process, filter theory is called an early selection theory of attention.

Source: Broadbent, 1958.

Broadbent suggested that people do so by occasionally switching the setting of the filter to other perceptual channels to sample the information there, as a shortwave radio fan might twist the dials to hear what Radio Moscow or Radio Beijing was proclaiming. On the other hand, contrary to Broadbent's filter theory, the words from another conversation might not be filtered out at a sensory level but might be unconsciously perceived. Important signals, such as your name, would break through into consciousness after their unconscious registration. If signals from the environment are registered without benefit of conscious attention, then it may be that the effect of attention does not occur at a sensory level (as Broadbent theorized), but later in the sequence of perceptual processes. This possibility is realized in late selection theories of attention.

LATE SELECTION MODELS. Broadbent's filter theory was important because it was the first model of attention. Also important was the theory's demonstration that mental processes could be conceived of as a flow of information. However, the validity of the idea is contradicted by evidence that not all information in ignored messages is screened out at the level of the senses.

The mind seems to process some signals automatically without conscious awareness. In one experiment Neville Moray (1959) delivered different messages to the subjects' two ears and required the subjects to repeat one of the messages; however, he occasionally instructed his subjects, through the headphones, to switch their attention from one message to the other. If the subjects were repeating the baseball message entering the right ear, they might be told to attend to the message about astronomy in the left ear. When Moray embedded the instruction in the accepted message, the subjects usually switched without trouble, but when the instruction was put in the rejected message, they missed it every time.

This part of the experiment supports filter theory. If the rejected message were filtered out before it had been processed beyond the sensory level, the listener would not perceive the instruction and so could not act on it. However, when the instruction to switch ears was placed in the rejected message and was preceded by the subject's name ("Mary, switch ears"), Moray found that it was followed 30 percent of the time. Thus it must be concluded that ignored information is not shut out at the level of the senses; some of it apparently seeps through, to be processed for meaning. A person's name is a particularly sensitive cue that seems to be perceived almost automatically.

Evidence thus mounts that ignored information is *not* filtered out at a sensory level. Instead, as with the example above, automatic processing occurs for some information of which people are unaware. This indicates the existence of unconscious perceptual processes, a topic discussed in the next section.

Most current theories of attention assume a *late selection,* that is, choosing information after a sensory level (e.g., Norman, 1968; Schneider & Shiffrin, 1977). These theories maintain that although people are still not conscious of the different signals at that point, some kind of decision making opens the door to consciousness for the most important or an expected signal. (See Figure 5–3 for a schematic outline of a late selection model of attention, contrasted with filter theory.) The basic difference between early

FIGURE 5–3
Two Models of Selective Attention

A. According to filter theory, a person selectively attends to information by filtering at a sensory level. The signal that receives perceptual analysis guides a person's response. B. According to late selection theories, all stimuli receive some perceptual processing, but only one is attended to and is used to make responses.

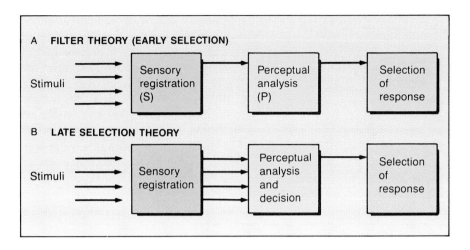

selection theories of attention (like filter theory) and the newer, late selection theories is the level at which attention is believed to have its effects. According to early selection theories, unattended information is screened out at the level of the senses, or early in the perceptual process. According to late selection theories, all information is processed through the early stages of perception, and attention to one source occurs much later, just before conscious awareness. If late selection theories are true, the exciting possibility exists that signals from the environment, of which we never become consciously aware, can register in our minds and affect our behavior.

Subliminal Perception

Can we be influenced by stimuli of which we are unaware? If so, can people attempt to use such unconscious influences to control our behavior? Consider a study conducted by James Vicary, who flashed messages very quickly during the showing of a movie (Naylor and Lawshe, 1958). One message, "Eat popcorn," was displayed at such rapid rates that the viewers were not aware of seeing it. The authors of the study reported that popcorn sales increased 58 percent during intermission when the message had been flashed during the movie. This study seemed to show that stimuli presented too fast to be consciously perceived could have an impact on behavior. Although the stimuli were not strong enough to be registered in the conscious parts of mind, they nonetheless were thought to register in the unconscious, which also controls behavior.

The popcorn study received wide publicity and generated concern (if not hysteria) among many people, who felt threatened by possible bombardment with subliminal messages from advertisers and others. However, the threat is overrated. Psychologists have studied the problem of *subliminal perception* for years, with mixed results (Dixon, 1981). (*Subliminal* means below the level of awareness, so subliminal perception refers to registration of information of which a person is never consciously aware, as in the popcorn study.) The case for subliminal perception depends on rather subtle effects in laboratory experiments conducted under carefully controlled conditions. Even so, demonstrating subconscious perception is extremely difficult. For one thing, if a stimulus such as a word is presented to the eyes or ears, it can be consciously identified very rapidly, probably in 200–300 milliseconds (or two-to-three-tenths of a second). Given that conscious perception is so quick, if a researcher shows some effect of a rapidly presented stimulus, how can a skeptic be convinced that the perceiver was unaware of its occurrence? Even assuming that the perceiver's ignorance of the stimulus could be assured, how can one measure the effects of a subliminal stimulus? Obviously, a researcher cannot ask a person to report it directly, because by definition—if it is truly subliminal—the person cannot do so. The effects of the subliminal stimulus must be measured on the processing of some other stimulus or on some other behavior. This is discussed further in "Research Frontier: Subliminal Perception."

Automatic and Controlled Processing

Many tasks that you do every day become easy and effortless. Consider reading, for example. In the first grade, reading each word took appreciable

---

RESEARCH FRONTIER

Subliminal Perception

An experiment reported by Anthony Marcel (1983) is one of the best attempts to overcome the difficulties inherent in studying subliminal perception. Marcel capitalized on a phenomenon known as **semantic priming** (to which we will return in Chapter 7) in one of his experiments. Briefly, semantic priming refers to the fact that if someone has just read a word such as *doctor*, identifying a related word such as *nurse* will be speeded up. The relation in meaning between *doctor* and *nurse* speeds (primes) the cognitive response to the second word. In Marcel's version of the task, people looked at a screen and received two items back to back. The person's task was to decide if the second item was a word or not. Thus they would have said yes to *nurse* and no to *narse*, or some other nonword. The interesting case is when both items were words that could be

either related in terms of meaning *(doctor-nurse)* or unrelated *(lawyer-nurse)*. As already mentioned, when the two are related, people can decide that the second is a word faster than when the two are unrelated.

Marcel wondered whether he could produce semantic priming when the first word in the related pair was presented so quickly that the viewer could not see it. That is, if *doctor* were presented in such a way that the subject would not detect it, would it still speed the processing of *nurse?* Four conditions of Marcel's experiment are relevant to this issue: either the two words were related or not related, and the first word was either visible or invisible to the viewers. When the first word was invisible, it was presented so quickly that the viewers could not even detect that a word had been shown, much less name it.

The results of Marcel's experiment showed evidence of subliminal perception because response to the second word *(nurse)* was speeded even when the related first word *(doctor)* was invisible. The findings are repre-

sented in Figure 5–4, where it can be seen that the semantic priming effect was almost as large when the first word was invisible as when it was visible. Even though people could not detect that the word had been presented, the information from it must have been unconsciously registered in the cognitive system because they processed the second word faster.

The implications of subliminal perception are profound. Our conscious perceptions may be determined by events outside of awareness. Marcel (1983) reported four other experiments that led him to similar conclusions. Other people have extended and replicated this work, too (e.g., Balota, 1983). Although not everyone is convinced by it (Holender, 1986; Merikle, 1982), evidence mounts that subliminal perception can be demonstrated, at least under controlled laboratory conditions (Dixon, 1981).

Assuming that subliminal perception occurs, does it pose a threat to the public, as some have assumed (Key, 1973)? Can advertisers and others use it to control our thoughts and be-time and effort, and you could be easily distracted and lose your place. But if you now picked up the book that seemed so hard when you were in the first grade, your reading would be quick and effortless. The thousands of hours you have practiced reading since the first grade have changed the nature of the task (Kolers, 1985).

Cognitive psychologists make a distinction between *controlled* and *automatic* mental processes (Posner and Synder, 1975; Schneider and Shiffrin, 1977). The basic idea is that some mental processes are under a person's conscious control, while others occur automatically—without one's awareness or attention. Controlled processing is that which (a) takes mental effort, (b) can be easily interrupted, and (c) is relatively slow. The perplexed state of the beginning reader reveals controlled processing. Automatic mental processes, on the other hand, are those that occur (a) effortlessly, or without conscious attention, (b) rapidly, and (c) in a way that makes them hard to interrupt. If the words *the boy* were flashed on a screen in front of you, your processing would likely be automatic (at least relative to a first grader) be-

FIGURE 5–4
Marcel's Results Showing Subliminal Perception

The graph shows the time taken by subjects to report whether or not letters flashed before them formed a word, after first being exposed to a "priming" word. The priming word was presented either so that it could be easily reported (visible condition) or so that it could not be seen (invisible condition). Subjects identified words faster when the words had been preceded by related words. For example, they responded faster that *nurse* was a word when it was preceded by the prime word *doctor* than when it was preceded by *lawyer.* This semantic priming effect was almost as great when the priming stimulus was invisible as when it was visible. Apparently, information about the first stimulus was registered in the invisible condition, even though people could not report the prime.

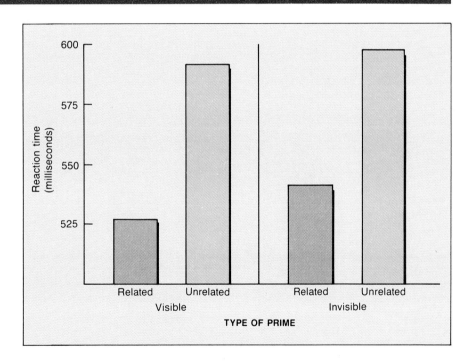

havior? The answer to both questions is almost certainly no. Subliminal priming effects are difficult to obtain and require sensitive measures to reveal their existence. For example, the effect that Marcel took as evidence for subliminal priming had to be measured in tens of milliseconds. Other research shows that the effects are short-lived (Balota, 1983). In all likelihood, if even a few seconds elapse between the subliminal stimulus and the measure of its effect, its impact will have vanished. In other words, even if advertisers did try to influence people with subliminal messages, the effects would probably be too small to notice.

cause your comprehension of the words would occur quickly, effortlessly, and probably unavoidably. (Try looking at a familiar word without thinking of its meaning.) As the example of reading makes clear, we can represent automatic and controlled processing as endpoints on a continuum, for a mental process that is under conscious control at first will probably become automatic when it has been practiced thousands of times (Logan, 1985).

An experimental situation that has been used for years to study mental processing is the Stroop color-naming task (Stroop, 1935). In this experimental situation people identify (name) colors as fast as they can. In one control condition they name patches of color, and in a second control condition words are written in different colors and people name the ink colors (not the words) as fast as possible. In a third condition, the one of greatest interest, people again name the ink colors of words, but this time the words are the names of other colors. So, for example, a person may see the word *red* written in blue ink and the task is to say "Blue." An example of the Stroop color-naming task is presented in Figure 5–5. Before reading any further, time yourself as you name the ink colors in each of the three columns there.

As you probably just discovered, people are much slower to name the colors in the third condition, in which the words represent the names of other colors. People are somewhat slower at naming the ink colors when they form unrelated words (the middle column) than at naming color patches (the first column), but this difference is quite small when compared to the case in which the words are other color names. Most people find naming colors in the third condition, requiring competing responses, a difficult and frustrating task.

The difficulty in performing the Stroop task is usually taken to indicate that people read words automatically. When a person sees the word *blue* and is supposed to respond with the name of the color of the ink—black in

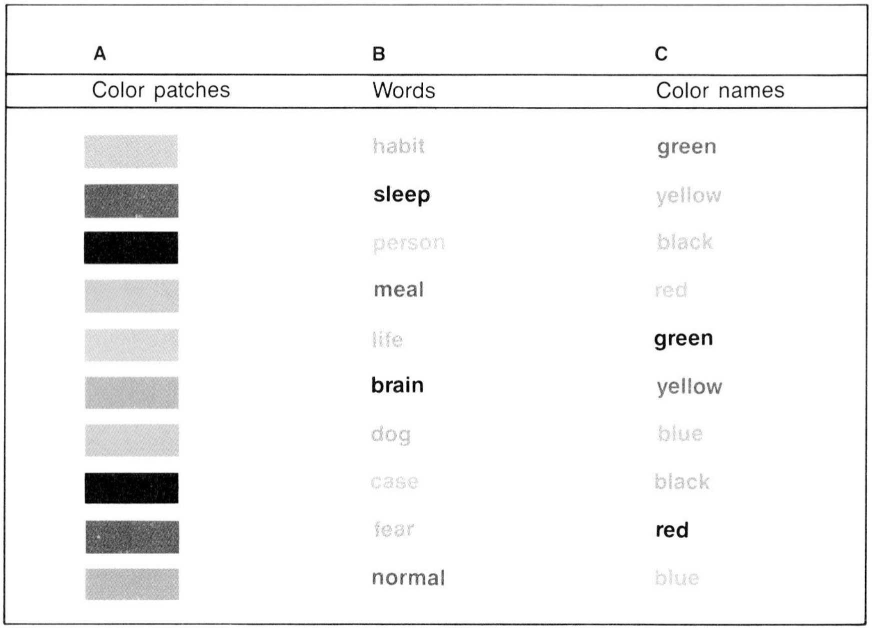

FIGURE 5–5
The Stroop Task

Time yourself as you name the ink colors for the items in each of the three columns. Column A is color patches, B is words, and C is words that name colors. People take much longer to name the colors when the words spell conflicting color names, as in C.

A	B	C
Color patches	Words	Color names
	habit	green
	sleep	yellow
	person	black
	meal	red
	life	green
	brain	yellow
	dog	blue
	case	black
	fear	red
	normal	blue

this case—the name of the word is automatically activated nonetheless. Even people who have been given extended practice at the Stroop task and have been told to try to suppress or ignore the printed word are still slower to name the colors in the third condition (Dyer, 1973). One theory explaining the Stroop effect is that there is a mental "horse race" between processes involved in naming the color and those in reading the word. Since people have much more practice in reading words than in naming colors, the reading response wins the race and slows color naming. The difficulty in performing the Stroop task is then attributed to automatic processes, which occur without a person's volition (or even contrary to it) and cannot be brought under conscious control. However, even when people's ability to name the words is greatly slowed down (say by printing the words upside down), the Stroop effect persists (Dunbar and MacLeod, 1984). That is, people are equally slow in calling the ink color of the following words "black": *red* and *pɒɹ*. Yet the word should be read much faster in the first case, and so according to the race theory the interference should be greater there. The fact that the Stroop effect is just as strong with both types of words seems to signal that the standard horse race theory may not be accurate.

Many tasks in life begin under slow, effortful, controlled processing but then become relatively automatic later. Consider walking, driving a car, or most athletic skills. The hallmark of a skilled athlete is that he or she can hit a baseball or dribble a basketball quickly, effortlessly, and without distraction—in a word, automatically. Of course, such performances usually take thousands of hours of practice. The same experience occurs for most of us in learning to drive. At first it is a challenging task, consuming our total attention as we gingerly motor about. However, after years of practice even driving becomes fairly automatic and we can listen to the radio or carry on a conversation without distraction. In fact, people driving on interstate highways often report that they will suddenly snap alert from some daydream or reverie to realize that they have not been paying conscious attention to the road for some time. They seem to have been driving on "automatic pilot."

Recently psychologists have become interested in studying *action slips*, the dumb things most of us do every day (misplace objects, forget why we went somewhere, and the like). One preliminary way to study such absent-mindedness is to ask people to fill out questionnaires and keep diaries on the circumstances in which they occur. Action slips occur more frequently when people are preoccupied with thoughts while their behavior seems to be automatic. Reason (1984) has summarized the evidence about action slips, which seems consistent with this view. One woman reported, "I went into my bedroom intending to fetch a book. Instead, I took off my rings, looked into the mirror, and came out again without my book." Many action slips are the result of the intrusion of habits appropriate in one circumstance into a similar, but inappropriate situation. For example, you might go to a friend's house and, upon arriving on the front porch, take out your key to open the door rather than ringing the bell or knocking. It seems especially hard to change some well-established routine that has been practiced thousands of times. As one of Reason's subjects reported, "I had decided to cut down my sugar consumption and wanted to have my cornflakes without it. But I sprinkled sugar on my cereal just as I had always done." The autopilot of everyday life had taken over.

Roger Sperry pioneered research on split-brain patients.

HEMISPHERIC SPECIALIZATION AND CONSCIOUSNESS

In Chapter 2 we discussed the different functions of the two hemispheres of the brain. In most people the left hemisphere is primarily responsible for comprehending and producing speech, and the right hemisphere controls many nonverbal abilities such as drawing, listening to music, and finding one's way with a map. Roger Sperry, who pioneered research on hemispheric specialization with special split-brain patients (see page 64), maintains that different types of consciousness are also associated with the two hemispheres. He writes, "Each hemisphere . . . has its own . . . private sensations, perceptions, thought, and ideas, all of which are cut off from the corresponding experiences in the opposite hemisphere. Each left and right hemisphere has its own private chain of memories and learning experiences that are inaccessible to recall by the other hemisphere. In many respects each disconnected hemisphere appears to have a 'mind of its own'" (1974). Here we consider some of the research that leads to these startling claims.

The Split-Brain Patient

In Chapter 2 we reviewed evidence about the cognitive functions of patients who had their corpus callosum—the bundle of fibers connecting the two hemispheres of the brain—severed surgically to help control epilepsy. The operation separates the two halves of the brain, which become functionally independent. The main evidence for different forms of consciousness comes from research on these patients. The split-brain subject is tested in a situation as portrayed in Figure 5–6, where information can be flashed either to the right or left of a fixation point, which is straight ahead. Information off to the right (that is, in the right visual field) goes to the left hemisphere, and that shown to the left visual field is transmitted to the right hemisphere (refer back to Figure 2–20 on page 65). For normal people with intact corpus

FIGURE 5–6
Testing a Split-Brain Patient

The patient fixates on a point straight ahead and words are flashed either to the left or to the right. A word flashed to the right is interpreted by the left hemisphere and can easily be named. (The left hemisphere has the capacity to produce speech.) A word flashed to the left, as in the picture, cannot be named by the right hemisphere, which cannot produce speech. However, in this case the person can pick out the object with the left hand (controlled by the right hemisphere), thus showing that the right hemisphere has some capacity to comprehend words.

Source: Gazzaniga, 1967, p. 27.

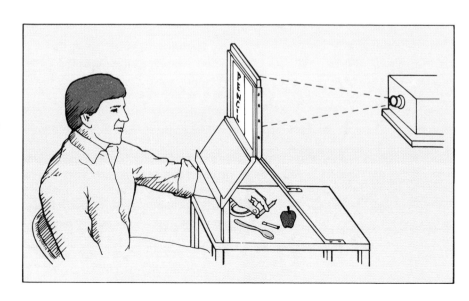

callosums, the information passes quickly to the other hemisphere as well; however, for split-brain patients the information is "trapped" in either the left or right hemisphere, thus permitting scientists to discover how it is processed. Michael Gazzaniga, a pioneer in this field, performed an experiment in which words were directed to one or the other hemisphere (Gazzaniga, 1970). If the word *pencil* was shown off to the right (transmitted to the left hemisphere), it could be named easily. But if it was shown off to the left, it could not be named, because the right hemisphere cannot produce speech. However, when the word was shown at the left and the patient was asked to pick out the object with the left hand from behind a screen, the patient could do so accurately since the right hemisphere controls the left hand. Apparently, then, the right hemisphere has some capacity for comprehending language, but it cannot produce it or translate it into conscious verbal experience.

In a similar experiment by Gazzaniga, a woman was shown a picture of a nude to the right hemisphere. She giggled with embarrassment, but when questioned did not know why. She remarked, "I don't know . . . nothing. . . . Oh—that funny machine." This is another case in which behavior is produced by a stimulus of which the verbal left hemisphere is unaware. Other studies have shown that when bodily reactions are provoked from split-brain patients by flashing pictures or commands to their right hemispheres, they will make up a story to explain their reaction. Depending on the reaction produced, their guess as to the true stimulus may be accurate or completely off target.

In other studies Gazzaniga (1970) observed split-brain patients who were given spatial tasks to perform, such as putting together simple jigsaw puzzles. If allowed to put the puzzles together with the left hand (controlled by the right hemisphere), the subjects had no trouble. The right hemisphere is specialized for such visual and spatial tasks. But when the patients were asked to solve the puzzles with their right hands and to keep their left hands under the table, their performance on the puzzles was dismal. The left hemisphere, which controls the right hand, is poor at such tasks. The patients often appeared frustrated, trying to bring their left hands out from under the table to solve the puzzle, as though the two halves of the brain were struggling to control behavior. The right brain observed the pathetic attempts of the right hand (and left hemisphere) to solve the puzzle. The right brain knew the solution and tried to order the left hand up from under the table to solve it.

The metaphorical war between two halves of the brain can be observed only in split-brain subjects. In normal people there is a smooth exchange between control of the two hemispheres because they communicate via the corpus callosum. But Sperry (1968) has shown that when the pathway is cut, the dual nature of consciousness is revealed. As with other topics in this chapter, we see evidence of an unconscious cognitive system processing information that is inaccessible to verbal report (which is usually equated with conscious awareness). Gazzaniga (1983) argues for a modular mind; that is, he claims that cognitive systems within the brain may operate as relatively independent modules controlling different aspects of behavior. He writes:

> The emerging picture is that our cognitive system is not a unified
> network with a single purpose and train of thought. A more accurate

metaphor is that our sense of subjective awareness arises out of our dominant left hemisphere's unrelenting need to explain the actions taken by any one of a multitude of mental systems that dwell within us. . . . These systems, which coexist with the language system, are not necessarily in touch with the language processor prior to a behavior. (p. 536)

Implications of the Two Types of Consciousness

The discovery that the two halves of the brain function differently and may be responsible for different forms of consciousness has been one of psychology's most exciting discoveries in the past 30 years. Some have argued that the implications are profound. Robert Ornstein (1977) believes that the different types of consciousness in the two halves of the brain may underlie some fundamental distinctions in human experience, such as individual differences among people and even global differences among cultures. People often differ markedly in their verbal and spatial skills. You probably have friends who write beautifully but cannot solve a simple puzzle, whereas others may be brilliant engineers or artists but poor writers and spellers. Although scant research has been conducted on the possible neurological underpinnings of differing cognitive abilities, it is possible that dominance of one hemisphere plays a role in such individual differences (Springer & Deutsch, 1985).

Even more speculatively, Ornstein (1977) proposes that the capabilities of the two hemispheres are differentially emphasized in Eastern and Western cultures. Western civilization has traditionally emphasized verbal, rational, analytic, scientific thought. Reading, writing, and mathematics are highly valued and are primary subjects in school. Thus our culture glories what may loosely be thought of as left hemisphere functions. Eastern cultures encourage a different form of consciousness based on the primacy of intuition, insight, music, and meditation. These may be considered right hemisphere functions, ones that do not depend heavily on language and verbalization.

Ornstein further argues that Westerners should try to educate the intuitive right hemisphere capacities to complement their predominantly verbal, rational ways of thought. The general argument is that both the analytic, rational consciousness of the left hemisphere and the intuitive, spatial capacities of the right hemisphere should be developed to the fullest. He believes that "Split- and whole-brain studies have led to a new conception of human knowledge, consciousness, and intelligence. All knowledge cannot be expressed in words, yet our education is based almost exclusively on its written or spoken forms" (1978).

Ornstein's speculations are provocative, but they have been criticized as being far removed from the research evidence on hemispheric specialization. Nevertheless, many books and devices have appeared on the market promising to teach the unwary (Western) purchaser methods of developing his or her right hemisphere capacities. Much more research is needed before such promises can be trusted.

SLEEP AND DREAMS

Thus far in this chapter we have been concerned with normal, everyday consciousness. In the remaining sections we will consider states in which consciousness is "lost" or altered. Every night you lose consciousness when you fall asleep, and later you enter an altered state when you dream. Sleeping and dreaming have been studied scientifically only for the last 40 or 50 years, which seems surprising since most of us spend almost a third of our lives sleeping. If you live to be 72, you will have slept for about 24 years.

Most adults average seven or eight hours of sleep nightly, but the need for sleep changes greatly in a lifetime. Newborn babies may snooze 20 hours a day, but after their first four weeks they stay awake for longer and longer periods. The time people sleep generally remains stable during adulthood, but it may decrease slightly in old age. The amount of sleep the elderly need, or can get, varies. Some people sleep more, but many sleep less.

Sleep is one of many bodily functions that occur in a regular pattern every 24 hours or so. Such patterns are called *circadian rhythms.* (*Circadian* is derived from the Latin, meaning "about a day.") Almost every physiological response exhibits circadian rhythms, as the body's internal clock regulates its functioning by complex sets of stimuli, some internal and some external. Even when animals or people are placed in controlled environments in which all cues about light and darkness in the outside world are removed, the body will continue to show circadian rhythms, although they may gradually drift away from actual day and night cycles. Most humans

A night of sleep involves continual change, both in physical movement, as seen here, and in the electrical activity of the brain (see Figure 5–9).

show a pattern that occurs every 25 hours rather than 24 in such controlled situations. The circadian rhythms seem to have evolved to maximize effectiveness of our biological systems, with natural lulls and peaks in performance occurring at various points in the day. Sleep is certainly the most drastic change in our daily pattern, leading to intense interest in its nature and purpose.

The Study of Sleep

The scientific study of sleep was given a dramatic boost by the development of electroencephalography, a procedure in which electrodes are attached to a person's scalp to permit measurement of changes in the electrical potentials of the brain (see Figure 5–7).

Before the use of the electroencephalogram (EEG), sleep had been regarded as a single state. EEG recordings first revealed distinct stages of sleep. Four of these have been labeled stages 1 through 4 (Dement & Kleitman, 1957a), and the brain waves that characterize them are pictured in Figure 5–8. At the top of the figure are brain waves obtained when a person is awake but resting (stage 0). The brain waves are of high frequency, low amplitude—that is, they are fast and short—and quite irregular. Drowsiness is marked by alpha waves, and when such waves are present, people usually report a pleasant feeling.

As a person drifts into stage 1, the brain waves remain fast, but they become more irregular. Theta waves appear. A person awakened in stage 1 will likely deny having been asleep. The brain waves in stage 2 are larger and slower, marked by occasional *spindles*, or short runs of rhythmic, low-frequency waves. It is more difficult to awaken a person from stage 2 sleep

FIGURE 5–7
An Electroencephalogram (EEG) Being Recorded

Electrodes are attached to certain points on the skull, and the combined electrical potentials are plotted against time to produce the EEG, or brain wave patterns such as those seen in Figure 5–8. The EEG has proved to be a useful measure, but it is still a crude one since electrical potentials from all over the brain are averaged together.

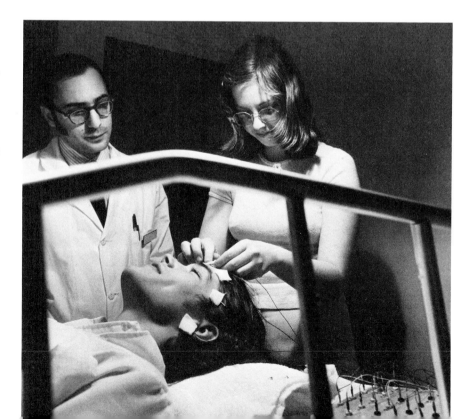

FIGURE 5–8
Brain Waves During Sleep

The figure shows how brain waves change systematically from when a person is awake (top) through drowsiness and the stages of sleep (stage 3 is not shown). Brain waves are measured in cycles per second (cps), which generally decrease with deeper sleep. However, notice that the brain waves of REM (dreaming) sleep at the bottom resemble those of the waking state at the top.

Source: Hauri, 1977.

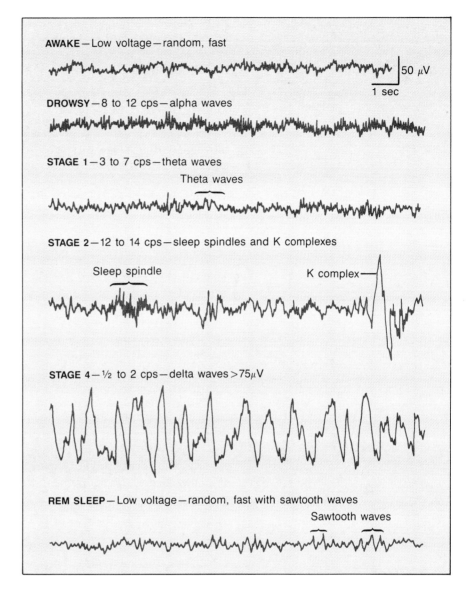

than from stage 1 sleep. Stage 3 is a deeper sleep. The brain waves are still irregular and have spindles, but the waves' amplitude is greater and occasionally large, slow waves, called delta waves, are interspersed. In the deepest stage of sleep, stage 4, the delta waves predominate.

A fifth stage of sleep, not numbered, is in some ways the most interesting. Researchers noticed that several times a night, while sleepers were cycling through other stages of sleep, their brain waves accelerated almost to the rate of the waking state. The sleepers seemed to enter stage 1, but their eyes moved rapidly underneath the eyelids, and other curious changes occurred. In this stage, males almost always have erections, and for both sexes, breathing and heartbeat become irregular. People awakened from this stage usually report they have been dreaming (Dement & Kleitman, 1957b), so the stage has been called dream sleep, or *REM* (for **R**apid **E**ye **M**ovement) *sleep* (stage REM). In this stage, sleepers seem, paradoxically, in some ways to be close to waking and in others to be in the depths of slumber. It is usually more difficult to awaken a person from REM sleep than from other stages, perhaps because of attention to the dream of the moment rather than to external stimuli.

A Night of Sleep

Sleep is not a simple "losing" of consciousness but a complicated pattern of movement from stage to stage. The sleep stages of one person on three successive nights are shown in Figure 5–9. The stages are on the vertical axis of each graph and the time spent in each stage is on the horizontal axis. The time spent in REM sleep is shown by dark bars. This person shows the normal pattern of cycling through the various sleep stages many times.

Although individual sleep patterns differ widely, a typical night of sleep can be constructed from averages. Usually sleepers progress quickly through stage 1 to stages 2 and 3 and often reach stage 4 within 30 minutes of having fallen asleep (Webb, 1975). In stage 4, sleepers are very relaxed and breathe slowly and evenly. Brain waves during stage 4 show a large response to external stimuli, even though the stimuli do not awaken the sleepers. The stimuli are making their way to central parts of the brain, but they are not being translated into conscious experience, which argues indirectly for a late selection process of attention, discussed on page 164. In one study experimenters spoke to sleeping subjects and recorded their EEG responses to each word. Among the words was the name of the person being tested; this evoked greater cortical arousal, as shown in the brain waves, than did other words, even though the subjects did not awaken (Oswald, Taylor, & Treisman, 1960). Apparently, people process information automatically while in the unconsciousness of deep sleep.

After sleepers have experienced stage 4 for a while, they start cycling to the other stages. Their first period of REM sleep begins after about an hour

FIGURE 5–9
Three Nights of Sleep

This diagram shows the amount of time one person spent in each stage of sleep over three successive nights. The sleep stage is shown on the vertical axis; the amount of time in each stage is on the horizontal axis. Notice how the person cycled among the different sleep stages and how periods of REM sleep (indicated by the dark bars) generally lasted longer toward morning.

Source: Webb & Agnew, 1968.

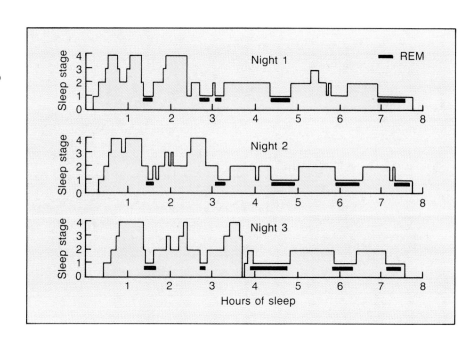

FIGURE 5–10
Typical Sleep Habits

The graph shows the average amount of time a group of young males spent in the different stages of sleep as well as individual variability in time spent in each stage. They spent most of the night in stage 2.

Source: Webb & Agnew, 1973.

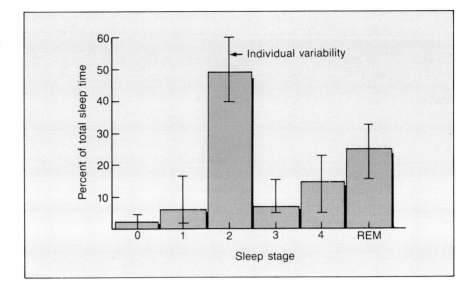

FIGURE 5–11
Stage 4 and REM Sleep Changes

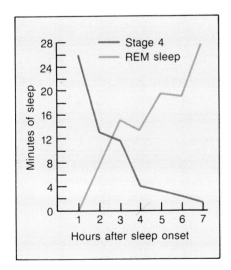

The graph depicts the changes in the amount of stage 4 and REM sleep during the course of a night. At first people spend much more time in stage 4 sleep than in REM sleep, but early in the morning REM sleep predominates.

Source: Webb & Agnew, 1973.

and a half of sleep, when they reenter stage 1. This is believed to coincide with the first dream; it is often marked by bodily movement, such as turning over. The first REM period is the shortest of the night, with a return to other stages in a matter of minutes. The sleeper continues to pass between stages through the night.

People average five distinct periods of REM sleep nightly, each usually longer than its predecessor and the time between them shorter. If it is assumed that REM sleep is associated with dreams, as it seems to be, then everyone dreams about five times a night with each dream period becoming increasingly longer. However, not all people react in exactly this way every night, as can be seen in Figure 5–10. During the long REM periods in the early morning, the temperature of the body reaches its lowest point. The autonomic nervous system produces the greatest changes in breathing and heart rate. Sleepers usually awaken after a dream period, and they remember only the last dream.

Just as REM periods grow longer during the night, the time spent in stage 4 becomes shorter (see Figure 5–11). However, together the two stages account for less than half the time spent sleeping. As Figure 5–10 shows, a great deal of the night is passed in stage 2.

Why Do We Sleep?

Most people assume that sleep has a restorative effect. It may be that when awake, people use up chemicals essential to the functioning of the brain, and sleep replenishes their supply. But no one really knows whether or not that is so. There are no firm answers to the questions of why people sleep, or how much sleep they require, or whether or not they even need sleep. Richard Thompson (1985) writes, "There is no obvious reason why humans should have to sleep. Sleep certainly does not provide the body with rest; as far as metabolism goes, sleep is little better than quietly reading a book. Nor does the brain rest during sleep. In [REM] sleep it is more active than when a person is awake but sitting quietly" (p. 279). Wilse Webb (1975) has proposed the novel theory that sleep evolved simply to keep us quiet at night. He suggests that night was a dangerous time for our ancestors because predators abounded; creatures that stayed home at night and slept had a better chance of surviving than nonsleeping wanderers.

Although the reason or reasons that people sleep remain to be determined, researchers have tried to discover the importance of sleep by studying what happens to people when they are deprived of it. We will consider two celebrated cases of sleep deprivation. The first is that of Peter Tripp, a 32-year-old New York disc jockey, who in January 1959 undertook to stay awake for 200 hours, or about eight days, in a glass booth in Times Square. The stunt was undertaken for the benefit of the March of Dimes and was supervised by doctors and scientists. The following fascinating description of Tripp's experience comes from a government report concerned with sleep:

> Almost from the first, the desire to sleep was so strong that Tripp was fighting to keep himself awake. After little more than 2 days and 2 nights he began to have visual illusions; for example, he reported finding cobwebs in his shoes. By about 100 hours the simple daily tests that required only minimal mental agility and attention were a torture for him. He was having trouble remembering things, and his visual illusions were perturbing: he saw the tweed suit of one of the scientists as a suit of fuzzy worms. . . . The daily tests were almost unendurable for Tripp and those who were studying him. "He looked like a blind animal trying to feel his way through a maze." A simple algebraic formula that he had earlier solved with ease now required such superhuman effort that Tripp broke down, frightened at his inability to solve the problem, fighting to perform. Scientists saw the spectacle of a suave New York radio entertainer trying vainly to find his way through the alphabet.
>
> By 170 hours the agony had become almost unbearable to watch. At times Tripp was no longer sure he was himself, and frequently tried to gain proof of his identity. Although he behaved as if he were awake, his brain wave patterns resembled those of sleep. In his psychotic delusions he was convinced that the doctors were in a conspiracy against him to send him to jail. . . . At the end of the 200 sleepless hours, nightmare hallucination and reality had merged, and he felt he was the victim of a sadistic conspiracy among the doctors. (Luce, 1966, pp. 19–20)

Some researchers have inferred from Tripp's and similar cases that sleep is critical to mental functioning and that if people are deprived of it for long periods they tend to exhibit symptoms associated with mental illness. But other cases have shown much less strain. In 1965 Randy Gardner, a San Diego high school student, decided to stay awake for 264 hours, or 11 days, as part of a high school science project. He also wanted to break the world record for sleeplessness. Gardner was watched at home by his parents, a doctor, and two sleep researchers. He whiled away the time talking to friends and family and playing pinball, among other activities. He became very tired, sometimes seemed a bit confused, and occasionally experienced the hatband illusion (a feeling of pressure around the head). But at the end of 11 days he appeared before TV cameras and comported himself perfectly naturally, manifesting none of the symptoms that had plagued Peter Tripp. The conclusion here would seem to be that sleep loss has little effect.

Why the discrepancy between the Tripp and Gardner cases? There is no certain answer, but one reason may have to do with their environments. Tripp was in a highly charged, emotional atmosphere, and he was tested and checked regularly with many people watching. Gardner was at home with family and friends and insulated from hoopla. Another possible reason is that Gardner was younger than Tripp and probably in better physical condition. Tripp also took drugs during his sleepless episode.

One noted researcher, William Dement (1976), has suggested that anyone who is young, highly motivated, and in good physical condition may be able to go without sleep more or less indefinitely. However, this conclusion is complicated a bit by the discovery that marathons of sleeplessness may be flawed by catnaps that have gone undetected because the napper's eyes remained open. Researchers call these periods *microsleeps*.

Participants in sleeplessness marathons seem to bounce back rapidly. After Randy Gardner had stayed awake for 264 hours and 12 minutes, he fell asleep and woke up a little under 15 hours later. The second night he slept 8 hours and his sleep cycle was pretty much back to normal. Peter Tripp also recovered quickly, after some 13 hours of sleep, although he complained of mild depression for about three months. Recent, well-controlled studies also lead to the conclusion that people can recover relatively rapidly from sleep deprivation (Rosa, Bonnet, & Warm, 1983).

How does lack of just some sleep affect normal people? The most common effects are extreme weariness, lapses in attention, hand tremors, irritability, and the hatband illusion. People also report being more depressed, less energetic, and less friendly. Very rarely will a person report hallucinations and disordered thought, as Peter Tripp did. Sleep loss sometimes has surprisingly little impact on task performance, especially if the task is brief, relatively easy and well practiced, and can be performed at a person's own pace. However, when a task is very challenging or very boring and must be done quickly and is paced by some external demand, then performance is likely to suffer.

How much sleep do we need? As mentioned at the outset, the average amount of daily sleep varies over people's life span from twenty or so hours for newborns to five to six hours for people in old age. Most college students sleep seven to eight hours, but many find themselves subjected to conditions in which sleep is restricted below those levels. Many studies have been conducted on the effects of sleep restriction. If people are permitted to sleep only two to five hours nightly and not at all during the day, their performance deteriorates over time on many tasks (Webb, 1975). Because REM sleep occurs in the latter part of the sleep cycle, such subjects at first lost a good deal of their REM sleep. However, later in the experiment they experienced more REM sleep than normal in the first hours of sleep, but this compensation took a week to develop in some cases.

Most people, even college students, probably average more than the two to five hours of sleep permitted in the experiment just described. In another study, researchers restricted young adults who normally slept eight hours to six hours of sleep a night for six weeks. (Control subjects were permitted to sleep the normal eight hours.) The subjects who experienced reduced sleep were deprived mostly of REM and stage 2 sleep. Surprisingly, their performance and feelings of fatigue did not differ much from those of the control subjects. The sleep-deprived subjects reported feeling worse than the control subjects in the morning and around lunchtime, but at other times the two groups did not differ. The only other important difference was that subjects who were deprived of sleep fell to sleep more quickly at night than did the control subjects (Horne and Wilkinson, 1985). In another study, in which subjects were permitted only five hours of sleep, the effects of sleep deprivation were much more pronounced (Carskadon and Dement, 1981).

There is no evidence about the effects of long-term partial sleep deprivation (such as during four years of college). However, if some nights are used for catching up on sleep, it seems likely that the impact is negligible. In fact, even during prolonged sleep deprivation an occasional nap will greatly benefit performance (Mullaney et al., 1983).

The amount of sleep people need varies greatly, despite the average of seven to eight hours. Benjamin Franklin apparently slept only three to four hours a night. More recently, sleep researchers have documented several cases in which people required as little as three hours of sleep to maintain normal functioning. The reasons for these large differences in need for sleep are not known.

Why Do We Dream?

Of the roughly 20 years that the average person will have slept by age 72, 5 years will have been devoted to dreaming. Dreams have fascinated humans since the dawn of recorded history, and probably long before. They have been used to foretell the future, to help make decisions, and, more recently in Freudian psychoanalysis, to chart the hidden workings of the unconscious mind. Dreams may even have led to belief in life after death. Primitive people, dreaming of their dead relatives and friends, could have believed that their loved ones still existed in this strange netherworld.

FREUD'S INTERPRETATION OF DREAMS. Modern dream analysis dates from publication of Sigmund Freud's monumental work *The Interpretation of Dreams* (1900/1938). For most of us, dreams seem bizarre, nonsensical, and meaningless. But Freud believed that "the interpretation of dreams is the royal road to a knowledge of the unconscious activities of the mind" (p. 540). By this view, dreams are an expression of repressed wishes of the individual, symbolizing ideas that provoke too much anxiety in conscious thought. Even in dreams these ideas must be disguised. When someone reports a dream, its true meaning is not immediately apparent but requires interpretation. Freud called a person's report of a dream its *manifest content.* This is what the person consciously remembers from the dream and may be subject to distortion as it is reported.

The true meaning of the dream is expressed in its *latent content*, which can be determined only by careful analysis. The latent content includes the individual's repressed wishes, which the dream both expresses and disguises. These repressed ideas are expressed symbolically in the dream.

Freud's interpretation of the latent content of dreams almost always revolved around two topics: sex and aggression. He believed that certain symbols were regularly used in dreams to stand for threatening thoughts and

Dreams have always puzzled people and have been a common theme in art and literature.

that the appropriate interpretation of dreams depends on the recognition of these symbols and their meaning. Freud was quite creative in his interpretation of symbols. Less charitably, some of his interpretations might be called farfetched. Here are a few excerpts from a section on symbols in dreams:

> The number of things which are represented symbolically in dreams is not great. . . . Parents appear in dreams as *emperor* and *empress, king* and *queen,* or other exalted personages. . . . Children and brothers and sisters are less tenderly treated, being symbolized as *little animals* or *vermin.* Birth is almost invariably represented by some reference to *water.* . . . An overwhelming majority of symbols in dreams are sexual symbols. . . . The male genital organ is symbolically represented in dreams in many different ways, with most of which the common idea underlying the comparison is easily apparent. In the first place, the sacred number *three* is symbolic of the whole male genitalia. Its more conspicuous and, to both sexes, more interesting part, the penis, is symbolized primarily by objects that resemble it in form, being long and upstanding, such as *sticks, umbrellas, poles, trees* and the like; also by objects which, like the thing symbolized, have the property of penetrating, and consequently of injuring the body,—that is to say, pointed weapons of all sorts: *knives, daggers, lances, sabres.* . . .

The peculiar property of this member of being able to raise itself upright in defiance of the law of gravity, part of the phenomenon of erection, leads to symbolic representation by means of *balloons* and *aeroplanes*. But dreams have another, much more impressive, way of symbolizing erection; they make the organ of sex into the essential part of the whole person, so that the dreamer himself flies. . . .

The female genitalia are symbolically represented by all such objects as share with them the property of enclosing a space or are capable of acting as receptacles: such as *pits, hollows* and *caves*, and also *jars* and *bottles*, and *boxes* of all sorts and sizes. . . . From the animal world, *snails* and *mussels* at any rate must be cited as unmistakable female symbols; . . . amongst buildings, *churches* and *chapels* are symbols of a woman. You see that all these symbols are not equally easy to understand. . . .

Gratification derived from a person's own genitals is indicated by any kind of *play*, including *playing the piano*. The symbolic representation of onanism [masturbation] by *sliding* or *gliding* and also by *pulling of a branch* is very typical. . . . Special representations of sexual intercourse are less frequent in dreams than we should expect after all this, but we may mention in this connection rhythmical activities such as *dancing, riding* and *climbing*, and also *experiencing some violence*, e.g. being run over. (Freud, 1924/1952, pp. 161–164)

It is difficult to know what to make of Freud's theory of dream interpretation. His is a rich and creative system, but there seems almost no way to verify or disprove it. Modern researchers have turned to other means to find out about dreams, mostly through studying the physiology and psychology of REM sleep.

MODERN THEORIES OF DREAMING. One basic question to be answered about dreams is whether or not there is a physiological need for REM sleep, the dream state. Is REM sleep necessary? One way to seek the answer is to deprive people of REM sleep, and William Dement (1960) performed one of the earliest such experiments. For five nights he allowed experimental subjects six hours of sleep, but he woke them at the first signs of REM sleep. (Dement monitored their EEGs and REMs [rapid eye movements] to determine when the patients were dreaming.) On recovery nights at the end of the treatment, subjects were allowed normal sleep. These same subjects were also tested in a control condition in which they were awakened an equal number of times over five nights, but always during non-REM sleep.

The findings from the experiment were dramatic. People deprived of REM sleep attempted to enter the REM state with increasing frequency over the five-night period. It was necessary to waken them about twice as many times on the fifth night as on the first. The same was not true in the control condition. Apparently, the REM-deprived subjects were trying to catch up on REM sleep to satisfy a need. In addition, they complained of more psychological discomfort when deprived of REM sleep. As a group they seemed more anxious, and one even quit the experiment. On recovery nights, when allowed to sleep through, subjects deprived of REM sleep spent about 50 percent more time in REM sleep than is normal. This increased REM sleep on recovery nights is called *REM rebound.*

The possibility that REM sleep is necessary for a person's physical and psychological well-being is interesting because it seems to confirm a part of

Freud's theory that dreams operate as a safety valve for repressed desires, especially sexual desires. Such a theory may be supported by the fact that males almost always have erections when they are dreaming. But these interesting speculations seem to be dashed by further research. A review of some 40 studies on REM deprivation revealed no systematic ill effects befalling the deprived subjects (Webb, 1975). These studies do confirm the increasing tendency for people who are REM-deprived to enter REM sleep as well as to experience the REM rebound phenomenon on later nights. But there is no clear-cut evidence for psychological disturbance produced by REM deprivation. Some studies have even shown that REM deprivation actually helps relieve depression in some people (Vogel, 1975). In addition, the erections in males do not depend on the content of the dreams; they occur in dreams of boring, everyday activities, as well as in dreams about sex.

A new theory of dreaming, put forward by J. Allan Hobson and Robert W. McCarley (1977), has attracted considerable attention and generated some controversy. The Hobson-McCarley hypothesis is basically a physiological explanation of REM sleep in which dreaming per se is considered of little importance. Some of the symptoms accompanying REM sleep were mentioned previously: rapid eye movements; high frequency, low amplitude brain waves resembling the waking pattern; temporary paralysis as motor control of the muscles is shut off; increased heart rate and respiration; and erections in males and vaginal engorgement in females. Hobson and McCarley argue that all these changes result from activation of brain cells in the pons, a part of the brain stem. Support for this idea comes from studies in which the same cells that control REM sleep in the brain stems of cats are supplied with the chemical neurotransmitter believed to instigate REM sleep. With their brains thus activated, all the symptoms for REM sleep appear, even though the cats are wide awake. The symptoms of REM sleep, then, are simply a consequence of physiological activation from the part of the brain stem that controls the physical responses.

But what do dreams represent? According to Hobson and McCarley, dreams are the desperate attempts of the higher centers in the brain to interpret the welter of conflicting signals that are passed along from the lower centers. Dreams are often bizarre because the signals from which they are constructed are basically random. This would also explain why dream sequences shift rapidly from one scene to another in disjointed ways. Edwin Kiester (1984) writes that Hobson and McCarley believe that "dreams are nothing more than the thinking brain's valiant efforts to weave a coherent plot out of disparate and contradictory signals from the lower brain centers during sleep" (p. 77). Although Hobson and McCarley do not deny that dreams are related to daily experiences and concerns, everyday matters are probably used only to structure the random signals and are not the prime reason for dreaming.

The Hobson-McCarley hypothesis fits well with many data collected by psychobiologists concerned with sleep in lower animals, but many researchers who seek the meaning of dreams have criticized the theory (Kiester, 1984). Even accepting the Hobson-McCarley hypothesis, why do dreams occur? What is their function? Francis Crick and Graeme Mitchison (1983) have proposed a bold, if speculative, theory that the function of REM sleep is essentially to clear the memory banks of the brain's cortex from unwanted

APPLYING PSYCHOLOGY

Sleep Disorders

Most people cherish their hours of slumber, but a sizable segment of the population dreads the night because of wakefulness. When opinion pollsters ask, "Do you often have trouble falling asleep and staying asleep?" some 14 percent of those questioned answer yes. Another 30 percent say sometimes. Sales of over-the-counter drugs and prescription drugs for sleeplessness total millions of dollars yearly.

The most common sleep disorder is **insomnia,** a term that embraces many types of sleep disturbance. The most frequent difficulty is in falling asleep, but there are often other symptoms. Some people go to sleep quickly but wake a number of times during the night. Others complain of sleeping lightly, which usually means they do a lot of stage 1

sleep and less than normal stage 4 sleep.

Situational insomnias have a sudden onset and seem to be due to circumstances, such as death in the family, a divorce, or loss of a job. The crisis will pass, and with it the insomnia. Physicians often prescribe sedatives during such an emergency.

Benign insomnias are those in which people complain of poor sleep or lack of sleep when in fact they sleep within the normal range. This occurs most often when people try to match their sleep to some imagined standard. Some people believe they sleep too little, others too much. The best therapy is reassurance that the person is in fact sleeping normally. Some therapists recommend the keeping of a "sleep diary" in which the amount of sleep is recorded for every night to bolster the reassurance.

Arrhythmic insomnias result from a disruption in the normal cycle of daily life. They may be caused by an altered work schedule, such as the "graveyard shift" from midnight to 8

A.M. in factories and other round-the-clock operations, or by jet travel and the resulting jet lag. Cues that signal sleep are disrupted, so the sufferer does not feel sleepy when it is "time to go to sleep." On a short-term basis, the only palliative lies in sedatives. For a long term, where the individual, say, takes a job demanding night work, the best solution is to establish regular routines and times for sleep: the body will eventually fall into a new sleep rhythm.

A final type of insomnia represents a relatively recent problem: *drug-related insomnias.* The regular use of most psychoactive drugs (chemicals that affect the central nervous system and produce changes in mood) results in sleep disorders. Sedatives and barbiturates suppress REM sleep and, while they may make it easier to sleep, probably lower the quality of sleep. Many people who use barbiturates to induce sleep become addicted to them, and they have to take increasing amounts.

information, a process they refer to as "reverse learning" or "unlearning." They argue that the cortex is a gigantic associative net containing millions of connections and that learning involves strengthening certain connections. However, learning also can produce many random or spurious connections. During REM sleep, they argue, these spurious associations are wiped clean. "Put . . . loosely, we suggest that in REM sleep we unlearn our unconscious dreams. 'We dream in order to forget' " (Crick & Mitchison, 1983, p. 112). Although some evidence can be interpreted as consistent with the theory, it must be regarded as highly speculative. Even its authors note that "a direct test of our postulated reverse learning mechanism seems extremely difficult" (p. 113).

Another recent theory maintains that REM sleep has a restorative function, involving regeneration of important brain chemicals, although as yet no specific neurotransmitter has been identified (Thompson, 1985). Other evidence even suggests—in direct contradiction of the reverse learning idea proposed by Crick and Mitchison—that REM sleep serves to consolidate

Insomnia and sleep disorders may be partly responsible for drug addiction. When prevented from using a drug, drug addicts suffer many withdrawal symptoms, including nervousness, "jitters," and insomnia. When addicts do sleep during withdrawal, they show large REM rebound effects. However, during these REM rebound periods, the addicts' sleep is often disrupted by terrifying nightmares. The addicts may in part be driven back to the drugs in order to stop the nightmares, creating a vicious cycle.

Other sleep disorders are relatively less frequent than insomnia. One is *sleep apnea* (Guilleminault & Dement, 1978), characterized by difficulty breathing or an actual inability to breathe while asleep (*apnea* means "cessation of breathing"). Most sufferers complain of sleeping too much and of being tired all day. They are typically unaware that they may wake themselves some 500 times during the night to breathe or that they are unable to breathe and sleep at the same time. Some researchers believe that apnea may be related to the mysterious crib death syndrome among infants.

Another serious sleep disorder is *narcolepsy,* which involves irresistible attacks of sleepiness during the day at inappropriate times; the narcoleptic may doze off when driving a car or even when making love. EEG recordings evidence that narcoleptics go directly from being wide awake to REM sleep, skipping the other sleep stages. This fact explains the terrifying hallucinations that sometimes occur at the onset of narcoleptic attacks. They are likely the dreams associated with the beginnings of REM sleep.

The cause of narcolepsy is unknown, but it may have a genetic origin because it tends to run in families; it usually occurs between 10 and 20 years of age. Some drugs reduce the frequency of attacks, but there is no known cure (Dement, 1976).

Three other sleep disorders—*sleeptalking, sleepwalking,* and *night terrors*—are poorly understood. One might think that they are associated with vivid dreams, but this is not the case. All three disorders occur when people are in stage 4 sleep, and all occur more in children than in adults. In sleepwalking and sleeptalking a person is vaguely conscious of the outside world. A sleepwalker can sometimes navigate through a room crowded with furniture, and sleeptalkers sometimes respond to questions and commands. Neither condition seems harmful, although one should try to arrange the house of a sleepwalker so that the person avoids injury. Awakening sleepwalkers is not harmful, contrary to legend, but they will usually be quite confused when wakened. Night terrors occur in children, who awaken with terrified screams. They usually do not report that they are dreaming at the onset of the terrors, nor do the terrors occur during REM sleep. (Nightmares or "bad dreams" do occur during REM sleep.) Night terrors seem to do no permanent harm and may not even be remembered in the morning.

memories of the previous day and makes them more resistant to forgetting (Scrima, 1982). As these various ideas show, we have much to learn about the nature of REM sleep and what purpose it serves. Certainly some important function of REM sleep seems likely: all mammals sleep and show REM sleep; newborn humans spend as many as eight hours a day in REM sleep; and when deprived of REM sleep people try to enter the state more frequently and show REM rebound when permitted undisturbed sleep.

HYPNOSIS

About 200 years ago a Frenchman named Anton Mesmer discovered a state of consciousness in which people were highly susceptible to suggestion. When Mesmer gave instructions to subjects in this state, they did many things they ordinarily could not do. Mesmer attributed this phenomenon to "animal magnetism," which he considered a mysterious force akin to magnetism in inanimate objects. At the time, the technique Mesmer employed was called *mesmerism;* today it is called *hypnosis,* a term derived from the Greek word for sleep.

Long controversial within the field of psychology, hypnosis is intensively investigated today, and a growing body of evidence shows that many claims concerning hypnosis over the years are true. For example, in the years before anesthetic drugs, hypnosis was used to block pain for surgical

CONTROVERSY

Does Hypnosis Improve Memory Retrieval?

Hypnosis is being used in some police departments (particularly in Los Angeles) as an aid in improving the memory of eyewitnesses to crimes. Sometimes a witness who has been repeatedly questioned may, when interrogated again under hypnosis, remember a critical fact that helps solve a crime (Reiser and Nielson, 1980).

One of the most dramatic instances of the use of hypnosis to refresh the memory of a witness occurred in a kidnapping case in Chowchilla, California (Kroger and Douce, 1979). Near this small town, 26 schoolchildren and their bus driver were ordered from their bus at gunpoint, crowded into vans, and taken to a remote rock quarry where they were trapped inside a large cavern. With heroic effort, the bus driver and two of the older boys were able to dig their way out and contact police to be rescued. When he was questioned later for fine details that might aid in the capture of the kidnappers, the bus driver's memory was rather hazy. He had tried to memorize the license plate numbers of the kidnappers' vans but could not recall them. He was hypnotized and given the suggestion that he should imagine himself sitting in his favorite chair and watching the drama unfold as if on television. Suddenly he recalled two numbers, one of which proved to be quite close to the license plate number of one of the vans (only a single digit was missing). This critical information helped solve the case,

which involved one of the largest dragnets in California's history.

The usual explanation for such dramatic recoveries is that the human brain contains faithful records of experience that can be "replayed" with accuracy under the right conditions. Although this is an appealing notion, it is contradicted by considerable evidence (described in Chapter 7). Often memories can be quite poor and error-prone, even when people are confident that their recall is accurate. In addition, many researchers have failed to find experimental evidence that hypnosis can be used to improve memory under laboratory conditions, although such studies do typically find that hypnotized people produce many memories that they judge to be authentic but that are not. Anecdotal reports, such as the Chowchilla case, are often not convincing because it is not usually possible (as it was in this case) to verify the remembered details. Orne (1979) reports that many license plate numbers that have been recalled under hypnosis have been found to belong to cars ruled out of any possible involvement by later investigation. In addition, these anecdotal studies do not have a control group that is not hypnotized to see if the same feat could be displayed by nonhypnotized subjects who are strongly motivated by task instructions similar to those given under hypnosis.

Marilyn C. Smith (1983) of the University of Toronto has reviewed the procedures. Although skeptics scoffed at the notion that pain from major surgery could be blunted by such means, recent studies (discussed below) show that hypnosis can indeed affect perception of pain. On the other hand, some claims for hypnosis have not been uniformly confirmed. Some maintain that under hypnosis people can retrieve seemingly forgotten experiences and provide detailed information about them. (See "Controversy: Does Hypnosis Improve Memory Retrieval?")

experimental evidence concerning effects of hypnosis on remembering and has concluded that there is little or no positive effect when hypnotized subjects are compared to proper controls. Some of the studies that Smith reviewed were conducted under artificial, laboratory conditions, but the same results occurred even when she considered studies using a more natural situation. In one study, people who thought they were really eyewitnesses to a crime and whose testimony (recall) was meaningful did no better than subjects who were simply asked to recall the scene (Malpass and Devine, 1980). Overall, differences between laboratory and natural conditions do not seem to account for the fact that hypnosis did not improve memory.

Some experiments have shown hypnosis to be effective in increasing recall, but often the improvement is accompanied by a large number of errors (Dywan and Bowers, 1983). Thus, hypnosis may not have truly improved memory but simply made people more willing to report whatever came to mind or to guess more wildly.

Other studies have shown that people under hypnosis are more confident in their judgments that what they recall is accurate, even when they are wrong (Nogrady, McConkey, & Perry, 1985). This is especially true for highly hypnotizable people. In addition, information suggested to people about a prior event while they are under hyp-

nosis will sometimes later be recalled as a true fact about the event (Laurence and Perry, 1983). Because of these problems, many states and Canadian provinces have passed laws stating that witnesses to crimes who have undergone hypnosis cannot testify in courts of law.

All the studies described so far have relied on procedures that are quite different from hypnotic interviews of witnesses conducted by police detectives. An ingenious study by Ralph E. Geiselman, Ronald P. Fisher, and their colleagues (1985) combined the controlled procedures of the laboratory with important facets of police interrogation. The subjects were undergraduate students who viewed films of violent crimes and were interviewed about the crimes two days later by police officers who had training in interrogation. The police interviewed students under one of three conditions, to which they were randomly assigned. In the standard interview the police questioned the subjects about the crime as detectives are taught to do, by first asking the "witnesses" to report as much as possible about the crime and then following up with specific questions. In the hypnosis interview the police again first asked subjects to recall as much as possible and then provided a hypnotic induction. Then the "witnesses" were again asked to report the crime in their own words before the police officer followed up with specific tech-

niques for improving memory. A third condition was called the cognitive interview and was based on the authors' expert knowledge derived from research about memory (to be discussed in Chapter 7). The police in this condition asked the subjects to describe the crime in their own words and then tried additional techniques to produce more memories.

The researchers found that witnesses in the hypnotic interview condition recalled more correct facts than did those in the standard police interview condition. However, witnesses in the cognitive interview condition recalled just as well as those under hypnosis! In addition, the good performance in the cognitive interview and in the hypnosis interview was not accompanied by an increase in errors. After analyzing transcripts of the interviews, the authors suggested that police in the hypnotic interviews had in fact often used techniques resembling those in the cognitive interview to improve memory. Thus the improved performance in the hypnotic interview may not have been caused by hypnosis per se, but instead by effective memory retrieval techniques. Because hypnosis has been shown to produce ill effects on later memory (overconfidence and introduction of false information as real), the cognitive interview may be a preferable strategy for questioning witnesses to a crime. It produces similar levels of recall and the testimony is admissible in court.

What exactly is hypnosis? The state is difficult to define precisely, and the means of inducing hypnosis are varied. In a typical experimental setting a hypnotist induces the hypnotic state by asking people to fix their attention on some object and suggesting that they are feeling relaxed and sleepy. The subjects do not actually go to sleep but seem to enter a trance in which they respond submissively to the hypnotist's directions. In general, people cannot be hypnotized against their will and cannot be made to perform antisocial or self-destructive acts while hypnotized. You should know that there are few regulations in most states about who may call themselves hypnotists or hypnotic therapists. Before submitting to hypnosis you should inspect the hypnotist's credentials. Under guidance of an inexperienced hypnotist, the procedure may provoke anxiety or stress.

Hypnosis does not work on everyone. Some 5 to 10 percent of the population is unresponsive to its effects, while about 15 percent are very easily hypnotizable. Most people fall between these extremes. Hypnotizability is measured on a scale consisting of various suggestions, and subjects are rated according to the number of suggestions to which they respond. For example, a subject might be told to hold out an arm for a long time, followed by the suggestion that the arm is growing heavy. If the arm drops noticeably after the suggestion, the person would have passed that item on the hypnotizability scale. People who follow many of the suggestions on the scale are considered easily hypnotizable. They respond more readily to hypnotic induction, and while under hypnosis their behavior is more readily influenced by the hypnotist's directions. In fact, Hilgard (1975) has suggested that the response obtained under hypnosis depends more on the person's hypnotizability than on the specific techniques used by the hypnotist. The measuring scales for hypnotizability are quite reliable, meaning that when given the tests repeatedly, people score roughly at the same level (Bowers, 1983). Surprisingly, hypnotizability is not highly correlated with other personality traits, although people who score high show an ability to control bodily functions—such as sleeping and napping (Evans, 1977)—better than others.

Most people who are easily hypnotized are susceptible to *posthypnotic suggestion,* a direction given by the hypnotist that impels them to certain behavior after a return to consciousness. Under hypnosis, subjects may be told to tap their feet three times after emerging from their trance. When they do, they are likely to explain, "My foot went to sleep." They do not recall the instruction. Though it is a popular theme of television programs, there is no evidence indicating that posthypnotic suggestion can be used to make people commit crimes (Coe, 1977).

Another interesting phenomenon is that of *posthypnotic amnesia,* in which the suggestion is made to the hypnotized subject that he or she will not be able to remember the events that transpired during hypnosis until a signal is given later. In a test given after the hypnosis is lifted, people do indeed show poor recall for the material. However, on a second test following the signal, recall improves. This phenomenon has occurred in many experiments, but the interpretation is still unclear (Kihlstrom, 1984; Spanos & Radtke, 1982).

As mentioned above, one of the most remarkable facets of hypnotic suggestion is in suppressing the experience of pain. In one remarkable study by Stern and his colleagues (1977), hypnosis was shown to be more effective

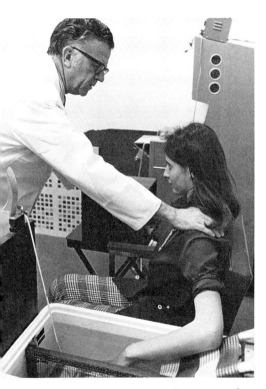

Ernest Hilgard is shown here measuring a hypnotized subject's pain reaction to having her hand placed in ice water. Hilgard discovered that often people will not report pain when asked directly but will indicate pain by other means such as automatic writing. Hilgard argues that there are different levels or types of awareness that can be separated, or dissociated, from one another. Pain reduction in hypnosis may operate by such a dissociation of a conscious level of awareness from others. The pain is felt but not consciously reported, according to Hilgard.

than aspirin, Valium, acupuncture, or even morphine in relieving pain. The pain was caused by the administration of intense cold, a standard laboratory technique used in hypnosis studies. (Immersion of a hand or arm in a bucket of ice water creates a very intense form of pain.) In Stern's study, highly hypnotizable subjects showed greater pain relief than others, as is usually found.

Exactly how hypnosis reduces pain is unknown. Some researchers have suggested that hypnotic pain reduction reflects a *dissociation,* in which the pain is actually registered in one cognitive system but is blocked from conscious awareness. Hilgard (1977) has developed a procedure that allows relatively direct observation of dissociation by the use of automatic writing, in which a hypnotized person writes without apparent knowledge of what he or she is writing. For example, if hypnotized subjects are instructed to place one hand into a bucket of ice water, they will say that they feel a little pain, but their automatic writing will describe great pain. It is as though their consciousness has been split (or dissociated) under hypnosis. In other words, subjects report feeling little pain, but when another level of consciousness is tapped through automatic writing, the "hidden observer" (to use Hilgard's term) reports pain. At some level the pain may be registered, but it seems blocked from conscious experience. These results have been replicated by others, but the interpretation in terms of a hidden observer divorced from conscious awareness is not universally accepted (Spanos, 1983).

Whatever the ultimate reason, researchers agree that hypnosis can reduce pain, and this has practical consequences. Hilgard and LeBaron (1984) found that hypnosis relieved the pain of highly hypnotizable children who were undergoing treatments for bone marrow cancer.

DRUGS AND CONSCIOUSNESS

Drugs have been used for thousands of years to produce altered states of consciousness, and there is no indication their popularity is waning. The most common drugs in North America are caffeine (found in tea, coffee, and some soft drinks), tobacco, and alcohol. More dangerous substances are hallucinogenics LSD and mescaline; the opiate narcotics heroin, opium, and morphine; stimulants of the central nervous system, amphetamines, and cocaine; and barbiturates such as Librium and methaqualone (Quaaludes).

Some of these drugs are considered acceptable in our society, others unacceptable. Acceptable drugs such as caffeine and nicotine were originally confiscated and condemned by societies into which they were introduced. After time these drugs became accepted, and marijuana may be following a similar route to acceptability. We describe the action of a few of these drugs briefly, with reference to their effects on conscious experience. Table 5–1 contains basic information about many controlled drugs.

Depressants

Alcohol is the most popular of the *depressants,* which generally reduce activity in the central nervous system. In small amounts depressants act as stimulants by producing relaxation and loosening inhibitions, but in larger

TABLE 5–1
Commonly Abused Substances and Their Effects

Classification	Drugs	Psychological Effects	Duration of Effects (in hours)	Dependence Potential Physical	Dependence Potential Psychological	Tolerance
DEPRESSANTS (SEDATIVES)	Alcohol (ethanol)	Relaxation; reduced inhibitions	3 to 6	High	High	Yes
	Barbiturates (e.g., Amytal, Seconal)	Relaxation, disorientation, sleep	1 to 16	High	High	Yes
	Mild tranquilizers (e.g., Librium, Valium)	Reduced anxiety, relaxation, sedation	4 to 8	Moderate	Moderate	Yes
OPIATES (NARCOTICS)	Codeine	Lack of feeling in the body, euphoria, drowsiness, nausea	3 to 6	Moderate	Moderate	Yes
	Heroin			High	High	Yes
	Opium			High	High	Yes
	Morphine			High	High	Yes
STIMULANTS	Amphetamines (e.g., Benzedrine, Dexedrine)	Increased alertness, excitation, decreased fatigue	2 to 4	Possible	High	Yes
	Caffeine (coffee, cola, tea)	Increased alertness, excitation, decreased fatigue	2 to 4	None	Moderate	Yes
	Cocaine	Euphoria, excitation, alertness, decreased fatigue	2 to 3	Possible	High	Yes
	Nicotine	Increased alertness	1 to 2	Possible	High	Yes
HALLUCINOGENS	Lysergic acid diethylamide (LSD) Mescaline, Psilocybin MDA	Distortions, illusions, hallucinations, time disorientation	1 to 8	None	Unknown	Yes
CANNABIS	Marijuana, Hashish	Euphoria, relaxed inhibitions, increased appetite, increased sensory sensitivity, disorientation	2 to 4	Unknown	Moderate	Yes

quantities they severely impair sensory functions and coordination. Concentrations of .10 to .15 percent of alcohol in the blood (10 to 15 parts in 10,000), which would result from imbibing three bottles of beer, can cause such impairment. At .20 percent a person is severely impaired, and at levels of .40 percent death can occur (see Table 5–2).

Small amounts of alcohol often produce a pleasurable, relaxed state of consciousness, but larger amounts may cause many people to become belligerent and angry as well as disoriented and confused. Severe abuse of alcohol may induce hallucinations, which are thought to occur by action of drugs (and their withdrawal) on the central nervous system (Siegel, 1977). Addicts who are withdrawn from alcohol often suffer *delirium tremens*, popularly known as the D.T.'s. Its most noticeable effect is hand tremors, but the addict also suffers hallucinations, usually visions of terrifying animals such as snakes or surreal monsters. The D.T.'s may be fatal.

Barbiturates are also depressants and are sometimes prescribed as relaxants for people under stress or as sleeping pills. If they are taken with alcohol, the combined effects on the central nervous system can cause death. Withdrawal from barbiturates is as harrowing as with alcohol. Because of awareness of these problems, physicians today are reluctant to prescribe barbiturates.

The *opiate narcotics* constitute another type of depressant. Opium comes from the juice of certain types of poppy, and its active ingredients are codeine and morphine, which are prescribed on occasion by physicians for control of pain for brief periods. Morphine is stronger than codeine, and heroin, which is derived from morphine, is the strongest narcotic of all. Addicts sniff or inject heroin. At first, heroin produces intense pleasure, similar to that of an orgasm, but its users develop *drug tolerance:* after repeated exposures, they must take ever-increasing amounts of the drug to achieve the same effect, so addiction usually results. (Tolerance is discussed in Chapter 6.) Unlike alcoholics, people addicted to opiate narcotics do not lose their sensory and motor functions, but they eventually destroy neural tissue and reduce production of the body's own opiates (the endorphins).

Stimulants

Caffeine and nicotine are the most popular *stimulants*. Coffee and tea, which contain caffeine, have long been enjoyed for their psychological lift, although they have been banned occasionally in some cultures, such as ancient Egypt. Many carbonated drinks, particularly colas, contain caffeine. The nicotine in tobacco is physiologically addictive, and cigarette smoking is one of the leading causes of disease and death in the United States. But nicotine may have a relaxing or stimulating effect, depending on the circumstances in which it is used and the expectations of the user, so many people continue smoking despite its widely publicized health hazards.

The concentration of alcohol in the blood depends on a person's sex and weight. Large people have more bodily fluid than small people, and men have more fluid than women of the same weight (because women have a greater amount of fat). Thus, four cans of beer or glasses of wine consumed during a one-hour period will produce a blood alcohol concentration of .18 in a 100-pound female, .15 in a 100-pound male, .12 in a 150-pound woman, and .10 in a 150-pound man (Ray, 1978). These concentrations would produce legal intoxication in most states, so people would be subject to arrest for driving a car. Even small amounts of alcohol can produce relatively grave impairments in judgments and reactions. Great amounts can kill a person.

Source: Ray, 1983.

TABLE 5–2
Blood Alcohol Levels and Behavior

Blood Alcohol Concentration (percent)	Behavioral Effects
0.05	Reduced alertness, often pleasurable feeling, release of inhibitions, impaired judgment
0.10	Slowed reaction times, impaired motor function, less caution; legal intoxication in many states
0.15	Large increases in reaction times
0.20	Marked depression in sensory and motor capability; decidedly intoxicated
0.25	Severe motor problems, such as staggering; sensory perceptions greatly impaired
0.30	Stuporous but conscious; no comprehension of the world around them
0.35	Surgical anesthesia (passed out); possible death at this point and beyond

Amphetamines are stronger stimulants, usually taken in the form of pills with brand names such as Dexedrine and Benzedrine. Popularly, they are known as "speed" or "uppers" because they heighten activity in the central nervous system, increase alertness, reduce boredom and fatigue, and suppress appetite. They were at one time widely prescribed for weight reduction. Used in moderation and only occasionally, these stimulants are not harmful. However, when taken in larger doses or for long periods, amphetamines can induce paranoid feelings. Withdrawal can produce a "crash" or a long period of severe depression and fatigue. A dangerous pattern may be established if a person uses sedatives to overcome the effects of the amphetamine and then needs the amphetamine to counter the use of the sedatives. This cycle can be difficult to break.

Cocaine, though illegal, is apparently increasing in popularity. Its effects are quite similar to those of amphetamines. In mild, occasional small doses it produces alertness and an increased capacity to work or think without fatigue. Cocaine is, however, addictive, and in large doses it can induce paranoid reactions of hostility and suspicion.

Hallucinogens

Hallucinogens take their name from the hallucinations, or alterations of perceptual experience, that they produce. One of the mildest hallucinogenics—and certainly the most common—is marijuana. Other, more potent varieties include the psychedelic drugs, which strongly affect visual perception and the experience of time, and some drugs that produce hallucinations but are not classed with the psychedelics. Among these nonpsychedelic hallucinogens is phencyclidene, or "angel dust," which may have dangerous side effects manifested in fits of wild rage.

Marijuana taken in small quantities produces euphoria in many people and may make listening to music and eating more pleasurable. However, large doses can lead to severe and frightening hallucinations.

The psychedelic drugs such as LSD (lysergic acid diethylamide) were once quite popular among college students for altering and "expanding" consciousness. LSD was discovered by Albert Hoffman, whose report of his experience on first taking the drug is quoted below:

> After 40 minutes, I noted the following symptoms in my laboratory journal: slight giddiness, restlessness, difficulty in concentration, visual disturbances, laughing. . . . Later: I lost all count of time, I noticed with dismay that my environment was undergoing progressive changes. My visual field wavered and everything appeared deformed as in a faulty mirror. Space and time became more and more disorganized, and I was overcome by a fear that I was going out of my mind. The worst part of it being that I was clearly aware of my condition. My power of observation was unimpaired. . . . Occasionally, I felt as if I were out of my body. I thought I had died. My ego seemed suspended somewhere in space, from where I saw my dead body lying on the sofa. . . . It was particularly striking how acoustic perceptions, such as the noise of water gushing from a tap or the spoken word, were transformed into optical illusions. I then fell asleep and awakened the next morning somewhat tired but otherwise feeling perfectly well. (As quoted in Ornstein, 1977, p. 94)

Increased knowledge of the dangers of LSD has greatly reduced its use. Its effects are unpredictable. Under its influence, people sometimes do irrational and injurious things. On the other hand, some users report hardly any effect, others have visions with semireligious qualities, and a few have terrifying hallucinations that may erupt days, weeks, or even months later.

A Caution

The drugs described here are often quite harmful, as can be seen from the general effects described in Figure 5–12 (and Table 5–1). However, the effects of most drugs are highly variable, and they seem to depend on the

FIGURE 5–12
Classification of Drugs

All drugs can be classified by the nature of their effect on the central nervous system: stimulating or depressing. The effects of different drug groups are shown in this chart.

Source: Robert W. Earle.

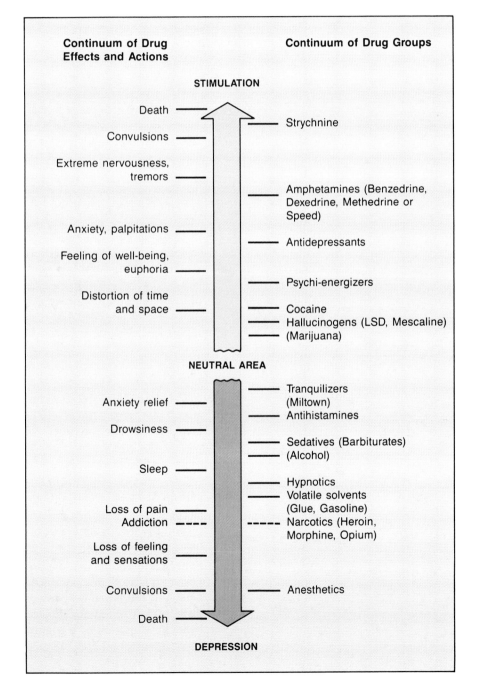

expectations of those who take them. People will often report relief from stress soon after taking a barbiturate, even before the drug itself could possibly work. So general statements about drugs cannot be made with certainty, but most of the ones listed here are extremely dangerous.

REPRISE: CONSCIOUS AWARENESS AND BEHAVIOR

The past three chapters—Sensation, Perception, and Consciousness—have all been broadly concerned with how information from the outside world is interpreted and used. The usual view of humans as rational beings is that we collect information from the outside world through our senses and that our higher brain centers sort it to arrive at a plan of action for dealing with our environment. In short, the view is one of bottom-up processing, to return to a distinction made in Chapter 3, with information processed by lower levels of the nervous system and passed along to higher cognitive centers. However, many phenomena and theories discussed in these three chapters reveal that this view, though quite logical, is probably wrong. Instead, many factors that people cannot describe exert strong effects on behavior. Because these factors escape conscious description, we may refer to them as unconscious. As a review, consider the following phenomena drawn from the previous three chapters:

□ In Chapter 3 we described how information from the senses traverses many neural pathways before arriving at the higher cortical centers where it is translated into conscious experience. In phenomena such as blindsight (page 83), brain damage to higher centers prevents the relay of information into conscious experience. A person knows the location of a scene at one level but is not aware of the knowledge and cannot report it. The same situation describes the cases of prosopagnosia that began this chapter, in which two women could not identify faces verbally but showed a heightened physiological response to them nonetheless.

□ In Chapter 4 illusions were described in which the perceiver automatically constructs a percept that does not correspond to the actual scene. The top-down, constructive processes in perception modify the information supplied by the senses in ways in which the perceiver is unaware.

□ In cases of automatic information processing, people respond quickly and unavoidably to information regardless of their expectations, strategies, or conscious intentions. In some cases they may even respond to information that is below the threshold of awareness (unconscious or subliminal perception).

□ Split-brain patients may be presented with information that is transmitted to their nonverbal right hemisphere and directs their behavior, but when asked about it their verbal left hemisphere cannot explain their actions or construct a plausible story about them. Again, behavior is guided by a cognitive system divorced from linguistic consciousness.

□ Highly hypnotizable subjects, when under hypnosis and guided by appropriate instructions, verbally report that they do not feel pain from a normally unpleasant stimulus. However, other responses indicate that the pain is registered at some level. The pain is dissociated from conscious awareness and verbal expression.

□ During sleep we are "unconscious," yet evidence exists that the brain continues to respond differentially to external stimuli. During stage 4 sleep people still respond on covert measures such as brain waves to the sound of their own name.

For all these reasons, unconscious forces can be said to guide our behavior. How do we think of these? As we discussed at the outset, many metaphors have been used to describe conscious experience—as a place in the mind, for example, or as a stream that runs through the mind. Perhaps a more appropriate analogy is of consciousness to a sense organ (Kolers and Roediger, 1984). Not all light or sound energy is detected by the eyes or ears. For example, infrared light cannot be perceived by humans, nor can we hear very high-pitched sounds (although other animals have sense organs capable of registering these stimuli). Consciousness may be similarly selective. People may be consciously aware of many factors that affect their behavior and be perfectly capable of verbalizing them, but other factors may escape conscious, verbal awareness altogether. The influence of unconscious forces does not mean that humans are irrational, as some would argue. Rather, just as the eye is incapable of detecting all electromagnetic radiation, conscious awareness does not extend to all factors that might influence behavior. Consciousness is obviously useful but (like other sensory and cognitive systems) selective and fallible.

SUMMARY

1. Consciousness is the current awareness of internal and external stimuli. Its capacity is limited; there is a limit to the number of stimuli of which individuals can be conscious at one time. Preconscious ideas can easily be called into consciousness, while unconscious thoughts cannot be easily retrieved. Nonconscious processes are those of which, in principle, we cannot be aware.

2. People often must deal with information overload, when more things happen to them than they can attend to. The problem of selective attention is how to concentrate on one stimulus and ignore others. Broadbent's filter theory maintains that people filter out ignored signals at the level of the senses. Experimental evidence has caused others to reject this view; they think that attention does not affect sensory processes and that information is selected for attention only after it has been processed by the senses. These are called late selection theories.

3. Two kinds of information processing can be distinguished: automatic and controlled. Automatic

processing occurs rapidly, does not depend on a person's expectations or strategies, and does not require conscious attention or cognitive resources. Controlled processing is the opposite: it is slower, depends on a person's strategy, and uses cognitive resources. These types should be considered as endpoints on a continuum. As a person takes up a new skill and practices it, controlled processing gives way to automatic processing.

4. Subliminal, or unconscious, perception refers to the effect on behavior of signals too weak to be noticed. Although demonstrations of the phenomenon exist under laboratory conditions, the practical implications (say, in advertising) are negligible. Subliminal effects are subtle and short-lived.

5. When information is flashed to the right hemisphere and provokes behavior, the split-brain patient may not be able to explain the behavior because the verbal centers in the left hemisphere are denied access to the stimulus that caused the behavior. The mind may be composed of various

systems that direct behavior but that are cut off from centers responsible for verbal consciousness.

6. An altered state of consciousness is experienced daily when people sleep and dream. Sleep is studied through analyzing patterns of brain waves. There are five stages of sleep. The stage that has attracted the most attention is rapid eye movement, or REM, sleep. In this stage, the brain gives off electrical signals similar to those emitted when people are awake. When awakened from this stage, people usually report having dreamt.

7. When people are deprived of sleep, they respond in widely different ways, so no firm conclusions currently can be drawn about the effects of sleep deprivation or the functions and purpose of sleep. The effects of sleep deprivation seem to be overcome relatively rapidly, after only a night or two of uninterrupted sleep.

8. The function of dreams is also not clear. However, if people are kept from dreaming, they dream more than normal on subsequent nights. This phenomenon is termed REM rebound. The Hobson-McCarley hypothesis maintains that REM sleep is caused by activation in the brain stem that spreads throughout neighboring systems and causes the physiological effects of that stage of sleep. Dreaming, according to this view, is the result of the desperate attempts of higher brain centers to interpret the blizzard of random signals generated by neural activity. The bizarre and disjointed nature of dreams is thus expected.

9. Insomnia embraces a variety of sleep disorders. Almost everyone occasionally suffers from situational insomnia, brought on by stress. Arrhythmic insomnia may occur after jet travel or be caused by working during other than the usual daylight hours. In sleep apnea, people stop breathing when asleep; in narcolepsy, they fall asleep uncontrollably no matter what they are doing.

10. The hypnotic trance may be a special state of consciousness in which people are quite responsive to others' suggestions. Often, hypnotized people can do things that they could not do—or would not try to do—when not hypnotized. People cannot be hypnotized against their will, and they will not perform antisocial acts under hypnosis. People differ greatly in their susceptibility to hypnotic suggestion. Highly hypnotizable people show considerably increased ability to tolerate pain under hypnosis. Effects of hypnosis on memory retrieval are more controversial. Many studies show no positive effect of hypnosis. When they are obtained, positive effects may be due to increased guessing under hypnosis or to good memory strategies suggested by the hypnotist, not to the hypnosis itself.

11. Drugs are frequently used to alter consciousness. Stimulants are used to perk people up, but strong ones or frequent use may lead to addiction. Depressants are used as relaxants, but they may affect coordination. When depressants such as sleeping pills and alcohol are combined, they may kill. Hallucinogens produce vivid hallucinations that some people believe reveal a hidden reality. Most strong drugs have negative effects on the physiology of the body and are addictive. Their use outside the field of medicine is usually illegal.

SUGGESTED READINGS

Bowers, K. S. (1983). *Hypnosis for the seriously curious* (2nd ed.). New York: Norton.
    This interesting book is written for people who have had little previous experience with hypnotic phenomena.

Keele, S. W. (1973). *Attention and human performance.* Pacific Palisades, Calif.: Goodyear.
    An introduction to research on the problem of attention, which also includes information on performance on many cognitive tasks.

Ornstein, R. E. (1977). *The psychology of consciousness* (2nd ed.). New York: Harcourt Brace Jovanovich.
    This popular book is based on the premise that the right side of the brain is responsible for the more intuitive and creative aspects of human thought. Ornstein argues for an ''education'' of intuitive consciousness and for serious study of meditation and Eastern philosophies. He has been criticized for uncritically accepting speculation about the specialization of the brain's hemispheres.

Springer, S. P., & Deutsch, G. (1985). *Left brain, right brain* (rev. ed.). New York: Freeman.
    A recent overview of what is known about hemispheric specialization. The last two chapters are concerned with implications for conscious experience.

Webb, W. B. (1975). *Sleep: The gentle tyrant.* Englewood Cliffs, N.J.: Prentice-Hall.
    This survey of what is known about sleep is written by one of the foremost sleep researchers. Webb focuses several chapters on dreams and sleep disorders.

Painting opposite: "Interior with a Girl Drawing, Paris, February 12, 1935" by Pablo Picasso. Nelson A. Rockefeller Bequest. The Museum of Modern Art, New York.

PART THREE
Learning, Memory, and Cognition

6

Conditioning and Learning

Habit is habit and not to be flung out the window by any [one], but coaxed downstairs one step at a time.

Mark Twain

IN THE EARLY PART OF THIS CENTURY, A REMARKABLE HORSE NAMED Clever Hans became an instant celebrity in Germany. The horse's owner, Herr von Osten, would read arithmetic problems to Clever Hans and the horse would tap out the correct answers with a forefoot. When asked to add "8 plus 3," Hans tapped his foot 11 times. The horse was about equally adept at addition, subtraction, multiplication, and division; he was also able to answer simple questions about spelling, reading, and musical harmony.

Needless to say, many Germans found Clever Hans's talents hard to believe. Yet von Osten seemed earnest, and he did not try to profit from his horse's notoriety. To satisfy the skeptics, the horse was tested in the absence of von Osten. Surprisingly, Hans performed his tasks about as well as ever.

Could Hans really understand language and do arithmetic? Two psychologists performed a series of experiments that finally convinced everyone that while Hans was in some ways a very clever horse, his talents did not extend to mathematics. Pfungst (1911) reported that Hans actually accomplished his feats by detecting subtle nonverbal signals that the questioners unconsciously provided. The researchers noted that when Hans tapped he would go quickly at first, then slow down, and then stop at the right place (or sometimes miss by a number or two). They discovered that the questioners tended to incline their heads as they gave Hans a problem, then to straighten up as he neared the correct answer. Hans also seemed to be sensitive to each questioner's eyebrow movements, dilation of nostrils, and tone of voice. When prevented from seeing or hearing his questioners while he tapped, Hans was no longer able to perform. The horse had simply learned covert signals from von Osten indicating when he should stop tapping.

Although Hans could not understand mathematics, he at least had the horse sense to outwit his human observers for a long while. Actually, the process by which Hans learned his trick is as interesting as the trick itself. Today psychologists would refer to this process as instrumental, or operant, conditioning, a process that we will describe in this chapter. From a cue, Hans learned to perform a response that was rewarded with attention and food. The same learning techniques are used by animal trainers to teach animals marvelous acts. Elephants stand on their front paws, dolphins caper about performing long series of tricks, and killer whales can even "kiss" their trainers. In these cases animals are explicitly trained to perform, whereas Hans had mastered his trick on his own.

This chapter is about learning; as you will see, instrumental learning is only one of several types. And although learning is considered here as a separate topic, it plays a role in almost every aspect of psychology. Learning is involved in how people perceive the world and form social attachments and in how events produce emotional reactions. Learning generates motivational and personality differences; for example, people learn to persist or not to persist in the face of frustration. We learn attitudes about issues,

Animals can be taught to perform incredible feats using the methods of instrumental conditioning. Elephants, despite their size, can be trained to lift a person gently without causing harm.

about ourselves and others, and about appropriate behavior in various situations. Many behavior disorders, from phobias (irrational fears) to sexual dysfunctions, also appear to be learned.

A general definition of *learning* that encompasses all these different examples is *a relatively permanent change in behavior or knowledge that occurs as a result of experience*. This definition carefully distinguishes learned changes from those produced by other processes such as fatigue or motivation. You may know perfectly well how to type but fail to perform as usual today because you are tired. After a good night's sleep your typing may improve tremendously, but not because you learned to type overnight. If you just tried harder tomorrow, your performance could improve, too, but that would not be a learned change. Not all changes in behavior reflect learning; the change must be a relatively permanent one resulting from experience.

Researchers interested in the fundamental processes of learning have generally employed two different procedures: classical conditioning and instrumental conditioning. In the first half of this chapter, we will describe the conditions in which learning occurs in each category.

In most of the early experiments with animals, learning was directly reflected in behavior, such as learning to make a response to get food. Sometimes, however, learning does not immediately produce any observable response. A student often learns not to talk in class by seeing another student criticized for doing so. The student's behavior potential has changed without any visible response on his or her part. Later in the chapter we will discuss learning by observing as well as other examples of learning that are not directly and immediately reflected in behavior.

In many experiments, learning researchers use nonhuman subjects. You may wonder why so much attention is paid to the learning abilities of cats, white rats, monkeys, and pigeons. This is because investigators can control such factors as experience, genetic background, and motivation in nonhuman animals, something not possible with human beings. The findings from animal laboratories have proved to be relevant for human behavior in many cases. For example, the principles derived from the learning laboratory have been successfully applied to therapy for emotionally disturbed patients. As we discuss the principles of learning in this chapter, we will make many connections between the animal laboratory and human behavior.

CLASSICAL CONDITIONING

Ivan P. Pavlov (1849–1936) is one of psychology's most famous scientists, yet he did no psychological work until late in life, and the important work for which he was awarded the Nobel Prize in 1904 concerned digestive physiology. Pavlov studied how secretions of gastric acids and other substances in the stomach varied depending on the food that was being digested. Working with dogs, for example, Pavlov discovered that meat greatly increased stomach secretions—one reason an ulcer patient may be advised to avoid beef or pork. Pavlov also noted that the mouth secretes more or less saliva in response to certain foods. A drop of an acidic substance (lemon, for example) elicits a large quantity of watery saliva that dilutes the acid.

FIGURE 6–1
Pavlov's Apparatus
for Classical Conditioning

As the dog is held in a harness, its saliva runs through a tube and the amount secreted is recorded by a stylus on a revolving drum. In one experiment a tone consistently preceded the arrival of food in the dish. After a number of pairings the dog salivated when the tone sounded.

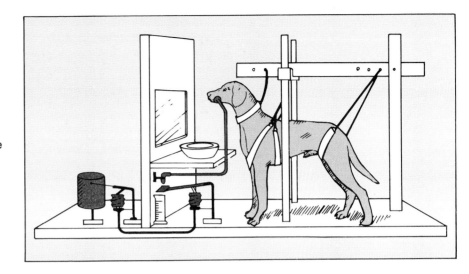

While studying salivary and gastric responses, Pavlov discovered a curious phenomenon. In one experiment he cut the esophagus of a dog and funneled it outside the animal's neck; the dog chewed and swallowed but food never reached its stomach. Despite the absence of food, stomach secretions still occurred! Then Pavlov found that even the sight of an empty food dish would trigger stomach secretions and salivation. Pavlov realized that these events represented a different kind of response than salivation and secretion in reaction to food. All dogs produce stomach secretions when food is placed in their stomachs and salivate when food is placed in their mouths. But only a dog that has had certain experiences will do so at the mere sight of a food dish. These responses result from learning: the responses are a relatively permanent change in behavior produced by experience, i.e., they are learned responses. Intrigued by this series of discoveries, Pavlov devoted years to studying such learned responses.

Pavlov's Experiments

Pavlov concentrated his experiments on salivary responses because they were easier to measure than stomach secretions. To study learned salivary responses, Pavlov provided a harnessed dog with a stimulus, such as a tone, before it was given food; then he measured the animal's salivation in response to the tone. To exclude all other stimulation, Pavlov isolated the dog in a soundproof room and conducted the whole experiment by remote control. Meat powder was automatically released into a dish in front of the hungry dog immediately after the tone sounded. Saliva ran through a tube connected to the dog's salivary gland, activating a device that recorded the flow of saliva (see Figures 6–1 and 6–2).

In a typical experiment, Pavlov consistently sounded the tone before releasing food into the dish. He discovered that after a number of tone-food pairings, the tone came to elicit salivation by itself. This outcome provides an impressive demonstration of how some neutral event in the environment, such as a tone, can gain control over behavior as a result of experience. Pavlov developed a terminology to describe his experimental situation.

FIGURE 6–2
Pavlov with His Laboratory Apparatus

In this photo Pavlov observes saliva flow in a dog subjected to a classical conditioning procedure in his laboratory.

He called the event that produces a response without prior learning the *unconditioned stimulus,* or *UCS.* Meat powder was the UCS in his experiment with the dog since meat powder automatically made the dog salivate when placed in the dog's mouth. The *unconditioned response,* or *UCR,* is the reaction to the unconditioned stimulus; it is a response that occurs automatically, without previous training.

The tone in Pavlov's situation is originally a neutral stimulus because at the beginning of the experiment it does not elicit the specific response to be conditioned, salivation. However, after being paired with food on several occasions, the tone by itself will become a *conditioned stimulus,* or *CS,* because it will then lead to the salivation response. Thus the conditioned stimulus does not bring out the specific response prior to training but does so after training. The reaction that is produced by the conditioned stimulus is called the *conditioned response,* or *CR.* In Pavlov's experiment the conditioned response was the salivation produced after the tone-food pairings when the tone was sounded by itself. Thus *classical conditioning* (or *Pavlovian conditioning*) is the procedure whereby a stimulus that does not initiate a reaction (the eventual CS) is paired with a stimulus (the UCS) that automatically produces a reaction. As a consequence of such CS-UCS pairings, the CS itself comes to elicit the response, the CR. The diagram in Figure 6–3 summarizes this procedure.

These terms may be a bit confusing at first, but you can use a rather simple rule to remember them. The unconditioned stimulus (UCS) operates to produce the unconditioned response (UCR) *without any prior experience or learning;* the reaction does not depend on (is not conditional on) prior training. On the other hand, the conditioned stimulus (CS) can produce the conditioned response (CR) *only after training.* Thus the reaction depends on (is conditional on) prior learning. And actually Pavlov's terms could just as easily have been translated unconditio*nal* stimulus for the UCS and conditio*nal* stimulus for the CS, a translation that might have made the terms easier for students to remember over the years.

FIGURE 6–3
Classical Conditioning Procedure

Before classical conditioning trials, food in the mouth (the unconditioned stimulus, UCS) elicits salivation (the unconditioned response, UCR). The tone (the conditioned stimulus, CS) does not induce salivation before conditioning. After the tone has preceded food a number of times (CS-UCS pairings), the tone by itself causes salivation (the conditioned response, CR).

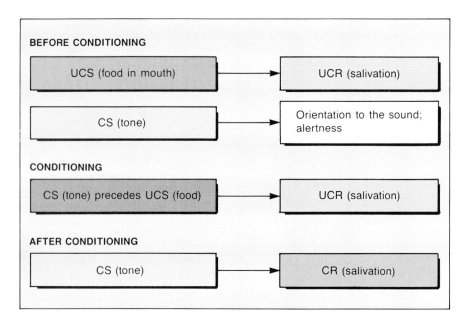

BEFORE CONDITIONING

UCS (food in mouth) → UCR (salivation)

CS (tone) → Orientation to the sound; alertness

CONDITIONING

CS (tone) precedes UCS (food) → UCR (salivation)

AFTER CONDITIONING

CS (tone) → CR (salivation)

Examples of Classical Conditioning in Human Behavior

Examples of classical conditioning abound in our everyday lives, but they are particularly evident in emotional reactions. If you have ever had a markedly embarrassing experience, you know that returning to the scene or seeing someone who witnessed your gaffe can renew your embarrassment. This is a result of the pairing of the place or person (CS) with the event (UCS).

HIGH BLOOD PRESSURE. High blood pressure is produced in part by stress, and this can be a result of classical conditioning. A stressful event, such as an electric shock, typically raises blood pressure. The shock can be considered a UCS, the elevated blood pressure a UCR. If a signal such as a light consistently precedes the shock, the light will become a conditioned stimulus and increase blood pressure whether or not the shock occurs (Bykov, 1957). These data suggest that classical conditioning may be the basis of many so-called psychosomatic illnesses. For example, a worker whose disagreeable supervisor (UCS) makes the worker tense (UCR) could be conditioned to be tense in any situation (CS) associated with that supervisor. If the supervisor's unpleasantness raises the worker's blood pressure on the job, ultimately the job itself will induce high blood pressure, even if the supervisor has been fired.

Learned fears can be long lasting. Many of the soldiers who fought in Vietnam still suffer from fears associated with the sights and sounds of battle.

FEAR. Overwhelming evidence indicates that people can learn to fear objects or places as a result of classical conditioning. In a well-known experiment, behaviorists John B. Watson and Rosalie Rayner (1920) induced fear of a white rat in a small boy named Albert, who showed no previous fear of rats. They paired the rat (CS) with a loud disturbing noise (the UCS). After a few such pairings, Albert would not approach a white rat and cried at the sight of one. Classical conditioning of fear in adults has also been demonstrated (e.g., Campbell, Sanderson, & Laverty, 1964). Many fears can be learned this way: fear of the dentist from a painful experience; fear of dogs from being bitten; fear of driving from being in a car accident. Learned fears can be quite long lasting. In a study of World War II veterans, researchers found a *galvanic skin response* (or *GSR*)—a change in the electrical potential of the skin that reflects anxiety or fear—to battle sounds as long as 15 years after the war (Edwards & Acker, 1972).

The Watson-Rayner experiment has been repeated several times, and some psychologists have had problems duplicating their results (Samuelson, 1980). One reason for failure to obtain their results is that fear conditioning in children will proceed rapidly only with certain CSs—those that are more likely to be feared (Kalish, 1981). Since children seem naturally more prepared to fear rats than toy ducks, fear conditioning is more difficult with a toy duck CS than with a rat CS.

DRUG TOLERANCE. Classical conditioning may also be involved in drug tolerance (Siegel, 1977). Often after a patient has had repeated exposure to a drug, doctors must prescribe increasingly larger dosages to produce the same effect. Morphine reduces pain, but if it is taken repeatedly, larger doses are required to reduce pain to the same level. Why does drug tolerance occur? One idea is that cues that precede administration of the drug, such as the sight of the needle, eventually elicit a conditioned response—hypersensitivity to pain—that opposes the unconditioned response to the drug and works against the drug's pain-reducing effect. The evidence for the role of classical conditioning in drug tolerance (e.g., Krank, Hinson, & Siegel, 1981; Siegel, et al., 1982) is of tremendous practical importance in treating drug addicts. One essential part of treatment for drug addiction should be eliminating the conditioned responses produced by drug-associated cues. These conditioned responses also can explain how drug overdoses can occur in experienced drug takers. If the drug is taken in a new location, the conditioned compensatory reaction may not occur. Thus the amount of drug necessary to produce a given effect will be less than that required in a familiar location, where the compensatory reaction is elicited. The drug user, not aware of this, can take the amount of drug appropriate to a familiar location in a new location, producing a drug overdose (Siegel et al., 1982).

PERSONAL ATTRACTION. Classical conditioning may even contribute to interpersonal attraction (Byrne, 1971). We tend to like people who agree with us and dislike those who disagree. Agreement (a UCS) seems inherently pleasurable; thus an agreeing person (CS) will be associated with pleasantness (UCS) and be liked (CR). Disagreement seems inherently unpleasant; thus a disagreeing person will be associated with unpleasantness and be disliked.

As you can see, through classical conditioning a wide array of neutral environmental stimuli can come to control a variety of responses in both animals and people. Indeed, Pavlov believed that classical conditioning could explain all learning, with complex behaviors composed of a series of simpler conditioned responses. Although there are many reasons to doubt Pavlov's initial enthusiasm, classical conditioning is a very important aspect of learning, and considerable effort has been devoted to identifying effective classical conditioning procedures, the topic to which we now turn.

Classical Conditioning Phenomena

Much of the information concerning the conditions governing the formation and persistence of conditioned responses was provided by Pavlov (1927), and his studies still constitute the fundamental basis of our knowledge. The phenomena discovered and named by Pavlov include *acquisition, extinction, spontaneous recovery, stimulus generalization, discrimination training,* and *higher-order conditioning.*

ACQUISITION. The process by which a conditioned stimulus comes to produce a conditioned response is called *acquisition.* To produce a conditioned response, a conditioned stimulus must consistently precede an unconditioned stimulus; however, conditioned responses vary in strength and the ease with which they can be conditioned. A person can be mildly fearful or scared to death; a dog can salivate a few drops or copiously. Two conditions that are important in determining the strength and ease of acquiring conditioned responses are the intensity of the unconditioned stimulus and the interval between the conditioned stimulus and the unconditioned stimulus.

UCS Intensity. The more intense the unconditioned stimulus, the stronger will be the conditioned response acquired in its presence. For example, greater conditioned fear results with higher rather than lower intensities of shock (Annau & Kamin, 1961). In one study using human subjects (Campbell, Sanderson, & Laverty, 1964), a drug called Scoline was the UCS. Scoline has a terrifying effect—it paralyzes the skeletal muscles, interrupting breathing for about two minutes. One conditioning trial of a tone CS with a Scoline UCS was sufficient to produce extreme fear to the tone.

A conditioned response is also generally acquired more *quickly* with increases in UCS intensity. For example, salivary conditioning is faster with a UCS of six food pellets than with one pellet (Wagner et al., 1964). As a rule, increasing the intensity of the UCS strengthens the CR and speeds the rate of conditioning for a wide variety of responses and species.

CS-UCS Interval. The time interval between the CS and the UCS is one of the most important factors affecting classical conditioning. The various possible temporal relationships between the CS and UCS are shown in Figure 6–4. Consider, as an analogy, flashing lights at a railroad intersection warning of an approaching train. The lights are the CS, the train the UCS. If the lights begin flashing before the train is in sight and stop flashing when the train arrives, they constitute an effective signal for preventing accidents. This relationship is called *delayed conditioning,* and it is the most effective procedure for acquisition of a CR. In delayed conditioning, the CS comes before the UCS and may stop when the UCS appears, during its occurrence, or after it has stopped. A very interesting phenomenon is associated with delayed conditioning. If the CS appears too long before the UCS, the CR does not occur until the time of the UCS draws closer (Pavlov, 1927). In real life, signals warning of a train often flash well before the train arrives, and people often ignore the signals when they first appear and cross the tracks, sometimes with disastrous results. If warning signals always began a short but adequate time before the train came and ceased when the train arrived, they would be more effective.

In *simultaneous conditioning,* the CS and UCS begin and end together. Not surprisingly, simultaneous conditioning often produces no CR (Smith, Coleman, & Gormezano, 1969). A warning signal for a train that began when the train came and ended when the train left would be of little use.

In *trace conditioning,* the CS begins and ends before the UCS occurs. A warning signal that goes on and off before the train arrives exemplifies trace conditioning, and, as you might imagine, this procedure is less effective than delayed conditioning (Schneiderman, 1966).

In *backward conditioning,* the CS begins after the UCS. Just as a warning signal that comes on after the train has gone by is of little use, backward conditioning is the least adequate procedure for acquisition of a CR. It is not totally ineffective, however (Spetch, Wilkie, & Pinel, 1981). In one experiment, rats that received a single shock followed by presentation of a toy hedgehog subsequently avoided the hedgehog (Keith-Lucas & Guttman, 1975). However, usually backward conditioning does not lead to the devel-

FIGURE 6–4
Temporal Relationships Between the CS and UCS in Classical Conditioning

The onset of a stimulus is represented by the rising vertical line; the stimulus stays on until the line returns to the horizontal. In delayed conditioning, the CS comes before the UCS and overlaps with it. In simultaneous conditioning, the CS and UCS begin and end together. In trace conditioning, the CS begins and ends before the UCS; in backward conditioning, the CS begins and ends after the UCS occurs.

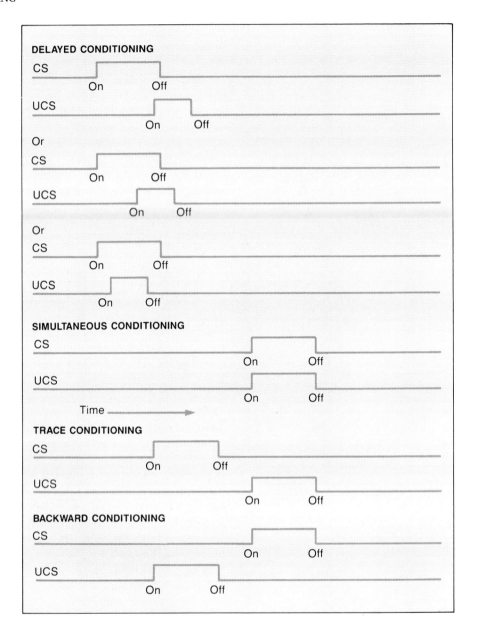

opment of new responses to the CS, and often animals learn to suppress or inhibit their response through backward conditioning (e.g., Maier, Rappaport, & Wheatley, 1976).

The length of the most effective interval between the delivery of the CS and the delivery of the UCS appears to depend on what CR is being conditioned. For example, the optimum interval seems to be a half-second for conditioning an eye-blink response using an airpuff UCS in humans (Ross & Ross, 1971), one to four seconds for conditioning a jaw movement response in rabbits (Gormezano, 1972), and six seconds for heart rate conditioning in rats (Fitzgerald & Martin, 1971). Why the optimum intervals vary with different CRs is not clear.

A popular recent procedure for studying classical conditioning is *taste-aversion learning.* In this procedure animals are given a flavored solution (CS) to drink and are then made ill by injection of a drug or by exposure to radiation (UCS). As a result of feeling sick (UCR), the animals acquire an aversion (CR) for the taste of the drink.

In taste-aversion learning, the interval between CS and UCS can be much longer than with the other classical conditioning techniques. Taste aversions can be formed even if several hours separate the CS and the UCS (Garcia, Ervin, & Koelling, 1966), although learned taste aversion is weaker the longer the interval between the presentation of the CS and the UCS (Best & Barker, 1977). We return to the phenomenon of taste-aversion learning a bit later in the chapter.

EXTINCTION. After a conditioned response is formed, if the unconditioned stimulus is no longer delivered following the conditioned stimulus, the conditioned response will weaken and ultimately disappear. Pavlov called this procedure *extinction.* Extinction is the procedure of presenting the CS without the UCS after the CS and UCS have been paired in conditioning. More recently, the term *extinction* has also been used to refer to the results of such a procedure: the weakening of the CR that occurs when the CS is presented repeatedly without the UCS (see Figure 6–5).

Fear can be eliminated by presenting the feared stimulus (CS) repeatedly without the UCS. *Systematic desensitization* is one such extinction procedure; it can be used, for example, to combat phobias (irrational fears). (Systematic desensitization is explained in more detail in Chapter 15.) It involves gradually exposing people to a series of stimuli (CS) that produce increasing fear. For example, a person with an abnormal fear of flying might (1) be required to sit in a airplane seat in a ground-floor room. When fear of this event had been extinguished, the patient later would sit in a plane (2) with the engines off, then (3) with them on, and finally (4) while the plane taxied. Because no UCS occurs, gradually fear will weaken. The individual would be led gradually through these steps until he or she could sit relaxed in a flying plane. Systematic desensitization is often highly effective. In one experiment (Lazarus, 1961), one month after therapy began, acrophobics—people who fear high places—climbed a fire escape to the third story of a building, proceeded to an eighth-floor roof, and counted the cars below for two minutes.

Why does systematic desensitization work? In part it works because the subject is exposed to the feared object (CS) with no bad consequences (no UCS), an extinction procedure. Fear (CR) weakens as a result. Although other processes also contribute to the effectiveness of systematic desensitization, extinction is an important element in weakening fear (Wilson & Davison, 1971).

SPONTANEOUS RECOVERY. After extinction has eliminated a CR, the CR is not necessarily gone forever. Often following a rest, the next presentation of the CS produces a CR. This increase in strength of the CR after extinction and a period of rest is called *spontaneous recovery.* Whenever extinction procedures are used to modify behavior, the possibility of spontaneous recovery must be taken into account. A conditioned response that appears to have been effectively extinguished may nevertheless reappear after some

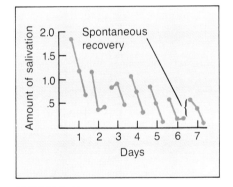

FIGURE 6–5
Extinction and Spontaneous Recovery

In this experiment, pairing of a CS with food conditioned dogs to salivate. The graph shows the amount of saliva secreted in response to the CS when the CS was presented with no UCS (extinction) three times on each of the seven days shown. The drops of saliva secreted decrease progressively with repeated presentations of the CS. More saliva was secreted on the first trial of each day of extinction than on the last trial of the day before—the response recovered overnight (spontaneous recovery).

Source: Wagner et al., 1964.

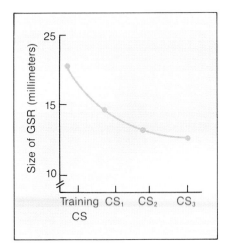

FIGURE 6–6
Stimulus Generalization

The graph shows the size of the galvanic skin response (GSR) for human subjects given tone and shock pairings. Subjects were first trained to give the response to a tone (training CS) when it was paired with an electric shock (UCS). Following training, the subjects were tested with three tones varying in pitch from the training CS. CS_1 was most similar to the training CS, CS_2 less similar, and CS_3 least similar. The GSR occurred with all three test stimuli (stimulus generalization), but the size of the GSR decreased as the stimuli became less similar to the training CS.

Source: Hovland, 1937.

time. Once revived, the response will recur repeatedly, but it will decrease in strength over repeated extinction sessions. Ultimately the spontaneous CR can be reduced to zero (see Figure 6–5).

STIMULUS GENERALIZATION. Another phenomenon discovered and named by Pavlov, *stimulus generalization,* refers to the phenomenon that a conditioned response formed with one conditioned stimulus will occur to other, similar stimuli. A dog will salivate not only to the tone that was paired with food but to other, similar tones. As a consequence of the pairing of the white rat with a loud noise, Albert feared not only the white rat but also a furry, white rabbit (Watson & Rayner, 1920).

Naturally the CR is stronger the *more similar* the test stimulus is to the original CS used in training. The results of a stimulus generalization experiment are shown in Figure 6–6. In this experiment, human subjects were given tone (CS) and shock (UCS) pairings. The CR was a galvanic skin response (GSR). In the test, experimenters sounded various tones and measured the strength of the GSR to each tone. As shown in the figure, the GSR decreased as the difference between the test stimulus and the original CS increased.

Stimulus generalization is clearly adaptive to an organism's survival. If generalization did not exist, a CR would occur only to the exact CS used in conditioning. For example, the fear of a large dog that bit you would not extend to other, similar dogs. On the other hand, overgeneralization can also present a problem: being bitten by a Doberman pinscher should not produce fear of a toy poodle. A third phenomenon, discrimination, also discovered and named by Pavlov, corrects for overgeneralization.

DISCRIMINATION TRAINING. **Discrimination training** consists of randomly intermixing trials in which one CS is followed by a UCS and another is not. If this is done, the CR will ultimately occur only to the CS that precedes the UCS (if the subject can tell the two CSs apart, of course). A discrimination is formed when the subject reacts differently to the two CSs. If you are bitten by a Doberman, you will fear it and similar dogs because of stimulus generalization. But if a large poodle is consistently friendly, ultimately you won't be afraid of it. The poodle does not bite, so your initial fear of the poodle will weaken because of extinction (presenting the CS without the UCS leads to weakening of the CR). In discrimination training one stimulus signals the absence of the UCS. Learning that a stimulus signals the absence of the UCS is called *inhibitory conditioning.* **Conditioned inhibition** refers to the subject's learning to inhibit or hold back responses. This is obviously as important as learning to make responses, and conditioned inhibition has commanded a great deal of experimental attention recently (e.g., Lysle & Fowler, 1985).

HIGHER-ORDER CONDITIONING. In general, any stimulus that elicits a reaction can serve as an unconditioned stimulus. This means that once a CR has been established to a CS, the CS can itself be used as a UCS. In one experiment rats were conditioned to fear a light by the pairing of the light with shock. Then a tone was paired repeatedly with the light, and no shock was given. Subsequently, the rats showed fear to the tone even though the tone had not been paired with shock (Rizley & Rescorla, 1972). This phe-

FIGURE 6–7
Second-Order Conditioning of Fear

Giving an animal a shock (UCS) causes pain (UCR). Consistently pairing a light (CS) with the shock produces fear (CR). If a second CS (tone) is then paired with the first CS, the second CS will eventually produce the CR, too. This phenomenon is higher-order conditioning. In this instance, second-order conditioning has been established because a second CS was conditioned to an original CS.

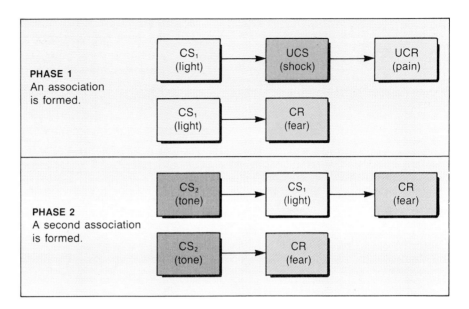

nomenon of using an old CS as a UCS for learning a new association is called *higher-order conditioning,* in this case second-order conditioning (see Figure 6–7). If the experimenter attempted to condition fear to a third stimulus, say a buzzer, by pairing the buzzer with the tone, the researcher would be attempting third-order conditioning. In animals, third-order conditioning is difficult to establish, although second-order conditioning is quite common. (If many repeated trials are given in a second-order conditioning experiment where light is paired with shock and the tone-light sequence means that no shock is given, ultimately the animals will learn that no shock follows the light when the tone is given and the tone will cause them to inhibit responding.)

When Does Classical Conditioning Occur?

Pavlov believed that classical conditioning would occur only if the CS and the UCS appeared in relatively quick succession; in other words, the *contiguity* of CS and UCS was both necessary and sufficient to produce a conditioned response. However, as we mentioned briefly above, an aversion (CR) to a flavored substance (CS) that is followed by a drug or irradiation (UCS) that produces sickness (UCR) can be formed even if several hours intervene between the flavor and the sickness. This shows that contiguity is *not* necessary for classical conditioning to occur. Why are such long delays possible in taste-aversion learning? It may be because there is a biological predisposition on the part of the animal to associate novel flavors with subsequent sickness. So even if a long delay intervenes between ingestion of the flavor and sickness classical conditioning will take place. In general, animals seem to have a biological predisposition to learn associations that have significance in their environments (Rozin & Kalat, 1971). Nausea is more likely to be related to substances that are eaten than to environmental events; thus the flavor-sickness association is formed even though environmental events occur in contiguity with the sickness while the flavor occurred earlier.

In general, classical conditioning proceeds more quickly if the CS and UCS are somehow appropriate to one another. In a well-known experiment demonstrating this connection, Garcia and Koelling (1966) gave different groups of rats saccharin-flavored water to drink while a light and clicker were presented. Thus the CS was a compound of three signals: a taste, a light, and a clicker. For one group this tasty, bright, noisy CS was followed by a shock UCS; for the other group the same CS was followed by nausea induced by poison or radiation. Afterward the rats were tested either with the saccharin taste alone (with no light or clicker), or with the light, the clicker, and unflavored water (no saccharin).

The researchers discovered that the nature of the UCS and UCR determined which components of the CS came to control the CR. The rats that had been sick following presentation of the CS later avoided the saccharin solution, but not the light or noise. An association between taste and sickness seems more appropriate than one between light or clickers and sickness because, as we have said, in the natural environment nausea is more likely to be related to substances that have been eaten than to environmental events like tones or lights. On the other hand, the rats that had been shocked in the presence of the CS later avoided the light and clicker, but not the saccharin. Externally produced pain (such as that from shock) is more likely to be related to external events (such as tones and lights) than to foods. It is possible for rats to connect visual and auditory cues with illness, but these associations are acquired with much more difficulty than those between taste cues and illness (Best, Best, & Henggeler, 1977).

The recent research on taste aversion has been very important theoretically in demonstrating the importance of biological predispositions in learning and also in showing that close contiguity in time between two stimuli is not necessary for them to be associated. Taste-aversion research has also had important practical implications (see "Applying Psychology: Taste Aversions and Cancer Patients").

CONTIGUITY IS NOT SUFFICIENT FOR CLASSICAL CONDITIONING. Consider again the flashing lights at a railroad intersection warning of an approaching train. Imagine that whenever the lights flash, the train arrives shortly thereafter, but on some occasions the train also comes when the lights do not flash. In this case the lights are not a perfectly reliable warning signal. As this example indicates, the pairing of a CS and a UCS may not be the important element in producing a CR; rather, the important factor may be whether the CS can be used to reliably predict the UCS. Recent research has shown this is indeed the case.

In one experiment confirming this relationship (Rescorla, 1968), several groups of rats were given the same number of pairings of a tone with shock, but the groups were given different numbers of shocks without a tone. The results showed that the CR to the tone was weaker in the groups of rats that had received shocks without tones. Even though the groups were given the same number of pairings of the CS and UCS, the strength of the CR differed among groups. Generally, the higher the percentage of UCSs received in the presence of a CS, the stronger the CR will be. This percentage is known as the ***relative validity of the CS,*** an indicator of how reliably the CS predicts the UCS. Another way to phrase this is in terms of *contingency*—

whether the occurrence of a UCS is likely to follow the occurrence of a CS (Rescorla, 1968). If the UCS is more likely to occur when the CS is presented than when there is no CS, then one can predict the occurrence of the UCS from the presence of the CS, and a positive contingency is said to exist between the CS and the UCS. If there is a positive contingency between CS and UCS, a CR will be formed; if there is no relationship between the occurrence of the CS and the UCS (they are randomly related), little or no learning will occur. So even if the CS and UCS are paired sometimes, if the occurrence of the UCS is not contingent on the CS, a CR will not be formed.

The fact that contiguity of two events is not sufficient for them to be associated is also shown by a phenomenon called *blocking*. Imagine that you have already learned that a flashing light warns of a train approaching a railroad intersection. Imagine now that a new signal—a beeping noise—is consistently added to the flashing light to also warn of the train's approach. Surprisingly, research suggests you would not learn about the relationship between the beeping noise and the train. It seems that once a reliable signal is found, learning about additional signals is "blocked" (Kamin, 1969). This work shows clearly that contiguity of two events is not a sufficient condition for them to be associated and for a CR to be formed.

APPLYING PSYCHOLOGY

Taste Aversions and Cancer Patients

Many cancer patients lose considerable weight during their illness. In part this weight loss can be due to lack of appetite, a result of taste aversions formed during the chemotherapy treatment for cancer. Chemotherapy normally produces severe nausea and vomiting in patients; thus foods eaten before these treatments are prime candidates for learned aversions.

Ilene Bernstein (1978, 1985) has done work suggesting an intervention technique that may prevent formation of the aversions and help reduce appetite problems associated with cancer. Her first study (1978) was done with children between the ages of 2 and 16 who were being treated with chemotherapy. The experimental group consumed a novel flavor of ice cream ("Mapletoff") shortly before their scheduled drug treatment, and a control group received drug treatment but no ice cream. A second control group received ice cream but no drug treatment or chemotherapy that did not produce nausea. Two to four weeks later patients were offered a choice between eating the Mapletoff ice cream and playing a game. Only 21% of the experimental group chose the ice cream, compared with 67% and 73%, respectively, in the two control groups. This shows an aversion to the ice cream in the experimental groups as a result of the ice cream–drug treatment association.

It is interesting to note that these aversions were formed in a single trial and that the experimental group ate the ice cream well before they suffered any nausea as a result of the chemotherapy. Also, most of the patients were old enough to understand that the cause of the symptoms was the drug therapy.

Using questionnaires, Bernstein also found aversions to familiar foods as a result of chemotherapy. The most interesting aspect of this part of the experiment was that aversions to familiar foods were formed only in the groups *not* given the novel Mapletoff ice cream. Taste-aversion experiments with animals are consistent in showing that aversions to novel flavors are greater than those to familiar flavors. Reasoning from the findings, Bernstein (1985) suggests that a novel food could be given to patients prior to chemotherapy as a "scapegoat" food. The aversion from the chemotherapy will accrue primarily to the scapegoat flavor, not to familiar foods. This strategy might prevent cancer patients from losing their appetites and further weakening their chances for recovery.

IF NOT CONTIGUITY, WHAT? There are many different explanations for the experiments we have been describing (Gibbon, 1981; Jenkins, Barnes, & Barrera, 1981; Rescorla & Wagner, 1972). Generally, however, the research supports the hypothesis that classical conditioning involves learning the predictive relationship between stimuli. Conditioning of a CR to a CS will occur only if the CS predicts the UCS better than the other stimuli in the situation predict it. This is a contingency view of classical conditioning rather than a contiguity view and is important on practical as well as theoretical grounds. Knowing that a person has experienced CS-UCS pairings tells us nothing about whether a CR will be produced. We need to know if the UCS is more likely to occur in the presence of the CS than its absence. This can explain why people who experience the same CS-UCS pairings may react quite differently depending on their experiences with the UCS independently of the CS.

INSTRUMENTAL CONDITIONING

In classical conditioning, the CS (the tone) and the UCS (the food) are presented to the subject regardless of the subject's behavior. The subject is not *required* to make a response to receive the tone or the food. We now turn to a second major procedure used to study learning which, in contrast to classical conditioning, does require the subject to respond. In *instrumental conditioning,* also called *operant conditioning,* a certain consequence will occur if and only if the subject makes the required response. Animal training exemplifies instrumental conditioning: the animal's response, such as leaping through a hoop, is instrumental in obtaining the reward. Watch closely and you'll often see the trainer reward the animal, usually with food, *after* it performs the tricks.

Thorndike's Puzzle Box

Edward L. Thorndike (1874–1949) was the first person to study instrumental conditioning systematically. In fact, the prototype for all subsequent instrumental conditioning research is the famous puzzle box experiment Thorndike completed as a part of his doctoral dissertation. Thorndike put a hungry cat in a box that had a door with a latch on the inside (see Figure 6–8), and he placed food outside the cage. When put in the box, the cat meowed and scratched at the walls trying to escape. Ultimately it accidentally hit a treadle (a pedal) that operated the latch, escaped, and got the food. The puzzle was thus "solved." Thorndike repeated this procedure a number of times and discovered that the length of time it took the cat to work the treadle decreased steadily. The cat had learned to make a response instrumental to obtaining food.

Today the runway and T-maze are often used to study instrumental learning. The runway is essentially a long wooden box, typically 4–6 feet long and 4–5 inches wide. The animal, usually a rat, is placed in one end (the startbox) and runs to the other, where it finds food or water. Time to traverse the runway is measured, and the time decreases with trials. The T-maze is a startbox and alley with a T shape and two goalboxes, one at each end of the T. In this apparatus, choice as well as running time can be measured. In these situations behavior is measured in discrete trials—the

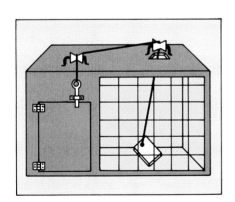

FIGURE 6–8
A Puzzle Box

This puzzle box is similar to those used by Thorndike. To get out of the box the animal must step on the treadle, which is attached to a rope that will open the latch on the door.

FIGURE 6–9
A Rat in a Skinner Box

The most commonly used apparatus for studying operant conditioning is the Skinner box, invented by B. F. Skinner. When the rat presses the lever, a pellet of food is delivered and the rate of responding is measured.

subject is removed from the apparatus and returned to the startbox for each trial.

The Skinner Box and Operant Behavior

The most widely used apparatus for studying instrumental learning and performance today is the *Skinner box*, or *operant conditioning chamber*, invented by B. F. Skinner (b. 1904). The apparatus contains a small lever on one wall that a rat can press (see Figure 6–9) to receive a reward, usually a small pellet of food, which drops into the small cup near the lever. The box can be adapted for different animals; for example, pigeons can peck a small illuminated disk on the wall (see Figure 6–10).

The repeated occurrences of the animal's response such as pressing the lever were recorded in early work with a *cumulative recorder* (see Figure 6–11). Every time the rat presses the lever, the recorder moves a pen one step up on a roll of paper that is moving at a constant speed. When the rat or pigeon does not respond at all, the pen remains where it last stopped and makes a horizontal line as the paper comes out of the machine. We will show you some results recorded with a cumulative recorder although in the modern laboratory data are collected and analyzed by a computer.

The main difference between the Skinner box and apparatus such as the runway or the T-maze is that the Skinner box measures behavior continuously. Skinner invented his box precisely because he wanted laboratory behavior to be representative of all naturally occurring behavior, and behavior outside the laboratory is continuous. To experimentally analyze behavior, however, one must break it into some meaningful units to measure it. Skinner proposed the concept of an operant, a term that denotes a specific unit of behavior. An *operant response* is a behavior that results in or is followed by a particular effect on the environment. For instance, a rat's press-

FIGURE 6–10
A Pigeon in an Operant Conditioning Chamber

The pigeon pecks a small illuminated disk on the wall of the box. The pecking response is reinforced by delivery of grain.

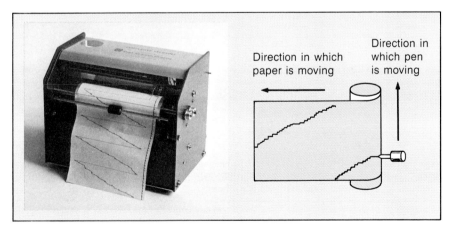

Direction in which paper is moving

Direction in which pen is moving

FIGURE 6–11
A Cumulative Recorder

A cumulative recorder consists of a roll of paper revolving at a constant speed on which a pen moves up a bit when the subject responds. If the subject does not respond at all the pen will not move up, and the line (cumulative record) will be horizontal. The more frequently the subject responds, the more frequently the pen will go up, and the steeper will be the incline of the cumulative record.

ing a lever to obtain food is defined as an operant response, regardless of whether the rat presses the lever with its nose or its paw. Behavior, in other words, is defined in terms of its effects on the environment, according to Skinner.

Behavior and Consequence

Based on his puzzle box experiments, Thorndike (1911) proposed that learning consists of associating a particular response with a particular stimulus. If the effect, or consequence, of the response satisfies the animal, then the strength of the stimulus-response association increases. By pushing the treadle, the cat obtained food, a satisfying effect. By what Thorndike termed the *law of effect,* the cat "learned" to push the treadle to escape the box and obtain the food.

Skinner refined the law of effect into a more general theory of behavior. Behavior can result in *reinforcement* (a positive, or satisfying, outcome) or *punishment* (a negative, or dissatisfying, outcome). Behavior that results in reinforcement is more likely to recur, whereas behavior that results in punishment is less likely to recur.

There are two varieties of reinforcement in Skinner's model: positive reinforcement and negative reinforcement. A *positive reinforcer* is any stimulus or event whose presentation increases the strength of the response that precedes it. In the Thorndike experiment, the food outside the cage acted as a positive reinforcer for the hungry cat. A *negative reinforcer* is any stimulus whose removal increases the likelihood of the preceding response. Suppose, for instance, that the floor of a Skinner box transmits a low voltage shock to the rat inside. When the rat presses the lever the shock stops. The shock in this experiment would be a negative reinforcer because its removal, or termination, increases the likelihood of the rat's pressing the bar. Reinforcers such as food for a hungry animal or removal of shock are referred to as *primary reinforcers.* Primary reinforcers exert their effect without prior association or experience. Not all stimuli, of course, are as intrinsically reinforcing as food. Money, for instance, is a reinforcer because we associate it with such things as food, relaxation, and shelter. Reinforcers that become reinforcers by means of association with primary reinforcers are called *conditioned reinforcers.*

To illustrate the concept of reinforcement a bit more concretely, suppose you are working with a Skinner box and wish to train a rat to push the lever. To do this you will use a method called *shaping by successive approximations.* Using this process you will gradually increase the requirements for delivering a reinforcer until your subject reaches the desired response. The rat will move around the box, at some point in the direction of the lever. As soon as you see it approach you will immediately release a pellet. Because responses followed by reinforcement increase in strength, soon the rat should move toward the lever again. Now the requirement for a reinforcement will be changed to approximate the desired response more closely. Perhaps the rat will have to touch the lever before you release the reinforcer. The process will be continued until the rat is pressing the lever to obtain more pellets. This is the same basic technique used by animal trainers to get whales to jump 15 feet in the air.

✓ Conditions of Reinforcement

The study of how various conditions of reinforcement affect performance is of tremendous theoretical and practical importance. Conditions of reinforcement that maintain behavior are of great concern to parents, teachers, and managers, all of whom want certain behaviors to continue to occur and others to cease.

SIZE AND TIMING OF REINFORCEMENT. Recall that classical conditioning proceeds faster and the CR is stronger when the UCS is more intense; in addition, if the interval between the CS and UCS is too long, no conditioning will occur. Analogously, instrumental conditioning generally is more effective when the reinforcer is larger and the delay between the response and the reinforcer is short (Meltzer & Brahlek, 1968; Renner, 1963; Wagner, 1961).

The effects of both size of reinforcement and delay of reinforcement are not absolute; they are relative to the size of reward and the delay of an expected reward. A reinforcer can affect performance negatively if it is smaller than one the subject previously received (Crespi, 1942). If rats get six food pellets for running an alley on a number of trials and then abruptly are reduced to one pellet, they temporarily run more slowly than a group of animals given one pellet all along (Crespi, 1942; Ehrenfreund, 1971). This is called a **negative contrast effect:** it seems that once experience has created an expectation that the response will produce a large reinforcer, the small reinforcer proves disappointing or frustrating (Amsel, 1958; Bower, 1961). Imagine that for a certain amount of work you usually receive $10; however, on one occasion, you toil as usual but are paid only $5. That $5 will not be particularly reinforcing. On the other hand, imagine you normally work for $1 and receive $5. The same $5 would be highly reinforcing. The point is that the effectiveness of a particular event as a reinforcer is relative to the anticipated outcome.

In instrumental conditioning, behavior that results in reinforcement increases in strength. Traditionally, psychologists believed that autonomic responses, such as heart rate and salivation, were not susceptible to instrumental conditioning. However, one reason that autonomic responses may not normally be affected by instrumental conditioning is that people are not aware of performing autonomic responses because they provide little feedback. You cannot tell when your blood pressure is high or low, or when your stomach creates too much acid. This situation can be changed with *biofeedback* techniques, in which some external cue is provided when an autonomic response is made. If this is done, instrumental conditioning procedures can affect autonomic responses.

The same principle is true for delay of reinforcement. A reinforcer that occurs later than expected is less potent than one that arrives on schedule (McHose & Tauber, 1972).

SCHEDULES OF REINFORCEMENT. What happens if reinforcement does not follow every response? In everyday life, it is rare for every response to be reinforced. A baby may cry for a long time before anyone picks the infant up. An actor doesn't land a part after every audition. A fisherman doesn't catch a fish with every try. When reinforcement occurs for fewer than 100 percent of responses, it is said to be *partial* or *intermittent reinforcement.* Surprisingly, partial or intermittent reinforcement can produce a stronger rate of responding than 100 percent or *continuous reinforcement.* To understand when and how this can happen, we must first describe the ways in which intermittent reinforcement can be given.

Two general ways of delivering intermittent reinforcement, or *intermittent reinforcement schedules,* are interval schedules and ratio schedules. In *interval schedules,* the first response after a certain length of time is reinforced, but any response occurring before that interval has passed is not. If the interval is set or fixed, the schedule is called a *fixed interval schedule.* To illustrate: in the laboratory a rat may be reinforced with a food pellet for the first response after one minute. After the rat responds, the next pellet will be presented following the first response that occurs one additional minute later, and so on. The rat will ultimately pause following each reinforcement and then gradually increase its response rate as time of reinforcement approaches. This pattern of responding is called a *fixed interval scallop* (see Figure 6–12A). A parent who offers a child a weekly allowance after a regular Saturday morning room inspection reinforces cleaning on a fixed interval schedule of reinforcement. The child might clean the room late on Saturday morning in a burst of activity, doing little the rest of the week. To be a true fixed interval schedule the child would have to be reinforced for the first cleaning after a week had passed. Thus even if the child waited until Sunday the allowance should still be given following the room cleaning.

On *variable interval schedules,* the period that precedes reinforcement varies. In the lab, the rat may be reinforced 30, 15, 60, 20, and 90 seconds after its last response, with the value varying randomly. On variable interval schedules, typically a steady low rate of responding occurs (see Figure 6–13). If a parent's room inspection is not predictable, the child might regularly keep the room relatively clean.

On *ratio schedules,* reinforcement is given only after a certain number of responses. On a *fixed ratio schedule,* for example, a specific number of lever presses are necessary to get food. If a worker is paid $1 for every ten baskets of tomatoes picked, the worker is, in effect, on a fixed ratio schedule of reinforcement. Fixed ratio schedules produce a high rate of responding. If the number of responses necessary to elicit reinforcement is high, a slight pause will follow reinforcement (see Figure 6–12B). This is called the fixed-ratio pause. On a *variable ratio schedule,* the number of responses necessary to produce reinforcement changes. This schedule also produces a high rate of responding (see Figure 6–13). A good example of this schedule is playing a slot machine—it pays off after some number of responses, but the number varies.

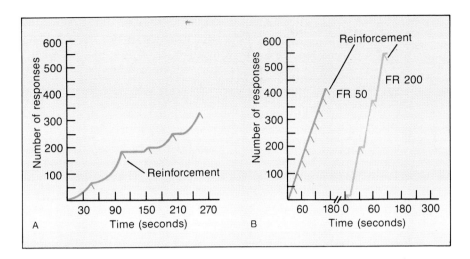

FIGURE 6–12
A Pigeon's Performance on Fixed Schedules of Reinforcement

A. The wavy line shows performance on a one-minute fixed interval schedule. Slash marks indicate when reinforcement was delivered. The response rate is low immediately following the reinforcer (the cumulative record is flat), and the rate of responding increases as the time of reinforcement approaches. This produces a cumulative record with a scallop shape; hence the name fixed interval scallop.

B. Representations of performance on two fixed ratio schedules. On the fixed ratio 50 (FR 50) schedule, the rate of responding is uniformly high; on a fixed ratio 200 (FR 200) schedule, there is a pause following reinforcement (fixed ratio pause).

Source: Reynolds, 1968.

EXTINCTION. After an instrumental response is conditioned, if the reinforcer is no longer delivered, the response will weaken and ultimately disappear. (The same thing happens in classical conditioning, where the conditioned response weakens if the unconditioned stimulus no longer follows the conditioned stimulus.) The procedure of stopping delivery of the reinforcer following conditioning is called *extinction.*

How long responding will continue in extinction depends on the schedule of reinforcement that was used to condition the response. If the response was conditioned using continuous reinforcement, responding ceases rapidly. Imagine a vending machine that no longer works (vending machines are supposed to pay off on a continuous reinforcement schedule). If we put money into one and fail to receive the product, we are unlikely to try again. The response is extinguished in one trial. In contrast, responding will continue in extinction much longer if reinforcement for the response has

FIGURE 6–13
Performance on Variable Schedules

This graph shows the cumulative records of responding of two pigeons. The first pigeon was reinforced on a variable ratio schedule; the second pigeon was reinforced whenever the first pigeon was, regardless of its number of pecks. This means that the second pigeon was reinforced on a variable interval schedule; its reinforcement depended not on its number of pecks, but on how long it took the first bird to complete the number of responses necessary to receive reinforcement. The bird on the variable ratio schedule responded nearly five times as fast as the bird on the variable interval schedule. (Slashes indicate when reinforcement was delivered.)

Source: Reynolds, 1968.

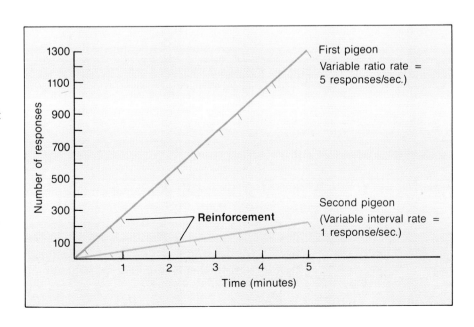

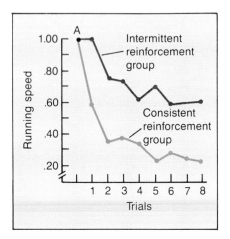

FIGURE 6–14
Resistance to Extinction

Intermittent reinforcement produces greater resistance to extinction than continuous reinforcement. This graph shows running speed in a straight alley runway for two groups of hungry rats. One was reinforced with food on all of its 60 previous runs down the alley (consistent reinforcement); the other was reinforced on only half of those 60 runs. Point A shows the running speed for each group at the end of the 60 runs. On trials 1–8, no reinforcement was given. The group previously given intermittent reinforcement continued to run fast. The group previously given consistent reinforcement stopped running fast very quickly.

Source: Wagner, 1961.

been intermittent. Imagine a broken slot machine that no longer pays off (slot machines pay off on a variable ratio schedule). A player would still insert many coins into a broken slot machine before the response extinguished. In general, variable ratio schedules produce greater *resistance to extinction*—many responses occur even when reinforcement is no longer forthcoming.

Almost any schedule of intermittent or partial reinforcement will produce greater resistance to extinction than continuous reinforcement. This is called the ***partial reinforcement extinction effect.*** Results of one study showing this effect are depicted in Figure 6–14. This phenomenon was surprising when it was first discovered; researchers had assumed that the more reinforcements an animal received, the greater the resistance to extinction. If this is so, why does a subject who received only 30 reinforcements and made 30 additional responses that were not reinforced persist without more reinforcement much longer than a subject who received 60 reinforcements and whose every response was reinforced? There are at least two reasons why intermittent reinforcement induces greater resistance to extinction than continuous reinforcement. One is that a subject trained with intermittent reinforcement has learned that reinforcement follows nonreinforcement. So when extinction begins, the subject trained with intermittent reinforcement continues to expect reinforcement in the face of nonreinforcement (Capaldi, 1967). A second reason is that a subject trained with intermittent reinforcement has learned to persist in the face of the frustration produced by absence of reinforcement, whereas a subject accustomed to consistent reinforcement has not (Amsel, 1958).

Generalization and Discrimination

Just as there are many parallels between the variables that affect classical conditioning and instrumental conditioning, there are many phenomena that the two procedures show in common. Extinction is one example. CRs weaken if the UCS is no longer given following the CS in classical conditioning, and responses weaken when the reinforcer is no longer forthcoming in instrumental conditioning. Two other phenomena that occur in both instrumental conditioning and classical conditioning are stimulus generalization and discrimination.

STIMULUS GENERALIZATION. In the laboratory, a bird trained to peck a red key for grain will peck other keys of similar hues. The less similar the color is to red, the less the bird will peck on those keys. This is termed *stimulus generalization:* a response reinforced in the presence of one stimulus will occur to other, similar stimuli. The same phenomenon, you may remember, occurs in classical conditioning (see page 208). Stimulus generalization in instrumental conditioning is widely used to measure the stimuli that control behavior (Honig & Urcuioli, 1981). If, for example, your classroom walls are repainted another color, your behavior probably will not alter appreciably. But if your teacher does not show up, your behavior will shift drastically—most students will leave the classroom within 15 minutes. The teacher is a more important stimulus controlling classroom behavior than is the room's color.

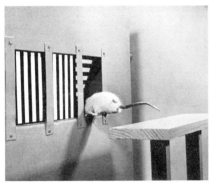

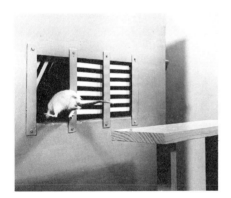

FIGURE 6–15
Picking the Odd Door

In this problem the rat is rewarded for jumping from the platform shown in the foreground to the door that differs from the other two. Food on the other side of the odd door serves as the reinforcer. This is an example of a discrimination procedure where responses are reinforced only if they are made to the correct stimulus.

DISCRIMINATION. Behavior appropriate in one situation is often inappropriate in another. Singing in a choir is expected; singing in class would be disapproved of. Sitting quietly and taking notes in class is proper; sitting quietly and taking notes at a party would be considered rude. Responses are associated with reinforcement only under certain stimulus conditions. In *discrimination learning,* responding in the presence of one stimulus is associated with reinforcement, while responding in the presence of a second stimulus is associated with no reinforcement. The subject will ultimately respond to a greater extent in the presence of the first stimulus than in the presence of the second. This phenomenon also occurs in classical conditioning (see page 208).

Given a choice, the subject in an experiment will choose the stimulus associated with reinforcement over the one associated with nonreinforcement. Using this method it is possible to determine what animals are capable of discriminating. For example, a researcher can use three striped doors, two with horizontal stripes and a third with vertical stripes. Can a rat learn to pick the door that is different? The answer is yes (see Figure 6–15).

Discrimination learning must be considered when attempts are made to modify behavior. The drug addict or alcoholic may avoid narcotics or liquor in therapy situations where punishment follows consumption, but outside of therapy, taking drugs or drinking liquor may still be reinforcing and therefore may continue. The patient has formed a discrimination: in the therapy situation the behavior is punished, while outside the therapy situation the behavior is reinforced. Such problems, however, are not insurmountable. Instrumental learning procedures are widely used successfully to modify behavior.

Negative Reinforcement

Thus far we have considered only positive reinforcement, events whose *onset* increases the strength of the preceding response. But remember that there are events whose *removal* is reinforcing; these are called negative reinforcers. The simplest situation in which to study the effects of negative reinforcement is escape conditioning.

ESCAPE CONDITIONING. In *escape conditioning,* some response terminates an aversive stimulus. Examples in everyday life include removing a pebble from your shoe or turning down the volume on a loud radio. In the laboratory a rat will learn to escape shock by running away from the shock site.

The effects of size and delay in negative reinforcement are the same as for positive reinforcement. Rats learn to escape shock more quickly if they can escape it completely. If they can only reach a place where shock is milder, they learn more slowly (Campbell & Kraeling, 1953). Elimination of shock is a more effective reinforcement than reduction of shock. Performance is also better if shock is reduced immediately rather than after a delay (Fowler & Trapold, 1962; Tarpy & Sawabini, 1974).

ACTIVE AVOIDANCE LEARNING. Negative reinforcement is also studied through *avoidance learning.* In active avoidance learning, some active response can prevent an aversive stimulus. Often escape learning precedes avoidance learning. If class is boring, you may fall asleep (your escape response terminates an aversive stimulus). Following a number of such experiences, you may no longer attend class (your avoidance response prevents the aversive stimulus).

In the laboratory, avoidance learning is often studied in an apparatus called a *shuttle box,* a box with a movable door or barrier in the middle that is controlled by the experimenter (see Figure 6–16). The subject (often a dog) is placed on one side of the door. A light (or other signal) comes on, the door opens, and some time later (say eight seconds), an electric shock is sent through the floor grid on the dog's side of the box. By jumping the barrier to the other side of the box, the dog can escape the shock. After eight seconds of safety, the light comes on again signaling that a shock will be sent to the dog through the second floor's grid. Once again the dog can escape the shock, this time by jumping back to the original side. Trials repeat in this manner. Ultimately the dog will learn to jump when the light comes on. Rather than waiting until shock occurs and leaping away from the shock, the dog has now learned to avoid shock by jumping to the other side when the light comes on. The dog will continue jumping even when the shock is stopped.

Avoidance learning is not well understood. One theory is that it involves two factors (Mowrer, 1947). First, the dog learns the association between the light and the shock by classical conditioning—the light is the CS; the shock is the UCS. This elicits a conditioned response, fear, to the light. So the first factor is learning fear. Then the dog learns that it can escape the CS and fear by jumping to the other side. Thus the second factor is instrumental learning: learning to escape fear by jumping. There are problems with this theory associated with the fact that fear and performance are often not well correlated in an avoidance learning situation (Mineka, 1979). After

FIGURE 6–16
A Shuttle Box

Overhead lights in the shuttle box are used as the signal for a shock. The dog is put in on one side of the box, the light comes on, and later—for example, in eight seconds—shock is delivered to the grid floor. The barrier is dropped when the light comes on. If the dog jumps when the light comes on, it can avoid the shock. Once the dog goes to the other side, the barrier is closed and another trial begins. The light comes on again after a few seconds, signaling that shock will be delivered again in eight seconds. Ultimately the dog learns to avoid shock by shuttling back and forth over the barrier when the light comes on.

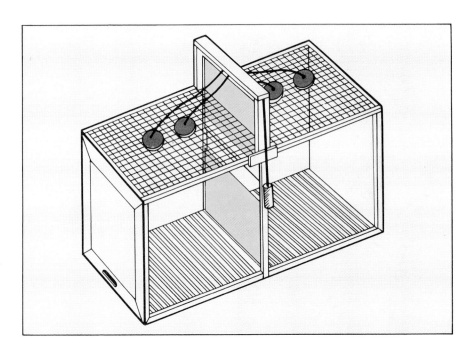

training for a number of trials, the dog does not look or act afraid; it just calmly jumps back and forth when the light comes on. Also, after hundreds of consecutive avoidance responses, the fear CR should gradually extinguish because the CS is being presented with no UCS (no shock). The avoidance response should also extinguish since it is supposedly fueled by fear; however, avoidance responding continues even when fear has weakened.

For these reasons, theorists of avoidance learning more recently have attributed the avoidance response to something other than fear. One of the many ideas proposed is that the dogs have learned they will not be shocked if they jump and that they will be shocked if they fail to jump. In well-learned avoidance, the expectancy of not being shocked for jumping continues to be confirmed, so the animals keep on jumping (Seligman & Johnston, 1973). As long as the animals jump, they cannot learn that no shock will occur if they do not jump. The persistence of some behavior disorders that are based on avoidance learning can be viewed similarly. For example, a person with a compulsion to wash his or her hands repeatedly to avoid illness will not learn that reducing hand washing does not increase disease unless hand washing is reduced for some other reason.

Sometimes avoidance learning is very slow; in other cases it is accomplished quickly. One case where avoidance learning is slow is discussed in "Controversy: Two Views on Helplessness" (page 224). Another time avoidance learning is very slow is when attempts are made to train a rat to press a bar to avoid shock. In contrast, a rat can learn in one or two trials to jump out of a box to avoid shock (Bolles, 1970). We know that rats are capable of pressing bars since they have done so for food in hundreds of experiments. So why do they find it difficult to avoid shock by bar pressing? One idea is that the shocked animals tend to make what have evolved as defense responses for their species, or *species-specific defense responses* (Bolles, 1970). Fleeing and freezing seem to be dominant responses for the rat in defensive situations. Thus it is easy to train a rat to jump out of a box to avoid shock but difficult to train it to stay there and press a bar. Pressing a bar does not allow the rat to flee the fear-producing predicament. If pressing the bar permits the rat to escape, the rat will learn to do so (Crawford & Masterson, 1978).

Punishment

Punishment consists of delivery of an unpleasant or aversive stimulus following a response. Common punishers parents use with children are disapproval, yelling, isolation ("go to your room"), and slapping. The threat of punishment is also often used. What constitutes justified punishment in child rearing, in the criminal justice system, and in the schools is a matter of great concern, especially in contemporary society.

The major effect of punishment is a quick reduction in responding. Note that punishment and negative reinforcement have opposite effects on behavior. Punishment suppresses the preceding response, negative reinforcement strengthens the preceding response.

Because punishment suppresses responding, its effects can be studied only if the response is likely to occur without punishment. Thus in the laboratory the punished response is reinforced first with a positive reinforcer such as food. The basic punishment procedure is to then present an aversive stimulus, such as a brief shock after the specified response. The intensity and immediacy of punishment determine how effectively the preceding response will be suppressed.

PUNISHMENT INTENSITY. The most commonly used punishment in the laboratory is electric shock. The higher the intensity of shock, the more a response is suppressed (Azrin & Holz, 1966). If shock is weak, a response is only mildly suppressed and may recover completely with repeated use of the weak shock punisher. With a high-intensity shock, a response can be suppressed completely for a very long time. If punishment begins with a weak shock that gradually become more intense, there will be much less suppression of behavior with the intense shock (Azrin, Holz, & Hake, 1963). One interpretation of this finding is that subjects learn to persist in the face of the low-intensity punishment and by doing so are less susceptible to the higher intensity. A practical implication of this is that if punishment is to be used, a high-intensity punisher should be used from the beginning.

DELAY OF PUNISHMENT. The delay between response and punishment is extremely important in determining how effectively the punishment will suppress a response. Increasing the interval between the response and the punisher greatly decreases the effectiveness of punishment (Baron, 1965). As parents or lawmakers know, it is often difficult or impossible to deliver punishment immediately following the response. The delay can render punishment ineffective. Punishment must also be used consistently for best results. To be maximally effective, punishment should be applied to every occurrence of the undesired behavior.

Operant conditioning techniques have been used successfully to treat autistic children. These children are difficult to treat by traditional psychotherapy because they refuse to speak or look at the psychotherapist. However, rewarding appropriate responses with candy and games and punishing inappropriate responses have been used successfully to teach socially acceptable behavior to autistic children.

Punishment can also be ineffective if it is associated with reinforcement. When this happens punishment can even *increase* responding. In one laboratory experiment (Azrin & Holz, 1966), key pecks by pigeons brought both food and mild shock. After key pecking had stabilized, the researchers stopped delivering both the food reinforcement and shock punishment, and responding declined. Later, they began the shock punishment again but not the food reinforcement. The key pecking response level *increased* as a result. On the face, this finding is highly paradoxical. Why would punishing the response increase its strength? To answer this puzzle, consider the setup once again. In phase 1 (when both shock punishment and food were given), the punishment apparently became a signal for positive reinforcement. Accordingly, in the final phase the punishment increased responding because it was a cue for food.

In everyday life what is meant as a punishment can function instead as a cue for reinforcement. If parents ignore their children except when they misbehave and then punish them by reprimand for their misbehavior, the reprimand may be ineffective because it is a form of attention. Misbehavior becomes a means of obtaining attention. This may lead the parents to believe punishment doesn't work, but actually they made punishment a signal that they care and are attending and so it is ineffective only because it is a cue for reinforcement.

USE OF PUNISHMENT OUTSIDE THE LABORATORY. There has always been considerable controversy on the use of punishment outside the laboratory. Books on child rearing often disagree: some advise no punishment, some recommend it. There is equal disagreement among social scientists, judges, and the public over whether punishment is an effective way to stifle criminal behavior.

One argument against the use of punishment has been that it simply does not work. It is said that prisons, for example, do not deter criminals. In the laboratory, as we have seen, punishment will effectively suppress responses if it is relatively intense, delivered immediately and consistently after the response, and unassociated with any form of positive reinforcement. Unfortunately, these conditions are often difficult to meet outside the laboratory. Therefore, the effect of punishment varies greatly from situation to situation and from person to person.

A second reservation about the use of punishment is that it produces undesirable side effects such as escape and aggression. It is true that laboratory studies have shown that shock punishers can produce aggression (Ulrich, Hutchinson & Azrin, 1965) and motivate escape (Azrin et al., 1965). When we use punishment in child rearing we do not want children to become aggressive or to run away from home.

A final problem involves the person delivering the punishment. It is a rare parent who can deliver punishment in a detached manner. Usually punishment is associated with being angry or upset, and under these conditions the punishment can be an aggressive act produced by the child's behavior. In extreme cases this can get out of control, producing child abuse.

Because punishment can be effective if used appropriately, it is a useful technique for suppression of undesirable behavior. However, the problems that are associated with the use of punishment are quite real and it is diffi-

CONTROVERSY

Two Views on Helplessness

Feelings of helplessness are a common fact of life. A difficult teacher, a stormy relationship, an uncertain future all contribute at times to the feeling that "nothing I do seems to matter." Helplessness is also characteristic of depression. Interviews with severely depressed patients often reveal their feelings of severe self-doubt and their inability to escape their own personal dilemmas.

Helplessness in the face of unpleasant, seemingly uncontrollable events has been carefully examined in the animal laboratory. The practical ramifications of this research are easy to see. If helplessness, like its opposite, avoidance, is the result of

learned behavior, then there may be ways to enable depression sufferers to break from their cycle of despair and resume constructive lives.

The laboratory study of helplessness began almost by accident. When psychologists were investigating the avoidance behavior of dogs (see page 220), they noticed that escape and avoidance learning became extremely retarded in animals that had been repeatedly shocked without any chance of escaping the shock. Researchers termed the effect **learned helplessness.** A brief demonstration will clarify what the term means.

In one of the first experiments showing the learned helplessness effect, three groups of dogs were placed in three different experimental settings. On the first day of the experiment, members of the first group ("escape" group) received 64 bolts of electric shock to their hind legs while

they were strapped in a harness. The dogs in this group could terminate or escape the shock by pressing a bar with their snouts. The second group ("no escape" group) also received 64 electric shocks to their legs, but they were given no opportunity to short-circuit the painful stimulus. The final control group was harnessed like the other groups but suffered no shocks at all.

The next day dogs from each group were moved to a two-way shuttle box (see Figure 6–16) and were given ten trials in avoidance training. Dogs from the "escape" group and dogs from the control group quickly learned to jump over the shuttle box barrier to avoid shock. Dogs from the "no escape" group, however, performed badly on the trials. After running in frantic circles, the dogs simply lay down and whimpered, appearing helpless to escape the pain (Seligman & Maier, 1967).

---

cult to meet all the conditions necessary for punishment to be effective. Accordingly, punishment should not be used indiscriminately.

COGNITIVE PERSPECTIVES ON LEARNING

Early experimenters studying learning, such as Pavlov (1927) and Thorndike (1911), dealt with learning that was directly reflected in behavior, such as learning to make a response to get food. Perhaps for this reason early theorists attributed all learning to a single process of associating a stimulus or a situation with an appropriate response.

In the study of cognitive processes psychologists are concerned with a much broader view of learning—how animals represent, store, and use information. Although Edward C. Tolman (1932) considered cognitive processes in animals decades ago, as we will discuss below, these concepts were not extensively used in the analysis of animal learning until recently. Research showing that an animal's behavior can be guided by internal representations of its past experiences has changed the nature of learning theories. Today these internal representations are central concepts used in the analysis of learning.

The learned helplessness effect caused a great deal of speculation among researchers. Did the repeated uncontrollable shock in the harnesses prevent the dogs from making new associations when they were placed in the shuttle box? In the research that followed, two general hypotheses attracted the most attention. According to the *learned helplessness hypothesis* (Maier & Seligman, 1976), animals exposed to uncontrollable events indeed learn that these events are uncontrollable. In other words, the dogs in the "no escape" group learned that the delivery of shock is completely unrelated to whatever response the animal might make to avoid it. Such an association has extremely powerful effects. First, it reduces the animal's motivation to escape. Since response has no effect on the pain, what incentive is there to respond? The association also has an effect on how well the

animal learns other associations. Learning that response and shock delivery are unconnected events interferes with later learning that there may be a possible connection between the two. In other words, the inescapable shock produces certain cognitive limitations in the dog.

The second explanation of the dogs' passive suffering is referred to as the *learned inactivity hypotheses* (e.g., Glazer and Weiss, 1976). According to this theory, dogs in the "no escape" group performed poorly in the shuttle box because they had learned to be inactive during their exposure to inescapable shock. The shocks were delivered to the animals in bursts that lasted about 5 seconds. While the shock persisted, the animals naturally responded with sudden movement. When the shock ended, the reflex movements also stopped. From the on-again, off-again pattern of shock

and movement, the animal learned an association between movement and shock and between inactivity and no shock. When placed in the shuttle box, this association persisted.

The controversy between these two views of how helplessness is produced in animals reflects a deeper controversy within the field of learning. The learned inactivity hypothesis is based on a traditional stimulus-response view of learning, a view that limits the study of learning to the range of observable behaviors (see Chapter 1, page 11). The learned helplessness view assumes that learning takes place whether or not it can be observed in behavior because learning includes forming cognitive representations of relationships between events. This cognitive perspective on learning is becoming increasingly important.

Insight

We begin with two examples of cognitive processing, the first where learning is reflected quickly in behavior, the second where it is delayed. Recall from earlier in the chapter Thorndike's cats who were placed repeatedly in a puzzle box and who learned to escape after trial and error. Such learning was reflected immediately in behavior, for each subsequent time the cat was placed in the puzzle box the response (stepping on the treadle) occurred much more rapidly. But now consider a different demonstration, one that was first observed by the Gestalt psychologist Wolfgang Köhler (1927) in his studies of problem solving in chimpanzees. Köhler provided his apes with a somewhat more challenging task than Thorndike gave his cats. The chimps were confined in a large enclosure with various objects strewn about, including boxes and sticks. Köhler tested the chimps' problem-solving abilities by hanging a bunch of bananas out of their reach and observing their attempts to get them.

At first the chimps proceeded in a trial-and-error fashion, like Thorndike's cats: they jumped for the bananas from the ground, leaped at them from nearby objects, and swung and threw sticks at them. But none of these simple strategies worked. Frustrated, the chimps gave up and ignored the

Initally these chimps tried jumping to get the banana and throwing sticks and other objects, but this did not work and the chimps gave up for a while. But then suddenly some of the chimps solved the problem and stacked boxes in order to reach the banana. This study was done by Wolfgang Köhler in 1925 and he named the process producing the sudden solution of a problem *insight*.

bananas, played with something else, or simply sat and rested. After a brief period, however, some of the chimps *suddenly* solved the problem, without any intervening physical effort: they stacked some boxes on top of one another, climbed them, and reached the bananas.

Köhler was naturally impressed by the chimps' sudden ability to solve the problem. To him such behavior reflected the operation of a cognitive process he termed *insight*. While a chimp was engaged in random activity (or no activity at all), it somehow suddenly conceived of the empty crates as related to the problem. With this insight, the solution was easy. This example illustrates how cognitive processes may occur between the time information is presented and the time the information is put to use.

Latent Learning and Cognitive Maps

The distinction between learning and performance was first identified in experimental research by Edward C. Tolman (1886–1959). Work in Tolman's lab in the 1920s and 1930s showed clearly that learning can occur that is not immediately reflected in performance. In one typical experiment (Tolman & Honzik, 1930) three groups of hungry rats were trained in a complex maze that required many turns for the rats to reach the food (see Figure 6–17). Only one trial was given each day. One group, the Rewarded Control Group, was always provided with food at the end of the maze, so these rats gradually learned to run directly to the food box. The rats in the Nonrewarded Control Group were tested with no food in the maze, so they just explored it. Members of the critical Experimental Group, like the Nonrewarded Control Group, were given no food in the maze, but only for the

"We're going to have to split those two up."

© 1982 Punch/Rothco

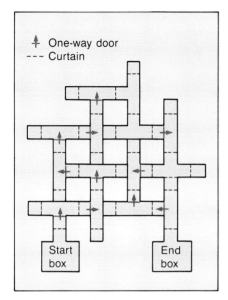

FIGURE 6–17 ▲
Tolman's Maze

In a typical latent learning experiment, food can be placed in the end box. The rat begins in the start box. Learning is measured by the number of errors (wrong turns) made by the rat as it goes through the maze toward the food.

first ten days; on the eleventh day food was put at the end of the maze for their run. The experimenters sought to find out if the Experimental Group would get to the food on day 12 with fewer errors than the control group. Such a result would mean that the rats had learned about the maze during the first ten days when they were unrewarded.

The results of this experiment are shown in Figure 6–18. As you can see, on day 12 the Experimental Group performed as well as the group that had food in the maze all along. Tolman believed this experiment showed that the Experimental Group rats had learned a *cognitive map* of the maze during the first ten days but had no reason to demonstrate or use their knowledge until food was put at the end. This learning is called *latent* or hidden, and experiments like Tolman's are termed ***latent learning*** experiments. These efforts demonstrate the need to distinguish between learning and performance, for animals (or humans) may well have learned something but fail to exhibit this knowledge because they have no occasion to use it. Thus researchers should always be wary about concluding that information was not learned on the basis of a behavior test, for the test may not permit the subject to exhibit all the knowledge he or she has acquired.

FIGURE 6–18 ▼
Latent Learning

The graph shows the number of errors for three groups of rats learning a complex maze. One group (Rewarded Control) was rewarded on every trial with food at the end of the maze. This group's errors decreased over trials. A second group (Nonrewarded Control) did not receive food and its members continued to make many errors (wrong turns) on all trials. The critical Experimental Group received no food until day 11. When food was put at the end of the maze for the Experimental Group on the next day they made as few errors as the group that had been rewarded all along. This shows that the Experimental Group "knew" the path through the maze but had no reason to show this knowledge until food was placed at the end of the maze. This learning was "latent."

Source: Tolman & Honzik, 1930.

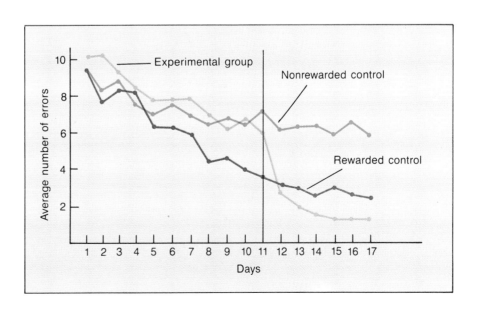

Recent work continues to support Tolman's conclusion that animals form cognitive maps. Menzel (1978), for example, showed this using chimpanzees. In one test an experimenter carried a chimp around a field following a second experimenter, who hid one piece of fruit in each of 18 randomly selected places. The animal was not allowed to do anything except cling to its carrier. Menzel wished to prevent instrumental conditioning, which would occur if the animal approached the food, and primary reinforcement, which would occur if it ate the food. Five control animals were not shown the food locations. Later all the animals were tested to see if they could find the food. The animal that had been shown the food locations ran directly to each piece of hidden food, consumed it, and ran to the next. The control animals, in contrast, found food mainly by searching around the test animal or begging food from the test animal directly. This experiment and others like it show that animals remember the locations of many pieces of food in a field just as if they had a map. Spatial memory (memory for loca-

RESEARCH FRONTIER

Spatial Memory

The study of memory in animals such as rats, pigeons, dogs, and chimpanzees has accelerated in recent years. Part of the reason for this revived interest in the capacity of animals to store information has been the gradual shift in learning theory toward internal, cognitive mechanisms. Memory itself is a fascinating topic, as you will discover in Chapter 7. But measuring the memory of animals poses some unique and interesting problems as well.

One apparatus used to study memory for locations in space, or spatial memory, is the radial maze, in which a number of arms extend from a central platform (see Figure 6–19). In a study by Olton and Samuelson (1976) each arm had food at its end and a rat could enter the arms and get the food in any sequence it wished. Obviously, the best, most efficient strat-

egy in this task is to enter each arm only once, because the food is gone after the first time. To do this, though, the rat must remember which arm it has already entered. Olton and Samuelson found that rats indeed ran down each arm only once in investigating the entire maze. They did not always make their selections in the same order, however, showing that they were not learning a particular chain of responses to obtain food. Nor did they go through successive arms systematically in a clockwise or counterclockwise direction. Were the rats able to remember which arm they had visited? Perhaps they could smell the food and were using odor as a cue to which arm to enter. To see, the researchers allowed rats to remove food from six of the eight radial arms in the usual fashion and then they replaced food in those six arms. If the rats were using the odor of food as a cue, this procedure should lead the rats to choose previously chosen arms. The rats did not do this. They ran directly toward previously unchosen arms. In other studies the maze has been

soaked with aftershave lotion, or surgery has removed the rats' sense of smell, and radial maze performance was not disrupted. These data are convincing eliminations of smell as a possible cue.

Other experiments have sought to see whether other characteristics of the maze arms such as tactile sensations are responsible for the radial arm performance. After entering a few arms of the maze, the rats were confined to the center platform and the researchers shifted the position of each arm, or they rotated the entire maze 45 degrees. Would the rats reenter arms in new locations (as they should if they are remembering locations), or would they enter new arms in old locations (as they should if they are using tactile cues)? All the studies are consistent in showing that the rats are responding on the basis of spatial location and not tactile cues (Olton, Collison, & Werz, 1977; Suzuki, Augerinos, & Black, 1980; for a review see Roberts, 1984). The rats do not reenter a particular location once they have removed food from that location

tions in space) has been studied in the laboratory with the use of the radial maze, as discussed in "Research Frontier: Spatial Memory."

Expectancies

While a cognitive map represents an animal's knowledge of the relationships between events in space, an expectancy represents the animal's knowledge of the relationships between events in time. Thus an *expectancy* is a mental representation that one event will follow another. Tolman (1932) was also the first psychologist to systematically study expectancies in animals. But only recently has the notion of expectancy become central to many other theories of learning (e.g., Dickinson & Mackintosh, 1978; Rescorla, 1978).

Evidence supporting the influences of expectancies on learning has come from a variety of sources. In classical conditioning, as you now know,

FIGURE 6–19
Eight-Arm Radial Maze.

Food is put in each arm and the rat is placed on the center platform. Optimal performance is to enter each arm only once.

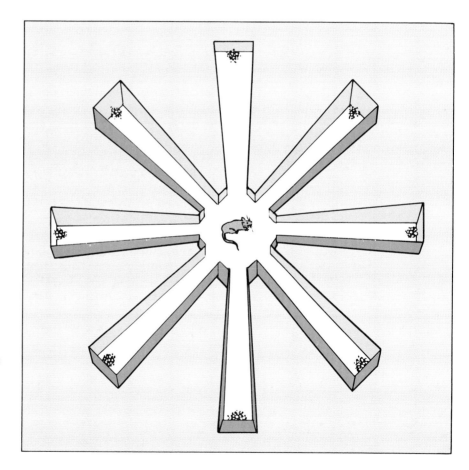

even if a new maze arm is placed there.

The radial maze performance of rats is rather remarkable. If following a series, the rat is placed on the central platform while food is replaced in the empty arms and then tested once more, it again manages not to enter any arms a second time. This means the rat can remember where it had been on its second time through *and* it did not confuse these memories with those from the first time. This work suggests that the memory capacity of rats is much greater than had been supposed. Recent data show that pigeons can perform as well as rats on the radial maze (Roberts & Van Veldhuizen, 1985).

a conditioned stimulus (CS) is paired with an unconditioned stimulus (UCS), and a conditioned response (CR) comes to be elicited by the CS. One hypothesis is that the organism is learning to *expect* the UCS in the presence of the CS, and the CR reflects this expectation. To test this idea, researchers have on many occasions performed experiments that try to surprise the animal or upset its expectations (Dickinson, Hall, & Mackintosh, 1976; Kamin, 1969). This research has shown that animals do indeed form expectancies.

Research involving reward size in instrumental conditioning provides other evidence that animals form expectancies (see page 215). If an animal receives a large reward for a response for a number of trials and then finds the reward reduced, the animal's performance is disrupted. One interpretation is that the animal expected a large reward and the small reward disappoints or frustrates it. In general, theories of learning today assume that animals form internal representations of events in their environment and make associations among those representations. Their behavior is therefore based on how the representations, or expectancies, are formed. Such theories help account for the fact that behavior is often controlled by stimuli not currently present or available. Rather, behavior is often controlled by internal representations of various past experiences.

OBSERVATIONAL LEARNING

As we said at the beginning, people and animals can learn by observing the consequences of others' behavior (Bandura, 1977; Sasvari, 1979). You may learn to say "please" by seeing your brother praised for doing so, or you may learn not to talk in class after seeing another student punished for doing so. Many of our behaviors are learned by observing the behavior of others who are models and by seeing the consequences of the behavior for those models, a process called *observational learning.*

In some of the earliest studies on observational learning, researchers concentrated on fear reduction. Mary Cover Jones (1924) taught children who were afraid of rabbits to be less afraid by having them watch other children playing with rabbits. Masserman (1943) had some success making cats that had been fearful of food less fearful by showing them normal cats eating. Bandura, Grusec, and Menlove (1967) demonstrated that children's fear of dogs could be reduced by exposing them to a model interacting with a dog. In this experiment, the effect of associating dogs with a pleasant situation—a party—was also evaluated. Four groups of children who were afraid of dogs were studied. One group watched a fearless boy play with a dog at a party (model plus positive context); a second group watched the same boy with a dog without the party (model plus neutral context); a third group saw the dog at a party (dog plus positive context); and the final group just attended the party (positive context). Results showed that groups that saw the model became substantially less fearful than the other groups, as later measured by their approach responses to a dog (see Figure 6–20). Whether the model was seen at the party or in a neutral context did not matter; either way, observing the model play with the dog reduced fear. This study shows that the fear associated with the response of approaching dogs (instrumental conditioning) can be weakened purely by observing that the response has safe consequences.

People can learn by observing the consequences of others' behavior. This girl's fear is reduced by seeing others play with the dog safely.

Fear can also be learned by observation. A child need never have been hurt by a dog to be afraid of one. Berger (1962) demonstrated that fear displayed by one person suffices to create it in another. Subjects in his study who saw other people shocked following the onset of a light increased their galvanic skin responses to the light even though they were never shocked. Their responses exemplify classical conditioning by observation.

Bandura and his associates have conducted several experiments showing an increase in aggressive responses by children who watched models beat up an inflated "Bobo" clown (Bandura, Ross, & Ross, 1963). Seeing a

FIGURE 6–20
The Effects of Observational Learning on Children Fearful of Dogs

The number of approach responses to a dog for children who observed a fearless model is greater than for children who did not observe the model, indicating that fear was reduced by observing a fearless model. It did not matter whether the model was observed in a positive context (at a party) or not. Also, observing a dog in a positive context without the fearless model did not reduce fear any more than simply observing the positive context.

Source: Bandura, Grusec & Menlove, 1967.

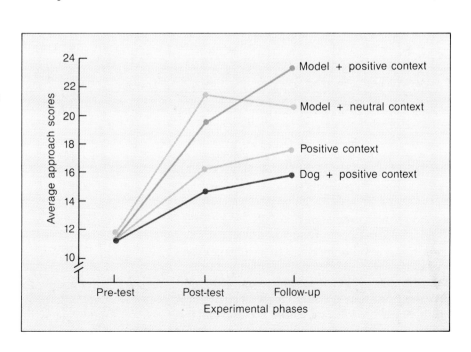

model being reinforced or punished has effects for subjects similar to those of actually receiving reinforcement or punishment. Children who observed a model being reinforced for aggressiveness later behaved more aggressively than those who had seen the model punished (Bandura, 1965). These experiments have obvious implications for the effects on behavior of violence seen on television, an issue discussed in more detail in Chapter 17. Bandura (1977) has described many other examples of observational learning and has given a general theoretical interpretation of these phenomena.

SUMMARY

1. Learning is defined as a relatively permanent change in behavior or knowledge that occurs as a result of experience.

2. There are four basic elements in the procedure of classical conditioning: an *unconditioned stimulus* (UCS), which elicits a response without any previous training; the *unconditioned response* (UCR), the response elicited by the UCS; the *conditioned stimulus* (CS), a neutral stimulus that is paired with the UCS; and the *conditioned response* (CR), the reaction the CS comes to elicit after pairing. Numerous responses can be conditioned by classical conditioning procedures, including many physiological reactions.

3. Classical conditioning is more effective with a strong UCS. Conditioning is also more effective if the CS precedes the UCS than if the CS begins and ends with the UCS (simultaneous conditioning) or if the CS follows the UCS (backward conditioning). Conditioning is usually most effective when the intervals between the presentation of the CS and the UCS are short, although the most effective interval varies depending on the nature of the CR.

4. After pairing the CS and the UCS in classical conditioning, presenting the CS alone will produce weakening of the CR (extinction); a CR will occur to other, similar CSs as well as to the original CS (stimulus generalization); and pairing a second CS with the first CS will produce a CR to the second CS (higher-order conditioning). Simultaneously pairing one CS with a UCS and a different CS with no UCS will produce a CR to the first CS and no CR to the second CS (discrimination).

5. In instrumental, or operant, conditioning a reinforcer is given only if the subject makes the appropriate response. Responses that produce reinforcement will increase in strength. Responses that produce punishment will decrease in strength. A positive reinforcer is one whose presentation increases the strength of the preceding response. A negative reinforcer is one whose *removal* strengthens the preceding response. Reinforcers can be unlearned (primary) or learned (conditioned).

6. Instrumental performance is better with large reinforcers given immediately than with smaller or delayed reinforcers. Schedules of intermittent reinforcement (when fewer than 100 percent of the responses are reinforced) include interval schedules and ratio schedules. In an interval schedule, the first response is reinforced after an interval has passed. On a ratio schedule, an organism must produce some number of responses to obtain reinforcement. Intermittent reinforcement produces greater resistance to extinction than continuous or 100 percent reinforcement.

7. Negative reinforcement procedures include escape learning, in which a response terminates an unpleasant stimulus; and active avoidance learning, in which an active response prevents an unpleasant stimulus.

8. Punishment consists of delivering an unpleasant stimulus following a response. Punishment suppresses the preceding response, but to be effective punishment must be intense, delivered immediately, and not associated with reinforcement.

9. The study of cognitive processes—how animals represent, store, and use information—has changed our understanding of how and when learning occurs. Animals, for example, are capable of forming cognitive maps of a maze and, by using internal representations, demonstrate learning. Animals can also form expectancies, the cognitive representation of how two events relate in time.

10. Animals and people can learn by observing others without showing their acquired knowledge through any overt performance. This demonstrates that learning (what we know) is not always immediately reflected in performance (what we do).

SUGGESTED READINGS

Bower, G. H., & Hilgard, E. R. (1981). *Theories of learning* (5th ed.). Englewood Cliffs, N.J.: Prentice-Hall.

   The latest edition of a classic in the field, this book offers excellent coverage of the theories of learning, including both historical background and recent developments.

Domjan, M., & Burkhard, B. (1982). *The principles of learning and behavior.* Monterey, Calif.: Brooks-Cole.

   A very up-to-date undergraduate text including topics we did not have space to cover here, such as the interaction between classical and instrumental conditioning.

Kalish, H. I. (1981). *From behavioral science to behavior modification.* New York: McGraw-Hill.

   An excellent coverage of current behavior-modification techniques, this book also describes the laboratory work that provided the basis for their development. It makes the connection between basic experimental work and application of this work very clear.

Miller, L. K. (1980). *Principles of everyday behavior analysis.* Monterey, Calif.: Brooks-Cole.

   Describes how to apply principles used in research in the animal laboratory to your everyday life.

Tarpy, R. M. (1982). *Principles of animal learning and motivation.* Glenview, Ill.: Scott, Foresman.

   A good undergraduate text that covers motivation and memory work related to learning in addition to learning research.

7

Remembering and Forgetting

The existence of forgetting has never been proved:
we only know that some things do not come to our
mind when we want them to.

Nietzsche

IN AN ARTICLE ENTITLED "WHAT COLLEGE DID TO ME," HUMORIST Robert Benchley facetiously tried to recall all of the things he had learned from his university education. In four productive years, Benchley felt that he had mastered some thirty-nine items, decreasing from twelve in his freshman year to eight in his senior year. Obviously, Benchley had a fairly typical college education, picking up the esoteric knowledge of both academics and everyday experience, as the following selection reveals:

*Things I Learned—Freshman Year**

1. Charlemagne either died or was born or did something with the Holy Roman Empire in 800.
2. There is a double l in the middle of "parallel."
3. French nouns ending in "aison" are feminine.
4. Almost everything you need to know about a subject is in the encyclopedia.
5. A tasty sandwich can be made by spreading peanut butter on raisin bread.
6. The chances are against filling an inside straight.
7. There is a law in economics called The Law of Diminishing Returns, which means after a certain margin is reached returns begin to diminish. This may not be correctly stated, but there is a law by that name.

Sophomore Year

1. A good imitation of measles rash can be effected by stabbing the forearm with a stiff whiskbroom.
2. You can sleep undetected in a lecture course by resting the head on the hand as if shading the eyes.
3. The ancient Phoenicians were really Jews, and got as far north as England where they operated tin mines.
4. You can get dressed much quicker in the morning if the night before when you are going to bed you take off your trousers and underdrawers at once, leaving the latter inside the former.

Junior Year

1. Pushing your arms back as far as they will go fifty times each day increases your chest measurement.
2. Marcus Aurelius had a son who turned out to be a bad boy.
3. Eight hours of sleep are not necessary.
4. Heraclitus believed fire was the basis of all life.
5. The chances are you will never fill an inside straight.

Senior Year

1. There is as yet no law determining what constitutes trespass in an airplane.
2. Six hours of sleep are not necessary.
3. Bicarbonate of soda taken before retiring makes you feel better the next day.
4. May is the shortest month of the year.

Source: Abridged from "What College Did to Me" in *Inside Benchley* by Robert Benchley. © 1921, 1922, 1925, 1927, 1928, 1942 by Harper & Row, Publishers, Inc. Reprinted by permission of the publisher.

REMEMBERING: AN OVERVIEW

Benchley's humor aside, what indeed do people remember from experience? Why are some things so easily recalled while others seem totally forgotten? Why can't people bring back memories of all that has happened to them?

In answering such questions, it is useful to distinguish among three stages in the memory process: *acquisition, storage,* and *retrieval* (Melton, 1963). To illustrate each stage, consider whether or not you can summon the following fact from memory: what is the capital of Ecuador? If you cannot, at which stage or stages in memory did a breakdown occur? Perhaps you have never heard of Ecuador's capital. In that case, you never acquired the information. *Acquisition* (or encoding) constitutes the first stage in the memory process and applies to initial learning. When a person attends to information, it is likely to be stored at least temporarily and perhaps permanently. *Storage* refers to the changes in the nervous system that allow information to be maintained, however briefly. The change is described as creation of a *memory trace.* If you once knew the capital of Ecuador but cannot recall it now, it may be that the memory trace has faded or decayed. Thus, forgetting can occur because of losses of stored information from memory.

Another possibility is that you forgot the capital because of a retrieval failure. *Retrieval* describes the process of getting at and using information in the memory store. You may have had the fact stored, but you were unable to retrieve it. If all three stages in the memory process—acquisition, storage, and retrieval—were completed, then you would correctly answer: Quito.

Approaches to Memory

Psychologists have two general approaches to the psychology of memory, psychological and physiological. In the psychological approach, to be emphasized in the first part of this chapter, theorists describe the workings of memory abstractly through the use of metaphors similar to those used to describe consciousness (see Chapter 5).

Psychologists typically discuss memory as though it were a container, which is where the idea of storing information in memory comes from (Roediger, 1980). Psychologists have also likened the workings of memory to human record-keeping in which the records—memories—are held in various depositories. They have compared memory to a record player, a tape recorder, a video recorder, a dictionary, a library, and a computer, among other things. For example, the terms *acquisition, storage,* and *retrieval* can be illustrated by analogy to similar processes in a library. If you go to search for a very old title, you may not find the book because the library never bought it (an acquisition problem), because it was so old that it decayed and fell apart (a storage problem), or because it has been misshelved and cannot be located (a retrieval problem). Of course, no one believes that human memory works exactly like the storage of books in a library, but the analogy is helpful. It is interesting to note that as the technology of record-keeping has improved, so have psychologists' theories of memory changed: many

Hermann Ebbinghaus originated the scientific study of human memory.

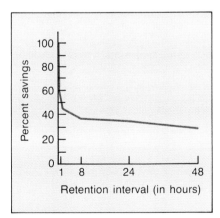

FIGURE 7–1
A Forgetting Curve

Ebbinghaus measured the savings in relearning a list of nonsense syllables after various periods of time had elapsed since original learning. Notice that forgetting is rapid at first and then levels off.

theorists now liken memory functions to the operation of computers (Gentner & Grudin, 1985).

In the physiological approach to memory (see Chapter 2), scientists seek to discover the neural underpinnings of memory. Later in the chapter we discuss the neuropsychology of memory underlying amnesia, severe cases of forgetting caused by damage to the brain.

The First Studies of Memory

Psychologists have been studying memory experimentally for about 100 years. Two primary questions were among the earliest to be addressed by researchers: if a person can no longer recall something, does it mean it is not stored? (Did Benchley's education really afford him only the scant knowledge he reported?) If information is stored, how can scientists measure the traces of memories that cannot be recalled? Hermann Ebbinghaus, whose pioneering studies were published in 1885 in a book titled (in translation) *Memory: A Contribution to Experimental Psychology* (1913), attacked these questions by performing numerous experiments with himself as the only subject. His contributions were truly original, and his experimental results have stood up over time (see Roediger, 1985; Slamecka, 1985). The materials he developed, called *nonsense syllables*, were a series of letters that usually did not form a word. Ebbinghaus often used syllables in which a vowel was sandwiched between two consonants: e.g., ZOK, KEP. Using these items Ebbinghaus hoped to minimize the influence of prior knowledge that would have been present had he relied on words, sentences, or (as he sometimes did), passages of poetry.

Ebbinghaus selected items from 2,300 such syllables and read them aloud at a fixed pace, then covered up the list and tried to recite it from memory. Of course, with a long list this proved impossible on the first attempt, but he could count the number of syllables he recalled correctly. Then he reread the list and repeated the procedure until he got everything right. One way Ebbinghaus measured the difficulty of a list was to count the number of study/test trials (or the amount of time) needed to achieve perfect recitation. This is called a *trials to criterion* measure of memory. For example, it takes more trials to get to the criterion of one perfectly correct performance for long lists than for short lists.

Ebbinghaus tested his memory of a list at various times after he learned it, often by providing himself with the initial syllable as a cue. But sometimes he was unable to recall any of the others. Did this mean that the series he had studied a month earlier, perhaps, was no longer stored in memory? Ebbinghaus developed a method to answer this question. He attempted to *relearn* the list with study/test trials just as he had originally. He then discovered that even when he could not recall any items on a list, he often needed fewer trials to relearn the list and could measure the resultant *savings*. This indicated that the original traces of the experience had not vanished from memory store. This **savings method** is still put to use today (e.g., Nelson, 1985).

One of Ebbinghaus's findings was that the longer the time between learning and relearning a list, the less savings occurred. This relation is expressed in a forgetting curve (see Figure 7–1). Forgetting is quite fast at first, but then it becomes more gradual, a phenomenon confirmed with other testing methods. One explanation is that the initial rapid forgetting reflects loss of information from a relatively short-term memory system, while the more gradual forgetting occurs from a more permanent, long-term system. We will turn now to this idea that there are different types of systems underlying memory.

STORAGE SYSTEMS

The most influential theory proposing a distinction among several different kinds, or types, of memory was articulated by Richard C. Atkinson and Richard M. Shiffrin (1968, 1971). They postulated three different memory storage systems: sensory stores, a short-term store, and a long-term store. *Sensory stores* hold information very briefly after it has reached the sense organs. The *short-term store* holds the data of which people are conscious at any one moment, such as the last few words in this sentence. (This system is sometimes equated with consciousness as it was discussed in Chapter 5.) The *long-term store* holds memories over lengthy periods. (For an overview of Atkinson and Shiffrin's theory, see Figure 7–2).

In the next few pages we will discuss the properties of these systems in more detail. But at the outset note that you should not take literally the idea that there are separate stores located in different places in the brain. The term "stores" is used in an abstract sense to refer to three systems with different properties.

The Sensory Stores

After information has reached the sense organs, it travels through the nervous system to the brain, which interprets it. The information must linger

FIGURE 7–2
Atkinson and Shiffrin's Model of Memory Storage

The relations among the sensory stores, the short-term store, and the long-term store are depicted in this flow chart. There is probably a sensory store for each sense. (*Haptic* refers to the sense of touch.) The short-term store may be thought of as a stage of conscious activity. It controls transfer of information to long-term store as well as retrieval from long-term store. It is also responsible for deciding which response should be made. The long-term store is the permanent memory store.

Source: Atkinson & Shiffrin, 1971.

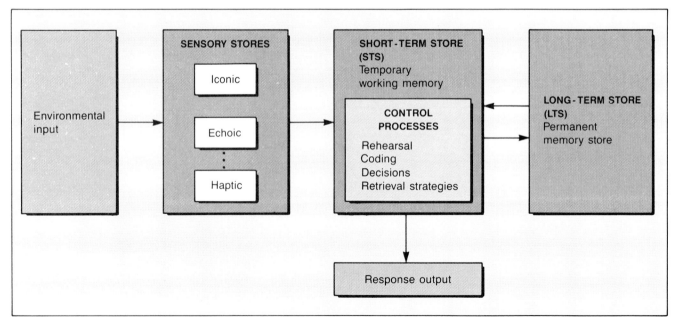

in the nervous system briefly for the brain to have time to interpret it. This "lingering," or persistence, is referred to as sensory storage. Atkinson and Shiffrin assumed that separate storage systems existed for each sense, but only the visual and auditory systems have been studied in any detail. The assumption of sensory stores is similar to the S-system (sensory system) Broadbent (1958) postulated in his theory of attention, discussed in Chapter 5. In fact, the Atkinson and Shiffrin theory is a grandchild of Broadbent's approach in which psychologists try to chart the flow of information through the mind.

You are familiar with the visual sensory storage. When someone takes your picture and uses a flashbulb, you usually see an afterimage of the flash for a few seconds. The technical term for this afterimage is *iconic storage,* the name of the sensory storage associated with vision (Neisser, 1967).

George Sperling (1960) developed a way to study iconic storage. He flashed an array of letters at a person through a device called a *tachistoscope* that controlled quite accurately how long the letters were displayed. Typically, Sperling used three rows of four letters and displayed them for 50 milliseconds, or ¹⁄₂₀ of a second. When he asked subjects to report as many letters as possible from the whole display—a situation referred to as the *whole report* condition—they averaged about 4.5 out of 12 items. This finding replicates the work of many others dating back to the 1880s.

Sperling's contribution was to introduce a *partial report* condition in which, as the name implies, a person was asked to recall only part of the display. Sperling instructed his subjects that if they heard a high-pitched tone just after a display was presented, they should report on the top row; if a medium-pitched tone, the middle row; and if a low-pitched tone, the bottom row. Sperling also varied the point at which a person would hear the tone: it would sound shortly before the display went off, simultaneously with the display going off, or at one of four times after the display went off.

A tachistoscope is a device for presenting visual information for brief periods of time. The person being tested stares down the tube and, in this experiment, pushes a button as quickly as possible when a stimulus is perceived. In Sperling's experiment the subjects reported as many letters as possible from a brief display.

FIGURE 7–3
A Typical Trial in Sperling's Experiment

Subjects fixated on a cross, and then a display of letters was flashed briefly on the screen. A tone sounded at various times to tell the person which row to report. The procedure was designed to answer two questions: (1) whether or not information can be retrieved from an afterimage (icon) of the display; and (2) if so, how quickly the image fades.

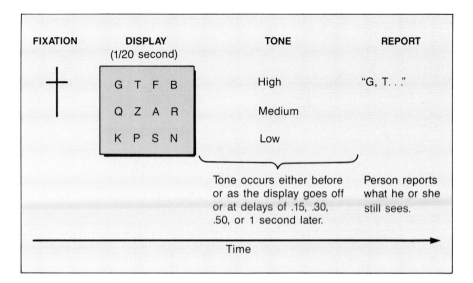

The tone was never delayed more than one second. The procedure for this experiment is illustrated in Figure 7–3.

Sperling found that when people were cued to report one row of a 12-letter display immediately after it went off, they averaged 3.3 letters. Since his subjects never knew which row they would be asked to recall (the rows were randomly cued), Sperling reasoned that they could have reported any of almost 10 letters (3 rows × 3.3 per row) just after the display was turned off. He thought people were reading the letters from an afterimage, the iconic store. If this were so, then the number of letters that could be reported from any row should decrease as the tone was delayed because the afterimage would be expected to fade. As you can see from Figure 7–4, the estimated number of letters the subjects could report decreased rapidly with

FIGURE 7–4
The Results of Sperling's Experiment

The graph shows that the number of letters available decreases with the delay of the signal to report the appropriate row. This outcome indicates the rate at which the image faded from the iconic store under the conditions of Sperling's experiment. After 1 second, the number of letters available has declined to the level of whole report (the right-hand color bar). The left bar indicates the time when the letters are displayed, while the dashed line shows when the letters disappeared from the display.

Source: Sperling, 1960.

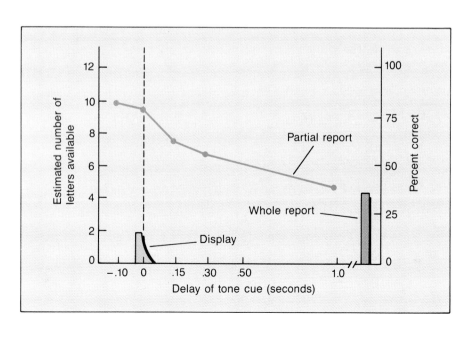

the delay of the tone. Apparently the image was fading from the iconic store. From this and other evidence, it has been estimated that the image in the iconic store typically lasts from a quarter to half a second, if it is not disturbed by other information shown to the eyes. However, as you know from your experience with camera flashes, the duration of an afterimage is determined in part by how strong the visual stimulus is in the first place (Long & Beaton, 1982). Some controversy exists over whether the iconic storage studied by Sperling is more complicated than a simple afterimage (e.g., Kolers, 1983).

The comparable storage system associated with hearing is called *echoic storage,* and it appears to last longer than iconic storage. For example, Darwin, Turvey, and Crowder (1972) used Sperling's partial report technique in a situation where people heard (rather than saw) information. They estimated that the "echo" of the information lasted from two to four seconds, which contrasts sharply with the fraction of a second the icon seems to last. On logical grounds, we might expect auditory information to persist longer in the sensory registers than visual information. Visual information is typically spread out in space—if you scan the environment and miss something, you can look back at it. Auditory information is usually spread out in time. If you miss something, you can't listen back. So it is not surprising that, on adaptive grounds, the auditory afterimage (the echo) should last a bit longer than the visual afterimage (the icon), because sounds have a greater chance of being missed.

The Short-term Store

Sensory storage is activated automatically by information coming in through the senses, and how long information lasts in the system is beyond conscious control. The case is quite different for short-term store, which holds the information of which people are currently aware, such as the last few words heard in conversation. For unrelated verbal material, such as words in a list, it has been estimated that the short-term store may hold from two to five items at a time (Watkins, 1974).

The display in Figure 7–2 illustrates Atkinson and Shiffrin's view of the relations among the various memory stores. Information passes through the sensory stores (or registers) to the short-term store. It can be retained as long as a person wants in the short-term store through *rehearsal,* or repeating it. Various *control processes* can also be used to transfer information from the short-term store to the long-term store. Rehearsal is one such process, but as we will see, other mental activities aid long-term memory much more than simple repetition. The short-term store also serves other functions, such as holding information that has been retrieved from the long-term store. It is sometimes called working memory, since is is responsible for much of the mental work that people do.

The short-term store is assumed to have a fairly small capacity; if information is not rehearsed, it will be lost. One way to find out how rapidly it will vanish is to give people a small amount of information and then prevent them from rehearsing it by requiring them to perform some other task, such as counting backward. After a certain time (the *retention interval*) they will be asked to recall the material. This technique is called the *Brown-Peterson method* after its inventors (J. Brown, 1958; Peterson & Peterson, 1959). The

FIGURE 7–5
A Trial in the Peterson and Peterson Experiment

Subjects were given three letters and then a three-digit number. They were to count backward by threes or fours until they were asked to recall the three letters. This procedure was followed on a number of trials, with the retention interval varying from 3 to 18 seconds. The results are presented in Figure 7–6.

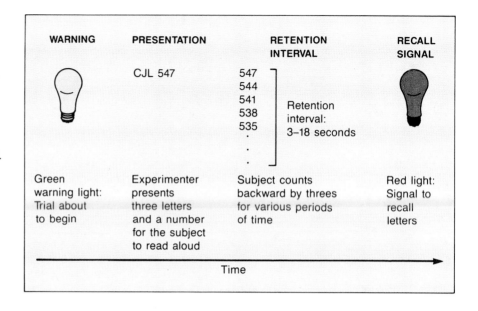

Petersons gave people nonsense syllables composed of consonants (e.g., KXS) to remember and then a number from which they were to count backward by threes. After differing lengths of time, the subjects got a signal to stop counting and to recall the letters. If you were in their experiment, you would have been given the sequence steps in Figure 7–5. Recall was delayed for 3, 6, 9, 12, 15, or 18 seconds by the mental arithmetic. The results of the Peterson and Peterson (1959) study are presented in Figure 7–6. Recall dropped quickly during the 18-second period. This is one piece of evidence that leads to the conclusion that information is kept only briefly in a short-term store if rehearsal is prevented. Muter (1980) has shown even more rapid forgetting in a slightly different situation.

Another technique used to study the short-term store is examination of serial position curves in memory experiments. A *serial position curve* is simply a graph that shows how well pieces of information can be remembered depending on where they were presented in a series (first, second, last, and so on). For example, Bennet Murdock (1962) presented people with lists that contained either 30 or 40 words. After hearing each list, each person's task was simply to recall the words as well as possible in any order. (This task is called *free recall* because no cues or hints are given and people are free to recall the words in any order.) The results are plotted in Figure 7–7. The most striking aspect is the very good recall of the last few words that were presented. This good recall of the last few things heard or seen is called the *recency effect* and is caused by recall from short-term store. Just after they have heard the list, people can recall the last four or five words that are still in short-term memory. (Note that recall of about the last five items is elevated in both the shorter and longer lists.) If recall is delayed even a few seconds by some distractor task (Glanzer & Cunitz, 1966), the strong recency effect vanishes, in agreement with the findings mentioned previously (see Figure 7–6).

Another point of interest in Figure 7–7 is the elevated recall of the first item or two in the list, which is called the ***primacy effect.*** The effect is rather

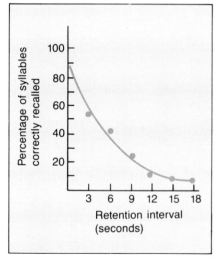

FIGURE 7–6
The Results of the Peterson and Peterson Experiment

Subjects who were prevented from rehearsing three letters rapidly forgot them.

Source: Peterson & Peterson, 1959.

FIGURE 7–7
The Serial Position Curve in Free Recall

After hearing word lists, people recalled them in any order. Recall was best for the last few items (the recency effect), which reflects recall from the short-term store. The better recall for the first few words relative to words in the middle of the list is the primacy effect.

Source: Murdock, 1962.

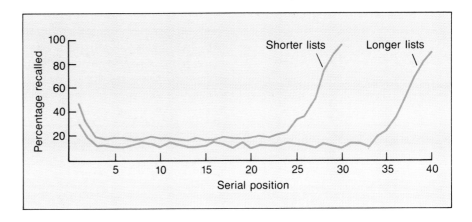

small in the free recall task Murdock used, but in other memory tasks the primacy effect can be quite large and often is even greater than the recency effect. The primacy effect (and recall of items in the middle positions) comes from the long-term memory store, which we consider next.

The Long-term Store

Unlike the short-term store, the long-term store is assumed to have almost unlimited capacity, and forgetting is believed to be quite slow. Three types of representation, referred to as *memory codes,* may be used to store information in long-term memory. Just as a signal may be sent in a code that will have to be deciphered, so people can think of their experiences as represented in memory codes that must be decoded when they remember the information. Three codes that represent information in the long-term store are *linguistic* (verbal), *imaginal,* and *motor.*

One of the most important codes is the **linguistic code.** People are freed from dealing only with concrete objects by being able to recode them in terms of relatively arbitrary symbols—words. There is usually no correspondence between a word, such as *iguana,* and what it stands for, except by the convention of language. If iguanas were called *dogs* and dogs were called *iguanas,* there would be no problem. Children would simply learn one term for the concept rather than another. Although several forms of linguistic coding occur, the most common coding of experience in terms of language is by meaning. Such **semantic coding** can be seen even in simple memory experiments. For example, suppose people study *chair* in a list of words. Later, they take a test on which they must pick out the studied words from among distractor words that were not studied. If *table* is a distractor, people will be more likely to pick it erroneously if the original list had contained *chair* than if it had not (Underwood, 1965). Such false recognitions indicate that people code even isolated words in terms of their meaning. Other evidence supports the idea that semantic coding is important in memory (e.g., Alba & Hasher, 1983).

Imaginal codes, unlike the linguistic codes, are thought to bear some resemblance to the experience they represent. Try to count from memory the number of windows in your house or apartment. Given this task, people usually say they form an image of their dwelling and then mentally walk through it. A good deal of evidence suggests that such an imaginal mode of thought has properties that differ from those of linguistic representation (Kosslyn, 1980; Paivio, 1975). Shepard (1978) has collected the accounts of many famous scientists and artists, who said that such imagery was an important part of their work. For example, the chemist Kekulé hit on the conception of the benzene ring, which revolutionized organic chemistry, by dreaming of a snake that bit its own tail. Telling people to form mental images of verbal material can greatly enhance their memory of it. In "Controversy: Does Photographic Memory Exist?" we consider whether or not

CONTROVERSY

Does Photographic Memory Exist?

To some degree everyone can form images of material when asked to do so. You can easily imagine a dog, a football, or your father's face. But are there people whose capacity for imagery most of us cannot hope to imitate? Do some people have photographic memories? The term *photographic memory* usually implies that a person can remember a scene in photographic detail, but how do we tell if someone has a true photographic memory, or just very good imagery?

The technical term for photographic memory is **eidetic imagery.** Psychologists have long debated its existence. The term sometimes refers to a constellation of abilities that does not necessarily imply the existence of a literal "mental photograph." German investigators in the 1930s reported that 30 percent of schoolchildren possessed eidetic imagery, but later researchers criticized the rather loose criteria used to identify them (Haber & Haber, 1964). Subsequent research reduced the estimate to about 5 percent of those tested (Leask, Haber, & Haber, 1969). But even the more stringent criteria rely on subjective accounts of

what those being tested said they saw. For example, researchers who have reported cases of eidetic imagery—almost always in children—have depended on the children's reports that they still "see" a picture after it has been taken away, with their descriptions of objects from the picture stating the right color and the proper locations (Haber, 1979a).

The real difficulty in confirming this ability lies in finding a more objective test for eidetic memory. If someone has an image something like a photograph, he or she should be able to perform tasks that would be easy with a picture but difficult or impossible to do from memory. For example, suppose you have a friend who claims to have a photographic memory for textbooks. Show your friend a textbook page to be studied and "mentally photographed." Then take away the book and say "Count up eight lines from the bottom of the page and read the letters from the right to the left side of the page." This would be easy with a photograph, but difficult without one.

As the criteria for proving eidetic imagery have become stricter, fewer people have passed the tests. People may say they still have images before their eyes, but when their memories are tested for the imagined scenes, they prove no more accurate than those of control subjects (Haber,

1979a). This leads to the question of whether anyone possesses a true photographic memory. Charles Stromeyer and Joseph Psotka (1970) have reported the case of a woman with seemingly incredible powers of imagery. Describing her as a 23-year-old teacher at Harvard and an artist, they said: "Her eidetic ability is remarkable for she can hallucinate at will a beard on a beardless man, leaves on a barren tree, or a page of poetry in a known foreign language which she can copy from bottom line to the top line as fast as she can write. These visions often obscure a real object. Thus the chin on a beardless man may disappear beneath the hallucinated beard."

In a test given to this woman, a complicated and meaningless random pattern of dots was shown to one eye and, sometime later, a slightly different random pattern to the other eye (see Figure 4–15 on page 138). If you looked at the patterns when they were presented separately, you would see only two meaningless patterns. But if you saw them simultaneously, with one shown to one eye and one to the other, they would fuse, and you would see a figure floating above the pattern, for example, a large *T*. The only way the woman could detect the figure when the two patterns were separated in time was to store an almost

some people have a strong form of imaginal coding known familiarly as photographic memory.

A third type of code is the *motor code,* the means of remembering physical skills, such as how to swim. But could a swimmer give a nonswimmer a description that would allow the latter to jump into the water and swim? Probably not. Knowledge of how to swim is not stored in a verbal code. Similarly, being able to picture swimming mentally probably has little to do with knowledge of how to swim. You likely can imagine or remember a breathtaking exhibition of ice skating even if you have never skated. How

---

FIGURE 7–8
Eidetic Imagery Test

Carefully examine the dot pattern in A for several minutes. Move your gaze about to inspect all details. Do not stare at one point. Shut your eyes and try to recall an image of the pattern. If you can build up a good image, look at B and superimpose your image on the dot pattern. Make the rectangular borders coincide exactly. Do you see any numbers or letters? Each pattern alone is a random array of dots, but when one is superimposed on the other, very clear figures will appear. The answer appears on page 275.

Source: Merritt, 1979.

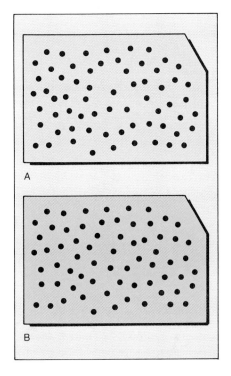

der laboratory conditions. None passed. Merritt concluded that eidetic ability, as indicated by the superimposition of one image on another, seems to be a "none-in-a-million phenomenon."

What are we to make of this research and its implications for eidetic imagery? Is there such a thing? If we define it as the fact that people report they still see things after the objects have been removed from before their eyes, the answer is definitely yes (Haber, 1979a). If we define it as having a literal photograph before the eyes that can be superimposed on another photo or reported with remarkable accuracy, the answer would seem to be no. There are too few demonstrated cases. Some people have suggested that psychologists are wasting their time studying eidetic imagery (Holding, 1979; Lieblich, 1979). Even Ralph Haber, who has done much of the research on the phenomenon, notes that between 1935 and 1965 "eidetic imagery must have ranked only marginally ahead of ESP and well behind hypnosis (to choose at random two other somewhat dicey subjects) as a legitimate topic for research in psychology" (1979b, p. 619). He believes, however, that matters have improved somewhat since 1965, and further work on the topic will be fruitful, so the debate continues.

---

exact image of the first pattern and superimpose it on the second pattern when it was presented later. Stromeyer and Psotka (1970) reported that she could do that even when 24 hours separated the two presentations. Stromeyer and Psotka appear to have designed a foolproof test of a very strong form of eidetic imagery.

But the report of one person may not convince the skeptics. Can other people pass the test? The Stromeyer

and Psotka study received widespread notice in newspapers and magazines some years ago, and many publications included a simpler test for readers. The test involved the two dot patterns presented in Figure 7–8, so you can test yourselves. (Follow the directions in the caption.) Dr. John Merritt (1979) reported that about 30 people of the millions who probably saw the test wrote in with the correct answer, and 15 were then tested unto perform these skills seems to be remembered differently from other knowledge (Fitts & Posner, 1967). It is necessary to learn most motor activities by doing them, and once learned well they seem particularly resistant to forgetting. Even if you have not been swimming or have not ridden a bicycle in years, with a little practice you could probably be as good as you ever were. Although motor codes are important, less is known about their properties than those of verbal and imaginal codes.

RECODING IN MEMORY

What is the best way to remember information for a later test? A clever response might be to tell you *not* to try to remember the information as it is given to you. Let us explain with an example. After the next sentence you will be given 15 numbers to remember. Read them once fairly slowly—aloud, if you prefer—and then close your eyes and try to recall the entire series in order. Here are the numbers: 1 4 9 1 6 2 5 3 6 4 9 6 4 8 1. Now repeat them. How did you do? Most people get only seven or eight after reading the series once. But you will be able to recall the series perfectly, even by the end of the chapter, when you realize the numbers are the squares of 1 through 9. If we had written them thus—1 4 9 16 25 36 49 64 81—you might have hit more easily on the hidden way of remembering the series.

You may think that is a trick for this particular case, but there is a general lesson here: it is often more efficient not to try to remember information just as it is given, but to change it or *recode* it to a form that will make it easier to recall. A difficult memorization task can become easy with an appropriate recoding strategy such as "squares of 1 to 9." We can think of these strategies within the model pictured in Figure 7–2 as control processes that allow information to be transferred from the short-term store (consciousness) to the long-term store.

The concept of *recoding* and its importance were introduced to psychologists by George Miller (1956a), who noted that memory is sometimes about as good for material that conveys a lot of information as for material that conveys little. He examined many experiments and discovered that in most cases people could recall about five to nine things. (Part of the title of his paper was "the magical number 7 ± 2" because the number of items people recalled so often fell within this range in the experiments he reviewed.) Surprisingly, the type of material to be remembered made little difference. For example, people can remember roughly as many words as they can isolated letters. If a group of people were given the letters *g r b s n y f t k w*, they would probably recall about seven of them in order. Similarly, they would remember about seven words from the list *bag, reap, ball, sleep, punk, you, fun, cat, quick*, and *crew*. But there is much more information in the words, since each contains several letters. The word list above recodes the letter list. (Each letter appears in order in the list of words.) If subjects can remember about seven things in order, then it is better to try to recode items having little information into items with more information. As Miller (1956b) put it, "To draw a rather farfetched analogy, it is as if we had to carry all our money in a purse that could contain only seven coins. It doesn't matter to the purse, however, whether these coins are pennies or silver dollars."

Recoding is an important tool in overcoming forgetting since it can be used to package information more economically. We will turn now to a consideration of some types of recoding.

Organization and Verbal Recoding

A great deal of research has been done to examine whether and how people organize information when faced with a memorization task. Much evidence indicates that people generally recode information, although they may not always be aware exactly how they are organizing it. Endel Tulving (1962) asked people to study and recall a list of unrelated words a number of times. Although the words were not associated in any obvious way and their presentation order was scrambled from trial to trial, Tulving discovered that people were building their own organization into the list because they tended to recall the words in the same order from one recall trial to the next. Since this ordering was not built into the list, the subjects must have been building it in themselves. Tulving referred to this type of recoding as *subjective organization,* or the tendency to impose organization on random events to remember them better. Memorization is an active process, with the rememberer taking the information and converting it to a form that can be more easily recalled.

Another way to study the effects of organization on memory is to give people material either with or without a good organizational scheme for recoding and remembering it. In one study (Bower et al., 1969), people were asked to remember 112 words in one of four common categories, among them minerals and animals. The words were presented either in organized fashion or at random. Figure 7–9 shows an example of the organized presentation of the minerals. In the random presentation people were given the same 112 words in tree structures like the one in Figure 7–9, but the words could appear in any of the five structures.

Recall was much greater when the information was organized. After seeing the items once, people who had the organized presentations aver-

FIGURE 7–9
A Tree Structure for Words That Represent Minerals

People given words in an organized structure remember them much better than the same words that are randomly arranged.

Source: Bower et al., 1969.

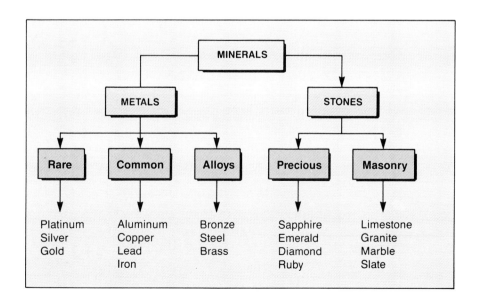

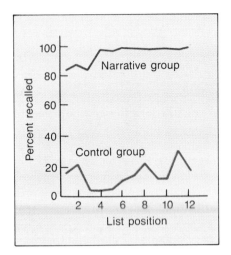

FIGURE 7–10
Story Recoding

One group of people was asked to recall 12 lists of words by constructing a story out of the words (the narrative condition). Another group was asked to recall the same lists, but these people were not given any special instructions (the control condition). The graph shows the percentages of words recalled across the lists for subjects in the two conditions. The people who constructed stories out of the words recalled an average of 94 percent of the list, while the control group averaged only 14 percent. Thus the story recoding led to almost seven times greater recall.

Source: Bower & Clark, 1969.

Gordon Bower, of Stanford University, has conducted important research about the effects of organization, imagery, and mood on memory.

aged 73 words while those who received the random presentation recalled 21. If you can organize information in terms of what you already know, you will remember it much better. This indicates that verbal recoding can prove to be effective for remembering information. Other research has shown that constructing a story (see Figure 7–10) can also be effective. Other techniques, to which we will now turn, depend on a different form of recoding.

Imaginal Recoding

As we have discussed, long-term memory includes imaginal codes as well as verbal codes. Allan Paivio (1969) has proposed that if information is represented in both codes rather than one it should be remembered better. He assumes that if we store two different sorts of information about some experience, the chances improve that one code or the other will support memory later. Much evidence agrees with this ***dual coding theory*** (Paivio, 1986). In one study, people were asked to rate on a scale of 1 to 7 a large number of nouns on how easy it was to form images of what the words referred to (Paivio, Yuille, & Madigan, 1968). Words such as *blood* or *hyena* rated high, at 6 or 7, since they stood for concrete objects. Words like *democracy* and *truth* ranked low because they represented abstract ideas. In a number of studies Paivio (1969) has compared the memorability of high-imagery words and low-imagery words and found that people are usually able to remember high-imagery words better than low-imagery words in many tasks. Why does this happen? According to the dual coding hypothesis, when people read either high- or low-imagery words they activate a verbal code since the items, after all, are words. But high-imagery words will tend to activate both verbal and imaginal codes since they are words and refer to concrete things. So high-imagery words should tend to be represented in two codes rather than one, as are low-imagery words. Thus the high-imagery words ought to be remembered better, as indeed they are. In addition, pictures of objects are better remembered than words naming the objects (e.g., Madigan, 1983). In experiments such as those cited here, people see a long series of pictures or of words representing the same objects and are asked to recall the objects in both cases. Even though subjects who see pictures must write down words, they actually do better than people who see only the words. According to dual code theory, presentation of pictures produces a strong trace in the imagery system but also arouses a verbal code because people label the pictures to recall them later.

In another test of the dual code theory, Gordon Bower (1972) gave people pairs of words (e.g., *thumbtack-pickle*) to remember. When tested, the people received the left-hand members of the pairs (*thumbtack*) and were asked to recall the right-hand members (*pickle*). The subjects learned five lists with 20 pairs in each list. One group was told to imagine the referents of the two words in interaction: a giant thumbtack, for example, being punched into a large pickle. The control group was instructed simply to learn the pairs. Each list was tested immediately after it was presented. The results (see Figure 7–11) illustrate the powerful effect of forming interacting images. The people told to form images recalled almost twice as many words as did the control subjects, who were not given any special instructions.

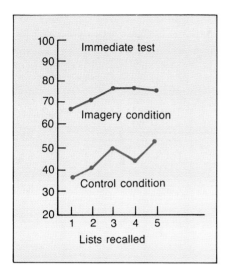

FIGURE 7–11
Effects of Imagery on Memory

In the imagery condition people were told to form interactive images of the objects the words referred to, while in the control condition people were not given any special instruction. People given the imagery instructions recalled the words much better than did people in the control condition.

Source: Bower, 1972.

Levels of Processing

Thus far we have presented verbal and imaginal recoding processes separately. The *levels-of-processing approach* to memory provides a unified view of coding processes. Fergus Craik and Robert Lockhart (1972) have advanced this theory as an alternative to the notion of various memory stores. The core of the idea is that memory is a by-product of perception, which can be considered to progress through stages, as discussed in Chapter 4. For example, when a person reads or hears a word, various mental operations must be performed for the word to be comprehended. First are relatively superficial sensory analyses of the features that make up the word: acoustic features for spoken language and letter features for written language. Then comes analysis of the word's sound or phonological features. Finally, the word must be analyzed for its meaning. Thus the processing of information can be considered to be carried out to different *depths* or *levels* depending on which stages in the perceptual sequence are completed. Craik and Lockhart proposed that memory is a by-product of depth of processing—the greater the depth, the better the memory for the material.

A number of experimental results are consistent with this general proposition, though there are difficulties, too. On the positive side, consider the findings from an experiment by Craik and Tulving (1975). They presented undergraduates with 60 words and had them answer questions about each word. The questions were designed to control the level of processing of the words. For example, people might see the word BEAR on a screen and be asked one of the following three questions: Is it in uppercase letters? Does it rhyme with *chair?* Is it an animal? In each case the person should answer *yes* but in doing so should process the words to different levels. In the first case only superficial characteristics of the letters need be checked; in the second case the sound of the word must be processed; in the third case the meaning must be discerned. The experimenters predicted that when memory is tested, it should be better for words that were processed to deeper levels.

Craik and Tulving's (1975) results confirmed this prediction impressively. They prepared a *recognition test* on which their subjects were given the 60 words about which they had answered questions, along with 120 new words. The subjects were told to try to recognize and circle exactly 60 words that they thought they had worked with before. Chance performance would have been 33 percent (60 out of 180). The results are shown in Figure 7–12 on the next page. Recognition increased from just above chance with superficial processing of the word's appearance to nearly perfect with a deep, semantic level. The only difference among conditions was the very brief mental process that occurred when the person answered the question, so this experiment shows the powerful effect of even rapid encoding (or recoding) operations on memory.

Craik and Tulving's experiment was concerned with the levels of processing in the verbal domain. The same concepts can be applied to the processing of nonverbal materials. Bower and Karlin (1974) showed people pictures and asked them to determine the sex of the person pictured or to judge how much they thought they would like the person. The researchers assumed that judging a person's likability would involve deeper, more semantic processing than judging a person's sex, and indeed the faces were

FIGURE 7–12
Effects of Levels of Processing

People in the experiment saw a word (e.g., BEAR) and answered one of three types of questions about it. "Is it in upper case?" required people to process only superficial (graphemic) features of the word. "Does it rhyme with *chair*?" caused people to use a phonemic or sound-based code to answer the question. "Is it an animal?" forced deep, semantic processing to provide the correct answer. In line with the levels-of-processing ideas, the deeper the level of original processing, the more accurate was recognition on the later test.

Source: Craik & Tulving, 1975.

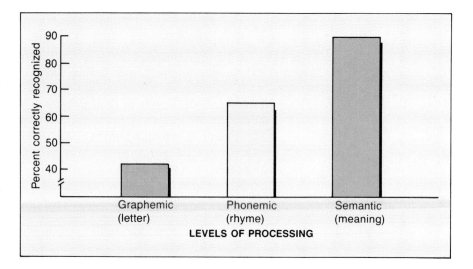

remembered better when judgments of likability were made. Thus the levels-of-processing ideas can be extended beyond the domain of verbal memory.

The levels-of-processing ideas were originally considered an alternative to the multistore view of memory (Craik & Lockhart, 1972). However, those ideas have attracted critics of their own (Baddeley, 1978), and some results are inconsistent with the ideas of a fixed level of processing and of memory improving with depth of processing (Cermak & Craik, 1979). For example, under some testing conditions information that is given "shallow" processing is better remembered than that receiving "deep" processing, as will be discussed later in the chapter (pages 256–257).

The results of research produced by the levels-of-processing approach drive home the importance of coding processes for memory. Other research has also shown that people recall information better when they have been actively involved in generating or constructing it at the time it is presented (Glisky & Rabinowitz, 1985; Slamecka & Graf, 1978). Paris and Lindauer (1976) asked children of different ages to remember sentences describing some actions, such as "The workman dug a hole in the ground." The children's memories were tested in some conditions by giving them a word implied but not used in the sentences, such as *shovel* in this example. Older children could use these cues to improve recall, while younger children (grades 1–3) could not. But when the young children were asked to act out the action described in the sentence during the presentation, they were able to use the implicit cues to aid recall.

Important practical points can be drawn from this research on recoding. When learning new material, you should not just read it but should try to recode it by relating it to your current knowledge. Seek a good organization—for example, by outlining new information. For some material, you might create mental images. When you come to the end of a section of a text, look away and try to summarize the main points. Paraphrasing the information in your own words will help, too. These forms of active recoding will aid your memory. In a later section we elaborate on this advice by discussing memory aids, or mnemonic devices.

DECAY AND INTERFERENCE

To review the major points made thus far, three separate memory stores can be distinguished: sensory, short term, and long term. The recoding techniques just described are the control processes that transfer information from short-term to long-term memory.

Now that we have a coherent model of memory to work with, we are in a better position to answer the two central questions of this chapter: How do we remember? Why do we forget? As we proceed with these questions, we will see how closely related they are.

Since Ebbinghaus derived his forgetting curve, a great deal of research has gone into explaining how experiences fade from memory. Two primary explanations for forgetting are decay and interference. Forgetting from sensory memories occurs in just a few seconds, or even fractions of a second (depending on the sense modality stimulated) through decay of information. *Decay* usually refers to physiological changes in the neural trace of the experience. Forgetting from short-term memory takes place over seconds, while any forgetting from long-term memory occurs over much longer periods—hours, days, weeks. What causes forgetting in these systems? The earliest and simplest answer is that decay of memory traces can explain forgetting from short- and long-term memory, too.

But decay of information from the memory store is not a satisfying explanation (McGeoch, 1932). For one thing, it does not tell us much unless it specifies some mechanism that causes forgetting. What actually decays? Also, decay theory would predict that the longer the interval between learning information and being tested on it, the worse memory should be. In many cases this is true, but when people are given two successive tests they almost always remember some material on the second test that they had forgotten on the first (Tulving, 1967). This is called *reminiscence,* and it is difficult to account for by decay. By the time of the second test, the memory traces should have decayed even more, yet the total number of items recalled is sometimes actually better on the second than on the first test (Erdelyi & Becker, 1974; Payne, 1986).

A third important observation—*interference*—also contradicts decay theory. According to decay theory, the most important determinant of forgetting is the time between learning and being tested on material. However, a number of experiments have shown that factors other than time since learning help determine forgetting.

In a classic experiment of this kind, Jenkins and Dallenbach (1924) taught people a list of nonsense syllables to the criterion of one perfect trial either late at night or early in the morning. Then they tested the subjects either one, two, four, or eight hours later. However, in one condition the people slept during the retention interval, whereas in the other they were awake. The researchers found greater forgetting for the people who had been awake (see Figure 7–13). Even following a constant period of time (say four hours) people recalled less in the awake condition than in the asleep condition. A simple decay theory would predict equal forgetting for the two. This finding suggests that interference from other activities produced additional forgetting in the awake condition.

Findings such as these have led many psychologists to postulate that the primary factor producing forgetting is interference rather than decay.

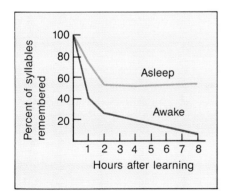

FIGURE 7–13
Forgetting After Sleeping or Staying Awake

The percentage of nonsense syllables subjects remembered decreased faster when they were awake than when they were asleep. Time alone is not the only important factor in forgetting; activities occurring between learning and testing also influence memory.

Source: Jenkins & Dallenbach, 1924.

FIGURE 7–14
Experimental Designs
for Studying Interference

In the retroactive interference design people learn some material (A) and then are tested on it. For the experimental group the test occurs after learning other material (B), which the control group does not learn. The amount of retroactive interference produced by learning B is shown by how much worse the experimental group does on the test of A relative to the control group. In the proactive interference design, people are tested on a set of material (B). In the control condition, B is the only material learned. In the experimental condition, people learn other material (A) before they learn B. The amount of proactive interference is shown by how much worse the experimental group recalls the B material relative to the control group.

RETROACTIVE INTERFERENCE

	Time ⟶			
Experimental group	Learn A	Learn B	Retention interval	Test A
Control group	Learn A	_____	Retention interval	Test A

PROACTIVE INTERFERENCE

Experimental group	Learn A	Learn B	Retention interval	Test B
Control group	_____	Learn B	Retention interval	Test B

Two general classes of interference are *proactive* and *retroactive;* the terms refer to activities occurring before (proactive) and after (retroactive) some event. Try to think back to your most recent psychology lecture. You can probably remember the topic and the main points the instructor made. But if you were asked to recall the same lecture at the end of the term you would likely find that you had forgotten it due to interference from so many other lectures. Interference from lectures before that particular one is proactive, from lectures after it is retroactive. These types of interference have been found for many different kinds of events.

The research designs in Figure 7–14 show how these types of interference are studied in experiments. In the top of Figure 7–14 is the simplest arrangement for studying retroactive interference. In an experimental condition people learn some material (called A here) and later other material (called B). The material in both A and B could be words, pictures, sentences, or stories. After some retention interval the people are tested on A. In the control condition people learn only the A, not the B, material, but are otherwise treated the same. (During the time the experimental group receives the B material, the controls would be given some simple task to prevent them from rehearsing the A material.) Typically, the experimental group performs worse than the control group on the test of the A material. The learning of the B material is said to interfere retroactively with the memory of the A material. For example, imagine that you and a friend had to learn the French equivalents for 100 English words, and then only you had to learn the German translations for the same words. Later, if both you and your friend were tested on the French names, you would probably do worse due to interference from having learned the German words.

For many years psychologists believed that retroactive interference was the primary source of forgetting (McGeoch, 1932); however, in 1957, Benton J. Underwood showed that proactive interference was also important in determining forgetting and that its influence had gone undetected in previous investigations. The experimental design to study proactive interference is shown in the bottom of Figure 7–14. In this case the interest centers on the effect of prior learning on memory for material learned later. By analysis of

FIGURE 7–15
**The Amount of Forgetting
in a 24-hour Period**

In all the studies listed that involved proactive interference, people learned a list perfectly and then were tested on it 24 hours later. What varied was the number of previous lists people had learned before they learned the last, critical list that was tested the next day. There was very little forgetting with few previous lists, and very much with 15 to 20 previous lists. Each point represents a different experiment.

Source: Underwood, 1957.

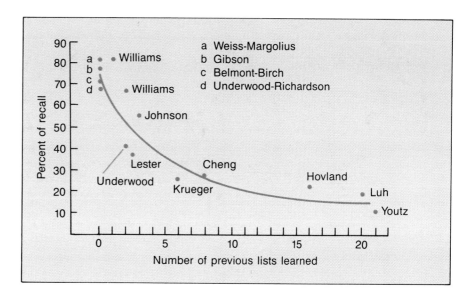

numerous studies, Underwood showed that 15 to 75 percent of material that a subject had learned perfectly might be forgotten over 24 hours, depending on the amount of proactive interference. The results of his analysis are shown in Figure 7–15 and confirm that proactive interference can be quite powerful.

The terms *proactive* and *retroactive interference* describe situations that produce forgetting, but they do not explain why the forgetting occurs. Is interference due to loss of information from storage or from inability to retrieve information? That question is difficult to answer with certainty, but some studies have shown that under appropriate retrieval conditions materials forgotten due to interference can be recovered (Tulving & Psotka, 1971). Thus at least some of the forgetting produced by interference is probably caused by retrieval factors, not loss of information. We turn next to a consideration of how retrieval cues revive dormant memories.

RETRIEVAL PROCESSES

Pause and try to recall all that you can about your year in the fifth grade: the names of your classmates, your teacher, the school layout, things you learned, occurrences. Chances are that you cannot remember very much. Yet this does not mean the experiences are totally forgotten. Suppose you were to return to the school with its familiar sights: the classroom, the small desks, the water fountains three feet off the floor, the auditorium. Seeing them, you would probably be reminded of things you had not thought of in years. The memories were obviously not lost, because with appropriate stimuli or cues you retrieved them.

Remembering depends not only on having information coded or stored in memory but on having an appropriate situation or cue that brings it back into consciousness. This point has been made most forcefully by Endel Tulving (1976, 1982), who argues that "recollection of an event is a joint function of information stored in memory about the event (the trace) and the information available to the rememberer at the time of attempted retrieval (the cue)." Up to this point in the chapter we have been primarily concerned with how information is coded or stored. We will turn now to consider retrieval processes.

Retrieval Cues

In experiments designed to study retrieval processes people are often tested either with or without external cues. In one experiment, the subjects were asked to remember words from common verbal categories such as *professions, weapons,* and *articles of furniture* (Tulving & Pearlstone, 1966). Both the category names and the words in the categories were presented so people heard long lists like "Professions—engineer, lawyer; Weapons—bomb, cannon; Furniture—bed, dresser." They were told they would have to recall only the items in the category, not the category names. In two conditions people heard 48 words from 24 different categories, two words from each category. In the free recall condition people were simply asked to recall the words in any order. They averaged 19 words, which means they forgot about 29. Were the memory traces for these forgotten words lost from the store?

The other condition helps to answer this question. In this condition people were given the category names to serve as retrieval cues for the list words. In this cued recall condition, the subjects averaged 36 words, or almost twice as many as in free recall. Thus we can conclude that the forgetting in the free recall condition was due largely to retrieval difficulties rather than to loss of information from storage.

The logic in this experiment essentially parallels your experience in remembering your fifth-grade year. If you have forgotten occurrences from that time but recover the memories when you get better retrieval cues, then the difficulty was in retrieval and not in the storage phase. In general, the way to separate retrieval from storage factors experimentally is to vary retrieval conditions while holding storage conditions constant. To the extent that recall changes, retrieval factors are involved. But even if retrieval processes are important in reversing forgetting, we can hardly ever rule out the possibility that some forgetting is due to information being lost from the memory store (Loftus & Loftus, 1980). Consider the experiment just described. People recollected about 19 words under free recall and about 36 when they were given retrieval cues. Thus some of the forgetting under free recall was due to retrieval factors. But even with strong retrieval cues, the subjects still missed about 12 out of the 48 words, on the average. Was information about these words lost from memory? Or, if we could give even stronger cues, could these words have been remembered, too? There is no way to answer this question, short of finding the stronger cues. In spite of this, an informal survey by Loftus and Loftus (1980) showed that a wide majority of psychologists polled tended to ascribe forgetting to retrieval failures. This is probably due in part to a number of experiments showing dramatic recoveries of "forgotten" information when strong retrieval cues are provided.

Striking, but controversial, evidence that seems to lead to the conclusion that memories are permanent was produced by a neurosurgeon, Wilder

Penfield (1958). He used local anesthetics while operating on epileptic patients so that they were conscious during surgery. Penfield discovered that when he touched electrodes to parts of the cortex, the patients sometimes responded with intense memories. One woman seemed to relive giving birth to a child; another heard an old song so vividly that she thought someone was playing it in the room.

These reports convinced Penfield that the brain permanently records all experiences and that if he could reactivate the right place, the memory of any occurrence would rush into consciousness. If this were the case, then all forgetting would obviously be due to retrieval failures. However, most scientists today regard Penfield's evidence with caution. For one thing, only a small percentage of his probes during surgery triggered vivid memories (Loftus & Loftus, 1980). More important, some have argued that many of the "memories" were fantasies or hallucinations, like dreams, resulting from the stimulation (Neisser, 1967). It was, of course, difficult to check the accuracy of patients' memories so many years later. Thus Penfield's experiments do not decisively determine whether or not memories are permanent.

Another situation in which people sometimes show dramatic recovery of memories is when they are questioned under hypnosis (see Chapter 5, pages 185–189). As with Penfield's evidence, some have used these cases to argue that all experiences leave a permanent record and that all forgetting is due to an inability to gain access to this information buried deep in the mind. However, careful examination of memories produced under hypnosis points up similar problems to those uncovered in Penfield's experiments. Highly hypnotizable people will often produce much erroneous information when questioned under hypnosis, and they are often unable to distinguish the true facts from the jumble of invented "facts." Thus the evidence from hypnosis also does not permit the conclusion that all memories are permanent.

Whether or not all memories are permanent, we can be sure that we usually have much more information stored about our experiences than we can call into consciousness in a free recall situation, or one in which no cues are given as aids. We turn now to the question of how cues cause people to remember things that are prompted by retrieval.

The Encoding Specificity Hypothesis

Appropriate retrieval cues can often bring back memories that seem completely forgotten. But why? What determines whether or not a retrieval cue will be effective? One idea is that effectiveness depends greatly on a cue's relation to the way information is coded or stored. Memory of an event will be aided to the extent that the information from the cue matches what is in the memory trace. Endel Tulving and Donald Thomson (1973) called this idea the *encoding specificity hypothesis.* When people experience something, they encode (learn and store) specific aspects of it. They may remember the time it happened, the context, and other points. The encoding specificity hypothesis states that a retrieval cue will prove effective to the extent that it helps tap this encoding. You may remember many more experiences when you return to your grade school because the familiar sights and sounds help to re-create the context in which you encoded them. The hypothesis is similar to the concept of stimulus generalization discussed in

Chapter 6; the more similar a stimulus is to the original conditioned stimulus, the greater the response will be to it.

One implication is that people should be able to remember information better if they acquire it and are tested on it in the same context. In an experimental test of this idea, subjects were given 80 words and were asked to recall them the next day in the same or a different context (Smith, Glenberg, & Bjork, 1978). In one context, subjects occupied a large equipment storeroom in the second floor of a building; the experimenter wore jeans and a T-shirt; and the test took place in the morning. The other context was a tastefully decorated and perfumed basement; the experimenter wore a shirt and tie; and the test was administered in the afternoon.

People either learned and were tested on the material in the same context or in different contexts on the two days. Those who learned and were tested in the same context recalled an average of 49 of the 80 words; those tested in a different context averaged only 35 words.

You may want to mention this study to your professor the next time you are asked to take an exam in a room other than your normal classroom. However, there are a couple of facts you should know. First, other studies have shown that poor recall caused by unfamiliar surroundings can be overcome by thinking about the original context (Smith, 1979). Second, unlike recall tests, change of context seems to have no effect on recognition tests. In a recognition test, such as the standard multiple-choice test, people are asked to decide which of several alternatives is correct. The recognition items constitute strong cues, so they may override the influence of external context (Eich, 1980). Indeed, some researchers have failed to find the room context effect even with recall tests (Fernandez & Glenberg, 1985). Thus, the practical effects of testing in different locations may not be too great when the tests themselves provide strong cues.

Another example of compatibility of cues to recall targets comes from research on levels of processing (Morris, Bransford, & Franks, 1977). People in this experiment studied words under conditions designed to produce either rhyme or semantic coding. For example, the word *eagle* might be given with one of the two following frames: "_____ rhymes with *legal*" or "_____ is a large bird." People responded *yes* or *no* to each statement. According to the depth-of-processing view, the second statement should provide for a deeper encoding of the word and therefore better memory of it than the first. This prediction was supported in a standard recognition test: for items with *yes* responses like the two above, people recognized rhyme items 63 percent of the time and semantic items 84 percent of the time, confirming past research (see Figure 7–16).

But the researchers also gave a novel rhyme recognition test. They asked people to recognize words that rhymed with the original study words, such as *beagle*. None of the actual studied words appeared on the test; only words rhyming with them appeared. People performed better on this rhyme test if they had studied words in the rhyme condition (49 percent correct) than in the semantic condition (33 percent). Thus the kind of processing an event receives is not inherently good or bad, but depends on the use to which the knowledge will be put. Morris, Bransford, and Franks (1977) proposed the concept of ***transfer-appropriate processing*** to replace the levels of processing notion: different types of processing will be useful depending on how well they transfer to the test situation. The subjects' performance on

FIGURE 7–16
Transfer Appropriate Processing

People answered questions about words (e.g., *eagle*) under conditions that were designed to make them think about the word's meaning (Is it an animal?) or its sound (Does it rhyme with *legal?*). Later they were given either a standard recognition test in which they had to choose the studied words from a long list of words, or a rhyme recognition test in which they had to identify words that rhymed with the studied words (e.g., *beagle*). The usual levels-of-processing effect was found on the standard recognition test, with semantic processing producing better recognition than rhyme processing. However, on the rhyme recognition test the case was reversed: rhyme encoding produced better performance than semantic encoding. Thus, types of processing are not inherently "deep" or "shallow" but depend on the way the information must be used. Poor processing for one type of test or activity may be good processing for another test.

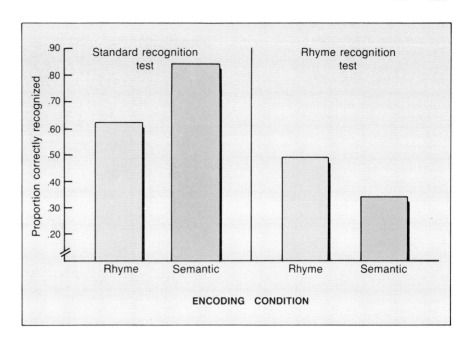

the rhyme recognition test also makes sense in terms of the encoding specificity hypothesis. Retrieval cues in the rhyme test match the rhyme encoding better than the semantic encoding, so performance was better in the rhyme encoding condition.

The lesson psychologists have learned from these examples is that how well some event will be remembered depends on at least two factors: how the event is encoded and how well the cues match the way the information was coded. Even something well represented in memory will not be remembered unless there is appropriate information (cues) in the retrieval environment. Recall from Chapter 1 research on state-dependent retrieval that makes the same point: information learned under the influence of a drug such as alcohol is better remembered if people are tested under the influence of alcohol than if they are tested sober (Eich, 1980). Moods seem to operate the same way: information learned while a person is happy is better retrieved later in a happy than in a sad mood (Bower, 1981).

Distinctiveness as an Aid to Retrieval

Bizarre or unusual events are often easily recalled. Everyone has had some unusual experience that stands out in memory. This phenomenon can also be studied experimentally. If you were asked to remember a three-digit number such as 237, it would prove difficult if the number were placed in the middle of a list of 100 three-digit numbers. But if 237 were put in the middle of 99 words, you would remember it well. This phenomenon is called the *von Restorff effect* after its discoverer (von Restorff, 1933). In general, events that are distinctive relative to others occurring at about the same time are well remembered. This is probably due to the role of retrieval factors. If a subject recalls that there were numbers in a recently studied list,

Most people remember with vivid clarity the explosion of the space shuttle Challenger in 1986. You may also have the flashbulb memory of where you were, who you were talking to, and other personal circumstances surrounding the event. Distinctive events that have high impact are well remembered.

this cue does not help summon 237 from among 99 other numbers. But if there is only one number, then the retrieval cue of "number" proves effective. Michael Watkins (1975) has proposed that a factor limiting the usefulness of retrieval cues is how overloaded they become. The more memories are associated with a specific cue, the poorer will be the recall of any one memory. Distinctive events may be memorable by reducing this *cue overload*.

This element of distinctiveness aiding memory can also be seen in personal experiences. People often can clearly remember ordinary occurrences that coincided with an important event. Brown and Kulik (1977) refer to these recollections as *flashbulb memories* since all the details stand out against the event. They asked people to recall what they were doing and thinking when they heard that President John F. Kennedy had been shot. Many readers of this book may have been too young to have a "flashbulb memory" of that event, but Brown and Kulik reported that older people could recount "with almost perceptual clarity" where they were, what they were doing, who told them, and what they thought. People also recalled all kinds of trivia related to that day. Of course, these memories cannot be checked directly, but assuming that they are generally accurate, they exemplify how unique events can be easily retrieved.

You may find a similar, if lesser, phenomenon by trying to recall where you were and what you did and thought last New Year's Eve. You can probably remember your activities quite well, at least relative to what you did December 1 or February 1. Events that occur on distinctive or surprising occasions are usually well remembered.

Retrieval from Semantic Memory

All of the memory situations we have talked about so far have related to information people have been given to learn, whether it consisted of words, sentences, stories, or pictures. Such situations constitute *episodic memory* because the subjects were tested on events or episodes they experienced. Episodic memories are those that depend on retrieving particular times and places in one's life. But there seems to be another kind of memory, known as *semantic memory* (Tulving, 1972, 1985), which refers to general knowledge. Comprehension of the meaning of *giraffe*, knowledge of what H_2O stands for, or of the names of the 50 states and thousands of other facts represent examples of retrieval from semantic memory. All these items are represented more or less permanently in people's memories. Most people have forgotten, no doubt, just when they learned these facts, so their recall does not depend on retrieving some specific episode from the past. Yet people summon up thousands of bits of information with amazing speed. (Semantic coding, described earlier, occurs when a new event arouses information in semantic memory.) In studies of semantic memory, psychologists often measure retrieval speed by having people respond to statements as rapidly as possible by pressing one button if the answer is true and another if it is false. Consider how fast you could respond to the following:

1. An oak has acorns.
2. Coca-Cola is blue.
3. A canary has wings.
4. Books contain words.
5. A dogwood is lazy.
6. A fish is a mineral.

Experiments show that subjects respond to such statements in a bit over one second, on the average, and much of that second is taken up in reading the question and pushing the button. Considering that humans can retrieve thousands of facts at that speed, we can gain some appreciation of how marvelous a device the brain must be for holding and retrieving information. Although computers perform some simple mental functions more rapidly and efficiently than humans can, many other aspects of human memory are unchallenged by computer memories and are likely to remain so (Estes, 1980).

Psychologists are just beginning to ask many fundamental questions about semantic memory. How must knowledge be stored and represented to be retrieved so fast? One popular theory sees knowledge in terms of large networks of associations (Anderson, 1976; Collins & Loftus, 1975). An example of an associative network for a fragment of knowledge (see Figure 7–17) comes from a theory of Allan Collins and Elizabeth Loftus (1975). Particular bits of memory are considered to be distributed in some conceptual space, with related concepts linked by associations. The length of a line between two concepts is intended to represent the strength of the association, with shorter lines indicating stronger associations. A number of important theories of memory are based on the concept of associative networks in memory, although not all have the same features as the one pictured in Figure 7–17 (Anderson, 1976; Raaijmakers & Shiffrin, 1981).

Collins and Loftus (1975) theorize that there is *spreading activation* among related concepts. They assume that, for example, if someone reads the word *car*, this concept is activated in semantic memory and the energy or activation spreads to related concepts, such as *truck* or *ambulance*. If this is so, it should be easier to activate these other concepts fully because they are already partly activated. Such spreading activation would prove useful

FIGURE 7–17
A Possible Representation of Concepts in a Fragment of Semantic Memory

The ellipses represent concepts; the lines represent associations. The strength of relation between two concepts is represented by the shortness of the line associating them. The assumption that memory can be represented as a gigantic network of associations is a central part of many theories of memory.

Source: Collins & Loftus, 1975.

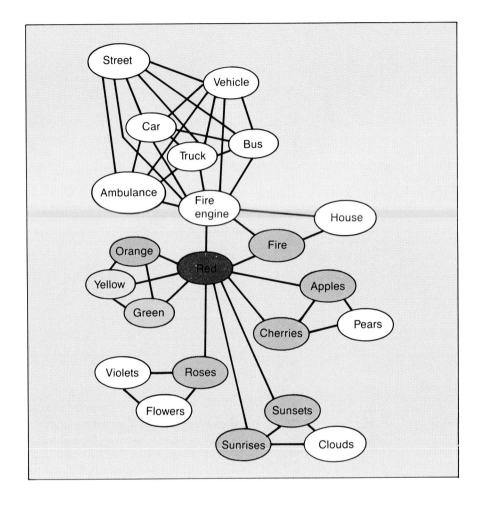

in reading because reading about one concept would make it easier to read about related topics.

Evidence for spreading activation comes from several different experiments. One is called the ***lexical decision task.*** In this test people are shown groups of letters at a relatively rapid rate and their task is to decide as quickly as possible whether or not each group forms a word. The items typically appear on a computer screen and subjects signal their response (*yes* or *no*) by hitting one of two keys. You can practice this task on the following list of stimuli. Rest your index fingers next to each other on your desk and move your right index finger down a bit if the item is a word and your left index finger if it is a nonword. Try to respond as rapidly as possible as you read each item.

□ groph
□ door
□ flummel
□ nurse
□ doctor
□ inglar
□ wooden

Many experiments have shown that people can make lexical decisions in well under a second. As mentioned before, part of this time is spent in perceiving the letters and part in making the response. We are capable of looking up words in our "mental dictionaries" at extraordinary rates, as we do in rapid reading.

The evidence for spreading activation comes from experiments in which two related words appear in a sequence, as was the case for *nurse* and *doctor* in the practice list. Many experiments have shown the *semantic priming effect* described in Chapter 5: people are faster to respond to the second word *(doctor)* if it is preceded by a related word *(nurse)* rather than by either an unrelated word *(chair)* or simply a neutral stimulus (XXX) (Meyer & Schvaneveldt, 1971; Neely, 1977). When the first word activates its node in the semantic memory network, the excitation spreads quickly to nearby nodes. The phenomenon of semantic priming fits well with the idea of spreading activation in the semantic network theories.

Priming effects do not occur in all situations, however (Roediger & Neely, 1982). Consider the tip-of-the-tongue state: you feel sure you know some fact, but you are temporarily incapable of producing it. This maddening mental block often occurs while playing Trivial Pursuit and similar games. Brown and McNeill (1966) attempted to study this phenomenon by giving students definitions of relatively rare words. For example, what is a "waxy, intestinal secretion produced by sperm whales and used in making perfumes"? Students received many such definitions, and most students either answered correctly or said they did not know the word. (The word in this example is *ambergris*, by the way.) On some rare occasions (about 5 percent overall) students said they were catapulted into a tip-of-the-tongue state. They were sure they knew the word but could not produce it. While in this helpless condition, students were asked to name the first letter of the word, estimate the number of syllables in it, and produce words that were related to it. Brown and McNeill discovered that their subjects could name the first letter and estimate the number of syllables far better than chance would predict. In particular, the words subjects produced while in the tip-of-the-tongue state were closely related in sound and meaning to the missing word after which they were groping.

The tip-of-the-tongue phenomenon seems to represent a failure of semantic priming and to contradict the spreading activation theory. Why didn't production of all the related words activate the missing word? One explanation is that closely related memories will sometimes compete at retrieval (Brown, 1981). If you are trying to recall a word and other related words have just been activated, the others block retrieval of the correct one. The mind is "clogged" by the related, but unwanted, information. This sort of retrieval road jam usually occurs in tests of recall. It is much less likely in tests of word identification (the lexical decision task) or word naming (Blaxton & Neely, 1983).

MNEMONIC DEVICES

Mnemonic (ni-**mon**-ik) *devices* are special techniques to improve the memory. We have described a number of factors that aid memory, and the specific techniques we will now consider combine several of these elements.

Some mnemonic techniques date back thousands of years, but the principles underlying their success have been uncovered only recently (Bellezza, 1981). Generally, all mnemonic devices employ two ingredients. First, they involve a good recoding technique so that a strong memory trace is constructed. Second, they provide effective retrieval cues.

The Link Method

The simplest mnemonic device is the *link method.* Suppose you had to remember a grocery list that included bread, eggs, bananas, and milk, among other items. If you wanted to remember them by the link method, you would try to recode each item into a mental image and link it to the others in some way. You might imagine a large loaf of bread with someone smashing eggs onto it. You might then imagine the eggs running off the bread and landing on a bunch of bananas, which are stuffed inside a milk carton, and so on. The idea is to convert each item into an image and then link it to the next one. Often the advice is given to make the images unusual or bizarre, but it is probably more important to make sure there are strong links between images. Bizarre images seem most effective if used for only a few of the things to be remembered (McDaniel and Einstein, 1986).

The linking images are designed to provide a good recoding of the information you want to remember and a good retrieval cue for each item on the list. When you remember one item, it should serve as a cue for the next. Although the link method is good, it has one problem: if one item is forgotten, it may be difficult to break back into the chain of images to recall the remaining items. At the least, you would probably lose track of the right order. This may not seem too important with a grocery list, but it could be important if you were trying to remember the points in a speech. The next two devices provide better systems for remembering things in order.

The Method of Loci

The *loci,* or *location, method* is one of the oldest memory techniques. It is attributed to Simonides, an early Greek who was called away from a large banquet to receive a message. In his absence, the roof of the hall collapsed, killing all who were inside. The dead were mutilated beyond recognition, but Simonides identified their bodies by where they had been sitting. He capitalized on this observation that locations can serve as effective cues and developed his technique for more general use.

To use the method of loci you first need to identify a set of places which occur in some natural order and which you know well. For example, you might choose 20 different locations in your house or apartment, or on a familiar path around your campus. Any number will do, depending on how many items you want to be able to remember. To use the locations in remembering a series, convert each item you want to remember to an image and store it in a location. So, for the grocery list, you would form an image of a loaf of bread and put it in the first location, eggs in the second, and so on (see Figure 7–18). The locations serve as excellent retrieval cues since you know them perfectly. The task then becomes one of "looking" in each place to "see" what is stored there (Bower, 1972).

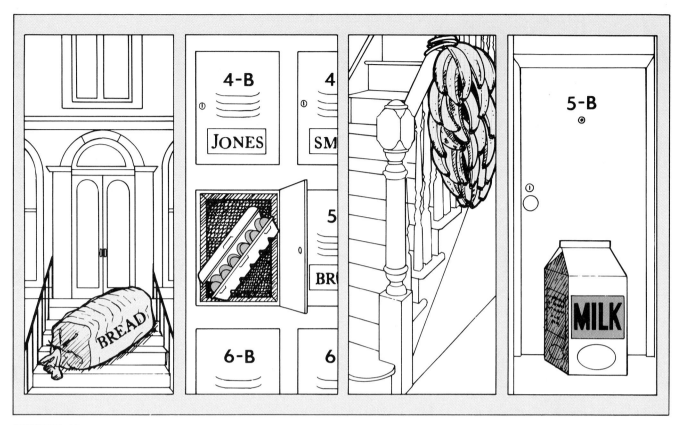

FIGURE 7–18
The Method of Loci

In using the loci technique people form mental pictures of items in familiar locations. Since the locations form a natural sequence, the order of events can be easily remembered.

Roman teachers of rhetoric, the art of public speaking, told students to use the technique for long speeches. Each idea was to be converted to an image and stored in a specific location. Studies have shown that the method of loci surpasses the link method by allowing people to keep track of the order of information better, since recall of an item does not depend on recollection of the previous item. The same is true of the peg method, discussed next.

The Peg Method

The *peg method* is based on the same principles as the method of loci, except that you memorize a set of pegs rather than a set of locations as cues. There are many peg systems, but in one of the easiest and most popular, you learn a set of objects that rhyme, more or less, with the numbers 1 to 20 (see Table 7–1). Each item to be remembered is converted to an image and then imagined to be interacting with the peg word. So to remember the grocery list, you would imagine a gun (the first peg) shooting a loaf of bread, a shoe smashing an egg, a big bunch of bananas hanging off a tree. Since the pegs have been learned perfectly, they can function as effective retrieval cues. The peg method allows you to recall particular items directly (e.g., what is number 13?) without going through the entire series, as you would probably have to do with the link and loci methods.

**TABLE 7–1
The Rhyme System of Pegs**

One is a gun
Two is a shoe
Three is a tree
Four is a door
Five is knives
Six is sticks
Seven is an oven
Eight is a plate
Nine is wine
Ten is a hen
Eleven is "penny-one," hotdog bun
Twelve is "penny-two," airplane glue
Thirteen is "penny-three," bumble bee
Fourteen is "penny-four," grocery store
Fifteen is "penny-five," big bee hive
Sixteen is "penny-six," magic tricks
Seventeen is "penny-seven," go to heaven
Eighteen is "penny-eight," golden gate
Nineteen is "penny-nine," ball of twine
Twenty is "penny-ten," ballpoint pen

These rhymes associate an object, or *peg word*, with the numbers from 1 to 20. Once you have learned the rhymes, you can remember a series of items (or points in a speech) by converting each item into an image and imagining it in interaction with each peg word. Thus, each peg allows you to "hang" a memory on it, providing an effective way of remembering things in order.

These mnemonic techniques, and others like them, are the bases for the remarkable memory feats people sometimes perform on television. Those demonstrations are not due simply to inherently "good memories" but to well-trained memories. The performers know how to recode information using mnemonic devices.

The PQ4R Method

The three mnemonic devices just described are most useful for remembering names, lists, or appointments or for preparing a speech. To improve memory for textbook material, the most suitable strategy is the PQ4R Method (Thomas and Robinson, 1972). PQ4R stands for Preview, Question, Read, Reflect, Recite, and Review. Research shows that these steps provide a useful program for improving reading and for learning course material (Anderson, 1985). Let us take the steps in order to show how you might read a chapter in this book most effectively.

1. *Preview.* In this important step you should survey the chapter. Look at the headings and identify the sections to be read as units. For example, in this text each chapter has about five or six main sections. You should apply the next four steps to each section as you read it.

2. *Question.* You should make up questions about each section, which you can often do just by changing the heading into a question. For example, for this section, you could have asked yourself, "What are mnemonic devices? What is the peg method? What is PQ4R?" and so forth. If you have questions in mind, then you can read with better purpose. You should write out the questions before reading.

3. *Reading.* Next you should read the section carefully, trying to answer your list of questions. The question-generating and question-answering aspects of PQ4R probably provide most of its effectiveness because they force people to ponder the meaning of the material and to encode it deeply as they read.

4. *Reflect.* As you are reading the material, you should think hard about it in addition to answering the questions. For example, try to think up additional examples to the ones the author provides in making some abstract point. Also, try to relate the material to things you already know whenever possible. One of the surest ways of incorporating new knowledge into memory is to see it as related to something you already know well.

5. *Recite.* After you have read each section of the book, look away and try to answer your questions again. If you cannot, then reread each part with which you had difficulty. (If you cannot remember it just after reading it, what chance do you have later on the test?)

6. *Review.* After you have read the entire chapter, you should go through it again trying to recall its main points. Try again answering the questions you constructed.

Tests of the PQ4R method have shown its value (Frase, 1975). Similar techniques have been shown to promote better reading in children (e.g., Paris, Cross, and Lipson, 1984). Although the PQ4R method has been shown to be quite effective, students are sometimes reluctant to use it because it slows reading rates. This is true enough, but it is much better to read a chapter once effectively than to rush through it a couple of times without understanding the material very well.

REMEMBERING AS RECONSTRUCTION

Throughout this chapter we have emphasized the accuracy (or inaccuracy) of memory. In most of the laboratory experiments we discussed, subjects were given a series of pictures, words, or sentences to remember and then were scored on how accurately they recalled or recognized them later. Accurate memories are crucial to everyday experiences, particularly education. But we also often rely on approximate, slightly inaccurate memories. For example, if a friend says, "Tell me what Gail said when you talked to her yesterday," the request is not for a verbatim record of Gail's remarks. The friend wants the gist, the main points of what Gail had to say.

Often our memories can play surprising tricks on us when we try to reconstruct past events. We may have a definite memory of events but find out later that our scenario could not possibly be correct. This happened to the famous child psychologist Jean Piaget:

> . . . one of my first memories would date, if it were true, from my second year. I can still see, most clearly, the following scene, in which I believed until I was about fifteen. I was sitting in my pram . . . when a man tried to kidnap me. I was held in by the strap fastened round me while my nurse bravely tried to stand between me and the thief. She received various scratches, and I can still see vaguely those on her face. . . . When I was about fifteen, my parents received a letter from my former nurse saying that she had been converted to the Salvation Army. She wanted to confess her past faults, and in particular to return the watch she had been given as a reward on this occasion. She had made up the whole story, faking the scratches. I therefore must have heard, as a child, the account of this story, which my parents believed, and projected it into the past in the form of a visual memory. . . . Many real memories are doubtless of the same order. (Piaget, 1962, pp. 187–188)

As a simple test of your own memory, try to draw the front side of a U.S. penny from memory. Give yourself one minute. Now look at Figure 7–19 and see if you can pick out the correct penny from among the representations there. Despite the fact that you have seen hundreds and probably thousands of pennies, the task is not easy. In one study in which a group of students was given the test in Figure 7–19, many picked the drawings labeled G and M. However, neither is correct. Altogether, fewer than half the people were able to choose the correct penny, which is A (Nickerson and Adams, 1979). How close is your drawing to it?

How are we to understand such errors of memory? Ideas presented earlier in the chapter can help. Recall that recoding processes are important in remembering; we translate experience into a form that can be more easily remembered, and we try to organize information according to our own knowledge. Information can be erroneously encoded or stored during this process. In addition, when we retrieve information, we may apply general knowledge of events or wishful thinking, so that the story we tell may bear little resemblance to the actual facts, as in Piaget's tale above. One analogy to remembering distant events is in terms of a *reconstruction* metaphor

FIGURE 7–19
Pick the Real Penny

Although you have seen hundreds of pennies, the task of recognizing the correct one is not easy. See the text on page 265 for the location of the real penny.

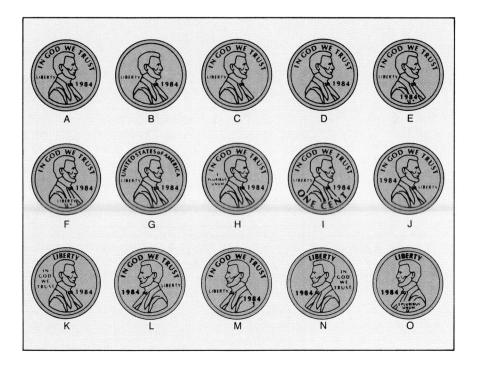

(Hebb, 1949; Neisser, 1967). Just as a paleontologist may take a few bits of fossilized bone from a dinosaur and construct an impressive model of what the beast might have looked like, so too a person remembering a distant event may take a few pieces of fact and weave them together into a coherent, plausible story. But in the process of reconstruction, errors easily creep in. In Chapter 4 we discussed how the constructive nature of perception accounts for perceptual illusions. In similar fashion, memories become distorted during recall as the rememberer smooths out the story with logical inferences.

Schemas

The idea that remembering is a constructive process was first forcefully presented by a British psychologist, Sir Frederic Bartlett, in his classic book *Remembering* (1932). He argued that people tended to remember experiences in terms of *schemas,* which are general themes that do not contain many specific details. In his experiments he gave English college students an American Indian folktale, called "The War of the Ghosts," to remember. The story involves two Indians who are invited by some ghost warriors to raid a neighboring village. The tale contains many implausible, supernatural elements. Bartlett discovered that his English students remembered the story differently from the way it was presented, especially after some time had passed. The students shortened and simplified the story and removed the supernatural elements. They tended to make it resemble a fairytale, a form with which they were more familiar. However, Bartlett noted that usually the main themes (the schemas) of the story were preserved. Schemas could operate during encoding and storage of information to cause people to elaborate on the information provided and store "facts" that were never actually presented. But schemas could also operate at retrieval to guide the reconstruction of the events. For example, if you tell a story about how a group entered a restaurant and ordered, you might fabricate details when recalling the story because behavior in restaurants usually occurs in a relatively fixed and orderly sequence of events (entering, being seated, ordering, etc.).

In an experiment designed to investigate these issues, Sulin and Dooling (1974) asked students to read and remember the following paragraph:

Carol Harris's Need for Professional Help

Carol Harris was a problem child from birth. She was wild, stubborn, and violent. By the time Carol turned eight, she was still unmanageable. Her parents were very concerned about her mental health. There was no good institution for her problem in her state. Her parents finally decided to take some action. They hired a private teacher for Carol.

A second group of students also received the same passage, except that Helen Keller's name was substituted for Carol Harris's throughout the passage. A week later both groups of subjects were given a recognition test. They were shown sentences and asked to decide whether or not each had been in the original story. One of the critical sentences was "She was deaf, dumb, and blind." Only 5 percent of the students who had read the Carol Harris version of the story said that this sentence had appeared in it, but 50 percent of the students given the Helen Keller version checked off the sentence as having appeared in the story. Their mistake seems natural. The name Helen Keller probably activated relevant schemas both when students read the story and when they tried to remember it later.

Do such errors arise through encoding and storage processes or during retrieval? This issue is usually difficult to decide, and probably processes operating at both times are important. However, in this case retrieval processes were likely important. In a later study students read the passages without a specific name and then were told a week later that the story had been about either Carol Harris or Helen Keller. In this experiment students tended to make the same pattern of errors. Since the critical information about the person was introduced just before testing, it must have affected retrieval processes (Dooling & Christiaansen, 1977).

The Soap Opera Effect

A related experiment by Owens, Bower, and Black (1979) showed how readers will elaborate on details of a story when they know the motives of one of the actors. They called their demonstration the "soap opera effect." In TV soap operas a character often utters some apparently inconsequential remark that nevertheless holds special significance for another character (and the viewer) because of their extra knowledge of the situation.

In the experiment subjects heard a story that contained a number of passages about a college student (Nancy) going about her typical daily activities: she made a cup of coffee, attended a lecture, went grocery shopping, and so forth. In one passage she went to a doctor's office:

Nancy went to the doctor. She arrived at the office and checked in with the receptionist. She went to see the nurse who went through the usual procedures. Then Nancy stepped on the scale and the nurse recorded her weight. The doctor entered the room and examined the results. He smiled

FIGURE 7–20
The Soap Opera Effect

People recalled the story about Nancy's day either after being given some statements describing her situation (the Nancy's plight condition) or with no prior information (the control condition). The people who were given information about Nancy's problem ahead of time had a schema around which to organize the facts. When the two groups were asked to recall the story, subjects in the plight condition recalled more correct facts than those in the control condition, as shown on the left of the figure. However, the plight subjects also generated many more errors than the controls, as indicated on the right. The prior schema aided recall of correct information but also led people to produce more erroneous "memories."

Source: Owens, Bower, & Black, 1979, Table 1.

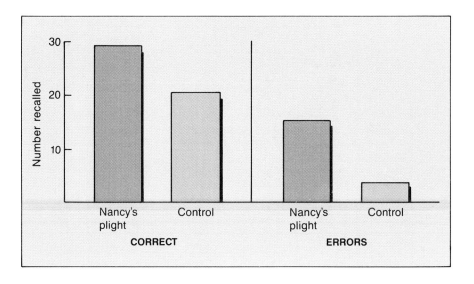

at Nancy and said, "Well, it seems my expectations have been confirmed." When the examination was finished, Nancy left the office.

One group of subjects was given the entire story with no further information, whereas a second group read a few other sentences as preamble: "Nancy woke up feeling sick again and wondered if she were really pregnant. How would she tell the college professor she had been seeing? And the money was another problem." Although it was not stated, most subjects interpreted the situation as one in which Nancy had been having an affair with her professor and was pregnant. The subjects were tested 24 hours later and the researchers measured the number of correct facts and incorrect "facts" recalled by both groups. The results are shown in Figure 7–20. On the left are shown the number of facts correctly recalled by the two groups. Those who had read the additional sentences about Nancy's worries recalled facts from the story more accurately than did the control group. On the right side of the graph are the number of incorrect statements subjects constructed about the story, which shows that these same subjects also recalled many more incorrect facts. Many of the inaccuracies were plausible given the subjects' beliefs of Nancy's plight, but they were erroneous nonetheless. For example, subjects recalled the doctor as saying, "Your fears have been confirmed."

The soap opera effect shows the dual effects of schemas quite well. If we read or hear information and have a plausible schema with which to organize the information, then our memory for the facts will be more accurate later. However, the schema-based processing can also lead us to introduce errors as we fill the gaps in the story and "remember" plausible events that actually did not occur. Probably the tendency toward reconstruction increases over time (Kintsch, 1977). If you were asked to recount what you did on Christmas day last year, you would probably accurately reproduce more facts than if you were asked to recall Christmas day in 1976. In the latter case your "memories" would more likely be reconstructions.

The reconstructive nature of memory has practical implications for the accuracy of eyewitness testimony, which is taken up in "Applying Psychology: Eyewitness Testimony." Also, remembering is similar to perceiving

Eyewitness Testimony

Examples of reconstructive processes indicate that even our most cherished memories may sometimes consist more of fiction than of fact. It may even be that the more often we recall something, the more opportunities we have to err, with possible practical consequences. Suppose you witnessed an automobile accident, and the police later questioned you to determine who was at fault. Would the type of questions you were asked, and your responses, change your recollection of the incident? If you were on the witness stand some time later, would you "remember" facts that never occurred?

Studies by Elizabeth Loftus (1979) suggest that the answer to these questions is yes. They have implications for how little trust we can sometimes put in eyewitness testimony. Eyewitness evidence is among the most convincing for jurors. But how reliable is it? Loftus and Palmer (1974) asked this question in a study in which people watched a film of a two-car accident and then were asked to fill out a questionnaire. There was one critical question. Some people were asked, "How fast were the two cars going when they hit each other?" For others *hit* was changed to *smashed, collided, bumped,* or *contacted.* Loftus and Palmer found that the verb used in the question determined to a great extent people's report of how fast the cars were going. The average speed estimate was 32 mph when the verb was *contacted,* 34 mph when it was *hit,* 38 mph when it

was *bumped,* 39 mph when it was *collided,* and 41 mph when it was *smashed.* Leading questions can greatly affect testimony, something police and lawyers have known intuitively for a long time (see Figure 7-21).

In another study, Loftus and Palmer (1974) showed 150 people a film of an automobile accident. On a questionnaire they asked 50 people, "About how fast were the cars going when they smashed into each other?" Fifty others were asked the same question, but with *hit* as the verb. The remaining 50, a control group, were not asked about speed. Once again, the estimate was higher when *smashed* rather than *hit* was the verb. But a week later the 150 people were asked, "Did you see any broken glass?" No broken glass was shown in the film, so *yes* answers were errors. Only 12% of the control group erred, and 14% of those who were asked the question with the verb *hit.* But 32% of the group members who heard the question with *smashed* in it answered *yes.* The leading question apparently caused people to recode the accident so that their memory of it changed. When asked about the event with *smashed,* they may have recoded the accident as being more serious. They integrated the information presented later into their earlier memory and altered it.

Other researchers have argued that memory for the event has not been altered in the eyewitness testimony experiment, but rather that retrieval conditions typically used in such experiments do not promote accurate memory (McCloskey & Zaragoza, 1985). Nonetheless, it is clear that distortions often will arise in reconstructing events from memory, espe-

About how fast were the cars going when they *smashed* into each other?

FIGURE 7–21
An Accident: From Bad to Worse

If a person is asked a leading question implying that an accident was more serious than it really was, the new information may be integrated into the memory of the original scene. Later the person might "remember" the accident to have been worse than it was.

cially when interfering activities occur between the events and their recall.

Think of what may happen to the eyewitness to a crime who is trying to be objective and truthful. First comes questioning by police, then by prosecution and defense attorneys before the trial. And of course, the witness will probably answer the repeated questions of family and friends. When the witness finally appears before a judge and jury months or even years later, how accurate do you think the testimony will be, especially for small details?

(Chapter 4) and thinking (Chapter 8) by involving active, inferential processes. We continue the story of active thought in the next chapter.

AMNESIA

The term *amnesia* covers a whole range of problems. For example, people who are involved in automobile collisions or other accidents in which the head receives a sharp blow often receive a concussion (swelling of the tissues surrounding the brain) and may lapse into unconsciousness. Upon recovery, they may suffer memory losses of one sort or another. *Retrograde amnesia* refers to loss of memory for events prior to the accident; *anterograde amnesia* refers to memory lapses for experiences after the accident. If the concussion is relatively mild, often these amnesias will lift. In the case of severe concussions, the events may be totally forgotten.

Neuropsychologists—those interested in discovering the neurological underpinnings of behavior—have spent years searching for clues to how the brain stores memories. The task is not a simple one. In 1915 Karl Lashley began a search for the locus of the engram (or memory trace) in animals. He removed various parts of the brain and then tested animals to see if they had forgotten responses learned prior to the operation or if their abilities to learn new responses were damaged. Summarizing decades of work in 1950, he wrote, "It is not possible to demonstrate the isolated localization of a memory trace anywhere in the nervous system. Limited regions may be essential for learning or retention of a particular activity, but . . . the engram is represented throughout the region" (p. 478). This animal work should caution against the simple notion that any one structure in the human brain is likely to be the seat of memory. However, damage to the temporal lobes, the frontal lobes, and the hippocampus often produce loss of memories (amnesia) in humans (Kolb & Whishaw, 1985). (Refer to Figure 2–14 on page 56 for the locations of these structures.) We will consider one case here, that of the most famous patient/subject studied by neuropsychological researchers, who is known by his initials—H.M.

The Case of H.M.

In 1953, just three years after Lashley had pronounced that the locus of the engram could not be found, neurosurgeon William Scoville inadvertently made a discovery that set researchers off on the trail once again. His patient, H.M., had epilepsy that was growing worse despite heavy medication. Scoville operated and removed large parts of H.M.'s temporal lobes in an attempt to cure the epilepsy. When H.M. recovered, he experienced severe anterograde amnesia. Although his intelligence was measured at well above normal, his vocabulary was good, his speech and language comprehension were normal, and he was able to remember events that had happened before his operation, he seemed incapable of learning new material. After more than 30 years he remains incapable of performing virtually any sort of memory task in which he is given verbal information and then asked to recall it after a brief delay. However, like other amnesic patients, he can recall the last few words from a list if he is tested immediately. This has led some researchers to explain amnesia in terms of the distinction between short-term and long-term memory. According to this view, the brain mechanisms damaged in amnesic patients prevent information from being transferred from a short-term state to a more permanent memory system (the long-term store).

H.M. is not poor only at laboratory memory tasks. For example, after his father's death he went to work at a rehabilitation center in which he performed monotonous tasks that usually are given to severely retarded people. Researchers reported that even after he had worked at the job every day (except weekends) for six months, he was still incapable of describing the place he worked, what he did there, or the route by which he was driven to and from work each day. On the other hand, H.M. did show some limited ability to learn the floor plan of the house in which he lived and had some idea of the two surrounding blocks in his neighborhood. Beyond that, he was lost (Milner, Corkin, & Teuber, 1968).

Korsakoff's Syndrome

Other patients also show profound amnesias, although none has been studied as thoroughly as H.M. Amnesia can be produced by other sorts of maladies besides direct injuries to the brain from surgery or accidents. For example, *Korsakoff's syndrome* is a condition that afflicts chronic alcoholics who (usually) have also been malnourished and have suffered irreversible brain damage. In the late 1800s the syndrome was first identified by a Russian physician, S. S. Korsakoff. Patients with the syndrome often seem perfectly normal on a first meeting because they can speak fluently and intelligently; their knowledge of events that occurred before their bouts with alcohol is normal. They also reason accurately and can even play cards and chess, if they knew these games beforehand. However, the patients will often ask the same questions repeatedly, even after hearing the answers, and tell the same stories over and over. Consider the following description of a person with Korsakoff's syndrome:

> Only after a long conversation with the patient, one may note that at times he utterly confuses events and that he remembers absolutely nothing of what goes on around him: he does not remember whether he had his dinner. . . . On occasion the patient forgets what happened to him just an instant ago: you came in, conversed with him, and stepped out for one minute, then you come in again and the patient has absolutely no recollection that you had already been with him. Patients of this type read the same page over and over again, sometimes for hours, because they are absolutely unable to remember what they had read. (Oscar-Berman, 1980, p. 410)

Amnesics' Hidden Memories

Although patients suffering from amnesia often seem incapable of new learning, particularly of verbal information, new discoveries indicate that amnesics may actually learn much more than anecdotal reports and previous research would suggest. On some tests, in fact, amnesics perform perfectly normally. Their difficulty may be traced to an inability to translate their knowledge into a consciously accessible form. They may know something, but not be aware that they do.

An experimenter (left) presents a patient suffering from Korsakoff's syndrome (right) with stimuli for brief intervals. Relative to normal subjects, Korsakoff patients require longer exposure to identify the stimuli. Thus mechanisms of perception, as well as those of remembering, are damaged in these patients.

The first such studies involved learning of motor skills. Milner, Corkin, and Teuber (1968) tested H.M. on a task in which he was asked to trace an outline on a sheet of paper in front of him while looking at the actual scene in a mirror. Because mirror-drawing involves a left-to-right reversal, the task is very difficult even for normal people. H.M. was tested across three successive days. He performed better on the task each day, showing that he was capable of learning. When he was brought back into the situation each day, he was asked if he had ever done the task before. He always declared that he had not but nonetheless showed strong improvements across the three days. Thus H.M. could obviously learn to perform the motor task, but he was unaware of his competence. Such a situation is referred to as a *dissociation;* a person's conscious knowledge is separated from other aspects of his or her behavior.

Some years later Cohen and Corkin (1981) demonstrated the same sort of phenomenon with H.M. on an even more complicated task. They gave him the Tower of Hanoi puzzle that is often used in research on thinking

RESEARCH FRONTIER

Normal Verbal Memory in Amnesics

Amnesics have traditionally been assumed to have virtually no memory for verbal material. They often fail to learn their doctors' names even after hundreds of introductions; they reread the same magazines without becoming bored; and they repeat the same comments and stories after very short delays. But recent research shows amnesics perform just as well as normals on some measures of verbal retention (Warrington & Weiskrantz, 1970).

Peter Graf, Larry Squire, and George Mandler (1984) tested 17 patients classified as amnesic. Seven suffered from Korsakoff's syndrome and eight others were severely depressed patients who were receiving electroconvulsive therapy (ECT). This ECT procedure, which is discussed more fully in Chapter 16, involves passing electric current briefly through electrodes attached to the scalp; it usually produces temporary anterograde amnesia. Two other subjects

were called "anoxic" amnesics because they had become amnesic following a period in which the oxygen supply to the brain was disrupted. Appropriate control groups were found for these amnesic patients. For example, the controls for Korsakoff patients were other chronic alcoholics who were hospitalized but who had not developed Korsakoff's syndrome. Twenty-six controls were tested.

All subjects were given several short lists of ten words to memorize, and after each list their memories were tested in two ways. First, the subjects were asked to recall as many words as they could in any order they wanted. This free recall test requires that subjects consciously recall the words. The second test, a word completion test, was not presented as a test of memory. In this task the subjects were given 20 sets of three-letter cues, such as *inf-*, and were instructed to write down the first word that came to mind beginning with those three letters (for example, *infant*). Half the three-letter cues represented words that had appeared in the study list, while the other half represented words that had not been

studied. However, subjects were told nothing about the relation of the cues to the words in the list, but simply to say the first word that popped into mind beginning with those letters. If patients completed the word stems with words from the list more often than for the nonstudied control words, then the word completion test measures retention for the words.

First let us consider the free recall results. As you can see from Figure 7–22, the amnesic subjects performed much worse than their controls on free recall (the two bars on the left). This is no surprise, of course, because by definition amnesics are poor at recalling information. The interesting data come from the word-completion task, the results of which are shown at the right side of Figure 7–22. Both groups performed much better than chance, and amnesics performed just as well as normal subjects (in fact, slightly better).

The word-completion test permits a measure of retention without awareness. That is, the test does not require people to recall recent events; rather it measures their learning indirectly. The conclusion is that when

(see Figure 8–4, page 281). The task takes many steps, and performance can be measured by the time or number of errors to completion. Cohen and Corkin asked H.M. to talk aloud while he was solving the puzzle, which they gave him repeatedly over several days. Each time he was given the problem, H.M. denied having seen it before; in addition, his commentary during his solution attempts always sounded as if he were solving the puzzle for the first time. Nonetheless, H.M.'s actual performance in solving the puzzle showed steady improvement.

These studies suggest that H.M. (and other amnesics, who show similar talents) may not be able to learn and remember new verbal information, but they are normal on tasks requiring learning of procedures. However, recent results challenge this conclusion because they show that on some tests amnesics reveal perfectly normal performance in retention of verbal information when their memories are tested indirectly (Jacoby & Witherspoon, 1982; Squire, 1982). Recent work demonstrating this point is described in "Research Frontier: Normal Verbal Memory in Amnesics."

---

amnesics' memories are tested on indirect tests that do not require conscious awareness, they show normal learning and retention. Other researchers have recently reported similar results and have even shown that amnesics can learn associations as well as normal control subjects when they are tested in this indirect way (Schacter & Graf, 1986). Put another way, the brain-damaged patients may be "amnesic" only on certain tests of retention; on others they are perfectly normal.

How best to explain these dissociations between memory measures reflecting conscious awareness of events (such as free recall) and those that do not (such as word completion) is currently a matter of hot debate (e.g., Hirst, 1982; Cermak, 1982). But the inescapable conclusion is that amnesics are not incapable of learning about verbal materials, as once thought. Instead, their difficulty resides in gaining conscious access to their tacit knowledge. H.M. once described his mental state as "like waking from a dream." Apparently the brain mechanisms underlying conscious awareness are disrupted in amnesia.

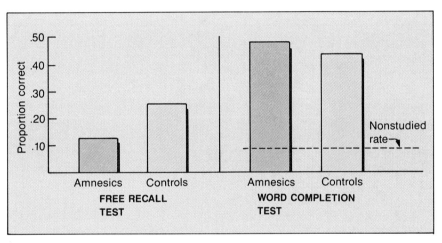

FIGURE 7–22
Verbal Memory in Amnesics

Amnesic patients and controls both received lists of words and then were given two tests after each list, free recall and then word completion. In free recall, which requires conscious recollection of the words from the list, the amnesics did much worse than the controls. In the word-completion test both groups were told to produce the first word to come to mind when given three-letter cues (e.g., *per-* for *permanent*). In this test the amnesics and normals did not differ. The word-completion test reflects learning because both groups did much better than if they had not studied the words (as indicated by the dashed line). Amnesics often show normal levels of retention, even for verbal materials, if the retention test does not require that they be consciously aware of the previous learning episode.

SUMMARY

1. Failures of memory may be due to inadequate acquisition, storage, or retrieval of information. Acquisition refers to initial learning, storage to retention of a memory trace over time, and retrieval to use of stored information.

2. Hermann Ebbinghaus was the first to study memory objectively. He measured the difficulty in learning lists of nonsense syllables by recording the number of trials taken to recite a series perfectly. He later measured retention by relearning the lists after some interval of time had passed and observing savings in the number of trials taken.

3. Some researchers believe that different types of memory are held in different "stores." Sensory stores hold information briefly while it is analyzed; the short-term store holds information for some seconds after it has been analyzed; and the long-term store holds information for longer periods, perhaps permanently.

4. The iconic store is the name of the sensory register for vision, while the echoic store is the sensory register for hearing, or audition. It is generally assumed that the echoic store holds information longer than the iconic store.

5. Recoding of information is a key to remembering. People can usually remember material better if they recode it in a form that matches their past knowledge. Effective forms of recoding involve recasting information in terms of both language and imagery. Few, if any, people have the ability to keep an image of photographic quality for a scene, but people do generally remember verbal information better if they try to recode it in mental images.

6. The levels-of-processing approach to memory conceives of events as being perceptually processed to different depths or levels depending on the degree of meaningful analysis they are given. Memory is thought to be related to the depth of processing, with deeper processing leading to less forgetting. However, whether or not a certain type of processing leads to good memory performance depends on the type of test used, so the concept of transfer-appropriate processing may be preferable to the depth-of-processing idea. The type of memory trace produced by a recoding process may lead to good or poor performance on a test depending on how appropriately the acquired knowledge transfers to the test.

7. One explanation for forgetting of information is interference from events that occur before or after the information is processed. Events that occur before the event provide proactive interference; those that occur later provide retroactive interference. The idea of trace decay has been discredited as a complete theory of forgetting.

8. When information is forgotten it can sometimes be recalled when people are given appropriate retrieval cues. Retrieval cues seem to be effective when they re-create the original learning context. This idea is referred to as the encoding specificity hypothesis: retrieval cues are effective to the extent that their information matches the information stored in the memory trace.

9. Research does not allow us to conclude that all memories are retained permanently, but we can show that many cases of forgetting can be reversed with appropriate cues or hints. Thus, forgetting is often due to failures in the retrieval process. But information may be permanently lost from memory, too. Retrieval cues are effective to the extent that they help re-create the context of original learning.

10. Episodic memory refers to memory for specific events, while semantic memory refers to memory for general knowledge. Concepts are linked according to the strength of their relation. Activation of one concept spreads to closely associated concepts.

11. Mnemonic devices are memory aids. Three effective devices are formed by linking images (the link method), placing images in imaginal locations (the method of loci), and "hanging" images on mental pegs (the peg method). All of these are more effective in remembering a series of points than the strategies most people normally use, but the peg and loci methods are better than the link method for allowing recall of items in order. The PQ4R method (Preview, Question, Read, Reflect, Recite, Review) is an effective method of studying text material.

12. Remembering can be viewed as a constructive activity, especially for distant events. People may remember some facts accurately but may weave them together and elaborate them with details that never actually occurred. Our recollections may represent some combination of fact and fantasy, especially when they have been repeatedly related on different occasions.

13. Amnesia refers to loss of memory, usually due to some injury to the brain. Retrograde amnesia is loss of memories before the damage; anterograde amnesia is the name for memory problems occurring

after the brain trauma. The most studied case of amnesia is that of H.M., who seemed incapable of learning new verbal material after the surgery that left him amnesic. However, H.M. and other amnesics can learn motor skills in a relatively normal manner, although they may deny ever having done a task more than once. Recent research shows that amnesics can even remember verbal materials if their memories are probed in ways that do not require them to be consciously aware of the prior experiences.

SUGGESTED READINGS

Anderson, J. R. (1985). *Cognitive psychology and its implications* (2nd ed.). New York: Freeman.
> A comprehensive text of cognitive psychology that includes the topics of perception, memory, language, reasoning, and cognitive development. The several chapters on memory are very good.

Higbee, K. L. (1977). *Your memory: How it works and how to improve it.* Englewood Cliffs, N.J.: Prentice-Hall.
> This memory improvement book draws heavily on academic research. A number of mnemonic devices are discussed, as well as the practical problems of remembering more from textbooks, remembering names and faces, and so on.

Luria, A. R. (1968). *The mind of a mnemonist.* New York: Basic Books.
> A fascinating account of a man with a phenomenally good memory, who seemed unable to forget. Besides trying to explain his unusual memory, the author discusses the personal problems created by the mnemonist's unusual capacity for imagery.

Neisser, U. (Ed.) (1982). *Memory observed: Remembering in natural contexts.* New York: Freeman, 1982.
> A collection of anecdotal observations and more rigorous studies of remembering of natural events.

Stern, L. (1985). *The structures and strategies of human memory.* Homewood, Ill.: Dorsey.
> Intended as a textbook for undergraduate courses, this book provides coverage of the field with many interesting examples and analogies.

Solution to Figure 7–8

Fusion of the two dot patterns on page 245.

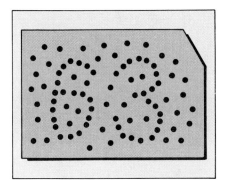

8

Thought and Language

Language is the light of the mind.

John Stuart Mill

I know that you believe you understand what you think I said, but I'm not sure you realize that what you heard is not what I meant.

Richard Nixon

T HINK FOR A MOMENT ABOUT THESE TWO SIMPLE PROBLEMS:

1. Take two apples from three apples. What have you got?
2. A shepherd had 17 sheep. All but nine died. How many did he have left?

The answers, of course, are two apples and nine sheep. If either of the two problems tripped you up, you might wonder why. What was it about the problems that led you astray? Did you seize upon an answer without carefully evaluating the question? Did the language of the problems trip you up?

Researchers often use brain teasers such as these to investigate the ways in which thought and language operate in everyday situations. How do we solve problems? How do we use concepts? What rules guide our reasoning? How do we make decisions? What role does language play in our thinking? These are only some of the questions that this chapter will examine. The questions are interesting not only from a psychological point of view but also from a very practical viewpoint. Thinking, or what psychologists call *cognition,* guides much of what we say and do every day. Without thought, our perceptions, our ability to learn, and our capacity for memory would amount to very little.

Yet thinking, like the notion of consciousness, is very hard to isolate and define. Is thinking in some way separate from our ability to recognize perceptual patterns, to focus our attention, to form expectations, or to construct our memories of past events? All of these abilities depend on some measure of cognition, and all of them, as we have seen up to now, are the objects of psychological research.

This chapter builds on earlier discussions of perception, consciousness, learning, and memory. At this point, we are ready to examine how our cognitive processes enable us to manipulate symbols and images, to organize information, and to use language. We begin with a topic familiar to any student who has wrestled with a midterm exam: problem solving.

PROBLEM SOLVING

Try to decipher this anagram—*ssoia*—and at the same time think about how you are trying to solve it. Did you experiment with various initial letters or did you just stare at the letters waiting for a word to appear? Sometimes problems can be solved by a sudden burst of *insight* rather than trial and error. (How did you discover *oasis* in this anagram?) A dramatic personal account of insight was recollected by Henri Poincaré (1913), the famous mathematician:

> For fifteen days I strove to prove there could not be any functions like those I have since called Fuchsian functions. I was then very ignorant;

every day I seated myself at my work table, stayed an hour or two, tried a great number of combinations and reached no results. One evening, contrary to my custom, I drank black coffee and could not sleep. Ideas rose in crowds; I felt them collide until pairs interlocked, so to speak, making a stable combination. By the next morning I had established the existence of a class of Fuchsian functions, those which come from the hypergeometric series; I had only to write out the results, which took but a few hours. (p. 58)

There are many varieties of problems, and not all of them are solved in the same way. Some solutions may be creative and rapid while others may follow considerable analysis. To reach some solutions may require days or even years of careful investigation. John Bransford and Barry Stein (1984) advocate five steps of IDEAL thinking to promote effective problem solving:

- □ I = identify the problem
- □ D = define and represent the problem
- □ E = explore possible strategies
- □ A = act on the strategies
- □ L = look back and evaluate the effects of your activities.

In this section we outline the methodology of problem solving by reducing Bransford and Stein's plan to three important topics: formulating the problem, generating possible solutions, and evaluating alternative solutions.

Formulating the Problem

The initial interpretation of a problem is the most important step to a successful solution. Suppose you have prepared an important presentation to be delivered to your new boss at 8 A.M. You pack your briefcase and get in your car, but the car won't start. Do you (a) lift the hood and get your toolbox, (b) ask your neighbor for help, or (c) phone for a taxi? Since the real problem is to reach work on time without getting grease on your clothes, (c) may be the best choice. People become sidetracked in their thinking if they do not identify the primary problem.

Sometimes people complicate simple problems unnecessarily. Figure 8–1 shows a circle with a radius of 5 inches. The problem is to figure out the length of line *c*. To solve this problem, do you need to recall the formula for the length of a right triangle's hypotenuse? Actually, no recall is necessary. First, visualize the *other* diagonal in the rectangle. This imaginary line, which forms a radius to the circle, is equal to 5 inches. Line *c* then is also 5 inches long.

Now look at the books shown in Figure 8–2 and solve this problem:

A set of ten books is arranged in orderly fashion on a shelf. Each book has 100 pages, making 1000 pages in all. A worm, starting on the first page of the first book, eats through to the last page of the last book. How many pages did it eat?

The answer is 802. Look again at the picture and you'll see why 99 pages in each of the first and last books were untouched. (The worm had to eat only one page in the first and last books because volumes I–X are arranged left to right.) These simple exercises illustrate why the initial steps in any problem-solving task are to identify and to define the problem accurately.

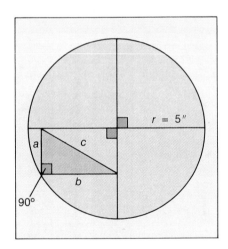

FIGURE 8–1
What Is the Length of Line c?

Initial representation of the problem is important. Many times we make problem solving difficult by overlooking the obvious. In this case, the length of line *c* does not need to be calculated since it is the same length as that of the second diagonal of the rectangle. Imagine the second diagonal from the middle of the circle to the right angle of the triangle. This line is a radius of the circle and the same length as line *c*.

FIGURE 8–2
The Worm Problem

Each volume on the shelf consists of 100 pages. If a worm eats through the volumes beginning at the first page of Volume I and ending at the last page of Volume X, how many pages does it eat?

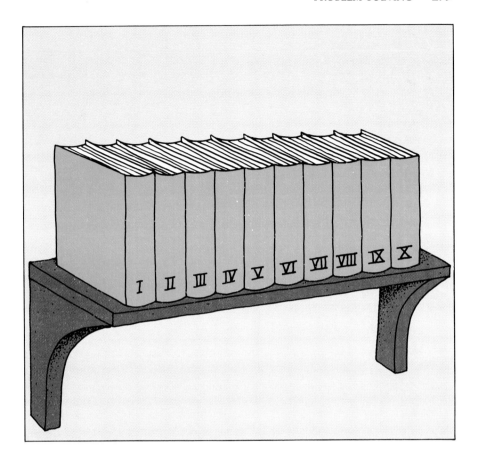

Generating Possible Solutions

Bransford and Stein (1984) posed this problem to a group of students:

> Generate as many reasons as you can to explain why, when my cousin comes to visit me, in my apartment, he always gets off the elevator five floors below my floor and walks the rest of the way.

Typical responses included "he needs the exercise," "he wants to surprise you," "he visits somebody else along the way," or "the elevator is broken." A seldom-mentioned possibility is that the cousin is so short that he can only reach the button for the floor five floors below his intended one.

Failure to generate diverse hypotheses as possible solutions can often thwart problem solving. The problems shown in Figure 8–3 are difficult because people usually do not consider unconventional solutions. They tend to think about (A) two-dimensional objects, (B) lines within the square of dots, or (C) same-sized boxes. The solutions appear simple as soon as these constraints are ignored. (The solutions appear on page 312.)

The tendency for people to be limited in their solutions by conventional uses of objects is referred to as *functional fixedness.* A classic problem (Duncker, 1945) involves giving a subject two long, thin pieces of wood, a clamp, and a coat. The subject is asked to hang the coat in a bare room without using the walls. One good—but uncommon—solution is to clamp

FIGURE 8–3
Mind Teasers

Solutions are on page 312.

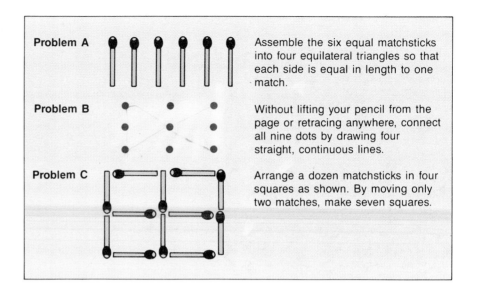

Problem A Assemble the six equal matchsticks into four equilateral triangles so that each side is equal in length to one match.

Problem B Without lifting your pencil from the page or retracing anywhere, connect all nine dots by drawing four straight, continuous lines.

Problem C Arrange a dozen matchsticks in four squares as shown. By moving only two matches, make seven squares.

the boards together, wedge them tightly between the floor and ceiling, and hang the coat on the clamp. Functional fixedness usually prevents subjects from envisioning these purposes for the objects.

In a similar study of creative problem solving, originally conducted by Karl Duncker (1945), people are given a candle, a box of tacks, and several matches and are asked to affix the candle upright to the wall so that its wax will not drip to the floor. Glucksberg and Weisberg (1966) modified Duncker's problem by telling one group of subjects to label the objects—box, tacks, candle, and matches—but giving no such instructions to another group. Those who used labels solved the problem in 30 to 40 seconds. The group that did not use labels averaged nearly 9 minutes; its members did not recognize that they could tack the box to the wall to hold the candle. Evidently, labeling the box helped students understand that it was more than a container for the tacks.

Evaluating Outcomes

After you generate various plans, strategies, or possible solutions, you must try them out and evaluate their effectiveness. As experienced chess players know, systematic checking of the consequences of various options helps to avoid impulsive actions or false solutions. Consider the Tower of Hanoi problem shown in Figure 8–4. The object of this game is to move three discs, one at a time, from the first peg to the third peg. A large disc can never cover a smaller disc. Can you find a way to do it in only seven moves? The seven-step solution requires planning, checking, and revising. When the problem is simplified, even four-to-six-year-olds can plan a sequence of moves to solve it (Klahr & Robinson, 1981). The important feature of evaluating outcomes is anticipation of the consequences of planned moves. If a given outcome does not bring you nearer to a solution, that outcome is ineffective and another tactic is required. (The solution to Figure 8–4 appears on page 312.)

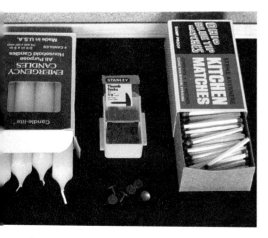

How can a candle be attached in an upright position so that no wax drips on the floor?

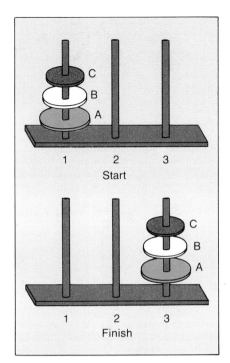

FIGURE 8–4
The Tower of Hanoi Problem

The object of this puzzle is to move the discs one at a time from peg 1 to peg 3 in the fewest moves possible. A large disc can never be placed on top of a smaller one. (The solution is on p. 312.)

"*Now* that desk looks better. Everything's squared away, yessir, squaaaaaared away."

Shortcuts to Problem Solving

Some of the strategies used for generating solutions are called *algorithms,* which are sets of rules that apply to particular types of problems. The optimal solution to the Tower of Hanoi problem is an algorithm; so are many mathematical solutions, such as finding the area of a circle by the formula $A = \pi r^2$. When properly applied, algorithms always lead to correct solutions, but they have two potential shortcomings. First, people often blindly depend on the rules and fail to check either the formulation of the problem or the correctness of the answer. Second, it is not always practical to follow logical steps of algorithms. If you were working a crossword puzzle with an entry __ a __ d __ __ __ a __ for "State bird of Illinois," you would not combine all possible letter combinations in algorithmic fashion. Instead, you would use a *heuristic,* or rule-of-thumb strategy, trying out only consonants in the first and last blanks. Or perhaps you would test some likely names of birds until you pounced on *cardinal.*

Heuristics are another type of mental shortcut. Instead of rules that always work, heuristics are informal cognitive strategies that experience teaches us to apply in particular situations. They do not always lead to correct answers, but they provide general guidelines about possible solutions. Every task has specific heuristics associated with it, and "troubleshooting" is based on experience with the problem. That is partly why "experts" isolate so quickly the most likely causes of such annoyances as stopped-up drains. Knowing heuristics is part of what makes a good coach, fisherman, golfer, plumber, or auto mechanic. But there are also general heuristics that help turn some people into good problem solvers. One general heuristic is *subgoal analysis,* the ability to reduce a complex problem to a series (or hierarchy) of smaller, more easily solvable problems. Consider how you might solve the following dilemma:

> Suppose you are a doctor faced with a patient who has a malignant tumor in his stomach. It is impossible to operate on the patient, but unless the tumor is destroyed the patient will die. There is a kind of ray that can be used to destroy the tumor. If the rays reach the tumor all at once at a sufficient high intensity, the tumor will be destroyed. Unfortunately, at this intensity the healthy tissue that the rays pass through on the way to the tumor will also be destroyed. At lower intensities the rays are harmless to healthy tissue, but they will not affect the tumor either. What type of procedure might be used to destroy the tumor with the rays, and at the same time avoid destroying the healthy tissue? (Gick & Holyoak, 1980, pp. 307–308)

This problem was devised by Karl Duncker (1945), who asked adults to think aloud as they tried to solve it. Several possible solutions are illustrated in Figure 8–5. Many of Duncker's subjects (40%) misinterpreted the problem and suggested an operation to expose the tumor. An additional 29% suggested that the best method would be to direct the rays to the stomach through an open route such as the esophagus or intestines. The best solution is to disperse the intensity of the rays by aiming several weak rays at the tumor from different points. Thus, rays would be weak when passing through healthy tissue, but strong at the affected organ. However, only 5% of subjects thought of this solution.

Would subjects be more able to solve the radiation problem if they had just learned the solution to a similar problem? Mary Gick and Keith Holyoak

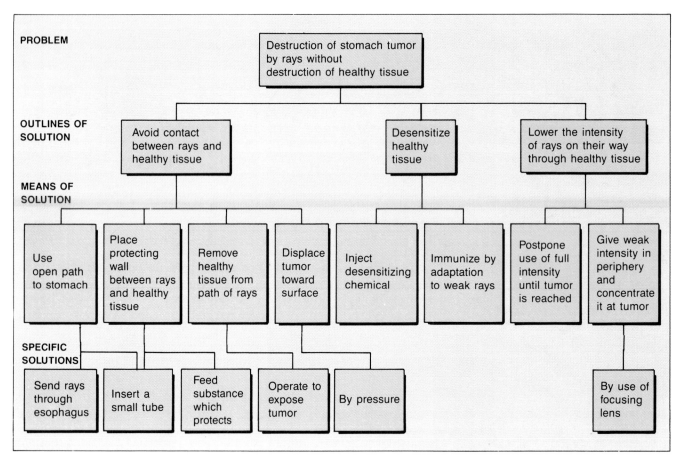

FIGURE 8–5
A Schematic Diagram of Possible Solutions to Duncker's (1945) Tumor Problem

Notice how different ideas are contained in each branch and the solutions become progressively more specific. The method of talking through a problem has been used often to reveal subjects' sequences of attempts to solve problems.

Source: Wortman & Loftus, 1981.

(1980) investigated how adults transfer general heuristics from one problem to another. In one study they read the following passage to ten subjects before giving them the radiation problem.

> A fortress was located in the center of the country. Many roads radiated out from the fortress. A general wanted to capture the fortress with his army. The general wanted to prevent mines on the roads from destroying his army and neighboring villages. As a result the entire army could not attack the fortress along one road. However, the entire army was needed to capture the fortress. So an attack by one small group would not succeed. The general therefore divided his army into several small groups. He positioned the small groups at the heads of different roads. The small groups simultaneously converged on the fortress. In this way the army captured the fortress. (p. 311)

This story is analogous to the radiation problem and provides a solution based on dispersion of the army (or rays). All ten subjects who heard this story suggested similar dispersion solutions to the radiation problem while no subjects in the control condition (those who did not hear the story of the army) thought of these options.

The repeated use of heuristics to solve similar problems builds up particular expectations and biases in the problem solver. These expectations and biases are called *mental set* and are partly responsible for the positive transfer of solutions in the Gick and Holyoak research. However, mental set

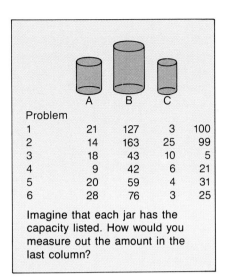

Problem

	A	B	C	
1	21	127	3	100
2	14	163	25	99
3	18	43	10	5
4	9	42	6	21
5	20	59	4	31
6	28	76	3	25

Imagine that each jar has the capacity listed. How would you measure out the amount in the last column?

FIGURE 8–6
Luchins's Water Jars

Try to solve each problem and you will see a general rule emerging. After solving the first five problems, most of Luchins's subjects could not solve the sixth. Why not?

Source: Luchins, 1946.

does not always facilitate problem solving; sometimes our biases prevent us from correctly identifying the problem. Here is a simple problem to illustrate mental set: "If 3 cats can kill 3 rats in 3 minutes, how long will it take 100 cats to kill 100 rats?" Did you say 100 minutes or 1 minute? Think again why the answer is actually 3 minutes.

The tendency to depend on heuristics even when they are no longer appropriate was illustrated by Abraham Luchins (1946). He presented subjects with three water jars of different sizes and a series of problems (see Figure 8–6). The goal was to measure out the amount of water shown in the chart using the hypothetical capacities of each jar. For example, in the first problem you can see that 100 quarts can be obtained by filling up jar B, then pouring 21 quarts into jar A and 3 quarts into C twice. Each of the first five problems can be solved in the same fashion. But the sixth problem requires only two jars (A and C). In fact, the apparent rule of B-A-2C yields the incorrect answer, and that may be why two-thirds of Luchins's subjects could not solve number 6. Clearly, problem solving requires flexibility to generate alternative solutions and to overcome "mental set."

We will return to the problem of mental bias when we discuss decision making later in the chapter.

REASONING SKILLS

We have seen that effective problem solving depends on general procedures for identifying problems, generating possible solutions, and evaluating the options. Mental algorithms and heuristics can facilitate problem solving, but care must be taken to avoid blind rule-following and functional fixedness. Psychologists have studied many kinds of thinking skills, some general and some quite specific. In the following sections, we briefly discuss four kinds of reasoning skills, but you should recognize that thinking about any particular problem often involves using several kinds of reasoning concurrently.

Concept Identification

We organize much of our knowledge about the world according to *concepts*, mental representations for categorizing information. Concepts can influence perception, memory, and language. They are a fundamental aspect of cognition, and, as we will see in Chapter 9, a great deal of children's development involves learning new concepts about objects and people.

Some concepts can be identified without any difficulty—for example, the people included in the category "Presidents of the United States." This kind of concept is well defined because each member of the category shares some critical attributes that define the concept. However, many concepts are difficult to pin down. For example, what are the differences between each of these pairs—chair-bench, cup-glass, and jacket-coat—and how can we define them as distinctive, nonoverlapping concepts? It is not easy to separate related objects; many concepts have uncertain boundaries.

To study how people form concepts, psychologists create situations in which subjects must devise rules that relate different stimuli. Imagine, for example, that you are given a deck of playing cards and asked to discover the rule for putting cards into two groups, the winners and the losers. You pick up each card, place it in one of the piles, and then are told if you are right or wrong. You pick up a four of hearts and put it in the winner pile

We can recognize a novel object by comparing certain salient features of the object to familiar concepts. This object rests on the floor, offers a surface for sitting, and has a back to lean against. Thus, it includes several prototypical characteristics of chairs and can be categorized as a chair, although it is an unusual and creative piece of furniture.

and you are told "wrong." Then you place a nine of clubs in the winner pile and are told "right." Do you know the rule? Probably not, but as you learn about the placement of successive cards, you can discover a rule—for example, any card in a black suit or odd number is a winner.

More complicated versions of such tasks were used by Bruner, Goodnow, and Austin (1956) in their study of concept learning. They also analyzed how people devised strategies to test their hypotheses about each concept. They presented adults with cards that portrayed geometric shapes in different colors. The number of shapes and the borders on the cards also varied. The task was similar to the playing card experiment just described. With so many features to consider, the subjects nevertheless focused on a single feature at a time and tested hypotheses by a rule of "win–stay, lose–shift," which means stick with your hypothesis until it is disconfirmed.

Recent research on concept formation (Murphy & Medin, 1985) has focused on how we know when two things are similar and, hence, members of the same conceptual class. If an oryx has four legs and eats grass, does it fall into the class of cows? No? Then how do you determine the necessary and sufficient defining features of a class or concept? Some psychologists have proposed that we use *prototypes* to define concepts. A prototype is a representative sample of a class of things. For example, *apple* is a representative type of *fruit*. When we form concepts, we arrive at a prototype and then compare objects on the basis of how closely they match our prototype. Cantor, Mischel, and Schwartz (1982) have shown, for example, that people perceive social situations such as parties, work, job interviews, and family dinners according to relatively orderly and easily recalled sets of prototypical features. The more an object bears a "family resemblance" to the prototypical concept, the more likely are people to classify it as a member of the concept. But other psychologists argue that concepts cannot be defined adequately by lists of features, by typical characteristics, or by prototypes (Murphy & Medin, 1985; Smith & Osherson, 1984).

One line of recent research on concepts suggests that some conceptual categories are *natural.* By this we mean that such concepts are familiar to us, entrenched in experience, simple, and easily characterized by prototypes (Sternberg, 1982). Frank Keil (1981) suggested that some basic categories, like "living things" or "intelligent beings," help establish the boundaries of natural concepts. (Thus, *thinking fish* or *talking refrigerators* are *un*natural concepts.) Children apparently learn natural concepts more easily than other concepts because they provide coherent frameworks for organizing their worlds (Carey, 1982; Markman & Callanan, 1984).

A second approach to concept learning is that concepts reflect people's beliefs and theories about the world. For example, it seems reasonable to claim that "a cheetah can outrun a man," but what about a newborn cheetah or an old one with arthritis? Ziff (1972) proposed that people understand the claim because we share certain intuitive notions of the relations involved. Barsalou (1983) showed that concepts are often based on people's actions. What is the conceptual relation shared by these objects: children, jewelry, money, heirlooms, and photograph albums? How about "things to carry out of the house if it catches on fire"? Barsalou found that people judged the typicality of each object by its relation to the behavioral goal, not by its similarity to other objects. He also found that natural concepts are organized along dimensions that reflect how people normally interact with objects. This approach to concept learning is consistent with research that compares novices and experts in different areas. Experts have more elaborate and coherent concepts than novices and they use this knowledge to solve problems more quickly and accurately. Cognitive expertise is discussed more fully in "Research Frontier: Cognitive Expertise."

Inductive Reasoning

Induction refers to the discovery or construction of a rule that links together elements or relations. For example, to solve a problem "x is to y as p is to t," you would need to induce a relation that is similar for both pairs. Both problem solving and concept learning can involve induction. Three common kinds of problems used to study *inductive reasoning* are based on classification, series completion, and analogies. Examples are illustrated in Figure 8–7. The classification problems involve identifying attributes that are

FIGURE 8–7
Inductive Reasoning Problems

Three kinds of problems are often used to test the ways that people induce relations among items. The problems can be presented verbally or visually, and they vary widely in difficulty. (Solutions are on page 312.)

Source: Pellegrino, 1985, p. 50.

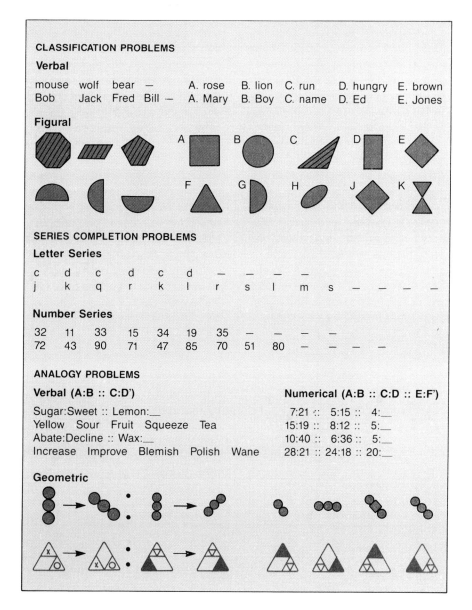

RESEARCH FRONTIER

Cognitive Expertise

Chess is a complicated game involving anticipation, strategies, and imagery. Accomplished chess players have amazing skills; they can see and remember patterns in a game that others do not. For example, Bill Chase and Herbert Simon (1973) allowed subjects to view for 5–10 seconds a chess board with about 25 pieces arranged in a game situation. Chess experts could reconstruct the positions of 90 percent of the pieces while unskilled players did well to replace five or six pieces correctly. Their understanding of the game allowed experts to group together in memory more chess pieces and spatial arrangements than could novices.

Cognitive scientists have begun intensive studies of expert-novice differences in several areas. The ways in which experts represent and solve problems can provide insight into efficient methods of structuring concepts and acquiring knowledge. Knowledge of cognitive expertise can also help

scientists to program computers more efficiently. We consider differences between novices and experts for physics problems as an illustration.

Michelene Chi, Paul Feltovich, and Robert Glaser (1981) asked subjects to sort 24 physics problems (taken from a college textbook) into categories based on the similarities of solutions. The problems included questions about forces on pulleys, the velocity of an object sliding down an inclined plane, and so forth. The experts were eight advanced Ph.D. students in physics, and the novices were eight undergraduates who had just completed a semester course on mechanics. The researchers collected data on the groups into which problems were sorted, response times, and subjects' reasons for their grouping arrangements.

Surprisingly, experts took longer to sort the problems. They spent an average of 45 seconds on each problem while novices required only an average of 30 seconds to categorize each one. On a second trial, however, both experts and novices required only 10–15 seconds to sort the problems. There were no differences in the number of groups formed. Both novices

and experts sorted the problems into about eight groups, but the categories differed significantly. Novices categorized them on the basis of superficial features such as whether the problems were based on inclined planes, friction, or revolving objects. Experts were not fooled by superficial features and instead categorized problems according to underlying physical principles such as the conservation of momentum or energy. Some even said explicitly, "These can all be solved by Newton's Second Law" or "$F = ma$" or "work-energy theorem."

In a second study, Chi, Feltovich, and Glaser (1981) devised 20 new problems that could be classified according to superficial features (such as pulleys or inclined planes) or grouped according to principles of force, energy, or momentum. An undergraduate novice categorized the problems by appearance while a graduate student and physics professor classified nearly all the problems according to the general principles. The researchers also observed how novices and experts described their own problem solving and hypothesis testing. Experts often analyzed problems more thoroughly than novices. Per-

shared by the words and figures. The series completion tasks require subjects to discover the rules. For example, the series 2, 3, 5, 9, 17 is produced by multiplying the previous number by 2 and subtracting 1.

Analogies have been studied extensively by researchers because they may reflect both intellectual and creative ability. For this reason, as we discuss in Chapter 11, analogy problems are often included on intelligence tests. Robert Sternberg (1985) has outlined three critical processes for solving analogy problems. First, *encode* the critical features of the left term, for example, *"Sugar* is to *Sweet"* (see Figure 8–7). Second, *combine* the items to discover conceptual relations between them. Third, *compare* the first pair of items and relations to the second pair of items, "Lemon is to _____" in this example. Mapping the relation of "object-taste" between the pairs of items yields "Sour" as the answer. Poor problem-solving procedures or the

Expert computer programmers organize knowledge according to programming principles.

while experts generated images, sketches, or representations of the problems. The results of both studies of how people categorize and solve physics problems reveal that experts have different conceptual knowledge about physical principles. This influences their perceptions of problem similarities as well as their actual problem-solving behavior.

Understanding cognitive expertise can be extended to many domains besides chess and physics problems. For example, McKeithen et al. (1981) compared novice and expert computer programmers. They found that expert programmers organize knowledge according to programming principles and can use the principles to chunk and recall more information than novices. As researchers explore other domains of cognitive expertise, we will gain fuller understanding of the knowledge organization and reasoning strategies of skilled performers.

haps that is why they took longer initially, too.

Larkin and colleagues (1980) noted four fundamental differences between novices and experts as they solved physics problems. First, experts solved the problems much faster and with fewer errors. (Notice that experts may take longer to analyze and *sort* the problems than novices, but the actual time required to *solve* the prob-lems is less.) Second, novices solved problems by working backward from the unknown to the given situation while experts worked forward (except for very difficult problems). Third, novices often mentioned equations explicitly and then substituted given values. Experts apparently did much of this automatically and simply stated the result. Fourth, novices tended to focus on the verbal statements of problems

inability to detect shared attributes or underlying relations can thwart analogical reasoning.

Deductive Reasoning

The ability to draw logical implications from statements or evidence is called **deductive reasoning.** The fictional detective Sherlock Holmes was famous for his power of deductive reasoning. He was able to solve difficult crimes by building logical conclusions from clues and small fragments of evidence. Deanna Kuhn, Erin Phelps, and Joseph Walters (1985) presented this problem to groups of students from grades 4 through 11 as well as to a group of college students:

> Last summer, I bought a new car. Around the time I bought it, I heard about a new product for cars that is supposed to help your car engine—it's called EngineHelp. One of the things that the makers of EngineHelp said in their ads was that EngineHelp helps your car run well. I wanted my car to run well, so I decided to use it. I was curious and decided to see what some other people's experience was with EngineHelp, so I went out and talked to some people. Six people I talked to said they used EngineHelp, and they all said their cars run well. Does EngineHelp have anything to do with whether a car runs well? How can you tell? (p. 87)

More than 80% of students below grade 7 responded "yes" and went on to explain that EngineHelp caused cars to run well. One-third of college students also said "yes," but two-thirds responded "can't tell." Next, the researchers provided more information to students.

> Two other people I talked to said that they use EngineHelp and that their cars run poorly.

Subjects were then asked the same questions as before. Next, they were told:

> Three other people I talked to said that they never use EngineHelp and that their cars run well. And one last person I talked to said that he never uses EngineHelp and that his car runs poorly.

Subjects were again asked if EngineHelp has anything to do with whether a car runs well.

In general, the additional information changed students' judgments from "yes" to "sometimes." But less than one-third of subjects answered "no," which is the correct answer. Even when all the data were presented together, the responses were similar. The researchers point out that students seemed to focus on the six people who used EngineHelp and whose cars ran well. Most ignored the disconfirming evidence from six other people.

What does this study tell us about reasoning skills? Kuhn, Phelps, and Walters (1985) point out that most children and adolescents (and a surprising number of adults) do not reason logically. The logical deduction of "If you use EngineHelp, then your car will run well" is falsified by the two people who used EngineHelp but still had poor-running cars. But most subjects did not take this into consideration. They focused instead on positive instances that confirm a relation. Using EngineHelp and having good-running cars was reported by six people and not using the product and having a poor-running car was reported by only one person. Therefore, subjects reasoned that there was a causal relation based only on a correlation (a problem discussed in Chapter 1). Such illogical thinking, or lack of deductive reasoning, is also involved in advertising lures and superstitious behaviors.

This study is an example of *conditional reasoning,* one kind of deduction. Conditional reasoning involves *syllogisms* of premises and conclusions of the form "If p, then q. p is true; therefore q is true." A more meaningful example from Mayer (1983) is the following:

1. If there is a solar eclipse, then the streets will be dark.
2. There is a solar eclipse.
3. Are the streets dark? (p. 138)

The answer is "yes." Most people have little difficulty with this syllogism, but what if premise (2) is now stated as "The streets are dark." Does this imply logically that (3) "There is a solar eclipse"? No. This is the *fallacy of affirming the consequence*. Many studies have shown that adults (as well as children) do not interpret conditional arguments in the way that formal logic dictates (Paris, 1975; Wason & Johnson-Laird, 1972). Instead of logical deduction, people often reason according to correlated outcomes or the meaning of the syllogism. The use of negative terms, complex language, and multiple comparisons also can interfere with logical deduction (Rips & Marcus, 1977).

A second kind of deductive reasoning is *categorical reasoning.* Categorical statements take four forms: "All *A* are *B*," "No *A* are *B*," "Some *A* are *B*," and "Some *A* are not *B*." A syllogism requiring categorical reasoning might read

- □ All magnificent things are preposterous.
- □ All syllogisms are magnificent.
- □ Therefore, all syllogisms are preposterous.

It is relatively easy to determine that this syllogism is true. However, the information can be complicated by juxtaposing terms *A* and *B* or switching the order of premises. Negative terms can be used, and any of the four conclusions can be reached about the *A:B* or *B:A* relations. In fact, there are hundreds of ways to state categorical syllogisms, but only a few are valid (Johnson-Laird & Steedman, 1978; Mayer, 1983).

A third type of deduction is called *linear reasoning.* Linear tasks involve reasoning about relations among elements. If John is taller than Fred, and Fred is taller than Max, who is the tallest? You can deduce that the answer is "John" because of the transitive relation among the heights of the men. But once again, the problem can be complicated by adding more elements in the series, changing terms (e.g., from taller to shorter), and by adding negative statements: "If John is taller than Fred, and Fred is not as short as Max, then who is the shortest?" (Max).

How do people reason about linear syllogisms? One view is that people construct spatial representations, or mental images, of the entire series by fitting each pair into one image (Potts, 1978; Scholz & Potts, 1974). Thus, a series of statements asserting that *A* is more than *B*, *D* is less than *C*, and *C* is less than *B* can be converted to a mental image of *A-B-C-D* ordered accordingly. When subjects are asked, "Is *A* more than *C*?" or "Is *C* less than *A*?" all they have to do is "read off" the right answer from the image. This example illustrates how logical thinking, language comprehension, and mental imagery can all influence reasoning.

Visual Thinking

Visual images can facilitate reasoning in many ways. Spatial representations of linear syllogisms offer one example. Drawings can aid problem solving, too. Try to solve the following problem in your head.

> There are three separate, equal-sized boxes, and inside each box there are two separate small boxes, and inside each small box there are 4 even smaller boxes. How many boxes are there altogether?

Now try to solve it with the aid of drawing. (Did you get 33 boxes both times?)

Imagery may play a key role in creative thinking with analogies. Seeing an image of one set of relations often helps create a similar set of relations. It is said that Gutenberg's invention of the printing press was developed partly by analogy from the presses used to make wine and coins. The personal reflections of August Wilhelm Kekule 25 years after he proposed the ring structure of the benzene molecule shows the vividness of visual, analogical thinking.

> I turned my chair to the fire and dozed. Again the atoms were gamboling before my eyes. This time the smaller groups kept modestly in the background. My mental eye, rendered more acute by repeated visions of this kind, could now distinguish larger structures, of manifold conformation; long rows, sometimes more closely fitted together; all twining and twisting in snakelike motion. But look! What was that? One of the snakes had seized hold of its own tail, and the form whirled mockingly before my eyes. (Cited in Koestler, 1964)

How does the "mind's eye" work? We saw in Chapter 4 that visual imagery has become an important area of investigation (e.g. Kosslyn, 1980). To investigate visual thinking for arithmetic, James Stigler (1984) observed how 11-year-old schoolchildren in Taiwan solved addition problems on an actual abacus and a "mental" abacus (see Figure 8–8). The subjects included some children who were beginners with the abacus, some who were experts with extensive training, and some who had intermediate skills. The addition problems included pairs of numbers with from two to five digits in each addend. (For example, the most complex problem could be 48,361 + 92,057.) Using the "mental" abacus, the 11-year-old experts took an average of less than 8 seconds to compute such problems! In fact, they calculated almost any of the problems in less than 5 seconds, which was several sec-

FIGURE 8–8
A Chinese Abacus

Numbers can be represented on the abacus by moving beads toward the dividing bar. Beads against the outside frame are not active. The five beads below the bar represent values 1–5 in each column. Each bead above the bar represents a value five times the value of a bead below the bar on the same rod. Thus, the number shown is 2,347. Adding and subtracting are performed by moving beads to or from the number actively represented along the dividing bar.

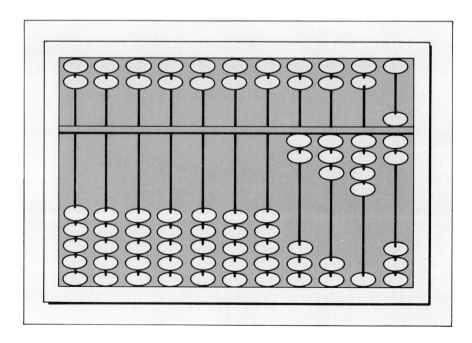

onds faster than experts could calculate on a real abacus. Less-skilled children required 10–30 seconds to perform the calculations and also made more mistakes than experts. It may be a small consolation to know that using the "mental" abacus resulted in more errors, especially with four- and five-digit problems. Stigler (1984) noted that as problems increase in difficulty, the accuracy and response times are roughly parallel for calculations with a real abacus and a "mental" abacus. Thus, the two forms of thinking appear analogous.

MAKING DECISIONS

We make decisions everyday. Should you study or should you go to the party? Should you buy new clothes now or wait for a sale? Should you major in psychology? A good decision maker might analyze the problem, list the alternatives, and weigh each option for its advantages and disadvantages. If we were to follow these logical and systematic steps for making decisions, we would operate like good statisticians to calculate the odds of different gains and losses of our various options. Leon Mann and Irving Janis (1982) labeled this kind of behavior as "vigilant" decision making. However, Mann and Janis suggest that emotional conflicts often lead us astray. Decision makers who are worried about their material gains and losses or their social esteem often are pressed to make less than optimal decisions. They propose that people adopt different coping patterns when faced with stressful decision making:

1. Continue previous behavior and ignore or dismiss information about potential gains and losses involved.

2. Accept uncritically a recommended course of action, usually in order to comply with the decisions of others.

3. Avoid decision making by procrastinating, shifting responsibility to someone else, or rationalizing the choice of the least objectionable alternative. Statements such as "I really didn't want that anyway" or "Nobody will find out" reflect this type of defensive coping.

4. Impulsively seize on a solution that promises immediate relief.

Cognitive Biases

Cognitive biases, as well as emotional conflicts, can affect decision making. Research by Daniel Kahneman and Amos Tversky (1973) has shown that people take mental shortcuts or use cognitive heuristics that can lead them to make poor choices. Many of these heuristics are misperceptions of statistical principles (Nisbett & Ross, 1980). Consider this example:

> A taxicab was involved in a hit-and-run accident. Two cab companies serve the city: Green, which operates 85% of the cabs, and Blue, which operates the remaining 15%. A witness identifies the hit-and-run cab as blue. When the court tests the reliability of the witness under circumstances similar to those of the night of the accident, he correctly identifies the color of the cab 80% of the time and misidentifies it 20%. What is the probability that the cab involved in the accident was blue as the witness stated?

Most people conclude that if the witness was 80% accurate, then the odds are 80% that the taxicab was blue. In fact, it is more likely that the cab was green. To understand this problem, imagine that the witness sees 100 accidents instead of just one. The laws of probability say that about 85 of those accidents would involve green cabs and 15 blue cabs (because that is the ratio of cabs). If the person mistakenly identified 20% of the green cabs as blue, he would misidentify 17 cabs. Conversely, if he correctly identified 80% of the blue cabs, he would spot only 12 of the 15 blue cabs. Thus, of the 29 times (17 + 12) the witness said he saw a blue cab, he is wrong on 17 occasions, an error rate of almost 60%. In other words, the odds are 60–40 that the witness has misidentified a green cab rather than correctly identified a blue one.

Statistical principles are often ignored or poorly understood by people when they make decisions. Consider two everyday examples. Tversky and Kahneman (1982) interviewed former Philadelphia 76ers coach Billy Cunningham and his players about basketball shooting and found that the players believed in the reality of a "hot hand." They believe they are more likely to make a shot after they have made one or two before. But examination of shooting records in games revealed little evidence to support such a belief. Indeed, the 76ers were slightly more likely to score a basket after a missed shot than after a previous score. Why the false belief in a "hot hand"? Tversky says it is because people forget that random sequences of numbers contain streaks. If you were to flip a coin 20 times, there is about a 50–50 chance of getting four heads in a row in any series. Five heads in a row comes up about 25% of the time, and there is a 10% chance of a streak of six. Tversky reasons that basketball players are more sensitive to the streaks of four, five, or six shots that they may make in a game than to the fact that it is just a chance occurrence.

A second common example is the *gambler's fallacy* (also discussed in the Appendix under Misuses of Statistics). Gamblers often believe that if they have been on a losing streak, their luck is bound to change and they will win on the next roll of the dice. Sometimes they use the same reasoning in reverse, believing that if they have been winning consistently they should quit because they are bound to lose soon. You can see that the gambler's fallacy and the basketball player's notion of a "hot hand" are exactly opposite. One believes that the string will continue and the other believes that the string must change. In both cases the players are neglecting statistical probability. (The gambler's fallacy and other important statistical principles are discussed on pages 693–695.)

Tversky and Kahneman (1982) say that such mental shortcuts are often based on availability. *Availability* refers to the accessibility of objects and events to the individual's thinking; it is based on experience and is thus colored by salience, imagination, and personal bias. For example, Paul Slovic, Baruch Fischhoff, and Sarah Lichtenstein (1976) have found that most of the people they interviewed overestimated the number of deaths that occur each year because of accidents and homicide. One reason for this misperception is media coverage. Each year cancer and heart disease claim about 16 times more lives than do accidents, yet the researchers found that newspapers offered more than six times as many articles about accidental deaths as about deaths caused by illnesses.

In another study, Slovic, Fischhoff, and Lichtenstein (1976) asked four groups of people—college students, members of the League of Women Voters in Oregon, business professionals, and experts at risk assessment—to rate 30 technologies and activities in terms of "the risk to society of dying." The items included handguns, pesticides, food coloring, nuclear power, and others. Many of the estimates of risk were similar among groups. However, some were dramatically different. Students and the League of Women Voters rated nuclear power as number one in riskiness; businesspeople ranked it eighth, and risk experts ranked it twentieth, below electrical power, railroads, and even bicycling. When the researchers looked at the actual risk statistics, they found that the experts were relying on actual data more than were other groups, who were probably influenced by media reports and their personal interests.

One final aspect of risk noted by the researchers concerns the cumulative effects of probable risk. For example, the chances of being killed in any one automobile trip are about 1 in 4 million, less than the chance of being killed in a year of mowing the lawn. But when you consider that people make more than 50,000 automobile trips in their lifetime, the probabilities add up to a risk that is considerably greater. Slovic and his colleagues argue that if motorists would think in terms of a lifetime of driving rather than each single automobile trip, they would perhaps be more inclined to buckle their seatbelts. Slovic and his colleagues watched the behavior of several hundred volunteers who witnessed the advertising about increased risks involved in not wearing seatbelts. Although people were more sensitive to the risks, when they were observed in the parking lot there was, unfortunately, no change in the likelihood that they would use their seatbelts.

Misconceptions of statistical principles are not the only ways that cognitive biases can influence decisions. Our choices are also influenced by the way situations are presented. Suppose that someone offers you to flip a coin for $10—heads you get $10, tails you get nothing. Now suppose someone asks you how much money you would accept as a sure thing instead of flipping the coin. What is the *least* amount of money you would take? Most people would settle for about $3.50 even though you have a 50–50 chance of winning $10. Now turn the situation around. Imagine that someone gives you $10 and asks if you are willing to flip a coin—heads you keep it all, tails you give it all back. How much money would you be willing to give back to avoid flipping the coin? Again, most people say they would give up about $3.50, even though the rational choice would be $5 (i.e., the probable amount you could win or lose on each flip).

The outcomes of the two situations are identical. Each one has a 50–50 chance of winning $10, but the presentations of the two situations are quite different. In the first, the choices are between two potential gains; in the second, the choices are between two potential losses. Kahneman and Tversky (1979) found that people react to these situations differently. When it comes to taking risks for gains, people are conservative; however, when faced with the possibility of two losses, people tend to gamble.

Kahneman and Tversky (1979) proposed a mathematical system that they called *prospect theory* to make sense of people's paradoxical attitudes toward risks. The main feature of prospect theory is that people tend to avoid losses. They are not afraid to take risks; rather, they are afraid to lose. To many people, the prospect of a gain often isn't worth the pain of a loss. Prospect theory calls attention to how problems are framed in terms of relative gains and losses, even though the probabilities of the choices remain equal. One implication of prospect theory is that people will continue an endeavor once they have invested time, money, or effort. Arkes and Blumer (1985) call this the "sunk cost effect" and present evidence that people often act contrary to economic considerations.

> Assume that you have spent $100 on a ticket for a weekend ski trip to Michigan. Several weeks later you buy a $50 ticket for a weekend ski trip to Wisconsin. You think you will enjoy the Wisconsin trip more and are looking forward to it. But you discover that both trips are for the same weekend. You can't return the tickets, and it is too late to sell them. You must use one ticket and not the other. Which trip do you go on? (p. 126)

Only 46% of the subjects studied chose the Wisconsin trip even though the total loss of money is the same and the Wisconsin weekend was expected to be more enjoyable. Apparently, subjects chose the option of greater investment to minimize perceived losses and to avoid appearing wasteful. This same type of reasoning underlies continued spending on projects that presently look like they may lead to potential losses. So aversive is the thought of the loss that people will "throw good money after bad." Prospect theory and the sunk cost effect have obvious relevance for decision makers in business, medicine, the military, and any other field in which choices must be made about gains and losses.

Cognitive biases, logic, and heuristic devices are all important aspects of thinking. In our discussion thus far, however, we have postponed mentioning an element that all of these thought patterns have in common—the relation between thinking and language. Solving many of the brain teasers and problems we have presented depends as much on our ability to use and comprehend language as on any other skill. In the remainder of this chapter we will explore the nature of language and its role in thinking.

THE NATURE OF LANGUAGE

As you read this chapter, you are comprehending written language and reasoning about the information, two complex cognitive processes. *Language* is a means of symbolic communication based on sounds, written symbols, and gestures. All languages have a *grammar*, a set of explicit or implicit rules that specify how sound, structure, and meaning are connected. *Linguistics* is the study of language and its rules. *Psycholinguistics* is the study of how language and its rules influence the ways in which people speak, write, and think.

Basic Units of Sound and Meaning

The basic units of any language are its sounds, called *phonemes.* Phonemes include vowels, consonants, and blends. Each language has a certain number of phonemes; English, for example, has 46. Other languages have many more, and some have considerably fewer. Each language also has rules for acceptable combinations of sounds. In English you are unlikely to hear the consonant sequence *pm*, while *mp* is common. Thus, *thump* is consistent with English sounds, but *pmet* is not. These rules of acceptability, called *phonological rules*, tell us how to combine the sounds of our language. They form part of our *linguistic competence*, our implicit knowledge about language.

Phonemes are produced by stopping or regulating the air flow in the mouth. Say the sounds *b, t, m,* and *l* aloud and you will notice how the lips, teeth, and tongue are used to form different sounds.

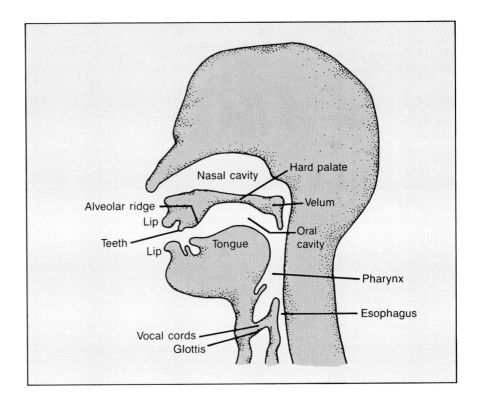

In speaking, we produce each phoneme in a distinctive manner. In English, vowel sounds are created by a continuous airflow through the vocal tract, and consonants are produced by stopping the airflow. Movements of the tongue, lips, and teeth modify the flow of air in the vocal tract to create the various sounds we hear (see Figure 8–9). The lips form the sounds *p* and *b,* for example, whereas *t* and *d* emerge when the tongue presses against the roof of the mouth against the teeth.

Phonemes are the basic sounds of language; ***morphemes*** are meaningful combinations of phonemes. The morpheme is the smallest unit of meaningful language. Some morphemes are words, but some words consist of more than one morpheme. Consider the word *sport.* It has one morpheme. Add *-s* to form *sports;* the result includes two morphemes. Now add other morphemes such as *un, man,* and *like* to generate *unsportsmanlike.* Many complex and compound words include several morphemes as combinations of stems, prefixes, and suffixes. Morphemes are combined in regular ways, such as by *inflection,* to modify the meanings of words. The primary English inflections include rules to form the following structures:

☐ Plural nouns:	apples = apple + s
☐ Third-person singular verbs:	jumps = jump + s
☐ Past-tense verbs:	kissed = kiss + ed
☐ Progressive verbs:	eating = eat + ing
☐ Comparative adjectives:	longer = long + er
☐ Superlative adjectives:	fastest = fast + est
☐ Possessive nouns:	Max's = Max + 's

The Structure of Language

Language includes more than just formulas for combining speech sounds and morphemes. It also depends on *syntax,* a classification system of words and rules for their combination. In English, words are classified as nouns, verbs, and adjectives, and rules govern their combination in sentences. For example, adjectives usually precede nouns in English sentences. One way to understand these relations among words is to diagram them. Consider the sentence shown in Figure 8–10: "The wicked vampire bites the girl." In this simple declarative sentence, articles precede nouns, adjectives precede and modify nouns, and the subject of the sentence comes before the verb. The tree diagram in Figure 8–10 shows the hierarchical relations among the parts of speech as well. The sentence has two main components—a noun phrase and a verb phrase. Each of these phrases has specific constituents (articles, adjectives, and nouns). Such tree diagrams can help us understand the structural relations among words. For example, consider the sentence "Visiting relatives can be a nuisance." It is ambiguous because you can be doing the visiting or *visiting* can be an adjective modifying *relatives.* These different syntactic relations are evident in Figure 8–11.

We usually remain unaware of the rules of grammar, but they are part of our linguistic competence. This means that even though you cannot easily state some rules of syntax, you can recognize well-formed sentences. Consider these two sentences:

1. Colorless green ideas sleep furiously.
2. Green furiously sleep ideas colorless.

Both (1) and (2) are nonsense, yet you can recognize (1) as acceptable syntax, while (2) is not.

Does syntax influence language processing? Yes. Both speed and accuracy of understanding are affected. For example, the effects of linguistic structure may be measured by giving people sentences to memorize and then determining which words they are likely to forget. Neal Johnson (1965)

FIGURE 8–10
A Tree Diagram of a Simple Sentence

The diagram specifies grammatical relationships among sentence parts.

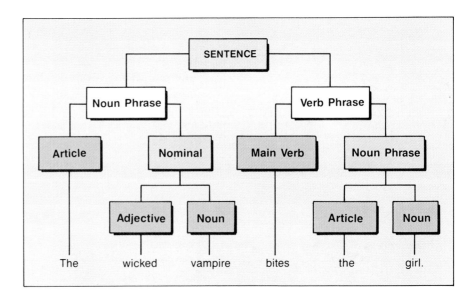

FIGURE 8–11
Ambiguous Sentences

Diagramming the syntactic relations among words in sentences can help to untangle the meanings. In A, *relatives* is the subject of the sentence; in B, *visiting* is the subject of the sentence. Thus, the ambiguity is whether to treat the word "visiting" as a modifier or as a noun.

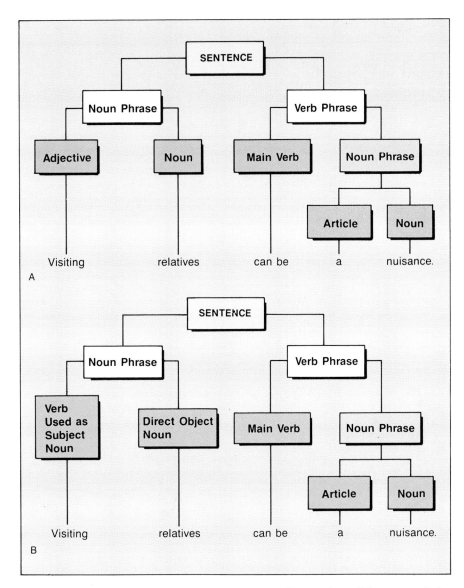

presented adults with such sentences to recall as "The tall boy saved the dying woman." Then each word was repeated for them as a cue to remembering the next word. If remembering sentences were like learning a list of words, errors would occur with equal frequency between all words. But errors turned up most often *between* syntactic boundaries, or grammatical units (for example, between the subject "the tall boy" and the predicate "saved the dying woman," and less often *within* phrases).

Perhaps the effect of syntax on our linguistic competence is more vivid when we consider the humor of linguistic ambiguity. A sign in a restaurant said, "Shoes are required to eat in the cafeteria." Underneath it, someone wrote, "But socks can eat wherever they like." Ambiguity can be an impediment to clear communication, a clever tool used by politicians and advertisers, or a source of amusement. "Applying Psychology: Humor in Linguistic Ambiguity" describes some research on the topic, and you will find many more examples in your local newspaper.

APPLYING PSYCHOLOGY

Humor in Linguistic Ambiguity

Sometimes a speaker or writer intends language to have multiple meanings, as in metaphors, analogies, and puns, but slips of the tongue and "bloopers" are, by definition, accidental. Newspaper writers occasionally allow unintended *linguistic ambiguity* in headlines. Consider the following examples that the *Columbia Journalism Review* found:

- Prostitutes Appeal to Pope
- Police Help Murder Victims
- Suicide More Common Than Thought
- Teenage Prostitution Problem Is Mounting
- American Sentenced to Life in Scotland

Verbal humor illustrates well the flexible use of language and the interaction between thinking and linguistic structure. One level of humor is based on *phonological ambiguity,* or the dual meanings of sounds. For example, children delight in knock-knock jokes such as:

Knock-knock.
Who's there?
Little old lady.
Little old lady who?
I didn't know you could yodel.

Double meanings of sound combinations produce, regrettably, puns like the following:

Mary: You have snew all over your sweater.
Sue: What's snew?
Mary: Not much, what's new with you?

Another kind of humor is based on *lexical ambiguity,* or the multiple meanings of words such as *draw*.

Joe, I like your picture of a horse but where's the wagon?
Oh, the horse is supposed to draw that.

I work as a baker because I knead the dough.

Verbal humor can also involve different inferences from grammatical relationships in the surface and the deep structure of sentences. *Syntactic ambiguity* and *semantic ambiguity* can both contribute to multiple interpretations of the same referent. Here are examples of each level:

John: I saw a man eating shark in the aquarium.
Mary: That's nothing, I saw a man eating herring in a restaurant.

Ralph: Call me a cab.
Fred: You're a cab.

The Meaning of Language

The grammatical rules presented so far describe the *surface structure* of sentences, a linguistic term that corresponds approximately to the actual words expressed in a sentence. Such structure can vary in expressing the same idea. For example, the following sentences all differ in form yet not in meaning:

- The old professor dropped his notes.
- The notes were dropped by the old professor.
- The professor, who was old, dropped his notes.

The linguist Noam Chomsky (1965), who revolutionized thinking about the structure of language, noted an abstract deep structure that did not always resemble the surface structure. *Deep structure* refers to the speaker's intended message and to the linguistic relations that constrain a sentence's

The fun of jokes, riddles, and puns often derives from their violation of our expectations or usual comprehension of language. If the incongruity is eliminated ("Call me a cab." "Yes, Ma'am"), no joke results. Children often do not arrive at dual interpretations and may laugh equally at riddles like "What do giraffes have that no other animal has?" (answer: baby giraffes) and nonriddles (answer: long necks). Shultz and Horibe (1974) found that children progressed during middle childhood from comprehending jokes based on phonological and lexical ambiguity to more subtle grammatical relationships involving syntax. Understanding of metaphoric uses of language also improves during childhood, and part of comprehending the humorous and creative aspects of language depends on interpreting linguistic ambiguity. Can you identify the linguistic bases of the jokes shown in these cartoons?

Cartoon sources: (top and middle) by permission of Johnny Hart and News America Syndicate. (bottom) TUMBLEWEEDS by Tom Ryan © King Features Syndicate, Inc. 1974. Permission of News America Syndicate.

meaning. In the preceding examples, each sentence has the same deep structure of ideas and grammatical relations, but the surface structures vary. Chomsky's theory of ***transformational grammar*** postulated that particular ***transformation rules*** are used to generate appropriate surface structures from deep structures. These rules enable us to insert words, change word order, or turn statements into questions or exclamations while systematically preserving the deep structure of meaning. Although some controversy exists over the best way to characterize the deep structure of a language, most psychologists and linguists agree that grammatical structure does reflect distinctive deep and surface structures.

The meaning expressed in language is called ***semantics***. A sentence can be formed from acceptable phonemes and morphemes and put together in proper syntactic order yet still be meaningless. "Colorless green ideas" defies semantic interpretation. But "My brother is an only child" is not uninterpretable; in fact, it is amusing. Semantic interpretation can be silly,

Noam Chomsky, the linguist, formulated new theories about the structure of language.

incomplete, contradictory, or anomalous. There are many levels of understanding for language and various criteria that we can apply to comprehension. The richness of semantics allows endless creative language expressions. We should also note that semantics applies to many levels of language, from morphemes to sentences to lengthy discourse.

Language communicates meaning, but meaning is not *in* words and sentences. Meaning is constructed in the mind. Declarations, questions, orders, and threats have meaning for both speaker and listener because each understands the words and social context. Language thus directs social exchanges by expressing the thoughts and intentions of the participants. In conversation or written text, a social interchange of information occurs between listeners and speakers or readers and authors. This exchange is termed a *speech act*, a social and linguistic unit of analysis that includes the message, the intent of the speaker, and the effect of the message on the listener. Each of the following sentences could be part of different kinds of speech acts:

☐ I now pronounce you husband and wife.

☐ I know who is buried in Grant's tomb.

☐ What was Zorro's real name?

☐ Please don't hit me with that!

☐ Give me all of your money—or else!

Because language is a shared medium, it demands a consensus between users about how words are employed to convey meaning. Without consensus, people would speak idiosyncratically like Humpty Dumpty in Lewis Carroll's *Through the Looking Glass:*

"When I use a word," Humpty Dumpty said, in a rather scornful tone, "it means just what I choose it to mean—neither more nor less." "The question is," said Alice, "whether you can make words mean so many different things." "The question is," said Humpty Dumpty, "which is to be master—that's all."

We consider the relation between language and thought in the following section on cognitive processes involved in understanding language.

COGNITIVE PROCESSES IN LANGUAGE COMPREHENSION

There are many cues to language meaning, such as gestures, facial expressions, the situation, topic, and prior utterances of the participants. People do not comprehend language in a vacuum nor do they interpret individual sentences and retain them in a mental file. Language comprehension requires generating, inferring, and consolidating meaning from speech or writing, guided by knowledge of the world and the context of language. For example, if a stranger tapped you on the shoulder and said, "There's no quiz this week," your comprehension would require more than linguistic analysis of the sentence. You might ask, "Who's he? Is he in my class? What quiz? You mean we've had quizzes the past weeks? Why is he telling me?" But if the tip came from a classmate and your class usually has weekly quizzes, you would readily understand the message.

We will briefly discuss some research findings that support a series of propositions about language comprehension:

1. People usually remember the meaning of sentences but forget the surface structure or form of the information.

2. A significant context and previous information about the topic of conversation facilitate comprehension and memory.

3. Language comprehension is a constructive process dependent on other knowledge.

Note that the generalizations in this list correspond well with our understanding of how memory works, as we discussed in Chapter 7.

Remembering the Meaning

Consider the first proposition. People seldom recall complex material word for word; instead, they remember the gist of the message. In other words, the ideas of the linguistic deep structure may be retained but the wording of the sentence is usually forgotten. To examine this notion, Jacquelyne Sachs (1967) tested the memories of adults for specific sentences immediately after they had read passages she had given them and 30 to 45 seconds later, after the subjects had continued reading. One sentence was "He sent a letter to Galileo, the great Italian scientist." When Sachs stopped her subjects, she gave them a recognition test that included either the original sentence, a sentence that meant the same thing but changed the word order (e.g., "He sent Galileo, the great Italian scientist, a letter about it"), or a sentence that changed the meaning (e.g., "Galileo, the great Italian scientist, sent him a letter about it"). When tested immediately after reading the sentence, subjects accurately identified both new sentences. After delays, they rejected the false sentence but frequently said that the new word order in the other choice was identical to what they had read previously. Thus, Sachs confirmed that people forget the surface-structure features of sentences while recalling the gist of the information.

The Role of Context

The second proposition says that the context in which one hears or reads something greatly affects how language is understood. The sentence "The haystack was important because the cloth ripped" is confusing until an additional cue is provided—"torn parachute." Now you can create a context (or perhaps a mental image) that makes the sentence easy to understand. Context can include prior knowledge, words, text, pictures, places, or people that help us understand language.

To demonstrate this point to yourself, read the following paragraph.

> If the balloons popped, the sound would not be able to carry since everything would be too far away from the correct floor. A closed window would also prevent the sound from carrying since most buildings tend to be well insulated. Since the whole operation depends on a steady flow of electricity, a break in the middle of the wire would also cause problems. Of course the fellow could shout, but the human voice is not loud enough to carry that far. An additional problem is that a string could break on the instrument. Then there would be no accompaniment to the message. It is

FIGURE 8–12
Context Aid for Language Comprehension

In the study by Bransford and Johnson (1972) adults could not recall or comprehend much of a story unless they were provided with the picture on the left before they heard the passage. Showing the left-hand picture after hearing the story or seeing the picture on the right before hearing the story did not aid understanding or memory for the passage.

Source: Bransford & Johnson, 1972.

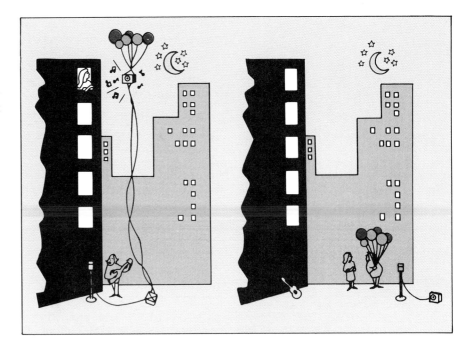

clear that the best situation would involve less distance. Then there would be fewer potential problems. With face-to-face contact, the least number of things could go wrong. (Bransford & Johnson, 1972, p. 11)

You probably rate this passage low on comprehensibility and would recall only a few ideas presented in it. However, if you looked first at the drawing in Figure 8–12, the passage would probably make more sense.

Bransford and Johnson (1972) read this passage to adults who had no picture to look at, to adults who had seen a picture with the same objects but in inappropriate positions, and to adults who had the correct picture displayed to them before or after they heard the passage. Only when the picture served as a map beforehand did the subjects judge the passage as sensible and remember ideas in it. Bransford and his colleagues have shown in many studies that context is a prerequisite for understanding pictures, sentences, and stories.

Context aids language comprehension because people base conversations on shared topics and understanding of the listener's point of view (although children sometimes have difficulty doing so). Thus new information is related to previous statements and comprehended according to relationships among sentences. Haviland and Clark (1974) referred to this as the *given-new contract;* that is, the speaker and listener specify the common topic (or "given" information) and add comments. For example, Haviland and Clark presented sentences like these to adults:

1. We got some beer out of the trunk. The beer was warm.
2. We checked the picnic supplies. The beer was warm.

They wanted to determine if subjects could comprehend the sentence "The beer was warm" more quickly in (1) than in (2). Subjects listened to the sentence and pushed a button as soon as they understood it. They were significantly faster at understanding the test sentence in (1) because it followed the "given" information. The phrase "some beer" provided an explicit context or shared knowledge that facilitated comprehension. Conversations and comprehension sometimes break down when participants do not share the same "given" information.

Understanding as a Constructive Process

According to the third proposition, expectations and knowledge guide interpretation of language. In Chapter 7, we showed how experience affects memory with examples from Elizabeth Loftus's experiments on eyewitness testimony. The same processes operate for linguistic comprehension. People interpret conversations or written messages according to their expectations of the characters and situations. (In Chapter 7, we referred to this as the "soap opera effect.") Many studies have shown that people interpret ambiguous sentences and discourse according to their beliefs about the context. For example, adults who read about Helen Keller reported later that they had seen sentences like "She was deaf, dumb, and blind" even though no such sentences had been in the passage (Sulin & Dooling, 1974). People often construct scenarios that can alter their comprehension of language in systematic ways (Anderson et al., 1977).

We also described in Chapter 7 how the presentation and organization of material can improve remembering. Language facilitates such "information packaging." For example, Carmichael, Hogan, and Walter (1932) showed adults 12 pictures (like those in Figure 8–13) and labeled each picture orally. By design, the pictures were ambiguous, but the labels biased the subjects of the experiment toward specific interpretations. Some heard the label "eyeglasses" for the first picture, others "dumbbell." Later, when they had to recall the pictures, the subjects drew objects resembling the labels that they had heard rather than the original pictures. The linguistic cues had influenced people to construct different mental representations of the objects.

The errors and distortions evident in these studies were not random. Their elaborations fit the topics appropriately and reveal how people construct meaning from linguistic and nonlinguistic cues. Children's language

FIGURE 8–13
Labels' Influence on Recall of Pictures

Adults were shown a series of pictures like those on the left, but with different labels. Some subjects were given the labels in the center column, while others were given the labels on the right. When subjects were later asked to recall the pictures, they drew pictures that were consistent with the labels, not with the pictures originally presented to them. Thus, language can influence the reconstruction of experiences.

Source: Carmichael, Hogan, & Walter, 1932.

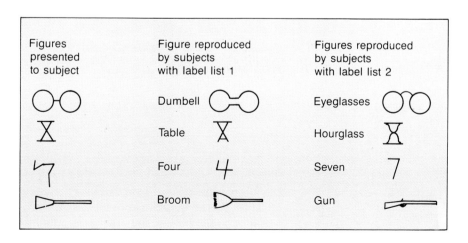

comprehension is also constructive and creative, yet children often do not know when or how to make some inferences. In one study, for example, short stories were read to children between 6 and 12 years of age (Paris & Upton, 1976). Later, children were asked yes-no questions about the stories and were also asked to recall the stories in their own words. Six- and seven-year-olds did not construct as many implied relations or link the main ideas together as much as older children. The ability to apply constructive processes to aid comprehension while reading, listening, or remembering improves with other problem-solving skills throughout childhood (Paris & Lindauer, 1982). We will discuss the linguistic competence of children more fully in Chapter 9.

LINGUISTIC DETERMINISM

All languages have sounds, syntax, meaning, and rules that specify how they are related. Yet the particular rules, like sounds and vocabulary, vary widely among languages. For example, the Chinese language has a much wider assortment of terms to indicate family relationships than English does, and Eskimos use 20 different words to describe kinds of snow.

A critical question asked by psychologists is whether this diversity of language reflects different forms of thinking. Does how we speak *determine* how we think? Because of their rich vocabulary, do Eskimos perceive their world of ice and snow differently than an outsider would?

Linguist Benjamin Whorf (1956) believed that language is the central force behind thought. He wrote,

> We dissect nature along the lines laid down by our native languages. . . . We cut nature up, organize it into concepts, and ascribe significances as we do, largely because we are parties to an agreement to organize it in this way—an agreement that holds through our speech community and is codified in the patterns of our language. (pp. 312–314)

Whorf deduced much of the evidence for this position by comparing American Indian languages with European languages. He argued that cultural differences in language produce culturally different ways of thinking. For example, in one anecdote Whorf compared two cultures' thinking about spring water:

> We might isolate something in nature by saying, "It is a dripping spring." Apache erects the statement on a verb *ga:* "be white (including clear, uncolored, and so on)." With a prefix *no-* the meaning of a downward motion enters: "Whiteness moves downward." Then "*to*," meaning both "water" and "spring," is prefixed. The result corresponds to our "dripping spring" but synthetically it is "as water, or springs, whiteness moves downward." How utterly unlike our thinking. (p. 241)

Granted that the literal translation is not everyday English, the utterance is comprehensible (perhaps poetic) and may not represent a different way of thinking. Contrary to Whorf and the *linguistic determinism* position, most people believe that language *reflects* general properties of human perception, thinking, and socialization rather than *determines* them. The evidence comes from studies of different language groups who have widely different vocabularies and grammar yet distinguish or "cut up nature" in similar ways. Let's consider a few examples.

For many years it was believed that every language divided the color spectrum in arbitrary ways because some languages have no names for colors commonly labeled in English. The Dani in New Guinea have only two basic terms, *mili* (black) and *mola* (white). But does color-naming limit perception to hues with names? Anthropologists Brent Berlin and Paul Kay (1969) discovered that all languages have basic color terms that come from only 11 color names; moreover, they found that these eleven names form a hierarchy (reading from left to right):

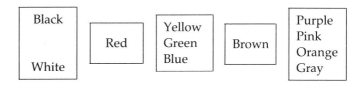

A language with two color names has black and white, a language with three names includes red, and so on. English includes all 11 terms.

These basic color names reflect how language mirrors perception. They represent *focal colors,* a fundamental category of light on the visible spectrum somewhat like the predominant hues perceived in rainbows. Eleanor Heider Rosch (Heider, 1972) showed how focal colors influenced thinking. When adults were shown a color chip for five seconds and later asked to pick out the same chip from among 160 chips, they demonstrated better memory for focal then for nonfocal colors. Even children matched focal colors to examples faster than nonfocal colors (Heider, 1971; Mervis, Catlin, & Rosch, 1975). Rosch (1973) also examined how fast the Dani could learn color names that were not in their vocabulary. They acquired names for focal colors quicker then for nonfocal colors. In other studies, the Dani were found to represent and remember colors the same way English-speaking people do (Heider & Oliver, 1972). So, in spite of great differences in the language terms available for color naming, and in contradiction to Whorf's theory, people's perception and memory are influenced by universal aspects of focal colors and not by their linguistic labels.

Other universal aspects of human thinking and socialization are reflected in language too. For example, languages seem to have different levels of abstraction for referring to things. English-speaking people might call an apple an apple, a Golden Delicious apple, a fruit, an object, something to eat, or a dessert. Why does the word *apple* seem most fitting? Roger Brown (1958) argues that the term is at a level of abstraction with the greatest utility, neither too general nor too specific.

Berlin and his colleagues (Berlin, 1972; Berlin, Breedlove, & Raven, 1973), studying how people around the world name plants and animals, discovered that the classification systems usually involve five levels of abstraction: (1) *unique beginner:* plant, animal; (2) *life form:* tree, bush, flower; (3) *generic name:* pine, oak, maple, elm; (4) *specific name:* Ponderosa pine, white pine; and (5) *varietal name:* Northern Ponderosa pine, Western Ponderosa pine. The levels become progressively more precise yet they do not overlap, and each lower level is included in the larger category hierarchically. Berlin and his coworkers found that level 3, or generic names, was the most common category of names in different languages. Rosch (1977) has suggested that these generic categories are the most common in language because the objects included in them share many attributes. General terms such as "tree" do not distinguish adequately among kinds of similar trees, nor do precise terms such as "white pine" describe the similarities of objects clearly. While languages may vary in their vocabulary for each level, the fact that diverse cultures rely most heavily on generic terms supports the notion that cognitive categories for objects help determine linguistic categories.

A similar effect has been observed for other dimensions of perception and cognition. All languages appear to refer to spatial dimensions such as height, weight, thickness, and distance. Most languages also specify directions (such as up-down, left-right, and front-back), time (such as present-past-future), and number. Even when languages do not include particular words for each characteristic, people process the basic cognitive and perceptual features similarly. For example, in Rosch's studies with the Dani (Rosch, 1973), she determined how they learned names for various shapes. The Dani had no appropriate vocabulary for circle, square, and triangle and resorted to "pig-shaped" or "fence-shaped" and the like. Rosch presented Dani subjects with figures that we regard as common—such as circle, square, and triangle—as well as with odd shapes. The Dani learned the names for "common" figures more easily than other shaped names. Thus, it seems that nonlinguistic features and categories help direct learning and language.

These studies and other evidence support the view that universal aspects of human perception and cognition appear to influence languages. But how do linguists account for the variations among languages: the plethora of Eskimo words for snow; the few color terms in some cultures; the lack of shape names among the Dani? Clark and Clark (1977) suggest that they reflect not different ways of thinking but adjustments to the environment. If you live in a world of snow or eat mostly rice, your language requires appropriate terms. Thus, people invent language to describe the important features of their environments and to communicate effectively.

NONHUMAN COMMUNICATION

Animals other than humans communicate with members of their own species in distinctive ways. The dancing patterns of a bee's flight can indicate the location of food. The gestures and odors of dogs can signal sexual and aggressive readiness. Whales, dolphins, and monkeys, among others, use specific sounds to warn of danger. Although animal communication is not a symbolic system (Clark & Clark, 1977) and does not have syntactic and semantic structures as flexible and creative as spoken human language, do other animal species besides ours have the capacity to learn and to use language?

Psychologists have been studying the communication of animals for more than 50 years. Much of this research has focused on members of the ape family, the species most closely related to humans in evolutionary terms. In one of the first attempts to teach language to animals, a chimpanzee named Gua was raised by two psychologists with their own infant son, Donald (Kellogg & Kellogg, 1933). Donald easily acquired language; Gua never produced sounds resembling human speech, and he could not understand language any better than a well-trained dog. Several years later, Keith and Cathy Hayes (Hayes, 1951) taught a chimp named Viki to say "papa," "mamma," and "cup," but that took three years and Viki comprehended little of the human speech directed toward her. One reason for these failures may be that neither the organization of chimps' brains nor the anatomy of their vocal tracts seems suited for verbal language (Lieberman, Crelin, & Klatt, 1972). Thus, more recent researchers have tried to teach *nonverbal* language to animals (see Figure 8–14).

One well-known animal communication study was done in Nevada by Beatrice and Allan Gardner (1978), who taught American Sign Language to

FIGURE 8–14
A Chimpanzee Learning to Imitate the Gestures of American Sign Language

Chimps' signs are often rapid and are not always perfect copies of human gestures.

To make the gesture that stands for "fruit," the fingers are loosely curled and the hand is drawn down the side of the cheek.

By pointing to the corner of its eye, a chimpanzee can signal "see." The same gesture is also used to signify "look."

a chimpanzee named Washoe. Since the sign language constitutes a symbolic and structured system and since chimps use their hands adeptly, this method is a better test of chimps' abilities to learn human language. When the experiment began, Washoe, a female, was a year old. She spent each day in the Gardners' house or yard and in her presence everyone communicated by sign language, never using oral speech. Dressing, feeding, and playing were accompanied by lots of signing, much like conversations between deaf-mute parents and children. In addition the Gardners used demonstration, imitation, and conditioning, with tickling as a frequent reward, to teach Washoe new signs.

After 7 months Washoe had mastered only four signs, but after 22 months she had a vocabulary of 34 different signs. She used the signs to refer to objects appropriately and correctly, even in new situations. Like a child, Washoe *generalized:* for example, she employed the signal for "open" to refer to the doors of the house, car, and refrigerator and the sign "pants" for diapers, rubber pants, and trousers. By five years of age, Washoe knew more than 160 distinctive language signs. Even more impressive, Washoe began to combine new individual signs into multiword utterances that could be translated as "you drink," "more tickle," "hurry open," and "hurry gimme toothbrush." Often, Washoe created novel word combinations to describe things. It has been reported that she signed "water bird" when she first saw a swan and called a nasty rhesus macaque a "dirty monkey."

There have been other approaches to teaching language to chimps. David and Ann Premack (Premack, 1971; Premack & Premack, 1972) raised a chimp named Sarah in a laboratory cage where she was given only periodic language training each day. Sarah was taught to manipulate plastic pieces that symbolized different words and relations (see Figure 8–15). Each piece varied in shape, size, and color and had a metal back so it could be placed on a magnetic board to answer questions and make requests. Sarah was taught the meaning of these tokens through shaping and conditioning. For example, an experimenter first provided a piece of banana for Sarah. Then the token signifying banana was placed closer to Sarah than another piece of banana. When Sarah stuck the token on the board, she got the piece

FIGURE 8–15
Plastic Shapes Used by Sarah the Chimp

The top row shows individual tokens, and the bottom row forms the sentence "Red is not the color of chocolate."

Source: Premack & Premack, 1972.

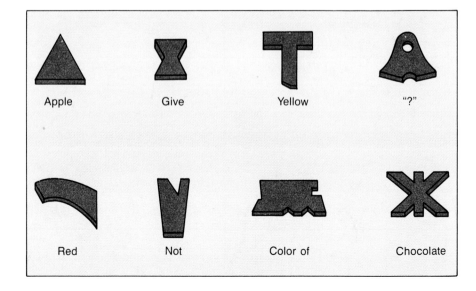

of banana to eat. In subsequent training, Sarah was presented the plastic shapes signifying apple, orange, and banana and was given the fruit only when she selected the correct token.

The Premacks also taught Sarah how to construct sentences and answer questions; the verb *be;* the conjunction *and;* and terms for color, shape, and size. Sarah learned to follow correctly the commands of a sentence that translates from the tokens as "Sarah, put the banana in the pail and the apple in the dish." When Sarah was shown two objects, such as a pencil and a key, and their corresponding tokens, she could, in response to a question, correctly pick the token indicating "same" or "not same" nearly 80 percent of the time.

The accomplishments of Washoe and Sarah stimulated others to train primates in symbolic communication. For example, Francine Patterson (1978) taught sign language to Koko, a lowland gorilla, and concluded triumphantly that "language is no longer the exclusive domain of man." Other projects have improved the technological aspects of teaching symbolic systems to chimpanzees. Duane Rumbaugh (1976) taught a chimp named Lana to communicate on a computer terminal by punching symbolic keys.

Recently, Sue Savage-Rumbaugh has begun to study a pygmy chimp named Kanzi (*New York Times*, 1985). Kanzi apparently first learned about symbols by watching other chimps being trained. Subsequently, Kanzi learned to combine new symbols, to make statements, and to request things. For example, when another chimp, named Austin, was removed from the compound, Kanzi was evidently lonely. He typed the symbols for "Austin" and "TV" and rested comfortably after watching a videotape of Austin. These studies suggest that other primates have more linguistic and conceptual competence than we suspected. But can they learn language as a symbolic system or do they only learn to manipulate objects and make gestures to receive rewards? This is an ongoing controversy that is not easy to settle.

At the heart of the controversy is the definition of key concepts. What is a word, what is a sentence, and, indeed, what is language? Premack (1985) argues that these terms are debatable but do not necessarily exclude chimpanzees' use of symbolic communication. He suggests that there are great similarities between children's language acquisition and the languages learned by nonhumans, similarities in grammatical form as well as semantic function. However, other scientists argue that chimpanzees do not learn symbolic language. We pursue this debate in "Controversy: Can Chimpanzees Learn to Use Language?"

SUMMARY

1. Effective problem solving depends on three steps: formulating the problem, generating possible solutions, and evaluating outcomes. Functional fixedness and mental set can block problem solving through inflexibility.

2. Mental shortcuts such as algorithms, which are specific rules that lead to solutions, and heuristics, which are general guidelines for what works for similar problems, can help people solve problems.

3. Identifying concepts involves recognizing critical attributes of objects and the rules that relate those attributes. Some concepts are defined more easily than others; some concepts can be defined by prototypical or natural characteristics.

4. Inductive reasoning includes the ability to classify objects, to solve analogy problems, and to complete series. Deductive reasoning includes logical thinking about syllogisms, categorical reasoning, and linear ordering.

5. Visual thinking involves mental manipulation

Can Chimpanzees Learn to Use Language?

Despite the excitement generated by Washoe, Sarah, and Lana, the issue remains as to whether language learned by other primates is qualitatively similar to human language. After five years of teaching sign language to a chimp, Herbert Terrace concluded, "I could find no evidence confirming an ape's grammatical competence, either in my own data or those of others, that could not be explained by simpler processes" (Terrace, 1979, p. 67).

Terrace points out a number of problems. First, how do we know that chimps produce sentences with an underlying knowledge of grammatical rules such as subject, verb, and object relations? Although the chimps constructed word strings such as "Washoe more eat," "Mary give Sarah apple," and "Please machine give Lana apple," did they actually create whole sentences as children do? Terrace suggests that the chimps may have only manipulated the symbol for rewards, such as apple or Coke, in a sequence of otherwise meaningless symbols. It is something like filling in the names of things in foreign phrases. If you didn't know French, you could still add to the imperative phrase "Donnez-moi _____ ("Give me _____") if you had learned that the first two symbols preceded the object symbol and led to reward. Terrace points out that chimps seldom spontaneously created sentences that followed rules for the order of words. The Gardners' Washoe, for instance, often signaled either "more drink" or "drink more," which were both recorded as "more drink." Terrace suggests that when Washoe made the signs for "water bird" on seeing a swan and being asked, "What's that?" she might have responded "water" and then "bird"—both appropriate but not necessarily grammatically creative.

Terrace (1979) trained a young male chimp named Nim Chimpsky (in a humorous twist on the name of the linguist Noam Chomsky) for four years beginning in Nim's infancy. Nim learned 125 signs, including a number of sign combinations that followed a fixed order. The sign for "more" oc-curred first 85 percent of the time (e.g., "more tickle," "more drink") and the sign for "give" in 78 percent of the two-sign combinations. Although this seemed to indicate a grammatical rule for Nim, Terrace concluded otherwise. He found, through detailed analyses of videotaped conversations, that Nim often imitated a trainer's signs while signing himself (see Figure 8–16).

Terrace describes similar problems in interpreting Washoe's creative utterances. One filmed conversation with Washoe "began with Gardner signing *eat me, more me,* after which Washoe gave her something to eat. Then she signed *thank you*—and only then asked *what time now?* Washoe's response *time eat, time eat* can hardly be considered spontaneous, since Gardner had just used the same signs and Washoe was offering a direct answer to her questions" (Terrace, 1979, p. 76).

Perhaps many of the chimps' symbolic expressions, rather than being novel, spontaneous, and grammatical, depend on training, reward, and imitation. The learning abilities of chimps are indeed impressive, but analyses and interpretations of their communication have induced skepticism about

of images, which can be rotated, moved, and scanned much like actual visual perceptions.

6. Decision making can be distorted by emotional stress and misconceptions about statistics. Judgments may be biased if based on readily available or representative information.

7. The basic units of sound in a language are phonemes; the basic units of meaning are morphemes. People are not usually aware of grammatical rules, but as part of linguistic competence they allow adults to judge when words and sentences are well formed.

8. Language has deep structure and surface structure. People usually remember the meaning of sentences, which is part of deep structure, more easily than exact words, part of surface structure.

9. Comprehending language is a constructive process that depends on prior knowledge, the social situation, and the context surrounding the utterance.

10. There is little evidence that people who speak different languages perceive and think about the world in radically different ways.

11. Chimpanzees can learn to use symbolic forms of communication, but they acquire only the rudiments of human language after considerable training.

FIGURE 8–16
Do Trainers Inadvertently Supply Extra Cues for Chimps to Sign Language?

Nim Chimpsky and a trainer, Susan Quinby, are shown conversing in sign language. Nim's hands indicate "me" (upper left), "hug" (upper right), and "cat" (lower left) and appear to be declaring "Me hug cat." But Terrace (1979, p. 71) suggests that the trainer may have provided cues to Nim without being aware she was doing so. He bases the idea on scrutiny of the pictures, which, he says, show Quinby making the sign for "you" while Nim is indicating "me," and Quinby signaling "who" while Nim is communicating "cat." "Cat" and "who" had frequently been linked in Nim's lessons. Whether the teacher's signs preceded or followed Nim's cannot be ascertained from the photos.

their capacity to comprehend and produce language. Indeed, when language tokens were left in Sarah's cage, she usually ignored them and did not initiate any "conversations" or practice her new skills.

Richard Sanders (1985) carefully analyzed all the videotapes of Nim's training and concluded that "the ape learned to use gestures as nonsymbolic instrumental responses." Sanders argues that neither Nim nor the training procedures were atypical of other studies, and thus earlier attempts to teach Washoe, Sarah, Lana, and other animals may have been confounded also. But as Premack (1985) points out, this does not mean that chimps are incapable of learning symbolic language. So despite the skepticism of Terrace and Sanders, the isssue of whether nonhumans can learn symbolic languages is an open, and fiercely debated, question.

SUGGESTED READINGS

Bransford, J. D., & Stein, B. S. (1984). *The IDEAL problem solver: A guide for improving thinking, learning, and creativity.* New York: Freeman.
> Presents a wealth of information in nontechnical language on problem solving, with many examples for inquisitive readers.

Clark, H. H., & Clark, E. V. (1977). *Psychology and language.* New York: Harcourt Brace Jovanovich.
> A thorough analysis of language with a strong linguistic orientation, written by two prominent researchers.

Mayer, R. E. (1983). *Thinking, problem solving, cognition.* New York: Freeman.
> An introduction to research and approaches in cognitive psychology.

Nisbett, R. E., & Ross, L. (1980). *Human inference: Strategies and shortcomings of social judgment.* Englewood Cliffs, N.J.: Prentice-Hall.
> Summarizes research and theories on errors in decision making and social judgment.

Whimbey, A., & Lochhead, R. (1982). *Problem solving and comprehension.* Philadelphia: Franklin Institute Press.
> A practical book with helpful suggestions for learning and studying.

◄ The solution to Duncker's functional fixedness problem demonstrates creative problem solving.

Solutions to Figure 8–3

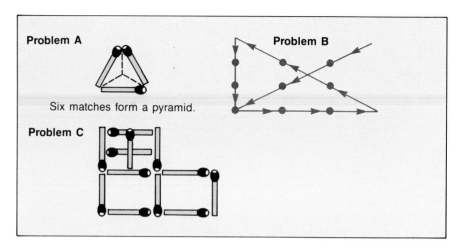

Problem A

Six matches form a pyramid.

Problem B

Problem C

Solution to Figure 8–4

Sequence of moves is C3, B2, C2, A3, C1, B3, C3.

Solutions to Figure 8–7

Verbal: B.; D.

Figural: C.; G.

Letter Series: c d c d; t m n t

Number Series: 23 36 27 37; 69 55 75 68

Analogy Problems

Verbal: Sour; Increase

Numerical: 12; 9; 20; 15

Geometric:

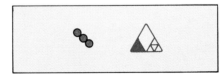

Painting opposite: (Detail) "Women Admiring a Child, 1904" by Mary Cassatt. The Detroit Institute of Arts, Gift of Edward Chandler Walker.

PART FOUR
Development and Intelligence

9

Infancy and Childhood

The frightening part about heredity and environment
is that we parents provide both.

—Notebook of a Printer

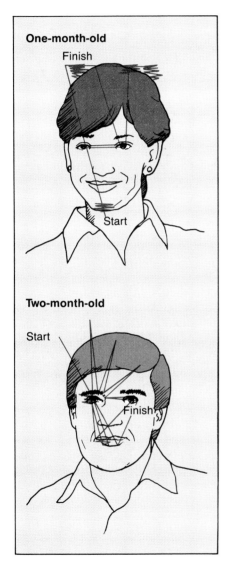

FIGURE 9–1
Infant Scanning of the Human Face

This illustration shows how one- and two-month-old infants scan the human face. Lines drawn across each face trace the eye movements of one- and two-month-old infants as they look at a human face. One-month-olds look mostly at the edges of faces while two-month-olds scan the eyes and mouth.

Source: Salapetek, 1975.

BABIES LOVE TO SMILE, COO, AND LOOK AROUND. THEIR CRIES OF hunger or joy are often easy to interpret, but sometimes they simply stare into your eyes or grasp your finger. What thoughts are running through their minds? How do they think about the world around them? For a long time, scientists and parents alike gave infants little credit for understanding the world. However, research during the past 20 years has shattered the myth that infants do not understand their world. For example, in the first few days following birth, newborns can discriminate some sounds of language. Babies who hear a recording of "pa, pa, pa" orient to the sound and suck a mechanical nipple vigorously as they listen. Gradually they suck less as they become more familiar with the sound. When the recording is switched to "ba, ba, ba," babies immediately orient to the sound and start to suck the nipple more strongly, indicating that they hear a distinctly new sound (Eimas, 1975).

Infants also quickly learn to examine human faces. In one study, the eye movements of one- and two-month-old infants were recorded as they scanned the faces of mothers or strangers (Maurer & Salapatek, 1976). One-month-olds looked mostly at the edges of the faces, regions of contour and contrast. Two-month-old babies, however, examined a wider area of the faces and looked more at internal features such as the eyes (see Figure 9–1). By two or three months, infants can distinguish facial features and mouth movements. By five to six months, infants can discriminate familiar from unfamiliar faces, masks from real faces, and parents from strangers (Gibson & Spelke, 1983). These abilities are remarkable because they reveal a depth of infant understanding that often goes unnoticed.

In this and the following chapter we will chart many of the changes and patterns of human development, beginning with the abilities of newborn infants and concluding with the adjustments of old age. The course of human development is a cumulative, continuous process of change involving both biological maturation and experience. The study of human development draws from all areas of psychology, including research on memory (discussed in Chapter 7), the principles of learning (covered in Chapter 6), and the study of the brain and the nervous system (introduced in Chapter 2). Because the topic of human development is so broad, we break our discussion into two chapters. This chapter covers development until puberty, about 11–13 years of age; Chapter 10 discusses adolescence, adulthood, and old age.

UNDERSTANDING HUMAN DEVELOPMENT

Developmental psychologists study how people change with age physically, mentally, and socially. They try to explain why people develop certain habits, talents, or disabilities. Developmental descriptions are like collections of

TABLE 9–1
Chronological Stages of Human Development

Stage	Approximate Time Frame
Prenatal	Conception to birth
Infancy	Birth to 2 years
Toddlerhood	2 to 3 years
Preschool	3 to 6 years
Middle childhood	6 years to adolescence
Adolescence	11–13 years puberty to young adulthood
Young adulthood	20–40 years
Middle age	40–65 years
Old age	Beyond 65 years

photographs showing what children can do at six months, two years, eight years, and so on. Uncovering the patterns and sequences that underlie the changes these pictures reveal is rather like the process of creating a film from a set of photographs.

Patterns Across the Life Span

Charting changes across the life span is not easy. Many factors affect development at different times, and they are often difficult to isolate. The major chronological periods of human development are listed in Table 9–1. Developmental theories provide guides to different patterns of growth across these age periods. For example, Sigmund Freud, the founder of psychoanalysis, offered a theory of distinct stages that children pass through in their sexual-emotional development. Jean Piaget, the pioneering Swiss psychologist, created a detailed and comprehensive theory of children's mental development that includes four broad periods. Other developmental theories based on physical or social stages have been devised to highlight distinctive developmental changes. Although *stage theories* call attention to relatively abrupt changes in behavior over the life span, other approaches, such as learning theory, stress the continuous nature of change in behavior as we mature and grow older.

As we discuss "ages" and "stages" of development, keep in mind three things. First, stages serve as a convenient way to divide the life course and to identify patterns, but they are not rigid timetables. People exhibit great variability in the ages at which they reach certain milestones. Second, there is no single theory of development or life stages. Each theory emphasizes different aspects of growth. Third, many theories have given inadequate attention to the roles of culture and history in development. Child rearing, adolescence, schooling, and old age, for example, differ profoundly around the world and throughout history. To understand development, we must consider the whole person and how individuals react to environmental, social, and historical forces (Rogoff, 1982).

The Emergence of Developmental Psychology

Until the nineteenth century, people's views of childhood were extremely narrow. Some philosophers, such as Thomas Hobbes (1588–1679), believed that children were inherently selfish and should be controlled by society, whereas others, such as Jean-Jacques Rousseau (1712–1778), believed that children had an intuitive sense of right and wrong but were often misdirected by adults. These philosophical arguments, as well as interest in pediatrics and education, eventually led to the first scientific studies of children. Society gradually began to view children as individuals valuable enough to care for (Kessen, 1965). However, academic centers for the study of children in the United States and Canada were not well established until the 1930s. Pioneers of the child study movement had to struggle to obtain funds and to convince politicians of the social and educational benefits from studying human development.

Shifting scientific and political attitudes were not the only reasons for expanding interest in human development. There were simply many more children, alive and healthy, than there used to be. For example, before 1750,

Sophisticated technology and research methods help psychologists unlock the mysteries of human development.

the odds were three to one against a child living to age five. As the risks of disease, infection, and abandonment declined, the brutally high rates of infant mortality have also decreased to one-tenth the level of 100 years ago.

Life expectancy has also changed dramatically, increasing from less than 30 years in 1800 to 47 years in 1900 to almost 75 years in 1987. (Expectancies are still slightly higher for women than men and for whites than blacks.) These trends, coupled with the "baby boom" following World War II, have created an aging population and larger numbers of retired people. One consequence of this population shift in recent years has been greater scientific interest in the study of development across the entire life span rather than just from infancy through adolescence.

Methods of Developmental Research

Several 19th-century scientists recorded their children's development in *baby biographies.* These observations were the first descriptions of the sequence of human development and were an important beginning to the scientific study of children. "Each father saw his own child—that is, the child that his prejudice or theory would predict—but sharing a common object of observation bound these men of divergent times and opinions to a set of common problems about human development" (Kessen, 1965, p. 1). Biographical accounts were often supplemented with questionnaires, interviews, and clinical reports.

Developmental psychologists today use many experimental procedures from other areas of psychology, but two methods are especially suited to test developmental hypotheses. *Longitudinal analysis* involves the repeated testing of the same individuals over time so that subtle changes can be analyzed over the course of their lives. Longitudinal research can be informal,

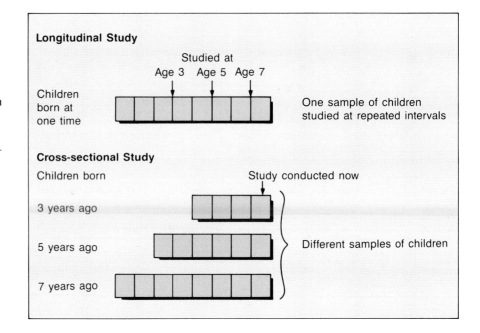

like some baby biographies, or it can be incredibly detailed, as were Jean Piaget's records of his own children's development. One disadvantage of the longitudinal method is that it takes a long time to collect data from a few individuals. *Cross-sectional analysis* is less time-consuming because it is conducted simultaneously on people of different ages. To follow language development in one child from his second to his fourth birthday would require a two-year longitudinal project, but cross-sectional comparisons of the language of two-, three-, and four-year-olds can be made concurrently. Of course, a combination of the two methods can be used. For example, a one-year longitudinal study of two-, three-, and four-year-olds could yield data for a cross-sectional analysis also. The two methods are summarized and compared in Figure 9–2.

Forces That Shape Development

Undoubtedly you have heard children being compared to their parents: "She has her mother's eyes," "She is as impatient as her father," or "Like father, like son." Whenever we try to explain a developmental outcome, we confront a basic, perplexing question: How much of a behavior or characteristic is due to heredity and how much is due to the environment? The debate is often referred to as *nature versus nurture,* a phrase you encountered in Chapter 4. Quite simply, *nature* refers to inherited, genetic characteristics: *nurture* refers to experiences such as parental care and the quality of the physical and social environment.

Throughout history, "nature" has been the more popular explanation for human behavior because people believed that qualities like wisdom, goodness, and strength were passed along biologically. Charles Darwin's (1859) theory about natural evolution fostered that view and the more particular view that each individual child passes through the same stages of development that characterized the evolution of the human species. By the turn of the twentieth century, Darwin's belief was so well established that G. Stanley Hall, the first American Ph.D. in psychology (Harvard, 1878) and the first president of the American Psychological Association (1892), suggested in 1904 that children would show better social behavior if they first were allowed to play as savages and then as barbarians and nomadic wanderers. Thus, he reasoned, they would eventually become socialized because they would have passed through all of the precivilized stages of human society. Arnold Gesell argued that biological *maturation* was the main principle of development. "All things considered, the inevitableness and surety of maturation are the most impressive characteristics of early development. It is the hereditary ballast which conserves and stabilizes growth of each individual infant" (Gesell, 1928, p. 378).

In contrast, many psychologists have stressed the ways in which learning in general and conditioning in particular can change how people behave. In 1928, the champion of behaviorism, John Watson, published *Psychological Care of Infant and Child,* which contained observations of behavioral development in children. In his book Watson opposed the views of Darwin, Hall, and Gesell. "The behaviorists believe that there is nothing from within to develop. If you start with a healthy body, the right number of fingers and toes, eyes, and a few elementary movements that are present at birth, you do not need anything else in the way of raw materials to make a man, be that a genius, a cultured gentleman, a rowdy, or a thug" (Watson, 1928, p. 41). He thought that human development depended so importantly on experience that from any dozen healthy babies he would "guarantee to take any one at random and train him to become any type of specialist I might select—doctor, lawyer, artist, merchant-chief, and yes, even beggar-man and thief, regardless of his talents, penchants, tendencies, abilities, vocations, and race of his ancestors (Watson, 1924, p. 104).

Nowadays, most psychologists refuse to accept the simple proposition of either nature or nurture. They look at the interaction of the two forces, the dynamic interplay between an individual's biological endowments and environmental opportunities. Sandra Scarr (1985) argues persuasively that scientists sometimes exaggerate the influences of nature and nurture and often overemphasize one or the other. She notes that interactionist theories emphasize how people evoke and experience different environments based on their own behavioral characteristics (e.g., age, skill, sex). To understand children's behavior, our scientific theories must consider how nature and nurture influence each other for particular individuals.

As we noted in Chapter 2, the science of behavior genetics helps us disentangle the relative contributions of nature and nurture. Selective breeding of nonhuman animals and studies of human families allow us to estimate the relative impact of nature and nurture. For example, *twin studies* allow researchers to compare identical twins (whose genetic makeup is the same) with fraternal twins (who share some, but not all, genetic characteristics). Another popular method is to study adopted children. If adopted children are more like their biological than their adoptive parents in a particular trait, then a genetic basis of transmission is suggested. If the children are more similar to their adoptive parents, then nurture appears to be the dominant factor.

Regardless of whether a developmental characteristic is more influenced by nature or by nurture, timing is important. In general, the earlier that a developmental problem is detected and remedial steps are taken, the better the chances for recovery. "Applying Psychology: Overcoming Early Disadvantages" describes how early risks to development can be minimized or overcome by timely intervention. In addition, psychologists have identified certain time frames that are *sensitive periods,* that is, periods in which development is proceeding rapidly with heightened susceptibility to external factors. If a particular behavior is not well established during the sensitive period, it may not develop to its full potential. For example, if a bond is not established between an infant and its caretaker during the first year, or if language is not encouraged during the first two years, serious problems may arise.

APPLYING PSYCHOLOGY

Overcoming Early Disadvantages

Many people believe that their entire lives are shaped by early childhood experiences and that the impact of parents and the environment is so great during infancy that the effects cannot be reversed. Children who survive war, family disintegration, or other calamities, however, reveal how extraordinarily flexible development can be. Psychologists have studied the resiliency of institutionalized or neglected children as well as the differences among cultures in child rearing to determine the influence of early experience.

Consider how children overcome the limitations of confinement and isolation. Hopi Indian infants are swaddled tightly to boards during infancy, but they learn to walk and develop physical coordination normally. In some Guatemalan villages, babies are kept in huts for the first year, and although their early development is retarded or delayed in comparison with that of American children, most differences in mental development disappear by ten years of age.

Infants raised in institutions usually have few toys and lack interaction with caretakers. By four months, they often appear listless and withdrawn. They vocalize little and are generally unresponsive. Some say that the babies have learned to be helpless because they cannot control the environment such as when they are fed, changed, or comforted. Such effects of institutionalization are reversible. Children in a Lebanese orphanage with IQ scores around 50 who were adopted before their second birthday later attained normal IQ scores. Those who were not adopted remained in the mentally retarded range (Dennis, 1973).

In the late 1930s, Harold Skeels and Marie Skodak began to study two groups of children from an Iowa orphanage. Because of overcrowding, 13 of the youngsters, whose average age was 19 months and whose average IQ score was 64, were transferred to an institution for the mentally retarded, where they were raised by the retarded female residents. Despite the fact that virtually the only adults with whom they had a bond of affection were of low intelligence, the children averaged gains of 28 points on an IQ test 18 months after entering the institution, while the IQ scores of those who remained in the orphanage de-

clined. The researchers followed the children for 30 years (Skeels, 1966). Eleven of the 13 were adopted, became self-supporting, married, and had children with normal IQ scores.

Perhaps the key to overcoming early social isolation lies in the child's ability to establish a personal relationship: what counts is not the amount of stimulaton provided but the quality of an emotional, caring adult's behavior. For example, one study (Saltz, 1973) compared one-to-six-year-old children developmentally from two model institutions. The institutions differed only in that one had a foster grandparent program. Elderly people from the community were employed to spend four hours a day, five days a week, with the children. Each foster grandparent was assigned two children; he or she fed the infants and changed their diapers or played games and read to the older ones. The IQ scores of the youngsters who received such attention rose significantly compared with those of the children at the other institution. Moreover, the foster grandparents felt useful and proud.

These important studies tell us that although isolation and deprivation may affect mental growth and behavior in early childhood, development can be modified substantially by caring adults and a nurturing environment.

PRENATAL DEVELOPMENT

The study of human development begins before birth because the infant carries a genetic heritage from both parents and distant ancestors. The genes that transmit this heritage are really combinations of chemicals along the *chromosomes,* the genetic material found in sperm and egg cells. Each sperm and egg cell carries 23 chromosomes, which unite during fertilization to form the full complement of 23 pairs. Each chromosome is a string of thousands of DNA (deoxyribonucleic acid) molecules arranged in a ladder-like spiral. During conception, one "leg" of the sperm's ladder combines with one leg of the egg's ladder to form a new spiral ladder, with half contributed from each parent. Since each molecule of DNA is made of gene pairs of highly complex sugar and phosphate molecules, the millions of new combinations in the chromosomes of the united sperm and egg yield an individual who is genetically unique.

Three Periods of Growth: Zygote, Embryo, and Fetus

At conception, usually a single male sperm cell fertilizes the female egg cell in one of the Fallopian tubes that connect a woman's ovaries to her uterus (see Figure 9–3). The united sperm and egg constitute a *zygote,* the first cell

FIGURE 9–3
Conception

The sperm cell usually meets and fertilizes the egg as it travels from the ovary to the uterus along a Fallopian tube. The developing zygote divides many times on the way to the uterus. Within two weeks after fertilization, the mass of cells, called a blastocyst, is embedded in the wall of the uterus. (The illustration is not drawn to scale.)

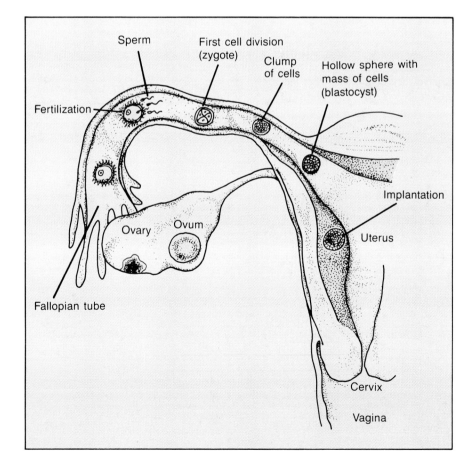

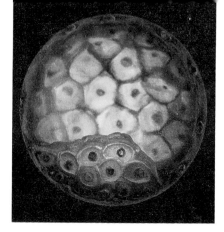

FIGURE 9–4
A Blastocyst

This mass of cells is produced when the fertilized egg divides repeatedly after conception.

FIGURE 9–5
Prenatal Growth

The shape of this 28-day-old embryo (left) already reveals a distinct head, tail, and limb buds. The embryo is still only 1/16 inch long. In the nine-week-old fetus (right), the rudimentary human form is quite apparent. Because the head and brain develop rapidly during the embryonic stage, the head is very large in proportion to the rest of the body. The internal organs, toes, and fingers are partially formed in this embryo—it is only a little more than one inch long.

containing all the genetic information necessary to form the new organism. The cell divides again and again to form a hollow ball of cells, a *blastocyst;* (see Figure 9–4), as it moves down the Fallopian tube. Usually it takes from seven to nine days to reach the uterus. The ball of cells, continually dividing, begins to shape the developing organism by first flattening and then folding its edges inward. The outer wall of cells inside the ball eventually becomes the *placenta,* a network of blood vessels attached to the mother's uterine lining that carries food and oxygen to the child and removes waste. The placenta starts growing by the end of the second week following fertilization, when the zygote embeds itself in the uterine lining. From this point, and for the next six weeks or so, the organism is called an *embryo.*

The embryo develops in a cushioned and protective environment called the *amniotic sac* and is connected to the placenta by an umbilical cord. During the *embryonic stage,* from approximately two to eight weeks after fertilization, three tissue layers form. By the end of the first month, the embryo has a heart that pumps blood. Soon after, the embryo generates a nervous system and a rudimentary abdomen. By the second month, the head becomes distinct and the face human-like. Arms and legs begin to appear, and muscles move reflexively. Still, the embryo is only one inch long and weighs one-fifteenth of an ounce.

During the *fetal period,* from approximately eight weeks after fertilization until birth, the organism is designated a *fetus.* The soft cartilage begins to harden to bone; nerves and muscles triple in number; the stomach manufactures digestive juices; and the reproductive system forms. The fetus takes on the appearance of a human baby (see Figure 9–5). By the sixth or seventh month, all major systems have been elaborated, and the fetus may

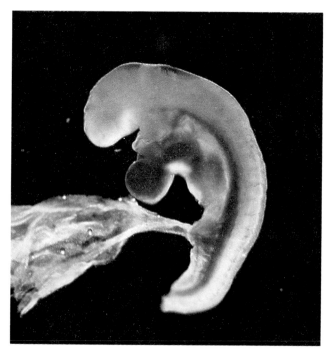

survive if born prematurely. However, the last months of pregnancy are important for the buildup of body fat, tissue, and antibodies and for refinements of other systems.

Complications During Prenatal Growth

Fetal growth can be complicated by inherited disorders, by the mother's age, and by stress during pregnancy. Inherited disorders can cause enzyme deficiencies or anemia. Women who have their first child after the age of 35 have a higher incidence of twins, mentally retarded children, and congenital abnormalities. Perhaps the most severe influences on fetal growth come from the mother's experiences during pregnancy. Disease, injuries, drugs, smoking, alcohol, and radiation during pregnancy can all affect the infant's physical and mental development.

Mother and child often share the burden unequally. A mild dose of radiation to the mother may cripple the embryo or fetus. Diseases such as rubella (German measles) in the mother can cause heart disorders, deafness, and mental retardation in infants, particularly if the mother is affected early in pregnancy. Smoking tobacco during pregnancy has been linked to increased risk of spontaneous abortion and fetal death. A synthetic hormone, DES (diethylstilbestrol), given to several million women between 1947 and 1970 to prevent miscarriage, has increased the incidence of cervical cancer and vaginal abnormalities in their daughters during adolescence. Also, undernourished pregnant women may bear babies of low weight who grow slowly and learn with difficulty (St. James–Roberts, 1979). Fortunately, medical supervision during pregnancy and parental awareness of prenatal development can reduce the incidence of these problems.

Several new methods are now available to help diagnose some complications during prenatal growth. *Amniocentesis* is a method in which a hollow needle is inserted through the woman's abdomen to remove a sample of amniotic fluid from the womb. Because the fluid contains discarded fetal cells, analyses can reveal any chromosomal abnormalities as well as the sex of the child. Amniocentesis carries some risk and cannot be used until the fourteenth to sixteenth week after conception. A new method, *chorionic villii biopsy,* can be done as early as the eighth week after conception, but it is slightly more risky. In this procedure, a tube is inserted into the pregnant woman's cervix and some fetal cells are suctioned off for analysis. A noninvasive technique, *ultrasound,* provides a measure of fetal growth. High-frequency sound waves are directed through the woman's abdomen, and the reflected waves provide an image of the fetus. Heart rate and movement can be observed directly. Bone growth, body proportions, and the sex of the child can also be determined.

The best advice for pregnant women is to stay in good health, to avoid drugs, tobacco, and alcohol, to exercise moderately, and to follow a balanced diet (Schuster & Ashburn, 1986). Pregnant women should eat at least three meals each day in order to gain the extra 20–25 pounds needed to support the fetus (see Figure 9–6). They should consult a physician early in pregnancy and continue regular checkups throughout pregnancy. Most hospitals and communities offer birthing classes that provide prospective parents with valuable information about prenatal development, maternal health, and birth procedures.

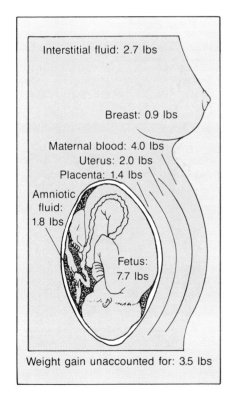

Interstitial fluid: 2.7 lbs

Breast: 0.9 lbs

Maternal blood: 4.0 lbs
Uterus: 2.0 lbs
Placenta: 1.4 lbs
Amniotic fluid: 1.8 lbs
Fetus: 7.7 lbs

Weight gain unaccounted for: 3.5 lbs

FIGURE 9–6
Average Weight Gain During Pregnancy

Women are encouraged to gain between 20 and 25 pounds during pregnancy to aid their own nutrition as well as the developing child's. Less than a third of the weight gain is due to the baby alone.

Source: Papalia & Olds, 1985, p. 397.

Childbirth

The process of childbirth usually begins about 266 days after conception. There are three distinct stages in the birth of a child. First, labor begins when the woman experiences uterine contractions and ends when her cervix is fully dilated to allow the baby's exit. This process lasts about 8–14 hours for a first child, but only half as long for subsequent children. The second stage involves the delivery of the baby, as illustrated in Figure 9–7. The head is usually delivered first, but occasionally the legs or buttocks emerge first (a breech delivery). The third stage is the delivery of the placenta.

Vaginal delivery is not always possible. When labor becomes stalled, when the fetus is not positioned well, or when there is a risk to mother or fetus, the baby is delivered surgically through the mother's abdomen. This procedure is called a caesarean section, and it occurs in about 15 percent of deliveries. Because birth can be a long and painful process, other medical interventions, such as pain medication, are often necessary. But medications during delivery can bring additional risks to the baby that may persist through the first year of life. One researcher (Brackbill, 1979) found that various kinds of pain medication can affect an infant's perceptual abilities during early months.

Because of the possible disadvantages of medicated deliveries, many people advocate natural childbirth techniques. The popular Lamaze method, for example, stresses the mother's control of breathing and muscular contractions to relieve the pain and to assist the delivery. Fathers can assist

FIGURE 9–7
Childbirth

As labor begins, the baby is positioned for delivery. Muscular contractions in the uterus during labor cause the cervix to dilate and the baby to pass through the birth canal.

Source: Shaffer, 1985, p. 142.

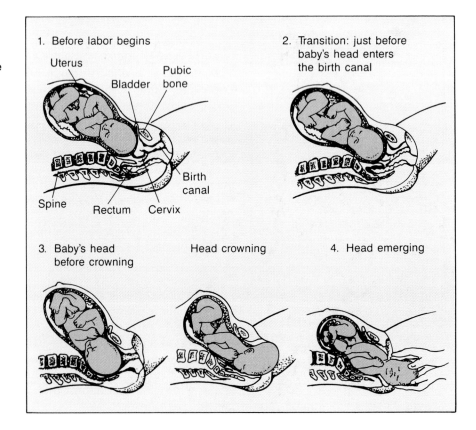

Drawing by Ziegler; © 1980 The New Yorker
Magazine, Inc.

mothers, acting as coaches for exercises in self-control both before and during childbirth. Some advocate giving birth at home or in comfortable surroundings with family members present. Some new techniques, such as the Leboyer method of gentle birth in a dimly lit, quiet room, are controversial. Critics point out the dangers of infection or poor observation in dim light as well as the lack of differences between babies born conventionally or by such methods (Nelson et al., 1980). No matter what birth method is preferred, recent obstetric advances have helped to educate future parents and make more options available.

PERCEPTUAL-MOTOR SKILLS AND PHYSICAL GROWTH

Newborn babies appear helpless. They sleep up to 20 hours each day, cannot crawl or even roll over, and communicate almost entirely by crying or gurgling. Yet babies are born with muscular and sensory responses that quickly adapt to the outside world. For example, an innate sucking reflex allows newborns to feed from a breast or bottle immediately. They find the nipple easily because another response, the rooting reflex, causes them to turn their heads toward any touch on their cheeks. One study showed that during the first few weeks after birth, babies learned to modify sucking patterns to obtain nourishment (Sameroff, 1968). In this study, babies received milk via a plastic nipple. The rate of delivery of the milk was controlled by the experimenter. The infants quickly adjusted the strength of their biting or sucking to keep the milk coming.

Perceptual Development

Babies are also born with several sensory responses ready for action. They can discriminate colors and brightness reasonably well by two months of age (Bornstein, 1979), but their visual acuity is not very good. Babies are nearsighted; their distance vision is approximately 20/600. They see objects best when 6–10 inches from their faces, but according to Martin Banks (1980), objects at any distance may appear blurred until six months of age because infants have difficulty accommodating (changing the shape of the lens in their eye) to focus.

Robert Fantz (1961; 1963; Fantz, Fagan, & Miranda, 1975) demonstrated that infants can discriminate visual patterns. He used an apparatus like the one shown in Figure 9–8. Placed in this equipment, infants lie on their backs and look at the ceiling of the chamber. Their eyes reflect the stimulus on which their gaze is fixed so an adult looking down through a peephole can determine which stimulus attracts the child's attention. Initially, Fantz (1961) showed that infants prefer to look at patterns rather than random figures. The contour, complexity, and curvature of shapes are important dimensions of infant visual preferences—one reason that infants often prefer to stare at faces. Despite this preference, infants cannot discriminate between their mother's and a stranger's face until three months of age, and memory for faces is not good until six months (Barrera & Maurer, 1981; Cohen, DeLoache, & Strauss, 1979). It is not just a coincidence that mother-infant bonds of attachment are beginning to form during the first six months.

FIGURE 9–8
Apparatus Used to Study Infant Perception

The adult is peering through a peephole into the infant's eyes so that she can determine where the baby's gaze is directed. Different objects are placed above the infant's head to measure attentional preferences.

Source: Shaffer, 1985, p. 209.

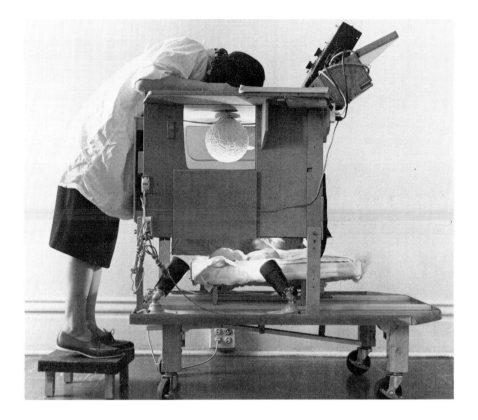

Infants also show a remarkable ability to perceive spatial depth. Eleanor Gibson and Richard Walk (1960) designed a *visual cliff* to test infants' depth perception (see Figure 9–9). The apparatus is actually like a glass table with a runway down the middle. On one side of the runway is a checkerboard pattern just below the glass surface. On the other side, the checkerboard is several feet below the glass, producing an illusion of a deep well. The question researchers posed was whether infants would be as likely to crawl from the runway onto the deep side, as onto the shallow side. Gibson and Walk observed that few six-month-old infants would cross the deep side, even with their mothers encouraging them. But the origins of depth perception may be even earlier. Campos, Langer, and Krowitz (1970) measured the heart rates of two-month-old infants placed on the deep and the shallow sides. They found that infants showed slower heart rates when placed on the deep side, presumably as an orienting, or attentional, response.

Babies also seem particularly sensitive to language. They can discriminate some speech sounds, such as "pa" and "ba," and prefer rhythmic sounds in the human voice range (Eimas, 1975). Condon and Sander (1974) observed two-day-old infants as they listened to tapping noises, vowel sounds, and natural language in English or Chinese. The newborns became alert and moved in synchrony with the languages but not with the other sounds. DeCasper and Fifer (1980) have even shown that three-day-old infants can recognize their mothers' voices and will suck harder on a mechanical nipple in order to hear it!

FIGURE 9–9
The Visual Cliff

The infant is coaxed to crawl on the glass over the "deep" side of the visual cliff apparatus.

Growth and Muscular Coordination

Average newborns weigh about 7½ pounds, but they can double their birth weight by six months and triple it by their first birthday. After age two and until puberty, children grow two to three inches in height and gain six to seven pounds in weight each year. Newborns have relatively large heads and small limbs. With increasing age, the body proportions change sharply, as shown in Figure 9–10.

At birth the brain is only 25% of its eventual adult size, but by age three it is 75% of its adult size (Schuster & Ashburn, 1986). Diet and stimulation are extremely important to an infant because half of the brain weight is added from the seventh prenatal month until the second birthday. Primary motor and sensory areas of the brain mature at this time and myelinization of neurons occurs. Speech and other functions located primarily in one hemisphere are not fully developed neurologically until adolescence or adulthood (Schuster & Ashburn, 1986).

Newborns cannot support their own body weight while standing, partly because their bones are so flexible. The skeleton grows and hardens with age. The soft spots in the skull join and harden by the age of two, while the leg bones continue to grow well into adolescence. Muscular development follows the same head-to-tail sequence of development as do other bodily systems. That is why babies can raise their heads before they can control

FIGURE 9–10 ▼
Body Proportions from Fetal Stage to Adulthood

The head represents 50% of body length at two months after conception but only 12–13% of adult stature. In contrast, the legs constitute about 12–13% of the total length of a two-month-old fetus but 50% of the height of a 25-year-old adult.

Source: Robbins et al., 1929.

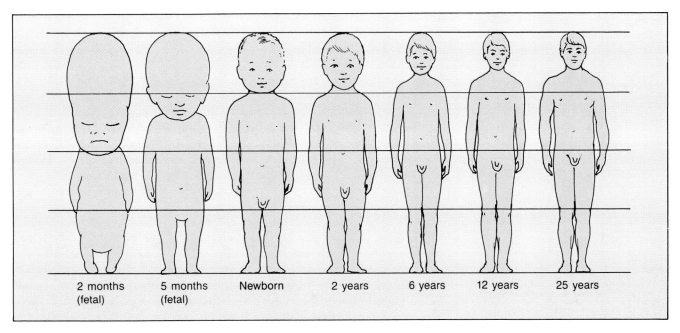

| 2 months (fetal) | 5 months (fetal) | Newborn | 2 years | 6 years | 12 years | 25 years |

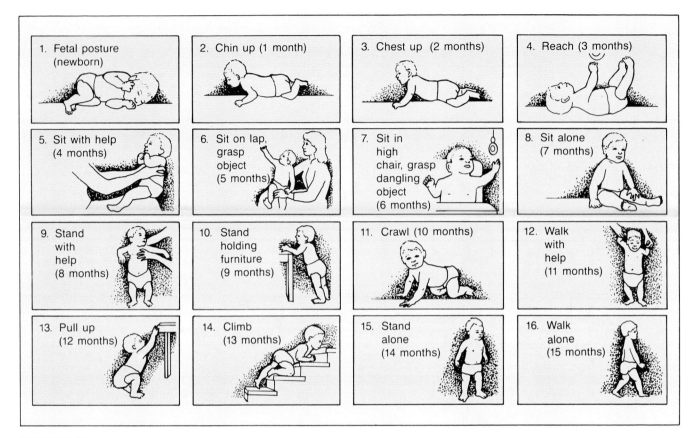

FIGURE 9–11
Sequence of Infant Growth

Physical growth during infancy is a gradual series of maturational changes that allow better control of actions and perceptions. Although there are differences among babies from different ethnic origins in terms of temperament, reactions, and rate of development, most infants follow this general sequence.

Source: Adapted from Shirley, 1923.

their arms and legs. The sequence of growth during infancy is rapid and uniform. Most American babies can sit in a highchair by 6 months, crawl by 10 months, and walk alone by 15 months (see Figure 9–11).

The two-year-old is a toddler who often falls down and appears clumsy. A four-year-old can skip, hop, run, dance, and catch a large ball with both hands. As children lose their baby fat and acquire more adult-like body proportions, they gain better balance. Maturation also brings better small-muscle coordination and eye-hand coordination. On the average, girls develop less muscle tissue and tend to be lighter and shorter than boys. After puberty, most girls are less strong, speedy, and agile than most boys (Tanner, 1978).

COGNITIVE DEVELOPMENT

When does thinking and the acquisition of knowledge begin? Infants recognize familiar stimuli, respond to cues, and show conditioned responses in the first months of life. Yet mental representation of events and manipulation of symbols seem to appear much later. Most theorists agree that intellectual development begins with an infant's understanding of actions, objects, and perceptions during the first year of life. The assessment of thinking during infancy is extremely difficult, however, because babies cannot answer questions, perform many complex responses, or stay awake and attentive very long. Older children can demonstrate their cognitive skills in many ways, and there is a wealth of information on how thinking develops beyond infancy. We will review two major perspectives on cognitive development: the stage theory of Jean Piaget and the information processing approach.

Piaget's Theory

Jean Piaget (1896–1980), the Swiss psychologist and philosopher was a pioneer in the study of children's thinking. After earning a Ph.D. in biology at the age of 21, Piaget became intrigued with children's mental development. More than 60 years ago, he began to record his observations of his own and other children as they solved simple problems. He viewed children as active seekers of knowledge who use their curiosity to discover regular characteristics of the world. Piaget believed that children construct ideas about their physical and social environments. He sought to understand how these ideas develop from the practical, action-oriented behaviors of infants to the reflective, logical thinking of adults.

Piaget's ideas about development were influenced by his biological training. His overarching concerns were with the *organization* of behavior and knowledge and the *adaptation* of the person to the environment. Piaget believed that every act—from grasping a rattle to solving a physics problem—is organized and that mental and behavioral organization are improved by two dynamic processes of adaptation: assimilation and accommodation. *Assimilation* is a process of taking in new information about the world and fitting it to existing ideas. For example, if a child has a concept of horses but not of cows, then the first time he sees a cow he may call it "horse." *Accommodation,* on the other hand, is a way of creating a new concept for new information. Children change their ideas about the world to fit new information. For example, young children often refer to all vehicles as "cars." When they see a van, they may point to it and say "car," a case of assimilating a new experience into their own concepts. As they are taught to discriminate vans, trucks, and other vehicles from cars, they establish new concepts by accommodating their previous notions. In Piaget's theory, the processes of assimilation and accommodation occur together, so children who experience something new are constantly trying to fit it into their existing ideas *and* to generate new concepts. This "push and pull" leads to a temporary balance, or *equilibrium,* that reflects children's reconciliation of new information with their previous levels of understanding. Piaget considered **equilibration,** the process of achieving equilibrium, the motivation for children's curiosity.

Piaget provided a systematic description of how the rules and content of thought changed throughout childhood. His theory divides cognitive development into four broad periods, shown in Table 9–2. In the following discussion of Piaget's stages, we try to illustrate how children's thinking improves in regular ways with each stage. The ages given for each stage and the characteristic behavior are only approximate; the quality of the child's thinking, not chronological age, determines the stage.

TABLE 9–2
Piaget's Periods of Cognitive Development

Period	Age	Characteristics
Sensorimotor period	Birth to 2 years	Recognize relations between perceptions and actions
		Manipulate objects, use tools, take active role in world
		Form basic concepts of object identity and permanence
		Begin to understand temporal, spatial, and cause-and-effect relations
Preoperational period	2 to 7 years	Acquire language, ability to use symbols
		Thinking dominated by perceptions of physical features of objects; cannot comprehend transformations that change appearance of objects
		Struggle to identify consistent properties and functions of events to construct cognitive rules that represent these regularities
Concrete operational period	7 to 11 years	Develop systematic operations that can be applied flexibly to a variety of physical problems; move beyond perceptions when solving problems
		Understand the reversible nature of transformations and appreciate the principle of conservation
		Develop enlarged social perspective
Formal operational period	11 years to adulthood	Become capable of solving abstract problems through logical operations
		Reasoning no longer limited to physical problems; function by means of deduction and hypothesis testing

Each of Piaget's stages of development emphasizes a special type of thought and behavior in children. The sequence of development is always the same, each successive accomplishment building on previous stages. The ages given are only approximate.

SENSORIMOTOR PERIOD: BIRTH TO TWO YEARS. During the *sensorimotor stage*, infants discover the relations between their perceptions and their actions (motor behavior). They often repeat actions that produce interesting sights and sounds. Infants learn to manipulate objects, use tools, and take active roles in their environment. Children also form basic concepts of objects and begin to understand relations based on time, space, and cause and effect.

Throughout the first year, infants learn to connect what they do with people and things around them. For example, they often stop crying when their mother pops into sight because they associate her with comfort. They learn how to react to and even to control changes in the environment. John Watson and Craig Ramey (1972) investigated this developing sense of control by placing two-month-old babies in special cribs for ten minutes a day. For one group of infants, a mobile above the crib turned every time the babies pressed their heads against the pillow. For another group, the mobile turned periodically regardless of what the babies did. A third group never saw the mobile turn. After two weeks, only infants in the first group were pressing against the pillow more frequently. The experimenters showed that these infants had learned to control the mobile by pressing the pillow.

Imagine that you are feeding applesauce to a four-month-old. You stop for a moment, put the spoon down, and slowly push it off the table. The

During the sensorimotor period, infants explore objects, discover their features, and learn to manipulate things in their environment.

child may smile or laugh but probably won't look to the floor. At that age, out of sight means out of mind. Four months later, if you drop the spoon, most likely the infant will look down to see where it has gone. At this stage, babies take to throwing things down themselves. (Drop-something-and-watch-somebody-retrieve-it is usually more fun for infants than for parents.) Around six months, babies begin to realize that things exist even when they are not in sight, a concept that Piaget labeled *object permanence.*

Object permanence indicates that infants possess mental representations for missing objects. Piaget provided an interesting vignette about a boy named Gerard who had rudimentary notions of object permanence:

> Gerard, at 13 months, knows how to walk, and is playing ball in a large room. He throws the ball, or rather lets it drop in front of him and, either on his feet or on all fours, hurries to pick it up. At a given moment, the ball rolls under an armchair. Gerard sees it and, not without some difficulty, takes it out in order to resume the game. Then the ball rolls under a sofa at the other end of the room. Gerard has seen it pass under the fringe of the sofa; he bends down to recover it. But as the sofa is deeper than the armchair and the fringe does prevent a clear view, Gerard gives up after a moment; he gets up, crosses the room, goes right under the armchair and carefully explores the place where the ball was before. (Piaget, 1954, p. 59)

Gerard searches for the ball in the most likely place, under the armchair where he found it before, not under the sofa. His ideas about locations of objects and how to search for them will develop significantly by age two.

PREOPERATIONAL PERIOD: TWO TO SEVEN YEARS. Children's thinking changes dramatically during the preschool and early school years. Two-year-olds who are just beginning to talk grow quickly into mobile, inquisitive explorers. The period between ages two and seven is a bridge between infantile sensorimotor actions and the logical thinking of later childhood. While infants are concerned mainly with exploration and play, preschoolers try to control and explain relations among events and to classify and conceptualize the phenomena that they discover. Piaget labeled this stage the ***preoperational period,*** a time in which the capacity for logical operations of thought is lacking. Striking limitations in thinking exist between ages two and seven years. Consider this example from Piaget's conversation with a six-year-old about the origin of the sun and moon. (Piaget's questions are in regular type. The child's answers are in italics.)

> How did the sun begin? *It was when life began.* Has there always been a sun? *No.* How did it begin? *Because it knew life had begun.* What is it made of? *Of fire.* But how? *Because there was fire up there.* How was the fire made in the sky? *It was lighted with a match.* Where did it come from, this match? *God threw it away.* How did the moon begin? *Because we began to be alive.* What did this do? *It made the moon get bigger.* Is the moon alive today? *No . . . Yes.* Why? *Because we are alive.* (Piaget, 1929, pp. 258–259)

Reasoning Based on Appearances. Children often have misconceptions about the world during the preoperational period. Three- and four-year-olds often think that inanimate objects are alive (Bullock, 1985). They do not eas-

Play can lead to important discoveries about measurement during the preoperational period.

ily understand chance or luck and believe that some person or force causes things to happen directly. Preoperational children's mental representations are confined mostly to concrete and immediate experiences. The children do not distinguish well the real from the imagined. Dreams are taken to be actual happenings, shared by other people. Preschoolers are easily fooled by appearances. They may believe that a girl is no longer a girl if she wears her brother's clothes and acts like him. DeVries (1969) tested three-to-six-year-olds' understanding of identity by having the children play with a cat, after which a dog's mask was placed on the animal. Then DeVries asked, "Now what animal is it? Can it bark? Would it rather eat cat food or dog food?" The three-year-olds believed the cat had turned into a dog, the four- and five-year-olds were confused but said the cat was a dog when it wore the mask, and the six-year-olds knew that the cat remained a cat.

Preoperational children often focus their attention on single aspects of objects—Piaget called this *centration*—so when a task requires simultaneous consideration of several aspects, they often make mistakes. For example, to decide whether or not a short, fat glass can hold as much liquid as a tall, thin one, children must *decenter* attention from a simple judgment based on height or width alone. Preoperational children do not take into account such trade-offs among dimensions and reason primarily on the basis of single features of their perceptions.

Nonlogical Thinking. Preschoolers' thinking frequently seems illogical to adults. When Piaget presented incomplete sentences ending with "because," the children typically confused cause and consequence when they completed the sentences. One exchange went as follows:

> I had a bath because . . . *afterwards I was clean.* I've lost my pen because . . . *I'm not writing.* He fell off his bike because . . . *he hurt himself.* (Piaget, 1926, pp. 17–18)

Besides lacking understanding of cause and effect, preschoolers do not realize that actions and relations can be *reversible*. For example, they do not realize that if you pour liquid from a full tall, thin glass into a squat one, you could return it to its first container and fill that glass to the same level again. Relationships do not extend in both directions. If you ask a five-year-old boy about his brother, the conversation might go as follows: "Do you have a brother? *Yes.* What's his name? *Jimmy.* Does Jimmy have a brother? *No.*"

Piaget thought that preschoolers are *egocentric,* that is, they think everyone sees what they do. They do not realize that other people have different points of view. However, research has shown that young children can appreciate someone else's visual or social perspective in at least a limited way. Jacques Lempers, Eleanor Flavell, and John Flavell (1977) designed some clever materials, such as a stick with pictures glued to each end and a box with a picture taped to the inside bottom. Even two-year-olds could turn the stick or tip the box to permit an adult to see what they were looking at. In this study and subsequent research it was found that preschoolers could share visual information, then show pictures to another person, and later hide or orient another's line of sight to objects (Flavell, 1985). They know that other people see things differently, but preschoolers still have difficulty explaining or imagining the differences.

Despite their limitations, preschoolers struggle to discover and conceptualize the regularities in the world. They may maintain contradictions, reason illogically, and cling to incorrect beliefs, but their cognitive and social stubbornness may simply reveal their efforts to construct order from a growing body of information. Their ability to understand symbols and their rapidly improving language skills facilitate their cognitive organization.

CONCRETE OPERATIONAL PERIOD: 7–11 YEARS. Sometime between five and seven years of age, most children seem to undergo an intellectual revolution that represents a turning point in several stage theories of development. Lev Vygotsky (1962), a Soviet psychologist, suggested that children learn how to direct their own thinking during this time by talking to themselves. Others have termed the developmental change a shift from perceptually based to conceptually based reasoning (Bruner, 1972; Flavell, 1985; White, 1965). Of course, the fact that most children begin school during this period plays a big role in the development of their cognitive abilities.

According to Piaget, during the early school years, children develop systematic mental rules (operations) that can be applied flexibly to a variety of physical problems. He termed this age the *concrete operational period* because thinking is applied to concrete, not abstract, problems. The mental rules permit children to overcome perceptual constraints when solving problems. They begin to understand that the rules themselves can be reversed. For example, multiplication and division, like subtraction and addition, undo the effects of each other. Actions can also be reversed. A lump of clay can be stretched or rolled out and then returned to the original shape. All of these transformations illustrate Piaget's notion of *reversibility,* the idea that one action can be undone by another. During this period, children also learn that operations can conserve properties of an object. Whether you roll out the clay or pinch some off, you could roll it back or add the pinched clay back again to have the same clay in the same amount in the same shape. Piaget studied how children learn about operations and how operations help children solve problems. We will briefly illustrate some of these accomplishments with Piaget's findings.

The concrete operational child develops rules for understanding mathematics and science.

Classification. If you present pictures of common objects to four-year-olds and ask them to put those that go together in piles, they might lump together the blue objects or the small ones. The ability to shift attention from such salient perceptual characteristics to more conceptual categories like animal, vegetable, and mineral, or furniture, toys, and food develops during the preschool years. As discussed in Chapter 8, concepts based on natural categories (e.g., living things) or generic terms (e.g., trees) are relatively easier for children to learn than other concepts (Carey, 1985). Sorting objects according to two dimensions simultaneously is more difficult, and that ability may not appear until middle childhood. Piaget found that until the concrete operational period, children do not understand class relationships thoroughly.

In one test of children's understanding of classification and hierarchical relations, Piaget showed them a picture containing seven tulips and four daisies and asked, "Are there more tulips or more flowers?" A preoperational five-year-old would characteristically say, "More tulips," whereas a child in the concrete operational stage would correctly reason that the whole class of flowers contains more than the two subclasses, tulips and daisies. The results are not as simple as they might seem, however. Researchers have found this verbal problem difficult to comprehend; children are not used to counting objects twice, once as tulips and again as flowers (e.g., Wilkinson, 1976). Nevertheless, categorizing and classifying objects conceptually seems to improve significantly in the concrete operational period.

Conservation. Perhaps the hallmark of Piaget's concrete operational period, and the most thoroughly investigated topic, is *conservation.* The critical question here is when children understand that an underlying physical dimension remains unchanged despite superficial changes in appearance. For example, when do children know that the number of objects in a collection remains the same whether the objects are neatly arranged or scattered about? Adults take conservation for granted, and our understanding of the physical world depends on it. Piaget asked questions of children regarding different physical dimensions (see Figure 9–12): "Which row of apples has more or are they the same?" "Which container has more liquid or do they have the same amount?" Children's correct answers and explanations for their choices reveal that conservation was not understood well until the concrete operational period. But once again, Piaget's claims are not accepted without criticism. Some types of conservation may not be fully understood by adults (Hall & Kingsley, 1968). Other researchers have shown that conservation can be learned by preoperational children when training is provided or when the task is simplified (Gelman, 1978).

FORMAL OPERATIONAL PERIOD: 11–15 YEARS. During the *formal operational period,* adolescents become capable of solving abstract problems through logical operations. For example, they can deduce logical conclusions and can test hypotheses to arrive at correct answers. However, there is some controversy about formal operations, and it may be that people acquire this kind of abstract reasoning only on some kinds of culturally specific tasks or with formal schooling. This cognitive stage is discussed more fully in Chapter 10.

Piaget's theory was popular and influential in the 1960s and 1970s, but it has come under increasing criticism. Some researchers have shown that Piaget considerably underestimated preschoolers' abilities (Gelman, 1978). Others have shown that his notions of egocentrism, centration, and conservation are too global. The terms encompass many different skills and knowledge. Still others have pointed out that many cognitive skills seem to develop independently and not in general stages. Information processing approaches that study continuous development of specific skills instead of global concepts avoid some of the problems of a stage theory like Piaget's. The research methods of information processing have provided fresh insights about children's thinking, and we consider them in the next section.

Information Processing Approaches

Information processing refers to a variety of viewpoints that regard people as symbol manipulators, much like computer systems. Stimuli from the environment are like input to the system, i.e., the person. As the person ana-

FIGURE 9–12
Typical Tasks to Measure Conservation

The child must realize that the physical dimensions remain unchanged despite the new appearances. Understanding conservation of number and length generally precedes understanding conservation of area and volume.

Source: Gardner, 1982.

Conservation of Number

Two equivalent rows of objects are shown to the child, who agrees that they have the same number.

One row is lengthened and the child is asked whether one row now has more objects.

Conservation of Substance

The experimenter shows the child two identical clay balls. The child acknowledges that the two have equal amounts of clay.

The experimenter changes the shape of one of the balls and asks the child whether they still contain equal amounts of clay.

Conservation of Length

Two sticks are aligned in front of the child. The child agrees that they are the same length.

After moving one stick to the left or right, the experimenter asks the child whether they are still equal in length.

Conservation of Area

Two identical sheets of cardboard have wooden blocks placed on them in identical positions. The child is asked whether the same amount of space is left on each piece of cardboard.

The experimenter scatters the blocks on one piece of cardboard and again asks the child whether the two pieces have the same amount of unoccupied space.

Conservation of Volume

Two balls are placed in two identical glasses with an equal amount of water. The child sees that the balls displace equal amounts of water.

The experimenter changes the shape of one of the balls and asks the child whether it will still displace the same amount of water.

lyzes the stimuli perceptually and cognitively, the processes he or she goes through are like the reorganization of information in a computer. Finally, the person's response is like the output from the computer system. Information processing approaches have emerged rapidly from advances in fields such as artificial intelligence, communications, and cognitive psychology,

Constructing a simple circuit requires causal reasoning, planning, memory, and other information-processing skills.

and they have begun to reshape the ways that psychologists study children. The general goal of information processing research aimed at children is to discover the child's emerging "mental programs." Researchers do this by breaking down the child's behavior on a particular task—such as adding sums or learning to solve problems—into a series of cognitive rules that resemble a computer program. Once these rules have been arranged in a coherent format, they constitute a testable model of how the child acquires and uses information (Klahr & Wallace, 1976). If a computer were "programmed" with the same set of rules shown by the child, would the computer duplicate the child's behavior? If it would, then the model could be used to demonstrate the capacity of the child's mental program, the complexity of the program, and the information base with which the child must work. This innovative approach, relying heavily on computer technology, has yielded several insights into how children acquire mathematical skills, language skills, and general reasoning ability. "Research Frontier: How Do Children Learn Addition?" offers a good illustration of information processing analysis.

DEVELOPMENTAL CHANGES IN INFORMATION PROCESSING. Information processing changes in four basic ways during cognitive development. First, children's knowledge becomes more organized to form richer hierarchical associations and thematic connections between concepts. These networks of knowledge help children understand and remember. In some cases, children's ability to organize and store information may surpass that of adults. When Michelene Chi (1978) compared chess experts with novice chess players, she found, not unexpectedly, that the experts were better able to remember the location of chess pieces on a board. The surprising feature of this study is that the experts were 8-to-12-year-old children and the novices were adults! In testing the same groups on their memory for numbers, the adults were superior. Thus, better knowledge leads to better recall. Other studies have shown that young children can recall familiar or meaningful items almost as well as older children and adults. Two- and three-year-olds, for example, can remember birthday parties, names of friends and relatives, and the locations of familiar toys with surprising accuracy (Bjorklund, 1985; DeLoache, Cassidy, & Brown, 1985; Lindberg, 1980). These studies suggest that the development of memory in children reflects changes in how they organize their developing knowledge (Ornstein & Naus, in press).

Second, information processing increases in speed as basic processes (such as scanning a stimulus, recognizing similarity) become automatic. As less and less attention is paid to these processes, children show a corresponding increase in the mental capacity to think about more things at the same time (Case, 1985). Third, children acquire a broader set of cognitive strategies to guide attention, learning, and memory. Even three-year-old children demonstrate a rudimentary form of the strategy called *memory rehearsal.* Before they are asked to recall the location of a hidden toy, young children will touch or stare at the object (Wellman, Ritter, & Flavell, 1975). Older children acquire more refined techniques to aid recall, such as rehearsing information by repeating it to themselves (Ornstein & Naus, 1978), grouping objects into related categories (Neimark, Slotnick, & Ulrich, 1971), and making inferences (Paris & Lindauer, 1976).

How Do Children Learn Addition?

Observing children as they perform ordinary tasks can often yield fascinating insights into their thinking processes. In a series of studies, Robert Siegler and his colleagues developed an information processing model of arithmetic skill. In one study (Siegler & Robinson, 1982) the researchers asked four-to-five-year-olds questions such as "If you had three oranges and I gave you one more, how many would you have?" In the course of their videotaped sessions, young children were asked to make 25 different calculations involving the numbers one through five. When the researchers analyzed the videotapes, they discovered that children relied on one of four different strategies to solve the problems. Sometimes they counted out the answers on their fingers. Sometimes they raised their fingers without counting on them. Sometimes they counted aloud. For about 25% of the problems, the children simply answered without using their fingers or without counting aloud. This last method was the quickest of all. Siegler also recorded the frequency of errors and noted that the choice of a counting strategy often depended on the difficulty of a problem. For instance, a child might quickly answer 1 + 1 = ? but use his fingers to answer 4 + 5 = ?

Next, Siegler tried to devise a mental program of how children answer arithmetic problems (Siegler & Shipley, in press). He assumed that children vary in the degree of confidence that they hold in their answers. In other words, each child has a particular "confidence criterion," and if the criterion is low, the child is more likely to accept the first answer that pops into his or her mind, even if it is an error. Children with a high confidence criterion are more likely to second-guess their response, even if they are correct. Siegler assumed that children vary in the length of time they are willing to spend searching for an answer before they resort to guessing. According to Siegler and Shipley (in press), here is how a preschooler might reason about the problem 4 + 3 = ?:

1. Retrieve an answer from memory.

2. If it exceeds the confidence criterion, state it.

3. If it falls below the confidence criterion and there is still time for searching, try a different strategy such as holding up fingers.

4. If there is no more time for searching, state an answer.

5. If the alternative strategy yields an answer that exceeds the confidence criterion, state it.

6. If the answer still falls below the confidence criterion, count by using fingers or objects and state the last number counted.

Is the model an accurate program for how children solve addition problems? Siegler believes so, for he has found that the sequence of steps he outlined correlates very well with the measured difficulty of arithmetic problems. He has used a computer to simulate the program and found that the computer responds with the same pattern of errors that he observed with children. Thus, information processing analyses help to confirm a sequence in cognitive development.

But why are some addition problems harder for some children? Why should 5 + 2 be harder than 3 + 2? Siegler and his colleagues identified three important influences on the development of counting skills. First previous associations that children learn from counting may interfere with addition. For example, in problems where the second number is larger than the first, children may add one more to the second number, or keep counting. They frequently say that 2 + 3 = 4, 3 + 4 = 5, or 2 + 5 = 6. Second, the size of the sum affects time and accuracy. Quite simply, the more objects that need to be represented and counted, the greater the likelihood of mistakes.

Siegler also conjectured that children may not be equally exposed to all forms of addition problems. Siegler and Shrager (1984) observed parents teaching two-to-four-year-olds addition problems and found striking differences among problems. Parents presented easy problems most often and they presented "ties," like 1 + 1 and 2 + 2, much more often than other pairs. Parents also presented "+ 1" problems like 3 + 1 and 4 + 1 five times more often than "1 +" problems like 1 + 3. Research into arithmetic skill has already yielded valuable information for improving the ways in which children are taught to add. Siegler (in press) has extended his research into other areas such as multiplication, subtraction, and spelling, and the information processing approach has yielded new insights into cognitive skill development in these areas also.

Finally, the development of information processing skills is usually accompanied by greater *metacognition* (Brown et al., 1983). Metacognition involves children's self-awareness and control of their own cognitive abilities. Planning, self-checking, and revising the solution to a problem are all evidence of metacognition. Research has shown that children find this kind of "mental pulse-taking" difficult. Before the age of seven many children may not use metacognition and cognitive strategies spontaneously to foster learning (Flavell, 1985). However, if young children are given information about the value and appropriateness of strategies, they are more likely to use them on their own (Paris, Newman, & McVey, 1982).

Growth in knowledge, strategies, automatic processes, and metacognition bears directly on how children learn in school. As John Holt (1964) said in his book *How Children Fail:*

> Part of being a good student is learning to be aware of one's own mind and the degree of one's understanding. The good student may be one who often says he does not understand, simply because he keeps a constant check on his understanding. The poor student, who does not, so to speak, watch himself trying to understand, does not know most of the time whether he understands or not. Thus the problem is not to get students to ask us what they don't know; the problem is to make them aware of the difference between what they know and what they don't. (pp. 28–29)

Learning to read exemplifies a cognitive skill of middle childhood that requires both cognitive strategies and metacognition. Some five-year-olds learning to read English understand so little about the skill that they are not sure whether they should "read" the words or the pictures or whether it makes any difference if they move from left to right or top to bottom of the page (Clay, 1973). In order to read, children must learn to convert print into sound, to interpret words, and to use the sentence context to comprehend meaning. Beyond that, they must relate the information throughout a passage, devote extra study to difficult parts, and check their own understanding (Paris, Lipson, & Wixson, 1983). These strategies are difficult to master, and poor readers sometimes resort to saying the words without knowing what they mean. Good readers, on the other hand, are more likely to notice inconsistencies in meaning and to correct their own errors while reading (Brown, Armbruster, & Baker, 1984).

LANGUAGE ACQUISITION

Acquisition of language is a unique human accomplishment that permits new kinds of cognitive and social interactions for young children. Most children use language moderately well by three or four years of age, although improvement continues for years. *Language competence,* the knowledge about language that all children seem to have, involves several related skills. Children must learn to analyze and combine the phonetic stream of speech sounds into language, to arrange words in correct order, to express ideas in multiple ways, and to converse. Why do babies around the world begin to talk at about the same age in similar ways? One key to understanding the similarity of language development across cultures and among children is to examine the similarity of development before language is acquired. Such research helps to explain why most infants learn to talk at the same age, about the same things, and in abbreviated sentences.

Language Precursors

Newborns are biologically prepared for speech. Infants are quite sensitive to sounds in the human voice range and prefer rhythmic tones 10 to 15 seconds long, such as the short sentences parents speak to children (Eimas, 1975). During infancy, the shape of the oral cavity changes. The larynx is in the right position to modulate air flow from the lungs. The cheeks lose some fat, and the tongue develops so that the passage of air can be regulated more easily. Muscular control of the lips, tongue, and cheeks, as well as the appearance of teeth at approximately six months of age, permit children to make a greater variety of sounds.

The extended period of infant dependency offers opportunities to learn through social interactions. In the first year, parents and infants communicate in many ways. Adults typically offer, name, and talk to babies about objects. When they are a year old, infants can offer, point to, and show objects to adults, establishing the primitive bases of speaker and listener. Crying, facial expressions, and intonation that may accompany gestures are also communicative.

Infants' gestures appear to fall into two categories (Clark & Clark, 1977). The first group consists of assertions such as "Look at X" or "Tell me about X"; the second group is a form of request such as "Show me X" or "Give me X." Pointing is a typical assertion and reaching is a typical request, and both gestures may be the nonverbal precursors to single-word utterances with the same function. Certainly, infants learn quickly that gestures, facial expressions, and intonation constitute clues about language, and they use that information to discern the meanings of words.

Children's early cooperation in communication represents both a cognitive and a social advance. The similarity in nonverbal knowledge and social activities among children during infancy may lead to similarities in language acquisition. Around the world, between one and two years of age, infants share similar concepts and topics of conversation. They discover the names of people and objects (e.g., Momma), descriptions of nonexistence (e.g., all gone), modifiers (e.g., big) and social terms (e.g., bye-bye) because most parents confront them with the same tasks—eating, playing with toys, commanding, requesting, describing.

From Babbling to Sentences

The varied vocalizations that babies emit in their first six months include babbling, which becomes a form of social play. The first language sounds are usually vowels because they are produced with a continuous airflow in which the lips and tongue change positions. Consonants usually require a "stop" in the air flow and greater muscular control. Some of the earliest consonants heard are those that are easy to articulate: p as in "Papa," g as in "go," and m as in "Momma." Ease of articulation, practice, muscular and anatomical development, and, of course, imitation of parents help the infant to generate a wide assortment of language sounds by ten months of age.

Long before infants use language, they learn to communicate with adults by using facial expressions and sounds.

FIRST WORDS. Many infants utter their first words between 10 and 12 months of age, and they usually acquire a vocabulary of 50 words by 20 months (Nelson, 1973). First words are often imitations of adult speech that accompany actions, such as "bye-bye" and hand waving. However, some first words are invented, and they function as idiosyncratic symbols.

Infants' first words vary a good deal in type and rate of production, as Katherine Nelson (1973) found in a longitudinal study of 18 children (see Table 9–3). One aspect of children's first words is obvious from her findings: they are not simply nouns and labels for objects. Nouns make up the largest category, accounting for 62% of all words in Nelson's study, but there were many other types such as action words, social expressions, and modifiers. The variety of first words shows the strong relationship between speech and sensorimotor knowledge. "Mommy," "Daddy," "doggie," "baby," and "milk" are common first words for most English-speaking children because they describe the infants' familiar world. "Look," "hi," "up," and "go" exemplify the first spatial, action-oriented relations infants comprehend. First words fit into existing nonverbal behavior and knowledge. Modifier words—such as "big," "red," and "hot"—describe perceptual characteristics. "All gone" and "more" reveal understanding of object permanence.

GRAMMATICAL RELATIONSHIPS. Between 18 and 24 months of age most children begin to combine words into short sentences. The word combinations permit us to analyze the rules—both syntactic and semantic—that children use to formulate their speech. (See Chapter 8 for a review of grammatical terms.) A striking feature of first word combinations is the way children use some words as anchors. Toddlers frequently say things like "all-gone milk," "all-gone cookies," "more boat," "more tickle," "here baby," and "here shoe." The first word in each utterance is combined with a noun, reflecting elementary syntactic and semantic relationships. Roger Brown (1973) found that although vocabulary and word order may vary between children, the *kinds* of meanings they express are often similar. For

---

TABLE 9–3
Types of Words Produced by Children with 50-Word Vocabularies

SPECIFIC WORDS	ACTION WORDS	MODIFIERS
People: mommy, daddy	Demand-descriptive:	Attributes: big, pretty
Animals: pet names	up	States: lot, all gone
Objects: car	Notice: look	Locative: there
		Possessives: mine
GENERAL WORDS	PERSONAL-SOCIAL EXPRESSIONS	
Objects: ball	Assertions: no, yes	
Animals and people: doggie	Social-expressives: please, ouch	
Letters and numbers: two		
Pronouns: she	FUNCTION WORDS	
	Question: what, where	
	Miscellaneous: is, to	

Source: Nelson, 1973. Adapted by permission.

TABLE 9–4		
Examples of Common Semantic Relations in Children's Speech		
Semantic Relation	Form	Example
Nomination	that + Noun	that book
Notice	hi + Noun	hi doggie
Recurrence	more + Noun	more milk
Nonexistence	all-gone + Noun	all-gone rattle
Attributive	adj. + Noun	big train
Possessive	Noun + Noun	mommy lunch
Locative	Noun + Noun	sweater chair
Locative	Verb + Noun	walk street
Agent-action	Noun + Verb	Eve read
Agent-object	Noun + Noun	mommy sock
Action-object	Verb + Noun	put book

Source: Brown, 1970.

example, children may regularly express reference, recurrence, and nonexistence through phrases such as "this cup," "more milk," and "all-gone doggie." Such word orders observed in early speech seem to be consequences of semantic regularities (see Table 9–4).

In their two- and three-word sentences, young children leave out prepositions, articles, and parts of verb phrases in "telegraphic speech." Two sorts of rules govern such utterances. First, the order of terms conveys meaning. So "shoe chair" indicates where a shoe is, while "daddy shoe" indicates whose shoe it is. Second, stress and intonation convey meaning. Stress on the first word in "Jeffie room" might indicate possession, while stress on the second word might be a response to "Where's Jeffie?" In short, early speech is characterized by regular stress patterns and a small number of semantic relationships that convey meaning according to rules.

GROWTH IN VOCABULARY. Three-year-olds expand their vocabularies with astonishing speed, sometimes learning two to four new words each day (Pease & Gleason, 1985). As you might expect, words that children hear frequently and that are easy to pronounce are acquired readily. A striking feature of early vocabulary development is that children often overextend the meanings of new words. For example, a child who learns the word "horse" may use it to refer to any large, four-legged animal. According to Clark (1973), children need to acquire knowledge of *semantic features* of words to avoid under- and overextending their meanings. The word "horse," for example, may be specified by features such as animal, domestic, large, long neck, long legs, no horns, long tail, and so forth. Knowledge of many features like these would help children distinguish horses from other animals and would allow them to use the word to refer only to horses.

BEYOND SIMPLE SENTENCES. Children gradually learn to talk in longer sentences that specify meaning more precisely than telegraphic utterances. But language development demands more than expansion of vocabulary. Children acquire many kinds of rules for generating longer sentences. Between the ages of two and five years, most children learn to use articles,

FIGURE 9–13
The Wugs Test

One way to test children's understanding of inflectional rules is to have children supply a missing word to describe pictures. Jean Berko devised a clever test with nonsense "words" to rule out imitation of natural words and word endings. If children supply the missing word "wugs" to the story as the experimenter's voice trails off, then they must know the general rule for adding -s to form plurals. The test contains many pictures for different kinds of rules. Try this one and then make up your own. "Three wugs went fribbing down the street. Yesterday they did the same thing. Yesterday they _____."

Source: Berko, 1958, p. 483.

past-tense endings, plurals, and other elements missing from telegraphic speech (Gleason, 1985). Children first imitate irregular forms, such as "did," "went," or "sheep," and later seem to regress when they say "doed," "goed," and "sheeps." In fact, these "errors" indicate that children have learned inflectional rules, such as adding -*ed* to form past tenses and -*s* to form plurals. But they overgeneralize the rules and need to learn the exceptions to them. Figure 9–13 illustrates one way to test children's understanding of inflectional rules.

Another way to increase sentence complexity is through transformational rules that rearrange word order, insert new words, and delete others, as in these examples:

Simple Sentence	*Transformation*	*Rule*
He is running.	Is he running?	Interrogative
Mary knows the answer.	Does Mary know the answer?	*Do* insertion plus interrogative
Jan rode the horse.	The horse was ridden by Jan.	Passive
Freddie is cheating.	Freddie is not cheating.	Negative

Transformational rules (see page 299) prove difficult for children to learn because they require changes in verbs and auxiliaries as well as alterations for number and tense agreement. Thus, grammatical complexity affects the course of language acquisition.

Children's Communication and Egocentric Speech

Understanding words and rules is not the same as knowing how and when to use language intentionally to influence other people. One of the earliest things children must learn about conversation is the give-and-take relationship between speaker and listener. Bruner (1975) suggests that prespeech "action dialogues" between parent and child are the foundation for these roles. Gradual progression from "role-rigid," turn-taking exchanges to "role-complementary" interactions (Bruner, 1975) occurs as the child begins to consider the other person's remarks and actions, a slow process that may not be completed until four or five years of age.

A second type of convention for communication that children learn is how to express meaning in alternative ways. Children's early speech—"hi," "bye-bye," "no, thank you"—is often ritualistic and varies little in form or context. Requests, denials, and assertions are often constrained by the child's inability to rephrase the utterance.

Reciprocal turn-taking and alternative ways of expressing meaning are part of a general progression between two and five years of age from *egocentric* to *socialized speech*, according to Piaget (1952). Piaget postulated that children do not overcome the limitations of egocentrism until they are seven or eight years old. But recent research has failed to bear him out. Younger children are not usually oblivious to the listener: they often try to get listeners' attention by calling to them or pointing to the object of conversation, and they frequently talk about listeners' activities and keep their conversations relevant to listeners' behavior.

Sometimes preschoolers do not consider the other person's point of view. While speaking on the telephone, they often refer to objects as if the listener could see them.

Young children are capable also of reformulating their speech to accommodate the listener. Shatz and Gelman (1973) recorded conversations of four-year-olds with two-year-olds, with other four-year-olds, and with adults. Four-year-olds talked in shorter, simpler sentences and used more attention-getting devices when talking to two-year-olds than when addressing their peers or adults. Other studies corroborate these findings and demonstrate that preschoolers consider the visual perspective, age, knowledge, and remarks of listeners in formulating messages to them (Schmidt & Paris, 1983). Consequently, some researchers suggest that speech is socialized even among three- and four-year-olds but that it continues to improve throughout childhood.

SOCIAL DEVELOPMENT

Most children grow up surrounded by their families and friends. These people help to establish emotional security in infancy and later to mold the personalities of young children. Adults provide care, model appropriate behavior, and set standards to follow. These principles of observational learning and conditioning promote social learning by children. Children, in turn, influence families by their behavior and development. The processes of socialization operate in both directions, and we must remember that families develop together in shared social and physical environments.

Erikson's Stages

A useful guide to children's social and emotional development is provided by the life span theory of *psychosocial development* proposed by Erik Erikson (1950), who built his theory on Freud's stages of psychosexual development (see Chapter 14, page 511). Each of the eight stages in Erikson's theory involves the resolution of a social crisis or challenge. We briefly describe his four stages of development in infancy and childhood here and examine the four stages of adolescence and adulthood in Chapter 10.

TRUST VERSUS MISTRUST. In the first stage infants make their initial encounters with a social world. They experience both trust and mistrust as they interact with their caretakers. To resolve this conflict they must develop a sense of confidence in the dependability of others. Of course, the parents' confidence in their own behavior is important for mutual trust to develop.

AUTONOMY VERSUS DOUBT AND SHAME. In this stage two- and three-year-olds exhibit a growing sense of independence. Toilet training and cleanliness are important, but, in a larger sense, children and parents must resolve conflicts between the parents' authority and the child's emerging autonomy. Adjustment to social rules without shame or self-doubt is the goal of this stage.

INITIATIVE VERSUS GUILT. From three to six years of age, children may imagine themselves in adult roles. Children also may "show off" their prowess by running, jumping, or throwing things. Parents attempt to harness this energy and redirect children's behavior into acceptable outlets. Learning these limitations to behavior without feeling guilty or losing self-initiative is a difficult task.

INDUSTRY VERSUS INFERIORITY. According to Erikson, this fourth stage is very important for self-development and feelings of competence. It covers growth from 6 to 11 years of age when children apply themselves to learning useful skills in school and outside of school. The focus of this stage is mastery of culturally relevant tasks (e.g., hunting, farming, cooking, schooling) without feeling inadequate.

Erikson's theory provides the broad outlines of social development across the life span. It helps to identify crucial hurdles of social development at different ages. In the following sections, we discuss the social relationships and experiences that foster social development and children's emerging realizations of who they are and how they should interact with others.

Social Interactions During Infancy

Watching parents play with their infants is almost like watching a ballet, with each partner acting and reacting to the movements of the other. When a parent wiggles the infant's arms and legs and talks and smiles, the baby reciprocates by laughing, cooing, and babbling. The responses are mutually satisfying. Dozens of such interactions occur daily as the baby is fed, bathed, and cradled in loving arms, and they afford the infant a chance to explore parental looks, sounds, and smells. Craig Peery (1980) recorded head movements of infants as a smiling female approached and withdrew from them and found that even one-day-old newborns seemed to coordinate their head movements with those of the adult.

EMOTIONAL BONDING. How does early experience contribute to the emotional relationship between mothers and their babies? About ten years ago, a startling hypothesis was offered by Marshall Klaus and John Kennell (1976). They argued that skin-to-skin contact between mother and child immediately after birth would stimulate later emotional bonding. This effect is important because bonding is part of the attachment relationship between

Babies depend on parents for comfort and love. Fathers as well as mothers can provide security and nurturance for their infants. As women with children continue to work, parents are more and more likely to share the responsibilities of childrearing.

mother and child. They suggested that during the first few hours after delivery, a sensitive period, mothers and children need direct physical contact or they will not become emotionally attached to each other later. These notions have been publicized widely and have influenced procedures in many hospitals, but there is little evidence to support them. Susan Goldberg (1983) reported that mothers who had early contact with their newborns were somewhat more responsive to them for the first three days, but the differences were small and disappeared a week later. Michael Lamb (1982) also concluded that there are no appreciable differences between mothers and infants who share early contact compared with those who are separated for several days after birth. This should be reassuring to adoptive parents and others who must be separated from their newborn babies because of illness or other complications.

ATTACHMENT. *Attachment* is a strong, emotional, reciprocal relationship established between an infant and a particular caregiver. It begins soon after birth but is not firmly established until about six months of age. Attachment is defined by three main characteristics. First, infants are likely to approach significant people, i.e., parents or other caregivers, for comfort when they are distressed or hungry. Second, they are most easily soothed by familiar caregivers: and third, they show little fear of them. For infants, familiarity breeds security.

But not all infants form social attachments to caregivers. In fact, only about 70% of one-year-old infants are securely attached to adults (Sroufe, 1985). Research by Mary Ainsworth has revealed three types of attachment relationships. Ainsworth (Ainsworth et al., 1978) created a staged sequence of events, called the "strange situation," which begins when a mother and her child enter a playroom. After a time, the mother leaves, and shortly thereafter a stranger enters and sits down. Next, the stranger leaves and the mother returns, and the whole sequence is repeated again. One-year-olds observed in this situation can be classified into three categories:

1. *Securely attached* infants use mothers as a base for exploring a new room but often return to the mothers for comfort.

2. *Avoidant* infants, who are insecurely attached, do not cry when mothers leave, nor do they approach them in the room.

3. *Anxious/resistant* infants appear upset when mothers leave *and* when they return. They may alternately seek out contact and resist mothers' efforts to hold or comfort them.

How do infants become attached to their caregivers? Ainsworth (1979) believes that mothers of securely attached infants are responsive to their infants' signals from the very beginning. They enjoy contact with their infants, express emotions openly, and encourage exploration. All these behaviors help to establish trust between the infant and the caregiver. Mothers of infants who are anxious/resistant try to provide physical comfort to their infants but often misinterpret the infants' signals. Mothers of avoidant infants may be impatient and frustrated with child rearing. These mothers may be self-centered, rigid individuals who regard their infants' needs as an interference with their own plans. These patterns of maternal rejection and infant avoidance can lead to cycles of child abuse (Egeland & Sroufe, 1981).

Changing Roles of Parents. As we have seen, attachment depends on the quality of interactions between infants and caregivers. These patterns, however, vary from culture to culture and throughout history. Seventy years ago, parents were told not to coddle or kiss their infants, yet today parents are encouraged to respond to their children's needs for physical contact and affection. The past few decades also have witnessed a historical change in maternal employment. Half of mothers who live with their husbands work outside the home, and the number of single-parent households is greater than ever before. Day care or other forms of child care are often necessary and many parents ask, "Will it affect my relationship with my children?" According to Lois Hoffman (1979), maternal employment is not likely to disrupt a child's emotional development because working mothers often compensate for their time away from home by interacting more with their children when they are at home. She concludes that high-quality day care provided by an adult other than the mother does not have negative effects on the mother-child relationship.

The role of fathers in child rearing has also changed dramatically in America. Traditionally fathers have accepted only minor roles in baby care, but, partly because more women work outside the home and partly because of changing attitudes, many fathers now change diapers, mix formulas, and otherwise share responsibilities for their children. Michael Lamb (1981) has shown that many infants establish attachment relationships with their fathers by 9 to 12 months of age. Even though fathers can soothe and nurture babies as well as mothers can, infants still prefer to be comforted by mothers (Parke, 1981). This may be because mothers usually spend more time feeding and nurturing babies while fathers often play with them.

A recent study by Ann Easterbrooks and Wendy Goldberg (1985) showed that families adapt to mothers' employment status. The researchers observed the parent-child interactions of 75 families with first-born 20-month-olds. They found that the security of attachment and the problem-solving skills of the toddlers were equal whether mothers were unemployed, employed part-time, or fully employed outside the home. Most employed women (67%) and their husbands (74%) viewed maternal employment as positive, whereas the majority of unemployed mothers and their husbands thought that maternal employment would have negative effects on mother-child relationships. The researchers concluded that maternal employment does not hurt mother-child relationships. When mothers were satisfied with their employment status (whether working outside the home or not) and when husbands were supportive, the families adapted well.

Consequences of Attachment. Two short-term consequences of attachment are commonly observed among infants. *Separation anxiety* is the distress experienced by infants when their parents leave them. It usually peaks between 12 and 15 months of age. When a mother puts a child to bed or leaves the room, a one-year-old may cry long and hard, while a five-month-old seems perfectly content. Fear of separation decreases as the infant learns that parents return and that crying does not prevent them from leaving. Children raised by many different adults may show relatively less distress when separated from parents, but separation anxiety troubles most youngsters of similar ages around the world (see Figure 9–14).

FIGURE 9–14
**Cross-Cultural Patterns
of Separation Anxiety**

Separation anxiety, measured by infant crying, increases quickly until 12 to 15 months of age. Similar patterns of infant distress are observed in many cultures, although the degree of crying may be more intense and longer in some.

Source: Mussen, Conger & Kagan, 1980.

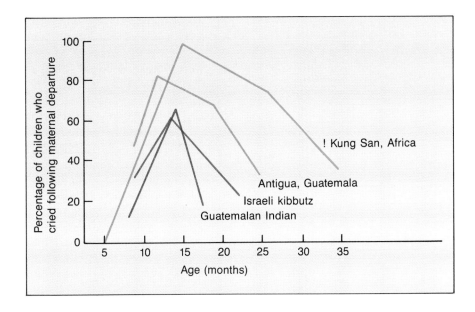

A second consequence of attachment may involve *stranger anxiety.* While the five-month-old happily accepts being picked up by grandparents or strangers, the one-year-old rejects the unfamiliar person and will cry to be back with Mommy or Daddy. This distress diminishes as the child is exposed to more people and learns that others besides parents can provide temporary security. In fact, reactions to strangers may be less severe among securely attached infants. Mary Main and Donna Weston (1981) observed infants as they interacted with a friendly but unfamiliar clown. The most socially responsive infants were those who were securely attached to both parents.

A securely attached infant will cry and protest when mother begins to leave.

Attachment also has long-term consequences. In a long-term longitudinal study, researchers found that infants who displayed the greatest anxiety to strangers at two years of age were socially anxious as five-year-olds and as adults (Kagan & Moss, 1962). Infants who are securely attached at 12 months of age are more obedient to their mothers and cooperative with strangers at 21 months of age than insecurely attached infants (Londerville & Main, 1981). Follow-up tests at two, three, and five years of age revealed that securely attached infants also are more curious and sociable with peers (Arend, Gove & Sroufe, 1979; Sroufe, 1985). Thus, early interactions between infants and caregivers can establish trust and confidence that have long-lasting benefits for children. This is consistent with Erikson's view of trust as the foundation of infant development.

Theories of Attachment. Researchers have proposed several explanations for attachment. Ethological theories suggest that the predisposition for attachment is an innate, species-specific relationship that helps protect the young and preserve the species (Bowlby, 1973). Biological factors, including innate influences and hormones, are important for establishing the emotional bonds (Cairns, 1979). Cognitive theories suggest that attachment depends on children's early abilities to discriminate and remember people. Research has shown that 9-to-12-month-olds who scored highly on tests of object permanence also protested more strongly when separated from their caregivers (Lester et al., 1974). Psychoanalytic theories explain attachment as a consequence of oral pleasure and security derived from being fed.

Finally, learning theories may help to explain attachment using principles of reinforcement and conditioning. Is attachment simply a conditioned response to one who feeds the infant? Harry Harlow and Robert Zimmerman (1959) conducted a classic study that did not confirm this hypothesis. They separated infant monkeys from their natural mothers and gave them the choice of one of two surrogate mothers. One surrogate was made of wire and the other was covered with terrycloth (see Figure 9–15). Regardless of which surrogate provided food, the infant monkeys preferred to stay in con-

FIGURE 9–15
**Preferences of Monkeys
for Surrogate Mothers**

Monkeys raised in social isolation prefer "contact comfort." Infant monkeys who were raised without contact with their mothers or other monkeys were offered two surrogates, one covered with wire and one covered with cloth. Regardless of which surrogate provided food to the infants, they preferred contact with the soft, cloth-covered surrogate. Thus, attachment bonds are not determined only by who feeds infants.

Source: Harlow and Zimmerman, 1959, pp. 421–432.

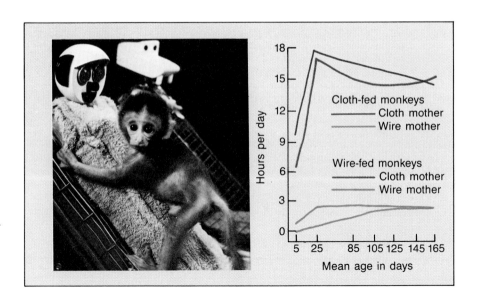

tact with the cloth-covered model. Harlow and Zimmerman concluded that the "contact comfort" provided by the cloth mother was more important than feeding and hunger reduction for establishing attachment.

Development of Self-Concept

Babies are not born with a sense of self, but by six months of age they begin to distinguish themselves from other people and objects. When do they recognize the "self"? Michael Lewis and Jeanne Brooks-Gunn (1979) studied the question by putting a spot of rouge on infants' noses and placing them in front of mirrors. They wanted to determine when infants would recognize themselves enough to try to rub the rouge off their noses. A few of the 15-month-old infants rubbed off the rouge, and nearly all the 18-to-24-month-olds did. Usually between the first and second birthdays, children begin to recognize themselves in pictures and mirrors. In the ensuing years, self-recognition leads to a distinct self-concept.

Preschoolers' ideas about themselves are concrete. When asked to describe themselves, three-to-five-year-olds usually give physical descriptions of what they look like or what they like to do (Damon & Hart, 1982). Rarely do they offer psychological descriptions of what they think or feel. These findings confirm the views of Erikson (1950). Three-year-olds strive to become independent and autonomous. They take great pride in their new skills and accomplishments. Five-year-olds who describe themselves according to their favorite activities are displaying a sense of initiative in their enthusiasm.

PARENTING STYLES. How do parents foster positive self-concepts in young children? Diana Baumrind (1967) investigated parenting styles and their influence on young children's personalities. She identified three distinct groups of children in a nursery school. Group I included independent, self-reliant youngsters who were friendly, curious, and energetic. Group II included children who were moody, insecure, and withdrawn. And group III were fearful, dependent, the least self-controlled, and the most immature. The question was whether their parents treated the members of the groups differently. Baumrind found that parents of the self-reliant children (group I) were firm yet loving, encouraged them to achieve, and communicated well with them. They presented clear goals and standards and promoted independent decision making. Accordingly, they were labeled authoritative. Parents of insecure children (group II) did not listen to their children's concerns often and imposed harsher discipline. They neither encouraged children to express disagreement, nor did they explain their decisions to them. They were categorized as authoritarian. Finally, the parents of immature children (group III) behaved warmly to them but demanded little initiative or achievement, and their discipline was lax or inconsistent. They were described as permissive. Thus, the most well-adjusted children came from authoritative families who were firm yet caring.

THE COMPETENT SELF. Parents encourage children to be independent. They also encourage them to be competitive and successful, whether the task is related to school, arts, or sports. *Achievement motivation* is a complex concept that signifies how much people strive for success (see

Chapter 12), and it contributes directly to children's developing self-concepts. Susan Harter (1981) believes that children can exhibit an *intrinsic orientation* toward achievement, meaning that they try to demonstrate their own mastery, or they can exhibit an *extrinsic orientation* to tasks, meaning that they try to succeed in order to obtain prizes and rewards. She suggests that children who are intrinsically oriented prefer challenging tasks and perceive themselves as more competent at schoolwork than children oriented to extrinsic incentives.

Children who achieve success feel proud of their accomplishments and increase their self-esteem. Harter (1982) developed a scale to test children's perceptions of their own abilities in four different areas: cognitive, social, and physical abilities and general self-worth. Harter (1982) gave the scale to more than 2,000 children from third to ninth grade and also asked teachers and classmates to rate the students on the same items. Even the youngest children had distinctive views of themselves in each area, thus showing that favorable or unfavorable views of self-competence can be established by eight years of age. Furthermore, children clearly discriminated their talents in different areas, such as performance on schoolwork and popularity among classmates. Were children's self-perceptions accurate? Although they improved with age, children's views of themselves generally matched the views of teachers and classmates. Children's knowledge and positive feelings about their own achievements contribute to the sense of industry stressed in Erikson's theory (1950) and help establish a healthy self-concept.

What factors promote achievement and self-esteem? One important factor is the stimulation provided at home. A team of researchers used a longitudinal design to study the relation between children's home environments and their school achievement (Van Doornick et al., 1981). The researchers visited the homes of 50 infants and classified them as stimulating or unstimulating according to an inventory of items. Five to nine years later, the researchers collected data on the children's school achievement. The majority of children from stimulating homes were achieving well at school, while 70% of the children from unstimulating environments were experiencing problems.

A second factor influencing achievement involves children's beliefs and expectations regarding their own abilities. Children who take responsibility for their own successes and failures are said to have an **internal locus of control.** These children usually achieve at higher levels than those who have an *external* locus of control and who attribute success and failure to luck, chance, or the behavior of others (Findley & Cooper, 1983). Children's expectancies about their own performances are shaped in part by their previous rate of success. Those children who have a history of failure in school often believe that they cannot succeed, and they quit trying while others who achieve well continue to have high expectations (Dweck & Elliott, 1983).

Parents' beliefs about their children's abilities can also influence children's expectations and motivation. For example, parents of students in fifth through eleventh grade believe that mathematics is easier, more important, and more enjoyable for boys than for girls (Parsons, Adler, & Kaczala, 1982). The researchers found that students' own expectations tended to follow their parents' sex-role stereotypes *even* when the males and females did not differ in prior school performance on mathematics. Thus, personal beliefs, parental expectations, and home environment can all influence children's views of their competence and self-esteem.

SEX TYPING. We have seen that independence and achievement are two important aspects of children's self-concepts. A third dimension is the sex role adopted by a child. *Sex typing* is the process by which a child acquires *gender identity,* the knowledge that he or she is a boy or a girl, and adopts socially appropriate male or female behaviors. The development of gender identity begins in infancy and is influenced by the way parents dress and speak to children. From the very beginning parents may refer to girls as "Honey" and boys as "Tiger" and dress them in pink and blue, respectively. As a result of this early experience, even two-year-olds can readily identify the sex of people in pictures (Thompson, 1975). By age three, most children can refer to themselves as either boys or girls, although they do not understand that one's gender is usually a permanent condition. The three-year-

Children adopt sex roles and sex-typed behavior from watching parents and others.

old boy who wants to grow up to be a mommy reveals this confusion in an amusing way. Three-to-five-year-olds can easily classify pictures of people according to sex and age (Edwards, 1984), and by age six or seven, children establish an enduring sense of their own gender identity as well as the genders of other people.

Children's awareness of stereotypic male and female behaviors develops along with gender identity. For example, when given a boy doll and a girl doll, even 2½-to-3½-year-olds know which doll is more likely to climb trees, play with dolls, fight, talk, cook, or sew (Kuhn, Nash & Brucken, 1978). Children also have different preferences for toys. Boys 14 to 22 months old prefer to play with trucks, while infant girls prefer dolls (Smith & Daglish, 1977). Preschoolers also develop preferences to play with other children of the same sex (Jacklin & Maccoby, 1978). Boys seem to acquire sex-typed behaviors more quickly than girls, perhaps because fathers are eager for their sons to conform to stereotypic *gender roles* (Fagot, 1978). From ages four to ten, boys also adhere to sex-typed activities more rigidly than girls. Despite their early interest in masculine activities, most girls begin to prefer and adopt traditional female roles as adolescence approaches. The question of sex roles and gender identity has been the focus of a great deal of psychological research and theory. We return to the issue of sexual identity in Chapters 12 and 14.

Social Roles and Rules

The development of social behavior involves more than the emergence of a child's self-concept. To participate in the world, children must become increasingly more considerate of others and less self-centered. Social behavior is a two-way street, in which each participant tries to understand the other person's point of view, thoughts, feelings, and intentions. Psychologists refer to this understanding as *social cognition.* During middle childhood, the child's social cognition undergoes significant change.

As we have seen, preschoolers think in very concrete terms and tend to describe other people according to their appearance, possessions, or activities. Gradually, however, this limited perspective begins to fade, and children develop appreciation of the less concrete, psychological qualities of those around them. Carl Barenboim (1981) divided this process into three distinct phases:

1. *The behavioral comparisons phase.* Between the ages of six and eight, children typically describe other people in reference to themselves. They might say "Marcy is the fastest," or "Fred has more toys than I have."

2. *The psychological constructs phase.* Beginning at about age eight or nine and often continuing into adolescence, children identify their friends with traits such as friendly, smart, kind, or stubborn.

3. *The psychological comparisons phase.* Usually by the age of 12, children compare and contrast other people in terms of how friendly, how smart, how kind, or how stubborn they are. This stage parallels

advances in cognitive development and shows deeper insight into why people behave as they do.

Thus, increased sensitivity to other people accompanies cognitive development during childhood.

SELF-CONTROL. Learning to control one's impulses is an important social lesson of early childhood. Infants learn early that they cannot always have things their own way when eating, playing, or getting dressed. Toddlers are admonished often not to pull the cat's tail, not to touch electrical outlets, not to play with sharp objects. Nevertheless, if you have ever tried to control rambunctious children, you know that they do not always follow your advice. In fact, one study found that three- and four-year-olds continued a behavior *more* as adults shouted louder not to do it (Saltz, Campbell, & Skotko, 1983).

When do children develop self-control? Like many other developmental accomplishments, it is difficult to pinpoint an exact age; it depends somewhat on how we define and measure self-control. Some psychologists have analyzed children's resistance to distraction, that is, how hard they will work at a task when other things compete for their attention. Walter Mischel and Charlotte Patterson (1978), for example, gave three-to-eight-year-olds a dull task to do while next to a noisy toy called Mr. Clown Box. Three- and four-year-old children were often distracted from the chore by the toy, but older children deliberately ignored the toy, often by talking to themselves with self-instructions. Young children can be taught strategies for avoiding distractions. Explaining *why* children should not be distracted and explaining how the child's performance affects someone else (e.g., "I'll be unhappy and have to do your work if you don't finish") helps children to exercise self-control (Kuczynski, 1983).

MORAL DEVELOPMENT. The many facets of social development that we have discussed converge in children's sense of morality. Their ideas about themselves, the way they view other people, and their abilities/inclinations to follow rules are all evident in their understanding of social standards of moral behavior. Knowing right from wrong is referred to as ***moral reasoning.*** One way that Piaget, and others since, have studied moral reasoning is to confront children with stories that posed dilemmas, such as the following:

1. John, who is in his room, is called to dinner. He goes downstairs and pushes open the diningroom door. Behind the door is a chair, and on the chair is a tray on which there are fifteen cups. John does not know that. He opens the door. The door hits the tray. Crash go the cups. All of them break.
2. Henry's mother is out and Henry tries to get some cookies in the cupboard. He climbs on a chair and while reaching for the cookie jar he knocks down a cup, which breaks.

Who was naughtier, John or Henry?

According to Piaget (1952), seven-to-eight-year-olds focus attention on the outcomes and reason that breaking 15 cups is a larger wrong than breaking only 1 cup. Not until 11 or 12 years of age do children reason clearly about other people's intentions and then judge guilt and punishment in re-

TABLE 9–5
Kohlberg's Six Stages of Moral Development

Level and Stage	What Is Right	Reasons for Doing Right	Social Perspective of Stage
LEVEL I: PRECONVENTIONAL			
Stage 1: Heteronomous morality	To avoid breaking rules backed by punishment and obedience for its own sake.	Avoidance of punishment, the superior power of authorities.	Doesn't consider the interests of others or relate two points of view.
Stage 2: Individualism, instrumental purpose, and exchange	Acting to meet your own interests and needs and letting others do the same.	To serve your own needs or interests in a world where you have to recognize that other people have their interests, too.	Aware that everybody has his or her own interest to pursue and these conflict, so that right is relative.
LEVEL II: CONVENTIONAL			
Stage 3: Mutual interpersonal expectations, relationships, and interpersonal conformity	Living up to what is expected by people close to you. "Being good" is important and means having good motives, showing concern about others.	Belief in the Golden Rule. Desire to maintain rules and authority which support stereotypical good behavior.	Relates points of view through the concrete Golden Rule, putting yourself in the other person's shoes. Does not yet consider generalized system perspective.
Stage 4: Social system and conscience	Fulfilling the actual duties to which you have agreed. Right is contributing to society, the group, or institution.	To keep the institution going as a whole.	Takes the point of view of the system that defines roles and rules.
LEVEL III: POSTCONVENTIONAL			
Stage 5: Social contract or utility and individual rights	Being aware that people hold a variety of values and opinions, that most values and rules are relative to your group.	Concern that laws and duties be based on rational calculation of overall utility, "the greatest good for the greatest number."	Integrates perspectives by formal mechanisms of agreement, contract, objective impartiality, and due process.
Stage 6: Universal ethical principles	Following self-chosen ethical universal principles of justice: the equality of human rights and respect for the dignity of human beings as individual persons.	The belief in universal moral principles and a personal commitment to them.	Perspective is that of any rational individual recognizing the nature of morality.

These stages show how moral reasoning can be based on different rules and justifications. Young children usually reason at the preconventional level while adults often use principled reasoning that considers humanistic values.

Source: Kohlberg, 1976.

lation to intentions. Recent evidence, though, has shown that Piaget underestimated children's moral reasoning. Nelson (1980) showed three-year-olds pictures of a child throwing a ball at another child and explained that the actor was either (a) playing catch with him or (b) angry at him. When asked to judge the "goodness" or "badness" of the child's ball throwing, even preschoolers could consider the actor's intentions.

Piaget's ideas have been refined by Lawrence Kohlberg (1976) into a stage model of moral development. Kohlberg studied children's moral reasoning by analyzing how they responded to moral dilemmas posed by vignettes. The following dilemma of Heinz is a good example.

In Europe, a woman was near death from a special kind of cancer. There was one drug that doctors thought might save her. It was a form of radium that a druggist in the same town had recently discovered. The drug was expensive, but the druggist was charging $2,000, or ten times the cost of the drug, for a small (possibly life-saving) dose. Heinz, the sick woman's husband, borrowed all the money he could, about $1,000, only half of what he needed. He told the druggist that his wife was dying and asked him to sell the drug cheaper or let him pay later. The druggist said no, so Heinz broke into the store and stole the drug.

Should Heinz have done that?

By studying how children reasoned about this dilemma and others like it, Kohlberg devised a stage theory to chart the course of moral development. The three levels of morality—preconventional, conventional, and post-conventional—are illustrated in Table 9–5. The preconventional level coincides with Piaget's preoperational period and reflects a self-centered viewpoint. The conventional level prescribes tangible rules much like Piaget's concrete operations. Finally, the postconventional level reflects abstract, principled reasoning not available until the formal operational period of adolescence.

Kohlberg's theory has been criticized because it represents a philosophical ideal rather than a developmental sequence through which most people pass. Others argue that moral reasoning is different from moral behavior, that is, acting in accordance with social rules of conduct. People may discuss dilemmas about morality at a high level, but when faced with actual choices to lie, steal, or cheat, they may act differently. Kohlberg's emphasis on reasoning as a basis for morality needs to be complemented with theories that emphasize socialization forces (Gibbs & Schnell, 1985). Further, some critics argue that few people progress beyond Kohlberg's conventional level and that progress may depend on formal schooling or a particular cultural viewpoint. Despite these criticisms, many children from diverse cultures do develop from the lower to higher stages of moral reasoning that Kohlberg described. Like Erikson's theory of general stages and crises across the life span, Kohlberg's views illuminate broad characteristics of children's developing moral reasoning and provide useful descriptions of developmental trends.

SUMMARY

1. Human development is a process of change that reflects the interaction of genetic and environmental factors. Developmental psychologists study how people change physically, mentally, and socially across the life span and why they develop particular habits, talents, and disabilities. Several theories help to identify distinctive developmental changes over chronological age periods. Stage theories focus on abrupt, qualitative shifts in behavior during development, while other theories, such as social learning theory, emphasize continuous, gradual changes in human behavior.

2. Over the past hundred years, significant changes in attitudes toward science, politics, and life expectancy have led to a greater scientific interest in human development. Today, two methods are especially suited to testing developmental hypotheses. The longitudinal method involves repeated testing of the same subjects over an extended time. The cross-sectional method involves testing subjects of different ages simultaneously.

3. There are three periods of prenatal growth, during which the organism becomes a zygote, then an embryo, and finally a fetus. As the organism passes through these stages, it gradually takes on the appearance of a human baby, and its major systems are refined. Prenatal growth can be impeded by such factors as inherited disorders, the mother's age, stress and diet during pregnancy. However, several new methods are available to help diagnose prenatal complications, including amniocentesis, chorionic villii biopsy, and ultrasound.

4. Birth usually occurs approximately 266 days after conception. Sometimes it is necessary to administer pain medication to the mother during the birth process, which may have adverse effects on the child through the first year of life. The disadvantages of medicated delivery and recent advances in obstetric education for parents have led to a more widespread practice of natural childbirth, during which fathers and other family members may be present.

5. Although newborn babies seem helpless, they have surprisingly good perceptual and motor abilities. By two months of age infants are able to perceive visual patterns and speech sounds and to distinguish colors and brightness to a reasonable degree.

6. Piaget's theory of cognitive development identifies four distinct stages of children's thinking: sensorimotor, preoperational, concrete operational, and formal operational. Cognitive abilities improve as children progress from stage to stage. For example, in the preoperational stage (2–7 years), children tend to focus on single aspects of stimuli and are fooled by the appearance of objects. However, when they reach the concrete operational stage (7–11 years), children achieve conservation, the understanding that properties such as number, weight, and volume can remain the same even when objects change appearance.

7. Information processing changes in four basic ways during cognitive development. First, children's knowledge becomes more organized. Second, information processing becomes faster as basic processes become more automatic. Third, the use of cognitive strategies to guide attention, language, and memory becomes deliberate. Fourth, children develop greater metacognition, increased awareness, and control of their own thinking.

8. Humans are biologically prepared to attend to and learn language. During infancy, babies learn to communicate through social interactions with adults. Children's early word combinations follow regular rules for expressing meaning in grammatical utterances. From two to three years of age, children begin to use language in nonegocentric ways to communicate effectively with other people.

9. Erik Erikson's theory of psychosocial development comprises eight stages, each of which involves the resolution of a social crisis. Four of these stages are concerned with social and emotional development in infancy and childhood: trust versus mistrust, autonomy versus doubt and shame, initiative versus guilt, and industry versus inferiority.

10. Attachment is a strong, emotional relationship between an infant and a particular caregiver. Early interactions between infants and caregivers can establish trust and confidence in children and can have long-term effects. For example, infants who are securely attached to their caregivers at one year of age tend to be more curious and sociable with their peers at five years than do insecurely attached infants.

11. Personal beliefs, parental expectations, and home environment influence children's achievement motivation and self-esteem. Another aspect of children's self-concept involves sex typing, a process by which children identify themselves as boys or girls and adopt socially appropriate male or female behaviors.

12. The development of social behavior includes not only a healthy self-concept but social cognition, the understanding of other people's points of view, thoughts, feelings, and intentions. Preschoolers characterize themselves and others in terms of appearances and possessions. As they grow older, children describe themselves and other people according to psychological attributes. Social development also reflects self-control, the ability to resist distraction and to delay gratification. Moral development represents a convergence of children's cognitive development, self-concept, and social role-taking.

SUGGESTED READINGS

Crain, W. C. (1985). *Theories of development: Concepts and applications.* Englewood Cliffs, N.J.: Prentice-Hall.
  Covers all the major viewpoints on human development including good historical coverage of Gesell, Werner, and others. Succinct summaries of theories of Piaget, Kohlberg, Erikson, Chomsky, and Bandura.

Flavell, J. H. (1985). *Cognitive development* (2nd ed.). Englewood Cliffs, N.J.: Prentice-Hall.
  The author has been a pioneer in cognitive development research for years and captures both the history and current enthusiasm in the field. Information processing, Piagetian theory, language, and memory are discussed in depth.

Kail, R. V. (1984). *The development of memory in children.* San Francisco: Freeman.
  An introduction to a wide range of developmental research methods, with emphasis on the central aspects of children's memory.

Perry, D. G., & Bussey, K. (1984). *Social development.* Englewood Cliffs, N.J.: Prentice-Hall.
  Detailed coverage of children's social behavior and interactions with families and peers, with in-depth discussions of research and social learning theories.

Shaffer, D. R. (1985). *Developmental psychology.* Monterey, Calif.: Brooks/Cole.
  An introductory textbook more thorough and up to date than most. Theories and research are evaluated, criticized, and synthesized in a scholarly way.

10

Adolescence and Adulthood

We are born twice over; the first time for existence,
the second for life; once as human beings and later as
men or as women.

Jean-Jacques Rousseau

WHEN DOES A CHILD BECOME AN ADULT? THERE ARE NO SHARP boundaries in our biological or cognitive development. The transition is usually gradual. Many cultures, however, define specific *rites of passage* from childhood to adulthood with elaborate rituals. For example, among the Mardudjara aborigines of Australia, when boys reach puberty they undergo nose-piercing, isolation, and eventually circumcision (Tonkinson, 1978). Anthropologist Ruth Benedict (1934) found that boys in a South African tribe were initiated by running through a gauntlet of older men who beat them with sticks. Then, during the coldest months of the year, the boys were forced to sleep without blankets and to swim in bitterly cold water. After months of such painful experience, the boys were accepted as adult members of the tribe in a special ceremony. Girls, too, often face initiation rites. The Carrier Indians of British Columbia feared and abhorred girls' puberty so much that they banished their young women to live in the wilderness for three or four years.

The passage to adulthood in contemporary American society is less clearly marked and more gradual than in these cultures. Our modern "rites of passage" to adulthood include the legal rights to drive, to marry, and to vote. We refer to the transitional development of the child into adulthood as the period of *adolescence.* Because this period is marked by transition to adult-like characteristics of cognitive, social, and biological functioning, the most significant characteristic of adolescence is change. Usually adolescence is signaled by the onset of puberty, which may be accompanied by ceremonies or rites of passage, (e.g., religious ceremonies such as baptism or a boy's Bar Mitzvah). The end of adolescence is difficult to pinpoint, but it is usually marked by social and cultural responsibilities such as marriage, parenting, work, or military service. During the past 100 years, the period of adolescence in American society has lengthened. Nowadays Americans remain in school longer, delay marriage, and join the work force later than our ancestors did. Many adult responsibilities are delayed as a consequence. This time of prolonged apprenticeship and education is sometimes referred to as the *adolescent moratorium.* The end of adolescence is therefore specified only loosely by the adoption of adult roles and responsibilities. Clearly, the period of adolescence varies among cultural groups and across history.

Popular movies, television series, and novels often portray adolescence as a troubled, rebellious phase of life. This picture of "storm and stress" derives from two historical viewpoints in psychology. G. Stanley Hall (1844–1924) wrote the first textbook on adolescents in 1904, and his notions of adolescence influenced both academic and public views for years. Hall believed that development from infancy to adolescence reflects the same kinds of changes as those involved in the evolution of societies from primitive savages to civilized people. He felt that enormous stress and conflict occur in this transition. Anna Freud (1958), daughter of the founder of psychoanalysis, also called attention to the turbulence of adolescence. She compared the inner emotional conflicts of adolescence with symptoms of psychological distress and even mental illness. But not all researchers define adolescence as a period of turmoil and stress. Anthropologists Margaret Mead (1935) and Ruth Benedict (1934) observed adolescents in many cultures more than 50 years ago and suggested that adolescence could be a relatively calm period depending on social customs. Psychologists Elizabeth Douvan and Joseph Adelson (1966) conducted a survey of American adolescents and concluded that most teenagers are somewhat conservative and conforming individuals. Only a minority suffer stress and emotional upheaval. As we will discover, adolescents confront remarkable physical changes and social challenges to their personal development, but most adolescents overcome these problems en route to adulthood.

In this chapter we survey the child's transition to adulthood. We begin with a discussion of puberty and the consequences of physical development during adolescence. Next we discuss how adolescents' increased cognitive abilities influence their reasoning and self-concepts. Then we consider some of the challenges and risks facing adolescents today, such as the availability and appeal of drugs. In the last half of the chapter we discuss stages of adulthood beginning with marriage and careers and ending with the challenges of old age and dying. We pay special attention to the intellectual and physical changes that accompany aging.

PHYSICAL AND SEXUAL DEVELOPMENT

Adolescence begins with a spurt in growth and a series of changes in sexual characteristics. *Puberty* is the period of development in which young people achieve sexual maturity and the capability for reproduction. Changes in body build, hormonal activity, and sexual maturity naturally inspire both joy and anxiety among boys and girls. Before we discuss how individuals respond to the changes of puberty, we briefly describe the biological mechanisms involved.

The Onset of Puberty

At the onset of puberty, the hypothalamus (see Chapter 2, Figure 2–11), located under the cortex and the thalamus, acts like a biological clock that signals the pituitary gland to become active. The pituitary gland then secretes several types of hormones that regulate puberty. The production of hormones in the body is part of a self-regulating feedback system often referred to as a *hypothalamic thermostat* (see Figure 10–1). The hypothalamus produces neurohormones that cause the pituitary gland to secrete other hormones called gonadotropins. These in turn stimulate production of sex hormones (estrogen, progesterone, and testosterone) in the male sex glands (testes) and female sex glands (ovaries). When the sex hormones reach a certain concentration in the blood system, the hypothalamus reduces its production of neurohormones, and this reduction in turn slows down the production of gonadotropins and sex hormones.

The feedback system changes as an individual matures, but it is relatively stable during childhood. During childhood, increases in gonadotropins and sex hormones occur only during sleep (Peterson & Taylor, 1980).

FIGURE 10–1
The Hypothalamic Thermostat

The hypothalamus regulates the production of hormones at puberty. It stimulates the pituitary gland, which in turn sends a signal to the sex glands to produce sex hormones. When these hormones reach a certain level in the blood system, the hypothalamus slows production of neurohormones, and the entire cycle slows.

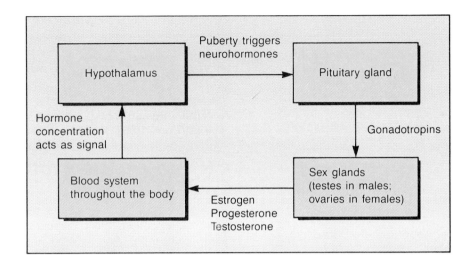

As children enter the adolescent years, the hypothalamus becomes less responsive to existing concentrations of sex hormones in the bloodstream. As a result, the pituitary gland secretes greater amounts of gonadotropins. This gradual process continues until some (as yet unknown) threshold is reached, whereupon rapid changes in hormonal production occur and puberty begins. Frisch and Revelle (1970) hypothesized that this sudden change in hormone production is triggered by a critical level of body fat, but the exact cause of puberty is still unknown (Brooks-Gunn & Peterson, 1983).

Physical Changes During Puberty

Some of the hormones produced by the pituitary gland influence physical growth and metabolism. The *adolescent growth spurt* is a rapid increase in the rate of physical development that accompanies puberty. The age at which children undergo a spurt in growth has changed over the years. A hundred years ago males did not reach full height until age 24; the average female kept growing until age 19. Fewer childhood diseases, better nutrition, and improved medical care have accelerated adolescent growth for both sexes. Recently, however, the trend has leveled off, particularly in Western cultures.

In our society, girls usually begin rapid growth around 11, boys at 13. For both sexes, growth rate usually peaks a year later and declines quickly during the following year. Males are about six inches taller than the average female following puberty (Tanner, 1973), partly because of the action of sex hormones on bone growth. Most growth of bones, particularly the long bones of the arms and legs, occurs at places called epiphyseal growing plates. These regions continue to grow until higher concentrations of sex hormones, particularly estrogen, increase the calcium deposits in the growing plates and slow down bone growth. Since girls usually begin puberty before boys, their bones have less time to grow before increasing levels of sex hormones slow bone growth. For both boys and girls, some parts of the body grow earlier and more rapidly than other parts; this is why adolescents may temporarily have disproportionately large hands and feet.

A junior high school dance illustrates that girls usually start their adolescent growth spurt one or two years before boys.

Weight changes dramatically during puberty. By age 11, boys have attained only 55 percent of normal adult weight and girls 59 percent. Although body fat decreases after puberty, females lose less than males and have more fat as adults in the pelvis, breasts, upper back, and upper arms. There is an opposite trend in muscular development. Boys have more muscle cells than girls after puberty, and the size of muscle cells continues to increase into adulthood, whereas girls achieve maximum muscle cell size by age 11 (Root, 1973). Sex-related changes in growth of bones and muscle and the distribution of fat lead to characteristic sex differences in body proportions. Males develop broad shoulders, narrow hips, and relatively long legs; females develop narrower shoulders, wider hips, and shorter legs in relation to the trunk.

Other changes are evident too. The heart increases in size and nearly doubles in weight. Blood pressure, the number of red blood cells, and the total blood volume increase at puberty, particularly for males (Katchadourian, 1977). The lungs increase in size, and respiratory capacity expands. The gains are greater for males, giving them a higher tolerance for exercise and a quicker recovery from fatigue. For both boys and girls, body odor becomes stronger, the skull becomes wider, the hairline recedes, the jaw and nose lengthen, and the skin pores enlarge, leading to acne in about 70 percent of adolescents (Tanner, 1978). But the most spectacular changes involve the sexual organs.

Primary and Secondary Sexual Development

Sexual development in adolescence involves both primary and secondary characteristics, as shown in Figure 10–2. *Primary sex characteristics* are related directly to reproduction. For males, the most noticeable primary change at puberty is the enlargement of the penis and scrotum, the structure that contains the testes. The tubes that carry sperm from the testes to the penis also develop; they enable the male to ejaculate sperm. The size and shape of the penis are *not* related to physique, race, or frequency of sexual activity (Katchadourian, 1977).

The primary changes in female genitalia are enlargement of the clitoris, labia, and vaginal opening. And like males, the female delivery system matures so that ova (eggs) can be transported to the uterus. The uterine wall becomes more muscular, the vaginal lining becomes thicker, and the interior of the vagina becomes acidic rather than alkaline. All of these changes enhance the likelihood of fertilization and impregnation. The ovaries also become somewhat larger and heavier during puberty, primarily because of the development of previously immature ova. At birth, the female's ovaries contain a lifetime supply of ova; males produce new sperm into old age. About 18 months after the growth spurt, girls usually experience their first menstrual period, or *menarche.* However, menarche does not signal the capacity for sexual reproduction; this may not occur for another one to two years.

Secondary sex characteristics include aspects of physical appearance that may or may not be related to sexual reproduction. As evident in Figure 10–2, many visible signs of puberty are secondary sexual characteristics. The growth of pubic hair early in puberty, for example, is a signal of other impending changes. Growth of body hair on the face, in the armpits, and on

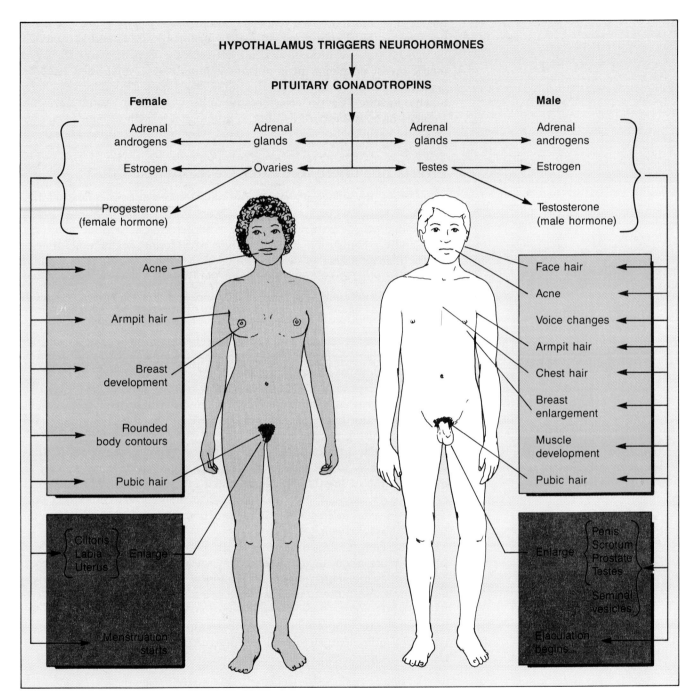

FIGURE 10–2
Primary and Secondary Sex Characteristics During Puberty

Puberty stimulates the production of hormones that prompt maturation and growth. The physical changes may continue for several years after puberty begins. Primary sex characteristics (shown in red) are related directly to reproduction. Secondary sex characteristics (shown in green) give distinctive physical appearances to males and females.

Source: Sarafino & Armstrong, 1980.

the chest occurs about two years later and is usually more evident in males. For females, breast development usually begins by age 11 and is completed by age 15, but it can occur anytime between the ages of 8 and 18. Asymmetric breast development is not uncommon, just as men often have one testicle larger than another (Garbarino, 1985). Other secondary sex characteristics include a deeper voice because of the enlargement of the larynx and changes in body proportions due to differential growth of bones, muscles, and fatty tissue.

Effects of Puberty on Later Development

All of these physiological changes can have important consequences for adolescents' self-concept, confidence, and social relationships (Brooks-Gunn & Peterson, 1983). A particular concern of adolescents is the first occasion of ejaculation or menstruation. These can be bewildering, frightening, or minor events in an adolescent's life depending on the person's level of understanding and parental communication about the subject. Likewise, teenagers are often preoccupied with concerns about their height, physique, or skin condition because of the rapid and often vaguely understood changes in these characteristics.

The age at which children experience changes in their primary and secondary sex characteristics varies greatly from child to child. Do children who undergo puberty at an earlier age realize any benefits in their social or personality development? The California Growth Study (Mussen & Jones, 1957) followed boys from infancy to adulthood in order to answer this question. Using X-rays to determine bone growth, the researchers identified early- and late-maturing boys from ages 14 to 18. The early-maturing boys looked more masculine as adolescents and were more relaxed. Late-maturing boys were more likely to feel rebellious against parents, rejected, and socially immature. Some of the differences persisted into adulthood. Other researchers, however, have observed some disadvantages for early-maturing boys. They often seem more somber and less curious than late-maturing boys (Peterson & Taylor, 1980).

Girls seem to react differently to the timing of puberty. Girls who mature early are often uncomfortable, less sociable, and less poised, perhaps because they are acutely aware of differences between their height, weight, and figures and those of their later-maturing peers (Jones & Mussen, 1958). Early-maturing girls, however, sometimes make better adjustments in adulthood, perhaps because parents have been stricter with them or perhaps because the girls learned to deal with social problems early in adolescence (Papalia & Olds, 1986).

COGNITIVE DEVELOPMENT

Although physical changes that accompany puberty are the most visible signs of adolescent development, significant cognitive changes occur as well. Adolescents are challenged by more difficult subjects in school (e.g., algebra, biology, chemistry), and they confront moral choices about drugs, sex, and crime. The ability to think abstractly and systematically about these issues develops during adolescence.

Abstract Thinking

As we saw in Chapter 9, children in middle childhood can classify objects into logical groups, solve problems involving conservation, and master several strategies in learning and remembering information, but they do not think abstractly. Pre-adolescents are limited primarily to reasoning about what they can perceive in the present. The adolescent, in contrast, can imagine not only what *is* but what *might be*. Thinking about imaginary and hypothetical events is characteristic of the formal operational period of thinking in Piaget's theory. An example of the shift from concrete to abstract thinking is evident in a well-known riddle. Imagine that you are sitting in a house with windows on all sides that face south and a bear walks by. What color is the bear? The concrete thinker may answer that he has never been in such a house and wouldn't know the answer. A formal, or logical thinker, might deduce that southern exposure on all four sides locates the house at the North Pole, and the bear must therefore be a polar bear, and white. Adolescents have a greater appreciation of logical deduction, symbolism, and irony. Abstract thinking also permits them to begin reasoning about science, religion, morality, and knowledge itself.

Adolescent reasoning is systematic and abstract, which facilitates hypothesis testing and scientific reasoning.

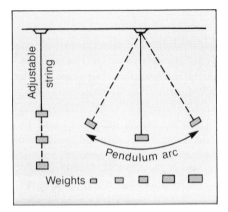

FIGURE 10–3
The Pendulum Problem

In this test of deductive reasoning, the child is given an adjustable string and a set of weights. The task is to find out what factors (such as the weight attached, length of the string, force of initial push) affect the speed of the pendulum's swing.

Source: Inhelder & Piaget, 1958.

As thinking becomes more adult-like during adolescence, it takes on three distinct characteristics. First, adolescents can form hypotheses about the world. They are not restricted to manipulating objects physically or actually observing the relations between events in order to understand them. Second, they can use deduction and inference to arrive at answers. Third, the process of generating and testing hypotheses becomes systematic. Rather than use trial and error, they test ideas in step-by-step logical combinations.

Many tasks have been devised to test formal operational thinking (Inhelder & Piaget, 1958). A task often used to measure deductive thought and systematic hypothesis-testing is the pendulum problem illustrated in Figure 10–3. Adolescents are given a pendulum, a weight swinging from a string, and are asked which factors determine the speed of the pendulum's swing. The string can be adjusted to different lengths and several different weights can be attached. The adolescents are shown that they can start the pendulum by pushing it or simply by releasing it. An adolescent with formal operational reasoning will approach this task by varying each factor in combination with the others (attaching each of the different weights to a short string and then to a long string). Through systematic hypothesis-testing, the adolescent can deduce that the length of the string determines the time it takes the pendulum to swing from one side to the other. The weight attached is irrelevant.

Piaget used many other tasks to measure formal operational thinking (Inhelder & Piaget, 1958). One task involves balancing different weights on a balance scale by varying the distance from the scale's midpoint, or fulcrum. Another involves calculating the angle a billiard ball will follow when it bounces off the side cushion of a billiard table. Have you ever been in a chemistry class where the teacher asked you to identify an unknown chemical substance? You probably made hypotheses about what the substance could have been and then tested the hypotheses by putting the chemical in water, in acid, over a flame, or through a filter. By generating hypotheses, testing them, keeping records, and arriving at a deductive conclusion, you were engaged in formal operational thinking.

Piaget believed that the stage of formal operations reflects mature thinking and that cognitive abilities change little in adulthood. In other words, experience and schooling could increase our knowledge, but our ability to reason or use knowledge is largely completed during adolescence. However, there has been considerable dispute over his claims. Some argue that thinking skills continue to change into adulthood (Arlin, 1975; Riegel, 1976). Others argue that many people do not always think logically according to Piaget's system (Keating, 1980). For example, Martorano (1977) presented children from ages 11 to 18 with ten different Piagetian tests of formal operations and found that performance varied greatly among the children. Although the quality of thinking improved with age, only 2 out of 80 subjects performed at the formal level on all ten tasks. Similarly, cross-cultural studies consistently fail to find evidence of formal operational thinking in societies without advanced formal schooling (Dasen, 1972). In response to these criticisms, Piaget modified his views about formal operations and explained that education and experience could promote formal operational thinking in specific subject areas. Thus, adolescents and adults continue to develop reasoning skills in particular areas of expertise, both practical and academic.

Academic Achievement

The ability to think abstractly and logically permits adolescents to study academic subjects such as science and mathematics in greater detail. They may establish favorite subjects and excel in particular classes. Such expertise may be motivated by an admired parent or teacher who is a model of academic success. Parents often express greater interest in their children's performance in school during adolescence, due in part to curriculum choices, academic tracking, and preparation for college or vocational training. Students' *academic achievement*—their relative standing compared to performance of their peers—becomes more stable by adolescence also. This is due to both cognitive and motivational influences and is illustrated well by studies of gifted students.

During the 1970s, Camilla Benbow and Julian Stanley conducted a series of talent searches to identify mathematically gifted students for their Study of Mathematically Precocious Youth. In 1980 they published a three-page article in the journal *Science* that summarized talented students' scores on the Scholastic Aptitude Test (SAT) for the previous six talent searches they had conducted. More specifically, they compared the mathematics (SAT-M) and verbal (SAT-V) test scores for the nearly 10,000 junior high school students who were mathematically gifted. To be classified as gifted, students had to score at least in the top 5 percent on the SAT-M. The striking result was that boys consistently scored higher than girls on the math part of the test, while boys and girls were equal on the verbal portion. The top scorers in all six searches were always boys, and in fact twice as many boys as girls scored over 500 on the SAT-M.

Benbow and Stanley (1980) considered various hypotheses that might account for the large differences in math scores. They ruled out the possibility that talented girls did not participate in the searches. They also rejected the possibility that boys and girls differed in math courses or informal experiences before seventh grade that would contribute to the differences. Thus, they concluded, "We favor the hypothesis that sex differences in achievement in and attitudes toward mathematics result from superior male mathematical ability, which may in turn be related to greater male ability in spatial tasks. This male superiority is probably an expression of a combination of both endogenous [produced from within] and exogenous [produced from without] variables" (p. 1264).

Despite the cautious language, Benbow and Stanley clearly suggest that males are biologically superior in math than females. Little attention was given to the generalizability of results from the talented sample to the other 95 percent of the population. Neither were data collected on spatial reasoning, attitudes, grades, or prior experiences. But the blow to sexual equality was struck, and the implication was clear when Camilla Benbow stated in an interview that women would be "better off accepting their differences" (Kolata, 1980). The ensuing debate, discussed in "Controversy: Why Do Males Excel in Math?," erupted when the media sensationalized the claims of sex differences in mathematical abilities.

CONTROVERSY

Why Do Males Excel in Math?

Immediately following the report in *Science* by Benbow and Stanley (1980), *Time* magazine reported the story under the headline "The Gender Factor in Math—A New Study Says Males May Be Naturally Abler Than Females" (1980). *Newsweek* asked, "Do Males Have a Math Gene?" (1980), while newspapers around the country publicized the issue.

The controversy over these findings does not concern the data Benbow and Stanley assembled. Researchers readily admit that boys score higher than girls on SAT-M and other math achievement tests in secondary school. The controversy centers on Benbow and Stanley's interpretation of their data and the role of the media in misinforming the public about the report. The outpouring of letters to *Science* have nearly all been critical. The four major problems were summarized by Beckwith (1983) and Eccles and Jacobs (1986). First, the SAT-M is *not* a pure measure of mathematical ability or reasoning. It is a psychometric instrument that measures achievement and aptitude and is also influenced by students' experiences, beliefs, anxiety, and expectations. (We will discuss the nature of psychometric testing in Chapter 11.) Second, Benbow and Stanley claim that the educational and informal math experiences of boys and girls are equivalent. Yet research on classroom interactions and out-of-school learning suggests that boys receive much more math-relevant instruction than girls (Eccles

& Jacobs, 1986). Third, Benbow and Stanley suggest that poorer ability leads girls to show less interest in math and to take fewer courses, but they provided no data linking ability, attitudes, and course selections. In fact, other analyses of the same data show no relation between SAT-M scores and course selections or attitudes. Fourth, Benbow and Stanley imply that male superiority is fixed by biological factors and cannot be altered. Whether or not the difference in scores is due to genetic factors, the implication is false because many behavioral traits with genetic bases can be modified.

Some researchers emphasize that social factors play an important role in the observed sex differences in math achievement. For example, Jacquelynne Parsons Eccles and her colleagues studied 250 students in seventh, eighth, and ninth grades and surveyed their parents and teachers. They interviewed each group about their attitudes toward math. They asked parents and teachers about their expectations for each child's success in math, and they collected information about students' grades and courses. Based on correlational research, the single best predictor of academic success in math was the mothers' beliefs and expectations about their own children's ability (Eccles & Jacobs, 1986; Parsons, Adler, & Kaczala, 1982). In fact, mothers typically had lower expectations for girls than for boys and more anxiety about girls' performance. So despite equivalent perceptions by teachers, equal homework, and comparable achievement before seventh grade, girls' scores slowly began to fall in junior high school below the level of boys' scores, and girls did not choose

to enroll in as many math courses as boys.

These social factors become even more important when one considers the role of the media in publicizing sex differences in math scores. Jacobs and Eccles (1985) surmised that parents in their study may have been influenced by media reports, so they sent all parents another questionnaire, 90 percent of which were returned. The questions again measured parents' attitudes and beliefs about math and their expectations for their own children. They also asked if parents had heard media reports about sex differences in math. About one quarter had; most had seen an article in a newspaper or magazine. Mothers who had read or heard that boys are superior to girls in math lowered their estimates of their own daughters' math abilities. Fathers who were exposed to these media reports, however, did not devalue their daughters' abilities. They apparently rushed to defend their daughters and subsequently reevaluated their abilities more highly than before. Why did mothers and fathers react differently? Jacobs and Eccles (1985) speculate that mothers of daughters project their own anxiety about math to girls, whereas fathers do not project negative images. Mothers' beliefs play a large role in shaping girls' attitudes toward math, and, thus, the pronounced effect of the media on them may perpetuate differences in math achievement. Future research must address the question of how much of the sex differences in math achievement is due to social and educational differences. But the role of parental beliefs on students' achievement should make us sensitive to the impact of media reports on education and development.

SOCIAL AND MORAL DEVELOPMENT

One of the consequences of abstract thinking during adolescence is the ability to reflect on the personal qualities of oneself and others. For example, when seven-to-eight-year-olds are asked to describe other people, they are likely to focus on what people look like, how they dress, what kind of car they drive, or other similar physical characteristics. Adolescents are more likely to mention more abstract attributes such as intelligence, sociability, or temperament. Adolescents show a growing appreciation for other people's motives, feelings, and social roles. As a result, they form deeper psychological impressions of people and understand the roles people play in different situations. For example, a teenager may act differently in different situations when he is clearly identified in a role such as brother, student, son, or boyfriend. This ability to understand other points of view and to adopt social roles is fundamental for acquiring emotional understanding and social relationships (Selman, 1980).

Social Cognition and Identity Development

The emergence of reflective, hypothetical thinking during adolescence also affects the teenager's self-understanding and *identity development.* According to Erik Erikson (1950), the establishment of an independent and positive view of oneself is a major goal of adolescence. One familiar example of identity development is the extreme self-consciousness and self-centeredness teenagers exhibit. Teenagers worry a great deal about how they dress. They imitate the dress and actions of movie stars, rock musicians, or sports figures. They are sensitive about their beliefs and attitudes and how other people regard them. The following excerpt from an interview with a 14-year-old girl illustrates teenage self-consciousness:

> I am a very temperamental person, sometimes, well, most of the time, I am happy. Then, now and again, I just go moody for no reason at all. I enjoy being different from everybody else, and I like to think of myself as being fairly modern. Up till I was about eleven, I was a pretty regular church-goer, but since then I have been thinking about religion and sometimes I do not believe in God. When I am nervous I talk a lot, and this gives some important new acquaintances the wrong impression, when I am trying to make a good one. I worry a lot about getting married and having a family, because I am frightened that I will make a mess of it. (Livesley & Bromley, 1973, pp. 239–240)

David Elkind (1967) suggested that adolescents often appear self-centered because they believe themselves to be under constant scrutiny. They act as though they are before an "imaginary audience," a product of their hypothetical reasoning and insecurity. Teenagers may also believe a "personal fable" whereby they are unique, powerful, immortal, or at least exceptions to the rule. This kind of belief, epitomized by thoughts such as "It won't happen to me" or "I can't get pregnant," underlies many teenagers' risk-taking behaviors.

According to Erikson (1950), whose theory of social development was introduced in Chapter 9, adolescents confront the challenge of their own identities during stage V, labeled identity versus role confusion. According to Erikson, individuals in this stage are seeking answers to questions such as Who am I? What will I become? How do I fit into my family and society? Erikson maintains that a strong sense of identity is necessary in order for a young person to choose a vocation and a marriage partner, two critical aspects of young adulthood.

How can we explain adolescent identity development? In Erikson's theory, identity formation is a process of **individuation,** differentiating self from others. It is a life-long process that begins in infancy and ends with integration in old age of self and humanity. During adolescence, teenagers form a sense of self that is not limited to one place or group such as home, school, or friends. Personal identity does not depend on how a few people regard an individual; it depends on the enduring characteristics that each person perceives in his or her own self. A stable sense of his or her competence helps the person to remove self-doubts and to avoid social withdrawal and thus promotes further individuation.

Moral Reasoning

The ability to reason about moral, religious, and ethical issues emerges during adolescence. Moral reasoning is partly a consequence of abstract, logical thinking and is partly due to the adolescent's newfound ability to consider other people's social roles and perspectives. Kohlberg's (1976) model of moral development (presented in Chapter 9, page 354) integrates developments in thinking and social cognition with the emergence of a moral sense.

In American society, many adolescents exhibit moral reasoning characteristic of Kohlberg's *postconventional stage* (see Table 9–5). In this stage of principled reasoning, people realize that individuals have certain rights and values that come before their social relationships (such as family and cultural ties). For example, advocates of nuclear disarmament often argue that individuals have the right to live without the threat of worldwide nuclear destruction carried out by one government against another. At the postconventional stage, people also recognize points of view other than their own and seek ways to resolve conflicts. Some studies have indicated that attending college may facilitate this development of moral reasoning. James Rest (1975) compared high school graduates who intended to go on to college with those who did not. Each group showed similar levels of moral reasoning, measured in terms of Kohlberg's developmental stages. Yet two years later, the group that had attended college included many more individuals at Kohlberg's highest stage of principled reasoning. Turiel (1974) observed the same advantage in moral reasoning among college students. It may be that attending college stimulates adolescents to think about a wider range of moral issues than those considered by people who do not attend college. Course work, peers, and campus activism may sensitize students to moral issues and encourage them to reconsider their own moral views. Alternatively, attending college may simply help students articulate moral dilemmas and options better than those who do not attend college. The differences were found in moral *reasoning*, not in actual behavior.

Political Ideology

Adolescents' *political ideology*—their set of beliefs and attitudes toward government and government policy—shows how logical, social, and moral thinking converge during adolescence. Five characteristics of adolescence are linked to the development of political ideology: abstract thinking, a better understanding of the past and future, a better understanding of political change, recognition of the costs and benefits of political decisions, and an understanding of social principles.

It is common to describe a "generation gap" in political ideology between adolescents and their parents. Adolescents, especially 16–20-year-olds, are often portrayed as more idealistic and optimistic than their mothers and fathers. They are often stereotyped as more open to change and less conservative. Does such a gap exist? Not really, according to research conducted by Richard Lerner and his colleagues. Lerner (1975) asked adolescents and parents to respond to 36 statements on a Contemporary Topics Questionnaire. In addition to offering their own opinions, adolescents told how they thought their parents would respond, and parents did the same for adolescents. Adolescents and parents basically agreed on most issues, although the strength of their beliefs often varied. Lerner found that adolescents tended to overestimate the differences between their parents' attitudes and their own views, whereas parents tended to underestimate these differences. This study suggests that the perceptions that adolescents and adults hold of each other may be the source of the popular conception of a "generation gap" in ideology.

CHALLENGES AND RISKS DURING ADOLESCENCE

Adolescence is sometimes portrayed as a time of rebellion and turbulence. Although this image is often exaggerated, there are many sources of adolescent anxiety: puberty, dating, parental discipline, and development of an individual identity. Abstract thinking skills help adolescents reason about these problems, but still they must negotiate a twisting road to adulthood that presents many obstacles. In this section, we discuss some of the risks that face adolescents today. Not all teenagers face these problems, and of those who do, the overwhelming majority successfully overcome them.

Substance Abuse

One of the major threats to health during adolescence is substance abuse. A wide range of legal and illegal substances is available to adolescents, including common items such as tobacco, caffeine, glue, paint vapors, alcohol, and pills. In a national survey commissioned by the National Institute on Drug Abuse, Johnston, Bachman, and O'Malley (1982) observed that 90% of the students they surveyed reported drinking alcohol within the past year. More than 20% got drunk frequently. More than 20% of high school seniors reported daily cigarette smoking, and 9% reported using marijuana daily. Thirty percent admitted using other illicit drugs such as amphetamines and cocaine. The survey concluded that drug use by adolescents is widespread; nearly two-thirds of high school students reported using illicit drugs. However, it must be noted that since 1975 there is a trend for more moderate drug use. The pattern of data reveals that adolescents are primarily recreational drug users rather than being drug addicts or abusers (Papalia & Olds,

1986). Two things may be contributing to a decline in adolescent substance abuse. First, peer pressure is a powerful inducement to experiment with drugs (see Chapter 15), but a growing number of adolescents avoid illicit substances. Thus, there may be less peer pressure today to use drugs than there was 10 years ago. Second, adolescents are becoming better informed about substance abuse, and they report an increased concern with the risks (Johnston, Bachman, & O'Malley, 1982).

Sexual Attitudes and Behavior

Nonconformity, thrill-seeking, and peer group pressure are all influential forces during adolescence. Coupled with an emerging sexual maturity, these forces often lead to sexual experimentation by adolescents. The period of adolescence presents many conflicting messages about sex. Adolescents are virtually bombarded by sexual suggestiveness in the media, while parents provide warnings and restrictions against sexual behavior. Adolescents must sort out these mixed messages and develop a sense of their own sexuality.

What attitudes do adolescents hold about sexual behavior? Several large surveys have sought to answer this question. Robert Sorenson (1973) collected data from more than 400 adolescents between the ages of 13 and 19, and Aaron Hass (1979) used questionnaires and interviews to assess the attitudes of 600 adolescents aged 15 through 18. Like all self-report measures, surveys are vulnerable to distortion, but the data reveal some general trends. Sorenson (1973) found that only 65% of the adolescents he interviewed agreed with the statement "I have a lot of respect for my parents' ideas and opinions about sex." Nearly 75% thought that premarital sex was acceptable when love was involved, but less than a fourth believed their parents would approve of premarital sex. Males generally had more positive feelings about their first sexual experience than did females. Almost half the males reported excitement about their first experience with intercourse, compared with 26% of females. Conversely, 17% of the males and 63% of females said they felt afraid.

Adolescents regard sexual morality as a personal matter based more on affection for the partner than on law or social standards. Females, however, feel more strongly than males that sex should be reserved for someone with whom they share a loving relationship. Hass (1979) observed that affection, love, and intimacy are reported by both sexes as more important reasons for having intercourse than was physical pleasure.

Sorenson (1973) observed that more than 90% of both sexes reported masturbating by the age of 15. Hass (1979) observed slightly lower rates but found among 16-to-19-year-olds that more than two-thirds of the boys and half of the girls masturbated at least once a week. Despite its common occurrence, Sorenson (1973) found that about half of adolescents have anxiety or guilt about masturbation. With regard to homosexuality, Hass (1979) found that homosexual contacts during adolescence are most frequent before age 15 and are more common among boys (14%) than girls (11%). He also found that 70% of 16-to-19-year-olds accept sexual relationships between two girls but that slightly less than 70% accept it between two boys. Finally, Hass (1979) observed that despite permissive attitudes, reported rates of adolescent homosexuality have not changed much in the past 30 years.

Physical attractiveness assumes greater importance for teenagers as they reach sexual maturity.

More liberal attitudes have been accompanied by changes in adolescent sexual behavior. Premarital sexual intercourse has increased during the past two decades, particularly for white, middle-class females (Dreyer, 1982). In fact, from 1971 to 1979 the percentages of 15-year-old females who reported intercourse rose from 11 to 23, while for 19-year-olds the frequency increased from 45% to 70% (Zelnick & Kantner, 1980). Sorenson's (1973) study revealed that half of all adolescents have had intercourse by age 16. But adolescents usually restrict their sexual encounters. Zelnick and Kantner (1977) found that over 90% of never-married 15-to-19-year-old women who were sexually experienced had had sexual intercourse with three or fewer partners by their twentieth birthday.

Increased sexual activity has been accompanied by modest increases in the use of contraception. In the early 1970s, less than half of sexually active teenagers used any type of contraceptive techniques (Sorenson, 1973); but by 1976, more than 60% of 15-to-19-year-olds reported using contraception (Zelnick & Kantner, 1977). The lag between initial sexual intercourse and use of contraceptive techniques may be six months or longer. Females who feel guilty about sexual behavior are the most reluctant to use birth control, while those who establish commitments are the most likely contraceptive users.

Finally, we note some of the consequences of increased adolescent sexual activity. Each year there are approximately one million teenage pregnancies, and almost 45% of those end in abortion (U.S. Department of Health and Human Services, 1980). The rate of abortion has increased dramatically, especially for teenagers under age 15, since the 1973 Supreme Court decision legalizing abortion. Between 1973 and 1977 more blacks than whites received abortions (Forrest, Sullivan, & Tietze, 1979), although Dreyer (1982) observed that many women who seek abortions come from middle- or upper-class backgrounds and have high career goals. The Dreyer study also revealed that adolescent abortion does not necessarily result in harmful psychological consequences for the adolescents.

Pregnancy is not the only consequence of adolescent sexual behavior. The rate of gonorrhea has tripled since 1956, mostly among young women. Part of the cause of gonorrhea's spread may be confusion about its symptoms. Males who contract gonorrhea exhibit symptoms, including painful urinary discharge, but 80% of females who contract the disease show no symptoms at all. If the disease goes untreated, it can cause infertility in females and sterility in males. Like syphilis, gonorrhea is easily treated with penicillin or tetracycline. Recently, there has also been an alarming increase in another sexually communicated disease, herpes simplex virus II. Its symptoms include irregular cycles of sores and blisters around the genital regions. Like gonorrhea, the herpes virus is potentially harmful. If babies are exposed to the active virus during birth, they are vulnerable to brain damage or even death. Women with herpes are eight times more likely than uninfected women to develop cervical cancer (Harvard Medical School Letter, 1981). At present, herpes is incurable, and the epidemic proportions of the disease may be curtailing the frequency of sexual experiences among young adults. The dramatic increase in AIDS (acquired immune deficiency syndrome), which can be transmitted by sexual intercourse, has also limited sexual promiscuity. Currently, AIDS is incurable.

Delinquents

It is difficult to chart the incidence of juvenile criminal activity because the rates of self-reported crimes and police records do not always agree. There are also many kinds of crime. Status offenders, such as school truants, violate laws that apply only to people their age. Juvenile delinquents violate laws that apply to adults as well as to minors. In a national survey of 1,400 youths between ages 11 and 18, Gold and Reimer (1975) observed a steady increase in the frequency of delinquent acts. The biggest jump occurred between ages 14 and 15, a finding consistent with other studies (Elliot & Ageton, 1980). The types of crime change with age. Crimes against property (such as burglary, theft, and arson) are committed most often by 13-to-15-year-olds, while crimes against people are committed most often by 18-to-20-year-olds. According to official arrest records, such as the Uniform Crime Reports, males commit more serious crimes than females, and adolescents from poor families commit more offenses than adolescents from middle- or upper-class families (Garbarino, 1985).

Why do adolescents turn to crime and violence? Some offenders act on spur-of-the-moment impulses, but for others, delinquency reflects a pattern of deviant behavior. Weiner (1982) identified three types of adolescent delinquency: sociological, characterological, and neurotic. Sociological delinquency occurs among members of a group; delinquent acts confirm the values and identity of the group and help each member feel accepted and secure among friends. Characterological delinquents are often labeled as sociopathic personalities (see Chapter 15). These delinquents seldom belong to a group. They are distrustful of others and selfish. Often they have low self-esteem and little respect for authority. They may have deficient moral reasoning and often come from broken or violent home situations. Neurotic delinquents are usually well-behaved adolescents who may break the law to get attention from family members or friends. We will discuss the issue of delinquent behavior in Chapter 15.

Runaways

Children and adolescents run away from home for many reasons. Some seek adventure; some try to escape their difficult relationships with parents; and some are lured away by lovers or friends. Whatever the reasons, about 12% of American youth, about 500,000 people, run away from home by age 18. Slightly more than half of this total are girls. The average age for runaways of both sexes is 15. Fewer than 20% of all runaways travel more than 50 miles from home, and 70% return within a week (Garbarino, 1985). Running away is often an impulsive act that provides only a temporary escape. Small incidents over dating or dress, for example, can be magnified and intensified and may become confrontations over parental control. Runaway girls report *excessive* parental control as a prime reason for leaving home, while boys say that *inadequate* control is a reason for running away.

A few adolescents run away to escape violent or intolerable home situations, and these people seldom return on their own. Long-term runaways face considerable risks. They usually have few skills or job opportunities and are vulnerable targets. Since most runaways have only enough money for a few days, their needs for food and shelter may force them to steal or to become prostitutes. Many runaways leave homes where drugs, crime, or sexual abuse was prevalent, and they become entrapped in similar problems in new locations.

Eating Disorders

Attention has been drawn recently to dramatic increases in eating disorders, particularly in adolescent females. In contemporary American culture, where a premium is often placed on physical attractiveness defined by thinness, girls may develop intense fears of becoming fat. This can lead to *anorexia nervosa,* a voluntary weight loss of at least 25 percent of original body weight along with other psychological symptoms. Anorexics often have poor body images and feel fat even when they are quite thin. They may feel inadequate or insecure and choose to deny themselves food as an expression of self-control. Most anorexics are females, often affluent and well educated. Anorexics are often obsessively concerned with food and cooking, and they hide or hoard food. They behave irritably, show wide swings of emotion, and lack sexual interest. Menstruation ceases in anorexic women. Most accounts of these symptoms stress their similarity to those symptoms present in people subjected to involuntary starvation (Bemis, 1978).

A second common eating disorder is *bulimia,* characterized by binge and purge cycles in which consumption of large quantities of food is followed by self-induced vomiting. Some people exhibit alternating patterns of anorexia and bulimia, and the two disorders reflect a similar concern for physical attractiveness, perfection, achievement, and personal control. Bulimics, however, tend to be better adjusted than anorexics. As might be expected, the problem seems especially prevalent among college women. One survey (Herzog, 1982) revealed that nearly half of college women reported that they occasionally binge and purge, but the incidence of compulsive bulimia is considerably less.

Suicide

Despite the array of conflicts and challenges faced by adolescents today, most overcome the problems and make a successful transition to adulthood. Extreme failures to cope, however, may end in suicide. The national rate of suicide among 15-to-19-year-olds has doubled in the last 20 years to the point that more than 2,000 adolescents kill themselves annually. Suicide is now the third leading cause of death among teenagers. Even more alarming is the fact that attempted suicides may outnumber actual suicides by 50 or even 100 to 1. Although more females attempt suicide than males, more than twice as many adolescent males actually take their own lives, perhaps because they choose more violent and certain means for self-destruction. Suicide victims frequently have a long history of maladjustment and depression, but specific crises such as pregnancy or academic problems may trigger suicide attempts. Social relationships among families and friends may help protect adolescents from potential conflicts. Fortunately, most teenagers successfully overcome threats to their health and well-being in their transition to adulthood.

Adolescence is filled with social and intellectual achievements that help prepare teenagers for adult roles.

STAGES OF ADULTHOOD

Throughout Chapters 9 and 10, we have referred to Erik Erikson's (1950) stages of psychosocial development. We have seen that at each stage, the person struggles with a basic conflict that, if resolved, successfully provides a transition to the next stage. The eight stages, conflicts, and positive outcomes are summarized in Figure 10–4. The resolutions of each developmental conflict persist throughout life. For example, hope that develops during infancy becomes faith in old age; autonomy during childhood influences future adult independence. Erikson's last three stages encompass development during young, middle, and older adulthood.

The main task of young adulthood, according to Erikson, is to establish love and intimacy in personal relationships. This requires mutual commitments and compromises and depends to some extent on the prior establishment of personal identities. During stage VI, young adults try to avoid social isolation and alienation that may lead to a lack of warmth or deep emotional exchange.

A central task of middle adulthood is creating and caring for a family. This joint activity builds on the mutual intimacy of marriage and extends to children, a home, and a stable future. According to Erikson, establishing a family provides a sense of *generativity* that is productive and satisfying. Feelings of generativity can also be expressed through one's work when it is directed to help other people or to improve society. Failure to generate a sense of caring during stage VII may lead to self-indulgence and boredom. It can also lead to pseudo-intimacy, in which couples analyze each other and their relationship without a commitment to nurture it.

The eighth and final stage of Erikson's theory is a struggle between integrity and despair. It is a time to accept one's life, to gain a broad perspective on the past, and to achieve satisfaction. Successful aging provides a sense of wisdom. When despair predominates, people may fear death and desperately seek another chance at life. Children can be influenced by the reactions of elderly people to the closing years of life. As Erikson (1950) said, "Healthy children will not fear life if their parents have integrity enough not to fear death" (p. 233).

Erikson's stages of development do not constitute the only theory of changes during adulthood. The occupations that people choose and the pat-

FIGURE 10–4
Erikson's Stages of Psychosocial Development

According to Erikson, each stage of life involves a fundamental conflict. The positive resolution of conflicts leads to a sense of hope, will, and so forth, that strengthens the individual and enhances subsequent development.

Source: Erikson, 1950.

DEVELOPMENTAL STAGE	CONFLICT	POSITIVE RESOLUTION
I Infancy	Basic trust versus mistrust	Hope
II Toddler	Autonomy versus shame, doubt	Will
III Early childhood	Initiative versus guilt	Purpose
IV School age	Industry versus inferiority	Competence
V Adolescence	Identity versus role confusion	Fidelity
VI Young adulthood	Intimacy versus isolation	Love
VII Adulthood	Generativity versus stagnation	Care
VIII Old age	Integrity versus despair	Wisdom

FIGURE 10–5
Developmental Periods in Early and Middle Adulthood

Levinson proposed three major stages of adult development—early, middle, and late—that each last about 25 years. The transitions to each stage may require up to five years and can be filled with self-examination, crises, and major changes in career orientations or family relationships.

Source: Levinson et al., 1978, p. 57.

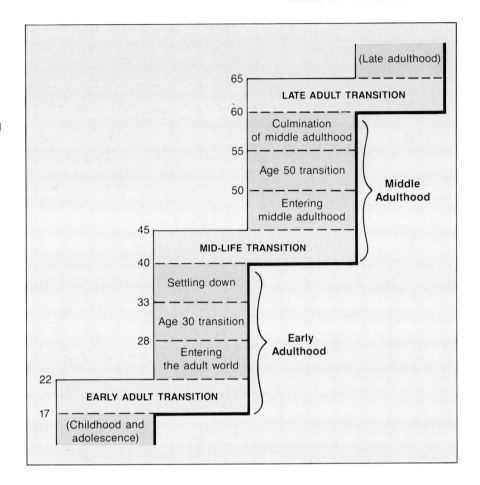

terns of their professional careers provide different insights into adult development. Daniel Levinson and his colleagues (1978) have identified stages of adulthood by analyzing patterns of men's lives. They interviewed in depth 40 men about their lives, aspirations, families, and backgrounds. The men (10 executives, 10 biologists, 10 factory workers, and 10 novelists) were all between 35 and 45 years of age. When the data from the many interviews and tests were analyzed, the researchers found similar patterns of development during early and middle adulthood. The men had progressed through several stable periods preceded by transitions that were often crucial turning points in their lives. Although Levinson collected data only from young and middle-aged adults, he projected three overlapping stages of adult development, illustrated in Figure 10–5. Each period is approximately 25 years long with transitional periods of about 5 years.

According to Levinson, early adulthood is begun by the early twenties. During this stage, the men in Levinson's study were characterized as "novices" in the workplace who tried to establish their career goals while working with other people. They were often guided by their "dreams" or idealized versions of their adolescent aspirations. Striving for these ideals is consistent with the search for identity emphasized in Erikson's theory. From 30 to 40 years of age, men tried to advance their careers, gain prestige, and settle down. As each man established his own career, he relied less and less on guidance from older workers, superiors, and mentors.

The midlife transition begins at about age 40, according to Levinson, and may involve radical changes in one's career and orientation to the family. Men may reevaluate their jobs, marriages, and goals and choose to change careers, to divorce, or to move to another city. In Levinson's study, most of the men experienced major emotional turmoil during midlife transitions. However, once the crises were over, middle adulthood to age 50 was often very satisfying and productive. The age 50 transition may be severe if there were few changes in lifestyle at age 30 or 40. But men usually find the years from 50 to 60 fulfilling because of career and family accomplishments.

Levinson's study does not provide data on further aging, although there may be several stages of development past age 60. Levinson's study included only a small number of men from the northeastern United States in the 1970s. Although his work popularized "the seasons of life" and "passages" (Sheehy, 1974) of adult development, the generality of the conclusions awaits further research.

Dividing the course of life into separate stages gives researchers a practical and systematic approach to studying continuity and change during adult development and aging. Realistically, however, it is difficult to clearly delineate one stage of adulthood from the next. Divisions occur differently from one person to another, from one culture to another, and throughout history. Even distinct classes within the same society view the stages of adulthood differently. For example, members of the working class in the United States tend to view a person as being middle-aged at 40 and old at 60, whereas members of the middle class do not view a person as being middle-aged until 50 and old until 70 (Neugarten, 1968). Age-defined stages may, in fact, be increasingly irrelevant in a society where there are no longer rigid expectations or time constraints for finishing an education, joining the work force, marrying, starting a family, seeking promotions, or retiring. Seventy-year-old college students and 50-year-old retirees have changed our views of adulthood and aging, and as Neugarten (1975) predicts, we may yet become an age-irrelevant society. Nevertheless, using the divisions provided by Levinson et al. (1978), we will briefly review the major events of adulthood.

Tasks of Early Adulthood

According to Robert Havighurst (1953), the major responsibilities of young adults are to select a mate, learn to live with a marriage partner, start a family, manage a home, adopt an occupation, take on civic responsibility, and find a congenial social group. But many of these tasks have changed over time. Today many young adults prefer to remain single or to live together rather than commit themselves to a traditional early marriage. Being single no longer carries the stigma of deviance that it did just 30 years ago. In 1957, women who remained single were considered sick, neurotic, or immoral by 80% of Americans surveyed (Yankelovich, 1981). By 1981, 75% felt that single women were simply those who had chosen an alternative lifestyle.

MARRIAGE AND FAMILY. Young adults today no longer feel obligated to have a family. Those who marry do so later, have fewer children, and start a family later. In 1960, 24% of married women between the ages of 20 and 24 and 13% of those between the ages of 25 and 29 were childless. Twenty years later the rates nearly doubled (U.S. Bureau of the Census, 1982). This trend toward postponing childbirth has resulted in a surge in the number of women in their thirties who give birth for the first time. Between 1980 and 1983, this number increased 15%. There are many reasons for these changes in lifestyle, including greater life expectancy, more career opportunities for women, wider use of contraception, and greater financial pressures. It has been estimated that it will cost $85,000 for a middle-class couple to raise a child born in 1980 to the age when the child enters college.

Unhappiness that married young adults experience often arises from the family. Marital conflicts over sexual dissatisfaction, money, children, and in-laws are common. The U.S. divorce rate has increased to the point that nearly 40% of young couples now married will probably part (Hetherington, 1979). Divorce usually occurs after six or seven years of marriage. The increased rate of divorce has changed our expectations of marriage. Sixty percent of Americans believe that young married couples have little or no expectations that the marriage will last until the death of one partner (Yankelovich, 1981). A number of factors increase the likelihood of divorce. Couples who come from divorced families or who marry while teenagers are much more likely to divorce. Divorce is also much more likely to occur if the woman is pregnant at the time of her marriage (U.S. Bureau of the Census, 1982).

The majority of people who divorce eventually remarry and do so, on the average, three years after their divorce. Men are more likely to remarry than women and often choose younger women. Women who remarry often

The responsibilities of family life are central concerns of young adults.

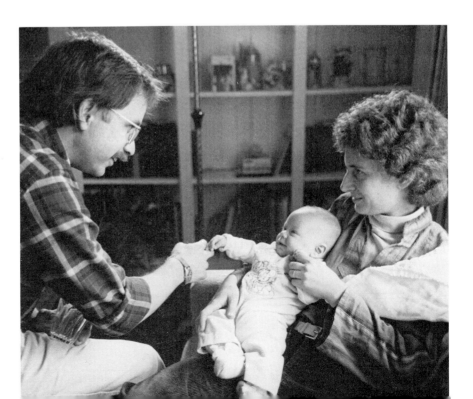

seek older men with secure positions and high income (Glick, 1980). Since women are less likely to remarry than men and since women often outlive their husbands, there has been an increase in the number of unmarried middle-aged and elderly women. Seventy-five percent of the remarriages that occur among older adults are due to the death of a spouse rather than divorce. When men are widowed before the age of 70, most remarry. However, remarriage occurs for only 5% of the women who are widowed after the age of 50 (Troll, Miller, & Atchley, 1979).

CAREERS. Compared to life at the turn of the century, young adults today begin working later, but they continue to work until later in life. A hundred years ago, the average laborer began working at 14 years of age, worked a 60-hour week without vacations, and had a life expectancy of 61 years. In 1970, the average laborer began working at the age of 20, worked a 40-hour work week with a 2-week annual vacation, and could be expected to live several years beyond the retirement age of 65. Over a lifetime, modern workers will earn four times the income for less work than their counterparts 100 years ago (Miernyk, 1975).

Today more than half of the women in the United States work full- or part-time outside the home, more than double the figure in 1900. Today's women are finding success in traditionally male-oriented fields despite barriers to advancement, which may be influenced by persistent negative stereotypes (Huston-Stein & Higgens-Trenk, 1978). Many working women are middle-aged women who return to the labor force after raising families. Today there are more mothers in the labor force than there are married women without children (U.S. Bureau of the Census, 1982). This increased percentage of working women with children is illustrated in Figure 10–6.

FIGURE 10–6
Mothers in the Labor Force

The percentages of working women with children under 18 years of age have increased dramatically since 1950.

Source: Papali & Olds, 1986, p. 390.

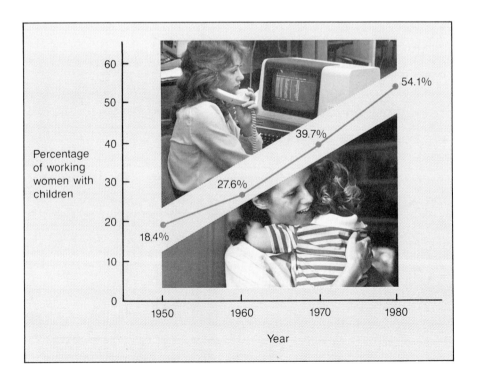

Midlife Transitions

Like the period of adolescence, middle age during adulthood is largely a twentieth-century phenomenon. Increased life expectancy means that people live beyond their fifties and adjust to new roles. For example, both parents usually live to see their children reach adulthood, and many become grandparents by age 60. Today's grandparents are often at the height of their careers and may not fit the stereotypic image of elderly grandmothers who knit between baking batches of cookies and grandfathers who whittle as they spin yarns to their grandchildren.

CHANGING ROLES. Part of the adjustment to aging involves accepting changes in family relationships. As children grow older, parents must adjust to their changing needs. For example, when children leave home for college or careers, parents are faced with an "empty nest." In the past, the children's departure has been viewed as a source of depression in middle-aged women. It was believed that men seldom experienced the departure with as much depression because their careers provided a sense of identity and meaning to their lives. This view of the traumatic impact of the "empty nest" has changed, however. Research indicates that this transition period is a time in life when satisfaction is greater than at any earlier stage of parenthood (Neugarten, 1970). As the final child departs the home, parents find more time and freedom to enjoy leisure activities and travel. Newfound privacy means that intimacy can be more spontaneous, and couples often enjoy the sense of being on a second honeymoon.

A second type of family adjustment during middle age is caring for one's aging parents. Because people live longer, more and more middle-aged adults must care for their parents. In 1980, it was estimated that 40 percent of all people in their late fifties had a living parent, and 10 percent of the people sixty-five and older had a child who was over sixty-five (Schaie & Willis, 1986). This trend will increase in the future, and many more middle-aged and elderly adults will care for their aging parents. Who provides the care? Usually the aging spouse, but since most older women are widows, the burden of care often falls on the closest relative, the eldest daughter (Cantor, 1983). But this may cause problems for the middle-aged daughter who may be working, caring for her own children, and coping with her own problems of middle age. Often, aging parents move into the homes of their children, sometimes referred to as "refilling the empty nest" (Brody, 1985). Have attitudes about caring for the elderly changed recently? Apparently not. In a study of three generations of women, Brody (1985) found strong commitments among all generations to provide care for aging family members. The majority of elderly and disabled adults are cared for by family members, and it is becoming a routine task of middle adulthood.

WORKPLACES AND CAREERS. A career is usually established during young adulthood—the realization of one's "dream," according to Levinson et al. (1978). Success is pursued vigorously, and achievement at work is highly valued. After several years on the job, however, these attitudes begin to change. In a classic study of managers begun in 1956 by American Telephone and Telegraph (AT&T), it was found that initially high expectations for job success became considerably lower and more realistic by the time the managers were in their early thirties (Howard & Bray, 1980). The men reported satisfaction in their jobs but often decided to meet their own personal standards or chose to devote more time to family and recreation. A second longitudinal study at AT&T begun in 1977 included women and minorities and revealed some interesting differences from the 1956 study (Howard & Wilson, 1982). The 1977 group had lower expectations for upward mobility and showed less interest in becoming corporate leaders. Their new values de-emphasized material rewards and placed greater weight on satisfaction derived from interpersonal relationships.

This shift in values at the workplace may reflect both historical and developmental changes in attitudes. It seems to be part of the realistic job appraisal and self-evaluation that occurs in middle age, a process termed "de-illusionment" by Levinson et al. (1978) because the unrealistic expectations are removed without bitterness. Desire for advancement at work declines, and many workers devote more and more time to family, leisure, and community activities. Howard and Bray (1980) observed this pattern for managers who held low- and mid-level positions. Paradoxically, the higher managers who enjoyed the most success at work actually valued work more

APPLYING PSYCHOLOGY

Perceptions of Aging

Researchers have investigated perceptions of the elderly by measuring people's attitudes, beliefs, and knowledge regarding aging. In a review of the literature, McTavish (1971) concluded that young adults tend to view the elderly as generally tired, ill, isolated, and sexually inactive. Such negative stereotypes can have profound implications for our daily interactions with elderly people and can also influence social policies concerning aging. Test your knowledge about aging on a selection from Erdman Palmore's (1977) Facts on Aging Quiz (FAQ). Answer each of the following 15 questions either True or False.

1. The majority of old people (past age 65) are senile.
2. All five senses tend to decline in old age.
3. Most old people have no interest in, or capacity for, sexual relations.
4. Physical strength tends to decline in old age.
5. At least 10% of the aged are living in long-stay institutions (i.e., nursing homes, mental hospitals, homes for the aged, etc.).
6. About 80% of the aged are healthy enough to carry out their normal activities.
7. Most old people are set in their ways and are unable to change.
8. The reaction time of most old people tends to be slower than the reaction time of younger people.
9. In general, most old people are pretty much alike.
10. The majority of old people are seldom bored.
11. Over 15% of the U.S. population are now 65 or over.
12. Most medical practitioners tend to give low priority to the aged.
13. The majority of older people have incomes below the poverty line (as defined by the federal government).
14. The majority of old people are seldom irritated or angry.
15. The health and socioeconomic status of older people compared to younger people in the year 2000 will probably be about the same as now.

To determine your score, count the number of questions marked correctly. Odd-numbered items are false; even-numbered items are true. If you answered 10 questions correctly, you scored about as well as the undergraduates in Palmore's (1977) study. It is surprising that college students do not know the answers to one-third of these questions, but the finding is reliable. In fact, Mary Luszcz (1982) replicated the study with Australian undergraduates and found a similar pattern with only slightly more errors and negative bias about aging. In a review of 25 studies that used the FAQ, Palmore (1980) concluded that the findings were relatively unaffected by race, sex, or age of the respondents. The one significant factor was level of education. People with the least education scored only 55% cor-

highly after 10 and 20 years at the job. These managers also become more involved in work and less sympathetic and helpful to coworkers.

Adjusting to the aging process is often difficult for middle-aged and older workers. Stereotypic beliefs held by the public and employers portray aging workers as less alert, less flexible, less efficient, and generally less capable than their younger counterparts (Harris, 1975). (See "Applying Psychology: Perceptions of Aging" to test your beliefs about aging and to discover common stereotypes of the elderly.) Such beliefs can lead to age discrimination in hiring and firing practices. Research indicates that older workers are often passed over for promotions, are less likely than younger workers to receive the education and retraining required to enhance skills, and are the first to be laid off and the last to be hired even when their work is comparable (Wanner & McDonald, 1983).

Career changes during middle age are becoming more frequent, partly because of the creation of new jobs and skills required by technology. In fact, most adults will have a variety of jobs rather than one kind of work for an entire career. Some of these changes are initiated by self-examination, discontent, or changing family relationships (e.g., divorce or children grow-

FIGURE 10–7
Effects of Education on Knowledge About Aging

The Facts on Aging Quiz (FAQ) measures people's perceptions of the effects of aging. Highly educated people score more highly on the FAQ. This shows that negative stereotypes and ignorance about aging are less evident among educated adults and perhaps that stereotypes can be reduced with education. (The total number of subjects tested at each educational level is shown inside each column, with the number of studies in parentheses.)

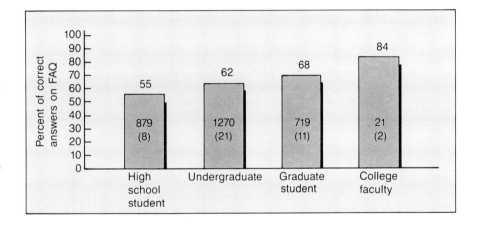

rect on the quiz, barely above chance levels, and held more negative stereotypes about aging. Figure 10–7 summarizes the average correct performance on the FAQ across many studies according to level of education. The figure suggests steady improvement with more education, although it is also possible that people with more education are more intelligent and less likely to believe stereotypes about the elderly.

Across many studies there is striking consistency in the items missed most often. The six most common misconceptions are:

most elderly people live in institutions (#5)

most old people cannot adapt to change (#7)

the majority of old people are bored (#10)

more than 15% of the population is 65 or older (#11)

the majority of elderly live in poverty (#13)

the majority of old people are often angry (#14)

Notice that five of these misconceptions are negative stereotypes of the aged. Because of the lack of knowledge and bias revealed by the FAQ, Palmore (1980) advocates using the quiz as a stimulus for group discussions in order to identify and correct erroneous perceptions of aging.

ing up). ''Burn-out'' is a popular term for the frustration that some workers feel. When feelings of helplessness and loss of control overcome people, they may quit a job, detach themselves from family and friends, and become depressed (Maslach & Jackson, 1985). But severe career changes due to burn-out or midlife crises are not very common. Even when people change careers in midlife, they often take on new jobs that require similar skills as their previous jobs (Schaie & Willis, 1986). Rarely do people in middle age switch to totally new careers.

MIDLIFE: CRISES OR TRANSITION? A popular image of middle age often portrays a balding father or harried housewife who is exasperated by work, children, and a boring future. Escape is provided by choosing a radical new lifestyle, and the crisis is solved. The romanticized scenario is derived in part from clinical studies of people confronting middle age. Inspired by Erikson's theory, Levinson et al. (1978) and Vaillant (1977) have described the crises faced in midlife as emotional conflicts about sexual relationships, family roles, and work values. George Vaillant (1977) conducted a longitudinal study of Harvard undergraduates from the classes of 1939 through 1944. He followed them into their fifties and concluded that the transitions to midlife were often stressful, not unlike a ''second adolescence.'' In the study by Levinson and colleagues (1978), 32 of the 40 men reported that the period from age 40 to 45 was a time of moderate or severe crisis.

In contrast, many researchers regard middle age as a transitional period that is not marked by emotional upheavals. Bernice Neugarten (1968) studied how middle-aged women reacted to events such as menopause and children leaving home. She found that few people perceived these changes as traumatic. Schaie and Willis (1986) suggest that the case studies have exaggerated midlife crises and that data on divorce, suicide, and admission to mental hospitals do not reveal middle age as a particularly turbulent time of life. Instead, it is a time of transition to new roles at work and at home that most people accept with responsibility and perceive as a challenge rather than a threat.

COGNITION AND AGING

One of the most common beliefs about adult development is that intellectual abilities slowly deteriorate with advancing age. Yet there are presidents, judges, and world leaders well past 60 and 70 years of age who work demanding schedules and make key decisions. Is cognitive decline with age just a cultural stereotype? Does it affect only some people? Researchers interested in cognitive development throughout the life span have tried to answer these questions by studying how thinking skills change from young adulthood to old age.

Stages of Adult Cognitive Development

Many people consider Piaget's theory to be the most comprehensive account of human intellectual development, but it ignores adult development en-

FIGURE 10–8
Stages of Adult
Cognitive Development

Schaie's stages of cognitive development reveal that adolescents acquire knowledge and that adults apply knowledge for different purposes. Young adults focus on achieving success in the workplace by demonstrating competence. Middle-aged adults direct their thinking to practical problems that may reflect responsibilities to family members as well as management skills in community or professional affairs. During old age, adults refocus their knowledge and skills on problems that are significant to their changing lifestyles, such as concerns about health or retirement.

Source: Schaie, 1977–78.

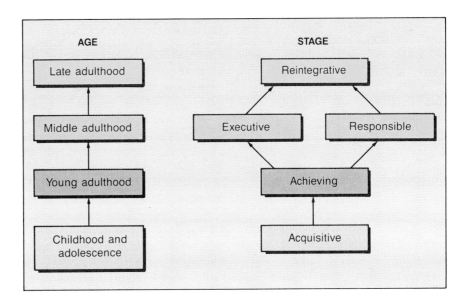

tirely. Piaget believed that the fundamental aspects of cognitive development are completed when adolescents acquire logical thinking during the formal operational period. Some researchers have argued that there are additional stages of development during adulthood (Arlin, 1975; Kramer, 1983; Riegel, 1976).

A provocative view of cognitive development during adulthood was offered by K. Warner Schaie (1977–1978). He proposed five stages of thinking, illustrated in Figure 10–8. The first stage is labeled *acquisitive* because Schaie believes that children and adolescents learn a great deal of information and skills for their own sake without regard for the uses of their new knowledge. The process of schooling reflects an emphasis on acquisition of knowledge. The *achieving stage* of young adulthood is concerned with the application of knowledge to relevant goals such as vocations, hobbies, or preparation for careers.

According to Schaie, the first stage is "freewheeling," and the second is "entrepreneurial and goal-directed." In contrast, the third stage of adult cognitive development (roughly from one's late thirties to early sixties) is called the *responsible stage.* During this stage, people solve practical problems and meet obligations that involve other people such as family members and co-workers. The fourth stage is labeled the *executive stage* because people need to apply their cognitive skills to managing groups or to thinking about community affairs that extend beyond the family. During the *reintegrative stage,* elderly adults may decrease their involvement in societal issues, business, and even family affairs. They become more selective about what they learn and where they apply their knowledge. These stages have not been confirmed by research, but they provide a good general description of how aging adults apply their knowledge and effort to different purposes. Schaie's stages are generally consistent with developmental changes outlined by Erikson (1950) and Levinson et al. (1978).

Information Processing Abilities During Adulthood

To examine directly how cognitive abilities change with age, researchers have given the same tasks to subjects of different ages. This kind of cross-sectional research has been used to compare the reaction times of young and old adults. A typical task used to measure speed of responding might involve pressing a button with the right hand when a red light appears and pressing a different button with the left hand when a green light appears. This task measures the speed required to process the perceptual information, make a decision, and respond. Adults in their sixties or seventies do considerably worse on speeded tasks than young adults in their twenties. This has led to the conclusion that the central nervous system functions at a slower rate with increasing age (Birren, 1974). In fact, recent evidence suggests that higher cognitive processes slow down with aging more than physical and perceptual processes (Cerella, 1985).

Does the ability to learn new information decline with age? Botwinick and Storandt (1974) studied how adults from 21 to 80 years of age learned lists of paired associates. They found little difference with age on easy lists but poorer performance by elderly subjects when there was interference from previous information. Elderly subjects may exhibit more caution, anxiety, and interference while learning, but there is no evidence that the general ability to learn declines with age (Schaie & Willis, 1986).

Elderly adults perform worse on some problem-solving tasks also. For example, Hartley (1981) devised a problem that required subjects to figure out which of several food combinations for dinner resulted in illness. The older subjects often focused on irrelevant information or useless hunches. In fact, elderly subjects do not approach a game of 20 questions as systematically as younger adults (Denney, 1980). It is important to note, however, that brief training can improve the information processing and problem solving of elderly adults (Willis, 1985). Thus, some differences in intellectual performance among adults are due to experience, education, motivation, and health rather than a decay of cognitive functioning with age.

Considerable research has investigated how memory abilities change with age. It appears that some aspects of remembering do not slowly deteriorate. For example, sensory recording of stimuli and short-term memory seem to change little with age (Craik & Rabinowitz, 1984). Likewise, adults' understanding of variables that influence memory does not decline with age (Perlmutter, 1978). Other researchers have examined how elderly adults retain common information. For example, Lachman, Lachman, and Thronesbery (1979) asked adults from 19 to 74 years of age 190 questions pertaining to geography, history, sports, news items, and so forth. Older adults recalled the same number of facts as young adults. One aspect of memory that does seem to decline with age is the effective use of cognitive strategies. Elderly adults do not often use good strategies for encoding and retrieving information without prompting (Craik & Rabinowitz, 1984; Poon, 1985). Memory and aging are discussed further in "Research Frontier: Does Memory Fail with Age?"

Reaction time, learning, and memory are three fundamental abilities, but other abilities include verbal comprehension, vocabulary, and perceptual

Fluid intelligence includes the perception, memory, and reasoning that are reflected in rapid decision-making, while crystallized intelligence includes the knowledge we gain from education and experience.

organization. These abilities may not change together with age. Several research studies have shown that specific mental abilities of adults vary according to different tasks (Baltes, Dittman-Kohli, & Dixon, 1984). John Horn has devised a theory to explain which abilities change with age and which do not (Horn & Cattell, 1966; Horn, 1982). Horn distinguished two kinds of mental abilities. *Fluid intelligence* refers to the speed and accuracy of processing information. It reflects incidental learning and is closely linked to the neurological status of the individual. *Crystallized intelligence* refers to facts and information that are accumulated as part of our general knowledge. This kind of intelligence reflects intentional learning of culturally relevant information. Horn (1982) argues that fluid intelligence declines gradually after young adulthood, a conclusion bolstered by the decline of processing on speeded tasks. Crystallized intelligence, in contrast, actually continues to increase throughout the life span. Horn and others argue that some tasks measure more of one kind of intelligence than another, and, thus, conclusions about whether mental abilities decline with age depend on the types of measures used.

Does Intelligence Decline with Age?

Although researchers have identified some stages, abilities, and processes that change with age (and some that do not), the big question is whether there is a general decline in intelligence with adult aging. To some extent, the answer depends on the tasks used to measure intelligence, an issue covered more fully in Chapter 11. The answer also depends on how the research study is designed. When researchers began to study adult intelligence and aging, they used a cross-sectional research design; that is, they tested various groups of adults across a broad age range. What they found was progressively lower scores by older adults, suggesting that intelligence slowly deteriorated with age. However, these findings have been contradicted by longitudinal research, the study of one group over a period of several years. Schaie and Hertzog (1985) report a program of research in which the same adults, ranging in age from 22 to 70, were tested four times between 1956 and 1977. The data from this study showed little decline in any of the mental abilities tested until age 60. For some abilities, there was only a modest drop by 80 years of age!

What can account for these different patterns? Historical changes are partly responsible. If we compare the reasoning of a 20-year-old and a 70-year-old in 1987, we would be comparing a person who went to school in the 1960s and 1970s with someone who went to school in the 1920s and 1930s. Education and cultural experiences have changed greatly over generations, and what appears to be a decline in intelligence may only reflect the fact that each successive generation is getting smarter (at least their performance on standardized tests improves). Education is not the only difference, though; health and medical care have also improved. Thus, some differences in intelligence scores between young and old adults in cross-sectional research is due to *age cohort* differences, that is, differences attributable to growing up in different historical eras. (Age cohorts are individuals who are born in the same year or whose lifespans coincide.)

Does Memory Fail with Age?

Some of the most common misconceptions about aging involve memory. These misconceptions often derive from stereotypes and folklore. We highlight here three myths about memory and aging that have been disproved by current research.

Myth 1: Everyone's memory slowly deteriorates during adulthood. Research shows that the sensory stores remain effective across the life span. The capacity of short-term memory does not diminish with age and the organization of stored knowledge is similar for young and old adults (Poon, 1985; Salthouse & Kail, 1983). For example, the recency effect (discussed in Chapter 7) is similar for young and old adults, and recognition memory for words continues to improve past age 60 (Schaie & Willis, 1986). Although disease and ill health certainly affect the older adult's memory, there is no uniform biological deterioration of memory capacity with aging.

Myth 2: Old people remember events in the distant past much better than recent events. Remote memory is not superior to recent memory, and it is not a special talent of the elderly. In one study, young and old adults were asked to recall events between the 1920s and 1970s (Poon et al., 1979). They did not recall the events from the 1920s better than recent events, and there were no memory differences between young and old adults. It may be that elderly people talk more about past events, which allows them to rehearse and elaborate some old memories, but "old memories" do not have some type of neurological advantage over "new memories."

Myth 3: Old people may not understand their memory abilities as well as do younger adults. Older adults can understand and monitor their memory behavior as well as young adults can (Lachman, Lachman, & Thronesbery, 1979; Perlmutter, 1978). They seem to understand how memory strategies operate, how task variables influence remembering, and how well they remember. In fact, elderly adults may be more sensitive than young adults to their memory abilities (Zelinski, Gilewski, & Thompson, 1980). Although elderly adults may complain more about

A second possible reason for the discrepancy between cross-sectional and longitudinal findings is that many subjects who drop out of longitudinal studies or who die are the same people who score below the group average. Thus, it may be that longitudinal research underestimates intellectual decline with age (Schaie & Willis, 1986). A third reason for the lower cross-sectional results is a "terminal drop" in performance that occurs just prior to death due to ill health. When older adults close to death are averaged into longitudinal performance scores, the data suggest an overall gradual decline in intelligence, some of which may be due to the terminal drop (Siegler, 1983). From the evidence collected so far, then, it seems unlikely that there is a significant gradual loss of cognitive ability during adulthood. Some speeded reasoning abilities may not be as good among the elderly as among young adults, but the decline, if any, is relatively small and does not affect everyone.

AGING AND HEALTH

One of the challenges for successful aging is coping with progressive physical changes. Appearance, perceptual sensitivity, strength, and coordination all change significantly during adulthood.

their memories and notice relative declines in their performance (Chaffin & Herrmann, 1983), they are accurate at evaluating their competence on memory tasks (Guttentag, 1985).

Does memory decline with age? Yes, it does for some people on some tasks. However, the decline is neither universal nor uniform. Poorer memory with age shows up mostly on laboratory tasks devoid of meaning and context. Waddell and Rogoff (1981), for example, gave groups of middle-aged (31–59) and elderly (65–85) women two kinds of memory tasks. In one the women had to remember objects arranged in a meaningless context, a plain box. In the other task, they had to remember the objects arranged in a natural, familiar setting outside the laboratory. In the first task, the elderly women remembered fewer items than the middle-aged women. In the second task, both groups performed equally well. Reder, Wible, and Martin (1986) asked young and old adults to read stories. Later they asked the subjects to judge whether an exact sentence had been presented before or whether a statement was plausibly true in the story. Elderly adults were slower and less accurate than young adults on the recognition test, but the groups performed equally on the plausibility judgments. The researchers conclude that reasoning about likely events is a more natural memory strategy and thus shows no decline with age.

Why do older adults show weaker performances in laboratory settings? It may be that elderly adults are "out of practice" with tasks requiring deliberate remembering. This could lead to either low motivation for the task or high anxiety that may interfere with memory. Another possibility is that elderly adults cannot process events as quickly (Salthouse & Kail, 1983), so they do not have adequate time to encode and retrieve information. Or it could be that the elderly only show declines for some kinds of information. Guttentag (1985) noted that elderly adults may not recruit and apply memory strategies as effectively as young adults. Some elderly adults may not have adequate attention or persistence to engage in strategic, deep, and effortful processing (Craik & Byrd, 1982). In sum, probably no single factor will explain the relation between memory and aging and we should be careful to avoid stereotypes and myths about dramatic declines in memory for old people.

Sixty-one-year old Paul Newman's furrowed brow and weathered skin are secondary characteristics of his aging. Primary characteristics include his graying hair.

Physical Changes During Adulthood

Primary aging refers to the gradual deterioration of the body's cells, tissues, and systems that ultimately results in the loss of the ability to adapt to environmental stress. It is considered normal because it affects everyone. For example, the sensitivity of all five senses is most keen between about 20 and 40 years of age and diminishes thereafter. A study of smell identification ability confirmed this developmental trend (Doty et al., 1984). The researchers tested nearly 2,000 people between 5 and 99 years of age and observed less sensitivity to odors among children and the elderly. Indeed, 80% of the people tested beyond 80 years of age had major impairment. The researchers note that the inability to smell may help to explain why elderly people complain about the flavor of food and avoid nutritional diets. It may also explain why so many elderly people do not detect gas leaks or fires in their homes. Thus, primary aging requires psychological and physical adjustments to routine activities.

Secondary aging refers to other physiological changes resulting from disease, disuse, or abuse that are correlated with chronological age and, as a result, are often confused with the effects of the normal aging process. Perlmutter and Hall (1985) have reviewed the effects of primary and secondary aging and have provided an excellent summary of those physiological changes associated with growing older.

PHYSICAL APPEARANCE. Most changes in the color, texture, and density of hair occur as a part of primary or normal aging, and, indeed, graying hair is considered the most reliable of all body indicators of aging (Damon et al., 1972). Changes in the skin that occur from primary aging include the loss of fat deposits in the epidermis, thinning and drying, and a marked slowing in the replacement rate of surface skin cells (Grove & Kligman, 1983). Together these effects may contribute to wrinkled skin, but in fact it is the secondary aging effects of abusive tanning that are most responsible for our etched and weathered countenances. The skeleton and teeth undergo changes in composition as well. After the age of 30 the bones lose calcium, and as fractures occur, repair becomes slower (Tonna, 1977).

THE CARDIOVASCULAR SYSTEM. The cardiovascular system eventually succumbs to the effects of primary aging because the cells of the heart, arteries, veins, and capillaries cannot divide and reproduce themselves. Thus, the system's efficiency decreases with age. The volume of blood pumped each minute decreases by 1 percent each year after the age of 20 (Kohn, 1977). During stress, the maximum heart rate decreases with age, and oxygen supply via arterial blood is slowed. Arteries become less flexible with age (hardening of the arteries, or arteriosclerosis, occurs), and they may become constricted with fatty deposits that restrict blood flow and raise blood pressure. When the blood supply to the brain is cut off, strokes may occur. Among the elderly, this is the third leading cause of death after heart disease and cancer.

THE RESPIRATORY SYSTEM. Shortness of breath occurs as a normal part of aging. With age, the rib cage stiffens, the cartilage in the trachea and bronchial tubes calcifies, and the alveoli within the lungs narrow, reducing the functioning gas exchange surface of the lungs. Secondary aging in the respiratory system can be seen in the increased incidence of respiratory diseases such as emphysema and lung cancer. These disorders occur more frequently in older people and are due to smoking and environmental pollutants rather than to primary aging.

THE ENDOCRINE SYSTEM. The pituitary, parathyroid, and thyroid glands remain virtually the same in anatomical structure and ability to function throughout adulthood. In the pancreas, the release of insulin is delayed and less insulin is released with age. This decrease in function leads to reduced glucose tolerance in most adults over the age of 65 and to diabetes in 10 percent of the adults in this age group (Rockstein & Sussman, 1979). Perhaps the gland most critically affected by the aging process is the thymus gland. With age, the gland shrinks in size and decreases its production of hormones. These changes result in decreased levels of antibodies in the blood and impaired function of the immune system. This renders the aged susceptible to infections, cancer, and many other disorders associated with secondary aging.

THE REPRODUCTIVE SYSTEM. It is clear that sperm production decreases with age, so by the forties, only 50 percent of the sperm-producing tubules have developing sperm, and after 80 years of age only 10 percent remain functioning. The prostate gland, which secretes the sperm-carrying fluid, becomes enlarged with age and may even double in size, making surgery necessary for many men (Rockstein & Sussman, 1979). In the female reproductive system, hormonal changes cause the menstrual periods to become shorter and irregular, and by age 50 most women cease to have periods at all. At this point *menopause* is said to occur, and many women experience hot flashes, headaches, and a variety of other symptoms associated with the change in hormone levels. The decrease in estrogen may also result in the shortening and thinning of the vaginal walls, and vaginal lubrication may diminish. Aging does not necessarily diminish sexual activity and enjoyment; only in cases of debilitative disease is sexual expression impossible (Solnick & Corby, 1983).

How Children View the Elderly

The signs of aging—wrinkled skin, reduced agility, increased physical complaints—are readily apparent to other people. We know that adults form stereotypes of the elderly, but how do children regard aging and the elderly? A study by Mitchell and coworkers (1985) investigated children's perceptions of aging by asking them questions about pictures of young and old adults. The 25 questions could be answered yes or no and included items such as "Is s/he fussy? Is s/he gentle? Is s/he lazy? Is s/he weak? Does s/he make you feel good? Would s/he do things with you that are fun?" The researchers tested 255 children from 5 to 13 years of age. Half were girls, half were boys; half were black and half were white; and half lived in a city while the other half lived in rural homes. The pictures that accompanied the questions showed black or white faces of females and males that children judged to be 17, 45, and 73 years old.

The researchers found that children's perceptions were not uniformly positive or negative. Instead, children distinguished among three principal characteristics of the elderly: their personalities, affective relations, and physical abilities. Each trait was judged independently of the others. Neither the age nor race of the children made any difference in their perceptions, but their gender did affect their responses. Girls had more positive evaluations than boys of elderly people's emotional relations and physical abilities. The gender of the person in the pictures also made a difference. Females were judged by all children to have more positive personality traits than males. In general, however, children viewed older adults as weaker, more likely to be ill, less aggressive, and nicer than younger adults.

Old Age and Dying

The last phase of human development includes dying and death. But when, where, and how people die have changed historically. Two hundred years ago, nearly half the children died before age 10, and one parent often died before his or her children had grown up (Perlmutter & Hall, 1985). Nowadays, death is most frequent among the elderly. Life expectancy in the United States has increased from 47 years for someone born in 1900 to 75 years for someone born in 1982. Because of these changes, old people often die apart from their families. In fact, more than 80 percent of all deaths in the United States occur in institutions or hospitals (Bok, 1978). Responsibility for care of the elderly has clearly shifted away from the family and has minimized our exposure to death and its painful effects.

Increased life expectancy and improved medical care have created a longer time period to anticipate death. Young adults tend not to think about death, but by middle age, adults often measure time by the number of years they have left to live (Neugarten, Crotty, & Tobin, 1964). As adults ponder death, they often compare the courses of their lives with the lives of friends and relatives. They may cope with impending death by adopting hedonistic strategies (Eat, drink, and be merry, for tomorrow we die), or they may become pessimistic and cynical about life. Many find strength in religious beliefs. According to Butler (1975), people often begin a *life review* as they anticipate death. They reflect on their past, sometimes to provide personal significance to their life events. Reminiscences of life help to integrate experiences and enhance self-esteem, processes that promote integrity, in Erikson's (1950) view.

Do people fear death? A survey of 1,000 adults in Los Angeles revealed that 63% were "not at all afraid" of death; only 4% responded "very afraid" (Bengston, Cuellar, & Ragan, 1977). Old people are less afraid of death than many young people, perhaps because they feel they have been given their allotted years or because declining health and income have made life less enjoyable or because they have prepared themselves more (Kalish, 1976). A psychiatrist who interviewed terminally ill elderly patients described five progressive reactions to death (Kübler-Ross, 1969). First was denial of death; second, anger, or a "Why me?" attitude. Next, patients tried to bargain with God, doctors, or family members to postpone death. Depression and finally acceptance of death followed. Although many people have some or all of these reactions to dying, research has not substantiated these general stages of dying as described by Kübler-Ross (Perlmutter & Hall, 1985).

There are many emotional reactions to impending death. Contrasting views of peaceful and angry anticipation are captured well by two famous poets.

> Though nothing can bring back the hour of splendour
>   in the grass, of glory in the flowers,
> We will grieve not, rather find
> Strength in what remains behind.
>   William Wordsworth
>
> Do not go gentle into that good night
> Old age should rave and burn at the close of day
> Rage, rage against the dying of the light.
>   Dylan Thomas

SUMMARY

1. Adolescence is a period of transition to adulthood marked occasionally by ceremonies or rites of passage. It is not stressful or stormy for many adolescents.

2. Puberty begins with increased hormone production triggered by the hypothalamus. The hormones stimulate the development of both primary and secondary sex characteristics and result in sexual maturity and the capacity for reproduction.

3. Adolescents acquire the ability to think abstractly and deductively. They can solve problems logically and develop cognitive expertise in particular

school subjects. Better reasoning skills allow adolescents to think more deeply about moral and political issues.

4. A fundamental part of adolescence is the development of social understanding about the self and others. Erikson's theory stresses the need to develop a stable identity during adolescence in order to avoid feelings of self-doubt and role confusion.

5. Risk-taking behaviors increase during adolescence as young people are confronted with opportunities to experiment with illegal substances, sex, and criminal activities. Most adolescents meet these challenges successfully, although the number of adolescent runaways and suicides is alarming.

6. Theories of adult development help identify crises encountered throughout adulthood. Erikson's theory emphasizes emotional development and progressive realization of love, caring, and wisdom. Young adults derive satisfaction from productivity at work and the creation of a family. Middle adulthood may involve reevaluating one's life and changing directions before settling down. Old age is a time to review one's life and to achieve a sense of integrity.

7. Cognitive abilities do not decline slowly with biological maturation. Although speed of processing information may slow down, accumulated knowledge increases with age. Compared to younger adults, poorer performance on cognitive tasks by elderly adults may be due to educational differences, lack of practice, or poor health.

8. Physical changes in appearance and functioning increase with age. The average life expectancy today is well over 70 years. Stereotypic views of the elderly are often held by children and adults.

9. Death is approached in different ways depending on individuals' personalities. Some become hedonistic, pessimistic, or angry, while others express little fear of death. A positive review of their lives and accomplishments, as well as support from family and friends, helps people face death with dignity.

SUGGESTED READINGS

Atchley, R. C. (1985). *The social forces in later life* (4th ed.). Belmont, Calif.: Wadsworth.
    Presents information on how family and community relationships affect the elderly.

Elkind, D. (1984). *All grown up and no place to go.* Reading, Mass.: Addison-Wesley.
    Describes the problems confronted by adolescents and their parents and argues that teenagers are often not prepared to meet the challenges of adulthood.

Garbarino, J. (1985). *Adolescent development: An ecological perspective.* Columbus, Ohio: Merrill.
    This textbook on adolescents provides descriptive data but also a unifying social and humanistic framework for understanding the transition to adulthood. Readable and interesting.

Perlmutter, M., & Hall, E. (1985). *Adult development and aging.* New York: Wiley.
    This textbook provides an excellent survey of issues in adult development; up to date and easy to read.

Schaie, K. W., & Willis, S. L. (1986). *Adult development and aging* (2nd ed.). Boston: Little, Brown.
    This new textbook updates the successful first edition with a wealth of new data. The authors are active researchers in the field who discuss their own studies and important research issues in depth.

11

Intelligence Tests and Mental Abilities

The error of youth is to believe that intelligence is a substitute for experience, while the error of age is to believe that experience is a substitute for intelligence.

Lyman Bryson

IN 1884, SIR FRANCIS GALTON, A COUSIN OF CHARLES DARWIN AND A pioneer in mental testing, established a laboratory at the International Health Exhibition in South Kensington, London. The purpose of the laboratory was to collect data ''by the best methods known to modern science,'' to describe individuals' physical stature, strength, and sensory abilities (Sternberg & Powell, 1982). For example, one of Galton's tests measured the strength of a hand squeeze, another gauged the highest pitch of a whistle that a person could hear, and other tests assessed reaction times to visual and auditory stimuli. Galton also measured physical attributes such as height, weight, head size, and length of limbs. During the 1880s and 1890s, more than 17,000 individuals of all ages from diverse walks of life were tested in Galton's laboratories. Re-analyses of Galton's data a century later revealed that his measures of physical attributes were quite reliable, while behavioral measures, such as reaction times, often were not (Johnson et al., 1985).

Why did Galton devise these measures? There are three main reasons. First, he believed that nearly all psychological characteristics—whether beauty, personality, or the power of prayer—could be measured. Thus, it was the role of science to analyze individual differences in sensory, psychomotor, and physical attributes. Second, Galton believed that intelligence could be predicted from basic human abilities such as quick reactions and a discriminating sense of hearing. Third, Galton, like many people of his time, thought that intelligence was an inherited trait. Intelligent parents were thought likely to have bright children, while intellectually dull parents were expected to have children who were less talented. Galton wanted to encourage gifted men to marry gifted women and to sire bright children, just as he wanted to discourage mating between less intelligent men and women (Galton, 1883).

Although Galton's ideas and methods now appear naive, his research identified issues that confront psychologists today. What is intelligence? How is it measured? Is intelligence inherited or acquired through experience? In this chapter we consider these questions and research that has tried to answer them. Is intelligence a general ability to reason or a composite of separate abilities such as memory skill, vocabulary, visual discrimination, and concept learning? Theorists have suggested both alternatives. Others simply define intelligence operationally as the score received on an intelligence test. Ideas about what intelligence is and how it should be measured have differed widely during the past 100 years, yet most ideas emphasize Galton's principle of quantitative measurement. This orientation to the study of intelligence is called the *psychometric* approach and has been the most popular approach historically. We begin with a discussion of intelligence tests—how they were designed, what they contain, and how they have been used. We discuss the hereditary and environmental bases of IQ scores and then consider cases of exceptional individuals who have high or

Sir Francis Galton was a nineteenth-century pioneer in psychophysical measurement.

Alfred Binet, with his daughters
Madeleine and Alice. Binet became
interested in measuring intelligence
when he noticed the two girls developed
their motor skills in different ways.

low amounts of measured intelligence and, finally, new ideas about the nature and measurement of intelligence.

THE DEVELOPMENT OF INTELLIGENCE TESTS

At the turn of this century, the French Ministry of Education wanted to identify slow learners who needed help. In 1904, Alfred Binet and a fellow psychologist, Theophile Simon, were hired to construct a test that would screen low-achieving students and predict degrees of academic success. Binet, who had been striving for a decade to determine how the human mind worked, was a sharp critic of tests like Galton's and an established scholar on children's thinking, so he was a particularly good choice for the task.

Binet and Simon devised a variety of puzzles for children of different ages to solve, questions to answer, and tasks to perform. They reasoned that a good test should include increasingly difficult items that older children could answer more easily than younger children. For example, a test item that few five-year-olds but most six-year-olds and nearly all seven-year-olds answered correctly was judged to be a good measure of an average six-year-old's ability.

Binet used the concept of *mental age (MA)* to describe an individual's test performance. If a six-year-old correctly answered questions like most eight-year-olds, then the child's mental age was eight. Thus, mental age was arrived at by comparing an individual's performance with average levels of performance by children of other ages. Wilhelm Stern, a German psychologist, elaborated this concept into an *intelligence quotient,* or *IQ score,* in the following formula, in which *CA* stands for chronological age:

$$\text{IQ} = \frac{MA}{CA} \times 100.$$

The ratio of *MA* to *CA* was multiplied by 100 to eliminate the decimal and to provide an average score of 100 if children's chronological and mental ages were equal. For example, suppose a 10-year-old performed as well as most 12-year-olds on Binet's tests. Her IQ score would be equal to 12/10 × 100, or 120. Although the method of calculating IQ scores has since changed and the early test has been modified, many of Binet's contributions to intelligence testing endure today.

Modern Intelligence Tests

Binet's pioneering work was introduced to America in 1916 by Louis Terman and his associates at Stanford University, where they adapted the Binet-Simon test to American children and culture. They set new norms for average performance by giving the revised version to 1,000 children and 400 adults. The original Binet-Simon test thus became the *Stanford-Binet test.* The 1916 Stanford-Binet exam was modified in 1937, 1960, and 1972, and the standards for average performance were changed in 1937 and 1972 so that test-takers would not be compared with people of different generations and varied educations.

The current version of the Stanford-Binet test includes tasks for different age levels from two to adulthood (see Table 11–1). The test is presented to individuals in a standard manner by an examiner. Tasks given to young children often involve copying, stringing beads, building with blocks, and answering questions about common activities. Older subjects may be directed to identify picture absurdities—specifying, for example, what is wrong with a depiction of a man trying to cut wood with a saw he is holding upside-down. In what is called the similarities test, the subjects are asked to tell what pairs of words such as *wood* and *coal, apple* and *peach,* and *ship* and *automobile* have in common. In other parts of the test, they have to complete sentences such as "The streams are dry _____ there has been little rain," to unscramble sentences such as "A defends dog good his bravely master," and to explain proverbs and analogies. Each task is designed to measure a different aspect of reasoning and judgment, but all are highly related to general intelligence and to each other. Many resemble schoolwork, which is partly why the tests predict academic success or failure.

The Stanford-Binet test contains six items for each mental test at each age level. The examiner starts by finding the level at which the subject answers all questions correctly and then presents more difficult problems until the subject cannot solve any. The examiner totals the points for the right responses and computes the IQ score as the test manual prescribes. These basic aspects of Binet's work remain unchanged.

TABLE 11–1
Representative Items from the Stanford-Binet Intelligence Test for Different Age Levels

TWO YEARS OLD

a. Identifies body parts such as hair, mouth, and ears on a doll.
b. Builds a tower of four blocks like a model that is presented.

FOUR YEARS OLD

a. Fills in the missing words when asked, "Brother is a boy; sister is a _____." and "In daytime it is light; at night it is _____."
b. Answers correctly when asked, "Why do we have houses? Why do we have books?"

NINE YEARS OLD

a. Answers correctly when asked, "In an old graveyard in Spain they have discovered a small skull which they believe to be that of Christopher Columbus when he was about ten years old. What is foolish about that?"
b. Answers correctly when asked, "Tell me the name of a color that rhymes with head. Tell me a number that rhymes with tree."

ADULT

a. Can describe the difference between laziness and idleness, poverty and misery, character and reputation.
b. Answers correctly when asked, "Which direction would you have to face so your right hand would be to the north?"

Source: Terman & Merrill, 1973.

Over the past 30 years, other widely used tests of intelligence have been devised by David Wechsler, a New York psychologist. He first prepared the Wechsler Bellevue Intelligence Scale because there were no satisfactory tests for adults, and he needed one for his work at Bellevue Hospital in New York City, which takes in patients who are alcoholics, derelicts, or feeble of mind as well as normal people in trouble. Later he refined this instrument into the Wechsler Adult Intelligence Scale (WAIS) and added the Wechsler Intelligence Scale for Children (WISC) and the Wechsler Preschool and Primary Scale of Intelligence (WPPSI). The *Wechsler tests,* like Binet's, are administered individually and range from easy to hard for a variety of skills. The examiner begins by asking readily answered questions and continues until the subject errs several times consecutively. The IQ score is calculated by comparing the subject's performance with the average of others of a similar age. The Wechsler tests differ from the Stanford-Binet test in that they include two separate scales for verbal and performance (i.e., nonverbal) tasks. The latter include completing pictures, assembling puzzles, and copying block designs, while the verbal aspects focus on general information, vocabulary, and similarities (see Table 11–2). One advantage of the different

---

TABLE 11–2
The Wechsler Intelligence Scale for Children

Verbal Scale	Performance Scale
1. *General information:* A series of questions involving a sample of information that most children will have been exposed to (for example, How many nickels make a dime? What is steam made of?).	1. *Picture completion:* The child is asked which part is missing in each picture in a series of 12 pictures of common objects (for example, a car with a wheel missing, a rabbit with an ear missing).
2. *General comprehension:* Items in which the child must explain why certain practices are desirable or what course of action is preferred under certain circumstances (for example, Why should people not waste fuel? What should you do if you see someone forget his book in a restaurant?).	2. *Picture arrangement:* A series of sets of pictures in which the pictures will tell a story if they are arranged in the correct order. These are rather like wordless comic-strip pictures.
3. *Arithmetic:* A series of arithmetic questions ranging from easy ones involving simple counting to more difficult ones involving mental computations and reasoning.	3. *Block design:* The child receives a set of small blocks having some white, some red, and some half-red and half-white sides. The child is shown a series of red and white designs which he or she must reproduce with the blocks.
4. *Similarities:* The child is asked to tell in what way a series of paired words are alike (for example, In what way are a shoe and a slipper alike? In what way are an hour and a week alike?).	4. *Object assembly:* The child must assemble jigsaw-like parts of common objects into the whole puzzle (for example, a chair, a foot).
5. *Vocabulary:* A series of increasingly difficult words are presented and the child is asked what each word means.	5. *Coding:* The child must match symbols with numbers on the basis of a code given to him or her.
6. *Digit span:* A series of numbers of increasing length are presented orally and the child is asked to repeat them either in the same order or in a reverse order.	6. *Mazes:* The child must trace the correct route from a starting point to home on a series of mazes.

These 12 tasks are used to assess children's intelligence. The WISC yields a total IQ score as well as separate performance and verbal scores.

Source: The examples given are similar but not identical to items on the Wechsler Intelligence Scale for Children. Used by permission of the publisher, The Psychological Corporation. All rights reserved.

scales is to help identify children with language problems. If a ten-year-old with a reading or language disability scores much lower on the verbal scale than on the performance scale, the examiner can use the difference to diagnose the child's strengths and weaknesses.

Lubin, Larsen, and Matarazzo (1984) analyzed the use of psychological tests in clinical settings in the United States between 1935 and 1982 and found that the WAIS was the most frequently mentioned test. The WISC test was fifth, whereas the Stanford-Binet, which had previously been in the top ten, was mentioned fifteenth. These rankings have remained relatively stable over the years. The survey reveals that tests of intelligence and mental abilities predominate among the most frequently administered psychological tests. Many kinds of intelligence tests are available, each designed for a particular group and a particular purpose. Some are for infants, handicapped people, or group testing. Some are based solely on nonverbal skills. The principles underlying their construction, however, remain the same.

Characteristics of Psychometric Tests

Intelligence tests are designed to measure relative performance, not absolute mental abilities. The group of subjects that forms the basis for comparison, called the *standardization sample,* must accurately represent the entire population that might be given the test. (*Population* is a statistical term in this context; it refers to a group from which a sample can be drawn and does not mean all the country's inhabitants.) The standardization sample that testers might choose for an admission test to medical school would be composed of people who had obtained or were about to obtain undergraduate degrees and should include representative numbers of graduates and undergraduates of large schools and small schools; eastern, midwestern, and western schools; men and women; whites and nonwhites. Often a standardization sample is selected by *stratified random sampling,* in which a variable such as family income is broken down into strata or levels (for example, $10,000 brackets) and people from each stratum are chosen randomly in equal numbers. Test designers thus can be confident that they have included a fair assortment of people by criteria that include sex, race, geography, income, and size of hometown.

Tests such as the Stanford-Binet are standardized according to age as well; that is, they compare individuals of the same age. The restandardization of the Stanford-Binet in 1937 and 1972 took into account advances in education, science, television, and other differences across generations. James Flynn (1984) has shown that each successive sample of people who served as the standards for the Stanford-Binet tests demonstrated improved performance over previous samples. Over a period of more than 40 years, the total gain amounted to nearly 14 IQ points! This could mean that Americans are getting smarter or better educated or that the sampling procedures are changing. Whatever the reason for the increase in IQ scores, an average eight-year-old today can answer more questions on the Stanford-Binet than could his or her counterpart in 1937. Because IQ scores are computed in relation to the standardization sample, however, each child, as an average child, would still have an IQ score of 100.

Both the Stanford-Binet and Wechsler tests have a *standard deviation* of approximately 15 points. (See the Appendix for a discussion of relevant statistical terms.) This means that the *variability* at each age is the same and that the IQ scores for each age resemble a *normal distribution* (see the bell curve in Figure 11–1). In a normal distribution of IQ scores, about 68 percent of the population is within one standard deviation (1SD), or 15 points, of the average score of 100, and 95 percent fall within two standard deviations, or 30 points, of the average.

A good test should yield consistent results. If the same person takes the same test on different occasions, the scores should be similar. The consistency of scores is called test *reliability,* and it can be calculated with a *correlation coefficient* statistic (see page 22). The reliability of IQ tests is often assessed by correlating the same people's scores on repeated tests, correlating half the test with the other half, or correlating scores on different forms of the test. Many IQ tests, thus measured, demonstrate great reliability, and the correlation statistics are often as high as +.9, indicating strong similarity

FIGURE 11–1
The Distribution of Intelligence

The psychometric model assumes that IQ scores are normally distributed with an average of 100. The standard deviations (SD) of the WISC and Stanford-Binet tests are approximately 15, so 68% of people score between 85 and 115. Ninety-five percent of the population have IQ scores between 70 and 130. The lower scale provides descriptive labels for people who achieve various IQ scores.

Source: Anastasi, 1976.

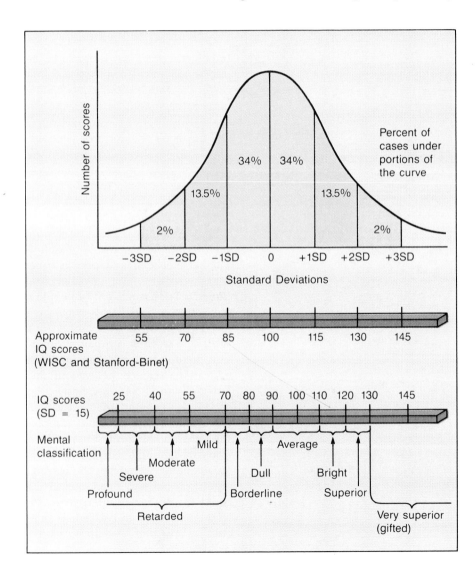

between scores. But motivation, fatigue, measurement error, and other factors can affect the consistency of results. Also, when considerable time and experience intervene between tests, scores may diverge more and be less reliable.

Finally, any good test must have *validity*, that is, it must measure what it claims to measure. Galton's measures of sensory thresholds and discriminations were precise, quick, and reliable, but they did not measure intelligence, so they were not valid.

There are several types of test validity. **Construct validity** refers to the accuracy with which a test measures the psychological processes specified by a theory. Unfortunately, not all test-makers agree on a single definition, theory, or measure of intelligence. Critics of intelligence tests often focus on the lack of uniform construct validity. Proponents counter that IQ tests have extremely good concurrent and predictive validity. **Concurrent validity** is the degree of correlation between two or more different tests given at approximately the same time to the same people. For example, IQ scores derived from the Stanford-Binet and WISC usually correlate highly. Arthur Jensen (1980), in a review of 47 studies in which different IQ tests were administered concurrently, reported that the range of correlations was +.43 to +.94, with a median correlation of +.80. Jensen reported that the average correlations among more than 40 popular intelligence tests ranged from +.67 to +.77.

Predictive validity is a measure of the test score's relation to other measures of aptitude or ability. How well do IQ scores predict other behavior? Quite well, and this is the strongest evidence for their usefulness. For example, IQ scores are correlated highly with scholastic achievement (usually measured as school grades). The correlations are approximately +.6 to +.7 during elementary school and +.4 to +.5 during college. The difference over time occurs because more factors influence scholastic performance during adulthood. Jensen (1980) reported a variety of additional data indicating that IQ scores are correlated highly with teachers' ratings of pupils' intelligence and sociability. It is evident that intelligence tests are reliable instruments and IQ scores are good predictors of later behavior, despite the fact that psychologists cannot agree on a single definition of intelligence.

Stability of IQ Scores

Do IQ scores change with development? Is intelligence, as measured by IQ, a stable characteristic? The answers depend on the conditions under which the tests are given, the kinds of tests, and the time between repeated tests. An examiner should not expect high reliability (i.e., similar scores on tests given at two different times) if the subject was fatigued during one of them or if the tests differed greatly. The examiner's behavior can also affect scores. Zigler and Butterfield (1968) tested 52 four-year-olds twice within one month on the Stanford-Binet. Half received the standard test both times. The other half got lots of encouragement on the second test, and easy and hard items were intermingled. The encouraged group averaged gains of more than ten points on the second test, more than twice as much as the control group. McCall, Appelbaum, and Hogarty (1973) conducted a longitudinal study of 140 middle-class children and found that their individual IQ scores fluctuated widely. Between ages 2½ and 17, individual IQ scores

"You did very well on your I.Q. test. You're a man of 49 with the intelligence of a man of 53."

© 1977 by Sidney Harris/American Scientist Magazine

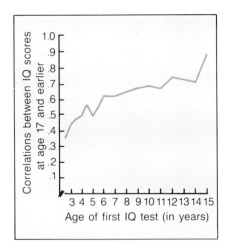

FIGURE 11–2
Stability of IQ Scores with Age

In this graph, the Stanford-Binet IQ scores obtained at age 17 are correlated with Stanford-Binet test scores obtained at an earlier age. Notice that the tests given at a very young age correlate poorly with adult performance. As the time between tests decreases, the correlations between IQ scores increase.

Source: Jensen, 1980.

varied by an average of 28.5 points. One out of three children changed IQ scores by more than 30 points, and a few changed by more than 70 points.

Does intelligence really vary that much with age? New evidence suggests that previous research underestimated the stability of IQ scores because the tests were based on measures of early development that are not related to the kinds of cognitive test items included in intelligence tests for older children. For example, IQ scores for preschoolers are often computed on the basis of tasks such as stringing beads or identifying body parts, tasks that may not be related to IQ test measures such as vocabulary and reasoning. Thus, researchers have suggested that the low stability of IQ scores may be due to the different kinds of items used in tests at various age levels and the changing nature of intelligence (Fagan & Singer, 1983; Ulvund, 1984).

Part of the problem in assessing stability of IQ scores, therefore, is the poor predictive validity of tests given to young children. As shown in Figure 11–2, the correlations between IQ scores at 17 years of age and scores measured at younger ages are much lower when the first test is given before 7 years of age. Indeed, predictions of IQ scores from tests given to infants are even worse. Fagan and Singer (1983) report that infant intelligence tests given from 3 to 8 months of age correlate poorly with IQ scores obtained at 6 or more years of age. IQ scores of high-risk infants are not predicted much better; nor are gifted children identified by infant intelligence tests. Willerman and Fiedler (1974) observed that performance levels of four-year-olds with IQ scores above 140 were not predicted by tests given at eight months of age.

Fagan and Singer (1983) argue that measures of infant memory abilities can predict later IQ scores better than measures of sensorimotor development. These researchers created 12 pairs of stimuli, such as geometric patterns and pictures of faces, and presented them to infants aged three to seven months. Each pair of stimuli included a novel stimulus along with a stimulus that the infant had seen before. The researchers obtained measures of preference for looking at the new stimulus and of the length of time spent looking at the novel picture. These simple measures of infant memory assess cognitive abilities and, thus, predict IQ scores better than do measures of sensorimotor coordination. Fagan (1984) reviewed 15 studies of the relation between early preference for new stimuli and later IQ scores. The correlations ranged from +.33 to +.66, with an average of +.45. Fagan (1984) also reported good concurrent validity for his procedure. Groups of high-risk infants who were expected to differ in intelligence later in life also showed differences in their preferences for novelty as infants. Thus, IQ scores based on infants' cognitive abilities may reveal more continuity in intelligence with age than previous research suggested.

IQ scores can change during adulthood. As many studies show, average IQ scores peak between 18 and 25 years of age, decline generally until approximately age 50, and then drop markedly (Horn, 1978). This pattern of growth, plateau, and decline is misleading, however, since it compares people of different generations, experience, and schooling, and it may include some elderly people who perform poorly due to health, fatigue, and other reasons (see Chapter 10, page 387).

In a longitudinal analysis of IQ changes in the same people from ages 65 to 85, Blum, Jarvik, and Clark (1970) found only a small decline in IQ scores from age 65 to age 73 and a steeper decline from age 73 to age 85.

However, the drop was uneven; vocabulary and general information did not deteriorate through age 85, while spatial reasoning and speed of responding fell off sharply. As described in Chapter 10, *fluid intelligence,* or processing speed and accuracy, declines with age, but *crystallized intelligence,* or general information and knowledge, increases or remains constant in adulthood (Horn, 1970). IQ scores decline most precipitously in the year or so before death, and when these figures are averaged with those of other elderly subjects, they create an illusion of slow slippage by everyone. The important points are that (1) IQ scores change considerably throughout life; (2) the type of test and its content are critical; (3) not all abilities improve or decline as a general factor of intelligence; and (4) IQ scores are most stable and predictive from late childhood to early adulthood.

APPLYING PSYCHOLOGY

Science, Politics, and Racism in Testing

When Lewis Terman at Stanford University, Robert Yerkes at Harvard University, and Henry Goddard at the Vineland Training School in New Jersey imported and enthusiastically revised Alfred Binet's test, they looked at it as a tool to be applied to such pressing problems as educational screening and military training. Since most Americans at the turn of the century considered intelligence to be an inherited, genetic trait, the first tests lent themselves to political purposes with racial-ethnic overtones. Consider some of the early statements about mental testing:

. . . in the near future intelligence tests will bring tens of thousands of these high-grade defectives under the surveillance and protection of society. This will ultimately result in curtailing the reproduction of feeble-mindedness and in the elimination of an enormous amount of crime, pauperism, and industrial inefficiency. (Terman, 1916, p. 6)

Who were these mentally defective people mentioned by Terman? Most were ethnic minorities or immigrants.

IQ scores in the 70 to 80 range were "very, very common among Spanish-Indian and Mexican families of the Southwest as also among negroes," Terman observed.

Their dullness seems to be racial, or at least inherent in the family stocks from which they come. . . . The whole question of racial differences in mental traits will have to be taken up anew and by experimental methods. The writer predicts that when this is done there will be discovered enormously significant racial differences which cannot be wiped out by any scheme of mental culture.

Children of this group should be segregated in special classes. . . . They cannot master abstractions, but they can often make efficient workers. . . . There is no possibility at present of convincing society that they should not be allowed to reproduce, although . . . they constitute a grave problem because of their unusually prolific breeding. (Terman, 1916, pp. 92–93)

The potential misuse of test results is still a problem today. Consider the decision reached in a California Federal District Court in 1979 after two years of testimony and deliberation. San Francisco schools were prohibited "from utilizing, permitting the use of, or approving the use of any standardized test . . . for the identification of black EMR [educable mentally retarded] children or their placement into

EMR classes, without first securing prior approval by this court" (Larry P. v. Riles, 1979, p. 989). The judge ruled that schools had shown intent to discriminate by using culturally biased intelligence tests as the primary criterion for assignment to EMR classes. Further, the judge ruled that "it doomed large numbers of black children to EMR status, racially unbalanced classes, an inferior and 'dead-end' education, and the stigma that inevitably comes from the use of the label 'retarded'" (p. 980). Years later there is still controversy about the court case and the implications for educational policies (Prasse & Reschly, 1986).

Intelligence tests, like other psychological assessments, have the potential for abuse and misinterpretation, for perpetuating racial prejudice, and for denying education to many children (Snyderman & Hernnstein, 1983). Yet these tests can provide valuable information for clinical diagnosis and educational intervention. Many psychologists are trying to improve the scientific accuracy of intelligence tests and to inform the public about the limitations and proper uses of test data so that mental tests do not become tools for political or racial discrimination (Samelson, 1975).

HEREDITY, ENVIRONMENT, AND IQ SCORES

The nature/nurture controversy is one of the enduring issues in the study of intelligence. Quite simply, the question is "How much of intelligence is due to heredity and how much is due to the environment in which a person is raised?" The construction of intelligence tests and IQ scores has allowed researchers to investigate this issue, but the results have not always been easy to interpret. The issue is not just philosophical. In 1969, Arthur Jensen argued that up to 80 percent of the variance in IQ scores among individuals is derived from heredity. Thus, compensatory and remedial educational programs, such as Head Start, he argued, have little chance of changing children's IQ scores. Jensen's views provoked outcries of indignation, proposals for social reform, and sharp scientific debate. Old studies have been re-analyzed, and a considerable amount of new research has been conducted. The basic research strategy has been to examine the similarity of IQ scores between groups of people who differ systematically in their genetic relationships or the environments in which they develop.

Family Resemblance

One would expect the IQ scores of family members to be similar. After all, they usually share similar genetic heritage *and* environments. Indeed, the IQ scores of parents and their offspring usually correlate at about +.5, the same degree of correlation found between IQ scores of siblings or fraternal twins. Other studies have looked at the IQ scores of family members raised in different environments or the correlations between IQ scores of biologically unrelated people raised in the same home.

A recent study conducted in Denmark analyzed the IQ scores of siblings reared together and those reared apart (Teasdale & Owen, 1984). IQ scores were compared among full siblings raised apart, half-siblings raised apart, full siblings raised together, and biologically unrelated individuals reared together (i.e., in adopted families). Full siblings showed strong correlations in their IQ scores whether they were raised together or apart. The IQ scores of full siblings raised apart were more similar than the scores of half-siblings raised apart. Individuals who were unrelated but were reared together showed no correlations in their intelligence test scores, although their levels of academic achievement were significantly correlated. Teasdale and Owen (1984) conclude that intelligence is most strongly correlated in full siblings and less correlated in half-siblings. Similar environments resulted in comparable achievement levels rather than similar intelligence scores.

Studies of Twins

Identical twins have identical genes. A strong hereditarian position would argue that their IQ scores should be very similar. But twins usually grow up together in the same environment, so identical twins raised in *different* environments are needed to test this genetic hypothesis. Hans Eysenck, a leading hereditarian, said in 1973, "IQs of identical twins reared apart . . . [are] perhaps the most cogent evidence in favor of the genetic determination of intelligence. . . . If the genetic case rested on just one kind of support, this would be the one chosen by the experts" (cited in Eysenck vs. Kamin, 1981,

Identical twins share more than identical genes. They often dress alike, participate in the same activities, and are treated the same way by other people.

p. 106). However, other experts disagree. Sandra Scarr and Robert Kidd (1983) suggest that identical twins reared apart are rare and unusual, the studies are difficult to interpret, and the results are not clear-cut. Only four studies of twins raised apart have been reported in the literature, and one of those (Burt, 1966) is now discredited.

Sir Cyril Burt, a British psychologist knighted for his scientific work, reported in 1966 that the scores on a group test of intelligence correlated +.94 for identical twins raised together, +.77 for identical twins raised apart, and +.55 for fraternal twins raised together. Eysenck (a student of Burt's) and other scientists cited these figures as solid evidence of the genetic contributions to intelligence. But the credibility of the data began to unravel when Kamin (1974) noticed that Burt was vague about his testing procedures. Also, the number of subjects fluctuated in different reports by Burt while the statistical values did not. No evidence could be uncovered of the actual twins studied, the tests used, or the examiners employed, and even Burt's official biographer concluded that Burt's data were fraudulent (Hearnshaw, 1979).

Each of the three other studies of twins raised apart found a high correlation between the twins' intelligence test scores. Newman, Freeman, and Holzinger (1937) reported that the IQ scores of 19 pairs of twins in the United States correlated at +.67. Shields (1962) studied 37 pairs of twins in England and found a correlation of +.77. Juel-Nielsen (1965) reported a correlation of +.62 for the intelligence scores of 12 pairs of Danish twins. The high correlations seem compelling. However, Leon Kamin points out that several problems arise in interpreting the data (Eysenck vs. Kamin, 1981). The most serious problem is that the twins in all the studies were often not separated by much time or experience. For example, 27 of the 37 pairs included in Shields's studies were raised by branches of the same family; typically, the mother raised one twin and her mother or sister cared for the other. Kamin points out that such twins had similar schooling, hometowns, and backgrounds. Their intelligence scores correlated at +.83 as opposed to +.51 for twins raised by unrelated families. Consider Ingegard and Monika, one of the separated Danish twin pairs who were raised "by relatives until the age of seven, then lived with their mother until they were fourteen. They were usually dressed alike and very often confused by strangers, at school, and sometimes by their stepfather" (Eysenck vs. Kamin, 1981, p. 112). Kamin points out that the environments of twins raised apart were often much alike and that such children shared more than similar genes.

Despite flaws in the design and procedures of the studies, proponents of the hereditarian view argue that genetic similarity between twins accounts for much of the similarity in their IQ scores. Thomas Bouchard (1983) re-analyzed data from these three studies of twins reared apart and concluded that environmental similarities cannot explain the similarity in IQ scores. A second source of data used to bolster the genetic side of the controversy is comparison between identical and fraternal twins. Fraternal twins are not more alike genetically than other brothers and sisters. They just happen to have been born at the same time. Fraternal twins can be of the same or opposite sex. If IQ is genetically determined, then identical twins should be more alike than fraternal twins. Bouchard and McGue (1981) reviewed 111 studies on family resemblance in intelligence and found that the IQ scores of identical twins usually correlated between +.70 and +.90, while the correlations for fraternal twins were between +.50 and +.70. The researchers found that in general "the higher the proportion of genes two family members have in common, the higher the average correlation between their IQ's" (Bouchard & McGue, 1981, p. 1055). This finding illustrates the importance of genetic contributions but does not diminish the role of environmental factors. Twins who are reared together, treated alike, and exposed to similar experiences exhibit more similar IQ scores than twins who are raised quite differently.

Adoption Studies

A third method of testing the relative influence of heredity and environment is to study adopted children. In Chapter 9 we discussed the dramatic changes in IQ scores of institutionalized infants who were adopted and cared for by institutionalized adult women. Marie Skodak and Harold Skeels (1949) followed such infants for 30 years and concluded that environmental enrichment can promote intellectual development. A more recent study in France supports this view (Schiff et al., 1978). The investigators compared the IQ scores of lower-class children adopted by well-off families with the scores of the children's siblings who had not been adopted. The adopted children's scores averaged 111; the scores of brothers and sisters raised by their biological mothers averaged 95. More than four times as many of the nonadopted children failed one year in school.

Recent studies of adopted children have examined the patterns of IQ correlations among children and other members of their natural and adoptive families. The environmental position predicts that unrelated children in the same family (who share an environment but not genes) will have similar IQ scores. The hereditarian position predicts that parents and their children put up for adoption (who share genes but not the same environment) will have similar IQ scores.

Many families today adopt children of different ethnic heritages. These interracial adoptions permit psychologists to study the relative contributions of nature and nurture to development.

FIGURE 11–3
Correlations of IQ Scores Among Adoptive Family Members

This figure shows that IQ scores of children are more strongly related to the IQ scores of their biological than adoptive parents. The correlations are shown on the lines connecting each set of relatives.

Source: Horn, Loehlin, & Willerman, 1979.

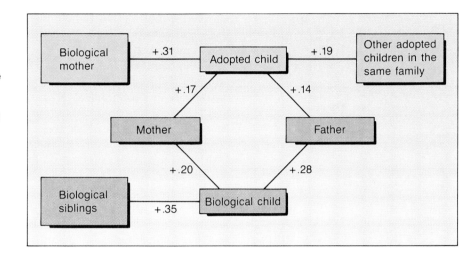

The Texas Adoption Study (Horn, 1983; Horn, Loehlin, & Willerman, 1979) collected extensive data on IQ scores and personality measures of adopted children, biological children, adoptive parents, and biological parents. The children in the Texas study were adopted within two weeks of birth. Therefore, they did not share the same environments as their biological parents. The critical question is "Did their IQ scores resemble more closely their biological or adoptive parents' IQ scores?" Figure 11–3 shows that the IQ scores of children are correlated more with their biological parents. Indeed, the correlation between the IQ scores of unwed mothers and their children put up for adoption is +.31, which indicates substantial similarity. Horn and his colleagues also analyzed the data according to the ages of the children. They found that correlations between the IQs of biological mothers and their adopted-away children decreased as children got older. Thus, they concluded that biological influences on IQ diminish with age and that environmental factors become more important.

Another major study of adopted children, the Minnesota Adolescent Study, was conducted by Sandra Scarr and her colleagues (Scarr & Weinberg, 1983). All the adopted children were placed in adoptive homes within their first year of infancy and were given a battery of IQ and personality tests as adolescents. No data were available from the biological parents of the adopted children, so the researchers compared IQ patterns from biologically related families and adoptive families. The IQ scores of mothers correlated +.41 with their biological children's IQs, whereas adoptive mothers' IQs correlated only +.09 with their adopted children's. Fathers' scores showed the same pattern. In biologically related families, fathers' IQs correlated +.40, while the correlation was only +.16 between IQs of fathers and their adopted children. In an extensive review of adoption studies, Scarr and Kidd (1983) acknowledge the importance of family environments but conclude, "greater genetic resemblance is associated with greater behavioral resemblance, quite strongly in the intellectual domain and to a lesser extent in personality and interests" (p. 418).

Scarr and Weinberg (1976) also conducted a study of transracial adoption that provides data relevant to the heredity/environment controversy. The researchers studied 101 white families in the Minneapolis area who had adopted a total of 176 nonwhite children, of whom 130 were classified as black and the other 46 as Asian, North American, or Latin American Indian. The families also had a total of 145 biological children. Parents and children took the appropriate WISC, WAIS, or Stanford-Binet tests. Most of the adopted children's biological parents had completed high school; the adoptive parents' educational level was on average four or five years higher. As a group, adoptive parents were middle class, their average age was 36, and their average IQ was 120; their biological children averaged 117 on IQ scores. The families seemed to provide stimulating environments.

Of the adopted children, 44 had been placed with their adoptive families by two months of age, and 111, including 99 black and interracial children, had been adopted within their first year. Black and interracial children were younger when adopted and had lived with their biological parents for less time than other adopted children. The adopted children averaged IQ scores of 106, significantly higher than those of nonadopted children of similar backgrounds but somewhat below those of the adoptive parents' biological offspring. Children adopted early surpassed the group average. Scarr and Weinberg concluded, "The dramatic increase in the IQ differences among the socially classified black children strongly suggest that IQ scores of these children are environmentally malleable" (1976, p. 173). However, the authors point out that the study cannot clearly separate the effects of race and social environment on intelligence, and they do not advocate placing black children in white homes. Their study supports the position that social and educational opportunities provided by the family can contribute greatly to children's IQs and academic success and that genetic heritage alone does not govern intelligence.

What can we conclude from studies of adopted children? First, heredity has a substantial effect on IQ scores. Plomin, DeFries, and McClearn (1980) conclude that "about half of the observed variation in IQ is due to genetic differences" (p. 338). Second, being raised in the same environment has a substantial effect on IQ. In the Texas study, unrelated children raised in the same families had IQs that correlated +.26. In the transracial study, the correlation was +.33. Although the correlations were slightly lower among genetically unrelated brothers and sisters, there was clearly an effect due to similar environments.

Family Characteristics and IQ Scores

Plomin, DeFries, and McClearn (1980) estimated that 36 percent of the variance in IQ scores is due to environmental influences within the family and that only 14 percent is due to environmental differences between families. Lois Hoffman (1985) believes that behavioral geneticists have underestimated the role of parenting styles and the impact of family interactions on IQ. Hoffman argues that most adoptive families have high IQs and stimulating homes; they are usually selected partly on these criteria. The narrow range of these enriched environments statistically reduces the impact of between-family differences and inflates the importance of genetic similarity. Hoffman suggests that better measures of family dynamics are needed to assess the influence of the home environment. The assumption made in most studies is that parents' IQ scores serve as good measures of the intellectual climate of the home. She points out that no socialization theory pos-

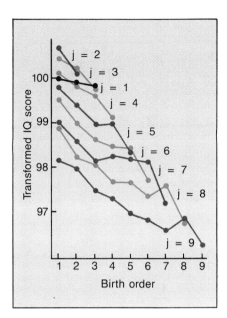

FIGURE 11–4
Intelligence and Birth Order

This graph shows how scores on a nonverbal intelligence test decrease for later-born children. The letter "*j*" indicates the number of children in the family. Notice how the last-born children of the largest families have the lowest scores.

Source: Zajonc & Markus, 1975.

tulates that parents, for example, with IQs of 115 provide more stimulating environments than parents with IQs of 110. More refined measures of intelligence, family dynamics, and home life are needed to clarify the relative influence of heredity and environment.

One measure of the family environment that has been related consistently to IQ scores is family size. Individuals from large families tend to have lower IQ scores than individuals from smaller families. Robert Zajonc (1983) observed this consistent pattern in 26 of 27 studies he reviewed. A survey of fertility and intelligence in the United States between 1894 and 1964 found a relation throughout the period between vocabulary scores (used as approximate measures of intelligence) and family size (Van Court & Bean, 1985). The more brothers and sisters a person has, the lower his or her vocabulary scores will be.

Birth order also is related to IQ scores. Later-born children usually have lower scores than early-born children. In the Netherlands, Belmont and Marolla (1983) compared the nonverbal intelligence scores of 400,000 men relative to family birth order and observed that later-born children, especially those in large families, had lower IQ scores than children born earlier (see Figure 11–4). Zajonc and Markus (1975) advanced the *confluence model* to explain how family characteristics influence IQ scores. This model is virtually the only environmental explanation of family influences yet proposed, but it has provoked sharp reactions. We discuss it more fully in "Controversy: Are IQ Scores Predicted by Family Size and Birth Order?"

IQ Within and Between Races

One of the most emotionally charged issues in the study of intelligence is the comparison of IQ scores between members of different racial groups. Science, politics, and opinion are difficult to separate when discussing the relative contributions of environment and heredity to the IQ scores of racial groups. The difficulty in separating these relative influences is intensified because of the history of racial prejudice that has accompanied intelligence testing. The evidence for differences in IQ scores between black and white Americans is straightforward. On the average, black Americans usually score lower than white Americans on standardized intelligence tests (Kennedy, 1969; Kennedy, Van de Riet, & White, 1963; Shuey, 1966). The difference in average scores is about 15 points, although the disparity is often less in northern than in southern states.

The 15-point difference in IQ scores is not disputed—the interpretation is. Some people argue that the intelligence tests themselves are unfair because they require information that is unfamiliar to poor, ghetto, or rural children. Although familiarity with testing procedures may in fact influence performance, test bias of the items does not seem to account for the difference in IQ scores. Mackenzie (1984) reviewed the evidence on the 15-point difference and did not dispute the conclusions emphasized by Jensen (1980) that "the difference is greater on nonverbal than on verbal tests, that it is greater on culture-reduced than on culture-loaded ones, and that item analyses reveal few, if any, significant race-by-item interactions" (p. 1215). Jensen (1985) reexamined data from 11 large-scale studies of black-white differences in IQ and concluded that the difference of 15 points is reliable and probably due to differences in rates of information processing rather than to any sort

CONTROVERSY

Are IQ Scores Predicted by Family Size and Birth Order?

A major factor in a child's intellectual development is the home environment. Some people grow up in large families; some are only children. Does it make any difference for intelligence if one grows up surrounded by brothers and sisters, is first born, or is last born? Some researchers believe that the birth patterns of families have considerable influence on intellectual development. Surveys of thousands of people revealed that later-born children of large families have lower IQ scores than earlier-born children or children from smaller families.

Robert Zajonc and Geoffrey Markus (1975) proposed the confluence model to explain these findings. This model does not rely just on parents' IQ scores as a measure of the intellectual environment of the family. Instead, the model is a set of equations that averages scores for all family members, considers their chronological ages, and includes a factor for the opportunity to teach younger siblings. Quite simply, Zajonc and Markus (1975) believe that the intellectual environment is diluted by more children and the arrival of new babies, partly

because family activities revolve around the youngest, most dependent members. As children mature, however, the family engages in more challenging cognitive tasks. Older brothers and sisters can also help teach their younger siblings, which benefits both "teacher" and "pupil."

The confluence model has been remarkably successful for predicting patterns of intellectual development among large samples of families, often explaining most of the variation in test scores (Zajonc, 1983). Several phenomena are explained well by the confluence model (Zajonc & Bargh, 1980). The model accurately predicts higher IQ scores for children of smaller families and for earlier-born siblings. It also predicts lower than expected scores for only and last-born children (because they have no siblings to teach). It also predicts depressed rates of intellectual growth following the birth of siblings. The confluence model even predicts the historical decline and rise in SAT scores as a function of family size.

However, some critics argue that the confluence model predicts not IQ but mental age, which is cumulative and inevitably predicted by equations that include maturation and chronological age (Rodgers, 1984). Critics argue that chronological age accounts for most of the predictive power of the

confluence model (McCall, 1985; Price, Walsh, & Vilberg, 1984). Some say it is a statistically inflated way of analyzing data (Galbraith, 1983). The controversy affects the interpretation of research. For example, Grotevant, Scarr, and Weinberg (1977) argue that the confluence model accounts for almost none of the variation in IQ scores of the transracial adoption study (Scarr & Weinberg, 1976). However, Berbaum and Moreland (1985) claimed that the wrong statistics were used, and when they reanalyzed the data, half of the variation was accounted for by the confluence model.

The controversy over the confluence model reveals two fundamental issues for research on intellectual development. First, psychologists need to devise better measures of the "environment" in order to understand how social, educational, and developmental forces influence intelligence scores. Characteristics of the family are good candidates but need to be elaborated to include the quality of interactions at home as well as the number and birth order of the children. Second, mathematical models of the relations between IQ and environmental variables can help identify the relative importance of different factors such as birth order. Future research will specify more precisely how family characteristics influence intellectual development.

of specific knowledge, training, or skill. The 29 commentaries by social scientists that follow Jensen's article reveal the broad range of issues and opinions on the topic. A large number of environmental hypotheses have been offered to account for the black-white IQ difference. Different social, economic, educational, cultural, motivational, nutritional, and medical opportunities in the United States doubtless contribute to the difference in IQ scores, although clear-cut data on many of these factors are lacking.

Other investigators have offered genetic hypotheses to account for the IQ differences. These inflammatory views have often been well publicized. Arthur Jensen is perhaps most well known for his views. His conclusion in 1969 that heredity accounts for up to 80 percent of the variation in IQ scores between blacks and whites provoked a great deal of controversy. The concept of *heritability*, a term that is vital to the interpretation of genetic influence on IQ differences between races, has often been misinterpreted.

HERITABILITY. Heritability is a statistic that can be calculated to reveal the variation in a characteristic, like IQ, that is accounted for by genetic factors. There are several ways to calculate heritability, but it is basically a measure of the similarity of characteristics among people who share similar genetic heritage. We have already seen that IQ scores are more highly correlated among family members who share genes. Heritability statistics provide an estimate of those relations. Plomin and DeFries (1980) concluded from their review that the heritability of IQ is approximately .50. This means that about 50 percent of the variation in IQ scores is due to similar genetic background. This estimate is considerably lower than Jensen's.

Keep in mind that heritability refers to the shared characteristics *within* the group; it does not indicate a genetic basis for *between*-group differences. This distinction has been ignored by some people who interpret differences between black and white Americans as due to heritability. Consider this parallel example: If a farmer has two varieties of corn to plant and each variety has been bred for distinctive characteristics, the separate strains have high heritability for these characteristics. But if the growing conditions in the fields where the corn is planted are different, then they would produce different yields. Thus, the more abundant yields of one strain of corn could be due to environmental differences even though there was a high heritability of characteristics in each strain. Although heritability was mistakenly used to explain differences in IQ scores between groups for many years, those errors have been clearly identified now.

FALLACIES. Mackenzie (1984) noted two other errors in reasoning that have plagued the analysis of racial differences in IQ. He labeled the first one "the sociologist's fallacy." This is the mistake of assuming that differences in IQ *must* be attributable to some environmental influence. For example, differences between individuals in socioeconomic status, education, or job opportunities may be due in part to selection of mates over generations rather than intelligence. The second mistake is called "the hereditarian fallacy." If an IQ difference cannot be given a detailed and specific environmental explanation, then some people wrongfully assume that the difference must be attributed to genetic causes. This is a fallacy because we cannot discount every possible environmental hypothesis. It is also an error because we may know that environmental influences are important without being able to specify exactly which factors are important and how they operate.

Mackenzie concludes that there is good evidence for an interactive model of genetic-environmental influences on IQ scores, but he stresses the need for new research designs. He also suggests that the oversimplified questions about the relative contributions of environment and heredity are fruitless. Even if we knew that a precise amount of IQ variation was due to heredity or environment, the statistic would not tell us how to promote the intellectual development of children, nor would it identify the specific environmental factors that underlie differences in intellectual achievement. The issue of nature *or* nurture may not be a fruitful question to pursue, especially in the area of racial differences in IQ scores.

AMERICAN AND JAPANESE IQ. Comparisons of academic achievement and intelligence in different countries also shed light on racial differences in mental abilities. British psychologist Richard Lynn (1982) compared IQ scores of 1,100 Japanese and 2,200 American schoolchildren between 6 and 16 years of age. The average IQ score of the Japanese children was 111, significantly higher than the average score of 100 for the American children. Lynn also investigated historical changes among Japanese IQ scores since 1910. Japanese born between 1910 and 1945 had mean IQ scores of 102 to 105 while those born between 1946 and 1969 had mean IQ scores of 108 to 115. Lynn points out that these dramatic increases give Japan the highest national average IQ score in the world. Lynn calculates from his study that fully 77 percent of the Japanese population have higher IQ scores than the average American or European.

Do these differences in IQ scores reflect genetic superiority? Some scientists think so. They point out that the IQ differences may not reflect consequences of education since the changes are observed in children as young as six and seven years of age. Alan Anderson (1982), an editor for *Nature*, reports that birth weights and life expectancy have increased dramatically in Japan since 1950 along with IQ scores. He suggests that the great migrations of rural people into urban centers that occurred between 1930 and 1960 contributed to more intermarriages among previously isolated groups. This outbreeding promoted changes in health and cognitive status through genetic mixing.

Of course, critics argue that nutrition, prenatal care, and other environmental factors changed in Japan to create healthier and smarter children. Indeed, Lynn suggests that environmental factors such as intensive educational training have encouraged Japanese children to achieve more than American and European children. For example, Japanese children may be better test-takers and be more academically prepared. Harold Stevenson and his colleagues (1982) compared children in the United States, Taiwan, and Japan on tests of mathematics and other general cognitive abilities (that is, the items were similar to those on standard intelligence tests). While the children in all three countries performed at similar levels on the general cognitive tests, Japanese children were far superior on the mathematical tests (Stevenson, Lee, & Stigler, 1986). The researchers also collected data from the children's parents and teachers. They found that Japanese children spend more time on mathematics in school and that they are encouraged to achieve more than other children. Thus, environmental differences including nutrition and schooling, as well as genetic factors such as interbreeding, may contribute to the different patterns of test scores among countries.

EXCEPTIONAL INTELLECTUAL DEVELOPMENT

Because of the many genetic and environmental influences on intelligence, the range of IQ scores is wide. At both ends of the distribution of IQ are individuals with exceptional mental abilities. Those who are more than 2 standard deviations below the average of 100 (i.e., IQ below 70) are often classified as mentally retarded. Those whose scores are beyond 130, two standard deviations above average, are labeled gifted. In the next few pages, we will describe these exceptional individuals and discuss problems with identifying and educating them.

Mental Retardation

Approximately 3 to 5 percent of the U.S. population, or almost 10 million people, are classified as mentally retarded, depending on the definitions and criteria used. The number is higher than should be expected by a normal distribution (see Figure 11–1) because of the many biological and environmental factors that can retard development.

Defining mental retardation is not easy. The mentally retarded do not all look alike or share the same handicaps. Their disability is not caused by just a few circumstances or genes. According to one definition, *mental retardation* refers to below-average general intelligence and poor adaptive behavior (Grossman, 1973). It can include physical and social difficulties as well as cognitive disabilities. The American Association on Mental Deficiency categorizes people with IQs between 55 and 70 as mildly, or educably, retarded, between 40 and 55 as moderately retarded, between 25 and 40 as severely retarded, and those with virtually immeasurable IQs below 25 as profoundly retarded (Hallahan & Kaufman, 1982).

Varying kinds of behavioral disturbances characterize retarded people at different ages (see Table 11–3). Not surprisingly, retardation is detected most often among schoolchildren, whose poor performance is revealed in IQ tests and schoolwork. Preschoolers and adults are less likely to be designated retarded unless their disabilities are extreme.

Mildly retarded adults can lead productive lives when given training and opportunity.

TABLE 11–3
Behavioral Characteristics of Mentally Retarded People Throughout the Life Span

Type	Characteristics from Birth to Adulthood		
	Birth through Five	Six through Twenty	Twenty-one and Over
Mild (IQ 53–69)	Often not noticed as retarded by casual observer but is slower to walk, feed himself, and talk than most children.	Can acquire practical skills and useful reading and arithmetic to a third- to sixth-grade level with special education. Can be guided toward social conformity.	Can usually achieve social and vocational skills adequate to self-maintenance; may need occasional guidance and support when under unusual social or economic stress.
Moderate (36–52)	Noticeable delays in motor development, especially in speech; responds to training in various self-help activities.	Can learn simple communication, elementary health and safety habits, and simple manual skills; does not progress in functional reading or arithmetic.	Can perform simple tasks under sheltered conditions; participates in simple recreation; travels alone in familiar places; usually incapable of self-maintenance.
Severe (20–35)	Marked delay in motor development; little or no communication skill; may respond to training in elementary self-help, such as self-feeding.	Usually walks, barring specific disability; has some understanding of speech and some response; can profit from systematic habit training.	Can conform to daily routines and repetitive activities; needs continuing direction and supervision in protective environment.
Profound (below 20)	Gross retardation; minimal capacity for functioning in sensorimotor areas; needs nursing care.	Obvious delays in all areas of development; shows basic emotional responses; may respond to skillful training in use of legs, hands, and jaws; needs close supervision.	May walk, need nursing care, have primitive speech; usually benefits from regular physical activity; incapable of self-maintenance.

Source: Kagan & Haveman, 1972, Table 14–15.

Many areas of development are affected in proportion to the severity of retardation. Mentally retarded children are often slow to begin to walk, talk, use the toilet, and engage in social interaction. Severely and profoundly retarded people seldom hold jobs, marry, or learn to care for themselves, and they usually require institutionalization or constant supervision. Moderately retarded people, on the other hand, can often perform unskilled labor satisfactorily and can manage their own lives. Mildly retarded children can attend school, but they may learn at a slower rate than normal children. The mildly retarded are not noticeable in appearance or behavior and may appear "slow" only when given a task requiring memory, reading, writing, or mathematical calculations.

Many of the cognitive difficulties of retardation involve problem-solving strategies. Given a series of words or pictures to remember, mildly retarded children and adolescents usually do not try to group the items, rehearse them, or test the accuracy of their memories (Campione & Brown, 1979). They often cannot plan, respond to feedback about their behavior, or control their attention; all these are fundamental learning skills. But recent studies have demonstrated that retarded children can be taught more effective learning strategies (see "Research Frontier: Metacognition and Intelligence" on page 424.) Current interpretations of the cognitive processes of the retarded emphasize a *slower rate* of development rather than a fundamental inability to learn (Weisz & Zigler, 1979).

What causes retardation? Genetic and biological factors can contribute. Among them is an inherited disorder known as **phenylketonuria (PKU)** that derives from a recessive gene. PKU involves an enzyme deficiency for metabolizing phenylalanine, an amino acid found in milk; absence of the enzyme results in a buildup of substances in the body that can harm the nervous system. If PKU is detected immediately after birth by blood or urine tests, the baby can be placed on a special diet to minimize the consequences of PKU. Other genetic factors have been identified as well. During early cell divisions of the ovum, sperm, or fertilized egg, the chromosomes may be rearranged or altered. These disorders, though based on genetic materials, are not inherited. The type of retardation called **Down's syndrome** results from such chromosomal aberrations. People afflicted with it usually have small heads, short necks, a fold over the eyelids, and distinctive appearance. Retardation can result also from accidents at birth such as extreme lack of oxygen (anoxia) and from diseases of the mother such as syphilis. Estimates are that genetic and biological factors identified so far account for 15 to 20 percent of mental retardation (Robinson & Robinson, 1976).

Many other causes remain unspecified, although it is clear that environmental variables are among them. Poor diet, poor health, and parental inattention can all lead to slower learning. The disadvantages of an environment can be subtle and varied, and it is difficult to relate particular factors directly to an individual's mental development. However, parents who cannot read or write and who do not value school achievement often have children who do poorly on IQ tests and, not surprisingly, are classified as mentally retarded. Poverty, low motivation, and poor education are often *family* characteristics that affect individual children. In one study, researchers observed that more than half of 200 mentally retarded people had another retarded individual in the family and 75 percent of the families were either disrupted or unable to provide necessities for living (Benda et al., 1963).

Whatever the cause of retardation, educators are concerned with improving the cognitive and social skills of its victims; their guiding philosophy seems to be that low intelligence indicated by IQ scores does not mean that retarded people cannot learn. Also, the label "retarded" should not become a stigma that fosters neglect or loss of personal rights. During the past 30 years educators have become more aware of the special needs of slow and retarded learners. From the late 1950s to the early 1970s the number of **special education** classrooms for the mildly retarded increased dramatically. One of the purposes of this change was to isolate children with learning problems so that they could be taught at a slower pace and with individual attention. Unfortunately, the curricula of these special classrooms were often diluted and boring versions of regular instruction and did not promote achievement as much as educators had hoped (Robinson & Robinson, 1976). In fact, classes often included a disproportionate number of disruptive children, members of ethnic minorities, and youngsters who did not speak English at home. The classes increased both the pupils' social isolation and the negative effects of the label "retarded."

An investigation of special education classes in California in the 1960s (Mercer, 1971) illustrated these consequences. The classes contained a disproportionately high percentage of blacks and Mexican-Americans. Mercer (1971), exploring the problem of placement in special classes for minorities, administered a behavioral test of social adaptation skills such as dressing, feeding, and shopping. She then compared the results with IQ test scores. The two tests were in general agreement for classifying the Anglo-American children in the special education classes. But the results changed for minority children. Ninety percent of the blacks and 50 percent of the Chicano children who had IQs below 70 nevertheless passed the social behavior test. One conclusion: minority children were more likely to be categorized as retarded when only an IQ test was used.

Because special education classes failed to improve retarded children's academic achievement and social integration, educators have attempted to provide special instruction to these children in regular classrooms. The Education for All Handicapped Children Act of 1975 (Public Law 94-142) mandated that children be given individualized instruction in the "least restrictive environment." This policy of *mainstreaming*, as it is called, means that many children now attend regular classrooms. It is too early to determine whether or not such changes will increase other children's acceptance of the mentally retarded and accelerate their intellectual achievement. Educational improvement, though, will not eliminate mental retardation. Retardation is a social category created by statistical divisions of IQ test scores that reflect the wide variability of human intelligence. Someone will always be at the bottom of any test score distribution. The aim of educators is to foster the development of retarded people's mental abilities and behavioral adaptation and to improve their lives.

Intellectually Gifted Children

People at the high end of the intelligence spectrum have not received much attention from psychologists. Some deemed it "elitist" to focus on the gifted. Others regarded the exceptionally bright as narrowly specialized geniuses who would grow up to be oddballs, in accord with the aphorism "Early ripe, early rot." However, the myth of social maladjustment and the reluctance to study gifted people are beginning to disappear.

One of the earliest and most ambitious studies of *gifted children* was undertaken by Lewis Terman in 1921 and subsequently carried on by Robert and Pauline Sears at Stanford (Goleman, 1980). Terman wanted to know what became of highly intelligent children when they grew up (Terman, 1954). He began by screening 250,000 California schoolchildren, from whom his staff identified 1,470 with IQs of 135 or higher. They averaged 11 years of age in 1922, and in 1928 Terman added 58 younger brothers and sisters so that the study included 1,528 in all, 857 boys and 671 girls. The sample was not typical of California children. Few members of minorities were represented, one-third of the children came from professional families, and more than 10 percent were Jewish. The subjects and some of their parents and teachers were interviewed and tested in 1922, 1928, 1940, 1950, 1955, 1960, 1972, and 1977. They were affectionately labeled "Termites" and have provided a wealth of data about intellectual development across the lifespan.

Intellectually gifted children often display sophisticated skills in science and mathematics at a young age.

The sample group grew up during a unique era in American history, including the Great Depression, World War II, and other vast social changes. Consequently, any comparisons drawn from the sample may confuse many differences found among generations. Despite this qualification, the study has provided compelling evidence that high IQs do not become handicaps in later life. Throughout school, Terman's subjects outpaced fellow students of the same ages by two to four grades and shone in all courses, refuting the belief that they would prove to be narrowly specialized. In general, bright children became successful and happy adults. In adulthood, 78 of the men earned Ph.D.s, 74 became college or university professors, 85 went into law, and 48 entered medicine. Of those who became scientists 47 were mentioned in American Men of Science for 1949. By the time they were 40 years old, in 1950, the men had published 93 books, 375 plays, novelettes, and short stories, and 2,000 scientific, technical, and professional articles. They also had registered more than 230 patents (Terman & Oden, 1959).

Not all, of course, achieved equally. In 1960, the 100 most and 100 least successful men were compared on the basis of income and job status. Fewer women were then employed full-time, so they were omitted in the study. In 1959 the median annual income in the United States was $5,000. The top 100, or A group, averaged $24,000; the bottom 100, or C group, $7,200. The A men differed socially and psychologically from the C's. A's had lower death rates and engaged more actively in physical sports and recreation. Their parents, and even grandparents, had higher educations than those of the C's. A's were more likely to marry and less likely to divorce. They had more and smarter children and happier family lives and reported fewer alcohol problems than C's. Perhaps A's and C's differed most in that A's had higher levels of aspiration, more drive, and longer persistence.

The study also measured, in 1972, satisfaction with life and attainment of goals (see Figure 11–5). Gifted men and women derived the greatest sense of well-being from their spouses and children. Men considered occu-

FIGURE 11–5
Life Satisfactions Reported by Gifted Men and Women in Terman's Life Span Study

These data were gathered in 1972 when most of the subjects were near retirement age. The source of greatest satisfaction was the family. Joy refers to overall pleasure with life. It is obvious that people with high IQs value and enjoy other things besides occupational success.

Source: Goleman, 1980.

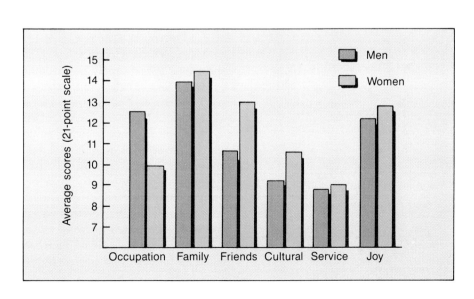

pational success much more important than did women, but they ranked friendships, status, and competence in work above income. Female heads of households—single, divorced, or widowed—found great rewards in work because of the challenge it presented and the sense of accomplishment it engendered. Men and women who reported highest satisfaction with life were also happy as children, respected their parents, had self-confidence, and were goal-directed.

MEASURING THE CREATIVITY OF THE GIFTED. The children in Terman's study were identified on the basis of IQ scores, which averaged 150. But does an IQ test alone suffice to define intellectual giftedness? Many scholars believe that it frequently proves inaccurate, and they advocate using additional criteria such as teacher ratings, achievement examinations, school grades, and special tests of talent and creativity. Children rarely perform equally well on all of these measures.

Defining giftedness is as difficult as defining retardation or intelligence in general. Some people argue that creativity and intelligence differ; others argue that the results of creativity tests and IQ tests often correlate highly. To distinguish creativity from intelligence, some investigators have postulated two kinds of thinking. One, *convergent thinking,* arrives at a proper—but conventional—answer. The other, *divergent thinking,* rides off in all directions to produce novel answers and solutions. One type is not better than the other. Similar to divergent thinking is *ideational fluency* (Wallach & Kogan, 1965), which refers to the number and kinds of ideas an individual can generate, e.g., how many different things can you do with a brick? Some typical tasks to measure creative thinking are shown in Figure 11–6. Judgments about creativity and novelty of answers obviously are subjective, and, in the absence of reliable measures of creativity, it is difficult to distinguish it from intelligence as measured on IQ tests.

EDUCATING THE GIFTED. Far fewer special educational programs have been provided for gifted children than for the retarded and learning disabled, but this is changing. Government programs, parents' interest groups, and psychological research focus more and more on examination of the gifted (Holden, 1980). This is exemplified by the Study of Mathematically Precocious Youth (SMPY) conducted at Johns Hopkins University by Julian Stanley and Camilla Benbow (1983). Since 1971, more than 7,000 students who reasoned extremely well in mathematics on the basis of their Scholastic Aptitude Test scores have participated in the program. From 1971 to 1981, SMPY discovered 100 twelve-year-olds whose SAT results surpassed 700 points, an achievement limited to one in 10,000 of their age. In a nationwide talent search in January 1981, Stanley's coworkers identified the 1,400 most gifted from a pool of more than 15,000 boys and girls whose test scores ranked in the top 3 percent. The purpose of SMPY is to foster the education of these gifted children, to promote their scientific accomplishments, and to avoid stifling their talents in unchallenging educational settings. The program includes intensive summer courses in science and mathematics coupled with accelerated university progress and family counseling. The SMPY will continue to investigate which children succeed in various kinds of enriched and accelerated science and mathematics programs.

FIGURE 11–6
**Examples of Tasks Used
to Measure Creativity**

To measure creativity, researchers provide children with simple tasks that can be solved in conventional or novel ways. The two paragraphs were written by different students in response to a photograph of a man in an office. Children's creative imagination is also measured in their drawings, shown by the two samples here. In the third task, children were asked what the jagged line looked like.

Source: Getzels & Jackson, 1962; Wallach & Kogan, 1965.

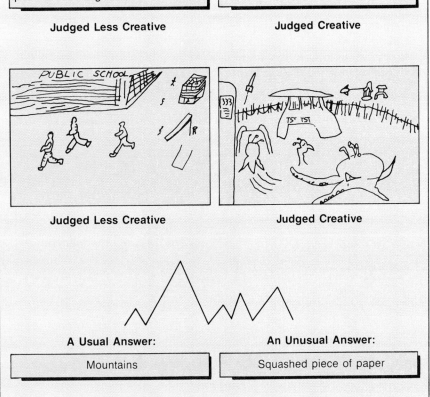

There's ambitious Bob, down at the office at 6:30 in the morning. Every morning it's the same. He's trying to show his boss how energetic he is. Now, thinks Bob, maybe the boss will give me a raise for all my extra work. The trouble is that Bob has been doing this for the last three years, and the boss still hasn't given him a raise. He'll come in at 9:00, not even noticing that Bob has been there so long, and poor Bob won't get his raise.

Judged Less Creative

This man has just broken into this office of a new cereal company. He is a private eye employed by a competitor firm to find out the formula that makes the cereal bend, sag, and sway. After a thorough search of the office he comes upon what he thinks is the current formula. He is now copying it. It turns out that it is the wrong formula and the competitor's factory blows up. Poetic justice!

Judged Creative

Judged Less Creative

Judged Creative

A Usual Answer:

Mountains

An Unusual Answer:

Squashed piece of paper

Other programs aim at improving educational opportunities for gifted children. Accelerated classes and enrichment programs have become more common. Psychologists like Stanley and his colleagues are investigating what educational alternatives prove most effective. However, some problems surrounding the study and education of gifted children resemble those encountered with the mentally retarded. What criteria are used to identify gifted children? How much should other kinds of information supplement IQ scores? Do the curricula for exceptional children really differ in quality or have they merely been adjusted to the youngsters' developmental levels? Does special treatment promote or impede social development and academic achievement? No clear answers to these questions appear, but special programs do seem to help both gifted and retarded children. Some people resist innovations in education for the gifted because they feel that such children need no help. Whether equal educational opportunity means treating all children the same or giving each the greatest opportunities remains a controversial question.

CONCEPTS OF INTELLIGENCE

So far we have discussed the characteristics and uses of intelligence tests. We have seen that IQ scores are widely used by educators to diagnose and place children in schools and by researchers to study the relative contributions of heredity and environment to development. But IQ scores are not equivalent to what we mean by intelligence. Indeed, there are many models of intelligence and many different ways of measuring it. For example, in Chapter 9 we saw that the cognitive developmental theory of Jean Piaget (Inhelder & Piaget, 1958) was a theory of intellectual development that did not rely on IQ scores. Besides the developmental approach, there are three other fundamental approaches to the study of intelligence: implicit theories, factor models, and cognitive processes.

Implicit Theories

One way to define intelligence is simply to ask people what they think it is. In 1921 the editor of the *Journal of Educational Psychology* asked 14 experts to give their views on the nature of intelligence (Sternberg, 1985). Their definitions included the following:

1. The power of good responses from the point of view of truth or fact
2. The ability to carry on abstract thinking
3. The ability to learn to adjust oneself to the environment
4. The ability to adapt oneself to relatively new situations in life
5. The capacity for acquiring knowledge and the knowledge already possessed
6. The capacity to learn or to profit by experience

These definitions and many others have been proposed over the years by experts. A more recent survey of expert opinions was conducted by Sternberg and his colleagues (1981). The researchers asked a large number of experts to rate the qualities of an intelligent person. Three factors emerged from the analysis—verbal intelligence, problem solving, and practical intelligence—characteristics that most of us would accept as key attributes of intellect.

But experts are not the only people who have been surveyed. Siegler and Richards (1982) asked a group of students in a psychology class to list five characteristics of intelligence in infants, children, and adults. They defined intelligence among infants as a matter of physical coordination, attachment, awareness of people, and verbal output. For children, learning, verbal facility, and understanding were mentioned frequently. For adults, language, problem solving, and logic were listed as key features. It seems that college students have developmental theories of intelligence that focus on different abilities at different ages. Yussen and Kane (1985) asked children from first, third, and sixth grades what their conceptions of intelligence are. They found that younger children tended to think of intelligence as a global characteristic, whereas older children viewed intelligence as more differentiated. Young children think that intelligence is clearly shown in behavior, whereas older children view intelligence as an internal characteristic. Younger children also overestimated their own intellectual abilities, while older children were more accurate in assessing their own intelligence.

What can we say about these commonsense theories of intelligence? First, the views of laypersons correlate remarkably well with the views of experts (Sternberg, 1985). Second, implicit theories reflect a broader range of abilities than typical IQ tests. Problem solving, planning, and understanding the world around us are often mentioned in implicit concepts that people have. Thus, they seem to be more relevant to the context of everyday behavior and to reflect the cognitive abilities that are important for daily interactions. Such implicit theories serve as rough guides for the creation of explicit theories. As Sternberg (1985) notes, implicit theories can enlarge our understanding about what constitutes intelligent behavior and what should be included in our explicit theories of intelligence.

Factor Theories

Psychometric theories are based on the study of individual differences among people. Psychometric tests are constructed to measure these differences. But how do we decide which abilities underlie the differences among people? Psychologists usually rely on a method called *factor analysis.* This technique starts with the measure of the correlations among test scores and tries to identify clusters of test scores that occur together. Then an ability that is common to these tests is inferred and called a *factor*. The basic strategy is to identify the primary factors that underlie the individual differences observed in the test scores. That is why these theories are sometimes called *differential* theories of intelligence.

Factor theorists vary greatly in the number of factors that they have identified as important. Indeed, in current theories the range goes from 1 to 150 factors! At one end of the extreme is the work of Charles Spearman (1927), who pioneered the use of factor analysis. He identified specific mental abilities associated with different tasks as well as a general ability, or "g factor," on mental tests. The general factor was so important on all tasks that Spearman concluded that it constituted *the* most important aspect of intelligence.

Other theorists have postulated that separate abilities characterize intelligence better. L. L. Thurstone (1938) identified seven primary mental abilities and constructed tests to measure each. The factors he identified are verbal comprehension, word fluency, number calculation, spatial reasoning, associative memory, perceptual speed, and general reasoning. Thurstone's research indicated that the primary mental abilities were not entirely independent, and he concluded, like Spearman, that a general intellectual factor seemed to underlie performance on many tasks.

Thurstone's primary mental abilities are not hierarchical; each is of equal importance. Other theorists have suggested hierarchical arrangements among factors. Perhaps the most ambitious work on the structural arrangement of factors of intelligence has been done by J. P. Guilford (1966, 1982). He proposed that intelligence is composed of 150 factors classified and arranged in a complex set of interconnections. Factor theorists have argued for years about the number of factors to include in their theories as well as the structural relations between factors. Perhaps as a response to controversies surrounding factor analysis, many theorists have turned to cognitive psychology for insight about the nature of intelligence.

Cognitive Theories

Several cognitive researchers have tried to identify fundamental cognitive processes as the basis of individual differences in intelligence. Raymond Cattell (1971) and John Horn (1978) have argued that intelligence is influenced by many primary mental abilities such as perceptual functions, speed of processing, and memory, but all of these abilities can be grouped into one of two categories: crystallized and fluid intelligence (see the initial presentation of these concepts on page 387). Crystallized intelligence involves the ability to understand relationships, make judgments, and solve problems. It is based on experience and information. Fluid intelligence is the general ability to perceive, encode, and reason about information. It derives more from biological and genetic factors and is less influenced by training and experience. The two may be highly related in children and young adults but less so in the elderly, who, as pointed out earlier, retain a high level of crystallized intelligence but not fluid intelligence.

In a similar vein, Jensen (1969) has proposed a two-dimensional theory of intelligence to explain why intelligence differs in social classes. On level I he places *associative* abilities such as digit recall, paired-associate learning, free recall, and trial-and-error learning. Level II embodies *conceptual* abilities such as problem solving, concept formation, and transformational reasoning. Level I abilities relate to biological maturation and differ little among social classes and races. Level II abilities may reflect education and ways of learning that contribute to observed differences in conceptual reasoning among social classes and races.

Another variant of the two-part system was developed by Joe Campione and Ann Brown (1979), who suggest that intelligence includes a biologically based architectural system and an environmentally influenced executive system. The architectural system incorporates such basics as memory capacity, durability (i.e., the rate at which information is lost), and efficiency (i.e., the speed of encoding, processing, and retrieving information). It changes mostly in preschoolers and the elderly. The executive system serves as the storehouse of knowledge, and it includes cognitive schemata, cognitive learning strategies, and metacognition (i.e., the awareness of an individual's abilities to plan, evaluate, and regulate learning). Many researchers believe that these skills may be poorly developed in retarded children, slow learners, people with low IQ scores, and the very young and very old. The system reflects training and experience and may indicate intellectual development derived from schooling. ''Research Frontier: Metacognition and

Intelligence" (on pages 424–425) elaborates on the relationship between executive thinking and retardation.

The most recent and comprehensive theory of intelligence has been proposed by Robert Sternberg (1985). It deserves special mention because it is based on an information processing approach to cognition and tries to relate social, developmental, and educational variables in the study of individual differences. Sternberg proposes three subtheories; hence the triarchic nature of his overall theory. The core of his approach is based on the ***components of intelligence.*** A component is an elementary information process that operates on internal representations of objects or symbols. Three kinds of components serve distinct functions. *Metacomponents* are higher-order executive processes used to plan, monitor, and regulate task performance. They include identifying problems, selecting strategies, monitoring possible solutions, and understanding feedback about performance. *Performance components* are the actual mental processes used to execute a task. They include perceiving aspects of the task, identifying concepts, and making responses. *Knowledge-acquisition components* are processes used to learn new information, such as combining old ideas in creative ways. Sternberg considers all three components to be basic aspects of intellectual functioning, yet he believes that metacomponents are the fundamental sources of individual and developmental differences in intelligence.

The second part of the triarchic theory is the experiential subtheory. Sternberg believes that intelligence requires the ability to deal with new tasks and situations and the ability to process information automatically. The purpose of the experiential subtheory is to identify specific tasks that are good measures of intelligence. The third part of the triarchic theory is the contextual subtheory. This subtheory goes beyond IQ tests and cognitive processes to deal with intelligence in relation to the external world of the individual. Sternberg considers intelligence as "mental activity directed toward purposive adaptation to, and selection and shaping of, real-world environments relevant to one's life" (1985, p. 45). This means that intelligence is functional and practical. Intelligent behavior helps the individual select and shape the environment. The three aspects of Sternberg's theory broaden cognitive approaches to intelligence by considering how individuals use their mental abilities in different settings to solve problems that are relevant to their everyday behavior.

SUMMARY

1. In France at the turn of this century, Alfred Binet constructed the forerunner of modern intelligence tests. Binet's test was designed to identify children who needed special educational help.

2. An IQ score is a measure of one person's performance relative to other individuals of the same age. It is *not* an absolute measure of intelligence or ability to learn.

3. There are many different kinds of intelligence tests. Some are designed for different age groups and some are created for people with particular handicaps. The Stanford-Binet and Wechsler tests of intelligence are widely used.

4. Many intelligence tests include a variety of tasks such as vocabulary, puzzles, arithmetic, sentence comprehension, and spatial reasoning. The tasks are administered and scored in a uniform manner.

5. Three important characteristics of intelligence

RESEARCH FRONTIER

Metacognition and Intelligence

What cognitive skills distinguish children with IQs of 70 or 90 from children who are more intelligent? If we knew the key processes that are problematic for low-achieving children, educational remediation could focus on them directly. This is one goal of research on intelligence: to discover basic cognitive processes that underlie individual differences in IQ scores. Recent research on intelligence has provided promising clues. One of the hallmarks of intelligent behavior is the ability to appraise and regulate one's own thinking. This is called *metacognition* and includes the same kinds of thinking skills included in Sternberg's (1985) theory of the metacomponents of intelligence and Campione and Brown's (1979) executive system.

How does metacognition influence children's thinking? Children with be-

low-average IQs have difficulty using and understanding cognitive strategies. For example, children who are labeled "learning disabled" do not use memory strategies effectively and independently to help organize and rehearse information (Newman & Hagen, 1981; Torgesen, 1977). They also have problems attending and concentrating (Traver et al., 1976) and summarizing the main ideas from text (Winograd, 1984). Bernice Wong (1985) reviewed many studies comparing average and learning disabled children and concluded that the underachieving children use learning strategies more poorly because they do not understand them well. Learning disabled children do not suffer deficits in basic perceptual and memory *abilities;* rather, they do not plan, evaluate, and regulate their own thinking as well as more intelligent children do (Paris & Lindauer, 1982).

Educators have expressed cautious enthusiasm about the role of metacognition because it may be possible to train students to control their own

thinking. Schumaker and colleagues (1984) taught reading strategies to learning disabled teenagers. Students learned to survey the text before reading, to examine the types of questions asked, and to reread the text by searching for information. Students mastered the strategies with a few hours of practice and improved their reading substantially. Palincsar and Brown (1984) created an instructional model called "reciprocal teaching" in which teachers and students talk about the strategies being learned and exchange roles. Students must understand the skills in order to help someone else use them properly. Palincsar and Brown (1984) taught learning disabled junior high school students four strategies: summarizing, self-questioning, asking for clarification, and predicting subsequent information. Together these strategies require students to think forward and backward as they read and to periodically check their understanding. Students learned these metacognitive strategies within a month of instruction, and the tech-

---

tests are the standardization sample, reliability, and validity.

6. IQ scores are not always stable. A person can easily vary by 10 points from one test to the next. IQ scores from infants and young children are not very good predictors of adult scores, but new measures of cognitive processes of infants provide remarkable correlations with later IQ scores. Intelligence does not show a general and gradual deterioration after early adulthood.

7. Approximately 50 percent of the variation in IQ scores is due to hereditary factors. Behavior geneticists and others argue that the environmental differences between families and groups account for relatively little of the variation in average IQ scores. Critics

counter that better measures of environmental influences are needed.

8. Research on adopted children reveals that their IQ scores are more highly related to the IQ scores of their biological parents and siblings than to those of the people who share the same home. However, enriched and nurturant environments do promote intellectual development.

9. Black Americans score lower on IQ tests than whites. The patterns of test scores for both groups are similar across test items, and the differences in levels of performance could be due to many factors. Differences among racial and ethnic groups on intelligence tests do *not* indicate genetic superiority of one group.

niques helped improve their reading comprehension significantly.

Metacognitive training has focused on helping students discover *what* cognitive strategies are critical for particular tasks, *how* they operate, *when* they should be applied, and *why* they are valuable (Paris, Cross, & Lipson, 1984). Such training has promoted academic performance on reading, spelling, writing, and arithmetic and is a promising avenue for educational remediation (Palincsar & Brown, in press). Other researchers have suggested that metacognition may help us understand black-white differences in IQ scores. Borkowski, Krause, and Maxwell (1985) analyzed the relative performance of black and white children on a variety of cognitive tasks. They suggest that racial differences between groups were much larger on metacognitive tasks than other tests measuring more basic skills such as the speed of perceptual processing. If this is true, and if these skills can be improved through training, it suggests that some of the IQ variation among people is due to understanding how to use one's cognitive resources and is thus not a fixed difference in abilities. Because of the importance for theories of intelligence and for educational practice, research on executive processes of thinking, or metacognition, will be pursued vigorously.

10. Exceptional children are usually defined according to statistical distance from average IQ scores, although many other behavioral characteristics are often used. The definition and classification of people as retarded or gifted present difficult problems. Early diagnosis and special educational programs appear to help exceptional children develop to their fullest potential.

11. The guiding concept of intelligence in psychology has been the psychometric model, which defines intelligence according to performance on standardized tests. This theoretical approach has been supplemented by various theories of information processing and mental abilities, but none has generated measures of intelligence that rival traditional psychometric tests.

SUGGESTED READINGS

Eysenck, H. J., vs. Kamin, L. (1981). *The intelligence controversy*. New York: Wiley.
A unique book of brief chapters that is really a debate in print; includes sharp criticism and commentary on many controversies.

Kail, R., & Pellegrino, J. W. (1985). *Human intelligence: Perspectives and prospects*. New York: Freeman.
The psychometric, information-processing, and cognitive developmental approaches to intelligence are summarized in this compact paperback. The

authors provide a scholarly yet readable introduction to the key issues involved in defining and measuring intelligence.

Resnick, L. B. (Ed.) (1976). *The nature of intelligence.* Hillsdale, N.J.: Erlbaum.
>   Contains chapters by many experts on theoretical aspects of cognitive abilities.

Robinson, N. M., & Robinson, H. B. (1976). *The mentally retarded child: A psychological approach.* New York: McGraw-Hill.
>   A compassionate and scientific analysis of retarded people and the study of mental retardation.

Sattler, J. M. (1982). *Assessment of children's intelligence and spatial abilities.* Boston: Allyn and Bacon.
>   This handbook for school psychologists provides a complete view of the history and problems of assessing children's mental abilities and instructions for administering and interpreting psychometric tests.

Sternberg, R. J. (1985). *Beyond IQ: A triarchic theory of human intelligence.* Cambridge: Cambridge University Press.
>   The first complete statement of Sternberg's theory, integrating a vast literature on intelligence with research on information processing and pointing the field in new directions.

12

Motivation

Call it what you will, incentives are what get people to work harder.

Nikita S. Khrushchev

ALBERT SCHWEITZER CAME FROM A WELL-TO-DO FAMILY AND WAS A musical prodigy, but he decided early in life to become a medical missionary. He became a doctor of medicine and in 1913 established a hospital in Africa that he rarely left until his death in 1965.

Two Japanese mountain climbers, Yasuo Kato and Tokiashi Kobayashi, became the first team to climb Mount Everest in winter. They reached the summit but became lost in attempting their descent and froze to death.

Adolf Hitler ordered the "Final Solution" for all Jews and other "undesirables" within the countries he controlled. By the end of World War II, some 11 million people had been slaughtered in German extermination camps, including about 6 million Jews.

The descriptions of these remarkable acts seem incomplete. In each case the reader naturally asks: why would someone do *that?* The same might be asked of people who enjoy hang gliding, sky diving, bullfighting, or any other behavior that seems extraordinary. In posing this question we raise the issue of *motivation,* of *why* behavior occurs. This question is appropriate not only for unusual behaviors but also for the most commonplace. Why are you attending a college or university? Why did you select the clothes you are wearing today? Why, for that matter, are you reading this book?

Most people at some time or another want to eat, want to drink, want to be liked, want to do well, want to hug someone, want someone to do what they say, want to be alone. Why do people want and like the things they do? Some desires are clearly biological. The desire to eat, for example, is partly a matter of our internal physiology. We are born with biological urges, called *drives* by some, that make us behave to satisfy these urges. The environment also directly affects our desires. The desire to eat is stronger when you enter a restaurant and smell a steak cooking, and the desire to succeed is greater when you are in competition. Moreover, some goals are more movitating than others; that is, some goals provide more of an *incentive* to the individual. The desire to eat is stronger in the presence of a plate of spaghetti than in the presence of a plate of worms, and the urge to compete is stronger against a good opponent than a weak one. In this chapter we will look closely at the psychological concepts of incentive, drive, and the motivation we have for eating, for drinking, for sex, for affiliating with others, and for achieving to the best of our ability. The concept of motivation is central to psychology and familiar to all of us. But what does motivation mean to a psychologist? To answer this question, we will outline several different approaches or theories of motivation.

THEORIES OF MOTIVATION

Before the advent of psychology, philosophers viewed humans as motivated primarily by *hedonism,* the desire to maximize pleasure and to minimize pain. Humans' ability to make conscious decisions between competing goals set them apart from other animals who were thought to act only in automatic, instinctive ways. The work of Charles Darwin helped change this view and led to the first theory of motivation in psychology: instinct theory.

Instinct Theory

In *Origin of the Species* (1859), Darwin devoted a chapter to the instinctive behavior patterns. In later books, he compared emotional expression in humans and other animals (1873) and mental powers and the moral sense of humans and other animals (1871). In these books, Darwin was satisfied that he had demonstrated that the difference between behavior in humans and in other animals "is certainly one of degree and not of kind" (1871, p. 101). Darwin's work opened the way for the idea that instincts may be important in humans (and for the idea that higher mental processes may be important in animals other than humans).

In the early days of psychology, *instinct theory* was the dominant theory of motivation. William James (1890, vol. 2) defined an instinct as "the faculty of acting in such a way as to produce certain ends without knowledge of the ends, without foresight of ends and without previous education in the performance" (p. 383). He believed that humans had the most instincts and that consciousness evolved to deal with all the conflicting instincts. Some of the instincts James suggested were modesty, cleanliness, jealousy, shyness, sociability, pugnacity, sympathy, rivalry, and fear. Ultimately the concept of instinct as an explanation of motivation was discredited because it was inherently circular—to say shy behavior occurred because of a shyness instinct is not really an explanation, but just a name for shy behavior. And there were ultimately too many instincts suggested (nearly 6,000 different instincts were proposed), many of them contradictory. Shyness and sociability are instincts included in James's list. When will a person be shy and when sociable? Instinct theory did not answer this question.

Today the word *instinct* has a much more specific meaning, and the concept has been revived in the work of ethologists, who compare instinctive behaviors among animals. Ethologists refer to instinctive behaviors as *fixed action patterns*, which they define as stereotyped, complex behavior shown by all appropriate members of a species, independent of the organism's experience. Ethologists investigate a wide variety of fixed action patterns, including those that involve courtship, aggressive displays, and maternal behavior.

Each fixed action pattern is elicited by a specific *sign stimulus.* For example, a male stickleback, a small freshwater fish, develops a red coloration on its body in the breeding season and attacks any other male stickleback intruding on its territory. A model of a stickleback that looks to a human remarkably like a stickleback will not be attacked by another stickleback if it lacks a red belly, but a model that looks to a human very unlike a stickleback will be attacked by another stickleback if it has one. The red belly is the sign stimulus. Male sticklebacks will attack a red-bellied model of a fish even if they have been reared in isolation and have never seen one before, indicating that the basis for the behavior must be encoded in the genes. Indeed, many instinctive behaviors occur automatically at the first opportunity. In

The red coloration of the stickleback fish is a sign stimulus that elicits attack in other sticklebacks. A model of a fish looking not at all like a stickleback will be attacked if it has a red belly, while a stickleback without the red belly will not be attacked.

one variety of spider, for example, the male must display the appropriate pattern toward the female the first time the male tries to mate or else it will be eaten by her.

In many cases, instinctive behavior is extremely stable and fixed in development. Altering the species' environment will exert little influence on the behavior. However, many fixed action patterns have been found to be more variable than originally thought. Instinctive behavior often evolves only in a certain range of environments or assumes differing forms depending on environment. For this reason, modern investigators describe how instinctive behaviors take shape as environments change rather than merely separating them into instinctive and noninstinctive patterns.

A good example of environmental variation is birdsong. Some birds, such as the ring dove, develop the ability to sing the song characteristic of their species even if the birds are reared in total isolation and even if they are deafened (Nottebohm & Nottebohm, 1971). In such species, birdsong unfolds in the same way regardless of environmental variation. Mynahs and parrots, in contrast, imitate sounds they hear; their vocalizations therefore vary with the environment, although of course their imitative capacity has a genetic basis. Song sparrows represent an intermediate case. If a group of song sparrows is reared in isolation from other birds, they will develop a normal song, but a deafened song sparrow reared in isolation will not (Mulligan, 1966). It appears that a genetic basis exists for recognizing the appropriate song, but the bird can perfect it only if it hears the song.

For many instinctive behaviors, there is a ***critical period*** when an organism reflects particular sensitivity to environmental influences. *Imprinting,* the tendency to follow or approach an object, is acquired early in life. The nursery rhyme "Mary Had a Little Lamb" deals with imprinting: "And everywhere that Mary went the lamb was sure to go." Imprinting has indeed been demonstrated in lambs (Sambraus & Sambraus, 1975), and comparable behavior has been systematically examined in dogs. Puppies of some breeds form lasting attachments to other dogs or people, but only in the third to seventh weeks after birth (Sluckin, 1965). Imprinting has been studied principally among fowl and birds (see Figure 12–1). The critical period when imprinting of a young chick or duckling may take place varies from 12 hours to about three days after hatching. In one experiment, during this critical time two groups of a species of young birds were put in two circular runways each with a different colored box that moved around the runway. Later, tested with the familiar box and a box of a different color, the birds approached, nestled against, and followed the box with which they had been reared (Bateson, 1973). In the birds' normal environment, the parent would be the most likely object of imprinting. Critical periods have also been observed in human development, particularly during the first year of life. In humans, these critical periods seem particularly important for language acquisition and emotional bonding.

Is instinct theory relevant to human behavior? Humans do indeed share behavior patterns with other animals. As shown in Figure 12–2, many mammals, including human babies, move their heads rhythmically to the left and right, a searching response for the nipple. The movement may recur either spontaneously or following a light touch on the cheek. Another example is the newborn infant's grasping reflex (see Figure 12–3). An infant's hand clutches an object in an ordered sequence of finger movements. The grasp-

FIGURE 12–1
Imprinting

Ethologist Konrad Lorenz is being followed by geese that have been imprinted. Animals are especially responsive to stimuli at certain periods in their lives. These geese were kept isolated from other geese early in life but were in the company of Lorenz. As you can see, they follow Lorenz as though he were their mother.

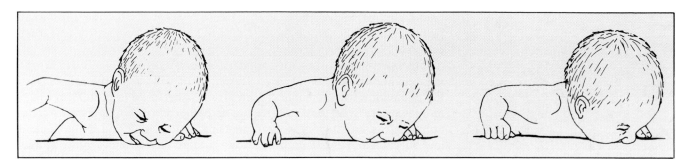

FIGURE 12–2
An Infant Showing the
Searching Response

With a touch on the cheek, human infants will move their heads from left to right in search of the breast. This behavior pattern is shared with other mammals.

ing reflex is especially strong while the infant is nursing, and ethologists suggest that its original (evolutionary) purpose was to hold on to the mother's fur. Although no longer necessary, the grasping reflex is so strong that a newborn can hang on by its hands from a clothesline. The grasping reflex is eventually replaced by voluntary grasping.

According to sociobiologists, the theory of natural selection explains why there may be a genetic basis for many behavioral traits, including aggression, altruism, and sexual behavior. The search for evolutionary causes for human behavior has been controversial, however. We discuss some aspects of sociobiological thinking in "Controversy: Sociobiology: Should We Look to the Genes?"

Drive Theory

The motivation to perform fixed action patterns is specific to the particular response. That is to say, a mynah bird's motive to imitate speech sounds begins and ends with its mimic and chatter. However, many motives seem not to be tied to specific responses. Drive theory is concerned with some of these. In *drive theory* the motive for performing is not tied to any specific response. Rather, the organism responds in reaction to internal cues, most often to maintain a stable internal state, or *homeostasis.* The body's homeostatic mechanism can be compared to that of a thermostat—when the temperature in a house deviates from the one set on the thermostat, a heater (in the winter) or air conditioner (in the summer) comes on to restore the temperature to the appropriate level. In drive theory, *drives* represent any state of tension that results from a breakdown in homeostasis. When the

FIGURE 12–3
The Grasping Reflex

A human infant will close his or her hand around an object such as a finger in an ordered sequence of finger movements. At first the middle finger closes, then the other fingers, with the thumb closing last. This grasping reflex, which presumably originated in the effort of the infant to hold on to the mother's fur, is eventually replaced by voluntary grasping.

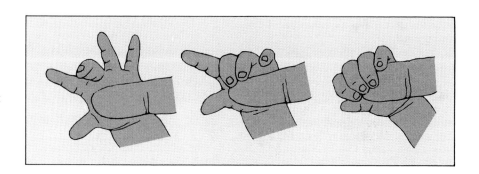

Sociobiology: Should We Look to the Genes?

Sociobiology has been defined as "the systematic study of the biological basis of all social behavior" (Wilson, 1975, p. 4). Its practitioners aim to understand all types of social behavior—including such complex behaviors as aggression, altruism, dominance, and sexual attraction—in evolutionary terms, by emphasizing how each behavior observes the principle of natural selection. We can clarify this theory by considering some applications to human social behavior.

The first application may be familiar to you: the conflict between parent and child as the child grows older. In mammals, including humans, there is a typical course of parent-offspring interactions. After birth, interactions are initiated primarily by the parent, but there is a gradual transition of roles,

so that later interactions are initiated primarily by the offspring. From a sociobiological perspective, this transition may represent the mother's changing perception of how much care the young need to survive. Parents will sacrifice their future reproductive capacity by attending their offspring only until the offspring are independent. However, the young may continue to demand attention to maximize their own survival. The genetic stake of the parents (more offspring) thus opposes the genetic stake of the young.

A second application is no doubt equally familiar: mate selection. In choosing mates, males and females often employ different strategies, and these differences are understandable on the basis of sociobiological principles. The female who must bear and care for the young must be sure that she mates with the best male available—best in the sense of producing more offspring that will survive or being able to care for offspring once they have arrived. The male, on the

other hand, has enough sperm to impregnate incredibly large numbers of females, and his best strategy to increase fitness is to impregnate as many females as possible. In many species, females mate with the winner of fights among males, that is, the stronger male. Some see a possible parallel in human behavior, where males often compete for a female. Likewise, some detect a possible sociobiological basis for a weaker monogamous tendency in males than in females.

Trivers (1972) speculates that each offspring a female produces should be of greater importance to her as a carrier for her genes than the same offspring is to the father because a male could produce so many more offspring. Mothers might thus be expected to be more altruistic than fathers toward their offspring.

Many researchers are currently concerned with developing other sociobiological explanations of human behavior (e.g., Freedman, 1979; Lumsden & Wilson, 1981). The verdict is not in, however. Attempts to explain behavior in sociobiological terms usually involve indirect arguments and analogies that may indeed be plausible. But contrary arguments or alternative explanations are often just as plausible. Gould (1977) argues that many comparisons of animal to human behavior capitalize on simple analogies of function rather than true homologies. If behaviors are homologous (descended from a common ancestor), the possibility of a genetic mechanism is plausible, but even then it is far from proven.

For this reason, whether or not sociobiological ideas provide an accurate account of human behavior is still an open question.

E. O. Wilson's highly influential 1975 book, *Sociobiology: The new synthesis* led to the tremendous upsurge in work on the biological basis of social behavior.

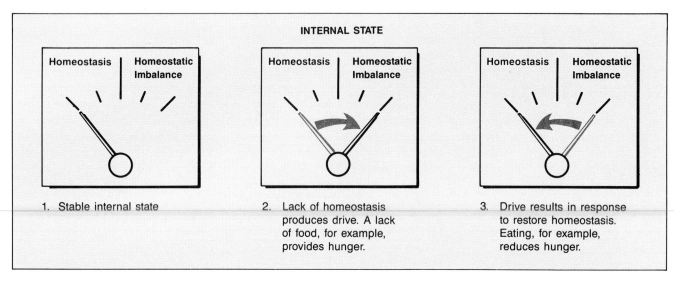

FIGURE 12–4
Basic Sequence of Motivation Outlined in Drive Theory

body's internal equilibrium is disturbed (when the drive occurs) the individual is motivated to eliminate the drive, to restore homeostasis. Many drives are related to biological needs. Humans need food and have a drive for food called hunger. They need water and have a drive for water called thirst. Drives are unpleasant, and people are motivated to reduce them—pleasure or reward is produced by reducing drives. (See Figure 12–4.)

Many behaviors are difficult to explain within drive theory. People play cards, doodle, shoot pool, ride roller coasters, and go to horror movies—all activities difficult to relate to biological needs or drives—and the pleasure produced by many of these activities seems to indicate that an increase in drive can be rewarding. The fact that people enjoy going to horror movies or riding roller coasters implies that fear can be pleasant. Yet within drive theory, fear is considered to be a drive that one wants to reduce. Some writers have attempted to account for the apparent absence of drives in some behaviors and the contradictions within drive theory by separating drive from biological need and by lengthening the list of drives (Fowler, 1967; Miller, 1957). Most, however, suggest that drive theory should be replaced by an alternative (Bolles, 1975). Two main alternatives have been proposed: cognitive theory and arousal theory.

Cognitive Theory

There are many varieties of *cognitive motivation theory* (Bolles, 1972; Mowrer, 1960; Tolman, 1932). All share the fundamental idea that *incentives* (also called "expectancies of goals") produce motivation. Expecting or anticipating something of value produces *positive incentive motivation*. Studying for good grades is an example of the motivating influence of positive incentives. On the other hand, expecting or anticipating something negative produces *negative incentive motivation*. Driving defensively late at night is an example of the motivating influences of negative incentives. As you can see, cognitive theory emphasizes the motivating effects of events in the environment and of goals or incentives. Some people describe this as a "pull" theory of motivation, in contrast to drive, which is a "push" theory.

Goals that motivate behavior are incentives.

Theorists of cognitive motivation often distinguish between two determinants of behaviors: *expectancy* and *value* (Feather, 1982). A positive incentive will motivate more effectively the more it is expected and the higher its value. A student will study to get good grades if the student values good grades and expects them as a consequence of study. On the other hand, if a student receives good grades without studying, the expectancy of receiving good grades for studying will be reduced; the student will have less motivation to study hard. In other words, incentives can prove ineffective if they are not valued or are not expected for the behavior being measured. Students may not study because they do not want good grades—which is low value—or they may want good grades but not expect them for studying—which is low expectancy.

Recent researchers have expanded the class of positive incentives to include not receiving an expected negative incentive. If you do not get a shock you anticipate, for example, you feel relief, which produces positive incentive motivation. And negative incentives have been expanded to include not receiving an expected positive incentive. For example, if you do not get the A grade you thought you would, you experience frustration, which induces negative incentive motivation, and you will be impelled to avoid a situation where that occurs. Finally, positive and negative incentive motivation inhibit one another; this means that to the extent that you are relieved by something, you cannot also feel frustrated. This theory has received extensive empirical support (Dickinson & Pearce, 1977).

Arousal Theory

A major difficulty with incentive theory and other theories of motivation is specifying in advance what a particular person will value positively and negatively. A theory that attempts to predict what people will find rewarding or pleasurable, and when, is *arousal theory.* The term *arousal* refers to the body's general level of activity, reflected in several physiological indices including muscle tension, galvanic skin response, patterns of electrical activity in the brain, and heart rate (Andrew, 1974; Appley, 1970; Campbell & Misanin, 1969). Generally speaking, arousal can vary along a continuum from deep sleep through normal wakefulness to extreme excitement.

There are four general sources of arousal. First, drives and incentives produce arousal. Hunger, thirst, and pain all contribute to arousal, as do anticipations of pleasure and pain. Second, environmental circumstances affect arousal. In general, the higher the intensity of stimuli such as noise and bright lights, the higher the arousal level. Color also affects arousal; a blue room is less stimulating than a red room. A third source consists of surprising or novel events, and a fourth is drugs. The caffeine in coffee heightens arousal, for example. Note that motivation and arousal are not the same. Motivation is only one source of arousal.

According to arousal theory, performance varies with arousal, and generally performance is best with intermediate levels of arousal. If you are too nervous about an exam, you may do poorly. On the other hand, if you fall asleep during the exam, you may also do poorly (see Figure 12–5). This idea has been substantiated in experiments with animals and humans. In one experiment (Belanger & Feldman, 1962) rats were trained to press a bar to get water following 24 hours of deprivation. After the rats had learned what

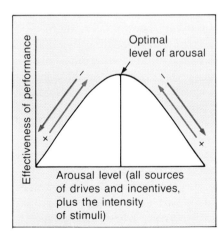

FIGURE 12–5
Basic Outline of Arousal Theory

According to arousal theory, for any particular task it is always pleasant to move toward the optimal level of arousal and unpleasant to move away from the optimal level.

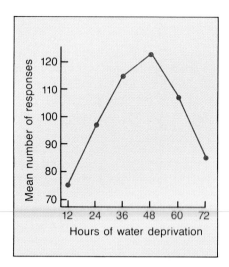

FIGURE 12–6
Rate of Bar Pressing for Water by Thirsty Rats

The highest rate of bar pressing occurred for rats that had been without water for 48 hours. They pressed at a higher rate than rats that had been without water for 12, 24, or 36 hours and at a higher rate than rats without water for 60–72 hours. The rats were not too weak to press the bar as hours without water increased. These findings support arousal theory, which states that performance should be best when arousal (in this case produced by water deprivation) is neither too high nor too low.

Source: Bélanger & Feldman, 1962.

to do, experimenters increased the rats' thirst by adding to their waterless hours, which was expected to increase arousal level. While the rats' heart rate continued to increase to the highest level of water deprivation (showing increased arousal), bar pressing did not. The highest rate of activity came after 48 hours of water deprivation; after that point it decreased with continued water deprivation (see Figure 12–6). This suggests that too high an arousal level interferes with performance.

Many studies have been done with humans to see if increasing arousal helps or hurts performance. In general, the studies show that increasing arousal helps performance on easy or boring tasks but hurts it on difficult tasks or those requiring concentration (Berlyne, 1967). For example, the Taylor Manifest Anxiety Scale has been used to select subjects high and low in anxiety from introductory psychology classes (see Table 12–1) (Taylor, 1953). Students high in anxiety perform better than those low in anxiety on easy verbal learning tasks, but on difficult tasks the subjects low in anxiety prove superior.

Before the advent of arousal theory, experimenters had found a similar relationship between optimal levels of motivation and task difficulty. Early psychological experiments led to formulation of the *Yerkes-Dodson law* (Yerkes & Morgulis, 1909), which says that there is an optimal degree of motivation for any task and that the more difficult the task, the lower the optimal degree. There is one critical difference, however, between the Yerkes-Dodson law and arousal theory. The more recent theory specifies degree of *arousal* as the crucial factor, rather than degree of *motivation*. (Keep in mind that motivation is only one source of arousal; degree of arousal does not mean degree of motivation.) In fact, recent studies using food deprivation as the source of motivation have shown that the Yerkes-Dodson law does not always hold. On many tasks, regardless of difficulty, higher levels of motivation lead to better performance (Fantino, Kasdon, & Stringer, 1970; Hochhauser & Fowler, 1975). The law does apply in cases where the source of motivation is much more unpleasant, such as air deprivation and shock. Naturally, in these cases the level of arousal would also be very high.

Sometimes arousal decreases are pleasant and rewarding: resting quietly, relaxing in a warm tub, sipping a drink of water; at other times arousal increases are rewarding: going to a disco, playing loud music. Arousal theory relates these differences to the individual's arousal level, sleep-wakefulness cycle, and the demands of the task being faced. So if you are a "night person," normally your arousal level is low in the morning. But if you are facing a morning exam, which requires a higher arousal level for optimum performance than your normal level at that time of day, you would be expected to take steps to increase your arousal level—perhaps a cup of coffee or a little test anxiety would be beneficial. Individual differences in motives, tastes, and preferences can be attributed in part to differences in arousal level. Loud music can be just the thing for someone whose arousal level is moderately high (awake and alert), but it can be unpleasant for a person who has just awakened and is in a low arousal state, for a person who is trying to concentrate, or for a person who is excited anyway and so is above the optimum level of arousal for that time of day.

As you might expect, there seem to be individual differences in optimal arousal level as well. Some people never enjoy loud music, horror movies, or fast driving, and they shudder at the thought of sky diving. Other people

TABLE 12–1
Representative Items from the Taylor Manifest Anxiety Scale

I am easily embarrassed. (True)

I am happy most of the time. (False)

I have nightmares every few nights. (True)

I sweat very easily even on cool days. (True)

I do not have as many fears as my friends. (False)

I certainly feel useless at times. (True)

I am very confident of myself. (False)

I practically never blush. (False)

I have very few headaches. (False)

I cannot keep my mind on one thing. (True)

The answer in parentheses indicates anxiety.

Source: Taylor, 1953.

The fact that people enjoy roller coasters, horror movies and other tension- or excitement-producing events was difficult to explain within drive theory but is understandable within arousal theory. According to arousal theory, increases in excitement are rewarding whenever a person's arousal level is beneath the optimum for the task or time of day.

seem to thrive on excitement. A sensation-seeking scale has been developed to measure these differences among people in their individual optimal levels of arousal (Zuckerman, 1979). High scores have been shown to be associated with alcohol use, smoking, sexual experience, risky activities, and voluntary participation in experiments, such as those involving drugs or hypnosis. High sensation-seekers become very restless in boring situations (Zuckerman, 1979).

Something novel will initially produce arousal, but with repetition it will become familiar and will no longer arouse, be pleasant, or be rewarding. Subjects first rated strange music played for them as an experiment as unpleasant because it overaroused. With repetition, when the music had become mildly novel, it was rated as pleasant; with continued playing, when it had become familiar and boring, it was rated as unpleasant (Berlyne, 1967). Arousal theory thus explains how new motives can be produced by experience. A recent theory that also is concerned with how new motives are acquired is opponent-process theory.

Opponent-Process Theory

Opponent-process theory (Solomon & Corbit, 1974) can be viewed as a homeostatic model, like drive theory. The theory states that increases in positive emotion (pleasure) always produce negative counterreactions afterward. Similarly, increases in negative emotion (displeasure) always produce positive reactions afterward. For example, a 12-hour-old infant will suck a nursing nipple, particularly if it contains sweet fluid. If the nipple is removed after 10–20 seconds, the baby will start crying. This, according to opponent-process theory, is because a negative after-reaction inevitably follows the end of a positive experience. Because the afterreactions are always opposite to the initial reaction, they are called *opponent processes*. Opponent processes are assumed to increase in strength each time they are elicited.

How does the theory explain the formation of new motives? Consider some examples. Why do people like sauna bathing when initially it is so unpleasant? Because the initial negative reaction produces a positive opponent process that increases in strength over repeated sauna baths. Likewise in sky diving, the initial fear and terror produce a positive afterreaction that grows stronger with repeated experiences. Opponent-process theory has also been applied to drug addiction. In drug addiction the initial "rush" and positive euphoria that can be produced by drugs such as heroin also produce a negative opponent process that grows with repeated drug use. This afterreaction is responsible for a craving for the drug—the drug removes the pain, fatigue, and depression associated with the negative opponent process. Notice that the motivation for taking the drug shifts then with repeated drug taking. Initially the drug is taken to obtain positive pleasure. After repeated doses, because of the growth of the opponent process, the drug is taken to remove the negative effects of no drug. A new motive has been produced. Thus, opponent process theory explains how new motives develop.

You should realize that the theories of motivation we have discussed are not incompatible. Each focuses on a different aspect of motivation. Instinct theory deals with biologically based specific responses, such as sucking in an infant. Drive theory deals with internal states that must be maintained, mostly related to biological needs such as those for water and food. Cognitive theory deals with the motivating effects of environmental events. Thus, in the case of feeding, for example, each theory focuses on a different aspect: instinct theory on the instinctive responses that constitute feeding, drive theory on hunger, and cognitive theory on the motivating effects of food. Arousal theory attempts to incorporate both internal and external motivating forces into one dimension of arousal.

The concept of homeostasis, as we have seen, is central to both drive theory and opponent-process theory. This concept has also been central in research on hunger and thirst, two of the physiological motives studied most closely and to which we now turn.

THIRST AND HUNGER

There is no doubt that body cells require very precise control of their environment: nutrients and oxygen are necessary; temperature must be kept within a small range. From a homeostatic point of view, the motives of hunger and thirst operate by means of feedback. An internal signal cues the organism that food or water is needed, and then feeding or drinking occurs until that signal is removed. This model is more correct for thirst than for hunger, as we will see.

Thirst

There are, generally, two ways for the body to become thirsty: by direct loss of fluid (e.g., sweating) or by excess consumption of salt. In each case the body's normal balance of water and minerals (particularly sodium chloride, or salt) within and outside the cells is disturbed. This disruption sets off a chain of events that produces thirst. Thirst, in other words, is based on a homeostatic system—an internal imbalance produces a signal that leads to behavior to restore balance.

The two types of thirst work slightly differently. When fluid is lost from the body through sweating, heavy bleeding, or diarrhea, there is a loss of extracellular fluid (fluid from outside the cell). When this occurs, receptors in the heart and kidney detect changes in blood pressure (Fitzsimons, 1971), and these receptors cause the kidneys to release the hormone *renin*. Renin initiates the synthesis of a substance called *angiotensin*, which acts on some cells in the brain to create thirst. This type of thirst is called **volumetric** because a change in the volume of extracellular fluid is being detected.

The body's normal water-and-sodium balance can also be disturbed by too much consumption of salt, as you know if you have ever eaten a large quantity of pretzels or other highly salted food. Once ingested, the sodium cannot enter the cells, so to maintain the sodium-water balance outside the cells, water leaves the cells. This dehydrates the cells, and the intracellular fluid must be replaced. This type of thirst is called **osmometric** (osmosis is the process by which fluid leaves the cell).

The brain is involved in volumetric and osmometric thirst in several ways. Surgical lesions of the brain's lateral hypothalamus (see Chapter 2, page 53) cause laboratory animals to stop drinking despite their thirst. Depending on where they are placed, these lesions can disrupt either volumet-

We regulate fluid intake to maintain a balance of water and minerals in our bodies.

ric or osmometric thirst or both (Blass & Epstein, 1971; Peck, 1973; Peck & Novin, 1971).

One way the hypothalamus regulates thirst is through indirect control of the kidneys. Receptors in a particular area of the hypothalamus that sense dehydration within the cell (osmometric thirst) regulate the release of the hormone ADH (antidiuretic hormone) by the pituitary gland (Hatton, 1976). Each day a person's kidneys filter approximately 45 gallons of water, most of which is reabsorbed into the body. (If this water were not reabsorbed, it would be passed out through the bladder. The fluid loss from constant urination would cause death.) ADH causes the kidneys to reabsorb more water in response to thirst. Its importance is demonstrated by the disease *diabetes insipidus,* which is produced by the absence of ADH. Without ADH approximately 26 quarts of urine have to be excreted each day, whereas normal excretion is about 2 quarts a day.

In addition to the hypothalamus, another structure in the brain, the septum, seems to play a role in thirst. Septal lesions in laboratory animals increase water intake (Blass, Nussbaum, & Hanson, 1974). So it appears that normally the septum helps to inhibit thirst.

In an animal with normal kidneys, volumetric and osmometric thirst generally work together. Between drinks, the body both retains salt and loses water through breathing, sweating, and urination. The loss of extracellular fluid makes the sodium concentration of the fluid higher, drawing water from inside the cells and producing osmometric thirst. A drink of water returns all of the fluid compartments to normal.

Hunger

Hunger is a more complicated motive than thirst. There are no cases of water addiction, but there are many cases of "food addiction," or obesity. There are also cases of self-starvation (anorexia nervosa), while no comparable cases of self-deprivation of water exist. Also, in many ways less is known about the brain mechanisms controlling hunger than about the mechanisms controlling thirst.

BRAIN MECHANISMS UNDERLYING HUNGER. In 1951 Anand and Brobeck established that surgical lesions made on both sides of the lateral hypothalamus (*LH lesions,* for short) caused rats and cats to stop eating and to die of starvation. Lesions in another part of the hypothalamus, the region of the ventromedial nucleus *(VMH lesions)* caused rats to overeat and become obese (see Figure 12–7). These findings led to a theory that the lateral hypothalamus was a hunger center and so LH lesions destroyed hunger and that the ventromedial hypothalamus was a satiety center and so VMH lesions destroyed the capacity to stop eating. Thus a VMH tumor could cause obesity in humans.

Subsequent research, however, has cast doubt on this theory. For one thing, LH lesions have shown effects other than causing rats to stop eating. Rats with LH lesions display a syndrome called *sensory neglect.* The rats ignore all stimuli, not just food. On the first day following an LH lesion, rats ignore pins stuck in them, the scent of ammonia and shaving lotion (unless the fluids are placed directly on their noses), and various visual stimuli (Marshall & Teitelbaum, 1974). Some investigators believe that the LH rats'

FIGURE 12–7
Effects of Lesioning in the VMH of a Rat

Lesioning in the ventromedial hypothalamus caused this rat to overeat and gain weight. It weighs 1,080 grams; a normal rat of the same age weighs 350 grams.

failure to eat is actually the result of sensory neglect—the food is simply ignored. Gradually, the rats recover from sensory neglect and at the same time feeding also recovers.

The effects of VMH lesions have also been a matter of debate. One hypothesis (Powley, 1977) is that VMH lesions exaggerate the body's initial responses of digestion, including the release of the hormone insulin. The excess insulin triggers overeating. Studies show that when extra insulin is administered to normal-weight animals, they overeat.

VMH lesions do not cause overeating if the vagus nerve is also cut. The vagus nerve has connections to the stomach and intestinal tract as well as the heart and other organs. This finding makes it appear that VMH lesions somehow affect the operation of the vagus nerve to produce more eating.

It is not known exactly how VMH and LH lesions produce the effects they do. We do know that somehow the hypothalamus is important. We also know that other areas of the brain and other hormones and organs also play a role in feeding. The intestinal tract releases several peptide hormones into the blood that affect feeding. At least two of them, bombesin and cholecystokinen (CCK) suppress eating behavior in animals when injected into the brain. So these gut hormones play some role in feeding. Normally when food enters the intestine, CCK is released and contributes to a feeling of satiety, and thus the cessation of eating.

THE ROLE OF THE LIVER. The liver also plays an important role in hunger. The independent roles of the liver and the brain can be examined by injecting insulin, which induces hunger, and then injecting nutrients such as fructose, which can be used by either the brain or the liver. Fructose, a form of sugar, cannot enter the brain because of the blood-brain barrier (described in Chapter 2). So the brain will still be "hungry" after fructose injections. But an animal given fructose after an insulin injection does not eat, indicating that receptors in the liver respond to the fructose and inhibit hunger. In contrast, an injection of a keto acid, a nutrient usable by the brain and not by the liver, does not halt eating after an insulin injection (Friedman et al., 1976; Stricker et al., 1976). These data show the liver's role in regulating food consumption. Liver diseases such as hepatitis may decrease appetite because the liver is not responding normally and so hunger signals are not being given.

WHAT IS REGULATED? Although we do not know exactly how the brain and other organs control hunger and feeding, we have come closer to understanding what is being regulated, i.e., what internal state is being maintained at a constant level (homeostasis). Recent data suggest that what is regulated is how large the fat cells become. We will trace the research leading to this conclusion.

The earliest research on the homeostatic regulation of hunger focused on the stomach since common sense suggests that an empty stomach triggers hunger and a full stomach inhibits hunger. Surprisingly, however, this is incorrect. People whose stomachs have been surgically removed still feel hunger (Ingelfinger, 1944). Also, animals fed a low-calorie diet eat *more* to maintain a relatively constant weight (Harte, Travers, & Savich, 1948). If each rat stopped eating when its stomach was full, it would eat the same amount of food, that necessary to fill its stomach, regardless of how many calories the food contained. The fact that animals eat more of low-calorie food to maintain constant weight suggests that the body somehow regulates calorie intake, not the amount of food (Adolph, 1947). An animal's stable weight is sometimes referred to as its *set point* (e.g., Keesey et al., 1976). Animals maintain their weight at their natural set point—if they are force-fed, they get fatter, but when the force-feeding stops, their weight returns to the set point. If they are deprived of food, they lose weight, but when given food, they regain weight to their set point. How do the animals keep themselves to a natural set point? There are basically three principal sources of food energy: glucose (sugar), lipids (fats), and amino acids (protein). Each source has been suggested as the substance whose regulation determines an animal's set point.

Glucostatic theory states that the level of blood sugar (glucose) may be the factor regulated to control consumption. It is true that a fall in blood glucose, brought about by an injection of insulin, produces hunger (Morgan & Morgan, 1940), whereas an injection of glucagon, which raises blood glucose, creates satiety (Mayer, 1955). Yet diabetics whose body cells cannot utilize blood sugar can have very high glucose levels and still feel hungry. Thus it seems that if glucose is regulated, it must be the extent to which it can be used that is controlled, a hypothesis suggested by Jean Mayer in 1955.

Aminostatic theory holds that amino acids are regulated. A high-protein meal satiates even though it results in a rather low blood-sugar level. (High-protein diets take advantage of this fact.) However, regulation of amino acids does not seem to be critical in food intake. The blood's amino acid level can be low without producing hunger, as in patients with hepatitis (Kassil, Ugolev, & Chernigovskii, 1970).

Lipostatic theory states that fat deposits are regulated. Any calories you consume above the level you need for your activities are converted to fat, whether you eat them as fat, protein, or carbohydrates. If you don't eat for a while and need calories for energy, your fat reserves are broken down and used. Since animals maintain their body weight at a relatively constant level and since changes in weight represent changes in fat deposits, fat deposits are logically involved in the maintenance of the set point. Long-term regulation of food intake does indeed involve regulation of fat deposits (Liebelt, Bordelon, & Liebelt, 1973).

Researchers now believe that fat-cell size is normally maintained at a constant level to regulate weight in normal people. In some obese people the normal signals may be disrupted because obese people tend to have fat cells that are 2 to 2½ times larger than normal. And if obese people are reduced to normal weight, their fat cells are not normal—they become tiny, so the caloric needs of the formerly obese are not normal, that is, they need 25 percent fewer calories to maintain body weight. They have low pulse rates and low blood pressure, and the women do not menstruate. They complain of being cold and are obsessed with food. These are also characteristics of people with anorexia nervosa, a disorder marked by loss of weight due to self-starvation (see Chapter 10, page 375). These findings suggest that the obese may have a naturally higher set point than normal-weight people (Nisbett, 1972); when they are at so-called normal weight, they are actually considerably below weight.

If indeed different people have different set points, the obese may be fighting a losing battle when they attempt to lose weight. And the skinny will have an equally difficult battle to gain weight. It is always difficult to rule out environmental influences with human data. However, the strong association between obesity in parents and their children make it appear likely that there is an hereditary influence on overweight. In a well-known study, Davenport (1923) found that in a sample of 37 children with very obese parents none were thin, and at least one third were very obese. In contrast, of 51 children of slim parents, none were of greater than average weight, and the great majority were themselves thin. A recent study of adopted children found a strong relation between the weight of adopted children and their biological parents, and no relation between the weight of adopters and their adoptive parents (Stunkard et al., 1986). This suggests an important genetic influence in determining human obesity.

The lesions in the hypothalamus we discussed above may affect the set point—VMH lesions may raise the set point and LH lesions lower it (Powley & Keesey, 1970). Consistent with this notion, VMH rats do not gain weight forever; they maintain body weight at a new, higher point after lesions. Also, LH rats do not always fail to eat. Animals reduced in body weight prior to LH lesions start eating immediately, perhaps because they are already at a new, low set point (Powley & Keesey, 1970).

OTHER FACTORS AFFECTING FEEDING AND BODY WEIGHT. A great number of factors other than the regulation of fat cells are involved in hunger and feeding; stress is one. Clinical investigations indicate that some obese people overeat when frustrated or tense or to reduce loneliness or boredom (Crisp, 1970; Mayer, 1968). And some studies have found that obese people

Recent data suggest there is a strong genetic influence on obesity. Adopted children's weights are strongly related to their biological parents' weights and not related to the weight of their adoptive parents (Stunkard et al., 1986).

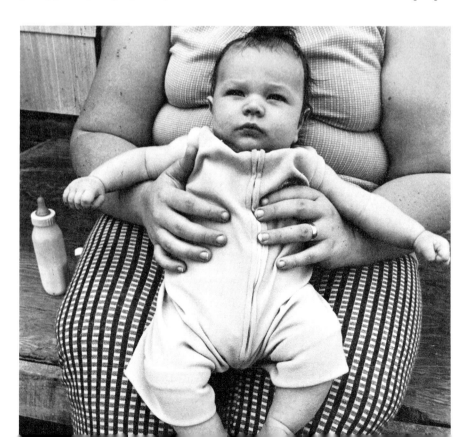

tend to eat slightly more when they are anxious (Herman & Polivy, 1975; Schachter, Goldman, & Gordon, 1968). In one study with rats, a mild and apparently not painful pinch of the tail six times a day caused daily caloric intake to increase 129 percent compared to the intake of unpinched control rats given access to the same food (Rowland & Antelman, 1976). These investigators suggest that stress produces a hyper-responsivity to environmental stimuli. Stress or arousal in general may make external cues such as food more noticeable (Rodin, 1981).

A second factor is that the more palatable the food, the more food is eaten. In our society, availability of a large variety of highly palatable food makes weight regulation difficult. Rats maintain normal weight on a lab chow diet, but they become obese when offered sausage, bananas, cake, cereal, and canned pet food (Stephens, 1980). Preferences for highly caloric food can contribute to overeating. We naturally prefer foods high in fat and foods that are sweet, and these foods are usually high in calories. In addition to the effect of palatability on the amount eaten, the greater the variety of different foods, the more total food is eaten. This may be because satiation occurs to particular tastes. If rats are given four different flavors of the same food, they will eat up to 270 percent more than if they are offered only one flavor (LeMagnen, 1956). Some diet plans borrow this information. When intake is restricted to particular foods, such as only grapes, satiety to taste will reduce consumption.

Eating can also occur just as a learned habit. Many habits, such as eating three meals a day at regular times, may interfere with regulatory mechanisms. Animals maintain a relatively constant weight by regulating the frequency of their meals (LeMagnen, 1956). Eating three times a day means intake must be regulated by the size of the meals rather than their frequency, and this may run counter to our nature. Animals trained to eat in a particular situation at a particular time of day will continue to do so from force of habit even if they are satiated (Capaldi & Myers, 1978). In general, eating can become associated with cues such as time of day or the appearance of a particular room. This is why many diet planners suggest that people record when and what they eat so that they can pay attention to their eating habits. Many diet planners also suggest that people avoid eating when they are engaged in something else such as watching TV, so that eating is not purely automatic. Overweight people tend to eat fewer meals and more food per meal than normal-weight people. This is a bad habit for weight control because one meal a day, as opposed to three or four, has different effects on the body's metabolism when the same number of calories is consumed. Most important, fat synthesis increases when calories are ingested in one large meal instead of several smaller ones (Bray, 1972). Developing the habit of spreading food over a number of meals instead of concentrating it in one large meal might aid in weight control.

Unfortunately, we have very little understanding of the physiological bases of these various factors and how they interact with each other and with the need for food to affect feeding. We do know that people have great difficulty maintaining normal weight, and perhaps this is not surprising given the many factors that produce eating. In "Research Frontier: Obesity and Dieting," we discuss one very interesting aspect of weight control currently being investigated.

RESEARCH FRONTIER

Obesity and Dieting

Exercise uses additional calories and also increases metabolic rate for hours afterward. This increase in metabolic rate also uses calories and can help counteract the decrease in metabolic rate that accompanies dieting.

Dieters often fight a losing battle. Despite the best intentions, people have difficulty sticking with a diet, and even if they lost weight successfully, they often have great difficulty keeping the weight off. Why is this? One reason is that it seems harder and harder to lose weight as a diet progresses. The second five pounds are much harder to lose than the first. And when a diet is over, it seems the weight comes back in no time. These differences in speed of weight loss and gain are not in the dieter's imagination. They are consistent with known changes in metabolic rate that operate to slow weight loss and promote regain. Energy expenditure can be divided into roughly three categories: basal metabolism (calories expended at rest or when fasting), the additional calories expended to support sedentary activity and metabolism of food, and the additional calories used in exercise. In most individuals, the largest portion of calories are used in the first two categories, with exercise using the least. Individuals at rest vary in basal metabolism and in the number of calories they utilize per day by as much as 100 to 500 (Wooley, Wooley, & Dyrenforth, 1979). Most people are aware of these differences in metabolic rate and are aware that these can be responsible for differences in weight among people. What you may not be aware of is that dieting reduces metabolic rate by from 15 to 30 percent and this can completely counteract the effects of reduced intake (Craddock, 1979). When food intake is restricted, it appears that the body responds defensively by lowering metabolic rate. As a result the rate of weight loss will decrease as dieting continues. In one study with humans (Jeffrey, Wing, & Stinkard, 1978), the amount lost on a fixed diet in successive four-week intervals was 6.3 pounds, 3.6 pounds, 2.1 pounds, and 1.7 pounds. Ultimately, as dieting continues, weight loss will be stopped by adaptive changes in energy expenditure induced by the restricted diet itself (Apfelbaum, Bostsarron, & Lacatis, 1971). If a person goes on and off a diet, metabolic rate falls more rapidly with each successive diet, and the return to pre-diet metabolism takes longer. Unfortunately, this means weight is lost more slowly with each diet and regained more rapidly afterward (Wooley et al., 1979). The enhanced rate of weight gain after a diet occurs because the reduced metabolic rate produced by dieting appears to persist after the fast is ended. In one study, rats starved to 20 percent below normal weight gained 29.6 grams during a period of refeeding, when they ate less than controls who only gained 1.6 grams, an 18-fold gain in efficiency (Boyle, Storlein, & Keesey, 1978). Also, metabolic changes associated with dieting predispose the system to excess storage of fat. One study with rats found that following deprivation and refeeding, they had 30–50 percent more adipose tissue than at baseline (Szepesi, 1978).

This does not mean dieting is hopeless. Increased exercise can help compensate for the decreased metabolic rate produced by dieting. Exercise not only uses calories but also accelerates the metabolic rate for hours afterward (Thompson et al., 1982).

SEXUAL MOTIVATION

Sexual motivation differs from hunger and thirst in many ways. If people do not eat or drink, they die; but however strong the urge, no one has ever died from lack of sex. Although sexual behavior and reproduction must occur if the species is to continue to exist, sex is not essential for any individual's survival. So sexual motivation may follow different laws from hunger and thirst (Beach, 1956). A second difference is that sexual behavior uses energy; eating and drinking restore needed resources. Thus the urge for sexual activity is not a homeostatic motive. A third difference is that sexual behavior does not appear to be strongly affected by deprivation. Immediately following sexual activity, there is a period when further sexual behavior will not occur; then sexual activity increases slightly with lengthening time without sex (Beach & Jordan, 1956). However, this effect is not nearly so strong or so clear as the effects of deprivation of food and water on eating and drinking. Last, each of us is sexually attracted to either males or females or, in the case of bisexuals, both. Thus there are important differences in the object of sexual desire.

In this section we will consider the various internal and external factors that affect sexual behavior and what determines each individual's feelings of maleness or femaleness. Information about sexual behavior is difficult to obtain because sex usually occurs in private. This is a serious handicap to researchers, but two notable scientists, William Masters and Virginia Johnson (1966), have observed human sexual behavior in a laboratory setting and provided a detailed description of the physiological sexual responses of men and women. Apart from their work, most information about human sexual behavior has come from questionnaires and interviews.

Questionnaire and Interview Data

The most comprehensive scientific survey ever undertaken on sexuality was conducted by Alfred Kinsey and his associates at Indiana University. Its results constitute the two-volume Kinsey report, *Sexual Behavior in the Human Male* (Kinsey, Pomeroy, & Martin, 1948) and *Sexual Behavior in the Human Female* (Kinsey et al., 1953), for which more than 5,300 American white males and 5,900 American white females were interviewed. (The results for blacks were not published because the sample was unrepresentative.)

The Kinsey report caused a stir because its findings proved surprising. The subjects reported much greater frequency and variety of sexual activities than had been expected. For example, 90 percent of males and 50 percent of females had engaged in premarital sex. The total orgasms reported per week were higher than generally expected (see Figure 12–8). More than 40 percent of college-educated couples indulged in cunnilingus (oral stimulation of the female genitals) and fellatio (oral stimulation of the penis). One-third of the males reported having experienced at least one orgasm with another male at some time past puberty. Kinsey also found that in general a man's first orgasm was brought on by solitary sex—spontaneous emission or masturbation—whereas a woman's first orgasm usually occurred with a partner. Masturbation was practiced earlier and more often by men than by women.

These findings were drawn from respondents in the 1940s and 1950s. Have people changed? Since the time of the Kinsey reports, two other large-

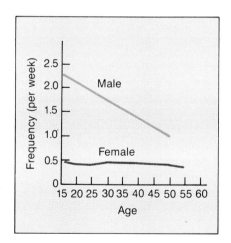

FIGURE 12–8
Kinsey Statistics

This graph shows the total number of orgasms per week from any source for single males and single females as a function of age, as described in the original Kinsey report.

Source: Kinsey et al., 1953.

scale sex surveys were done that provide us with more recent information. One was commissioned by the Playboy Foundation with the primary aim of updating Kinsey's data, and the results were published in a series of articles in *Playboy* magazine and subsequently in *Sexual Behavior in the 1970s* (Hunt, 1975). Hunt's sample of 982 males and 1,044 females was obtained by random selection from telephone book listings in 24 American cities. Twenty percent of those contacted actually provided data. Another study by two sociologists, Philip Blumstein and Pepper Schwartz (1976) distributed questionnaires to about 11,000 couples, with a return rate of about 55 percent. This study included 4,314 heterosexual couples, 969 gay male couples, and 788 lesbian couples. The study was published in a book, *American Couples* (1983). Both these recent studies can be criticized for not having representative samples, yet they provide the best data available on sexual practices. Hunt's study found that two-thirds of women had engaged in premarital intercourse, a significant increase over the number reported by Kinsey. Today premarital intercourse occurs on the average at an earlier age and is more frequent among teenagers than it was three decades ago. Another recent survey (Zelnick & Kanter, 1977) found that by age nineteen, 49 percent of unmarried white females and 84 percent of black females have engaged in intercourse. The comparable figure for white females in the Kinsey report was 19 percent. In Kinsey's time and today, college-educated men and women marry later and start their coital experiences later than those with less education. But the difference between the age at which college-educated and non-college-educated people first experience intercourse has decreased from about five years to about two years (Gebhard & Johnson, 1979).

Reading these statistics, you will tend to compare yourself to averages, but any average is not necessarily right, desirable, or relevant to you. You should realize also that the range of frequencies for most of these behaviors is wide. Consider the incidence of premarital intercourse for the college-educated. It varies from 28 to 82 percent for men and from 29 to 86 percent for women, depending on the year in college (intercourse is more frequent in later years) and the school sampled.

Sexual intercourse in married couples is now more frequent. Kinsey reported that married couples around 20 years old averaged intercourse about three times a week. A 1974 survey (Westoff, 1974) put the incidence at about 3.5 times a week at that age. Data from various years are shown in Figure 12–9. It is not clear why sexual intercourse among married couples is now more frequent, although less fear of pregnancy because of the availability of the birth-control pill may be involved. Greater openness toward sexual behavior also could be a factor (Luria & Rose, 1979).

Data on frequency of extramarital sex are contradictory for men. Kinsey (1948, 1953) estimated that half of all married men and 26 percent of married women had had extramarital coitus. Hunt's (1975) report showed about the same percentages, while Blumstein and Schwartz (1983) found that only 26 percent of husbands and 21 percent of wives had any form of extramarital involvement. One reason for the discrepancies in the data for men may be the reluctance of many to admit to extramarital relations.

As you can see, some patterns of sexual behavior have remained stable since the publication of the Kinsey report, while others have changed. The changes suggest that societal influences may be important in determining

FIGURE 12–9
Frequency of Intercourse

This graph shows the average frequency of intercourse in the four weeks before interview for married white American women by age.

Source: Trussell & Westoff, 1980.

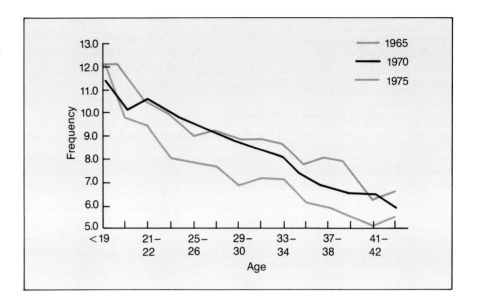

human sexual behavior. This conclusion is supported strongly by comparisons across cultures.

Cross-Cultural Comparisons

Studies of cultures other than our own show a wide variety of sexual behavior. In a classic inquiry, Ford and Beach (1951) compared practices in 190 societies, some of them preliterate. The most frequent sexual behavior across the world is heterosexual intercourse, but it varies tremendously in technique and preferred circumstances. Some cultures regard intercourse during the day as dangerous; others prefer it. Most groups seek privacy, but there are exceptions. Different positions are favored by different societies. The Kamasutra, a Hindu love manual written in the eighth century, lists more than 35 positions, with names such as "Union of the Elephant with Its Mates." In most societies the preferred position is man on top of woman, but some favor others. Generally each culture prefers only one or two positions (Gebhard, 1971).

Frequency of intercourse varies widely as well. Among the Dani of New Guinea, both men and women observe a four-to-six-year period of sexual abstinence after the birth of a child, and it does not appear that other sexual behavior, such as masturbation, occurs in the meantime (Heider, 1976). Couples do not begin sexual intercourse until two years after marriage, and weddings take place only every four to six years. Premarital and extramarital sex are rare. As you might expect, the birth rate among the Dani is low, barely achieving replacement. In contrast, in the Kinsey report (1948) some young husbands reported an average of 3.5 coital episodes within 24 hours.

Large cultural differences exist in what is considered sexually desirable. The female breast ranks as an important attraction in our society, whereas in many cultures it has no particular sexual significance. In at least one culture, black gums are highly favored (Ford & Beach, 1951). In the United

States thin women are viewed as desirable, while in parts of Africa unmarried women are placed in "fattening huts" where they are given high-calorie food to gain weight and increase their attractiveness (Gregersen, 1983). Although the effects of culture and learning modify expression of the sexual drive, the underlying basis for sexual motivation is, of course, biological. The primary biological influence is believed to be hormonal.

Hormones and Sexual Behavior

The important sex hormones are *estrogens,* the "female" sex hormones, and *testosterone* and *androgens,* the "male" sex hormones. Males and females produce both types of hormones, but the male has a much higher percentage of testosterone and androgen than the female.

Sex hormones have two basic effects on the body: organizational and activational. Organizational effects refer to the effects of hormones on tissue development and differentiation. In humans the sex chromosomes—female XX and male XY—determine whether the fetus's sex glands will develop into testes (male) or ovaries (female). And secretion of sex hormones by the fetus's sex glands determines whether the fetus's external genitalia will be male or female. At puberty, the increased secretion of sex hormones causes development of the secondary sex characteristics (see Chapter 10, page 362).

Activational effects refer to the effects of sex hormones in directing sexual behavior. Animals exhibit stereotyped sexual behaviors that differ for male and female. A female rat given androgen will increase mounting of male rats and will reject advances from males. The effects are greater if the female is given androgen at birth (Harris & Levine, 1965). Sex hormones produce some activational effects in humans, but these effects are much weaker than in other animals. Also, whereas in other animals each sex is activated by the hormones appropriate to it, in humans androgen underlies sex drive in both men and women.

In men, androgen can be removed by castration (removal of the testes), which eliminates erection and ejaculation in most, but not all, cases. Some castrated men lose their potency immediately, and a gradual decline occurs in others (Ford & Beach, 1951). Androgen seems to have an all-or-none effect. If there is enough androgen, men are potent and fertile; otherwise they are not. Beyond the critical level, extra androgen seems to have no effect on potency (Money & Ehrhardt, 1972).

Androgen seems to affect sexual behavior in women in the same direction as in men. Its removal appears to weaken a female's sex drive (Waxenberg, Drellich, & Sutherland, 1959), and administration of extra androgen appears to increase it (Money & Ehrhardt, 1972). But removal of estrogen does not lessen a woman's sex drive (Money & Ehrhardt, 1972). For this reason androgen has been called the libido hormone for both sexes in humans. However, keep in mind that the relationship between hormones and sexual behavior in humans is not as strong or as direct as it is in other animals.

Situational and External Factors

Thus far we have seen that both cultural and physiological forces play a part in sexual behavior. Now we look at a variety of other factors affecting sexual

Some species, including swans, pair for life.

arousal. These situational and external factors are probably more important for humans than the activational effects of hormones.

As you might expect, one critical factor for sexual behavior is the availability of a partner. Psychologists do not understand exactly what underlies sexual attraction, why some people have the right chemistry and others do not. One hypothesis concerns smell. Certain smells convey sexual readiness for many animals, and there is evidence that smells play a strong part in sexual attraction between insects (Hassett, 1978). The possible role of smell in both animal and human sexual activity is being investigated.

Among many animals, a new partner proves arousing. After intercourse with one partner, introduction of another can renew activity. This is called the *Coolidge effect,* and the story behind the name, which may or may not be true, goes as follows: Calvin Coolidge and his wife were visting a farm when Mrs. Coolidge asked the farmer whether the continual sexual activity of the flock of hens was really the work of just one rooster. The reply was yes. "You might point that out to Mr. Coolidge," she said. Mr. Coolidge then asked the farmer whether a different hen was involved each time. The answer again was yes. "You might point that out to Mrs. Coolidge," he said. The Coolidge effect has been demonstrated in a number of animals such as guinea pigs, monkeys, and bulls, and also in humans. A new partner does not seem as arousing to women as to men (Masters, Johnson, & Kolodny, 1985). The difference may be culturally learned since women traditionally have been expected to be more monogamous than men, or it may be biologically determined.

Particular stimuli—such as romantic music, a dimly lit private place, erotic photographs—can also be important for some people. The list of desirable circumstances and features varies considerably from person to person and, as we have seen, from culture to culture. In the extreme, a person can develop a sexual *fetish,* in which an ordinary object such as a shoe abnormally triggers arousal, as will be further discussed in Chapter 15.

One topic we have omitted from our list of physiological, situational, and external arousal factors is emotion, which in all types of animals (including humans) can override hormones, the Coolidge effect, and other factors. Species such as swans and geese pair for life (Dewsbury, 1978). For human relationships, love and jealousy, two topics not well understood by psychologists, play an essential role, a topic to which we will return to Chapter 17.

Gender Identity

Males and females have different chromosomes, different hormonal balances, different reproductive systems, and distinct physical appearances. Furthermore, the rearing that males and females receive is often quite different. Boys and girls are taught to behave in ways considered appropriate to their sex. An important issue in the study of sexuality is the origin of a boy's or girl's *gender identity,* the private conviction of a male or female sexual identity. To what extent is a boy's masculine behavior and masculine identity a product of his biological makeup? To what extent does the child's rearing and early developmental experience determine his gender identity?

There is no simple answer to this question. Evidence, however, suggests that rearing and upbringing play a very important role in the development of gender identity. John Money and Anke A. Ehrhardt (1972) have done a great deal of research on the effects of social influence and gender identity. One of their case studies involved identical twin boys who were given a normal upbringing for the first 7 months of their lives (Money & Ehrhardt, 1972). At 7 months, one of the twins suffered a tragic accident. During surgery for circumcision, a device malfunctioned and his penis was severed. The physicians advised the parents to rear the injured boy as a girl, and when the child was 17 months old, doctors performed surgery to give him the genital anatomy of a female. Money and Ehrhardt followed the development of the two children until they reached puberty. During this time, the parents followed their doctor's advice and treated the children differently, one as a boy and one as a girl. The effects of this rearing on the injured child's behavior was quite strong. For example, when the boy-turned-girl was four and a half, her mother reported:

> She likes for me to wipe her face. She doesn't like to be dirty, and yet my son is quite different. I can't wash his face for anything. . . . She seems to be daintier. Maybe it's because I encourage it. . . . One thing that really amazes me is that she is so feminine. I've never seen a little girl so neat and tidy as she can be when she wants to be. . . . She is very proud of herself, when she puts on a new dress or I set her hair. (1972, pp. 119–120)

This dramatic case demonstrates that masculine or feminine behaviors can develop from the same set of genes, depending on upbringing. Until the surgery performed at 17 months, the two children shared identical biological characteristics. From that point on, they differed only in their hormonal balance. (The injured child was administered dosages of female hormones as a part of the sex-change operation.)

Money and Ehrhardt also reported several case studies involving hermaphrodites. A *hermaphrodite's* genital structure is ambiguous. That is, from birth onward, a hermaphrodite possesses a combination of male and female genitals. In Money and Ehrhardt's (1972) cases, hermaphrodite children consistently identified with the gender in which they were reared, even if that identity did not match their chromosomes, their hormonal balance, or their appearance. For example, one hermaphrodite had female XX chromosomes, ovaries, female sex hormones, and breasts that appeared at puberty. Despite all of these female characteristics, the hermaphrodite had a masculine gender identity. His parents had raised him as a boy because at birth he also had a small penis.

All the evidence, however, does not support the thesis that gender identity is purely a product of upbringing. Some research, for example, suggests that hormones and hormonal balance can contribute to gender identity. When pregnant rhesus monkeys were injected with the male sex hormone testosterone, their female offspring developed external genitals and social behavior that closely resembled that of the male rhesus monkey (Young, Goy & Phoenix, 1964). Similar effects have been observed in humans. Money and Ehrhardt (1972) investigated several case studies of women who were administered a drug similar to testosterone during their pregnancy to prevent miscarriage. Some of these women gave birth to children who had the internal reproductive systems of females but the external appearance of males. (This form of ambiguous sexual appearance is referred

Dr. Richard Raskind (top) became Dr. Renée Richards (bottom) after a sex-change operation. This sex-change led to a court case to determine if Dr. Richards could play in women's tennis matches. The judge ruled she can; she is legally a female.

to as *pseudohermaphroditism.*) Money and Ehrhardt followed the development of these children after surgery was performed to modify their external male appearance to conform to their internal female physiology. Despite the surgery and their upbringing, these girls exhibited many more masculine behavioral traits than their sisters and female peers.

Another set of cases involving pseudohermaphroditism occurred in the Dominican Republic (Imperato-McGinley et al., 1974). The males were born with male XY chromosomes and testes, but with female genitalia. They were raised as females. At puberty, however, their voices deepened, their muscle mass increased, and no breasts appeared. The researchers reported that at puberty, the gender identity of these children changed from female to male. They attributed this change to the influence of hormones.

The Dominican study has caused some controversy, however. Money and Ehrhardt (1972) suggest that these children were not given a strictly female upbringing. The peculiarity of their genitals at birth may have affected how their parents treated them. Thus, their ability to change gender identity at puberty could have resulted from the effects of rearing in addition to the influence of hormones.

A third form of gender reversal involves *transsexuals,* individuals whose gender identity contradicts their physiology. Many transsexuals undergo sex change operations. A famous case involved Dr. Richard Raskind, who became Dr. Renée Richards. Transsexualism has been less common in women than in men, but the number of women seeking to change their sex has been increasing (Pauly, 1974). The origins of transsexualism, like those of earlier cases involving gender reversal, are not clear. In transsexuals chromosome structure and hormone levels are not unusual. Money and Ehrhardt (1972) believe that transsexualism occurs as a result of ambiguous rearing, a pattern of social influence that leads these people to feel that their sexual physiology must be changed.

Homosexuality

In all known cultures, heterosexuality is the most common sexual preference, although homosexuality seems to exist in all cultures as well. Performing homosexual acts should be distinguished from having a homosexual identity. In a Melanesian culture that Davenport (1965) called East Bay to protect the inhabitants, homosexual acts are expected of males prior to marriage, but heterosexuality is the norm after marriage. Thus, despite participation in homosexual acts, the males do not develop a homosexual identity.

Throughout history, different cultures have reacted differently to homosexuality. In ancient Greece, it was an accepted part of male life. About two-thirds of twentieth-century societies seem to approve of some homosexuality, at least tacitly (Ford & Beach, 1951). In the early 1950s the Kinsey report estimated that 4 percent of males and 2 to 3 percent of females were exclusively homosexual throughout adulthood, and these figures seem to be accurate today as well (Paul et al., 1982).

The origins of homosexuality are not well understood. Some studies have shown higher estrogen or lower testosterone levels in homosexual men than in heterosexual men, but this is not replicable (Tourney, 1980). Many researchers believe that either an excess or deficiency in prenatal hormones

Throughout history different cultures have reacted differently to homosexuality. In the United States, homosexuality is expressed more openly now than in past eras.

may be important in producing homosexuality. In animals, treatments with hormones prenatally can lead to male or female homosexual behavior patterns (Hutchison, 1978). And there is some evidence for an effect in humans, but only in cases of hermaphroditism (cases where prenatal hormones produce ambiguous sexual features) (Money & Schwartz, 1977). Learning could also be involved in the development of homosexuality. Either pleasant homosexual experiences or unpleasant heterosexual experiences could produce tendencies toward homosexuality. Some researchers believe that "tomboyish" girls and "sissy" boys are more likely to become homosexual (Money & Russo, 1979), but there is as yet no firm evidence for this hypothesis.

Bisexuality

Kinsey and his colleagues (Kinsey, Pomeroy, & Martin, 1948) developed a seven-point scale to describe the inner psychological feelings and overt sexual experience of people (see Table 12–2). Ratings of 2, 3, or 4 on this scale indicate bisexuality. Very little research has been done on bisexuality. Some bisexuals have long-term unitary relationships, a homosexual one followed by a heterosexual one. Other bisexuals are concurrently involved with both a man and a woman. A common reason given by women bisexuals for their bisexuality is that they have different emotional needs, some of which are best met by women and some best met by men (Blumstein & Schwartz, 1976).

NEED FOR ACHIEVEMENT

Apart from hunger, thirst, and other biologically based motives present in all people, there are motives that some people do not share, that are not present in all cultures, and that result from learning. The most extensively studied of these is the achievement motive, known as the **need for achievement.** It was first defined by Henry Murray in 1938 as the desire

> To accomplish something difficult. To master, manipulate, or organize physical objects, human beings, or ideas. To do this as rapidly and as independently as possible. To overcome obstacles and attain a high standard. To excel one's self. To rival and surpass others. To increase self-regard by the successful exercise of talent. (p. 164)

Murray developed the **Thematic Apperception Test,** or **TAT,** to measure need for achievement, and McClelland and his colleagues refined the test for use as a research tool (McClelland et al., 1953). In this test a subject is asked to write stories about ambiguous pictures (see Figure 12–10). Experimenters then analyze the stories to find indications of the achievement motive. There is some difficulty obtaining consistent results, and controversy has arisen about whether this means the test is not useful (Atkinson & Raynor, 1974; Entwisle, 1972). Attempts to create an objective test are not fully developed, and the TAT remains the major yardstick of the need for achievement.

People who score high in need for achievement on the TAT differ in a number of ways from those who score low. For example, high scorers appear better able to delay gratification (Mischel, 1961) and to attain higher

**TABLE 12–2
Kinsey's Heterosexual-Homosexual Rating Scale**

0 Exclusively heterosexual

1 Predominantly heterosexual: only incidentally homosexual

2 Predominantly heterosexual: more than incidentally homosexual

3 Equally heterosexual and homosexual

4 Predominantly homosexual: more than incidentally heterosexual

5 Predominantly homosexual: only incidentally heterosexual

6 Exclusively homosexual

Source: Adapted from Kinsey, Pomeroy, & Martin, 1948.

FIGURE 12–10
Thematic Apperception Test

This picture was used in the original research to develop a test for need for achievement. The following examples of stories elicited by the photograph reflect achievement imagery. The sections in bold type reflect the critical achievement-oriented statement.

"3. The boy is taking an examination. He is a college student. He is trying to recall a pertinent fact. He did not study this particular point enough, although he thought it might be on the examination. He is trying to recall that point. He can almost get it but not quite. It's almost on the tip of his tongue. Either he will recall it or he won't. If he recalls it, he will write it down. **If he doesn't, he will be mad.**"

"11. **The boy is thinking about a career as a doctor. He sees himself as a great surgeon performing an operation.** He has been doing minor first aid work on his injured dog, and discovers he enjoys working with medicine. He thinks he is suited for this profession and sets it as an ultimate goal in life at this moment. He has not weighed the pros and cons of his own ability and has let his goal blind him of his own inability. An adjustment which will injure him will have to be made."

"7. The boy is a student and during a boring lecture his mind is going off on a tangent, and he is daydreaming. The instructor has been talking about medieval history, and his reference to the knights of old has made the lad project himself into such a battle arrayed with armor and riding a white stallion. The boy is thinking of riding out of the castle, waving goodbye to his lady fair, **and going into the battle and accomplishing many heroic deeds.** The boy will snap out of it when the instructor starts questioning the students on various aspects of the lecture, and the boy will become frantic realizing he has not been paying attention."

Source: McClelland et al., 1953.

grades in school in courses that are essential to their long-term career goals (Raynor, 1970).

A theory of achievement motivation proposed by John Atkinson (1957, 1964) deals with the tendency to approach achievement situations where a person "knows that his performance will be evaluated (by himself or by others) in terms of some standard of excellence" (Atkinson, 1964, p. 240). Atkinson suggested that this tendency depends also, in each case, on how unpleasant it would be to fail and how pleasant it would be to succeed. This theory is one variety of the cognitive theories discussed earlier that relate motivation to expectancy and value. Atkinson suggested that succeeding represents no particular accomplishment if the task is too easy. On the other hand, success is unlikely on a very difficult task. The main point of this theory is that individuals high in need to achieve will prefer tasks of intermediate difficulty. A person low in need to achieve, in contrast, is afraid of failure. This type of person would prefer either very easy tasks (where failure is unlikely) or very difficult tasks (where it is not embarrassing to fail).

One experiment to determine if high- and low-need achievers would react to tasks in that way involved ring tossing (Atkinson & Litwin, 1960). Degree of difficulty was defined by the distance each subject chose to stand from the target stick. As you can see in Figure 12–11, high-need achievers preferred intermediate distances. Low-need achievers showed a lesser preference for intermediate distances, but they did not prefer very long or very short distances either, as had been expected. These subjects, however, were college students, among whom need for achievement is high in general, so perhaps the low-need achievers were not very low. Another explanation of the low-need achievers' performance is that other motives can account for it. Need for achievement is not the only reason people want to succeed. For example, they may desire to impress friends, in which case even low-need achievers would have some desire to achieve and so would tend to choose tasks of intermediate difficulty.

When real-life choices are measured, high-need achievers tend to choose goals of moderate difficulty, while low-need achievers tend to choose

APPLYING PSYCHOLOGY

Training the Achievement Motive

Because need for achievement is a learned motive, it should be possible to train people to acquire more of it. And because successful entrepreneurs (small-businessmen) tend to be high in achievement motivation, perhaps training small-businessmen in this way would make them more successful.

The first attempt to increase need for achievement in small-businessmen was made in India by McClelland and Winter (1969–1971). Two Indian cities were chosen to be as similar as pos-

sible, and achievement training was provided to business leaders in one city and not the other. Each businessman was given 10 or more hours of training per day for two weeks. (Training was given to small groups of 14 members or so at a location where they all stayed.) In the training the businessmen were taught how to think, talk, and act like a person high in achievement motivation. They participated, for example, in a game where they learned how to set goals of medium difficulty, how to use feedback to change their goals as necessary, and how to seek new ways of achieving their goals when necessary. At the end of the training they were asked to set specific goals for themselves as they reentered their jobs.

Business activities were monitored for several years before, during, and after the training. Measures were taken of income, profit, and amount invested. Achievement motivation training was effective in increasing the level of business activity when measured in this way. The changes were much larger for those who were in charge of a business and so had greater opportunity to change some behavior of importance than for those who worked for someone else, as would be expected. Also, training was not effective for everyone. For some trainees, it appeared that need for power—i.e., to have impact and be recognized as a success—was increased, which will not necessarily increase moderate risk taking nec-

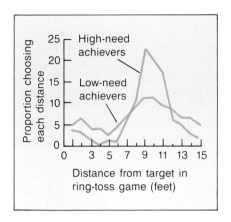

FIGURE 12–11
Testing Need for Achievement

In this experiment subjects chose how far from a stick they wished to stand in a ring-toss game. The graph shows the proportion of high-need achievers and low-need achievers who chose each distance. As you can see, high-need achievers chose intermediate distances over very near or very far distances to a greater extent than did low-need achievers.

Source: Atkinson & Litwin, 1960.

goals that are too easy or too difficult. High-need achievers are more realistic about career goals, setting goals that are neither too easy nor too difficult for their abilities, while low-need achievers tend to choose career goals either too easy or too difficult for their abilities (Mahone, 1960; Morris, 1966).

High-need achievers may prefer tasks of intermediate difficulty because the tasks inform them about their own capacities (Weiner & Kukla, 1970). When a task is very difficult, failure is usually attributed to that; when it is easy, success is laid to that. Only in tasks of intermediate difficulty may failure or success be attributed to the individual's abilities and effort. A recent study supported this idea. Subjects could choose between easy tasks that provided information about their capacities and those of intermediate difficulty that did not. The subjects could opt for a task at which, they were told, 90 percent of high-ability subjects and 60 percent of low-ability subjects succeeded or for one at which 52 percent of the high-ability and 48 percent of the low-ability subjects succeeded. Both high- and low-need subjects preferred the easy, informative task, but the preference was stronger among high-need achievers (Trope, 1975).

A successful program for inculcating need for achievement has been given to American and Indian businessmen and male high school students (e.g., McClelland & Winter, 1969). This program involves teaching people to think and act like high-need achievers and to set specific, realistic goals for themselves. When people achieve these realistic goals, they experience the rewarding effects of succeeding, and this experience should encourage achievement-oriented behavior to increase. "Applying Psychology: Training the Achievement Motive" discusses this training program in more depth.

FIGURE 12–12
Results of Achievement Training for Minority Business People

After a group of 67 minority entrepreneurs underwent training in achievement motivation, their monthly sales, personal income, and business profits increased dramatically.

Source: Miron & McClelland, 1979.

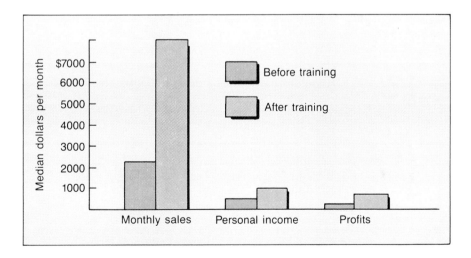

essary for improved business activity scores.

The training program has also been given to black and Hispanic businesspeople in nine different U.S. cities (Miron & McClelland, 1979). Figure 12–12 shows that monthly sales, personal income, and profits all increased significantly following training. These changes were much larger than changes in the general economy or in the economy in the regions where the training took place. Thus, it seems training in need for achievement can indeed improve the business performance of small-businesspeople.

INTERACTION OF MOTIVES

Thus far we have looked at four separate motives: hunger, thirst, sex, and the need for achievement. Behavior, however, is composed of many motives at work simultaneously. How do motives combine to produce behavior? Psychologists have not yet defined a complete answer, but we do have some principles.

Hierarchies of Motives

Clearly, some motives—such as hunger and thirst—must be satisfied before others. Recognizing this situation, researchers have proposed a variety of hierarchies of motives to describe these levels of needs. In a hierarchy of motives, those at the first level must be satisfied before those at the next, and so on. The most influential of these hierarchies, shown in Figure 12–13, was suggested by Abraham Maslow (1954). On the first level Maslow posited physiological needs, such as those for food and water. The next level is safety from crime, from fire, from extremes of heat and cold, from wild animals, and from financial disaster (prevented by buying insurance, having a savings account, etc.). On the third level are love needs, which include affection, belonging with people, and having a place in a group. Next comes esteem, the requirement for a stable, firmly based evaluation of oneself. This category embraces need for achievement, power, and self-respect. Only when all these are satisfied can the final level be reached—self-fulfillment, whether it involves being a parent, an athlete, a musician, or whatever one is suited for.

FIGURE 12–13
Maslow's Hierarchy of Needs

In Maslow's proposed hierarchy of motives, those at the first level must be satisfied before those at the next and so on.

Source: Maslow, 1943.

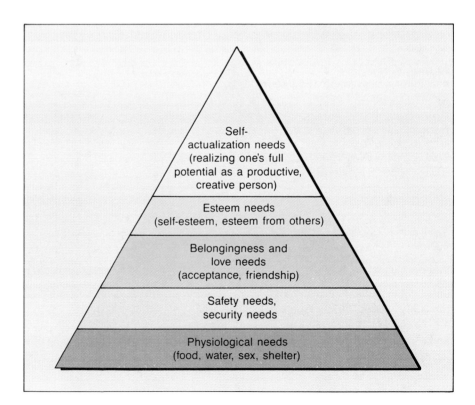

Maslow's hierarchy of motives is very useful as an organizational device, but its levels should not be considered rigid. For example, Maslow reasonably suggests that physiological needs must be satisfied before social and other learned motives. Nevertheless, people have starved to death to make a political point (as Irish Republican Army activists have done in Northern Ireland), so hunger does not always dominate other motives, as Maslow himself has pointed out (1970). Also in humans, satisfying a particular need does not reduce the need's importance, contrary to the premise of Maslow's and all of the other proposed hierarchies of motives. The opposite seems to be true: the greater the satisfaction a person has obtained with a particular need, the more important that need is to that person (Hall & Nougaim, 1968). So although some motives are more important than others, the hierarchy is not inflexible.

Reciprocal Inhibition of Motives

Recent data suggest that at a particular time almost any motive can be stronger than any other motive. Once a single motive has been activated, it seems to dominate and inhibit all other motives. Hunger can inhibit fear (Dickinson & Pearce, 1977), as is indicated by the idea that physiological needs are stronger than those for safety. Conversely, fear can inhibit hunger (Dickinson & Pearce, 1977). Motives block or interfere with one another, a concept called *reciprocal inhibition.* A fearful animal will feel less hunger under the same degree of food deprivation than one who is unafraid. The reverse is also true: a hungry animal given food will feel less fear in a frightening situation than an animal that is not hungry and given food. Which motive dominates depends in part on which is aroused first. A hungry animal will not be easy to arouse sexually. But once sexual activity has begun, thus triggering sexual motivation, it is not disturbed by increasing hunger (Sachs, 1965). Although there may be a fundamental hierarchy of motives, at any given time in a situation one particular motive can dominate all others, even if that motive would normally be relatively low in the hierarchy.

One practical implication of this pattern is that knowing a person's motivation hierarchy is quite valuable if you want to motivate him or her to do something. For example, if you want to motivate someone to donate blood, do you offer that person money? If the person is more motivated by the mere act of helping others, offering money can actually defeat the person's motivation (Upton, 1974). The issue of motive hierarchies and intrinsic motivation is particularly important in the workplace, where the motive to work is the employer's chief concern.

WORK MOTIVATION

Most adults spend a good portion of their day at work. Why do people work? One incentive is money, of course. Money enables people to buy food, shelter, and many of the enjoyable things in life. And money is a measure of status in our culture, so to some extent earning more money is a way to earn prestige. The field of *work motivation* is concerned with what motivates workers and how managers can arrange the work situation to satisfy the goals of both workers and management.

The earliest model of work motivation came from Frederick W. Taylor (1911), who began the scientific study of business management. Taylor believed it was management's job to find suitable workers for a job, train them to do the job, and then use a wage incentive system to maintain maximum productivity. Taylor's approach to work motivation was oversimplistic. He believed that workers were essentially lazy, aimless, and motivated solely by money. He also felt that workers would tolerate the boring, routine jobs of the factory for a price.

As this model was increasingly applied, problems arose. First, the relation between a worker's output and a worker's income became less direct. Mass production made factories more efficient, but the incentive system changed very little, so workers' income did not increase as much as their productivity did. As a result of this and other problems associated with the industrial setting, more and more workers joined unions to enforce their demands about pay, work safety, and job security (Steers & Porter, 1979). These developments led some to reexamine Taylor's assumptions about workers' motivation. Although money is still seen as the primary incentive for work, newer approaches stress additional motivational factors.

The human relations approach to work motivation is based on the assumption that Taylor's scientific management model failed to consider the whole person and by doing so helped produce low morale and poor performance (e.g., Mayo, 1933). Efforts in the 1940's and 50's were started to make workers feel important and part of the organization. Companies gave workers more leeway to make routine decisions regarding their own jobs and to suggest improvements to management. Many incentives were based on group, rather than individual, performance to encourage teamwork.

The human resources approach to management moves even further from "scientific management" and tries to avoid any direct manipulation of worker incentives. In the human resources approach people are viewed as self-motivated, as wanting to contribute to the job. This approach leads to efforts to make the job more meaningful and to give employees real decision-making authority.

Job Satisfaction and Work Motivation

Most approaches to work motivation assume that an employee's performance will improve according to the amount of job satisfaction or need fulfillment a job offers. If a job satisfies the worker's need to belong to a group (one of the fundamental ideas behind the human relations model), then the employee will have greater motivation to work, and productivity will improve. Jobs can also satisfy the worker's need for status and self-esteem, achievement, power, and self-fulfillment.

What factors determine job satisfaction? The basic theory of job satisfaction involves reinforcement. A worker who is given consistent and immediate reinforcement—money, praise, and other rewards—for achieving specific goals will be satisfied by the job. This theory is based, of course, on B. F. Skinner's model of reinforcement discussed in Chapter 6. The best-selling book *One Minute Manager* (Blanchard & Johnson, 1985) is essentially built on reinforcement theory. The book gives practical advice for managers in setting worker goals and delivering reinforcement.

In some individuals, so-called "workaholics," the motivation to work dominates many other motives. Because the motivation to work is really composed of many different motives, individuals who work very hard to the exclusion of other pleasures can be doing so for many different reasons.

Another important factor in job satisfaction is the degree to which a worker feels he or she is being treated equitably (Adams, 1979). If some workers are receiving less compensation for performing the same work as others, they are likely to become dissatisfied. Two-tier pay schemes, for instance, which compensate some employees at wage rates below their colleagues although all do the same work, violate a worker's sense of equity and contribute to poor morale. Equity does not mean that all employees should receive the same salary. Workers accept the notion that a worker who produces more should receive more in return. Also, a worker who has been employed longer at a job should receive more pay than one who is recently hired.

A final element in job satisfaction involves expectations. When taking on a job, people naturally develop expectations about what rewards the job will offer. They also develop beliefs about what matters most in their job performance. Any mismatch between worker expectations and real job experience will foster dissatisfaction. A bank teller might think, for instance, that personal appearance is unimportant, only to discover that bank management insists on good grooming. This conflict naturally creates resentment on both sides. To resolve a potential source of dissatisfaction, the employer should make special efforts to recruit employees who accept the job's goals and requirements and to inform them of the job's present and potential rewards.

Intrinsic Motivation

Not all approaches to work motivation assume that job satisfaction is crucial to success. The human resources approach, for example, assumes that the reverse is true; that is, if a job allows a person to perform well, then job satisfaction will naturally result.

Many studies support the view that job performance determines job satisfaction (e.g., Locke, 1979). One conclusion from these studies is that job performance and its extrinsic rewards, such as pay, are usually only indirectly related. People nevertheless perform well, despite the fact that it may take a long time for them to be rewarded for their efforts.

How do we explain the motive to perform without external or extrinsic rewards? One concept that has become increasingly important to the study of work motivation is called *intrinsic motivation,* which is the desire to do something for its own sake, to enjoy the activity without the reward. Doing something in order to receive something else is called *extrinsic motivation* (Deci, 1975).

Experiments on intrinsic motivation have produced interesting results. Counter to what many theorists, including Frederick Taylor, believed, providing extrinsic rewards to experimental subjects can actually decrease their future performance. Lepper, Greene, and Nisbett (1973) demonstrated this result in a study involving nursery school children. Three groups of children were given colored marking pens. One group was told beforehand that they would receive a "good player" award for playing with the pens. The second group was told about the reward only after their play period was over, and the third group was not offered any reward at all. A week later, each group was given the pens again, but this time none of the groups was offered any reward. Surprisingly, the group that was previously offered the extrinsic "good player" award before their play period showed the least interest of any of the groups in playing with the pens. Deci (1971) obtained similar findings with college students; those paid to solve puzzles at one dollar per puzzle subsequently showed less interest in the puzzles than unpaid students.

Initially this effect was difficult to explain because it seemed inconsistent with the general rule that rewards improve performance. One possible explanation is that people attribute their performance on a task to the extrinsic reward, if one is present. If the extrinsic reward is later removed, motivation to perform grows weaker (Lepper, Greene, & Nisbett, 1973). Also, the promise of an extrinsic reward often focuses the person's attention on merely obtaining the reward, causing other aspects of performance to deteriorate (Lepper & Greene, 1978). The process of determining to what we attribute performance on tasks is further discussed in Chapter 17.

Extrinsic rewards do not always reduce subsequent performance. Unless the task has a high amount of interest for the subject, that is, unless it is intrinsically rewarding, extrinsic rewards will foster more effort (Calder & Staw, 1975; Upton, 1974). Also, if the extrinsic reward is given for a specific level of performance, it will not interfere with later performance (Boggiano & Ruble, 1979; Karniol & Ross, 1977). In this case, the extrinsic reward provides information to the worker about the level of competence he or she needs to do the job. But giving an external reward regardless of performance provides no such information about competence and deprives the subject of this sort of satisfaction. The reduction in performance that sometimes results from offering extrinsic rewards may occur, then, because the *total* psychological reward available in the task has been lessened. Therefore, to predict an extrinsic reward's effect on performance, it is important to understand as much as possible about the individual's other sources for reward, whether they are extrinsic or not (Lepper & Greene, 1978). This also seems to be a general conclusion from the studies of work motivation discussed above. Money, an extrinsic reward, is the main reason why people work, but there are many other motives involved, too, and to maximize worker performance and satisfaction these other motives must be taken into account.

SUMMARY

1. The science of motivation is concerned with why behavior occurs. The answer to the question why often involves internal physiological determinants, for example, the physiological mechanisms of hunger and thirst can explain feeding and drinking. Drive theory emphasizes internal needs as explanations of behavior.

2. External determinants of behavior are emphasized by cognitive theory, which deals with expectancies of goals as motivating forces. Positive incentive motivation is produced by anticipating something an individual wants or likes; positive incentives are approached. Negative incentive motivation is produced by anticipating something not wanted; it produces avoidance.

3. Arousal theory suggests that people are motivated to be at the optimal level of arousal for a particular task or at a particular time of day. Depending on an individual's current arousal, it can be pleasant to have an increase or a decrease in arousal. Arousal is a state of physiological activation

produced by drives and incentives, external stimulation, surprising or novel events, and drugs.

4. Opponent-process theory suggests that any movement from a neutral state is automatically counteracted by an opponent process, opposite in sign to the initial disturbance. Opponent processes grow in strength with repeated elicitation, accounting for pleasure produced by initially negative experiences such as sauna bathing and for the negative afterreaction that follows the termination of positive events.

5. Regulation of water intake is accomplished by receptors sensing the disruption of water-sodium balance both within the cell (osmometric thirst) and outside the cell (volumetric thirst). These receptors are located in the heart, kidney, and brain. Thirst is a homeostatic motive because the motive is to maintain an internal state at a particular level, called homeostasis.

6. Animals regulate food intake to maintain a relatively constant body weight. There is evidence that glucose availability and size of fat cells are regulated. Receptors involved in the control of food intake are located in the liver and in the brain.

7. Sexual motivation is also biologically based, but it is not a homeostatic motive. A minimum level of sex hormones seems to be necessary for sexual motivation and behavior in humans, but the relationship between hormones and sexual behavior is not very strong in humans. Sexual behavior is strongly affected by culture and learning.

8. Some motives are learned, such as need for achievement. People high in need for achievement tend to prefer tasks of intermediate difficulty and have greater pride in accomplishment and less fear of failing than people low in need for achievement.

9. In general, biologically based motives are satisfied before other motives such as need for achievement. However, for any one person in a particular situation any motive can dominate and inhibit all other motives, even biologically based motives.

10. Money is the primary reason people work, but other motives are also very important. Job satisfaction is produced by achievement of reinforcements, according to reinforcement theory; by a belief that fairness exists, according to equity theory; and by receiving the rewards expected.

SUGGESTED READINGS

Franken, R. E. (1982). *Human motivation*. Monterey, Calif.: Brooks/Cole.

An excellent overview of motivation including more detail than possible here. Covers both animal and human data, with an emphasis on applications to human behavior.

Masters, W. H., Johnson, V. E., & Kolodny, R. C. (1985). *Human sexuality* (2nd ed.). Boston: Little, Brown.

Covers many facets of human sexuality, written by leading researchers in the field.

McClelland, D. C. (1985). *Human motivation*. Glenview, Ill.: Scott, Foresman.

An in-depth coverage of the approach to motivation through measuring individual differences, as exemplified in this chapter by the study of need for achievement.

Money, J., & Ehrhardt, A. A. (1972). *Man & woman, boy & girl*. Baltimore: Johns Hopkins University Press.

A fascinating description of the work of John Money and associates with hermaphrodites.

Polivy, J., & Herman, C. P. (1983). *Breaking the diet habit*. New York: Basic Books.

Intended for the nonspecialist; provides a wealth of information on how people regulate food intake. The authors are critical of the "diet habit" of so many people.

13

Emotion and Stress

When angry, count ten before you speak, if very
angry, a hundred.

Thomas Jefferson

When angry, count four; when very angry, swear.

Mark Twain

Having finally located your car in the crowded parking lot, you put it in reverse and back quickly from your spot. Unfortunately, so does the person directly behind you. You both slam on the brakes and ease around one another, glowering and muttering. After waiting in a long line, you finally make it to the stoplight. A car full of tough-looking teenagers pulls up next to you. As the light changes, one casually flicks a cigarette directly at your car. Annoyed, you accelerate, but come up behind an elderly lady going 20 mph in a 40-mph zone. After you endure her dawdling for five minutes, she finally signals left and turns right, almost smashing into you as you speed around her. Furious, you slam your foot onto the accelerator and your car rockets ahead. A child suddenly appears between two parked cars and, desperately braking, you narrowly avert an accident.

If you have never experienced this precise scenario, you have probably endured or witnessed others like it. A series of events produces a strong emotional reaction, and this reaction affects behavior. *Emotions,* one of the key topics of this chapter, are a large part of what it means to be human. Imagine, for a moment, living a life free of emotion. Such an experience would be relentlessly boring, empty of joy, heartache, surprise, or fear. Furthermore, how people *feel* often determines what they do. In other words, emotions have a great deal to do with what motivates our behavior. Positive emotions such as happiness or negative emotions such as grief often serve as incentives for behavior since in general people seek what is pleasant and avoid what is unpleasant. To a large degree, then, the study of emotion is closely related to the study of motivation.

Our language is full of words that communicate emotion. Words such as *love, ecstasy, elation, contentment,* and *warmth* reflect positive emotions, those that are pleasant and enhance our lives. Words such as *sadness, anger, terror,* and *disgust* reflect negative emotions, which are generally unpleasant and diminish our well-being. Aside from this general classification, how can emotions be defined? First, emotions involve a complex subjective experience, a combination of feeling and thought. All of the words listed above communicate different subjective states, which vary in intensity. Second, emotions involve physiological changes. When we are emotionally excited, our hands may begin to sweat, our heart to race, or our face to become pale. These reactions constitute emotional arousal and normally accompany our subjective feelings. Finally, emotion involves expressive gestures and facial movements. Smiling, frowning, trembling, and tensed shoulders all communicate our emotions in specific ways.

In this chapter, we will look at all three components of emotion and how they relate to one another. We will also look at a variety of explanations for emotions. Where do our emotions come from? Why do we express our emotions in particular ways? How do we respond to emotional arousal? Then we will turn to one of the most important medical applications of psychology: the control of stress. When emotional reactions lead to stress, the effects can be dangerous to health. We will explore the relation between stress and disease, and we will look at a few ways in which people can learn to cope with stress to avoid its potential harm.

EXPRESSION OF EMOTION

The scientific study of emotion has gone on for more than a hundred years. In 1872 Charles Darwin (1872/1965) published a book that proposed that emotions and emotional expression are biological traits shaped by evolutionary history. Darwin stressed that emotions perform an extremely useful function for an animal's survival. Emotional expressions such as bared fangs on a wolf, for example, signal hostile intentions to other animals. Animals whose faces convey fear to other animals when danger approaches increase the chances of survival of their fellow animals who see their fear and increase their own chances of survival if their communication of fear brings aid to themselves.

Darwin also pointed out that animals and humans share a great number of similar facial expressions. A dog's smile communicates the same friendly intentions as a human smile. A downturned mouth conveys sadness in both a human and a dog.

The strong similarity of facial expressions among animals, including humans, has continued to attract interest among scientists since Darwin's time. Facial expressions represent one important clue that emotions may have an evolutionary function.

Facial Expression of Emotion

Paul Ekman has done a great deal of work on the importance of facial expressions in emotion. Borrowing from the early work of Darwin, Ekman

In 1872 Charles Darwin published a book describing the great similarity in emotional expressions in animals and humans. The bared fangs of a hostile wolf, for example, are similar to the signs of anger in a human.

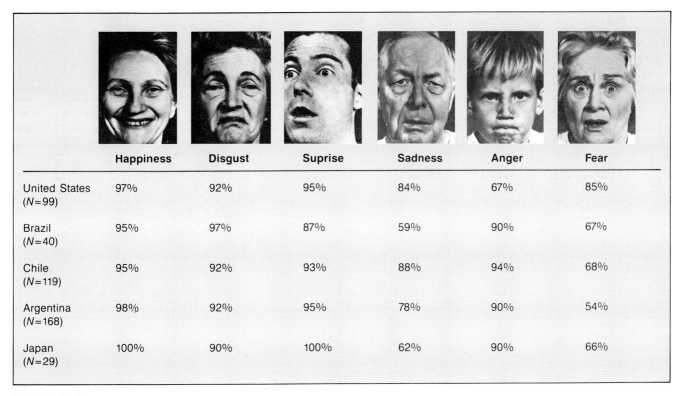

	Happiness	Disgust	Suprise	Sadness	Anger	Fear
United States (N=99)	97%	92%	95%	84%	67%	85%
Brazil (N=40)	95%	97%	87%	59%	90%	67%
Chile (N=119)	95%	92%	93%	88%	94%	68%
Argentina (N=168)	98%	92%	95%	78%	90%	54%
Japan (N=29)	100%	90%	100%	62%	90%	66%

FIGURE 13–1
Expressions of Emotions

Photographs of facial expressions were shown to people in five different cultures: United States, Brazil, Chile, Argentina, and Japan. Beneath each photograph are the percentages of people in each culture who identified the photograph with the emotion listed under the photograph.

Source: Ekman, 1973.

has sought evidence to prove that our ability to communicate emotion through facial expression is largely innate, or genetically determined.

In a series of cross-cultural studies, Ekman and his colleagues (Ekman, Sorenson, & Friesen, 1969; Ekman, 1972) presented photographs of different facial expressions to individuals living in various parts of the world, including citizens of Brazil, the United States, Argentina, and Japan. Despite their cultural differences, most of the people tested matched the faces with the same emotion (see Figure 13–1). This remarkable similarity of facial expression across cultures suggested to Ekman that smiling, frowning, and other such facial expressions are a result of genetics rather than learning. Critics pointed out, however, that all of Ekman's sample populations had been exposed to similar influences, such as mass media, and it could be possible that the facial expressions were in some degree transmitted culturally.

To deal with this criticism, Ekman performed another study in which he presented photographs of facial expressions to members of the South Fore tribe, a preliterate culture in remote New Guinea. Members of this tribe had had only minimal contact with outside cultures. None of them had ever seen a movie, and none of them either spoke or understood English. Despite their isolation, the South Fore tribespeople matched faces and emotions in much the same way as did people from other cultures. They were not able to distinguish a look of fear from a look of surprise, but they were able to distinguish these faces from those showing anger, sadness, happiness, and disgust. In another experiment, Ekman asked the South Fore to make faces reflecting how they would feel if they were a character in a story

FIGURE 13-2
Facial Expressions Posed by the South Fore

At the time of this study, the South Fore tribe of New Guinea had had minimal contact with outside cultures. Nevertheless, their facial expressions are quite similar to those in many other cultures of the world. The instruction for the top left photograph was, "Your friend has come and you are happy"; for the top right, "Your child has died"; for the bottom left, "You are angry, about to fight"; and for the bottom right, "You see a dead pig that has been lying there for a long time."

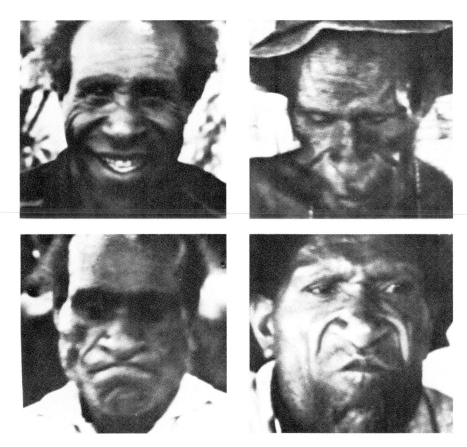

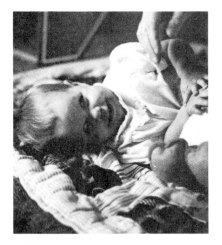

FIGURE 13-3
A Blind Child's Smile

Although this two-month-old girl has been blind since birth, she smiles like a normally sighted child. Emotional expressions such as laughing, crying, fear, and sadness seem to be inborn.

about sadness or happiness (see Figure 13–2). He showed videotapes of their expressions to a group of American college students, and most of the students had no trouble identifying the emotions expressed by the tribespeople.

Ekman's evidence for the universality of certain facial expressions is bolstered by studies conducted with blind and deaf children (Eibl-Eibesfeldt, 1973). Obviously, blind children cannot learn facial expressions by observing others, yet their smiles are very much like those of normally sighted children (see Figure 13–3).

Ekman's evidence that certain emotions such as sadness, happiness, disgust, fear, and surprise—what Ekman terms "primary emotions"—are expressed in universal ways through facial movements does not rule out the influence of learning. Many of our facial movements are voluntary. Indeed, later in the chapter we will review evidence that shows that women are much more expressive in their facial gestures than men. Expressions in certain cultures are seldom found in others. Yet Ekman's research, collected almost 100 years after Darwin, lends support to the notion that our emotional behavior is to some degree a result of evolutionary forces.

From the surface features of emotion, we move next to its internal features, the body's emotional arousal. After considering these physiological changes, we can further investigate how and why certain events in our environment produce emotional feelings.

The Body's Emotional Response

Imagine yourself in any situation where you are concerned and unsure, perhaps just before having to address a group. You probably can name easily the bodily changes that you would experience: pounding heart, sweaty palms, dry mouth, tense stomach. The English language reflects this relationship between emotions and bodily reactions with expressions such as "cold sweat," "trembling with fear," and "butterflies in the stomach."

Of primary importance in the body's emotional reaction is the *autonomic nervous system*. As described in Chapter 2, the autonomic nervous system consists of the sensory and motor nerves serving the heart and the glands and the smooth muscles of the internal organs. The system has two branches: the *sympathetic nervous system* and the *parasympathetic nervous system*. The first tends to function more actively during strong emotion and the second to operate during relaxation and rest. Table 13–1 compares the two systems.

Table 13–2 shows the effects of sympathetic and parasympathetic control. Some organs, such as the sweat and adrenal glands, are associated only with the sympathetic nervous system, but most are controlled by both the sympathetic and parasympathetic nervous systems. In these cases, the bodily reactions produced by the two branches are opposites. The reactions associated with the sympathetic nervous system and emotional arousal consist of increased heart rate, increased blood pressure, pupil dilation, inhibition of salivation (causing dryness of the mouth), sweat secretion (resulting in clammy hands), constriction of blood vessels in the periphery of the body (producing cold hands and feet), and impeded digestion. The parasympathetic nervous system decreases heart rate and blood pressure, constricts pupils, and increases salivation and digestive processes. The parasympathetic and sympathetic nervous systems work together and complement each other. So you can simultaneously digest a meal, governed primarily by parasympathetic activity, while sweating if you are too hot, a reaction governed by the sympathetic nervous system.

TABLE 13–1
Comparison of Sympathetic with Parasympathetic System

Characteristic	Sympathetic System	Parasympathetic System
General effect	Prepares body to cope with stressful situations	Restores body to resting state after stressful situation; actively maintains normal body functions
Extent of effect	Widespread throughout body	Localized
Transmitter substance released at synapse	Norepinephrine and epinephrine	Acetylcholine
Duration of effect	Lasting	Brief

Source: Villee, Solomon, & Davis, 1985, p. 868.

TABLE 13–2
Comparison of Sympathetic and Parasympathetic Actions on Selected Organs and Glands

Organ and Gland	Sympathetic Action	Parasympathetic Action
Heart	Increases rate and strength of contraction	Decreases rate; no direct effect on strength of contraction
Bronchial tubes	Dilates	Constricts
Iris of eye	Dilates pupil	Constricts pupil
Sex organs	Constricts blood vessels; ejaculation	Dilates blood vessels; erection
Blood vessels	Generally constricts	No stimulation for many
Sweat glands	Stimulates	No stimulation
Intestine	Inhibits digestion	Stimulates digestion and secretion of gastric fluids
Adrenal medulla	Stimulates secretion of epinephrine and norepinephrine	No effect
Salivary glands	Inhibits watery saliva	Stimulates profuse, watery secretion

Source: Villee, Solomon, & Davis, 1985, p. 869.

The two branches differ significantly as well in the nature of the neurotransmitter substance that is active at the synapse. The major transmitter in the parasympathetic system is acetylcholine (ACh), and synaptic transmission using ACh is categorized as *cholinergic transmission.* In the sympathetic nervous system, the major synaptic transmitter is norepinephrine. Synaptic transmission using norepinephrine is designated as *adrenergic.* Norepinephrine and the closely related epinephrine, once called adrenaline, are both released in the bloodstream by the adrenal glands. Once in action, they maintain the arousal initiated by the sympathetic nervous system. This is reflected in the phrase "your adrenaline is flowing" to indicate excitement.

Because the sympathetic nervous system is active in emotion, one way to measure emotion is to measure physiological responses associated with the sympathetic nervous system. This is the idea behind the *polygraph,* or lie detector. Various parts of the machine record heart rate, blood pressure, palm conductance (which is affected by sweating on the palm), and breathing rate. The subject's response is measured when he or she is calm and answering neutral questions such as name and address. The critical questions that an investigator wants answered are interspersed. If the subject is lying, an emotional reaction to the lie will show up on the machine. But the machine doesn't measure lying; it measures physiological reactions associated with emotion, so anyone who can lie with no emotional reaction can fool the machine. And a person who is reacting emotionally to certain questions but is not lying will be wrongly judged a liar.

In general, physiological reactions do not unequivocally measure emotion because the exact physiological reaction may differ from person to person (Grings & Dawson, 1978). One individual may show increased heart rate and little change in palm conductance, while in another individual palm

The polygraph, or lie detector, measures various responses that increase with sympathetic nervous system arousal and heart rate: blood pressure, breathing rate and palm conductance (affected by sweating on the palm). The idea is that a person who is lying will react emotionally and so sympathetic nervous system activity will increase. A person who can lie unemotionally will fool the machine and a person who reacts emotionally but is not lying will be wrongly judged a liar.

conductance may change but not heart rate (e.g., Lacey & Lacey, 1958). Also, people vary in overall level of physiological reactivity in emotion. In addition, facial expression is not an infallible guide to emotion. People can smile without feeling happy and can feel happy without smiling. The best way to determine another person's emotion is to combine measures—facial expression, physiological measures, and behavior.

THEORIES OF EMOTION

Now that we have some technical understanding of emotion, how do we explain what we call an emotional experience? Darwin, as we said, argued that emotions are shaped by our natural history. Each of us has the capacity to respond emotionally in particular ways because of our biological heritage. But this explanation fails to address the issue of whether the emotions we feel in any particular situation are caused by physiological arousal, subjective feelings or thoughts, or a combination of these factors. Some theorists propose that emotions are mostly physiological events that we label with familiar terms such as "anger" or "fear." Others contend that the emotion we experience depends in part on how we respond to and interpret situations. If we encounter a vicious dog, we know enough to be fearful, and this response in turn directs our physiological arousal. In the following sections, we will survey various interpretations of emotional experience.

The James-Lange Theory of Emotion

Theorists who analyze emotion in strictly physiological terms generally choose to confine "emotional experience" to a limited set of universal physiological responses. Paul Ekman (1984), for example, has identified six "universal" or *primary* emotions: fear, anger, happiness, disgust, surprise, and sadness. He believes that each of these emotions is expressed by a distinct pattern of activity within the autonomic nervous system. (Earlier we discussed how each of these primary emotions is also expressed in similar facial expressions among members of different cultures.)

RESEARCH FRONTIER

It Hurts Less When You Laugh

According to the James-Lange theory of emotion, we feel sad *because* we are crying, we feel afraid *because* we are trembling, and we feel happy *because* we are smiling. Is there any evidence that our emotions are captive to our physiological response?

A recent experiment by Paul Ekman, Robert Levenson, and Wallace

FIGURE 13–4
Actor Following Directions to Contort His Face

The fear prototype instructions were the following: A. "Raise your brows and pull them together"; B. "Now raise your upper eyelid"; C. "Now also stretch your lips horizontally, back toward your ears."

Friesan (1983) showed that changes in facial expressions could produce subjective feelings of happiness or fear. They directed their subjects to contort their faces in specific ways. Figure 13–4, for example, shows how one subject was instructed to raise his brows and eyelids and to move his mouth. Even though these facial movements are characteristic of fear, the subject was not told to express fear; he was simply given directions for muscle contortions. After performing these exercises for six different facial expressions, each subject was asked to relive a past emotional experience involving fear, happiness, disgust, sadness, anger, and surprise. As subjects contorted their faces and relived their emotional episodes, the researchers carefully measured changes in heart rate and finger temperatures, both signs of emotional arousal. They found greater arousal from the facial muscle movements than from the emotional recollections, suggesting that feedback from our expressions

can affect our moods. "Put on a happy face" is probably good advice to someone who is sad!

The James-Lange theory proposed that physiological responses precede emotional experience. The idea that sensations produced by movements of facial muscles produce a physiological response which in turn produces subjective feeling was proposed by a French physician, Israel Waynbaum, in 1907, and it has recently been revived by Bob Zajonc (1985). The results of the Ekman, Levenson, and Friesan (1983) experiment support this theory. Ekman and colleagues also found that the subjects' autonomic arousal differed according to which emotion was being expressed or relived. Heart rate, for example, increased more in fear than in happiness. If in fact different emotions are related to different autonomic nervous system responses (as suggested by the James-Lange theory), then these scientists have uncovered the very first evidence of this link.

FIGURE 13–5
James-Lange Theory of Emotion

According to the James-Lange theory, emotion is a result of our sensing the body's physiological reaction to an event that arouses the autonomic nervous system.

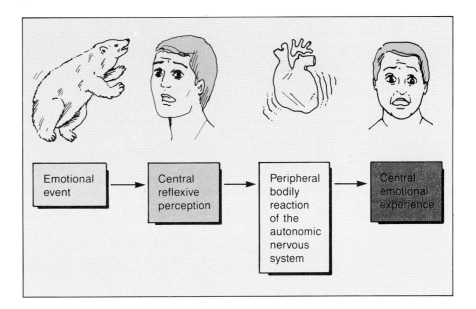

The identification between emotion and physiological response actually began with the *James-Lange theory of emotion,* developed independently by the American psychologist William James (1885/1968) and the Danish physiologist Carl Lange (1885–1967). The James-Lange theory of emotion proposes that what we normally call emotion is actually a result of our sensing the body's physiological reaction to an event that arouses the autonomic nervous system (see Figure 13–5). In other words, when a person encounters a vicious bear, that event produces a reflexive action, such as a pounding heart. When the person senses the pounding heart, he or she experiences emotional "fear." This theory therefore assumes that if no sympathetic arousal takes place, no emotion takes place either. If you saw a vicious bear and your heart didn't pound, then you would not be afraid. (See Figure 13–5.)

One way to test the James-Lange theory is to study whether emotions can be produced by physiological arousal. Some recent research has done this by manipulating facial expressions to produce physiological reactions. If feedback from these reactions can induce emotional feelings, then this evidence would support part of the James-Lange hypothesis. In other words, if putting on a happy face can indeed make us happier, then our experience of emotion is in some measure controlled by our physiological responses. "Research Frontier: It Hurts Less When You Laugh" describes some of this research.

Problems with the James-Lange Theory

The James-Lange theory of emotion has not met universal acceptance. As early as 1927, Walter B. Cannon carried out a set of experiments that demonstrated several problems with the James-Lange approach.

If the James-Lange theory is correct, then in order for emotion to occur, the sympathetic nervous system must be intact. However, when Cannon, Lewis, and Britton (1927) surgically destroyed the sympathetic nervous system of a cat, the cat still showed a normal emotional reaction to a barking dog. This experiment was not as conclusive as it may seem, since the researchers failed to destroy all of the important nerve fiber pathways leading to the sympathetic nervous system (Fehr & Stern, 1970). Even so, the important question is not whether the cat acted angrily without its sympathetic nervous system but whether it *felt* angry. Cats, of course, cannot report their feelings. When humans who suffer spinal cord injuries affecting the sympathetic nervous system are asked to report their feelings, they generally show reduced emotional experience, but not its disappearance, as the James-Lange theory would predict. As one unfortunate patient reported:

> Sometimes I act angry when I see some injustice. I yell and cuss and raise hell, because if you don't do it sometimes, I learned people will take advantage of you, but it just doesn't have the heat to it that it used to. It's a mental kind of anger. (Hohmann, 1966, p. 151)

This evidence would support the view that physiological reactions play some part in emotional feeling, but they are not necessary for *all* emotional feeling.

A second criticism made by Cannon of the idea that autonomic activity produces emotional experience is that these reactions are too slow. Have you ever been afraid, then acted, and *then* started trembling? Autonomic nervous system changes often do not occur until one or two seconds after an event. This delay contradicts the basic sequence outlined in the James-Lange theory.

Another problem with the strict interpretation offered by the James-Lange theory is that emotions are often complex mixtures of physiological and cognitive states. An emotion such as disappointment, for example, includes elements of sadness produced by not receiving an expected event. Thus, the ability to represent future expected events and other cognitive processes such as memory play a role in emotional experience.

To get around this problem, Ekman and other theorists prefer to speak of only a limited number of primary emotions, each with a distinctive physiological component. Nevertheless, there are at least 200 different terms in the English language for various emotional experiences (Scott, 1980), and most of these are in some degree influenced by cognitive processes. In answer, theorists can argue that complex emotions such as envy and jealousy are merely combinations of primary emotions. This is possible. Because complex emotions are not yet well understood, we do not know if it will be feasible to understand them as combinations of simpler emotions.

The Role of the Central Nervous System

If Cannon's criticisms of the James-Lange theory are valid, then emotions must be directed in part by the brain, without the indirect influence of the autonomic nervous system. Research into the brain's role in emotion has focused on many different areas. Cannon, for instance, proposed that the critical brain mechanism in emotion was the thalamus. Later research ruled out his theory, however. In 1937 James Papez brought forth evidence pointing to the limbic system as the critical component in emotion. Today the brain circuit he identified, known as the *Papez circuit*, is accepted as one of the keys to the control of emotion. Subsequent research has focused on the cerebral cortex—the outermost layer of the brain where most higher functions seem to be organized. Removal of the cerebral cortex in lower animals will produce a highly excitable animal. Animals fly into a rage at the slightest provocation. Bard (1934) called this "sham rage" because it was short-lived, not clearly directed at the provocation, and seemingly without conscious control. One interpretation of this finding is that the cerebral cortex normally inhibits emotion.

Emotions are also controlled by the hypothalamus. Stimulation of a particular portion of the hypothalamus elicits rage and provokes attack that can be well directed toward the provoking stimulus (Flynn et al., 1970; Panskepp, 1971). Electrical stimulation of particular portions of the hypothalamus can produce strong pleasure reactions as well. In sum, Cannon's criticism of the James-Lange hypothesis and subsequent research have redefined our understanding of what determines emotional experience. Today, central cognitive processes as well as physiological responses are seen as vital components to emotion. The first theory to accommodate the role of both elements appeared a little over 20 years ago.

Cognitive-Physiological Arousal Theory

In 1962 Stanley Schachter and Jerome Singer proposed a theory of emotion that contradicted the idea that specific physiological responses produced specific emotions. Instead they argued emotions are determined in part by the situation and the person's evaluation of the situation. That is, two things are necessary for an emotion to be experienced: general autonomic arousal and a cognitive interpretation of why the arousal takes place (see Figure 13–6). This theory is referred to as the *two-component theory* of emotion.

FIGURE 13–6
The Schachter-Singer Model of Emotional Experience

According to the Schachter-Singer model, two things are necessary for an emotion to be experienced: general autonomic arousal and a cognitive interpretation of the situation consistent with emotion.

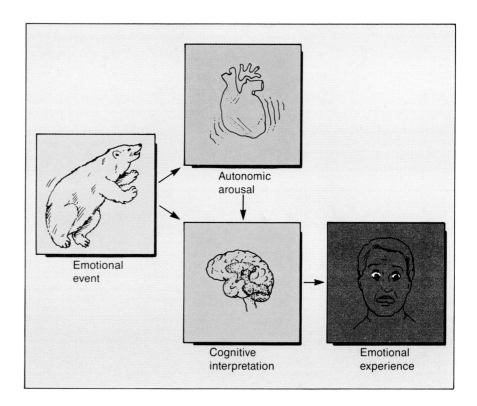

Emotional event

Autonomic arousal

Cognitive interpretation

Emotional experience

To test this theory Schachter and Singer (1962) administered epinephrine, which causes trembling and speeds the heart rate, reactions similar to those of natural sympathetic nervous system arousal, to one group of subjects and correctly informed them that "your hand will start to shake, your heart will start to pound, your face may get warm and flushed." A second group was told nothing about the drug's effects, and a third was misinformed and warned to expect itching, numbness, and headache.

If the Schachter-Singer theory is correct, the specific emotion experienced by each group would depend on the appropriate situational cues. So the group that was told the epinephrine would produce arousal should not feel emotional. That is, they should interpret the sympathetic arousal as an effect of the drug, not as an emotional reaction. The other groups should feel emotional if they have a good reason to do so. Schachter and Singer set up the experiment so that these other groups would have appropriate reasons to "explain" the emotional arousal produced by the drug.

Every subject waited in a room with another person who supposedly was also a participant in the experiment and had received the epinephrine. The other person actually had been hired by the experimenter to behave in particular ways, providing the subject with situational cues. In one condition the hired subject—or model—threw paper airplanes, shot wads of paper, and was generally cheery. In the other condition, the model simulated anger, complained about the experiment, and displayed aggressiveness. The subjects were watched through one-way mirrors, and those uninformed and misinformed about the drug's effects acted angrier with the angry model than those who were informed about the drug. Thus, as expected, emotion was produced in these people by combining an unexplained physiological arousal with situational cues appropriate to emotion. Results with the happy model were the same. With the happy model, uninformed and misinformed subjects reported they were happier and tended to act happier than subjects who were informed about the drug's effects. Thus Schachter and Singer concluded that two factors are involved in the experience of emotion: physiological arousal and a situational cue. The arousal produced by the epinephrine was inferred to be emotional arousal from the situation.

Although Schachter and Singer's paper became highly influential, this theory remains controversial. Some experiments, for example, have contradicted Schachter and Singer's view that autonomic nervous system arousal is one of two elements necessary for emotional experience. Some studies find that increasing arousal frequently intensifies emotional experience but it is not essential for emotional experience (Shaver & Klinnert, 1982). The presence of arousal can actually prevent the induction of certain emotions (Reilly & Morris, 1983).

Other recent data suggest that situational factors do not totally determine the interpretation of arousal. Contrary to what Schachter and Singer found in 1962, it appears that physiological arousal (produced by epinephrine) is more likely to be interpreted as negative emotion rather than positive (Marshall & Zimbardo, 1979; Maslach, 1979). In other words, it is not yet clear to what extent autonomic physiological responses determine emotion and whether physiological arousal is necessary to produce emotion.

In any event, some recent theorists have moved beyond the Schachter-Singer model altogether and eliminated arousal as a critical determining fac-

CONTROVERSY

Are Men or Women More Emotional?

One popular accepted belief is that females are more "emotional" than males. Research suggests that females do indeed react more intensely to the same level of emotional stimuli than men (Diener, Sandvik, & Larsen, 1985). For example, females are more likely than males to disagree with the statement "I would characterize my happy moods as closer to contentment than to joy." Females also show more facial expression of emotion than do males. In some studies (Buck et al., 1972), male and female subjects were shown color slides of seminude men and women, pleasant landscapes, a mother and child in a tender scene, repellent facial injuries and burns, and strange photographic effects. Observers watched each subject's face over television and tried to judge which of the five kinds of slides the subject was seeing. When women were viewing the slides, observers proved to be correct much more often

than when men were viewing the slides, indicating that women were revealing more emotion in their faces than were men. So you might think females have greater emotional reactivity than males.

But emotional reaction can be measured physiologically as well. In a similar study that measured galvanic skin response (GSR), females had fewer responses than males (Buck et al., 1972). Craig and Lowrey (1969) found greater GSR changes for males than for females who were watching someone receiving shock, but males rated themselves as experiencing less stress than females did. It appears that when overt responses such as facial expressions and verbal report are measured, males show less emotional reactivity than females, but when physiological measures are taken, males exceed females.

One explanation is that open expression of emotion is more socially acceptable for females than for males. So males learn to inhibit their openly emotional reactions, causing them to increase their physiological expression (Jones, 1950). In other words, the emotion must manifest itself some-

how, and if open expression is inhibited, physiological expression will increase.

Some observers have argued that blocking of emotional expression can produce stress within the body, which may result in illness. It is indeed true, for example, that ulcers and heart disease are much more common among men than among women. If these illnesses occur because men inhibit open expression of their emotions, then perhaps they should be encouraged not to suppress their emotions. However, free expression of emotion is not always beneficial. It can foster socially undesirable behavior such as aggression (Berkowitz, 1973). Also, there are other explanations of the differences between men and women in incidence of ulcers and heart disease. For one, female sex hormones appear to provide protection against these diseases.

The controversy over whether the male's more inhibited style of emotional expression contributes to illness is currently attracting a great deal of attention. We may expect to see some significant new research in this area over the next few years.

tor in emotion (e.g., papers in Izard, Kagan, & Zajonc, 1984). Although these theorists vary widely in specifics, generally they believe that emotional reactions occur primarily when the self is implicated in some way, i.e., when a person interprets an event in terms of his or her own plans and goals (Branscombe, 1985). Generally these theorists believe that the same stimulus-processing mechanisms occur in emotion and cognition, the difference being that emotion is produced by events interpreted with reference to the self. This recent view moves totally away from the James-Lange emphasis on autonomic physiological reactions as primary in emotion, farther than the Schachter-Singer position where autonomic physiological arousal plus cognition and central processes determines emotion. An important area for future research is understanding the interactions between affective reactions (a term used more frequently now than emotion) and cognition.

FRUSTRATION AND ITS EFFECTS

Whatever its ultimate cause, emotion is a strong motivator of behavior. Much of what we do every day depends on how we feel. We seek out situations that make us happy and avoid situations that make us feel upset or distressed. Emotion can also result when our motivations are blocked or frustrated. *Frustration* is a negative emotional state that occurs whenever we are prevented from attaining a goal. Because frustration is unpleasant, it motivates new reponses to reduce it. In this section we will look at the emotion of frustration in detail. We will see that our responses to frustration depend a great deal on learning. In the next section we will consider the effects of frustration, particularly the problem of stress.

Frustration appears to be an inevitable part of life. Indeed, it is difficult to imagine a life without disappointments, where every goal is achieved. From the moment we are born we are confronted with limits, and much of growing up seems to involve learning to live with frustrations. Since it is virtually impossible to avoid frustration, we must learn to respond to it. *How* we learn to do so has many psychological consequences, for there are many possible responses to frustration, including aggression, increased persistence, escape and avoidance, and depression. Each of these responses has been carefully analyzed in behavioral experiments. As we will see, the choice of response depends on the situation and the probable consequences.

Aggression

In certain situations, frustration can motivate aggression. In one experiment, ten-year-olds were stacking bottle caps to earn money. When they had almost finished, the table was shaken and their stack toppled, an obviously frustrating experience. The youngsters became aggressive toward the person they thought responsible. Pigeons, rats, monkeys, and humans all have shown an inclination to attack when they do not receive an expected reward (Hutchinson, 1972), although aggression does not always follow frustration (see Figure 13–7). For aggression to occur, there must be no reason to think it will worsen the situation. If an individual has seen other people punished for aggression or has learned nonaggressive responses in similar situations, aggression will be less likely. That is, organisms learn not to become aggressive when they are frustrated if aggression invites negative consequences, and aggression is also less likely if they have learned other responses to frustration. (The relationship between frustration and aggression is discussed in more detail in Chapter 17.)

FIGURE 13–7
Stereotyped Fighting Postures of Rats

In this case fighting was produced by delivering shock to the floor the rats are standing on. Fighting will also occur if the rats are frustrated, for example, by not receiving an expected reward. However, they will not fight even if frustrated if they have learned to make other responses when frustrated.

Increased Vigor of Reaction

A second response to frustration is persistence, usually referred to as "increased vigor of reaction." When animals are frustrated and they have nothing to attack, the vigor of their response increases. Pigeons accustomed to receiving food for pecking keys will peck harder and faster for a while when food does not appear. Children who have been rewarded for pushing a window to get marbles will push the window harder following a trial when no marble appears (Holton, 1961). Sometimes increases in vigor of response do yield rewards: if study for an exam earns a grade less than that expected and the resulting frustration induces harder studying, the desired grade might be achieved next time.

One reason for this increase in vigor may be the fact that frustration seems to make a blocked goal more desirable. Animals that expect a certain food but do not receive it subsequently prefer that food over milk more than before; animals that expect milk but are denied it later favor milk over food more than before (Gaffan & Keeble, 1976). When a film that children were watching was interrupted and they thought it would not resume, they rated it as much better than did children who saw it uninterrupted (Mischel & Masters, 1966). There are other familiar examples of this phenomenon. Spurned lovers yearn and mope for the girlfriend or boyfriend who eludes them while others equally attractive are neglected. Adolescents forbidden to haunt certain hangouts or to belong to certain cliques often value them beyond their actual worth.

Escape and Avoidance

Because frustration is unpleasant, denial of customary pleasures can be used as punishment; sending children to their rooms, for example, deprives them of their customary free play. Because it is unpleasant, frustration motivates *escape* or *avoidance*, efforts to find more effective paths to rewards. Animals will devise a new response to get away from a place where they have been frustrated because they did not receive an expected reward (Daly, 1974). Many such different responses can be learned.

If no alternative path to the goal is available, frustration can interfere with performance because it produces a tendency to avoid the goal. Rats trained to run a straight-alley runway—a long box with food at the end— will race faster for a larger reward. Thus a group of rats that get six pieces of food will outpace a group that receives only one piece. After the rats have gone through a number of such trials, if the six pieces are reduced to one, the effect of the rats' resulting frustration evidences itself dramatically (see Figure 13–8). The animals on lowered reward now proceed more slowly than the other group. The goalbox has become unpleasant for them and they show reluctance to run down the alley. Called a *negative contrast effect*, this phenomenon was also discussed in Chapter 6. In this case, frustration interferes with performance. But the animals do adjust ultimately, and they run as rapidly for one piece of food as the group that had received one piece all along. This is probably because they become used to and expect only one piece and no longer find it frustrating.

Depression

Recent evidence has shown that the psychological state of depression may be a way some people react to frustration. When 332 college students were asked to describe any situation in which they had been depressed, their replies primarily related to loss of rewards (Izard, 1972). The top five situations described were: (1) academic failure or pressure (failing a course, doing poorly on an exam for which "I thought I was prepared," too little time for too much work); (2) female-male problems (being at school away from a girlfriend or boyfriend, breaking up with a girlfriend or boyfriend); (3) loneliness, being left out (being dropped from a fraternity rush list); (4)

FIGURE 13–8
Results of Frustration: Negative Contrast Effect

Two groups of rats were run through a straight-alley runway with food at the end. The black line shows the speed of the group that received one piece of food on all of the trials. The red line shows the speed of the group that received six pieces of food up to the point where the arrow is. Then they began receiving only one piece. As you can see, the rats decreased in speed when they received one piece and ran more slowly than the group receiving one piece all along. This happened in part because receiving a reward less than that expected produced frustration and made the rats unwilling to run to the place where they were frustrated.

Source: Ehrenfreund, 1971.

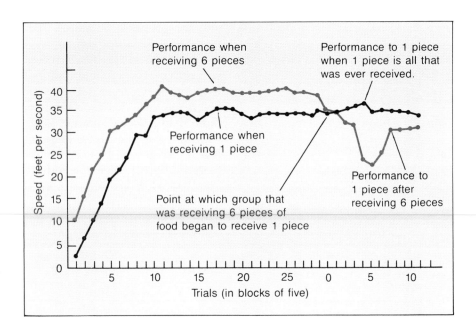

loss or failure in nonacademic competition (losing an important athletic contest); (5) death or illness of a loved one or friend. One explanation of these and related results is that repeated frustrations with no intervening rewarding events can produce depression and apathy (Klinger, 1977).

While the responses described all may occur with initial frustration, repeated frustration can still increase persistence if some reward follows frustrating experiences. As we saw earlier, if an animal is trained to make a response for a reward and then gets no reward, it will be frustrated. If a suitable target is available, the animal will attack; if no reward appears, the animal will stop responding. But suppose that after reward is denied for a few responses, one is presented, and this sequence is repeated—sometimes reward, sometimes not. An animal thus trained will put up with many more nonrewards in a row without ceasing to respond than will an animal that has never been frustrated before. This effect was discussed in greater detail in Chapter 6. Part of the reason is that when an animal has been rewarded and not rewarded for the same response, it learns to continue responding when frustrated; it will respond longer in the face of frustration than an animal not thus conditioned (Amsel, 1958). Some people relate this to spoiled children's intolerance of frustration; they throw tantrums when they do not get what they want because they have not been trained to persist in the face of frustration. As you can see, how an individual responds to frustration depends on experiences with the frustration and what he or she has learned from these experiences.

SOURCES OF STRESS

When emotions such as frustration are prolonged or excessive, the associated physiological changes can become detrimental to health. *Stress* is a general term that refers to physiological and psychological reactions to certain events in the environment, those that create a perceived threat to an individual's physical or psychological well-being, and the feeling that he or she is unable to deal with it (Glass, 1977; Sarason & Spielberger, 1979). The list of things that bring on stress varies widely from individual to individual. Some events, such as the death of a loved one, cause stress for almost everyone; otherwise, the context of the event and the individual's appraisal of the event determine whether or not stress occurs. Retirement, for instance, threatens self-esteem and induces great stress in some people; it presents a welcome opportunity to do different things for others. Keeping the importance of the individual's perceptions in mind, we will consider the most common sources of stress.

Life Changes

One general source of stress is a major change or adjustment in life, such as beginning a new job, moving to a new city, or suffering a death in the family. Any change in life that requires a person to adapt to new circumstances can cause stress, whether or not the change has beneficial effects. A new job can mean greater pay, for example, but it still requires some stressful adjustment. In general, the greater the degree of change and adaptation, the greater the stress will be.

The effects of life change have been carefully analyzed by Thomas Holmes and Richard Rahe (1967), who developed a scale to measure the impact of 43 major life events, called the Social Readjustment Rating Scale. They asked 394 men and women of different ages and backgrounds to rate the amount of readjustment required by each life event. Using marriage as a benchmark, they posed the following questions about each event: "Is this event indicative of more or less readjustment than marriage? Would the readjustment take longer or shorter to accomplish?" If the event caused greater adjustment, it was assigned a proportionally higher value than marriage; if less severe, a lower value. The events were than ranked according to a 100-point scale, as shown in Table 13–3. On this scale marriage was assigned a middle value, 50 points. As you can see, "death of a spouse" was considered the most serious event, followed by divorce and marital separation. But while older adults ranked sex difficulties thirteenth, adolescents put them fifth.

Life changes take place at all ages but, naturally, how often each kind occurs differs at each age. Illness and death in the family, for example, become more frequent as one grows older. At some time most people will experience most of the stress-producing life changes. Studies have found that high life-change scores—totaling 300 or greater—are related to increased frequency of ailments, accidents, and athletic injuries (Rahe, 1974).

Some theorists suggest that modern society produces more stress than did earlier periods of human life, in part because of the large number and rapidity of changes people now endure. Alvin Toffler coined the term "future shock" and wrote a best-selling book to describe the stress and disorientation that result when people are subject to too much change at too rapid a pace. More people change homes now than ever before; more than 36 million Americans may move in a single year. More and more switch jobs. Changing physical location, relationships, and employment all involve stress. Divorce is more frequent than in previous eras. The U.S. divorce rate

Any change can produce stress. When asked to rate events for their seriousness both adolescent and adult raters placed marriage in the top ten.

TABLE 13–3
Ranking and Item Scale Scores from the Social Readjustment Rating Scale

Life Event	Adult Group		Adolescent Group	
	Rank Given Event	Life Change Score	Rank Given Event	Life Change Score
Death of spouse	1	100	1	69
Divorce	2	73	2	60
Marital separation	3	65	3	55
Jail term	4	63	8	50
Death of a close family member	5	63	4	50
Major personal injury or illness	6	53	6	50
Marriage	7	50	9	50
Fired from work	8	47	7	50
Marital reconciliation	9	45	10	47
Retirement	10	45	11	46
Major change in family member's health	11	44	16	44
Pregnancy	12	40	13	45
Sex difficulties	13	39	5	51
Gain of a new family member	14	39	17	43
Business readjustment	15	39	15	44
Change in financial state	16	38	14	44
Death of a close friend	17	37	12	46
Change to a different line of work	18	36	21	38
Change in number of marital arguments	19	35	19	41
Mortgage or loan over $10,000	20	31	18	41
Foreclosure of mortgage or loan	21	30	23	36
Change in responsibilities at work	22	29	20	38
Son or daughter leaving home	23	29	25	34
Trouble with in-laws	24	29	22	36
Outstanding personal achievement	25	28	28	31
Wife begins or stops work	26	26	27	32
Begin or end school	27	26	26	34
Change in living conditions	28	25	24	35
Revision of personal habits	29	24	35	26
Trouble with boss	30	23	33	26
Change in work hours or conditions	31	20	29	30
Change in residence	32	20	30	28
Change in schools	33	20	34	26
Change in recreation	34	19	36	26
Change in church activities	35	19	38	21
Change in social activities	36	18	32	28
Mortgage or loan less than $10,000	37	17	31	28
Change in sleeping habits	38	16	41	18
Change in number of family get-togethers	39	15	37	22
Change in eating habits	40	15	40	18
Vacation	41	13	39	19
Christmas	42	12	42	16
Minor violations of the law	43	11	43	12

Adult and adolescent subjects rated the seriousness of various life events. The life change score indicates degree of seriousness of the change.

Source: Ruch & Holmes, 1971.

is the world's highest and, as you can see, divorce was ranked second in degree of necessary adjustment by both groups of raters. A marriage that isn't working also can create stress, so there may be less stress from divorce than from staying together. Whether the stress of modern life is greater or less than in the supposedly good old days is difficult to judge, but it does seem that the sources of stress today differ from those of the past. Some stress-producing events, such as moving and divorce, now come more frequently, but illness and early death of a parent or spouse occur less often. And some stress-producing physical discomforts are less common now; for example, air conditioning has reduced the stress produced by heat.

Irwin G. Sarason and his colleagues recently modified the Holmes-Rahe scale by having subjects rate the severity of the impact of each relevant event (Sarason & Spielberger, 1979). It also appears that life changes do not have inevitable effects since other variables may moderate their impact. To predict whether or not life change will be related to illness in an individual, it is necessary to know the context of the change and how the individual appraises and copes with it.

Minor Annoyances

Recent work by Richard Lazarus (1981) suggests that the minor hassles, or annoyances, of everyday life may influence our psychological and physical health more than the major life changes on the Holmes-Rahe scale. Lazarus created a scale to measure the intensity and frequency of hassles by asking white middle-class men and women what they considered their most common annoyances. Samples of items on this scale include "You have had to care for a pet," "You have had sexual problems other than those resulting from physical problems," "You are concerned about your use of alcohol," "You have had to plan meals." The top three for this group were concerns about weight, about health of a family member, and about economic conditions such as inflation. Among college students, the top three were anxiety over wasting time, anxiety over meeting high standards, and loneliness. Over a year, physical and mental health measured by questionnaires was reported as poorer when these and other hassles had been frequent and intense (Lazarus, 1981). Major life changes in the two and a half years preceding the measurement also had effects. Emphasizing minor hassles rather than major life events as a source of stress helps explain some puzzling data. For example, as people grow older they experience fewer and fewer major "events" in their lives (Lazarus & DeLongis, 1983), yet they do not experience less stress. Major life events, Lazarus and his colleagues believe, do not necessarily produce stress; rather, their effect depends on the individual's appraisal of the event. If the person construes the significance of an event as harmful, threatening, or challenging, this appraisal will produce stress. If the event is seen as benign or irrelevant, little or no stress results. Also, Lazarus and DeLongis suggest the traditional "life events" approach to stress is too narrow because the list of major life events excludes many important experiences, such as loneliness, limited energy, reaching the plateau of one's career, or being passed over for a promotion. Lazarus suggests that major life change may have long-term impact but that the short-term effects of minor hassles on physical and psychological health may be even more important. In part, major life changes may indirectly affect psycholog-

Recent work by Richard Lazarus suggests that the stress produced by the minor hassles of everyday life also has detrimental effects on psychological and physical health.

Some situations are so stressful that they would cause anyone to experience stress. Other situations produce different reactions in different people and so are not stressful for all. The situation shown is a highly stressful one that is part of the occupation of fireman.

ical and physical health by bringing about minor hassles that can be a source of stress. For example, divorce may mean having to learn to cook for oneself.

Chronic Discomfort

Besides life change, chronic or relatively long-term unpleasantness can prove stressful. Environmental stress such as the barrage of noise in modern urban environments is an example of this type of problem. Another example is occupational stress. Work and responsibility do not induce stress until they exceed the individual's capacity to control a situation: it is the reaction that counts. On the other hand, some occupations involve so much tension that almost everyone engaged in them experiences a great deal of stress. Air traffic controllers, for example, are keyed up almost constantly, and they have a very high incidence of peptic ulcers and hypertension (Glass, 1977).

Conflict

Unresolved conflict is a major source of stress. Many of the things people desire prove to be incompatible. For example, you may want to be thin but also eat a lot. Kurt Lewin (1935) originally described different types of conflict, and Neal Miller (1959) made a detailed analysis of three kinds of conflict and how they can be resolved: approach-approach conflict, avoidance-avoidance conflict, and approach-avoidance conflict. Because unresolved conflict produces stress, resolution of conflict prevents stress. It is important, then, to understand the varieties of conflict.

APPROACH-APPROACH CONFLICT. The first type is the easiest to resolve: a conflict between two desirable goals. This is termed an ***approach-approach conflict.*** Should I have the chocolate or the vanilla ice cream? Buy the blue or the green suit? Go swimming or play tennis? An approach-approach conflict is shown in Figure 13–9A, in which the height of the lines represents how strong the approach tendency is. As you can see, the nearer the goal is, the more you are drawn toward it. Nearness can signify physical distance. As you get closer to the vanilla ice cream, dip your spoon in it, and lift it to your mouth, it becomes increasingly desirable. Nearness can also be measured in terms of time: the closer the time comes for eating ice cream, the more you look forward to it. And nearness can also be seen in terms of similarity: the more something is like your most desired goal, the stronger your approach tendency to it will be. The person in Figure 13–9A is in conflict because only goal 1 or goal 2 is attainable, but not both. But this conflict is easy to resolve. Anything that increases the desirability of either goal slightly will pull the person toward that goal and resolve the conflict in its favor.

AVOIDANCE-AVOIDANCE CONFLICT. The second kind of conflict, ***avoidance-avoidance conflict,*** occurs between two undesirable things. You don't want to study for a test, but you don't want to do badly on it either. As you can see in Figure 13–9B, the avoidance tendency strengthens near the goal and weakens as distance from it increases. Again, distance can be represented as physical, in time, or as similarity. The closer you are to something

FIGURE 13–9
Three Different Kinds of Conflict

In each kind of conflict the strengths of two response tendencies are about equal, making a choice difficult. In A, a person is attracted to both goals (approach-approach conflict). The lines represent how desirable the goal seems. As soon as the person moves toward one goal, conflict will be resolved in favor of that goal. In B a person wants to avoid each goal but has to choose (avoidance-avoidance conflict). This conflict is difficult to resolve because the undesirability of the goal increases as the goal gets nearer (degree of undesirability is represented by the color lines). In C a person wants to approach and avoid the same goal (approach-avoidance conflict). This conflict can be resolved if desire to approach the goal increases or if desire to avoid the goal decreases.

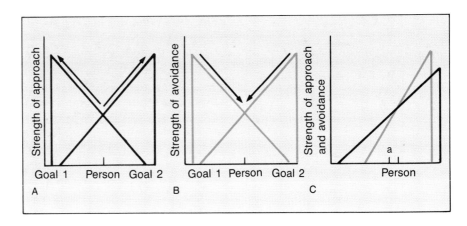

you don't want to do, the worse it seems, so resolving the problem looks difficult. To resolve an avoidance-avoidance conflict, some other factor must present itself, determining for you in favor of goal 1—a friend comes in and says "Let's study together"—or in favor of goal 2—the friend says "Let's go get a pizza."

APPROACH-AVOIDANCE CONFLICT. The approach-avoidance conflict describes the most common dilemma. An ***approach-avoidance conflict*** involves a single goal for which there is a tendency to approach and a tendency to avoid—you may want dessert, but not want to get fat; to enjoy drinking, but not to suffer a hangover; to live in an exciting big city, but to avoid crime and noise.

Let us consider an approach-avoidance conflict (see Figure 13–9C). Approach and avoidance, it is evident, are both strongest at the goal. The strength of the tendency to approach minus the strength of the tendency to avoid determines the observed response. The gradients of approach and avoidance are drawn in Figure 13–9C so that the person will stop at point A and not reach the goal. Before that point, approach is stronger than avoidance, so the person will approach to that point; beyond that point, avoidance is stronger than approach, so the person will not go closer to the goal than point A. This happens because the gradient of avoidance is steeper than the gradient of approach. In other words, as you get closer to a goal, its disadvantages begin to outweigh its advantages. Imagine you want to telephone somebody to meet you for a cup of coffee, perhaps on a first date. You worry that you may get a "no thanks." So you are in conflict: to call or not to call. Preparing to call may be easy; because it is far from the goal, approach is stronger than avoidance. But as you get closer to the phone, calling will be harder and harder, and if avoidance is stronger than approach near the goal, you'll never complete the call—you may dial, perhaps even let the phone ring or be answered, but then you'll hang up.

The gradients of approach and avoidance have been measured in rats by running them in a straight-alley runway with food and shock at the end. They are hungry so they want the food (approach), but they don't want the shock (avoidance). Appropriate levels of shock, hunger, and amount of food can be established so that the animal will run partway down the alley and

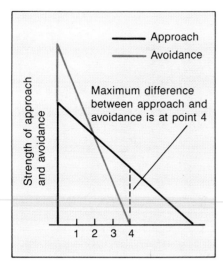

FIGURE 13–10
An Approach-Avoidance Conflict

This approach-avoidance conflict shows the net tendency to choose each goal as goals become less similar to the original goal. This tendency to choose a goal is equal to strength of approach minus strength of avoidance. As you can see, the person should choose a goal that is of intermediate similarity to the original goal.

stop. Observers can literally see the point at which avoidance starts to outweigh approach.

How is approach-avoidance conflict resolved? One way is to raise the approach gradient by increasing the desirability of the goal. Rats, for example, will go to the goal when they get hungry enough and approach is strong enough to overcome avoidance.

Another solution is to reduce the avoidance gradient, perhaps using alcohol or some other drug. If alcohol or a tranquilizer such as sodium amobarbital is given to an animal that is in a pure approach situation—hungry and running for food—the drug will, if anything, make the animal run slower. But if alcohol is given to an animal caught in an approach-avoidance conflict, it will run faster and get closer to the goal than a nondrugged animal. Alcohol also reduces avoidance of a place associated with shock. So it is clear that alcohol prompts a faster response in an approach-avoidance conflict by lessening avoidance. The everyday observation that alcohol reduces your inhibitions is essentially correct: people who are drunk are likely to do things they would normally want to do but would avoid because of the probable negative consequences.

Another way approach-avoidance conflict is resolved is by making an approach response to a different goal, but one that is similar to the original. Remember that the element of nearness can be viewed in terms of similarity, as well as distance or time. As you can see in Figure 13–10, response strength in the approach-avoidance conflict will be greatest at point 4, where the approach gradient minus the avoidance gradient produces the largest number. If, for example, you would like to yell at your boss, you might yell at someone else who is similar, but not too similar, to him. Your boss's assistant, for example, will probably not do. A response should be made to a stimulus of moderate similarity to the original.

Generally, when conflict prevents a direct response to the original goal, goals that are moderately similar to the original will elicit the strongest response. This contrasts with the situation when absence of the original goal precludes a response. In the case of pure approach, if the goal is not present, the response should be made to the most similar goal available. As Neal Miller (1959) suggested, a woman whose fiancé has died and who has recovered from grief will be expected to prefer to marry someone who is most like him. But a woman who is prevented from marrying her fiancé because of a violent quarrel would be expected to prefer someone not completely similar, but not completely different either.

If conflict cannot be resolved by these methods, stress develops. In animals, unresolved approach-avoidance conflict produces ulcers (Lovibond, 1969; Sawrey, Conger, & Turrell, 1956) as does unresolved avoidance-avoidance conflict (Weiss, 1971b). Physical problems can result from prolonged stress in human beings as well.

EFFECTS OF STRESS

Physiological Reaction

When an individual undergoes stress, physiological reactions occur in a pattern called the *stress reaction.* This is an innate response that is triggered by a wide variety of stressors, including burns, surgery, bone fractures, loud

Hans Selye initially decribed the body's reaction to stress, which he hypothesized was the same regardless of the source of stress.

noises, temperature extremes, food deprivation, fear, crowding, and sometimes exposure to an unfamiliar situation (Levi & Kagan, 1980). The immediate physiological reaction to stress basically parallels the reaction to emotion. Autonomic arousal increases the rate and strength of heartbeat, raises blood pressure, accelerates respiration, increases muscle tension, and lowers skin resistance. The hypothalamus responds to stress by initiating activity in the endocrine system to secrete the corticotropin-releasing factor (CRF), which stimulates the pituitary. The pituitary in turn secretes the adrenocorticotropic hormone (ACTH) about ten seconds after a stressful event. ACTH stimulates the release of fatty acids and the utilization of glucose, which are important in providing energy for dealing with a stressor. In addition, ACTH stimulates the adrenal cortex (the outermost portion of the adrenal glands), which then secretes glucocorticoid hormones, whose effects are discussed below. These responses, initially described by Hans Selye (1956), are important in the body's reaction to long-term stress.

In 1953, Selye was studying the effects of injecting hormones into rats, and he found that the rats suffered ulcers, enlarged adrenal glands, and shrunken thymus and lymph nodes. The effects were the same from different mixtures of hormones (regardless of their concentration) and from simple irritants as well. Selye hypothesized that any impurities irritated the organism. This idea gained support when other stressors, such as exposure to severe cold, produced the same results. Selye called this the "stress syndrome," a nonspecific bodily reaction common to all stress. He believed, and his view is now widely accepted, that any situation may prove stressful if the organism cannot adapt to it.

There are three stages in the body's reaction to stress, together called the *general adaptation syndrome* (see Figure 13–11). The first stage is the *alarm reaction*, which includes the effects of autonomic nervous system activation and which is characterized by a drop in bodily resistance to the stress. The autonomic nervous system stimulates the adrenal medulla,

FIGURE 13–11
The General Adaptation Syndrome

The graph shows resistance to stress as the stress continues over time. The first reaction is one of alarm. Then resistance to the original stress increases while resistance to other stresses decreases (stage of resistance). However, if the original stress continues, the body's resistance to all stress will ultimately decrease (stage of exhaustion).

Source: Selye, 1956.

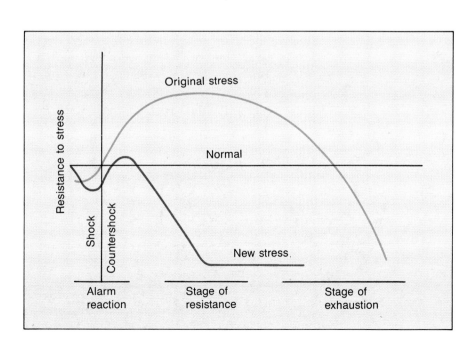

which secretes norepinephrine and epinephrine. The pituitary secretes ACTH, which stimulates the adrenal cortex to release glucocorticoids. If the initial stress is too severe, the organism may die in this stage. If it doesn't die, the second phase, the *resistance stage,* begins. In this stage, the pituitary continues to secrete ACTH, which goes on stimulating the adrenal cortex to secrete glucocorticoids, important in resistance to stress. The glucocorticoid hormones stimulate the conversion of fats and proteins to sugars, providing energy to deal with the stressor. Simultaneously, though, these hormones delay the growth of new tissue around a wound, inhibit formation of antibodies, and decrease the formation of white blood cells, increasing susceptibility to disease and injury. The adrenal glands actually expand in size in the resistance stage, reflecting their heightened activity. During this phase, resistance to the specific stress increases, and, accordingly, the generalized response disappears. After a few days of exposure to stress, experimental animal subjects appear to adapt. The adrenal glands return to normal size and begin to renew their supply of steroids. Things may appear to be normal, but they're not. If a second stress is introduced at this point, death can occur, indicating that general resistance is low despite increased specific resistance to the original stress.

Selye (1974) has noticed that many stress-related diseases develop in the resistance stage. Some may relate to the effects of the glucocorticoid hormones described above. Another part of the resistance stage of the general adaptation syndrome is the suppression of many of the bodily functions related to sexual behavior and reproduction. In males, sperm production drops, as does secretion of male sex hormones; in females, the menstrual cycle is disrupted or suppressed. Lessened sexual interest is a well-known psychological effect of stress as well.

If the specific stress continues, the body's ability to contain it and to resist other stresses ultimately collapses and the *exhaustion stage* sets in. Under prolonged stress, then, bodily mechanisms are geared to defend the body. The mechanisms also prepare for corresponding reductions in the activities promoting reproduction and an associated weakening of resistance to disease and infection. This pattern manifests itself regardless of the source of stress: external, such as extreme cold; internal, such as illness or surgery; or emotional, involving frustration, conflict, or fear.

Stress and Disease

Specific diseases related to stress include high blood pressure, headaches, insomnia, sinus attacks, heart and kidney diseases, and ulcers. Recent evidence suggests that stress is also related to cancer (Sklar & Anisman, 1981). The strongest evidence links stress and heart disease and stress and ulcers, although why one person may develop ulcers and another heart disease from stress remains unclear. It is possible that the organ that stress affects and the illness it produces depend on individual predispositions. Sickness may develop in the weakest area of the body's system. So someone with a high natural rate of gastric secretion may be predisposed to peptic ulcer, while another who has a natural high cholesterol level may be predisposed to stress-produced coronary disease.

Researchers relate stress and coronary artery disease in part because the two often occur together. Stressful events also produce physiological effects

TABLE 13-4
Sample Questionnaire Items Measuring the Tendency Toward Pattern A (Type A) or Pattern B (Type B) Behavior in College Students

1. "Has your spouse or some friend ever told you that you eat too fast?" A Pattern A response is "yes, often"; Pattern B responses are "yes, once or twice" or "no, no one has told me this."

2. "Do you maintain a regular study schedule during vacations such as Thanksgiving, Christmas, and Easter?" Here "yes" is a Pattern A answer; "no" and "sometimes" are B answers.

3. "How would your spouse (or closest friend) rate you?" Pattern A responses are "definitely hard-driving and competitive" and "probably hard-driving and competitive"; B responses are "probably relaxed and easygoing" and "definitely relaxed and easygoing."

4. "How would your spouse (or best friend) rate your general level of activity?" An A response is "too active, needs to slow down"; B responses are "too slow, should be more active" and "about average, is busy most of the time."

Source: Glass, 1977.

such as elevated serum cholesterol level, an important risk factor for coronary artery disease (Friedman, 1969).

Because of the relationship between stress and coronary artery disease, a stress-prone person is also coronary-prone. The coronary-prone behavior pattern has been described by Friedman (1969) as characterized by a constant struggle to achieve poorly defined goals in the shortest possible time. People who act thus are referred to as type A; calm, serene, relaxed people are called type B. A questionnaire can distinguish the types (see Table 13–4). Of course, this classification is a continuum, and whether you are type A or type B depends on how many of the characteristics composing the pattern you possess. A determination of type A has been shown to be a good predictor of coronary artery disease; the higher incidence appears even when other risk factors such as smoking, diet, and blood pressure are controlled. In competitive situations, higher serum cholesterol and higher secretion of norepinephrine have been found in type A than in type B people. Thus a type A personality may lead to more heart disease because of these factors (Glass, 1977).

The relationship between stress and disease is under study in a new interdisciplinary field called *behavioral medicine,* which is concerned with the integration of knowledge and techniques relevant to health and illness discovered by both behavioral and biomedical science (Schwartz & Weiss, 1978a, 1978b). Researchers in this field aim to apply new knowledge and techniques to prevent illness and to aid in diagnosis and treatment.

COPING WITH STRESS

Our understanding of the different ways people cope owes much to Richard Lazarus. Coping, he states, "is best considered as a form of problem-solving in which the stakes are the person's well-being and the person is not entirely clear about what to do." By coping an individual tries to master situations experienced as stressful (1966, 1976).

In general, according to Lazarus, there are two categories of coping: direct action and palliation.

Direct Action

Direct action involves behavior aimed at changing the person's relationship to the stressful event. There are many different kinds of direct action possible to deal with stress, including preparation against harm, escape, and avoidance. A person can reduce the stress of an impending exam, for example, by studying (preparing against the harm of failure). If the person fails to study enough, he or she might employ another coping strategy. For example, the student could deny the importance of the exam (a defense mechanism, see below and pages 513–514), or the student may become physically ill (preventing the anticipated harm of taking the exam) (Cox, 1978).

Palliation

Palliation refers to moderating the negative consequences of stress. In other words, palliation means dealing with the symptoms of stress rather than the source of stress. Use of drugs such as alcohol or tranquilizers is one palliative technique. Other techniques include muscle relaxation and exercise. Palliation can also involve many *intrapsychic* techniques, through which a person tries to change the meaning of a stressful situation by reinterpreting it. Lazarus has done many studies showing how the interpretation of a threatening event can affect the stress the event produces. These studies showed that the same event can prove stressful or not, depending on the person's cognitive appraisal. In one study (Speisman et al., 1964) a film showing a circumcision-like ritual performed on adolescent Australian aborigines was screened for three different groups and accompanied by three different commentaries. In one, harm to the adolescents was denied (denial). In the second, a technical description was given (intellectualization). A third emphasized the horror and pain (trauma). A fourth group heard no commentary. The denial and intellectualization commentaries reduced the degree of autonomic arousal compared to that of the group that heard no commentary. Lazarus's recent work has consistently shown that emotional reaction and stress are strongly affected by cognitive appraisal (Lazarus, Kanner, & Folkman, 1980).

Another factor that can affect your ability to cope with stress is the degree to which you gain sympathetic support from family, friends, and others. Having a confidant helps significantly (Miller & Ingham, 1979). Also, there is some evidence that confiding in someone such as a community professional (a counselor, a lawyer, or a police officer, for example) is more useful than confiding in relatives or friends (Lindenthal & Myers, 1979).

In general, we also know that being able to predict and control a stressful event reduces the resultant stress (e.g., Glass & Singer, 1972). Making efforts to increase predictability and control are other coping mechanisms.

Predictability

Stress-producing events have been found to be more stressful if they are unpredictable rather than predictable. Ulcers are produced in rats that receive unpredictable shocks to a greater extent than in rats that receive predictable shocks signaled by a tone (Weiss, 1970).

Being informed beforehand and being able to predict stressful events have proved beneficial in real-life situations. Students who have written for course catalogues, spoken with potential roommates, or visited the campus before going to college adjust better during their freshman year than those who have no advance information (Silber et al., 1976). Patients undergoing operations required fewer painkilling drugs and a shorter hospital stay when informed than when not informed about the operation (Egbert et al., 1964). So one technique for dealing with stress is to learn what to expect.

Control

Another factor that affects the intensity of stress is whether or not a person controls the situation. An early experiment that used four pairs of monkeys seemed to show that control produced more stress than noncontrol (Brady et al., 1958). A pair of such monkeys is shown in Figure 13–12. In each pair, one monkey, called the "executive" monkey, was able to press a lever to avoid a strong shock. Each lever press postponed shock for 20 seconds, so if the monkey pressed often enough, it would never get shocked. The other monkey, called the "yoked" monkey, got shocked whenever the executive monkey did, but it had no control over the shocks. In all four pairs of animals the executive monkeys developed ulcers, while the yoked monkeys did not. Being in control seemed to be more stressful. But in this experiment, the monkeys that had the highest rate of responding were put into the executive group, and it is now known that ulcers are more likely in animals selected for a high rate of responding (Weiss, 1971b).

FIGURE 13–12
Experimental Setup in the Executive Monkey Study

The monkey on the left can avoid shock by pressing the lever; the monkey on the right cannot avoid shock and gets shocked whenever the executive monkey does. In the original experiment the "executive monkey" developed stomach ulcers, while the other monkey did not. Subsequent experiments have shown, however, that being in control produces less stress and less likelihood of stomach ulcers than not being in control.

APPLYING PSYCHOLOGY

Stress and Relaxation

One effect of stress is muscle tension, which can produce tension headaches, insomnia, hypertension, and other negative effects. One skill to control muscle tension is called progressive relaxation. The first work on relaxation therapy was done by Dr. Edmund Jacobson beginning in 1908. In 1938 he published *Progressive Relaxation,* a book in which he established an important principle: physiologically, relaxation is the direct opposite of tension. The original relaxation program proposed by Jacobson was very time-consuming, and modifications since then by Joseph Wolpe (1969) and many others have produced a less difficult series of steps to progressive relaxation.

Relaxation is an active coping skill, and practice is essential (Beech, Barnes, & Sheffield, 1982). In the early phases, relaxation should be practiced at least 30 minutes a day. Later this can be reduced to 15–20 minutes. To practice progressive relaxation it is best to find a quiet, peaceful place with indirect light in which you can sit or recline. (Lying in

bed is not a good idea—you want to be deeply relaxed while wide awake, not asleep.) It is not a bad idea, though, to practice relaxation an hour or so before going to bed as sleep will be facilitated by relaxation.

The basic technique of progressive relaxation is to proceed through all the major muscle groups tensing and then relaxing them until total relaxation is achieved. Contracting and then releasing the muscles produces deeper relaxation than just relaxing. We will give the beginning of the basic training program here. Students who wish to read the entire sequence should see Beech, Burns, and Sheffield (1982, pp. 48–54). The following is just a sample of the instructions that could be used by a professional guiding you in progressive relaxation.

Relaxation of the arms.
Sit back in your chair as comfortably as possible, breathe in and out normally, close your eyes and relax—relax completely.
Keep relaxed but clench your right fist.
Make the muscles of your lower arm and hand even tighter.
Monitor the feelings of tension.
Now relax; let all the tension go.
Allow the muscles of your lower arm and hand to become completely limp and loose.

Notice the contrast in the feelings.
Again clench your right fist—tighter and tighter.
Hold the tension and monitor the feelings.
Relax. There should be no signs of tension in your hand or lower arm.
Notice the feelings of relaxation again.
Keeping your right hand and lower arm as relaxed as possible, bring your right elbow into the back of the chair and press downward, contracting the bicep muscles (between your elbow and shoulder). Press harder—make the muscles more tense.
Monitor the feelings of tightness.
Relax. Now let the tension dissipate immediately.
Observe the difference. Let the muscles relax further.
Now tense the right biceps again.
Make the muscles harder, tighter, more tense.
Monitor the feelings of tension.
Relax. Let the tension go completely.
Concentrate on the whole of your right arm. Relax it now, more and more deeply; relax it further and further.

The exercises for the left hand, lower arm, and biceps are exactly the same, and these are followed by instructions for relaxing the facial muscles, neck muscles, shoulders, chest, lower back and stomach, thigh, calves, and feet.

As in the connection between type A behavior and heart disease, it seems that personal characteristics relate to susceptibility to ulcers. Experiments with animals that did not differ in activity level have demonstrated that control over shock produces less stress than noncontrol; it results in less severe ulcers. It also appears that the monkeys in the original studies must have been highly vulnerable to ulcers because subsequent research has found much less susceptibility to the disease among like animals (Foltz & Millett, 1964; Natelson, 1976). Generally, such studies have determined that shock itself is relatively unimportant as a cause of ulcers: whether or not the animal can control and predict shock is much more significant. Psychological factors can outweigh physical stress.

In an experiment with human subjects, two groups were exposed to loud noise (Glass & Singer, 1972). People in one group could turn off the noise by pressing a button, but they were asked not to do so unless they felt it was absolutely necessary. None pressed the button. The second group had no control over the noise, which was of the same intensity. Subsequent performance at proofreading was better for the group that had had control, suggesting that the noise had disturbed the group less. Similar findings have been obtained with other stressors (Cohen, 1980). So in both people and animals another factor affecting degree of stress is whether or not they can control the stressor.

SUMMARY

1. Facial expressions and physiological reaction can indicate emotion. There seems to be an innate basis for facial expressions that are produced by emotion. There is great similarity in emotional expressions among many different cultures and animals. All infants, including those born blind, show the same emotional expressions at about the same age.

2. In emotional arousal, reactions associated with the sympathetic nervous system dominate. These include acceleration of heart rate, heightened blood pressure, inhibition of salivation, pupil dilation, constriction of blood vessels in the periphery of the body, and inhibition of digestive processes.

3. The James-Lange theory of emotion suggests that the subjective experience of emotion is produced by sensing your own body's reaction to something you perceive that is emotion-producing. While feedback from facial muscles can produce physiological arousal and emotional experience, neither this feedback nor peripheral physiological arousal seems necessary for emotional experience. The Schachter-Singer hypothesis is that cognitive and situational factors also play an important part in determining whether our physiological reaction is interpreted as emotional or nonemotional and in determining what emotion we experience.

4. Frustration is an emotion produced by being blocked from an expected goal. Frustration can produce aggression, but it will not follow if aggression has failed in the past or if nonaggressive responses have been learned. Frustration can also increase the vigor of responding, perhaps because the value of blocked responses increases. Persistence in the face of frustration can be developed, but repeated frustrations with no intervening reward lead to cessation of response and perhaps depression.

5. Stress is caused by a perceived threat to physical and psychological well-being, together with the feeling that the individual cannot cope with the threat. Life changes, minor hassles, chronic unpleasantness, occupational tensions, environmental conditions such as noise, and intemperate climate, prolonged or intense emotional reactions such as frustration, and unresolved conflict all induce stress.

6. Conflict is produced when two incompatible response tendencies appear to be equally strong. Three kinds of conflict are approach-approach, avoidance-avoidance, and approach-avoidance. The approach-avoidance type is probably the most common. It can be resolved by increasing the strength of approach, decreasing the strength of avoidance, or shifting the blocked response to a different but similar goal.

7. A clear relationship exists between stress and illness, particularly ulcers and heart disease; it seems to originate in the body's physiological reaction to stress. Stages of the body's physiological reaction to stress constitute the general adaptation syndrome.

8. Two categories of coping are direct action to change the person's relationship to the stressful event and palliation, which involves dealing with the symptoms of stress. An event produces less stress if it is predictable and if the subject is informed about it beforehand. Less stress results also if the individual has control over the event. Social support from friends, family, or professional counselors moderates the negative effects of stress. In addition, cognitive evaluations of stressful events can increase or decrease the amount of stress the events produce.

SUGGESTED READINGS

Beech, H. R., Burns, L. E., & Sheffield, B. F. (1982). *A behavioral approach to the management of stress: A practical guide to techniques.* New York: Wiley.

An explicit coverage of techniques for dealing with stress.

Ekman, P. (1973). *Darwin and facial expression: A century of research in review.* New York: Academic Press.

A study of the similarity of emotional expression in children, adults, and infrahuman species. Some of Darwin's original notes and drawings are included.

Glass, D. C. (1977). *Behavior patterns, stress and coronary disease.* Hillsdale, N.J.: Erlbaum.

Glass, D. C., & Singer, J. E. (1972). *Urban stress: Experiments on noise and social stressors.* New York: Academic Press.

The two preceding books give excellent coverage of the recent work on stress and disease, with an emphasis on experimental work with human beings.

Izard, C. E., Kagan, J., & Zajonc, R. B. (Eds.) (1984). *Emotion, cognition, and behavior.* New York: Cambridge University Press.

Scherer, K. R., & Ekman, P. (Eds.) (1984). *Approaches to emotion.* Hillsdale, N.J.: Erlbaum.

The two preceding books contain papers by the major figures working today in the field of emotion.

PART SIX

Personality and Abnormal Psychology

14 ▫ Personality

15 ▫ Abnormality and Deviance

16 ▫ Therapies

14

Personality

People have one thing in common: they are all different.

Robert Zend

AT THE AGE OF 99, THE GREEK PHILOSOPHER THEOPHRASTUS (ca. 372–ca. 287 B.C.), wrote a book entitled *Characters,* in which he posed the question that has motivated all efforts to study personality and individual differences ever since: "Why is it that while all Greece lies under the same sky and all the Greeks are educated alike, nevertheless we are all different with respect to personality?"

Consider yourself for a moment. What type of person are you? Imagine the following:

> You are at a party. An attractive person of the opposite sex turns and smiles at you. Do you blush and become self-conscious or do you return the smile and say "hello"?

> You get a C grade on a paper you thought was worth an A. Do you become angry and threaten your professor with physical violence? Do you become anxious and depressed and consider dropping out of college? Or do you shrug it off and resolve to do better the next time?

> You are in an elegant restaurant with a date. An elderly person is having difficulty walking to the exit, and no one seems to be paying attention. Do you get up out of your seat and offer assistance, or do you too pretend not to notice?

> You see an unusual-looking person holding signs warning "The end of the world is at hand." Do you take a leaflet he offers? Do you detour around him and give him no more thought? Or do you wonder how and why he came to do what he does?

Quite likely you have been able to answer these questions and recognize yourself in them. In every case, how you respond depends on your personality. Quite probably, no one else in your class would react exactly the same way you would. Indeed, even brothers and sisters raised in the same family would likely differ. This chapter explores how our personalities help distinguish us as individuals.

To draw a complete picture of the individual, the field of ***personality psychology*** integrates many of the topics studied in earlier chapters, especially psychobiology, learning, development, intelligence, and motivation. In turn, the study of personality has important implications for understanding topics we have not considered yet, especially abnormal psychology, social psychology, and social issues such as aggression.

Investigators of personality study how and why people, who all share a common human nature, are all unique individuals. The first part of that question can be rephrased as "What is human nature?" or "What is the structure of the human personality that everyone shares?" The second part can be phrased as "How do important differences among people arise?" The science of personality is thus concerned with the way our character, our intellect, our temperament, and our behavior determine our individual adjustments to the environment (Allport, 1937). In this chapter, we will describe four major approaches to personality: trait, psychoanalytic, humanistic, and social learning. Each set of theories has value and was developed independently, so we will consider them separately. At the end of the chapter we will synthesize them because we believe that the phenomenon of personality is captured more fully by a combination of approaches than by each in isolation.

THE TRAIT APPROACH

Analyzing personality according to types, or *traits,* is a commonsense approach that predates the ancient Greeks. People often describe and explain behavior in terms of enduring characteristics such as persistence, shyness, and friendliness and invoke the existence of types, such as the "student type," the "intellectual type," and the "sociable type." Trait psychologists believe there is truth in such folk wisdom; they have set about to measure traits and to see whether such assessments can be used to predict how well people will adjust to various situations. Measuring personality and predicting behavior are the greatest contributions the trait approach has made to the understanding of personality. Personality consists, according to this approach, of a number of traits, defined as "any distinguishable, relatively enduring way in which one individual varies from others" (Guilford, 1959, p. 6).

Identifying Traits

Gordon W. Allport (1897–1967), a leading trait theorist for more than 40 years, noted that an unabridged dictionary contained 18,000 words that people could use to describe each other (1937). If synonyms were ignored, nearly 5,000 such words remained. Which among these thousands of attributes represent the most basic elements of personality? Some trait theorists use factor analysis to reduce the many to an essential few.

Factor analysis was introduced in Chapter 11 as the method used to answer such questions as whether mathematical and verbal skills are separate aspects of "intelligence." It is a statistical technique for analyzing and grouping a large number of variables. In factor analysis variables that are related are grouped into clusters and separated from other clusters whose variables correlate. You might suspect, for example, that people who score high on a trait such as "warm" would tend to do so too on "sociable," "agreeable," and even "talkative." That cluster would be set apart from another cluster of terms such as "touchy," "restless," "moody," and "excitable."

Raymond B. Cattell, one of the most famous factor analysts, whose work has spanned five decades, has proposed 16 basic trait dimensions to describe the ways in which people differ (1973, 1982). These 16 dimensions appear in the right and left columns in Figure 14–1. Cattell regarded three of these dimensions—outgoingness, intelligence, and emotional stability—as the most important.

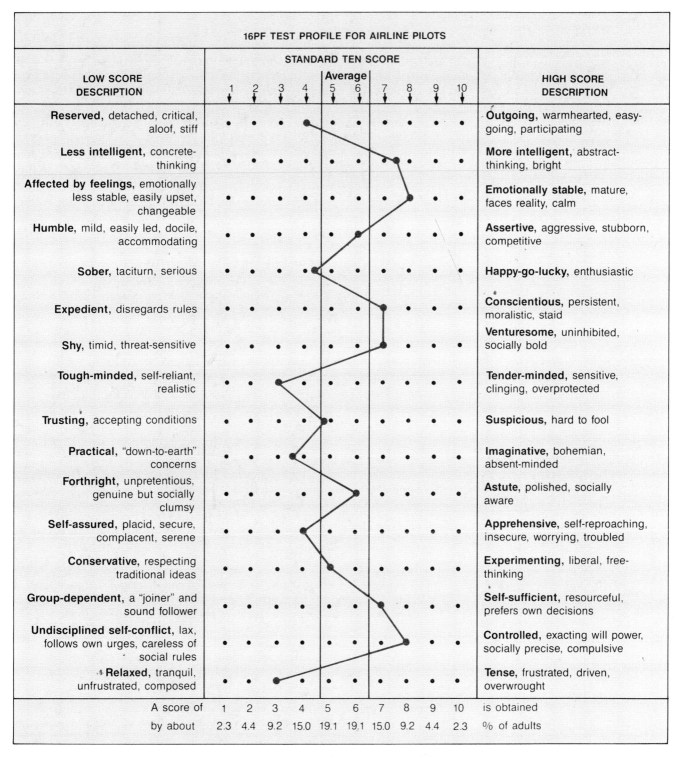

FIGURE 14–1
Cattell's Sixteen Personality Factor Questionnaire (16PF)

The chart lists Cattell's 16 personality dimensions and the personality profiles for airline pilots. Note the pilots' distinctive scores on traits of intelligence, emotional stability, tough-minded self-reliance, self-control, and composure, among other characteristics.

Source: Cattell, 1973.

Cattell also created a questionnaire to measure these 16 dimensions: the *Sixteen Personality Factor Questionnaire,* or *16PF.* It consists of several hundred multiple-choice questions by which subjects describe their own personalities. For example, one question asks the subjects whether they generally prefer others who (a) are somewhat reserved, (b) are in between, or (c) are somewhat outgoing. From the answers given, psychologists can construct a personality profile of the test-taker. Figure 14–1 presents the personality profile for airline pilots. They appear to have the traits most plane passengers would find reassuring. They are relaxed, controlled, tough-minded, emotionally stable, self-assured, and practical. Cattell has long believed that such personality profiles can be a valuable source of information in choosing a career.

Cattell (1982) has given his 16PF to many groups of people, with interesting results. In comparing stable and unstable marriages, Cattell has found that couples with stable marriages have greater similarities of personality than couples with unstable marriages. Because of research such as this, computer dating services often make personality profiles of their clients.

Hans Eysenck, another trait theorist, also used factor analysis to reduce the hundreds of possible traits to a few basic concepts (Eysenck & Eysenck, 1985). He went beyond Cattell's ideas, however, and cut them down to three basic dimensions, or *types,* defined as groups of correlated traits. Eysenck's three types are *extraversion* (as opposed to introversion), *neuroticism* (as opposed to emotional stability), and *psychoticism* (as opposed to impulse control). About extraversion, Eysenck says,

> The typical extravert is sociable, likes parties, has many friends, needs to have people to talk to, and does not like reading or studying by himself. He craves excitement, takes chances, often sticks his neck out, acts on the spur of the moment, and is generally an impulsive individual. He is fond of practical jokes, always has a ready answer, and generally likes change; he is carefree, easygoing, optimistic, and "likes to laugh and be merry." He prefers to keep moving and doing things, tends to be aggressive and loses his temper quickly; altogether his feelings are not kept under control, and he is not always a reliable person.

> The typical introvert is a quiet, retiring sort of person, introspective, fond of books rather than people; he is reserved and distant except to intimate friends. He tends to plan ahead, "looks before he leaps," and mistrusts the impulse of the moment. He does not like excitement, takes matters of everyday life with proper seriousness, and likes a well-ordered mode of life. He keeps his feelings under close control, seldom behaves in an aggressive manner, and does not lose his temper easily. He is reliable, somewhat pessimistic, and places greater value on ethical standards. (Eysenck & Eysenck, 1975, p. 5).

Eysenck recognizes that these descriptions may seem almost like caricatures because they portray "perfect" extraverts and introverts while in fact most people's personalities blend both types, falling in the middle rather than at the extremes.

The second major dimension of Eysenck's scheme consists of emotional instability–emotional stability, or neuroticism. This dimension embraces at one end people who tend to be moody, touchy, anxious, or restless and at the other people who are stable, calm, carefree, even-tempered, and reliable. The final dimension is psychoticism. People who score high on this

FIGURE 14–2
Two of Eysenck's Three Dimensions of Personality and the Classic Four Temperaments

The inner ring shows the "four temperaments" proposed by the second-century Greek physician Galen; the outer ring shows the results of modern factor analytic studies of the intercorrelations between traits by Hans Eysenck.

Source: Eysenck & Eysenck, 1985.

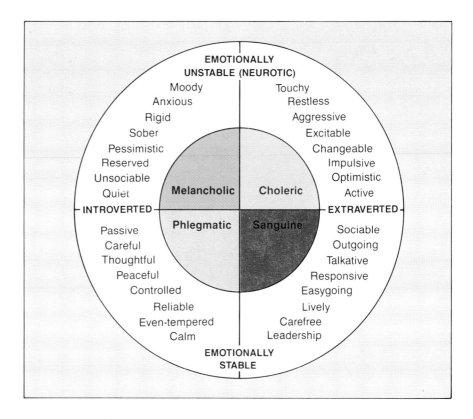

concept are described as aggressive, cold, egocentric, impersonal, and impulsive. People who score low in psychoticism are more empathic and less adventurous and bold. Eysenck uses the terms neuroticism and psychoticism partially because he believes that extreme scores on these two dimensions may predispose to psychiatric disorder.

Eysenck points out that his scheme closely resembles those put forward since antiquity. Galen, the Greek physician, medical writer, and philosopher (129–199 A.D.), suggested that people fell into four main types: *melancholic* (gloomy), *choleric* (angry), *sanguine* (cheerful), and *phlegmatic* (stolid). The relationship of Galen's types to Eysenck's introversion-extraversion and emotional stability–instability dimensions is illustrated in Figure 14–2. Eysenck developed a personality questionnaire to measure traits, called the *Eysenck Personality Questionnaire* or *EPQ* (Eysenck & Eysenck, 1975). It consists of 90 items requiring "yes" or "no" responses and includes a "lie" scale to attempt to detect people who answer untruthfully.

Cattell and Eysenck approve of one another's techniques; they disagree on how many trait dimensions best account for human personality. Cattell contends that reliance on three dimensions is unnecessarily restrictive and fails to consider the enormous complexity of individuality. Eysenck believes that his three types capture the most important dimensions of personality.

Measuring Traits

The 16PF and the EPQ are both examples of psychological measurement. Various ways of assessing personality traits have been developed, but two

A number of organizations use psychological test profiles of people's values, needs, and personalities either to provide useful feedback to the individual about himself (e.g., for human resource managers) or for selection purposes (e.g., to become an astronaut or fighter pilot).

methods stand out as the most frequently used and most popular: *objective personality questionnaires* and *rating scales.* They provide psychologists with a personality profile of an individual and can be employed for a variety of purposes, including predicting vocational success, judging personality change, and comparing groups (e.g., leaders and nonleaders).

OBJECTIVE PERSONALITY QUESTIONNAIRES. Cattell's Sixteen Personality Factor Questionnaire and the Eysenck Personality Questionnaire are objective personality questionnaires. There are many others. Some may measure a single aspect of personality, such as anxiety; others may assess several aspects simultaneously. All, however, contain statements about how people might feel, think, or behave in given situations. The respondents indicate whether or not a particular response is characteristic of themselves.

One of the earliest objective personality questionnaires, the *Minnesota Multiphasic Personality Inventory,* or *MMPI,* was created in 1942 to help clinical psychologists diagnose mental illness. It remains among the most widely known and used of such clinical tests. The MMPI consists of 550 statements such as the following:

1. I do not tire easily.
2. My bowel movements are irregular.
3. I am in touch with flying saucers.
4. When I get bored I like to stir up some excitement.
5. There are those out there who want to get me.

The respondent checks "true," "false," or "cannot say" to the questions. The answers determine scores on ten clinical scales that diagnose mental illness and on four validity scales designed to check that the respondent is answering truthfully (see Table 14–1).

Considerable evidence shows that the greater the number of scales on which a person's scores deviate from the norm (an average person's score), the more likely the person is to be severely disturbed. Unfortunately, evidence also indicates that a high score on any one scale does not predict a particular type of mental disorder. Thus a high score on the schizophrenia scale does not necessarily indicate the presence of schizophrenia. Several other problems have arisen with the MMPI, including low test-retest reliability and the fact that it was standardized on a nonrepresentative sample. (For a discussion of the terms *standardization* and *reliability,* see Chapter 11, pages 399 and 400). Although often criticized today, at the time it was developed the MMPI constituted a valuable instrument, for it served as the basis for the development of many other widely used tests.

Another well-known personality test is the *California Psychological Inventory,* or *CPI* (Gough, 1956). One of the earliest large-scale questionnaires for those not mentally ill, it consists of 480 items, half of them from the MMPI. The CPI provides scores on 15 personality traits such as dominance, sociability, self-acceptance, responsibility, socialization, achievement orientation, and masculinity/femininity. It was standardized on 13,000 people from many different socioeconomic backgrounds and geographical regions. To test the validity of the scores, psychologists asked high school and university students to nominate those among their classmates who were particularly high or low on many traits. (Such "peer" nominations are widely used to validate scores.) Hundreds of studies have now been carried out with the

TABLE 14–1
The Validity and Clinical Scales of the MMPI

Scale Name	Interpretation
Validity Scales	
1. Cannot say scale (?)	High scorers were evasive in filling out the questionnaire.
2. Lie scale (L)	High scorers attempt to present themselves in a very favorable light and possibly tell lies to do so.
3. Infrequency (F)	High scorers are presenting themselves in a particularly bad way and may well be "faking bad."
4. Correction (K)	High scorers may be very defensive in filling out the questionnaire.
Clinical Scales	
1. Hypochondriasis (Hs)	High scorers reflect an exaggerated concern about their physical health.
2. Depression (D)	High scorers are usually depressed, despondent, and distressed.
3. Hysteria (Hy)	High scorers complain often about physical symptoms with no apparent organic cause.
4. Psychopathic Deviate (Pd)	High scorers show a disregard for social and moral standards.
5. Masculinity/femininity (Mf)	High scorers show "traditional" masculine or feminine attitudes and values.
6. Paranoia (Pa)	High scorers demonstrate extreme suspiciousness and feelings of persecution.
7. Psychasthenia (Pt)	High scorers tend to be highly anxious, rigid, tense, and worrying.
8. Schizophrenia (Sc)	High scorers tend to be socially withdrawn and to engage in bizarre and unusual thinking.
9. Hypomania (Ma)	High scorers are highly emotionally excitable, energetic, and impulsive.
10. Social introversion (Si)	High scorers tend to be modest, self-effacing, and shy.

Source: Minnesota Multiphasic Personality Inventory Manual, 1970.

CPI, and its scales have been found useful for predicting behavior. For example, high school students scoring low on socialization have a greater chance of becoming delinquent and of dropping out of school, while those scoring high on achievement orientation do very well in school and beyond.

A more recently devised personality test is the ***Personality Research Form,*** or ***PRF*** (Jackson, 1984). Based on the most up-to-date methods of test construction, it was created to measure 20 essential "needs" postulated as the basis of human motivation by Henry A. Murray (see Chapter 12, page 452). In Murray's view (1938), needs such as the need for achievement constitute motives that arouse and maintain activity until the needs are satisfied. As with other tests, the PRF requires the respondent to check a box to agree or disagree with a written statement.

RATING SCALES. Rating scales are a means to record responses from standardized tests, interviews, and other assessment techniques. Table 14–2 shows some sample rating scales for the trait dimensions used in Cattell's 16PF. If a scale involves a dimension of outgoingness, one end of the scale might be labeled "extremely outgoing," while the other end is labeled "extremely reserved." A check mark somewhere between these extremes locates an individual along that dimension. Unlike objective personality questionnaires, rating scales are often filled out by professionals, using the information supplied by respondents in interviews. Sometimes the raters are clinical psychologists and psychiatrists, personnel managers, teachers, or

TABLE 14–2
Rating Scales Based on the 16 Personality Traits Identified by Cattell (1973)

	Average	
Reserved	:____:____:____:____:____:____:____:	Outgoing
Less intelligent	:____:____:____:____:____:____:____:	More intelligent
Affected by feelings	:____:____:____:____:____:____:____:	Emotionally stable
Submissive	:____:____:____:____:____:____:____:	Dominant
Serious	:____:____:____:____:____:____:____:	Happy-go-lucky
Expedient	:____:____:____:____:____:____:____:	Conscientious
Timid	:____:____:____:____:____:____:____:	Venturesome
Tough-minded	:____:____:____:____:____:____:____:	Sensitive
Trusting	:____:____:____:____:____:____:____:	Suspicious
Practical	:____:____:____:____:____:____:____:	Imaginative
Forthright	:____:____:____:____:____:____:____:	Shrewd
Self-assured	:____:____:____:____:____:____:____:	Apprehensive
Conservative	:____:____:____:____:____:____:____:	Experimenting
Group-dependent	:____:____:____:____:____:____:____:	Self-sufficient
Uncontrolled	:____:____:____:____:____:____:____:	Controlled
Relaxed	:____:____:____:____:____:____:____:	Tense

Construct your own (or a friend's) profile. See where you fall on each of these dimensions. Place an X in the middle category if you are "average" on the trait. Place the X to one side of the average to the degree to which you are "higher" or "lower" than the average.

school counselors, but the scales are so easy to administer that almost everybody can use them. Try completing the scales in Table 14–2 for yourself to see where you fall on each of the dimensions. Or ask a friend who knows you well to complete them. Now you can compare your own profile to that of the airline pilots in Figure 14–1. Of course, you may get a somewhat biased picture if you have only one person fill out the scales (especially if that one person is you!). One way around this problem is to ask several people to make the ratings and then to take an average. This is a procedure often used by psychologists when carrying out research to see how predictive personality can be (see "Controversy: Do People Behave Consistently?" on pages 504–505).

Biological Origins of Traits

Where do our personality traits come from? Do we learn to be shy or is there a genetic source? The idea that different personality types are based on biological factors is in fact one of the oldest views in the study of personality. Biological approaches to personality historically have taken two main paths. One considers body build, while the other focuses on inheritance. We will discuss environmental forces at work in personality later in the chapter.

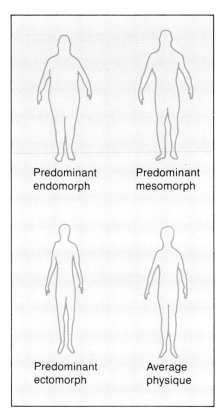

FIGURE 14–3
Body Types

Do different body types have different personalities? Research suggests that endomorphs are easygoing; mesomorphs are assertive; and ectomorphs are intense.

Predominant endomorph

Predominant mesomorph

Predominant ectomorph

Average physique

PHYSIQUE AND TEMPERAMENT. It is now widely accepted that you inherit much of your physique. Your genes determine a good deal of your bone structure, including height and girth. And since antiquity, thinking people have wondered whether bodily physique was somehow related to personality. Shakespeare, for example, had Julius Caesar comment:

> Let me have men about me that are fat;
> Sleek-headed men and such as sleep o' nights.
> Yond Cassius has a lean and hungry look;
> He thinks too much; such men are dangerous.
>   Julius Caesar; act 1, scene 2

One biological approach to personality focuses on body types (see Figure 14–3). Using complex scaling techniques and photographs, William Sheldon (1940, 1954) analyzed the body types of thousands of male college students and typed them predominantly as endomorphs (fat), mesomorphs (muscular), or ectomorphs (thin). Sheldon then compared ratings on more than 60 personality characteristics with the three body types and found three corresponding temperaments. *Endomorphs* tended to be easygoing, relaxed, sociable, and fond of good food and physical comfort. *Mesomorphs* were by and large more aggressive, bold, energetic, and fond of physical activity. *Ectomorphs* were intense, quiet, private, shy, and restrained in posture, movement, and social activity. Later studies showed that physique, as objectively measured, had predictive value. One study found dental and medical students more mesomorphic and less ectomorphic than those in chemistry and physics (Parnell, 1953). Another observed that research workers were more ectomorphic and less mesomorphic than factory workers in the same organization (Garn & Gertler, 1950). Many have reported that delinquents are more likely to be mesomorphic (Horn, 1983; Wilson & Herrnstein, 1985). Sheldon's theory of body types is currently out of favor among psychologists, and little research is being carried out. Sheldon, however, does have supporters, who argue that his theory has not been given a fair chance (Horn, 1983; Lindzey, 1973; Hall & Lindzey, 1985).

There may indeed be a core of truth in the long-held belief that physique and temperament are related; however, the link is fairly weak and its origins are a matter of speculation (Stager & Burke, 1982). Biologically inclined psychologists have suggested that the genes that determine body build independently determine the personality; others propose that body build shapes the personality by fostering one behavior pattern rather than another or by evoking stereotypic expectations in others. For example, from a sociobiological perspective, it may be adaptive for those who inherit thin bodies and thus are less fitted for physical interaction also to inherit a preference for solitude and intense thinking. An alternative view is that thin people develop the personalities they do because interaction with others reinforces one behavior pattern over another; for example, social interaction fosters the conduct that makes leaders of large and active body types. Another hypothesis suggests that the relationship is a by-product of stereotypes. If a chubby boy learns that others consider him easygoing, he may act accordingly. This does not explain how the stereotype originated, but it suggests how it is perpetuated.

GENES AND PERSONALITY. Can we use research to discover whether personality differences have a significant genetic component? It would not do

CONTROVERSY

Do People Behave Consistently?

For the trait approach to be valid, behavior that it describes must display a substantial amount of consistency. If people are to be characterized predictably as shy or persistent, they should demonstrate shyness or persistence across a number of diverse situations—at school, at work, at leisure. Should someone's shyness vary so much that it is not predictable from one circumstance to another, it is misleading to ascribe a trait of shyness to him or her.

Do people behave consistently across situations, or is their behavior specifically tailored to the demands of individual situations? A classic study of this issue was carried out in the 1920s by Hugh Hartshorne and Mark May (1928; Hartshorne, May, & Maller, 1929; Hartshorne, May, & Shuttleworth, 1930). They gave 11,000 elementary and high school students 33 different behavioral tests of their altruism, self-control, and honesty in various situations: at home, in the classroom, at church, and in athletic competition. In one of the tests of honesty, children were given a paper-and-pencil exam, and the test papers

were collected and duplicated. Later the original tests were returned to the children, who were told to score their own answers using an answer key supplied by the researchers. Whenever children changed their answers by copying answers from the key, the researchers were able to note their dishonesty. In another test, the children were tested twice. On one occasion, conditions permitted deception; on the other, strict supervision allowed no opportunity to deceive. This procedure also was applied to athletics: the achievement of a child on such activities as push-ups, chinning, sit-ups, and broad jumps was measured when the test was supervised by the examiner and when it was self-administered. Any difference in scores became evidence of cheating. Coincidental with the tests, teachers and classmates rated the children's reputations. Altogether 170,000 observations were collected.

By examining the relationships among the children's scores on all of the tests, the researchers were able to discover whether the children's behavior was specific to situations or consistent across situations. If behavior is specific to situations, then cheating in class should not predict cheating in the gym. If honesty is a consistent trait, then results from one test should predict how a person will behave on

the next. The degree of correlation across situations serves as the measure of consistency.

What were the results from this extremely large and intensive study? Measures of honesty correlated at an average of $+.23$, such a low correlation that it led Hartshorne and May to favor the specificity viewpoint. They stated, "neither deceit nor its opposite, 'honesty,' are unified character traits, but rather specific functions of life situations. Most children will deceive in certain situations and not in others. Lying, cheating, and stealing as measured by the test situations in these studies are only very loosely related" (1928, p. 411).

Other writers have subsequently sided with these experimenters. In a widely influential review of the literature subsequent to Hartshorne and May's study, Walter Mischel (1968) supported the notion of specificity, pointing out that the average correlation of behaviors across different situations is $+.30$.

Critics of trait theory have argued that correlations between $+.20$ to $+.30$ are too low to support the idea that people are consistent in their behavior. Trait theorists have responded to this criticism by pointing out that adding up several individual responses from a person and using this total score to predict aggregate scores

simply to examine how much offspring are like their parents, for similarities may be transmitted socially. To sort out the relative effects of heredity and environment, psychologists would somehow have to hold one of them constant so that the impact of the other could be detected. Twin studies and adoption studies, which were explained in Chapter 2, help us do just that.

As discussed in Chapter 2, twins are of two kinds: monozygotic, or identical, twins, who have 100 percent of their genes in common; and dizygotic, or fraternal, twins, who have 50 percent of their genes in common,

Is the child who is altruistic in this situation also likely to help in others, or is there little consistency to behavior?

in another situation give behavioral correlations closer to +.60, evidence that clearly supports the validity of trait theory (Epstein, 1980; Epstein & O'Brien, 1985; Rushton, Brainerd, & Pressley, 1983).

Why is consistency upheld when the focus is on total scores rather than individual examples? The answer is that there is always a certain amount of random variability in any one measure. Consider, for example, how inappropriate it would be for your professor to assess your achievements in this course on the basis of one or two multiple-choice questions. The correlation between individual items on a test of educational achievement averages around +.20.

A truer picture emerges when an individual's answers to several questions are combined. The randomness of any one score is averaged out when many scores are added together. For example, in the Hartshorne and May study we have just described, when the children's scores on the classroom honesty tests were added into a total and this total was correlated with other total scores of honesty in other situations, the correlation proved to be +.72. This indicates considerable consistency of honest behavior. Tests of altruism yielded similar results. Hartshorne and May found correlations of +.20 for altruistic behavior across situations. When the results of individual tests were incorporated into

a total score, however, they showed much higher correlations. For example, teachers' perceptions of students' altruism agreed extremely highly (+.80) with those of the students' classmates. Correlations greater than +.60 are quite high and, as trait theorists argue, support the trait approach to personality. In fact, recent evidence suggests that when aggregate scores are used, traits not only are stable over a situation but also prove to be stable over time, even decades (Block, 1981; Epstein, 1980).

The evidence, then, supports both specificity and consistency, depending on whether the focus is on the relationship between individual behavioral measures or on the broader connection among averaged groups of situations. Which of these two focal points—specific behavior or generalized trait—is more useful? The answer depends on the purpose at hand. If the goal is to modify certain behaviors in specific situations, then a specificity viewpoint is appropriate. If more general predictions are to be made, such as predicting a person's overall adjustment to new situations, it is more suitable to focus on the consistency of behavior across situations. This view now represents a consensus, including Walter Mischel, who was originally critical of the trait perspective (e.g., Mischel & Peake, 1982).

the same as nontwin siblings. Identical and fraternal twins can be compared to estimate the genetic influence on a particular characteristic. The results are called *heritability coefficients*. Although many disagreements exist about the practicalities of computing heritability scores for humans, some rough estimates are possible (Plomin, DeFries, & McClearn, 1980).

Numerous studies of twins were compiled in *The Study of Twins* (Mittler, 1971) using the *concordance method*. This involves finding a twin in a clearly established behavioral category (in a mental hospital, for example) and then studying the co-twin for evidence of the same behavior. If identical twins are more similar to each other than fraternal twins, then the similarity or difference can be attributed to genetic effects, assuming environments for both types of twins are equal in influence. Some have argued that the equal environment assumption is not valid because identical twins may be treated more alike by their parents than fraternal twins. A review by Scarr and Carter-Saltzman (1979) suggests that this criticism is of limited importance: in cases where parents have incorrectly classified their identical twins as fraternals, the degree of twin similarity typically remains unaffected. Moreover, Loehlin and Nichols (1976) showed that when measures of the differences that do exist in the treatment of twins are related to their personality, there is no evidence that differences in treatment have any effect. Table 14–3 summarizes the findings of several studies involving concordance rates for identical and fraternal twins. The evidence shown here supports the view that many of these behavioral categories have a significant genetic component.

Quite remarkable evidence on the heritability of personality is currently being gathered at the University of Minnesota (Bouchard & Segal, in press). Only adult identical twins who were separated at birth are being studied. One pair, the "Jim Twins," were adopted as infants into separate working-class families in Ohio. Both liked math and did not like spelling in school. Both chose law enforcement training and worked part-time as deputy sheriffs. Both vacationed in Florida, both drove Chevrolets. Incredibly, their lives have been marked by a trail of similar names. Both had dogs named Toy. Both married and divorced women named Linda and had second marriages with women named Betty. They named their sons James Allen and James Alan. Finally, although the emotional environments in which they were brought up differed notably, their profiles on objective personality questionnaires are very similar.

TABLE 14–3
The Heritability of Behavior

Category	Number of Studies	Number of Twins	Type of Twin	
			Identical	Fraternal
Adult crime	6	225	71%	34%
Alcoholism	1	82	65%	30%
Childhood behavior disorder	2	107	87%	43%
Male homosexuality	1	63	100%	12%
Manic-depressive psychosis	5	518	74%	12%
Mental subnormality	2	586	96%	56%
Neurosis	10	1,267	22%	11%
Schizophrenia	13	1,251	53%	11%

The table shows the percentage of identical and fraternal twins falling into the same category as their co-twins. The larger the discrepancy between identical and fraternal twins, the greater the importance of genetic influence.

Source: Rushton, 1984.

A study comparing identical and fraternal twins reared apart shows an interesting difference between the pairs. Here, the top row shows identical twins while the bottom shows fraternal (all reared apart). Note that, although told merely to stand against the wall, the identical twins unconsciously assumed similar postures, while the fraternal twins did not.

The 47-year-old Oskar and Jock are another twin pair. One was raised as a German Catholic and a Nazi; the other lived as a Jew in Trinidad, Israel, and the United States. Both arrived at the research center wearing wire-rimmed glasses and mustaches. Both like spicy foods and sweet liqueurs, flush the toilet before using it, store rubber bands on their wrists, and have domineering relationships with women. Both are absentminded. They also have extremely similar profiles on objectively measured personality tests. Of course, individual cases, however striking, do not tell us much. More quantifiable procedures are needed to gain estimates of heritability.

The most widely used method for estimating heritabilities involves comparing trait scores of identical and fraternal twins raised together. One of the most extensive twin studies compared 514 pairs of identical twins with 336 pairs of fraternal twins who as high school students had competed in the National Merit Scholarship test. Each participant took a wide variety of personality, attitude, and interest tests and answered questionnaires. Identical twins proved twice as much alike as fraternal twins on the personality measures, including many of the traits we have discussed—such as extraversion-introversion—exactly as would be predicted by genetic theory (Loehlin & Nichols, 1976). It appears that people may inherit a great deal more of their personalities than has often been realized (see "Research Frontier: Genetic Influence on Personality").

Evaluation of the Trait Approach

The traditional wisdom of the trait approach has contributed greatly to the understanding of personality. The approach has provided the trait as the unit of analysis and has demonstrated that consistency exists in the way

RESEARCH FRONTIER

___

Genetic Influence on Personality

Currently an enormous amount of research is going on in the field of behavior genetics, much of it concerned with personality. Different teams of researchers in different countries using a variety of techniques are finding that a great deal more of normal personality functioning is due to genetic influences than was previously believed. Consider some of the wide range of topics that have been investigated.

Vocational Interests

In a study of 850 twin pairs raised together, Loehlin and Nichols (1976) provided initial evidence that vocational interests, including those for sales, blue-collar management, teaching, banking, literary, military, and social service, and sports, have a significant genetic component. Supporting evidence for this position has come from the study of twins raised apart. Bouchard and Segal (in press) report that, on measures of vocational interests, their 34 identical twins raised apart are four to five times more similar than genetically unrelated individuals who are reared in the same home. Indeed, the twins raised apart were almost as alike in their job performance as twins raised together. Moreover, both types of identical twins were twice as similar in vocational interests as related individuals who share only half their genes and live together, such as parents and offspring or fraternal twins. Adoption studies also confirm the importance of genetic factors in vocational interests. Grotevant,

Scarr, and Weinberg (1977) contrasted 194 adopted with 237 biological siblings, all of whom had spent an average of 18 years in their families. While biological siblings shared similar interests, adoptive siblings did not.

Altruism and Aggression

A recent study examined the extent to which heredity influences individual differences in altruism and aggression, or the willingness to help or hurt others. The study compared 573 identical and fraternal adult twin pairs who had been reared together. All of the twins completed separate questionnaires measuring altruistic and aggressive tendencies. (The questionnaires included a 20-item self-report altruism scale, a 33-item empathy scale, and a 16-item nurturance scale, and many items measuring aggressive dispositions.) A variety of statistical analyses performed on the data revealed that about half of the differences between people in the tendency to behave altruistically are inherited and the other half of the differences are due to environmental influences (Rushton et al., 1986).

Political Attitudes

It has generally been thought that political attitudes are for the most part environmentally determined. However, in a twin study of social and political attitudes, Eaves and Eysenck (1974) found that dimensions of radicalism-conservatism, tough-mindedness (associated with ideological commitment), and the tendency to voice extreme views irrespective of right- or left-wing bias were partially attributable to genetic influence. In an Australian study of 4,000 twin pairs, researchers found

evidence for genetic influence on quite specific conservative political beliefs, such as those toward capital punishment, abortion, and nuclear disarmament (Martin et al., 1986). Finally, Scarr (1981) reported an adoption study of middle-aged parents and their adolescent children in which authoritarianism (the tendency to go along with political authorities) appeared to be genetically transmitted from parents to their children rather than to be the result of learning from the family.

Sexuality

A study of twins found evidence that inheritance plays a role in accounting for individual differences in the strength of one's sex drive (Eysenck, 1976). Differences in sex drive were found to be predictive of many phenomena, including age of first sexual intercourse (itself shown to be under genetic influence), intercourse frequency, and total number of partners. Human sexuality has also been related to genetically influenced personality traits. Thus, compared to introverts, the more outgoing extraverted person typically has intercourse earlier, more frequently, and with more different partners (Barnes, Malamuth, & Check, 1984).

A major review of some of the literature concerning the genetics of personality was made by Goldsmith (1983), who stated: "With substantial confidence, it can be concluded that theories of personality development ignore the action of genetic factors at some risk. Across age, across traits, and across methods, moderate genetic influences on individual differences have been demonstrated" (p. 349).

people behave, both over time and across situations. Most important, it has shown that personality can be measured in ways that allow behavior to be predicted. Trait theorists have also shown the importance of heredity in shaping personality. The chief weakness of the trait approach is that it does not address itself to the question of how behavior develops and changes with experience. The other three approaches do address these questions.

THE PSYCHOANALYTIC APPROACH

The psychoanalytic approach to personality was created and articulated by Sigmund Freud (1856–1939) and elaborated by others. Freud's was the first major theory of psychological development; he attempted not only to account for the origins of traits and other behavior but to provide a complete explanation of psychological functioning. This approach actually had its beginnings as a theory of mental illness based on Freud's analyses of his patient's cases.

Freud was born in Freiburg, Moravia, in the heart of the Austro-Hungarian Empire that sprawled across central Europe until its breakup following World War I. His father, a Jewish wool merchant, led the family to Vienna when Freud was a young boy. Freud grew up in the cosmopolitan capital and entered the University of Vienna's medical school at age 17.

Highly ambitious and gifted, Freud wanted to devote his life to the study of human physiology, which was in its infancy. But Jews had limited opportunities in the academic world, and the married young man had to earn his own way. So, reluctantly, he set up practice as a physician specializing in nervous disorders. In that role, Freud came to realize that many of his patients' problems were psychological. That realization and his efforts at treatment accordingly led, over decades, to his wide-ranging theories about the structure and function of the human psyche.

Perhaps Freud's most important intellectual breakthrough occurred when he postulated the existence of a powerful unconscious that was the source of a number of potent biological motivations such as sex and aggression. Once Freud had fully grasped that idea, it was a relatively small step for him to view these unconscious motivations as being in conflict with each other and with the conscious mind, thus generating anxiety over the unacceptability of these motives. Freud believed that unconscious motives revealed themselves indirectly in slips of the tongue and in dreams. Freud's first great work, published in 1900 when he was 46 years old, was titled *The Interpretation of Dreams* (1900/1964). (For selections from *The Interpretation of Dreams*, see Chapter 5.) This and Freud's later writing shocked the world. People were not ready to concede that deep-rooted forces to which they had no conscious access shaped their behavior. Neither were they pleased with Freud's emphasis on sex as one of the strongest unconscious drives. Within a few years, however, Freud had a sizable following. A full-fledged international psychoanalytic school developed with Freud at its head. Although some early disciples later broke away and founded alternative schools, Freud's brand of psychoanalysis has had the most impact on psychology. Indeed, Freud is one of the most influential psychologists of all time.

Freud's Theory of Personality Structure

Freud conceptualized the mind, or the *psyche,* as consisting of three levels of consciousness: the conscious, the preconscious, and the unconscious. As you will recall from Chapter 5, the conscious mind consists of what we are aware of at any time. Consciousness, however, is only the tip of the iceberg, to use Freud's metaphor. Freud described most cognitive functioning as taking place beneath the surface of consciousness. The preconscious consists of the parts of the mind of which people are not aware but which can be brought to consciousness without much effort—for example, if they are asked what they did two summers ago. The unconscious embodies the parts of the mind that cannot be brought directly to consciousness. Within the unconscious lie the basic instincts and drives, particularly those that motivate aggression and sex. Freud conceptualized the psyche as having a fixed amount of *psychic energy,* the dynamic source of all motivation, the sexual part of which is called *libido.* Freud divided the psyche into three parts: the id, the ego, and the superego. While the id is completely unconscious, the ego and superego span all three levels of awareness (see Figure 14–4).

THE ID. The *id* is the original reservoir of psychic energy and is present from birth. Aggressive, sexual, and other impulses from the id always demand immediate gratification. Thus, the id is said to operate on the *pleasure principle,* continually pressing for the immediate discharge of any bodily tension. One way the id reduces tension is to create an image of what it wants. This image, which cannot be distinguished from reality, is known as *wish fulfillment,* but wish-fulfilling mental images themselves cannot reduce tension. After all, hungry people cannot eat images. This failure of the id to deal with reality opens the way for the ego.

THE EGO. The ego comes into existence to deal with the objective, outside world and to satisfy the id's wishes and instinctive demands. For example, it seeks food when the id calls for appeasement of hunger drives. The ego eventually becomes capable of self-reflection and deserves the name Freud gave it: *ego,* or self. Until self-reflection occurs there is no "I" but only a mass of undifferentiated strivings (appropriately named after the Latin im-

FIGURE 14–4
Relationship Between Id, Ego, and Superego to the Freudian Unconscious

The ego, which is partly conscious and partly unconscious, tries to balance the entirely unconscious desires from the id against the superego's demands and the realities of the world. Note that the superego, like the ego, is partly conscious. The id is entirely unconscious.

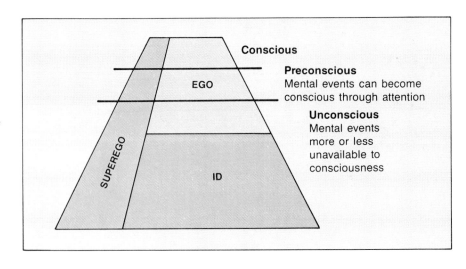

personal pronoun *id*, literally "it"). The ego obeys the ***reality principle*** in contrast to the id's pleasure principle. The reality principle, because it has to deal with the objective, "real" world, aims to suspend the pleasure principle until satisfaction—food in this example—is found. The ego is thus the executive of the personality. It controls actions and chooses outcomes. A person with a weak ego may be dominated by the wish-fulfilling fantasies of the id and fail to deal effectively with objective reality, spending instead a disproportionate amount of time in fantasy and daydreaming.

THE SUPEREGO. The *superego* is concerned with morality, with what is "right" and what is "wrong." It consists of two distinct parts: the ego-ideal and the conscience. The *ego-ideal's* primary interest pertains to what is right and virtuous. It holds up an image of ideal behavior and perfection and says "yes" to morally good things. *Conscience,* on the other hand, watches primarily over what is bad. It says "no" to wishes that are morally wrong. Indeed, it attempts to censor certain impulses from the id and prevent them from entering the consciousness of the ego.

The Development of Personality

Freud believed that the first few years of life are most important for development of a child's character. He conceptualized several distinct stages of development, which he called the *psychosexual stages;* each is concerned with a major biological function, and each influences personality development.

THE ORAL STAGE. The *oral stage* occurs from birth to 18 months and centers on eating, biting, and sucking. Psychoanalytic theory holds that if people are either overindulged or frustrated at this stage they become orally *fixated* and develop oral personalities. According to the psychoanalytic tradition, an oral fixation may last a lifetime and may manifest itself symbolically. Orally fixated people may be too gullible (they will swallow anything) or they may be sarcastic (verbally biting). They may also enjoy oral activities—smoking, eating, talking, and so on.

THE ANAL STAGE. The *anal stage* begins at about two years of age and is concerned with toilet training and eliminating and holding feces. In the psychoanalytic tradition, if parents are very strict during toilet training a child may become anally fixated and develop an anal personality. For example, a child may retain the feces and subsequently develop a stingy or too orderly and neat personality. If the parents, on the other hand, thank the child for "the gift," the youngster may become compulsively generous or highly creative and productive.

During the anal stage, the ego-ideal part of the superego becomes formed. Children are said to develop tremendous dependence on their mothers and in their absence become anxious. To relieve this anxiety, they introject the mothers into themselves as images of perfection. This is the origin of the ego-ideal, and people are doomed to strive forever to attain its high standards and to seek love from it fruitlessly.

THE PHALLIC STAGE. The *phallic stage* occurs by the fifth year. The male child is said to have sexual desires for his mother and to wish to possess her totally. He is intensely jealous of his father and of any siblings who are rivals for his mother's love. This, however, generates fear that the father will find out and punish the child by castration. *Castration anxiety* engenders more fear, even terror. Males are said to resolve their fear of their fathers by identifying with them. This is known as *identification with the aggressor.* They internalize images of their fathers and subsequently desire to be as much like them as possible. It is at this point that the conscience forms. The punitive father has become the forbidding part of the self. Desire for the mother and fear of the father become repressed from memory. Failure to identify with a father is said to cause problems later, including a lack of conscience. In addition, since a form of sex-role identification is made at this time, a lack of identification also results in poor sex-role development. Freud called this whole process, culminating in identification with the aggressor, the *Oedipus complex* after the ancient Greek tragedy *Oedipus Rex,* which is about a son who inadvertently kills his father and marries his mother. In Freudian theory, when the son's identification with the father occurs, the Oedipus complex is said to be resolved.

Freud described a different pattern of development for females; he called it the *Electra complex* after a Greek play about a woman who plotted her mother's death. At age two, females love their mothers, but they soon notice that little boys have penises while they do not. This is considered a traumatic discovery and they blame their mothers who, they believe, must have castrated them. They develop *penis envy* and desire sexual intercourse with their fathers so that they can share the fathers' penises. In some manner or other—Freud was uncertain how—females subsequently reidentify with their mothers in order to have intercourse with their fathers vicariously. This identification resolves the Electra complex.

LATENCY STAGE. Latency is the period from age five to the onset of puberty. After the turmoil of the Oedipus and Electra stages, this is a time of relative sexual calm. Boys and girls tend to avoid the opposite sex but are not totally asexual during this time since there is some interest in masturbating and in sex-oriented jokes.

GENITAL STAGE. The *genital stage,* from puberty on, occurs because of the hormonal changes that accompany puberty and marks the entry into mature sexuality and the development of a strong interest in forming heterosexual relationships with people outside the family. Ultimately, the desire to marry and raise a family appears and increases.

This general description of Freudian theory is oversimplified, but the chronology and outline of psychosexual development are as Freud conceptualized them. Freud's emphasis on oral, anal, and sexual sensation and gratification led many of his contemporaries to express moral outrage and denounce him as a pervert. Freud's basic purpose, however, was to emphasize that all people are born with biological drives, even erotic ones.

The Dynamics of Personality

Freud conceived of the id, ego, and superego as being in continual conflict. Since the id is totally hedonistic and demands immediate reduction of tension, a clash with the environment becomes inevitable. The superego wishes to deny gratification to the id's impulses. Thus, perpetual war is waged between the id and the superego, with the ego attempting to mediate. One view of the mental life depicted by Freud is that it resembles a house in which an aggressive, sex-crazed gorilla (the id) lives in the basement, and a harsh, puritanical spinster (the superego) dominates in the attic—with the battle between them being refereed by a nervous bank clerk (the ego) dwelling on the first floor!

ANXIETY. Anxiety originates in the personality because of this id-ego-superego conflict. Freud described three basic types of anxiety: neurotic, moral, and objective. *Neurotic anxiety* develops when people fear that their instincts will get out of control. Here a strong id dominates a weak ego. *Moral anxiety,* sometimes called guilt, occurs when people punish themselves for minor transgressions. Here a strong superego controls a weak ego. In *objective anxiety,* the ego perceives a genuine danger in the real world.

DEFENSE MECHANISMS. Anxiety is unpleasant, and Freud believed people developed *defense mechanisms* for dealing with it. Part of the unconscious, these are entirely normal and effective coping mechanisms when used appropriately even if they do serve to deny, falsify, or distort reality. Among the most common of them are denial, repression, projection, reaction formation, rationalization, displacement, and sublimation.

Denial constitutes a massive negative reaction rather than a specific response. For example, the death of someone close may cause shock and disbelief. *Repression* is a particular form of denial in which unacceptable impulses are pushed into the unconscious. A person may be unable to remember a painful experience or be unaware of feelings that at one time had been freely expressed. People cannot remember, for example, the sexual desire felt for the parent of the opposite sex. In *projection* an individual attributes to others the inner urges he or she disapproves of. For example, those who engage in sexual self-denial are said to see sexual irresponsibilities in others. A little boy may talk about how much his sister hates him instead of how much he hates her. *Reaction formation* involves doing or feeling the opposite of what one wants to do or feel. Thus someone may say, vehemently, after a lover has caused pain, "I hate you," when really he or she feels love. How can we distinguish a reaction formation from the real thing? Usually by the compulsiveness and the extreme behavior that tend to mark the reaction formation. When a person overreacts, we are alerted to the fact that things may not be what they seem. *Rationalization* finds a "perfectly reasonable" reason for behavior that isn't the real reason. A student who fails a psychology course, for example, may rationalize, "Well, I didn't really work for it because I didn't want to take any more psychology courses anyway."

Freud considered two defense mechanisms, *displacement* and *sublimation,* to be the healthiest. He believed that displacing unacceptable desires into more acceptable forms was sounder than repressing them altogether. Thus, if you want to hit the professor, but it seems wiser not to, then you go to the gym for a workout. Sublimation represents a displacement that produces a higher cultural achievement. According to the psychoanalytic tradition, sublimated sadistic urges may lead one to become a surgeon, and

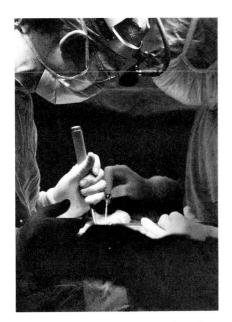

Psychoanalytic approaches tend to view surface behaviors as outlets for libidinal energy. Are these "altruistic" surgeons sublimating unconscious sadistic urges?

incestual sexual desires may lead one to paint or write creatively. Freud believed that the very advance of civilization depends on the mechanism of sublimation.

Psychoanalytic Assessment

Freud believed that much of the psyche could not be measured directly because most of it was unconscious. There would be little point in asking someone to describe his personality, for he cannot answer accurately—he does not know, for his ego does not have access to unconscious motives and conflicts. Thus, psychoanalytic personality assessment uses indirect methods, including *dream analysis, free associations, symbols,* and *projective personality tests.* All of these methods generate responses that are not under the ego's direct control.

Dream analysis is important to psychoanalysts because dreams are full of symbols. For example, the number 3 and elongated objects such as snakes, tree trunks, and even neckties are sometimes thought to represent the penis. Balloons and airplanes can be considered to symbolize erections, and climbing a ladder represents sexual intercourse. Particular interpretations are said to depend on the joint insights of therapist and patient, but a large number of such symbols in the dreams of a person who professes a happy and sexually satisfying marriage may suggest frustration and the desire for another partner.

Free associations and the presentation of other **symbols** may be interpreted in ways similar to dream analysis. In a free association test the analyst says a word and the patient counters with the first word that pops into mind. More elaborate projective personality tests are the ***Rorschach inkblots*** and the ***Thematic Apperception Test,*** or ***TAT.*** Each presents the subject with ambiguous images, and the structure the subject imposes on the image is said to reflect the subject's personality.

THE RORSCHACH. The Rorschach is one of the most popular projective techniques. Developed by the psychiatrist Herman Rorschach in 1921, the test uses complex, bilaterally symmetrical inkblots on ten separate cards (see a sample in Figure 14–5). Five blots are black and white; five are colored. The subject looks at the inkblots one at a time and names everything that the blot resembles. Responses may be scored on a number of dimensions, including location (the place on the card to which the response refers); whether movement was seen; whether the response was original; and so on. The interpreter seeks to relate these scores to aspects of the subject's personality.

THE THEMATIC APPERCEPTION TEST (TAT). As we first discussed in Chapter 12, the TAT was developed by H. A. Murray in the Harvard Psychological Clinic research program in the 1930s. The test consists of a series of pictures presented one at a time (see Figure 12–10, p. 453). Subjects usually are told that it is a storytelling test and that they are to make up as dramatic or interesting a story as they can for each picture. They are encouraged to be imaginative and to say whatever comes to mind. It is expected that subjects will project into the stories the basic themes that are of concern to their unconscious.

FIGURE 14–5
A Rorschach Inkblot

Interpretation of Rorschach responses is a complex process. Any response is always viewed in relation to other responses made by the subject. Nonetheless, certain examples can be provided. Thus, if a subject uses the entire blot for a concept, one interpretation might be that he or she has the ability to organize and integrate material. If small detail is used, then the interpretation might be that the subject needs to be exact and accurate. Animal responses are often given and have significance. Thus, if the outline looks like a bear, the subject may have a strong degree of emotional control; flying hawks, on the other hand, suggest a high level of ego functioning. It is important to bear in mind that these interpretations often derive from "clinical experience," and little in the way of hard evidence justifies any one view.

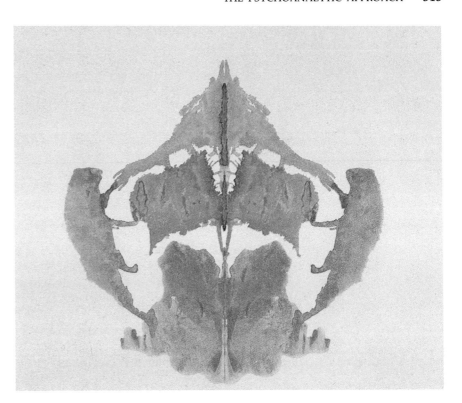

Other Psychoanalytic Theorists

Since Freud articulated his philosophy, a number of psychoanalytic theorists, some called *neo-Freudians,* have proposed modifications to his original theory. Most believed that Freud overemphasized sexual and aggressive urges. In Freud's account, for example, the ego arises out of the id, and its primary purpose is to deal with reality to satisfy the id's impulses. Later psychoanalysts viewed the ego as much more autonomous and capable of higher-level motives such as creativity, pursuit of knowledge for its own sake, and formation of self-fulfilling goals. Others have de-emphasized biological drives in personality development in favor of social factors. Still others have offered alternative basic drives. Among the best known neo-Freudians are Carl Jung, Alfred Adler, Karen Horney, and Erik Erikson.

CARL JUNG. Carl Jung (1875–1961), an admirer and one-time associate of Freud, broke with Freud and developed his own theory of psychoanalysis and method of psychotherapy, known as *analytic psychology.* Although Jung's theory retained Freud's unconscious processes, Jung also posited a *collective unconscious.* This is an inherited "racial unconscious" dominated by a set of symbols called *archetypes,* or "primordial images." Archetypes include God, the young, potent hero, the wise old man, rebirth (resurrection), the Earth Mother, the Fairy Godmother, and the hostile brethren, to list a few from among the many in legends and literature. Jung believed that all these archetypes owed their existence to the individual's heredity. His view of the unconscious differed from Freud's also in that he conceived of

The psychoanalyst Carl Jung.

it as the repository of broader and more positive images and urges in addition to dark, forbidden ones.

Jung also expanded on Freudian theory by writing about personality types, including the introvert and extravert varieties discussed in the context of trait theory. Jung also believed that people engage in characteristic ways of experiencing the world. One individual may rely primarily on sensing, or knowing through the sensory systems; others may rely on intuition, or feeling or thinking. Finally, in Jung's view, for every conscious or dominant side to personality, there is an unconscious side. He believed that every female's unconscious includes a masculine, assertive element; every male's a feminine, passive element. The process of personal growth involves an unfolding of the personality into a coherent life pattern in which the opposites are balanced.

ALFRED ADLER. Alfred Adler (1870–1937) was, like Jung, a student of Freud's who broke away to found his own school of psychoanalysis, known as *individual psychology.* He disagreed most strongly with Freud about the importance of the need for power as opposed to sexual need. Adler suggested that, because they are born weak and helpless, people develop *inferiority complexes* that produce a will to power, dominance, and interpersonal superiority. Like other neo-Freudians, Adler stressed the importance of the social environment; for him, feelings of inferiority and strivings for superiority manifest themselves in social interaction. For this reason there is a sense in which people create their own personalities. Adler also believed that people have social interests and a feeling of responsibility toward others. They will not be happy unless they are actively engaged in improving life for everyone and in helping to construct the best possible society.

KAREN HORNEY. Karen Horney (1885–1952) was born in Germany, trained in Europe with one of Freud's students, and emigrated to the United States shortly before World War II. Like Freud, Horney saw adult personality as shaped largely by childhood experiences. But unlike Freud, she believed that personality development is a product of social relationships rather than an expression of innate sexual and aggressive drives. In particular, Horney argued that when parents' behavior toward a child is indifferent, belittling, and erratic, the child feels helpless and insecure. Horney called this *basic anxiety.* Deep resentment toward the parents, or *basic hostility,* accompanies the anxiety. This hostility cannot be expressed directly because the child needs and fears the parents and wants their love. So the hostility is repressed, engendering increased anxiety and feelings of unworthiness. Such conflict between basic anxiety and basic hostility leads the child, and later the neurotic adult, into difficulties in all social interactions.

Horney was a pioneer in the psychology of women. As one of the first women to be admitted to a medical school in Germany, she came to see that women's feelings of inferiority resulted from their powerless position in the society of the 1920s. Horney believed that masculine influences have a distorting effect on feminine development. Within the family this might occur through the favoritism shown a brother or the punishment of a young girl's sexual curiosity. Outside the family, women experience harmful effects from the greater social value placed on maleness. Such social favoritism contributes to a woman's sense of inferiority and lack of self-esteem.

The psychoanalyst Karen Horney.

Horney's work also focused on the nature of the sexual relationships between men and women. She believed that women were subjugated and debased by the male's need to reaffirm his dominance and need for conquest. Why, Freud had asked, did men often choose inferior and submissive women to be their wives or turn to prostitutes to satisfy their sexual drives? Freud's answer: sexuality can be expressed only to one who is inferior to the "pure" mother idealization. Horney believed that a superior woman would pose too great a threat to masculine pride, and therefore debasement becomes the male solution to the problem.

ERIK ERIKSON. Erik Erikson (b. 1902) studied psychoanalysis with Freud's daughter, Anna, in Austria, moved to the United States, and began work on a developmental theory of personality. He stressed the development of the ego and the social nature of the human being and thus the great importance to personality development of the person's interactions with the social environment. As discussed in Chapters 9 and 10, Erikson also extended the development of personality well into the life cycle and proposed that the solution of specific problems at each of eight psychosocial stages (rather than Freud's five psychosexual stages) determines the kind of adults people would become. Erikson's focus on psychosocial development reflects the growing neo-Freudian emphasis on broad social and cultural forces rather than on instinctual drives alone.

Evaluation of the Psychoanalytic Approach

Psychoanalytic theory has had enormous impact on psychology and our self-concepts. One of Freud's greatest contributions was to establish the first scientifically deterministic model of human personality. Previously people had believed in free will and the overwhelming importance of the rational conscious mind. After Freud, it became respectable to ask questions such as why people behaved the way they did and to expect answers at a level deeper than what was accessible to direct conscious experience. Freud's second contribution was to point out that many causes of human behavior are biological and hidden from awareness. A third contribution was his emphasis on the importance of early childhood. Unfortunately, these positive aspects of his theorizing are often overlooked because the theory's defects make it less acceptable to modern psychologists. Freud's vagueness of terminology is a primary example: concepts such as id, ego, superego, Oedipus complex, repression, and psychic energy prove difficult to study scientifically. Many academic psychologists go so far as to say that psychoanalytic theory is primarily of historical interest (Eysenck, 1985). Many modern psychologists, however, scrutinize in detail the phenomena and topics that Freud first identified, but their theories and methods differ a good deal from Freud's.

THE HUMANISTIC APPROACH

The approaches to personality that we have considered so far have been deterministic. The trait and psychoanalytic approaches have emphasized that biological forces from within largely govern personality. Although neo-Freudians have sought to balance these extreme deterministic positions with a greater emphasis on the ego and on cognitive functioning, the humanistic approach has advanced further in this direction.

According to *humanistic psychology,* a person's conscious experience, what he or she feels and thinks, forms the basic structure of personality. Indeed, according to this approach, what people experience constitutes the only meaningful data for a psychology of personality. The external world is important only to the degree that it has meaning for the individual. For example, you may see everyone smiling and laughing and realize that that is the objective situation, but how you interpret it is vital. Do you assume that they are laughing at you or with you and that the circumstances accordingly are hostile or friendly? Hence, to understand somebody and to predict what that person is going to do on a particular occasion, humanists assert that psychologists have to know how the person thinks and feels. Two highly influential thinkers whose ideas are representative of humanistic perspectives are Carl Rogers and Abraham Maslow.

Carl Rogers and Self-Theory

Carl Rogers (b. 1902), a clinical psychologist, developed his theory of personality from observations he made while practicing psychotherapy. At the heart of Rogers's (1970b) theory is the self-concept. In his clinical experience, Rogers came to realize that his clients (a term he prefers to "patients") usually expressed their problems in terms of a sense of themselves as an "I" or "me." Such statements led Rogers to conclude that the self—the body of perceptions we think of as "I" or "me"—is a vital part of human experience. Rogers defines *self* or *self-concept* as an organized pattern of perceived characteristics along with the values attached to those attributes. People can have positive self-concepts, in which they feel good about themselves, or negative self-concepts, in which they may actually dislike themselves. How people view themselves, according to the humanistic approach, is the single most important aspect of personality functioning. The self-concept need not reflect "objective reality"; an individual may be at the top of her profession and appear happy and successful yet view herself as a failure. In fact, the self-concept comes in two parts: the *actual-self* and the *ideal-self.* The ideal-self is similar to Freud's concept of the ego-ideal. A positive self-concept arises when close agreement exists between the actual and the ideal selves. A large discrepancy between the two results in an unhappy, dissatisfied individual.

DEVELOPMENT OF THE SELF-CONCEPT. As a child grows, his or her self-concept emerges. Rogers (1970b) assumes that within each person there is an innate, biologically given drive toward growth in the self-concept. This drive can lead ultimately to *self-actualization,* the fulfillment of all of an individual's capabilities and the achievement of all of his or her potential. The drive toward growth in self-concept can manifest itself at a number of levels. At a low level, it is basically a desire for food, water, and physical growth and comfort. At a higher level are the needs for autonomy, self-efficiency, experience, and creativity. This motivation for actualization serves as a criterion by which all experiences are evaluated. An event is good or bad, by this criterion, in terms of whether or not it leads to self-actualization.

Rogers (1970b) views childhood as crucial for personality development. He stresses the importance of early social relationships. In this account, people need positive regard, warmth, and acceptance in order to grow and develop positive self-concepts. To enhance growth, in Rogers' opinion, children engage in a wide variety of acts. Herein lies a potential problem. Children may distort or deny their own perceptions, emotions, sensations, and thoughts and come to judge an event as good or bad on the grounds of whether it leads to approval or disapproval rather than to growth. Indeed, children may even internalize what Rogers calls *conditions of worth,* strong feelings about what kind of behaviors will bring them approval from others. Internalized, the conditions of worth serve a function similar to that of the superego of psychoanalytic theory.

Thus, to Rogers, all experiences are evaluated on two criteria, one that leads to self-actualization and one that leads to social approval. Often the two conflict; a typical example is when children wish to play with the household pots and pans. From a self-actualization perspective this would be good for children, enabling them to experience and grow. From a social approval perspective, parents may object because such play makes noise and annoys others. Parents' disapproval may then cause the children not to play with the pots, thus limiting their growth toward self-actualization. To promote growth, therefore, Rogers believes that parents and teachers should give children unconditional acceptance and love so that they do not become ashamed of their experiences and thoughts. By being unconditionally loved and accepted, Rogers suggests, people come to accept themselves and to achieve self-actualization. Being able to accept themselves is a major step toward becoming autonomous.

Rogers has extended these ideas to therapy. He views people who have internalized conditions of worth to be psychologically restrictive, anxious, defensive, conforming, unrealistic in self-demands, and feeling manipulated rather than free. To help such people find their way back toward self-actualization, Rogers (1970a) has developed what he calls *person-centered therapy.* In this approach the therapist's role is not to judge the client but to empathize with and to construe the world from the client's point of view. Most important, the therapist offers the client *unconditional positive regard;* that is, the therapist supports the client regardless of what the client says or does. In this warm, sympathetic, and accepting environment, the client can be freed from internalized conditions of worth and can grow again to self-actualization.

Abraham Maslow and Self-Actualization

How can we recognize a self-actualized person? Abraham Maslow (1908–1970) (see Chapter 12), studied 49 apparently self-actualized persons whom he admired. These included two of his professors and such historical figures as Eleanor Roosevelt, Albert Einstein, Spinoza, and Abraham Lincoln. He gathered his data by obtaining biographical information and, when possible, by questioning friends, relatives, and in some cases the subjects themselves. He concluded that these exemplary human beings shared the 16 characteristics shown in Table 14–4.

From studying self-actualized people and isolating their characteristics, Maslow developed a theory of personality with a key concept called the

TABLE 14–4
The Characteristics of Self-Actualized Individuals

1. Are able to perceive reality accurately.
2. Are able to accept reality readily.
3. Are natural and spontaneous.
4. Can focus on problems rather than on their self.
5. Have a need for privacy.
6. Are self-sufficient and independent.
7. Are capable of fresh, spontaneous, nonstereotyped appreciation of objects, events, and people that they encounter.
8. Have peak experiences and attain transcendence.
9. Identify with humankind and experience shared social bonds with other people.
10. May have few or many friends but will have deep relationships with at least some of these friends.
11. Have a democratic, egalitarian attitude.
12. Have strongly held values and do not confuse means with ends.
13. Have a broad, tolerant sense of humor.
14. Are inventive and creative and able to see things in new ways.
15. Resist the pressures of conformity to society.
16. Are able to transcend dichotomies, bring together opposites.

Source: Maslow, 1962.

hierarchy of needs (see Figure 12–13). At the bottom of the hierarchy are the physiological necessities and safety. Next come the psychological needs for belongingness and love, then self-esteem, and then self-actualization. In an ideal world, Maslow felt, everyone would become totally self-actualized.

Evaluation of the Humanistic Approach

Rogers's and Maslow's work has served the valuable purpose of forcing psychologists to focus on the study of private experience and the role of self-esteem in the functioning of personality. In addition, it has spotlighted some of the more positive aspects of human personality. The major criticism of the humanistic approach is that (like the psychoanalytic) its terms are rather vague and not immediately testable. There is, however, no reason why this should not change. Carl Rogers has called for extensive research into his ideas, and experimenters seem to be responding. Further, there is no reason why researchers could not attempt to measure some of the dimensions that Maslow has identified to see if there are generalized traits that differentiate the self-actualized person from the person who is not self-actualized.

THE SOCIAL LEARNING APPROACH

Shortly after the turn of the century, while Freud was developing his theory of psychoanalysis in central Europe, a brilliant young American psychologist, John B. Watson (1913), was sparking the behaviorist revolution. As described in Chapter 1, behaviorism aimed to apply scientific rigor to the study of human beings. Behaviorism has also been enlisted to investigate personality; behavioral psychologists insist that research should center on what people do rather than on what they feel or experience. Since their focus is on behavior, these researchers assert, they can directly assess personality both objectively and systematically. Behaviorists would argue that there is no need to look within the organism for unconscious processes, as the psychoanalytic approach does. They would not deny that people have feelings or intentions, but they would suggest that science might progress more in understanding personality if psychologists concentrated on studying its observable aspects. Because behaviorists focus on the modifiability of personality through learning, they also differ from trait psychologists who tend to see personality as relatively stable and unchanging.

The Learning of Personality

Besides observable behavior, behaviorists emphasize learning in explaining personality; therefore, they are much concerned with development and change in personality. To a behaviorist, if someone is described as having an aggressive personality, this means the person behaves aggressively and does so because he or she has learned aggressive behavior. Similarly, if a person is said to be an anxious type, then to a behaviorist this means that the person shows anxious behavior as a result of having learned to be anxious. Of course, what has been learned in the past can be unlearned in the future. Behaviorists hold an optimistic view of human nature since they believe that people can alter their personalities. In this view the aggressive, anxious, or shy can become nonaggressive, calm, or outgoing.

In recent years a schism between radical behaviorism and neo-behaviorism, or social learning theory, has split the behaviorist camp. Radical behaviorists, who are associated with the psychologist B. F. Skinner, deny the necessity of ever looking for internal mediators of behavior within the organism. Instead, radical behaviorists believe that events in the environment, particularly rewards and punishments, shape and control all human actions. The causes of behavior, they believe, lie totally outside the organism. Over more than four decades, Skinner's behavioral ideas have enhanced our insights of the functioning of human personality. Skinner has written extensively on the implications of his ideas for education, psychotherapy, and the organization of society (Skinner, 1953, 1978).

To distinguish themselves from Skinner's perspective, behavioral personality theorists such as Albert Bandura and Walter Mischel refer to their approaches as *social learning theory.* This thinking differs in two ways from traditional or radical behaviorism. First, it refers to an explicit attempt to add cognitive processes to learning theory. Second, it refers to particular ways of learning, such as observing others in a social context. It should be noted, however, that both social learning theory and radical behaviorism tend to emphasize the importance of concentrating on overt, objective behavior as the phenomenon to be accounted for and the role of learning in behavior.

We will examine some ways in which learning theorists explain human personality development by looking at three types of learning procedures: (1) classical conditioning, (2) instrumental learning, and (3) observational learning, all of which were explained in Chapter 6.

CLASSICAL CONDITIONING: THE ACQUISITION OF EMOTIONAL MEANING. How we think and feel about the world is an important part of our

Some of the most powerful sources of reinforcement originate from the approval and affection of other people.

personality. Social learning theorists believe that we acquire many of our emotional responses and our attitudes through classical conditioning. Our tastes for food, for example, may be acquired through the pairing of an unknown food (a neutral stimulus) with a positive stimulus or a negative stimulus. The same process may be at work in how we acquire our attitudes about national or ethnic groups. One study (Staats and Staats, 1963) showed that feelings about national names—Swedish and Dutch names, in this case—and familiar masculine names (Tom and Bill) could be changed simply by associating them several times with positive and negative words such as *sacred* and *happy* or *ugly* and *failure*. In this way, we acquire positive or negative attitudes about groups and people, or for that matter consumer products, even before we experience them directly.

INSTRUMENTAL LEARNING. The fundamental principle in instrumental learning is that of reinforcement: responses that result in reinforcement will increase in strength. This principle applies to such behaviors as an infant's smiles when caressed, interaction in a nursery school, criminal delinquency, and adult sexual conduct. Reinforcement can consist of an almost endless myriad of such things and events as information, money, approval, and removal of aversive stimuli. Some of the most powerful sources of reinforcement originate from other people.

Some applications of instrumental conditioning are very important. In one study (Allen et al., 1964), investigators went to a nursery school to see if they could make a child more sociable. Ann, a bright four-year-old, almost always played by herself and rejected social advances. Using reinforcement procedures, her teachers gave her much attention and approval whenever Ann spontaneously played with someone and ignored her when she chose to play by herself. After several days, Ann's sociability level increased significantly and remained high even when the teachers no longer gave her special attention. Positive reinforcement in the form of attention and approval had transformed Ann's personality from the most withdrawn in the school to that of a quite normal, socially interacting child.

Reinforcement analyses can be used to shed light on all kinds of personality problems, such as those caused by unwitting reinforcement. Parents who ignore their children's mild demands for attention and only reinforce their intense demands unintentionally produce loud, strident youngsters. Thus, it is argued that traits such as dependency, aggressiveness, achievement orientation, altruism, sexual behavior, and many others are learned, maintained, and changed through positive and negative reinforcement.

OBSERVATIONAL LEARNING. Numerous studies have indicated that much of personality is acquired by observing others. Some of the most important work in this area has been carried out by Albert Bandura (1977, 1986) and his colleagues.

In one early study Bandura and Mischel (1965) demonstrated that control of impulses and delay of gratification could be increased or decreased as a result of observational experiences. In the experiment, children were first offered a choice between a small candy bar they could eat immediately or a larger one they could eat in a week. On the basis of this and other similar testing, children were divided into groups designated as having

Observational learning asserts that much of our behavior, including sex-role learning and social skills, is acquired by watching others.

(a) little ability to delay gratification (they chose the immediately available candy) or (b) high ability to delay gratification (they chose the larger but delayed bar). The two groups then separately watched an adult model who was asked if he would prefer a small reward immediately or a larger one subsequently. If the children watching him had demonstrated a low ability to delay gratification, the adult simulated high ability, and vice versa with the other group. Subsequently, the children were again given the choice. In both groups, they now were likely to choose as the model had. Altered behavior persisted over four weeks. The experiment demonstrates the potential power of significant role models to modify such personality traits as self-control.

In another study (Grusec et al., 1979), kindergarten children were tempted to abandon their work to play with attractive toys. Whether they gave in to or resisted the lure depended on what they had seen a model person do. If the model spurned the temptation, the children proved better able to do so, and if the model succumbed, so did the children. Furthermore, these results endured and generalized to a different situation. The experiment (see Figure 14–6) shows that self-control and resistance to temptation can be acquired by observation.

Vicarious Conditioning and Reinforcement. Observational learning also accounts for the acquisition of emotional responses. If a child sees someone show fright at the sight of a snake crossing a path, the child may acquire a fear of snakes. Similarly, you might form a liking or disliking for particular ethnic groups (or future psychology courses) by observing how others feel about them. In this way people can build up stocks of emotional reactions to objects or people without any direct experience of them. This phenomenon has been labeled ***vicarious conditioning*** because stimuli are paired by observational rather than actual impact on the subjects (Bandura, 1986).

FIGURE 14–6
Temptation and Resistance

The figure shows the amount of time children played with the forbidden toy (instead of working) as a function of what the children saw the model do. The well-behaved "resisting model" led the children to play less with the forbidden toy in comparison with the control group, while the naughty "yielding model" led the children to neglect their work and play more with the forbidden toy.

Source: Grusec et al., 1979.

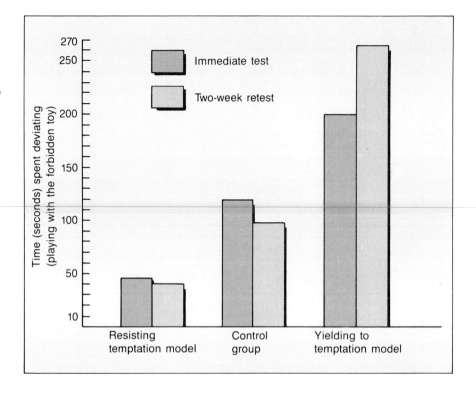

Through watching models, people are also able to observe the outcomes for the models, a phenomenon labeled *vicarious reinforcement* (Bandura, 1986). Vicarious reinforcement is said to have effects similar to those of direct reinforcement in increasing or decreasing the probability of any behavior. For example, if you see someone with a new hair style, you may do your hair that way too, depending on whether the other person wins admiration or criticism.

Social Learning Assessment

Because the social learning approach to personality stresses the importance of learning, it also emphasizes the situation in which any behavior is learned. You might assume that aggressiveness, for example, occurs far more on the football field than in a schoolroom and more in a schoolroom than in a church or synagogue. In other words, different situations elicit different responses, an aspect of learning referred to as *discrimination.* If sociability in one setting brings reward and in another meets rebuff, you would behave socially in the first but not in the second case. This of course raises the question of whether we demonstrate general, consistent traits in our behavior or whether we act as each situation demands. Many learning theorists play down the importance of traits and instead focus on situations and the previous learning experiences people have had in them.

Social learning theorists therefore assess personality by measuring behavior in a specific situation and analyzing its consequences. For example, a widely used situational testing procedure in industry is the "in-basket" technique in which people have to complete tasks similar to the ones they will subsequently perform on the job. Each job candidate is given an in-basket full of memos, phone messages, reports, and letters similar to those actually encountered on the job. After the candidate has responded to each of these items, the examiner rates the candidate on a specially designed scale and compiles an overall assessment of the candidate's likely success on the job. The method has proved quite effective, particularly for predicting managerial success (Howard, 1975).

Consider another example. Suppose psychologists wished to know how assertive a personality someone had. They would first need to know under what circumstances the person was and was not assertive. A behavioral assessment might require that the subject keep a diary for a few weeks, recording all occasions on which, in the subject's view, his or her behavior had been either satisfactorily assertive or insufficiently so. A pattern would emerge from the diary. The subject might be quite assertive with certain individuals in some situations and timid with people in other situations. He or she might be assertive with friends but not enough so with coworkers or, perhaps, with a professor. Once having isolated the circumstances in which nonassertiveness occurred, social learning theorists might then devise a program to help the person learn to deal with those situations more effectively (see Chapter 16 for a discussion of behavioral therapy).

Another means of behavioral assessment is physiological. This has proved to be effective, for example, with sex offenders who molest children. Using an instrument called a *phallic plethysmograph,* psychologists can measure changes in blood flow through the penis and can detect sexual arousal. By showing photographs of sexual stimuli to subjects, it is possible to determine their sexual preferences. Child molesters, for example, might be expected to exhibit sexual arousal at the sight of young children; homosexuals at the portrayal of members of the same sex; and heterosexuals for members of the opposite sex. It is then possible to pinpoint features that subjects find most attractive, such as hair and eye color, height, bust measurements, or age.

Evaluation of the Social Learning Approach

The social learning approach to how people acquire and alter their personalities and how our behaviors vary from situation to situation has added tremendously to psychological knowledge. Furthermore, because learning theory has been avowedly scientific and experimental from the beginning, it has forced all personality theorists to become generally more scientific in the way they study their field. Learning theorists have been criticized, however, for overemphasizing the importance of situational factors in behavior while neglecting the consistent patterns of individual differences in behavior. In addition, they have neglected and to some extent disavow the importance of genetic factors. Furthermore, some have been criticized for neglecting the cognitive and emotional sides of the personality, particularly conscious experience. Albert Bandura and other social learning theorists have responded to these criticisms by proposing a model of personality and behavior that integrates the social learning approach with other approaches.

INTERACTIONISM: TOWARD AN INTEGRATION OF APPROACHES

Each approach to personality that we have discussed—trait, psychoanalytic, humanistic, and social learning—has emphasized quite different aspects of personality. The trait approach focuses primarily on behavioral consistencies; the psychoanalytic on unconscious motives; the humanistic on the contents of consciousness; and the social learning on acquired variability. There is no need to view these approaches as conflicting; rather, they all stress different, but complementary, aspects of personality. Some might think that the trait approach, which emphasizes consistency, cannot be compatible

---

APPLYING PSYCHOLOGY

Assessing Vocational Interests and Aptitudes

Personality assessment is widely used in business and industry. Vocational counselors, for example, use tests to help guide people toward occupations suited to their interests. In addition, a variety of tests are used by employers to screen job applicants. And when a job requires specific skills (typing, for instance), special performance tests are often given.

One way to increase certainty about your own career preferences is to take a vocational interest test. The most widely used is the Strong-Campbell Interest Inventory (Campbell & Hansen, 1981), which includes information on 162 occupations, 99 of them added since 1977 and almost all of them coded for both males or females. Another popular test is the Jackson Vocational Interest Survey (Jackson, 1977). Your college counseling or career service or a psychologist who specializes in testing could provide you with information about these tests.

When taking vocational tests, you first answer "true" or "false" to a series of questions such as "I would rather be a lighthouse keeper than a

head waiter" and "I enjoy taking young people under my wing." The test manual then matches up the profile of your answers to that of a representative group of people successfully employed in various occupations. If your interests are typical of people holding particular occupations, then these are the jobs that are likely to appeal to you. For example, the interests of psychologists are associated with investigative (i.e., intellectual, scientific), artistic, and social themes (Jackson, 1977). Just as useful is the information concerning how dissimilar your interests are to various occupations. Interests in engineering and social work, for example, tend to be negatively related.

The strength and direction of an individual's vocational interests often overlap other aspects of personality, including values and work style preferences. Accountants tend to value orderliness and prefer working in environments in which activities occur in an expected sequence (Jackson, 1977). Entertainers, on the other hand, tend to value independence and prefer working in environments free from restraints and close supervision. Many of the tests provide this type of information.

Of course, tests of vocational interests cannot predict whether you will

succeed in a profession. Therefore, knowing your aptitudes, abilities, and personality can help determine the suitability of a particular job. To be successful as either a computer programmer or a computer salesperson requires the ability to think in mathematical ways. Each job, however, suits different temperaments when it comes to dealing with people. An accurate assessment of your strengths and weaknesses (e.g., shy versus interpersonally confident) can be a useful first step in planning a career. The example of Anne C., adapted from Jackson (1977), provides a case in point.

Anne C., a 22-year-old female college student, arranged for counseling during the final year of a college secretarial science course. She reported that she was sorry her education had taken this direction because she did not want to be a secretary but said that she might consider teaching business courses.

Her Scholastic Aptitude Test scores were at the 76th percentile in verbal and the 50th in quantitative. Personality information suggested that she was high in extraversion and low in neuroticism. She impressed the counselor as being outgoing, vivacious, talkative, and quite purposeful in planning her career.

Her JVIS (Jackson Vocational Interest Survey) profile [Figure 14–7] showed high scores on Author-Journalism, Academic

with a social learning approach, which emphasizes variability. Closer examination, however, reveals that both consistency and variability operate in human personality. It would be wrong to emphasize one at the expense of the other. Similarly, the fact that the humanistic approach focuses on the contents of consciousness does not mean that unconscious motives do not exist. In short, there is no reason why these approaches cannot be used in conjunction with one another, as they often are for assessment. Indeed, there is no reason why these approaches could not be integrated.

One conceptual scheme has tried to do so. *Interactionism* suggests that human behavior results from exchanges between ongoing, consistent personality dispositions, including both conscious and unconscious motiva-

FIGURE 14–7
Vocational Case History of Anne C.

Anne C.'s vocational interest profile shows high scores on Technical Writing, Author Journalism, Sales, Academic Achievement, Independence, and Interpersonal Confidence, among others. She had low scores in Math/Science Interests, Stamina, Accountability, and Need for Job Security.

Source: Jackson, 1977.

Achievement, Independence, Sales, and Interpersonal Confidence, among others. In terms of her similarity to college groups, she was most similar to liberal arts students. In terms of similarity to a classification of occupations, she was most similar to occupations in writing. She reported that she had always been interested in writing. As a child she had a fantasy of becoming a writer of children's stories. After exploring opportunities both with the counselor and on her own, she narrowed her career alternatives to two, teaching and journalism, at which point formal counseling ended. Followup two years later revealed that she was employed by an FM radio station working on a variety of tasks, including her own interview program. She was quite happy with her work but hoped to break into newscasting.

```
                              VERY              STANDARD SCORE            VERY
                       P/C- LOW         LOW       AVERAGE      HIGH       HIGH
                       TILE 10   15    20    25   30   35   40   45   50    55
                 SCORE  F   M .
. . . . . . . . . . . . . . . . . . . . . . . . . . . . . . . . . . . . . . . . . . . . .
CREATIVE ARTS        12 60 74 XXXXXXXXXXXXXXXXXXXXXXXXXXXX
PERFORMING ARTS      14 91 93 XXXXXXXXXXXXXXXXXXXXXXXXXXXXXXXXXXXXXX

MATHEMATICS           1  4  2 XXXXXXX
PHYSICAL SCIENCE      2 10  3 XXXXXXX
ENGINEERING           3 19  4 XXXXXXXXX
LIFE SCIENCE          6 29 22 XXXXXXXXXXXXXX
SOCIAL SCIENCE       13 74 82 XXXXXXXXXXXXXXXXXXXXXXXXXXXXXXXX

ADVENTURE             6 17  6 XXXXXXXXX
NATURE-AGRICULTURE    3 10  8 XXXXXXXXX
SKILLED TRADES        4 50 38 XXXXXXXXXXXXXXXXXX

PERSONAL SERVICE      7 27 50 XXXXXXXXXXXXXXXXX
FAMILY ACTIVITY       8 22 41 XXXXXXXXXXXXXXXX
MEDICAL SERVICE       5 36 28 XXXXXXXXXXXXXXX

DOMINANT LEADERSHIP   6 62 41 XXXXXXXXXXXXXXXXXXXXX
JOB SECURITY          4 18 13 XXXXXXXXXXXX
STAMINA               7 26 19 XXXXXXXXXXXXXX
ACCOUNTABILITY        8 11 10 XXXXXXXXXX

TEACHING             10 42 65 XXXXXXXXXXXXXXXXXXXXXXX
SOCIAL SERVICE        7 10 47 XXXXXXXXXXXXX
ELEMENTARY EDUCATION 10 38 77 XXXXXXXXXXXXXXXXXXXXXXXX .

FINANCE               6 45 27 XXXXXXXXXXXXXXXXX
BUSINESS              8 40 42 XXXXXXXXXXXXXXXXXXX
OFFICE WORK           7 50 62 XXXXXXXXXXXXXXXXXXXX
SALES                14 96 96 XXXXXXXXXXXXXXXXXXXXXXXXXXXXXXXXXXXXXXXXXXXX

SUPERVISION           8 51 44 XXXXXXXXXXXXXXXXXXXX
HUMAN RELATIONS MGT  10 48 53 XXXXXXXXXXXXXXXXXXXX
LAW                   9 47 45 XXXXXXXXXXXXXXXXXXX
PROFESSIONAL ADVISING 9 46 52 XXXXXXXXXXXXXXXXXXX

AUTHOR-JOURNALISM    16 93 95 XXXXXXXXXXXXXXXXXXXXXXXXXXXXXXXXXXXXXXX
ACADEMIC ACHIEVEMENT 13 83 82 XXXXXXXXXXXXXXXXXXXXXXXXXXXXXXXX
TECHNICAL WRITING    15 98 99 XXXXXXXXXXXXXXXXXXXXXXXXXXXXXXXXXXXXXXXXXXXXX

INDEPENDENCE         15 95 93 XXXXXXXXXXXXXXXXXXXXXXXXXXXXXXXXXXXXXX
PLANFULNESS           8 33 32 XXXXXXXXXXXXXXXXX
INTERPERSONAL
   CONFIDENCE        15 78 87 XXXXXXXXXXXXXXXXXXXXXXXXXXXXXXXX
. . . . . . . . . . . . . . . . . . . . . . . . . . . . . . . . . . . . . . . . . . . . .
THE BAR GRAPH PRINTED NEXT TO EACH SCALE NAME INDICATES HOW YOUR STANDARD
SCORES COMPARE WITH THOSE OF A LARGE GROUP OF MALE AND FEMALE STUDENTS
AND YOUNG ADULTS.  THE COLUMN LABELED `SCORE' TO THE LEFT INDICATES THE
NUMBER OF ACTIVITIES RELATED TO THAT AREA FOR WHICH YOU HAVE INDICATED A
PREFERENCE.  THE PERCENTILE (P/C-TILE) INDICATES THE NUMBER OF FEMALES (F)
AND MALES (M) OUT OF 100 WHO WOULD RECEIVE A SCORE LOWER THAN YOUR SCORE.
A HIGHER SCORE INDICATES GREATER RELATIVE INTEREST.
```

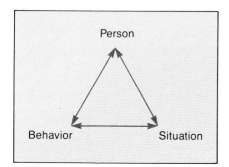

FIGURE 14–8
Schematic Representation
of an Interaction

Within the person can be found the self-concept and conscious and unconscious experiences and the biological basis from which they emerge. The situation includes reinforcements and other situational contingencies that affect behavior, attitudes, and self-concepts. Behavior represents behavioral competencies and characteristic ways of behaving. The arrows suggest that each of the focal points affects each other.

tions, and the situations people find themselves in (Bandura, 1978, 1986; Endler & Edwards, 1986). Thus, even the most aggressive person will behave relatively peaceably in church or synagogue, while the least aggressive will behave more aggressively playing football. One way of conceptualizing this interaction (see Figure 14–8) was suggested by Bandura (1978).

Bandura's formulation analyzes the interaction in three separate components. These are (1) aspects about or events occurring within each individual as a *person*, (2) overt *behavior*, and (3) the *situation*. Within the person can be found all of an individual's conscious and unconscious experiences and genetic makeup. Included here as well are the self-concept as outlined in Rogers's theory and the unconscious biological drives outlined by psychoanalytic views. In Figure 14–8, the arrow going from person to behavior suggests that these factors all contribute to create behavior. Behavior, of course, is the part of personality that learning theorists have focused on. Learning theorists would particularly stress the arrow going from the situation to behavior. The situation includes whatever models and reinforcement shape behavior. At the same time the situation has an arrow going to the person because these reinforcement and other situational aspects cause attitudes, self-concepts, and needs to alter. According to the figure, however, it is important to note that after someone behaves in a certain way, he or she changes the situation. This requires the arrow going from behavior to situation. Thus, if you have developed good social skills, you will change a social situation to make it more compatible with your personality. On the other hand, if you behave in a socially unacceptable way you will cause negative consequences from the situation. Finally, the arrow going from behavior to the person indicates that as you behave so you also change your conception of the kind of person you are. In short, Bandura's interactionist position requires all three components to be seen as an interlocking chain. Although at any one point each of the three components can be viewed as having independent effects, they actually operate only in reciprocal interaction.

An understanding of human personality requires us to comprehend how each of these three components can have both independent and interactive effects. It is also important not to denigrate any one approach but to accept that each of us owes his or her personality to genetic inheritance, consistent behavior, unconscious motives, conscious experiences, and previous learning experiences.

SUMMARY

1. Personality is the study of individual differences in behavior and experience. Four major approaches to personality have been developed: trait, psychoanalytic, humanistic, and social learning.

2. Traits may be defined as "any distinguishable, relatively enduring way in which one individual varies from others" (Guilford, 1959, p. 6). The underlying assumption of trait theory is that such traits are fundamentally consistent over time and situations.

3. There may be thousands of traits by which people differ from each other. Factor analysis is a statistical technique that has been used by trait theorists such as Raymond Cattell and Hans Eysenck to reduce the many to a manageable few. Cattell measured 16 traits using the Sixteen Personality Factor Questionnaire. Eysenck reduced traits to three on the Eysenck Personality Questionnaire: extraversion, neuroticism, and psychoticism.

4. Other objective personality questionnaires include the Minnesota Multiphasic Personality Inventory (MMPI), standardized on a psychiatric sample, and the California Psychological Inventory

(CPI) and Personality Research Form (PRF), standardized on normal (nonpsychiatric) samples.

5. The concept of stable personality traits has been seriously challenged by the theory of specificity, which argues that people behave much less consistently than a trait theory would predict. If the principle of aggregation is used to assess personality, however, consistency is indeed found.

6. The biological approach to personality focuses on the genetic inheritance of personality. One procedure is to build a taxonomy by relating personality traits to bodily physique. The major example is Sheldon's classification according to the dimensions of endomorphy, mesomorphy, and ectomorphy. Sheldon suggested that these dimensions of body type relate to three clusters of personality traits—easygoing, energetic, and intense.

7. Another approach centering on genetic factors embraces the studies showing that scores on many personality questionnaires are more similar for identical than for fraternal twins or for biological than adoptive families.

8. The psychoanalytic model assumes that people are primarily motivated by drives and instincts over which they have little control; these motivations exist, for the most part, in the unconscious. Personality is made up of three processes, or systems: the id, the ego, and the superego. A person's behavior is the product of the interaction, and often conflict, of these three systems.

9. According to Freud, personality development takes place during five psychosexual stages: oral, anal, phallic, latency, and genital.

10. The psychoanalytic approach to assessing personality uses projective techniques. Two prominent examples are the Rorschach Inkblot Test and the Thematic Apperception Test (TAT). While the tests are often used in clinical practice, they have been criticized because of their poor reliability, standardization, and validity.

11. The humanistic perspective stresses the individual's unique experience of the world and a belief in human potential. Carl Rogers has developed a theory of the self according to which each person is engaged in a lifelong striving for self-actualization, the process of achieving individual potential.

12. Abraham Maslow also believed in the self-actualized person, who he postulated must fulfill a hierarchy of needs before reaching the goal of realizing his or her unique potential.

13. According to Rogers, a strong, positive self-concept and eventual self-actualization are likely to occur if an individual receives unconditional love. Conditional love can result in a negative self-concept.

14. According to learning theorists, personality is a set of patterns of behavior that people learn to make in response to specific stimuli. People's behavior depends on how their responses have been reinforced in the past or on how they have seen successful models behave in similar situations.

15. Interactionism is a growing consensus in the psychology of personality. Interactionism suggests that human behavior is the result of an interaction between people's ongoing consistent personality dispositions, including both conscious and unconscious motivations, and the situations they find themselves in.

SUGGESTED READINGS

Anastasi, A. (1982). *Psychological testing* (5th ed.). New York: Macmillan.
  A classic introductory textbook that covers the basics of the functions and history of psychological testing and the importance of norms, standardization, reliability, and validity; also covers many of the important personality tests.

Hall, C. S., & Lindzey, G. (1985). *Introduction to theories of personality*. New York: Wiley.
  A classic textbook on the various theories of personality, particularly strong in its coverage of both classical psychoanalytic theory and later neo-Freudian conceptions.

Mischel, W. (1986). *Introduction to personality* (4th ed.). New York: Holt, Rinehart & Winston.
  Another good introduction to personality. Attempts to be a little more evaluative and integrative, primarily from the perspective of social learning theory and interactionism.

Phares, E. J. (1984). *Introduction to personality.* Columbus, Ohio: Merrill.

  Another excellent undergraduate textbook giving in-depth coverage of the basic approaches. A novel feature in the last part of the book is the application of the different approaches to various specific topics of interest.

Richman, J. (Ed.) (1957). *A general selection from the works of Sigmund Freud.* Garden City, N.Y.: Doubleday Anchor.
  A paperback edition of excerpts from the writings of Sigmund Freud. For those who want to read Freud in the original, this is an excellent introduction to his work.

15

Abnormality and Deviance

> Everybody is a moon, and has a dark side which [is never shown] to anybody.
>
> *Mark Twain*

THE PSYCHOLOGISTS MET WITH THE THREE MEN ON JULY 1, 1959, IN A large room at the Ypsilanti State Hospital in Michigan. The first patient, a 58-year-old, introduced himself: "My name is Joseph Cassell." When asked if he had anything else to say, he responded, "Yes, I'm God." Then it was the turn of the tall, 70-year-old man, who spoke with a low, rumbling voice: "My name is Clyde Benson. That's my name straight." When asked if he had other names, he answered, "Well, I have other names, but that's my vital side and I made God five and Jesus six." "Does that mean you're God?" "I made God, yes. I made it seventy years old a year ago. Hell! I passed seventy years old!"

The last man to speak was 38 and named Leon Gabor. But he denied his real name and refused to deal with anyone who attempted to use it. The psychologists referred to him as Rex. To introduce himself, Leon said, "Sir, it so happens that my birth certificate says that I am Dr. Domino Dominorum et Rex Resarum, Simplis Christianus Pueris Mentalis Doktor. [This is all the Latin Leon knows: "Lord of Lords and King of Kings, Simple Christian Boy Psychiatrist."] It also states on my birth certificate that I am the reincarnation of Jesus Christ of Nazareth, and I also salute, and I want to add this. I do salute the manliness in Jesus Christ also, because the vine is Jesus and the rock is Christ, pertaining to the penis and testicles; and it so happens that I was railroaded into this place because of prejudice and jealousy and duping that started before I was born, and that is the main issue why I am here."

This scenario is not from some movie or novel but was actually played out under the watchful eye of Milton Rokeach, a psychologist. Each of the three men unswervingly believed himself to be Jesus Christ. Each had been diagnosed as schizophrenic and had spent years in the Ypsilanti State Hospital. Rokeach decided to bring them together in an attempt to break into their delusional worlds and return them to reality. If all three were brought together, he believed that it was possible that they would undermine each other's belief system. The fascinating tale is told in *The Three Christs of Ypsilanti* (1964).

In the end, Rokeach did not succeed in lifting the three Christs from their tragic state. They quarreled and argued theology, and each one invented reasons why the other two were lying. Each was convinced that he was the only true Christ. Clyde dismissed the others' claims by arguing, "They are not really alive. The machines in them are talking. Take the machines out of them and they won't talk anything. You can't kill the ones with machines in them. They're dead already" (Rokeach, 1964, p. 50).

The three Christs had developed incredibly strong belief systems (along with other symptoms) that greatly interfered with their lives and the lives of those around them. This chapter is about the variety of such maladies that befall people and lead to their being considered abnormal or deviant. First, however, we must define what we mean by these terms.

WHAT IS ABNORMAL BEHAVIOR?

It is impossible to say exactly how many people are "abnormal," although some researchers estimate that virtually 100 percent of the population will suffer some psychological problem, such as anxiety or depression, at some time, with 25 percent encountering serious psychological difficulties. The U.S. Surgeon General (1979) predicted that one out of every eight individuals would actually require mental health care. In terms of individual suffering and the loss of human potential, the costs of these problems are enormous. The financial burdens of mental illness alone are put in the tens of billions of dollars annually; if the price of crime and other deviances is added, the figures quintuple. Table 15–1 provides a list of just some of the mental health problems in the United States in the 1980s. There is considerable debate among psychologists about how to define the subject matter of abnormal psychology. No single definition exists, but most approaches use one or more of the following criteria: statistical, cultural, and personal.

Statistical abnormality includes any substantial deviation from the average or typical behavior of the group to which an individual belongs. (The diagnosis of mental retardation is based on this assumption; see Chapter 11.) Thus, any behavior that is sufficiently rare or unusual statistically is designated as abnormal. By this definition, abnormality would include Larry Bird's remarkable basketball skills or Michael Jackson's unusual dancing ability. The statistical criterion does not distinguish between desirable and undesirable behavior.

Cultural abnormality involves any deviation from a societal standard or norm. To be considered normal, behavior must be socially acceptable. This perspective emphasizes value judgments. What one person considers abnormal, another may view as perfectly sensible. Indeed, the "abnormal" at one time can become the "normal" at some later time. For example, in 1973 the American Psychiatric Association removed homosexuality from its list of

---

TABLE 15–1
The Mental Health Picture in the United States in the 1980s

45 to 55 million Americans suffer from mild to moderate depression.
20 to 30 million Americans need mental health care at any one time.
20 million individuals suffer from neurotic disturbance.
10 million people have an alcohol problem (1 million are being treated for such).
10 million juveniles and adults are arrested in connection with serious crimes.
 7 million individuals are considered mentally retarded.
 6 million children and teenagers are considered emotionally disturbed.
 2 million youth have specific learning disabilities.
 2 million people suffer profound depression.
 2 million Americans are or have been schizophrenic.
 1 million Americans suffer from an organic mental disorder.
 1 million students withdraw from college each year as a result of emotional problems.
 ½ million people are addicted to heroin.
200,000 child abuse cases are reported annually.
200,000 people attempt suicide (26,000 individuals die from suicide).
 1 of every 3,000 children is autistic.

Source: U.S. Surgeon General, 1979.

disorders: a sexual deviance now became by implication a sexual choice. The fact that abnormality involves a cultural value judgment reveals something else about these behaviors: they differ only by degree. Most psychologists accept the idea of a *normality-abnormality continuum* in which behavior well within the norms of society falls at one end while abnormal behavior is at the other end.

A third criterion, *personal,* considers abnormality in terms of the individual's subjective feelings. For example, several studies have demonstrated that thousands of young people have problems controlling their weight and consequently view themselves as unattractive. Similarly, most people at times feel anxious or depressed or suffer from aches, pains, and other psychosomatic problems. These problems are not abnormal statistically, for they occur frequently. They are abnormal, however, in an ideal sense because they cause unhappiness to the sufferer.

None of these criteria—statistical, cultural, or personal—is completely satisfactory for diagnosing abnormality. In most instances of diagnosis, all three are considered. A fourth criterion—*the legal definition of abnormality*—declares a person insane largely on the basis of his or her ability to judge between right and wrong or to exert control over his or her behavior. This approach is even less useful for diagnostic purposes. **Insanity** is a legal term meaning not legally responsible for actions because of a deranged mind (see "Applying Psychology: The Plea of Insanity and Criminal Responsibility," page 561). The term insane is not employed by psychologists in discussing abnormality.

Approaches to Abnormality and Deviance

Words such as "abnormal" and "deviant" are emotionally powerful. We would not like to use them to refer to ourselves or members of our families. Some psychologists prefer terms such as "behavior disorder," "emotional disturbance," "mental illness," and "psychological problem." In this chapter we consider these terms, for most purposes, to be interchangeable. They have in common that they pertain to behavior sufficiently outside the norm to warrant attention. To psychologists, however, they differ in what they imply about the origins and treatment of abnormalities. For example, a behavior disorder suggests a highly specific problem, such as learning to sit still and listen while a teacher is talking, whereas emotional disturbance suggests deeper-lying difficulties, such as hyperactivity. As we saw in Chapter 14, psychologists have differing conceptions of normal personality. These differences recur in the study of abnormality.

How did psychology's modern ideas of abnormality evolve? We will first consider the historical development of the different approaches to abnormality. These include: (1) the superstitious, (2) the medical, (3) the psychoanalytic, and (4) the behavioral. We will also discuss modern approaches to the classification of abnormal behavior.

THE SUPERSTITIOUS APPROACH. Some of the earliest explanations of abnormal behavior attributed it to supernatural powers. During the Middle Ages, for example, all natural phenomena were perceived as manifestations of God or Satan. Thus, a person who acted abnormally was thought to be possessed by a god or devil. For eviction of a satanic spirit, treatment might

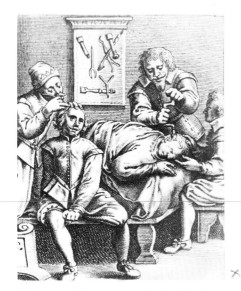

This superstitious approach, trephination of the skull, is thought to date back to the Stone Age, when it was believed that abnormal behavior could be cured by cutting a hole in the disturbed person's head to release evil spirits.

consist of torture, even execution. As late as 1692, in Salem, Massachusetts, 19 women were put to death publicly as witches. The fear and fascination of possession by devils linger: many contemporary rock videos and movies feature satanic themes.

The more fortunate abnormal individual, of course, was possessed by a god. In ancient Greece, people visited oracles such as Delphi to hear a priestess make divine prophecies. Some of these priestesses may have heard voices and if they had lived at other times might have been burned as witches.

Moral wickedness was another pervasive explanation for bizarre conduct throughout the Middle Ages. This resulted partly from strong religious feeling and partly from people's limited knowledge and education. Up to the late 1700s, the treatment for people who acted bizarrely consisted of locking them up in horrendous institutions where they often died from malnutrition and abuse.

THE MEDICAL APPROACH. Attitudes began to change in the late 1700s and early 1800s. With the Enlightenment came renewed interest in human rationality and thus the power of experiment and observation. Slowly, explanations for behavior based on reason replaced religious accounts. The idea developed that people in asylums were ill, not evil. In Paris, the physician Philippe Pinel (1745–1826) promoted this view and removed the inmates' shackles and ensured that they had sufficient food, fresh air, and exercise.

This medical perspective gained much support when it was found that some bizarre behaviors were due to brain damage and identifiable physical causes. Classic among these causes was the discovery that syphilis, a sex-

Pinel at the hospital of Salpêtrière removing the inmates' shackles, an example of the "medical approach."

ually communicated microorganism, produced aberrant behavior through deterioration of the brain 10 to 20 years after initial infection.

The medical model remains very important in the diagnosis of psychological distress. Scientists now know that a number of diseases other than syphilis, as well as the intake of certain substances, can cause mental disturbances. Excessive use of alcohol or other drugs damages the brain. Ingestion of lead or mercury has been linked to delusions, hallucinations, and a lack of emotional control in industrial workers and in people who have consumed fish taken from industrially polluted waters. Finally, the medical model focuses research attention on the genetic inheritance of illness. Heredity has been implicated in a number of mental disorders, particularly schizophrenia.

THE PSYCHOANALYTIC APPROACH. Not all physicians accepted the medical model's biological version of the origin of abnormal behavior. Sigmund Freud elaborated his view that psychological problems could be traced to childhood conflicts (see Chapter 14). These conflicts, if not resolved, could lead to a fixation at the stage of development where they occurred. Thus, for the distressed adult, problems are assumed to be due to unconscious, unresolved conflicts from childhood. Impulses that have not been completely discharged and instead have been dealt with inadequately by defense mechanisms become transformed into the symptoms of the *neuroses* and *psychoses.* According to Freud, "Neurosis is the result of a conflict between the ego and its id, whereas psychosis is the analogous outcome of a similar disturbance in the relation between the ego and external world" (1959, p. 250). Fundamental to the psychoanalytic view, therefore, is the idea of an inner core of emotional or mental disturbances, i.e., disease, from which the observed symptoms spring.

Freud's ideas have profoundly affected how psychologists think about adjustment and the healthy personality. From the psychoanalytic perspective, well-adapted individuals possess insight into their unconscious motives and a strong ego, and they do not waste psychic energy in distorting either wishes or reality itself (Meissner, 1980).

THE BEHAVIORAL APPROACH. In contrast to the medical and psychoanalytic models, which view abnormal behavior as a surface manifestation of underlying problems, the behavioral approach regards the behavior itself as the problem. Its major aspect is its claim that abnormality and deviance are explained just like other behaviors through the laws of learning and conditioning. According to this perspective, one person may have learned from the environment to be a hard-working business executive and another to be an easygoing teacher; still another may have learned to become alcoholic or schizophrenic.

One of the differences between the behavioral and medical perspectives lies in the labels the practitioners apply to abnormality and deviance. Behaviorally oriented psychologists prefer to use such terms as "behavior problem." This is partly to avoid stigmatizing the whole individual as "mentally ill" or "emotionally disturbed." (The issue of whether or not the diagnostic labels of abnormal psychology contribute to a person's personal distress is covered in "Controversy: Is Mental Illness a Myth?")

CONTROVERSY

Is Mental Illness a Myth?

Critics of DSM-III have been concerned that this classificatory system increases the danger of labeling and stigmatizing as "abnormal" people who have relatively mild difficulties. Certainly any classificatory system can be misused if professionals allow a diagnostic label to carry too much weight. They run the risk of overlooking the unique features of each case and of expecting the person to conform to the classification. Another danger is forgetting that naming or classifying is only a first and tentative step in scientific understanding.

The most radical criticism is that the whole notion of classification is misguided. Critics with this point of view argue that there is no such thing as mental illness. Psychiatrist Thomas Szasz (1961, 1970, 1974) has been a leading exponent of this view for some years. Szasz has argued that abnor-

mal behaviors often reflect "problems in living," which are *not* comparable to physical disease. He suggests that a term like "depression" simply describes an unhappy human being. To elevate depression to a medical diagnosis turns a person with problems into a patient with a sickness, thereby condoning all sorts of restrictive practices in the name of making the patient well.

Furthermore, an approach called *labeling theory* argues that the very use of diagnostic labels has a profoundly negative effect on a person's ability to resolve problems. In this view, once someone who is unhappy is diagnosed as suffering from depression, the individual begins to assume the role of a sick person. Others also begin to treat the person as ill. After people are labeled "sick," they manifest even more symptoms. In addition, the psychiatric labels are hard to get rid of. Imagine meeting someone who told you that a few years ago he had a "schizophrenic breakdown." Would your reaction be the same as if he had told you he had pneumonia?

In a well-known study, "On Being Sane in Insane Places," Rosenhan (1973) examined the effects of being labeled schizophrenic. Over three years, Rosenhan arranged for 12 normal people to arrive at a psychiatric hospital under pseudonyms and to complain of hearing voices that kept saying "empty," "hollow," and "thud." The patients responded truthfully to all questions except for their names. On the basis of one reported symptom and without any confirming evidence, all were diagnosed as either "schizophrenic" or "manic-depressive" and admitted for inpatient care. Hospitalization ranged from 3 to 52 days, averaging 19, even though the pseudo-patients stopped manifesting symptoms and wanted to leave. When discharged, most were diagnosed "schizophrenia, in remission," which implies that they were still schizophrenic but did not show signs of the disorder at the time of release. In no instance did any hospital staff member detect that any of the pseudo-patients was quite normal. Labeling theorists argue from such evidence that terms

Classifying Abnormal Behavior

Before diagnosticians can say whether or not a particular behavior problem is a mental illness, let alone isolate its origins, they must first describe it adequately. Classification is an important part of any science. The periodic table in chemistry, for example, has been revised as new elements have been discovered. Much of our understanding of evolutionary theory would not be possible without reliable classification of various species of animals and plants. Psychologists studying abnormal behavior are still in the early stages of developing a classificatory system.

A good clinical classification scheme for behavior has three particular values (Goldstein, Baker, & Jamison, 1986):

1. to predict the future course of a pattern of abnormal behavior—to make a *prognosis;*
2. to develop different *treatment* plans for distinct disorders;
3. to study the causes, or etiologies, of specific disorders.

These photographs show an Eskimo and an African in an "altered state of consciousness." Is either of these two persons crazy? His peers judged the Eskimo not to be crazy because he controlled his altered state of consciousness; the African tribesman's peers judged him insane because his altered states controlled him.

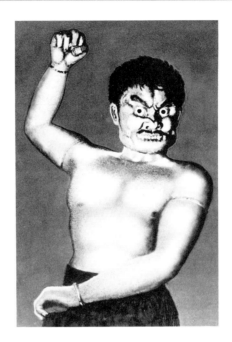

such as "schizophrenia" could become self-fulfilling prophecies.

Defenders of the view that mental illness is real and deserves labels point to how difficult it is to change abnormal behavior back to normal—an achievement that should be easy if it is just a matter of relabeling. They also point to cross-cultural studies that find the same evidence and pattern of abnormalities in such diverse cultural groupings as North American Eskimos and the Yoruba tribe of West Africa (Murphy, 1976). Eskimos and Yoruba

could clearly distinguish between someone in a religious "trance" and someone who was "crazy." In the former case, the person was said to be in control of the altered state of consciousness, while in the latter the altered state was said to be in control of

the person. Furthermore, the number of Eskimos who manifested a schizophrenic-like syndrome of behavior was 8.8 per 1,000. This figure is directly comparable to incidence rates reported as early as the 1940s in places such as rural Sweden.

The German physician Emil Kraepelin (Kraepelin, 1896) set up much of our present-day system of classifying abnormal behavior. Kraepelin was clearly influenced by the writings of others, dating back to Hippocrates, the ancient Greek philosopher and physician. Many modern disorders, such as mania and depression, are recognizable in the ancient writings. In the United States, the standard psychiatric classification system is the *Diagnostic and Statistical Manual of Mental Disorders,* published by the American Psychiatric Association (1980). Since 1952, three editions of the manual, referred to as the DSM, have appeared: DSM-I, 1952; DSM-II, 1968; and the most recent edition, *DSM-III,* 1980. The first two editions reflected the theories of Freud along with Kraepelin and others. By contrast, DSM-III places more emphasis on simply describing the categories of mental disorders. The focus is on what is wrong, and there is little theorizing about the causes of the disorder. DSM-III was designed to spell out in great detail specific behavioral definitions for many of the more severe mental disorders. This attention to detail has paid off in terms of increased reliability and validity of diagnosis—at least in contrast to what went before (Eysenck, Wakefield, & Friedman, 1983).

But each revision also gives up some categories that have become widely familiar. DSM-III has dropped the distinction between neuroses and psychoses that was a major feature of DSM-II, for example. (DSM-III still refers to some disorders as psychotic but no longer uses the term *neurotic*.) You are still likely to encounter these terms, however, and should be familiar with them. In DSM-II, neuroses were disorders that were generally considered less severe; patients were said to remain in touch with reality but to have difficulty managing anxiety. Psychoses were more severe disorders, typically with some break from reality.

DSM-III

The DSM-III volume, which names and classifies mental disorders, is used by virtually all clinical psychologists and psychiatrists in North America. To produce it, the American Psychiatric Association worked closely with the World Health Organization to make the DSM-III similar to the International Classification of Diseases. In this way clinicians and research investigators around the world have a common language.

DSM-III consists of five axes, or dimensions (see Table 15–2). The patient is rated on each axis by a *psychiatrist* or *psychologist* (see Chapter 16 for a discussion of the difference), who uses clinical training and experience to make the judgments. Axis I indicates the primary diagnosis for 15 major disorders. Most serious disorders, such as major depression and schizophrenia, are on Axis I. Axis II describes maladaptive personality traits as well as specific developmental disorders that may be occurring in addition to the major mental disorders of Axis I. Axis III identifies any physical disorders that may be important to the understanding or treatment of the patient. Some drugs, for example, should not be administered to people with a heart problem. Axis IV provides a rating of the severity of any current stress that may be contributing to the disorder. Axis V gives criteria for rating the highest level of adaptive functioning achieved by the individual during the previous year. This rating is based on functioning in three areas: social, occupational, and leisure activities. In general, the higher the level of functioning, the better the likelihood of recovery. As mentioned, most psychologists and psychiatrists recognize DSM-III to be an improvement over previous classificatory schemes, although additional improvements will be looked for in future editions (Eysenck, Wakefield, & Friedman, 1983).

To become familiar with the DSM-III system, consider the following case study taken from the DSM-III (1980, p. 30). A 62-year-old man who is slated for early retirement is manifesting a high rate of absenteeism due to depression. His employer knows this worker used to be absent often because of a drinking problem but thinks that the man is not drinking now and feels that there are other problems. The man is referred to a clinician, who offers the following diagnosis:

□ *Axis I:* Major depression, single episode with melancholia. Alcohol dependence, in remission.

□ *Axis II:* Dependent personality disorder (provisional, rule out borderline personality disorder).

**TABLE 15–2
DSM-III Multiaxial Classification System**

AXIS I: The Major Mental Disorders

1. Disorders Usually First Evident in Infancy, Childhood, or Adolescence
   Example: Conduct Disorder
2. Organic Mental Disorders
   Example: Senility
3. *Substance Use Disorders
   Example: Alcoholism
4. *Schizophrenic Disorders
   Example: Schizophrenia
5. Paranoid Disorders
   Example: Paranoia
6. Psychotic Disorders Not Elsewhere Classified
   Example: Brief Reactive Psychosis
7. *Affective Disorders
   Example: Depression
8. *Anxiety Disorders
   Example: Phobia
9. *Somatoform Disorders
   Example: Conversion Disorder
10. *Dissociative Disorders
    Example: Multiple Personality
11. *Psychosexual Disorders
    Example: Sexual Masochism
12. Factitious Disorders
    Example: Hysteria
13. Disorders of Impulse Control Not Elsewhere Classified
    Example: Pathological Gambling
14. Adjustment Disorder
    Example: Inability to work
15. Psychological Factors Affecting Physical Condition
    Example: Migraine Headache

AXIS II: Personality Disorders

1. Paranoid Personality Disorder
   Example: Unwarranted suspiciousness and mistrust of people
2. Schizoid Personality Disorder
   Example: Emotionally cold, unable to form social relationships
3. Schizotypal Personality Disorder
   Example: Having oddities of thought, perception, speech not severe enough to meet the criteria for schizophrenia

4. Histrionic Personality Disorder
   Example: Overly dramatic leading to disturbances in interpersonal relationships
5. Narcissistic Personality Disorder
   Example: Grandiose sense of self-importance or uniqueness
6. *Antisocial Personality Disorder
   Example: Continuously antisocial, violating the rights of others.
7. Borderline Personality Disorder
   Example: Impulsively unpredictable with unstable mood and self-image
8. Avoidant Personality Disorder
   Example: Hypersensitive to rejection
9. Dependent Personality Disorder
   Example: Passively dependent on others
10. Compulsive Personality Disorder
    Example: Preoccupied with trivial details
11. Passive-Aggressive Personality Disorder
    Example: Indirectly resisting demands
12. Atypical, Mixed, or Other Personality Disorder
    Example: Immature

AXIS II: Specific Developmental Disorders

1. Reading
2. Arithmetic
3. Language
4. Articulation

AXIS III: Physical Disorders

AXIS IV: Psychosocial Stressors

1. None
   Example: No apparent psychosocial stressor
2. Minimal
   Example: Small bank loan
3. Mild
   Example: Argument with neighbor
4. Moderate
   Example: New career
5. Severe
   Example: Marital separation

6. Extreme
   Example: Death of close relative
7. Catastrophic
   Example: Multiple family deaths
0. Unspecified
   Example: No information

AXIS V: Highest Level of Adaptive Functioning in Past Year

1. Superior: usually effective in social relations, occupation, and use of leisure time
   Example: Single parent in reduced circumstances takes excellent care of children, has warm friendships and a hobby.
2. Very good: better than average in job, leisure time, and social functioning
   Example: Retired person does volunteer work, sees old friends.
3. Good: no more than slight impairment in either occupational or social functioning
   Example: Individual with many friends does a difficult job extremely well but finds it a strain.
4. Fair: moderate impairment in either social or occupational functioning or some impairment in both
   Example: Lawyer has trouble carrying through assignments, has almost no close friends.
5. Poor: marked impairment in either social or occupational functioning or moderate impairment in both
   Example: Man with one or two friends has trouble holding a job for more than a few weeks.
6. Very poor: marked impairment in social and occupational functioning
   Example: Woman is unable to do any housework and has violent outbursts.
7. Grossly impaired: gross impairment in virtually all areas of functioning
   Example: Elderly man needs supervision in maintaining personal hygiene, usually incoherent.

*Disorders with an asterisk are discussed in the text.

    □ *Axis III:* Alcoholic cirrhosis of liver.

    □ *Axis IV:* Psychosocial stressors: anticipated retirement and change in residence with loss of contact with friends. Severity: Moderate.

    □ *Axis V:* Highest level of adaptive functioning past year: Good.

In the remainder of this chapter we will spell out many of the features of DSM-III diagnosis.

SEVEN MAJOR DISORDERS

Because DSM-III is the most widely used classificatory system, we will use it here to describe seven major disorders from Axis I in Table 15–2. (Note that we do not consider all categories given by DSM-III.) Besides listing the symptoms and offering case examples, we will also selectively apply the major approaches to the mental disorders outlined earlier in the chapter. After completing the discussion of the seven disorders, we will also consider the topic of crime and delinquency and illustrate one of the DSM-III personality disorders: the antisocial personality (from Axis II).

Anxiety Disorders

Everybody suffers from anxiety at some time. You probably do not have to think very hard to remember a recent episode of mild anxiety: an awkward moment with a new acquaintance, a difficult test, the sight of a police car in your rearview mirror. But what about extreme anxiety, the kind that sometimes seems to border on panic? Although it may be less common, strong anxiety is seldom totally absent from a person's life. Indeed, to feel no anxiety would be extremely maladaptive, for anxiety warns of danger.

    Some people suffer from more anxiety than others. Estimates are that 2 to 4 percent of the population have had at some time what DSM-III classifies as an *anxiety disorder.* DSM-III subdivides anxiety disorders into phobic disorder, generalized anxiety disorder, panic disorder, and obsessive-compulsive disorder.

PHOBIAS. Phobias constitute intense fears of objects or activities that seem out of proportion to the dangers involved. Most people have minor phobias (such as discomfort in the presence of snakes or atop a ladder). The usual response to phobias is to avoid their source.

CASE STUDY
Little Hans's Phobia

In 1909, Freud reported the classic case of Little Hans, a five-year-old whose phobia about horses prevented him from leaving his mother and going outdoors. According to Freud, the boy's anxiety about horses was secondary. Hans's primary fear was of his father, as the result of an Oedipus conflict. Hans desired his mother sexually and feared castration by his father—a punishment his mother had once threatened when

This girl appears to have a phobia, but it is not clear whether she is suffering from acrophobia (fear of high places), hydrophobia (fear of water), or a combination of the two.

she found him with his hand on his penis. Freud felt that Hans dealt with this threat by symbolically displacing his fear onto horses. Behaviorists Wolpe and Rachman (1960) note, however, that the child experienced a traumatic exposure to horses during the time his phobia developed; they suggest that the aversive encounter explains Hans's phobia better than Freud does.

Where do phobias originate? They tend to be limited to a number of common stimuli. For example, few people develop phobias about books, clothing, or the color red, whereas phobias involving naturally occurring phenomena such as heights, snakes, or open spaces are relatively common (see Table 15–3). This might suggest that phobias have an evolutionary, biological basis (Seligman, 1972); fears of heights, snakes, or even open spaces have obvious survival value. Learning is important, however, and learning theorists provide a number of explanations for the development of phobias (Bandura, 1986; see also Chapter 6). First, they may be acquired through a frightening experience. If you are attacked by a dog, it would not be surprising for you to develop a fear of dogs. Most phobias, however, may be learned through observation; parents who fear particular objects often serve as models for their children who grow up to share their dreads (Bandura, Blanchard, & Ritter, 1969). Phobias can also originate, or be enhanced, if they result in positive reinforcement. If going to school or work results in stress for someone, staying at home may be so rewarding that he or she develops agoraphobia. Psychoanalytic theory also provides an explanation for fears. It assumes that phobias evolve as defenses against impulses that an individual fears. Thus, if going outside leads to an increase in unconscious aggressive or sexual urges, and if a person unconsciously fears these urges, one way to stave them off is to develop agoraphobia and stay indoors.

GENERALIZED ANXIETY DISORDER AND PANIC. Generalized anxiety disorders are characterized by broad, overall tension that lasts at least a month and lacks the specificity of the phobias. It is commonly marked by general apprehensiveness and physical complaints such as upset stomach and fre-

TABLE 15–3
Types of Phobias

Acrophobia	Fear of high places
Agoraphobia	Fear of open places
Astraphobia	Fear of thunder and/or lightning
Cardiophobia	Fear of heart attack
Claustrophobia	Fear of closed spaces or confinement
Hematophobia	Fear of the sight of blood
Hydrophobia	Fear of water
Lalophobia	Fear of (public) speaking
Mysophobia	Fear of dirt, germs, or contamination
Phobophobia	Fear of fear
Thanatophobia	Fear of death
Xenophobia	Fear of strangers
Zoophobia	Fear of animals (usually specific kinds)

quent diarrhea and urination. Extreme irritability may also occur. This kind of anxiety, which Freud called "free-floating," is not associated with any particular situation, and the victims who experience the disorder don't know why they are anxious.

People subject to anxiety disorders may also experience *panic disorders* (or panic attacks) involving intense fear or terror. During an attack the victim may suffer from palpitations, trembling, choking or smothering sensations, and feelings of unreality. Attacks usually last only minutes, but long after they have passed apprehensiveness and a sense of helplessness persist. Unlike phobias, these attacks are not associated with particular stimuli, so the sufferer cannot choose to avoid whatever is likely to bring on an attack. A common complication is the development of anticipatory fears; consequently, people will often stay home, afraid of a panic attack if they go out.

CASE STUDIES
Generalized Anxiety and Panic Attacks

Many case studies have been reported of people suffering from generalized anxiety disorders with panic, demonstrating the debilitating effects of this terror for the victim. One patient described the symptoms this way:

> When I experience an anxiety attack, I often feel dizzy and off balance. If the attack is particularly severe, I have difficulty concentrating and understanding things. Words, physical objects, and people may come to seem unreal, almost like in a dream. I sometimes don't know where I am or what I'm doing. The attacks are often followed by profound exhaustion. Shaking and trembling are common and I often feel hot afterwards. (Adapted from Nemiah, 1980)

In another case a patient felt as though he were having a heart seizure, with chest pains, palpitations, numbness, and shortness of breath. During the attack he felt a tightness over his eyes and had difficulty focusing. He feared he would not be able to swallow. As attacks became more frequent, he began to worry about when the next one would occur, and that made him still more anxious. He began to note the location of doctors' offices and hospitals wherever he happened to be and became extremely anxious if medical help was not close by. If he could not bring his attack under control himself, his only recourse was to seek a physician for a tranquilizer injection (Leon, 1977).

Is this compulsive behavior? This man collected thousands of pieces of tin foil to create this incredible ball.

OBSESSIVE-COMPULSIVE DISORDER. Obsessions are recurring thoughts that are troublesome and that persist uncontrollably. Compulsions are behaviors that the victim feels compelled to repeat over and over. Most obsessions and compulsions do not give pleasure, but yielding to them appears to reduce anxiety. A sense of mounting tension connected with the obsessing thought can be immediately relieved by giving in to the compulsion; thus the title *obsessive-compulsive disorder.* This disorder is equally common to males and females and usually begins in adolescence or early adulthood.

> **CASE STUDY**
> **Obsessive Thoughts of Sexual Jealousy**

Stuart Sutherland, a well-known British experimental psychologist, wrote an autobiographical account of his brief bout with madness. He called his book *Breakdown* (1976). Sutherland had been happily married for several years and was a highly successful research psychologist and teacher. When his wife revealed she had been having an affair with another man (but had no wish to end their married life), he was at first able to accept the situation. Indeed, he found that the resultant increase in communication and honesty improved his marriage. He even liked himself better because of his broadminded attitude. He asked his wife for further details of the affair. But suddenly he became obsessed with vivid images of his wife in moments of sexual passion with her lover. He could not purge the thoughts from his mind, by day or night. Eventually he had to leave his teaching and research duties. Only after several months and many different types of therapy was he able to reduce the disturbing thoughts to a low enough frequency to be able to return to work.

Somatoform Disorders

The essential features of *somatoform disorders* are physical symptoms for which no physical causes are apparent. Unlike psychosomatic illness, where emotional stress causes bodily changes (see Chapter 12), somatoform disorders have no physical basis. Nevertheless, the victim is not faking and believes the disorder is real. There are several different types of somatoform disorders, but we will discuss just one: *conversion disorder.*

Freud believed that anxiety could be "converted" into loss of sensory or motor functioning. Individuals may awaken to find that they cannot hear or see or speak or move their legs or arms. No actual biological change is involved, however, for people with the conversion reaction of blindness do not bump into objects and those with apparently paralyzed muscles can move them during sleep.

> **CASE STUDY**
> **Jean G.**

A 24-year-old woman known to one of the authors of this textbook illustrates this disorder. Her symptoms began with feelings of dizziness and a ringing sound in her ears. Then she awoke one morning experiencing major difficulties in hearing. A thorough medical examination revealed no medical basis for her hearing loss. Neither tranquilizers nor short-term conventional psychotherapy restored her hearing. After a week of concern by her friends and her relatives, Jean began a scheduled holiday. The first morning of her holiday, Jean's hearing returned, as mysteriously as it had disappeared.

Several theories attempt to explain these disorders. Freud argued that they are defenses against forbidden impulses. A woman who wished to leave her husband for another man, for example, might develop paralysis of the leg; a soldier tempted to flee battle may go blind. Learning theorists tend to see conversion disorders as means of escaping anxiety and stress and of gaining attention.

Dissociative Disorders

Psychological rather than physical impairment offers another escape route from anxiety. In *dissociative disorders,* one major part of a person's consciousness or personality becomes, in a sense, separate from other parts. This dissociation can take one of three forms.

Functional amnesia is a failure of memory that is not brought about by such causes as a blow on the head. An amnesia victim usually appears perplexed and disoriented and wanders purposelessly. Functional amnesia usually begins suddenly, often immediately following severe psychological stress. This stress may derive from something the victim has done, such as commission of a crime, or from an event such as losing a job unexpectedly. Amnesia typically ends abruptly. Recovery is complete and recurrence is rare.

Fugue manifests itself in the assumption of a new identity while away from home or work. Victims cannot recall who they truly are, but fugue is unlike amnesia in that there is little confusion or disorientation. Usually the fugue is brief, lasting hours to days rather than weeks, and often it occurs following severe stress brought on by natural disasters, military conflicts, and, occasionally, marital quarrels. Recovery is rapid and recurrence is, once again, rare.

In *multiple personality disorders* the victim shows two or more distinct integrated personalities, each of which dominates at particular times. The original personality is usually not aware of the other, although the second may be partly aware of the first. Often the personalities are distinctly different from each other: if the original personality is quiet and sexually inhibited, the second may be loud and sexually promiscuous. Shifts from one personality to another may be sudden and dramatic, as in the novel *Dr. Jekyll and Mr. Hyde.* One case study became both a popular book and a film, *The Three Faces of Eve* (Thigpen & Cleckley, 1954). It should be noted, however, that documented cases of full-blown multiple personality are extremely rare. As Coleman, Butcher, and Carson (1980) point out, there are only about 100 cases in the psychological and psychiatric literature.

Substance Use Disorders

Throughout history, humans have used chemical agents to alter their moods. Drugs such as alcohol and coffee are taken for granted by most people; more than 93 percent of adults have used both. However, wide subcultural variations affect usage. Some groups frown on alcohol and caffeine consumption while others accept illegal substances such as marijuana.

In recent years the pharmaceutical industry has added many powerful mind-altering substances to the available array. The frequency of use of various drugs among U.S. high school students can be estimated from Figure 15–1. A classification of some commonly abused drugs is shown in Table 5–1 on page 190.

FIGURE 15–1
Drug Use in the United States

The chart shows the percentage of the U.S. high school class of 1982 using various types of drugs. These data were collected in a nationwide study of high school students, focusing on a pivotal point in their life: their final year in high school.

Source: Johnston, Bachman, & O'Malley, 1982.

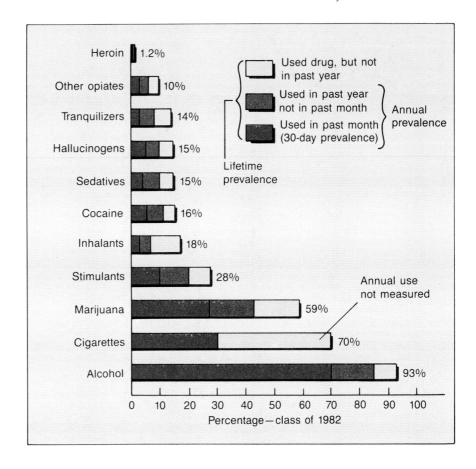

DSM-III judges excessive drug use as a mental disorder. It distinguishes between different degrees of "excessive," ranging from "abuse" at the milder end to "dependence" at the more serious extreme. Alcoholism constitutes the most prevalent abuse; it is estimated that alcoholics or problem drinkers today number 10 million people in the United States, and alcohol consumption appears to be steadily increasing (Akers, 1985). Alcohol abuse has been estimated as a factor in more than 10 percent of all deaths in the United States, totaling about 200,000 per year. It is associated with half of all traffic deaths, many involving teenagers. This fact has spurred many state legislatures to raise the legal drinking age from 18 to 20 or 21. Prolonged abuse can damage virtually every system of the body, and it is the primary cause of cirrhosis of the liver, one of the ten major killers (U.S. Surgeon General, 1979).

Alcohol has almost paradoxical effects on the psychological state. It acts as a depressant, but the first parts of the brain it depresses are the inhibitory centers. Thus, briefly, alcohol raises spirits and releases inhibitions. But continued drinking depresses the systems that keep the body efficient and impairs reaction times, speech, and fine-motor coordination. Eventually even walking becomes difficult, and finally the drinker falls asleep.

Why do people drink to excess? The most frequent reason cited currently is that alcohol consumption reduces anxiety and tension (Akers, 1985). Extreme problem drinkers may even desire the oblivion it produces.

More psychoanalytically oriented theorists, however, view alcoholism as due to deep-rooted unconscious impulses. Freud considered drinking a symptom of fixation at the oral stage of psychosexual development; Adler suggested it was caused by feelings of inferiority.

THE ROLE OF THE PEER GROUP IN DRUG USE. Sociologist Ronald Akers (1985; Akers et al., 1979) investigated whether such important social learning variables as observational learning and reinforcement were responsible for substance abuse by teenagers.

The researchers gave questionnaires to 3,065 boys and girls attending grades 7 through 12 in seven communities in three midwestern states. They personally interviewed 106 of these students two to eight weeks later. The questionnaire measured both use and abuse of alcohol and marijuana. The frequency of use scale, for example, ranged from "never" to "nearly every day." To measure drug abuse, the researchers asked the students whether they had experienced any of several problems while, or soon after, using the drug, including accidents, and whether or not they could later remember what they had done.

The study also measured observational learning and reinforcement. For instance, the researchers asked students to count all the "admired" models—parents, friends, other adults—they had seen consuming alcohol or drugs. Another question asked how many of the students' best friends used drugs. In terms of reinforcement, one item assessed the degree to which friends, parents, or both discouraged the teenagers from using drugs; another asked whether friends praised, punished, or were indifferent to drug taking. Finally, the respondents reported on the effects drugs usually had on them: from none, to mostly good, to mostly bad.

The results showed that observational learning and reinforcement accounted for much of the adolescents' behavior. Those teenagers who observed friends or admired adults using the drugs and/or whose use of drugs resulted in pleasurable feelings and encouragement and praise from their peers were the ones who most used (and abused) the drugs. It would appear from these results that social learning represents a powerful theory in explaining drug use.

Psychosexual Disorders

Although sexual urges and gratifications can obviously be extremely pleasant, they also can cause unhappiness. According to DSM-III, there are three basic categories of *psychosexual disorder:* (1) those involving gender identity; (2) those involving paraphilias, or sexual deviations; and (3) those involving sexual dysfunction (see Table 15–4). All of these disorders are assumed to have psychological, rather than organic, origins. Thus, for example, a male who cannot attain an erection because of a spinal cord injury would not be given a psychiatric classification.

In the *gender identity disorders,* individuals show dissatisfaction with their anatomic sex, desire to become members of the opposite sex, and frequently dress and behave like the opposite sex. This disorder is apparently rare and includes males more commonly than females.

Once again, there are major differences of opinion between the psychoanalytic and learning theory points of view on the causes of gender dis-

TABLE 15–4
DSM-III Categories of Psychosexual Disorder

Category of Psychosexual Disorder	Example
GENDER IDENTITY OR ROLE DISORDER	
Transsexualism	The wish to be rid of one's own genitals and to have those of the opposite sex
Transvestism	Wearing the clothes of the opposite sex
Gender identity or role disorder of childhood	Strong preference for the clothes, toys, activities, and companionship of the other sex
PARAPHILIAS (SEXUAL DEVIATIONS)	
Fetishism	Sexual arousal to inanimate object, usually clothing (e.g., rubber boots, underclothes)
Zoophilia	The use of animals as the preferred method of achieving sexual excitement
Pedophilia	The use of a young child as the choice of sexual excitement
Dyshomophilia	The act or fantasy of homosexual activity where such activity produces distress or guilt
Exhibitionism	Gaining sexual excitement by exposing the genitals to an unsuspecting stranger
Voyeurism	Spying on a member of the opposite sex while that person undresses, is nude, or engages in sexual activity
Sexual masochism	Deriving sexual gratification from behaviors that are painful or symbolic of punishment
Sexual sadism	Deriving sexual gratification from inflicting pain or suffering on another
Other paraphilias (a residual category)	E.g., intercourse with a corpse (necrophilia); rubbing against others in elevators (frottage); sex with a sibling or parent (incest)
PSYCHOSEXUAL DYSFUNCTIONS	
Inhibited desire	Persistent lack of interest in sex
Inhibited sexual excitement (frigidity in females; impotence in males)	Frequent inability to achieve full sexual excitement
Inhibited female orgasm	The (more or less complete) inability to have an orgasm
Inhibited male orgasm	The inability to ejaculate
Premature ejaculation	Too speedy ejaculation due to absence of voluntary control
Functional dyspareunia	Painful intercourse
Functional vaginismus	Involuntary and intense contractions of the outermost portion of the vagina

Source: American Psychiatric Association, 1980.

orders. Freudians emphasize early stages of psychosexual development and the nonresolution of the Oedipus complex at age five. They view gender disorders as resulting from unconscious conflicts.

Learning theorists stress the "laws of learning," including specific learning experiences, usually during adolescence, that resulted in inappropriate conditioned emotional responses. This is perhaps the most viable account of the processes involved in the development of psychosexual disorders (Akers, 1985; Masters, Johnson, & Kolodny, 1985). One dramatic experiment supported the behavioral conditioning model, demonstrating how fetishes could be acquired. Adult males were shown slides of women's boots together with slides of attractive nude women. After repeated pairings, the women's boots elicited sexual arousal by themselves as measured by the phallic plethysmograph (see Chapter 14), a device for detecting even minor changes in the size of the penis (Rachman & Hodgson, 1968). Other deviations may be learned through associating images with the sexual arousal that occurs in masturbation. One concern recently highlighted by such groups as Women Against Pornography is the increase in pornography in which sex is linked with violence. Pictures of alluring women in torn clothes chained to beds or chairs while men hold guns or knives may encourage development of sadistic sexual fantasies. Even some advertising links sex with violence. Many other sexual problems may be due to excessive conditioning of anxiety to sexual behavior and thoughts (Eysenck, 1979; Masters, Johnson, & Kolodny, 1985).

Affective Disorders

Affect is a synonym for "emotional feeling," and *affective disorders* include disabling disturbances of moods and feelings. A changed mood may come to dominate a person's subjective life and functioning and even result in loss of contact with reality. Two emotional extremes characterize the affective disorders: the excessive energy of mania and the debilitating lethargy of depression, or both.

MANIA. *Mania* is a state of intense euphoria or sense of well-being. In its mild forms, the person suffering from mania simply appears happier, more optimistic, more talkative, and more energetic than usual. Its more extreme form is marked by an endless stream of talk that runs from one topic to another, a total lack of inhibition in relationships, intense activity, spending sprees, heightened sexuality, decreased sleep, irrepressible good humor, and, almost invariably, increased sociability, which includes phone calls to friends at all hours of the night and efforts to renew old acquaintances. There are usually unwarranted optimism and grandiosity, reckless driving, or foolish business investments. Speech becomes loud, rapid, and difficult to understand. Typically the individual does not recognize the intrusive, domineering, and demanding nature of the behavior. Slowly but surely, sufferers exhaust themselves and everyone around them.

DEPRESSION. *Depression* describes a wide range of complaints from a mild sadness to a state in which the victim loses all interest in normal activities, becomes extremely gloomy, and often spends a great deal of time in bed. The sufferer may be overwhelmed with feelings of hopelessness and worthlessness. Physical symptoms often include sad face, lack of appetite, inability to sleep, uncontrollable crying, and loss of energy. Speech is usually slow and emotionless, and it generally expresses suffering and suicidal desires. In this phase, the patient may well attempt suicide and must be watched carefully.

Many famous people have suffered from depression. Winston Churchill wrote about the "black dog" that followed him through his life.

Depression is a major form of human distress. Seligman (1975) has described it as "the common cold of mental illness," and a report to the National Institute of Mental Health (NIMH) concluded that "depression now rivals schizophrenia as the nation's number one [mental] health problem" (Secunda, Friedman, & Schuyler, 1973). According to the NIMH report, at any given time, 15 percent of the population may be experiencing "significant depressive features." In the investigators' estimation, one out of every ten people may, at some point, experience depression severe enough to warrant therapy. This figure is ten times higher than the risk of schizophrenia.

Who gets depressed? In one sense, of course, everyone—depression is a universal experience. All of us have times when we feel "down" and discouraged, lonely, sad, and empty and when life seems an effort. We say we are depressed. Usually, however, we expect the feeling to go away soon. Perhaps, therefore, it would be better to rephrase the question as: "Who gets depressed severely enough to warrant therapy?" This varies according to who is making the judgment. There is no clear criterion for distinguishing between mild and severe depression. Generally, however, debilitating depression has been a more severe problem for the middle-aged (i.e., those between 40 and 55); there is, though, a recent trend toward earlier onset. Depression can be found at all levels of society. In the upper and middle classes, depression hospitalizes females twice as frequently as males; in the lower socioeconomic class the difference is reversed (Wing & Bebbington, 1985).

CAUSES OF DEPRESSION. Psychologists disagree about the causes of depressive disorders. The psychoanalytic tradition sees them as symptoms of unconscious pathological processes. The medical model attributes them to chemical imbalance perhaps due to genetic transmission. The learning tradition views them as problems of faulty learning. We consider each tradition in turn.

Psychoanalytic Formulations. The early psychoanalytic writers tended to endorse an aggression-turned-inward hypothesis to account for depression. More recent contributors have focused on a weak ego and loss of self-esteem (Bemporad, 1985). Often this is asserted to be due to early childhood deprivation. In what is termed *anaclitic depression,* a child may become despondent and depressed over the loss of a person, perhaps a parent, on whom the child has been dependent. According to this view, such traumas as death, adoption, and divorce may scar children for life, making them susceptible to depressive reactions. The supporting evidence, however, has not been strong (Bemporad, 1985).

Biomedical Perspective. Heredity seems to be important in predisposing people to mood disorders. Mendlewicz (1985) reviewed data from twin, family, and adoption studies demonstrating the role of genetics in transmitting the mood disorders. For example, adopted children are more at risk for depression if their biological parents have the disorder than they are if their adopting parents have it (Mendlewicz & Rainer, 1977). Furthermore, twin and other family studies demonstrate that a person's risk increases directly as a function of the degree of genetic similarity to an affected family member. The fact that mood disorders are partly inherited has inspired scientists

FIGURE 15–2
Lewinsohn's Model of Depression

In this formulation, predisposing characteristics in both the person (e.g., genetic biases) and the environment (e.g., disruptions) affect the individual's mood, depending on the rate of positive reinforcement. Decreases in positive reinforcement lead to depression. This in turn can lead to a reduced rate of activity, which can cause a downward cycle and still further depression.

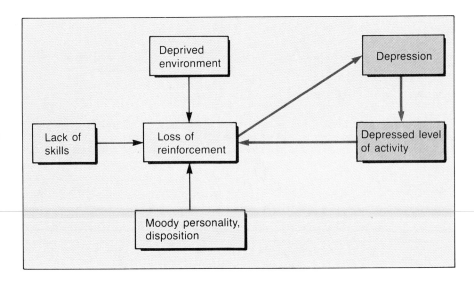

to search for biochemical defects. Much research has centered on the role of neurotransmitters, particularly norepinephrine, dopamine, and serotonin (see Chapter 2 for a detailed discussion of neuronal transmission). One value of research in this area is that it could lead to significant advances in biomedical types of therapies.

Learning Theories. Only in the last decade and a half have behavioral researchers turned their attention to depression. Several important theories have been put forward, and this is currently a major area of research.

Lewinsohn's behavioral theory. Peter Lewinsohn (1974; Lewinsohn et al., 1985) proposes that depression results from a lack or loss of reinforcement, particularly positive reinforcement. This view implies that someone with many sources of reinforcement is much less susceptible to depression than one whose behavior has been maintained by relatively few sources. It also suggests that depressed people can be taught skills that will earn them reinforcement. Figure 15–2 represents some of the variables involved in Lewinsohn's model of depression.

Beck's cognitive social learning theory. An important model of human adaptation was developed by Aaron T. Beck and his colleagues. Trained as a psychoanalyst, Beck soon abandoned the psychoanalytic approach for cognitive learning theory. His observations and research on depression culminated in a classic book, *Depression: Clinical, Experimental, and Theoretical Aspects* (Beck, 1967). According to Beck, depression results from the development and dominance of a set of beliefs, fantasies, and expectancies that individuals form about themselves, their world, and their future, often called the "cognitive triad." These cognitive blueprints or schemata cause people to construe themselves as inadequate, unworthy, and helpless. Moreover, they see the world as insensitive, ungratifying, and generally empty or unpleasant. To make matters worse, depressed people tend to see their futures as unpromising; there is little hope for improvement, let alone happiness.

CASE STUDY

Consider Tom, a recent college graduate, who applies for his first job and fails to get it. If Tom is prone to depression, he is likely to interpret this to mean it was his fault because he was unattractive, socially unskilled, and incompetent. He dislikes himself for these presumed inadequacies and believes this rejection proves he will never find a job that will suit him. According to Beck, thinking of this sort can actually make people depressed.

Research has supported Beck's theory. Depressive individuals, for example, have been shown to underrate their own abilities even when they are equal to those of nondepressed persons (Hamilton & Abramson, 1983). This negative view flavors all later decisions, behaviors, emotions, and interactions, thus locking in a pattern of depression (Sacco & Beck, 1985). The extent to which Beck's formulations work alongside those of Lewinsohn and other behaviorists remains to be decided. It seems clear, however, that both Beck and Lewinsohn have touched on issues that may be critically important in the development and maintenance of depressive patterns.

Seligman's learned helplessness. Martin Seligman's (1975) model of *learned helplessness* provides a theory of how negative beliefs might come about. Seligman proposed that depressed people believe themselves unable to influence and control events. Thus they develop negative symptoms, including hopelessness, passivity, and depressed and negative expectations, when faced with stressful situations. In his original studies, Seligman demonstrated that if animals were given a large number of extremely painful electric shocks, they would exhibit "depressed behavior" only if there was nothing they could do about it. If they could escape from the shock, the depressed behavior did not occur. Seligman equated depression, then, with "learned helplessness" (see Chapter 6, page 224, for a fuller explanation of the learned helplessness effect). In laboratory research with college students, Seligman (1975) found that both depressed students and students who were not depressed but were made helpless show the same sort of performance deficits. Seligman also extended this conception to reactive depression, theorizing that the common core is the development of a belief in the futility of active responding. This theory therefore includes a cognitive component (e.g., belief in the futility of active responding) as well as a behavioral component. The depressed person becomes passive only with repeated lack of positive reinforcement for responding.

Subsequently, Seligman and his associates have modified their theory (Abramson, Seligman, & Teasdale, 1978; Peterson & Seligman, 1984, 1985). The reformulation suggests that it is not uncontrollable outcomes themselves but a person's explanations for these outcomes that determine the nature and magnitude of depression. People who attribute an undesirable outcome to their own inadequacies will experience guilt and self-blame. Those who attribute an undesirable outcome to external factors may feel depressed, but they will not feel self-blame. This reformulation incorporates both reinforcement theory and cognitive theory. For example, if Tom in the preceding case study attributed his situation to the harsh competition for

According to Beck, depression arises when people view themselves as unworthy, see their world as empty, and see their situation as hopeless.

good jobs rather than to his own inadequacies, he would be much less likely to suffer depression. Recent evidence provides support for this perspective: students, patients, and other subjects who attributed bad events in the classroom, therapy, and elsewhere to their own inadequacies were more likely to suffer mood swings than those who did not (Brewin, 1985; Peterson & Seligman, 1985).

Schizophrenic Disorders

A whole class of disorders known as *schizophrenic disorders* (or schizophrenia) remains one of the major challenges facing psychological researchers. Although it is the most frequent diagnosis among institutionalized adult mental patients, schizophrenia is also among the least understood problems in the whole field of abnormal psychology. One out of a hundred persons will be hospitalized at some point as schizophrenic; about 40 percent of all mental patients bear that label.

The term *schizophrenia* was contrived in 1911 by a Swiss psychiatrist, Eugen Bleuler, from the Greek words for "split" and "mind." It does not mean multiple personality disorders like those in *The Three Faces of Eve* mentioned earlier. The "splitting" refers to the patient's departure from social reality. According to DSM-III, schizophrenia has three essential features— thought disorders, delusions, and hallucinations—and a person must exhibit at least one of them to warrant the diagnosis.

THOUGHT DISORDERS. Almost all schizophrenics suffer from some disorder of thought, emotion, or perception. These are usually inferred from the individual's language, which may be bizarre and incomprehensible. The schizophrenic often displays loose associations and may shift the focus of a sentence abruptly. Neologisms (invented words) are not uncommon, and the patient may repeat the same phrase over and over for no apparent reason. Logical thinking is greatly impaired, and no connection may be apparent between parts of a schizophrenic's argument (Lehmann, 1980).

The case of the patient who thought he was dead exemplifies schizophrenic logic. Frustrated in his efforts to dissuade the patient from this belief, a psychiatrist decided to force him to confront evidence to the contrary. He asked the patient, "Do dead people bleed?" "No, of course not" came the reply, at which point the psychiatrist pricked the patient's finger with a scalpel. A tiny drop of blood trickled from the incision. After a long silence, the patient said, "I'll be damned! Dead people do bleed!" (Mahoney, 1980).

A fragment of a letter written by a schizophrenic patient provides another example of thought disorders: "I wish you, therefore, a very happy, pleasant, healthy, blessed and fruit-crop-rich year; and also many good wine-harvest years thereafter, as well as good potato-crop years; as well as fine potato years, and sauerkraut years, and sprouts years, and cucumber years, and nut years; a good-egg year, and also a good cheese year" (Bleuler, 1911/1950, p. 28).

DELUSIONS. Once having broken with social reality, many schizophrenics experience delusions. Typical is the feeling that an external force is directing the patient's thoughts, actions, or emotions. Often the force becomes God,

These colorful paintings of nature covered the walls of Walter Anderson's home in Mississippi. Following treatment for schizophrenia, Anderson lived as a recluse and communed with the creatures of ponds and woods. He recorded his vivid impressions in notebooks and in literally thousands of paintings.

the Communists, or the CIA. The three Christs of Ypsilanti, whose story opened this chapter, were all victims of schizophrenia.

Roger Brown, an eminent Harvard psychologist, reports an encounter with a high school friend who looked him up eight years after they had graduated from high school:

> We had half an hour or so of pleasant chatter about old friends, and then I noticed that my guest was looking at me in a rather curious "knowing" way that seemed to suggest that he did not mind playing this game of reunion after a long separation if I had a taste for it, but the guest was not "taken in" by this pretense. Then he came out with the remark, "I saw you in Cleveland last week, you know." That rocked me a bit as I had not been in Cleveland. And then it all came out. My guest believed that his entire circle of high school friends—who had, in fact, gone their separate ways for years—had had him under surveillance since high school. (Brown & Herrnstein, 1975, p. 631)

HALLUCINATIONS. The schizophrenic patient hears imagined voices or, less commonly, sees imagined persons or objects. The voices may be of God, the devil, relatives, or neighbors. Quite often the voices talk about the patient, sometimes threatening, sometimes commanding, sometimes emit-

David Berkowitz, the "Son of Sam" killer, is thought by many to be suffering from schizophrenia.

ting obscenities. The best guess is that such hallucinations reflect a person's inability to distinguish between his or her own memory images and perceptual experiences that originate without.

The longest and most difficult manhunt in the history of New York ended in August 1977, when police arrested David Berkowitz, the "Son of Sam," who killed or maimed 13 young people. Berkowitz attributed his crimes to commands from an outside voice that came to him through Sam, a neighbor's dog. Although hallucinations are the hallmark of schizophrenia, most schizophrenics do not commit such atrocities. Rather, they are fairly helpless and need to be looked after.

In his 1976 book, *The Eden Express*, Mark Vonnegut recounted vividly the sequence of his schizophrenic episode. It all began with disorders of perception and emotion:

> Small tasks became incredibly intricate and complex. It started with pruning the fruit trees. One saw cut would take forever. I was completely absorbed in the sawdust floating gently to the ground, the feel of the saw in my hand, the incredible patterns in the bark, the muscles in my arm pulling back and then pushing forward. Everything stretched infinitely in all directions. Suddenly it seemed as if everything was slowing down and I would never finish sawing the limb. Then I found myself being unable to stick with any one tree. I'd take a branch here, a couple there. It seemed I had been working for hours and hours but the sun hadn't moved at all.

> I began to wonder if I was hurting the trees and found myself apologizing. Each tree began to take on personality. I began to wonder if any of them liked me. (p. 99)

Later, delusions appeared while Vonnegut was in a cafe:

> I started falling very deeply in love with the waitress and everyone else in the place. It seemed that they in turn were just as deeply in love with me. It was like something I couldn't get out of my eye.

> I didn't understand it, but I recognized it. There were all those little things that had happened occasionally between me and lovers before, but never this strong, never so lastingly, never with so many. I was completely in love, willing to die for or suffer incredibly for whatever they might want. A rush of warmth and emotion, spiritual and physical attraction, a wanting of oneness, a feeling of already oneness. (p. 117)

And finally came the hallucinations:

> The Voices. Testing one, two, testing one. Checking out the circuits: "What hath God wrought. Yip di mina di zonda za da boom di yaidi yoohoo."

By this time the voices had gotten very clear:

> At first I had to strain to hear or understand them. They were soft and working some pretty tricky codes. Snap-crackle-pops, the sound of the wind with blinking lights and horns for punctuation. I broke the code and somehow was able to internalize it to the point where it was just like hearing words. In the beginning it seemed mostly nonsense, but as things went along they made more and more sense. Once you hear voices, you realize they've always been there. It's just a matter of being tuned to them. (p. 136)

Some schizophrenics may adopt catatonic poses. In a condition known as "waxy flexibility," another person can place the patient's limbs in odd positions, which the schizophrenic will maintain like a statue.

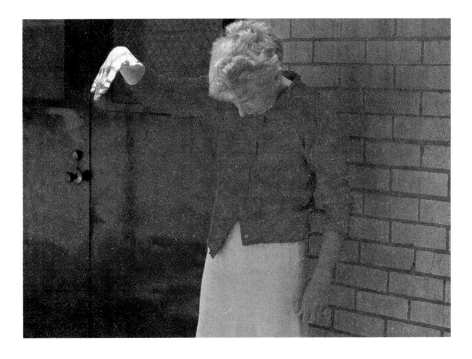

TYPES OF SCHIZOPHRENIA. Although all schizophrenics have some of the symptoms described above, they differ enough in detail so that diagnosticians have recognized a number of varieties of the condition. DSM-III lists four types of schizophrenic reactions: disorganized, paranoid, catatonic, and undifferentiated.

Disorganized types of schizophrenics are the most likely to be labeled "crazy." Their speech is often unorganized and nonsensical. The emotion they express is often silly and includes smiling and laughing for no reason. Their behavior is often bizarre, ranging from social withdrawal to ostentatiously taking showers with clothes on. This type is usually associated with extreme social impairment. The *catatonic* type demonstrates unusual physical activity ranging from wild and uncontrolled to stuporous; in a condition known as "waxy flexibility," another person may place the patient's limbs in odd positions which the catatonic schizophrenic will maintain statue-like. *Paranoid* schizophrenics prove less likely to be seen immediately as "crazy," but they are often full of bizarre delusions of persecution or grandeur. Finally, many schizophrenics are diagnosed as *undifferentiated:* they have so many overlapping symptoms that it isn't clear in what subtype they should be categorized.

CAUSES OF SCHIZOPHRENIA. Partly because of its relatively high frequency, schizophrenia has generated many theories and therapies. Unfortunately, none has yet made a truly significant breakthrough. Many investigators believe schizophrenia is a disease in the biomedical sense, although no complete medical explanation has been found. Nonetheless, the biomedical model presents the most promising perspective.

Biomedical Model of Schizophrenia. The biomedical position is strongly supported by evidence on the inheritance of schizophrenia. It has long been

TABLE 15–5
Biological Risk of Developing Schizophrenia

Relationship to Person	Morbidity Risk (risk of developing schizophrenia) (%)
No blood relationship	0.8–1.5
Second-degree relatives (e.g., grandparent, uncle, niece, half-sibling)	2.4–4.2
First-degree relatives	
Parent	5.6
Sibling	10.1
Child	12.8
One sibling and at least one parent	16.7
Both parents	46.3
Monozygotic (identical) twin	50.0

As the number of relatives or their genetic similarity to a person increases, so does the person's risk of developing schizophrenia.

Source: Gottesman, et al., 1982.

known that schizophrenia tends to run in families. The probability of a person developing schizophrenia increases dramatically if family members and other relatives also manifest schizophrenia (see Table 15–5). These findings suggest that people inherit a potential for the disorder. The most compelling evidence for the role of genetic factors in schizophrenia comes from adoption studies. When the offspring of a schizophrenic parent are adopted by a normal parent and reared in a foster home, they still have the same risk for the disorder as they would if they had been brought up by the biological parent (Gottesman, Shields, & Hanson, 1982). In addition, adopted children who are schizophrenic have significantly more relatives with schizophrenic disorders among their biological kin than among their nonbiological, or adoptive, families (Gottesman, et al. 1982).

Does this mean, then, that schizophrenia is inherited? The answer is "probably yes, but not directly." Most schizophrenics do not have schizophrenic parents or siblings. In fact, the risk of developing schizophrenia is only 50 percent even among identical twins. In other words, in half of these cases, only one member of the pair develops schizophrenia; the other twin never does. Schizophrenics do, however, have parents and siblings who suffer a wider range of psychological disorders than other persons. The consensus, therefore, suggests that what people inherit are degrees of vulnerability to exhibit schizophrenic symptoms; whether or not they will exhibit them depends on environmental stress (Zubin & Spring, 1977).

Another line of research supporting the biomedical perspective focuses on the chemical imbalance implicated in the disease. If there is a single dominating hypothesis about the biochemistry of schizophrenia, it would have to be the dopamine hypothesis (Snyder, 1976, 1981). This hypothesis asserts that schizophrenics suffer from excessively high concentration of the transmitter substance dopamine in their brains. Dopamine is an inhibitory transmitter involved in the synaptic transmission of neural signals. It is concentrated in certain areas of the brain, particularly in the limbic system, which is involved in regulating emotional behavior. The evidence associating schizophrenia with an excess of dopamine comes from at least three sources. First, animals sometimes exhibit stereotyped behavior similar to catatonia when they are injected with chemicals that increase brain dopamine (Bernheim & Lewine, 1979). Second, some evidence indicates that the psychotic experiences reported in amphetamine overdose may be due to elevation of brain dopamine levels. (Amphetamine psychoses closely resemble the paranoid features of some forms of schizophrenia.) Finally, one of the most widely prescribed drug treatments for schizophrenia employs a class of the antipsychotic drugs called phenothiazine. According to pharmacological studies, the phenothiazines block dopamine receptors in the brain, thereby reducing the amount of dopamine present (Turkington, 1983). The chemical imbalance hypothesis has promise, but it has many scientific hurdles to jump before it can be declared highly probable.

Other Models of Schizophrenia. Psychoanalytic approaches view schizophrenia and other psychoses as examples of extensive regression in which the patient substitutes a fantasy world for the real one. Thus, hallucinations and delusions are thought to be imagined surrogates for an unacceptable reality (Lehmann, 1980).

Learning theorists also offer explanations for schizophrenia. From one perspective, for example, schizophrenic behaviors, bizarre as they may be, are rewarded by the environment, notably by the attention they elicit. Proponents of this explanation point to research and treatment programs which show that schizophrenic behaviors can be increased or decreased by training the nursing staff to attend differentially to bizarre and normal behaviors (Haughton & Ayllon, 1965; Ullman & Krasner, 1965). A similar learning perspective argues that schizophrenics have lost their ability to attend to appropriate objects effectively because for some reason they are no longer rewarded by their environment for doing so (Ullman & Krasner, 1969).

Most environmental models of schizophrenia today involve the influence of *stress*. While some people may be biologically more vulnerable than others to develop schizophrenia, life stress may be necessary to set off a schizophrenic episode (Rosenthal, 1970). Thus, persistently disturbed family relationships or a temporary but powerful negative event such as the loss of a loved one may be required to trigger a breakdown. Vulnerable individuals are those who are less equipped to handle the stresses of life. Longitudinal studies are currently in progress in Denmark (Mednick et al., 1982) and in the United States (Erlenmeyer-Kimling et al., 1984) to test this approach. The research strategy involves locating children with a vulnerability for developing schizophrenia (for example, being the relative of a schizophrenic) and following these children through adulthood, when the appearance of symptoms is likely to occur. Tests of their vulnerability to stressors and measurement of the amount of ongoing stress are made throughout. While stress was found to be predictive of schizophrenia in one study (Mednick et al., 1982), it was not in the other (Erlenmeyer-Kimling et al., 1984). The subjects in these studies are still quite young, however, so we will have to wait a few more years before more definitive results will be possible.

RESEARCH FRONTIER

Scanning the Brain

For many years, scientists sought to identify brain abnormalities among hardened criminals and victims of schizophrenia. Scientists typically dissected the brain after death and made careful microscopic comparisons between the neural tissue of a normal person and that of an abnormal individual. These studies yielded few conclusive results; only minor differences in the structure of the brains were found, and even these meager differences could not be replicated in later studies.

One reason for the lack of success could possibly be that the brain tissue was dead by the time it was dissected. However, new advances in technology permit a variety of ways to study the living brain. Some techniques produce full-color images of the brain, as shown in Figure 15–3. Others rely on more indirect procedures, such as recording brain waves from electrodes placed on the outside of the skull. What have these new methods revealed about the brain structures of victims of mental disorders?

In *CAT (computer-assisted tomography) scans*, many low-energy X-ray pictures are taken at different levels of the living brain and integrated by a computer into pictures. These pictures provide detailed images of underlying brain tissue. A number of recent CAT scan–based reports (Weinberger, Wagner, & Wyatt, 1983) have revealed that 20–25% of schizophrenic patients show enlarged ventricles,

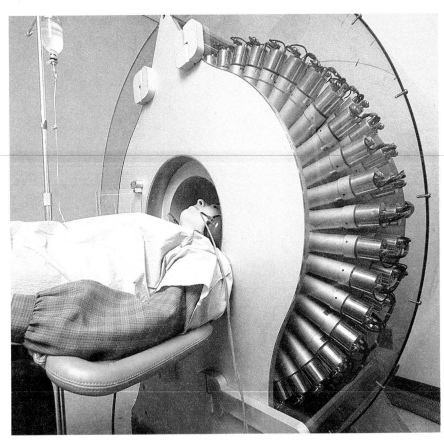

 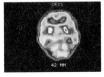

 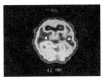

FIGURE 15–3
PET Scanner and Scans of Four Schizophrenic Sisters: Nora, Hester, Iris, and Myra

In the large photograph is a patient undergoing a PET scan. The smaller photographs are the scans for four quadruplets with schizophrenia. The scans show the variability in glucose use among the sisters. Lower glucose use is indicated by blue or green colors, higher use by red or orange. The PET technique is still largely too experimental to be able to lead to firm conclusions about brain disturbances in schizophrenia, although it may in the future, when the chemical and behavioral technology is improved.

Source: Mirsky, following Buchsbaum et al., 1984.

large, fluid-filled chambers located in the brain. Enlarged ventricles occur in many different forms of brain disease. For example, they can sometimes be found in people who have long histories of alcoholism or who have experienced viral or bacterial infections.

Many observers feel that the CAT scan is the least informative technique for studying the living brain. A CAT scan can reveal only a picture of the size and shape of different brain structures (the cortex, cerebellum, hypothalamus, and so on). It tells little about how brain structures are functioning. The *PET (positron emission tomography) scan,* on the other hand, measures metabolic activity in several areas of the brain and provides researchers with a color-coded view of how active various parts of the brain are at any given moment. Orange to red colors on the PET scan indicate normal to high use of energy; and green to blue colors indicate low activity. (See Figure 15–3.)

PET scans can measure, compare, and contrast brain activity in people suffering from various psychological disorders. If it can be shown, for example, that schizophrenics reliably differ from depressives in their brain activity, diagnosis would become a more exact and easier process. A diagnosis could be made by comparing a patient's brain scan with that of different patient groups, a procedure that takes only a few hours. Some preliminary evidence from PET scans suggests that schizophrenics, in particular, show decreased activity in the frontal lobes (Buchsbaum et al., 1984). (See Figure 15–3 for a sample of PET scans of four schizophrenic sisters.)

Some investigators have used electroencephalogram (EEG) measures to examine people with the antisocial personality disorder to see if there were abnormalities in the brain. Reviewers have concluded that 50–60% of these individuals showed abnormal brain waves compared with 10–15%

in normal controls (Mednick et al., 1982). The most common abnormality is widespread, excessively slow brain wave activity (5 to 8 cycles per second). In one study of 11-to-13-year-olds, Mednick and colleagues (1981) found that those who six years later were multiple offenders exhibited slower brain waves than either noncriminals or one-time offenders. This pattern resembles that generally found in children, leading some to suggest that the antisocial personality's higher brain centers mature more slowly.

Brain wave patterns have also been used recently in the study of multiple personality. Braun (1983) reported the case of a woman, who, at one point in her treatment, manifested four personalities. Brain wave measurement showed that each had a distinct pattern of brain function. After her successful treatment, when these four personalities were blended into a single, integrated one, the remaining pattern was distinct from any one of the previous four (see Figure 15–4).

FIGURE 15–4
Four Brain Wave Patterns of Jan G.

Each of the four subpersonalities (Susan, Jan. L., Joan, and Jan G.) exhibited by Jan G. was found to have a distinct brain wave pattern. Over the course of therapy, the personalities merged. First Susan and Jan L. formed a composite, Jan; Joan and Jan G. merged into Lucy. Finally, the new, fully integrated Jan G. emerged from the combination of Jan and Lucy.

Source: Braun, 1983.

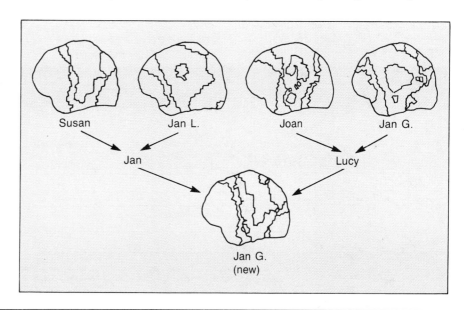

Finally, what has been referred to as a humanistic perspective has been proposed by Laing (1967). Laing argues that schizophrenics are inwardly reaching to discover their true selves and to recapture their wholeness. Because they have been subjected to intolerable pressures and contradictory demands from their environment, particularly from their families, they are less whole and less aware of their inner selves than normal people. Their schizophrenia simply represents a withdrawal from others in order to make an inward search which, if allowed to continue, will result in a strong, well-adjusted person. Laing is strongly opposed to conventional therapies for schizophrenia, particularly drug therapies, which he views as interfering with self-discovery.

CRIME AND DELINQUENCY

Americans are experiencing violent crime—and their fear of it—as a critical epidemic. Some years ago a *Newsweek* poll (1981) showed that nearly 60 percent of Americans believed their neighborhoods were becoming increasingly dangerous and 53 percent were afraid to walk alone at night within a mile of their own homes. Official statistics appear to make these fears quite reasonable. More than 12 million offenses were reported in America in 1984 (Federal Bureau of Investigation, 1985). Violent crimes, which raise the greatest public concern, accounted for 10 percent of these; the average likelihood of any one person being the victim of a reported violent crime during that year was 1 in 190. Although victims are almost twice as likely to be attacked by their spouses, other members of their family, friends, or acquaintances as by strangers, roughly one-third of murders are committed by someone the victims had never met.

Some experts on crime argue that "victimization" studies, in which U.S. Justice Department researchers use scientific polling techniques to sample the population, are more reliable than the FBI's annual counts. The department's studies, in which people are asked to respond anonymously to their personal encounters with violence, are hardly comforting. They showed, for example, a 14 percent increase in rape from 1970 to 1984 (Federal Bureau of Investigation, 1985).

Young people commit most of the violent crimes in American society. Nearly 60 percent of all arrests for such offenses in 1984 were of persons under age 25; one-fifth were under 18. Although the female prison population doubled through the 1970s, women accounted for only about 10 percent of the violent crime arrests in 1984. Blacks are disproportionately involved both as offenders and as victims. Although they constitute only 12 percent of the U.S. population, they make up 48 percent of the prison population. They are also the main victims of crime. For example, over 60 percent of all homicide victims are black.

There are, of course, many different types of crime and many types of criminals (Akers, 1985; Wilson & Herrnstein, 1985). Most crime is committed by individuals who knowingly and intentionally set out to break the law for individual gain. Sociologists classify them as professional criminals, organized criminals, and white-collar criminals. We will concentrate here primarily on individuals whose antisocial behavior has particularly interested psychologists.

APPLYING PSYCHOLOGY

The Plea of Insanity and Criminal Responsibility

In June 1982, John W. Hinckley, Jr., was found not guilty of attempted murder "by reason of insanity" for his shooting of President Reagan and three other men. The defense doctors found him to be schizophrenic. The decision aroused deep feelings of outrage in many people, and the insanity defense itself is now on trial. What was once routinely regarded as a standard part of the legal system has since been denounced in Congress and many state legislatures. Idaho has abolished the insanity defense. Bills in two dozen other states would replace it with a new plea—guilty but mentally ill.

Insanity pleas, of course, do not always win freedom for the defendant. In 1968 Sirhan Sirhan assassinated Robert Kennedy in the presence of many witnesses. His defense at trial was that he had been "in a dissociated . . . state" at the time of the shooting and therefore was not guilty. The jury, however, was not convinced. Sirhan was convicted of first-degree murder and received a death sentence, which was later commuted to life imprisonment. Two other publicized killers who tried the insanity plea, Jack Ruby (who murdered Lee Harvey Oswald) and John Wayne Gacy (who murdered 33 young boys in Chicago), also failed. "Son of Sam" David Berkowitz, Charles Manson, Mark David Chapman—all colloquially "certifiable"—never even used the defense.

Whether successful or not, the insanity defense raises fundamental is-

John W. Hinckley, Jr., was found not guilty of attempted murder "by reason of insanity" for his shooting of President Reagan and three other men. His parents have recently written a book about their son's experience—*Breaking Point* (Hinckley & Hinckley, 1985).

sues for psychology and its relation to the legal system. From the purely deterministic, scientific point of view of psychology, all behavior may derive ultimately from forces beyond an individual's control—e.g., genes, upbringing, socioeconomic status, peers, and psychological stressors. The legal system, however, assumes that people behave with free will and do wrong because they choose to. It is justifiable, then, to punish lawbreakers.

The major exception is if the offender is judged to be "insane." It is important to note that insanity is a legal concept, not a psychological one, although psychologists are often called to make judgments about it in trials. Criminals are considered insane if they appear not to be responsible for their acts.

The defense by reason of insanity was first clearly outlined in Britain in 1843 in the trial of a Scot, Daniel McNaughten, who today would probably be diagnosed as a paranoid schizophrenic. McNaughten attempted to assassinate the British prime minister in the belief that he, McNaughten, was being persecuted by members of the Conservative Party. He missed but killed somebody else. He was acquitted on "the grounds of insanity" and confined to an asylum for life. The case established the **McNaughten rule** for judging insanity on the basis of whether or not the accused was capable of knowing that the act was wrong. Since then, another criterion has often been added: could the person have controlled the behavior or was he or she directed by an "irresistible urge"? The American Law Institute suggests:

A person is not responsible for criminal conduct if at the time of such conduct, as a result of mental disease or defect, he lacks substantial capacity either to appreciate the criminality (wrongfulness) of his conduct or to conform his conduct to the requirements of the law. (*Model Penal Code,* 1962)

Recently, attempts have been made to broaden the range of social deviances, including dependence on alcohol and other drugs, that come under the purview of mental health rather than criminal justice. For example, criminal sex offenders are often handled by both systems: special psychological inpatient facilities increasingly are provided in prisons in an attempt to combine custody with rehabilitation.

The Antisocial Personality Disorder

The DSM-III personality disorders include a wide variety of enduring, inflexible, and maladaptive personality traits. DSM-III lists a number of specific personality disorders (see Table 15–2, Axis II); they are generally recognizable by adolescence or earlier and continue throughout most of adult life, although they become less obvious in middle and old age. We will cover one major personality disorder, *antisocial personality disorder,* in detail. This disorder is marked by "a history of continuous and chronic antisocial behavior in which the rights of others are violated, persistence into adult life of a pattern of antisocial behavior that began before the age of 15, and failure to sustain good job performance over a period of several years" (American Psychiatric Association, 1980, pp. 317–318). This disorder, then, includes both criminal behavior and delinquency. Some 10 percent of adult criminals are classifiable as *antisocial,* or what used to be referred to as *psychopathic* and *sociopathic.*

A number of characteristics mark the criminal psychopath (Cleckley, 1964). Psychopaths usually are superficially charming and make a good initial impression. They tend to impulsivity and a disregard for social convention. Perhaps their most notable characteristic is their lack of empathy, love, guilt, and shame. Their relationships with others incline to be exploitative and manipulative. Finally, psychopaths fail to learn from experience. Some evidence indicates that psychopaths have a very low level of reactivity in their autonomic nervous systems, which makes them insensitive both to conditioning and to learning to feel the same emotions as other people (Hare, 1978).

Charles Manson is an example of a person with antisocial personality disorder.

CASE STUDY
An Antisocial Personality

Charles Manson was born November 11, 1934, to a teenage prostitute. When he was five years old, his mother was arrested for robbery and was sent to jail; Manson went to live with an aunt and uncle in West Virginia. He remembered his aunt as being very strict, his uncle as kind and compassionate. When the boy was 13, his mother, now out of jail, took him home to Indianapolis. She drank heavily and often left him alone all night. At 14 he departed, supporting himself by taking odd jobs and by petty theft. His mother felt he was uncontrollable and turned him in to the police, who placed him in a juvenile detention center. He ran away after three days and robbed a grocery store. Arrested, he was sent to a reformatory but escaped. In the next four years he escaped from 18 juvenile correction institutions. Manson's life became a series of imprisonments and crimes. In 1967, at age 33, after release from yet another jail, he drifted to the Haight-Ashbury section of San Francisco, then teeming with "flower children" and "hippies." He was superficially charming, even charismatic, and gained a small following of young men and women. The Manson Family, as they became known, moved to southern California, where they intimidated an old, blind rancher into allowing them to live with him. In August 1969, Manson and his family entered an expensive Hollywood home and murdered five persons, including the pregnant movie star Sharon Tate. The bodies were horribly mutilated. When police arrived, they found a brief message—the word "pig" written in blood on the front door.

Causes of Crime and Delinquency

Both genetic predispositions and social learning underlie antisocial behavior. Recall that concordance studies examining the incidence of criminal behavior among identical and fraternal twin pairs show a significant discrepancy in favor of identical twins being most similar (Table 14–3, page 506). Such statistical evidence suggests a heritable predisposition for criminality. Adoption studies in both Denmark and the United States also show a role for genetic factors (Crowe, 1972, 1974; Hutchings & Mednick, 1975; Schulsinger, 1972). A summary of the studies shows that even though they were adopted and reared by noncriminals, 25 percent of the biological children of criminals still ended up either having criminal records or being diagnosed as psychopaths. Only 13 percent of a control group—biological children of noncriminals adopted and reared by noncriminals—had similar fates.

One of the studies allowed a more detailed analysis. Four groups of male children were involved: (1) those whose biological fathers and adopted fathers were not criminal; (2) those whose biological fathers were not criminal but whose adopted fathers were; (3) those whose biological fathers were criminal but whose adopted fathers were not; and (4) those whose biological and adopted fathers were criminal. The results showed that having a biological father who was a criminal increased the son's likelihood of being criminal, but being adopted by a criminal father did not (see Table 15–6). When both the genetic and the environmental factors were present, the rate of criminal behavior was highest.

One large adoption study was carried out by Mednick, Gabrielli, and Hutchings (1984) with 14,427 children separated from their biological parents at birth. They found that the children were more at risk for criminal conviction if their biological parents had been so convicted than if their adopting parents had. Moreover, brothers and sisters who were adopted into different homes had equal criminal tendencies. These results and many others reviewed by Wilson and Herrnstein (1985) imply that a predisposition toward criminality is inherited.

Social learning theory also accounts for the acquisition of antisocial behavior (Akers, 1985; Wilson & Herrnstein, 1985). According to this approach, people learn to be criminal—partly because of a lack of discipline in the home and the school and partly because of reinforcement and modeling

TABLE 15–6
The Criminality of Adopted Children and Their Fathers

Fathers' Criminality	Adoptees' Criminal Rates (%)
Neither biological nor adoptive father criminal	10.4
Adoptive father criminal, biological not a known criminal	11.2
Biological father criminal, adoptive not a known criminal	21.0
Both biological and adoptive fathers criminal	36.2

Source: Goldstein, Baker, & Jamison, 1986, p. 527.

of antisocial behavior patterns. Earlier in the chapter, for example, we discussed the role of the peer group in the acquisition of substance abuse. In Chapter 18 we will discuss the role of the mass media in shaping aggressive behavior.

HOPE FOR THE FUTURE

We have seen that mental disorders encompass an enormous range of conditions, some quite common. There are also many different explanations for these varied problems. Research has sometimes clarified a particular type of abnormal functioning, but more often it has simply given us clues that lead us further into the puzzle. Under these circumstances, we must not expect to find one set of principles that accounts for all conditions that clinical psychologists deal with. One set may underlie schizophrenia, others depression, still others drug addiction, and so on. In the future, psychologists will better understand the processes involved in the development of personality and will be able to reduce the incidence of mental disturbance. The methods of treating these disturbances will also improve to the point where the disturbances can be more readily cured. We turn to the methods of treatment in the next chapter.

SUMMARY

1. The field of abnormal psychology, or psychopathology, deals with a wide assortment of behavioral conditions that differ from the appropriate or ideal. Three criteria for deciding whether a behavior is abnormal are (1) deviation from a statistical norm, (2) deviation from an ideal standard, and (3) personal distress.

2. A number of theoretical conceptions have been developed in attempts to explain the origins or causes of abnormal behaviors. In certain periods of history, the superstitious approach prevailed, and abnormal behavior was seen as a form of demonic possession. In others, as in our own, the medical model, probably the most influential perspective, has seen abnormal behavior as similar to physical illness. The psychoanalytic approach, pioneered by Sigmund Freud, views abnormal behavior as resulting from unconscious conflicts between the individual's impulses and socially and personally acceptable behavior. The behavioral approach suggests that people learn abnormal behaviors much as they learn normal ones—through modeling, classical conditioning, instrumental learning, and so on.

3. The third and current edition of the *Diagnostic and Statistical Manual of Mental Disorders* (DSM-III)

represents an attempt to provide reliable descriptions of patterns of abnormal behavior. It provides 15 separate classifications of disorder.

4. Some psychologists have suggested that mental illness is really a myth and that abnormal behaviors more often reflect problems in living. Furthermore, an approach called labeling theory argues that the use of diagnostic labels has a negative effect on a person's ability to resolve problems. Although diagnosis has its critics, it is hard to imagine treatment of the mentally ill without it.

5. The anxiety disorders are characterized by high levels of apprehension in the presence of certain objects or situations and by the development of behavior patterns to avoid these stimuli. The most prevalent types of anxiety disorders are phobias, generalized anxiety disorders, and obsessive-compulsive disorders.

6. Somatoform disorders involve physical symptoms that suggest physical disorder but for which there are no apparent organic causes. The most common form of these disorders is conversion disorder.

7. Dissociative disorders involve a splitting off (dissociation) of a part of the individual's personality

so that memory or identity is disturbed. In amnesia, there is a loss of memory. In a fugue, a person takes on a new identity. In multiple personality, the person shows two or more distinct, integrated personalities, each of which dominates at a particular time.

8. Susbtance use disorders involve excessive use of drugs. Alcohol is the most widely used drug. It is estimated that in the United States today, about 10 million people are alcoholics or problem drinkers.

9. According to DSM-III, there are three basic sexual disorders. Gender identity disturbance involves a confusion between anatomic and psychological sexuality. Paraphilias (sexual deviations) involve focusing on particular sexual practices, such as fetishism or exhibitionism, as the sole means of sexual release. Psychosexual dysfunctions, such as impotence, involve difficulties in the initiation or completion of the sexual cycle. There is a clear trend away from labeling the individual who engages in homosexual behavior as emotionally disturbed.

10. Affective disorders involve disturbances of mood or emotion. People suffering from these disturbances are unrealistically depressed, inappropriately joyful, or both. Learning theorists focus on reduced positive reinforcement and learned helplessness to explain depression.

11. Schizophrenic disorders are the most serious type of abnormal behavior and the most likely to require hospitalization. Schizophrenics experience thought disorder, delusions, and hallucinations. DSM-III lists four types of schizophrenic reactions: disorganized, paranoid, catatonic, and undifferentiated. Most scientists agree that some combination of genetic and environmental factors works to produce schizophrenia. Strong evidence for a genetic factor is provided by studies of children of schizophrenic mothers adopted shortly after birth and from studies of identical and fraternal twins.

12. Crime and delinquency are reaching epidemic proportions in American society. About 10 percent of adult offenders are classified as psychopathic or sociopathic, known to DSM-III as antisocial personality disorder. These individuals demonstrate a lack of empathy, love, guilt, and shame. The psychopath's relationships with others tend to be exploitative and manipulative.

SUGGESTED READINGS

Freud, S. (1933). *New introductory lectures on psychoanalysis.* New York: Norton.
> An introduction to the psychoanalytic approach to abnormal personality, written by the master himself.

Goldstein, M. J., Baker, B. L., & Jamison, K. R. (1986). *Abnormal psychology: Experiences, origins, and interventions* (2nd ed.). Boston: Little, Brown.
> A thorough survey of all aspects of abnormal behavior, covering all of the DSM-III categories.

Meyer, R. G. & Osborne, Y.V.H. (Eds.) (1982). *Case studies in abnormal behavior.* Boston: Allyn and Bacon.
> Fascinating case histories are presented, including all of the DSM-III categories described in this chapter.

> Especially good sections on anxiety, depression and the antisocial personality.

Sutherland, N. S. (1976). *Breakdown.* New York: Stein & Day.
> An autobiographical account of a mental breakdown written by a leading British experimental psychologist.

Wilson, J. Q., & Herrnstein, R. J. (1985). *Crime and human nature.* New York: Simon & Schuster.
> Integrates all the major research findings and theories about crime into one source; a major achievement at cross-disciplinary research by two of America's leading social scientists.

16

Therapies

Mental health problems do not affect three or four out of every five persons but one out of one.

Karl Menninger

IN THE SUMMER OF 1977, NORMAN S. ENDLER, A WELL-KNOWN PSYCHOLogist at York University in Toronto, suffered a profound depression that brought his normal mode of life to a halt and disrupted the lives of his family and friends. He tells the story of his depression in *Holiday of Darkness* (1982).

As a psychologist, Endler knew the varieties of treatment available. He went to a traditional psychiatrist who, after talking the problem over with Endler, suggested that he try antidepressant drugs, which in many cases overcome depression quite successfully. However, this therapy did not bring Endler out of his depression. Another psychiatrist suggested that Endler try electroconvulsive therapy (ECT), a procedure in which electrodes are attached to a person's head and electric current is passed through the brain. This controversial treatment seems to reduce depression in many cases, but for reasons not well understood. Its serious side effects include temporary confusion, memory loss, and, in some cases, physical injury. In fact, when he was a psychology graduate student, Endler had seen ECT break a patient's back. Endler mulled over his choices. He recounts, "In late 1977 when it was suggested that I consider ECT as a possible course of treatment for my depression, I was repelled. The alternatives were hospitalization or the misery of depression, both of which were highly repugnant to me. . . . At that time I was so desperate that if Dr. Persad had suggested that walking down Yonge Street (the main street in Toronto) nude would be beneficial to me, I would probably have tried it. Therefore, I agreed, although reluctantly, to ECT as a course of treatment for my depression" (1982, p. 72).

Over a two-week period in September 1977, Endler had seven ECT sessions. Remarkably, he felt much better. He resumed his duties as chairman of the psychology department and taught his classes. He writes, "A miracle had happened in two weeks. I had gone from feeling like an emotional cripple to feeling well . . . my holiday of darkness was over" (p. 83). Today Endler has recovered from his depression and he has resumed his very successful research program.

As this dramatic example indicates, there are several types of therapy available to combat mental disorders. Many people are helped with treatments far less extreme and controversial than ECT. This chapter will discuss the types of treatments used and their effectiveness. First we provide some historical background.

THERAPIES: SOME HISTORY AND BACKGROUND

People have been trying for centuries to correct behavior that societies deem abnormal or deviant. Once it became apparent that madness constituted an

William Hogarth's engraving, Bedlam, depicts conditions in the Hospital of St. Mary of Bethlehem (Bedlam) in London in 1770. Note the chains on two of the patients.

illness rather than a manifestation of wickedness or possession by demons, asylums, or institutions to house those afflicted with madness, were established. But their conditions of confinement were awful. Patients were chained to the cell walls by iron collars and treated as little better than criminals. One such institution, St. Mary of Bethlehem, founded in London in 1547, was the source of the word *bedlam.* (The local Cockney accent slurred the pronunciation.) For a small fee, Londoners could watch the tragic antics of the inmates, who were required to perform in plays and sketches for the audience.

After Philippe Pinel (see Chapter 15) became director of an asylum in Paris in 1792 and treated inmates with compassion, similar humanitarians achieved some success in other countries. In the United States, Dorothea Dix, a Massachusetts schoolteacher, almost single-handedly roused the nation to the needs of the mentally disturbed. In 1840, mental hospitals housed only about 15 percent of those who needed care; by 1890, the figure was almost 70 percent, largely because of Dix's efforts. For the first time, "treatments" were provided, although most of them consisted of traumas intended to bring patients "back to their senses." If patients became unruly, devices were available to restrain them. As late as the 1950s locked rooms, straightjackets, and impoverished conditions persisted as aspects of treatment. Although tremendous progress has been made, room for improvement remains. Loneliness and boredom continue to be problems even in well-run institutions.

In the mid-1950s, the introduction of a range of "wonder drugs" initiated a revolution in patient management and eventually to a decline in the number of people kept in mental institutions. By the 1970s the closing of

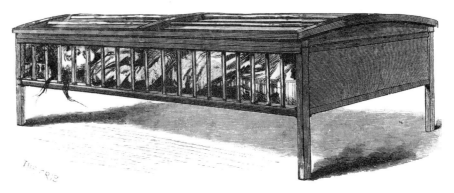

THE DOCTOR THINKS THAT "NO WELL-REGULATED INSTITUTION SHOULD BE
UNPROVIDED WITH THE CIRCULATING SWING." 1818.

Restraining devices were common in
nineteenth-century mental hospitals.
Many early "treatments" assumed that
physical traumas would restore patients
to their senses.

mental hospitals was in full swing, but the "deinstitutionalization" of the
mentally ill has created a new set of dilemmas, as we discuss later in the
chapter.

Types of Therapy

There are two major categories of therapy available for treating psychological disorders. The first is the *somatic* or *physical therapies,* such as drug
and shock therapy. These therapies are based on physiological and biochemical views of mental disorder, and we discuss these at the end of the chapter. We begin with the second group, the *psychotherapies,* which are based
on psychological theories of mental disorder, such as Sigmund Freud's psychoanalytic approach.

In recent years, a variety of other psychological techniques has developed. Foremost among the newer psychological approaches is *behavior therapy*, a treatment based on learning principles. Proponents of behavior

therapy share a belief that abnormality and deviance are best considered as problems in coping with life rather than as illness. Their assumption is that the same processes apply to abnormal behavior and deviance as to normal behavior. *Cognitive therapies* attempt to restructure the way people think about themselves and the world in which they live. *Humanistic therapies* aim to alter the way people feel about themselves and also to emphasize improvement of interpersonal relationships among healthy people. Finally, and perhaps most recent of all, *group and community therapy* attempts to help people in the family or community group to which they belong rather than in mental hospitals and to prevent abnormality by working against harmful social conditions such as child abuse, poor nutrition, loneliness, and neglect.

So many different types of therapy are available—from the traditional to the avant-garde and "pop" varieties—that it would be impossible to list them all in one chapter. Most, however, fall into a few distinct categories, based primarily on the personality theories presented in Chapter 14 and the approaches to the mental disorders described in Chapter 15. Therapies are also constantly evolving and giving birth to new versions, some of which will be described in this chapter.

Despite differences, each of the psychotherapies aims to help the client acquire more useful ways of feeling, thinking, and behaving. It is also worth pointing out that most contemporary therapists do not adhere rigidly to one form of treatment. As a recent survey of psychologists showed, most are to some extent "eclectic," borrowing approaches and techniques from other schools of thought to supplement their own perspectives (Smith, 1982). This overlap should be kept in mind as you read the sections that follow.

Types of Therapists

Those who practice psychotherapy can be divided into five groups, largely on the basis of their training. After earning a medical degree, a *psychiatrist* usually completes three years of residency training in psychiatry. Psychiatrists take medical as well as psychotherapeutic responsibility for patients; they are the only psychotherapists permitted to prescribe psychoactive drugs, electroshock treatment, or other biological intervention techniques. Psychiatrists are often thought to be the best trained of the psychotherapists, but this is not necessarily so. In fact, few of the courses they take to become medical doctors involve psychological knowledge. *Clinical psychologists* have completed four years of undergraduate work and have earned doctorate degrees in psychology. The Ph.D. typically involves four to five years of intensive training in research and clinical skills as well as a one-year internship under professional supervision. A *counseling psychologist* has had graduate training somewhat similar to that of the clinical psychologist, usually to the Ph.D. level, but typically with less emphasis on research. This training differs slightly in that it is concerned with problems of adjustment rather than abnormal functioning and often concentrates on specific areas such as student, marriage, or family counseling. A *psychiatric social worker* usually has a master's degree in social work and special training in treatment procedures, with emphasis on the family or community. A *psychiatric nurse* is a registered nurse with special training for work in a mental hospital.

PSYCHOANALYTIC THERAPIES

As we saw in Chapter 14, Freud attempted to explain the development of personality in terms of how the individual resolves conflicts among the unconscious biological instincts in the id, the constraints of reality imposed on the ego, and the moral strictures of the conscience imposed by the superego. Freud considered the development of the defense mechanisms and the individual's characteristic ways of dealing with conflicts to be heavily influenced by early childhood experiences. According to Freudian theory, abnormal behavior is largely the result of unresolved conflicts occurring deep in the unconscious. The cause of conflict is, therefore, far below the patient's level of awareness; indeed, the person may be using a great deal of psychic energy to keep the conflict repressed. The goal of Freudian therapy, called *psychoanalysis,* is to uncover and bring to the surface the unconscious conflict, to free the repressed energies of the psyche so it can deal more effectively with the environment.

In Freud's method, the client lay on a couch, relaxed, and talked about dreams, early relationships with parents, and other topics that came to consciousness. Typically the therapist, in order not to provide a distraction, sat behind the person, listening. Although contemporary procedures vary, the emphasis on the client talking to the therapist about early relationships with parents and current relationships with loved ones remains the same.

From Free Association to Catharsis

The course of psychoanalysis might typically run through several phases.

FREE ASSOCIATION. Sometimes a therapist might begin with free association, a technique described in Chapter 14. During this phase, the client simply reports whatever comes to mind. With the help of the therapist, the client allows thoughts to move freely from one association to another even if the associations make little sense or are painful or embarrassing. The goal of free association is to lower the client's defense mechanisms so that unconscious material may emerge into consciousness.

DREAM ANALYSIS. Freud thought dreams an especially good way of tapping the unconscious, referring to them as "the royal road to the unconscious." He distinguished between the *manifest* (obvious, visible) *content* and the *latent* (hidden, underlying) *content* of dreams. Freud interpreted dream symbols. For example, elongated objects such as snakes, sticks, guns, tree trunks, and pencils are symbols of the penis, and balloons and airplanes are symbols of erections. Suppose a student reports a dream in which he is busy writing with a fountain pen when it suddenly breaks, sending ink all over the page. In the background, his friend starts to laugh at him. Freud might see this dream as an indication of repressed feelings of sexual impotence. Note that the validity of such psychoanalytic translation remains questionable to many non-Freudian psychologists.

RESISTANCE. As defenses weaken, anxiety emerges; to deal with this, clients often attempt, unconsciously, to block treatment. They may miss therapy appointments, report they have no dreams to relate, or lapse into monologues of little relevance to therapy. According to psychoanalytic theory, such *resistance* protects the clients' neuroses; unconsciously, they want to avoid the anxiety evoked by facing repressed impulses. To overcome resistance, the analyst provides an interpretation of the client's behavior, attempting to make the client aware of just what is being avoided. Analysts must offer interpretation only when they have developed a reasonably clear picture of the dynamics of the client's personality. Analysts believe that, when timed correctly, their interpretations can lead to emotional insights on the client's part, and client and analyst can begin working through the client's problems, uncovering the repressed thoughts and desires.

TRANSFERENCE. As analysis progresses, clients may make a *transference* to the therapist of the unconscious feelings of love or hatred they have toward their parents, lover, or some other person who has been at the center of an emotional conflict in the past. The transference is called *positive transference* when the feelings attached to the therapist are those of love or admiration and *negative transference* when the feelings consist of hostility or envy. Often the client's attitude is *ambivalent*, including a mixture of positive and negative feelings.

Freud first noticed the transference phenomenon when he realized that patients ascribed to him characteristics of God (or the devil) or professed love for him. Therapists do not allow their clients to continue those feelings. They remain impersonal and professional and attempt to direct patients back to themselves. For instance, therapists may ask, "What do you see when you imagine my face?" Clients may reply that they see the therapist with an angry, frowning, unpleasant face. But therapists do not take this sort of response personally. Instead, they may calmly say, "What does this make you think of?" Gradually, it becomes clear to the clients that they are reacting to the neutral figure of the therapist as though the therapist were a threatening father or some other childhood figure of authority. Interpretation of the transference is the key to successful psychoanalysis for it enables the client to raise the most repressed emotions to consciousness and to begin to deal realistically with them.

CATHARSIS. Resolving transference may trigger *catharsis,* a major emotional release in which clients gain sudden insight into the nature not only of their relationship with the therapist but, more important, of their previous relationships with their parents. This "unlocking" of repressed memories represents an important milestone in therapy, often leading to further exploration of repressed memories and desires. In serious cases where there may be more than one or two repressed conflicts, the same procedure continues until all the unconscious conflicts are resolved.

Psychoanalysis can be an involved, time-consuming, and expensive undertaking. It may require patient-therapist meetings several times a week and can go on for years. It is difficult for psychoanalysis to be effective for those who are unable to articulate their feelings and thoughts well (such as those suffering from psychotic disorders). Indeed, whether or not it has been beneficial even to the affluent few who can afford it has been hotly contested.

Psychoanalysis Since Freud

As Freud was working on his own theories of personality, some of his followers were carving out theories of their own and developing variations on classical psychoanalysis (see Chapter 14, pages 515–517). Jung's therapy aimed at uncovering patients' unconscious desires for artistic expression and religious experience. Adler emphasized gaining insight into feelings of inferiority and exploring the various stratagems people use to achieve power and dominance and to hide unconscious feelings of weakness. The ego theorists, such as Karen Horney and Erik Erikson, de-emphasized the unconscious and stressed the relative importance of ego functioning and, in particular, the patient's self-concept, current anxieties, and interpersonal relationships. Like Freud, however, they believe that the key to mental distress is unconscious conflict and that successful therapy requires insight into unconscious processes.

Therapeutic techniques also have undergone changes. One change has been to reduce the number of sessions per week and generally to attempt to condense the whole process into a few months or a year (Strupp, 1983). Another has been the disappearance of the psychoanalytic couch. Still another has altered the role of the therapist from a noninvolved figure sitting behind the patient to a more human, interacting, and supportive figure. Finally, the modern versions of psychoanalysis play down the need to recall repressed childhood memories in favor of highlighting current conflicts and defenses in the patient's life (Strupp, 1983).

All psychoanalytic approaches involve helping the patient to achieve insight into the dynamics of his or her personality and the release of repressed tensions, a process known as *abreaction.* Abreaction is a fancy name for "getting it out of your system." The basic assumption is that everybody suffers from frustrations and unhappiness, some of which result

Although some modern psychoanalysts have dispensed with the couch and become more interactive and supportive, some still practice using Freud's original method.

from childhood experiences and others from day-to-day pressures. These frustrations are assumed to accumulate deep in the unconscious, almost festering there, rising to the surface in a variety of maladaptive ways. The cure is to remove this psychic tension and gain insight into the patient's problems.

BEHAVIORAL THERAPIES

Whereas psychoanalytic therapy tries to change abnormal behavior indirectly by releasing unconscious energies, behavioral approaches to therapy try to change the behavior directly by applying the laws and principles of learning theory (see Chapter 14). Hans Eysenck coined the term *behavior therapy* in 1952, and B. F. Skinner used it almost immediately afterward, in 1953. Subsequently behavior therapy has also been known as *behavior modification,* and the two terms can be used interchangeably (Eysenck & Skinner, 1980). We will discuss a variety of behavior modification or therapeutic techniques based on classical conditioning, instrumental or operant conditioning, biofeedback, and observational learning.

Classical Conditioning Techniques

In psychotherapy, classical conditioning is referred to as *counterconditioning.* This therapy presents essentially two possibilities: (1) to alter an emotional response from an inappropriately negative one (e.g., anxiety) to a neutral or even positive one or (2) to alter an inappropriately positive emotional response (e.g., to heroin) to a negative one. The first process occurs either through systematic desensitization therapy or, alternatively, implosion therapy, and the second through aversion therapy.

SYSTEMATIC DESENSITIZATION THERAPY. Systematic desensitization therapy is used primarily to treat anxiety disorders such as those described in Chapter 15. In this treatment an individual learns to make a response, such as relaxation, to a stimulus that normally elicits anxiety. The first study to use systematic desensitization therapy was conducted by Mary Cover Jones in 1924. She presented a young child with a delicious food (unconditioned stimulus) that the child enjoyed (unconditioned response), while a rabbit (conditioned stimulus) that the child feared (conditioned response) was kept in a cage in the far corner of the room. Over a number of days, while the child ate the food, the rabbit was brought closer and closer until it no longer elicited a fear response even when sitting on the child's chest. The unconditioned response of eating and digesting the food was incompatible with being fearful.

Jones's pioneering efforts had relatively little impact on psychotherapeutic practice. Although she anticipated and developed many contemporary methods, her work remained relatively unrecognized for several decades. The popularization of counterconditioning techniques must be credited instead to Joseph Wolpe, who published a landmark book, *Psychotherapy by Reciprocal Inhibition,* in 1958. Since then, the therapy has been developed extensively (Wolpe, 1982).

Don't shoot. I am Dr. Cranish, and this is my patient. I am a pioneer in excitement therapy.

© 1979 Sidney Harris

**TABLE 16–1
Sample Anxiety Hierarchy
for an Agoraphobic**

1. Walking down to the garden gate
2. Walking down an empty sidewalk with a friend
3. Walking down an empty sidewalk alone
4. Walking down a sidewalk with a few people on it
5. Walking down a crowded sidewalk
6. Walking into a crowded store with a friend
7. Walking into a crowded store alone
8. Getting on a crowded bus with a friend
9. Getting on a crowded bus alone
10. Going onto the New York subway in rush hour

In systematic desensitization, the conditioned fear response must be kept at a weaker level than the unconditioned incompatible response. Consider a young woman who is agoraphobic, afraid of going outside. A therapist might first ask her to construct a stimulus *anxiety hierarchy,* a list of activities ranging from the least to the most threatening (see Table 16–1). The next step is to teach the client how to relax, since relaxation is incompatible with anxiety.

Wolpe used muscle relaxation techniques in which the client is taught to become aware of and control specific muscle groups throughout the body by successively tensing and relaxing each of them. Deep and slow breathing coupled with the relaxation of more and more muscle groups can lead to very deep relaxation.

Once the stimulus hierarchy is constructed and relaxation learned, the client is asked to imagine the first item in the hierarchy—in our example, walking down to the garden gate. The therapist may vividly describe the scene for the client. While relaxing, the client concentrates until she is certain that her imagined walk no longer elicits fear. Then she and the therapist move on to the next scene, and so on. After the client can envision all the various situations while she is deliberately relaxed, she repeats the hierarchy in reality—she places herself physically in each successive situation. This general procedure can be applied to a variety of phobias and anxiety-producing situations, including fear of public speaking, of snakes, and of sexual intercourse. We will return to these examples later in this chapter.

IMPLOSION THERAPY. Instead of beginning with the first scene in the hierarchy of Table 16–1, the one that arouses the least anxiety, *implosion therapy* begins with the most fear-arousing, hair-raising stimulus imaginable in an effort to provide intensive and dramatic extinction. Implosion therapists believe that patients will never overcome anxiety or their maladaptive behavior as long as they are allowed to avoid the anxiety-arousing stimulus situations. Implosion therapy forces the client to experience a full-blown anxiety reaction without suffering any harm. The therapist may describe to the client an extremely frightening situation and ask the client to try to experience his fear as fully as possible. In a variant of this procedure, the individual is exposed to a real situation rather than an imagined one. In either case, the inner explosion (implosion) of anxiety is extinguished, and the stimulus loses its power to elicit anxiety.

A case study from Isaac Marks (1978), a well-known British behavioral psychiatrist illustrates implosion therapy:

A young male student had failed an exam because of a panic-attack. The therapist with the student's collaboration decided to have the client experience his examination anxiety fully without providing an escape from it. The student was made to sit up in bed and try to feel his fear. He was asked to imagine all the consequences that would follow his failure— derision from his friends, disappointment from his family, and financial loss. At first as he followed the instructions, his sobbings increased. But soon his tremblings ceased. As the effort needed to maintain a vivid imagination increased, the emotion he could summon began to ebb. Within half an hour he was calm. He was instructed to repeatedly experience his fears. Every time he felt a little wave of spontaneous alarm he was not to push it aside but was to enhance and try to experience it

FIGURE 16–1
Treatment of a Child Molester

The man on the couch has volunteered for this procedure. The therapist presents slides of young girls. A phallic plethysmograph, attached to the man's penis, measures any sexual arousal. An electric shock is then given to the man in an attempt to reverse his tendency to associate children with sexual pleasure.

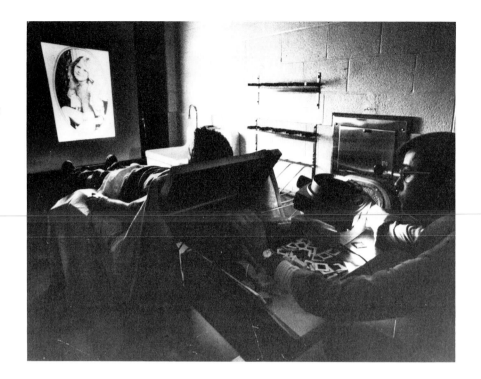

more vividly. The patient was intelligent and practiced his exercises methodically until he became almost unable to feel frightened. He passed his examinations without difficulty. (p. 212)

AVERSION THERAPY. Aversion therapy constitutes the opposite of desensitization. It involves transforming an undesirable positive stimulus into a negative one. For example, an alcoholic may be given a drug which, in interaction with liquor, makes the person violently ill; it is hoped that nausea will become associated with drinking. Because classical conditioning involves careful timing of the pairing of the unconditioned and the conditioned stimuli, the therapist may ensure that many liquor bottles are in sight while the client is being ill (Callner, 1975; Gotestam, Melin, & Ost, 1976).

Aversion therapy has also been used to treat sexual aberrations such as exhibitionism, voyeurism, and child molestation (see Figure 16–1) and to change the sexual orientation of homosexuals who desire to change (Adams, Tollison, & Carson 1981; Brady, 1980). In each case the client is exposed to the inappropriate attraction by slides, verbal descriptions, or real activities. These stimuli are then paired with unpleasant stimuli such as electric shock, nauseating chemicals, or disgusting images that the client is asked to picture. The theoretical underpinning is that the inappropriate stimuli elicit aversive emotional responses through association with the aversive stimuli (Brady, 1980).

Operant Conditioning Techniques

Operant or, as it is often known, *instrumental conditioning,* discussed in Chapters 6 and 14, can be described fairly simply. The central principle is the *law of effect,* which states that positive consequences following a behavior increase the future probability of that behavior, whereas negative consequences, such as punishment, decrease its future probability. This theory has been applied with great ingenuity to both an understanding of "irrational" abnormal behavior and its modification. There are essentially two possible treatments: (1) the provision of positive reinforcement to increase desired behaviors and (2) the use of punishment and nonreward to decrease undesired behavior.

POSITIVE REINFORCEMENT. Positive reinforcement often manifests itself inadvertently during therapy in the form of the therapist's nods of agreement, smiles, verbal encouragement, and sheer presence of attention. Thus it must be operating in all therapies in which a client interacts with a therapist. Therapists who do not adhere to a behavioral school of thought may deny that they are simply positively reinforcing certain ways of thinking and feeling in their clients; rather, they believe they are giving their patients insights. From a behavioral perspective, however, it is clear that the kinds of "insights" a client achieves are better predicted by the therapist's theoretical orientation than by the client's particular problems (Bandura, 1969). Thus the clients of Freudian therapists uncover unresolved Oedipal complexes; those of Adlerians find inferiority striving; and those of Jungians find archetypes.

If therapists' reinforcements inadvertently shape clients' behavior, then why not use them contingently to increase the behaviors explicitly desired? We will describe three studies that used positive reinforcement to modify behavior in autistic children, psychotic adults, and university students frustrated by their inability to study.

Autistic children are difficult to treat by traditional psychotherapy. They refuse to speak or even to make eye contact with the therapist. Often they engage in self-stimulatory behavior such as waving their hands in front of their eyes or rocking back and forth for hours. Ivor Lovaas (1973, 1977), a behavior therapist at UCLA, developed a program to change these children's behavior from withdrawal to attending, talking, and engaging in affectionate demonstrations and social interaction. At first he rewarded appropriate responses with chocolate candy. Later, when the children were proving responsive to being cuddled, cuddling became the reinforcement contingent on good behavior. Later still, reinforcement could consist of the the praise "well done" and "good boy." While such reinforcement produced short-term positive effects, it is questionable whether the behavior changes endure when the contingencies are removed (Lovaas, 1977).

As described in the opening section of Chapter 15, psychotic adults in wards often engage in bizarre behavior, such as arguing that they are Napoleon reincarnate or the God of the Old Testament. Other patients sit relatively quietly, reading newspapers and playing chess. In one study it was found that the nursing staff gave far more attention—positive reinforcement—to bizarre or disruptive behavior than to constructive but quiet behavior (Ayllon & Haughton, 1964). Under the psychologists' instructions, this pattern was reversed; bizarre behavior was ignored but any constructive behavior was immediately lavished with attention and praise. The results of this study, shown in Figure 16–2, demonstrate that psychotic

FIGURE 16–2
The Influence of Reinforcement on Psychotic and Neutral Verbal Behavior

The baseline (left) represents the rate of neutral and psychotic talking in the institution before the experiment began. Over the next several days, psychotic behavior was reinforced by social attention while neutral talk was ignored. As the graph illustrates, the rate of psychotic talk increased and that of neutral talk decreased. Then the experimenters reversed the procedure. Neutral talk was reinforced by attention and psychotic talk was ignored. As a result, neutral talk increased while psychotic talk dropped. The experiment demonstrates that psychotic "symptoms" can to some extent be brought under environmental control.

Source: Ayllon & Haughton, 1964.

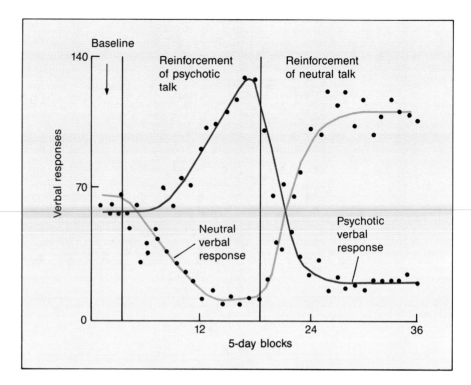

talk could be increased or decreased through the reinforcement provided by social attention.

Our final example of the power of positive reinforcement comes from procedures variously known as *contingency contracting* or *self-management.* Imagine that a male university student finds it difficult to devote the number of hours to study that he feels he should. In contingency contracting, the student draws up a contract with himself, to be witnessed by others, in which he specifies the hours that he is to study and the reinforcements he is accustomed to (e.g., a financial allowance from a parent, a date with a steady girlfriend, attendance at sports events with friends) that will not be delivered unless he fulfills the contract. To work best, such programs require friends' active participation. They allow an individual, however, to control his or her own behavior (Mahoney, 1980).

PUNISHMENT. In ancient times, Roman doctors recommended putting snakes and other unpleasant things in wine cups to discourage alcohol abuse. Punishment today takes many forms. Courts hand out prison terms for criminals, parents scold children, and teachers impose penalties for unruly behavior. Punishment is behind the simple technique used by many people who try to quit smoking by snapping a rubber band on their wrists whenever they crave a cigarette. The use of punishment in therapy has been open to controversy. Usually, punishment therapy has been directed at extremely destructive or dangerous behavior. When punishment is used, an unpleasant stimulus, such as a loud shout or a mild electric shock, is presented following specific behaviors, such as urinating on the floor. The punishment decreases the probability that the undesirable behavior will occur again and may provide an opportunity to teach and reward an alternative response (such as asking to go to the bathroom).

The power of punishment in controlling behavior has been demonstrated by Lovaas (1977) in his work with autistic children. Some autistic children are self-destructive, biting their arms and banging their heads against a wall so that they must be physically restrained; some must be tied to their beds. Lovaas (1977) showed that brief electric shocks eliminated self-mutilation in severely autistic children. Behavior therapists have been sharply criticized for using such procedures, however. This is a thorny ethical issue, and most behavioral therapists agree that such methods should be used only when other procedures are unavailable, inappropriate, or have failed.

"Time out" from positive reinforcement is a more acceptable punishment procedure that is used in many classrooms and homes. With this procedure, whenever a child behaves inappropriately (for example, hits another child), he or she is isolated for a few minutes in a "time-out" chair or room. Afterward, the child is returned to the original environment and asked to correct the misbehavior. When properly used, time out can be a very helpful procedure for correcting problem behaviors and eliminates the necessity of yelling at children.

Punishment can also be applied to self-management. A graduate student in psychology was having difficulty completing his doctoral thesis. In desperation, the student, who was Jewish, wrote a series of postdated checks payable to an anti-Semitic political organization. He told his supervisor to mail each check on the appropriate date if the student did not de-

Autistic children are often socially withdrawn and engage in self-stimulatory behavior such as rocking back and forth for hours.

liver a chapter of the thesis by that time. Only one such check was mailed; the student completed all the other chapters, and his thesis, before the deadline.

Biofeedback

Studies during the 1960s demonstrated that rats and monkeys can increase or decrease salivation, heart rate, and blood pressure when their autonomic responses are reinforced (Harris & Brady, 1974). Such studies spurred research into ways to train people to control their biological processes, particularly responses associated with psychological and medical problems. These methods are known as *biofeedback.* The idea behind biofeedback techniques is that if clients are informed by special instruments about specific bodily processes, such as blood pressure, they may attempt to modify their physiological activities (Miller, 1980).

For example, the therapist attaches electrodes to the heart region of the client's body. These electrodes convey electrical charges to an apparatus that monitors the client's heart rate and feeds it back to him or her via a visual or auditory display (see Figure 16–3). The client then uses relaxing strategies suggested by the therapist to lower his or her heart rate. The feedback showing the client's success in modifying the behavior usually is the reinforcer, but praise from the therapist may also be reinforcing. Psychologists and physicians widely employ biofeedback techniques to manipulate stress-related problems including asthma, headaches, elevated blood pressure, and tension. Biofeedback practitioners are highly optimistic that their procedures

FIGURE 16–3
A Biofeedback Therapy Situation

Through the use of monitoring instruments to give a person a continuous flow of information about his or her own biological state, a person can experiment with various ways of altering his or her physiological functioning.

will create major breakthroughs in treatment; researchers remain more reserved (Miller, 1983).

Modeling Therapy

In previous chapters we examined the role of *observational learning* in the development of normal personality. Since observing other models is a principal way in which humans learn, watching people who are displaying appropriate and adaptive behavior should teach people with maladaptive responses better coping strategies. The model may be observed live or on videotape. Modeling therapy has been used effectively both to eliminate unwanted behaviors and to build new behavioral competencies.

ELIMINATING ANXIETY THROUGH MODELING. Many studies illustrating the importance of modeling in the treatment of phobias have been carried out by Albert Bandura and his colleagues at Stanford University (Bandura, 1969, 1986; Rosenthal & Bandura, 1978). One dramatic sequence dealt with snake phobias (Bandura, Blanchard, & Ritter, 1969). Only subjects whose fear of snakes was intense were permitted to participate; the phobia had to interfere seriously with their ability to go camping or to do gardening. The study began with the subjects being tested to see how closely they would approach a glass tank with a live snake inside. Then the treatment group watched a film in which both children and adults enjoyably interacted with a large king snake, while a control group did not watch the film (see Figure 16–4). In early scenes the models handled only plastic snakes. In later

FIGURE 16–4
A Lesson in Overcoming Fear of Snakes

Children and adults are shown in films modeling interactions with a king snake. Victims of snake phobias watch these films to learn fearless behavior in the presence of the objects they fear.

scenes the models allowed the large king snake to crawl over their shoulders and around their necks. Subjects could stop the film whenever they wanted to, reverse it, see it again, and so on. After they had watched the film, the subjects were tested again to see how closely they would approach the live snake in the tank. The findings were clear. People in the treatment group, who had watched the film, significantly reduced their fears, and many actually held the snake. The ultimate test, which 33 percent of the subjects in the treatment group performed, included allowing the snake to lie in their laps while their hands hung at their sides. People in the control group, however, showed no such improvement.

The therapeutic value of film modeling has been demonstrated in a number of other studies. In one effort, 60 children aged 4 to 12 who were about to undergo surgery were shown one of two films. One film consisted of scenes of events encountered by most children hospitalized for surgery. The other was a control film unrelated to the hospital. Children who saw the first film showed substantially less anxiety than those who had seen the control film. Furthermore, parents reported fewer post-surgery problem behaviors in the children in the first group (Melamed & Siegel, 1975). Other studies have demonstrated that special films can reduce fear of dental treatment in both children and adults. Shaw and Thoresen (1974) showed adults who were phobic about dental treatment films of people enjoying a visit to the dentist. Actual visits to the dentist by the fearful ones substantiated the success of the effort. Sexual dysfunction in women has been treated somewhat similarly. Women who have been unable to achieve orgasm are taught to masturbate to climax by watching another woman do so on videotape (Wincze & Caird, 1976).

An extensive review of this literature indicates that modeling films have great therapeutic potential for eliminating a variety of anxieties and fears (Rosenthal & Bandura, 1978).

BUILDING NEW COMPETENCIES THROUGH MODELING. Modeling procedures have also been used to help people cope with problems of social interaction. Perhaps the best example of this is *assertivness and social skills training* (Argyle, Furnham, & Graham, 1981). In a variety of situations, many people feel they cannot stand up for their rights and say "no" to unreasonable requests, particularly when they come from authority figures such as a boss, a parent, or a professor. Such people often lack self-esteem. Assertiveness training provides people with the social skills to say "no" pleasantly but firmly.

The therapy may well begin with the therapist and the client collaborating to reconstruct scenarios in which the client felt exploited. An example may include a boss asking the client to work late, although the client had made other plans. The therapist may play the boss and, after seeing how the client behaves, may model a more assertive and useful response. The client then practices the new response on the therapist. The general procedure can be used in teaching social skills for a variety of situations, from coaching shy students how to ask for dates to training overaggressive individuals in how to deal with police who stop them for speeding (Argyle, Furnham, & Graham, 1981). One of the most dramatic applications of modeling therapy and behavior modification generally is sex therapy, the focus of "Applying Psychology: Overcoming Sexual Disorders."

APPLYING PSYCHOLOGY

Overcoming Sexual Disorders

For most people, sexual behavior with a loved one can be a source of tremendous pleasure and joy. But some do not gain as much gratification as they should because of sexual dysfunctions. From a behavioral perspective, such dysfunctions result from faulty learning about sexuality: they endure because of fear of failure, worry about pleasing a partner, fear of rejection, or inability to express to a partner sexual likes and dislikes.

Successful ways of treating sexual dysfunction have grown rapidly over the last decade, due in large part to the pioneering work of William Masters and Virginia Johnson (1966, 1970). In the early Masters and Johnson procedure (1966), a couple with a problem stayed at a therapeutic residence for several days while they relearned sexual behavior. A controversial aspect was the provision of a co-therapy team, consisting of a male and female therapist, who sat in with the husband and wife to offer understanding, to undergo frank and

open questioning, and to share information.

One of the biggest problems attending sexual dysfunctions is anxiety, which often makes people want to avoid the whole question of sex. In therapy, therefore, the first goal is to remove this anxiety. Talking to a therapist about sex can in itself be difficult, but once talking starts, anxiety will begin to dissipate. Relaxation procedures and cotherapy modeling can greatly speed up the anxiety reduction. Masters and Johnson recommend several exercises that couples can engage in together. Under strict instructions not to attempt intercourse, couples lie together naked in bed and take turns giving each other relaxing massages. They neither demand nor expect that either partner will become aroused, which reduces any anxiety about performance.

Many people experience guilt about erotic thoughts and fantasies. This, too, can readily be overcome through gradual exercises. In treatment of women who are inorgasmic, for example, many procedures encourage self-stimulation. Women can learn to explore their own bodies visually and tactually, ultimately focusing on pleasure-producing sensations in the cli-

toral area. When a woman can achieve orgasm by self-stimulation, she learns to teach her partner to stimulate her by giving him verbal directions and physically guiding his hands. Both partners can be encouraged to use erotic fantasy during mutual masturbation, sometimes with the help of erotic books and films.

The problem of the male having an orgasm "too soon" is fairly common. A series of exercises can help. One is the squeeze technique, designed to help the male achieve voluntary control over the ejaculatory reflex. While his partner masturbates him, he is instructed to focus on the sensations. When the excitement mounts and he approaches orgasm, he tells his partner, who then firmly squeezes the erect penis just below the glans. The ejaculatory urge abates and the erection subsides. Moments later, the couple repeat the process. After several repetitions, the man is permitted to ejaculate. Masters and Johnson (1970) reported a 98 percent success rate with a sample of nearly 200 men after several days of such exercises. It appears that the new sex therapies have significantly improved the lives of many men and women (Masters, Johnson, & Kolodny, 1985).

COGNITIVE THERAPIES

One of the clearest trends in therapy today involves techniques that aim to alter not behavior directly but the client's subjective cognitions and perceptions of the world (Bandura, 1986; Mahoney, 1977; Meichenbaum, 1977). One of the first of the cognitive therapies was rational-emotive therapy.

Rational-Emotive Therapy

Rational-emotive therapy (RET) was pioneered by Albert Ellis (1962). Ellis believed that an aggressive, even belligerent, approach by the therapist was necessary to ensure that a client adequately confronted his or her own way

**TABLE 16–2
Common Irrational Beliefs**

1. One should be loved by everyone for everything one does.
2. It is horrible when things are not the way one would like them to be.
3. Human misery is produced by external causes, outside persons, or events rather than by one's view of these conditions.
4. If possible, it is better to avoid life's problems than to face them.
5. One needs something stronger or more powerful than oneself to rely on.
6. One should be thoroughly competent, intelligent, and achieving in all respects.
7. Because something once affected one's life, it will indefinitely affect it.
8. One must obtain and perfect self-control.
9. Happiness can be achieved by inertia and inaction.
10. One has virtually no control over one's emotions and cannot help having certain feelings.

Albert Ellis considers the core of most people's maladjustments to be irrational beliefs. Common irrational beliefs people hold, according to Ellis, are those above.

of thinking and gained a more rational perspective of the world. Ellis suggested that most people operate on a number of serious fallacies that lead them to engage in irrational behavior. Among the fallacies, Ellis listed the ideas that people's unhappiness is not their own responsibility because the causes lie outside of them, that they have to strive to be liked by everybody, that they have to be perfect in every way, and that they are responsible for other people (see Table 16–2).

To help people change their thinking, therapists practicing RET may verbally attack their client whenever the client expresses statements that seem to reflect these irrational beliefs. Rid of the beliefs, clients may learn to accept themselves more and reduce their neurotic self-blaming and hypercritical attitudes and practice new, more adaptive ways of behaving.

Suppose a young woman complains of being unable to say "no" to dates with men she does not find attractive. She reports that she is bored on these dates but does not want to hurt men's feelings or make them dislike her. A RET therapist would probably attack her for preserving other people's feelings at the expense of her own and then have her practice more useful thinking (for example, "I don't have to please everyone—I'll spend my time as I please") and start behaving accordingly.

Cognitive Behavior Modification

Practitioners of *cognitive behavior modification* often have two goals: (1) to learn what the client is thinking while engaging in undesired behavior and (2) to teach the client more appropriate thoughts. For example, as we discussed in Chapter 15, Aaron Beck's theory of depression is that depressives are always thinking about how worthless they are and dwelling on the pointlessness of carrying on with their lives. This view has led to a number of influential treatment programs (Beck et al., 1979; Sacco & Beck, 1985). The first goal may simply be to make depressives say "stop" to themselves whenever they become aware of these self-defeating thoughts. Thought-stopping techniques can reduce the unpleasantness people deliver to themselves. A second step is for the depressed people to learn to say good things to themselves about themselves or their lives. The "power of positive thinking" appears to have something going for it in the new ideas of cognitive therapy.

Donald Meichenbaum (1977) makes the power of positive thinking explicit in his treatment programs, in which clients are provided with self-instructional training. If you were to seek cognitive behavior modification therapy for anxiety, you would first be made aware of the way "talking to yourself" influences your level of arousal, that is, that you inadvertently increase your own distress by focusing on it. You might be asked to "listen for" and record some of your own private monologues and to evaluate their effect on your comfort. Next you might be taught some alternative coping dialogue, such as "Okay. It's almost time. I'm starting to feel 'different' but that's okay—I can make it work for me. It is my cue to cope. Just relax; I can handle this situation. Let me take a deep breath and go slowly. . . . Good! I'm doing fine; still nervous but I'm keeping it in bounds. Got to concentrate on what it is I have to do; don't think about fear. Hey, this isn't so bad—I'm doing a good job!"

The evidence is beginning to accumulate that strategies such as this, particularly when combined with modeling and reinforcement therapy, are going a long way toward alleviating anxiety and depression (Bandura, 1986).

HUMANISTIC THERAPIES

The humanistic approach to personality was described in Chapter 14. From this perspective the important data for psychology are people's conscious experiences and feelings, especially their self-concepts. A humanistic approach to abnormality focuses on how an individual thinks, feels, and experiences in the present. Several therapies have arisen within this perspective. Here we will consider person-centered therapy and Gestalt therapy.

Person-Centered Therapy

Client-centered therapy, or, as expressed more recently, ***person-centered therapy,*** stems from the work of Carl Rogers (e.g., 1970a, 1980). This approach has also been called "humanistic" because it emphasizes the potential for good in clients and "nondirective" because the therapist's role is to place the primary responsibility for solving a problem with the person who has the problem. (Hence the reference to "client" or "person" rather than "patient.")

The other essential features of Rogerian therapy include an emphasis on the immediacy (the "here and now") of the person's experience; the empathy of the therapist; and the use of unconditional positive regard, or acceptance, of the client regardless of what the client may say or do. The emphasis on here and now helps clients gain insight into their current thinking and feeling. Little conversation centers on childhood experiences or traumatic past events. The focus is on what the client currently feels, not what may be causing the feelings.

Empathy is considered vital in this therapy. If a therapist does not feel able to empathize adequately with a client, it is the therapist's moral obligation not to engage in therapy with that client. Empathy manifests itself in the therapist's reflecting back to the client the emotional quality of the things that the client says. One advantage of this procedure is that it ensures that the therapist fully attends to and understands the client and that the client can either correct any misperception of the therapist or gain insight into what the client actually feels as a result of hearing it restated in slightly different ways. An example of a client-therapist interaction is shown in Figure 16–5.

The final aspect of the Rogerian approach is unconditional positive regard, in which the therapist accepts as wholly valid and important the feelings that clients express about themselves and others. If a client reports that he thinks of hurting others, the therapist would not be judgmental.

In addition to gaining insight into current feelings, the central goal of Rogerian therapy is the improvement of the client's self-concept: to get the client to accept his or her *actual self* more and to stop striving for the unobtainable *ideal self* (see Chapter 14). The goal of therapy is reached when there is a greater congruence between these two self-concepts and the client is

FIGURE 16–5
A Rogerian therapist Interacting with a Client

In Rogerian therapy, the therapist attempts to understand the client's perception of the world through empathy and reflecting back to the client the emotional quality of the things the client says.

Client:	I'm not coming any more. It doesn't do any good. I don't like you. I hate you! I wish you never were born.
Therapist:	You must hate me very bitterly.
Client:	I think I'll throw you in the lake. I'll cut you up! You think people like you, but they don't. . . . You think you can attract women, but you *can't*. . . . I wish you were *dead*.
Therapist:	You *detest* me and you'd really like to get rid of me.
Client:	You think my father did bad things with me, but he didn't! You think he wasn't a good man, but he *was*. You think I want intercourse, but I *don't*.
Therapist:	You feel I *absolutely misrepresent* all your thoughts.
Client:	. . . You think you can get people to come in and tell you everything, and they'll think they're being helped, but they're *not!* You just like to make 'em suffer. You think you can hypnotize them, but you *can't!* You think you're good, but you ain't. I hate you, I hate you, I *hate* you!
Therapist:	You feel I really like to make 'em suffer, but that I *don't* help them.
	(Later in the hour)
Client:	I knew at the office I had to get rid of this somewhere. I felt I could come down and tell you. I knew you'd understand. I couldn't say I hated myself. That's true but I couldn't say it. So I just thought of all the ugly things I could say to you instead.
Therapist:	The things you felt about yourself you couldn't say, but you could say them about me.
Client:	I know we're getting to rock bottom. . . .

Source: Rogers, 1951.

perceived as further on the way toward self-actualization. The Rogerian approach has had an enormous impact on both the methods and the theory of psychological counseling. It tends to be the dominant method used in university counseling services and in many child guidance clinics. It is used primarily with those who have only mild disturbances, not more serious disorders.

Gestalt Therapy

Another humanistic approach, *Gestalt therapy* was pioneered by Fritz Perls (1893–1970). A psychoanalyst of German birth, Perls created his own procedures. He settled at Esalen, Big Sur, in California in 1963, and many people seeking an alternative therapy were attracted to work with him there. Gestalt therapy quickly became fashionable.

The use of the word *Gestalt* is unfortunate because it implies a connection with the Gestalt theory of perception discussed in Chapter 4. The only link is the emphasis on the concept of the "whole" or "totality." The goal of the therapy is to make people more aware of themselves so that they can move toward self-actualization (Perls, 1970). There is little theory in Gestalt therapy; rather, there are various "exercises." One of them is called the Empty Chair. In this exercise clients move back and forth between two chairs. In one chair, they are themselves. In the other, they assume the roles of other people, perhaps parents or spouses. Clients gain insight and self-awareness by being able to "observe" how they interact with these others. Another exercise consists of speaking only in the present tense to emphasize the here-and-now aspects of awareness. In the Game of Dialogues, patients personify different facets of their personalities, such as their dominant and submissive sides or their nice or nasty sides.

One way of becoming more aware is to remove blocks to emotional expression. Marriage partners, for example, confront one another and tell how they feel by completing such sentences as "What annoys me most about you is. . . ." Unfortunately, few studies have evaluated the effectiveness of this therapy.

GROUP AND COMMUNITY THERAPY

All the therapeutic techniques discussed so far have involved a one-on-one relationship between the client and therapist. In recent years the practice of treating people in groups has increased enormously. Group therapy has advantages over individual therapy. First, there are obvious economies of cost, effort, and time. Second, patients may learn quickly and effectively whether their fellow group members share their perceptions of themselves and others. Finally, since human beings almost invariably live in groups, many psychologists believe that abnormal and deviant behavior should be treated at that level. Here we discuss three types of therapy conducted in a social setting: group, family, and community.

Group Therapy

In the most usual form of *group therapy,* several unrelated individuals with similar problems (for example, alcoholics) meet with a therapist once a week in groups of from 6 to 12 (Sadock, 1980). Typically they discuss the nature of their problems and how they are coping with them. By doing so, they reveal to themselves and to their therapist distorted or erroneous ways in which they perceive and deal with everyday challenges. The group can also provide emotional support for an individual undergoing a major readjustment, such as withdrawal from alcohol.

There are as many forms of group therapy as of individual therapy. A psychoanalytically oriented group might stress the "group as family" and the release of pent-up emotions. One popular form of psychoanalytically inspired group therapy is *transactional analysis.* Based on a 1964 book by Eric Berne entitled *Games People Play,* transactional analysis suggests that most human interactions involve social "games." In these exchanges an individual behaves either as a fun-loving but somewhat irresponsible *child,* which is something like the Freudian id; as the rather stern and forbidding *parent,* corresponding to the superego; or as a reasonable and sensible *adult,* corresponding to the ego. In transactional analysis, the therapist helps the group members become more aware of the three parts of their personalities and to recognize when they behave as the child, the adult, or the parent.

A behavioral group might focus on the modeling and practice of social skills. Group assertiveness training currently constitutes one popular form of group behavior therapy. The group judgment of what is or is not appropriately assertive may be better than that of a single therapist in a one-to-

Much psychotherapy today goes on in groups. In the photo, marriage counseling is taking place. In many cases of family therapy, both marital partners see the same therapist.

CONTROVERSY

Does Psychotherapy Work?

During the past 20 years there has been an enormous growth in the number and variety of therapies available to people. Many of these programs are as concerned with promoting personal growth as with helping people overcome debilitating problems. Indeed, some orientations are as much cults and secular religions as they are therapies since they aim to engender happiness, give meaning to life, and enhance peace of mind.

In recent years behavioral psychologists have leveled strong criticisms against the "unscientific" nature of many of these therapies and ideas-systems. In 1952, Hans Eysenck published a now-famous article contending that patients treated by psychotherapy were no better off than those who had not undergone therapy. Eysenck argued that over a two-year period some 66 percent of neurotic problems cleared up spontaneously even if patients received no therapy, a rate not surpassed by psychotherapy. Indeed, some types of psychotherapy, and in particular psychoanalysis, appeared to retard patients' progress. Needless to say, Eysenck's review and his conclusion were highly controversial and stirred up considerable interest in research on the outcome of therapy.

After another decade and a half of research, Albert Bandura (1969) concluded that Eysenck's estimates were generally accurate except that they may have overestimated the effectiveness of psychoanalytic programs. If measurements are based on specific changes in behavior instead of on therapist ratings, the data, said Bandura, yield success rates substantially below 66 percent, the rate Eysenck claimed was possible with no therapy at all.

Bandura based his conclusions on what have since become classic studies of the relative effectiveness of different therapies for anxiety. Perhaps the most famous was carried out by Gordon L. Paul (1966). Paul's "patients" were 96 undergraduates who suffered from severe anxiety when they had to talk in front of others. All accepted an offer of six weeks of free treatment and were randomly assigned to one of four therapy groups: *insight therapy,* in which insight-oriented psychotherapists worked individually with subjects; *behavior therapy desensitization,* in which patients were led systematically through a behavior modification program; an *attention-placebo* control group, in which subjects were supposedly given a tranquilizer; and a *no-treatment* control group.

After treatment, the subjects were required to talk in public. They were rated by (1) the amount of anxiety they themselves reported; (2) the signs of anxiety (e.g., trembling hands and quivering voice) observed by others; and (3) their sweating and pulse rates. The two groups that received psychotherapy treatment improved significantly over the no-treatment control. But the placebo control group also improved, although its members had been given only bicarbonate of soda. Paul's results demonstrate a **placebo effect** in psychotherapy. People get better because they believe they will and because someone pays special attention to them. Of particular interest in the results, however, was the finding that desensitization therapy produced considerably more improvement than the placebo treatment, but insight treatment did not. These effects were still present on a follow-up two years later in which all the subjects were again questioned about their speech anxiety. Relative to the statements they had made two years earlier, improvement was shown by 85 percent of the desensitization subjects and by 50 percent of both the insight and placebo subjects (Paul, 1967) (see Table 16–3).

The behaviorists' arguments and data have not been accepted by everyone, however. In 1978 the *Handbook of Psychotherapy and Behavior Change* reviewed all of the treatment procedures and outcome studies to date. Allen Bergin, one of the editors, and Michael Lambert criticized much of the data used by Eysenck in his early critique of psychotherapy. Bergin's and Lambert's (1978) analysis of the data suggested that the "spontaneous recovery" rate was 43 percent, not 66 percent, and that psychotherapy, including psychoanalysis, was, therefore, effective. They conceded, however, that some psychotherapies made people worse than if they had not undergone treatment. Eysenck remains unrepentant, and a subsequent review purports to provide additional evidence for his position (Rachman & Wilson, 1980).

In 1980, the publication of *The Benefits of Psychotherapy* by Mary Lee Smith, Gene Glass, and Thomas Miller rekindled the question of whether psychotherapy is better than no therapy at all. The authors examined more than 500 studies comparing

TABLE 16–3
Improvement Percentages for Public Speaking After Different Treatments

	Self-Report Anxiety (%)	Behavior Ratings (%)	Physiological Arousal (%)
Behavioral desensitization	100	100	87
Insight therapy	53	60	53
No-treatment placebo	47	73	47
No-treatment control	7	24	28

Source: Adapted from Paul, 1966.

some form of psychological therapy with a control condition. Based on this extensive review of evidence, they reported that psychological therapy is significantly more effective than no therapy at all. Furthermore, Smith and her colleagues found no significant differences between the effectiveness of behavioral and nonbehavioral (e.g., psychoanalytic, humanistic) therapies, a surprising finding in view of their totally different approaches.

The Smith, Glass, and Miller study provoked a spirited counterattack from behaviorists, who criticized both its methods and its conclusions (Bandura, 1986; Eysenck, 1985; Prioleau, Murdock, & Brody, 1983). In terms of method, many of the 500 studies Smith and her colleagues included in their review did not include a placebo control group and relied instead on a "no-treatment" control condition. Although some psychologists contend that placebos are themselves a form of treatment (Butler et al., 1984), the lack of placebo control is normally regarded as unacceptable practice. When the data from Smith, Glass, and Miller were reanalyzed, excluding the studies involving "no-treatment" controls, the overall rating for the effectiveness of psychotherapy versus no therapy diminished significantly (Eysenck, 1985; Prioleau, Murdock, & Brody, 1983), falling more in line with the original estimates provided by Eysenck (1952) and Bandura (1969).

Behaviorists have also criticized the conclusion that behavioral and nonbehavioral therapies differ little in their effectiveness. They point to evidence showing marked differences even between different behavioral therapies. Modeling procedures, for example, are demonstrably better than desensitization programs for removing dog and snake phobias (Rosenthal and Bandura, 1978). If this is the case, they ask, then how is it that Smith and her colleagues could find therapies, behavioral and nonbehavioral, equally effective?

One big problem in resolving this controversy is that different therapeutic approaches demand different criteria for a "cure." Behaviorists require an actual change in behavior, as when phobics pick up snakes. Psychoanalysts, however, are not quite so interested in altering overt behavior as they are in releasing pent-up feelings deep in the unconscious (which some behaviorists deny even exist). Humanistic therapists, on the other hand, stress how the client feels about a problem. If the client can learn to live with and not be unhappy about a snake phobia, then this "cure" may suffice to a humanistic therapist. Given such widely differing goals of psychotherapy, it is not surprising that practitioners disagree on how effective their respective therapies are. For example, has psychotherapy been effective for an individual who reports being considerably happier despite no improvement in social adjustment? If therapists accept as their data a client's subjective reports about feeling better, then it does appear as though most treatments work. If, however, the more stringent criterion of actual behavior change is required before the therapy can be viewed as successful, then behavioral therapies do seem more effective than humanistic or psychoanalytic therapies, with cognitive approaches falling in between (Rachman & Wilson, 1980; Shapiro, 1985).

Certainly the last word has not been said on the subject. Many more refined studies will be needed to work out how to help people most economically, effectively, and compassionately. As we saw at the beginning of the last chapter, behavior disorders are a public health problem of the highest magnitude. Much work remains to be done on all fronts. In "Research Frontier: Comparing Psychotherapy and Drug Therapy" at the end of this chapter we discuss a major new effort to assess the contributions of psychotherapy.

one setting. The group can also give collective reinforcement for effective or assertive behavior by a member. Exercises such as exchanging compliments and making small talk would be more awkward in one-to-one therapy (Franks & Barbrack, 1983).

A humanistic group might emphasize the sharing of experiences and the development of group togetherness within the context of personal growth. Today's *encounter groups* were begun by Carl Rogers as part of the humanistic movement. Their purpose was not so much to serve as therapy as it was to increase awareness and sensitivity and help normal growth toward self-actualization (Rogers, 1970c). Rules governing encounter groups require absolute honesty, readiness to be open (and vulnerable), expression of feelings, including hostility, and willingness to touch and be touched. Marathon encounter groups are longer, more intense versions of regular encounter groups; they may go on virtually nonstop for a weekend or more.

Family Therapy

A form of psychotherapy that is receiving a good deal of recent attention is *family* and marital *therapy* (Jacobson & Bussod, 1983). Part of the reason for interest in marital and family therapy has been the finding that marital discord often accompanies childhood disorders. It is not always clear whether marital discord causes disruptive behavior in children or whether children's misbehavior causes marital discord, or some combination of the two. Nevertheless, an increasing number of psychotherapists now argue for the need to intervene in the family system rather than focus on the child alone.

Several types of family therapy exist. In most cases, both marital partners see the same therapist. The goal is often to make the couple aware of the interpersonal cycle in which they have become entrapped and to foster more adaptive ways of communicating. When psychotherapy is conducted at the family level, all members become involved and participate in the therapy sessions. Different combinations of individual, group, marital, and family therapy are often used depending on the circumstances and needs of the case (Jackson & Bussod, 1983).

Community Therapy

There are many different types of therapy aimed at helping people cope better at the community level. Some involve treatments within institutions themselves, such as the *token economy systems.* Others are at the level of the *community halfway house.* Still others are more preventive in nature and occur directly in the community.

TOKEN ECONOMIES. Behavior therapists have been at the forefront of the movement to restructure institutions so that they reinforce desired behaviors. From the behavioral perspective, all the staff and the other inmates act as constant sources of observational learning and as dispensers of reinforcement. If the goal of institutionalization is to change behavior rather than simply to provide custodial care or punishment, the staff must give close attention to the inmates' inadvertent learning experiences. The best-known behavioral approach to the residential therapeutic community is the *token economy* or its variation, *social milieu therapy.* Token economies and social milieu therapy contrast markedly with traditional institutional policies. Both programs treat inmates as responsible human beings, "residents." Often the physical setting is remodeled to provide home-style amenities, and staff and residents wear ordinary clothes. All participate in "town meetings" to decide on rules, activities, schedules, problems, and similar matters. Residents are expected to work, socialize, and follow rules. Many behavioral goals are targeted for improvement, including, for example, holding down a job, solving problems independently, caring for others, and so on. If a resident's behavior is at a very low level of competence, the target goals can be as simple as getting dressed, making the bed, or getting to meals on time.

Token economies are based on principles of positive reinforcement, and they provide external incentives—at least initially—to motivate the desired behavior. For completing tasks or goals, residents receive poker chips or coupons, which can be exchanged for goods or privileges. Later the tokens can be phased out, and praise and social pressure can be substituted as motivators. Residents who hold regular jobs can be paid. Progress reports are kept and the residents know explicitly what the rules of the game are so they can work harder to progress. When various criteria have been met successfully, the residents can be released into the outside community.

COMMUNITY HALFWAY HOUSES. Often located in a city, a *community halfway house* serves as a treatment facility and a residence for those who have just been released from a mental hospital or prison or for those who fear they may need hospitalization. Halfway houses tend to be run by small, nonprofessional staffs who consult mental health experts regularly. In the typical halfway house, about ten residents live in a family-style atmosphere. Residents participate in the daily life of the larger community, going to jobs or school and finding recreation away from the house. The residents contribute a small fee for room and board and are expected to keep their rooms clean and to complete chores. Some residents have improved to an extent where they move on to manage their own halfway houses.

Within the past decade, more former patients from mental hospitals have been placed in some form of so-called care in the community. The goal of this effort was to free patients from institutionalization. In practice, many mental patients have landed in rather unhelpful board-and-care facilities run for private profit while the patients are on welfare (Jones, 1975). In many cases, patients drift into skid-row rooming houses and single-room occupancy hotels and often become street derelicts. These are not the halfway houses involving community support and professional care that were intended when the patients were released. Some researchers have suggested that the government has washed its hands of responsibility for some of its most dependent citizens (Jones, 1975). (See Figure 16–6.)

COMMUNITY MENTAL HEALTH CENTERS. During the 1960s community mental health centers were established with federal aid. They were located in the hearts of communities, often in storefronts, and were supposed to supply a variety of psychological services. Three kinds of services are offered.

Primary services (often referred to as primary prevention) are directed toward eliminating the causes of patients' problems. Efforts to eradicate poverty and disease, racial discrimination and injustice, and loneliness and

A modern mental hospital provides a humane physical and psychological environment. The homestyle amenities can themselves be considered therapeutic in leading patients to interact in socially adaptive ways which are useful in the outside world.

FIGURE 16–6
Halfway Houses

While some patients do very well in halfway houses (left), others end up as street derelicts (right).

Many altruistic community volunteers, such as the telephone hotline workers shown, devote long hours to staffing crisis centers and other community mental health projects. These secondary services have expanded the range of facilities available to people in need.

social isolation are examples of primary prevention. The theory is that by identifying potential social stressors and eliminating them or educating people to handle them, future behavior problems can be prevented. Although there may be great potential for primary prevention in the future, to date it has not been applied in a major way.

Secondary services (also called secondary prevention) focus on providing immediate treatment of existing psychological problems in a wider range of situations than traditional treatment programs. Crisis intervention is an example of a secondary service; it is based on the assumption that people can best be helped when there is an emergency in their lives. Such help may last over four or five sessions, after which the person can return to normal functioning. One example of crisis intervention is a suicide hot line that provides a phone number to connect potentially suicidal people with counselors at a suicide prevention center. Such centers are sometimes staffed 24 hours a day, often by paraprofessionals including undergraduate psychology majors who have had special training.

Tertiary services (also called tertiary prevention) are concerned with the aftereffects of emotional problems. This type of treatment is generally referred to as rehabilitation. People who have had severe emotional problems may have lost their jobs or families and need counseling to get back into the community. This may involve job training, counseling on how to get a job, and development of social skills.

BIOLOGICAL APPROACHES TO THERAPY

Biological or somatic therapies are based on a medical model of abnormal behavior. These therapies assume that mental illness has a biological cause and that by treating the body directly one can alleviate or even end the symptoms. Biological approaches can be used for all kinds of problems, from anxiety to depression, as we discuss in the section on chemotherapy. Historically, however, and still often in the public mind, biological interventions are viewed as quite drastic, to be used only with severely psychotic patients.

Psychosurgery

The most drastic form of biological intervention involves surgery to destroy or remove brain tissue to change behavior. *Psychosurgery* is the most controversial of the medical approaches, in part because it is irreversible. Once nerve fibers have been cut, they cannot be repaired.

During the 1940s and 1950s, the most frequent psychosurgery was the *prefrontal lobotomy.* This operation destroys the fibers connecting the brain's frontal lobes with the emotional control centers in the thalamus. The operation was carried out primarily on severely disturbed psychotics who tended to be extremely emotional or violent or had hallucinations. The purpose was to reduce the turbulence raging within these patients. Early reports appeared to demonstrate that the operation was an amazing success, and the physician who originated the procedure in 1937, Egas Moniz of Portugal, was awarded the Nobel Prize in medicine. In the United States, it is estimated, some 50,000 patients underwent prefrontal lobotomies. But later studies found that a high proportion of lobotomized patients had been permanently disabled. Many of them showed little or no intellectual function. Today the procedure is extremely rare, used only after every possible alternative has been tried (Donnelly, 1980). Fortunately, the development of a variety of drugs is helping to make psychosurgery obsolete.

One organic brain disorder that produces severe distress in otherwise normal people is epilepsy. This electrical discharge in the brain, of unknown origin, causes a person to lose consciousness and the body to alternate between rigidity and jerking movements. Although various chemotherapies have been effective, psychosurgery is used in severe cases. Such surgery severs the *corpus callosum,* the bridge of fibers between the hemispheres of the brain, to prevent electrical overactivity in one hemisphere from transferring to the other. The surgery often decreases the severity of epileptic attacks. Patients who have undergone such split-brain surgery are often studied by psychologists interested in finding out how each hemisphere directs our thoughts and actions, a topic we discussed in Chapters 2 and 5.

Electroconvulsive Therapy

Popularly known as "shock therapy," *electroconvulsive therapy (ECT)* has become a controversial and unpopular therapy. ECT involves passing an alternating 110 to 115 volts of electricity across the patient's temples for a fraction of a second. The patient has been anesthetized and has been given a muscle relaxant. The shock produces a convulsion that lasts about a minute and amnesia that can persist for an hour or so following treatment. Typically 5 to 12 treatments over 10 to 30 days are required for the severely psychotically depressed.

Potential negative side effects exist, as with biological procedures of any kind. Before muscle relaxants were available, patients might suffer broken

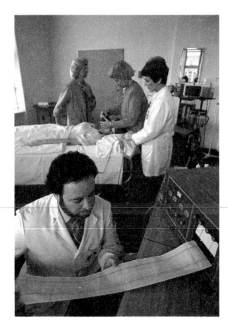

A patient undergoes electroconvulsive therapy (ECT). Note the number of hospital staff in attendance.

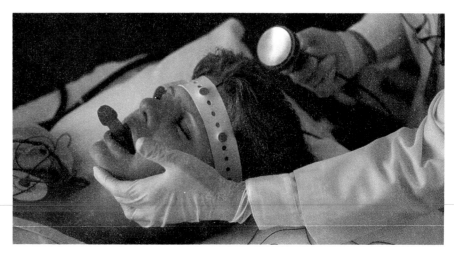

bones as a result of the convulsion. There are still bruising of the temples, disorientation following therapy, fear and social stigma, and the chance of memory impairment lasting several months (Weiner, 1984). These risks, however, have to be compared with those of not treating the patient—danger of suicide and other physical, social, and psychological problems—or of the risks involved in chemotherapy.

Holden (1985) recently described the deliberations of a panel assembled by the National Institute of Health to evaluate the treatment for cases of severe depression. The panel concluded that ECT is effective in treating severe depression that has not responded to drug therapy. Moreover, the panel noted that complications arise in only about 1 in 1,700 treatments, with the mortality risk not different from that associated with the use of anesthetics alone. Even the research on memory loss seemed to indicate that the widespread belief in the harmful effects of ECT are misplaced. One panelist found that memory problems completely clear up within seven months following treatment. Despite the research findings, however, the panel observed a persistent and fierce opposition to ECT among both the general public and many professionals. They cited a 1978 survey by the American Psychiatric Association, for example, finding one-third of psychiatrists "generally opposed" to ECT. In 1982, the city of Berkeley, California, took the unusual step of outlawing the use of ECT within its community.

Although there is increasing evidence for the effectiveness of ECT as a mode of treatment, there is little certainty on how it works. Given that ECT produces massive changes in the endocrine glands, neural transmission systems, and biochemical balance of the brain, it is difficult to research which of the changes has the beneficial effect. Much of the current interest is focused on the potential similarity of action between ECT and antidepressant drugs.

Chemotherapy

During the 1950s a variety of new drugs transformed treatment procedures in mental hospitals. *Chemotherapy,* or drug treatment, markedly decreased psychosurgery and use of ECT. It also led to unlocking of wards and abandoning of straightjackets, padded cells, and other forms of physical restraint and reduced the number of mental patients confined in hospitals. Some expect mental hospitals to be phased out altogether eventually, partly as a result of the ability of drugs to control behavior. We will look briefly at two sets of drugs commonly used for treatment.

ANTIANXIETY DRUGS. In treatment of the anxiety disorders, the most frequently used drugs are the minor tranquilizers such as Librium, Valium, Equanil, and Miltown. Although we have no firm figures on the number of people who use them, estimates reach the millions. Many estimate that Valium is one of the most widely prescribed drugs in the world (Caplan et al., 1983). *Antianxiety drugs* such as Valium work primarily by depressing the activity of the central nervous system. Controlled studies have indicated that they reduce anxiety and tension. Unfortunately, people often learn to depend on them instead of finding ways to cope with situations that cause distress.

ANTIPSYCHOTIC DRUGS. Antipsychotic drugs are the major tranquilizers, such as *chlorpromazine,* which belongs to the family of drugs called phenothiazines. These drugs tend to stabilize agitated and overactive patients and to eliminate hallucinations and paranoid symptoms among schizophrenics. They have done the most to improve the situation of the severely psychotic and to allow more and more psychotics to be treated in the community rather than in mental hospitals (Noll, Davis, & DeLeon-Jones, 1985). However, they can produce side effects ranging from drowsiness and fatigue to low blood pressure and ulcers.

Another major set of antipsychotic drugs consists of the *antidepressants* such as Tofranil and Elavil. They seem to be effective for about 50 to 70 percent of depressed patients (Noll, Davis, & DeLeon-Jones, 1985). Some antipsychotic drugs appear to have quite specific effects on one type of disorder and little or none on other disorders. In the affective disorder of depression with mania, for example, Lithium has had an estimated success rate of 70 to 80 percent within 14 days of treatment on the basis of 60 controlled studies (Noll, Davis, & DeLeon-Jones, 1985). As with any powerful drug, there are potentially harmful side effects. Excessive dosages can result in coma and convulsions. Less extreme effects often include diarrhea, vomiting, and tremor.

Evaluating ECT and Chemotherapy

Researchers have studied the effectiveness of various biological therapies for many years. A good study normally must meet each of the following criteria: the use of a placebo control group, random assignment of patients to treatment groups, and double-blind research design.

If we are to investigate whether ECT or a particular drug alters behavior, patients in the *placebo control group* must experience all of the aspects of the treatment except the essential one. Thus, control group patients for ECT must believe they are undergoing ECT. They must be given the same diet, the same injections, the same waiting period, and the same posttreatment care as the actual ECT group. This sham ECT rules out the effects of suggestion. Similarly, in a drug treatment the control group must be given pills they believe will cause them to get better.

Random assignment is an experimental design in which each individual has an equal chance of being placed in any treatment condition. Unfortunately, in the real world of patients and doctors, it is not always practical or ethical to assign people randomly to a no treatment, placebo, or control. Thus, many of the published studies must be excluded from consideration if this criterion is to be met. It is a necessary criterion, however, for otherwise any differences later found between the treated and nontreated groups may be due entirely to the characteristics of the samples before they were treated and not to the treatment. For example, perhaps only the best (or the worst) patients were assigned to the experimental treatment.

Double-blind procedures require that both the person who receives the treatment and the person who assesses it do not know whether the treatment is actual therapy or a placebo. This is necessary to avoid the effects of subtle suggestions between patients and doctors.

A knowledge of appropriate procedures helps us to understand why most studies fall short on one or another criterion. Nonetheless, enough have met all the requirements so that some conclusions can be drawn for both ECT and chemotherapy.

We have already discussed the literature on ECT (Holden, 1985; Weiner, 1984). Many studies compared ECT with a variety of placebo alternatives including psychotherapy, chemotherapy, and simulated ECT, in which the patient undergoes all aspects of the ECT procedure except that no elec-

RESEARCH FRONTIER

Comparing Psychotherapy and Drug Therapy

As a result of scientific debate (see "Controversy: Does Psychotherapy Work?" earlier in the chapter), the National Institute of Mental Health (NIMH) is carrying out a broad study comparing the results of various therapeutic methods (Elkin et al., 1985). Two hundred and forty patients suffering a major depressive disorder were randomly assigned to one of four treatment programs: cognitive therapy, interpersonal therapy, (a program based on psychoanalytic and humanistic techniques), antidepressant drug therapy, or a placebo, no treatment control group. Treatments lasted 16

weeks, with a total of 16 to 20 sessions.

The preliminary results of the study offer significant evidence in the controversy over the relative effectiveness of individual therapies. Irene Elkin (1986), coordinator of the project, reported that all three therapies eliminated serious symptoms in 50 to 60 percent of the patients treated for the 16 weeks, while fewer than 30 percent of those given the placebo reached full recovery. One important goal of the study was to compare the effectiveness of psychotherapies with that of drug therapies. Elkin said there was no evidence so far in the study that the standard drug therapy for depression was more effective than the two forms of psychotherapy. Although the drug treatment started to work somewhat more rapidly than the other treatments, by the end of 16 weeks the

two psychotherapies had caught up and were as effective. She cautioned that important questions remained unanswered, including whether the patients would continue to do well long after treatment was completed. Additional evaluations are to be conducted over an 18-month period to determine if there is any relapse or recurrence.

The NIMH study may shed light on another long-standing controversy involving psychotherapy. The therapists were taped as they treated their patients, and this record may provide evidence that those using the different approaches do treat patients in distinctly different ways. Psychologists who do not know what approach each therapist followed will hear tapes of the therapy sessions and will try to distinguish the cognitive behavioral from the interpersonal therapists.

trical current is passed through the brain and therefore no seizure is induced. The benefits of ECT are directly related to clinical diagnosis. For psychotic-depressive syndromes and in mania, success rates of 60 to 90 percent are reported (Scovern & Kilmann, 1980) with suicide being found less frequent in ECT-treated patients than among those treated by psychotherapy alone. Patients other than depressives, however, appear to be poorer candidates for ECT (Scovern & Kilmann, 1980).

Morris and Beck (1974) reviewed the efficacy of antidepressant drugs. They examined 146 well-controlled double-blind studies carried out between 1958 and 1972 and found the drugs tested to be significantly more effective than placebos in 60 percent of the studies. Not one study reported a placebo to be more effective than the antidepressant. More recent studies, including those on the new generation of antidepressants, confirm these conclusions (Noll, Davis, & DeLeon-Jones, 1985).

Overall it appears that more well-controlled outcome studies are being carried out on the biological therapies than on the psychotherapies. It seems also that many of these biological interventions are a great boon to distressed people. It should be noted, however, that most biological procedures are supplemented by some form of psychotherapy.

SUMMARY

1. Through the centuries, society has attempted to deal with abnormal behavior in many ways. Several treatment approaches have come into being over the last few decades, and extensive training has been provided to the professionals who treat disordered behavior. These professionals are classified principally according to their educational backgrounds. Psychiatrists are physicians who have spent a postgraduate residency training in psychiatry. Clinical psychologists hold Ph.D.'s in psychology, and they have had extensive training in research and therapeutic techniques. Counseling psychologists have graduate training similar to that of clinical psychologists, but typically with less emphasis on research. Psychiatric social workers hold master's degrees in social work and have special training in treatment procedures that emphasize the home and community. Psychiatric nurses are registered nurses with special training.

2. Classical psychoanalysis focuses on unconscious conflict as the source of disturbing symptoms. The goal of therapy is to help the client uncover these conflicts so that they may come under conscious and rational awareness. In this method, the primary techniques are free association and the interpretation of the client's resistance to recognizing influences. One important form of resistance is the transference to the therapist of the client's

unconscious feelings about parents. An understanding of resistance and transference enables the therapist to help the client work through the conflict. Working through involves bringing to consciousness previously repressed wishes and memories. These may trigger catharsis, a major emotional release in which the client gains sudden insight into the dynamics of his or her personality.

3. There are several variations on classical psychoanalysis. Modern methods attempt to condense the whole process into a few months or a year and highlight current rather than historical conflicts in the client's life. All psychoanalytic models, though, involve helping the client achieve insight and/or abreaction, the release of repressed tensions.

4. Behavior therapies are generally based on principles of learning and conditioning. The approach based on classical conditioning is known generally as counterconditioning. It involves systematic desensitization, in which the goal is to reduce anxiety, and aversion therapy, in which undesired behavior patterns are coupled with unpleasant stimuli. Operant approaches stress the modifiability of abnormal behavior through the use of contingent reinforcement. One interesting aspect of the operant approach is biofeedback. Finally, modeling therapy, based on observational learning, has been used effectively both

to eliminate unwanted behaviors and to build new behavioral competencies.

5. Recently principles of behavior therapy have been applied to cognition, where it is known as cognitive behavior modification, and the goal is to modify thought patterns. Much of this therapy takes place with depressives, where an attempt is made to help them stop thinking continuously about how worthless they are by substituting more positive thinking. Cognitive approaches to therapy are fast becoming the most widely used. One early cognitive approach is Ellis's rational-emotive therapy (RET), in which the therapist verbally confronts the client to make him or her accept reality.

6. Humanistic approaches focus on people's phenomenology: their currently conscious experiences and feelings and especially their self-concepts. In Carl Rogers's person-centered therapy, the important elements are a nondirective stance, emphasis on the here and now of the person's experience, the empathy of the therapist, and the unconditional positive regard, or acceptance, of the client. In Gestalt therapy, developed by Fritz Perls, part-playing techniques and exercises are employed to make the client more self-aware.

7. A recent trend is the provision of therapy at the level of the group, family, or community. In group therapy, several unrelated individuals with similar problems meet with a therapist once a week in groups of from 6 to 12 people. In family therapy, couples or parents and children meet with a therapist jointly. The role of the community in treating and preventing mental illness has grown enormously in the past 20 years. Community resources that offer help include residental therapeutic communities, token economy systems, halfway houses, and various forms of crisis intervention and prevention programs.

8. There is considerable controversy over whether psychotherapy works and whether some therapies are more effective than others. Hans Eysenck argues that two-thirds of neurotic problems clear up spontaneously over a two-year period and that most psychotherapies do no better than this rate. Others argue that the spontaneous recovery figure is 43 percent and that compared to this figure most therapies are effective. Evaluation of the effectiveness of the different psychotherapies is hampered by numerous research problems, including the fact that each therapeutic approach demands different criteria for a cure.

9. Biological treatments for mental disorders are based on the assumption that the condition is due in part to physical causes. Psychosurgery calmed patients, but because it seemed to rob them of all other emotions it is no longer used. ECT appears to be a very useful treatment for severe depression, although it has been replaced to some extent by drug therapy. A variety of antianxiety and antipsychotic drugs are widely used and have been helpful in alleviating anxiety, depression, and schizophrenia.

SUGGESTED READINGS

Beck, A. T., Rush, A. J., Shaw, B. F., & Emery, G. (1979). *Cognitive therapy of depression*. New York: Guilford Press.
 A thorough presentation of the analysis and treatment of depression, focusing on Beck's cognitive theory of depression.

Endler, N. S. (1982). *Holiday of darkness: A psychologist's personal journey out of his depression*. New York: Wiley.
 A readable account of a well-known psychologist's personal battle with depression. He discusses from firsthand experience the effects of various treatments.

Garfield, S. L., & Bergin, A. E. (Eds.) (1978). *Handbook of psychotherapy and behavior change* (2nd ed.). New York: Wiley.
 This large book has twenty-three different chapters by renowned practitioners and researchers in the treatment of abnormality. Every major orientation is represented, and the flavor is decidedly empirical and scholarly.

Goldstein, M. J., Baker, B. L., & Jamison, K. R. (1986). *Abnormal psychology: Experiences, origins, and interventions* (2nd ed.). Boston: Little, Brown.
 A first-class introduction to all types of therapy for all types of abnormality and deviance.

Rogers, C. R. (1970). *Client-centered therapy* (2nd ed.). Boston: Houghton Mifflin.
 An extremely readable and enjoyable "classic" in the humanistic tradition, written by the master of the therapy.

Spiegler, M. D. (1983). *Contemporary behavioral therapy*. Palo Alto, Calif.: Mayfield Publishing.
 An up-to-date, well written overview of the behavioral therapies, including numerous case studies and exercises.

Painting opposite: (Detail) "Subway" by Mimi Gross & Red Grooms from Mimi Gross and Red Grooms, *Ruckus Manhattan*, 1976. Courtesy of Marlborough Gallery.

PART SEVEN

Social Behavior

17

Social Psychology

Those of us who keep our eyes open can read
volumes into what we see going on around us.

E. T. Hall

IN PLANNING AND CONDUCTING THE CAMPAIGN THAT RESULTED IN HIS landslide reelection victory in 1984, Ronald Reagan and his advisers faced several tasks.

- [] They had to create or maintain public perceptions of the candidate as strong, capable, confident, and "presidential."
- [] They had to persuade voters through Reagan's speeches and advertisements that his positions on the issues were correct and that his opponent's were wrong.
- [] They had to motivate hundreds of thousands of volunteers to perform the work of the campaign, ringing doorbells and sending out campaign materials.
- [] The top-level campaign staff had to meet to make daily decisions, such as allocating campaign funds, planning Reagan's campaign trips, and countering his opponent's strategies.
- [] President Reagan himself had to exercise leadership, setting overall direction for both the nation and the campaign and encouraging and motivating his subordinates to perform well.

The tasks confronting Reagan's campaign managers illustrate some major concerns of social psychology, the topic of this chapter. Social psychologists study how people form impressions of others, including how people perceive basic character traits from another person's behavior and from their own self-presentations. They investigate persuasion and attitude change, including the effectiveness of advertising. They study the social influence of groups, including the pressures group members feel to conform to the group's standards and the processes that underlie group problem solving and decision making. All of these topics form part of our discussion in this chapter. Before moving to them, however, we begin with a brief overview of the field of social psychology.

THE SOCIAL PSYCHOLOGICAL APPROACH

Social psychology is the systematic study of how social influences affect individual behavior. Most human behavior, after all, is carried out in a social context. Consider how much time you have spent today in the company of other people. Even time spent alone may well involve social influences: for example, you may spend time studying or exercising because you wish to create a good impression on your professors or acquaintances. Thus, behavior can be affected by the implied, rather than actual, presence of others. Social influences on human thought and behavior, the subject matter of social psychology, are pervasive.

Ronald Reagan's 1984 campaign for reelection illustrates many issues that have been studied by social psychologists.

Other fields of psychology, such as personality or developmental psychology, typically look for the causes of a person's behavior within that person—in personality traits or learning histories that make the person different from others. For example, an explanation of why Fred voted for Reagan in the election might be sought in his particular personality structure or in the types of parental treatment he experienced in childhood. Social psychologists instead tend to emphasize the social situation and to look for factors in the situation that influence individual behavior regardless of the type of person involved. For example, they might investigate the particular ways in which Fred perceived and interpreted Reagan's actions, what advertisements he was exposed to, or whether he might have adopted his friends' or parents' political preferences.

The effects of social situations begin with the individual's perceptions of other people. Using research on cognitive processes, social psychologists investigate how people form impressions of others. An important aspect of perceiving other people is assigning causes to their behavior. For example, if someone pays you an extremely flattering compliment, do you decide that the person is sincere or that they are "buttering you up" because they are planning to ask you for a favor? Beginning at the level of initial impressions, social psychologists study the development of relationships—from feelings of attraction among strangers to romantic love and long-term, close relationships. Other types of social influence on individuals include the formation of attitudes as people are persuaded by information coming from others. Finally, the influence of groups is a major topic, for the groups in which people participate can shape individual behavior. Since much work in businesses and other large organizations is accomplished by groups, the effects on the individual of membership in a group have important implications. The goal of this chapter and the next is thus to provide an understanding of some of the main topics studied by social psychologists.

SOCIAL COGNITION

Social cognition is a major branch of social psychology concerned with how the individual comes to know other people. Researchers study how we perceive other people, how we remember their actions, and how we attribute—assign causes to—their behavior.

Of course, many of the principles of perception, memory, and thinking discussed in earlier chapters apply to the perception and memory of information about other people as well. However, people, unlike objects, have beliefs, wishes, desires, and personality traits. Also, our perception of other people can affect their behavior, as when Mary decides that John is really unfriendly and John then tries to act more warmly toward her. For these reasons, social perception involves more complex processes than does perception of nonsocial objects (Ostrom, 1984). We begin our survey of social cognition with the study of *person perception.*

Person Perception

People form impressions of others on the basis of many cues (Ross & Fletcher, 1985). Sometimes we may know something about an individual's

What characteristics would you guess these people have? Research shows that attractive people are assumed to be stronger, kinder, and more sociable than less attractive people. If you had to guess, which of these two belongs to a fraternity? Which is a computer science major?

past behaviors, personality, or other characteristics. On other occasions we may have to rely on cues—such as skin color, sex, age, attractiveness, dress—that are evident at first sight. Such cues may elicit the perceiver's stereotypes (Ashmore & Del Boca, 1981). A *stereotype* is a belief that people in a certain group are likely to possess certain characteristics. You may think that stereotypes apply only to certain specific minority groups, such as blacks, Chicanos, or Poles. But stereotypes can apply to any identifiable group of people: football players, college professors, and sorority members all call forth a set of characteristics that would constitute a stereotype of the group. Stereotypes can be accurate, as when we believe that football players are likely to be larger than other people, but they can also be erroneous. To use the concepts of Chapters 7 and 8, we can say that stereotypes function as schemas for social groups.

Stereotypes can operate at various levels of specificity. For example, people typically believe that men are more competent and independent than women, while women are warmer and more expressive (Spence & Helmreich, 1978). However, recent research shows that more specific stereotypes for women exist, too (Rothbart & John, 1985). A person may not have a strong stereotype of women in general, but may have a stereotype of various subtypes of women, such as the businesswoman, the grandmother, or the flirt. The characteristics of these subtypes certainly differ, and a businesswoman, for instance, can be perceived as assertive and independent, even though these traits may not be part of the general stereotype of women. The work discussed in "Research Frontier: When Do Stereotypes Break Down?" (page 606) shows that stereotypes often depend on the mix of information we have about other people.

What triggers a stereotype? Research shows that people often infer a great deal from an individual's physical features. Attractive people are generally judged to be more modest, more sociable, kinder, stronger, and more sexually responsive than unattractive people (Dion, Berscheid, & Walster, 1972). Even people's first names can cue positive or negative stereotypes; Harari and McDavid (1973) found that teachers evaluated essays written by 10-year-olds more positively when the children were named David or Lisa than when the names Hubert and Bertha were used.

Stereotypes often accurately reflect group characteristics, as when we think of football players as large. However, we can form erroneous stereotypes, too, especially when we observe a very limited sample of a group's behavior and overgeneralize the traits observed to the whole group. Even when stereotypes do not reflect reality very well, they can be quite resistant to change. A stereotype may lead the perceiver to make inferences that in turn support the stereotype. For example, if I know that Sam and Nancy worked together on a highly successful project, I may infer (based on my stereotype of male competence) that Sam was primarily responsible for the work. Over time, the memory of this episode may help perpetuate the stereotype, even if it is completely false. In addition, perceivers may treat counterstereotypic behaviors as exceptions, thereby maintaining the original stereotype. A person who believes that women are not assertive, if reminded of Margaret Thatcher, may decide that female politicians are atypical and thus irrelevant to beliefs about women. As previously discussed, the person may form a more specific stereotype for female politicians. Stereotypes also resist change because someone with a negative stereotype about a particular group may simply avoid encounters with members of that group, eliminating the possibility of learning new information that might prove the stereotype wrong.

Finally, a stereotype may persist because it acts as a self-fulfilling prophecy: treating a stereotyped individual in accordance with a stereotype may cause him or her to act that way in reality. Imagine, for example, how it might affect you if people treated you as basically hostile and unfriendly. Might you not begin to act that way? Mark Snyder, Elizabeth Tanke, and Ellen Berscheid (1977) found that a male subject's belief that a female was physically attractive caused the female to behave in more likable ways in a brief telephone interaction. The male was shown a photograph of a very attractive or unattractive woman and was told that he was about to interact with this person on the telephone. The female on the other end of the phone was actually just another subject, but her side of the conversation was later rated by judges as being more friendly and likable if she was interacting with a male who thought she was beautiful. Stereotypes can actually affect the course of social interaction. We turn next to consider how people form impressions of others on the basis of descriptions and other information.

FORMING IMPRESSIONS. Researchers have examined how people form impressions about others on the basis of brief descriptions. If you are going on a blind date, the friend arranging it will likely describe your prospective partner and you will gain an impression in advance ("Well, he is not the greatest-looking person, but he is really warm and fun and has a great personality"). In a pioneering study on impression formation, Solomon Asch (1946) provided descriptions of a hypothetical person to students. For one group the person was described as "intelligent, skillful, industrious, warm, determined, practical, and cautious." For another group, "warm" was replaced by "cold." Asch asked the students to write a paragraph about what they thought the person was like and to rate the person on a number of dimensions.

Asch discovered that the single change of terms from "warm" to "cold" greatly affected the impressions that the students formed. In Figure 17–1, you can see how the students rated various characteristics of the hypothetical person. If the person was described as "warm," he was judged more likely to be generous, wise, happy, and good-natured than when he was labeled "cold."

In a follow-up to Asch's study, Harold Kelley (1950) tested the warm-cold variable in the formation of impressions of a real person. A psychology instructor described a guest lecturer in advance to students, using several adjectives in the course of the description. Most were identical for the entire class, but a randomly selected half of the students were told the speaker was warm, and the other half were told he was cold. After the guest lecturer spoke, students were asked for their impressions of him. Those who had been told that he was cold rated the speaker as more self-centered, formal, irritable, humorless, and unpopular than did those given the term "warm." Asch's and Kelley's studies show that a relatively small change in a description can greatly alter impressions of a person, at least on dimensions to which the change is relevant (Wishner, 1960).

FIGURE 17–1
Asch's Impression-Formation Experiment

Students participating in this experiment read the description of a person and were then asked to select traits that would best characterize the individual. The description was either "intelligent, skillful, industrious, *cold,* determined, practical, cautious"; or "intelligent, skillful, industrious, *warm,* determined, practical, cautious." As shown here, the simple variation between the adjectives *warm* and *cold* produced large differences in judgments of the traits of generosity, wisdom, happiness, and good-naturedness. The traits of reliability and importance were not affected very much by the warm-cold dimension.

Source: Asch, 1946.

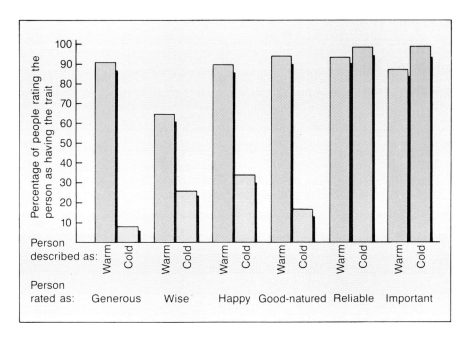

COMBINING INFORMATION. You might receive descriptions of a prospective blind date or a new professor independently from several different friends. How might you combine these several items of information to come up with an overall impression? The order in which information is given shapes the impression. In general, the first information a person receives carries the most weight. The warm versus cold difference in judgments would likely be even greater if the two terms appeared at the beginning of the description rather than in the middle (Luchins, 1957). Thus, there is a *primacy effect* in impression formation, just as there usually is in remembering lists (as we discussed in Chapter 7). One natural assumption from these similar effects is that the first term used weighs most heavily in forming impressions because it is best remembered. That may be the case, but some evidence seems inconsistent with the idea (Anderson & Hubert, 1963; Dreben, Fiske, & Hastie, 1979).

One theory that has enjoyed a good deal of success in explaining the effects of the order of terms on the forming of impressions is the *change-of-meaning hypothesis* first suggested by Asch (1946). The premise of the theory is that the meaning of a term depends on its context. Meaning may vary depending on the term's place in a sequence, and the first term's meaning may color that of later terms. If the warm or cold term occurs early, it may change the meaning inferred from the later terms. Thus the effect of the warm-cold variable will be greater when the term appears early rather than late. When it appears late, the prior terms will have more influence on the impression given by the sequence of adjectives, and the effect of the warm-cold variable will be watered down. Yet even when the adjective occurs in the middle of the sequence, as in Asch's study, the effect can be strong.

A striking example of how prior information can affect social judgments is seen in an experiment conducted by Thomas Srull and Robert Wyer (1980). In the first part of their experiment people constructed simple sen-

RESEARCH FRONTIER

When Do Stereotypes Break Down?

When will stereotypes influence how we perceive other people? What factors can override stereotypic beliefs? Recent research shows that group stereotypes may have little effect on judgments if the perceiver has additional information about the individual that has clear implications for the judgment. That is, if we know only that someone is a truck driver, we will assume that the person is male and probably likes country music, relying on our stereotype for lack of any better information. But if we also know that the trucker loves Mozart, we may base our impression of the individual's musical taste on that clearly relevant information and ignore the group stereotype. However, if the perceiver has additional information that is unclear or mixed in its implications, the stereotype may still have an effect. If you think that fraternity members like to party, and you meet some fraternity members who do and some who do not, you may interpret this mixed information in a biased fashion and end up basing your judgments on the stereotype.

Anne Locksley and her colleagues (Locksley et al., 1980) tested the first idea, using the common stereotype that men are more assertive than women. Subjects in some conditions learned only that a character was named Paul or Susan and rated the likelihood of that person's behaving assertively. Not surprisingly, Paul was rated more likely to be assertive than Susan, reflecting general stereotypes about males and females. Other subjects received a description of a *single* episode in which Paul or Susan behaved relatively assertively. For example, Paul or Susan interrupted a student who was completely dominating a class discussion in order to make a point. Even this minimal additional information overrode the stereotype: subjects in this condition no longer judged Paul and Susan differently. Both were now seen as fairly likely to behave in assertive ways in the future. These results, then, support the idea that stereotypes are applied when there is little or no relevant information about a person but are ignored when relevant information is available. In other cases, individuals seem to use both their stereotype and the new information to arrive at their judgments, with the weight given to each probably depending on the situation (Rasinski, Crocker, & Hastie, 1985).

Another study examined the more complex situation where the additional information about a stereotyped indi-

tences from 50 sets of four words given in a random order (for example, leg break arm his). In one condition, 15 of the 50 sets of words referred to hostile actions, as in this example. In another condition, 35 of the 50 sets represented hostile actions. After constructing the sentences subjects were then asked to read a passage describing the behavior of a stranger. The passage was relatively neutral with regard to hostile behaviors. Then the subjects were asked to judge the stranger on many different traits, a few of which pertained to hostility. For example, subjects were asked to rate the stranger on how unfriendly, unlikable, and hostile he was. This rating task occurred either immediately after the subjects read the passage or one day or seven days later for different groups of subjects.

vidual is mixed and has unclear implications (Darley & Gross, 1983). In this experiment, subjects viewed a videotape of a fourth-grade girl. The first part of the tape gave background information about the child's home and neighborhood. For subjects in one condition, the videotape showed a modest house on a somewhat dilapidated street, a schoolyard surrounded by a chain-link fence, and other material intended to convey a lower- or working-class environment. Other subjects saw a magnificent house in a huge, parklike lawn, a beautiful suburban school with a completely equipped schoolyard, and so on: an upper-middle-class environment. Some subjects saw only this background information, which was intended to elicit stereotypes about the girl's academic ability. For other subjects, the tape went on to show the girl's performance on an achievement test. She sat across a table from an examiner and answered 25 problems, with mixed results that conveyed an unclear impression of her ability. She answered some difficult questions correctly but missed other questions, even some easy ones.

How will subjects rate the child's academic ability under these conditions? Results showed that those who

observed only the lower-class or upper-class background information did not differ much in their ratings; see Figure 17–2. Perhaps they were reluctant to rely on their stereotypes since they recognized that they did not have any performance information on which to base judgments. But subjects who saw the mixed results of the achievement test did rate the child in accordance with the stereotype evoked by the background information—despite the availability of much information (the achievement test responses) directly relevant to the ratings.

In summary, people who receive *consistent* information about an individual—even if it is minimal, such as a single behavior—may feel confident in ignoring their stereotype and basing their judgments on the other information. People who have *mixed* information about an individual will likely still base their judgments on their stereotypes because some other information agrees with them. We should point out that when additional information overcomes stereotypes, it probably does so only for the individual case that is observed. Overcoming general stereotypes that happen to be erroneous is doubtless much harder.

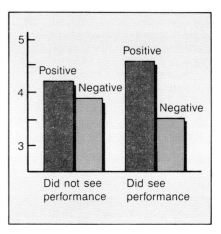

FIGURE 17–2
Effects of Stereotypes in Person Perception

Subjects saw background information intended to convey a positive or negative expectancy of a child, and then (in some conditions) saw mixed performance as the child took a test. Subjects rated the child's ability by estimating the child's grade in school. The graph shows ratings of the child's ability (in grade-level placements). Stereotypes had only a small effect when subjects did not view the performance. However, when subjects saw the child perform, stereotypes determined how much ability they thought the child had, as reflected in the school grade they assigned.

Source: Darley & Gross, 1983.

The results in Figure 17–3 show a *priming effect:* people who had read 35 sentences pertaining to hostile behaviors rated the stranger as more hostile than did those who had read only 15 statements referring to hostility. This happened even though subjects believed that the two parts of the experiment—reading the sentences and rating the person—were unrelated. The results show that the priming of a category can affect later social perception. If a person is prepared to see the behavior of a stranger as hostile, the stranger will indeed appear more hostile. Notice too from Figure 17–3 that the effect actually seems to grow stronger over time; the subjects judged the stranger as more hostile when they rated him either a day or a week after reading the passage than when they rated him immediately. So-

FIGURE 17–3
Priming of Hostility

Subjects were given sets of words with which to construct sentences. When most of their sentences referred to hostile actions, the subjects had a greater tendency to view a stranger as hostile. In addition, the tendency to view the stranger as hostile grew over time. These results show how activating a schema can affect people's perception of a "neutral" person.

Source: Data from Srull & Wyer, 1980; figure from Baron & Byrne, 1984, p. 105.

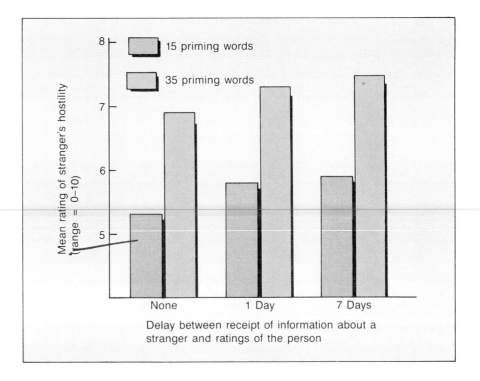

cial judgments depend on the perceiver's frame of mind—what schema are currently active—as well as the actual characteristics of the person being judged.

Another important question about how people form impressions is how they respond when confronted with mixed information. For example, suppose you are thinking of applying to graduate school and must ask your professors for letters of recommendation. You need only three letters, but you may submit up to five. You know three professors very well and feel sure that they will write strong letters for you. You know two other professors less well. You think that they will write good letters but that their letters will probably not be as strong as the first three.

Should you ask those two professors? If you have three strong letters, will the material in the two mildly positive letters strengthen or dilute the other information? Will all the positive information add together? Or will the committee members who read the application average the information? A number of studies indicate that people form impressions by averaging rather than by adding information (Anderson, 1965). So it is better to go with just the three strong letters and forget the two professors you do not know well.

Norman Anderson (1974) has studied the "cognitive algebra" of how people form impressions and concludes that they do it according to a *weighted averaging model,* in which they average pieces of information but do not give all the pieces equal weight. Some pieces, such as the first in a sequence, are assumed to weigh more than others in determining an impression, just as in many courses the final exam may be weighted more heavily than other tests in determining a student's average performance.

The weighted averaging model provides a good account of impression formation in many situations where separate items of information must be combined to give an overall impression.

Attribution: Perceiving the Causes of Behavior

A central aspect of person perception involves making *attributions,* or explaining why people behave in a particular way. If a friend does extremely well on a difficult test, you may wonder why. Is she smart or just lucky, or did she study especially hard? An unexpected compliment from someone you do not know well may lead you to wonder about the person's motives: Why did he say that? Your reaction to the compliment may depend on your judgment that it is sincere or just intended as flattery (Jones, 1964). In general, we react not so much to the specific behaviors of other people as to what we infer or assume their underlying motives or true natures are. A particular behavior, such as a kindly action, might have many different causes, so it becomes meaningful for the observer only when it is taken as evidence that the person is basically kind. Such questions about the causes of behavior form the subject matter of *attribution theory.*

Fritz Heider, whose work inspired much of modern attribution theory, assumed that people act as "naive psychologists" in explaining behavior (Heider, 1944; 1958). When people witness a behavior, they try to assign a cause for it. Heider suggested that causes are of two basic types: *dispositional* and *situational*. **Dispositional causes** are within the actor: the behavior occurred because of the person's basic character, motives, or abilities. **Situational causes** are external factors that surround the behavior. If a person does well on a test, it might be because he or she studied hard or has a lot of ability (dispositional) or because the test was easy (situational) or both.

Harold Kelley (1967) elaborated some of Heider's ideas and sought general rules by which people make attributions of causality. He proposed that when people witness an event or behavior, they seek additional information to allow them to make an attribution with confidence. For example, suppose that Professor Neely summons your friend Madelyn to his office and criticizes her work in his course. You are naturally interested in why Professor Neely took such a step. Kelley's theory holds that you are likely to use information about other occurrences of the behavior to answer this question. Specifically, Kelley points to certain critical information that would help determine whether the professor or student is more likely the cause of the professor's critical remarks. One possibility is that you learn that Professor Neely criticizes every other student in the class as well; that no other professors criticize Madelyn; and that Professor Neely has criticized Madelyn often in the past. This pattern of information would suggest that something dispositional about Professor Neely caused the behavior (perhaps he is just a mean professor). On the other hand, you might discover that most other professors also criticize Madelyn, while Professor Neely has criticized Madelyn consistently but does not criticize other students. This information would suggest that something about Madelyn caused the behavior. She might be lazy. A third possibility is that Professor Neely has never criticized Madelyn before and neither have other professors. This would suggest that the action should be attributed to some particular circumstances and not to any disposition of either Madelyn or Professor Neely. For example, she might have said something that he misinterpreted.

Several studies have generally confirmed Kelley's analysis. McArthur (1972) gave students descriptions of events along with additional information and found that the students perceived the causes of behaviors in line with Kelley's theory as just outlined.

OTHER INFLUENCES ON ATTRIBUTIONS. The extensive additional information that Kelley's theory discusses may not always be available when a person wants to assign a cause to an observed behavior. In such cases research has shown that other factors influence attributions. One factor is what Kelley (1972) calls the *discounting principle.* If a behavior can be explained by several plausible causes, observers cannot be confident that any particular cause produced the behavior. In this case, they discount any one factor as causing the behavior. For example, suppose you were to approach a professor just after the final exam (but before grades were given) to tell her how much you enjoyed the course. When she tries to explain your behavior, one possibility is that you sincerely liked the course. However, another possibility is that you were simply flattering her to try to improve your grade in the course. Given that the alternative interpretation might be true, the professor may well discount your opinion of the course. However, if you approached your professor after you received your grades and told her how much you enjoyed the course, she would be more likely to believe you. The alternative cause of flattery has been ruled out. Research has shown that people are quite sensitive to social factors in assigning causes in line with the discounting principle (e.g., Jones, Davis, & Gergen, 1961).

Edward Jones (Jones & Davis, 1965; Jones & McGillis, 1976) has also investigated the general factors that lead people to make dispositional attributions, particularly inferences of others' underlying characteristics or motives. Jones and McGillis (1976) distinguish two types of situations in which we may wish to infer dispositions based on behaviors that depart from our

Unusual actions usually elicit attributions about the people involved. Are these people a nun and a priest with a fondness for alcohol? Or are they people stopping to buy liquor on the way to a costume party?

expectations. If a person behaves differently from what we would normally expect of that type of person or of someone in that situation, we tend to feel that the action discloses something about the person's true characteristics or dispositions. The behavior is contrary to what we might normally expect, so observers believe it tells something about the person's true nature.

On the other hand, we might have expectations about the *specific person* based on his or her past behaviors. Behavior that violates those expectations is not likely to be attributed dispositionally but will be attributed to someone else or to the circumstances. If we have seen someone behave kindly on a number of occasions but now observe him act very cruelly toward another person, we are likely to attribute the behavior not to him but to the other person or to the circumstances. In general, behaviors that violate our expectations are likely to be informative. But the specific inferences we make from them depend on whether the expectations are general (based on the situation) or specific (based on the person's past behavior).

Robert Wyer (1981) has proposed a general theory of how people make attributions, with a somewhat different emphasis. Wyer finds that people often use the first information that comes to mind in assigning causes. Information may be accessible (easily retrieved from memory) for many reasons, including its having been used in the recent past. Wyer and Carlston (1979, pp. 40–41) report a study in which groups of students were given differing information about a basketball team's performance over the first ten games of a season. The record showed that the team had either improved or deteriorated steadily over the ten games. The students also received information about the improvement (or decline) of a different team during a past season, with an explanation of that team's performance as due to one of several causes such as luck, the team's ability, or the difficulty of their schedule. The information about the other team was logically irrelevant to attributions about the original team, but when students were asked to make attributions about the original team, their judgments were strongly affected by the irrelevant information. Wyer concluded that the information about the other team was readily accessible to the students (because they had just read it), so it influenced their judgments despite its objective irrelevance. As we saw in Chapter 8, people often respond to complex problems with the first idea that comes to mind rather than analyzing the situation more carefully.

Attributional Biases

The principles we have discussed thus far may leave you with the impression that people always determine causes for behavior accurately. Fortunately, people usually do, but sometimes people make attributions without all the relevant information or are misguided in other ways. Just as visual illusions can tell us about normal mechanisms of perception, so too can attributional biases tell us about normal processes of assigning causes. We can identify two types of bias: cognitive (or perceptual) and motivational. Often these interact, but we will discuss each separately.

COGNITIVE BIASES. The salience of objects often affects attributions. Salient objects are those that are perceptually distinct and to which attention is easily drawn. Shelley Taylor and her colleagues (Taylor & Fiske, 1978;

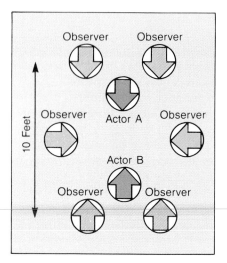

FIGURE 17–4
The Seating Arrangement in Taylor and Fiske's Experiment

Observers who faced an actor attributed his or her influence on the conversation to be greater than that of the other actor. Observers who sat to the side perceived the actors as equally influential. The perceptual salience of a person or object in the environment affects the attributions observers make.

Source: Taylor & Fiske, 1975.

Taylor et al., 1979) have shown in a number of studies that, other things being equal, people tend to assign the cause of some behavior to salient situational factors. In one study Taylor and Fiske (1975) arranged a situation in which two people (actors) conversed while several other people (observers) looked on. The observers could see either one actor (A), the other actor (B), or both actors equally (see Figure 17–4). Later the observers were asked how much each actor had determined the course of the conversation. Those who had faced actor A tended to judge this person as having dominated the discussion, those who had faced actor B said the opposite, and those who had a view of both actors believed they had contributed equally. The conclusion from this experiment, as well as others, is that the perceptual salience of objects helps determine observers' causal attributions.

Another attributional bias reflects the tendency of observers to overemphasize the actor's role in an event and to underestimate environmental causes, an error so pervasive that Ross (1977) has referred to it as the *fundamental attribution error.* If someone scores poorly on a test, you as observer may assume that the individual is not very bright, a *dispositional cause.* But if you yourself score poorly, you might be likely to say that the test was hard, a *situational cause.* Even an observer who can hear the questions and thus knows that a test is difficult will still attribute poor performance to a person's level of intelligence rather than to the test's nature (Jones & Nisbett, 1972).

In one experiment testing the fundamental attribution error, a researcher assigned students to write essays favoring or opposing Castro's Cuba (Jones & Harris, 1967). The students had no choice about which side they were assigned to. Later other people were asked to read the essays to determine whether or not the writers were really pro- or anti-Castro. Though the readers knew that the writers had been assigned their political postures, they still assumed that those who had written the pro-Castro essays were favorably disposed to the Cuban leader and the others negatively disposed. This finding has even been obtained in experiments designed to make the required essays unconvincing and forced (Snyder & Schneider, 1974; Jones & Miller, 1975). "All in all, it appears that the tendency to take a speaker's position as his true attitude seems amazingly resilient, even in conditions when he has no choice, is unenthusiastic, gives weak arguments, and is simply presenting someone else's speech" (Freedman, Sears, & Carlsmith, 1981, p. 155). One way to explain the tendency is to relate it to salience. Relative to environmental features, the actor's behavior is salient to observers, who tend to assume that the actor caused the behavior.

While observers overattribute behavior to the actor's disposition, actors tend to attribute their own behavior to situational causes. Edward Jones and Richard Nisbett (1972) point out that the actor and observer view a social situation quite differently. To the observer, the actor's behavior is salient; to the actor, the environment is salient. If you trip going upstairs, you might blame environmental causes such as haste or wobbly heels, but an observer might fault you for clumsiness.

When college males were asked to explain in a paragraph their reasons for choosing their major subjects and for liking their girlfriends (Nisbett et al., 1973), the students tended to write equal amounts about their own qualities and those of their majors (or girlfriends). But when they were instructed to write about their best friends' reasons for similar choices, the pattern of answers differed. The friends' characteristics were given much more weight than those of the friends' majors or girlfriends. The friends' characteristics were overemphasized, the environmental factor (major, girlfriend) de-emphasized.

These biases in attribution sometimes distort the way people assign causes to events. Similar biases may affect other types of human inference and judgment, both in social situations and in others (e.g., Nisbett & Ross, 1980; Tversky & Kahneman, 1981).

The three cognitive biases in attribution that we have described here are the tendencies (1) of observers to attribute behavior to salient events, (2) of observers to attribute behavior to actors' dispositions, and (3) of actors to attribute their own behavior to environmental causes. However, the latter two may simply be special cases of the salience bias since the actor's behavior is salient for the observer, while the environment is salient for the actor.

MOTIVATIONAL BIASES. Attributions can also be affected by the personal involvement or vested interests of the perceiver, based on his or her motives. Two general types of motivational biases have been uncovered, labeled attributional egotism and defensive attribution.

Attributional egotism refers to a tendency to take credit for successes (or other good outcomes) but to avoid blame for failures, and it has been demonstrated in a study by Mark Snyder and his colleagues (Snyder, Stephan, & Rosenfield, 1976). The researchers had two students play a competitive game, which was rigged so that one student was randomly chosen to succeed (winning seven of the nine trials) and the other to fail (winning only two of the nine trials). The students were then asked about the causes of their own and their opponent's performance. In accounting for the losing performance, the losers (as actors) blamed their sorry performance more on bad luck and less on lack of skill than did their opponents (in the role of observers). On the other hand, the winners attributed their good performance more to skill and less to good luck than did their opponents when judging causes of the winners' behavior. The study shows clear evidence of egotism. Note that the subjects who were randomly chosen to win in this experiment reversed the normal actor-observer difference in attributions: they were more likely to assign a dispositional cause for their winning performance than were the observers.

In general, research has shown that attributional egotism will appear when people find themselves apparently responsible for good or bad outcomes and when the success or failure is important to the individual's self-concept (Snyder, Stephan, & Rosenfield, 1978). You may lose at a card game, for example, and feel that the loss is due to your lack of skill (the first condition), but you still might not engage in egotistical attributions because card-playing skill is not important to the way you view yourself (the second condition).

Defensive attribution refers to attributions that serve to protect the perceiver's self-concept or view of the world. One type of defensive attribution involves the "belief in a just world" (Lerner & Miller, 1978). People are motivated to believe that the world is a just place where people generally get what they deserve. This belief serves to protect the perceiver from a fear of negative outcomes (fatal diseases, unforeseen accidents); if the world is just, such outcomes happen only to people who are basically bad and thus de-

If John McEnroe feels responsible for his loss and if tennis is important to his self-image, he may tend to engage in egotistical attributions. He may blame the photographers in the crowd, the referees, or some other external factor for his poor performance.

serve them. The belief in a just world may cause people to respond negatively to victims of accidents, diseases, or crimes; perceivers make the attribution that the victims brought it on themselves in some way. Interestingly, just-world beliefs will result in *more negative* reactions to victims who are clearly innocent and undeserving (say, a pedestrian who is struck by an out-of-control car) than to those who carry some objective responsibility for their fate (say, the driver who lost control and was injured in the same accident). This is because the idea of innocent people suffering unjustly is more threatening to the belief in the just world—and thus to the perceiver's sense of personal control and safety—than the idea that the responsible driver might suffer from his or her own actions. This prediction has been tested and found to be accurate (Lerner & Miller, 1978).

Self-Perception

It is logical to ask, based on the research on person perception discussed above, how people perceive *themselves* and what the effects of self-knowledge are. People certainly do not have direct and immediate knowledge about all aspects of themselves simply by engaging in introspection, or "looking inward" (Nisbett & Wilson, 1977). For example, to answer a question such as "Are you shy with strangers?" you might have to recall your past behaviors in situations with strangers and reflect on them to arrive at an overall conclusion, in much the same way you might go about answering the same question about a friend.

Daryl Bem (1967, 1972) has proposed that we often do not directly perceive our own attitudes but infer them indirectly from surveying our own behavior. For example, if someone asks if you are hungry, you probably think that you answer by checking your internal physiological state. But you may often answer by checking external events rather than your physiological state. You may look at your watch to see if it is time to be hungry. Or you may eat two sandwiches rather than one and say, "I guess I was hungrier than I thought." In these cases and many others, you determine your feelings, attitudes, or beliefs by checking your behavior. Your self-knowledge seems to derive from your external behavior, just as your knowledge of others is determined from their behavior. Other research has shown that people make attributions about their own behavior in much the same way that they attribute dispositional or situational causes to others' behavior (Smith, 1984).

People typically go through most of the day without thinking directly about themselves, focusing their attention on their surroundings (especially their social surroundings). On occasion, though, people stop to reflect about themselves, directing attention inward. Perhaps a hungry, rumbling stomach or a compliment on your appearance or someone's nonverbal message that you are "coming on too strong" in your interaction may trigger such reflection on your self. A theory first offered by Duval and Wicklund (1972) and refined by Charles Carver and Michael Scheier (1981) has elaborated on the causes and consequences of self-directed attention.

Carver and Scheier first make the point that the self can be divided into two separate facets. The **private self** includes the aspects perceptible only to you, including your inner attitudes, feelings, beliefs, and values. The **public self** refers to the aspects of your self that others can observe, such as phys-

Deep inside, Brian wondered if the other guys really listened to his ideas or regarded him only as comic relief.

ical appearance, overt behaviors, and interactions with others. People can direct attention toward either of these aspects of the self. Several stimuli can cause shifts in attention. A view of yourself in a mirror or internal stimuli like hunger pangs or a pounding heartbeat cause attention to be focused on the private self. On the other hand, stimuli suggesting public observation, such as a video camera or the presence of an audience watching you, focus attention on the public self (Carver & Scheier, 1981). In addition, people differ in their general tendency to focus attention on the different aspects of the self, tendencies that are referred to as *private self-consciousness* and *public self-consciousness* (Fenigstein, Scheier, & Buss, 1975) and can be measured with personality scales (see Chapter 14).

Self-attention has complex and interesting consequences, and research has generally shown that its effects are similar whether attention is directed by environmental stimuli (say a mirror) or by a person's general tendency to be high or low in private self-consciousness. When asked to describe themselves, people high in private self-consciousness list many dispositions or traits, as one would expect if they have thought a lot about what they are like. Focusing attention on the self also leads to more attributions of causality to the self. Subjects in a study by Buss and Scheier (1976) had various hypothetical events described to them and reported their perceptions of what caused the events. Those who were high in private self-consciousness and those making their ratings while confronted with a mirror (which also induces self-focused attention) were more likely to rate themselves as causing the events.

Self-focused attention also produces more accurate perceptions of physical symptoms and sensations (such as the intensity of taste). In one study (Scheier, Carver, & Gibbons, 1979) subjects received tastes of solutions of peppermint extract, which differed only slightly in strength. After tasting one sample, subjects were given a second, which the experimenter casually mentioned was "a little stronger" or "a little weaker" than the first one. This statement was incorrect in some cases, and the experimenters wanted to see whether subjects would go along with the misleading comment by the experimenter or would accurately perceive the taste difference. Twelve of 17 subjects high in private self-consciousness were accurate in judging the difference in taste intensity, while 15 of 20 low-self-consciousness subjects were inaccurate, agreeing with the experimenter's misleading comment.

Finally, a study by Carver (1975) examined attitude-behavior consistency. Carver reasoned that self-attention (produced by a mirror) would cause people to examine their attitudes more closely as guides to behavior, increasing attitude-behavior consistency. He selected subjects based on their attitudes toward the use of physical punishment as a teaching technique; some favored it and some opposed it. Several weeks later, the subjects participated in a bogus learning study in which they gave shocks to another person while trying to teach a concept to that person. They were free to select the intensity of the shocks they used. Under conditions of low self-focus (no mirror present), subjects with positive and negative attitudes toward punishment did not differ at all in the intensity of shocks they used—their behaviors had little relationship to their attitudes. However, when the mirror was present to induce self-attention, those with a positive attitude toward punishment used more intense shocks and those with negative attitudes used less intense ones. It appears that paying attention to the private self increases subjects' tendencies to use their personal attitudes to guide their behavior.

In general, self-focused attention—whether caused by mirrors or other external stimuli or by a person's general level of self-consciousness—has a variety of important effects on social judgment and social behavior, including the amount and type of self-knowledge, responsiveness to internal stimuli, and attitude-behavior consistency. In some cases the effects differ depending on whether attention is focused on the private or public aspects of the self, as the theory predicts (Carver & Scheier, 1981).

ATTRACTION AND PERSONAL RELATIONSHIPS

As we form an initial impression of another person, one of the most important questions we seek to answer is, Will I like this person? Positive or negative feelings about other people are extremely important, for interpersonal relationships are the source of some of the deepest joys and the most painful miseries in human experience. Social psychologists have studied the factors that lead to attraction between strangers or in relatively short-term relationships and also the development of romantic love and the nature of long-term close relationships (Berscheid, 1985).

Attraction

Many factors determine liking or attraction for another person. We focus on three: physical attractiveness, proximity, and similarity.

PHYSICAL ATTRACTIVENESS. Most of us would like to think that we are not so shallow as to let appearance affect whether or not we like someone. Most of us would be dead wrong. Research shows that physical attractiveness strongly influences liking: in general, the more attractive people are, the more we like them.

In one experiment (Walster et al., 1966), researchers staged a dance in which partners were supposedly selected by computer, although in actuality males and females were randomly paired. At intermission, the dancers filled out questionnaires that asked, among other things, how much each person liked his or her partner. The researchers found that the partner's attractiveness was the main determinant for liking; personality factors, intelligence, and social skills did not matter. Of course, the participants in this experiment had virtually no time to learn each other's inner qualities, but at the level of first impressions, physical attractiveness greatly affected liking.

Some evidence indicates that men and women differ on the importance of physical attractiveness in their liking of others. Several studies have shown that frequency of being asked for a date in college is more strongly determined by appearance for women than for men (Berscheid et al., 1971). Apparently men decide whether or not to ask for a date mainly on the basis of a woman's physical attributes. Women are more likely to take into account other factors, such as social skills. These principles agree with stereotypes that everyone grows up believing, but they are also supported by research (Morse, Gruzen, & Reis, 1976).

PROXIMITY. People tend to like others with whom they interact regularly, and this often means people who are physically near. A classic study by Festinger, Schacter, and Back (1950) found that residents of an apartment complex tended to interact with—and like—those who lived on the same floor more than those who lived on other floors or in other buildings. Students are more likely to be friends with people who share the same last initial than with those who are more distant in the alphabet when they are in classrooms where seating is alphabetical (Byrne, 1961).

There are two major explanations for the effects of proximity on liking. The first is simple availability. Perhaps most people are basically nice and would be likable if we got to know them. Proximity simply increases chances for interaction, and liking naturally follows (in most cases). People may even come to tolerate disagreeable neighbors when they know that they must live with them (Tyler & Sears, 1977).

The second explanation is more interesting theoretically. Research in a number of areas has shown that simple familiarity with a person or object can increase liking for it. This ***mere exposure effect*** (Zajonc, 1968) has been demonstrated in the laboratory with nonsense syllables, for example. People rate syllables as more pleasing when they have read them several times before than when they are novel. Recent studies have even demonstrated that the mere exposure effect can occur even when the stimuli are flashed so briefly on a screen that subjects cannot report having seen them! Though people are later unable to recognize which stimuli they have seen before, they reliably prefer those that have been flashed (Zajonc, 1980; Seamon, Brody, & Kauff, 1984). (Recall the research on subliminal perception described in Chapter 5.) The mere exposure effect may account for part of the effect of proximity on interpersonal liking because we will generally have more frequent encounters with people who are near us.

SIMILARITY. People may be most attracted to others of great beauty, but they usually wind up with someone about as attractive as they are (Berscheid & Walster, 1978). In one study, judges provided independent ratings of attractiveness for each person in 99 married couples. The judges did not know who was married to whom. But married couples were rated much more similar in attractiveness than were the same people when randomly paired (Murstein, 1972). We tend to expect attractive people to have attractive mates, and we are surprised when a couple seems greatly mismatched.

Considerable evidence indicates that, apart from physical similarity, similarity in other dimensions also affects attraction and liking. In a number of studies, Donn Byrne (1971) has shown that if all you know about someone is his or her opinions and attitudes, the more they resemble your own the more you think you will like the person. Although you may believe your friends differ from you a good deal, they probably have fairly similar attitudes, beliefs, habits, and manners of dress.

You may now be thinking that what you have just read confirms some of your suspicions about psychologists: they busily do studies showing what everyone knew all along, such as that "birds of a feather flock together." Since many of our commonsense beliefs derive from observation, it would be remarkable if psychological research always disagreed with them. But often, as in this case, common observations lead us to diametrically opposed principles. You have probably also heard that "opposites attract," a state-

And then, from across the room, their eyes met.

"The Far Side" cartoon by Gary Larson is reprinted by permission of Chronicle Features, San Francisco.

People tend to like others who are similar in age, dress, looks and attributes.

ment that the evidence just reviewed (and much other evidence) contradicts. Is the second adage ever right? There are situations in which people with opposite characteristics do seem attracted to one another (Winch, 1958). For example, in a marriage, a domineering woman may be happier with a meek, passive man than with one who is strong-willed like herself. Thus, for happier relationships, certain people may seek others with complementary personality characteristics. However, this principle does not necessarily contradict the notion that attitude similarity is important in liking. Two dissimilar people could have quite similar attitudes and values and be equally attractive (Aronson, 1980).

The role of attitude similarity in liking and attraction is more apparent in long-term relations than in first impressions. It takes time to get to know someone and his or her opinions and attitudes. In many studies of dating and other situations of relatively short duration, similarity of attitudes plays much less of a role than does physical attractiveness (Curran & Lippold, 1975).

Romantic Love

Love is one of the most important human emotions, yet it is poorly understood. Every year in the United States, hundreds of thousands of marriages take place. Surely most of the people marrying believe they are in love and that their love will last all their lives. Yet about half of today's marriages will end in divorce. Many people marry several times. Do they understand love and how to maintain it? Do those who stay married understand love? In the last 20 years psychologists have become involved in learning more about love but research is just beginning and many questions remain unanswered.

Human beings experience many types of love. You may love your parents, grandparents, brothers and sisters, and friends, each in a specific way. Psychologists have been most interested in studying *romantic love,* the special feeling that two people, usually of opposite sex, develop toward one another. To study a phenomenon, it must be possible to define and measure it. Although finding a generally acceptable definition of romantic love is difficult, behaviorally oriented psychologists assume that everything that exists can be measured. Zick Rubin (1970, 1973) has made a promising beginning to measuring love by developing the *love scale,* which consists of 13 statements about the beloved (e.g., "I would do almost anything for _____" and "I find it easy to ignore _____'s faults"). People rate the truth of each statement on a scale from 1 to 9. The total score can vary from 117 (9 points on all 13 items) to 13 (1 on each item). Rubin has also developed a similar "liking scale" (e.g., "I would highly recommend _____ for an important job" and "_____ is the sort of person I myself would like to be").

Rubin (1970) tested his love scale on 158 unmarried but dating couples at the University of Michigan. They were asked to fill out both the love and the liking scales twice, once with their dating partners in mind and once with a close friend of their own sex in mind. The average scores shown in Figure 17–5 indicate that love and liking for the partner were quite high for both men and women. The score on the love scale correlated fairly highly with reports of whether or not the couples intended to marry. The higher the love scale score, the more likely the people were to say they would wed. The liking scale did not correlate as highly with marriage plans.

In Rubin's study, love for the friend of the same sex was lower than that for the partner, and in this regard men's and women's ratings differed.

FIGURE 17–5
The Scores of 158 Dating Couples on Rubin's Love and Liking Scales

When the couples rated each other on the scales, the scores for how much they liked and loved each other were about the same. However, when the couples rated how much they liked and loved a close friend of their same sex, there was a great difference between men and women in how much love they expressed toward that friend. Men rated their love as being much less than did women. This agrees with our cultural taboo against heterosexual men expressing their love for other men. Less loving and liking were also expressed for the friend than for the partner. Rubin's love scale has been shown to have some validity. People who rate each other high on the love scale spend more time gazing into each other's eyes than do those who score low on the love scale.

Source: Rubin, 1970.

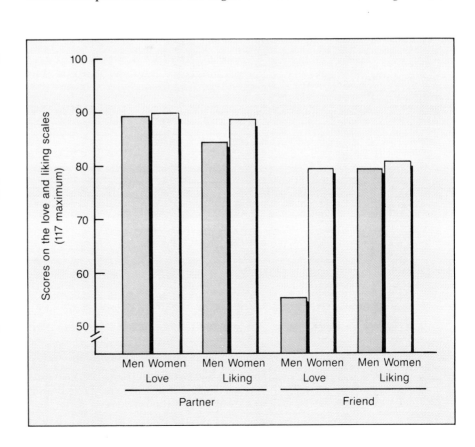

Women expressed greater love for the friend than men did. Cultural norms make it more permissible for women than for men to say they love friends of the same sex. Women also expressed more liking for their partners than men did. Other research shows, perhaps contrary to expectations, that men fall in love faster (after fewer dates) than women do (Kanin, Davidson, & Scheck, 1970) and are more depressed and lonely after a relationship breaks up (Hill, Rubin, & Peplau, 1976).

Rubin's (1970, 1973) work represents a beginning toward measuring romantic love, but how are we to explain love theoretically? One approach is to use the theories discussed in Chapter 13 in explaining other emotions.

Schachter and Singer (1962) articulated one influential theory of emotion. They proposed that emotions consist of a physiological component, an arousal reaction, and a cognitive component, an appropriate labeling of the arousal. If you are studying in the library and a fire alarm goes off, you may undergo a great deal of physiological arousal: pounding heart, rapid breathing, trembling, perspiration, excitement. You would probably label the emotion as fear.

Psychologists Elaine Walster and Ellen Berscheid (Berscheid & Walster, 1978; Walster, 1971) have proposed a comparable theory for romantic love. When a person is in the presence of a loved one, similar physical reactions occur, such as pounding heart and fast breathing, but with the addition of sexual excitement. So, according to Walster and Berscheid, we can think of love as the emotion felt when this complicated pattern of physiological arousal occurs in the presence of another person. Love is then an attribution we make, the label we apply to that emotion: "If I feel like this every time I see him (her), it must be love."

This theory has some interesting implications. For one thing, excitement from negative feelings—jealousy, frustration, loneliness—is likely to be attributed to love and can fuel the emotion. Even arousal at being spurned may strengthen love. Walster (1971, p. 87) quotes a man who kidnapped his former lover: "The fact that she rejected me made me love her all the more." Experimental evidence is needed to test these ideas. In a series of studies, Dutton and Aron (1974) investigated the effects arousal from fear had on attraction. In one, men participated in an experiment that purportedly was to investigate the effects of shock on learning. Some men were led to believe they would receive mild shocks; others expected strong shocks. Beforehand, they were asked to rate how much they were attracted to their partner in the experiment, a beautiful woman. (They were told that this was to determine their mental state so that it could be taken into account in the learning results.) Dutton and Aron found that the men who expected strong shocks reported that they were more attracted to the woman than the men who expected mild shocks. Presumably the men mistook their fear for attraction to the woman, a finding replicated in other studies. In a different study, males who were aroused by physical exercise were more attracted to a female whom they observed on a videotape (and expected to meet) than were males who had exercised less strenuously (White & Kight, 1984). Once again, the males may have misattributed arousal to love. "If I am all excited while watching her, then I must really be attracted to her."

It is much too early to say if the Walster-Berscheid theory will stand up. Not all of the relatively few tests conducted so far have supported it (Walster et al., 1973). Yet the theory may also help explain falling out of love. Let us return to the fire alarm in the library. Imagine that it went off ten times a day as you sat there. After a while, you would no longer be aroused. Is the same mechanism responsible for feelings of falling out of love? If physical sensations accompany your love, they will likely extinguish or fade over time. Try as you may, you will not feel the same tingling thrill that you did on your first date or the first time you made love. You might then say, "I don't feel the same way when I'm with her (him). I must not be in love anymore." Unfortunately, if romantic love is based on attributions to physical sensations and these sensations go away, then you might think that romantic love has gone, too.

Many writers distinguish between romantic (or passionate) love and conjugal (or companionate) love (e.g., Berscheid & Walster, 1978). The latter is the deep affection that people feel for those who are important in their lives and whom they see repeatedly. It may be that when the special sensations of romantic love wane or vanish, romantic love develops into conjugal love.

Close Relationships

Long-term close relationships (including marriage, but also relationships with close friends, parents, and siblings) are among the most significant social influences on individuals. Social psychologists, influenced particularly by the theoretical contributions of Kelley (1979; Kelley & Thibaut, 1978), have studied such relationships. Three concepts are central to Kelley's theory. First is *interdependence* between the partners in the relationship. That is, each partner cares what the other does; each partner's behavior (praise or indifference, giving or withholding affection) affects the other's feelings.

Romantic love changes to companionate love in most close personal relationships.

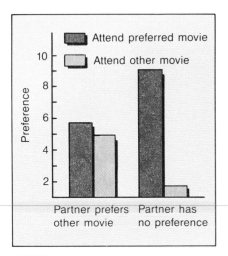

FIGURE 17–6
Interdependence in Close Relationships

People in this study were asked to rate their preference (on a scale from −10 to +10) for one of two alternatives: going with their partner to a movie they preferred or going with the partner to a different movie. When the partner has no particular preference, subjects express a strong desire to go to their preferred movie rather than the other one. But when it is specified that the partner prefers the other movie, the difference in preference nearly vanishes. People take account of others' preferences in close relationships.

Source: Kelley, 1979, p. 64.

The second is *responsiveness to the other's feelings.* In close relationships each partner shares the other's desires and preferences. In a study reported by Kelley (1979, pp. 64–65), students were given a description of a hypothetical situation in which there are two movies available for the student and a partner to attend: "(1) a movie that *you* very much want to see, and (2) a movie that you don't care about." Students rated their satisfaction with the situation of going with the partner to movie (1) or (2). In a condition where the partner was said to have no preference between the two movies, the ratings (on a scale from −10 to +10) showed a large difference in satisfaction, as Figure 17–6 illustrates. However, if the partner was said to have a preference for the movie the subject did not want to see, the ratings changed dramatically. Now subjects had very little preference for going to their favored movie; they took account of their partner's desires as well as their own. Kelley concluded that his subjects typically "evaluate events in terms of their combined consequences—that is, *both* own and partner's outcomes should be as high as possible" (1979, p. 67).

The final element of Kelley's approach is *dispositional attributions* made by the partners concerning each other's actions. Each partner wants to know that the other's actions are due to their love, commitment, and other stable dispositions and attitudes toward the relationship. In one study, when students were asked about things they wanted their relationship partner to stop doing or continue doing, both the positive and negative responses often involved stable dispositions. People wanted their partners to continue displaying understanding and support and positive attitudes in general. Things they wanted their partners to stop also tended to be dispositions, such as passivity or impulsiveness (Kelley, 1979, pp. 95–97). Instances of attributional conflict, where the partners made different attributions for a specific behavior (usually a negative behavior), were also common in the couples studied by Kelley. A typical pattern might be that partner A failed to fulfill a request that B had made, and this behavior was attributed to a lack of caring by B ("You don't care about my feelings at all") but to simple forgetfulness or distraction by A. Such conflicts may be important sources of stress in relationships. They clearly point to the importance of dispositional attributions in close relationships, for it is only at that level that the partners disagree. They presumably agree that the specific behavior is undesirable, but the behavior itself is of relatively minor importance. The central disagreement concerns the disposition (specifically, the attitude toward the partner) that the two feel the behavior reveals.

Kelley's theoretical framework and the research that it has inspired may have many implications, including effective counseling to overcome conflict in relationships (Christensen, 1983). Analysis of relationships and their problems in terms of interdependence, responsiveness to others' outcomes, and attributed dispositions is proving to be quite fruitful (Kelley et al., 1983).

PERSUASION AND ATTITUDE CHANGE

People constantly try to persuade others to do all kinds of things. Advertisers blitz consumers with urgings to buy their products. Parents try to mold their children's beliefs and attitudes. Religious leaders and teachers attempt to shape the ways people think. Friends often convince others to do the same things they do. Sometimes these influences are overt, but more often they are subtle. In this section we will consider the methods used in conscious efforts to change attitudes and beliefs and the effects of attitudes on behavior.

An *attitude* is a consistent tendency to evaluate particular people, objects, or situations positively or negatively. Everyone has attitudes toward a host of objects; for example, do you favor or oppose capital punishment? A nuclear freeze? What is your attitude toward abortion? This psychology course? Attitudes are logically distinct from both *beliefs*—for example, the belief that capital punishment does or does not deter crime—and *behaviors*—for example, signing a petition in favor of capital punishment. We do generally expect, of course, that attitudes, beliefs, and behaviors are related, and the question of attitude-behavior relationships will be examined at the end of this section.

Persuasive Messages

We will focus on three aspects of persuasion: the source of the message (who is trying to do the persuading), the characteristics of the message, and the characteristics of those to whom the message is directed. Much of our discussion will relate to practices in advertising, although most of these practices were developed independently of research by social psychologists.

CHARACTERISTICS OF THE SOURCE. In most radio and television advertising, someone—not just a disembodied voice—urges you to buy something. It should be clear to you that the speaker is being paid by the advertiser and may not be expressing genuine opinions. But recall the fundamental attribution error: observers tend to attribute actions to the actor rather than to environmental influences. Even though you know the person is endorsing the product for money, you are still likely to think the approval is sincere. What characteristics of the source affect the persuasiveness of the message?

Advertisers go to a good deal of trouble to foster the illusion that the person in the ad—the source—is *credible* and *trustworthy*. Communicators who are perceived as unbiased experts have greater impact than do less credible people presenting the same arguments (Hovland & Weiss, 1951). In one study (Aronson, Turner, & Carlsmith, 1963), researchers asked students to evaluate some little-known poems. The researchers then had each student read a strongly favorable evaluation of a poem the student did not like. The favorable evaluation was attributed either to T. S. Eliot or to one Agnes Stearns, described as a student at Mississippi State Teachers College. Later, students reevaluated the poems. There was much more change toward favoring a poem when the encomium was attributed to Eliot, a high-credibility source, rather than to Stearns, a low-credibility source.

Other aspects of the communicator are also important in determining how persuasive the person will be. Other things being equal, physically attractive people seem to be more persuasive (Snyder & Rothbart, 1971). And people who are similar to the person to whom the message is directed are also more effective (Brock, 1965).

The practical implications for ad campaigns are clear. The communicator who hawks a product should be credible and trustworthy, well-liked, attractive, and similar to those in the target audience. It may not be possible to

Michael Jackson was reported to have received $15 million in his most recent contract with Pepsi. Companies will pay large sums to have popular entertainers endorse their products. Despite the audience knowing that the celebrity is endorsing their product for money, such campaigns seem to work.

find all these qualities in one person. A "scientist" in a white lab coat might foster credibility; a sports figure might be well liked and attractive; a family sitting around the breakfast table would encourage identification.

CHARACTERISTICS OF THE COMMUNICATION. The art of persuasion definitely depends on more than the characteristics of the persuader. Elements of the communication are also important. One important aspect is the *medium* by which the message is delivered. Is a live message better than a videotaped message? In turn, is a visual message better than an audio message or a written message? Obviously this question greatly affects whether advertisers should invest their money in television, radio, or magazines and newspapers. Although some early evidence suggested that live and video communications were more persuasive, later research has not uniformly confirmed this finding. The issue is much more complicated than "one medium is better and one worse." At the very least, the answer depends on the need to distinguish between comprehending and being persuaded by the message (Chaiken & Eagly, 1976). For a complicated argument, a written communication may be more comprehensible and eventually do more to change attitudes; for a simple message where the focus is on persuasion rather than comprehension, a high-impact video message may be more appropriate.

Is it better to present only the favorable argument or to present the opposite view as well? Evidence indicates that when the audience is friendly or predisposed to the argument, a one-sided message is preferable to a two-sided message. But if the audience is indifferent or opposed to the position advocated, it is better to have a two-sided communication in which the competing viewpoint can be attacked (Deaux & Wrightsman, 1984).

Another factor important in some types of persuasive messages is the use of emotional appeals. Is it better to couch an appeal in terms of logical arguments or gut-level emotions? Public service announcements designed to get people to stop smoking or drinking often rely on fear-inducing pictures. Are these campaigns more effective than efforts making the same points logically? People can be told that smoking frequently leads to lung cancer without seeing pictures of cancerous lungs; however, the evidence demonstrates that inducement of fear often works better than the presentation of the same information in other ways (Higbee, 1969; Leventhal, 1970). Fear has the greatest impact when the message suggests specific measures for dealing with a problem.

AUDIENCE CHARACTERISTICS. A message's impact also depends on characteristics of its audience. The important element here is the *discrepancy* between the belief held by the audience and the action urged in the message. Suppose you had to talk to an anti-abortion group to try to change its members' opinions. Would you be better off making extreme pro-choice arguments or only moderate ones?

Up to some limit, the greater the discrepancy between the audience's initial position and that of the message, the greater the potential change of attitude can be. However, "up to some limit" is a critical qualifier, because statements that greatly differ from the audience's original beliefs may cause no attitude change. With a wildly discrepant message, it is easy to discredit and ignore the source. In general, it is best to have a communication that

A fear appeal used by the American Cancer Society encourages smokers to quit. The most effective fear appeals arouse fear but then tell how it can be reduced or avoided. The text of the ad specifies the benefits that will result if the reader quits smoking, explaining that the body will begin to reverse damage done by cigarettes.

Mark Waters was a chain smoker. Wonder who'll get his office?

Too bad about Mark. Kept hearing the same thing every-one does about lung cancer. But, like so many people, he kept right on smoking cigarettes. Must have thought,

"been smoking all my life... what good'll it do to stop now?" Fact is, once you've stopped smoking, no matter how long you've smoked, the body begins to reverse the damage done by cigarettes, provided cancer or emphysema have

not developed. Next time you reach for a cigarette, think of Mark. Then think of your office—and your home.

American Cancer Society

deviates only moderately from the audience's viewpoint, if this is known (Eagly & Telaak, 1972). But if the speaker has great credibility with the audience, other research has shown that he or she can make more extreme statements and still change attitudes because the source is more difficult for listeners to reject (Bochner & Insko, 1966).

One critical factor in this process is the *commitment* of the audience toward an attitude. Talking to the members of the National Rifle Association to urge gun control will not accomplish much. (Even after President Ronald Reagan was shot with a handgun, he still opposed control of handguns.) Freedman (1964) has shown that the more committed someone is to a position, the smaller the discrepancy must be between that position and the message for maximum change of attitude. For a strongly committed individual, attitude change occurs in small steps, if at all.

A number of researchers have examined individual differences among audiences in how easily attitudes can be changed. Are women more easily persuaded than men? They may be slightly so (McGuire, 1985), but this difference is more often reported in studies conducted by men than by women (Eagly & Carli, 1981)! Are people of low intelligence more easily persuaded than the highly intelligent? Eagly and Warren (1976) determined that people of high intelligence are actually more easily persuaded when the message is complex because people of low intelligence may not be able to follow the argument as well. With uncomplicated arguments, the less intelligent may be more readily persuaded, but the important point is that there is no simple, universal relationship between many individual differences among people (gender, intelligence) and attitude change.

CENTRAL VERSUS PERIPHERAL PROCESSING. People do not always carefully analyze an argument or other persuasive message to uncover its implications for their attitudes and beliefs. Approaching a message logically and focusing on its implications is called *central processing* (Petty & Cacioppo, 1984), and it typically occurs in people who are highly motivated. For example, if you plan to spend several hundred dollars for a new stereo system, you might well spend time studying advertisements and product information, carefully deciding which model is best for you. But with lower levels of motivation, perceivers may use another strategy, *peripheral processing.* They may respond not to the logical nature of the arguments in the message but to its more superficial aspects. You might buy a particular brand of suntan lotion because you like the appearance of the model in its ads, not because you think the lotion itself has superior properties. The type of communication that will be effective in persuading the target audience may differ, depending on whether the audience processes it by the central or peripheral route. It may be hard to motivate an audience to perform central processing, but attitude change thus achieved will generally be longer lasting and more strongly related to later behavior (Petty & Cacioppo, 1984).

Cognitive Dissonance

People often say things they do not really mean. You go to a boring party and, on leaving, declare to the host: "I had a terrific time." If a friend believes in capital punishment, you might, for fun, argue against it. Will your attitude toward capital punishment change if you take a position contrary to your true beliefs?

In the jargon of social psychology, situations such as these are described as *counterattitudinal behavior:* people behave in a way that runs counter to their actual attitudes or beliefs. In one well-known experiment (Festinger & Carlsmith, 1959) students were required to perform a series of dull tasks that seemed meaningless, such as placing empty spools on a tray, dumping them, and starting over. Afterward the experimenter asked each student to tell the next subject that the task was interesting and fun. Half of them were paid $20 to lie; the other half were paid $1. Later both groups were asked to evaluate the experiment in a questionnaire. The people who had been paid $1 said they had liked the task more than those who had been paid $20! They also liked the task more than the control subjects who had not been paid anything and had not been asked to lie. The average attitude ratings toward the task are shown in Figure 17–7.

The results seem surprising: people asked to perform counterattitudinal behavior changed their attitudes, but only when they were paid very little. Why? This finding and many others can be accounted for through a novel theory of attitude change introduced in 1957 by Leon Festinger called *cognitive dissonance theory.* Festinger's basic assumption is that people want consistency among their cognitions (defined as attitudes and beliefs), and they work to maintain that consistency. If inconsistency occurs, a force will emerge to push the attitudes or beliefs back in line. Festinger refers to this force as *cognitive dissonance.* The state of cognitive dissonance is unpleasant and arousing. You are motivated to change your cognitions to make them consistent again. Reducing cognitive dissonance in this way is normally called rationalization.

These ideas are quite simple and straightforward. But how do they apply to the Festinger and Carlsmith (1959) experiment in which only the subjects who were paid $1 changed their attitudes? Think of the subjects'

FIGURE 17–7
Cognitive Dissonance at Work

People were either given a small reward ($1) or a large reward ($20) to tell someone else that a boring task was really interesting. Later these people were asked how much they liked the task and how willing they would be to take part in a similar experiment. Other people performed the same ratings after doing the tasks, but without lying to incoming subjects. The results showed that those people who were paid the small amount for lying rated the tasks more favorably than did both the $20-reward and the no-reward groups. The paltry payment was insufficient justification for telling a lie, so the subjects rated the tasks more favorably to reduce cognitive dissonance: "It really wasn't much of a lie. The tasks were pretty interesting."

Source: Baron & Byrne, 1975, p. 140.

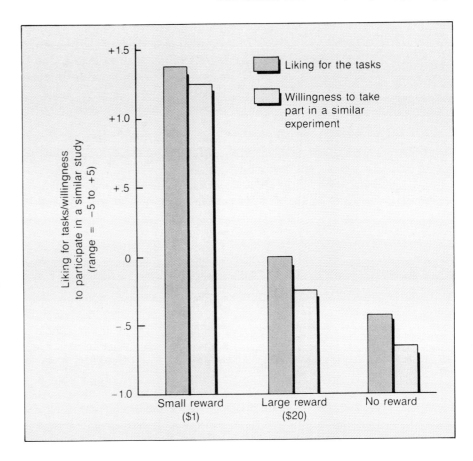

mental state after they lied. Since people do not like to believe that they ever lie without good reason, the subjects would be asking themselves why they lied. One group had a good reason—the $20. Thus no cognitive dissonance should have been aroused in them. But for those paid $1 this probably did not seem enough. They were left with the incompatible ideas of "The task was dull" and "I lied and told someone it was interesting." How might they reduce the resultant cognitive dissonance? One way would be to say, "I guess the tasks weren't really so boring after all." That is apparently what they did, since later they rated the experiment as more interesting.

Further research has refined the situation in which dissonance leads to attitude change after people engage in counterattitudinal behavior (Kiesler & Munson, 1975). The most change takes place (1) when people freely choose to do the act for little external reward, (2) when they are publicly committed to their course of action, and (3) when similar people refuse to go along with that course (Haney, 1978). To restate the situation a bit differently: little cognitive dissonance occurs (1) when people feel they had no choice, (2) when the act is not made public, and (3) when other people act in the same way. Another important factor in producing attitude change through cognitive dissonance seems to be tension or arousal; people given tranquilizers in such situations show little attitude change (Cooper, Zanna, & Taves, 1978).

Cognitive dissonance can be reduced in various ways. Since a choice between different products or courses of action commonly produces cognitive dissonance, easing the conflict is especially important when decisions are required. Which college should you choose? If you decide to go to college A rather than college B, the positive things about B will create dissonance. So will the negative things about A. One way to reduce dissonance is to exaggerate the good things about A and downgrade those about B. After you decide, the choice will seem quite clear. By the time you have graduated, you will probably wonder how the choice could ever have seemed so difficult. After four years you would have rehearsed all the good things about where you chose to go and all the bad things about where you did not go.

One field experiment tested this prediction about the reduction of dissonance after a decision (Knox & Inkster, 1968). Since bettors at a racetrack are picking one alternative from among many, conditions are ripe for them to experience dissonance. Once they have placed their bets (a public commitment), they should reduce dissonance by favoring their horse over the others even more than they did before the bet was made. The researchers tested this prediction by questioning people who were either about to make a $2 bet or had just made one. They asked the bettors to rate on a scale from 1 to 7 how confident they were of winning their bet. Those questioned before placing their bets responded with an average rating of 3.5, a slightly better than fair chance to win. Those asked after their bets were down gave an average rating of 4.8, a good chance to win. After deciding—and committing themselves—the bettors appeared to reduce dissonance by strengthening their beliefs that their horses would win.

Dissonance reduction turns up in many situations. When smokers face the overwhelming evidence that smoking is a major cause of lung cancer and other health problems, they often refuse to quit smoking. In fact, they often seem to reduce cognitive dissonance by *increasing* their liking for smoking. Knowing that the habit may be killing them, they say, "I must really like it."

Bettors are more confident in their choice just after they have placed a bet, relative to just before, in accord with predictions from the theory of cognitive dissonance.

Attitudes and Behaviors

Advertisers and others attempt to change attitudes because they believe that by changing attitudes they can also change behavior. In the early days of social psychology, it was often assumed that attitudes had a simple, direct relationship to behavior. For example, it would be assumed that a person with a positive attitude toward preserving the environment would be very likely to contribute money to pro-environmental groups and very unlikely to toss litter from a car onto the highway. This commonsense assumption was challenged by a series of studies that questioned the link from attitude to behavior. For example, Corey (1937) measured students' attitudes toward cheating and then gave them several chances to actually cheat on their schoolwork under conditions where he could tell who succumbed to the temptation. Attitudes toward cheating were virtually unrelated to the students' actual cheating behavior. Wicker (1969) reviewed a number of such studies and concluded that attitudes were very poor predictors of subsequent behavior.

In response to these challenges, many researchers have sought to determine when attitudes will predict behavior and when they will not (Cialdini, Petty, & Cacioppo, 1981). The amount of a person's *direct experience* with the attitude object influences attitude-behavior consistency. Regan and Fazio (1977) examined attitudes and behavior toward a student housing crisis on a college campus. Students who had direct experience with the crisis (those who had been put in crowded temporary quarters) showed a much higher level of correspondence between their attitudes and their behaviors (such as petition-signing) than students who had no direct experience. The correlations between attitudes and behavior were $+.42$ and $+.04$ in the two groups. It appears that without direct experience, attitudes may be rather ephemeral and unstable, not reliable predictors of future behavior.

A similar factor is *vested interest:* whether the attitude in question will have a direct impact on the perceiver. Sivacek and Crano (1982) measured students' attitudes and behaviors toward a referendum on increasing the state drinking age from 19 to 21. Some students would be personally affected by this possible change, while others (those who would be over 21 when the new law became effective) would not be. Attitude-behavior consistency was much higher for students who had a vested interest in the issue because it could affect them personally.

Another important factor is the *correspondence* between the attitude measure and the behavior: whether the attitude and behavior match in type, time, and context (Ajzen & Fishbein, 1977). A common sort of mismatch is to try to use a very general attitude to predict a specific behavior, a project that is unlikely to succeed. For example, one study (Weigel, Vernon, & Tognacci, 1974) measured people's attitudes toward the environment and toward more specific objects (such as the Sierra Club). The researchers later gave people a chance to sign up for Sierra Club activities. Though there was almost no relationship between a person's general attitude toward the environment and his or her willingness to join the club, the more specific attitude items did strongly predict who would sign up. That is, people who thought highly of the Sierra Club were more likely to join it, irrespective of their general attitudes.

APPLYING PSYCHOLOGY

Attitudes, Issues, Candidates, and Voting

The processes of forming attitudes and making judgments about other people affect us all in one sphere: the political system. Citizens evaluate the performance of candidates and office-holders, form impressions of their traits and other characteristics, and develop attitudes toward them. Along with such factors as political party loyalties, these attitudes may affect actual votes in elections. Can social psychology help us understand the processes involved in *political* person perception and attitude formation?

One topic that has recently been investigated involves public perceptions of important issues facing the country. Perceptions of issue importance shift over time, as poll data reveal. Most people named inflation as the most important problem in the late 1970s, for example, but it was replaced by recession and unemployment in the early 1980s. Views of issue importance have significant political consequences because people's votes are closely related to their feelings about which candidate can best handle the important issues (RePass, 1971). What influences the public's definition of an issue as important? Major wars or economic catastrophes (like the Great Depression of the 1930s) have an impact on almost everyone, so it is no puzzle why they are viewed as important. But what accounts for shifts in public concern about issues like the environment or energy conservation, whose impact is less dramatic?

News coverage may shape perceptions of issue importance. Indeed, the amount of coverage given to particular issues increases and decreases over time as public concern rises and falls—but this does not demonstrate that news coverage shapes public perceptions. It is equally plausible that the news media increase coverage of an issue *because* the public has come to see it as important. Now, however, a study by Shanto Iyengar and colleagues (1984) helps pin down the cause-and-effect link between news coverage and the perceived importance of an issue in evaluating presidential performance.

In the study, conducted in 1981, subjects watched about 40 minutes of a TV "news broadcast" assembled from stories recorded in 1979 and 1980 on a variety of current issues. People in different conditions saw either no coverage or some coverage (8 minutes or more) of issues related to energy. After viewing the broadcast, the subjects filled out a questionnaire on several political topics, including then-President Carter's performance in several issue areas (including energy policy) and his overall performance as president.

The news coverage did influence the relative impact of the energy issue on subjects' judgments. The impact of the energy issue on ratings of Carter's overall performance was much greater (nearly three times as great) among subjects who saw the energy stories as among those who did not. In a political situation where the public generally perceives a candidate as strong on issue X but weak on issue Y, then, the media could indirectly influence opinion, and perhaps an election outcome, by giving more prominence to one or the other of these issues. As Cohen (1963) stated, "the mass media may not be successful much of the time in telling people what to think, but the media are stunningly successful in telling their audience what to think about" (p. 16).

Social psychologists have also shed light on the factors that influence the voting decision itself. For example, voting is related to a person's feelings of identification with a political party and to views on the issues as well as on candidates' "images" (Kinder & Sears, 1985). All these factors determining a political decision seem quite rational and, in a way, impersonal. We decide which candidate agrees with us on the issues and which is more honest and competent, and we cast our vote. But research by Robert Abelson and others (Abelson et al., 1982) shows that this picture of a coolly calculating, emotionally uninvolved voter is incomplete. In a survey of political opinions in the 1980 presidential campaign, these researchers asked a series of questions about emotional reactions to the candidates. People were asked whether Carter and Reagan had ever made them feel angry, happy, hopeful, or frustrated. Abelson and his colleagues found that these emotional reactions influenced actual preferences for the candidates as powerfully as perceptions of the candidates' traits, and more strongly even than party loyalties or opinions about the issues!

Responses to a political candidate, like responses to another person, are often based on emotional reactions. Feelings of anger, disgust, or pride about a candidate—in response to the candidate's decisions, actions, or even physical appearance—may outweigh more rational factors in many voters' choices during an election. Pause to consider the implications of these findings for the workings of a democracy.

Most researchers today reject both the old commonsense idea that attitudes are almost always directly related to behavior and the conclusion of Wicker (1969) that attitudes almost never predict behavior. When attitudes are important to people (when they concern objects with which the person has direct experience, and matters in which the person has a vested interest), and when they are measured with an appropriate degree of correspondence, strong and reliable attitude-behavior relationships can be found.

SOCIAL INFLUENCE

Human beings are among the most social of all animals, and a large part of social psychology is concerned with the effects of groups and other people on the behavior of individuals. Social influence can affect behavior in a variety of ways (Moscovici, 1985). Throughout this section we will point to implications of social influence for businesses and other organizations.

Social Facilitation and Group Performance

Sometimes the presence of a group can help individual performance, an effect referred to as *social facilitation.* Social facilitation is one of the oldest topics in psychology. In fact, the study that is generally recognized as the first in social psychology (Triplett, 1897) investigated social facilitation. Triplett found that children performed a simple task (winding fishing reels) faster in competition with other children than they did alone. Other studies by Allport (1920, 1924) measured how well individuals did five tasks when either five people or only one were in the room. The tasks included crossing out vowels in a newspaper article, multiplying, and writing refutations of logical arguments. Although the subjects worked individually, they performed better among others than when alone.

Social facilitation should make groups perform better (at least on some types of task) than individuals do. Other factors may also contribute to group performance. For example, if solving a particular problem requires several separate items of information, with no one individual likely to know them all, then a group is more likely to be able to put together all the necessary pieces from among its members to solve the problem. Consistent with this idea, the amount of new information exchanged has been found to be among the most important features of group interactions that lead to effective group problem solving (Steiner, 1972). This idea was recently tested in a nonlaboratory study of medical experts serving on government panels to evaluate new medical technologies (Vinokur et al., 1985). The exchange of new information among the panel members and the *absence* of strong disagreements among them were found to be related to the quality of the decision produced by the group. Disagreements probably have a negative impact because they disrupt effective information exchange. Additional findings in this study suggest that the group leader's role is crucial. An effective leader can facilitate information exchange, producing both better-quality decisions and more satisfaction among the group members. Similar social facilitation effects have been found in other animal species, too.

Robert Zajonc (1965) has proposed that having others around increases the individual's motivation. As you will recall from Chapter 12, increasing

Offices without walls might be expected to produce social facilitation of workers' performance if the work of each individual is monitored. However, other factors, such as greater distraction from work by the activities of others, may limit any benefit of the wall-less office.

motivation above an optimal level can prove harmful, especially for tasks that are difficult or not well practiced. In line with Zajonc's theory, other researchers have found that the presence of an audience improves performance on easy tasks but hampers it on difficult ones (Geen & Gange, 1977).

Conformity

One major force on people to change their attitudes and behavior comes from others' tacit social pressure. *Conformity* is yielding to group pressure when there is no direct request or order to do so. Every group has *social norms,* or implicit rules, that its members obey. These rules describe what is normal for the group, and rarely does behavior diverge importantly from them. People may not like to think of themselves as conformists, but typically they are. Groups such as the Mafia or Hell's Angels may take pride in deviating from the standards of society, but even these groups have rigid rules that prescribe what their members must do. Your parents may often find that your behavior is nonconformist, and you may like to regard it that way, too. But chances are that you are deviating from the norms of your parents' group, not those of your close friends.

Experiments have shown that the pressure of other people's opinions can greatly change individual behavior. In one series, Muzafer Sherif (1935) studied the effect of others' opinions on a perceptual phenomenon known as the *autokinetic effect.* When a person is placed in a totally dark room and a small spot of light is shown on a wall, the light will appear to move though it does not; it seems to "move itself." (The word autokinetic means "self-moving.")

We normally think of police as conformists and punk rockers as nonconformists. But individuals in both groups generally conform to the appearance, attitudes, and behaviors appropriate to their groups.

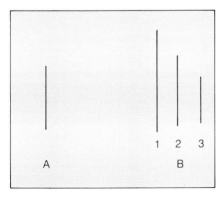

FIGURE 17–8
Asch's Challenge

The people in Asch's experiment on conformity were asked to compare several comparison lines, B, to a standard stimulus, A. They were to pick the line in B that was the same length as A. What would you do if five people ahead of you had picked 3 as the correct answer?

Sherif asked whether other people's opinons and judgments about the light would cause it to be perceived differently. He discovered that the motion a subject saw could be determined by what others led him or her to expect. If a subject expected the light to move in a wide arc, then it would appear to do so. These experiments showed the power of others' opinions to affect individual perceptions, or at least the report of those perceptions.

Sherif used a stimulus that was ambiguous. The subject could not be sure of the movement, since the phenomenon was illusory. An even more powerful example of conformity was shown by Solomon Asch some years later (1956). He asked, "Granting the great power of groups, may we simply conclude that they can induce persons to shift their decisions and convictions in almost any desired direction, that they can prompt us to call true what we yesterday deemed false?" His experiments led him to believe that the answer should be a qualified yes.

The basic procedure Asch used involved a perceptual discrimination task. People had to decide which of several comparison stimuli was the same as a standard stimulus. An example of the task is shown in Figure 17–8. The subjects saw three comparison lines and had to say which was equal in length to the standard. In one experiment there were seven people, one a bonafide subject, the others confederates of the researcher. The entire group was shown the lines and then answered one by one, with the subject always speaking next to last.

Asch conducted 18 trials with different groups, and in each case one comparison line was clearly equivalent to the standard. The confederates were instructed to give the right answer on the first six trials, and identical wrong answers on the last 12. The perceptual evidence clearly pointed to the conclusion that they were mistaken. Would the real subjects conform to the group judgment, even though it flew in the face of what they saw? A large percentage of the subjects (75 percent) did in fact conform on one or more trials. Since control subjects hardly ever erred, Asch's experiment showed how group pressure could lead people to go against their own best judgment and conform to the group response. The group here was made up of strangers. The power for conformity might be even greater when friends are involved.

Why do people conform? A number of factors have been found to influence conformity in experimental situations. First, having an ally helps a person to resist pressures to conform. When someone else refuses to bow, one is much less likely to yield. Second is the size of the group. Not surprisingly, the greater the number of people who supply pressure for conforming, the greater the amount of conformity that results. However, in small groups, the effects of group size on conformity seem to level off when the group exceeds six or seven members (Wilder, 1977). Another important factor involves ambiguity, with more ambiguous situations producing greater conformity. Conformity is not necessarily bad—when someone does not know how to react, it is sensible to take the lead from another who moves confidently and may be better informed. Thus, a fourth factor affecting conformity is the expertise of the people the situation embraces. The more expert the group in terms of the judgments being made, the more likely an individual is to conform (Crano, 1970).

In some of the earliest studies, experimenters found that women conformed more than men (Crutchfield, 1955), but the conclusion that there is a sex difference in conformity now appears to have been an oversimplification. The tasks used in the experiments were ones that men might be expected to do better on than women. Thus the women may have conformed more because they felt less confident. If the assigned tasks were familiar to women but unfamiliar to men, greater conformity might be obtained among men than women (Eagly, 1978). In fact, just this result has been found. In one experiment (Sistrunk & McDavid, 1971) the tasks could be perceived as masculine, feminine, or neutral. Women conformed more to group opinion on the masculine tasks, as did men on the feminine tasks; on the neutral tasks, the sexes reacted alike. Thus men and women do not seem to differ overall in conformity, but they may vary according to the situation.

The tendency to conform to social pressure may differ depending on the individual's level of self-consciousness. William Froming and Charles Carver (1981) performed a study modeled on that of Asch (1956), in which subjects made perceptual judgments while a number of "other subjects" gave incorrect responses. (The other subjects were not physically present in this study but were represented by tape-recorded voices that the subject heard). Subjects high in private self-consciousness were more accurate in reporting the correct responses despite the social pressure toward conformity, while subjects high in public self-consciousness were slightly more likely to conform and to give the wrong responses. These results are to be expected if one recalls that private self-consciousness implies a greater sensitivity to one's own perceptions and sensations, while public self-consciousness is linked to a concern over other people's reactions.

Conformity may occur not only with groups that are physically present, as in the situations studied by Asch (1956) and Sherif (1935). People may conform to *reference groups*—groups that they evaluate positively and use as a standard for attitudes or beliefs—whether or not they are a member of the group. Peer groups or high-status groups to which a person aspires to belong may serve this function. For example, "social climbers" may shape their attitudes to match those of "high society," their reference group, while adolescents may adopt the attitudes and behaviors of the peer group at school or of the latest punk rock band. Theodore Newcomb (1943) studied the effects of reference groups at Bennington College, a small, very liberal college, during the Depression years. Though most students arrived at Bennington from well-to-do, conservative families, some adopted the college faculty and other students as a reference group and changed their attitudes in a liberal direction during college. Others retained their family as a reference group and kept more conservative attitudes. Conformity to reference groups may thus occur even when the group is not physically present, reminding us that social influences on attitudes and behavior go far beyond the situation of face-to-face interaction.

Compliance

Compliance occurs in situations involving a request. With conformity, the pressure to go along with the group is indirect, but in compliance it is direct. For example, a professor asks you to stop by after class, or a salesperson asks you to buy something.

Salespeople believe that the best way to make a sale is to "get a foot in the door," a bit of advice that dates back to house-to-house peddling. The general idea is that a person who agrees to some small request—"May I come in?"—will be more likely to assent to a larger request—to buy something—later. Freedman and Fraser (1966), testing the *foot-in-the-door effect*, had two undergraduates approach housewives in a California suburb with various requests. One of the student experimenters asked the women to place small signs in their windows or to sign a petition about keeping California beautiful. Two weeks later the other student asked if the women would allow a large and unsightly billboard promoting auto safety to be put on their lawns for a few weeks. Housewives in a control group were requested only to permit placement of the billboard. Just 17 percent of the control subjects were willing, but 76 percent of the women who had agreed to the lesser request assented. This study and similar ones (Pliner et al., 1974) confirm the effectiveness of the foot-in-the-door technique to obtain compliance.

Why does the foot-in-the-door work? One explanation that enjoys a good deal of support is couched in terms of self-perception. When you agree to a request, you think of yourself as somebody who does that sort of thing, and this change in self-concept will lead you to agree later to other similar requests, even when they are bothersome. Much evidence backs this interpretation, as long as two criteria are met (DeJong, 1979). First, the initial request must be large enough to make people think about the implications of their behavior, to change their self-concept. And second, the actor must believe that he or she exercised free choice in agreeing, so that an internal attribution will be made about the behavior. If people are paid in connection with the first request, they will attribute the behavior to the money, and they will not comply to a greater degree than a control group to a large request (Zuckerman, Lazzaro, & Waldgair, 1979).

Obedience

Obedience involves orders, rather than requests. An order is the most direct form of social influence, and obedience is essential if societies are to run efficiently; for example, chaos would ensue if motorists did not obey traffic regulations. However, obedience can become destructive when orders are blindly followed.

In the 1930s and 1940s millions of Jews and Eastern Europeans were murdered in concentration camps in Nazi Germany. The slaughter was directed by Adolf Hitler and a few other German leaders, but it took hundreds of other people to run the death camps. At the Nuremberg war crime trials that followed World War II, most of these people defended themselves by saying that "I was only following orders."

Why do people obey such orders? This question was raised in some experiments by Stanley Milgram (1963, 1974). He advertised in a newspaper for subjects, and a number of people from all walks of life responded. At the lab, the subjects were told that they were participating in a study of the effects of punishment on learning. Their task was to monitor someone who was trying to master certain material and to punish him with shock when he erred. The subjects were shown an imposing shock generator; they were given sample shocks themselves to demonstrate that it was working. The generator had 30 switches, marked from 15 to 450 volts. Beneath groups of four switches were labels: Slight Shock, Moderate Shock, Strong Shock,

FIGURE 17–9
The Learner in Milgram's Studies of Obedience

Do you think you would give this man painful shocks and risk seriously injuring him if an experimenter told you to? Milgram's results suggest that you would.

Very Strong Shock, Intense Shock, Extreme Intensity Shock, and Danger: Severe Shock. Two switches at the end were simply identified by XXX.

The experimenter was a seemingly severe 31-year-old male biology teacher. The confederate was a 47-year-old accountant who had been trained for his role as the learner (see Figure 17–9) and appeared to be mild-mannered and likable. The confederate was strapped into a chair to prevent movement, and electrodes were placed on his wrists.

The experiment began with the "learner" making few errors and the monitor, the actual subject of the study, having to give him few shocks. But as the learner made more frequent errors, the subject was required to give him supposedly ever-increasing amounts of shock. (The shocks actually were simulated.)

In the original study the "learner" was out of sight of the monitor and the experimenter. His responses were standardized on tape. "Starting with 75 volts the learner begins to grunt and moan. At 150 volts he demands to be let out of the experiment. At 180 volts he cries that he can no longer stand the pain. At 300 volts he refuses to provide any more answers. . . . The experimenter (then) instructs the naive subject to treat the absence of an answer as a wrong answer, and to follow the usual shock procedure" (Milgram, 1965, p. 246). The subjects turned and frequently asked the experimenter what to do. At first he said merely, "Please go on." But later he said things like "It is absolutely essential that you continue" or "You have no other choice. You *must* go on."

Milgram was interested in seeing how much obedience he would obtain. His results are remarkable. Of the original 40 people tested, 65 percent (26) delivered the entire sequence of shocks to the "learner" and 14 broke off the experiment and refused to continue. The results are portrayed in Figure 17–10. Milgram's subjects were not torturers, but normal people who experienced a great deal of conflict: they sweated and trembled; many

FIGURE 17–10
Milgram's Results

The graph shows the percentage of people who continued shocking the learner in Milgram's obedience study at increasing levels of shock intensity. Even when the learner cried out in pain and stopped responding to the task, nearly two-thirds of the subjects obeyed the experimenter and continued to administer shocks beyond the danger point.

Source: Baron & Byrne, 1977, p. 292.

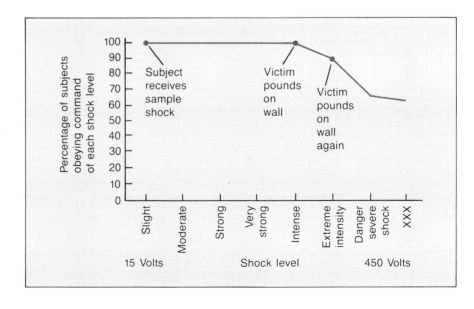

FIGURE 17–11
"Learner" Being "Shocked"

A subject in Milgram's experiment is shocking the learner while holding his arm to the shock plate.

laughed nervously, a few uncontrollably. One viewer of the experiment commented:

> I observed a mature and initially poised businessman enter the laboratory smiling and confident. Within 20 minutes he was reduced to a nervous, stuttering wreck, who was rapidly approaching a point of nervous collapse. He constantly pulled on his earlobe and twisted his hands. At one point he pushed his fist into his forehead and muttered: "Oh God, let's stop it." And yet he continued to respond to every word of the experimenter, and obeyed to the end. (Milgram, 1963, p. 377)

Milgram's findings show clearly how ordinary people can be led to commit acts under orders that violate their best judgments. They are all the more surprising because the experimenter really had no power over the subjects, who could have walked out at any time. In most real-life situations, those giving orders have actual control, so obedience may be even greater.

On a more hopeful note, some of Milgram's research did show that there are several ways to decrease subjects' obedience. When the subject who had to administer the shock could actually see the "learner," obedience to the experimenter's commands dropped greatly (Milgram, 1965). In one condition of another experiment, the victim was in the other room, as in the original study, so that his protests could only be heard. In a second condition, the learner sat across the room, but he was visible to the subject. In a third, the subject actually had to hold the learner's arm on the shock plate. The number of subjects willing to complete the whole series of shocks decreased from 74 percent to 40 percent to 30 percent in the three conditions. But it seems incredible that even 30 percent were willing to hold the victim's arm on the shock plate against his protests (Figure 17–11).

Obedience also drops in Milgram's situation when a confederate defies the experimenter. As in conformity research, a disobedient model produces disobedience in real subjects. These results are portrayed in Figure 17–12.

FIGURE 17–12
Reducing Blind Obedience

When a confederate refused to obey the experimenter in the obedience situation, the subject also refused to go along. Blind obedience can be reduced when there are appropriate models. (But isn't this a sort of conformity?)

Source: Baron & Byrne, 1977, p. 292.

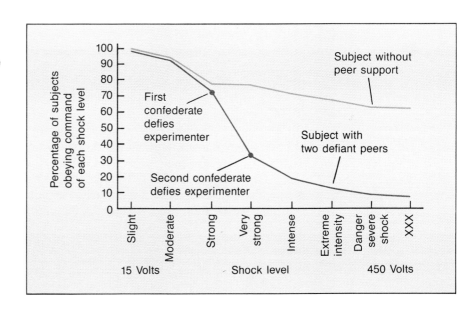

CONTROVERSY

Are Deception Experiments Ethical?

Milgram's experiments on obedience (1963, 1974) have raised many thorny ethical issues. Some have argued that the procedures he used are unethical (Baumrind, 1964). The major criticisms are the following:

1. The subjects could have suffered from stress in the studies, possibly even suffering a heart attack, or their self-concept could have been changed to that of a cold, heartless person ("What kind of person must I be if I did this?")

2. The subjects were deceived into participating, and the experimenter lied to them about the experiment's purpose.

In Milgram's study, it is certainly true that stress or other negative effects of the study might have done lasting damage to the subjects. However, Milgram did not know ahead of time that this would be the case. In fact, psychiatrists and psychologists with whom he discussed the experiment beforehand all predicted much lower levels of obedience than Milgram found. Milgram also made a special effort to follow up his subjects to examine the possibility of long-term psychological harm. About 83 percent of those completing questionnaires later said that they were "glad" or "very glad" to have participated (Milgram, 1964). Only 2 percent regretted their participation. (But remember the effects of cognitive dissonance. If people chose to take part in a stressful event, how might this decision affect their attitude toward it when measured later?)

Even if subjects in Milgram's study may not have been permanently harmed, researchers must take the possibility of harm seriously and deal with it in at least two ways. First, the researcher considers whether the knowledge to be gained is more important than harm to a few people. This argument may be persuasive for medical research, where the discovery of an important new drug (for instance) may justify experimental treatments that may have unforeseen negative side effects on a few patients. The same argument can be used for Milgram's research since its

Some experiments have revealed lower levels of obedience than those found by Milgram (Kilham & Mann, 1974). But, as has been mentioned, the forces for obedience are probably much greater in natural situations because the power of the leader who commands obedience is much greater. Milgram's studies point out how easily blind obedience to authority can be brought about. It is a lesson that should not be taken lightly. When Milgram's experiment is described and people are asked whether or not they would obey the experimenter as did his subjects, almost all say no. But most people probably would. When Milgram conducted his experiment with Yale University undergraduates, he got roughly the same levels of obedience as he did with people from the community. This leads us back to the fundamental attribution error. People systematically tend to underestimate the power of environmental or social forces on human behavior. They may deride those who conform or are obedient to others, but they do not stop to think how they might have acted in their places. Aronson (1980, p. 39) reports that when he asked his social psychology class if they would have continued giving shocks to Milgram's learner, only one person raised his

results are important. But this argument cannot be pushed too far. Certainly most psychological investigations cannot be said to be matters of life and death, as can those in medicine.

The second precaution against possible harm to research participants involves the use of *informed consent.* In medical research today, for example, those participating in a study would have the nature of the experiment and any known side effects of the treatment fully explained to them. They would then sign a legal consent form authorizing the research. This brings us to the second criticism of Milgram's study: the use of deception. Obviously subjects who are deceived about the purpose of a study are unable to give informed consent to their participation or to evaluate the possible harm or stress that they might encounter. Besides preventing the possibility of informed consent, deception has other problems. Some people argue that deception itself is unethical, even if it is used in a study where there is no

other likelihood of harm to subjects (Kelman, 1968).

Psychologists use deception because they believe that if the subjects knew the purposes of the study, they might behave differently. For example, would a subject who knew that Milgram was studying destructive obedience be as likely as a deceived subject to obey all the way to the end of the experiment? Kelman (1968) and others have suggested that people need not be deceived, even in studies of sensitive topics, because they can be asked to *role-play* their responses. For instance, someone might be shown the Milgram shock generator, introduced to the smiling confederate, and have the experimental procedure explained to him. He would then be asked to play the role of a naive subject and (in effect) to predict how much shock he would use. However, research on the validity of role-playing subjects is not encouraging. Recall that even the psychologists consulted by Milgram failed to predict the high levels of obedience displayed by Mil-

gram's actual subjects. Role-played results often fail to duplicate more subtle aspects of findings obtained with subjects deceived into thinking the situation is real (Miller, 1972).

Unfortunately, it therefore seems that valid results in some important areas of research depend on the use of deception. Researchers generally acknowledge the ethical questions about deception by (1) considering all possible alternatives before choosing to use deception in a study, (2) minimizing the deception that is used, not going beyond what is necessary to carry out the study, and (3) *debriefing* the subjects (admitting the deception and explaining why it had to be used) as soon as practicable. Most universities and psychology departments have committees that must approve research involving human subjects. These committees endorse the ethical guidelines of the American Psychological Association, which require informed consent from subjects whenever the experiment will involve stress or the possibility of harm.

hand. The others were confident that they would not have done so. The lone exception was a veteran of the Vietnam war; probably he knew, first-hand, the power of situations over behavior.

SUMMARY

1. Social psychology is the systematic study of how social influences affect individual behavior. It encompasses social cognition (how we come to know other people and think about them), interpersonal relationships, persuasion and attitude change, and other forms of social influence.

2. Person perception refers to the processes involved in forming impressions of other people and explaining their behavior. People make snap judgments on the basis of easily visible characteristics such as looks, age, and sex. They assume that these features allow them to predict other things about people, but often these judgments are based on stereotypes that may be erroneous but hard to change.

3. Attribution theory is concerned with how people assign causes to behavior. People use information about the relation of a behavior and its

possible causes to make an attribution to the person performing the act or to some other cause. When this information is not available, people may use other rules to make attributions, such as simply choosing the most readily accessible explanation.

4. People do not always assign causes in a purely rational manner; biases creep into the attribution process. People are more likely to attribute behavior to perceptually salient events in the environment. Actors tend to attribute their behavior to situational causes, while observers tend to attribute the same actions to the actor's inherent disposition. This latter tendency has been called the fundamental attribution error, but the name may be a misnomer because the actor's and observer's attributions may be determined by what is salient in their environments. Thus the salience bias may be the truly fundamental one.

5. Other biases are motivational. Attributional egotism is a tendency for an actor to take personal credit for success and deny blame for failures (relative to the attributions that an observer would make). Defensive attributions serve to protect the perceiver's self-image or view of the world.

6. The primary factors that determine attraction to another person are looks, similarity (on a number of dimensions), and propinquity. People also tend to like people who like them.

7. Close personal relationships depend on a number of social psychological processes. The partners are dependent on each other's behaviors, are sensitive to the other's outcomes, and make dispositional attributions about each other. Conflicts as well as stable relationships are related to these factors (or their absence).

8. Attitudes and beliefs may be changed in many ways. A persuasive appeal works best when it comes from a person who is perceived as credible and trustworthy. Emotional appeals based on fear may be effective, especially if they allow people to reduce the fear by following some specific steps. With sympathetic audiences, one-sided messages are most effective, but in skeptical audiences two-sided messages produce more attitude change. A message must differ somewhat from an audience's prior beliefs to produce attitude change, but if it differs too much it may produce no change because the source will lose credibility. People may process a persuasive message in different ways, analyzing it logically if they are motivated to do so but responding only to simple features (such as its attractiveness) if the motivation is absent.

9. According to cognitive dissonance theory, there is a general tendency for people to keep their attitudes and beliefs in harmony with each other. When inconsistent beliefs are held, they arouse dissonance, an unpleasant state of tension that motivates attempts to reduce it. Dissonance occurs particularly in situations involving decisions in which people freely and publicly commit themselves to one course of action among alternatives. After such a decision there is a tendency to favor the chosen alternative over the others even more strongly than before.

10. Attitudes and behaviors are strongly related under some circumstances. Attitudes that concern objects with which the person has behavioral experience and a vested interest tend to predict behaviors quite well.

11. Social facilitation refers to an improvement in performance that often occurs with simple tasks when other people are present. Other factors are also responsible for group performances that surpass those of isolated individuals, including the sharing of information that is possible in a well-functioning group.

12. Conformity, compliance, and obedience are forms of social influence. In each case other people exert influence on the behavior of the individual. Conformity refers to the individual's behavior in situations in which there is no direct pressure to go along with others. Compliance refers to situations in which a request is made. Obedience refers to situations in which one is given an order.

SUGGESTED READINGS

Aronson, E. (1980). *The social animal* (3rd ed.). San Francisco: Freeman.
    A well-written and entertaining introduction to the main topics in social psychology; the book covers conformity, persuasion, attraction, aggression, and prejudice.

Baron, R. A., & Byrne, D. (1987). *Social psychology: Understanding human interaction* (5th ed.). Boston: Allyn and Bacon.
    A leading textbook on social psychology, covering all of the topics in this chapter and many more.

Deaux, K., & Wrightsman, L. S. (1984). *Social psychology in the 80s* (4th ed.). Monterey, Calif.: Brooks/Cole.

An excellent social psychology text that covers all the standard topics and in addition has novel chapters on communication and intergroup relations.

Fiske, S. T., & Taylor, S. E. (1984). *Social cognition.* Reading, Mass.: Addison-Wesley.

A text that focuses on topics of person perception, attribution, and social inference from a unified theoretical perspective, by two noted researchers in social cognition.

Milgram, S. (1974). *Obedience to authority.* New York: Harper & Row.

Milgram discusses the problem of obedience to authority and recounts findings from his famous experiments. He includes discussion of the ethical issues surrounding his research and retrospective interviews with some of his subjects.

18

Social Issues

There's nothing as practical as a good theory.

Kurt Lewin

ON DECEMBER 26, 1982, 20-YEAR-OLD NEVELL JOHNSON, JR., STOPPED off at a video game arcade on his way home from work in a Dade County government office in Miami, Florida. While he was engrossed in a game called Eagle, two policemen came in to observe the arcade and its 30 customers. The two policemen were Hispanic, and the customers were mostly young blacks. One of the officers, Luis Alvarez, questioned Johnson about a suspicious bulge under his shirt. What happened in the next few moments is in dispute: police say that Johnson made a sudden move, but a relative of Johnson's present at the time claimed he made no resistance. Whatever the circumstances, Alvarez fired his pistol into Johnson's face at point-blank range and the youth died 24 hours later. His shooting set off a two-day riot of violence and looting in the poor, black Overtown neighborhood of Miami. Police were attacked, and several whites driving through the area were pulled from their cars and beaten.

As sad as it is, this incident represents only a minor skirmish in the stormy history of racial relations in the United States. Just two years earlier Miami had endured a worse riot in which 18 people died. Commenting on the Overtown violence, Miami's police chief said, "It is a tragic situation, but not a major circumstance."

The research of psychologists is often relevant to many pressing social issues. How can discrimination, prejudice, and aggression—root causes of many social problems—be better understood? How can altruism—people's concern for others—be increased? What is the impact of the environment and of crowding on social behavior? In this chapter we will survey several areas of social concern and psychological application: aggression, altruism, prejudice, the effects of the mass media, environmental psychology, and industrial psychology.

AGGRESSION

Aggression—behavior intended to cause harm—is a pervasive characteristic of human society. In western Europe alone, a war erupted an average of every two years between 275 and 1025 A.D. (Wilson, 1975). Recent history shows little change in that pattern. Since World War II, the United States has engaged in major wars in Korea and Vietnam; the Arabs and Israelis have fought five times; the U.S.S.R. has battled in Afghanistan and China. Today there are bloody conflicts in Nicaragua, El Salvador, Angola, Ethiopia, Lebanon, and many other regions of the world.

Aggression, of course, involves much more than armed warfare. It also includes verbal abuse, vandalism, and crimes of violence. Such acts of aggression are familiar to anyone who reads a daily newspaper or watches television. Indeed, the rate of violent crimes (murder, forcible rape, aggravated assault, and robbery) in the United States has climbed dramatically over the past 20 years. The FBI's Uniform Crime Reports figures placed the violent crime rate in 1970 at 361 per 100,000 people; it reached 540 in 1979 and may now have stabilized with a similar rate for 1984. Even in European countries, where street crimes used to be rare, delinquency and violence are reaching record highs.

Aggression as Innate

Because of the pervasiveness of aggression, many theorists have suggested that the will to aggression is part of our biological inheritance. The best-known theories of innate aggression are the psychoanalytic theory of Sigmund Freud and the evolutionary theories of ethologists and sociobiologists such as Konrad Lorenz (1966) and Edward O. Wilson (1975).

According to Freud (1930/1962), aggressive instincts are lodged deep in the unconscious id (see Chapter 14 for a review of terms) and are constantly being generated within the body. These impulses, kept from entering consciousness by the superego, nevertheless greatly influence behavior. Typically the impulses are released in small amounts and in socially acceptable ways. People with highly aggressive personalities might enter occupations (the military, politics, athletics) that allow their aggressive drives, suitably disguised, free play. One implication of Freudian theory is that if the aggressive energy lodged within is not allowed reasonable expression it will eventually overflow into violent behavior. The evidence for this part of the psychoanalytic perspective, however, is not very strong.

In recent years, theorists have looked at aggression from an evolutionary perspective. Evolutionists believe that the tendency to respond aggressively when attacked may be a direct result of the way the human brain and nervous system are structured (see the discussion of the amygdala and limbic system in Chapter 2). As such, these inclinations are part of our genetic inheritance. The Nobel Prize–winning ethologist Konrad Lorenz (1966) carried out many observational studies of aggression in animals and argued that aggression is part of our inheritance, describing it as "an essential part of the life-preserving organization of instincts." The reasons for its value include hunting, defense of territories, and competition among males for females (Wilson, 1975). Evolutionists propose that through the course of evolution, people—especially men—developed a tendency toward aggressiveness because aggressiveness was useful for survival. The aggressive man, they claim, controls territory, women, food, and other resources. The adult males in a troop of baboons, for example, constantly challenge each other for dominance. The result is a fairly stable hierarchy in which the most dominant males gain greatest access to females and father the most offspring. Certainly aggression is common and apparently instinctive among lower animals. Even if a rat is raised in isolation—without any chance to observe and learn aggression from others—it will immediately show hostility toward any other rat that enters its cage. It uses the same aggressive tactics employed by other members of its species.

One implication of the evolutionary perspective on aggression is that aggressive tendencies vary from individual to individual according to genetic and biological influences. In both humans and animals, for example, males of most species are more aggressive, on average, than females. This may be due in part to the early influence of sex hormones on the brain.

The aggressive adult males in a troop of baboons constantly challenge each other for dominance. The result is a fairly stable hierarchy in which the most dominant males gain greatest access to females and father the most offspring.

Female animals that have been injected with male sex hormones often display increased aggressive behavior (Hines, 1982). Behavior genetic studies of humans, comparing identical and fraternal twins, suggest that up to 50 percent of individual differences in aggressiveness are inherited, with the remainder being due to the environment (see Chapter 14 for more detailed discussion).

The Frustration-Aggression Hypothesis

One variation on the innate-drive theory of aggression that incorporates environmental variables is the *frustration-aggression hypothesis,* first formulated more than 40 years ago (Dollard et al., 1939). This theory proposed that frustration always leads to aggression and that aggression is always the result of frustration. But as research has demonstrated, frustration does not always lead to aggression; it can, for example, cause depression and lethargy (Seligman, 1975). Likewise, aggression is not always the result of frustration. Not all criminals who engage in aggression to make money do so because they are frustrated.

Leonard Berkowitz (1962, 1969, 1979) has proposed a *revised frustration-aggression hypothesis:* frustration leads to anger, not aggression. Anger can easily instigate aggression if suitable aggressive cues exist in the environment. In one experiment to test this hypothesis, Berkowitz and LePage (1967) had a colleague anger their male subjects. The men then were given the opportunity to administer electric shocks, a form of aggression, to the colleague. Significantly more shocks were delivered when aggressive cues—a rifle and a revolver—were nearby than when neutral objects such as badminton rackets were present. Several other researchers have replicated and extended this *weapons effect*. A Belgian experiment (Leyens & Parke, 1975) has demonstrated that even photographs of guns can intensify the attacks that insulted men want to inflict on the tormentor.

According to the revised frustration-aggression hypothesis, pain and other unpleasant stimuli can also stimulate aggression (Berkowitz, 1979). This is true for many animal species as well as humans (Moyer, 1976; Ulrich, 1966). If two animals cooped up in a small chamber are shocked electrically or hit, they often fight. Since the aggression occurs with some regularity, emerges without training, and persists even without reward, some psychologists believe that aggression is an unlearned response to pain, a reflexive reaction (Ulrich & Azrin, 1962).

Many experiments have demonstrated that pain is a fairly reliable stimulus to aggression among humans. In one, Berkowitz, Cochrane, and Embree (1979) had university women sit with one of their hands in a tank of water. For half of them the water was quite cold (6°C, 42°F), and for the others it was warmer (18°C, 63°F). During this time, each subject, by pushing one of two buttons, delivered either rewards—five-cent coins—or punishments—blasts of noise—to a partner she believed she was supervising in the next room. The women whose hands were in the cold water delivered the most "hurt" to their partners. Stimuli other than pain can also sometimes elicit aggressive inclinations. In one experiment, subjects were more hostile in their ratings of a stranger of their own sex when they were in a foul-smelling room than when they were in a normal atmosphere (Rotton et al., 1978).

Social variables affect aggression in humans. Research has shown that even the presence of weapons can help elicit aggression, especially when people feel frustrated in meeting their needs.

Social Learning Theory and Aggression

Regardless of whether humans have an evolutionary history that predisposes them to aggression, social learning theorists point to how susceptible aggressive behavior is to learning experiences. *How* to be aggressive, *whom* to be aggressive toward and whom not to, and *when* aggression can succeed—all these rules are learned. From a social learning perspective, there is nothing inevitable about wars and violence. In cultures that teach and value peaceful cooperation, cooperation rather than aggression becomes the social norm.

In addition, according to social learning theory, there is nothing inevitable about the frustration-aggression relationship. Through learning experiences, people can acquire a variety of other responses to frustration, anger, and pain, varying from constructive problem solving to depression and self-anesthetization through drugs. Let us consider the acquisition of aggression from the perspectives of instrumental conditioning and observational learning, both of which are defined in Chapter 6.

INSTRUMENTAL CONDITIONING. According to the principle of *instrumental conditioning*, aggressive behavior increases in frequency to the degree to which it results in reinforcing consequences. For a study of the reinforcement of aggressive behaviors, Bandura and Walters (1963) constructed an inflatable Bobo clown doll that recorded the frequency and intensity of punches inflicted on it. Children who were given marbles for hitting the clown frequently and hard increased the quantity, direction, strength, and persistence of their punching.

Differences in reinforcement, i.e., in the payoff, affect the direction of behavior. Once well-aimed punches are in a child's repertoire of behavior, they are available for use on other occasions, against, for example, a young neighbor who is playing the tease. If a punch stops the teasing, the punching behavior is reinforced. However, if the child lands a punch on the parent's nose, swift retaliation will reduce the probability of such behavior's recurrence. Through differential rewards and punishment, the child learns which targets are safe subjects for blows.

Many peer groups provide reinforcement in the form of social approval to members who fight well; they look on an inability to do so as indicating a lack of virility and scorn the failures. So it is not surprising that some people devote considerable energy and time to improving their capacities for combat. If aggression pays, we can hardly expect people not to engage in it.

The influential role of social reinforcement was revealed in a field study by Yablonsky (1962) of delinquent gangs. He found that assaults executed in a "cool" and apparently indifferent manner won status and social approval for the gang member. The point is made in an excerpt from an interview with one of the boys studied by Yablonsky. The youth had been involved in a gang killing: "If I would of got the knife, I would have stabbed him. That would have got me more of a buildup. People would have respected me for what I've done and things like that. They would say, 'There goes a cold killer' " (Yablonsky, 1962, p. 8).

A similar reinforcement analysis explains the practice of a gang that required novices to attack people without provocation. Each assault, which had to be observed by a gang member, was accorded 10 points; 100 points were required for full-fledged membership (*San Francisco Chronicle*, 1964). Such subgroups value and reward skillful "stomping" as the norm rather than, say, good grades, athletic prowess, or musical virtuosity.

OBSERVATIONAL LEARNING. Humans can learn aggressive responses by observing aggression in others. The experiments by Albert Bandura and his coworkers, mentioned in Chapter 6, demonstrated how quickly and completely children can learn new forms of aggression. In a typical study (Bandura, Ross, & Ross, 1963), one group of nursery school children was shown a film of an adult hitting a large rubber Bobo doll on the head with a hammer, punching it in the face, kicking it about a room, and throwing things at it, at the same time saying "Pow!" "Right on the nose!" or "Bang!" (Figure 18–1). A second group of children did not see the film. Afterward, both groups were allowed to play with similar sorts of toys in a playroom. The children who had seen an adult behave violently beat up and kicked the Bobo doll; other youngsters showed little inclination to beat up the Bobo doll.

It was evident that most of the aggression had been learned simply by watching the adult. These results have been replicated in many similar experiments (Bandura, 1973). When the children were tested again after six months without further exposure to the film, they engaged in about 40 per-

FIGURE 18–1
Effects of Observational Learning on Children's Aggression

In the top panel an adult models the behavior; in the bottom two panels the children demonstrate their imitative learning.

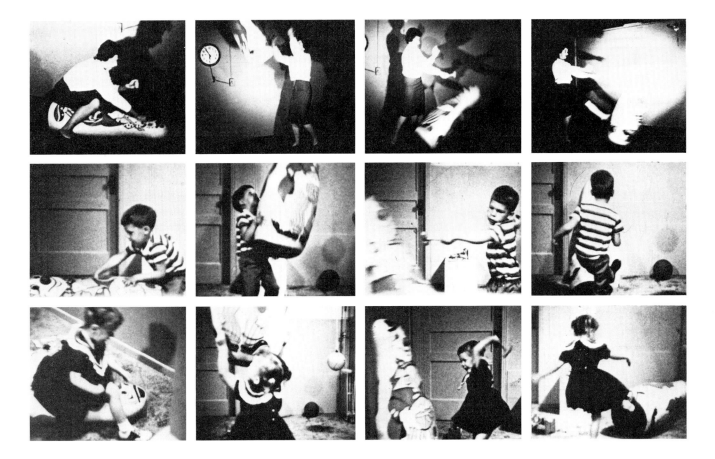

cent of the aggressive acts they had seen. The effects of such imitation are, unfortunately, also to be found in real life, and we will shortly consider some of these in our discussion of the mass media.

Comparing and Integrating Theories of Aggression

Both the biological and the social learning approaches to aggression help explain important data. Both theories are probably correct in much of what they assert but wrong in what they leave out. Biological and social learning approaches are often pitted against one another as though behavior is either an innate tendency or a learned response. It might, however, be more useful to consider biological and social learning approaches as complementary. We will first focus on how each approach deals with the important issue of the motivation for aggression, and then consider whether synthesizing them provides an even fuller account.

In the biologically oriented approaches such as psychoanalytic theory and some versions of ethological theory (e.g., Lorenz, 1966), aggressive energy builds up gradually and eventually demands discharge; there is little requirement for any particular stimulus to elicit aggression. In both versions of the frustration-aggression hypothesis, there is some focus on the stimuli that elicit aggression: frustrating circumstances lead to the buildup of an aggressive drive that culminates in aggression. For example, the wife who has been rebuked by her boss at work shouts at her husband for a trivial reason at home that evening.

The social learning perspective focuses on both the stimuli that precede aggression and the reinforcing consequences of the aggression. Essentially, social learning theorists view aversive stimuli as leading to emotional arousal, which in turn leads to a variety of potential responses including aggression, dependency, depression, self-anesthetization through drugs and alcohol, and constructive problem solving. The particular response selected depends on the person's learning experiences. Bandura (1973), writing from a social learning perspective, has depicted the different theories of aggression as shown in Figure 18–2. In Bandura's social learning theory formula-

FIGURE 18–2
Comparison of Three Theories of Aggression

In psychoanalytic theory, the drive directly leads to aggressive behavior with little requirement for any stimulus to elicit it. In the frustration-aggression theory, there is some focus on stimuli, such as frustration. The social learning approach focuses on both the stimuli that precede aggression and the reinforcing consequences of the aggression.

Source: Modified from Bandura, 1973, p. 54.

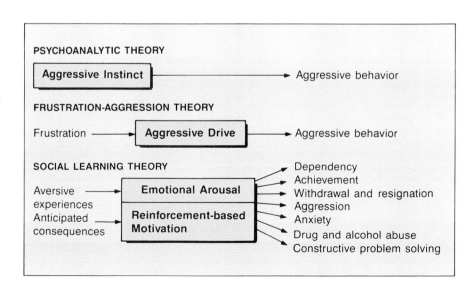

FIGURE 18-3
A Combined Model of Aggression

The diagram synthesizes the biological and social-learning theories. In this model, stimuli that cause pain and frustration lead to arousal or anger, in addition to general arousal. The anger arousal is probably genetically programmed (through neural and chemical circuits) to lead to "fight or flight." Depending on very important learning experiences, however, individuals may acquire alternative ways of responding. But more learning may be required to teach individuals to solve problems constructively rather than to fight. Further, some individuals may be more biologically prepared to fight than others.

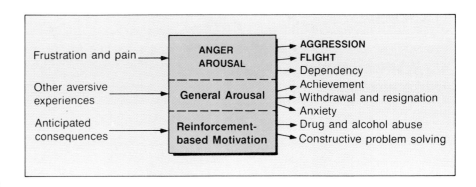

tion, the emotional arousal is a general rather than a specific arousal, such as anger. Moreover, each of the possible outcomes is equally learnable.

A synthesis of the biological approaches with social learning theory is depicted in Figure 18–3. In the synthesis, fighting is a biologically prepared response to frustration. Alternative responses can replace the fighting response if there are strong social influences present. Figure 18–3 also helps explain individual differences in aggression. Since evolutionary theory implies that there are individual differences in the genetic basis of aggression; some individuals are expected to be more genetically disposed than others to act aggressively. For example, males prove to be consistently more aggressive than females (Maccoby & Jacklin, 1974). Does this mean, however, that males are inevitably going to be more aggressive than females? The answer is no, for social learning could intervene to alter the relationship drastically. If males were taught to respond to frustration with passivity and females to respond with aggression, the patterns might well be reversed. This is illustrated with hypothetical data in Figure 18–4. Here each individual's "aggressiveness" score begins with a contribution from his or her

FIGURE 18-4
Social Learning Stretching Genetic Dispositions to Aggression

This hypothetical chart summarizes the interaction of biological and social influences on aggression. The three individuals on the left have a larger genetic predisposition to behave aggressively than do the three individuals on the right. The "stretching" effects of social learning, however, have in fact caused one of the individuals on the right to manifest the most aggression of the six and one of the individuals on the left to display the least amount of aggression. Note, however, that *both* the individual's genes *and* social learning history contribute to the total amount of aggressiveness displayed. Adding to (or reducing) either the genetic or environmental contribution will alter the total amount of individual aggression.

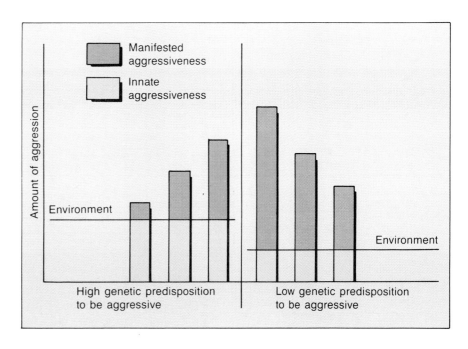

CONTROVERSY

Do We Need to Vent Our Aggression?

Will attending a boxing match reduce the aggressive urges of the audience, or will it provide increments in aggressive tendencies?

Many people hold the view that it is harmful to "bottle up" feelings, including aggressive feelings. Accordingly, either the aggressive drive will build up until it explodes into violence or it will emerge in other disorders, such as alcohol abuse. Psychoanalytic psychiatrists and psychologists sometimes encourage people to discharge their dammed-up aggressive feelings by ventilating hostility. This process is referred to as *catharsis.* Catharsis can take the form of verbal expressions ranging from stating feelings through swearing and yelling. Or it can take the form of pummeling a pillow. Some therapists provide padded "encounter bats" for use in group therapy; people can use them to strike others without hurting them. Some employers in Japan have adopted this technique to avoid tension between managers and workers.

From a social learning perspective, however, such demonstrations of aggression are often characterized as counterproductive and dangerous (Bandura, 1973, 1986). People's experiences in these ventilating sessions could serve inadvertently to reinforce aggressive tendencies; indeed, by

being encouraged to engage in aggression, people may improve their aggressive skills and become even more effective aggressors.

There are, then, two opposing views on whether it's good to get aggression "out of your system." The best available evidence, however, appears to indicate that participation in aggressive activities either increases aggressive behavior or maintains it at the same level (Tavris, 1983). For example, when given repeated opportunities to shock another person who can't retaliate, college students be-

come more punitive the more they aggress. Subjects who are made angry beforehand give even more shocks on successive attacks than subjects who are not angry (Bandura, 1973; Baron, 1977; Berkowitz, 1979). If aggression were cathartic, the angry subjects should be reducing their aggressive drives by giving shocks. This, however, has not been shown to occur. It currently appears, then, that there is little evidence for the catharsis view and more support for a social learning theory perspective on aggression (Tavris, 1983).

genes, which is then modified by social learning and other environmental variables. Given that both genetic and environmental factors operate together; we must look in both directions for the answer.

ALTRUISM

By this point in your study of psychology, you may be thinking that behavioral scientists study only the negative sides of human behavior: aggression, violence, delinquency, anxiety, fear, and mental illness. Psychologists, however, are interested in all of human nature, not merely its darkest tendencies. We all know, for instance, that people are capable of mercy as well as violence. How do we identify and encourage humanity's good nature? This question is certainly as important to our lives as the problem of aggression.

The Prevalence of Altruism

Altruism—behavior intended to benefit another—might be considered a universal value among human societies. It appears as a basic tenet of many of the world's great religious, social, and political movements. From Christianity there are pronouncements such as "Do unto others as you would have them do unto you" and "Greater love hath no man than this, that a man lay down his life for his friend." According to Article 73 of the United Nations Charter, "Members of the United Nations which have or assume responsibility for . . . territories whose people have not yet attained a full measure of government . . . accept as a sacred trust the obligation to promote to the utmost . . . the well-being of the inhabitants of the territories."

Often extreme examples of the lack of altruism capture attention. In one incident that gained headlines several years ago, a woman named Kitty Genovese was repeatedly assaulted and finally murdered while 38 witnesses failed to help her. Such lack of caring is still with us. But perhaps it is because people tend to be prosocial, or altruistic, that cases such as that of Kitty Genovese fill them with horror.

At the other end of the spectrum, dramatic instances of self-sacrifice occur. In 1904 the Carnegie Hero Fund was established to reward "outstanding acts of selfless heroism performed in the United States and Canada." One example from the commission's annual report illustrates contemporary altruism:

> *Bronze Medal awarded to Billie Joe McCullough, who helped to save Bradley T. VanDamme from burning, Fulton, Ill., October 10, 1975.* In a one-car accident at night, VanDamme, aged nineteen, unconscious from injuries received, was in the right front seat of a station wagon on which flames burned across the rear and along the passenger side. McCullough, aged twenty-two, laborer, and another man ran to the vehicle, where the driver's door had been torn off. Flames had spread into the front seat area. Kneeling on the seat, McCullough and the other man with some difficulty freed VanDamme, who was afire, and removed him from the vehicle, which soon afterward was engulfed in flames. VanDamme was hospitalized for injuries and extensive burns. He recovered.

Much altruistic behavior, neither heroic nor dramatic, manifests itself every day and is taken for granted. For example, an overwhelming majority of passersby will give someone the time, street directions, and even money on request. Even on the New York subway, people are altruistic: in one study, an investigator fell to the floor pretending to have hurt a knee. At once, 83 percent of the people in the subway car offered to help (Latané & Darley, 1970). Three-to-five-year-old children also engage in altruistic behavior toward both peers and teachers. Strayer, Wareing, and Rushton (1979) videotaped more than 30 hours of free-play activity by 26 preschool children. They found that each child engaged in an act of sharing, cooperation, helping, or comforting on average about 15 times per hour. Furthermore, the prosocial acts outnumbered those that might be considered antisocial, such as aggression (Strayer, 1980). The behavior occurred within the gener-

Boston fireman Walter McGinn is altruistic. He tumbled 40 feet from a highway overpass while saving a would-be suicide jumper. Cited for bravery, McGinn said matter-of-factly, "I didn't let go because I didn't want him to fall."

ally benign atmosphere of a university preschool; in another environment the pattern might differ. Nonetheless, it is clear from these data that even very young children often conduct themselves altruistically. Other evidence suggests that forms of sharing and comforting appear as early as the second year of life (Radke-Yarrow, Zahn-Waxler, & Chapman, 1983).

Altruism as Innate

Psychologists, as you know well by now, emphasize both genetic and environmental influences on human nature, and altruism has similar origins. It may seem strange to posit an evolutionary basis for behavior that appears to be uniquely human. But other animals risk their lives to defend their offspring and mates. Various birds and waterfowl feign injury by drooping one wing or paddling in circles to draw a predator away from their nests. Some species, such as honey bees, which die after stinging their enemies, are altruistic to the point of self-sacrifice.

Instances of altruism in animals have been widely documented (Wilson, 1975), and even Darwin recognized the problem they presented for his theory of natural selection (1871, p. 130). The problem is this: if the most altruistic members of a group sacrifice themselves for others, they run the risk of leaving fewer offspring to carry forward their genes for altruistic behavior. Hence, altruism would be selected out, and selfishness would be selected in. How could altruistic behavior possibly evolve according to Darwin's principle of "survival of the fittest individual" when such behavior would appear to diminish personal fitness? (*Fitness*, you may remember

Springboks emit warning signals when alarmed. Is this altruism? Springboks, a type of gazelle living in southern Africa, get their name because of a habit of springing into the air when alarmed. Some sociobiologists speculate that this behavior may be altruistic, serving to warn other members of the pack that a predator is close. It would be considered altruistic if by adopting this behavior the individual springbok lost precious ground in the process of running away, while individuals with whom it shared genes were better able to avoid the predator (Caro, 1986).

from Chapter 2, is the ability to produce offspring that subsequently reproduce themselves.)

Altruistic acts appear paradoxical if one focuses on the fitness of the individual, but this paradox can be resolved if the idea of *individual fitness* is replaced by the concept of inclusive fitness (Hamilton, 1964). *Inclusive fitness* is the sum of an individual's own fitness plus the fitness of relatives who share a high percentage of the same genes.

An individual may actually make a greater contribution of its own genes to the next generation's gene pool by sacrificing itself to save its relatives. Because an individual shares, at minimum, an average of 50 percent of his or her genes with brothers and sisters, 50 percent with children, 25 percent with uncles, aunts, nephews, and nieces, and 12 percent with first cousins, more of the individual's genes can survive if enough relatives are saved by self-sacrifice. For example, if a man dies for the sake of three brothers, at least one and one-half times his genes will survive. Among social bees, wasps, and ants, sister workers share 75 percent of their genes. This may explain how social systems have evolved in insects in which individuals forsake their ability to reproduce in favor of helping their mother, the queen, do so (Trivers & Hare, 1976; Trivers, 1985).

By focusing on genes as the fundamental unit of evolution, sociobiology provides an answer to the riddle of altruism in animals. But how much of behavior, particularly human social behavior, can be explained by sociobiology? Answers to this question are controversial. Critics might question, for example, how such behavior as crawling into a burning automobile to rescue strangers is explained by this theory. One answer from sociobiology lies in human history: one and a half million years ago, when human altruism presumably evolved, such rescue behavior might have helped propagate an individual's own genes because people lived in tribes in which everyone was related to everyone else. Thus, from a sociobiological perspective a person's genes today are still fulfilling the same function, as though strangers were more genetically similar than they truly are.

One prediction from the sociobiological approach, then, is that people should be most altruistic to those who are genetically similar to them, that is, to close family rather than distant family and, to the degree to which friends are genetically similar, to close friends rather than distant friends (Rushton, Russell, & Wells, 1984). Although there is little direct evidence that altruism is correlated with genetic similarity in humans as it is in other species, we do know that *perceived* similarity directly increases physiological signs of empathy as well as willingness to aid victims (Krebs, 1975; Stotland, 1969). Since perceived similarity correlates with genetic similarity, at least among twins and other siblings (Scarr & Grajek, 1982), these findings offer some support for the sociobiological prediction.

Another example of the sociobiological perspective concerns altruism between ethnic groups. Since two individuals within an ethnic group are, on average, more genetically similar than two from different ethnic groups, there is a biological basis for ethnic groups to favor their own members (van den Berghe, 1981). Ethnic favoritism may reveal itself in many ways: through charity work, hiring practices, etc. Several studies have found stronger patterns of altruism among fellow members of a race or country than among members of different races or countries (Brigham & Richardson, 1979; Feldman, 1968).

Keep in mind that human sociobiology is a controversial approach. Indeed, some critics argue that it is pure speculation and that its ideas are essentially untestable (Kitcher, 1985). Also bear in mind that although there might well be a biological basis to human altruism, as with aggression, much of human behavior is acquired through environmental influences. Indeed, people are altruistic in part because they have learned to be so in the same way that they learn to be honest, generous, helpful, and compassionate. Studies done by social learning theorists support the connection between altruism and learning.

Social Learning Theory and Altruism

Social learning theorists assume that it is important for children to have altruistic models to foster the development of altruistic behavior. If this is so, we might expect that the modeling effects discussed in experiments on aggression (Figure 18–1) would manifest themselves elsewhere, and it appears that they do.

Midlarsky and Bryan (1972) found that a model who donated tokens to a charity favorably affected children's donations of candy to the same charity ten days later, even though the children's donations took place in a different setting and were solicited by a stranger. Rushton (1975) showed children models who practiced either charity or selfishness. Two months later, the children were given an opportunity to share valuable tokens with a group very unlike the altruistic model's beneficiaries; moreover, the donations were solicited in a different locale by a different experimenter. Children who had observed the altruistic model gave far more generously than those in a control group, and youngsters who had been exposed to the selfish model gave far less generously.

If the observational learning process studied in the laboratory really is important for the development of altruistic behavior, we should be able to find it operating in natural settings, such as the family. Several studies have discovered this to be the case. In one study, Hoffman (1963) observed the naturally occurring play behavior of 22 nursery school children and coded it into two categories of altruism. The first, *consideration for others,* involved a child's demonstration of concern for the feelings of fellows in a variety of ways while interacting socially. The second category, *giving affection,* involved the child's hugging and kissing of others and offering of friendly greetings.

Once the children's prosocial behavior toward their peers had been measured, the next step was to determine what parental disciplinary techniques correlated with it. In-depth interviews with parents revealed, essentially, that parents who demonstrated lots of affection had children who bestowed affection on their playmates, a finding predicted by modeling theory.

In another study, Hoffman (1975a) observed 80 ten-year-old boys and girls from an affluent Detroit suburb. They were rated by both their teachers and their classmates on measures of altruism. This consisted, for example, of asking each child which of his or her classmates would care about how other children felt and would stick up for a child the others were making fun of. When all of the measures were combined into a total rating of each child's altruism, it turned out that the children and their teacher agreed on who were the most altruistic children.

Hoffman then interviewed the children's parents, who were asked to describe their own value systems by ranking 18 values in order of importance. These included "showing consideration of others' feelings," "putting work before play," and "going out of one's way to help other people." Those who embraced altruistic values most strongly were parents of children judged by both their teachers and classmates to be the most considerate. Many other studies have been carried out to examine the naturally occurring socialization of altruism in the family (Radke-Yarrow, Zahn-Waxler, & Chapman, 1983), and the evidence consistently agrees with the view that the family system acts as a primary socializer of children's altruistic behavior, the effects apparently showing up years later when the children are adults (London, 1970; Rosenhan, 1970).

Situational Influences on Altruism

In addition to altruistic tendencies acquired from genetic and social learning backgrounds, it seems that situational pressures also play a part in determining whether altruism occurs. Many social psychologists have sought to discover the conditions in people's lives that encourage or inhibit the helping response.

THE EFFECTS OF GROUP SIZE. The murder of Kitty Genovese, which we mentioned earlier as an example of the lack of altruism, also demonstrates the effect of group size on altruism. At about 3 A.M. in a middle-class area of New York City, Kitty Genovese was savagely attacked outside her apartment building as she arrived home from work. As she screamed for help, at least 38 of her neighbors looked out of their windows, but no one came to her aid. The attack continued for more than half an hour before she died of stab wounds. No one so much as called the police.

The Genovese murder caused a sensation in the press. How could people be so callous and indifferent to the fate of another human being? Yet investigation revealed that the witnesses to Kitty Genovese's murder had been far from indifferent. They had stood and watched in horror, "unable to act but unwilling to turn away" (Latané & Darley, 1976, pp. 309–310). What prevented them from acting? Two psychologists, Bibb Latané and John Darley, examined a number of cases like that of Kitty Genovese and came up with a simple but surprising hypothesis. They proposed that the greater the number of people who saw an emergency, the *less* likely it was that any person would intervene. We might think that with more people present, the chances would be greater that at least one person would help, since aid from others could be expected. However, if we see someone who seems to need assistance and others are not helping, we may dismiss the occurrence as something other than an emergency. Or, we may not intervene for fear of appearing foolish. We may also infer that noninterference is the socially appropriate behavior. This process can be thought of as the modeling of *inaction*, a mirror image of the modeling of altruistic action, discussed earlier. Finally, we may yield to ***diffusion of responsibility:*** if oth-

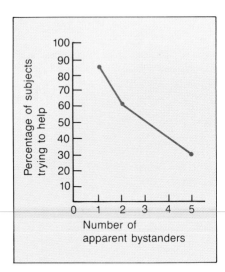

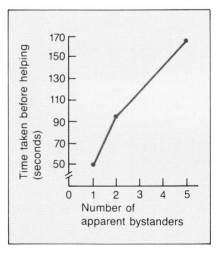

FIGURE 18–6
Time Taken for Response
of Bystanders

When there are bystanders, individuals are less likely to intervene in a crisis. This graph shows that even when they do help, they are slower to do so. When alone, a person assisted in 52 seconds, but when four others were thought to be present, people took almost 3 minutes (166 seconds) to provide aid!

Source: Darley & Latané, 1968.

FIGURE 18–5
Percentages of Bystanders Helping Victims

The results in this figure show that a person is less likely to help someone in trouble if others are believed to be witnessing the emergency. When people thought they were alone, 85 percent helped, but when four others were present only 31 percent helped. The more people there are, the less responsible any one person feels for helping.

Source: Darley & Latané, 1968.

ers are present, we feel less accountable for taking any action. If your professor asks a question in class, and 50 people are in the room, you would feel less compelled to raise your hand than if there were only two others. These are some of the reasons that bystanders might not intervene in emergencies (Latané & Nida, 1981).

To test their idea of why bystanders do not intervene in emergencies, Darley and Latané (1968) directed male college students to a cubicle and told them that they would be communicating with either one, two, or five other students via an intercom. Actually, only one person was tested at a time, and the voices that a subject heard over the intercom were tape-recorded. The discussion began with the students (the subject and the taped voices) introducing themselves to one another. Several minutes into the discussion, one of the students on the tape made sounds as though he were having an epileptic seizure. Would the subject's tendency to help or report the emergency be affected by the number of other people (one, two, or five) he believed to be present in the situation? Darley and Latané measured people who helped in each of the conditions and the amount of time that elapsed before a person began to help. The results of the first measure are shown in Figure 18–5. Subjects who thought they were the only one present besides the victim intervened 85 percent of the time; subjects who believed one other person was present helped 62 percent of the time; and those who thought five others were in the group went to the person's aid only 31 percent of the time. According to the second measure, subjects who helped when they thought there were two or five others present were slower than those who thought there was only one other present (see Figure 18–6). This finding has been confirmed many times (Latané & Nida, 1981). Altruistic behavior often depends on situational factors such as the number of people present.

GOOD MOODS AND ALTRUISM. Many studies have demonstrated our tendency to behave more altruistically when we are in a good mood and less generously when in a bad one. Berkowitz (1972) summarized an early series of experiments in which people were observed for altruistic behavior after they had experienced either success or failure on a task. Subjects who succeeded on a task later offered help more than an average person; subjects who had failed on the same task offered less help than average. The positive effects of good moods have also been observed in children. In a series of studies reviewed by Rosenhan and colleagues (1981), children were either put into a happy mood (for example, "think about a time something good happened to you") or a sad mood (for example, "think about a time something bad happened to you"). Those who reminisced about happy experiences contributed more to a charity than control children who were told simply to count, whereas children who thought about sad experiences contributed less than controls did.

THE PSYCHOLOGY OF PREJUDICE

People are capable of forming deep attachments to each other, to the groups to which they belong, and even to inanimate objects and idea systems. They also, however, have the capacity to develop strong and implacable hatreds.

Most of us have biases, or preferences, whether we are aware of them or not. Many of our biases are irrational since they are based on only partial information or rumors and they resist change even in the face of contradictory information. We sometimes refer to these biased attitudes as *prejudices* because, strictly speaking, *prejudice* simply means "prejudgment," a judgment based on little or no information about something. Social psychologists, however, have often used the term *prejudice* in a more specific sense: the forming of hostile, negative feelings toward an individual on the basis of his or her group membership. Prejudice as such exists against people of virtually every racial and ethnic group (racism), the elderly (ageism), women (sexism), the poor and uneducated (elitism), the handicapped, and people who pursue unpopular lifestyles. Prejudice is not just a prerogative of the well-to-do against the underprivileged but can be found in all walks of life.

While prejudice is primarily an attitude, a negative feeling, it is usually associated with stereotyping and discrimination. Stereotyping, as discussed in Chapter 17, involves oversimplified beliefs about the characteristics of members of a group, beliefs that do not allow for individual differences. The term *discrimination* refers to prejudiced *behavior*, favoring one group or person over another as a result of biased feeling.

Origins of Prejudice

PREJUDICE IS LEARNED. One prominent view of the origins of prejudice is that such attitudes are learned—particularly during childhood and adolescence—and such attitudes can be modified throughout the life span (Cook, 1978). All the main types of learning discussed earlier—classical conditioning, instrumental conditioning, and observational learning—seem to be involved in the formation of prejudice. Classical conditioning produces prejudice whenever a particular group becomes associated with a negative event; for example, a black child seeing his father harassed by a Chinese landlord might develop negative attitudes toward Asians in general or Chinese in particular. Prejudice may become the social norm, with racism reinforced, even institutionalized, by law. In a place such as South Africa, the social consequences for not acting in a racist manner may include ostracism, fines, imprisonment, and continual police surveillance.

PREJUDICE AS PART OF PERSONALITY. Some people nurture more prejudice than others because of learning experiences or, as Freud suggested, because of deep-rooted personality traits. According to the psychoanalytic view, personality dynamics such as aggression, frustration, or even neuroticism impel people to vent their feelings onto others. A classical study from

Racism may be be institutionalized by law. This toilet for non-whites only is on the outskirts of Johannesburg, South Africa. The sign indicates, in English, Afrikaans, and Tswana, for whose use the toilet is intended. Individuals who break these legal norms face fines and imprisonment.

this perspective is *The Authoritarian Personality* written by T. W. Adorno and his coworkers in 1950. Working at the University of California at Berkeley, the investigators evolved a portrait of the prejudiced personality which they ultimately called the **authoritarian personality.** Such individuals were thought to have been reared by harsh parents who created in their offspring a pattern of submissive obedience to authority and harsh rejection of groups other than their own. High-authoritarian individuals see the world in uncompromising terms of black and white: either you are a member of their group and for them or you are a member of some other, rejected group and against them. These suggestions have been examined over the decades since publication and many studies (but certainly not all) have supported the view that strongly negative prejudices are related to certain personality characteristics (Cherry & Byrne, 1976). Not all prejudice results from deep-seated personality dynamics, however. Much of it conforms to social norms, and if the norms were changed, so would attitudes change.

PREJUDICE AS A NATURAL RESULT OF SIMILARITY AND GROUP MEMBERSHIP. A commonsense approach to prejudice suggests that we like people whom we perceive as similar to us and dislike a racial group because we see them as very different. There is some support for this proposal. If we know that we share knowledge and beliefs with a person of another race, this knowledge of similarity can help override our stereotyping (Silverman, 1974; Wilder, 1986).

Many studies have demonstrated that by age four or five, children prefer playmates of their own nationality and race and form groups on that basis. Similarity continues to be a base for group formation during adult years too (van den Berghe, 1981). When groups form, however, positive feelings for the in group ("us") tend to intensify, as do hostile, rejecting feelings for the out group ("them"). This tendency is so strong that Henri Tajfel has been able to show that merely putting people randomly into two groups and giving each a label ("Klee" group and "Kandinsky" group in one study) produces discriminatory behavior (Tajfel, 1982). Many group conflicts, of course, are over life-and-death issues—who will have the land to farm, who will have the jobs. People of one ethnic or racial group often become violently prejudiced against the members of any group vying for the same land or jobs. This has shown up between Americans and Mexicans in the American Southwest, between blacks and whites in large urban areas, and among the different ethnic groups on the West Coast.

Reducing Prejudice

From a social learning perspective, one way to reduce prejudice is to provide new learning experiences, as the fluctuations of prejudices over the last 40 years demonstrate. For example, many Americans who today are in their sixties and who fought against the Germans and Japanese in World War II once shared extremely negative attitudes toward anyone, even Americans, of German or Japanese ancestry. The Russians, on the other hand, were admired and valued allies. Today the political situation has reversed, and old enemies are allies. Most of those 60-year-old Americans also have reversed their attitudes. Why? Because of new learning experiences related to world events.

Other prejudicial attitudes have been harder to change. Racism, sexism, and attitudes toward the elderly remain problems in our society, as in other societies, despite substantial progress. How can these prejudiced behaviors be reduced further?

One solution is to change the social norms legally. A historic U.S. Supreme Court decision (*Brown v. Board of Education of Topeka*, 1955) made it illegal to segregate public schools on the basis of race. Since that decision, numerous desgregation laws have been enacted, and with the change in laws has come some change in attitudes. Once the old norms of discrimination are legislated out of existence, whites' attitudes toward blacks become more favorable (Middleton, 1976).

From a social learning perspective, favorable attitudes grow among members of different ethnic, racial, or religious groups to the degree to which there have been favorable contacts with each other (Cook, 1978). A study carried out shortly after World War II found that blacks and whites occupying integrated public housing developed more favorable attitudes toward each other than those who remained in segregated projects (Deutsch & Collins, 1951). But, obviously, to the degree to which contacts are unfavorable, negative feelings develop. In one series of studies in newly integrated schools, Elliot Aronson and his coworkers directed groups of fifth- and sixth-grade Chicanos, blacks, and Anglos to work cooperatively on teachers' assignments (Aronson & Osherow, 1980). Each pupil had one part of the task and all had to pool their segments of information if they were to pass the exams, a procedure known as the "jigsaw" method of learning. The evidence suggested that the cooperation created more positive social interactions.

Sexism

Men have dominated most societies throughout history because they have possessed the political power. As a result, women often have been treated unfairly. The sacred texts of the great religions refer to the supposed inferiority of women. Philosophers of classical Greece, Aristotle among them, took male superiority for granted. So did scientists throughout the nineteenth and early twentieth centuries, who attributed lesser intellectual and psychological powers to females. Alphonse de Candolle, for example, remarks in his 1885 work on the history of science that the female mind "takes pleasure in ideas that are readily seized by a kind of intuition; a mind in which the slow method of observation and calculation by which truth is surely arrived at are not pleasing." Candolle's ideas were not exceptional in their time (Cole, 1981). Indeed, even Freud believed that women developed poorer consciences than men and thus were doomed to a sort of moral inferiority (Freud, 1925/1961, p. 258).

In the past two decades, men's and women's roles in the spheres of work and family have changed dramatically. More and more women fill traditionally male jobs, while men are becoming airline attendants, telephone operators, and nurses. Furthermore, men are assuming larger roles in the care of children. Despite the changes, economic discrimination persists. For

The number of women and men who are working in "non-traditional" roles is on the increase.

every dollar that men were paid in the mid-1970s, women earned an average of 59 cents (Treiman & Terrell, 1975). Since then, the economic situation has improved little and men continue to be more frequent in most of the high-status, high-paying jobs in our society (Steinberg & Shapiro, 1982).

During the past decade, however, there has been a marked shift toward more egalitarian attitudes about sex roles on the part of both men and women, and stereotypes about the supposed traits of females and males are the subject of a great deal of research attention (Eagly & Steffen, 1984). The total picture is as yet incomplete. Evidence gathered to date does suggest that stereotypes overstate the differences between the sexes. Males and females do indeed differ in several respects, but the number and size of such differences may not be nearly as great as prevailing stereotypes portray them.

Sandra Bem (1975) suggested that psychological *androgyny* might be the healthiest and best-adjusted state of mind, at least among university students in contemporary America. Androgyny, from the Greek words for "man" and "woman," represents a combination of "masculine" and "feminine" traits. Bem measured androgyny by asking students whether various adjectives applied to them. Some of the adjectives were traditionally masculine ("ambitious," "self-reliant," "independent") and some traditionally feminine ("affectionate," "gentle," "sensitive"). Subjects were categorized as androgynous if they described themselves on about an equal number of masculine and feminine terms. Bem found that androgynous students of both sexes behaved more effectively in various laboratory situations than those who were highly masculine or highly feminine. Highly masculine men lacked the ability to express warmth and playfulness; they were not responsive to a kitten, a baby, or another student who was emotionally troubled. Highly feminine women showed concern for others, but they were not independent or assertive; they conformed more to others' opinions and found it difficult to turn down unreasonable requests. In contrast, the androgynous men and women could be both independent and assertive when they needed to be, as well as warm and responsive (Bem, 1975).

Is androgny the wave of the future? There is evidence that American parents are treating their sons and daughters more alike in some ways than they used to: they encourage girls to participate in competitive sports and assign boys to more domestic tasks (Klemesrud, 1980). Despite criticisms of Bem's methodology (Jackson & Paunonen, 1980), the concept of androgyny is likely to continue to be a source of research interest for some time.

EFFECTS OF THE MASS MEDIA

If social learning theorists are correct in assuming that people learn norms of behavior by observing others, then people should learn a great deal from television, which provides access to a wide range of observational learning experiences.

How pervasive is this influence? Investigations have shown that almost every family in the United States has at least one television set; the set is on for almost six hours per day in the average household; both children and adults see, on the average, more than three hours of programs daily; about 40 percent of leisure time is devoted to television; and television ranks third, behind sleep and work, as a consumer of time (U.S. Department of Health and Human Services, 1982). Children entering kindergarten at age five already have spent more hours watching television than liberal arts students spend in classrooms throughout four years of college (U.S. Department of Health and Human Services, 1982).

There has been extensive research on the effects of television ever since the medium made its appearance in the 1950s. We will review what this research has told us about TV's effects on antisocial behavior, prosocial behavior, and occupational, ethnic, and sex-role behavior.

Portraying Antisocial Behavior

Throughout the 1970s and 1980s, researchers have monitored the amount of violence of prime time and weekend daytime (children's) shows. Over the years there has been a remarkable consistency in the levels of violence portrayed (Liebert, Sprafkin, & Davidson, 1982). Typically, eight out of ten American television programs and nine out of ten children's hour shows contain violence. Between the ages of 5 and 15, researchers estimate, the young viewer witnesses the violent destruction of more than 13,400 characters. Even many situational comedies contain verbal aggression in the form of abuse and sarcasm (Williams, Zabrack, & Joy, 1977). These alarming statistics have provoked considerable concern. Investigators examining the relationship between aggression and violence on television and the social behavior of viewers have employed four techniques: case studies, experimental laboratory studies, experimental field studies, and correlational studies. We will consider at least one example of each method and its results.

CASE STUDIES. Many examples of direct imitations from television were collected by Stanley and Riera (1977). One case involved a seven-year-old in Los Angeles who was caught putting ground glass into the family meal. He had seen the act perpetrated on television. Another Los Angeles case involved individuals who robbed banks by attaching bombs to themselves, threatening to detonate the explosives if not given money. At least five separate robbery attempts were carried out in this fashion only a few days after three different television programs aired in Los Angeles had depicted similar crimes. (The three programs were "The Rookies," "Ironsides," and "Hawaii Five-O.") No bank robberies of this sort had been reported in Los Angeles before these five incidents.

EXPERIMENTAL LABORATORY STUDIES. Some people remain unpersuaded by such case studies; they argue that such imitators are mentally unbalanced or have criminal tendencies to begin with. But the relationship between television violence and antisocial behavior in ordinary viewers has been confirmed by experimental investigators. One study used programs such as "The Untouchables," a crime drama, and assessed their effects on children's willingness to intervene in the belligerent actions of younger children. Those who had witnessed "The Untouchables" were slower to act than others in a control group who had watched nonaggressive films; indeed, those children who viewed the TV show waited to intervene until the disruptive behavior had escalated into potentially serious assault (Drabman & Thomas, 1974).

EXPERIMENTAL FIELD STUDIES. Parke and colleagues (1977) carried out field experiments with adolescent male Belgian and American juvenile delinquents who were living in small-group cottages in minimum-security institutions. The boys' normal rate of aggressive behavior was coded into such categories as physical threats, expressed by fist waving; verbal aggression, in the form of taunting and cursing; and assault, carried out by hitting, choking, or kicking someone. The researchers also coded various kinds of aggression that were not directed at people, such as the wanton destruction of inanimate objects and cursing at no one in particular. In the first study of a series, a three-week baseline rate was established for each boy. Then the boys in one cottage were exposed over a one-week period to a diet of five commercial movies that embodied violence. The boys in a second cottage saw five nonviolent films. Those who had viewed the aggressive movies showed significant increases in aggressive behavior over their original rate on most of the categories of aggression. The control group subjects showed no similar tendencies.

CORRELATIONAL STUDIES. The great advantage of the experimental studies is that they imply causality; that is, television violence causes viewers to behave more aggressively. Correlational studies do not allow for causal statements, but they do enable researchers to make broad generalizations of the experimental findings to natural settings. If it is true, as the experimental studies suggest, that the average person who views a great deal of television violence will be more aggressive than one who does not, then there should be a direct, positive correlation between television viewing and violence in the real world. Many correlational studies were conducted to examine this question, and most of them bear out the experimental hypotheses.

In one large study, Eron, Huesmann, Lefkowitz, and Walder (1972; Huesmann, 1983) obtained peer ratings of aggressiveness in a large number of eight-year-old children as well as preferences for various kinds of television, radio, and comic books. Researchers found a weak but significantly positive $+.21$ correlation between the children's preference for violent media and their aggressive behavior. Ten years later, when the same youngsters had reached 18, the investigators again obtained measures of aggressive behavior and television preferences. The question now became: could aggressive behavior at 18 be predicted from knowledge of viewing habits in early childhood? The answer was yes. There was a significant correlation of $+.31$ between preference for violent television programs at age 8 and aggression at age 18. Furthermore, the positive correlation remained significant when the level of childhood aggression was statistically taken out, thus reducing the possibility that initial aggressiveness determined both child viewing preferences and adult conduct. Other statistical controls were introduced to ensure that the results were not due to a range of background and family characteristics such as socioeconomic status and IQ. In all cases, the significant positive correlation between viewing at age 8 and being aggressive at age 18 remained.

David Phillips (1986) has reviewed a remarkable series of findings from natural experiments linking mass media portrayals with subsequent fluctuations in suicide and homicide. In an analysis of suicides, for example, he showed that U.S. suicides increase after publicized suicide stories; that the more publicity given to a suicide story, the higher the suicide rate there-

"I can watch as much crime and violence as I like as long as they keep their clothes on."

after; and that the rise occurs mainly in the geographic area where the suicide story is publicized. With respect to homicides, one analysis showed that homicide rates increased following highly publicized heavyweight prizefights. Moreover, the more publicized the fight, the greater the increase in the rate of homicides. Additional analyses revealed that the relationship between prizefight and homicide rate persisted after statistically controlling for day of the week, seasons, and other extraneous variables.

OVERVIEW OF STUDIES INTO TELEVISION VIOLENCE. The combined findings from case studies, laboratory experiments, field studies, and naturalistic investigations offer substantial testimony that viewing violence on television tends to foster aggressiveness. Only a handful of the major studies have been reviewed here, but voluminous literature demonstrates this apparently causal link between television violence and viewers' aggressive behavior. There are still dissenters who argue that an insufficient number of field studies have been carried out in natural settings demonstrating a link between viewing violence and behaving aggressively (Freedman, 1984). The general view of most researchers, however, is that television violence has effects on viewers.

Vicarious Catharsis

Earlier we discussed catharsis as the act of engaging in aggression to "get it out of your system." A similar concept, *vicarious catharsis,* suggests that watching others be aggressive (e.g., watching television, a play, a boxing match) will also help "get it out of your system." The idea was introduced by Aristotle to explain the *decrease* in unhappiness among depressed persons after they had seen a tragic play. Aristotle suggested that the spectator's unhappiness became drained off as a result of seeing others in even greater distress. Aristotle's ideas were elaborated by Sigmund Freud and some modern writers, such as Konrad Lorenz (1966), and the general idea of "getting it out of your system" has gained fairly common acceptance. The research evidence, however, appears to be at odds with this viewpoint (Tavris, 1983).

Typical testing of the vicarious catharsis hypothesis involves angering one group of subjects and not angering a control group. The anger is usually incited by having a confederate of the experimenter insult the subject. Next, half of the experimental group and half of the control group are shown violent television shows, while the other halves of both groups see nonviolent films. Finally, all the subjects are ostensibly given an opportunity to deliver electric shocks to the confederate who insulted them. The results of several experiments reveal that regardless of the level of anger aroused, subjects who witness aggression deliver more electric shocks than subjects who view nonaggressive television; anger-aroused viewers generally respond more punitively than nonaroused viewers; and angered subjects who witness aggressive fare respond most aggressively of all. This last finding contradicts the vicarious catharsis hypothesis and, instead, supports a social learning perspective (Hartmann, 1969; Mallick & McCandless, 1966).

How, then, are we to explain Aristotle's observations? Perhaps the answer is that the spectators were temporarily distracted from their own feelings. The same lessening of unhappiness would have occurred if the same ancient Greeks had seen a nontragic, action-packed adventure. Viewing violence apparently does not drain off violent emotion; it increases the probability that the spectator will engage in violence. Apart from the research evidence, the idea of vicarious catharsis doesn't suit common sense. Do hungry people feel satisfied watching others enjoy a gourmet dinner? Do sexually aroused people feel less sexy after seeing an erotic movie? Will watching others engage in helpful behavior drain off our own tendencies to altruism? Quite the contrary: those who have watched these events find that their appetites for the activities have increased.

Portraying Prosocial Behavior

If television can have effects on aggression, can it also encourage altruism? A number of studies suggest that it can. David Moriarty and Ann McCabe (1977) carried out a particularly ambitious and realistic investigation to see if television influenced altruistic behavior. They studied 259 children and youths engaged in organized team sports—Little League baseball, lacrosse, and ice hockey. They measured the prosocial behavior of the players on the field before, during, and after experimental treatment. The treatment consisted of providing prosocial and control video presentations of the relevant sport. The prosocial material embodied altruism—helping, encouraging, and team work; sympathy—compassion, pity, and caring for another's plight; courtesy—displays of respect; reparation—correcting a wrong or apologizing; and (e) affection—expressing positive feelings toward another. The level of prosocial behavior on the part of hockey and lacrosse players heightened following exposure to prosocial television content; no effects were found for baseball players.

O'Connor (1969) conducted a dramatic and potentially important study to see if television programs could be used to increase social interaction among nursery school "loners," children who tended to isolate themselves. Thirteen youngsters who were "difficult cases" were chosen for the study. The subjects interacted on fewer than 5 of 32 possible occasions over eight days. One group of them was then shown, on a television console, a specially prepared sound-color film that portrayed 11 scenes in which children in a nursery school interacted with reinforcing consequences. Those who saw the film increased from their baseline score of an average of nearly 2 interactions out of 32 to an average of nearly 12; the control group showed no change. In a follow-up at the end of the school year investigators found that the improvements had persisted.

In another large study, over a four-week period, 93 four-year-old nursery school children were shown the prosocial television program "Mister Rogers' Neighborhood," the aggressive "Superman" and "Batman," or neutral fare (Friedrich & Stein, 1973), and their free-play behavior was observed. Three categories of the children's self-control behavior were recorded: obedience to rules, tolerance of delay, and persistence at tasks. Whereas aggressive films decreased obedience in relation to neutral films, the prosocial films increased it. The aggressive films also made children less able to tolerate delay. These effects endured in a test taken two weeks later. Finally, the prosocial television content increased persistence at tasks over the neutral and aggressive films on both immediate and later observations.

Television programs such as Sesame Street have been demonstrated to influence children's social and emotional development in a positive way. Prosocial consequences have included increases in altruism, cooperation, self-esteem, and the expression of positive feelings toward others.

It would appear, then, that television and films can modify viewers' social behavior for good or bad. In the words of a recent U.S. government report, "Television has become a major socializing agent of American children" (U.S. Department of Health and Human Services, 1982, vol. 1, p. 7). Television is not only a form of entertainment but also a source of observational learning experiences, a setter of norms.

Occupational, Ethnic Group, and Sex-Role Behavior on Television

To what extent are people's conceptions about occupations, ethnic groups, and sex roles influenced by how they see them portrayed on television? Only recently has some research been directed at answering this particular question (Greenberg, 1982).

In one analysis of program content, researchers found police portrayed as powerful, interesting, satisfied with their lives, and emotionally stable (Williams, Zabrack, & Joy, 1977). This was similar to a finding by Dominick (1978), who in addition reported that the police officers portrayed on television were far more efficient than real ones. Dominick also discovered that portrayal of law enforcement situations on prime time had increased from 7 percent of general content in 1953 to 27 percent in 1977.

In regard to ethnic groups, the characters portrayed on North American television are overwhelmingly young, white, middle class, and American (Berry & Mitchell-Kernan, 1982). Most ethnic minorities and foreigners have been ignored or made to look ridiculous or villainous, although black Americans are now portrayed both more frequently and in higher-status positions. Donagher and colleagues (1975) found that black males, for example, were usually presented as nonaggressive, persistent, altruistic, and more likely to make reparation for injury than any other group. Black women expressed a high ability to explain feelings in order to increase understanding, resolve strife, and reassure others.

In regard to sex roles, some observers have expressed concern about the way females have been depicted on television. Sternglanz and Serbin (1974) analyzed a number of children's programs that had high Nielsen ratings (reflecting wide popularity). They found that males were portrayed nearly twice as often as females and were shown as aggressive and constructive, while females were presented as passive. But women do get credited as being "interesting" and "emotionally stable" (Williams, Zabrack, & Joy, 1977). These trends have continued well into the 1980s (Durkin, 1985a).

Finally, in an analysis of sexual behavior on prime time, Silverman, Sprafkin, and Rubinstein (1979) found that sexually suggestive remarks increased from about one per hour in 1975 to about seven per hour in 1977. White females were disproportionately responsible for these suggestive behaviors. (Black females affectionately touched children; males, particularly white ones, engaged in aggression.)

It appears that commercially produced television programs are carrying quite different messages about behavior considered appropriate for males and females; they may well be an important source in the learning of stereotyped sex roles.

Can TV Overcome Prejudice?

If blacks, women, and other disadvantaged groups are shown in an attractive manner on television, will these positive images result in a decrease in prejudice? Few studies have been carried out to determine whether or not such changes as have occurred on television are mirrored in viewers' perceptions (Berry & Mitchell-Kernan, 1982). But there have been at least four reports, and their findings are encouraging.

In one early British study, researchers reported that television changed children's perceptions of foreigners: The more documentary programs that British children saw about the Germans, Italians, and French, the more favorable their attitudes became and the more facts they knew about those groups (Himmelweit, Oppenheim, & Vince, 1958). An American study of the effects of "Sesame Street" suggested that two years of viewing—but not one year—seemed to produce somewhat more favorable attitudes toward children of other races (Bogatz & Ball, 1971).

A Canadian study has produced the clearest evidence to date that television can produce favorable attitudes toward children from other races (Gorn, Goldberg, & Kanungo, 1976). That investigation was carried out with more than 200 upper-middle-class, white, English-speaking Canadian boys and girls from two nursery schools in Montreal. They ranged in age from three and a half to five and a half. The children were tested in their nursery schools in groups of approximately ten. The children watched "Sesame Street," as usual, but it was a "Sesame Street" in which scenes had been inserted showing whites and nonwhites—Asians and American Indians—playing together. Each insert lasted from two to three minutes and the investigators varied the number of such inserts the children observed. The total viewing time was 12 minutes. Immediately after viewing the inserts, each child was approached by one of ten interviewers and shown two sets of four photos taken from the inserts. One set contained white children, the other Asians and Indians. The children were then asked which group of kids they would like to meet at school the next day. In the control group that did not see the television inserts, 67 percent preferred to play

with whites. Of the children who had been exposed to the multiracial inserts, only 33 percent expressed a preference for the white children.

Gorn, Goldberg, and Kanungo (1976) accept that their study capitalized to some extent on novelty. Exposure to the nonwhites may have stimulated the youngsters' curiosity and interest. Nonetheless, the researchers concluded that even minimal television exposure produced clear short-term changes in attitude toward children of other racial groups.

Some investigators have conducted interviews with young children (four and a half to nine and a half years old) who watched a series of short excerpts of television material portraying male or female counterstereotypes (for example, an aggressive female police officer, a nurturant male nurse). The children revealed a spontaneous ability to relate what they had seen to their broad existing knowledge of sex-role stereotypes (for example, "that lady is like a man"). On retests, however, children who had seen these excerpts were less likely to endorse traditional stereotypes as often as children who had not seen the excerpts (Durkin, 1985a, 1985b, 1985c). Further research will likely yield new insights into this use of television.

ENVIRONMENTAL PSYCHOLOGY

Environmental psychology has emerged in recent years as a branch of social psychology concerned with the way in which the environment influences behavior. One of the main concerns of environmental psychologists has been the effects on people of living in physically dense and noisy cities. Here we consider the effects of both crowding and noise on behavior.

Urban Density and Crowding

A widespread belief is that overcrowding leads to psychological stress, poor physical and mental health, crime and delinquency, aggression, and family

The psychological effects of a noisy environment are still being investigated. Here on New York City's 5th Avenue, noise is inescapable.

disruption. Some of this belief derives from a study of animal crowding conducted by Calhoun (1962). Norway rats were enclosed in connecting pens and their population was allowed to increase to twice its normal size. The animals were observed for 16 months. Disruptions occurred in mating and maternal behavior; for example, nest building was neglected. Infant mortality and aborted pregnancies reached high levels. Abnormal sexual behavior became common. Some animals attacked others viciously, but a portion of the population manifested extreme passivity. Would the results be the same with people? Before we consider some of the research carried out with humans, we should deal with some definitions.

Crowding, or overcrowding, should not be considered synonymous with *density*. The amount of space available per person is the reference for density; crowding refers to the stress that high density produces (Stokols, 1972). Thus, crowding is a psychological state with motivational properties: the individual tries to cope with the negative experience that high density imposes.

DENSITY AND SOCIAL PATHOLOGY IN HUMANS. In a study carried out in Chicago, Galle, Gove, and McPherson (1972) investigated the relation between density and mortality, fertility, public assistance (a measure they considered indicative of inadequate care of the young), delinquency, and mental hospital admissions rate, all of which served as estimates of the behavioral pathologies found in Calhoun's rats (1962). Density, as measured by the number of inhabitants per acre, was related to all the measures of pathology. When even more sensitive measures of density were used, such as number of people per room, number of rooms per housing unit, number of housing units per structure, and number of structures per acre, even stronger relations appeared between density and the social pathology measures. Furthermore, the relationship held up even when statistical techniques were introduced to control for social class and ethnicity (see Table 18–1).

In a follow-up study, a large, stratified random sample of persons from Chicago were examined (Gove, Hughes, & Galle, 1979). The sample varied

TABLE 18–1
Correlation of Population Density (Persons per Room) with Social Pathologies

	Social Pathologies				
	Standard Mortality Ratio	General Fertility Rate	Public Assistance Rate	Juvenile Delinquency Rate	Admissions to Mental Hospitals
Correlation with density	.87	.86	.89	.92	.69
Correlation with density controlling for ethnicity and social class	.48	.37	.58	.50	.51

Source: Galle, Gove, & McPherson, 1972.

widely in terms of socioeconomic status, race, and density. By extensive interviewing, information was amassed on the number of persons per room, on subjective crowding, and on several behavioral measures. The number of persons per room was strongly associated with the subjective experience of crowding, and crowding was shown to be related to poor mental and physical health, inadequate child care, psychological and physical withdrawal, and poor social relationships in the home. The effect of crowding on behavior continued to be found when race, education, income, age, and sex had been controlled statistically.

LABORATORY STUDIES OF CROWDING. All the studies we have described in this section were correlational, for crowding was not experimentally manipulated. The researchers simply looked at the real world to see if density and pathology were positively related. However, we cannot conclude a cause-and-effect relationship based on a correlation because some unknown and unmeasured variable may have been present. Psychologists, therefore, have carried out experimental studies in the laboratory to try to disentangle the complexities of crowding in the real world and to answer the question of causality. Despite much experimental research, however, it appears that to date, at any rate, the negative effects of crowding have not been reliably demonstrated in the experimental laboratory (Freedman, 1979). This may have been due simply to the fact that ethical constraints restricted the degree of unpleasantness that the experimenters could create with their manipulations. Some researchers, however, believe that density just does not have the negative effects other researchers claim it does (Freedman, 1979).

There is no reason to believe that density always results in a negative human experience. Tokyo has one of the highest population densities in the world. In its subways men are employed to stand outside train doors and

High density is a feature of urban life in many cities of the world. High density doesn't necessarily lead to social pathologies, however. Tokyo, for example, has a very low crime rate.

pack in as many people as possible by sheer force. Some passengers wear coats of slippery material to ease their entrance. Yet crime rates are remarkably low in Tokyo. Determining the conditions under which density and crowding do cause social pathologies (and when they do not) remains a challenging issue for environmental psychologists.

Noise

Noise has often been studied as a major variable by environmental psychologists; it is especially important because so much of industrial life creates noise. Perhaps the most striking difference among rural, suburban, and urban communities is the almost constant din that pervades the city.

ADAPTATION TO MODERN NOISE. Anyone who moves from the city to the country or vice versa is usually aware immediately of the change in noise level. Country residents find it difficult to accustom themselves to the squeaks and roars of traffic in the city, and city folk in the countryside find they are kept awake by the quiet or the racket of crickets and the like.

One important finding from research on noise is that people adapt to it quickly as long as it is predictable (Glass and Singer, 1972). In experiments, subjects have been asked to proofread texts while they heard no noise, noise that recurred exactly once a minute, or noise that occurred randomly. Only when the noise was unpredictable did the proofreaders make errors.

The experimental research becomes more difficult to interpret, however, when louder noise is used or more complex tasks are involved or both conditions are present. Sometimes the noise proves distracting and impedes work; sometimes noise seems to enhance performance, perhaps by keeping the individual more alert. On still other occasions, noise seems to have no effects at all. Something of a controversy surrounds these data (Broadbent, 1978; Poulton, 1977, 1978).

EFFECTS OF LONG-TERM NOISE. Some researchers have argued that laboratory experiments cannot tell us much about the real world in this context because in a laboratory setting people are not exposed to noise over long periods. Sheldon Cohen and his colleagues have been studying the effects of persisting noise on elementary school students for several years, with very disturbing results. In one study, the subjects had lived at least four years in a large New York City apartment house built over a highway (Cohen, Glass, & Singer, 1973). The investigators assessed their reading achievements and their ability to discriminate among sounds. The lower the floor on which the children lived and, therefore, the closer to the noise, the poorer they did on both tests. The study suggests that constant noise may contribute directly or indirectly to poor mental functioning.

Later, Cohen and colleagues (1980) studied 271 Los Angeles children, some of whom attended schools near a busy airport, others schools in quiet neighborhoods. Care was taken to match the two groups of children on a number of dimensions including age, ethnicity, race, sex, and social class. The results showed that the children from the noisy schools had higher blood pressure, were more easily distracted, and gave up more quickly in trying to solve puzzles than the children from the quiet schools. One year later, in a follow-up study, the results were entirely replicable (Cohen et al.,

1981). Indeed, children who had been in the noisy classrooms earlier but who had shifted to quieter ones showed no significant improvement. One interpretation of this finding is that harmful effects of early exposure to noise may be long-lasting. Continuing research on the effects of noise, as on crowding and other environmental stressors, is an important and potentially extremely useful direction for environmental psychologists to pursue.

INDUSTRIAL/ORGANIZATIONAL PSYCHOLOGY

Industrial/organizational psychologists, or I/O psychologists, as they are called, work for businesses, labor organizations, or governments or teach at universities as members of psychology or business departments. Traditionally the main concern of industrial/organizational psychology has been to identify ways to make a business or industry more efficient and effective. I/O psychology began with time-motion studies in which workers' movements were carefully analyzed during the work day for speed and efficiency. From there, the field expanded to consider the great range of variables that influence worker productivity and business success. The three major areas of concern among I/O psychologists are the creation and operation of organizations (typically business organizations), the selection and training of personnel and staff, and job performance and productivity.

Organizational Behavior

Organizational behavior includes the policies and procedures of managers, the way managers interact with workers, the tasks of jobs, and the structure of organizations. Of course, no one organizational arrangement is best suited for all businesses, all jobs, and all individuals. The goal of I/O psychology is to help a company achieve its goals by pointing out possible improvements in the way workers and managers cooperate.

One of the best-studied organizational behaviors is leadership or supervisory capability. Studies conducted by researchers at Michigan State and Ohio State universities more than 25 years ago provide the foundation of our modern understanding of leadership and supervision. In these studies, carried out in different industries, government agencies, hospitals, and volunteer organizations, leaders and supervisors were examined according to two dimensions, "employee-centered" and "job-centered." Employee-centered supervisors were those who were most concerned with their workers' problems. They were supportive of the workers and friendly, they helped instill in the employees a sense of pride, and personally made sure that the workers met their quotas. Job-centered supervisors, on the other hand, tended to focus on work production more directly, ignoring the human relations involved. The studies indicated that employee-centered supervisors and leaders were more effective and more likely to increase production (Likert, 1961).

Employee-centered and job-centered approaches are not necessarily mutually exclusive. Supervisors and leaders who are interested in their employees in a friendly and personal sense and also emphasize job production are also likely to be successful (Anastasi, 1979). Of course, studies of this kind are correlational, and it is difficult to establish a cause-and-effect rela-

Industrial/organization psychologists aim to increase job performance and productivity.

tionship between a supervisor's style and his or her employees' performance. For example, if production falls significantly, supervisors may become exceptionally concerned about productivity and therefore become job-centered. This, of course, is different from saying that job-centered supervisors cause lower production. On the whole, however, current research supports the finding that employee-centered supervisors are more successful. Many organizations have set up training programs to teach managers how to get along with others. Such behavior is not necessarily easily taught. Most employee-centered managers are such because of their personalities prior to becoming managers (Anastasi, 1979).

Personnel Selection

The personnel selected to run an organization may determine the organization's success or failure. I/O psychologists have been instrumental in developing valid personnel selection techniques and in devising the best ways for organizations to select successful employees.

The first important step in developing a personnel classification and selection system is job analysis. Before selecting someone for a job, an organization must know which tasks are required for a job and what those tasks entail. They must also identify the intellectual and personality traits required for the job. Perhaps the best way to give you a flavor of job analysis in personnel selection, the way an I/O psychologist would see it, is to have you do this kind of analysis yourself. Let's imagine that you are an I/O psychologist who has been called in by the Air Force to help select the best fighter pilots from hundreds of applicants.

It costs a tremendous amount of money to train a fighter pilot. It seems that everybody in the Air Force wants to be one, although few actually have the necessary skills. Let's assume that you have 1,000 applicants. Is there some way to choose the best 100? After carefully analyzing the job requirements, you may delineate certain traits and skills that are needed: excellent eye-hand coordination, intelligence, courage, loyalty, good vision, rapid orientation, good physical condition, and a host of other abilities. To do proper personnel selection, you then want to develop assessment devices that would allow you to measure the personal characteristics identified in the job analysis.

There are many kinds of tests to measure the traits you've selected. One method is to develop a test that cannot be passed but that applicants feel they must pass in order to be admitted. As each applicant starts to fail at the impossible task, you can watch how this frustration affects the test-taker. Since good jet pilots need to stay cool and not panic, those who become extremely agitated in their frustration may be less suitable for the job. Other tests might measure eyesight, balance, or ability to maintain a sense of direction. Such a battery of tests will likely yield a range of scores from very high to very low and provide a basis for selecting the top 100 applicants.

To be effective, personnel tests should be both valid and reliable. Each test must measure the skill it claims to measure, and if a candidate took the test over again, he or she should get the same or a close score each time. Any of the tests that fails to predict fairly well can be eliminated, while those that are good predictors can be retained. In this way, you will eventually build a valid test for fighter pilot selection.

Air Force pilots may seem an exotic example, but there are hundreds of such personnel selection tests that show a certain amount of validity—that is, a high score on the test indicates that the applicant is likely to do well in a job that requires the skills measured by the test.

Of course, no test is perfect. Personnel may be selected who shouldn't have been, and some may be turned away who should have been selected. The point is that a valid test will make an accurate selection most of the time. As you might imagine, such a selection device can be of great benefit to any organization.

Motivation and Performance

The two most valuable techniques for increasing employees' motivation to produce are behavior modification and goal setting (Staw, 1984). Behavior-modification techniques (see Chapter 6) include the use of reinforcers for appropriate behavior. Workers who produce are given houses, promotions, better offices, more prestigious titles, or verbal praise in an effort to maintain and reinforce their successful behavior within the corporation (Landy, 1985). Much research has shown that workers perform better if they have specific goals to aim for than if they are simply told, "Do your best." Knowing the exact goal required seems to help create within each worker an internal structure or organization for achieving that end. This simple technique is one of the most powerful ways to increase worker motivation.

One form of motivation that has been extensively researched is job commitment (Coombs, 1979). A worker is committed to an occupation to the extent that he or she feels involved, loyal, and able to identify with the company. Commitment increases when workers have a high need to achieve and are given some degree of responsibility in the firm (Landy, 1985). Commitment is also enhanced by the company's success and by symbols and activities that involve identification. Japanese firms have traditionally done an excellent job in creating such commitment in their workers, and some American companies have borrowed their techniques (Peters & Austin, 1985).

Does job satisfaction lead to greater worker productivity? Early studies found a poor relation between job satisfaction and productivity. Vroom (1964), for example, reported a median correlation of only $+.14$ from the studies he reviewed. This remains the general conclusion of researchers in this area (Iaffaldano & Muchinsky, 1985). Job satisfaction does, however, seem to play a role in absenteeism. It is often difficult to separate the influence of job satisfaction on absenteeism from all the other variables, but because of one very interesting field study, we know that it probably makes a difference. The study concerned salaried employees who were working for the Sears Roebuck Company in Chicago. When a snowstorm crippled the city, the Sears employees were told they didn't need to come to work unless they wanted to. It turned out that those in the study who reported highest job satisfaction were also many of the same people who voluntarily reported to work. This study shows that in situations in which attendance is mostly voluntary, high job satisfaction is a good indicator of low absenteeism (Smith, 1977).

I/O psychology is a growing area. For instance, many I/O psychologists are now working to see if managerial techniques that have been so effective in Japan and other countries are culturally transferable to the United States (Ouchi, 1981). Such cultural applications are relatively new to American I/O psychology because, for the first time, Americans are seeing other nations with higher productivity than their own.

Research has shown that job commitment increases when an employee feels involved, loyal, and able to identify with the company. Many firms have fostered this commitment by providing job security, identification with the company, and sensitivity toward their employees.

SUMMARY

1. Social psychology is increasingly being used to study social issues. For example, how can we better understand aggression and prejudice? What are the origins of altruism and the tendency to care for others? What are the effects of television on the attitudes and behavior of viewers? How is social psychological knowledge applied in environmental psychology and industrial/organizational (I/O) psychology?

2. Aggression—behavior intended to harm—is a pervasive characteristic of human society, and many theorists have addressed the issue. Biological theories of aggression emphasize an innate tendency for humans to be aggressive. Among the most influential of the biological theories is the innate drive hypothesis of Sigmund Freud. The more modern ethological and sociobiological theories, such as the ones associated with Konrad Lorenz and Edward O. Wilson, emphasize the adaptive value and evolutionary origins of the behavior.

3. The frustration-aggression hypothesis of Dollard and Miller (original version) and Leonard Berkowitz (revised version) proposes a biological tendency for frustration to create a drive to aggression, first by making the person angry.

4. Social learning theories of aggression emphasize the importance of reinforcement and observational learning in influencing the norms that govern aggressive behavior. The work of Albert Bandura has been particularly significant in this regard.

5. Biological theories and social learning theories can often be viewed as complementary rather than as opposing. Thus social learning can be thought of as modifying, perhaps quite markedly, an underlying disposition. Sometimes the two approaches offer conflicting views of how to deal with aggression. For example, the Freudian view of catharsis is to encourage expressions of the aggressive drive to limit the drive's buildup. Social learning theorists, however, suggest that encouraging expressions of aggression will increase, not decrease, aggression. The research evidence to date favors the social learning perspective.

6. Altruism constitutes a positive side to human nature. Humans engage in helpful, cooperative, empathic, loving, and considerate behavior toward each other. Altruistic behavior is found as early as the first two years of childhood and in many aspects of daily life.

7. Sociobiological theories of altruism emphasize that it can be found in many other animal species beside humans and that self-sacrifice is a way to propagate one's own genes, so long as the sacrifice benefits others who share the genes.

8. Social learning theorists stress the importance of learning altruistic norms from observation of others. Many different types of investigation, including laboratory experiments and naturalistic studies of the family, suggest the importance of observational learning in the transmission of such norms.

9. Whether we display altruism in any particular situation depends on many factors, including the number of other people present and whether circumstances have led us to be in a good or a bad mood. Thus, acts of altruism arise from external circumstances as well as from internal dispositions.

10. Prejudice is a negative attitude toward an individual because of his or her membership in a particular group. Many psychologists believe that prejudiced attitudes are learned—particularly during childhood and adolescence or as a result of group membership—although such attitudes can be modified throughout life.

11. If social learning theorists are correct in assuming that one of the ways in which people learn norms of appropriate behavior is by observing others, then it follows that people should learn a great deal from viewing others on television. Research has demonstrated that this is the case. If antisocial behavior and uncontrolled aggression are shown, then these actions are what viewers take to be the norm. If, on the other hand, altruistic helping and kindness make up the content of television programming, then these may be learned by viewers as appropriate, normative behaviors.

12. Environmental psychology is concerned with the way in which the environment influences behavior. Evidence has shown that people who live in big cities demonstrate a greater number of social pathologies than people who live in small towns. Other researchers have suggested that noise can have detrimental effects on work performance.

13. Industrial/organizational psychologists work for businesses, organizations, or governments or teach at universities. Their main concern has been to

improve the functioning of business and industry and to investigate ways to make an organization efficient and effective. The three major areas of concern for I/O psychologists are the creation and operation of organizations, the selection and training of personnel, and job performance and productivity.

SUGGESTED READINGS

Baron, R. A. (1983). *Behavior in organizations.* Boston: Allyn and Bacon.

> A comprehensive and up-to-date introduction to the field of organizational behavior. It describes how basic psychological principles such as learning, personality, perception, attitudes, and motivation are relevant to behavior in the organizational setting.

Baron, R. A., & Byrne, D. (1987). *Social psychology: Understanding human interaction* (5th ed.). Boston: Allyn and Bacon.

> A comprehensive introduction to the field written by two leading social psychologists.

Liebert, R. M., Sprafkin, J. N., & Davidson, E. S. (1982). *The early window: Effects of television on children and youth* (2nd ed.). New York: Pergamon.

> Covers the research on whether TV instigates antisocial behavior in children; discusses TV portrayals of minorities and women; considers the role of TV commercials in influencing behavior; and is generally one of the most comprehensive and compelling texts ever published on the effects of television (especially on children).

Skinner, B. F. (1978). *Reflections on behaviorism and society.* Englewood Cliffs, N.J.: Prentice-Hall.

> Essays by one of the most influential psychologists of the twentieth century deal with the application of behavioral science to social issues and raise challenging thoughts on the control of human behavior.

Staub, E., Bar-Tal, D., Karylowski, J., Reykowski, J. (Eds.) (1984). *Development and maintenance of prosocial behavior: International perspectives on positive morality.* New York: Plenum.

> This collection of chapters by researchers in the field of prosocial behavior discusses the ways in which altruism develops, the effects of various circumstances surrounding the helping incident, and the relationship of individual characteristics to helping behavior.

Trivers, R. (1985). *Social evolution.* Menlo Park, CA: Benjamin Cummings.

> Beautifully illustrated, this book introduces the field of sociobiology. The issues of altruism, aggression, kin-selection, sex, and reproductive strategy are developed within the framework of modern evolutionary biology by one of the pivotal figures in the field.

APPENDIX

An Introduction to Statistics

Statistical thinking will one day be as necessary for efficient citizenship as the ability to read and write.

H. G. Wells

WE HAVE SEVERAL GOALS IN WRITING THIS APPENDIX. FIRST, WE hope to show that the study of statistics has important implications for your knowledge and evaluation of psychological research. Statistical reasoning is an essential part of psychological research, and almost all research reports in psychology contain some statistics. Second, we hope to illustrate, through examples, that you already know some things about statistics, and it is worth your while to learn more. Third, we hope to convince you that studying statistics can be, if not fun, at least relatively painless.

You often encounter statistics in your daily life, for example, when you hear that a public opinion poll shows one candidate leading another by 50 to 42 percent, with 8 percent undecided. In other instances you might read about the median annual income for people of different occupations; that the Consumer Price Index went up 12 percent last year; or that a weather forecaster predicts a 60 percent chance of rain tomorrow. The probability-of-rain figure is particularly interesting. The forecaster is saying that meteorologists, with all their instruments, charts, and knowledge of weather patterns, cannot forecast tomorrow's weather with certainty. Psychologists are usually in a similar situation; they cannot predict behavior with certainty, but only with some probability.

There are two branches of statistics: descriptive statistics and inferential statistics, which we will consider in turn. *Descriptive statistics* summarize or describe a set of scores, whereas *inferential statistics* help researchers to decide what conclusions (or inferences) to draw from the scores.

DESCRIPTIVE STATISTICS

Psychologists do research to discover the principles underlying behavior. Typically, they will devise a hypothesis to account for some behavior and then try to collect evidence that will bear on the truth or falsity of the hypothesis. The evidence is usually in the form of measures of the behavior. In doing the research, investigators may collect hundreds, or even thousands, of observations. How are they to make sense of them? Descriptive statistics are useful for summarizing and describing a great amount of *data,* or observations. They are used to describe the main features of the observations that have been collected.

To understand how statistics can be useful, let us consider results that might be obtained from an experimental situation of interest to social psychologists called the *bystander intervention* experiment. You have probably read newspaper accounts in which numerous people, usually in large cities, witness a robbery or murder without intervening to help the victim. Social psychologists became interested in this phenomenon and sought to discover what caused it. Are people callous? Don't they care? (Research on bystander intervention is described in Chapter 18.) After analyzing a number of cases, two social psychologists came up with a paradoxical idea: a person is less likely to assist in a crisis the more other people are present in the situation (Darley and Latané, 1968). This hypothesis seems implausible because one might expect that with other people present, a person would be more likely to intervene because additional help could be expected. However, Darley and Latané reasoned that any individual person might actually be less likely to give aid because he or she would feel less responsible when in a group. The feeling of responsibility for acting is weak when many others are present. (If a professor asks a question in a class of 100, you would feel less pressure to volunteer an answer than if only three people were present.)

One way to test this *diffusion of responsibility* hypothesis is to set up a laboratory experiment testing individuals in which an emergency occurs. In one condition people should think they are alone; in the other condition they should think three others are present. Participants should be randomly assigned to one condition or the other. During the course of the experiment an accident would occur to the experimenter, who is out of sight in the other room. For example, she might be shocked, cry out in pain, and fall on the floor with a loud thud. Let us assume that in this situation most participants would come to the aid of the victim. The test of the hypothesis is that people should take longer to come to the experimenter's aid when they think three other people are present than when they think they are alone.

The independent variable, or the factor manipulated, is the number of bystanders besides the subject who are believed to witness the crisis (zero or three). The dependent variable, or what is measured, is the amount of time before the subjects begin helping. Variables to be controlled are the time of day during testing, the type of crisis, the experimenter, and so forth. All of the control variables should be the same for the two conditions. Let us suppose that 15 people are tested in each condition (Alone and Three Bystanders) and that the numbers in Table A–1 represent the amount of time the people take to begin to help.

As you can see by reading through the numbers in the two conditions, the time elapsed before helping seems to be greater for people in the Three

Hypothetical time measures indicating how long subjects might take to respond in two conditions of a bystander intervention experiment. Thirty people would have been randomly assigned to the two groups, so each group would have 15 people.

TABLE A–1
Response Times

	Alone		Three Bystanders	
Subject	Time to Respond (in seconds)	Subject	Time to Respond (in seconds)	
Subject 1	30	Subject 1	45	
Subject 2	42	Subject 2	37	
Subject 3	20	Subject 3	55	
Subject 4	58	Subject 4	75	
Subject 5	45	Subject 5	50	
Subject 6	102	Subject 6	90	
Subject 7	40	Subject 7	125	
Subject 8	24	Subject 8	81	
Subject 9	55	Subject 9	71	
Subject 10	31	Subject 10	60	
Subject 11	44	Subject 11	85	
Subject 12	68	Subject 12	70	
Subject 13	38	Subject 13	103	
Subject 14	21	Subject 14	54	
Subject 15	38	Subject 15	90	
Total (ΣX)	656	Total (ΣX)	1091	
Mean ($\overline{X}$)	43.73	Mean ($\overline{X}$)	72.73	

Bystander condition than for those in the Alone condition. But precisely how much did the two conditions affect the time it took subjects to respond? Two primary types of descriptive statistics help researchers at this point by providing convenient summaries of the scores. *Measures of central tendency* locate the center of a set of scores. *Measures of dispersion* show how scores are spread out (or dispersed) from their center.

Measures of Central Tendency

A group of scores can be analyzed by several measures of *central tendency,* but the one most frequently used is the mean. (You know this term as the average score, but often the term *average* is used for any measure of central tendency, so the term *mean* is preferred.) The **mean** is the total of all the scores divided by the number of scores. In the Alone condition the total of the scores of all subjects is 656 seconds. Since there are 15 scores, the mean is 656 ÷ 15, or 43.73 seconds. The totals of the times for the 15 people tested in each condition are listed in Table A–1 along with the mean for the condition. As you can see, the mean scores of the two conditions differ by almost 30 seconds. The mean time that elapsed before a person helped in the Alone condition was 43.73 seconds, while the comparable figure for the Three Bystanders condition was 72.73 seconds.

The mean is the measure of central tendency that is almost always given in reports of experiments, but in some cases another common measure of central tendency is used. The **median** is the middle score in the set of scores; half the scores lie above the median score and half below it. The median of the scores in the Alone condition is 40 seconds, and in the Three Bystanders condition it is 71 seconds. Finding the median is easy: put the scores in order from highest to lowest and count down through half of them. When there is an odd number of scores, it is the middlemost score. When there is an even number of scores, the median is simply the mean of the two scores nearest the middle. If there were 20 scores and the tenth score was 30 and the eleventh score was 32, then the median would be 31.

Why is the median ever used in place of the mean? The primary reason is that the median is less sensitive than the mean to extreme scores, and sometimes this can be desirable. Suppose that one person tested in the Alone condition of the hypothetical experiment never helped in the crisis but just sat there for 30 minutes until the experimenter gave permission to leave. How would the experimenter record that person's time? One way would be to enter the maximum time allowed, in this case 30 minutes, or 1,800 seconds. If the uncooperative person was subject 6 of the Alone condition in Table A–1, and 1,800 seconds replaced the 102 seconds there, the mean of the scores in the Alone condition would be 156.93 seconds instead of 43.73 seconds. This would indicate to someone who knew only the mean scores of the two conditions that people were more than twice as slow in the Alone condition as in the Three Bystanders condition. Obviously there is something wrong with this conclusion, since it is based almost completely on the score of only one person who reacted atypically. One extreme score is distorting the results of the experiment.

In cases when one score or a few scores are extreme, the median often provides a more useful measure of central tendency than does the mean. In fact, in this example the median will be the same—40 seconds—in the Alone condition, whether the sixth subject helped after 102 seconds or after 1,800 seconds. Since it is the middlemost score, the median is not sensitive to great extremes in the set of scores. Changing the most extreme score will not change the median at all. So in cases where one quite deviant score causes the mean to give an unrepresentative measure of the central tendency, the median should be used instead.

The third measure of central tendency is the *mode,* which is simply the most frequent score in a set of scores. In the Alone condition the mode would be 38 seconds, while in the Three Bystanders condition it would be 90 seconds. These are the only scores in each set of figures that appear more than once. The mode is rarely used as a measure of central tendency because it can be misleading, especially when there are only a few scores in a set. For example, if a student's five test scores were 63, 55, 84, 40, and 84, the mode would be 84. Obviously, this measure of central tendency when used as the average would misrepresent the student's performance. The mean score (65.2) better reflects the central tendency in this case. (What would be the median in this set?)

Measures of Dispersion

Measures of central tendency indicate the center of a group of scores, while *measures of dispersion,* or variability, indicate the spread of the scores about that center. As their names imply, measures of central tendency indicate the point that tends to be in the center of a distribution of scores, while measures of dispersion indicate how scores spread away (disperse, as a crowd might disperse) from this center point. The simplest measure of dispersion is the *range,* which is the difference between the highest and the lowest scores in the set of scores. For the Alone condition in our hypothetical experiment, the range is $102 - 20$, or 82 seconds. The range in the Three Bystanders condition is $125 - 37$, or 88 seconds. Since the range is based solely on the most extreme scores in the group, it is rarely used, because only one extreme score can greatly affect the range. The range shows how much difference there is between the highest and lowest scores, but it does not tell how much most scores vary from one another.

The most common descriptive statistic of variability is the *standard deviation,* which indicates the size of the average differences of individual scores from the mean. The standard deviation is more difficult to compute than the range, but it has mathematical properties that make it more useful. The standard deviation for a sample of scores is obtained by first taking the difference of each score from the mean and squaring it. Second, these squared values are added together and divided by the number of scores minus one. Finally, the square root of this value is taken. This procedure can be represented by a simple formula:

$$s = \sqrt{\frac{\text{Sum of } d^2}{n - 1}}.$$

TABLE A–2
Computation of Standard Deviations for the Bystander Intervention Experiment

		Alone					Three Bystanders		
Subject	Time	Mean	d	d^2	Subject	Time	Mean	d	d^2
1	30	43.73	−13.73	188.51	1	45	72.73	−27.73	768.95
2	42	43.73	−1.73	2.99	2	37	72.73	−35.73	1276.63
3	20	43.73	−23.73	563.11	3	55	72.73	−17.73	314.35
4	58	43.73	14.27	203.63	4	75	72.73	2.27	5.15
5	45	43.73	1.27	1.61	5	50	72.73	−22.73	516.65
6	102	43.73	58.27	3395.39	6	90	72.73	17.27	298.25
7	40	43.73	−3.73	13.91	7	125	72.73	52.27	2732.15
8	24	43.73	−19.73	389.27	8	81	72.73	8.27	68.39
9	55	43.73	11.27	127.01	9	71	72.73	−1.73	2.99
10	31	43.73	−12.73	162.05	10	60	72.73	−12.73	162.05
11	44	43.73	0.27	0.07	11	85	72.73	12.27	150.55
12	68	43.73	24.27	589.03	12	70	72.73	−2.73	7.45
13	38	43.73	−5.73	32.83	13	103	72.73	30.27	916.27
14	21	43.73	−22.73	516.65	14	54	72.73	−18.73	350.81
15	38	43.73	−5.73	32.83	15	90	72.73	17.27	298.25

sum of $d^2 = 6{,}218.89$ sum of $d^2 = 7{,}868.89$

$$s = \sqrt{\frac{6{,}218.89}{14}} \qquad\qquad\qquad s = \sqrt{\frac{7{,}868.89}{14}}$$

$$s = \sqrt{444.21} \qquad\qquad\qquad\qquad s = \sqrt{562.06}$$

$$s = 21.08 \qquad\qquad\qquad\qquad\quad s = 23.71$$

$$s = \sqrt{\frac{\text{sum of } d^2}{n - 1}}$$

where s is the standard deviation
d is the difference between each score and the mean
n is the number of scores

In this formula, *s* stands for the standard deviation, *d* stands for the difference between each score and the mean, and *n* stands for the number of scores in the set. Table A–2 shows the computations for finding the standard deviations of the scores in Table A–1. The standard deviation in the Alone condition is 21.08 seconds, and in the Three Bystanders condition it is 23.71. In actual practice, there are simpler formulas for obtaining the standard deviation than the one shown in Table A–2, but the one we have chosen provides a better understanding of the concept of the standard deviation. With many hand calculators you can automatically obtain the mean and standard deviation when you punch in a series of scores.

Frequency Distributions

In the bystander intervention example, the dispersion of scores about the mean is roughly the same for the two conditions. But this is not always the case. Consider the two graphs in Figure A–1. These graphs depict *frequency distributions,* because they show the number (frequency) of people scoring at different levels for a group of scores. They show the distribution of the scores, or how scores pile up at different points, or spread out. The frequency distributions in Figure A–1 are the hypothetical scores of two groups of entering university students on the verbal part of the Scholastic Aptitude Test (SAT) taken by U.S. high school students. In both cases the mean of the distribution is just below 500, but in one case (represented in blue) there is not much spread of the scores around the mean. Students at this school

FIGURE A–1
Hypothetical Verbal SAT Scores for Students at Two Universities

At one school (represented in blue) the students come from a much narrower range in terms of ability than at the other school (represented in black). The mean score of the entering students would be the same in the two cases, but the standard deviations would differ considerably.

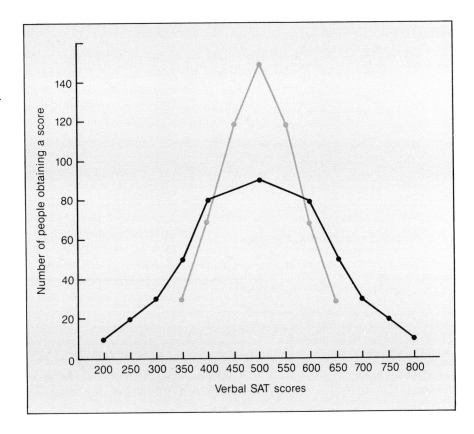

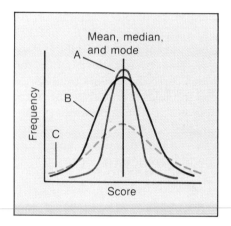

FIGURE A–2
Symmetrical Distributions

Three examples of symmetrical curves that differ in variability. C has the greatest variability and A the least. In these symmetrical distributions, the mean, median, and mode all fall at the same point. B is a normal curve.

would come from a rather narrow range in terms of their test scores. On the other hand, students at the other college (in black) have much more variable SAT scores, even though the mean is the same. In this case the scores are dispersed more greatly around the mean. The standard deviation of the students' scores would be much greater in the second case than the first. This is what a large standard deviation reveals; the scores are distributed quite widely about the mean. This knowledge is important. A professor at the college with students who vary widely in SAT scores would know to adopt teaching methods for a wide range of intellectual abilities.

The Normal Curve

The graphs of the hypothetical SAT scores in Figure A–1 show that the scores pile up in the middle but tail off toward the extremes (tails) of the distribution of scores. Although these numbers were hypothetical, this sort of distribution has a property that occurs for most measures of behavior: that is, for most phenomena that are measured, scores cluster in the center of the distribution. This commonly found shape of behavioral measures is called the *normal curve,* an example of which is presented in Figure A–2 (the curve labeled B). When put on a graph, psychological data typically are most numerous in the middle of the set of scores; they decline in frequency with distance from the middle in a symmetrical way. A score ten points below the center of the distribution occurs about as frequently as a score ten points above the center.

The three curves shown in Figure A–2 are all symmetrical. In such distributions of scores the mean, median, and mode of the distribution all fall at the same point or score. Curves with the same mean, median, and mode may differ in their variability, as do the curves in Figure A–2. The tall, thin curve labeled A would have a smaller standard deviation than the other two. Similarly, the broad, flat curve would have a greater standard deviation than the other two.

The normal curve (labeled B in Figure A–2) has a very useful property. It turns out that a specific proportion of scores falls under each part of the normal curve. This feature is illustrated in Figure A–3. For normal curves, about 68 percent of the scores fall within one standard deviation of the mean score (34 percent on each side). Similarly, almost 96 percent of the scores are contained within two standard deviations of the mean, while 99.74 percent of all the scores fall within three standard deviations. These properties are true of all normal curves. This feature allows test-givers to figure an individual's relative rank based on his or her score and the mean and standard deviation of the distribution of scores. For example, the Scholastic Aptitude Test was originally devised to have a mean score of 500 and a standard deviation of 100. So 68 percent of all of the test-takers score between 400 and 600; 96 percent score between 300 and 700; and almost everyone scores between 200 and 800. If you know your own score, you can roughly figure out what *percentile* you are in (that is, what percentage of people scored lower than you did). If your score was 400, about 16 percent of the other students scored worse and 84 percent better. You would be in about the 16th percentile. If your score was 700, then you scored higher than all but about 2 percent of the people taking the test! You would be in the 98th percentile. (Actually these figures are no longer quite accurate, since

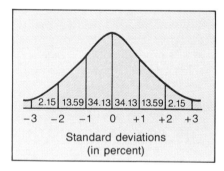

FIGURE A–3
The Normal Curve

Proportions of scores in specific areas under the normal curve. About 68 percent of the scores fall within ±1 standard deviation of the mean, 96 percent within ±2 standard deviations, and almost all within ±3 standard deviations.

the mean scores on the verbal and quantitative parts of the SAT have dropped from 500 over the years. But this example serves as a good approximation to introduce the useful properties of the normal curve.)

CORRELATION AND PREDICTION

As we discussed in the first chapter, in one type of research psychologists employ the correlational approach. Correlational research attempts to determine whether or not two variables are related. Is smoking related to lung cancer? Is IQ related to grades in high school? Are sons' heights related to their fathers' heights? Any two variables can be correlated. The amount of ice cream consumed in every country in the world can be correlated with the incidence of malaria in each country. Although the result may not tell much about either variable, the calculations for computing correlations can be carried out on any two sets of scores.

Consider, for example, the question of whether or not sons' heights are related to their fathers' heights. After compiling the heights of 1,000 20-year-old men and the heights of their fathers, you could read down the list and try to determine if tall fathers tend to have tall sons and short fathers tend to have short sons. Unfortunately, reading through this list would not be an easy way to see if there is a relation between the heights. It would be much easier to construct a *scattergram* by putting the fathers' and sons' heights in a single graph. In a scattergram one variable is represented on the *y*-axis, the other is placed on the *x*-axis, and a point is placed in the graph for each pair of scores.

A scattergram with the heights of 1,078 sons and their fathers is plotted in Figure A–4. To enter a score in the scattergram you would find the height of the son on the *y*-axis (the vertical one), then the height of the father on the *x*-axis (the horizontal one), and place a point there. So if a son is 66 inches tall and his father is 68 inches tall, one point will be entered in the graph for this pair.

The Correlation Coefficient

It is obvious in Figure A–4 that as fathers' heights increase, so do their sons'. As statisticians would say, there is a *positive association*, or *positive correlation*, between the two measures of height. A statistical calculation known as the *correlation coefficient* is used to measure more precisely the relation between two variables. The computational details that go into this measure are beyond the scope of this appendix, but the values of the measure can range from -1.00 through 0 to $+1.00$. If two scores are completely unrelated, so that as one measure changes the other changes only haphazardly, there is a zero correlation between them. For example, there is probably a zero correlation between weight and intelligence in adults. If the intelligence of people of different weights were measured by having them take IQ tests, no relation probably would be found between the two factors. The scores would then look like those in the top left panel of Figure A–5, which shows two scores that have a zero correlation.

The positive correlation between fathers' and sons' heights that is shown in Figure A–4 is not a perfect correlation. Positive correlations can vary from 0 to $+1.00$, where $+1.00$ is a perfect positive correlation. If the

FIGURE A–4
Heights of Fathers and Sons

A scatter diagram (or scattergram) plots the heights of 1,078 fathers and their sons. Each point represents a father-son pair. If sons always grew to the heights of their fathers, then all the points would fall along the straight line. This would indicate a correlation of +1.00. But most points fall off the line, indicating how much the sons' heights differ from their fathers'.

Source: Freedman, Pisani, & Purves, 1978.

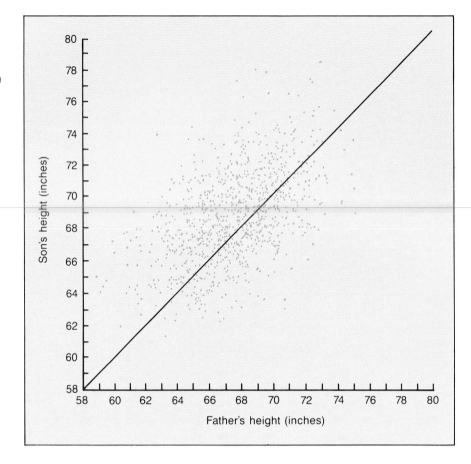

correlation is perfect, then sons' heights would always be directly related to the heights of their fathers. The diagonal line represents a perfect positive correlation in Figure A–4. If all the scores fell on this line, the correlation between the two measures would be +1.00. Obviously, the positive correlation between fathers' and sons' heights is far from perfect. There are few perfect positive correlations in nature, and most positive correlations measured in psychology are in the range of +.30 to +.80. Two panels on the left-hand side of Figure A–5 show positive correlations of different magnitudes.

The three other panels in Figure A–5 show negative correlations. A negative correlation occurs when increases in one measure are associated with decreases in the other measure. A hypothetical example would be if tall fathers tended to have short sons, the reverse of the actual case. Negative correlations vary between 0 and −1.00. An example of a negative correlation is the negative association between the education of parents and the number of children they have. Parents with more education tend to have fewer children. However, the correlation is not great, about −.30.

Prediction

How are correlations useful? One important use is in making predictions. If we know a father's height and we want to predict how tall his son will be

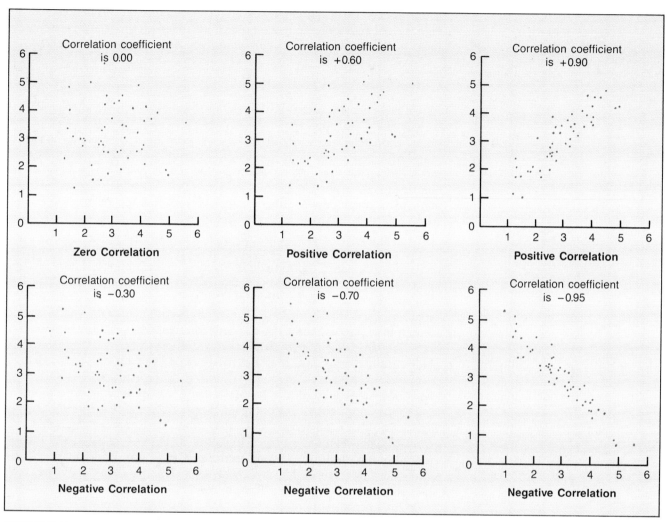

FIGURE A–5
Varying Correlation Coefficients

These scattergrams represent six different correlation coefficients. A zero correlation (upper left) indicates no relation between the two variables; the points are strewn about randomly. Positive correlations (two upper-right graphs) tend to run from the lower left to upper right of the graph. As one variable increases, so does the other. Negative correlations (the three graphs in the bottom row) run from the upper left to lower right. As one variable increases, the other decreases.

when the son is grown, we could base the prediction on the correlation between the two variables. Looking at Figure A–4, we could say with some confidence that if the father were 72 inches tall the son would be between 68 and 74 inches tall. *The nearer the correlation coefficient is to 1, the more nearly certain a researcher can be in making a prediction.* If all the points in Figure A–4 fell on the straight line so that the correlation between heights of fathers and sons were +1.00, then we could predict a son's height precisely from knowing his father's. If all the points fell on this line, if the father were 72 inches tall, we could predict with certainty that the son would be 72 inches tall, too. Even if each son were exactly 2 inches taller than his father, the correlation coefficient would be a perfect +1.00, and prediction would be completely accurate. Alas, life is hardly ever so precise as in these hypothetical cases.

Predictions can also be made, of course, from negative correlations, but in this case as one score increases the other score decreases. The closer the negative correlation is to −1.00, the more confident would be the prediction. You can see how this case is exactly comparable to that of predictability from positive correlations by examining the graphs on the bottom half of Figure A–5. If you had to make predictions based on the relations shown in these panels, in which prediction would you have the most confidence?

Correlation and Causation

As we have shown, knowing the relationship between two variables allows us to make predictions about one variable when we know the value of the other, especially when the association between the two variables is great. However, even a very high correlation between two variables does not permit a conclusion that one caused the other. *Correlation does not imply causation.* If fathers' and sons' heights are correlated, this fact by itself does not allow us to conclude that fathers' heights cause the sons' heights, any more than sons' heights cause fathers' heights. (Of course, other evidence links fathers' and sons' heights. They share similar genes.)

A great number of variables may be correlated. Since 1950 the number of people graduating from medical school and the amount of alcohol consumed in the United States have increased yearly. There is a high positive correlation between these variables. Did the increased number of doctors cause people to drink more? Of course not. Both trends are due to other factors; they just happen to be strongly correlated. Whenever a high correlation is reported in a study, caution is in order. Observers can never conclude simply on this basis that the change in one variable caused the change in another variable.

Many medical studies of factors causing disease begin with the observation of a correlation. For example, concern about the bad effects of smoking on health began during the 1950s when a researcher computed the correlation between the average number of cigarettes consumed and the incidence of lung cancer in eleven countries (Doll, 1955). He found a correlation of +.70 between the two measures. Thus a suspicion arose that smoking causes lung cancer. But one cannot conclude that smoking does cause lung cancer only on the basis of this correlation. Some hereditary defect distributed differently across populations may make people want to smoke and also may make them get lung cancer. Or it could be that smoking occurs only in more developed countries and that pollution in more developed countries causes lung cancer. In other words, the correlation between smoking and lung cancer could be due to other factors, just like the accidental correlation between the number of new doctors and the amount of alcohol consumed. Of course, in the case of smoking most medical researchers agree with the conclusion that smoking causes lung cancer on the basis of other evidence. But it is worth pointing out that the positive correlation between smoking and cancer is not the only information that leads to this conclusion.

To gain better evidence about the effect of one factor on another, it is necessary to conduct an experiment in which the factor can be manipulated directly in a controlled manner, as described in Chapter 1. To review, in an experiment the independent variable is the one that is manipulated, the dependent variable is the one that is measured, and control variables are factors that are held constant. For example, to study the effects of the number of people in a group (the independent variable) on how quickly bystanders intervene in a crisis, researchers could just watch groups of different sizes and see if a person in a large group is less likely to intervene than one in a small group. This is the correlational approach. The researcher would be looking for a negative correlation: the more people in the group, the less likely the person is to intervene. But since other factors are uncontrolled in correlational studies, something else about the group besides its size might actually cause differences in giving help. We would find much more trustworthy information by conducting an experiment and randomly assigning people to small or large groups while holding all other factors constant, as in our hypothetical example. We will return to the bystander intervention experiment now to illustrate how another branch of statistics is used to draw conclusions.

INFERENTIAL STATISTICS

Descriptive statistics are used to describe or summarize data. The results from our hypothetical experiment on bystander intervention can be summarized by saying that people in the Alone condition took a mean time of 43.7 seconds to intervene (with a standard deviation of 21.08), while those tested in the Three Bystanders condition took a mean of 72.7 seconds to intervene (with a standard deviation of 23.71). Thus the people in the Three Bystanders condition reacted more slowly to the crisis than people in the Alone condition, on the average. The difference was about 30 seconds. But should this difference be taken seriously? Can we infer (conclude) that the independent variable of number of people really caused the difference in times taken to intervene?

You might be tempted to say yes, since there was almost a 30-second difference in the times. However, this difference may just be due to random or chance factors rather than to a true difference created by the conditions. Notice that the variability in the two conditions was quite wide (look back at Table A–1). Some people in the Alone condition responded fairly slowly (especially subject 6), while other people in the Three Bystanders condition actually responded quite quickly (subjects 1 and 2). How can we judge the likelihood that the difference in times between the two conditions is "real" or reliable, that it is not a fluke? How large must the difference be between two conditions before we can conclude that it is unlikely to have occurred by mere chance alone?

Inferential statistics are used to answer this question. As the name implies, inferential statistics are those used by researchers to determine what conclusions (or inferences) can be drawn from their research. We will introduce two important concepts to help you understand inferential statistics: populations and samples of scores.

Population and Sample

In statistics, a *population* is a complete set of scores or measures. A population might be all U.S. citizens of voting age, the number of words that all college sophomores could recall from a 50-word list, or the speed with which all university students would react to give aid in a crisis. These are all populations that might interest psychologists for one reason or another. However, it is almost always impossible or impractical to study an entire population of observations. What researchers do instead is to study a *sample,* or part, of observations from the entire population. The best procedure is to select a random sample, or one in which each member of the population has an equal chance of being chosen. It is nearly always impossible to sample randomly from the relevant population. Typically, the individuals who serve as subjects are randomly assigned to the various conditions of the experiment, so that, on average, people of the same ability participate in all conditions. In our hypothetical experiment on bystander intervention, the 30 subjects would have been randomly assigned to the two conditions.

Inferential statistics are concerned with the conclusions that can be drawn about populations based on the observation of differences in the sample studied. If researchers are interested in the effect of the number of bystanders on how quickly a person will react in an emergency, they would really like to know the effect on all people (the population). However, they have to settle for studying the effect on small samples of people. Inferential statistics help experimenters determine if what was found for samples holds true for populations.

You should be familiar with this sort of logic from listening to reports of public opinion polls. Several organizations routinely survey public opinion on a number of issues. In election years, there are weekly reports of how presidential candidates are faring. Reports like "Candidate A was preferred by 43 percent of the sample surveyed, candidate B was preferred by 37 percent, and 20 percent of the people were undecided" are typical polling results. What the researchers would really like to know are the preferences of all U.S. voters on the candidates. Since it is impractical to survey all voters, the pollsters survey perhaps 2,000 or so, selected in an unbiased way, and then infer the preferences of the entire population on the basis of this sample.

The danger in this procedure is that errors can creep into the sampling process, with the result that figures found from the sample are not representative of the population at large. Accurate news reports about the polls will also announce the level of sampling error to be expected. You have probably heard statements to the effect that "these figures are subject to an error of 4 percent in either direction." What this means is that the pollster is reasonably confident that from 39 percent to 47 percent of people in the population prefer candidate A but that the true value could fall anywhere in this range. The 43 percent is the midpoint. The range for candidate B is then 33 percent to 41 percent due to possible sampling errors. Because of sampling error there is then some chance that the preference is actually different from what the poll sample shows. It is possible, though unlikely, that candidate B is actually preferred to candidate A by the population at large. Fortunately, pollsters and statisticians can measure this probability.

In making inferences from experiments researchers are interested in answering the following question: are the differences observed between conditions on the dependent variable due to the operation of the independent variable, or are they due merely to sampling error and other random factors? Is the difference between conditions great enough so that chance factors can be ruled out as having produced the difference? In the bystander intervention experiment there is a 30-second difference in the time it took to help in the Alone and Three Bystanders conditions. Is this difference large enough

| TABLE A–3 |
| A Population of Scores |

75	83	66	92
91	60	76	70
80	74	79	78
46	91	73	80
101	59	84	75
81	65	68	78
78	74	90	68
72	72	57	68
69	84	72	90
70	98	82	83
95	75	65	71
84	64	69	74
68	70	75	70
75	68	78	81
84	88	80	69
90	80	73	80
75	78	77	75
71	79	85	85
56	59	91	65
68	48	68	77
74	59	70	70
77	65	66	76
80	75	78	82
69	83	85	60
91	80	59	74

The list contains 100 hypothetical scores with a mean of 75.1 and a standard deviation of 10.12.

to be attributed to the number of people present (the independent variable) rather than to chance factors?

There is a slightly different way to approach this question. We can hypothesize that the two sets of scores from our experiment come from two different populations of scores; that is, there is a population of scores for people tested in the Alone condition and a population of scores for people tested in the Three Bystanders condition. Of course, the times to help of the 15 people tested in each condition do not represent the population of scores, but rather a sample from that population. The means of the two samples differ, but is the difference great enough to assume that the different times come from two different populations of scores? The other possibility is that both sets of scores came from the same population and that the only difference between them is due to sampling error and measurement error. Since the difference between the two means is so great—30 seconds—you might be tempted to conclude that this second possibility can be ruled out and that the two samples do come from different populations. But you should realize that measures based on two small samples from even the same population will differ somewhat because of variability in individuals and measurement error.

An example here will be useful: There are 100 numbers listed in Table A–3. Consider these figures as a complete population of scores. The mean of the population is 75.1, and the standard deviation is 10.12. Now randomly select five numbers from those listed there. This is a sample of the numbers. You will probably find that when you calculate the mean of your random sample of five numbers, it is not the same as the mean of the population. Here are the *means* of five samples of five numbers randomly selected from the population in Table A–3: 83.6, 76.2, 69.4, 78.6, and 83.2. None is right on the true population mean of 75.1, though some are reasonably close. Suppose you had taken one sample of five numbers and found a mean of 69.4, then taken another sample of five numbers and found a mean of 83.6. Then you asked yourself, "Do these two sets of numbers come from the same population?" There is a fairly large average difference between the two sets (about 14), so you might be tempted to say no. After all, the means are different. But, as is obvious from this example, it is possible to find a fairly large difference between two samples of observations that are in fact drawn from the same population.

You can convince yourself of another important point concerning sample statistics by taking larger samples from the numbers in Table A–3. If you took a sample of ten observations, the chances are that the mean based on this sample would be closer to the true mean of the population than your mean based on only five observations. Here are five means calculated on random samples of ten observations per sample: 77.2, 76.7, 74.8, 79.8, and 78.0. Notice that these values are generally much closer to the population mean of 75.1 than the sample means in the previous paragraph that were based on only five observations per sample. In general, the larger the size of the sample that is selected in a random manner, the closer the sample statistics that are obtained will be to the true values of the population. We can place more faith in a public opinion poll that randomly sampled 100,000 people from the whole U.S. population than one in which only 1,000 people were sampled.

What statistical tests do is help researchers decide if two samples of scores come from the same population or from different populations. As a loose rule, the greater the difference between the mean values of two groups of scores, the more likely it is that they come from different populations. But this depends on the variability in the scores, which is indexed by the standard deviation. The greater the dispersion, or variability, of the scores about the mean, the less confidence we can have about the difference between the two means indicating that they are from different populations. It is like the level of confidence in the polling example used earlier. If candidate A is preferred to candidate B by 44 percent to 40 percent, those who read the poll can be more nearly certain that this is the real preference of the population if the estimated "error" associated with each figure is 2 percent rather than 10 percent.

Statistical Tests

Statistical tests are used to decide whether a difference between sets of scores from an experiment is due to the operation of the independent variable or to chance factors. In practice, it is not too difficult to answer the question. The researcher chooses an appropriate statistical test, performs some straightforward computations on a calculator (or uses a computer), and then consults a table designed to be used with that test. The table tells the researcher the likelihood that the differences uncovered in the research are due to chance factors. If the outcome is quite unlikely to have occurred by chance, then the investigator concludes that the difference among conditions is a real one produced by the independent variable. It is said to be a *reliable* difference, or one that has ***statistical significance.***

A great variety of statistical tests is used to infer whether or not differences among experimental conditions are reliable. We will try here to give you some understanding of the rationale behind these tests without going into all the computational details or characteristics of particular tests.

In testing hypotheses with inferential statistics, it is important to distinguish between the ***null hypothesis*** and the ***alternative hypothesis.*** Imagine, as in the case of the hypothetical bystander intervention experiment, that a researcher has performed an experiment with two conditions and found some difference between them on the dependent variable. The null hypothesis is that there is no true difference between the two samples of scores in the conditions of the experiment; they were not produced by the independent variable but came about only because of chance factors. The alternative hypothesis is the one in which the researcher is really interested, since the experiment was designed to test it. The alternative hypothesis is that the difference between the two conditions was produced by the independent variable. In the bystander intervention case the alternative hypothesis is that the mean difference in time taken to help in the two conditions is due to the number of people believed to be present.

A critical assumption is that *it is impossible to prove the alternative hypothesis conclusively* since there is always some chance that the two samples came from the same population no matter how different they appear. What inferential statistics allow us to do, though, is to determine how confident we can be in rejecting the null hypothesis. The alternative hypothesis is thus tested indirectly; if we can be quite confident in rejecting the null hypothesis, then we assume that the alternative hypothesis is correct and that there is a real difference between scores in the different conditions. Statisticians have agreed, by convention, that if calculations from a statistical test show that there is less than a .05 probability (a 5 percent chance) that the null hypothesis is correct, we can reject it and accept the alternative hypothesis.

We will describe the concept of probability briefly in this context. Consider the following problem: what is the probability that, if we randomly draw a card from a deck of 52 cards, it will be a spade? Since there are 13 spades in a deck, the probability of drawing a spade is $13 \div 52$, or $\frac{1}{4} = .25$. In general, if there are r ways that an event can occur and a total of N possibilities, then the probability of the event is r/N. What is the probability that a fair coin will come up heads when flipped? There are two ways a coin can come up, so $N = 2$. One of them is heads, so $r = 1$. So the probability of heads is $\frac{1}{2}$, or .50.

Now we can more precisely describe what the conventional level of .05 for statistical significance means. If the null hypothesis were actually true, a researcher would obtain such a large difference between conditions less than 5 times in 100. If the chances are this slight in making an error by rejecting the null hypothesis, then it is deemed safe to do so and to opt for the alternative hypothesis. The .05 criterion is referred to as the .05 *level of confidence* since a mistake will be made only 5 times in 100. When the null hypothesis is rejected, researchers conclude that the results are *reliably different* or *statistically significant*. In other words, the researchers can be quite confident that the difference obtained between the conditions is trustworthy and that if the experiment were repeated the same outcome would result.

In practice, when a statistical test is used it is possible to get a more exact probability for rejecting the null hypothesis. For example, when applying one statistical test to the hypothetical data from the bystander intervention experiment in Table A–1, it was determined that the null hypothesis could be rejected with less than 1 percent chance of an error ($p < .01$). So we can be confident that there is less than 1 chance in 100 that these data would occur if the null hypothesis were true.

In summary, inferential statistics allow researchers to test their hypotheses or ideas in an indirect manner. They test the alternative hypothesis by rejecting the null hypothesis at a certain level of confidence. If the statistical test does not permit rejection of the null hypothesis, then a researcher cannot conclude that there is a reliable difference produced by the independent variable.

MISUSES OF STATISTICS

Statistics are used so often that it seems possible to bolster any argument with them. They are employed by politicians, economists, advertisers, psychologists, and many others to support various views, so it is little wonder that people have gained the impression that statistics can be bent to any purpose. But an old adage has it that "Statistics don't lie, statisticians do." Actually, there is probably little to fear from statisticians themselves, because their sophistication permits them to differentiate a true argument based on statistics from a false one. Nonetheless, statistics can be misused to create a false impression. You should be aware of some common misuses so that you will not be misled by them.

Use of Small or Biased Samples

Many television commercials implicitly mislead us with one or both of these techniques. Viewers see a woman who is asked to test two brands of detergent on the wash of her husband's greasy, grass-stained clothes. She is pitting her usual product, BAF, against new Super Dirt Remover. BAF goes into one washer, Super Dirt Remover goes into the other, and then later the woman is shown exclaiming over the better job that SDR did. Announcer: "Are you convinced?" Woman: "Why, yes. I will always use Super Dirt Remover from now on. It really gets the dirt off my clothes."

Even making the unlikely assumption that the whole demonstration was not rigged, observers should know better than to be convinced by such a small sample (one case). If the "experiment" were repeated honestly with 100 women, would all of them pick Super Dirt Remover? The ad tries to leave us with the impression that because this one woman prefers the product, everyone (the population) will. But we should be careful about assuming something to be true of the population at large from a sample of one.

Another problem is that a sample of individuals surveyed for such an ad might be deliberately biased. Advertisers are always surveying groups that are likely to be predisposed in their favor anyway, such as people who already own the product. They ask consumers, "How well do you like your Bass-o-matic?" and then show a small sample of interviews that went well from the company's point of view. It would be more convincing to sample people who had never used the product and to test it against its main rivals. Since more advertising claims on television must now be based on facts, this type of study and commercial is becoming more widely used. In one interesting case, owners of one type of luxury car are asked to test it against a competitor. Here is a case in which the sample tested is expected to be biased *against* the new product and for their old product, so if a preference is found for the new product it seems to argue much more strongly for the new product.

Whenever you hear about preferences that people have exhibited, you should ask two questions about the sample: How large was it? How were people chosen to be in it?

The Exaggerated Graph

This is a common device to show or hide differences in graphs. It involves changing the scale on the graph to show off a difference or (more rarely) to hide a difference. Suppose that the number of murders in a city increased over three years from 72 to 80 to 91. The next year the mayor is running for reelection and is eager to show that the city has been safe for the past three years under her administration. So her campaign workers prepare the graph in the top of Figure A–6. By making the scale on the y-axis very long, they create the impression that the murder rate is fairly steady. In the same year

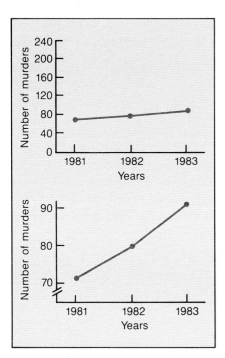

FIGURE A–6
Variation in Scales

The graph at the top seems to show the murder rate increasing only slightly, while the one at the bottom shows the rate going up dramatically. Yet both graphs actually show the murder rate accurately—the difference is in the scale on the y-axis. It is important to examine a graph carefully and note the scale of measurement since scale changes can make small differences look large and vice versa.

the city police may be arguing that they need higher staffing levels. They want to show how the city is becoming more unsafe, so they depict the murder rate as increasing steeply, as in the bottom panel of Figure A–6, by changing the scale.

The facts are shown accurately in both graphs; however, the top graph gives the impression that the murder rate is increasing very gradually, hardly worth worrying about. (Hasn't the mayor done a good job leading the city?) The bottom panel creates the impression that the murder rate is increasing dramatically. (Don't we need more police?)

These graphing techniques are common. In fact, you will see exaggerated scales in some of the graphs in this book to show patterns of results more clearly. You should always look carefully to see what the scale is in a graph. With experimental data it is more important to determine if a difference is statistically reliable than to see if it looks to be "large" when graphed.

Absent or Inappropriate Comparisons

A common ploy used in advertising is to say that some product has x percent more of something good or y percent less of something bad. "Buy the new Thunderbolt since it gives 27 percent better gas mileage." This sounds convincing until you stop to ask yourself, "27 percent better than what?" A missing comparison here makes the statistic completely meaningless. Perhaps the Thunderbolt gets 27 percent better mileage than a two-ton tank, which is hardly an argument for buying it.

Even when a comparison is made specific, it is often still inappropriate. The claim is often made in advertising that a product is better than last year's model. "Buy the new, improved Thunderbolt. It gets 27 percent better mileage than last year's model." Of course, it could still be a real dog, even if better than last year's dog. What the consumer would really like is a comparison of the mileage efficiency of the new Thunderbolt with other new cars in roughly the same class, as is now provided by government testing.

Another problem in making comparisons is that often there is no information on the reliability of differences. In a recent commercial two cars of the same make and year were filled with one gallon of gas and test driven at a constant speed around a track. The difference in the test was the type of gasoline used. One car stops before the other, and the viewers are supposed to conclude that the sponsor's gasoline is superior to the other brand. But only after a long series of comparisons could a researcher statistically test for a reliable difference between the two types of gas. This is the same problem as in the case of BAF versus Super Dirt Remover; the sample of observations is too small.

In general, watch to make sure that in statements involving a comparison, the object of comparison is described and is appropriate. There should also be some statement about whether or not any differences are statistically reliable.

The Gambler's Fallacy

Statistical tests are based on *probability theory*, the theory of expectations about the likelihood of random events. Probability theory was discussed briefly in the section on inferential statistics, where we considered the probability of drawing cards from a deck and of getting heads when flipping coins. It is interesting to note that people's perceptions of the randomness of events do not agree in some important respects with ideas from probability theory. Thus, people often make conclusions that seem irrational when judged by the logic of probability theory. There is much interesting research on this phenomenon (for example, Tversky & Kahneman, 1971, 1974). Here we will examine one of the most common mistakes in judgments of probability.

Imagine the case of a person flipping a coin 1,000 times. If it is a fair coin, it should come up heads about 500 times and tails about 500 times. The probability of its coming up heads over a large number of trials is 0.50, but of course even a fair coin would probably not come up heads exactly 500 times in 1,000 flips. It might come up 490 or 505, yet the result would be fairly close to half and half.

Let us now take the case of a person betting on whether or not the coin will come up heads or tails. If the situation is truly random, a gambler has a probability of 0.50 on any particular trial of winning. Imagine that on five trials in a row the gambler bets $5 that the coin will come up heads, and each time it comes up tails. Of course, the fact that the coin comes up tails five times in a row is unusual, and the chances of such an event are quite low (.03). The gambler notes this odd occurrence and, on the next bet, he doubles his bet to $10 and again bets on heads. Now he is more certain that the coin will come up heads.

The logic the gambler uses is as follows. "The coin is a fair coin. On the average it will come up heads half the time and tails half the time. The coin has just come up tails five times in a row. Therefore, it is due to come up heads soon now to even things up, because on the average it will come up heads half the time. So I should bet on heads and even increase my bet." More generally, the logic is that if the game is truly random and I am losing, then I should keep playing because my luck is bound to change for the better. It is this kind of logic that keeps gambling casinos at Las Vegas and Atlantic City humming and wipes out the fortunes of otherwise intelligent people.

The fallacy of the argument is that applications of the laws of probability—such as a fair coin coming up heads half the time—hold only over tremendously large numbers of events. The laws cannot be applied to small runs. What the gambler overlooks is that the flips of the coin are *independent events;* what happened on previous flips does not influence what happens next. If the coin came up tails five times in a row, this does not increase the probability of heads on the next throw. It is still 0.50. The coin does not have a memory for previous trials, as the gambler seems to assume implicitly. The gambler should not feel any more certain on the sixth trial than he or she did on the first five. The probability of heads showing has not changed.

In some sense the gambler's mistake is natural. There is a ring of truth to the argument, and it is based on true laws of probability. Over a very large series of throws, a fair coin will come up heads 50 percent of the time. The error comes in applying what is true over a very large series of events to a small series. The laws do not apply to small series of random events as well. With, say, 10,000,000 coin flips, heads will come up almost exactly 50 percent of the time. But if a gambler takes a small series of the larger number, say 5 flips, heads could come up either 0 or 5 times with a probability of 0.06. These outcomes (all heads or all tails) are not terribly likely, but they are not vanishingly small, either.

SUMMARY

1. Statistics serve two primary purposes. Descriptive statistics are used to summarize or describe a large number of observations. Inferential statistics are employed to make a generalization about some population based only on scores of a sample from the population. Most generalizations ("laws") in psychology are probabilistic; they do not hold in every case, but with a certain probability over a large number of cases.

2. The two primary types of descriptive statistics of a set of scores are measures of central tendency and measures of variability or dispersion.

3. Measures of central tendency include the mean (the arithmetic average), the median (the middlemost score), and the mode (the most frequent score). The mean is the most generally used measure, but if there are one or a few extreme scores the median may be the preferred measure.

4. The range and standard deviation are the most common descriptive measures of dispersion or variability. The range is the difference between the highest and lowest score, and so depends simply on the most extreme scores. The standard deviation, though more complex in formulation, is the more useful measure of variability.

5. Correlations are measures of association between two variables. If as one measure increases, so does another, the two variables are said to be positively correlated. If one variable decreases as the other increases, the variables are said to be negatively correlated. The correlation coefficient can vary from -1.00 to $+1.00$, with negative and positive values indicating negative and positive correlations, respectively. A zero correlation coefficient indicates that there is no systematic relation between the two variables. The sign ($+$ or $-$) of a correlation indicates the direction of the relation; the size of the number indicates its magnitude or strength. Strong correlations (whether positive or negative) are useful for predictions. If height and weight are strongly correlated, knowing a person's height would permit prediction of weight. Correlation of two variables does not necessarily mean that one caused the other; correlation does not imply causation.

6. A population is a complete collection of observations or scores. A sample is a subset of the population. In psychological research, samples of observations are taken and conclusions about populations are drawn through the logic of inferential statistics.

7. In testing to see if a difference between samples of scores can be generalized to population differences, it is common to consider a null hypothesis and an alternative hypothesis. The null hypothesis is that the two samples actually come from the same population, or that no real difference exists between the samples. The alternative hypothesis is that the samples really did come from different populations. Statistical tests provide researchers with information about how likely it is that the null hypothesis is wrong. Thus the alternative hypothesis is tested indirectly. If the test provides the information that the obtained result would only occur with a probability of .05 or less if the null hypothesis were true, the researchers can reject the null hypothesis and conclude in favor of the alternative hypothesis of a real difference between the samples of scores.

8. Mark Twain wrote, "There are three kinds of lies—lies, damned lies, and statistics." Some ways in which statistics can be misused include drawing conclusions from small or biased samples; exaggerating the scales on graphs for effect; making inappropriate comparisons; and assuming that the laws of probability which hold for huge samples of observations can be generalized to small samples (as in the gambler's fallacy). Statistics themselves do not lie, but they can often be manipulated to give misleading impressions.

SUGGESTED READINGS

Freedman, D., Pisani, R., & Purves, R. (1978). *Statistics.* New York: Norton.

> An excellent introduction to statistical concepts and reasoning. The material is presented in nontechnical language, and many interesting examples are used to illustrate the concepts.

Huff, D. (1954). *How to lie with statistics.* New York: Norton.

> This entertaining and very simply written book is about misuses of statistics.

Kimble, G. (1978). *How to use (and mis-use) statistics.* Englewood Cliffs, N.J.: Spectrum Books.

> This brief book is written for people with limited backgrounds in mathematics. The author shows how statistics are used in many practical tasks, and he also illustrates their misuse.

Pagano, R. L. (1986). *Understanding statistics in the behavioral sciences* (2nd ed.) St. Paul, MN: West.

> A very good introduction to the basic elements of statistics for behavioral scientists.

Tanur, J. M., Mosteller, F., Kruskal, W. H., Link, R. F., Pieters, R. S., Rising, G. R., & Lehman, E. H. (1978). *Statistics: A guide to the unknown* (2nd ed.). San Francisco: Holden-Day.

> This fascinating series of essays on diverse topics illustrates the usefulness of a variety of statistical techniques.

Glossary

abreaction. In psychoanalysis, an intense emotional outburst; more generally, any procedure in which repressed impulses are released. **16**

absolute threshold. The minimum amount of physical energy needed for a stimulus to produce a sensation. For research purposes, the absolute threshold is defined as the minimally effective stimulus that will elicit a sensation on 50 percent of trials. See also *difference threshold*. **3**

accommodation. (1) The process by which the lens of the eye changes to focus an object on the retina; it becomes more spherical for near objects and flatter for distant objects. (2) Piaget's term for adapting actions to respond to new stimuli. **3**

acetylcholine (ACH). A neurotransmitter that elicits contraction of skeletal muscles in response to motor nerve activity; it is also a transmitter of impulses in other parts of the nervous system. **2**

achievement motivation. See *need for achievement*.

acquisition. (1) In classical conditioning, the formation of a conditioned response. (2) In instrumental conditioning, the strengthening of a reinforced response. (3) In memory theory, the first of three stages in the memory process. See also *storage, retrieval*. **6**

action potential. The stage during which a neuron fires (or sends) its impulse to the next neuron; it involves the rapid reversal of electrical charge between the inside and outside of the cell membrane. See also *resting potential*. **2**

actualizing tendency. See *self-actualization*.

actual self. In Rogerian therapy, the half of the self-concept that corresponds to a person's current view of himself or herself. See also *ideal self*. **14**

adolescence. The period of transition from childhood into adulthood. The period usually begins at the onset of

puberty and ends when the adolescent takes on social responsibilities such as work and marriage. **10**

adolescent growth spurt. A rapid increase in the rate of physical development that accompanies puberty. **10**

adolescent moratorium. By social conventions, a time for personal development and education before the responsibilities of work and family begin. **10**

adrenal cortex. The outer portion of the adrenal glands; it generates a large number of chemicals, some of them sex hormones. **2**

adrenal glands. Endocrine glands lying just above the kidneys and consisting of a central core; the adrenal medulla, and an outer portion, the adrenal cortex. **2**

adrenaline. See *epinephrine*.

adrenal medulla. The central core of the adrenal gland; it secretes the hormones epinephrine and norepinephrine. **2**

adrenergic transmission. Synaptic transmission using noradrenalin (norepinephrine), the major neurotransmitter in the sympathetic nervous system. **13**

Adrian's rate law. A theory proposing that the greater the intensity of stimuli, the greater the increase in the firing rate of action potentials. **2**

affective disorders. A group of disorders, including mania and depression, characterized by extremes of mood and emotion. **15**

afferent nerves. Nerve fibers bearing sensory information into the central nervous system from sensory receptors and the peripheral nervous system. See also *efferent nerves*. **2**

afterimage. Sensory experience that persists after a stimulus is removed. In color vision, positive afterimages have the same color as the original stimulus. Negative afterimages have approximately the complementary color of the original stimulus. **3**

age cohort. A group of individuals who are born in the same year or period. **10**

aggression. Behavior intended to harm another. **18**

algorithm. A well-defined set of procedures or rules for solving a particular type of problem. **8**

all-or-none law. The principle that a neuron's action potential triggers either completely or not at all. Once an action potential is triggered, it continues down an axon to its end. **2**

alternative hypothesis. In statistics, the hypothesis that samples of scores are from different populations. See also *null hypothesis.* **Appendix**

altruism. (1) In sociobiology, behavior that benefits the inclusive fitness of others. (2) In general terms, behavior that benefits others. **18.**

aminostatic theory. A theory that suggests that hunger is caused by low levels of amino acids in the blood, and satiety is produced by high levels of amino acids. **12**

amnesia. A dissociative disorder, usually caused by some injury to the brain, characterized by either total or partial memory loss. Anterograde amnesia is loss of memory for events that occurred prior to the cerebral shock. Retrograde amnesia is memory loss for experiences occurring after the brain trauma. **7**

amniocentesis. A method used to diagnose prenatal complications in which a hollow needle is inserted through a pregnant woman's abdomen to remove a sample of amniotic fluid from the womb. **9**

amniotic sac. A thin membrane that surrounds the fetus in the womb. **9**

amphetamine. Any one of a class of drugs such as benzedrine, dexedrine, or methedrine, which act as central nervous system stimulants. **5**

amplitude. The difference in sound waves from the maximum to minimum levels of pressure. **3**

amygdala. A part of the limbic system that appears to be involved in aggressive behavior. See also *limbic system.* **2**

anaclitic depression. Depression associated with loss of a parent. **15**

anal stage. In Freudian theory, the second stage of psychosexual development, corresponding roughly to the period of toilet training during the first or second year, during which the anal region is the source of sensual pleasure. See also *genital, latency,* and *phallic stages.* **14**

analytic introspection. In structural psychology, the rigorous classification of experience into its components. **1**

analytic psychology. The system of psychoanalytic psychology begun by Carl Jung, an early disciple of Freud. Jung's view of the unconscious differs from Freud's in that Jung conceived of the unconscious as the repository of both good and evil images and urges. See also *archetype; collective unconscious.* **14**

androgen. Sex hormone secreted to a larger degree by males than by females. Androgen determines male structural development. See also *testosterone.* **12**

androgyny. Possession of both masculine and feminine personality traits. **18**

anorexia nervosa. A disorder defined by marked loss of body weight due to self-starvation. **10**

anterograde amnesia. See *amnesia.*

antianxiety drugs. Central nervous system depressants. Examples include Valium and Librium. **16**

antidepressant drugs. Drugs used to relieve symptoms of extreme sadness and withdrawal, characteristics of depressed individuals. **16**

antipsychotic drugs. Drugs used to relieve several mental disorders such as schizophrenia. **16**

antisocial personality disorder. A type of personality disorder characterized by repetitive, impulsive, and purposeless antisocial behavior displayed with emotional indifference and without guilt. In the past, individuals classified as antisocial were referred to as psychopaths or sociopaths. **15**

anxiety. (1) In Freudian theory, the feeling of dread and/or apprehension about the future caused by id-ego-super-ego conflict. (2) In behavior theory, a feeling of tension or dread. **14**

anxiety disorders. A class of dysfunctions characterized by heightened tension, anxiety, worry, or fear without any realistic reason or cause. **15**

anxiety hierarchy. Any list or sequence of events that is increasingly anxiety-provoking for the individual. In systematic desensitization therapy, the individual becomes conditioned to reduce anxiety at each step of the hierarchy. **16**

apparent motion. The perception of movement created by stationary stimuli that are flashed on and off at appropriate intervals. **4**

applied research. Research directed toward understanding and solving behavioral and social problems. See also *basic research.* **1**

approach-approach conflict A conflict in which an individual is drawn toward two equally satisfying but incompatible goals. By attaining one goal, the other is lost. **13**

approach-avoidance conflict. A conflict in which an individual faces a single goal, but the goal possesses both positive and negative factors. **13**

archetype. In Jung's theory, a universal, primordial image found in the collective unconscious. Examples include God, Mother Earth, and rebirth. **14**

arousal. The general level of alertness and activation of the body, reflected in several physiological responses, including muscle tension, heart rate, and galvanic skin response. **12**

arousal theory. The theory that behavior can be explained by the desire to maintain an optimal arousal level for the task at hand, or for a specific time of day. **12**

assertiveness and social skills training. A type of behavior therapy in which people are trained in social skills that enable them to be more direct and effective in resolving interpersonal conflicts. See also *behavior therapy.* **16**

assimilation. In Piaget's theory, absorbing new information and fitting it with existing knowledge. **9**

association areas. Areas of the cerebral cortex that appear to be involved in the storage and processing of information. **2**

astigmatism. A defect in which visual images are not sharply focused on all parts of the retina. **3**

attachment. The process of forming and maintaining an emotional bond during infancy with parents, caregivers, and significant objects in the environment. **9**

attention. In perception, the active selection of and focus upon one object or component of a complex experience. The organism thereby responds to a more narrow range of stimuli. **5**

attitude. A fairly stable disposition toward particular people, objects, institutions, or issues. **17**

attribution theory. A theory concerning how an individual tries to explain people's behavior, including his or her own. Such explanations may link the behavior to situational or personal qualities, to a combination of both, or to some other factor such as luck. **17**

attributional egotism. The tendency to attribute success to dispositional factors and failure to external factors. It generally appears when people feel themselves responsible for good or bad outcomes and when success or failure is important to the individual's self-concept. **17**

auditory canal. The tubelike passageway that guides sound waves from the outer opening of the ear to the tympanic membrane or eardrum, of the middle ear. **3**

auditory localization. The ability to know the direction from which a sound originates. **3**

auditory nerve. The nerve that connects the inner ear with the brain. It transmits information concerned with hearing and balance. **3**

authoritarian personality. A personality type that views the world in uncompromising terms, with highly prejudiced attitudes. Harsh and punitive experiences during childhood are thought to develop such personalities. **18**

autokinetic effect. The apparent movement of a spot of light in a dark room. **17**

automatic processing. Mental processing that is effortless, rapid, and difficult to interrupt. **5**

autonomic nervous system. The collection of sensory and motor nerves serving the heart and glands and smooth muscles of the internal organs. **2**

availability. (1) The ready and spontaneous use of a learning strategy. (2) Information stored in memory, but not necessarily retrievable. **8**

aversion therapy. Therapy in which a positive response to an event is changed to a negative response by associating the event with something negative, such as a shock. **16**

avoidance-avoidance conflict. A conflict in which an individual must choose between two equally undesirable alternatives. **13**

avoidance learning. In instrumental conditioning, the learning of a response that prevents the occurrence of a noxious stimulus. **6**

axon. The part of a neuron shaped like a long slender tube that extends outward from the cell body. The axon carries the signal from one neuron on to other neurons. **2**

baby biographies. Detailed records of children's development, such as those kept by early developmental scientists. **9**

backward conditioning. In classical conditioning, a procedure in which the conditioned stimulus begins after the unconditioned stimulus. **6**

barbiturates. A class of drugs that act as central nervous system depressants, including drowsiness and muscular relaxation. Examples include phenobarbital, Nembutal, and Seconal. **5**

basic anxiety. In Karen Horney's psychodynamic theory of personality, deep-seated feelings of insecurity and anger originating in childhood that determine how a person will respond to others. **14**

basic hostility. See *basic anxiety*.

basic research. Systematic study directed toward establishing fundamental principles of behavior; it need not be related directly to social or behavioral problems. See also *applied research*. **1**

basilar membrane. A membrane located in the cochlea of the inner ear. Vibrations of fluid in the cochlea stimulate the hair cells on the basilar membrane which in turn send neural impulses to the brain via the auditory nerve. See also *auditory nerve, cochlea, hair cells*. **3**

behavioral medicine. A field that integrates knowledge and techniques of behavioral and biomedical science. **13**

behavior genetics. A field of study that analyzes genetic and environmental contributions to behavior. **2**

behaviorism. A school of psychology founded by John B. Watson in which psychology is defined solely as the study of behavior; all data therefore must come from observable behavior. See also *neobehaviorism*. **1**

behavior modification. See *behavior therapy*.

behavior therapy. Psychotherapy, based on principles of learning, that seeks to change undesirable behavior. See also *cognitive behavior modification; counterconditioning*. **16**

binocular disparity. The slight difference between the two retinal images of an object in view that is caused by the separation of the two eyes and the consequent difference in viewing angles. It is an important depth cue. See also *stereoscopic image*. **4**

biofeedback. A technique for monitoring autonomic responses, such as heart rate or the galvanic skin response, through conditioning procedures. **16**

biological approach. An approach to psychology that emphasizes the biological structures and processes that underlie behavior. See also *psychobiology; ethology*. **1**

bipolar cells. Cells located in the retina that pass information from the rods and cones to the ganglion cells. See also *cones; ganglion cells; rods*. **3**

blastocyst. In prenatal development, a hollow ball of cells enclosing the developing zygote that continually divides as it travels down one of the fallopian tubes. **9**

blind spot. The portion of the retina where the optic nerve exits from the eye and which contains no receptor cells. **3**

blindsight. The ability of some cortically blind patients to indicate the location of a stimulus they claim they cannot see. **3**

blocking. In classical conditioning, the failure of an animal to learn about a second stimulus presented in compound with a conditioned stimulus, that already has been associated with the unconditioned stimulus. **6**

blood-brain barrier. The general term for various features of brain tissue that slow or prevent the passage of substances from the bloodstream into the brain. **2**

bottom-up theories. A class of theories that describe perception as a strictly passive process; information passes from receptor organs to higher levels of the nervous system in stages of increasing complexity. See also *top-down theories*. **4**

brain stem. The part of the brain located inside the skull directly above the spinal cord. **2**

brightness. The perceived intensity of visual stimuli. Brightness depends primarily on the amplitude of light waves. **3**

Broca's aphasia. Difficulty in speaking after damage to Broca's area, indicated by slow, labored speech. **2**

Broca's area. A certain part of the brain's left hemisphere that, when damaged, causes speech to become slow and labored. **2**

bulimia. An eating disorder involving cycles of high consumption followed by self-induced vomiting and self-starvation. **10**

bystander intervention. Reaction to a crisis or emergency involving a stranger. **18**

California Psychological Inventory (CPI). A personality questionnaire designed for measuring 15 dimensions of normal personality, including self-reliance, personal worth, and sense of freedom. **14**

case study. The intensive study of one particular instance of some behavior. **1**

castration anxiety. In Freudian theory, a boy's unconscious fear that he will be castrated by his jealous father for having sexually desired his mother. See also *Oedipus complex; phallic stage*. **14**

catatonic schizophrenia. A disorder marked by unusual physical activity—from wild and uncontrolled tantrums to stupor. See also *schizophrenic disorder*. **15**

categorical reasoning. A type of deductive reasoning in which statements take four forms: all *A* are *B*, no *A* are *B*, some *A* are *B*, and some *A* are not *B*. **8**

catharsis. In psychoanalytic theory, the relief from tension that is brought about through psychotherapy or through expressing and acting out feelings. **16**

cell body. The part of the neuron containing the nucleus and cytoplasm, where the cell's chemical reactions are regulated, ensuring the cell's survival. See also *axon; dendrites*. **2**

cell membrane. The membrane enclosing the neuron which protects the cell and regulates the concentration of chemicals inside and outside the cell. **2**

central fissure. The major fissure of the cerebral cortex; it separates the frontal lobe from the parietal lobe. **2**

central nervous system. The brain and spinal cord. See also *peripheral nervous system.* **2**

central processing. An individual's careful attention to the meaning and logical implications of a message or argument. **17**

central tendency. In statistics, measures of the tendency of scores in a frequency distribution to cluster around a central value. See also *mean; median; mode.* **Appendix**

centration. Directing attention to only limited aspects of a stimulus. **9**

cerebellum. The part of the brain in the lower back region of the brain stem that helps to make movements smooth and precise. **2**

cerebral cortex. The surface layer of gray matter—unmyelinated axons of the cell bodies—over the cerebral hemispheres. **2**

cerebral hemispheres. The two large structures on the top of the brain—one on the left, one on the right—which are separated by the longitudinal fissure; fibers joining the hemispheres over this fissure are called the *corpus callosum.* See also *hemispheric specialization; split-brain patient.* **2**

cerebrospinal fluid. Fluid filling all the area surrounding the brain and spinal cord inside the skull that helps to support and to cushion the brain and spinal cord. **2**

cerebrum. The white matter—myelinated axons of the cell bodies—and subcortical structures, on the inside of the cerebral cortex. **2**

change-of-meaning hypothesis. The hypothesis that the meaning of a word may be changed depending on the word's context; it has been used to explain the effects of word order in impression formation. **17**

character disorder. A broad, somewhat old-fashioned term to describe behavioral problems such as delinquency, habitual criminality, drug abuse, and sexual deviancy. **15**

chemotherapy. The use of drugs in the treatment of mental disorders. **16**

cholinergic transmission. Synaptic transmission using acetylcholine (ACH), the major neurotransmitter in the parasympathetic nervous system. **13**

chorionic villii biopsy. A procedure to diagnose prenatal complications in which a tube is inserted into a pregnant woman's cervix to suction off fetal cells for analysis. **9**

chromosomes. Thread-like cell molecules that carry genes, the elementary units of heredity. **2**

ciliary muscles. Muscles in the eye that stretch and release the lens, thereby controlling its thickness. **3**

circadian rhythm. A cycle or pattern that occurs approximately every 24 hours; sleep is one bodily function that follows a circadian rhythm. **5**

classical conditioning. The procedure whereby a neutral stimulus is paired with a stimulus that automatically produces a response. As a consequence, the neutral stimulus comes to elicit the response. See also *conditioned stimulus, conditioned response, unconditioned stimulus, unconditioned response.* **6**

client-centered therapy. See *person-centered therapy.*

clinical psychologist. A person with a Ph.D. in psychology whose graduate work involved four to five years of intensive training in research and clinical skills, as well as a one-year internship under professional supervision. **16**

clinical psychology. A branch of applied psychology that deals with research and practice in the treatment of personality problems and mental disorders. **1**

cochlea. A small, bony, snail-shaped organ of the inner ear that contains the receptors for hearing. **3**

cocktail party phenomenon. The ability to attend selectively to one of many simultaneous conversations. See also *selective attention.* **5**

cognition. The process of thinking, encompassing perception, consciousness, learning, and memory. **8**

cognitive behavior modification. A type of psychotherapy, based on principles of learning, which seeks to change beliefs, thoughts, and self-perceptions underlying behavior. See also *behavior therapy.* **16**

cognitive biases. Mental shortcuts or cognitive heuristics, such as misperceptions of statistical principles, that can affect decision making. **8**

cognitive dissonance theory. A theory that explains changes in beliefs and attitudes. People want consistency in their beliefs and attitudes, and whenever beliefs and attitudes conflict with each other tension motivates changes in behavior or cognition. **17**

cognitive map. An internal representation, or mental picture, or information about events and their spatial relationship. **6**

cognitive motivation theory. A group of theories that share the idea that motivation is produced through positive and negative incentives. In cognitive theory, incentives are usually referred to as expectancies of goals. **12**

cognitive psychology. The study of how people acquire, store, and use information. **1**

collective unconscious. In Jung's theory, an inherited unconscious dominated by a set of symbols or archetypes. See also *archetype.* **14**

color circle. A diagram representing the colors of the spectrum. Colors are arranged around the circumference in the order of the spectrum. Complementary colors appear opposite each other on the circle. See also *complementary colors.* **3**

community halfway house. A treatment facility and a residence for people recently discharged from a mental hospital or a prison, or for people who feel they may require hospitalization. **16**

complementary colors. Any two colors which, in an additive mixture, produce either gray or an unsaturated version of the hue of the stronger color. **3**

compliance. A form of social influence in which a person abides by a direct request. **17**

components of intelligence. Basic elements involved in processing information. Sternberg's theory of intelligence identifies three categories of components: metacomponents, performance components, and knowledge-acquisition components. **11**

concepts. Mental representations for classifying information. **8**

concordance rate. The percentage of twins who share a trait, such as schizophrenia. **2**

concrete operational period. In Piaget's theory of cognitive development, a stage in which children approximately seven to eleven years of age use rules and strategies to understand physical laws and social relationships. **9**

concurrent validity. The degree to which two measures taken together yield similar evidence of a phenomenon. See also *predictive valdity, validity.* **11**

conditional reasoning. A type of deductive reasoning based on syllogisms. **8**

conditioned inhibition. A learned tendency to inhibit or hold back responses. **6**

conditioned reinforcer. An event that becomes a reinforcer through learning. See also *primary reinforcer.* **6**

conditioned response (CR). In classical conditioning, the learned response to a conditioned stimulus. See also *conditioned stimulus, classical conditioning.* **6**

conditioned stimulus (CS). In classical conditioning, a previously neutral stimulus, or a stimulus that does not elicit the response to be conditioned. By pairing with an unconditioned stimulus, the conditioned stimulus comes to elicit some response. See also *classical conditioning, unconditioned stimulus*. **6**

conditions of worth. In Roger's theory of personality, children's strong feelings about what kind of behaviors will bring them approval from others. **14**

cones. Receptor cells located in the retina of the eye that are capable of transforming light energy into neural impulses. The cones are responsible for color vision. See also *rods*. **3**

confluence model. An hypothesis which predicts that later-born children of large families have lower I.Q.s than earlier-born children. **11**

conformity. Yielding to individual or group pressure when there is no direct request to do so. **17**

confounding. In experimental and correlational research, the simultaneous variation of two independent variables, only one of which is the variable of interest. As a result, the researcher cannot attribute with certainty any effect on the dependent variable to the independent variable of interest. **1**

conscience. See *superego*.

consciousness. A general term referring to current awareness of internal and/or external stimuli. **5**

conservation. In Piaget's theory, the understanding that certain properties of matter, such as number, length, and volume, remain constant despite superficial changes in appearance. **9**

construct validity. The accuracy with which a test measures what it is intended to measure. **11**

contingency contracting. Behavior therapy involving a written agreement between therapist and client. See also *self-management*.

continuous reinforcement. In instrumental conditioning, providing reinforcement for every instance of desired behavior. See also *partial reinforcement*. **6**

control processes. In the multistore model of memory, mental processes that regulate the flow of information between short- and long-term memory. **7**

control variable. A potential independent variable that is held constant in an experiment. **1**

controlled processing. Mental processing that is consciously controlled, relatively slow, and easily interrupted. **5**

convergent thinking. Using information to arrive at a standard correct answer. See also *divergent thinking*. **11**

conversion disorder. A disorder in which the individual manifests a severe physical impairment such as paralysis, blindness, or deafness, that has no organic cause. See also *somatoform disorder*. **15**

Coolidge effect. The stimulating effect of a new partner after sexual intercourse with another. **12**

cornea. The transparent outer membrane of the eye covering the iris and the pupil. The cornea admits light into the eye and bends it for focusing on the retina. **3**

corpus callosum. A large fiber bundle joining the areas of cortex on each side of the brain. **2**

correlation. A measure of the extent to which two variables are related. A correlation may not be used to infer causality. **1**

correlation coefficient. A numerical index of the degree of relationship between two variables. Correlation coefficients range between .00 and 1.00 and may be either negative or positive. Positive correlations indicate that high rank on one variable is associated with high rank on the other variable. Negative correlations indicate that high rank on one variable is associated with low rank on the other variable. **Appendix**

counseling psychologist. A trained psychologist who specializes in marital, vocational, or other personal problems not associated with specific illness. **16**

counterattitudinal behavior. Behavior that opposes the person's beliefs or attitudes. **17**

counterconditioning. Psychotherapy based on classical conditioning procedures, in which an event that produces a positive reaction is associated with something negative and so comes to produce a negative reaction (aversion therapy), or an event that produces a negative response is associated with something positive and so comes to produce a positive response (systematic desensitization). **16**

critical period. A time of particular sensitivity to certain environmental influences during development. **12**

cross-sectional analysis. Experimental design for simultaneously testing subjects of many different ages. See also *longitudinal analysis*. **9**

crowding. Negative feeling and perception of too many people in too little space. See also *density*. **18**

crystallized intelligence. The ability to make decisions and solve problems based on culturally-given information and skills. See also *fluid intelligence*. **10**

cued recall test. A method for studying retrieval processes in memory. Subjects are given lists of words to recall and provided with specific cues or hints to aid their recall. See *free recall*. **1**

cumulative recorder. A machine that records responding in operant conditioning. A roll of paper revolves at a constant speed, while a pen moves up a bit each time the subject responds. **6**

dark adaptation. The process by which the eye becomes increasingly sensitive to illumination during periods of darkness. See also *light adaptation*. **3**

data. Observations drawn from experiments or other research. **Appendix**

deactivation. A process whereby enzymes in the postsynaptic membrane destroy a large number of transmitter substances. **2**

decay theory. A theory of memory which views the cause of forgetting as the weakening of the memory trace over time. **7**

deductive reasoning. The ability to draw logical conclusions from statements or evidence. **8**

deep structure. Grammatical relationships and intentions which underlie words in sentences (the surface structure) and follow structural principles. **8**

defense mechanisms. In Freudian theory, unconscious means to deny, falsify, or distort reality. See also *denial, displacement, projection, rationalization, reaction formation, repression, sublimation*. **14**

defensive attribution. Attributions that serve to protect the perceiver's self-concept or view of the world, for example, the belief in a just world. **17**

delayed conditioning. A classical conditioning procedure in which the conditioned stimulus comes on before the unconditioned stimulus and terminates with the onset, during, or with the offset of unconditioned stimulus. **6**

delirium tremens. A state of confusion and hallucination exhibited by chronic alcoholics. **5**

dementia. Progressive deterioration of the ability to think abstractly, make judgments, and control impulses. **15**

dendrites. The fibers branching out from a neuron that receive signals from other neurons. **2**

denial. In psychoanalytic theory, a defense mechanism involving refusal to acknowledge certain aspects of reality. See also *defense mechanisms*. **14**

density. The objective number of people in a given space. Density may or may not give rise to a feeling of crowding. See also *crowding*. **18**

dependent variable. The variable in research which is measured; changes in it are attributable to variation in the independent variable in a properly controlled experiment. See also *control variable, independent variable*. **1**

depressants. A class of drugs that suppress the activity of the central nervous system. **5**

depression. An affective disorder characterized by intense sadness and feelings of hopelessness and worthlessness. **15**

depth cues. Binocular and monocular cues to the distance of an object from the observer, or the distance between two objects. **4**

descriptive statistics. A summary of measurements made on a sample or population. **Appendix**

developmental psychology. Study of the processes of growth and maturation, from conception to death. **1**

Diagnostic and Statistical Manual. See *DSM-III*.

dichromats. People with partial color blindness. Perceived hues are matched with only two primary colors, instead of three. See also *monochromats, trichromats*. **3**

difference threshold. The smallest change in a physical stimulus that can be perceived. See also *absolute threshold*. **3**

diffusion of responsibility. The tendency of individual members of a group to avoid direct action in a situation because of the presence of others. **18**

discounting principle. A principle used in making causal attributions of another's behavior. In situations where some behavior has many possible causes, an observer will tend to dismiss any one cause as the only explanation. **17**

discrimination training. Training in which responding in the presence of one stimulus (S+) is reinforced while responding in the presence of another stimulus (S−) is not.

disorganized schizophrenia. Schizophrenic condition marked by unorganized and nonsensical speech, unprovoked emotion, and bizarre behavior. **15**

displacement. The psychoanalytic defense mechanism by which feelings toward one object are refocused on a substitute object. See also *defense mechanisms*. **14**

dispositional cause. As an observer, attributing behavior to the person, rather than the situation. See also *situational cause*. **17**

dissociation. The process in which ideas, feelings, or activities operate automatically, or independently of consciousness. **5**

dissociative disorder. Behavior characterized by separating one's self-identity from the remainder of one's personality. See also *amnesia, fugue, multiple personality*. **15**

distal stimuli. Objects in the environment that give rise to proximal stimuli, those that strike the sense organs. **4**

divergent thinking. Reasoning that generates novel ideas by pursuing many new directions, none of which can be judged as the single correct answer. See also *convergent thinking*. **11**

dizygotic twins (DZ). Fraternal twins, or twins which arise from separate eggs. **2**

dopamine (DA). A neurotransmitter found in various brain structures. Schizophrenia may be related to an excess of dopamine. **2**

Doppler effect. The shift in perceived hue or pitch that occurs when a source of light or sound is moving rapidly. **4**

Down's syndrome. Mental retardation caused by genetic abnormality. Characteristic physical appearance includes thick eyelid folds. **11**

dream analysis. In Freudian therapy, the interpretation of dream symbols to uncover unconscious motives. **14**

drive. A motivational state that energizes behavior until it is removed. Many drives are produced by physiological needs, e.g., the hunger drive. **12**

drive theory. The assumption that all motivated behavior arises from drives and that responses which satisfy drives are reinforced. **12**

drug tolerance. In repeated drug use, the requirement for higher and higher dosages of drugs to produce the same effect. **5**

DSM-III (Diagnostic and Statistical Manual III). The latest classification system developed by the American Psychiatric Association. The DSM-III specifies behavioral criteria for determining diagnosis of abnormal behavior from clinical observation. **15**

dual coding theory. Proposition that the human memory system can store both pictorial/imaginal information and verbal/linguistic information. **7**

early selection theory. In theories of attention, the hypothesis that one sensory signal is selected early in the sensory system for further processing. All unattended signals are presumed to be lost from the system and therefore unavailable to the perceiver. See also *filter theory, late selection theory*. **5**

echoic storage. A peripheral memory system that maintains auditory information for approximately 2–4 seconds. **7**

ectomorph. See *Sheldon's theory of body types*.

educational psychology. The branch of psychology concerned with the application of psychological principles to the education of children and adults in schools. **1**

efferent nerves. Nerves conducting signals away from the central nervous system to the peripheral nervous system. See also *afferent nerves*. **2**

ego. In Freud's three-part division of the personality, the ego corresponds most closely to the conscious self. The ego attempts to reconcile the conflicting demands of the id, the superego, and external reality. See also *id, superego*. **14**

egocentrism. The naive belief that your point of view or visual perspective is shared by others. **9**

ego-ideal. See *superego*.

eidetic imagery. Sometimes referred to as photographic memory, it is uncommonly vivid imagery, as though the person were perceiving rather than remembering. **7**

Electra complex. In Freudian theory, a girl's intimate attachment to her father and hostility to her mother, occurring during the phallic stage. See also *Oedipus complex*. **14**

electroconvulsive therapy (ECT). A controversial form of shock treatment used mainly for alleviating depression. Electric current is passed briefly through the patient's head, producing temporary convulsions. **16**

electroencephalogram (EEG). The recording of wavelike electrical activity in the brain. These recordings are useful in the study of sleep and other states of consciousness. **2**

embryo. The developing organism during early differentiation of anatomical structures (from conception to six to eight weeks). **9**

embryonic stage. The period lasting six to eight weeks after fertilization. **9**

emotion. Complex physiological and cognitive states that people describe in subjective terms, such as joy, anger, or fear. **13**

empirical test. A test based on observation and experiment used to determine the truth or falsity of a hypothesis.

empiricism. The philosophical view that all of our knowledge of the world comes from experience, as opposed to innate knowledge. See also *nativism*. **4**

encoding specificity hypothesis. The theory that memory for an event is improved to the extent that the information present at the time of retrieval matches the way information is stored in memory. **7**

encounter groups. A general term for a large variety of groups set up to develop greater social and personal awareness in members. Procedures used in groups vary widely. **16**

endocrine system. A chemical communication system within the body. Endocrine glands secrete hormones that have specific effects on other body organs. **2**

endomorph. See *Sheldon's theory of body types.*

endorphins. Opiate-like substances within the body. **3**

engineering psychology. The branch of applied psychology concerned with the design of equipment and systems to fit the size, strength, and capabilities of the people who will use them. **1**

enkephalins. See *endorphins.*

environmental psychology. The branch of social psychology dealing with the way in which environment influences behavior. Environmental psychologists are often concerned with the problems of an expanding industrial and technological society. **1**

epinephrine. A hormone that increases the liver's sugar output and accelerates the heart rate and surge of blood to the skeletal muscles. **2**

episodic memory. Memory dependent upon retrieving the particular time, place, or context in which a particular event or episode took place. See also *semantic memory.* **7**

equilibration. In Piaget's theory, the process of achieving equilibrium, a temporary balance between existing knowledge and perceived information. **9**

equilibratory senses. Sense organs in the middle ear that help maintain balance. **3**

equilibrium. See *equilibration.*

escape conditioning. The learning of a response that terminates a noxious stimulus. **6**

estrogens. Hormones, secreted to a larger degree in females, that influence female physical development. **12**

ethology. The field of inquiry concerned with the study of the behavior of animals in natural settings. **1**

expectancy. A cognitive representation of an event predicted to follow an event currently being processed. **6**

experimental psychology. The laboratory study of psychological phenomena. Such research is characterized by careful control over experimental and environmental variables. See also *field research.* **1**

experimental research. The creation of a situation that allows controlled observation. The experimenter varies some aspect of the situation, controls all others, and then observes the effects of the variation on the behavior of interest. **1**

external validity. The generalizability of conclusions to a range of conditions, populations, and environmental settings not included in research. **1**

extinction. (1) In classical conditioning, stopping presentation of the unconditioned stimulus. (2) In instrumental conditioning, discontinuing reinforcement for a response. **6**

extrasensory perception (ESP). A controversial category of perception which allegedly occurs without any physical stimulation of the sensory receptors. Varieties of ESP include clairvoyance (awareness of objects not present to the senses), telepathy (transmission of thought between two minds), precognition (ability to foresee events), and psychokinesis (the ability of the mind to move or bend objects). **3**

extrinsic motivation. Doing something in order to obtain an external reward. See also *intrinsic motivation.* **12**

Eysenck Personality Questionnaire (EPQ). A paper-and-pencil personality test designed to measure three dimensions of normal personality: introversion-extraversion, neuroticism-stability, and psychoticism. **14**

factor analysis. A statistical technique used to identify and analyze the underlying dimensions, or factors, in a large variety of measures, such as those gained from a battery of tests. **11**

family studies. A method used to measure the influence of genetics on behavior by examining the pattern of a trait over several members of one family. **2**

family therapy. A form of psychotherapy in which problems are addressed by the family members as a group rather than by an individual. **16**

feature detectors. Cells in the visual cortex that selectively respond to particular stimuli. **3**

fetal period. The prenatal stage lasting from about two months after conception until birth in humans; during this time the fetus becomes capable of sustaining life independently of the mother. **9**

fetus. The name of the unborn organism in the womb as it develops its species characteristics from about two months until birth. See also *fetal period.* **9**

figure-ground segregation. A principle of perceptual organization in which viewers of a complex two- or three-dimensional scene perceive part of it as being closer (the figure) than the rest (the ground). **4**

filter theory. In theories of attention, the hypothesis that the perceptual system selects one signal from the many sources of information available to it for further perceptual analysis. See also *early selection theory, late selection theory.* **5**

firing. The conduction of an action potential through the neuron. **2**

fissures. Natural divisions in the surface of the cortex. The *central fissure* separates the frontal lobe from the parietal lobe; the *lateral fissure* constitutes the boundary of the temporal lobe; the *longitudinal fissure* separates the two hemispheres. **2**

fixed action pattern. A stereotyped, complex behavior that is instinctive, usually elicited by a specific sign stimulus (for example, the tongue flick with which a frog catches flies). See also *sign stimulus.* **12**

fixed interval scallop. The name of the cumulative record of performance by a subject on a fixed interval schedule, so-called because responding slows greatly after each reinforcement and increases when the next reinforcement is due. **6**

fixed interval schedule. A pattern of intermittent reinforcement in which a reward is provided following the first response made after a certain (or fixed) period of time has passed, and the time period remains constant for each trial. **6**

fixed ratio schedule. A pattern of intermittent reinforcement in which a reward is given only after a certain number of responses have been made, for example, five lever presses. **6**

flashbulb memory. Clear recollections that people sometimes have of the events surrounding a momentous event, for example, when they first learned President Ronald Reagan had been shot. **7**

fluid intelligence. The capacity to analyze and solve problems. **10**

focal colors. Certain basic colors that are salient to all observers regardless of the particular labels used to describe them. **8**

foot-in-the-door effect. A method for increasing compliance to a large request by first inducing someone to agree to a much smaller request. (The phenomenon is also called foot-in-the-door technique.) **17**

formal operational period. In Piaget's theory, the period during which children acquire logical thinking skills, usually after eleven or twelve years of age. **9**

fovea. A small region in the retina that contains the highest concentration of cones and provides the greatest visual acuity. **3**

fraternal twins. See *dizygotic twins.*

free association. (1) In psychoanalysis, a technique in which the patient simply reports everything which comes to awareness. (2) A form of testing in which an analyst provides a stimulus and the patient counters with the first word or thought that comes to mind. **14**

free recall test. A technique used in the study of short-term memory which involves asking people to recall a list of words to the best of their ability in any order they like. **1**

frequency. The number of complete cycles per second of a sound wave. See also *hertz*. **3**

frequency distribution. A table or graph indicating the number of individuals scoring at different levels on some measure. **Appendix**

frequency theory. A theory of pitch perception which suggests that when a hair cell fires, its rhythm or tempo of firing is in synchrony with the frequency of the sound entering the ear. See also *place theory, volley theory*. **3**

frontal lobe. One of four natural sections of each cerebral hemisphere, positioned in front of the central fissure. See also *occipital lobe, parietal lobe, temporal lobe*. **2**

frustration. The blocking of or interference with goal-directed activity, or the absence of a reward when one is expected. **13**

frustration-aggression hypothesis. The hypothesis that frustration induces an aggressive drive which, in turn, motivates aggressive behavior. See also *revised frustration-aggression hypothesis*. **18**

fugue. A dissociative disorder in which an individual leaves home and establishes a different existence in another place. Although the former life is blocked from memory, other abilities are unimpaired and the individual appears normal. See also *amnesia, dissociative disorder, multiple personality disorder*. **15**

functional amnesia. Failure of memory that often occurs immediately following severe conflict or psychological stress. Unlike amnesia caused by cerebral shock, this type of amnesia may be unconsciously willed by individuals in order to forget certain events or actions. **15**

functional fixedness. A tendency to consider only one use for familiar objects, or more generally always to view problems in the same way. **8**

functionalism. A school of psychology which emphasized mental processes as the proper subject matter for psychology. Functionalists argued that the mind should be studied in terms of its usefulness to the organism in adapting to its environment. **1**

fundamental attribution error. The tendency to underestimate situational influences on behavior and to assume instead that some personal characteristic of the individual is responsible, or a bias toward dispositional rather than situational attributions. See also *attribution theory*. **17**

GABA. The most common inhibitory neurotransmitter. **2**

galvanic skin response (GSR). A change in the electrical resistance of the skin. The GSR measure is commonly used as an indicator of arousal or anxiety. **6**

gambler's fallacy. Willingness to make irrational bets in probabilistic situations due to the failure to recognize the independence of some events that occur in sequence, such as the successive flips of a coin. **8**

ganglion cells. In the retina, groups of nerve cells that collect information from the bipolar cells and pass it along to the brain via the optic nerve. **3**

gate-control theory. In the study of pain, a theory that sensations result from the activation of nerve fibers that lead to specific centers of the brain responsible for pain perception. **3**

gender identity. The personal conviction that one is male or female. **9**

gender identity disorder. A psychosexual disorder in which the individual lacks a clear identification with his or her physiological gender. **15**

gender role. A type of behavior that is culturally sanctioned as appropriate for males or females. **9**

gene. The basic unit of inheritance that is located on and transmitted by the chromosome and develops into a hereditary character as it reacts with the environment and other genes. **2**

general adaptation syndrome. A series of reactions that occur under stress, beginning with alarm and progressing through resistance and exhaustion. **13**

generality of results. The assumption that findings in one experimental situation will generalize to others. **1**

generalized anxiety disorder. An anxiety disorder characterized by general apprehensiveness, tension, and physical complaints that last at least a month and lack specific focus. See also *panic disorder, phobia, obsessive-compulsive disorder*. **15**

genetics. The study of the inheritance of traits and the mechanisms of this inheritance. **2**

genital stage. The fifth and final psychosexual stage, according to Freud, which occurs during adolescence and in which the individual obtains pleasure from sexual contact with others. See also *anal, latency, oral, and phallic stages*. **14**

genotype. The genetic composition of an individual. **2**

Gestalt psychology. A theoretical approach that emphasizes the role of organized wholes ("gestalten") in perception and other psychological processes. **1**

Gestalt therapy. A form of psychotherapy based on the ideas of Fritz Perls which emphasizes the individual's positive and creative aspects. Gestalt methods are directed at externalizing the patient's feelings so they can be confronted and if necessary changed. See also *psychotherapy*. **16**

Gestalts. Patterns of sensation so arranged as to affect the nature of perceptual experience. **1**

gifted children. Children who are performing at levels many years beyond their chronological ages, as defined by high scores on tests. **11**

given-new contract. A linguistic principle describing how new information is understood by being related to previous statements that can be readily comprehended (the "given" information). **8**

glial cells. Cells that provide services to neurons. **2**

glucostatic theory. The hypothesis that level of blood sugar (glucose) is regulated by feeding behavior. Feeding occurs when blood glucose is too low; satiety occurs when blood glucose is raised. **12**

grammar. A set of linguistic principles that describe how classes of words are connected in sentences. **8**

group therapy. Psychotherapy undertaken by several people simultaneously. **16**

habituation. A research procedure in which a stimulus (such as a red light) is repeatedly presented until the subject no longer reacts to it (thus, habituates). Afterward some aspect of the stimulus (such as its color) is altered to determine if the change can be detected, as evidenced by attention to the new stimulus. **4**

hair cell. A cell known as a receptor which lines the basilar membrane of the ear. Hair cells convert the mechanical pressures of air waves into neural impulses. **3**

hallucinogens. Psychoactive drugs that usually produce altered perceptual experiences. **5**

hedonism. The theory that individuals are motivated primarily by the desire to seek pleasure and avoid pain. **12**

hemispheric specialization. The tendency for certain psychological functions (such as language and spatial processing) to be controlled more by one hemisphere of the brain than the other. **2**

Hering's grid. A retinal illusion in which lateral inhibition causes the viewer to perceive nonexistent gray spots. **4**

heritability. The proportion of variance in a trait (within a population) that is attributable to genetic factors. **11**

hermaphrodite. A person whose genital structure is internally or externally ambiguous. **12**

hertz (Hz). A unit of frequency of a wave equal to cycles per second (cps); i.e., 10 Hz = 10 cps. **3**

heuristic. A rule-of-thumb strategy that serves as a guide to problem solving. **8**

hierarchy of needs. A ranking of levels of needs in which the first level must be satisfied before the second, and so on. The most influential is Maslow's hierarchy of needs. **14**

higher-order conditioning. A form of conditioning in which a conditioned stimulus from earlier training serves as an unconditioned stimulus. **6**

hippocampus. A nerve tract that is part of the limbic system, located in the temporal lobe of the brain, that may be involved in the formation and consolidation of memory. **2**

homeostasis. Literally, "equal state," which cells of the body maintain. **12**

homosexuality. Sexual feeling for a person of the same sex. Facultative homosexuality describes occasional same-sex acts in particular situations, but with a customary preference for the opposite sex. Obligative homosexuality refers to exclusive preference for the same sex, with a corresponding identity. **12**

hormones. The chemical secretions of the endocrine glands that are distributed by body fluids and activate specific receptive organs. **2**

hue. The dimension of visual sensation that is most closely related to the color of the perceived object. It derives primarily from the wavelength of the stimulus. **3**

humanistic psychology. An approach to psychology that emphasizes the consciousness of human beings. Humanistic psychology is concerned with the qualities that distinguish human beings from other animals (e.g., desires for dignity, self-worth). See also *phenomenological approach.* **1**

hyperopia. A common condition referred to as farsightedness. Hyperopia results when the image of the object being viewed is focused beyond the retina. See also *myopia.* **3**

hypnosis. A sleeplike but responsive state achieved artificially by a hypnotist. The hypnotic state is typically characterized by relaxation, exaggerated suggestibility, and focused attention. **5**

hypothalamic thermostat. A self-regulating feedback system that controls the body's production of hormones. **10**

hypothalamus. A tiny structure lying beneath the thalamus that has tremendous importance in the regulation of emotion and motivation. **2**

hypothesis. A tentative assumption advanced to explain or predict certain facts. **1**

iconic storage. The peripheral memory system that maintains visual information for very brief periods of time. **7**

id. In Freud's three-part theory of personality, the most primitive part which provides instinctive energy that demands immediate gratification of aggressive and sexual needs and desires. See also *ego, pleasure principle, superego.* **14**

ideal-self. The composite of ideas, feelings, and attributes people would like to have about themselves. See also *actual-self, self-actualization, self-concept.* **14**

ideational fluency. The ability to generate many ideas about the same stimulus or problem. **11**

identical twins. See *monozygotic twins.*

identification with the aggressor. In Freudian theory, the process that occurs in boys during the phallic stage in which they internalize their father's values to form a conscience. See also *castration anxiety, ego-ideal, phallic stage, superego.* **14**

identity development. The establishment of an independent and positive view of oneself. **10**

imaginal code. An internal representation or memory code for previously perceived visual sensory information. Imaginal codes are presumed to bear some resemblance to the experiences they represent. **1**

implosion therapy. A type of behavior therapy in which patients are encouraged to imagine or engage in anxiety-arousing stimulus situations and to experience their anxiety as fully as possible. Since these situations do not pose any objective harm to the patients, the inner explosion (implosion) of anxiety abates and the stimulus loses its power to elicit anxiety. **16**

imprinting. The tendency acquired early in life to follow or approach an object. Geese, for example, will follow any large moving object they are exposed to during a *critical period* shortly after birth. This tendency persists throughout life. **12**

incentive motivation. Motivation produced by anticipation of events in the environment. Positive incentives increase performance; negative incentives decrease performance. **12**

inclusive fitness. The sum of an individual's fitness plus the fitness of its relatives. See *individual fitness.* **18**

independent variable. In a controlled experiment, the factor or potential cause of behavior under investigation. The independent variable is the element manipulated by the experimenter. See also *control variable, confounding, dependent variable.* **1**

individual fitness. The extent to which an individual produces viable offspring that also successfully reproduce. **18**

individual psychology. The school of psychoanalysis founded by Alfred Adler in which feelings of inferiority and the need for power are considered important. **14**

individuation. In Erickson's theory of psychosocial development, the process of identity development. **10**

induced motion. The illusion that a stationary object is moving when in fact some object nearby is actually in motion, e.g., when your car is stopped but appears to move backward as your neighbor's car edges forward. **4**

inductive reasoning. The ability to determine or construct a rule that links together elements or relations. **8**

industrial/organizational psychology. The branch of psychology concerned with the application of psychological phenomena to industrial problems. Industrial/organizational psychologists are mainly concerned with the selection and training of personnel and staff, job performance and productivity, and the ways in which organizations operate. **1**

inferential statistics. Techniques used for determining the reliability and generality of a particular experimental result. **Appendix**

inferiority complex. Alfred Adler's term for feelings of inadequacy. **14**

information processing. An approach to thinking that measures and defines the flow of information through a person. The approach borrows much of its terminology from computer technology. **9**

innate-drive theory of aggression. The theory that humans are aggressive because they have an inborn drive to be that way. See also *aggression.* 18

inner ear. The portion of the ear containing the cochlea and the semicircular canals. 3

insanity. A legal term for a mental disorder, implying that someone is not responsible for his or her actions. See also *McNaughten Rule.* 15

insight. The perception of relationships followed by a solution, as in problem-solving. 6

insomnia. The class of disorders characterized primarily by consistent or prolonged inability to obtain enough sleep. 5

instinct theory. The theory that proposes that motivation is based on innate, internal forces, which are characteristic of a species. 12

instrumental conditioning. A type of conditioning in which reinforcement is contingent upon the subject providing a particular response; also called operant conditioning. 6

intelligence quotient (IQ). An index of a subject's level of achievement relative to others on a standardized test that purportedly measures intelligence. I.Q. = Mental Age ÷ Chronological Age × 100. 11

intensity. The amount of energy in light waves. Generally, the more intense the source of light, the brighter the light will appear. 3

interactionism. In modern personality theory, a framework in which behavior is seen as resulting from the interaction between consistent personality dispositions and the situations in which people find themselves. 14

interference. See *proactive* or *retroactive interference.*

intermittent reinforcement. See *partial reinforcement.*

internal locus of control. A child's sense of responsibility for personal success or failure. 9

internal validity. Refers to the state in which an observed effect on a dependent variable can be safely attributed to the experimenter's manipulation of the independent variable. See also *external validity.* 1

interneurons. Neurons that connect one neuron to another. 2

interposition. A monocular depth cue resulting from the fact that when one object blocks another from view the eye tends to perceive the former object as closer than the later. 4

interval schedules. Schedules in which reinforcement is given for the first response made after a certain period of time (interval) has passed. On *fixed interval schedules* the period of time is always the same; on *variable interval schedules* the period of time fluctuates. 6

interview. A meeting between a researcher and a respondent at which information about the respondent is obtained through personal questions and answers. 1

intrinsic motivation. The desire to do something for its own sake and the pleasure of doing it. 12

ions. Electrically charged particles that pass through the cell membrane changing its electrical state from positive to negative or vice versa. 2

iris. The colored, circular muscle in the eye that regulates the size of pupil to control the amount of light entering the eye. The iris gives eyes their distinctive color. 3

James-Lange theory of emotion. A theory that emotion is the subjective experience of peripheral physiological reactions that occur when an emotional stimulus is perceived. Thus a stimulus leads to physiological responses, and awareness of the responses causes the emotion. 13

just noticeable difference (j.n.d.). The amount of increase or decrease in a stimulus that an observer can reliably detect. See also *difference threshold.* 3

kinesthetic sense (kinethesis). The muscle, tendon, and joint sense that, along with sensations from the inner ear, provide information about the position of the body in space. 3

Korsakoff's syndrome. An amnesiuc condition afflicting some chronic alcoholics, many of whom have suffered malnutrition and irreversible brain damage. 7

labeling theory. The theory that "mental illness" or other social deviances are brought into being by the application of a title or label. Once the label is applied, deviant people's expectations of themselves, as well as others' expectations of them, are purported to cause the display of behaviors associated with the label. Theorists suggest the behaviors would not be apparent without the label. 15

language. A means of symbolic communication based on sounds, written symbols, and gestures. 8

language competence. An inborn knowledge about language all children seem to possess. 9

latency stage. The fourth of Freud's psychosexual stages of development, occurring roughly between the ages of six and the onset of puberty, when drive activity subsides, allowing the ego to consolidate the changes that have occured to that point. See also *anal, genital, oral,* and *phallic stages.* 14

latent content. The underlying meaning of a dream, such as the individual's repressed wishes expressed symbolically in the dream. 16

latent learning. Learning that is not shown immediately in performance. For example, in a latent learning experiment an animal is exposed to a maze with no reinforcement; the reinforcement is introduced at a later time to determine if the animal learned anything about the maze. 6

lateral fissure. One of the natural divisions in the surface of the cortex, it constitutes the boundary of the temporal lobe. 2

lateral geniculate nucleus. A portion of the thalamus that receives neural impulses from the retina and passes them on to the visual cortex. 3

lateral inhibition. The tendency for stimulated receptors in the visual system to inhibit adjacent receptors. 3

late selection theory. The view that all incoming sensory signals receive some processing initially, and then one signal is chosen by the nervous system for further processing. See also *early selection theory.* 5

law of effect. Behavioral law stating that responses followed by reinforcement tend to increase in frequency, while responses not followed by reinforcement become less frequent. 6

learned helplessness. A condition hypothesized to develop after an organism is exposed to a repeated, inescapable stimulus. Later, learning to escape aversive stimuli is impaired. 6

learning. A relatively permanent change in behavior or knowledge that occurs as a result of experience. 6

lens. The flexible, transparent structure located at the front of the eye that changes shape in order for images of near or distant objects to focus on the retina. 3

letter detectors. Mechanisms hypothesized in the visual system to identify letters from their visual features. 4

level of confidence. A probability statement concerning the decision to reject the null hypothesis. It specifies the probability that the decision to reject the null hypothesis was incorrect and in actuality that no difference existed among the population means. **Appendix**

levels-of-processing approach. In this approach, memory is considered a byproduct of perceptual processing where perception of a stimulus is conceived as involving stages of coding that lead to comprehension. Deeper codes lead to better memory. **7**

lexical ambiguity. The multiple meanings of words. **8**

lexical decision task. An experimental procedure in which subjects view strings of letters and must decide which form words. Reaction time and errors are the key measure. **7**

LH lesions. Damage to the lateral hypothalamus. Rats with these lesions eat and drink less than a nonlesioned rat. **11**

libido. In Freudian terminology, the energy of the sexual instinct in the functioning of the personality. **14**

life review. The reflection on life's accomplishments that occurs as a person nears death. **10**

light adaptation. The rapid adjustment made by the eye when it is exposed to bright light. See also *dark adaptation*. **3**

lightness. The reflected light from an object. **3**

limbic system. Groups of similar cell bodies located in the thalamus and hypothalamus and in part of the brain above these structures that appear to form a border around the lower fore-brain. Parts of the limbic system are involved in emotional behavior. **2**

linear perspective. A monocular depth cue that is based on the fact that as objects recede they appear to converge or grow smaller in size (e.g., railroad tracks). **4**

linear reasoning. A type of deductive reasoning requiring the ability to discern relations among a series of elements. This may be accomplished by constructing spatial representations, or mental images, of the entire series by fitting each pair into one image. **8**

linguistic ambiguity. Multiple interpretations of language that may be produced at several levels: phonological (sounds), lexical (words), syntactic (word order), and semantic (meaning). **8**

linguistic codes. Memories based on verbal recoding. **7**

linguistic competence. The potential to produce and comprehend language. **8**

linguistic determinism. The view that diverse language terms, grammars, and linguistic abilities cause people to think differently. **8**

linguistics. The study of language, its rules, forms, and functions. **8**

link method. A memory device in which the learner forms mental images of the items to be remembered thus linking the items together. See also *mnemonic devices*. **7**

lipostatic theory. The theory that the level of fat deposits is regulated by feeding behavior, particularly with respect to long-term regulation of food intake. **12**

loci method. See *method of loci*.

longitudinal analysis. An experimental method of studying the same subjects for long time periods with repeated observations. **9**

longitudinal fissure. See *fissures*.

long-term store. According to the three-store model of memory, the relatively permanent component of the system that is presumed to have a very large capacity for holding information. See also *sensory store, short-term store.* **7**

loudness. The psychological attribute of sounds corresponding to their intensity and primarily related to the amplitude of soundwaves. **3**

love scale. A paper-and-pencil test developed in an attempt to measure romantic love. **17**

magnitude estimation. A research procedure used to construct psychophysical scales. For example, in magnitude estimation of loudness an observer is presented a number of tones and asked to give each a numerical value indicating how loud each tone sounds. **3**

mainstreaming. The educational practice of placing handicapped children in regular rather than special classes. **11**

mania. An affective disorder characterized by intense euphoria or sense of well-being. See also *affective disorder, depression.* **15**

manifest content. The part of a dream that is remembered and reported. **16**

Maslow's hierarchy of needs. Physiological needs must be satisfied prior to the need for safety, which in turn be satisfied before love needs, then esteem; when all these needs are satisfied the final level, self-actualization, can be reached. **12**

McCollough effect. A visual illusion caused by the sensitivity of cortical feature detectors to combinations of color and orientation. **4**

McNaughten rule. A standard of legal responsibility for actions; an accused is judged to be sane or insane on the basis of whether he or she was capable of knowing that an act was wrong at the time it was being committed. See also *insanity.* **15**

mean. The most commonly used measure of central tendency of a frequency distribution, it is the arithmetic average of all scores in the distribution. **Appendix**

measures of central tendency. In descriptive statistics, a value used to indicate the midpoint of the frequency of scores in a distribution. See also *mean, median, mode.* **Appendix**

measures of dispersion. In descriptive statistics, a measure of how scores in a distribution spread away from a center point. See also *range, standard deviation.* **Appendix**

median. A measure of central tendency equal to a score that divides a distribution into two equal parts, with half the scores being larger than the median and half smaller. **Appendix**

medulla. The portion of the brain in the lower rear section adjacent to the spinal cord that controls some vital functions, such as breathing. **2**

memory codes. Forms of representation in memory, e.g., imaginal and verbal codes. **7**

memory trace. The inferred change in the nervous system that persists between the time something is learned and the time it is retrieved. **7**

menarche. The first menstrual period. **10**

menopause. The point at which women cease to undergo menstrual periods. **10**

mental age (MA). An individual's intellectual level of performance relative to others as opposed to his or her chronological age. **11**

mental retardation. An impairment in thinking and social skills that can range from slightly below average to profoundly handicapped. The degree of retardation is usually judged on the basis of test scores and behavior. **11**

mental set. The tendency to view new problems in the same fashion as previous problems. **8**

mere exposure effect. The tendency to like a person or an object more with increased exposure. **17**

mesmerism. An early name for hypnosis, from Anton Mesmer, a practitioner who used the phenomenon for varied purposes. See also *hypnosis.* **5**

mesomorph. See *Sheldon's theory of body types.*

metacognition. Awareness of one's own knowledge and mental abilities. **8**

method of loci. A memory technique in which the items to be recalled are transformed into mental images, which are then located at successive positions along a visualized route, such as an imagined walk down a familiar street. It is a useful technique for remembering lists of items in specific order. See also *mnemonic devices*. 7

midbrain. The upper portion of the brain stem which is the conduit for all neural information passing between the brain and the spinal cord. 2

middle ear. The portion of the ear extending from the tympanic membrane to the cochlea and containing the ossicles. 3

mnemonic devices. Any technique or strategy used to improve memory. See also *link method, method of loci, peg method*. 7

modality effect. The finding that when subjects are required to remember lists of items, the last few are better remembered when presented auditorily than visually. 7

mode. A measure of central tendency equivalent to the most frequently occurring score (or class of scores) in a frequency distribution. **Appendix**

monochromats. People who are completely colorblind and see objects as varying only in brightness. See also *dichromats*. 3

monocular cues. In vision, the factors that can be used by only one eye to allow judgment of distance. See also *interposition, linear perspective, motion parallax, texture gradients*. 4

monozygotic twins (MZ). Twins developed from the division of a single fertilized egg. Also called identical twins. See also *dizygotic twins*. 2

moon illusion. A phenomenon in which the moon appears to be larger when it is on the horizon than when it is directly above the observer. 4

moral anxiety. In Freudian theory, a condition that develops when people punish themselves too severely for often minor transgressions; sometimes also called guilt. In this condition a strong superego dominates a weak ego. See also *neurotic anxiety, objective anxiety*. 14

moral reasoning. The ability to distinguish between right and wrong. 9

morpheme. The smallest unit of speech sound that has meaning in a given language; for example, prefixes, suffixes, and single syllable words. 8

motion parallax. In perception, a depth cue in which the images of nearby objects sweep across the field of vision faster than objects at a distance. 4

motivation. A theoretical construct that is used to explain initiation, direction, vigor, and persistence of behavior. 12

motor codes. The representation that is assumed to support memory for physical (motor) activities. 7

motor cortex. The areas of the cortex involved in controlling bodily movements. 2

motor neuron. Nerve cell that carries signals from the brain and spinal cord to the muscles, organs, and glands of the body. 2

Müller-Lyer illusion. A spatial distortion in which two parallel lines of equal length appear to be unequal because of pairs of angular lines drawn at the ends of the parallel lines. 4

multiple personality disorder. A dissociative disorder in which an individual expresses two or more distinct personalities that have varying degrees of awareness of each other. See also *amnesia, dissociative disorder, fugue*. 15

myelin sheath. A segmented tube of glial cells that insulates many axons. 2

myopia. A condition commonly referred to as nearsightedness. It results when the image of the object being viewed is focused in front of the retina. See also *hyperopia*. 3

nanometer (NM). A unit of measure corresponding to one-billionth of a meter. 3

narcolepsy. A sleep disturbance characterized by a continual feeling of sleepiness and an uncontrollable tendency to fall asleep for brief periods at inappropriate times. 5

nativism. (1) As a philosophy, the position that humans are born with some innate knowledge. (2) As a theory of perception, the view that humans are born with the ability to perceive stimuli, and that learning plays a relatively small role in perceptual development. See also *empiricism*. 4

natural concepts. Concepts that are familiar to us, rooted in experience, simply and easily characterized by prototypes. 8

naturalistic observation. The viewing and recording of events as they occur in nature. It is used frequently for ethological studies of animals. 1

natural selection. A theory of evolution describing a process by which species with traits that enable them to survive and reproduce pass on fitness to succeeding generations. Over time, the changes can become so great they constitute a new species that alters the characteristics of a general population. 2

nature versus nurture. A philosophical controversy about the source of knowledge and the causes of behavior. The "nature" position argues that people are born with some inherited knowledge that guides behavior. The "nurture" position argues that knowledge is acquired and behavior is shaped by experiences in the world. See also *empiricism, nativism*. 4

need for achievement. One of twenty basic human motives suggested by Henry Murray; in brief, the desire to do things as well as possible, better than they have been done before. 12

negative contrast effect. The exaggerated suppression in performance obtained when the reward a subject customarily receives suddenly diminishes. 6

negative reinforcer. An event that increases the likelihood of the preceding behavior when it is removed, e.g., removal of shock. 6

neobehaviorism. A theoretical approach that continues the behaviorists' traditional emphasis on behavior and objective methodology, it also employs some unobservable constructs (such as hunger, thirst) to explain behavior. 1

neo-Freudian psychoanalysis. Schools of thought and therapy based on modifications of Freud's theories, including the ideas of such theorists as Jung and Adler. See also *psychoanalysis*. 14

neomentalism. The objective study of the structure, function, and development of mental representations by making inferences from objective measures. 1

nerve. A collection of axons. 2

nerve cell membrane. A molecular substance that protects the neuron and is the key to communication among cells. 2

neuron. A nerve cell, usually consisting of a cell body, axon, and dendrites. 2

neuropsychology. A branch of psychology that studies the nervous system and how it mediates behavior. 1

neuroses. A broad term once used to describe a wide range of nonpsychotic mental disorders whose primary symptoms were anxiety or various defenses against anxiety. See also *character disorders, DSM-III, mental disorder, psychoses*. 15

neurotic anxiety. In Freudian theory, a condition that develops when people fear their instincts will get out of control; a strong id dominates a weak ego. See also *moral anxiety, objective anxiety*. 14

neurotransmitter. A chemical released by a neuron when an axon fires to transmit a signal from one neuron to the next. Also known as transmitter substance. 2

nodes of Ranvier. The bare portions between segments of myelin sheath on the axons of neurons. 2

noise. The constant background of randomly varying signals in the sensory system caused by firing nerve cells. 3

nonconscious processes. The mental or physical operations that cannot be brought to consciousness, such as the processes occurring in the retina during visual perception. 5

nonreactive observations. Behavioral observations made by detracting attention away from the researcher. 1

norepinephrine (NE). A neurotransmitter that has an inhibitory effect on the brain and spinal cord, but an excitatory effect on heart muscles and smooth muscles of the blood vessels, intestine, and urogenital system. 2

normal curve. See *normal distribution.*

normal distribution. A symmetrical, bell-shaped frequency distribution that roughly describes many events in nature. The greatest number of scores fall in the middle of the curve, with fewer found at the extremes on each end. 11

null hypothesis. In statistics, the hypothesis that any difference observed among treatment conditions is merely a chance fluctuation and that the true mean difference between conditions is zero. **Appendix**

obedience. In social psychology, behaving in accord with the requests or demands of an authority figure. 17

object permanence. The understanding that objects continue to exist even when they are no longer observed, usually acquired by six months of age in humans. 9

objective anxiety. In Freudian theory, perception by the ego of a genuine danger in the real world. See also *neurotic anxiety, moral anxiety.* 14

observational learning. Learning that results from watching the behavior of others and seeing the consequences of the behavior for them. Sometimes called vicarious learning. See also *vicarious conditioning, vicarious reinforcement.* 6

obsessive-compulsive disorder. An anxiety disorder characterized by anxiety or apprehension, persistent unwanted thoughts, and/or the compulsion to repeat ritualistic acts such as washing hands. See also *anxiety disorder, generalized anxiety disorder, panic disorder, phobias.* 15

occipital lobe. One of the four natural sections of the cerebral hemisphere, it is the rear portion containing the vision centers. See also *frontal, parietal,* and *temporal lobes.* 2

Oedipus complex. In Freudian theory, a young boy's intimate attachment to his mother and jealousy of this father, occurring during the phallic stage. See also *castration anxiety, Electra complex, phallic stage.* 14

olfactory epithelium. The patches of mucous membrane located at the top of the nasal cavity and containing the olfactory receptors. 3

operant conditioning. A type of conditioning in which reinforcement is contingent upon the subject's providing a particular response; also called *instrumental conditioning.* 6

operant conditioning chamber. A box with a device (such as a small lever on the wall) that an animal can operate in order to receive reinforcement. It is sometimes called a *Skinner box.* 6

operant response. A response resulting in or followed by a particular effect on the environment. 6

opiate narcotics. The group of drugs comprising the various naturally occurring alkaloids of the opium poppy, including morphine, codeine, and heroin. These drugs produce analgesic effects and have complex psychological effects. 5

opponent-process theory. (1) In perception, a theory that explains color vision by postulating three types of color cells: white-black, yellow-blue, and green-red. The perception of color is the result of the combined action of these pairs. See also *trichromatic theory.* (2) In motivation, a theory that any affective reaction, whether pleasant or unpleasant, automatically produces the opposite reaction. 3

optic nerve. The bundle of nerve fibers that relays information from the ganglion cells of the retina to the lateral geniculate nucleus of the thalamus. 3

oral stage. The first of Freud's psychosexual stages of development, through the first year of life, during which the mouth is the source of sensual pleasure. See also *anal, latency, genital,* and *phallic stages.* 14

organizational psychology. See *industrial/organizational psychology.*

osmometric thirst. A temporary cellular fluid imbalance in which sodium is prevented from leaving the cells so water leaves to maintain the sodium-water balance outside the cell; the resulting dehydration causes thirst. 12

ossicles. The set of three tiny interconnecting bones (malleus, incus, and stapes) that connect the tympanic membrane (eardrum) to the cochlea. 3

outer ear. The portion of the ear containing the pinna (the flap of skin protruding from both sides of the head) and the auditory canal. 3

oval window. A flexible membrane on the outer surface of the cochlea (of the ear) to which the stapes is attached. 3

ovaries. The female organ that produces the egg for fertilization and the female sex hormone, estrogen. Each of the two ovaries is connected to the uterus by the Fallopian tubes. 2

palliation. A means of coping with stress by dealing with its symptoms rather than its source. Palliative techniques include drugs, muscle relaxation, or intrapsychic methods. 13

panic disorder. An anxiety disorder characterized by intense fear or terror. Attacks usually last only minutes but long after they have passed apprehension persists. Unlike phobias, panic attacks are typically not associated with particular stimuli. See also *generalized anxiety disorder, obsessive-compulsive disorder, phobias.* 15

paranoid schizophrenia. A schizophrenic disorder characterized by delusions of persecution or grand importance, with hallucinations and a loss of contact with reality. See also *schizophrenic disorder, catatonic schizophrenia.* 15

parasympathetic nervous system. The division of the autonomic nervous system that serves vegetative functions and conserves energies. Associated reactions include increased salivation and digestive processes, and decreased heart rate and blood pressure. 2

parietal lobe. One of the four sections of the cerebral hemisphere, the middle region of the top of the skull, which contains somesthetic centers. See also *frontal, occipital,* and *temporal lobes.* 2

partial reinforcement. Any schedule of reinforcement where fewer than 100 percent of the responses are rewarded. Also called intermittent reinforcement. 6

partial reinforcement extinction effect. The result that almost any schedule of intermittent or partial reinforcement will produce greater resistance to extinction than continuous reinforcement. 6

pattern recognition. The cognitive and perceptual processes by which people are able to perceive groups of features as unified patterns. See also *bottom-up theories, top-down theories.* 4

Pavlovian conditioning. See *classical conditioning.*

peg method. A memory technique utilizing a rhyme scheme and mental imagery (one is a bun, two is a shoe, etc.), in which the item to be remembered is coded in an interactive image with object in the rhyme. See also *mnemonic devices.* 7

penis envy. In Freudian psychosexual development, the alleged envy of girls, who are in the phallic stage, of the male genital organ; it is accompanied by attraction for the father. See also *Electra complex, phallic stage.* 14

perception. The process of interpreting and understanding sensory information. **3**

perceptual constancy. The fact that objects are normally perceived as remaining constant in size and shape, despite the fact that the retinal images of the objects may be constantly changing as the perceiver or objects move. **4**

perceptual grouping. A principle of perceptual organization that refers to the tendency to perceive independent spatial patterns as groups or units. **4**

perceptual illusions. Misleading images of the relationships among stimuli, that do not conform to physical reality. **4**

perceptual organization. The processes by which elementary sensations are organized into perceived objects; thus three lines joined together end-to-end are perceived as a triangle, not simply as three lines. **4**

peripheral nervous system. All of the nervous system outside the brain and spinal cord. **2**

peripheral processing. An individual's superficial appraisal of an argument's logic. **17**

peripheral vision. Vision away from the center of focus. **3**

personality disorder. A well-established maladaptive behavior pattern such as self-defeating personal habits and forms of social deviance. The DSM III classification system estimates that individuals may suffer from one of ten forms, in addition to serious mental disorders. See also *DSM III.*

person-centered therapy. A form of psychotherapy proposed by Carl Rogers which views human nature as fundamentally good and every individual as capable of adjustment and self-realization. The client must identify and solve problems; the therapist provides a supportive environment. See also *psychotherapy.* **14**

person perception. The processes by which individuals perceive others' behavior. Social psychologists study person perception to explain the impressions we form of others. **17**

personality psychology. The branch of psychology concerned with individual differences among people and with why people in the same situations often behave differently. **1**

Personality Research Form (PRF). A paper-and-pencil personality test designed to measure twenty essential "needs" postulated as the basis of human motivation by Henry A. Murray. **14**

phallic plethysmograph. An instrument used by psychologists to measure changes in blood flow through the penis and to detect sexual arousal. **14**

phallic stage. Freud's third psychosexual stage of development, roughly from the third to fifth year, during which the genitals are the source of sensual pleasure. Oedipal and Electra complexes occur during this stage. See also *anal, genital, latency,* and *oral stages.* **14**

phenomenological approach. An approach to psychology that emphasizes the importance of consciousness and feelings in human beings. See also *humanistic psychology.* **1**

phenotype. Characteristics or traits of the individual that are visible and measurable (such as eye color). **2**

phenylketonuria (PKU). An enzyme deficiency caused by a genetic disorder that can lead to severe mental retardation. **11**

phobia. An anxiety disorder characterized by an intense fear of a specific object or situation. The individual may realize that the fear is irrational but be unable to control it; he or she thus avoids the object or situation. See also other forms of *disorders: anxiety, generalized anxiety, obsessive-compulsive, panic.* **15**

phoneme. The smallest unit of sound in a language. **8**

phonological ambiguity. The dual meaning of sounds (such as often occurs in children's jokes). **8**

phonological rules. Procedures for combining sounds into words appropriate to a given language. **8**

physical therapies. See *somatic therapies.* **16**

pinna. The projecting flap of skin of the outer ear located on both sides of the head. **3**

pitch. The qualitative dimension of hearing that corresponds to the frequency of the sound waves comprising the stimulus. **3**

pituitary gland. Sometimes called the master gland, it secretes hormones that stimulate the production and release of hormones by other endocrine glands. See also *endocrine system, hormones.* **2**

placebo. A substance, usually in pill form, that has no active ingredients (it may be sugar) but is believed by subjects or patients to contain drugs. It acts as a control in an experimental situation. **1**

placebo control condition. A condition in which the control group of an experimental test believe they are taking active drugs, but in fact are not. **1**

placebo effect. The finding that expectation of treatment produces a benefit (e.g., relief of pain), even when no active substance is provided in the treatment. **16**

placenta. Connecting tissue between a mother and her prenatal organism that is rich in blood vessels and allows exchange of maternal nutrients and discharge of fetal wastes. **9**

place theory. In hearing, a theory that human perception of pitch depends on the fact that different frequency sound waves produce maximal vibrations at various locations along the basilar membrane. The location of the maximal vibration is thus used to code the pitch of the sound wave. See also *frequency theory.* **3**

pleasure principle. According to Freud, the motive to seek immediate pleasure and gratification which governs the id. See also *id.* **14**

polygraph. Also called a lie detector, this device is used to record a number of physiological stress reactions such as heart rate and blood pressure. **13**

pons. A swelling at the base of the brain that contains the neural connections between the cerebrum and the cerebellum. **2**

population. All of the members of a defined group from which a small sample may be drawn and about which an investigator wishes to draw conclusions. **Appendix**

positive reinforcer. An event (reward) whose onset increases the likelihood of the preceding behavior when it is presented (e.g., food for a hungry organism). **6**

postconventional stage of moral reasoning. In Kohlberg's theory of moral development, the stage at which individuals recognize the rights and values of society members. **10**

posthypnotic amnesia. A form of posthypnotic suggestion in which the hypnotized subject does not recall the events that occurred during hypnosis until a signal is later given. **5**

posthypnotic suggestion. A proposal made to an individual in a hypnotic state which usually urges a prescribed behavior (in response to a prearranged signal) after awakening. **5**

preconscious. The mental state that refers to ideas or memories an individual is currently unaware of but, which can be brought to consciousness easily. **5**

predictive validity. A measure of a test's relation to a criterion of behavior in the future; for example, the degree to which I.Q. scores predict college grades. **11**

prefrontal lobotomy. A form of psychosurgery in which the nerve fibers connecting the hypothalamus with the prefrontal lobes are severed to reduce the effects of emotions on intellectual processes. The procedure is not used as widely as in earlier years. **16**

prejudice. A preconceived feeling or opinion of worth on the basis of little or no evidence. The word is often used in the context of attitudes of an unreasonable or hostile nature. See also *authoritarian personality, stereotyping.* **18**

preoperational period. In Piaget's theory, the period from approximately two to seven years when children use few cognitive strategies or rules for reasoning and are easily fooled by appearances. **9**

presbyopia. A visual defect common in elderly people, it is a progressive hardening of the lens which makes the eye less able to change its shape (or accommodate) to bring objects close at hand into focus. **3**

primacy effect. (1) In impression formation, the fact that attributes noted early are given greater weight than attributes noted at a later time. (2) In memory, the tendency for initial items on a list to be recalled better than other items on the list. See also *recency effect.* **7**

primary aging. General deterioration of the body's cells. **10**

primary colors. The three colors—red, green, and blue—which, when combined in the correct proportions, produce any of the colors of the spectrum. **3**

primary reinforcer. An event that increases the strength of preceding responses even if the event has never been experienced before. **6**

primary services. Also called primary prevention, these community mental health assistance programs aim to eliminate the causes of potential social stressors. See also *community psychology.* **16**

primary sex characteristics. Physical attributes that relate directly to reproductive capacity, e.g. the male's penis and scrotum. **10**

principle of reinforcement. The rule that responses that produce reinforcement will increase in strength. Also called the law of effect. **6**

private self. The aspects of your self perceptible only to you, including your inner attitudes, feelings, beliefs, and values. **17**

proactive interference. The interference of earlier learning with the learning and recall of new material. See also *retroactive interference.* **7**

probability theory. A mathematical theory of the likelihood that random events will occur. **Appendix**

projection. A psychoanalytic defense mechanism by which the individual attributes his or her own motives to others, especially when these thoughts are considered undesirable. See also *defense mechanism.* **14**

proprioceptive feedback. The neural impulses arising in the limbs that allow determination of their position. **4**

prospect theory. A mathematical system designed to make sense of people's paradoxical attitudes towards risks. **8**

prototype. A representative sample of a class of things. **8**

proximal stimuli. The patterns of physical energy that strike the receptor organs and cause them to fire neural impulses. See also *distal stimuli.* **4**

pseudohermaphroditism. A congenital condition of some males in which the sex chromosomes are XY and testes are present but the external genitalia are usually more female than male. **12**

psyche. The mind, mental life, and personality as a whole. **14**

psychiatric nurse. A registered nurse with special training for work with patients in mental hospitals. **16**

psychiatric social worker. A social service professional with a master's degree and training in treatment procedures with emphasis on the family and community. **16**

psychiatrist. A medical doctor who specializes in the treatment of psychotherapy. Psychiatrists take medical as well as therapeutic responsibility for their patients; they are the only therapists who can prescribe psychoactive drugs, shock treatment, or other biological intervention methods. **16**

psychic energy. In Freudian theory, the origin of the dynamic forces guiding motivation and causing behavior. **14**

psychoanalysis. A Freudian approach to therapy emphasizing free association, dream interpretation, and transference. **1**

psychobiology. A branch of psychology that emphasizes study of the mechanisms of the brain and nervous system that control behavior. **1**

psycholinguistics. The study of how people understand and use language. **8**

psychological tests. Paper-and-pencil tests that measure and describe people's mental aptitudes, personality characteristics, and interests. **1**

psychology. The scientific study of the mind and behavior. **1**

psychometric model of intelligence. The model of intelligence constructed on statistical measures of performance such as intelligence tests. **11**

psychopath. See *antisocial personality disorder.*

psychophysical function. The relationship between changes in physical stimulation and their psychological functions. **3**

psychophysical scaling. The process of measuring the relationship between the physical intensity of a stimulus and its perceived intensity. **3**

psychophysics. The branch of psychology concerned with how changes in physical stimuli are translated into psychological experience. **3**

psychoses. A broad term once used to describe the more severe mental disorders in which a person has lost touch with reality, often suffering hallucinations or delusions. See also *character disorder, DSM-III.* **15**

psychosexual disorder. A mental disorder in which potentially harmful or unusual sexual actions become the primary mode of arousal. See also *gender identity disorders.* **15**

psychosocial development. An individual's thoughts and feelings about the relationship between self and others. **9**

psychosurgery. The most drastic form of biological intervention which involves surgery to destroy or remove brain tissue to change behavior. **16**

psychotherapy. Treatment of mental or emotional disorders through specialized techniques, all of which involve close communication between the patient and a therapist trained in psychological problems. **16**

puberty. For humans, a time of physiological and psychological change from about age ten to fifteen when sexual characteristics and reproductive systems mature. **10**

public self. The aspects of your self others can observe, such as physical appearance, overt behaviors, and interactions with others. **17**

punishment. The delivery of an aversive stimulus contingent on some response; its major effect is to suppress the response. **6**

pupil. The opening in the iris through which light passes as it enters the eye. **3**

random assignment. The assignment of research participants to a control or an experimental group according to a procedure in which participants have an equal chance of being appointed to either group; eliminates confounded variables. **1**

range. A statistic indicating the variability of a distribution that is computed by subtracting the lowest score from the highest score; the resulting difference is the range of the distribution. **Appendix**

rating score. A form of assessing personality traits in which respondents are asked to judge others on scales. **14**

Rational-Emotive Therapy (RET). A form of psychotherapy based on the work of Albert Ellis in which the therapist takes an active role by attempting to confront the client about his or her inappropriate cognitions regarding self-concept and relations with others. See also *psychotherapy.* **16**

rationalization. The psychoanalytic defense mechanism in which acceptable "reasons" are invented for unacceptable attitudes, beliefs, feelings, and behavior. See also *defense mechanisms.* **14**

ratio schedule. A program of reinforcement in which a certain number of responses are necessary in order to produce the reward. See also *fixed* and *variable ratio schedules.* **6**

reaction formation. The psychoanalytic defense mechanism by which a person behaves or feels in a manner opposite his or her unconscious impulses. See also *defense mechanisms.* **14**

reactive observations. Behavioral observations influenced by the obvious presence of the researcher. **1**

reality principle. In Freud's theory, the tendency to behave in such a way as to conform to the demands of reality. This principle governs the ego. **14**

recency effect. In memory experiments, the tendency for subjects to recall the items at the end of a list more readily than those in the middle. See also *primacy effect.* **7**

receptor cells. Specialized neurons that receive information directly from the environment and carry it to other neurons. **2**

recessive gene. A gene, or unit of heredity, that does not produce an observable effect unless it is paired with another recessive gene of the same type. **2**

reciprocal inhibition of motives. The idea that once aroused, any motive can inhibit or interfere with other motives. **12**

recoding. The process of transforming information into a form other than its original one, e.g., forming a mental image of a collie when the letters D-O-G are presented for study. **7**

reductionism. An approach to explaining psychological phenomena in which all of the factors—including cognitive and social ones—are explained in terms of their biological underpinnings. **1**

reference group. A group that an individual uses as a standard for beliefs or attitudes. **17**

reflex. An automatic response to a stimulus. **2**

rehearsal. The process of recycling information in short-term store. It can facilitate the short-term retention of information as well as the transfer of that information to long-term store. See also *long-* and *short-term store.* **7**

reinforcement. An event that increases the likelihood of behavior that precedes it. Also called reinforcer. **6**

reinforcement schedules. Different means of delivering reinforcement or rewards. See also *interval schedules, ratio schedules.* **6**

relative validity of a CS. The percentage of UCSs that occur in the presence of a CS; indicates how reliably the CS predicts the UCS. **6**

reliability. The stability of test scores after the repetition of the test on the same group. **11**

reminiscence. The recovery of information on a later test that could not be recalled on an earlier one. **7**

REM rebound. A sleep phenomenon exhibited by people who are deprived of REM sleep over a period of several nights. When finally allowed to sleep undisturbed, these people spend a greater proportion of their sleep time in REM sleep than nondeprived sleepers. **5**

REM sleep. A stage of sleep characterized by rapid eye movements (REMs) and an EEG pattern somewhat similar to that of a waking state. It usually coincides with periods of dreaming. **5**

renin. A substance released by the kidney when extracellular fluid is lost, initiating the synthesis of angiotensin, which acts on some cells in the brain to produce thirst. **12**

repression. In psychoanalytic theory, a defense mechanism by which memories, feelings, or impulses that might provoke

guilt feelings are denied by being pushed from conscious awareness. See also *defense mechanisms.* **14**

resistance. In psychoanalytic therapy, an unwillingness or reluctance on the part of a client to disclose material fully and accurately to the therapist; lack of cooperation. **16**

response. Any behavior of an organism. **1**

resting potential. The electrical state of a neuron that is at rest. **2**

reticular activating system. A network of cells in the center of the brain stem involved in activation or arousal of other parts of the brain. See reticular formation. **2**

retina. The membrane at the back of the eye containing the photoreceptors (rods and cones) that images are focused on. **3**

retrieval. The process of bringing stored information into consciousness. **7**

retrieval cues. Environmental or internal stimuli that affect the retrieval of an experience. **7**

retroactive interference. The effect of subsequent learning on the recall of information learned earlier. See also *proactive interference.* **7**

retrograde amnesia. See *amnesia.*

reuptake. The process whereby those substances not deactivated are reabsorbed into the terminal button. **2**

reversibility. A term used by Piaget to refer to actions that can be performed in two ways with opposite effects.

revised frustration-aggression hypothesis. Leonard Berkowitz's proposal that frustration leads to anger, not aggression. See also *frustration-aggression hypothesis.* **18**

rites of passage. Various rituals used in different cultures to signify the passage into adulthood. **10**

rods. Photoreceptors located outside the fovea of the eye that function primarily under low levels of illumination. They produce only monochromatic (black and white) vision. **3**

romantic love. A special emotion that two people, usually of the opposite sex, develop toward each other, often characterized by sexual attraction, tenderness, yearning, and strong attachment. **17**

Rorschach inkblots. A projective personality technique developed by Herman Rorschach which uses complex, bilaterally symmetrical blots of ink on ten cards and scores subjects' responses on a variety of measures. **14**

sample. A selection of items from a total set known as the population. If selection is random, an unbiased sample results; if selection is based on some criteria, the sample may be biased and unrepresentative of the population. **Appendix**

saturation. The apparent purity of a color. The more saturated a color is, the more it appears as a hue that is pure and free of white (e.g., pink is less saturated than red). **3**

savings method. The memory measurement technique which compares how long it takes to relearn some material with how long it took to learn the same material originally. If it takes less time to relearn the material the inference is made that the memory traces of the experience had not completely vanished. **7**

scattergram. A diagram that plots two variables against each other in order to show their relationship (or lack of relationship). **Appendix**

schema. A hypothetical memory structure that organizes and preserves information relevant to some event or concept. **7**

schizophrenic disorder. Also called schizophrenia, this group of severe disorders is characterized by generalized withdrawal, apathy, thought disorder, emotional disturbance, delusions, and hallucinations. There are several types of schizophrenia. See also *catatonic schizophrenia, paranoid schizophrenia.* **15**

school psychologist. Specialists in learning and education who are usually employed in primary and secondary schools to help classify students, provide counseling and guidance, and evaluate learning problems. **1**

secondary aging. Physical changes related to primary aging. Diseases such as emphysema are secondary effects of the general deterioration of the body's respiration system. **10**

secondary services. Also called secondary prevention, these community mental health assistance programs focus on immediate treatment of psychological problems through techniques such as crisis intervention counseling (e.g., hotlines). See also *community psychology*. **16**

secondary sex characteristics. Physical attributes that accompany primary sex characteristics but may not be related to sexual reproduction, e.g. the growth of pubic hair during puberty. **10**

selective attention. The ability to choose one of many stimuli attracting the senses for further perception and analysis. **5**

selective breeding. The choices of animals for mating on the basis of some observable characteristic; usually done through several generations. **2**

self-actualization. Abraham Maslow's term for an individual's striving to realize his or her greatest potential, including maximizing feelings of love and acceptance of the actual-self. **14**

self-concept. The composite of ideas, feelings, and attitudes that people have about themselves. **14**

self-management. See *contingency contracting.*

semantic ambiguity. Multiple interpretations or meanings of the same word, phrase, or sentence. See also *lexical ambiguity*. **8**

semantic code. The memory systems based on meaning that are used to store verbal information. See also *imaginal codes, motor codes*. **7**

semantic memory. Recall of general knowledge that does not depend on retrieving the time and place in which the information was learned. See also *episodic memory*. **7**

semantic priming effect. The tendency to respond more quickly to a second word if it is preceded by a related word, rather than by an unrelated word or a neutral stimulus. **5**

semantics. The principles by which meaning is expressed through language. **8**

sensation. The reception of stimulation from the environment involving the transduction of environmental or internal events into neural impulses. **3**

sensitive periods. Time periods in which development proceeds rapidly with increased susceptibility to external factors. **9**

sensorimotor stage. In Piaget's theory, the first two years of life during which infants learn to coordinate actions and perceptions. The period culminates in the attainment of symbolic representation. **9**

sensory cortex. The three regions of the cortex (somasensory, visual, and auditory) that function as receptors of information from other parts of the body or the environment. **2**

sensory neuron. Nerve cell that receives information from receptor cells about the environment and conveys this information to other neurons. **2**

sensory storage. The portion of the memory system that maintains representations of sensory information for very brief intervals. See also *long-term store, short-term store*. **7**

separation anxiety. A common fear infants have of being apart from their mothers or others to whom they are strongly attached. See *stranger anxiety*. **9**

septum. A region in the midline area of the brain that seems to inhibit thirst, and, in some species, aggressive behavior. **2**

serial position curve. The curve that results from plotting the accuracy of retention as a function of the position of the items in a studied list. **7**

set point. A hypothetical point around which organisms maintain their body weight. **12**

sex typing. The process by which children learn to identify themselves as boys or girls, and adapt socially appropriate male or female behaviors. **9**

shaping by successive approximations. A procedure in which an animal is rewarded for performing behaviors that progressively resemble a target behavior until that behavior is reached. **6**

Sheldon's theory of body types. A theory that there are three basic somatotypes (body types), each associated with certain clusters of personality traits; *ectomorphs* have thin, delicate builds and are intense and shy in personality; *endomorphs* have soft, round builds and are easy going and sociable; *mesomorphs* have strong, muscular builds and are aggressive and bold. **14**

short-term store. A limited capacity component of the memory system that retains information for a relatively short period of time. See also *long-term store, sensory store*. **7**

shuttle box. An apparatus used in the study of avoidance learning. **6**

signal detection theory. A theory of the sensory and decision processes which asserts that there are no fixed absolute thresholds; rather, a person decides about the presence of a sensory signal against a background of "noise" in the nervous system. **3**

sign stimulus. An ethological term for the particular aspect of a stimulus that releases a fixed action pattern. See also *fixed action pattern*. **12**

simultaneous conditioning. A procedure in classical conditioning where the conditioned stimulus and the unconditioned stimulus begin and end together. **6**

simultaneous contrast. In visual perception, the fact that the color or brightness of an object is affected by, and in turn affects, any other object near or surrounding the object. **3**

sine wave. A wave which rises and falls in a regular, rhythmic manner. **3**

situational cause. Attributing behavior or results to the environment, rather than to the individual. See also *dispositional cause*. **17**

Sixteen Personality Factor Questionnaire (16PF). A paper-and-pencil personality inventory developed by Raymond B. Cattell to measure sixteen dimensions of normal personality. **14**

Skinner box. See *operant conditioning chamber.*

skin senses. The four types of sensation—pressure, pain, cold, warmth—that are typically referred to as touch. **3**

sleep apnea. A sleep disorder characterized by difficulty in breathing. **5**

social cognition. Knowledge and thoughts about other people's points of view, thoughts, feelings, and intentions. **17**

social facilitation. The energizing effect of other people on the motivation and behavior of an individual. **17**

social learning theory. A theoretical approach that is midway between behavior theories such as Skinner's and cognitive approaches. It emphasizes particular ways of learning, such as observing others in a social context. **14**

socialization. Processes by which people learn the attitudes, values, roles, and behavior of a given social or cultural group. **9**

social milieu therapy. Treatment based on learning principles that aims to alter behavior in the setting in which it occurs. See also *behavior therapy, psychotherapy*. **16**

social norm. A group or community's unwritten rules that govern its members' attitudes, beliefs, and behavior. **17**

social psychology. The branch of psychology concerned with the study of the effects of social factors on individual behavior, as well as behavior in groups. **1**

sociobiology. The systematic study of the biological bases of social behavior, employing evolution as the basic explanatory tool. 1

sodium-potassium pump. A set of mechanisms that force sodium out of neurons and potassium into it. 7

somatic nervous system. Part of the peripheral nervous system; these efferent fibers activate skeletal muscles; afferent fibers come from the major receptor organs (eyes, ears, etc.). 2

somatic therapies. Therapies based on biochemical and physiological methods of treatment, such as drug and shock therapy. 16

somatoform disorder. A pattern of behavior characterized by complaints of physical symptoms in the absence of any real illness. Conversion disorder is a classical example. 15

spatial illusions. Systematic errors in the perception of objects in space, usually caused by central perceptual processes. 4

special education. Classrooms and curricula designed to meet the particular needs of handicapped populations. 11

species-specific defense responses. Reactions that are readily produced in a species in a particular situation. 6

speech act. A unit of communication comprised of a speaker who intends to influence a listener with a verbal message. 8

speech shadowing. A research procedure in which subjects are simultaneously presented with two or more spoken messages; they are required to repeat (or shadow) one of the messages. Subjects' memories for the shadowed messages are usually very good, while their memories for the others are poor. See also *selective attention*. 5

split-brain patient. One who has had the corpus callosum surgically severed, thus isolating the functions of the two cerebral hemispheres. 2

spontaneous recovery. The return of an extinguished response following a rest period, when an animal is replaced in the original circumstances of conditioning. 6

spreading activation. In memory, the theory that when a concept is activated in semantic memory by a word (e.g., *car*), the energy or activation travels to related concepts *truck* or *ambulance*) and partially arouses them. 7

S-R approach. The theory that the basic components of learning are stimulus (S) and response (R) bonds. 1

stage theories. Theories of development concerned with relatively abrupt changes in behavior across the life span. 9

standard deviation. A measure of the dispersion or variability of a distribution. It is equivalent to the square root of the variance. 11

standardization sample. In psychometric testing, the group that forms the basis for comparison of relative performance. It must accurately represent the entire population. 11

Stanford-Binet test. A widely used, standardized intelligence test. 11

state-dependent retrieval. The finding that information a subject learns in a drug-induced state is better recalled at a later time when the person is under the influence of the same drug than when he or she is tested in a nondrugged state. 1

statistical significance. The reliability of measures based on samples as a statement about population characteristics. If a difference between groups of scores is quite unlikely to have occurred by chance it is said to be statistically significant. **Appendix**

stereochemical theory. A theory that explains sense of smell by postulating that the receptors in the nose are configured to match the variety of shapes of the molecules in the air. When the shape of a molecule matches the shape of a receptor (the way a key matches a lock), the receptor fires a neural impulse. 3

stereoscopic image. The apparently three-dimensional image that is formed when one views—with two eyes—two photographs that were taken from two slightly different viewpoints. See also *binocular disparity*. 4

stereotype. An overgeneralized or commonly held belief or attitude about an identifiable group. 17

stimulants. Chemical agents that produce temporary excitation of the body and/or nervous system. 5

stimulus. Any external event. 1

stimulus generalization. The principle that when a subject has been conditioned to make a response to a stimulus other similar stimuli will evoke the same response, though to a lesser degree than the original stimulus would have. 6

stimulus-response approach. See *S-R approach*.

storage. The second of three stages in the memory process, it is responsible for the retention of information over a period of time. See also *acquisition, retrieval*. 7

stranger anxiety. A common fear infants have of unfamiliar people. It may appear at the end of the first year and disappear sometime around the second birthday. 9

stratified random sampling. The selection of subjects by chance within levels of different attributes. 11

stress. The collection of physical and physiological reactions an organism forms to a perceived threat to its well-being. 13

stress reaction. An innate response triggered by a wide variety of stressors consisting of autonomic system arousal and release of various stress-related hormones. 13

striate cortex. The visual cortex located at the occipital lobe at the rear of the brain. Projection fibers from the lateral geniculate nucleus carry signals from the optic nerve to the striate cortex. 3

structuralism. A school of psychology which held that the primary task of psychologists was the analysis of the structure of conscious experience through analytic introspection. 1

subgoal analysis. The ability to break down a complex problem into a series (or hierarchy) of smaller, more easily solvable problems. 8

subjective colors. Various patterns of hues that are visible when a black and white disk is rotated very rapidly. 3

subjective contour. The phenomenon of an outline or contouring appearing in a visual display when no such thing is physically present. 4

subjective organization. In memory, a recoding process in which people impose order on randomly presented events so they can remember them better. 7

sublimation. A psychoanalytic defense mechanism in which unacceptable impulses are channeled into socially approved forms of expression. See also *defense mechanism*. 14

subliminal perception. The effect of stimuli below the threshold (or linen) of awareness that are not perceived consciously but may influence behavior. 5

superego. In Freud's theory of personality, a two-part structure: the harsh *conscience* that attempts to forbid aggressive and sexual gratification; and the *ego-ideal* that holds the individual to a standard of future development. See also *ego, id*. 14

surface structure. The actual words and their organization in a sentence. See also *deep structure*. 8

survey. The sampling of opinions of a small proportion of the population in order to gather information representative of the population as a whole. 1

syllogism. A sequence of three statements consisting of a major and a minor premise that lead to a conclusion. 8

symbols. Anything that stands for or represents something other than itself. In psychoanalytic personality assessment the symbols found in dreams and free associations may signify unconscious motives. 14

sympathetic nervous system. The division of the autonomic nervous system that is active in emotion and arousal.

Associated reactions include increased heart rate and blood pressure. See also *parasympathetic nervous system*. **2**

synapse. The place where the boutons of one neuron adjoin the dendrites of another neuron. **2**

synaptic cleft. The space that separates the presynaptic and postsynaptic membranes of two neurons. **2**

synaptic transmission. The sending of information from one neuron to another. **2**

synaptic vesicles. Small, membrane-enclosed spherical bodies located in the bouton. **2**

syntactic ambiguity. A violation of the usual rules of syntax that is often the source of jokes and puns. See also *lexical ambiguity, syntax*. **8**

syntax. The ways in which words are connected to form phrases and sentences. **8**

systematic desensitization therapy. Conditioning procedure in which a patient is presented a sequence of greater and greater anxiety-producing situations, and learns to relax in the presence of each. **6**

tachistoscope. A mechanical instrument capable of flashing visual displays on a screen for very short periods of time and used in perceptual testing. **7**

taste-aversion learning. A procedure for studying classical conditioning in which animals are given a flavored solution (CS) to drink and are then made ill by drugs or radiation (UCS), resulting in sickness (UCR) and thus aversion for the taste. **6**

telepathy. The hypothesized ability for one person to transmit thoughts to another with no sensory communication. See also *extrasensory perception*.

temporal lobe. One of the four sections of the cerebral hemisphere, it lies below the lateral fissure and between the occipital and frontal lobes. See also *frontal, parietal, occipital lobes*. **2**

terminal button. The small swelling at the end of an axon branch. See also *axon*. **2**

tertiary services. Also called tertiary prevention, these community mental health assistance programs are concerned with rehabilitative treatment for those with emotional problems. Services include job training, employment counseling and development of social skills. See also *community psychology*. **16**

testosterone. A male sex hormone that influences development of the genitals and secondary sexual characteristics. It is secreted by the testes. **12**

thalamus. A part of the brain forming a bulge on the top of the brain stem; sensory information is exchanged throughout the brain from this relay station. **2**

Thematic Apperception Test (TAT). A projective test used to measure need for achievement and other motives. The subject is asked to tell stories about a series of ambiguous pictures, thus being able to project his or her needs, motives, etc., into the tales. **12**

theory. A set of formal statements advancing concepts and relationships among them in order to explain a phenomenon or a body of data. **1**

theory of natural selection. A theory originated by Charles Darwin stating that selective survival could be a mechanism for changes in the characteristics of a population of organisms, eventually resulting in a new species. **2**

threshold of excitation. The point at which an action potential is produced in a neuron. **2**

token economy. A form of behavior modification treatment in which a formal system of secondary reinforcement (and punishment, via withdrawal of tokens) is used to encourage desired behaviors and discourage undesired ones. See also *behavior therapy*. **16**

top-down theories. The view that perception is an active process guided in part by high-level mental processes such as expectancies. See also *bottom-up theories*. **4**

trace conditioning. A procedure used in classical conditioning where the conditioned stimulus begins and ends before the unconditioned stimulus comes on. **6**

trait. An inherited or acquired characteristic that is considered consistent, persistent, and stable. In personality theory each individual's traits determine his or her behavior in a unique way. **14**

transfer-appropriate processing. The idea that different ways of processing information will lead to better or worse memory performance depending on how well the processing transfers to the specific test situation in which performance is measured. **7**

transference. In psychoanalytic theory, the process during therapy by which the client attributes to the therapist qualities belonging to a significant person in his or her life, such as a parent, and responds to the therapist accordingly. **16**

transformation rules. See *transformational grammar*.

transformational grammar. A set of linguistic principles elaborated by Noam Chomsky to describe how the surface structure of language can be changed and interpreted according to rules that operate to produce the deep structure of language. See also *deep structure*. **8**

transsexual. An individual whose gender identity does not match his or her biological sex. **12**

transvestite. A person, usually male, who enjoys dressing in the garb of the opposite sex. **15**

trichromatic theory. A theory of color vision which postulates that there are three types of photoreceptors which are maximally sensitive to three colors (red, blue, and green). Colors are "coded" according to the relative activity levels of these three receptor types. See also *opponent process theory*. **3**

trichromats. People who can see all three primary colors: red, green, and blue. **3**

twin studies. A method used to measure genetic influences on behavior; if genes strongly influence a trait identical twins should be more similar in behavior related to that trait than fraternal twins. **2**

two-component theory. A theory developed by Schacter and Singer (1962) which suggests that emotion is determined by the interaction of two processes: general autonomic arousal and cognitive interpretation of the arousal. **13**

two-point threshold. The minimum physical separation between two points placed simultaneously on the skin which allows them to be perceived as two points and not a single one. **3**

tympanic membrane. The membrane stretching across the end of the auditory canal. It is typically referred to as the eardrum. **3**

types. In personality theory, types refer to a class of people grouped together because they share certain personality *traits* or characteristics. **14**

ultrasound. A technique used to measure fetal growth in which high-frequency sound waves are directed through the woman's abdomen, the reflected waves providing an image of the fetus. **9**

unconditional positive regard. The term given to the warm, sympathetic and accepting environment provided by therapists to clients in Carl Rogers's person-centered therapy. **14**

unconditioned reponse (UCR). A response that is elicited by a stimulus prior to any learning or conditioning. **6**

unconditioned stimulus (UCS). A stimulus that is capable of evoking a response by itself, without learning or conditioning; for example, presentation of food (UCS) causes salivation (UCR) in dogs. **6**

unconscious. The part of a person's mind which contains ideas and memories that the person cannot easily bring into consciousness. **5**

undifferentiated schizophrenia. A diagnosis for certain schizophrenics who have so many overlapping symptoms that the appropriate subtype category is difficult to determine. See also *schizophrenic disorder.* **15**

validity. The degree to which a test actually measures what it is designed to measure. **1**

value. A theoretical construct representing the degree of affect or worth—either positive or negative—produced by an event. **12**

variability. In statistics, an amount that represents the dispersion of scores found in a group of measurements. See also *range, standard deviation.* **11**

variable. One of the factors that is manipulated, measured, or controlled in an experiment. See also *control variable, dependent variable, independent variable.* **1**

variable interval schedule. A schedule of partial reinforcement in which a reward (reinforcement) follows the first response made after a certain time period has lapsed, and the time period varies from trial to trial. See also *fixed interval schedule.* **6**

variable ratio schedule. A schedule of partial reinforcement in which the reward (reinforcement) occurs following a certain number of responses, and the number varies from trial to trial. See also *fixed ratio schedule.* **6**

veridical perception. The aspect of experience in which our perceptions of the world are accurate and in accord with objective reality. **4**

vestibular sacs. The sacs at the base of the semicircular canals in the inner ear in which the movement of fluid signals motion and the tilt of the head to help maintain balance. **3**

vestibular sense. The inner maintenance of balance with respect to gravity. **3**

vicarious catharsis. The hypothesis that aggressive drives and feelings can be released by observing other people who are behaving aggressively. **18**

vicarious conditioning. The establishment of a conditioned response (often an emotional one) by observing the reactions of another person to a particular stimulus. See also *observational learning, vicarious reinforcement.* **14**

vicarious reinforcement. Reinforcement that is obtained from watching someone else being rewarded for a particular behavior. See also *observational learning, vicarious conditioning.* **14**

visible spectrum. The only region of the electromagnetic spectrum to which our eyes are sensitive. Different light wavelengths in the visible spectrum create our perception of various colors. **3**

visual cliff. A research apparatus used to examine depth perception in young children and animals. An apparent cliff is covered with a clear piece of glass and the infant is tempted to cross the "cliff." **9**

visual deprivation. A condition in which an organism is deprived of visual experience, typically from birth, to determine the role early experience plays in later visual perceptual skills or deficits. **4**

visual form agnosia. The inability to recognize visual patterns. **3**

VMH lesions. Intentional injuries to tissue in the region of the ventromedial nucleus of the hypothalamus; rats with these lesions overeat and become obese. **12**

volley theory. A version of frequency theory that holds that when one hair cell proves unable to fire in the process of determining pitch, another cell pops away to keep pace with the frequency. See also *frequency theory; place theory.* **3**

von Restorff effect. The finding that if one item in a list is very different from other list items, the unique one will be recalled better than the remaining items. **7**

volumetric thirst Type of thirst caused by lack of extracellular fluid. **12**

waterfall illusion. The visual phenomenon that occurs after watching moving objects, such as the water in a waterfall, for a period of time. Stationary objects seem to move in a reverse direction from the moving item(s). **4**

wavelength. The distance between two adjacent peaks of a wave; long waves are slower and short waves are faster. **3**

weapons effect. In aggression research, the phenomenon in which the presence of aggressive cues (such as guns) has caused subjects to deliver angrier responses. See also *revised frustration-aggression hypothesis.* **17**

Weber's law. The principle that the difference threshold between two stimulus magnitudes is a certain constant fraction of the total magnitude. The relationship is given in Weber's Fraction: $\Delta I/I = $ Constant, where I is the stimulation of the standard simulus and ΔI is the difference in stimulation that is just noticeable. **3**

Wechsler test. A variety of intelligence test developed by David Wechsler. Wechsler tests include two separate scales for measuring performance, a verbal scale and a performance (nonverbal) scale. **11**

weighted averaging model. The view that people form impressions by averaging information available to them, with some information getting more weight than others. **17**

Wernicke's area. An area in the left hemisphere of the brain which, when damaged, produces a speech disorder. **2**

Wernicke's aphasia. A disorder characterized by speech that is rapid and articulate but has little meaning. **2**

wish fulfillment. In Freudian terminology, a process by which the id forms mental images of the objects or acts that will satisfy its demands. See also *id; pleasure principle.* **14**

work motivation. The field concerned with what motivates workers and with how managers can arrange the work situation to satisfy the goals of both workers and management. **12**

Yerkes-Dodson law. By this principle there is an optimal degree of motivation for any task; the more difficult the task is, the lower the optimum will be. **12.**

Young-Helmholtz trichromatic theory. See *trichromatic theory.*

zygote. The fertilized egg produced by the union of a male sperm and a female egg cell. **9**

References

Abelson, R. P., Kinder, D. R., Peters, M. D., & Fiske, S. T. (1982). Affective and semantic components in political person perception. *Journal of Personality and Social Psychology, 42,* 619–630.

Abramson, L. Y., Seligman, M. E. P., & Teasdale, J. D. (1978). Learned helplessness in humans: Critique and reformulation. *Journal of Abnormal Psychology, 87,* 49–74.

Adams, H. E., Tollison, C. D., & Carson, T. P. (1981). Behavior therapy with sexual preventive medicine. In S. M. Turner, K. S. Calhoun, & H. E. Adams (Eds.), *Handbook of Clinical Behavior Therapy.* New York: Wiley.

Adams, J. S. (1979). Inequity in social exchange. In R. M. Steers & L. W. Porter (Eds.), *Motivation and work behavior.* New York: McGraw-Hill.

Adolph, E. F. (1947). Urges to eat and drink in rats. *American Journal of Physiology, 151,* 110–125.

Adorno, T., Frenkel-Brunswik, E., Levinson, D., & Sandord, R. (1950). *The authoritarian personality.* New York: Harper & Row.

Ainsworth, M. D. S. (1979). Attachment as related to mother-infant interaction. In J. S. Rosenblatt, G. A. Hinde, C. Beer, and & M. Busnel (Eds.), *Advances in the study of behavior* (Vol. 9). New York: Academic Press.

Ainsworth, M. D. S., Blehar, M., Waters, E., & Walls, S. (1978). *Patterns of attachment.* Hillsdale, N.J.: Erlbaum.

Ajzen, I., & Fishbein, M. H. (1977). Attitude-behavior relations: A theoretical analysis and review of empirical research. *Psychological Bulletin, 84,* 888–918.

Akers, R. L. (1985). *Deviant behavior: A social learning approach* (3rd ed.). Belmont, Calif.: Wadsworth.

Akers, R. L., Krohn, M. D., Lanza-Kaduce, L., & Radosevich, M. (1979). Social learning and deviant behavior: A specific test of a general theory. *American Sociological Review, 44,* 636–655.

Alba, J. W., & Hasher, L. (1983). Is memory schematic? *Psychological Review, 93,* 203–231.

Allen, E. K., Hart, B. M., Buell, J. S., Harris, F. R., & Wolf, M. M. (1964). Effects of social reinforcement on isolate behavior of a nursery school child. *Child Development, 35,* 511–518.

Allport, F. H. (1920). The influence of the group upon association and thought. *Journal of Experimental Psychology, 3,* 159–182.

Allport, F. H. (1924). *Social psychology.* Boston: Houghton Mifflin.

Allport, G. W. (1937). *Personality: A psychological interpretation.* New York: Holt.

American Psychiatric Association. (1980). *Diagnostic and statistical manual of mental disorders: DSM-III* (3rd ed.). Washington, D.C.: American Psychiatric Association.

American Psychological Association. (1981). Ethical principles of psychologists. *American Psychologist, 36,* 633–638.

Amsel, A. (1958). The role of frustrative nonreward in noncontinuous reward situations. *Psychological Bulletin, 55,* 102–119.

Anand, B. K., & Brobeck, J, R. (1951). Hypothalamic control of food intake in rats and cats. *Yale Journal of Biology and Medicine, 24,* 123–140.

Anastasi, A. (1979). *Fields of applied psychology* (2nd ed.). New York: McGraw-Hill.

Anderson, A. (1982). The great Japanese IQ increase. *Nature, 297,* 180–181

Anderson, J. R. (1976). *Language, memory, and thought.* Hillsdale, N.J.: Erlbaum.

Anderson, J. R. (1985). *Cognitive psychology and its implications* (2nd ed.). New York: Freeman.

Anderson, N. H. (1965). Adding versus averaging as a stimulus combination rule in impression formation. *Journal of Experimental Psychology, 70,* 394–400.

Anderson, N. H. (1974). Cognitive algebra: Integration theory applied to social attribution. In L. Berkowitz (Ed.), *Advances in experimental social psychology* (Vol. 7). New York: Academic Press.

Anderson, N. H., & Hubert, S. (1963). Effects of concomitant verbal recall on order effects in personality impression formation. *Journal of Verbal Learning and Verbal Behavior, 2,* 379–391.

Anderson, R. C., Reynolds, R. E., Schallert, D. L., & Goetz, E. T. (1977). Frameworks for comprehending discourse. *American Educational Research Journal, 14,* 367–381.

Andrew, R. J. (1974). Arousal and the causation of behavior. *Behaviour, 51,* 135–165.

Anisman, H. (1975). Time-dependent variations in aversively motivated behaviors: Non-associative effects of cholinergic and catecholaminergic activity. *Psychological Review, 82,* 359–385.

Anisman, H., Hamilton, M., & Zacharko, R. M. (1984). Cue and response-choice acquisition and reversal after exposure to uncontrollable shock: Induction of response preservation. *Journal of Experimental Psychology: Animal Behavior Processes, 10,* 229–243.

Annau, Z., & Kamin, L. J. (1961). The conditioned emotional response as a function of intensity of the US. *Journal of Comparative and Physiological Psychology, 54,* 428–432.

Apfelbaum, M., Bostsarron, J., & Lacatis, D. (1971). Effect of caloric restriction and excessive caloric intake on energy expenditure. *American Journal of Clinical Nutrition, 24,* 1405–1409.

Appley, M. H. (1970). Derived motives. *Annual Review of Psychology, 21,* 485–518.

Arbuthnott, G. W., & Ungerstedt, U. (1969). *Acta Physiological Scandinavia Supplement, 330,* 117.

Arend, R., Gove, F. L., & Sroufe, L. A. (1979). Continuity of individual adaptation from infancy to kindergarten: A predictive study of ego resiliency and curiosity in preschoolers. *Child Development, 50,* 950–959.

Argyle, M., Furnham, A., & Graham, J. A. (1981). *Social situations.* New York: Cambridge University Press.

Arkes, H. R., & Blumer, C. (1985). The psychology of sunk cost. *Organizational Behavior and Human Decision Processes, 35,* 124–140.

Arlin, P. K. (1975). Cognitive development in adulthood: A fifth stage? *Developmental Psychology, 11,* 602–606.

Aronson, E. (1980). *The social animal* (3rd ed.). San Francisco: Freeman.

Aronson, E., & Osherow, N. (1980). Cooperation, prosocial behavior, and academic performance: Experiments in the desegregated classroom. In L. Bickman (Ed.), *Applied social psychology annual* (Vol. 1). Beverly Hills, Calif.: Sage.

Aronson, E., Turner, J. A., & Carlsmith, J. M. (1963). Communicator credibility and communication discrepancy as a determinant of opinion change. *Journal of Abnormal and Social Psychology, 67,* 31–36.

Asch, S. E. (1946). Forming impressions of personality. *Journal of Abnormal and Social Psychology, 41,* 258–290.

Asch, S. E. (1956). Studies of independence and conformity: 1. A minority of one against a unanimous majority. *Psychological Monographs, 70* (Whole No. 546).

Ashmore, R. D., & Del Boca, F. K. (1981). Conceptual approaches to stereotypes and stereotyping. In D. L. Hamilton (Ed.), *Cognitive processes in stereotyping and intergroup behavior.* Hillsdale, N.J.: Erlbaum.

Atkinson, J. W. (1957). Motivational determinants of risk-taking behavior. *Psychological Review, 64,* 359–372.

Atkinson, J. W. (1964). *An introduction to motivation.* Princeton, N.J.: Van Nostrand.

Atkinson, J. W., & Litwin, G. H. (1960). Achievement motive and test anxiety conceived as motive to approach success and motive to avoid failure. *Journal of Abnormal and Social Psychology, 60,* 52–63.

Atkinson, J. W., & Raynor, J. O. (Eds.). (1974). *Motivation and achievement.* Washington, D.C.: Winston.

Atkinson, R. C., & Shiffrin, R. M. (1968). Human memory: A proposed system and its control processes. In K. W. Spence & J. T. Spence (Eds.), *The psychology of learning and motivation: Advances in research and theory* (Vol. 2). New York: Academic Press.

Atkinson, R. C., & Shiffrin, R. M. (1971). The control of short-term memory. *Scientific American, 224,* 83–89.

Ayllon, T., & Haughton, E. (1964). Modification of symptomatic verbal behavior of mental patients. *Behaviour Research and Therapy, 2,* 87–97.

Azrin, N. H., Hake, D. F., Holz, W. C., & Hutchinson, R. R. (1965). Motivational aspects of escape from punishment. *Journal of Experimental Analysis of Behavior, 8,* 31–44.

Azrin, N. H., & Holz, W. C. (1966). Punishment. In W. K. Honig (Ed.), *Operant behavior: Areas of research and application.* New York: Appleton-Century-Crofts.

Azrin, N. H., Holz, W. C., & Hake, D. F. (1963). Fixed-ratio punishment. *Journal of the Experimental Analysis of Behavior, 6,* 141–148.

Baddeley, A. D. (1978). The trouble with levels: A reexamination of Craik and Lockhart's framework for memory research. *Psychological Review, 85,* 139–152.

Balota, D. (1983). Automatic semantic activation and subliminal episodic encoding. *Journal of Verbal Learning and Verbal Behavior, 22,* 88–104.

Baltes, P. B., Dittmann-Kohli, M., & Dixon, R. A. (1984). New perspectives on the development of intelligence in adulthood: Toward a dual-process conception and a model of selective optimization with compensation. In P. B. Baltes & O. G. Brim, Jr. (Eds.), *Life-span development and behavior* (Vol. 6). New York: Academic Press.

Bandura, A. (1965). Influence of a model's reinforcement contingencies on the acquisition of imitative responses. *Journal of Personality and Social Psychology, 1,* 589–595.

Bandura, A. (1969). *Principles of behavior modification.* New York: Holt, Rinehart & Winston.

Bandura, A. (1973). *Aggression: A social learning analysis.* Englewood Cliffs, N.J.: Prentice-Hall.

Bandura, A. (1977). *Social learning theory.* Englewood Cliffs, N.J.: Prentice-Hall.

Bandura, A. (1978). The self-system in reciprocal determinism. *American Psychologist, 33,* 344–358.

Bandura, A. (1986). *Social foundations of thought and action: A social cognitive theory.* Englewood Cliffs, N.J.: Prentice-Hall.

Bandura, A., Blanchard, E. B., & Ritter, B. (1969). Relative efficacy of desensitization and modeling approaches for inducing behavioral, affective, and attitudinal changes. *Journal of Personality and Social Psychology, 13,* 173–199.

Bandura, A., Grusec, J. E., & Menlove, F. L. (1967). Vicarious extinction of avoidance behavior. *Journal of Personality and Social Psychology, 5,* 16–23.

Bandura, A., & Mischel, W. (1965). Modification of self-imposed delay of reward through exposure to live and symbolic models. *Journal of Personality and Social Psychology, 2,* 698–705.

Bandura, A., Ross, D. A., & Ross, S. A. (1963). Imitation of film-mediated aggressive models. *Journal of Abnormal and Social Psychology, 66,* 3–11.

Bandura, A., & Walters, R. H. (1963). *Social learning and personality development.* New York: Holt, Rinehart & Winston.

Banks, M. S. (1980). The development of visual accommodation during early infancy. *Child Development, 51,* 646–666.

Barash, D. P. (1977). *Sociobiology and behavior.* New York: Elsevier.

Bard, P. (1934). On emotional expression after decortication with some remarks on certain theoretical views, Parts I and II. *Psychological Review, 41,* 309–329; 424–449.

Barenboim, C. (1981). The development of person perception in childhood and adolescence: From behavioral comparisons to psychological constructs. *Child Development, 52,* 129–144.

Barnes, G. E., Malamuth, N. M., & Check, J. V. P. (1984). Personality and sexuality. *Personality and Individual Differences, 5,* 159–172.

Baron, A. (1965). Delayed punishment of runway response. *Journal of Comparative and Physiological Psychology, 60,* 131–134.

Baron, R. A. (1977). *Human aggression.* New York: Plenum.

Baron, R. A., & Byrne, D. (1977). *Social psychology: Understanding human interaction* (2nd ed.). Boston: Allyn and Bacon.

Baron, R. A., & Byrne, D. (1987). *Social psychology: Understanding human interaction* (5th ed.). Boston: Allyn and Bacon.

Barrera, M. E., & Maurer, D. (1981). Discrimination of strangers by the three-month-old. *Child Development, 52,* 558–563.

Barsalou, L. W. (1983). Ad hoc categories. *Memory and Cognition, 11,* 211–227.

Bartholow, R. Experimental investigations into the functions of the human brain. *American Journal of Medical Science* (new series), *67,* 305–313.

Bartlett, F. C. (1932). *Remembering: A study in experimental and social psychology.* Cambridge, England: Cambridge University Press.

Bateson, P. P. G. (1973). Internal influences on early learning in birds. In R. A. Hinde & J. Stevenson-Hinde (Eds.), *Constraints on learning.* London: Academic Press.

Baumrind, D. (1964). Some thoughts on ethics of research: After reading Milgram's "Behavioral study of obedience." *American Psychologist, 19,* 421–423.

Baumrind, D. (1967). Child care practices anteceding three patterns of preschool behavior. *Genetic Psychology Monographs, 75,* 43–88.

Beach, F. (1967). Cerebral and hormonal control of reflexive mechanisms involved in copulatory behavior. *Physiological Review, 47,* 289–316.

Beach, F. A. (1956). Characteristics of masculine "sex drive." In M. Jones (Ed.), *Nebraska symposium on motivation.* Lincoln: University of Nebraska Press.

Beach, F. A., & Jordan, L. (1956). Sexual exhaustion and recovery in the male rat. *Quarterly Journal of Experimental Psychology, 8,* 121–133.

Beck, A. T. (1967). *Depression: Clinical, experimental and theoretical aspects.* New York: Harper & Row.

Beck, A. T., Rush, A. J., Shaw, B. F., & Emery, G. (1979). *Cognitive therapy of depression.* New York: Guilford Press.

Beckwith, J. (1983). Gender and math performance: Does biology have implications for educational policy? *Journal of Education, 165,* 158–174.

Beech, H. R., Burns, L. E., & Scheffield, B. F. (1982). *A behavioral approach to the management of stress: A practical guide to techniques.* New York: Wiley.

Beecher, H. K. (1956). Relationship of significance of wound to the pain experienced. *Journal of the American Medical Association, 161,* 1609–1613.

Beecher, H. K. (1959). Generalization from pain of various types and diverse origins. *Science, 130,* 267–268.

Belanger, D., & Feldman, S. M. (1962). Effects of water deprivation upon heart rate and instrumental activity in the rat. *Journal of Comparative and Physiological Psychology, 55,* 220–225.

Bell, A. P., & Weinberg, M. S. (1978). *Homosexualities.* New York: Simon & Schuster.

Bell, A. P., Weinberg, M. S., & Hammersmith, S. K. (1981). *Sexual preference: Its development in men and women.* Bloomington: Indiana University Press.

Bellezza, F. S. (1981). Mnemonic devices: Classification, characteristics, and criteria. *Review of Educational Research, 51,* 247–275.

Belmont, L., & Marolla, F. A. (1973). Birth order, family size, and intelligence. *Science, 182,* 1096–1101.

Bem, D. J. (1967). Self-perception: An alternative interpretation of cognitive dissonance phenomena. *Psychological Review, 74,* 183–200.

Bem, D. J. (1972). Self-perception theory. In L. Berkowitz (Ed.), *Advances in experimental social psychology* (Vol. 6). New York: Academic Press.

Bem, S. L. (1975). Sex-role adaptability: One consequence of psychological androgyny. *Journal of Personality and Social Psychology, 31,* 634–643.

Bemis, K. M. (1978). Current approaches to the etiology and treatment of anorexia nervosa. *Psychological Bulletin, 85,* 593–617.

Bemporad, J. R. (1985). Long-term analytic treatment of depression. In E. E. Beckham & W. R. Leber (Eds.), *Handbook of depression: Treatment, assessment, and research.* Homewood, Ill.: Dorsey Press.

Benbow, C. P., & Stanley, J. C. (1980). Sex differences in mathematical ability: Fact or artifact? *Science, 210,* 1262–1264.

Benchley, R. W. (1937). The early worm. In R. W. Benchley, *Inside Benchley.* New York: Harper.

Benda, C. E., Squires, N. D., Ogonik, N. J., & Wise, R. (1963). Personality factors in mild mental retardation: 1. Family background and sociocultural patterns. *American Journal of Mental Deficiency, 68,* 24–40.

Benedict, R. (1934). *Patterns of culture.* Boston: Houghton Mifflin.

Bengston, V. L., Cuellar, J. E., & Ragan, P. K. (1977). Stratum contrasts and similarities in attitudes toward death. *Journal of Gerontology, 32,* 76–88.

Benson, D. F., & Greenberg, J. P. (1969). Visual form agnosia. *Archives of Neurology, 20,* 82–89.

Berbaum, M. L., & Moreland, R. L. (1985). Intellectual development within transracial adoptive families: Retesting the confluence model. *Child Development, 56,* 207–216.

Berger, S. M. (1962). Conditioning through vicarious instigation. *Psychological Review, 69,* 450–466.

Bergin, A. E., & Lambert, M. J. (1978). The evaluation of therapeutic outcomes. In S. L. Garfield & A. E. Bergin (Eds.), *Handbook of psychotherapy and behavior change* (2nd ed.). New York: Wiley.

Berko, J. (1958). The child's learning of English morphology. *Word, 14,* 150–177.

Berkowitz, L. (1962). *Aggression: A social psychological analysis.* New York: McGraw-Hill.

Berkowitz, L. (1969). The frustration-aggression hypothesis revisited. In L. Berkowitz (Ed.), *Roots of aggression: A re-examination of the frustration-aggression hypothesis.* New York: Atherton Press.

Berkowitz, L. (1972). Social norms, feelings, and other factors affecting helping and altruism. In L. Berkowitz (Ed.), *Advances in experimental social psychology* (Vol. 6). New York: Academic Press.

Berkowitz, L. (1973, July). The case for bottling up rage. *Psychology Today,* pp. 24–31.

Berkowitz, L. (1979). *A survey of social psychology* (2nd ed.). New York: Holt Rinehart & Winston.

Berkowitz, L., Cochrane, S., & Embree, M. (1979). Influence of aversive experience and the consequences of one's aggression on aggressive behavior. Reported in L. Berkowitz, *A survey of social psychology* (2nd ed.). New York: Holt, Rinehart & Winston.

Berkowitz, L., & Donnerstein, E. (1982). External validity is more than skin deep: Some answers to criticisms of laboratory experiments. *American Psychologist, 37,* 245–257.

Berkowitz, L., & LePage, A. (1967). Weapons as aggression-eliciting stimuli. *Journal of Personality and Social Psychology, 7,* 202–207.

Berlin, B. (1972). Speculations on the growth of ethnobotanical nomenclature. *Language in Society, 1,* 51–86.

Berlin, B., Breedlove, D. E., & Raven, P. H. (1973). General principles of classification and nomenclature in folk biology. *American Anthropologist, 75,* 214–242.

Berlin, B., & Kay, P. (1969). *Basic color terms: Their universality and evolution.* Berkeley: University of California Press.

Berlyne, D. (1967). Arousal and reinforcement. In D. Levine (Ed.), *Nebraska symposium on motivation.* Lincoln: University of Nebraska Press.

Berne, E. (1964). *Games people play.* New York: Grove Press.

Bernheim, K. F., & Lewine, R. R. J. (1979). *Schizophrenia: Symptoms, causes, treatments.* New York: Norton.

Bernstein, I. L. (1978). Learned taste aversions in children receiving chemotherapy. *Science, 200,* 1302–1303.

Bernstein, I. L. (1985). Learned food aversions in the progression of cancer and its treatment. In N. S. Braverman & P. Bernstein (Eds.), *Experimental assessments and clinical application of conditioned food aversions. Annals of the New York Academy of Sciences,* Vol. 443.

Berry, G. L., & Mitchell-Kernan, C. (1982). *Television and the socialization of the minority child.* New York: Academic Press.

Berscheid, E. (1985). Interpersonal attraction. In G. Lindzey & E. Aronson (Eds.), *Handbook of social psychology* (3rd ed.) (Vol. 2). New York: Random House.

Berscheid, E., Dion, K., Walster, E., & Walster, G. W. (1971). Physical attractiveness and dating choice: A test of the matching hypothesis. *Journal of Experimental Social Psychology, 7,* 173–189.

Berscheid, E., & Walster, E. (1978). *Interpersonal attraction* (2nd ed.). Reading, Mass.: Addison-Wesley.

Best, M. R., & Barker, L. M. (1977). The nature of "learned safety" and its role in the delay of reinforcement gradient. In L. M. Barker, M. R. Best, & M. Domjan (Eds.), *Learning mechanisms in food selection.* Waco, Tex.: Baylor University Press.

Best, P. J., Best, M. R., & Henggeler, S. (1977). The contribution of environmental non-ingestive cues in conditioning with aversive internal consequences. In L. M. Barker, M. R. Best, & M. Domjan (Eds.), *Learning mechanisms in food selection.* Waco, Tex.: Baylor University Press.

Biederman, I. (1981). On the semantics of a glance at a scene. In M. Kubovy & J. Pomerantz (Eds.), *Perceptual organization.* Hillsdale, N.J.: Erlbaum.

Birren, J. E. (1974). Transitions in gerontology—from lab to life: Psychophysiology and speed of response. *American Psychologist, 29,* 808–815.

Bjorklund, D. F. (1985). The role of conceptual knowledge in the development of organization in children's memory. In C. J. Brainerd & M. Pressley (Eds.), *Basic processes in memory development.* New York: Springer-Verlag.

Blanchard, K. H., & Johnson, S. (1985). *One minute manager.* Berkeley, Calif.: Berkeley Books.

Blaxton, T. A., & Neely, J. H. (1983). Inhibition from semantically related primes: Evidence of category specific inhibition. *Memory & Cognition, 11,* 500–510.

Blass, E. M., & Epstein, A. N. (1971). A lateral preoptic osmosensitive zone for thirst. *Journal of Comparative and Physiological Psychology, 76,* 378–394.

Blass, E. M., Nussbaum, A. I., & Hanson, D. G. (1974). Septal hyperdipsia: Specific enhancement of drinking to angiotensin in rats. *Journal of Comparative Physiological Psychology, 87,* 422–439.

Bleuler, E. (1950). *Dementia praecox, or the group of schizophrenias* (J. Zinkin & N. D. C. Lewis, Trans.). New York: International Universities Press. (Original work published 1911)

Block, J. (1981). Some enduring and consequential structures of personality. In A. I. Rabin, J. Aronoff, A. M. Barclay, & R. A. Zucker (Eds.), *Further explorations in personality.* New York: Wiley.

Blum, J. E., Jarvik, L. F., & Clark, E. T. (1970). Rate of change on selective tests of intelligence: A twenty-year longitudinal study. *Journal of Gerontology, 25,* 171–176.

Blumstein, P. W., & Schwartz, P. (1976). Bisexuality in women. *Archives of Sexual Behavior, 5,* 171–181.

Blumstein, P. W., & Schwartz, P. (1983). *American Couples.* New York: Morrow.

Bochner, S., & Insko, C. (1966). Communicator discrepancy, source credibility, and influence. *Journal of Personality and Social Psychology, 4,* 614–621.

Bogatz, G., & Ball, S. J. (1971). *The second year of Sesame Street: A continuing evaluation*. Princeton, N.J.: Educational Testing Service.

Bogen, J. E. (1969). The other side of the brain: An appositional mind. *Bulletin of the Los Angeles Neurological Society, 34*, 73–105.

Boggiano, A. K., & Ruble, D. N. (1979). Competence and overjustification effect: A developmental study. *Journal of Personality and Social Psychology, 37*, 1462–1468.

Bohannon, J. N., & Warren-Leubecker, A. W. (1985). Theoretical approaches to language acquisition. In J. B. Gleason (Ed.), *The development of language*. Columbus, Ohio: Merrill.

Bok, S. (1978). *Dying: Moral choice in public and private life*. New York: Pantheon.

Bolles, R. C. (1970). Species-specific defense reactions and avoidance learning. *Psychological Review, 77*, 32–48.

Bolles, R. C. (1972). Reinforcement, expectancy, and learning. *Psychological Review, 79*, 394–409.

Bolles, R. C. (1975). *Theory of motivation* (2nd ed.). New York: Harper & Row.

Bolles, R. C., & Fanselow, M. S. (1980). A perceptual-defensive recuperative model of fear and pain. *Behavioral and Brain Sciences, 3*, 291–323.

Bolles, R. C., & Fanselow, M. S. (1982). Endorphins and behavior. *Annual Review of Psychology, 33*, 87–101.

Boring, E. G. (1950). *A history of experimental psychology*. (2nd ed.). New York: Appleton-Century-Crofts.

Borkowski, J. G., Krause, A., & Maxwell, S. E. (1985). On multiple determinants of racial differences in intelligence: A reply to Jensen. *Intelligence, 9*, 41–49.

Bornstein, M. H. (1979). Perceptual development: Stability and change in feature perception. In M. Bornstein & W. Kessen (Eds.), *Psychological development from infancy: Image to intention*. Hillsdale, N.J.: Erlbaum.

Botwinick, J., & Storandt, M. (1974). *Memory, related functions and age*. Springfield, Ill.: Charles Thomas.

Bouchard, T. J. (1983). Do environmental similarities explain the similarity in intelligence of identical twins reared apart? *Intelligence, 7*, 175–184.

Bouchard, T. J., & McGue, M. (1981). Familial studies of intelligence: A review. *Science, 212*, 1055–1059.

Bouchard, T. J., Jr., & Segal, N. L. (Eds.) (in press). *Twins raised apart*. New York: Harcourt Brace Jovanovich.

Bower, G. H. (1961). A contrast effect in differential conditioning. *Journal of Experimental Psychology, 62*, 196–199.

Bower, G. H. (1972). Mental imagery and associative learning. In L. W. Gregg (Ed.), *Cognition in learning and memory*. New York: Wiley.

Bower, G. H. (1981). Mood and memory. *American Psychologist, 36*, 129–148.

Bower, G. H., & Clark, M. C. (1969). Narrative stories as mediators for serial learning. *Psychonomic Science, 14*, 181–182.

Bower, G. H., Clark, M. C., Lesgold, A. M., & Winzenz, D. (1969). Hierarchical retrieval schemes in recall of categorized work lists. *Journal of Verbal Learning and Verbal Behavior, 8*, 323–343.

Bower, G. H., & Karlin, M. B. (1974). Depth of processing pictures of faces and recognition memory. *Journal of Experimental Psychology, 103*, 751–757.

Bowers, K. S. (1983). *Hypnosis for the seriously curious* (2nd ed.). New York: Norton.

Bowlby, J. (1973). *Attachment and loss: Vol. 2. Separation*. London: Hogarth Press.

Bowles, N., & Hynds, F. (1978). *Psi Search: The comprehensive guide to psychic phenomena*. New York: Harper & Row.

Boyle, P. C., Storlein, H., & Keesey, R. E. (1978). Increased efficiency of food utilization following weight loss. *Physiology and Behavior, 21*, 261.

Brackbill, Y. (1979). Obstetrical medication and infant behavior. In J. D. Osofsky (Ed.), *Handbook of infant development*. New York: Wiley.

Bradley, D. R., Dumais, S. T., & Petry, H. M. (1976). Reply to Cavonias. *Nature, 261*, 77–78.

Brady, J. P. (1980). Behavior therapy. In H. I. Kaplan, A. M. Freeman, & B. J. Sadock (Eds.), *Comprehensive textbook of psychiatry: III*. Baltimore: Williams & Wilkins.

Brady, J. V., & Nauta, W. J. H. (1953). Subcortical mechanisms in emotional behavior: Affective changes following septal forebrain lesions in the albino rat. *Journal of Comparative and Physiological Psychology, 46*, 339–346.

Brady, J. V., Porter, R. W., Conrad, D. G., & Mason, J. W. (1958). Avoidance behavior and the development of gastroduodenal ulcers. *Journal of the Experimental Analysis of Behavior, 1*, 69–72.

Branscombe, N. R. (1985). Conscious and unconscious processing of affective and cognitive information. Unpublished manuscript, Purdue University.

Bransford, J. D. (1979). *Human cognition: Learning, understanding, and remembering*. Belmont, Calif.: Wadsworth.

Bransford, J. D., & Johnson, M. K. (1972). Contextual prerequisites for understanding: Some investigations of comprehension and recall. *Journal of Verbal Learning and Verbal Behavior, 11*, 717–726.

Bransford, J. D., & Stein, B. S. (1984). *The IDEAL problem solver: A guide for improving thinking, learning, and creativity*. New York: Freeman.

Braun, B. G. (1983). Neurophysiologic changes in multiple personality due to integration: A preliminary report. *American Journal of Clinical Hypnosis, 26*, 84–92.

Bray, G. A. (1972). Lipogenesis in human adipose tissue: Some effects of nibbling and gorging. *Journal of Clinical Investigation, 51*, 537–548.

Brecher, E. M. (1972). *Licit and illicit drugs*. Boston: Little, Brown.

Brewin, C. R. (1985). Depression and causal attributions: What is their relation? *Psychological Bulletin, 98*, 297–309.

Bridgeman, B., & Staggs, D. (1982). Plasticity in human blindsight. *Vision Research, 22*, 1199–1203.

Brigham, C. C. (1923). *A study of American intelligence*. Princeton, N.J.: Princeton University Press.

Brigham, J. C., & Richardson, C. G. (1979). Race, sex and helping in the marketplace. *Journal of Applied Social Psychology, 9*, 314–322.

Broadbent, D. E. (1957). A mechanical model for human attention and immediate memory. *Psychological Review, 64*, 205–215.

Broadbent, D. E. (1958). *Perception and communication*. N.Y.: Pergamon.

Broadbent, D. E. (1978). The current state of noise research: Reply to Poulton. *Psychological Bulletin, 85*, 1052–1067.

Brock, T. C. (1965). Communicator-recipient similarity and decision change. *Journal of Personality and Social Psychology, 1*, 650–654.

Brody, E. M. (1985). Parent care as a normative family stress. *The Gerontologist, 25*, 19–29.

Brooks-Gunn, J., & Peterson, A. (1983). *Girls at puberty*. New York: Plenum.

Brown v. Board of Education of Topeka (1955). 98 F. Supp. 797 (1951), 347 U.S. 438 (1954), 349 U.S. 294.

Brown, A. L. (1978). Knowing when, where, and how to remember: A problem of metacognition. In R. Glaser (Ed.), *Advances in instructional psychology*. Hillsdale, N.J.: Erlbaum.

Brown, A. L., Armbruster, B. B., & Baker, L. (1984). The role of metacognition in reading and study. In J. Orasanu (Ed.), *A decade of reading research: Implications for practice*. Hillsdale, N.J.: Erlbaum.

Brown, A. L., Bransford, J. D., Ferrara, R. A., & Campione, J. C. (1983). Learning, remembering, and understanding. In J. H. Flavell & E. M. Markman (Eds.), *Handbook of child psychology: Vol. 3. Cognitive development* (pp. 71–166). New York: Wiley.

Brown, A. S. (1981). Inhibition in cued retrieval. *Journal of Experimental Psychology: Human Learning and Memory, 7*, 204–215.

Brown, J. (1958). Some tests of the decay theory of immediate memory. *Quarterly Journal of Experimental Psychology, 10*, 12–21.

Brown, R. (1958). How shall a thing be called? *Psychological Review, 65*, 14–21.

Brown, R. (1970). *Psycholinguistics*. New York: Free Press.

Brown, R., & Kulik, J. (1977). Flashbulb memories. *Cognition, 5*, 73–99.

Brown, R. A. (1973). *A first language: The early stages*. Cambridge, Mass.: Harvard University Press.

Brown, R. A., & Herrnstein, R. J. (1975). *Psychology*. Boston: Little, Brown.

Brown, R., & McNeill, D. (1966). The tip-of-the-tongue phenomenon. *Journal of Verbal Learning and Verbal Behavior, 5*, 325–337.

Brown, R., et al. (1962). *New directions in psychology*. New York: Holt.

Bruner, J. S. (1972). The nature and uses of immaturity. *American Psychologist, 27*, 687–701.

Bruner, J. S. (1975). The ontogenesis of speech acts. *Journal of Child Language, 2*, 1–19.

Bruner, J. S., Goodnow, J. J., & Austin, G. A. (1956). *A study of thinking*. New York: Wiley.

Buchsbaum, M. S., Mirsky, A. F., Delisi, L. E., Morihisa, J., Karson, C. N., Mendelson, W. B., King, A. C., Johnson, J., and Kessler, R. (1984). The Genain quadruplets: Electrophysiological, positron emission, and x-ray tomographic studies. *Psychiatry Research, 13*, 95–108.

Buck, R., Savin, V. J., Miller, R. E., & Caul, W. F. (1972). Nonverbal communication of affect in humans. *Journal of Personality and Social Psychology, 23*, 362–371.

Bullock, M. (1985). Animism in childhood thinking: A new look at an old question. *Developmental Psychology, 21,* 217–225.

Burt, C. (1966). The genetic determination of differences in intelligence: A study of monozygotic twins reared together and apart. *British Journal of Psychology, 57,* 137–153.

Buss, D. M., & Scheier, M. F. (1976). Self-awareness, self-consciousness, and self-attribution. *Journal of Research in Personality, 10,* 463–468.

Butler, R. W. (1975). *Why survive? Being old in America.* New York: Harper & Row.

Butler, S. F., Schact, T. E., Henry, W. P., & Strupp, H. H. (1984). Psychotherapy versus placebo: Revisiting a pseudo issue. *Behavioral and Brain Sciences, 7,* 756–757.

Bykov, K. M. (1957). *The cerebral cortex and the internal organs* (W. H. Gantt, Trans.). New York: Chemical Publishing.

Byrne, D. (1961). The influence of propinquity and opportunities for interaction on classroom relationships. *Human Relations, 14,* 63–70.

Byrne, D. (1971). *The attraction paradigm.* New York: Academic Press.

Cain, W. S. (1982). Odor identification by males and females: Predictions versus performance. *Chemical Senses, 7,* 129–142.

Cairns, R. B. (1979). *Social development: The origins and plasticity of interchanges.* San Francisco: Freeman.

Calder, B. J., & Staw, B. M. (1975). Self-perception of intrinsic and extrinsic motivation. *Journal of Personality and Social Psychology, 31,* 599–605.

Calhoun, J. B. (1962). Population density and social pathology. *Scientific American, 206,* 139–148.

Callner, D. A. (1975). Behavioral treatment approaches to drug abuse: A critical review of the research. *Psychological Bulletin, 82,* 143–164.

Campbell, B. A., & Kraeling, D. (1953). Response strength as a function of drive level and amount of drive reduction. *Journal of Experimental Psychology, 45,* 97–101.

Campbell, B. A., & Misanin, J. R. (1969). Basic drives. *Annual Review of Psychology,* 57–84.

Campbell, D., Sanderson, R. E. & Laverty, S. G. (1964). Characteristics of a conditioned response in human subjects during extinction trials following a single traumatic conditioning trial. *Journal of Abnormal and Social Psychology, 68,* 627–639.

Campbell, D. P., & Hansen, J. C. (1981). *Manual for the SVIB-SCII Strong-Campbell interest inventory* (3rd ed.). Stanford, Calif.: Stanford University Press.

Campione, J. C., & Brown, A. L. (1979). Toward a theory of intelligence: Contributions from research with retarded children. *Intelligence, 2,* 279–304.

Campos, J. J., Langer, A., & Krowitz, A. (1970). Cardiac responses on the visual cliff in prelocomotor human infants. *Science, 170,* 196–197.

Candolle, M. A. de. (1974). *Histoire des sciences et des savants depuis deux siècles.* In H. J. Mozans, *Women in science* (p. 392). Cambridge, Mass.: MIT Press. (Original work published 1913)

Cannon, W. B. (1927). The James-Lange theory of emotions: A critical examination and an alternative. *American Journal of Psychology, 39,* 106–124.

Cannon, W. B., Lewis, J. T., & Britton, S. W. (1927). The dispensability of the sympathetic division of the autonomic nervous system. *Boston Medical Surgery Journal, 197,* 514.

Cantor, M. H. (1983). Strain among caregivers: A study of experience in the United States. *The Gerontologist, 23,* 597–604.

Cantor, N., Mischel, W., & Schwartz, J. C. (1982). A prototype analysis of psychological situations. *Cognitive Psychology, 14,* 45–77.

Capaldi, E. D., & Myers, D. E. (1978). Resistance to satiation of consummatory and instrumental performance. *Learning and Motivation, 9,* 179–201.

Capaldi, E. J. (1967). A sequential hypothesis of instrumental learning. In K. W. Spence & J. T. Spence (Eds.), *The psychology of learning and motivation* (Vol. 1). New York: Academic Press.

Caplan, R. D., Abbey, A., Abramis, D. J., Andrews, F. M., Conway, T. L., & French, J. R. P. (1983). *Tranquilizer use and well being: A longitudinal study of social and psychological effects.* Ann Arbor: Institute for Social Research, University of Michigan.

Carey, S. (1982). Semantic development: The state of the art. In E. Wanner & L. R. Gleitman (Eds.), *Language acquisition: The state of the art* (pp. 347–389). Cambridge, England: Cambridge University Press.

Carey, S. (1985). *Conceptual change in childhood.* Cambridge, Mass.: MIT Press.

Carlson, N. R. (1986). *Physiology of behavior* (3rd ed). Boston: Allyn and Bacon.

Carmichael, L. L., Hogan, H. P., & Walter, A. A. (1932). An experimental study of the effect of language on reproduction of visually perceived form. *Journal of Experimental Psychology, 15,* 73–85.

Caro, T. M. (1986). The functions of stotting: A review of the hypotheses. *Animal Behavior, 34,* 649–662.

Carskadon, M. A., & Dement, W. C. (1981). Cumulative effects of sleep restriction on daytime sleepiness. *Psycho-physiology, 18,* 107–113.

Carver, C. S. (1975). Physical aggression as a function of objective self-awareness and attitudes toward punishment. *Journal of Experimental Social Psychology, 11,* 510–519.

Carver, C. S., & Scheier, M. F. (1981). *Attention and self-regulation: A control theory approach to human behavior.* New York: Springer-Verlag.

Case, R. (1985). *Intellectual development: Birth to adulthood.* New York: Academic Press.

Cates, J. (1970). Psychology's manpower: Report on the 1968 national register of scientific and technical personnel. *American Psychologist, 25,* 254–264.

Cattell, R. B. (1971). *Abilities: Their structure, growth, and action.* Boston: Houghton Mifflin.

Cattell, R. B. (1973, July). Personality pinned down. *Psychology Today,* pp. 40–46.

Cattell, R. B. (1982). *The inheritance of personality and ability.* New York: Academic Press.

Cerella, J. (1985). Information processing rates in the elderly. *Psychological Bulletin, 98.* 67–83.

Cermak, L. S. (Ed.) (1982). *Human memory and amnesia.* Hillsdale, N.J.: Erlbaum.

Cermak, L. S., & Craik, F. I. M. (Eds.). (1979). *Levels of processing in human memory.* Hillsdale, N.J.: Erlbaum.

Chafetz, M. E. (1979, May–June). Alcohol and alcoholism. *American Scientist.*

Chaffin, R., & Herrmann, D. J. (1983). Self-reports of memory abilities by old and young adults. *Human Learning, 2,* 17–28.

Chaiken, S., & Eagly, A. H. (1976). Communication modality as a determinant of message persuasiveness and message comprehensibility. *Journal of Personality and Social Psychology, 34,* 605–614.

Chapman, C. R., Gehrig, J. D., & Wilson, M. E. (1975). Acupuncture, pain and signal detection theory. *Science, 189,* 65.

Chase, W. G., & Simon, H. A. (1973). Perception in chess. *Cognitive Psychology, 4,* 55–81.

Cherry, E. C. (1953). Some experiments on the recognition of speech with one and two ears. *Journal of the Acoustical Society of America, 25,* 975–979.

Cherry, F., & Byrne, D. (1976). Authoritarianism. In T. Blass (Ed.), *Personality variables in social behavior.* Hillsdale, N.J.: Erlbaum.

Chi, M. T., Feltovich, P. J., & Glaser, R. (1981). Categorization and representation of physics problems by experts and novices. *Cognitive Science, 5,* 121–152.

Chi, M. T. H. (1978). Knowledge structures and memory development. In R. Siegler (Ed.), *Children's thinking: What develops?* Hillsdale, N.J.: Erlbaum.

Chomsky, N. (1957). *Syntactic structures.* The Hague: Mouton.

Chomsky, N. (1965). *Aspects of the theory of syntax.* Cambridge, Mass.: MIT Press.

Christensen, A. (1983). Intervention. In H. H. Kelley et al. (Eds.), *Close relationships.* San Francisco: Freeman.

Cialdini, R. B., Petty, R. E., & Cacioppo, J. T. (1981). Attitude and attitude change. In M. R. Rosenzweig & L. W. Porter (Eds.), *Annual Review of Psychology, 32,* 357–404.

Clark, E. V. (1973). What's in a word? On the child's acquisition of semantics in his first language. In T. E. Moore (Ed.), *Cognitive development and the acquisition of language.* New York: Academic Press.

Clark, H. H., & Clark, E. V. (1977). *Psychology and language.* New York: Harcourt Brace Jovanovich.

Clay, M. M. (1973). *Reading: The patterning of complex behavior.* Auckland, New Zealand: Heineman Educational Books.

Cleckley, H. (1964). *The mask of sanity.* St. Louis: Mosby.

Coe, W. C. (1977). The problem of relevance versus ethics in researching hypnosis and antisocial conduct. *Annuals of the New York Academy of Sciences, 296,* 90–104.

Cohen, B. (1963). *The press and foreign policy.* Princeton, N.J.: Princeton University Press.

Cohen, L. G., DeLoache, J. S., & Strauss, M. S. (1979). Infant visual perception. In J. Osofsky (Ed.), *Handbook of infant development.* New York: Wiley.

Cohen, N. J., & Corkin, S. (1981). The amnesic patient, H.M.: Learning and retention of a cognitive skill. *Society for Neuroscience Abstracts, 7,* 235.

Cohen, S. (1980). Aftereffects of stress on human performance and social behavior: A review of research and theory. *Psychological Bulletin, 88,* 82–108.

Cohen, S., Evans, G. W., Krantz, D. S., & Stokols, D. (1980). Physiological, motivational, and cognitive effects of aircraft noise on children: Moving from the laboratory to the field. *American Psychologist, 35,* 231–243.

Cohen, S., Evans, G. W., Krantz, D. S., Stokols, D., & Kelly, S. (1981). Aircraft noise and children: Longitudinal and cross-sectional evidence on adaptation to noise and the effectiveness of noise abatement. *Journal of Personality and Social Psychology, 40,* 331–345.

Cohen, S., Glass, D. D., & Singer, J. E. (1973). Apartment noise, auditory discrimination, and reading ability in children. *Journal of Experimental Social Psychology, 9,* 407–422.

Cole, J. R. (1981). Women in science. *American Scientist, 69,* 385–391.

Coleman, J. C., Butcher, J. N., & Carson, R. C. (1980). *Abnormal psychology and modern life* (6th ed.). Glenview, Ill.: Scott Foresman.

Collins, A. M., & Loftus, E. F. (1975). A spreading activation theory of semantic processing. *Psychological Review, 82,* 407–428.

Condon, W. S., & Sander, L. (1974). Neonate movement is synchronized with adult speech: Interactional participation and language acquisition. *Science, 183,* 99–101.

Conrad, R., & Hull, A. J. (1968). Input modality and the serial position curve in short-term memory. *Psychonomic Science, 10,* 135–136.

Cook, S. W. (1978). Interpersonal and attitudinal outcomes in cooperating interracial groups. *Journal of Research and Development in Education, 12.*

Coombs, L. C. (1979). The measurement of commitment to work. *Journal of Population, 2,* 203–223.

Cooper, J. C., Zanna, M. P., & Taves, P. A. (1978). Arousal as a necessary condition for attitude change following induced compliance. *Journal of Personality and Social Psychology, 36,* 1101–1106.

Cooper, R. M., & Zubek, J. P. (1958). Effects of enriched and restricted early environment on the learning ability of bright and dull rats. *Canadian Journal of Psychology, 12,* 159–164.

Cornsweet, T. N. (1970). *Visual perception.* New York: Academic Press.

Coren, S., & Girgus, J. S. (1978). *Seeing is deceiving: The psychology of visual illusions.* Hillsdale, N.J.: Erlbaum.

Corey, S. M. (1937). Professed attitudes and actual behavior. *Journal of Educational Psychology, 28,* 271–280.

Cosgrove, J. M., & Patterson, C. J. (1977). Plans and the development of listener skills. *Developmental Psychology, 13,* 557–564.

Cowart, B. J. (1981). Development of taste perception in humans: Sensitivity and preference throughout the life span. *Psychological Bulletin, 90,* 43–73.

Cox, T. (1978). *Stress.* Baltimore, Md.: University Park Press.

Craddock, D. (1979). *Obesity and its management.* London: Churchill Livingstone.

Craig, J. D. (1979). Asymmetries in processing auditory nonverbal stimuli? *Psychological Bulletin, 86,* 1339–1349.

Craig, K., & Lowrey, H. J. (1969). Heart rate components of conditioned vicarious autonomic responses. *Journal of Personality and Social Psychology, 11,* 381–387.

Craik, F. I. M. (1977). Age differences in human memory. In J. E. Birren & K. W. Schaie (Eds.), *The handbook of the psychology of aging.* New York: Van Nostrand Reinhold.

Craik, F. I. M., & Byrd, M. (1982). Aging and cognitive deficits: The role of attentional resources. In F. I. M. Craik & S. E. Trehub (Eds.), *Aging and cognitive processes.* New York: Plenum.

Craik, F. I. M., & Lockhart, R. S. (1972). Levels of processing: A framework for memory research. *Journal of Verbal Learning and Verbal Behavior, 11,* 671–684.

Craik, F. I. M., & Rabinowitz, J. C. (1984). Age differences in the acquisition and use of verbal information. In J. Long & A. Baddeley (Eds.), *Attention and performance* (Vol. 10). Hillsdale, N.J.: Erlbaum.

Craik, F. I. M., & Tulving, E. (1975). Depth of processing and retention of words in episodic memory. *Journal of Experimental Psychology: General, 104,* 268–294.

Crano, W. D. (1970). Effects of sex, response order, and expertise in conformity: A dispositional approach. *Sociometry, 33,* 239–252.

Crawford, M., & Masterson, F. (1978). Components of the flight response can reinforce bar-press avoidance learning. *Journal of Experimental Psychology: Animal Behavior Processes, 4,* 144–151.

Crespi, L. P. (1942). Quantitative variations of incentive and performance in the white rat. *American Journal of Psychology, 55,* 467–517.

Crick, F., & Mitchison, G. (1983). The function of dream sleep. *Nature, 304,* 111–114.

Crisp, A. H. (1970). Premorbid factors in adult disorders of weight, with primary reference to primary anorexia nervosa: A literature review. *Journal of Psychosometric Research, 14,* 1–22.

Crowder, R. G. (1976). *Principles of learning and memory.* Hillsdale, N.J.: Erlbaum.

Crowe, R. R. (1972). The adopted offspring of women criminal offenders: A study of their arrest records. *Archives of General Psychiatry, 27,* 600–603.

Crowe, R. R. (1974). An adoption study of antisocial personality. *Archives of General Psychiatry, 31,* 785–791.

Crutchfield, R. A. (1955). Conformity and character. *American Psychologist, 10,* 191–198.

Curran, J. P., & Lippold, S. (1975). The effects of physical attraction and attitude similarity on attraction in dating dyads. *Journal of Personality, 44,* 528–539.

Daly, H. B. (1974). Reinforcing properties of escape from frustration aroused in various learning situations. In G. H. Bower, *The psychology of learning and motivation: Advances in research and theory* (Vol. 8). New York: Academic Press.

Damon, A., Seltzer, C. C., Stoudt, H. W., & Bell, B. (1972). Age and physique in healthy white veterans at Boston. *Aging and Human Development, 3,* 202–208.

Damon, W., & Hart, D. (1982). The development of self-understanding from infancy through adolescence. *Child Development, 53,* 841–864.

Darley, J. M., & Gross, P. H. (1983). A hypothesis-confirming bias in labeling effects. *Journal of Personality and Social Psychology, 44,* 20–33.

Darley, J. M., & Latané, B. (1968). Bystander intervention in emergencies: Diffusion of responsibility. *Journal of Personality and Social Psychology, 8,* 377–388.

Darwin, C. (1859). *On the origin of species by means of natural selection, or the preservation of favoured races in the struggle for life.* London: John Murray.

Darwin, C. (1871). *The descent of man and selection in relation to sex.* London: John Murray.

Darwin, C. (1965). *The expression of the emotions in man and in animals.* Chicago: University of Chicago Press. (Original work published 1872)

Darwin, C. J., Turvey, M. T., & Crowder, R. G. (1972). An auditory analogue of the Sperling partial report procedure: Evidence for brief auditory storage. *Cognitive Psychology, 3,* 255–267.

Dasen, P. R. (1972). Cross-cultural Piagetian research: A summary. *Journal of Cross-Cultural Psychology, 3,* 23–29.

Davenport, W. (1965). Sexual patterns and their regulation in a society of the Southwest Pacific. In F. A. Beach (Ed.), *Sex and behavior.* New York: Wiley.

Davison, A. N., & Dobbing, J. (1966). Myelination as a vulnerable period in brain development. *British Medical Bulletin, 22,* 40–44.

Deaux, K., & Wrightsman, L. S. (1984). *Social psychology in the 80s* (4th ed.). Monterey, Calif.: Brooks/Cole.

DeCasper, A. J., & Fifer, W. P. (1980). Of human bonding: Newborns prefer their mothers' voices. *Science, 208,* 1174–1176.

DeCasper, A. J., & Prescott, P. A. (1984). Human newborn perception of male voices: Preference, discrimination, and reinforcing value. *Developmental Psychobiology, 17,* 481–491.

Deci, E. L. (1975). *Intrinsic motivation.* New York: Plenum.

DeFries, J. C., Hegmann, J. P., & Halcomb, R. A. (1974). Response to 20 generations of selection for open-field activity in mice. *Behavioral Biology, 11,* 481–495.

DeJong, W. (1979). An examination of self-perception mediation of the foot-in-the-door effect. *Journal of Personality and Social Psychology, 37,* 2221–2239.

DeLoache, J. S., Cassidy, D. J., & Brown, A. L. (1985). Precursors of mnemonic strategies in very young children's memory. *Child Development, 56,* 125–137.

Dember, W. N., Jenkins, J. J., & Teylor, T. J. (1984). *General psychology.* Hillsdale, N.J.: Erlbaum.

Dement, W. C. (1960). The effect of dream deprivation. *Science, 131,* 1705–1707.

Dement, W. C. (1976). *Some must watch while some must sleep.* New York: Norton.

Dement, W. C., & Kleitman, N. (1957a). Cyclic variations in EEG during sleep and their relations to eye movement, body motility, and dreaming. *EEG Clinical Neurophysiology, 9,* 673–690.

Dement, W. C., & Kleitman, N. (1957b). The relation of eye movements during sleep to dream activity: An objective method for the study of dreaming. *Journal of Experimental Psychology, 53,* 339–346.

Denney, N. W. (1980). Task demands and problem-solving strategies in middle-age and older adults. *Journal of Gerontology, 35,* 559–564.

Dennis, W. (1973). *Children of the creche.* Englewood Cliffs, N.J.: Prentice-Hall.

Dermer, M., & Pyszczynski, T. A. (1978). Effects of erotica upon men's loving and liking responses for women they love. *Journal of Personality and Social Psychology, 36,* 1302–1309.

Desor, J. A., Greene, L. S., & Maller, O. (1975). Preference for sweet and salty in 9- to 15-year-old and adult humans. *Science, 190,* 686–697.

Deutsch, M., & Collins, M. E. (1951). *Interracial housing: A psychological evaluation of a social experiment.* Minneapolis: University of Minnesota Press.

DeVries, R. (1969). Constancy of generic identity in the years three to six. *Society for Research in Child Development Monographs, 34*(3, Serial No. 127).

Dewsbury, D. A. (1978). *Comparative animal behavior.* New York: McGraw-Hill.

Diaconis, P. (1978). Statistical problems in ESP research. *Science, 201,* 131–136.

Dickinson, A., Hall, G., & Mackintosh, N. J. (1976). Surprise and the attenuation of blocking. *Journal of Experimental Psychology: Animal Behavior Processes, 2,* 213–222.

Dickinson, A., & Mackintosh, N. J. (1978). Classical conditioning in animals. *Annual Review of Psychology, 29,* 587–612.

Dickinson, D., & Pearce, J. M. (1977). Inhibitory interactions between appetitive and aversive stimuli. *Psychological Bulletin, 84,* 690–711.

Diener, E., Sandvik, E., & Larsen, R. J. (1985). Age and sex effects for emotional intensity. *Developmental Psychology, 21,* 542–546.

Dion, K. K., Berscheid, E., & Walster, E. (1972). What is beautiful is good. *Journal of Personality and Social Psychology, 24,* 285–290.

Dixon, N. F. (1981). *Preconscious processing.* New York: Wiley.

Dobelle, W. H. (1977). Current status of research on providing sight to the blind by electrical stimulation of the brain. *Journal of Visual Impairment and Blindness, 71,* 290–297.

Doll, R. (1955). Etiology of lung cancer. *Advances in Cancer Research, 3,* 1–50.

Dollard, J., Doob, L., Miller, N., Mowrer, O., & Sears, K. (1939). *Frustration and aggression.* New Haven: Yale University Press.

Do males have a math gene? (1980, December 15). *Newsweek.*

Dominick, J. R. (1978). Crime and law enforcement in the mass media. In C. Winick (Ed.), *Sage annual reviews of studies in deviance: Vol. 2. Deviance and mass media.* Beverly Hills, Calif.: Sage.

Donagher, P. C., Poulos, R. W., Liebert, R. M., & Davidson, E. S. (1975). Race, sex and social example: An analysis of character portrayals on interracial television entertainment. *Psychological Reports, 37,* 1023–1034.

Donnelly, J. (1980). Psychosurgery. In H. I. Kaplan, A. M. Freedman, & B. J. Sadock (Eds.), *Comprehensive textbook of psychiatry: III.* Baltimore: Williams & Wilkins.

Dooling, D. J., & Christiaansen, R. E. (1977). Episodic and semantic aspects of memory for prose. *Journal of Experimental Psychology: Human Learning and Memory, 3,* 428–436.

Doty, R. L., Green, P. A., Ram C., & Yankell, S. L. (1982). Communication of gender from human breath odors: Relationship to perceived intensity and pleasantness. *Hormones and Behavior, 16,* 13–22.

Doty, R. L., Shamon, P., Applebaum, S. L., Giberson, R., Siksorski, L., & Rosenberg, L. (1984). Smell identification ability: Changes with age. *Science, 226,* 1441–1442.

Douvan, E. K., & Adelson, J. (1966). *The adolescent experience.* New York: Wiley.

Drabman, R. S., & Thomas, M. H. (1974). Does media violence increase children's toleration of real life aggression? *Developmental Psychology, 10,* 418–421.

Dreben, E. K., Fiske, S. T., & Hastie, R. (1979). The independence of evaluative and item information: Impression and recall order effects in behavior-based impression formation. *Journal of Personality and Social Psychology, 37,* 1758–1768.

Dreyer, P. H. (1982). Sexuality during adolescence. In B. Wolman (Ed.), *Handbook of developmental psychology.* Englewood Cliffs, N.J.: Prentice-Hall.

Droscher. (1969). *The magic of the senses.* New York: Dutton.

Dunbar, K., & MacLeod, C. M. (1984). A horse race of a different color: Stroop interference with transformed words. *Journal of Experimental Psychology: Human Perception and Performance, 10,* 622–639.

Duncker, K. (1929). Über induzerte Bewegung. *Psychologische Forschung, 12,* 180–259. In W. Ellis (1955) (Trans. and Condenser), *Source book of Gestalt psychology.* London: Routledge and Kegan Paul.

Duncker, K. (1945). On problem-solving. *Psychological Monographs, 58* (Whole No. 270).

Durkin, K. (1985a). Television and sex-role acquisition: 1. Content. *British Journal of Social Psychology, 24,* 101–113.

Durkin, K. (1985b). Television and sex-role acquisition: 2. Effects. *British Journal of Social Psychology, 24,* 191–210.

Durkin, K. (1985c). Television and sex-role acquisition: 3. Counter-stereotyping. *British Journal of Social Psychology, 24,* 211–222.

Dutton, D. G., & Aron, A. P. (1974). Some evidence for heightened sexual attraction under conditions of high anxiety. *Journal of Personality and Social Psychology, 30,* 510–517.

Duval, S. & Wicklund, R. A. (1972). *A theory of objective self-awareness.* New York: Academic Press.

Dweck, C. S., & Elliott, E. S. (1983). Achievement motivation. In P. H. Mussen (Ed.), *Handbook of child psychology* (Vol. 4). New York: Wiley.

Dyer, F. N. (1973). The Stroop phenomenon and its use in the study of perceptual and cognitive and response processes. *Memory and Cognition, 1,* 106–120.

Dywan, J., & Bowers, K. (1983). The use of hypnosis to enhance recall. *Science, 222,* 184–185.

Eagly, A. H. (1978). Sex differences in influenceability. *Psychological Bulletin, 85,* 86–116.

Eagly, A. H., & Carli, L. L. (1981). Sex of researchers and sex-typed communications as determinants of sex differences in influenceability: A meta-analysis of social influence studies. *Psychological Bulletin, 90,* 1–20.

Eagly, A. H., & Steffen, V. J. (1984). Gender stereotypes stem from the distribution of women and men into social roles. *Journal of Personality and Social Psychology, 46,* 735–754.

Eagly, A. H., & Telaak, K. (1972). Width of the latitude of acceptance as a determinant of attitude change. *Journal of Personality and Social Psychology, 23,* 388–397.

Eagly, A. H., & Warren, R. (1976). Intelligence, comprehension, and opinion change. *Journal of Personality, 44,* 226–242.

Easterbrooks, M. A., & Goldberg, W. A. (1985). Effects of early maternal employment on toddlers, mothers, and fathers. *Developmental Psychology, 21,* 774–783.

Eaves, L. J., & Eysenck, H. J. (1974). Genetics and the development of social attitudes. *Nature, 249,* 288–289.

Ebbinghaus, H. (1913). *Memory: A contribution to experimental psychology.* New York: Columbia University Press.

Eccles, J. S., & Jacobs, J. E. (1986). Social forces shape math attitudes and performance. *Signs, 11,* 367–380.

Edwards, A. E., & Acker, L. E. (1972). A demonstration of the long-term retention of a conditioned GSR. *Psychosomatic Science, 26,* 27–28.

Edwards, C. P. (1984). The age group labels and categories of preschool children. *Child Development, 55,* 440–452.

Egbert, L. D., Battit, G. E., Welsh, C. E., & Bartlett, M. K. (1964). Reduction of postoperative pain by encouragement and instruction of patients. *New England Journal of Medicine, 270,* 825–827.

Egeland, B., & Sroufe, L. A. (1981). Attachment and early maltreatment. *Child Development, 52,* 44–52.

Ehrenfreund, D. (1971). Effect of drive on successive magnitude shift in rats. *Journal of Comparative and Physiological Psychology, 76,* 418–423.

Ehringer, H., & Hornykiewicz, O. (1960). *Klin. Wochenschr., 38,* 1236.

Eibl-Eibesfeldt, I. (1973). The expressive behavior of the deaf-and-blind-born. In M. von Cranach & I. Vine (Eds.), *Social communication and movement.* New York: Academic Press.

Eich, J. E. (1980). The cue dependent nature of state dependent retrieval. *Memory and Cognition, 8,* 157–173.

Eich, J. E., Weingartner, H., Stillman, R. C., & Gillin, J. C. (1975). State dependent accessibility of retrieval cues in the retention of a categorized list. *Journal of Verbal Learning and Verbal Behavior, 14,* 408–417.

Eimas, P. (1975). Speech perception in early infancy. In L. B. Cohen & P. Salapatek (Eds.), *Infant perception*. New York: Academic Press.

Eimas, P. D., Siqueland, E. R., Jusczyk, P., & Vigorito, J. (1971). Speech perception in infants. *Science, 171,* 303–306.

Ekman, P. (1972). Universals and cultural differences in facial expressions of emotion. In J. K. Cole (Ed.), *Nebraska symposium on motivation.* Lincoln: University of Nebraska Press.

Ekman, P. (1973). Cross-cultural studies of facial expression. In P. Ekman (Ed.), *Darwin and facial expression: A century of research in review.* New York: Academic Press.

Ekman, P. (1984). Expression and the nature of emotion. In K. R. Scherer & P. Ekman (Eds.), *Approaches to emotion.* Hillsdale, N.J.: Erlbaum.

Ekman, P., Levenson, R. W., & Friesen, W. V. (1983). Autonomic nervous system activity distinguishes among emotions. *Science, 221,* 1208–1210.

Ekman, P., Sorenson, E. R., & Friesen, W. V. (1969). Pan-cultural elements in facial displays of emotion. *Science, 164,* 86–88.

Elkin, I. (1986). *The NIMH study of psychotherapeutic effectiveness.* Paper presented at the Annual Meeting of the American Psychiatric Association, Washington, D.C., May 14, 1986.

Elkin, I., Parloff, M. B., Hadley, S. W. & Autry, J. H. (1985). NIMH Treatment of Depression Collaborative Research Program. *Archives of General Psychiatry, 42,* 305–316.

Elkind, D. (1967). Egocentrism in adolescence. *Child Development, 38,* 1025–1034.

Elliot, D. S., & Ageton, S. (1980). Reconciling differences in estimates of delinquency. *American Sociological Review, 45,* 85–110.

Ellis, A. (1962). *Reason and emotion in psychotherapy.* New York: Lyle Stuart.

Endler, N. S. (1982). *Holiday of darkness: A psychologist's personal journey out of his depression.* New York: Wiley.

Endler, N. S., & Edwards, J. M. (1986). Interactionism in personality in the twentieth century. *Personality and Individual Differences, 7,* 379–384.

Engen, T. (1982). *The perception of odors.* New York: Academic Press.

Entwistle, D. R. (1972). To dispel fantasies about fantasy-based measures of achievement motivation. *Psychological Bulletin, 77,* 377–391.

Epstein, S. (1980). The stability of behavior: II. *American Psychologist, 35,* 790–806.

Epstein, S. (1986). Does aggregation produce spuriously high estimates of behavior stability? *Journal of Personality and Social Psychology, 50,* 1199–1209.

Epstein, S., & O'Brien, E. J. (1985). The person-situation debate in historical and current perspective. *Psychological Bulletin, 98,* 513–537.

Erdelyi, M. H., & Becker, J. (1974). Hypermnesia for pictures: Incremental memory for pictures but not words in multiple recall trials. *Cognitive Psychology, 6,* 159–171.

Erdelyi, M. H., & Goldberg, B. (1979). Let's not sweep repression under the rug: Toward a cognitive psychology of repression. In J. F. Kihlstrom & F. J. Evans (Eds.), *Functional disorders of memory.* Hillsdale, N.J.: Erlbaum.

Erickson, E. H. (1950). *Childhood and society.* New York: Norton.

Erlenmeyer-Kimling, L., Marcuse, Y., Cornblatt, B., Friedman, D., Rainer, J. D., and Rutschmann, J. (1984). The New York high rise project. In N. F. Watt, E. J. Anthony, L. C. Wynne, & J. Rolf (Eds.), *Children at risk for schizophrenia: A longitudinal perspective.* New York: Cambridge University Press.

Eron, L. D., Huesmann, L. R., Lefkowitz, M. M., & Walder, L. O. (1972). Does television violence cause aggression? *American Psychologist, 27,* 253–263.

Estes, W. K. (1980). Is human memory obsolete? *American Scientist, 68,* 62–69.

Evans, E. F. (1982). Functional anatomy of the auditory system. In H. B. Barlow & J. D. Mollon (Eds.), *The senses.* London: Cambridge University Press.

Evans, F. J. (1977). Hypnosis and sleep: The control of altered states of awareness. *Annals of the New York Academy of Sciences, 296,* 162–174.

Eysenck, H. J. (1952). The effects of psychotherapy: An evaluation. *Journal of Consulting Psychology, 16,* 319–324.

Eysenck, H. J. (1976). *Sex and personality.* London: Open Books.

Eysenck, H. J. (1979). The conditioning model of neurosis. *Behavioral and Brain Sciences, 2,* 155–199.

Eysenck, H. J. (1985). *The rise and decline of the Freudian empire.* London: Pelican.

Eysenck, H. J., & Eysenck, M. W. (1985). *Personality and individual differences.* New York: Plenum.

Eysenck, H. J., & Eysenck, S. B. G. (1975). *Manual of the Eysenck personality questionnaire.* San Diego: Educational and Industrial Testing Service.

Eysenck, H. J., & Kamin, L. J. (1981). *The intelligence controversy.* New York: Wiley.

Eysenck, H. J., & Skinner, B. F. (1980, September). *Behavior modification, behavior therapy, and other matters: Invited dialogue.* Paper presented at the 88th Annual Convention of the American Psychological Association, Montreal.

Eysenck, H. J., Wakefield, J. A., Jr., & Friedman, A. F. (1983). Diagnosis and clinical assessment: The DSM-III. In M. R. Rosenzweig and L. W. Porter (Eds.), *Annual reivew of psychology* (Vol. 34). Palo Alto, Calif.: Annual Reviews.

Fagan, J. F. (1984). The intelligent infant: Theoretical implications. *Intelligence, 8,* 1–9.

Fagan, J. F., & Singer, L. T. (1983). Infant recognition memory as a measure of intelligence. In L. P. Lipsitt (Ed.), *Advances in infancy research* (Vol. 2). Norwood, N.J.: Ablex.

Fagot, B. I. (1978). The influence of sex of child on parental reactions to toddler children. *Child Development, 49,* 459–465.

Fahn, S., & Calne, D. B. (1978). Consideration in the management of Parkinsonism. *Neurology, 28,* 5–7.

Fanselow, M. S. (1984). Shock-induced analgesia on the formalin test: Effects of shock severity, naloxone, hypophysectomy, and associative variables. *Behavioral Neuroscience, 98,* 79–95.

Fantino, E., Kasdon, D., & Stringer, N. (1970). The Yerkes-Dodson law and alimentary motivation. *Canadian Journal of Psychology, 24,* 77–84.

Fantz, R. L. (1961). The origin of form perception. *Scientific American, 204,* 66–84.

Fantz, R. L. (1963). Pattern vision in newborn infants. *Science, 140,* 296–297.

Fantz, R. L., Fagan, J. F., & Miranda, S. B. (1975). Early visual selectivity as a function of pattern variables, previous exposure, age from birth and conception, and expected cognitive deficit. In L. B. Cohen & P. Salapatek (Eds.), *Infant perception: From sensation to cognition.* (Vol. 1). New York: Academic Press.

Feather, N. T. (1982). *Expectations and actions: Expectancy-value models in psychology.* Hillsdale, N.J.: Erlbaum.

Fechner, G. (1966). *Elements of psychophysics* (H. E. Adler, Trans., D. H. Howes & E. G. Boring, Eds.). New York: Holt, Rinehart & Winston. (First German edition 1860)

Federal Bureau of Investigation (1985). *Uniform crime reports for the United States.* Washington, D.C.: U.S. Department of Justice.

Fehr, F. S., & Stern, J. A. (1970). Peripheral physiological variables and emotion: The James-Lange theory revisited. *Psychological Bulletin, 74,* 411–424.

Feldman, R. E. (1968). Response to compatriots and foreigners who seek assistance. *Journal of Personality and Social Psychology, 10,* 202–214.

Fenigstein, A., Scheier, M. F., & Buss, A. H. (1975). Public and private self-consciousness: Assessment and theory. *Journal of Consulting and Clinical Psychology, 43,* 522–527.

Fernandez, A., & Glenberg, A. M. (1985). Changing environmental context does not reliably affect memory. *Memory & Cognition, 13,* 333–345.

Festinger, L. (1957). *A theory of cognitive dissonance.* Stanford, Calif.: Stanford University Press.

Festinger, L., & Carlsmith, J. M. (1959). Cognitive consequences of forced compliance. *Journal of Abnormal and Social Psychology, 58,* 203–210.

Festinger, L., Schacter, S., & Back, K. (1950). *Social pressures in informal groups: A study of human factors in housing.* New York: Harper.

Findley, M. J., & Cooper, H. M. (1983). Locus of control and academic achievement: A literature review. *Journal of Personality and Social Psychology, 44,* 419–427.

Fischer, M., Harvald, B., & Hauge, M. S. (1969). Danish twin study of schizophrenia. *British Journal of Psychiatry, 115,* 981–990.

Fitts, P. M., & Posner, M. I. (1967). *Human performance.* Belmont, Calif.: Brooks/Cole.

Fitzgerald, R. D., & Martin, G. K. (1971). Heart-rate conditioning in rats as a function of interstimulus interval. *Psychological Reports, 29,* 1103–1110.

Fitzsimons, J. T. (1971). The physiology of thirst: A review of the extraneural aspects of the mechanism of drinking. In E. Stellar & J. M. Sprague (Eds.), *Progress in physiological psychology* (Vol. 4). New York: Academic Press.

Flavell, J. H. (1985). *Cognitive development.* Englewood Cliffs, N.J.: Prentice-Hall.

Flynn, J., Vanegas, H., Foote, W., & Edwards, S. (1970). Neural mechanisms involved in a cat's attack on a rat. In R. F. Whalen, M. Thompson, M. Verzeano, & N. Weinberger (Eds.), *The neural control of behavior.* New York: Academic Press.

Flynn, J. R. (1984). The mean IQ of Americans: Massive gains 1932 to 1978. *Psychological Bulletin, 95,* 29–51.

Foltz, E. L., & Millett, F. E. (1964). Experimental psychosomatic disease states in monkeys: 1. Peptic "ulcer-executive" monkeys. *Journal of Surgical Research, 4,* 445–453.

Ford, C. S., & Beach, F. A. (1951). *Patterns of sexual behavior.* New York: Harper & Row.

Forrest, J., Sullivan, E., & Tietze, C. (1979). Abortions in the United States, 1977–1979. *Family Planning Perspectives, 11,* 329–341.

Fowler, H. (1967). Satiation and curiosity: Constructs for a drive and incentive-motivational theory of exploration. In K. W. Spence & J. T. Spence (Eds.), *The psychology of learning and motivation: Advances in research and theory* (Vol. 1). New York: Academic Press.

Fowler, H., & Trapold, M. A. (1962). Escape performance as a function of delay of reinforcement. *Journal of Experimental Psychology, 63,* 464–467.

Franks, C. M., & Barbrack, C. R. (1983). Behavior therapy with adults: An integrative perspective. In M. Hersen, A. E. Kazdin, & A. S. Bellack (Eds.), *The Clinical Psychology Handbook.* New York: Pergamon Press.

Frase, L. T. (1975). Prose processing. In G. H. Bower (Ed.), *The psychology of learning and motivation* (Vol. 9). New York: Academic Press.

Freed, C. R., & Yamamoto, B. K. (1985). Regional brain dopamine metabolism: A marker for the speed, direction and posture of moving animals. *Science, 229,* 62–65.

Freedman, D., Pisani, R., & Purves, R. (1978). *Statistics.* New York: Norton.

Freedman, J. L. (1964). Involvement, discrepancy, and change. *Journal of Abnormal and Social Psychology, 64,* 290–295.

Freedman, J. L. (1979). Reconciling apparent differences between the responses of humans and other animals to crowding. *Psychological Review, 86,* 80–88.

Freedman, J. L. (1984). Effect of television violence on aggressiveness. *Psychological Bulletin, 96,* 227–246.

Freedman, J. L., & Fraser, S. C. (1966). Compliance without pressure: The foot-in-the-door technique. *Journal of Personality and Social Psychology, 4,* 195–202.

Freedman, J. L., Sears, D. O., & Carlsmith, J. L. (1981). *Social psychology* (4th ed.). Englewood Cliffs, N.J.: Prentice-Hall.

Freud, A. (1958). Adolescence. *Psychoanalytic Study of the Child, 13,* 255–278.

Freud, S. (1938). *The basic writings of Sigmund Freud.* New York: Modern Library.

Freud, S. (1952). *A general introduction to psychoanalysis.* New York: Washington Square Press. (Original work published 1924)

Freud, S. (1959). *Collected papers* (Vol. 5). New York: Basic Books.

Freud, S. (1961). Some psychical consequences of the anatomical distinction between the sexes. In *The standard edition of the complete psychological works of Sigmund Freud* (Vol. 19). London: Hogarth Press. (Original work published 1925)

Freud, S. (1962). *Civilization and its discontents* (James Strachey, Ed. and Trans.). New York: Norton. (Original work published 1930)

Freud, S. (1964). *The interpretation of dreams.* New York: Basic Books. (Original work published 1900)

Friedman, M. (1969). *Pathogenesis of coronary artery disease.* New York: McGraw-Hill.

Friedman, M. I., Rowland, N., Saller, C., & Stricker, E. M. (1976). Different receptors initiate adrenal secretion and hunger during hypoglycemia. *Neuroscience Abstracts, 2,* 299.

Friedman, M. I., & Stricker, E. M. (1976). The physiological psychology of hunger: A physiological perspective. *Psychological Review, 83,* 409–431.

Friedrich, L. K., & Stein, A. H. (1973). Aggressive and pro-social television programs and the natural behavior of preschool children. *Monographs of the Society for Research in Child Development, 38*(4, Serial No. 151).

Frisby, J. P. (1980). *Seeing.* New York: Oxford University Press.

Frisch, R. E., & Revelle, R. (1970). Height and weight, menarche and a hypothesis of critical body weight and adolescent events. *Science, 169,* 397–399.

Froming, W. J., & Carver, C. S. (1981). Divergent influences of private and public self-consciousness in a compliance paradigm. *Journal of Research in Personality, 15,* 159–171.

Gaffan, E. A., & Keeble, S. (1976). The effect of frustrative nonreward on the attractiveness of the omitted reward. *Learning and Motivation, 7,* 50–65.

Galanter, E. (1962). Contemporary psychophysics. In R. Brown and others (Eds.), *New directions in psychology* (Vol. 1). New York: Holt, Rinehart & Winston.

Galbraith, R. C. (1983). Individual differences in intelligence: A reappraisal of the confluence model. *Intelligence, 7,* 185–194.

Galle, O. R., Gove, W. R., & McPherson, J. M. (1972). Population density and pathology: What are the relationships for man? *Science, 176,* 385–389.

Galton, F. (1883). *Inquiry into human faculty and its development.* London: Macmillan.

Garbarino, J. (1985). *Adolescent development: An ecological perspective.* Columbus, Ohio: Merrill.

Garcia, J., Ervin, F. R., & Koelling, R. A. (1966). Learning with prolonged delay of reinforcement. *Psychonomic Science, 5,* 121–122.

Garcia, J., & Koelling, R. A. (1966). Relation of cue to consequences in avoidance learning. *Psychonomic Science, 4,* 123–124.

Gardner, H. (1975). *The shattered mind: The person after brain damage.* New York: Knopf.

Gardner, H. (1982). *Developmental psychology: An introduction* (2nd ed.). Boston: Little, Brown.

Gardner, R. A., & Gardner, B. T. (1978). Comparative psychology and language acquisition. *Annals of the New York Academy of Sciences, 309,* 37–76.

Garfield, L. S., & Bergin, A. E. (Eds.) (1978). *Handbook of psychotherapy and behavior change* (2nd ed.). New York: Wiley.

Garn, S. M., & Gertler, M. M. (1950). An association between type of work and physique in an industrial group. *American Journal of Physical Anthropology, 8,* 387–397.

Garner, W. R. (1972). The acquisition and application of knowledge: A symbiotic relation. *American Psychologist, 27,* 941–946.

Gazzaniga, M. (1967). The split brain in man. *Scientific American, 217,* 24–29.

Gazzaniga, M. S. (1970). *The bisected brain.* New York: Appleton-Century-Crofts.

Gazzaniga, M. S. (1983). Right hemisphere language following commissurotomy: A twenty-year perspective. *American Psychologist, 38,* 525–537.

Gazzaniga, M. S., & Sperry, R. W. (1967). Language after section of the cerebral commissures. *Brain, 90,* 131–148.

Gebhard, P. H. (1971). Human sexual behavior: A summary statement. In D. S. Marshall & R. C. Suggs (Eds.), *Human sexual behavior.* Englewood Cliffs, N.J.: Prentice-Hall.

Gebhard, P. H., & Johnson, A. B. (1979). *The Kinsey data: Marginal tabulations of the 1938–1963 interviews conducted by the Institute for Sex Research.* Philadelphia: Saunders.

Geen, R. G., & Gange, J. J. (1977). Drive theory of social facilitation: Twelve years of theory and research. *Psychological Bulletin, 84,* 1267–1288.

Geiselman, R. E., Fisher, R. P., Mackinnon, D. P., & Holland, H. L. (1985). Eyewitness memory enhancement in the police interview: Cognitive retrieval mnemonics versus hypnosis. *Journal of Applied Psychology, 70,* 401–412.

Gelman, R. (1978). Cognitive development. *Annual Review of Psychology, 29,* 297–332.

Gender factor in math: A new study says males may be naturally abler than females. (1980, December 15). *Time.*

Gentner, G., & Grudin, J. (1985). The evolution of mental metaphors in psychology: A 90-year retrospective. *American Psychologist, 40,* 181–192.

Gescheider, G. E. (1985). *Psychophysics: Method, theory, and application.* (2nd ed.). Hillsdale, N.J.: Erlbaum.

Gesell, A. (1928). *Infancy and human growth.* New York: Macmillan.

Geshwind, N. (1972). Language and the brain. *Scientific American, 226,* 76–83.

Gibbon, J. (1981). The contingency problem in autoshaping. In C. M. Locurto, H. S. Terrace, & J. Gibbon (Eds.), *Autoshaping and conditioning theory.* New York: Academic Press.

Gibbs, J. C., & Schnell, S. V. (1985). Moral development "versus" socialization. *American Psychologist, 40,* 1071–1080.

Gibson, E. J., & Spelke, E. S. (1983). The development of perception. In

J. H. Flavell & E. M. Markman (Eds.), *Handbook of child psychology: Vol. 3. Cognitive development.* New York: Wiley.

Gibson, E. J., & Walk, R. D. (1960). The "visual cliff." *Scientific American, 202,* 64–71.

Gibson, J. J. (1950). *The perception of the visual world.* Boston: Houghton Mifflin.

Gick, M. L., & Holyoak, K. J. (1980). Analogical problem solving. *Cognitive Psychology, 12,* 306–355.

Gilinsky, A. S. (1984). *Mind and brain: Principles of neuropsychology.* New York: Praeger.

Glanzer, M., & Cunitz, A. R. (1966). Two storage mechanisms in free recall. *Journal of Verbal Learning and Verbal Behavior, 5,* 351–360.

Glass, D. C. (1977). *Behavior patterns, stress and coronary disease.* Hillsdale, N.J.: Erlbaum.

Glass, D. C., & Singer, J. E. (1972). *Urban stress: Experiments on noise and social stressors.* New York: Academic Press.

Glazer, H. I., & Weiss, J. M. (1976). Long-term interference effect: An alternative to "learned helplessness." *Journal of Experimental Psychology: Animal Behavior Processes, 2,* 201–213.

Gleason, J. B. (1985). *The development of language.* Columbus, Ohio: Merrill.

Glendenning, K. K. (1972). Effects of septal and amygdaloid lesions on social behavior of the cat. *Journal of Comparative and Physiological Psychology, 80,* 199–207.

Glick, P. C. (1980). Remarriage: Some recent changes and variations. *Journal of Family Issues, 1,* 455–478.

Glisky, E. L., & Rabinowitz, J. (1985). Enhancing the generation effect through repetition of operations. *Journal of Experimental Psychology: Learning, Memory, and Cognition, 11,* 193–205.

Glucksberg, S., & Cowan, G. N. (1970). Memory for nonattended auditory material. *Cognitive Psychology, 1,* 149–156.

Glucksberg, S., & Weisberg, R. W. (1966). Verbal behavior and problem solving: Some effects of labeling in a functional fixedness problem. *Journal of Experimental Psychology, 71,* 659–664.

Gold, M., & Reimer, O. J. (1975). Changing patterns of delinquent behavior among Americans 13 through 16 years old: 1967–1972. *Crime and Delinquency Literature, 7,* 483–517.

Goldberg, S. (1983). Parent-infant bonding: Another look. *Child Development, 54,* 1355–1382.

Goldsmith, H. H. (1983). Genetic influences on personality from infancy to adulthood. *Child Development, 54,* 331–355.

Goldstein, A., & Hilgard, E. R. (1975). Lack of influence of the morphine antagonist naloxone on hypnotic analgesia. *Proceedings of the National Academy of Sciences (USA), 72,* 2041–2043.

Goldstein, E. B. (1984). *Sensation and perception* (2nd ed.). Belmont, Calif.: Wadsworth.

Goldstein, M. J., Baker, B. L., & Jamison, K. R. (1986). *Abnormal psychology: Experiences, origins and interventions* (2nd ed.). Boston: Little, Brown.

Goleman, O. (1980, February). 1,528 little geniuses and how they grew. *Psychology Today,* pp. 28–53.

Gormezano, I. (1972). Investigations of defense and reward conditioning in the rabbit. In A. H. Black & W. F. Prokasy (Eds.), *Classical conditioning II: Current theory and research.* New York: Appleton-Century-Crofts.

Gorn, G. J., Goldberg, M. E., & Kanungo, R. N. (1976). The role of educational television in changing the intergroup attitudes of children. *Child Development, 47,* 277–280.

Gotestam, K. G., Melin, L., & Ost, L. (1976). Behavioral techniques in the treatment of drug abuse: An evaluative review. *Addictive Behaviors, 1,* 205–225.

Gottesman, I. I., & Shields, J. A. (1976). A critical review of recent adoption, twin, and family studies of schizophrenia: Behavioral genetics perspectives. *Schizophrenia Bulletin, 2,* 360–461.

Gottesman, I. I., Shields, J., & Hanson, D. R. (1982). *Schizophrenia: The epigenetic puzzle.* New York: Cambridge University Press.

Gottlieb, G. (1985). On discovering significant acoustic dimensions of auditory stimulation for infants. In G. Gottlieb & N. A. Krasnegor (Eds.), *Measurement of audition and vision in the first year of postnatal life: A methodological overview.* Norwood, N.J.: Ablex.

Gough, H. G. (1956). *California psychological inventory.* Palo Alto, Calif.: Consulting Psychologists Press.

Gould, S. J. (1977). *Ever since Darwin: Reflections in natural history.* New York: Norton.

Gove, W. R., Hughes, M., & Galle, O. R. (1979). Overcrowding in the home. *American Sociological Review, 44,* 59–80.

Graf, P., Squire, L. R., & Mandler, G. (1984). The information that amnesic patients do not forget. *Journal of Experimental Psychology: Learning, Memory, and Cognition, 10,* 164–178.

Grau, J. W. (1984). Influence of naloxone on shock-induced freezing and analgesia. *Behavioral Neuroscience, 98,* 278–292.

Gray, C. R., & Gummerman, K. (1975). The enigmatic eidetic image: A critical examination of methods, data, and theories. *Psychological Bulletin, 82,* 383–407.

Green, D. M. (1976). *An introduction to hearing.* Hillsdale, N.J.: Erlbaum.

Green, D. M., & Swets, J. A. (1966). *Signal detection theory and psychophysics.* New York: Wiley.

Greenberg, B. S. (1982). Television and role socialization: An overview. In U.S. Department of Health and Human Services, *Television and behavior: Ten years of progress and implications for the eighties: Vol. 2. Technical reviews.* Washington, D.C.: U.S. Government Printing Office.

Gregersen, F. (1983). *Sexual practices.* New York: Watts.

Gregory, R. L. (1978). *Eye and brain: The psychology of seeing* (3rd ed.). New York: McGraw-Hill.

Grings, W. W., & Dawson, M. E. (1978). *Emotions and bodily responses: A psychophysiological approach.* New York: Academic Press.

Grossman, H. J. (1973). *Manual on terminology and classification in mental retardation.* Washington, D.C.: American Association on Mental Deficiency.

Grotevant, H. D., Scarr, S., & Weinberg, R. A. (1977). Intellectual development in family constellations with adopted and natural children: A test of the Zajonc and Markus model. *Child Development, 48,* 1699–1703.

Grotevant, H. D., Scarr, S., & Weinberg, R. A. (1977). Patterns of interest similarity in adoptive and biological families. *Journal of Personality and Social Psychology, 35,* 667–676.

Grove, G. L., & Kligman, A. M. (1983). Age associated changes in human epidermal cell renewal. *Journal of Gerontology, 38,* 137–142.

Grusec, J. E., Kuczynski, L., Rushton, J. P., & Simutis, Z. M. (1979). Learning resistance to temptation through observation. *Developmental Psychology, 15,* 233–240.

Guilford, J. P. (1959). *Personality.* New York: McGraw-Hill.

Guilford, J. P. (1966). Intelligence: 1965 model. *American Psychologist, 21,* 20–26.

Guilford, J. P. (1982). Cognitive psychology's ambiguities: Some suggested remedies. *Psychological Review, 89,* 48–59.

Guilleminault, C., & Dement, W. C. (Eds.) (1978). *The sleep apnea syndrome.* New York: Alan R. Liss.

Gur, R. C., Gur, R. E., Obrist, W. D., Hungerbuhler, J. P., Younkin, D., Rosen, A. D., Skilnick, B. E., & Reivich, M. (1982). Sex and handedness differences in cerebral blood flow during rest and cognitive activity. *Science, 217,* 659–661.

Guttentag, R. E. (1985). Memory and aging: Implications for theories of memory development during childhood. *Developmental Review, 5,* 56–82.

Haber, R. N. (1979a). Twenty years of haunting eidetic imagery: Where's the ghost? *The Behavioral and Brain Sciences, 2,* 583–629.

Haber, R. N. (1979b). Author's response. *The Behavioral and Brain Sciences, 2,* 619–624.

Haber, R. N., & Haber, R. B. (1964). Eidetic imagery: 1. Frequency. *Perceptual and Motor Skills, 19,* 131–138.

Hall, C. S., & Lindzey, G. (1985). *Introduction to theories of personality.* New York: Wiley.

Hall, D. T., & Nougaim, K. E. (1968). An examination of Maslow's need hierarchy in an organized setting. *Organizational Behavior and Human Performance, 3,* 12–35.

Hall, G. S. (1904). *Adolescence.* New York: Appleton.

Hall, V. C., & Kingsley, R. C. (1968). Conservation and equilibration theory. *Journal of Genetic Psychology, 113,* 195–213.

Hallahan, D. P., & Kauffman, J. M. (1982). *Exceptional children: Introduction to special education.* Englewood Cliffs, N.J.: Prentice-Hall.

Hamilton, E. W., & Abramson, L. Y. (1983). Cognitive patterns and major depressive disorder: A longitudinal study in a hospital setting. *Journal of Abnormal Psychology, 92,* 173–184.

Hamilton, W. D. (1964). The genetical theory of social behavior: I, II. *Journal of Theoretical Biology, 7,* 1–52.

Haney, C. (1978). Consensus information and attitude change. Unpublished Ph.D. dissertation, Stanford University.

Hansel, C. E. M. (1980). *Science and parapsychology: A critical reevaluation.* Buffalo: Prometheus Books.

Harari, H., & McDavid, J. W. (1973). Name stereotypes and teachers' expectations. *Journal of Educational Psychology, 65*, 222–225.

Hare, R. D. (1978). Electrodermal and cardiovascular correlates of psychopathy. In R. D. Hare & D. Schalling (Eds.), *Psychopathic behavior: Approaches to research* (pp. 103–143). New York: Wiley.

Harlow, H. F., & Zimmerman, R. R. (1959). Affectional responses in the infant monkey. *Science, 130*, 421–432.

Harris, A. H., & Brady, J. V. (1974). Animal learning: Visceral and autonomic conditioning. *Annual Review of Psychology, 25*, 107–133.

Harris, C. S. (1965). Perceptual adaptation to inverted, reversed, or displaced vision. *Psychological Review, 72*, 419–444.

Harris, G. W., & Levine, S. (1965). Sexual differentiation of the brain and its experimental control. *Journal of Physiology, 181*, 379–400.

Harris, L. (1975). *The myth and reality of aging in America.* Washington, D.C.: National Council on Aging.

Hart, B. (1969). Gonadal hormones and sexual reflexes in the female rat. *Hormones and Behavior, 1*, 65–71.

Harte, R. A., Travers, J. A., & Sarich, P. (1948). Voluntary caloric intake of the growing rat. *Journal of Nutrition, 36*, 667–679.

Harter, S. (1981). A new self-report scale of intrinsic versus extrinsic orientation in the classroom: Motivational and informational components. *Developmental Psychology, 17*, 300–312.

Harter, S. (1982). The perceived competence scale for children. *Child Development, 53*, 87–97.

Hartley, A. (1981). Adult age differences in deductive reasoning processes. *Journal of Gerontology, 36*, 700–706.

Hartmann, D. P. (1969). Influence of symbolically modeled instrumental aggression and pain cues on aggressive behavior. *Journal of Personality and Social Psychology, 11*, 280–288.

Hartshorne, H., & May, M. A. (1928). *Studies in the nature of character: Vol. 1. Studies in deceit.* New York: Macmillan.

Hartshorne, H., May, M. A., & Maller, J. B. (1929). *Studies in the nature of character: Vol. 2. Studies in self-control.* New York: Macmillan.

Hartshorne, H., May, M. A., & Shuttleworth, F. K. (1930). *Studies in the nature of character: Vol. 3. Studies in the organization of character.* New York: Macmillan.

Harvard Medical School Health Letter. (1981, April). Cambridge, Mass.: Department of Continuing Education, Harvard Medical Shcool.

Hass, A. (1979). *Teenage sexuality: A survey of teenage sexual behavior.* New York: Macmillan.

Hassett, J. (1978, March). Sex and smell. *Psychology Today, 11*, 40–42.

Hastorf, A. H. (1950). The influence of suggestion on the relationship between stimulus size and perceived distance. *Journal of Psychology, 29*, 195–217.

Hatton, G. I. (1976). *Nucleus circularis: Is it an osmoreceptor in the brain?* Brain Research Bulletin, 1, 123–131.

Haughton, E., & Ayllon, T. (1965). Production and elimination of symptomatic behavior. In L. P. Ullman & L. Krasner (Eds.), *Case studies in behavior modification* (pp. 268–284). New York: Holt, Rinehart & Winston.

Hauri, P. (1977). *The sleep disorders.* Kalamazoo, Mich.: Upjohn.

Havighurst, R. J. (1953). *Human development and education.* New York: Longmans.

Haviland, S. E., & Clark, H. H. (1974). What's new? Acquiring new information as a process in comprehension. *Journal of Verbal Learning and Verbal Behavior, 13*, 512–521.

Hayes, C. (1951). *The ape in our house.* New York: Harper & Row.

Hearnshaw, L. S. (1979). *Cyril Burt: Psychologist.* Ithaca: Cornell University Press.

Hebb, D. O. (1949). *The organization of behavior.* New York: Wiley.

Hefner, R. S., & Hefner, H. E. (1983). Hearing in large and small dogs: Absolute thresholds and size of the tympanic membrane. *Behavioral Neuroscience, 97*, 310–318.

Heidbreder, E. (1933). *Seven psychologies.* New York: Appleton.

Heider, E. R. (1971). "Focal" color areas and the development of color names. *Developmental Psychology, 4*, 447–455.

Heider, E. R. (1972). Universals in color naming and memory. *Journal of Experimental Psychology, 93*, 10–20.

Heider, E. R., & Oliver, D. (1972). The structure of the color space in naming and memory for two languages. *Cognitive Psychology, 3*, 337–354.

Heider, F. (1944). Social perception and phenomenal causality. *Psychological Review, 51*, 358–374.

Heider, F. (1958). *The psychology of interpersonal relations.* New York: Wiley.

Heider, K. G. (1976). Dani sexuality: A low energy system. *Man, 11*, 188–201.

Held, R., & Hein, A. (1963). Movement-produced stimulation in the development of visually guided behavior. *Journal of Comparative and Physiological Psychology, 56*, 872–876.

Herman, C. P., & Polivy, J. (1975). Anxiety, restraint and eating behavior. *Journal of Abnormal Psychology, 84*, 666–672.

Herzog, D. B. (1982). Bulimia in the adolescent. *American Journal of the Diseases of Children, 136*, 985–989.

Heston, L. L. (1970). The genetics of schizophrenic and schizoid disease. *Science, 167*, 249–256.

Hetherington, E. M. (1979). Divorce: A child's perspective. *American Psychologist, 34*, 851–858.

Higbee, K. L. (1969). Fifteen years of fear arousal: Research on threat appeals, 1953–1968. *Psychological Bulletin, 72*, 426–444.

Hilgard, E. R. (1975). Hypnosis. *Annual Review of Psychology, 26*, 19–44.

Hilgard, E. R. (1977). *Divided consciousness: Multiple controls in human thought and action.* New York: Wiley.

Hilgard, E. R., & LeBaron, S. (1984). *Hypnosis in the treatment of pain and anxiety in children with cancer: A clinical and quantitative investigation.* Los Altos, Calif.: Kaufmann.

Hill, C. T., Rubin, Z., & Peplau, L. A. (1976). Breakups before marriage: The end of 103 affairs. *Journal of Social Issues, 32*(1), 147–168.

Himmelweit, H., Oppenheim, A. N., & Vince, P. (1958). *Television and the child: An empirical study of the effects of television on the young.* London: Oxford University Press.

Hinckley, J., & Hinckley, J. (1985). *Breaking points.* Grand Rapids, MI: Zondervan.

Hines, M. (1982). Parental gonadal hormones and sex differences in human behavior. *Psychological Bulletin, 92*, 56–80.

Hirst, W. (1982). The amnesic syndrome: Descriptions and explanations. *Psychological Bulletin, 91*, 435–460.

Hobson, J. A., & McCarley, R. W. (1977). The brain as a dream state generator: An activation-synthesis hypothesis of the dream process. *American Journal of Psychiatry, 134*, 1335–1348.

Hochberg, J. E. (1978). *Perception* (2nd ed.). Englewood Cliffs, N.J.: Prentice-Hall.

Hochhauser, M., & Fowler, H. (1975). Cue effects of drive and reward as a function of discrimination difficulty: Evidence against the Yerkes-Dodson law. *Journal of Experimental Psychology: Animal Behavior Processes, 1*, 261–269.

Hoff-Ginsberg, E., & Shatz, M. (1982). Linguistic input and the child's acquisition of language. *Psychological Bulletin, 92*, 3–26.

Hoffman, L. W. (1979). Maternal employment: 1979. *American Psychologist, 34*, 859–865.

Hoffman, L. W. (1985). The changing genetics/socialization balance. *Journal of Social Issues, 41*, 127–148.

Hoffman, M. L. (1963). Parent discipline and the child's consideration for others. *Child Development, 34*, 573–588.

Hoffman, M. L. (1975a). Altruistic behavior and the parent-child relationship. *Journal of Personality and Social Psychology, 31*, 937–943.

Hoffman, M. L. (1975b). Moral internalization, parental power, and the nature of parent-child interaction. *Developmental Psychology, 11*, 228–239.

Hohmann, G. W. (1966). Some effects of spinal cord lesions on experienced emotional feelings. *Psychophysiology, 3*, 143–156.

Holden, C. (1985). A guarded endorsement for shock therapy. *Science, 228*, 1510–1511.

Holding, D. H. (1979). Does being "eidetic" matter? *The Behavioral and Brain Sciences, 2*, 604–605.

Holender, D. (1986). Semantic activation without conscious identification in dichotic listening, paraforeal vision, and visual masking: A survey and appraisal. *The Behavioral and Brain Sciences, 9*, 1–66.

Holmes, T. H., & Rahe, R. H. (1967). The social readjustment rating scale. *Journal of Psychosomatic Research, 11*, 213–218.

Holt, J. H. (1964). *How children fail.* New York: Dell.

Holton, R. B. (1961). Amplitude of an instrumental response following the cessation of reward. *Child Development, 32*, 107–116.

Honig, W. K., & Urcuioli, P. J. (1981). The legacy of Guttman and Kalish (1956): Twenty-five years of research on stimulus generalization. *Journal of the Experimental Analysis of Behavior, 36*, 405–445.

Horn, J. L. (1970). Organization of data on life-span development of human abilities. In L. R. Goulet & P. B. Baltes (Eds.), *Life-span developmental psychology: Research and theory.* New York: Academic Press.

Horn, J. L. (1978). The nature and development of intellectual abilities. In R. T. Osborne, C. E. Noble, and N. Weyl (Eds.), *Human variation.* New York: Academic Press.

Horn, J. L. (1982). The theory of fluid and crystallized intelligence in relation to concepts of cognitive psychology and aging in adulthood. In F. I. M. Craik & S. E. Trehub (Eds.), *Aging and cognitive processes.* New York: Plenum.

Horn, J. L., & Cattell, R. B. (1966). Age differences in primary mental ability factors. *Journal of Gerontology, 21,* 210–220.

Horn, J. L., Loehlin, J. C., & Willerman, L. (1979). Intellectual resemblance among adoptive and biological relatives: The Texas adoption project. *Behavior Genetics, 9,* 177–207.

Horn, J. M. (1983a). Delinquents in adulthood. *Science, 221,* 256–257.

Horn, J. M. (1983b). The Texas adoption project: Adopted children and their intellectual resemblance to biological and adoptive parents. *Child Development, 54,* 268–275.

Horne, J. A., & Wilkinson, S. (1985). Chronic sleep reduction: Daytime vigilance performance and EEG measures of sleepiness, with particular reference to "practice" effects. *Psychophysiology, 22,* 69–78.

Hovland, C. I. (1937). The generalization of conditioned responses: 1. The sensory generalization of conditioned responses with varying frequencies of tone. *Journal of General Psychology, 17,* 125–148.

Hovland, C. I., & Weiss, W. (1951). The influence of source credibility on communication effectiveness. *Public Opinion Quarterly, 15,* 635–650.

Howard, A. (1975). An assessment of assessment centers. *Academy of Management Journal, 17,* 115–134.

Howard, A., & Bray, D. W. (1980). Career motivation in mid-life managers. Paper presented at the annual meeting of the American Psychological Association, Montreal.

Howard, A., & Wilson, J. A. (1982). Leadership in a declining work ethic. *California Management Review, 24,* 33–46.

Hubel, D. H., & Wiesel, T. N. (1968). Receptive fields and functional architecture of the monkey striate cortex. *Journal of Physiology (London), 195,* 215–243.

Hubel, D. H., & Wiesel, T. N. (1979). Brain mechanisms of vision. *Scientific American, 241,* 150–162.

Huesman, L. R. (1983). On Sohn's accusations. *American Psychologist, 38,* 117–119.

Hughes, J., Smith, T. W., Kosterlitz, H. W., Fothergill, L. A., Morgan, B. A., & Morris, H. R. (1975). Identification of two related pentapeptides from the brain with potent opiate agonist activity. *Nature, 258,* 577–579.

Hunt, M. (1974). *Sexual behavior in the 1970s.* Chicago: Playboy Press.

Hurvich, L., & Jameson, D. (1957). An opponent process theory of color vision. *Psychological Review, 64,* 384–404.

Hurvich, L., & Jameson, D. (1974). Opponent processes as a model of neural organization. *American Psychologist, 29,* 88–102.

Huston, A. C. (1985). The development of sex-typing: Themes from recent research. *Developmental Review, 5,* 1–17.

Huston-Stein, A., & Higgins-Trenk, A. (1978). Development of females from childhood through adulthood: Career and feminine role orientations. In P. B. Baltes (Ed.), *Life-span development and behavior* (Vol. 1). New York: Academic Press.

Hutchings, B., & Mednick, S. A. (1975). Registered criminality in the adoptive and biological parents of registered male criminal adoptees. In R. R. Fieve, D. Rosenthal, & H. Brill (Eds.), *Genetic research in psychiatry.* Baltimore: Johns Hopkins University Press.

Hutchinson, R. R. (1972). The environmental causes of aggression. In J. K. Cole & D. D. Jensen (Eds.), *Nebraska symposium on motivation* (pp. 155–181). Lincoln: University of Nebraska Press.

Hutchison, J. B. (Ed.) (1978). *Biological determinants of sexual behavior.* New York: Wiley.

Hyman, R. (1977, May/June). Uri Geller at SRI. *The Humanist.*

Iaffaldano, M. T., & Muchinsky, P. M. (1985). Job satisfaction and job performance: A meta analysis. *Psychological Bulletin, 97,* 251–273.

Imperato-McGinley, J., Guerrero, L., Gautier, T., & Peterson, R. (1974). Steroid 52-reductase deficiency in man: An inherited form of male pseudohermaphroditism. *Science, 186,* 1213–1215.

Ingelfinger, F. J. (1944). The late effects of total and subtotal gastrectomy. *New England Journal of Medicine, 231,* 321–327.

Inhelder, B., & Piaget, J. (1958). *The growth of logical thinking from childhood to adolescence.* New York: Basic Books.

Ittelson, W. H., & Kilpatrick, F. (1951, August). Experiments in perception. *Scientific American,* pp. 50–55.

Iversen, S. D., & Iversen, L. L. (1981). *Behavioral pharmacology* (2nd ed.). New York: Oxford University Press.

Iyengar, S., Kinder, D. R., Peters, M. D., & Krosnick, J. A. (1984). The evening news and presidential evaluations. *Journal of Personality and Social Psychology, 46,* 778–787.

Izard, C. E. (1972). *Patterns of emotions: A new analysis of anxiety and depression.* New York: Academic Press.

Izard, C. E. (1977). *Human emotion.* New York: Plenum.

Izard, C. E., Kagan, J., & Zajonc, R. B. (Eds.). (1984). *Emotion, cognition, and behavior.* New York: Cambridge University Press.

Jacklin, C. N., & Maccoby, E. E. (1978). Social behavior at 33 months in same-sex and mixed-sex dyads. *Child Development, 49,* 557–569.

Jackson, D. N. (1974). *The personality research form manual.* Port Huron, Mich.: Research Psychologists Press.

Jackson, D. N. (1977). *Jackson vocational interest survey manual.* Port Huron, Mich.: Research Psychologists Press.

Jackson, D. N. (1984). *The personality research form manual.* Port Huron, Mich.: Research Psychologists Press.

Jackson, D. N., & Paunonen, S. V. (1980). Personality structure and assessment. In M. R. Rosenzweig & L. W. Porter (Eds.), *Annual review of psychology* (Vol. 31). Palo Alto, Calif.: Annual Reviews.

Jackson, R. L., Maier, S. F., & Rappaport, P. M. (1978). Exposure to inescapable shock produces both activity and associative deficits in the rat. *Learning and Motivation, 9,* 69–98.

Jacobs, J. E., & Eccles, J. S. (1985). Gender differences in math ability: The impact of media reports on parents. *Education Researcher, 14,* 20–25.

Jacobson, N. S., & Bussod, N. (1983). Marital and family therapy. In M. Hersen, A. E. Kazdin, & A. S. Bellack (Eds.), *The clinical psychology handbook.* New York: Pergamon.

Jacoby, L. L., & Witherspoon, D. (1982). Remembering without awareness. *Canadian Journal of Psychology, 36,* 300–324.

James, W. (1890). *The principles of psychology.* New York: Holt.

James, W. (1902). *The varieties of religious experience.* New York: Modern Library.

James, W. (1968). What is an emotion? (*Mind,* 1885, *9,* 188–205.) Reprinted in M. Arnold, *The nature of emotion.* Baltimore: Penguin.

Jaynes, J. (1976). *The origin of consciousness in the breakdown of the bicameral mind.* Boston: Houghton Mifflin.

Jeffrey, R. W., Wing, R. R., & Stinkard, A. J. Behavioral treatment of obesity: The state of the art 1976. *Behavior Therapy, 9,* 189–199.

Jenkins, H. M., Barnes, R. A., & Barrera, F. J. (1981). Why autoshaping depends on trial spacing. In C. M. Locurto, H. S. Terrace, & J. Gibbon (Eds.), *Autoshaping and conditioning theory.* New York: Academic Press.

Jenkins, J. G., & Dallenbach, K. M. (1924). Oblivescence during sleep and waking. *American Journal of Psychology, 35,* 605–612.

Jensen, A. R. (1969). How much can we boost IQ and scholastic achievement? *Harvard Educational Review, 39,* 1–123.

Jensen, A. R. (1980). *Bias in mental testing.* New York: Free Press.

Jensen, A. R. (1985). The nature of the black-white difference on various psychometric tests: Spearman's hypothesis. *The Behavioral and Brain Sciences, 8*(2), 193–219.

Johansson, G. (1975). Visual motion perception. *Scientific American, 232,* 76–88.

Johnson, C. L., Stuckey, M. K., Lewis, L. D., & Schwartz, D. M. (1983). Bulimia: A descriptive survey of 509 cases. In P. L. Darby, P. E. Garfinkel, D. M. Garner, & D. V. Coscina (Eds.), *Anorexia nervosa: Recent developments* (pp. 159–172). New York: Allen R. Liss.

Johnson, N. F. (1965). The psychological reality of phrase-structure rules. *Journal of Verbal Learning and Verbal Behavior, 4,* 469–475.

Johnson, R. C., McClearn, G. E., Yuen, S., Nagoshi, C. T., Ahern, F. M., & Cole, R. E. (1985). Galton's data a century later. *American Psychologist, 40,* 875–892.

Johnson-Laird, P. N., & Steedman, M. (1978). The psychology of syllogisms. *Cognitive Psychology, 10,* 64–99.

Johnston, L. D., Bachman, J. G., & O'Malley, P. M. (1982). *Student drug use, attitudes, and beliefs: National trends 1975–1982.* Rockville, Md.: National Institute on Drug Abuse. Washington, D.C.: U.S. Government Printing Office.

Jones, E. E. (1964). *Ingratiation: A social-psychological analysis.* New York: Appleton-Century-Crofts.

Jones, E. E., & Davis, K. D. (1965). From acts to dispositions: The attribution process in person perception. In L. Berkowitz (Ed.), *Advances in experimental social psychology* (Vol. 2). New York: Academic Press.

Jones, E. E., Davis, K. E., & Gergen, K. J. (1961). Role playing variations and their informational value for person perception. *Journal of Abnormal and Social Psychology, 63,* 302–310.

Jones, E. E., & Harris, V. A. (1967). The attributions of attitudes. *Journal of Experimental Social Psychology, 3,* 1–24.

Jones, E. E., & McGillis, D. (1976). Correspondent inferences and the attribution cube: A comparative reappraisal. In J. H. Harvey, W. J. Ickes, and R. F. Kidd (Eds.), *New directions in attribution research* (Vol. 1). Hillsdale, N.J.: Erlbaum.

Jones, E. E., & Nisbett, R. E. (1972). The actor and observer: Divergent perceptions of the causes of behavior. In E. E. Jones, E. E. Karouse, H. H. Keeley, R. E. Nisbett, S. Valins, & B. Weiner, *Attribution: Perceiving the causes of behavior.* Morristown, N.J.: General Learning Press.

Jones, H. E. (1950). The study of patterns of emotional expression. In M. Reymert (Ed.), *Feelings and emotions.* New York: McGraw-Hill.

Jones, M. (1975). Community care for chronic mental patients: The need for a reassessment. *Hospital and Community Psychiatry, 26,* 94–98.

Jones, M. C. (1924). The elimination of children's fears. *Journal of Experimental Psychology, 7,* 382–390.

Jones, M. C., & Mussen, P. H. (1958). Self-conceptions, motivations, and interpersonal attitudes of early- and late-maturing girls. *Child Development, 29,* 491–501.

Juel-Nielsen, N. (1965). Individual and environment: A psychiatric-psychological investigation of twins reared apart. *Acta Psychiatrica et Neurologica Scandinavica* (Monograph Supplement 183).

Julesz, B. (1971). *Foundations of Cyclopean perception.* Chicago: University of Chicago Press.

Juscyzk, P. W. (1985). The high amplitude sucking technique as a methodological tool in speech perception research. In G. Gottlieb & N. A. Krasnegor (Eds.), *Measurement of audition and vision in the first year of postnatal life: A methodological overview.* Norwood, N.J.: Ablex.

Kagan, J., & Haveman, E. (1972). *Psychology: An introduction.* New York: Harcourt Brace Jovanovich.

Kagan, J., & Moss, H. (1962). *Birth to maturity.* New York: Wiley.

Kahneman, D., & Chajczyk, D. (1983). Tests of the automaticity of reading: Dilution of Stroop effects by color-irrelevant stimuli. *Journal of Experimental Psychology: Human Perception and Performance, 9,* 497–509.

Kahneman, D., & Tversky, A. (1973). On the psychology of prediction. *Psychological Review, 80,* 237–251.

Kahneman, D., & Tversky, A. (1979). Prospect theory: An analysis of decision under risk. *Econometrica, 47,* 263–291.

Kalish, H. I. (1981). *From behavioral science to behavior modification.* New York: McGraw-Hill.

Kalish, R. A. (1976). Death in a social context. In R. H. Binstock & C. Shanas (Eds.), *Handbook of aging and the social sciences.* New York: Van Nostrand Reinhold.

Kallmann, F. J. (1946). The genetic theory of schizophrenia: An analysis of 691 schizophrenic twin index families. *American Journal of Psychiatry, 103,* 309–322.

Kamin, L. J. (1969). Predictability, surprise, attention and conditioning. In B. A. Campbell & R. M. Church (Eds.), *Punishment and aversive behavior.* New York: Appleton-Century-Crofts.

Kamin, L. J. (1974). *The science and politics of IQ.* Potomac, Md.: Erlbaum.

Kanin, E. J., Davidson, D. K. D., & Scheck, S. R. (1970). A research note on male-female differentials in the experience of heterosexual love. *The Journal of Sex Research, 6,* 64–72.

Kanizsa, G. (1976, September). Subjective contours. *Scientific American,* pp. 48–52.

Karniol, R., & Ross, M. (1977). The effect of performance-relevant and performance-irrelevant rewards on children's intrinsic motivation. *Child Development, 48,* 482–487.

Kassil, V. G., Ugolev, A. M. & Chernigovskii, V. N. (1970). Regulation of selection and consumption of food and metabolism. *Progress in Physiological Sciences, 1,* 387–404.

Katchadourian, M. (1977). *The biology of adolescence.* San Francisco: Freeman.

Kaufman, L. (1974). *Sight and mind.* New York: Oxford University Press.

Kaufman, L., & Rock, I. (1962). The moon illusion. *Scientific American, 207,* 120–132.

Keating, D. P. (1980). Thinking processes in adolescence. In J. Adelson (Ed.), *Handbook of adolescent psychology.* New York: Wiley.

Keesey, R. E., Boyle, P. C., Kemnitz, J. W., & Mitchell, J. S. (1976). The role of the lateral hypothalamus in determining the body weight set point. In D. Novin, W. Wyrwicka, & G. Bray (Eds.), *Hunger: Basic mechanisms and clinical applications* (pp. 243–255). New York: Raven Press.

Keil, F. C. (1981). Constraints on knowledge and cognitive development. *Psychological Review, 88,* 197–227.

Keith-Lucas, T., & Guttman, N. (1975). Robust single-trial delayed backward conditioning. *Journal of Comparative and Physiological Psychology, 88,* 468–476.

Kelley, H. H. (1950). The warm-cold variable in first impressions of persons. *Journal of Personality, 18,* 431–439.

Kelley, H. H. (1967). Attribution theory in social psychology. In D. Levine (Ed.), *Nebraska symposium on motivation.* Lincoln: University of Nebraska Press.

Kelley, H. H. (1979). *Personal relationships.* Hillsdale, N.J.: Erlbaum.

Kelley, H. H., Berscheid, E., Christensen, A., Harvey, J. H., Huston, T. L., Levinger, G., McClintock, E., Peplau, L. A., & Peterson, D. R. (1983). *Close Relationships.* San Francisco: Freeman.

Kelley, H. H., & Thibaut, J. W. (1978). *Interpersonal relations: A theory of interdependence.* New York: Wiley-Interscience.

Kellogg, W. N., & Kellogg, L. A. (1933). *The ape and the child.* New York: McGraw-Hill.

Kelman, H. C. (1968). *A time to speak: On human values and social research.* San Francisco: Jossey-Bass.

Kennedy, W. A. (1969). A follow-up normative study of Negro intelligence and achievement. *Monographs of the Society for Research in Child Development, 34*(2, Serial No. 126).

Kennedy, W. A., Van de Riet, V., & White, J. C. (1963). A normative sample of intelligence and achievement of Negro elementary school children in the southeastern United States. *Monographs of the Society for Research in Child Development, 28*(6, Serial No. 90).

Kessen, W. (1965). *The child.* New York: Wiley.

Key, W. B. (1973). *Subliminal seduction: Ad media's manipulation of a not so innocent America.* New York: Signet.

Kiesler, C. A., & Munson, P. A. (1975). Attitudes and opinions. In M. R. Rosenzweig & L. W. Porter (Eds.), *Annual review of psychology* (Vol. 26). Palo Alto, Calif.: Annual Reviews.

Kiester, E. (1984). Images of the night. In M. G. Walraven and H. E. Fitzgerald (Eds.), *Psychology 84/85.* Guilford, Conn.: Dushkin.

Kihlstrom, J. F. (1984). Hypnosis. In M. R. Rosenzweig & L. W. Porter (Eds.), *Annual Review of Psychology, 36,* 385–418.

Kilham, W., & Mann, L. (1974). Level of destructive obedience as a function of transmitter and executant roles in the Milgram obedience paradigm. *Journal of Personality and Social Psychology, 29,* 696–702.

Kimura, D. (1961). Cerebral dominance and the perception of verbal stimuli. *Canadian Journal of Psychology, 15,* 166–171.

Kimura, D. (1964). Left-right differences in the perception of melodies. *Quarterly Journal of Experimental Psychology, 14,* 335–338.

Kimura, D. (1983). Sex differences in cerebral organization for speech and praxic functions. *Canadian Journal of Psychology, 37,* 19–35.

Kinder, D. R., & Sears, D. O. (1985). Public opinion and political action. In G. Lindzey & E. Aronson (Eds.), *Handbook of social psychology* (3rd ed.) (Vol. 2). New York: Random House.

Kinsey, A. C., Pomeroy, W. B., & Martin, C. E. (1948). *Sexual behavior in the human male.* Philadelphia: Saunders.

Kinsey, A. C., Pomeroy, W. B., Martin, C. E., & Gebhard, P. H. (1953). *Sexual behavior in the human female.* Philadelphia: Saunders.

Kintsch, W. (1977). *Memory and cognition.* New York: Wiley.

Kitcher, P. (1985). *Vaulting ambition: Sociobiology and the quest for human nature.* Cambridge, Mass.: MIT Press.

Klahr, D., & Robinson, M. (1981). Formal assessment of problem solving and planning processes in preschool children. *Cognitive Psychology, 13,* 113–148.

Klahr, D., & Wallace, J. G. (1976). *Cognitive development: An information-processing view.* Hillsdale, N.J.: Erlbaum.

Klaus, H. M., & Kennell, J. H. (1976). *Maternal-infant bonding.* St. Louis, Mo.: Mosby.

Klemesrud, J. (1980, March 13). Survey finds major shifts in attitudes of women. *New York Times.*

Klinger, E. (1977). *Meaning and void: Inner experience and the incentives in people's lives.* Minneapolis: University of Minnesota Press.

Knox, R. E., & Inkster, J. A. (1968). Postdecision dissonance at post time. *Journal of Personality and Social Psychology, 8,* 319–323.

Koestler, A. (1964). *The act of creation.* New York: Macmillan.

Kohlberg, L. (1976). Moral stages and moralization: The cognitive-developmental approach. In T. Lickona (Ed.), *Moral development and behavior.* New York: Holt, Rinehart & Winston.

Köhler, W. (1927). *The mentality of apes.* London: Routledge & Kegan Paul.

Köhler, W. (1929). *Gestalt psychology.* New York: Liveright.

Kohn, R. R. (1977). Heart and cardiovascular system. In C. E. Finch & L. Hayflick (Eds.), *Handbook of the biology of aging*. New York: Van Nostrand Reinhold.

Kolata, G. B. (1980). Math and sex: Are girls born with less ability? *Science, 210*, 1234–1235.

Kolb, B., & Whishaw, I. Q. (1985). *Fundamentals of human neuropsychology* (2nd ed.). New York: Freeman.

Kolers, P. A. (1983). Perception and representation. *Annual Review of Psychology* (Vol. 33). Palo Alto, Calif.: Annual Reviews.

Kolers, P. A. (1985). Skill in reading and memory. *Canadian Journal of Psychology, 39*, 232–239.

Kolers, P. A., & Roediger, H. L. (1984). Procedures of mind. *Journal of Verbal Learning and Verbal Behavior, 23*, 425–449.

Kosslyn, S. M. (1980). *Image and mind*. Cambridge, Mass.: Harvard University Press.

Kosslyn, S. M., Ball, T. M., & Reiser, B. J. (1978). Visual images preserve metric spatial information: Evidence from studies of image scanning. *Journal of Experimental Psychology: Human Perception and Performance, 4*, 47–60.

Kosslyn, S. M., & Pomerantz, J. R. (1977). Imagery, propositions and the form of internal representations. *Cognitive Psychology, 9*, 52–76.

Kowler, E., & Martins, A. J. (1982). Eye movements of preschool children. *Science, 215*, 997–999.

Kraepelin. E. (1896). *Lehrbuch der Psychiatrie* (5th ed.). Leipzig: Barth.

Kramer, D. (1983). Post-formal operations? A need for further conceptualization. *Human Development, 26*, 91–105.

Krank, M. D., Hinson, R. E., & Siegel, S. (1981). Conditional hyperalgesia is elicited by environmental signs of morphine. *Behavioral and Neural Biology, 32*, 148–157.

Krebs, D. L. (1975). Empathy and altruism. *Journal of Personality and Social Psychology, 32*, 1134–1146.

Krech, D., & Crutchfield, R. S. (1958). *Elements of psychology*. New York: Knopf.

Kroger, W. S., & Douce, R. G. (1979). Hypnosis in criminal investigation. *International Journal of Clinical and Experimental Hypnosis, 27*, 358–374.

Kübler-Ross, E. (1969). *On death and dying*. Toronto: Macmillan.

Kubovy, M., & Pomerantz, J. R. (Eds.), *Perceptual organization*. Hillsdale, N.J.: Erlbaum.

Kuczynski, L. (1983). Reasoning, prohibitions, and motivations for compliance. *Developmental Psychology, 19*, 126–134.

Kuhl, D. E., et al. (1982). *Annals of neurology, 12*, 425.

Kuhn, D., Nash, S. C., & Brucken, L. (1978). Sex-role concepts of two- and three-year-olds. *Child Development, 49*, 445–451.

Kuhn, D., Phelps, E., & Walters, J. (1985). Correlational reasoning in an everyday context. *Journal of Applied Developmental Psychology, 6*, 85–97.

Lacey, J. I., & Lacey, B. C. (1958). Verification and extension of the principle of autonomic response stereotype. *The American Journal of Psychology, 71*, 50–73.

Lachman, J. L., Lachman, R., & Thronesbery, C. (1979). Metamemory throughout the adult life span. *Developmental Psychology, 15*, 543–551.

Laing, R. D. (1967). *The politics of experience*. New York: Pantheon.

Lakoff, G., & Johnson, M. (1980). *Metaphors we live by*. Chicago: University of Chicago Press.

Lamb, M. (1982). The bonding phenomenon: Misinterpretations and their implications. *Journal of Pediatrics, 101*, 555–557.

Lamb, M. E. (1981). The development of father-infant relationships. In M. E. Lamb (Ed.), *The role of the father in child development*. New York: Wiley.

Landy, F. J. (1985). *Psychology of work behavior* (3rd ed.). Homewood, Ill.: Dorsey Press.

Landy, F., & Trumbo, D. A. (1980). *Psychology of work behavior*. Homewood, Ill.: Dorsey Press.

Lange, C. J. (1967). The emotions (Translation of Lange's 1885 monograph). In C. J. Lange & W. James (Eds.), *The emotions*. New York: Hafner Publishing Co. (Facsimile of 1922 edition)

Larkin, J., McDermott, J., Simon, D. P., & Simon, H. A. (1980). Expert and novice performance in solving physics problems. *Science, 208*, 1335–1342.

Larry, P., v. Riles (1979). 495 F. Supp. 96 (N.D. Cal. 1979).

Lashley, K. S. (1929). *Brain mechanisms and intelligence*. Chicago, Ill.: University of Chicago Press.

Lashley, K. S. (1950). In search of the engram. *Symposia of the Society for Experimental Biology, 4*, 454–482.

Latané, B., & Darley, J. M. (1970). *The unresponsive bystander: Why doesn't he help?* New York: Appleton-Century-Crofts.

Latané, B., & Darley, J. M. (1976). *Help in a crisis: Bystander response to an emergency*. Morristown, N.J.: General Learning Press.

Latané, B., & Nida, S. A. (1981). Ten years of research on group size and helping. *Psychological Bulletin, 89*, 308–324.

Laurence, J. R., & Perry, C. (1983). Hypnotically created memory among highly hypnotizable subjects. *Science, 222*, 523–524.

Lawler, E. E. III. (1979). Expectancy theory. In R. M. Steers & L. W. Porter (Eds.), *Motivation and work behavior*. New York: McGraw-Hill.

Lazarus, A. A. (1961). Group therapy of phobic disorders by systematic desensitization. *Journal of Abnormal and Social Psychology, 63*, 504–510.

Lazarus, R. S. (1966). *Psychological stress and the coping process*. New York: McGraw-Hill.

Lazarus, R. S. (1976). *Patterns of adjustment*. New York: McGraw-Hill.

Lazarus, R. S. (1981). A cognitivist's reply to Zajonc on emotion and cognition. *American Psychologist, 36*, 222–223.

Lazarus, R. S., Kanner, A. D., & Folkman, S. (1980). Emotions: A cognitive-phenomenological analysis. In R. Plutchik & H. Kellerman (Eds.), *Emotion: Theory, research and experience: Vol. 1. Theories of emotion*. New York: Academic Press.

Lazarus, R. S., & Delongis (1983). Psychological stress and coping in aging. *American Psychologist, 38*, 245–254.

Leask, J., Haber, R. N., & Haber, R. B. (1969). Eidetic imagery in children: 2. Longitudinal and experimental results. *Psychonomic Monograph Supplements, 3*(3, Whole No. 35).

Lehmann, H. E. (1980). Schizophrenia: Clinical features. In H. I. Kaplan, A. M. Freedman, & B. J. Sadock (Eds.), *Comprehensive textbook of psychiatry: III*. Baltimore: Williams & Wilkins.

LeMagnen, J. (1956). Hyperphagie provoquée chez le rat blanc par altération du mécanisme de satiété périphérique. *Comptes Rendus des Séances de la Société de Biologie, 150*, 32.

Lempers, J. D., Flavell, E. R., & Flavell, J. H. (1977). The development in very young children of tacit knowledge concerning visual perception. *Genetic Psychology Monographs, 95*, 3–53.

Leon, D. (1969). *The kibbutz: A new way of life*. London: Pergamon.

Leon, G. R. (Ed.). (1977). *Case histories of deviant behavior* (2nd ed.). Boston: Holbrook Press.

Lepper, M. R., & Greene, D. (1978). *The hidden costs of reward: New perspectives on the psychology of human motivation*. Hillsdale, N.J.: Erlbaum.

Lepper, M. R., Greene, D., & Nisbett, R. E. (1973). Undermining children's intrinsic interest with extrinsic rewards: A test of the overjustification hypotheses. *Journal of Personality and Social Psychology, 23*, 129–137.

Lerner, M. J., & Miller, D. T. (1978). Just world research and the attribution process: Looking back and ahead. *Psychological Bulletin, 85*, 1030–1051.

Lerner, R. M. (1975). Showdown at generation gap: Attitudes of adolescents and their parents toward contemporary issues. In H. D. Thornburg (Ed.), *Contemporary adolescence: Readings*. (2nd ed.). Belmont, Calif.: Brooks/Cole.

Lester, B. M., Kotelchuck, M., Spelke, E., Sellers, M. J., & Klein, R. E. (1974). Separation protest in Guatemalan infants: Cross-cultural and cognitive findings. *Developmental Psychology, 10*, 79–85.

Levanthal, H. (1970). Findings and theory in the study of fear communications. In L. Berkowitz (Ed.), *Advances in experimental social psychology* (Vol. 5). New York: Academic Press.

Levi, L., & Kagan, A. (1980). Psychosocially induced stress and disease: Problems, research strategies, and results. In H. Selye (Ed.), *Selye's guide to stress research* (Vol. 1). New York: Van Nostrand Reinhold.

Levinson, D. J., Darrow, C. N., Klein, E. B., Levinson, M. H., & McKee, B. (1978). *The seasons of a man's life*. New York: Knopf.

Levy, J. (1980). Cerebral asymmetry and the psychology of man. In M. C. Wittrock (Ed.), *The brain and psychology*. New York: Academic Press.

Levy, J., & Trevarthen, C. (1974). Perceptual, semantic and phonetic aspects of elementary language processes in split-brain patients. *Brain, 95*, 61–78.

Levy, J., Trevarthen, C. B., & Sperry, R. W. (1972). Perception of bilateral chimeric figures following hemispheric deconnection. *Brain, 95*, 61–78.

Lewin, K. (1935). *A dynamic theory of personality*. New York: McGraw-Hill.

Lewin, R. (1980). Is your brain really necessary? *Science, 210*, 1232–1234.

Lewinsohn, P. M. (1974). A behavioral approach to depression. In R. M. Friedman & M. M. Katz (Eds.), *The psychology of depression: Contemporary theory and research.* New York: Wiley.

Lewinsohn, P. M., Hoberman, H. M., Teri, L., & Hautzinger, M. (1985). An integrative theory of depression. In S. Reiss & R. Bootzin (Eds.), *Theoretical issues in behavior therapy.* New York: Academic Press.

Lewis, J. W., Cannon, J. T., & Liebeskind, J. C. (1980). Opioid and nonopioid mechanisms of stress analgesia. *Science, 208,* 623–625.

Lewis, M., & Brooks-Gunn, J. (1979). *Social cognition and the acquisition of self.* New York: Plenum.

Leyens, J. P., & Parke, R. D. (1975). Aggressive slides can induce a weapons effect. *European Journal of Social Psychology, 5,* 229–236.

Liebelt, R. A., Bordelon, C. B., & Liebelt, A. G. (1973). The adipose tissue system and food intake. In E. Stellar & J. M. Sprague (Eds.), *Progress in physiological psychology.* New York: Academic Press.

Lieberman, P., Crelin, E. S., & Klatt, D. H. (1972). Phonetic ability and relaxed anatomy of the newborn and adult human, Neanderthal man, and the chimpanzee. *American Anthropologist, 74,* 287–307.

Liebert, R. M., Sprafkin, J. N., & Davidson, E. S. (1982). *The early window: Effects of television on children and youth* (2nd ed.). New York: Pergamon.

Lieblich, I. (1979). Eidetic imagery: Do not use ghosts to hunt ghosts of the same species. *Behavioral and Brain Sciences, 2,* 608–609.

Likert, R. (1961). *New patterns of management.* New York: McGraw-Hill.

Lindberg, M. (1980). The role of knowledge structures in the ontogeny of learning. *Journal of Experimental Child Psychology, 30,* 401–410.

Lindenthal, J. J., & Myers, J. K. (1979). The New Haven longitudinal survey. In I. G. Sarason & C. D. Spielberger (Eds.), *Stress and anxiety: Vol. 6. The Series in Clinical and Community Psychology.* Washington, D.C.: Hemisphere Publishing.

Lindsay, P. H., & Norman, D. A. (1977). *Human information processing* (2nd ed.). New York: Academic Press.

Lindzey, G. (1973). Morphology and behavior. In G. Lindzey, C. S. Hall, & M. Manosevitz (Eds.), *Theories of personality: Primary sources and research.* New York: Wiley.

Livesley, W. J., & Bromley, D. B. (1973). *Person perception in childhood and adolescence.* London: Wiley.

Locke, E. A. (1979). The supervisor as a motivator: His influence on employee performance and satisfaction. In R. M. Steers & L. W. Porter (Eds.), *Motivation and work behavior.* New York: McGraw-Hill.

Locksley, A., Borgida, E., Brekke, N., & Hepburn, C. (1980). Sex stereotypes and social judgment. *Journal of Personality and Social Psychology, 39,* 821–831.

Locke, J. (1950). *Essay concerning human understanding.* New York: Dover. (Original work published 1690)

Loehlin, J. C., & Nichols, R. C. (1976). *Heredity, environment, and personality.* Austin: University of Texas Press.

Loftus, E. F. (1979). The malleability of human memory. *American Scientist, 67,* 312–320.

Loftus, E. F., & Loftus, G. R. (1980). On the permanence of stored information in the brain. *American Psychologist, 35,* 409–420.

Loftus, E. F., & Palmer, J. C. (1974). Reconstruction of automobile destruction: An example of interaction between language and memory. *Journal of Verbal Learning and Verbal Behavior, 13,* 585–589.

Logan, G. D. (1985). Skill and automaticity: Relations, implications, and future directions. *Canadian Journal of Psychology, 39,* 367–386.

Londerville, S., & Main, M. (1981). Security of attachment, compliance, and maternal training methods in the second year of life. *Developmental Psychology, 17,* 289–299.

London, P. (1970). The rescuers: Motivational hypotheses about Christians who saved Jews from the Nazis. In J. Macaulay & L. Berkowitz (Eds.), *Altruism and helping behavior.* New York: Academic Press.

Long, G. M., & Beaton, R. J. (1982). The case for peripheral persistence: Effects of target and background luminance on a partial-report task. *Journal of Experimental Psychology: Human Perception and Performance, 8,* 383–391.

Lorenz, K. (1966). *On aggression.* New York: Harcourt Brace Jovanovich.

Loro, A. D., & Orleans, C. S. (1981). Binge eating in obesity: Preliminary findings and guidelines for behavioral analysis and treatment. *Addictive Behaviors, 6,* 155–166.

Lovaas, O. I. (1973). *Behavioral treatment of autistic children.* Morristown, N.J.: General Learning Press.

Lovaas, O. I. (1977). *The autistic child: Language development through behavior modification.* New York: Halsted Press.

Lovibond, S. H. (1969). Effect of patterns of aversive and appetitive conditioned stimuli on the incidence of gastric lesions in the immobilized rat. *Journal of Comparative and Physiological Psychology, 69,* 636–639.

Lubin, B., Larsen, R. M., & Matarazzo, J. D. (1984). Patterns of psychological test usage in the United States: 1935–1982. *American Psychologist, 39,* 451–453.

Luce, G. G. (1966). *Current research on sleep and dreams* (Public Health Service Publication No. 1389). Washington, D.C.: Public Health Service.

Luchins, A. S. (1946). Classroom experiments on mental set. *American Journal of Psychology, 59,* 295–298.

Luchins, A. S. (1957). Primacy-recency in impression formation. In C. Hovland (Ed.), *The order of presentation in persuasion.* New Haven: Yale University Press.

Lumsden, C. J., & Wilson, E. O. (1981). *Genes, mind, and culture: The coevolutionary process.* Cambridge, Mass.: Harvard University Press.

Luria, Z., & Rose, M. D. (1979). *Psychology of human sexuality.* New York: Wiley.

Luszcz, M. (1982). Facts on Aging: An Australian validation. *The Gerontologist, 22,* 369–372.

Lynn, R. (1982). IQ in Japan and the United States shows a growing disparity. *Nature, 297,* 222–223.

Lysle, D. T., & Fowler, H. (1985). Inhibition as a "slave" process: Deactivation of conditioned inhibition through extinction of conditioned excitation. *Journal of Experimental Psychology: Animal Behavior Processes, 11,* 71–91.

Maccoby, E. E., & Jacklin, C. N. (1974). *The psychology of sex differences.* Stanford, Calif.: Stanford University Press.

Mackenzie, B. (1984). Explaining race differences in IQ: The logic, the methodology, and the evidence. *American Psychologist, 39,* 1214–1233.

Madigan, S. (1983). Picture memory. In J. C. Yuille (Ed.), *Imagery, memory, and cognition: Essays in honor of Allan Paivio.* Hillsdale, N.J.: Erlbaum.

Mahone, C. H. (1960). Fear of failure and unrealistic vocational aspiration. *Journal of Abnormal and Social Psychology, 60,* 253–261.

Mahoney, M. J. (1977). Reflections on the cognitive learning trend in psychotherapy. *American Psychologist, 32,* 5–13.

Mahoney, M. J. (1980). *Abnormal psychology: Perspectives on human variance.* New York: Harper & Row.

Maier, S. F., & Jackson, R. L. (1979). Learned helplessness: All of us were right (and wrong): Inescapable shock has multiple effects. In G. H. Bower (Ed.), *The psychology of learning and motivation: Advances in research and theory.* New York: Academic Press.

Maier, S. F., Rappaport, P. M., & Wheatley, K. L. (1976). Conditioned inhibition and UCS-CS interval. *Animal Learning and Behavior, 4,* 217–220.

Maier, S. F., & Seligman, M. E. P. (1976). Learned helplessness: Theory and evidence. *Journal of Experimental Psychology: General, 105,* 3–46.

Maier, S. F., Sherman, J. E., Lewis, J. W., Terman, G. W., & Liebeskind, J. C. (1983). The opioid/nonopioid nature of stress-induced analgesia and learned helplessness. *Journal of Experimental Psychology: Animal Behavior Processes, 9,* 80–90.

Main, M., & Weston, D. R. (1981). The quality of the toddler's relationship to mother and father: Related to conflict and the readiness to establish new relationships. *Child Development, 52,* 932–940.

Mallick, S. K., & McCandless, B. R. (1966). A study of catharsis of aggression. *Journal of Personality and Social Psychology, 4,* 591–596.

Malpass, R. S., & Devine, P. G. (1980). Realism and eyewitness identification research. *Law and Human Behavior, 4,* 347–357.

Mann, L., & Janis, I. (1982). Conflict theory of decision making and the expectancy-value approach. In N. Feather (Ed.), *Expectations and actions: Expectancy value models in psychology* (pp. 341–364). Hillsdale, N.J.: Erlbaum.

Maratsos, M. (1973). Nonegocentric communication abilities in preschool children. *Child Development, 44,* 697–700.

Marcel, A. J. (1983). Conscious and unconscious perception: Experiments on visual masking and word recognition. *Cognitive Psychology, 15,* 197–237.

Marg, E., Freeman, D. N., Pheltzman, P. & Goldstein, P. J. (1976). Visual acuity development in human infants: Evoked potential estimates. *Investigative Ophthalmology, 15,* 150–153.

Markman, E. M., & Callanan, M. S. (1984). An analysis of hierarchical classification. In R. Sternberg (Ed.), *Advances in the psychology of human intelligence* (Vol. 2, pp. 345–365). Hillsdale, N.J.: Erlbaum.

Marks, I. M. (1978). *Living with fear.* New York: McGraw-Hill.

Marr, D. (1982). *Vision.* San Francisco: Freeman.

Marshall, G. D., & Zimbardo, P. G. (1979). Affective consequences of inadequately explained physiological arousal. *Journal of Personality and Social Psychology, 37,* 970–988.

Marshall, J. F., & Teitelbaum, P. (1974). Further analysis of sensory inattention following lateral hypothalamic damage in rats. *Journal of Comparative and Physiological Psychology, 86,* 375–395.

Martin, N. G., Eaves, L. J., Heath, A. C., Jardine, R., Feingold, L. M., & Eysenck, H. J. (1986). The transmission of social attitudes. *Proceedings of the National Academy of Sciences (USA), 83,* 4364–4368.

Martorano, S. C. (1977). A developmental analysis of performance on Piaget's formal operations tasks. *Developmental Psychology, 13,* 666–672.

Maslach, C. (1979). Negative emotional biasing of unexplained arousal. *Journal of Personality and Social Psychology, 37,* 953–969.

Maslach, C., & Jackson, S. E. (1985). Burnout in health professions: A social psychological analysis. In G. Sanders & J. Suls (Eds.), *Social psychology of health and illness.* Hillsdale, N.J.: Erlbaum.

Maslow, A. H. (1943). A theory of human motivation. *Psychological Review, 50,* 370–396.

Maslow, A. H. (1954). *Motivation and personality.* New York: Harper & Row.

Maslow, A. H. (1962). *Toward a psychology of being.* Princeton, N.J.: Van Nostrand.

Maslow, A. H. (1970). *Motivation and personality* (2nd ed.). New York: Harper & Row.

Masserman, J. H. (1943). *Behavior and neurosis: An experimental psychoanalytic approach to psychobiologic principles.* Chicago: University of Chicago Press.

Masters, W. H., & Johnson, V. E. (1966). *Human sexual response.* Boston: Little, Brown.

Masters, W. H., & Johnson, V. E. (1970). *Human sexual inadequacy.* Boston: Little, Brown.

Masters, W. H., Johnson, V. E., & Kolodny, R. C. (1985). *Human sexuality* (2nd ed.). Boston: Little, Brown.

Maurer, D., & Salapatek, P. (1976). Developmental changes in the scanning of faces by young infants. *Child Development, 47,* 523–527.

Maurer, D. M. (1975). Infant visual perception: Methods of study. In L. B. Cohen & P. Salapatek (Eds.), *Infant perception: From sensation to cognition* (Vol. 1). New York: Academic Press.

Mayer, J. (1955). Regulation of energy intake and body weight: The glucostatic theory and the lipostatic hypothesis. *Annals of the New York Academy of Science, 63,* 15–43.

Mayer, J. (1968). *Overweight: Causes and control.* Englewood Cliffs, N.J.: Prentice-Hall.

Mayer, R. E. (1983). *Thinking, problem solving, cognition.* New York: Freeman.

Mayo, E. (1933). *The human problems of an industrial civilization.* New York: Macmillan.

McArthur, L. A. (1972). The how and what of why: Some determinants of consequences of causal attribution. *Journal of Personality and Social Psychology, 22,* 171–193.

McCall, R. B. (1985). The confluence model and theory. *Child Development, 56,* 217–218.

McCall, R. B., Appelbaum, M. I., & Hogarty, P. S. (1973). Developmental changes in mental performance. *Monographs of the Society for Research in Child Development, 38*(3, Serial No. 150), 1–84.

McClelland, D. C., Atkinson, J. W., Clark, R. W., & Lowell, E. L. (1953). *The achievement motive.* New York: Appleton-Century-Crofts.

McClelland, D. C., & Winter, D. G. (1969). *Motivating economic achievement.* New York: Free Press. (Paperback 1971)

McClelland, J. L., & Rumelhart, D. E. (1981). An interactive activation model of the effect of context in perception: Part 1. An account of basic findings. *Psychological Review, 88,* 375–407.

McCloskey, M., & Zaragoza, M. (1985). Misleading postevent information and memory for events: Arguments and evidence against memory impairment hypotheses. *Journal of Experimental Psychology: General, 114,* 1–16.

McCollough, D. (1965). Color adaptation of edge-detectors in the human visual system. *Science, 149,* 1115–1116.

McDaniel, M. A., & Einstein, G. O. (1986). Bizarre imagery as an effective memory aid: The importance of distinctiveness. *Journal of Experimental Psychology: Learning, Memory and Cognition, 12,* 54–65.

McGeoch, J. A. (1932). Forgetting and the law of disuse. *Psychological Review, 39,* 352–370.

McGill, T. E. (1962). Sexual behavior in three inbred strains of mice. *Behaviour, 19,* 341–350.

McGlone, J. (1980). Sex differences in human brain asymmetry: A critical survey. *Behavioral and Brain Sciences, 3,* 215–263.

McGuire, W. J. (1985). Attitudes and attitude change. In G. Lindzey & E. Aronson (Eds.), *Handbook of social psychology* (3rd ed.) (Vol. 2). New York: Random House.

McHose, J. H., & Tauber, L. (1972). Changes in delay of reinforcement in simple instrumental conditioning. *Psychonomic Science, 27,* 291–292.

McKeithen, K. B., Reitman, J. S., Rueter, H. H., & Hirtle, S. C. (1981). Knowledge organization and skill differences in computer programmers. *Cognitive Psychology, 13,* 307–325.

McTavish, D. G. (1971). Perceptions of old people: A review of research methodologies and findings. *The Gerontologist, 11,* 90–101.

Mead, M. (1935). *Sex and temperament in three primitive societies.* New York: Morrow.

Mednick, S. A., Gabrielli, W. F., & Hutchings, B. (1984). Genetic influences in criminal convictions: Evidence from an adoption cohort. *Science, 224,* 891–894.

Mednick, S. A., Pollock, V., Volavka, J., & Gabrielli, W. F. (1982). Biology and violence. In M. E. Wolfgang & N. A. Weiner (Eds.), *Criminal violence.* Beverly Hills, Calif.: Sage.

Mednick, S. A., Venables, P. H., Schulsinger, F., & Cudeck, R. (1982). The Mauritius project: An experiment in primary prevention. In M. J. Goldstein (Ed.), *Preventive intervention in schizophrenia: Are we ready?* (pp. 287–296). Washington, D.C.: Government Printing Office.

Mednick, S. A., Volavka, J., Gabrielli, W. F., & Itil, T. (1981). EEG as a predictor of antisocial behavior. *Criminology, 19,* 219–231.

Meichenbaum, D. H. (1977). *Cognitive-behavior modification: An integrative approach.* New York: Plenum.

Meissner, W. W. (1980). Theories of personality and psychopathology: Classical psychoanalysis. In H. I. Kaplan, A. M. Freedman, & B. J. Sadock (Eds.), *Comprehensive textbook of psychiatry: III.* Baltimore: Williams & Wilkins.

Melamed, B. G., & Siegel, L. J. (1975). Reduction of anxiety in children facing hospitalization and surgery by use of filmed modeling. *Journal of Consulting and Clinical Psychology, 43,* 511–521.

Melton, A. W. (1963). Implications of short-term memory for a general theory of memory. *Journal of Verbal Learning and Verbal Behavior, 2,* 1–21.

Meltzer, D., & Brahlek, J. A. (1968). Quantity of reinforcement and fixed-interval performance. *Psychonomic Science, 12,* 207–208.

Melzack, R., & Wall, P. D. (1965). Pain mechanisms: A new theory. *Science, 150,* 971–979.

Melzack, R. D. (1970, October). Phantom limbs. *Psychology Today,* 63–68.

Melzack, R. D. (1973). *The puzzle of pain.* New York: Basic Books.

Mendlewicz, J. (1985). Genetic research in depressive disorders. In E. E. Beckham & W. E. Leber (Eds.), *Handbook of depression: Treatment, assessment, and research.* Homeword, Ill.: Dorsey Press.

Mendlewicz, J., & Rainer, J. D. (1977). Adoption study supporting genetic transmission in manic-depressive illness. *Nature, 268,* 327–329.

Menzel, E. W. (1978). Cognitive mapping in chimpanzees. In S. H. Hulse, H. Fowler, & W. K. Honig (Eds.), *Cognitive processes in animal behavior.* Hillsdale, N.J.: Erlbaum.

Mercer, J. R. (1971). Sociocultural factors in labeling mental retardates. *Peabody Journal of Education, 48,* 188–203.

Merikle, P. M. (1982). Unconscious perception revisited. *Perception and Psychophysics, 31,* 298–301.

Merritt, J. O. (1979). None in a million: Results of mass screening for eidetic ability using objective tests published in newspapers and magazines. *Behavioral and Brain Sciences, 2,* 612.

Mervis, C. B., Catlin, J., & Rosch, E. (1975). Development of the structure of color categories. *Developmental Psychology, 11,* 54–60.

Middleton, R. (1976). Regional differences in prejudice. *American Sociological Review, 41,* 94–117.

Midlarsky, E., & Bryan, J. H. (1972). Affect expressions and children's imitative altruism. *Journal of Experimental Research in Personality, 6,* 195–203.

Miernyk, W. H. (1975). The changing life cycle of work. In N. Datan & L. H. Ginsberg (Eds.), *Life-span developmental psychology: Normative life crises.* New York: Academic Press.

Milgram, S. (1963). Behavioral study of obedience. *Journal of Abnormal and Social Psychology, 67,* 371–378.

Milgram, S. (1964). Issues in the study of obedience: A reply to Baumrind. *American Psychologist, 19,* 848–852.

Milgram, S. (1965). Some conditions of obedience and disobedience to authority. *Human Relations, 18*, 57–76.

Milgram, S. (1974). *Obedience to authority: An experimental view.* New York: Harper & Row.

Miller, A. G. (1972). Role playing: An alternative to deception? *American Psychologist, 27*, 623–636.

Miller, G. A. (1956a). The magical number seven plus or minus two: Some limits on our capacity for processing information. *Psychological Review, 63*, 81–97.

Miller, G. A. (1956b). Human memory and the storage of information. *IRE Transactions on Information Theory*, Vol. IT-2, pp. 129–137.

Miller, G. A. (1962). *Psychology: The science of mental life.* New York: Harper & Row.

Miller, N. E. (1957). Experiments on motivation. *Science, 126*, 1271–1278.

Miller, N. E. (1959). Liberalization of basic S-R concepts: Extensions to conflict behavior, motivation, and social learning. In S. Koch (Ed.), *Psychology: A study of a science* (pp. 196–292). New York: McGraw-Hill.

Miller, N. E. (1980). Applications of learning and biofeedback to psychiatry and medicine. In H. I. Kaplan, A. M. Freedman, & B. J. Sadock (Eds.), *Comprehensive textbook of psychiatry: III.* Baltimore: Williams & Wilkins.

Miller, N. E. (1983). Behavioral medicine: Symbiosis between laboratory and clinic. In M. R. Rosenzweig & L. W. Porter (Eds.), *Annual Review of Psychology.* Palo Alto, Calif.: Annual Reviews.

Miller, N. E. (1985). The value of behavioral research on animals. *American Psychologist, 40*, 423–440.

Miller, P. McC., & Ingham, J. G. (1979). Reflections on the life-events-to-illness link with some preliminary findings. In G. Sarason & C. D. Spielberger (Eds.), *Stress and anxiety: Vol. 6. The series in clinical and community psychology.* Washington, D.C.: Hemisphere.

Milner, B., Corkin, S., & Teuber, H. H. (1968). Further analysis of the hippocampal amnesic syndrome: 14-year follow-up study of H.M. *Neuropsychologia, 6*, 215–234.

Mineka, S. (1979). The role of fear in theories of avoidance learning, flooding, and extinction. *Psychological Bulletin, 86*, 985–1010.

Miron, D., & McClelland, D. C. (1979). The impact of achievement motivation training on small business performance. *California Management Review, 1979, 21*(4), 13–28.

Mischel, H. N., & Mischel, W. (1983). The development of children's knowledge of self-control strategies. *Child Development, 54*, 603–619.

Mischel, W. (1961). Delay of gratification, need for achievement, and acquiescence in another culture. *Journal of Abnormal and Social Psychology, 62*, 543–552.

Mischel, W. (1968). *Personality and assessment.* New York: Wiley.

Mischel, W. (1974). Processes in the delay of gratification. In L. Berkowitz (Ed.), *Advances in experimental social psychology* (Vol. 7). New York: Academic Press.

Mischel, W., & Masters, J. C. (1966). Effects of probability of reward attainment on responses to frustration. *Journal of Personality and Social Psychology, 3*, 390–396.

Mischel, W., & Patterson, C. J. (1978). Effective plans for self-control in children. In W. A. Collins (Ed.), *Minnesota symposium on child psychology* (Vol. 11). Hillsdale, N.J.: Erlbaum.

Mischel, W., & Peake, P. K. (1982). Beyond déjà vu in the search for cross-situational consistency. *Psychological Review, 89*, 730–755.

Mitchell, D. E. (1980). The influence of early visual experience on visual perception. In C. S. Harris (Ed.), *Visual coding and adaptability.* Hillsdale, N.J.: Erlbaum.

Mitchell, J., Wilson, K., Revicki, D., & Parker, L. (1985). Children's perceptions of aging: A multidimensional approach to difference by age, sex, and race. *The Gerontologist, 25*, 182–187.

Mittler, P. (1971). *The study of twins.* Harmondsworth, Middlesex, England: Penguin.

Model Penal Code: Proposed Official Draft. (1962). Philadelphia: American Law Institute.

Money, J., & Ehrhardt, A. A. (1972). *Man & woman, boy & girl.* Baltimore: Johns Hopkins University Press.

Money, J., & Russo, A. J. (1979). Homosexual outcome of discordant gender identity/role in childhood: Longitudinal follow-up. *Journal of Pediatric Psychology, 41*(1), 29–41.

Moray, N. (1959). Attention in dichotic listening: Affective cues and the influence of instructions. *Quarterly Journal of Experimental Psychology, 9*, 56–60.

Money, J., & Schwartz, M. (1977). Dating, romantic and nonromantic friendship and sexuality in 17 early-treated adrenogenital females,

aged 16–25. In P. A. Lee et al. (Eds.), *Congenital adrenal hyperplasia.* Baltimore, Md.: University Park Press.

Morgan, C. T., & Morgan, J. D. (1940). Studies in hunger: 2. The relation of gastric denervation and dietary sugar to the effect of insulin upon food intake in the rat. *Journal of General Psychology, 57*, 153–163.

Moriarty, D., & McCabe, A. E. (1977). Studies of television and youth sport. In *Ontario: Royal commission on violence in the communications industry, Report: Vol. 5. Learning from the media (research reports).* Toronto: Queen's Printer for Ontario.

Morris, C. D., Bransford, J. D., & Franks, J. J. (1977). Levels of processing versus transfer appropriate processing. *Journal of Verbal Learning and Verbal Behavior, 16*, 519–533.

Morris, J. B., & Beck, A. T. (1974). The efficacy of antidepressant drugs: A review of research (1958–1972). *Archives of General Psychiatry, 30*, 667–674.

Morris, J. L. (1966). Propensity for risk taking as a determinant of vocational choice: An extension of the theory of achievement motivation. *Journal of Personality and Social Psychology, 3*, 328–335.

Morse, S. J., Gruzen, J., & Reis, H. (1976). The "eye of the beholder": A neglected variable in the study of physical attractiveness? *Journal of Personality, 44*, 209–225.

Moscovici, S. (1985). Social influence and conformity. In G. Lindzey & E. Aronson (Eds.), *Handbook of social psychology* (3rd ed.) (Vol. 2). New York: Random House.

Mowrer, O. H. (1947). On the dual nature of learning: A reinterpretation of "conditioning" and "problem-solving." *Harvard Educational Review, 17*, 102–148.

Mowrer, O. H. (1960). *Learning theory and behavior.* New York: Wiley.

Moyer, K. E. (1976). *The psychobiology of aggression.* New York: Harper & Row.

Mullaney, D. J., Kripke, D. F., Fleck, P. A., & Johnson, L. C. (1983). Sleep loss and nap effects on sustained continuous performance. *Psychophysiology, 20*, 643–651.

Mulligan, J. A. (1966). Singing behavior and its development in the song sparrow. *Melospiza Melodia University of California Publications in Zoology, 166*(81), 1–76.

Murdock, B. B., Jr. (1962). The serial position effect of free recall. *Journal of Experimental Psychology, 64*, 482–488.

Murphy, G. L., & Medin, D. L. (1985). The role of theories in conceptual coherence. *Psychological Review, 92*, 289–316.

Murphy, J. M. (1976). Psychiatric labeling in cross-cultural perspective. *Science, 191*, 1019–1028.

Murray, H. A., et al. (1938). *Explorations in personality.* New York: Oxford University Press.

Murstein, B. I. (1972). Physical attractiveness and marital choice. *Journal of Personality and Social Psychology, 22*, 8–12.

Mussen, P. H., & Jones, M. C. (1957). Self-conceptions, motivations, and interpersonal attitudes of late- and early-maturing boys. *Child Development, 28*, 243–256.

Mussen, P. H., Conger, J. J., & Kagan, J. (1980). *Essentials of child development and personality.* New York: Harper & Row.

Muter, P. M. (1980). Very rapid forgetting. *Memory and Cognition, 8*, 174–179.

Natelson, B. (1976). The "executive" monkey revisited. Paper presented at the Symposium on Nerves and the Gut, Philadelphia.

Natsoulas, T. (1983). Addendum to "Consciousness." *American Psychologist, 38*, 121–122.

Naylor, J. C., & Lawshe, C. H. (1958). An analytical review of the experimental basis of subception. *Journal of Psychology, 46*, 75–96.

Nebes, R. D. (1974). Hemispheric specialization in commissurotomized man. *Psychological Bulletin, 81*, 1–14.

Neely, J. H. (1977). Semantic priming and retrieval from lexical memory: Roles of inhibitionless spreading activation and limited capacity attention. *Journal of Experimental Psychology: General, 106*, 226–254.

Neimark, E., Slotnick, N. S., & Ulrich, T. (1971). Development of memorization strategies. *Developmental Psychology, 5*, 427–432.

Neisser, U. (1967). *Cognitive psychology.* New York: Appleton-Century-Crofts.

Neisser, U. (1968). The processes of vision. *Scientific American, 219*, 204–214.

Nelson, H., Erkin, M., Saigal, S., Bennett, K., Milner, R., & Sackett, D. (1980). A randomized clinical trial of the Leboyer approach to childbirth. *New England Journal of Medicine, 302*, 655–660.

Nelson, K. (1973). Structure and strategy in learning to talk. *Monographs of the Society for Research in Child Development, 38* (No. 149).

Nelson, S. A. (1980). Factors influencing young children's use of motives and outcomes as moral criteria. *Child Development, 51*, 823–829.

Nelson, T. O. (1985). Ebbinghaus' contribution to the measurement of retention: Savings during relearning. *Journal of Experimental Psychology: Learning, Memory, and Cognition, 11*, 472–479.

Nemiah, J. C. (1980). Neurotic disorders. In H. I. Kaplan, A. M. Freedman, & B. J. Sadock (Eds.), *Comprehensive textbook of psychiatry: III.* Baltimore: Williams & Wilkins.

Netter, F. H. (1983). *CIBA collection of medical illustrations: Vol. 1. Nervous system. Part 1. Anatomy and physiology.* CIBA Pharmaceutical.

Neugarten, B. (1968). Adult personality: Toward a psychology of the life cycle. In B. Neugarten (Ed.), *Middle age and aging.* Chicago: University of Chicago Press.

Neugarten, B. L. (Ed.) (1968). *Middle age and aging.* Chicago: University of Chicago Press.

Neugarten, B. L. (1970). Adaptation and the life cycle. *Journal of Geriatric Psychiatry, 4*, 71–87.

Neugarten, B. L. (1975). The future and the young-old. *Gerontologist, 15*, 4–9.

Neugarten, B. L., Crotty, W., & Tobin, S. (1964). Personality types in an aged population. In B. L. Neugarten (Ed.), *Personality in middle and late life: Empirical studies.* New York: Atherton.

Newcomb, T. M. (1943). *Personality and social change.* New York: Dryden.

Newman, H. H., Freeman, F. N., & Holzinger, K. J. (1937). *Twins: A study of heredity and environment.* Chicago: University of Chicago Press.

Newman, J., & McCauley, C. (1977). Eye contact with strangers in city, suburb, and small town. *Environment and Behavior, 9*, 547–557.

Newman, R. S., & Hagen, J. W. (1981). Memory strategies in children with learning disabilities. *Journal of Applied Developmental Psychology, 1*, 297–312.

Nickerson, R. S., & Adams, M. J. (1979). Long term memory for a common object. *Cognitive Psychology, 11*, 287–307.

Nisbett, R. E. (1972). Hunger, obesity and the ventromedial hypothalamus. *Psychological Review, 79*, 433–453.

Nisbett, R. E., & Ross, L. (1980). *Human inference: Strategies and shortcomings of social judgment.* Englewood Cliffs, N.J.: Prentice-Hall.

Nisbett, R. E., & Wilson, T. D. (1977a). Telling more than we can know: Verbal reports on mental processes. *Psychological Review, 84*, 231–259.

Nisbett, R. E., & Wilson, T. D. (1977b). The halo effect: Evidence for unconscious alteration of judgments. *Journal of Personality and Social Psychology, 35*, 250–256.

Nisbett, R. E., Caputo, G. C., Legant, P., & Mareck, J. (1973). Behavior as seen by the actor and the observer. *Journal of Personality and Social Psychology, 27*, 154–164.

Nogrady, H., McConkey, K. M., & Perry, C. (1985). Enhancing visual memory: Trying hypnosis, trying imagination, and trying again. *Journal of Abnormal Psychology, 94*, 195–204.

Noll, K. M., Davis, J. M., & DeLeon-Jones, F. (1985). Medication and somatic therapies in the treatment of depression. In E. E. Beckham & W. R. Leber (Eds.), *Handbook of Depression: Treatment, Assessment, and Research.* Homewood, Ill.: Dorsey Press.

Norman, D. A. (1968). Toward a theory of memory and attention. *Psychological Review, 75*, 522–536.

Nottebohm, F., & Nottebohm, M. (1971). Vocalizations and breeding behavior of surgically deafened ring doves. *Streptopelia Risoria Animal Behaviour, 19*, 313–328.

O'Connor, R. D. (1969). Modification of social withdrawal through symbolic modeling. *Journal of Applied Behavior Analysis, 2*, 15–22.

Olton, D. S., Collison, C., & Werz, M. A. (1977). Spatial memory and radial arm performance of rats. *Learning and Motivation, 8*, 289–314.

Olton, D. S., & Samuelson, R. J. (1976). Remembrance of places passed: Spatial memory in rats. *Journal of Experimental Psychology: Animal Behavior Processes, 2*, 97–116.

Orne, M. T. (1979). The use and misuse of hypnosis in court. *International Journal of Clinical and Experimental Hypnosis, 27*, 311–374.

Ornstein, P. A. & Naus, M. J. (1978). Rehearsal processes in children's memory. In P. Ornstein (Ed.), *Memory development in children.* Hillsdale, N.J.: Erlbaum.

Ornstein, P. A., & Naus, M. J. (in press). Effects of the knowledge base on children's memory strategies. In H. W. Reese (Ed.), *Advances in child development and behavior* (Vol. 19). New York: Academic Press.

Ornstein, R. (1978). The split and whole brain. *Human Nature, 1*, 76–83.

Ornstein, R. E. (1977). *The psychology of consciousness* (2nd ed.). New York: Harcourt Brace Jovanovich.

Oscar-Berman, M. (1980). Neuropsychological consequences of long-term chronic alcoholism. *American Scientist, 68*, 410–419.

Ostrom, T. M. (1984). The sovereignty of social cognition. In R. S. Wyer & T. K. Srull (Eds.), *Handbook of social cognition* (Vol. 1). Hillsdale, N.J.: Erlbaum.

Oswald, I., Taylor, A. M., & Treisman, M. (1960). Discriminative responses to stimulation during sleep. *Brain, 83*, 440–453.

Ouchi, W. G. (1981). *Theory Z: How American business can meet the Japanese challenge.* Reading, Mass.: Addison-Wesley.

Owens, J., Bower, G. H., & Black, J. (1979). The "soap opera" effect in story recall. *Memory & Cognition, 7*, 185–191.

Paivio, A. (1969). Mental imagery in associative learning and memory. *Psychological Review, 76*, 241–263.

Paivio, A. (1975). Neomentalism. *Canadian Journal of Psychology, 29*, 263–291.

Paivio, A. (1986). *Mental representations: A dual coding approach.* New York: Oxford University Press.

Paivio, A., Yuille, J. C., & Madigan, S. (1968). Concreteness, imagery, and meaningfulness values for 925 concrete nouns. *Journal of Experimental Psychology Monograph Supplement, 76* (1 Pt. 2).

Palincsar, A. S., & Brown, A. L. (1984). Reciprocal teaching of comprehension fostering and comprehension monitoring activities. *Cognition and Instruction, 1*(2), 117–175.

Palincsar, A. S., & Brown, A. L. (in press). Advances in the cognitive instruction of handicapped students. In M. Wong, H. Walberg, & M. Reynolds (Eds.), *The handbook of special education: Research and practice.* New York: Pergamon.

Palmore, E. (1977). Facts on aging: A short quiz. *The Gerontologist, 17*, 315–320.

Palmore, E. (1980). The facts on aging quiz: A review of findings. *The Gerontologist, 20*, 669–672.

Panskepp, J. (1971). Aggression elicited by electrical stimulation of the hypothalamus in albino rats. *Physiology and Behavior, 6*, 321–329.

Papalia, D. E., & Olds, S. W. (1985). *Psychology.* New York: McGraw-Hill.

Papalia, D. E., & Olds, S. W. (1986). *Human development.* New York: McGraw-Hill.

Papez, J. W. (1937). A proposed mechanism of emotion. *Archives of Neurology and Psychiatry, 38*, 725–743.

Paris, S. G. (1975). *Propositional logical thinking and comprehension of language connectives.* The Hague: Mouton.

Paris, S. G., Cross, D. R., & Lipson, M. Y. (1984). Informed strategies for learning: A program to improve children's reading awareness and comprehension. *Journal of Educational Psychology, 76*, 1239–1252.

Paris, S. G., & Lindauer, B. K. (1976) The role of inference in children's comprehension and memory for sentences. *Cognitive Psychology, 8*, 217–227.

Paris, S. G., & Lindauer, B. K. (1982). The development of cognitive skills during childhood. In B. Wolman (Ed.), *Handbook of developmental psychology.* Englewood Cliffs, N.J.: Prentice-Hall.

Paris, S. G., Lipson, M. Y., & Wixson, K. K. (1983). Becoming a strategic reader. *Contemporary Educational Psychology, 8*, 293–316.

Paris, S. G., Newman, R. S., & McVey, K. A. (1982). Learning the functional significance of mnemonic actions: A microgenetic study of strategy acquisition. *Journal of Experimental Child Psychology, 34*, 490–509.

Paris, S. G., & Upton, L. R. (1976). Children's memory for inferential relationships in prose. *Child Development, 47*, 660–668.

Parke, R. D. (1981). *Fathers.* Cambridge, Mass.: Harvard University Press.

Parke, R. D., Berkowitz, L., Leyens, J. P., West, S., & Sebastian, R. J. (1977). Some effects of violent and nonviolent movies on the behavior of juvenile delinquents. In L. Berkowitz (Ed.), *Advances in experimental social psychology* (Vol. 10). New York: Academic Press.

Parnell, R. W. (1953). Physique and choice of faculty. *British Medical Journal, 2*, 472–475.

Parsons, J. E., Adler, T. F., & Kaczala, C. M. (1982). Socialization of achievement attitudes and beliefs: Parental inferences. *Child Development, 53*, 310–321.

Patterson, F. G. (1978). The gestures of a gorilla: Language acquisition in another pongid. *Brain and Language, 5*, 72–97.

Paul, G. L. (1966). *Insight vs. desensitization in psychotherapy: An experiment in anxiety reduction.* Stanford, Calif.: Stanford University Press.

Paul, G. L. (1967). Insight versus desensitization in psychotherapy two years after termination. *Journal of Consulting Psychology, 31,* 333–348.

Paul, W., Weinrich, J. D., Gensiorek, J. C., & Hotvedt, M. E. (1982). *Homosexuality: Social, psychological and biological issues.* Beverly Hills, Calif.: Sage.

Pavlov, I. P. (1927). *Conditioned reflexes* (G. V. Anrep, Trans.). London: Oxford University Press.

Payne, D. G. (1986). Hypermnesia for pictures and words: Testing the recall level hypothesis. *Journal of Experimental Psychology: Learning, Memory, and Cognition, 12,* 16–29.

Pease, D., & Gleason, J. B. (1985). Gaining meaning: Semantic development. In J. B. Gleason (Ed.), *The development of language.* Columbus, Ohio: Merrill.

Peck, J. W. (1973). Discussion: Thirst(s) resulting from bodily water imbalances. In A. N. Epstein, H. R. Kissileff, & E. Stellar (Eds.), *The neuropsychology of thirst: New findings and advances in concepts.* Washington, D.C.: Winston.

Peck, J. W., & Novin, D. (1971). Evidence that osmoreceptors mediating drinking in rabbits are in the lateral preoptic region. *Journal of Comparative and Physiological Psychology, 74,* 134–147.

Peery, J. C. (1980). Neonate and adult head movement: No and yes revisited. *Developmental Psychology, 16,* 245–250.

Pelligrino, J. W. (1985, October). Anatomy of analogy. *Psychology Today,* pp. 49–54.

Penfield, W., & Jasper, H. H. (1954). *Epilepsy and the functional anatomy of the human brain.* Boston: Little, Brown.

Perlmutter, M. (1978). What is memory aging the aging of? *Developmental Psychology, 14,* 330–345.

Perlmutter, M., & Hall, E. (1985). *Adult development and aging.* New York: Wiley.

Perls, F. S. (1970). Four lectures. In J. Fagan & I. L. Sheperd (Eds.), *Gestalt therapy now.* Palo Alto, Calif.: Science and Behavior Books.

Perry, T. L., Hansen, S., & Kloster, M. (1973). Huntington's chorea: Deficiency of 5-aminobutyric acid in brain. *New England Journal of Medicine, 288,* 337–342.

Pert, C. B., Snowman, A. M., & Snyder, S. H. (1974). Localization of opiate receptor binding in presynaptic membranes of rat brain. *Brain Research, 70,* 184–188.

Peters, T., & Austin, N. (1985). *A passion for excellence: The leadership difference.* New York: Random House.

Petersen, R. T., Beecher, M. D., Zoloth, S. R., Moody, D. B., & Stebbins, W. C. (1978). Neural lateralization of species-specific vocalizations by Japanese macaques (Macaca fuscata). *Science, 202,* 324–327.

Peterson, A., & Taylor, B. (1980). The biological approach to adolescence: Biological change and psychological adaptation. In J. Adelson (Ed.), *Handbook of adolescent psychology.* New York: Wiley.

Peterson, C., & Seligman, M. E. P. (1984). Causal explanations as a risk factor for depression: Theory and evidence. *Psychological Review, 91,* 347–374.

Peterson, C., & Seligman, M. E. P. (1985). The learned helplessness model of depression: Current status of theory and research. In E. E. Beckham & W. R. Leber (Eds.), *Handbook of depression: Treatment, assessment, and research.* Homewood, Ill.: Dorsey Press.

Peterson, L. R., & Peterson, M. J. (1959). Short-term retention of individual items. *Journal of Experimental Psychology, 58,* 193–198.

Petty, R. E., & Cacioppo, J. T. (1984). The effects of involvement on responses to argument quantity and quality: Central and peripheral routes to persuasion. *Journal of Personality and Social Psychology, 46,* 69–81.

Pfaffman, C. (1955). Gustatory nerve impulses in rat, cat, and rabbit. *Journal of Neurophysiology, 18,* 429–440.

Phelps, M. E., & Mazziotta, J. C. (1985). Positron emission tomography: Human brain function and biochemistry. *Science, 228,* 799–809.

Phillips, D. P. (1986). Natural experiments on the effects of mass media violence on fatal aggression: Strengths and weaknesses of a new approach. In L. Berkowitz (Ed.), *Advances in experimental social psychology* (Vol. 19). New York: Academic Press.

Piaget, J. (1926). *Judgment and reasoning in the child.* New York: Harcourt & Brace.

Piaget, J. (1929). *The child's conception of the world.* New York: Harcourt & Brace.

Piaget, J. (1954). *The construction of reality in the child.* New York: Basic Books.

Piaget, J. (1962). *Play, dreams, and imitation in childhood.* New York: Norton.

Pliner, P., Hart, H., Kohn, J., & Saari, D. (1974). Compliance without pressure: Some further data on the foot-in-the-door technique. *Journal of Experimental Social Psychology, 10,* 17–22.

Plomin, R., & DeFries, J. C. (1980). Genetics and intelligence: Recent data. *Intelligence, 4,* 15–24.

Plomin, R., DeFries, J. C., & McClearn, G. E. (1980). *Behavioral genetics: A primer.* San Francisco: Freeman.

Plutchik, R. (1980). *Emotion: A psychoevolutionary synthesis.* New York: Academic Press.

Poggio, T. (1984). Vision by man and machine. *Scientific American, 250,* 106–116.

Poincaré, H. (1913). Mathematical creation. In G. H. Halstead (Trans.), *The foundations of science.* New York: Science Press.

Polivy, J., & Herman, C. P. (1985). Dieting and binging: A causal analysis. *American Psychologist, 40,* 193–201.

Pomerantz, J. R. (1981). Perceptual organization in information processing. In M. Kubovy & J. R. Pomerantz (Eds.), *Perceptual organization.* Hillsdale, N.J.: Erlbaum.

Poon, L. (1985). Differences in human memory with aging: Nature, causes, and clinical implications. In J. E. Birren & K. W. Schaie (Eds.), *Handbook of the psychology of aging* (2nd ed.). New York: Van Nostrand Reinhold.

Poon, L., Fozard, J., Paulschock, D., & Thomas, J. (1979). A questionnaire assessment of age differences in retention of recent and remote events. *Experimental Aging Research, 5,* 401–411.

Posner, M.I., & Snyder, C. R. R. (1975). Attention and cognitive control. In R. L. Solso (Ed.), *Information processing and cognition: The Loyola Symposium.* Hillsdale, N.J.: Erlbaum.

Potts, G. R. (1978). The role of inference in memory for real and artificial information. In R. Revlis & R. Mayer (Eds.), *Human reasoning.* Washington, D.C.: Winston/Wiley.

Poulton, E. C . (1977). Continuous intense noise masks auditory feedback and inner speech. *Psychological Bulletin, 84,* 997–1001.

Poulton, E. C. (1978). A new look at the effects of noise: A rejoinder. *Psychological Bulletin, 85,* 1068–1079.

Powley, T. L. (1977). The ventromedial hypothalamic syndrome satiety, and a cephalic phase hypothesis. *Psychological Review, 84,* 89–126.

Powley, T. L., & Keesey, R. E. (1970). Relationship of body weight to the lateral hypothalamic feeding syndrome. *Journal of Comparative and Physiological Psychology, 70,* 25–36.

Prasse, D. P., & Reschly, D. J. (1986). Larry P.: A case of segregation, testing, or program efficacy? *Exceptional Children, 52,* 333–346.

Premack, A. J., & Premack, D. (1972). Teaching language to an ape. *Scientific American, 227,* 92–99.

Premack, D. (1971). Language in chimpanzee? *Science, 172,* 808–822.

Premack, D. (1985). ''Gavagai!'' or the future history of the animal language controversy. *Cognition, 19,* 207–296.

Pribram, K. H. (1971). *Languages of the brain.* Englewood Cliffs, N.J.: Prentice-Hall.

Price, G. G., Walsh, D. J., & Vilberg, W. R. (1984). The confluence model's good predictions of mental age beg the question. *Psychological Bulletin, 96,* 195–200.

Prioleau, L., Murdock, M., & Brody, N. (1983). An analysis of psychotherapy versus placebo studies. *Behavioral and Brain Sciences, 6,* 275–310.

Pygmy chimp readily learns language skill (1985, June 24). *New York Times,* p. C1.

Pylyshyn, Z. (1973). What the mind's eye tells the mind's brain: A critique of mental imagery. *Psychological Bulletin, 80,* 1–24.

Raaijmakers, J. G. W., & Shiffrin, R. M. (1981). Search of associative memory. *Psychological Review, 88,* 93–134.

Rachman, S., & Hodgson, S. (1968). Experimentally-induced ''sexual fetishism'': Replication and development. *Psychological Record, 18,* 25–27.

Rachman, S. J., & Wilson, G. T. (1980). *The effects of psychological therapy.* London: Pergamon.

Radke-Yarrow, M., Zahn-Waxler, C., & Chapman, M. (1983). The development of prosocial behavior. In P. Mussen (Ed.), *Handbook of child psychology.* New York: Wiley.

Rahe, R. H. (1974). The pathway between subjects' recent life changes and their near future illness reports: Representative results and methodological issues. In B. S. Dohrenwend & B. P. Dohrenwend (Eds.), *Stressful life events: Their nature and effects.* New York: Wiley.

Rasinski, K. A., Crocker, J., & Hastie, R. (1985). Another look at sex stereotypes and social judgments: An analysis of the social perceiver's use of subjective probabilities. *Journal of Personality and Social Psychology, 49,* 317–326.

Ray, O. S. (1983). *Drugs, society, and human behavior* (3rd ed.). St. Louis: Mosby.

Raynor, J. O. (1970). Relationships between achievement-related motives, future orientation and academic performance. *Journal of Personality and Social Psychology, 15,* 28–33.

Read, J. A., & Miller, F. C. (1977). Fetal heart rate acceleration in response to acoustic stimulation as a measure of fetal well-being. *American Journal of Obstetrics and Gynecology, 129,* 512–517.

Reason, J. T. (1984). Absent-mindedness and cognitive control. In J. E. Harris & P. E. Morris (Eds.), *Everyday memory, actions and absent-mindedness.* London: Academic Press.

Reder, L. M., Wible, C., & Martin, J. (1986). Differential memory changes with age: Exact retrieval versus plausible inference. *Journal of Experimental Psychology: Learning, Memory, and Cognition, 12,* 72–81.

Reed, C. F. (1984). Terrestrial passage theory of the moon illusion. *Journal of Experimental Psychology: General, 113,* 489–500.

Regan, D. T., & Fazio, R. H. (1977). On the consistency between attitudes and behavior: Look to the method of attitude formation. *Journal of Experimental Social Psychology, 13,* 38–45.

Reicher, G. M. (1969). Perceptual recognition as a function of meaningfulness of stimulus materials. *Journal of Experimental Psychology, 81,* 275–280.

Reilly, N. P., & Morris, W. N. (1983). The role of arousal in the induction of mood. Paper presented at the meeting of the American Psychological Association, Anaheim, Calif.

Reiser, M., & Nielson, M. (1980). Investigative hypnosis: A developing specialty. *American Journal of Clinical Hypnosis, 23,* 75–83.

Renner, K. E. (1963). Influence of deprivation and availability of goal box cues on the temporal gradient of reinforcement. *Journal of Comparative and Physiological Psychology, 56,* 101–104.

RePass, D. E. (1971). Issue salience and party choice. *American Political Science Review, 65,* 389–400.

Rescorla, R. A. (1968). Probability of shock in the presence and absence of CS in fear conditioning. *Journal of Comparative and Physiological Psychology, 66,* 1–5.

Rescorla, R. A. (1978). Some implications of a cognitive perspective on Pavlovian conditioning. In S. H. Hulse, H. Fowler, & W. K. Honig (Eds.), *Cognitive processes in animal behavior.* Hillsdale, N.J.: Erlbaum.

Rescorla, R. A. & Wagner, A. R. (1972). A theory of Pavlovian conditioning: Variations in the effectiveness of reinforcement and nonreinforcement. In A. H. Black & W. F. Prokasy (Eds.), *Classical conditioning II: Current research and theory.* New York: Appleton-Century-Crofts.

Rest, J. R. (1975). Longitudinal study of the defining issues test of moral judgment: A strategy for analyzing developmental change. *Developmental Psychology, 11,* 738–748.

Reynolds, G. S. (1968). *A primer of operant conditioning.* Dallas: Scott, Foresman.

Riegel, K. (1976). The dialectics of human development. *American Psychologist, 31,* 689–699.

Riesen, A. H. (1960). The effects of stimulus deprivation on the development and atrophy of the visual sensory system. *American Journal of Orthopsychiatry, 30,* 23–26.

Riesen, A. H. (1965). Effects of early deprivation of photic stimulation. In S. Osler & R. Cooke (Eds.), *The biosocial bases of mental retardation.* Baltimore: Johns Hopkins University Press.

Rips, L. J., & Marcus, S. L. (1977). Suppositions and the analysis of conditional sentences. In M. A. Just & P. A. Carpenter (Eds.), *Cognitive processes in comprehension.* Hillsdale, N.J.: Erlbaum.

Rizley, R. C., & Rescorla, R. A. (1972). Associations in second-order conditioning and sensory preconditioning. *Journal of Comparative and Physiological Psychology, 81,* 1–11.

Robbins, W. J., et al. (1929). *Growth.* New Haven: Yale University Press.

Roberts, W. A. (1984). Some issues in animal spatial memory. In H. L. Roitblat, T. G. Bever, & H. S. Terrace (Eds.), *Animal cognition* (pp. 425–443). Hillsdale, N.J.: Erlbaum.

Roberts, W. A., & Van Veldhuizen, N. (1985). Spatial memory in pigeons on the radial maze. *Journal of Experimental Psychology: Animal Behavior Processes, 11,* 241–260.

Robinson, N. M., & Robinson, H. B. (1976). *The mentally retarded child: A psychological approach.* New York: McGraw-Hill.

Rock, I. (1984). *Perception.* New York: Scientific American Library.

Rockstein, M. J., & Sussman, M. (1979). *Biology of aging.* Belmont, Calif.: Wadsworth.

Rodgers, J. L. (1984). Confluence effects: Not here, not now! *Developmental Psychology, 20,* 321–331.

Rodin, J. (1981). Current status of the internal-external hypothesis for obesity: What went wrong? *American Psychologist, 36,* 361–372.

Roediger, H. L. (1980a). The effectiveness of four mnemonics in ordering recall. *Journal of Experimental Psychology, 6,* 558–567.

Roediger, H. L. (1980b). Memory metaphors in cognitive psychology. *Memory and Cognition, 8,* 231–246.

Roediger, H. L. (1985). Remembering Ebbinghaus. *Contemporary Psychology, 30,* 519–523.

Roediger, H. L., & Neely, J. H. (1982). Retrieval blocks in episodic and semantic memory. *Canadian Journal of Psychology, 36,* 213–242.

Roediger, H. L., & Stevens, M. C. (1970). The effects of delayed presentation of the object of aggression on pain-induced fighting. *Psychonomic Science, 21,* 55–56.

Rogers, C. R. (1970a). *Client-centered therapy* (2nd ed.) Boston: Houghton Mifflin.

Rogers, C. R. (1970b). *On becoming a person.* Boston: Houghton Mifflin.

Rogers, C. R. (1970c). *On encounter groups.* New York: Harper & Row.

Rogers, C. R. (1980). Client-centered psychotherapy. In H. I. Kaplan, A. M. Freeman, & B. J. Sadock (Eds.), *Comprehensive textbook of psychiatry: III.* Baltimore: Williams & Wilkins.

Rogoff, B. (1982). Integrating context and cognitive development. In M. E. Lamb & A. L. Brown (Eds.), *Advances in developmental psychology* (Vol. 2). Hillsdale, N.J.: Erlbaum.

Rokeach, M. (1964). *The three Christs of Ypsilanti: A psychological study.* New York: Knopf.

Root, A. W. (1973). Endocrinology of puberty: 1. Normal sexual maturation. *Journal of Pediatrics, 83,* 187–200.

Rorschach, H. (1921). *Psychodiagnostics.* Berne: Hans Huber.

Rosa, R. R., Bonnet, M. H., & Warm, J. S. (1983). Recovery of performance during sleep following sleep deprivation. *Psychophysiology, 20,* 152–159.

Rosch, E. (1973). On the internal structure of perceptual and semantic categories. In T. E. Moore (Ed.), *Cognitive development and the acquisition of language.* New York: Academic Press.

Rosch, E. (1977). Human categorization. In N. Warren (Ed.), *Advances in cross-cultural psychology* (Vol. I). London: Academic Press.

Rosenhan, D. L. (1970). The natural socialization of altruistic autonomy. In J. Macaulay & L. Berkowitz (Eds.), *Altruism and helping behavior.* New York: Academic Press.

Rosenhan, D. L. (1973). On being sane in insane places. *Science, 179,* 250–258.

Rosenhan, D. L., Salovey, P., Karylowski, J., & Hargis, K. (1981). Emotion and altruism. In J. P. Rushton & R. M. Sorrentino (Eds.), *Altruism and helping behavior: Social, personality, and developmental perspectives.* Hillsdale, N.J.: Erlbaum.

Rosenthal, D. (1970). *Genetic theory and abnormal behavior.* New York: McGraw-Hill.

Rosenthal, T. L., & Bandura, S. (1978). Psychological modeling: Theory and practice. In S. L. Garfield & A. E. Bergin (Eds.), *Handbook of psychotherapy and behavior change.* New York: Wiley.

Rosenzweig, M. R., & Lieman, A. L. (1982). *Physiological psychology.* Lexington, MA: Heath.

Ross, L. D. (1975). The intuitive psychologist and his shortcomings: Distortions in the attribution process. In L. Berkowitz (Ed.), *Advances in experimental social psychology* (Vol. 2). New York: Academic Press.

Ross, L. D., Amabile, T. M., & Steinmetz, J. L. (1977). Social roles, social control, and biases in social perception processes. *Journal of Personality and Social Psychology, 35,* 485–494.

Ross, M., & Fletcher, G. J. O. (1985). Attribution and social perception. In G. Lindzey & E. Aronson (Eds.), *Handbook of social psychology* (3rd ed.) (Vol. 2). New York: Random House.

Ross, S. M., & Ross, L. E. (1971). Comparison of trace and delay classical eyelid conditioning as a function of interstimulus interval. *Journal of Experimental Psychology, 91,* 165–167.

Rothbart, M., & John, O. P. (1985). Social categorization and behavioral episodes: A cognitive analysis of the effects of intergroup contact. *Journal of Social Issues 41,* 81–104.

Rotton, J., Barry, T., Frey, J., & Soler, E. (1978). Air pollution and interpersonal attraction. *Journal of Applied Social Psychology, 8,* 57–71.

Rowland, N. E., & Antelman, S. M. (1976). Stress-induced hyperphagia and obesity in rats: A possible model for understanding human obesity. *Science, 191,* 310–312.

Rozin, P., & Kalat, J. W. (1971). Specific hungers and poison avoidance as adaptive specializations of learning. *Psychological Review, 78,* 459–486.

Rubin, Z. (1970). Measurement of romantic love. *Journal of Personality and Social Psychology, 16,* 265–273.

Rubin, Z. (1973). *Liking and loving: An invitation to social psychology.* New York: Holt, Rinehart & Winston.

Ruch, L. E., & Holmes, T. H. (1971). Scaling of life change: Comparison of direct and indirect methods. *Journal of Psychosomatic Research, 15,* 221–227.

Rumbaugh, D. M. (1976). *Language learning by a chimpanzee: The Lana project.* New York: Academic Press.

Rushton, J. P. (1975). Generosity in children: Immediate and long-term effects of modeling, preaching, and moral judgment. *Journal of Personality and Social Psychology, 31,* 459–466.

Rushton, J. P. (1984). Sociobiology: Toward a theory of individual and group differences in personality and social behavior. In J. R. Royce & L. P. Mos (Eds.), *Annals of Theoretical Psychology* (Vol. 2). New York: Plenum.

Rushton, J. P., Brainerd, C. J., & Pressley, M. (1983). Behavioral development and construct validity: The principle of aggregation. *Psychological Bulletin, 94,* 18–38.

Rushton, J. P., Fulker, D. W., Neale, M. C., Nias, D. K. B., & Eysenck, H. J. (1986). Altruism and aggression: The heritability of individual differences. *Journal of Personality and Social Psychology, 50,* 1192–1198.

Rushton, J. P., Russell, R. J. H., & Wells, P. A. (1984). Genetic similarity theory: Beyond kin selection. *Behavior Genetics, 14,* 179–193.

Russell, M. J. (1976). Human olfactory communication. *Nature, 260,* 520–522.

Rychlak, J. F. (1977). *The psychology of rigorous humanism.* New York: Wiley-Interscience.

Sacco, W. P., & Beck, A. T. (1985). Cognitive therapy of depression. In E. E. Beckham & W. R. Leber (Eds.), *Handbook of depression: Treatment, assessment, and research.* Homewood, Ill.: Dorsey Press.

Sachs, B. D. (1965). Sexual behavior of male rats after one to nine days without food. *Journal of Comparative and Physiological Psychology, 60,* 144–146.

Sachs, J. S. (1967). Recognition memory for syntactic and semantic aspects of connected discourse. *Perception and Psychophysics, 2,* 437–442.

Sackheim, H. A., Gur, R. C., & Saucy, M. C. (1978). Emotions are expressed more intensely on the left side of the face. *Science, 202,* 434–436.

Sadock, B. J. (1980). Group psychotherapy, combined individual and group psychotherapy, and psychodrama. In H. I. Kaplan, A. M. Freedman, & B. J. Sadock, (Eds.), *Comprehensive textbook of psychiatry: III.* Baltimore: Williams & Wilkins.

St. James–Roberts, I. (1979). Neurological plasticity, recovery from brain insult, and child development. In H. W. Reese & L. P. Lipsitt (Eds.), *Advances in child development and behavior* (Vol. 14). New York: Academic Press.

Salapatek, P. (1975). Pattern perception in early infancy. In L. B. Cohen & P. Salapatek (Eds.), *Infant perception: From sensation to cognition* (Vol. 1). New York: Academic Press.

Salthouse, T. A., & Kail, R. (1983). Memory development throughout the life span: The role of processing rate. In P. B. Baltes & O. G. Brim, Jr., *Life-span development and behavior* (Vol. 5). New York: Academic Press.

Saltz, E., Campbell, S., & Skotko, D. (1983). Verbal control of behavior: The effects of shouting. *Developmental Psychology, 19,* 461–464.

Saltz, R. (1973). Effects of part-time "mothering" on IQ and SQ of young institutionalized children. *Child Development, 9,* 166–170.

Sambraus, V. H. H., & Sambraus, D. (1975). Prägung von Nutztieren auf Menschen. *Zeitschrift für Tierpsychologie, 38,* 1–17.

Samelson, F. (1975). On the science and politics of the IQ. *Social Research, 42,* 467–488.

Sameroff, A. J. (1968). The components of sucking in the human newborn. *Journal of Experimental Child Psychology, 6,* 607–623.

Samuelson, F. J. B. (1980). Watson's Little Albert, Cyril Burt's twins, and the need for a critical science. *American Psychologist, 35,* 619–625.

Sanders, R. J. (1985). Teaching apes to ape language: Explaining the imitative and nonimitative signing of a chimpanzee (*Pan troglodytes*). *Journal of Comparative Psychology, 99,* 197–210.

San Francisco Chronicle. (1964, November 26), p. 3.

Sarason, I. G., & Spielberger, C. D. (Eds.). (1979). *Stress and anxiety* (Vol. 6). The Series in Clinical and Community Psychology. Washington, D.C.: Hemisphere.

Sasvari, L. (1979). Observational learning in great, blue and marsh vits. *Animal Behavior, 27,* 767–771.

Sawrey, W. L., Conger, J. J., & Turrell, E. S. (1956). An experimental investigation of the role of psychological factors in the production of gastric ulcers in rats. *Journal of Comparative and Physiological Psychology, 49,* 457–461.

Scarr, S. (1981). The transmission of authoritarianism in families: Genetic resemblance in social-political attitudes? In S. Scarr (Ed.), *Race, social class, and individual differences in IQ.* Hillsdale, N.J.: Erlbaum.

Scarr, S. (1985). Constructing psychology: Making facts and fables for our times. *American Psychologist, 40,* 499–512.

Scarr, S., & Carter-Saltzman, L. (1979). Twin methods: Defense of a critical assumption. *Behavior Genetics, 9,* 527–542.

Scarr, S., & Grajeck, S. (1982). Similarities and differences among siblings. In M. E. Lamb and B. Sutton-Smith (Eds.), *Sibling relationships.* Hillsdale, N.J.: Erlbaum.

Scarr, S., & Kidd, K. K. (1983). Developmental behavior genetics. In P. H. Mussen (Ed.), *Handbook of child psychology: Vol. 2. Infancy and developmental psychobiology.* New York: Wiley.

Scarr, S., & Weinberg, R. A. (1976). IQ test performance of black children adopted by white families. *American Psychologist, 31,* 726–739.

Scarr, S., & Weinberg, R. A. (1983). The Minnesota adoption studies: Genetic differences and malleability. *Child Development, 54,* 260–267.

Schacter, D. L., & Graf, P. (1986). Effects of elaborative processing on implicit and explicit memory for new associations. *Journal of Experimental Psychology: Learning, Memory, and Cognition, 12.*

Schachter, S. (1971). Some extraordinary facts about obese humans and rats. *American Psychologist, 26,* 129–144.

Schachter, S., Goldman, R., & Gordon, A. (1968). Effects of fear, food deprivation, and obesity on eating. *Journal of Personality and Social Psychology, 10,* 91–97.

Schachter, S., & Singer, J. E. (1962). Cognitive, social and physiological determinants of emotional state. *Psychological Review, 69,* 379–399.

Schaie, K. W. (1977–1978). Toward a stage theory of adult cognitive development. *Aging and Human Development, 8,* 129–138.

Schaie, K. W., & Hertzog, D. (1985). Toward a comprehensive model of adult intellectual development: Contributions from the Seattle Longitudinal Study. In R. J. Sternberg (Ed.), *Advances in human intelligence* (Vol. 3). New York: Academic Press.

Schaie, K. W., & Willis, S. L. (1986). *Adult development and aging* (2nd ed.). Boston: Little, Brown.

Scheier, M. F., Carver, C. S., & Gibbons, F. X. (1979). Self-directed attention, awareness of bodily states, and suggestibility. *Journal of Personality and Social Psychology, 37,* 1576–1588.

Schiff, M., Duyme, M., Dumaret, A., Steward, J., Tomkiewicz, S., & Feingold, J. (1978). Intellectual status of working class children adopted early into upper middle-class families. *Science, 200,* 1503–1504.

Schiff, W. (1980). *Perception: An applied approach.* Boston: Houghton Mifflin.

Schiffman, H. R. (1976). *Sensation and perception: An integrated approach.* New York: Wiley.

Schmidt, C. R., & Paris, S. G. (1983). The development of children's verbal communication skills. In H. Reese & L. Lipsitt (Eds.), *Advances in child development and behavior* (Vol. 18). New York: Academic Press.

Schneider, D. J., & Miller, R. S. (1975). The effects of enthusiasm and quality of arguments on attitude attribution. *Journal of Personality, 43,* 698–708.

Schneider, W., & Shiffrin, R. M. (1977). Controlled and automatic information processing: 1. Detection, search, and attention. *Psychological Review, 84,* 1–66.

Schneiderman, N. (1966). Interstimulus interval function of the nictitating membrane response of the rabbit under delay versus trace conditioning. *Journal of Comparative and Physiological Psychology, 62,* 397–402.

Scholz, K. W., & Potts, G. R. (1974). Cognitive processing of linear orderings. *Journal of Experimental Psychology, 102,* 323–326.

Schulsinger, F. (1972). Psychopathy: Heredity and environment. *International Journal of Mental Health, 1,* 190–206.

Schumaker, J., Deshler, D., Alley, G., Warner, M., & Denton, P. (1984). Multipass: A learning strategy for improving reading comprehension. *Learning Disability Quarterly, 5*(2), 295–304.

Schuster, C. S., & Ashburn, S. S. (1986). *The process of human development* (2nd ed.). Boston: Little, Brown.

Schwartz, G. E., & Weiss, S. M. (1978a). Yale conference on behavioral medicine: A proposed definition and statement of goals. *Journal of Behavioral Medicine, 1,* 3–12.

Schwartz, G. E., & Weiss, S. M. (1978b). Behavioral medicine revisited: An amended definition. *Journal of Behavioral Medicine, 1,* 249–251.

Scott, J. P. (1980). The function of emotions in behavioral systems: A systems analysis. In R. Plutchik & H. Kellerman (Eds.), *Emotion, theory, research, and experience* (Vol. 1). New York: Academic Press.

Scovern, A. W., & Kilmann, P. R. (1980). Status of electroconvulsive therapy: Review of the outcome literature. *Psychological Bulletin, 87,* 260–303.

Scrima, L. (1982). Isolated REM sleep facilitates recall of complex associative information. *Psychophysiology, 19,* 252–259.

Seamon, J. G., Brody, N., & Kauff, D. (1983). Affective discrimination of stimuli that are not recognized: Effects of shadowing, masking, and cerebral laterality. *Journal of Experimental Psychology: Learning, Memory, & Cognition, 9,* 544–555.

Secunda, S. K., Friedman, R. J., & Schuyler, D. (1973). *The depressive disorders: Special report, 1973* (DHEW Publication No. HSM-73-9157). Washington, D.C.: U.S. Government Printing Office.

Segal, S. J. (1971). Processing of the stimulus in imagery and perception. In S. J. Segal (Ed.), *Imagery: Current cognitive approaches.* New York: Academic Press.

Sekuler, R., & Blake, R. (1985). *Perception.* New York: Knopf.

Seligman, M. E. P. (1975). *Helplessness: On depression, development and death.* San Francisco: Freeman.

Seligman, M. E. P., & Hager, J. L. (1972). *Biological boundaries of learning.* Englewood Cliffs, N.J.: Prentice-Hall.

Seligman, M. E. P., & Johnston, J. (1973). A cognitive theory of avoidance learning. In F. J. McGuigan & D. B. Lunsden (Eds.), *Contemporary approaches to conditioning and learning.* New York: Wiley.

Seligman, M. E. P., & Maier, S. F. (1967). Failure to escape traumatic shock. *Journal of Experimental Psychology, 74,* 1–9.

Selman, R. L. (1980). *The growth of interpersonal understanding: Developmental and clinical analyses.* New York: Academic Press.

Selye, H. (1956). *The stress of life.* New York: McGraw-Hill.

Selye, H. (1974). *Stress without distress.* Philadelphia: Lippincott.

Shaffer, D. R. (1985). *Developmental psychology.* Monterey, Calif.: Brooks/Cole.

Shapiro, D. A. (1985). Recent applications of meta-analysis in clinical research. *Clinical Psychology Review, 5,* 13–34.

Shatz, M., & Gelman, R. (1973). The development of communication skills: Modifications in the speech of young children as a function of the listener. *Monographs of the Society for Research in Child Development, 38*(5, No. 152).

Shaver, P., & Klinnert, M. (1982). Schachter's theories of affiliation and emotion: Implications of development research. In L. Wheeler (Ed.), *Review of Personality and Social Psychology, 3,* 37–72.

Shaw, D. W., & Thoresen, C. E. (1974). Effects of modeling and desensitization in reducing dentist phobia. *Journal of Counseling Psychology, 21,* 415–420.

Sheldon, W. H. (1940). *Varieties of human physique.* New York: Harper & Row.

Sheldon, W. H. (1954). *Atlas of man: A guide for somatotyping the adult male of all ages.* New York: Harper & Row.

Shepard, R. N. (1978). Externalization of mental images and the act of creation. In B. S. Randhawa & W. E. Goffman (Eds.), *Visual learning, thinking, and communication.* New York: Academic Press.

Shepard, R. N. (1981). Psychophysical complementarity. In M. Kubovy & J. R. Pomerantz (Eds.), *Perceptual organization.* Hillsdale, N.J.: Erlbaum.

Sherif, M. (1935). A study of some social factors in perception. *Archives of Psychology,* No. 187.

Sherrod, D. R. (1974). Crowding, perceived control, and behavioral aftereffects. *Journal of Applied Social Psychology, 2,* 171–186.

Shields, J. (1962). *Monozygotic twins brought up apart and brought up together.* London: Oxford University Press.

Shirley, M. M. (1923). *The First Two Years: A Study of Twenty-Five Babies,* Vol. II. Minneapolis: University of Minnesota Press.

Shore, C., O'Connell, B., & Bates, E. (1984). First sentence in language and symbolic play. *Developmental Psychology, 20,* 872–880.

Shuey, A. M. (1966). *The testing of Negro intelligence.* New York: Social Science Press.

Shultz, T. R., & Horibe, F. (1974). Development of the appreciation of verbal jokes. *Developmental Psychology, 10,* 13–20.

Siegal, S. (1977). Morphine tolerance acquisition as an associative process. *Journal of Experimental Psychology: Animal Behavior Processes, 3,* 1–13.

Siegal, R. K. (1977). Hallucinations. *Scientific American, 237,* 132–140.

Siegel, S., Hinson, R. E., Krank, M. D., & McCully, J. (1982). Heroin "overdose" death: Contribution of drug associated environmental cues. *Science, 216,* 436–437.

Siegler, I. C. (1983). Psychological aspects of the Duke longitudinal studies. In K. W. Schaie (Ed.), *Longitudinal studies of adult psychological development.* New York: Guilford Press.

Siegler, R. (1978). The origins of scientific reasoning. In R. Siegler (Ed.), *Children's thinking: What develops?* Hillsdale, N.J.: Erlbaum.

Siegler, R. S. (in press). Unities in thinking across domains. In M. Perlmutter (Ed.), *Minnesota symposia on child psychology.* Hillsdale, N.J.: Erlbaum.

Siegler, R. S., & Richards, D. D. (1982). The development of intelligence. In R. J. Sternberg (Ed.), *Handbook of human intelligence.* Cambridge, England: Cambridge University Press.

Siegler, R. S., & Robinson, M. (1982). The development of numerical understanding. In H. Reese & L. P. Lipsett (Eds.), *Advances in child development and behavior.* New York: Academic Press.

Siegler, R. S., & Shipley, C. (in press). The role of learning in children's strategy choices. In L. Liben & D. Feldman (Eds.), *Development and learning: Conflicts or congruence?* Hillsdale, N.J.: Erlbaum.

Siegler, R. S., & Shrager, J. (1984). A model of strategy choice. In C. Sophian (Ed.), *Origins of cognitive skills.* Hillsdale, N.J.: Erlbaum.

Silber, E., Hamburg, D. A., Coelho, G. V., Murphey, E. B., Rosenberg, M., & Pearlin, L. I. (1976). Adaptive behavior in competent adolescents: Coping with the anticipation of college. In R. H. Moss (Ed.), *Human adaptation: Coping with life crises* (pp. 111–127). Lexington, Mass.: Heath.

Silverman, B. I. (1974). Consequences, racial discrimination, and the principle of belief congruence. *Journal of Personality and Social Psychology, 29,* 497–508.

Silverman, L. T., Sprafkin, J. N., & Rubinstein, E. A. (1979). Physical contact and sexual behavior on prime-time TV. *Journal of Communication, 29,* 33–43.

Sistrunk, F., & McDavid, J. W. (1971). Sex as a variable in conforming behavior. *Journal of Personality and Social Psychology, 17,* 200–207.

Sivacek, K., & Crano, W. D. (1982). Vested interest as a moderator of attitude-behavior constancy. *Journal of Personality and Social Psychology, 43,* 210–221.

Skeels, H. (1966). Adult status of children with contrasting early life experiences. *Monographs of the Society for Research in Child Development, 31*(No. 3).

Skinner, B. F. (1948). *Walden two.* New York: Macmillan.

Skinner, B. F. (1953). *Science and human behavior.* New York: Macmillan.

Skinner, B. F. (1957). *Verbal behavior.* Englewood Cliffs, N.J.: Prentice-Hall.

Skinner, B. F. (1978). *Reflections on behaviorism and society.* Englewood Cliffs, N.J.: Prentice-Hall.

Skinner, B. F. (1979). *The shaping of a behaviorist.* New York: Knopf.

Sklar, L. S., & Anisman, H. (1981). Stress and cancer. *Psychological Bulletin, 89,* 369–406.

Skodak, M., & Skeels, H. M. (1949). A final follow-up study of one hundred adopted children. *Journal of Genetic Psychology, 75,* 85–125.

Slamecka, N. J. (1985). Ebbinghaus: Some associations. *Journal of Experimental Psychology: Learning, Memory, and Cognition, 11,* 414–435.

Slamecka, N. J., & Graf, P. (1978). The generation effect: Delineation of a phenomenon. *Journal of Experimental Psychology: Human Learning and Memory, 4,* 592–604.

Slotnick, B. M., McMullen, M. F., & Fleischer, S. (1974). Changes in emotionality following destruction of the septal areas in albino mice. *Brain, Behavior and Evolution, 8,* 241–252.

Slovic, P., Fischoff, B., & Lichtenstein, S. (1976). Cognitive processes and societal risk taking. In J. S. Carroll & J. W. Payne (Eds.), *Cognition and social behavior.* Hillsdale, N.J.: Erlbaum.

Sluckin, W. (1965). *Imprinting and early learning.* London: Methuen.

Smith, D. (1982). Trends in counseling and psychotherapy. *American Psychologist, 37,* 802–809.

Smith, E. E., & Osherson, D. N. (1984). Conceptual combination with prototype concepts. *Cognitive Science, 8,* 337–361.

Smith, E. R. (1984). Attributions and other inferences: Processing information about self versus others. *Journal of Experimental Social Psychology, 20,* 97–115.

Smith, F. J. (1977). Work attitudes as predictors of attendance on a specific day. *Journal of Applied Psychology, 62,* 16–19.

Smith, M. C. (1983). Hypnotic memory enhancement of witnesses: Does it work? *Psychological Bulletin, 94,* 387–407.

Smith, M. C., Coleman, S. R., & Gormezano, I. (1969). Classical conditioning of the rabbit's nictitating membrane response at backward, simultaneous and forward CS-US intervals. *Journal of Comparative and Physiological Psychology, 69,* 226–231.

Smith, M. L., Glass, G. V., & Miller, R. L. (1980). *The benefits of psychotherapy.* Baltimore: Johns Hopkins University Press.

Smith, P. K., & Daglish, L. (1977). Sex differences in parent and infant behavior in the home. *Child Development, 48,* 1250–1254.

Smith, S. M. (1979). Remembering in and out of context. *Journal of Experimental Psychology: Human Learning and Memory, 5,* 460–471.

Smith, S. M., Glenberg, A. M., & Bjork, R. A. (1978). Environmental context and human memory. *Memory and Cognition, 6,* 342–355.

Snyder, F. W., & Pronko, N. H. (1952). *Visual with spatial inversion.* Wichita: University of Kansas Press.

Snyder, M., & Jones, E. E. (1974). Attitude attribution when behavior is constrained. *Journal of Experimental Social Psychology, 10,* 585–600.

Snyder, M., & Rothbart, M. (1971). Communicator attractiveness and opinion change. *Canadian Journal of Behavioral Science, 3,* 377–387.

Snyder, M., Tanke, E. D., & Berscheid, E. (1977). Social perception and interpersonal behavior: On the self-fulfilling nature of social stereotypes. *Journal of Personality and Social Psychology, 35,* 656–666.

Snyder, M. L., Stephan, W. G., & Rosenfield, D. (1976). Egotism and attribution. *Journal of Personality and Social Psychology, 33,* 435–441.

Snyder, M. L., Stephan, W. G., & Rosenfield, D. (1978). Attributional egotism. In J. H. Harvey, W. Ickes, & R. F. Kidd (Eds.), *New directions in attribution research* (Vol. 2). Hillsdale, N.J.: Erlbaum.

Snyder, S. H. (1976). The dopamine hypothesis of schizophrenia. *American Journal of Psychiatry, 133,* 197–202.

Snyder, S. H. (1981). Dopamine receptors, neuroleptics, and schizophrenia. *American Journal of Psychiatry, 138,* 460–464.

Snyderman, M., & Herrnstein, R. J. (1983). Intelligence tests and the Immigration Act of 1924. *American Psychologist, 38,* 986–995.

Solnick, R. L., & Corby, N. (1983). Human sexuality and aging. In D. S. Woodruff & J. E. Birren (Eds.), *Aging: Scientific perspectives and social issues.* Monterey, Calif.: Brooks/Cole.

Solomon, R. L. (1980). The opponent-process theory of motivation: The costs of pleasure and the benefits of pain. *American Psychologist, 35,* 691–712.

Solomon, R. L., & Corbit, J. D. (1974). An opponent-process theory of motivation: 1. Temporal dynamics of affect. *Psychological Review, 81,* 119–145.

Southwick, C. H., & Clark, L. H. (1968). Interstrain differences in aggressive behavior and exploratory activity of inbred mice. *Communications in Behavioral Biology, 1,* 49–59.

Spanos, N. P. (1983). The hidden observer as an experimental creation. *Journal of Personality and Social Psychology, 44,* 170–176.

Spanos, N. P., & Radtke, H. L. (1982). Hypnotic amnesia as strategic enactment: A cognitive, social-psychological perspective. *Research in Community Psychology, Psychiatry and Behavior, 7,* 215–231.

Spearman, C. (1927). *The abilities of man: Their nature and measurement.* New York: Macmillan.

Speisman, J. C., Lazarus, R. S., Mordkoff, A. M., & Davidson, L. A. (1964). Experimental reduction of stress based on ego-defense theory. *Journal of Abnormal and Social Psychology, 68,* 367–380.

Spence, J. T., & Helmreich, R. L. (1978). *Masculinity and femininity: Their psychological dimensions, correlates, and antecedents.* Austin: University of Texas Press.

Sperling, G. (1960). The information available in brief visual presentations. *Psychological Monographs, 74*(Whole No. 11).

Sperry, R. W. (1968). Hemisphere deconnection and the unity of conscious experience. *American Psychologist, 23,* 723–733.

Sperry, R. W. (1974). Lateral specialization in surgically separated hemispheres. In F. O. Schmitt & F. G. Worden (Eds.), *The neurosciences* (Vol. 3). Cambridge, Mass.: MIT Press.

Spetch, M. L., Wilkie, D. M., & Pinel, J. P. J. (1981). Backward conditioning: A re-evaluation of the empirical evidence. *Psychological Bulletin, 89,* 163–175.

Spilton, D., & Lee, L. D. (1977). Some determinants of effective communication in four year olds. *Child Development, 48,* 968–977.

Springer, S. P., & Deutsch, G. (1985). *Left brain, right brain* (rev. ed.). San Francisco: Freeman.

Squire, L. R. (1982). The neuropsychology of human memory. *Annual Review of Neuroscience, 5,* 241–273.

Sroufe, L. A. (1985). Attachment classification from the perspective of infant-caregiver relationships and infant temperament. *Child Development, 56,* 1–14.

Srull, T. K., & Wyer, R. S. (1980). Category accessibility and social perception: Some implications for the study of person memory and interpersonal judgments. *Journal of Personality and Social Psychology, 38,* 841–856.

Staats, A. W., & Staats, C. K. (1963). *Complex human behavior: A systematic extension of learning principles.* New York: Holt, Rinehart & Winston.

Stager, S. F., & Burke, P. J. (1982). A reexamination of body build stereotypes. *Journal of Research in Personality, 16,* 435–446.

Stanley, J., & Benbow, C. (1983). Studying the process and results of greatly accelerating (especially in mathematics and science) the educational progress of youths who reason well mathematically. In S. Paris, G. Olson, & H. Stevenson (Eds.), *Learning and motivation in the classroom.* Hillsdale, N.J.: Erlbaum.

Stanley, P. R. A., & Riera, B. (1977). Replications of media violence. In *Ontario: Royal commission on violence in the communications industry. Report: Vol. 5. Learning from the media* (Research reports). Toronto: Queen's Printer for Ontario.

Stapp, J., & Fulcher, R. (1981). The employment of APA members. *American Psychologist, 36,* 1263–1314.

Staw, B. M. (1984). Organizational behavior: A review and reformulation of the field's outcome variables. *Annual Review of Psychology, 35,* 627–666.

Steers, R. M., & Porter, L. W. (1979). *Motivation and work behavior* (2nd ed.). New York: McGraw-Hill.

Steinberg, R., & Shapiro, S. (1982). Sex differences in personality traits of female and male master of business administration students. *Journal of Applied Psychology, 67,* 306–310.

Steiner, I. (1972). *Group process and productivity.* New York: Academic Press.

Stephens, D. N. (1980). Does the Lee obesity index measure general obesity? *Physiology and Behavior, 25,* 313–315.

Stern, C. (1949). *Principles of human genetics.* San Francisco: Freeman.

Stern, J. A., Brown, M., Ulett, G. A., & Sletten, I. (1977). A comparison of hypnosis, acupuncture, morphine, valium, aspirin, and placebo in the management of experimentally induced pain. *Annals of the New York Academy of Sciences, 296,* 175–193.

Sternberg, R. J. (1982). Natural, unnatural, and supernatural concepts. *Cognitive Psychology, 14,* 451–466.

Sternberg, R. J. (1985). *Beyond IQ: A triarchic theory of human intelligence.* Cambridge, England: Cambridge University Press.

Sternberg, R. J., Conway, B. E., Ketron, J. L., & Bernstein, M. (1981). People's conceptions of intelligence. *Journal of Personality and Social Psychology, 41,* 37–55.

Sternberg, R. J., & Powell, J. S. (1982). Theories of intelligence. In R. J. Sternberg (Ed.), *Handbook of human intelligence.* Cambridge, England: Cambridge University Press.

Sternberg, S. (1966). High-speed scanning in human memory. *Science, 153,* 652–654.

Sternglanz, S. H., & Serbin, L. A. (1974). Sex role stereotyping in children's television programs. *Developmental Psychology, 10,* 710–715.

Stevenson, H. W., Lee, S. Y., & Stigler, J. W. (1986). Mathematics achievement of Chinese, Japanese, and American children. *Science, 231,* 693–699.

Stevenson, H. W., Stigler, J. W., Lucker, G. W., Lee, S. Y., Hsu, C. C., & Kitamura, S. (1982). Reading disabilities: The case of Chinese, Japanese and English. *Child Development, 53,* 1164–1181.

Stigler, J. W. (1984). "Mental abacus": The effect of abacus training on Chinese children's mental calculation. *Cognitive Psychology, 16,* 145–176.

Stokols, D. (1972). On the distinction between density and crowding: Some implications for future research. *Psychological Review, 79,* 275–277.

Stotland, E. (1969). Exploratory investigations of empathy. In L. Berkowitz (Ed.), *Advances in experimental social psychology* (Vol. 4). New York: Academic Press.

Stratton, G. M. (1897). Vision without inversion of the retinal image. *Psychological Review, 4,* 341–360.

Strayer, F. F. (1980). Social ecology of the preschool peer group. In W. A. Collins (Ed.), *Minnesota symposium on child psychology: Vol. 13. Development of cognition, affect, and social relations.* Hillsdale, N.J.: Erlbaum.

Strayer, F. F., Wareing, S., & Rushton, J. P. (1979). Social constraints on naturally occurring preschool altruism. *Ethology and Sociobiology, 1,* 3–11.

Stricker, E. M. (1973). Thirst, sodium appetite, and complementary physiological contributions to the regulation of intravascular fluid volume. In A. N. Epstein, H. R. Kissileff, & E. Stellar (Eds.), *The neuropsychology of thirst: New findings and advances in concepts.* Washington, D.C.: Winston.

Stricker, E. M., Rowland, N., Saller, C. F., & Friedman, M. I. (1977). Homeostasis during hypoglycemia: Central control of adrenal secretion and peripheral control of feeding. *Science, 196,* 79–81.

Stromeyer, C. F., & Psotka, J. (1970). The detailed texture of eidetic images. *Nature, 225,* 346–349.

Stroop, J. R. (1935). Studies of interference in serial verbal reactions. *Journal of Experimental Psychology, 18,* 643–662.

Strupp, H. H. (1983). Psychoanalytic psychotherapy. In M. Hersen, A. E. Kazdin, & A. S. Bellock (Eds.), *The clinical psychology handbook.* New York: Pergamon.

Stunkard, A. J., Sorensen, T. I. A., Hanis, C., Teasdale, T. W., Chakraborty, R., Schull, W. J., & Schulsinger, F. (1986). An adoption study of human obesity. *The New England Journal of Medicine, 314,* 193–198.

Sulin, R. A., & Dooling, D. J. (1974). Intrusion of a thematic idea in retention of prose. *Journal of Experimental Psychology, 103,* 255–262.

Surwit, R. S., Pilon, R. N., & Fenton, C. H. (1978). Behavioral treatment of Raynaud's disease. *Journal of Behavioral Medicine, 1,* 323.

Sutherland, N. S. (1976). *Breakdown.* New York: Stein & Day.

Suzuki, S., Augerinos, G., & Black, A. H. (1980). Stimulus control of spatial behavior on the eight-arm maze in rats. *Learning and Motivation, 11,* 1–18.

Szasz, T. S. (1961). *The myth of mental illness: Foundations of a theory of personal conduct.* New York: Harper & Hoeber.

Szasz, T. S. (1970). *The manufacture of madness.* New York: Harper & Row.

Szasz, T. S. (1974). *Ceremonial chemistry: The ritual persecution of drugs, addicts, and pushers.* Garden City, N.Y.: Doubleday.

Szepesi, B. (1978). A model of nutritionally induced overweight: Weight "rebound" following caloric restriction. In G. A. Bray (Ed.), *Recent advances in obesity research* (Vol. 2). London: Newman.

Tajfel, H. (1982). Social psychology of intergroup relations. *Annual Review of psychology, 33,* 1–39.

Tanner, J. M. (1973). Growing up. *Scientific American, 229,* 34–43.

Tanner, J. M. (1978). *Fetus into man: Physical growth from conception to maturity.* Cambridge, Mass.: Harvard University Press.

Tarpy, R. M., & Sawabini, F. L. (1974). Reinforcement delay: A selective review of the last decade. *Psychological Bulletin, 81,* 984–987.

Tavris, C. (1983). *Anger: The misunderstood emotion.* New York: Simon & Schuster.

Taylor, F. W. (1911). *Scientific management.* New York: Harper & Brothers.

Taylor, J. A. (1953). A personality scale of manifest anxiety. *Journal of Abnormal and Social Psychology, 48,* 285–290.

Taylor, S. E., Crocker, J., Fiske, S. T., Sprinzen, M., & Winkler, J. D. (1979). The generalizability of salience effects. *Journal of Personality and Social Psychology, 37,* 357–368.

Taylor, S. E., & Fiske, S. T. (1975). Point of view and perceptions of causality. *Journal of Personality and Social Psychology, 32,* 439–445.

Taylor, S. E., & Fiske, S. T. (1978). Salience, attention, and attribution: Top of the head phenomena. *Advances in Experimental Social Psychology* (Vol. 2). New York: Academic Press.

Teasdale, T. W., & Owen, D. R. (1984). Heredity and familial environment in intelligence and educational level: A sibling study. *Nature, 309,* 620–622.

Terenius, L., & Wahlström, A. (1975). Morphine-like ligand for opiate receptors in human CSF. *Life Sciences, 16,* 1759–1764.

Terman, L. M. (1916). *The measurement of intelligence.* Boston: Houghton Mifflin.

Terman, L. M. (1954). The discovery and encouragement of exceptional talent. *American Psychologist, 9,* 221–230.

Terman, L. M., & Merrill, M. A. (1973). *Stanford-Binet intelligence scales: 1973 norms edition.* Boston: Houghton Mifflin.

Terman, L. M., & Oden, M. H. (1959). *Genetic studies of genius: The gifted at mid-life: Thirty-five years follow-up of the superior child* (Vol. 5). Stanford, Calif.: Stanford University Press.

Terrace, H. S. (1979, November). How Nim Chimpsky changed my mind. *Psychology Today, 13,* 65–76.

Thigpen, C. H., & Cleckley, H. (1954). *The three faces of Eve.* Kingsport, Tenn.: Kingsport Press.

Thomas, E. L., & Robinson, H. A. (1972). *Improving reading in every class: A sourcebook for teachers.* Boston: Allyn & Bacon.

Thompson, J. K., Jarvie, G. J., Lahey, B. B., & Cureton, K. J. (1982). Exercise and obesity: Etiology, physiology, and intervention. *Psychological Bulletin, 91,* 55–79.

Thompson, R. F. (1985). *The brain: An introduction to neuroscience.* New York: Freeman.

Thompson, S. K. (1975). Gender labels and early sex-role development. *Child Development, 46,* 339–347.

Thompson, W. R. (1953). The inheritance of behavior: Behavioral differences in fifteen mouse strains. *Canadian Journal of Psychology, 7,* 145–155.

Thorndike, E. L. (1911). *Animal intelligence.* New York: Macmillan.

Thurstone, L. L. (1938). *Primary mental abilities.* Chicago: University of Chicago Press.

Toffler, A. (1970). *Future shock.* New York: Random House.

Tolman, E. C. (1932). *Purposive behavior in animals and men.* New York: Appleton-Century-Crofts.

Tolman, E. C., & Honzik, C. H. (1930). Introduction and removal of reward and maze performance in rats. *University of California Publications in Psychology, 4,* 257–275.

Tomkins, S. S. (1980). Affect as amplification: Some modifications in theory. In R. Plutchik & H. Kellerman (Eds.), *Theories of emotion.* New York: Academic Press.

Tonkinson, R. (1978). *The Mardudjara aborigines.* New York: Holt, Rinehart & Winston.

Tonna, E. A. (1977). Aging of skeletal-dental systems and supporting tissue. In C. E. Finch & L. Hayflick (Eds.), *Handbook of the biology of aging.* New York: Van Nostrand Reinhold.

Torgesen, J. K. (1977). The role of nonspecific factors in the task performance of learning-disabled children: A theoretical assessment. *Journal of Learning Disabilities, 10,* 27–34.

Tourney, G. (1980). Hormones and homosexuality. In J. Marmon (Ed.), *Homosexual Behavior* (pp. 41–58). New York: Basic Books.

Tranel, D., & Damasio, A. R. (1985). Knowledge without awareness: An automatic index of facial recognition by prosopagnosics. *Science, 228,* 1453–1454.

Townsend, J. T. (1971). Theoretical analysis of an alphabetical confusion matrix. *Perception & Psychophysics, 9,* 40–50.

Traver, S. G., Hallahan, D. P., Kauffman, J. M., & Ball, D. W. (1976). Verbal rehearsal and selective attention in children with learning disabilities: A developmental lag. *Journal of Experimental Child Psychology, 22,* 375–385.

Treiman, D., & Terrell, K. (1975). Sex and the process of status attainment: A comparison of working men and women. *American Sociological Review, 40,* 174–200.

Trevarthen, C. (1980). Functional organization of the human brain. In M. C. Wittrock (Ed.), *The brain and psychology.* New York: Academic Press.

Triplett, N. (1897). The dynamogenic factors in pacemaking and competition. *American Journal of Psychology, 9,* 507–533.

Trivers, R. L. (1972). Parental investment and sexual selection. In B. Campbell (Ed.), *Sexual selection and the descent of man.* Chicago: Aldine.

Trivers, R. (1985). *Social evolution.* Menlo Park, Ca.: Benjamin/Cummings.

Trivers, R. L., & Hare, H. (1976). Haplodiploidy and the evolution of social insects. *Science, 191,* 249–263.

Troll, L. E., Miller, S. J., & Atchley, R. C. (1979). *Families in later life.* Belmont, Calif.: Wadsworth.

Trope, Y. (1975). Seeking information about one's own ability as a determinant of choice among tasks. *Journal of Personality and Social Psychology, 32,* 1004–1013.

Trussell, J., and Westoff, C. F. (1980). "Contraceptive Practice and Trends in Coital Frequency." *Family Planning Perspectives, 12,* 246–249.

Tucker, D. M. (1981). Lateral brain function, emotion, and conceptualization. *Psychological Bulletin, 89,* 19–46.

Tulving, E. (1962). Subjective organization in the free recall of "unrelated" words. *Psychological Review, 69,* 344–354.

Tulving, E. (1967). The effects of presentation and recall in free recall learning. *Journal of Verbal Learning and Verbal Behavior, 6,* 175–184.

Tulving, E. (1972). Episodic and semantic memory. In E. Tulving & W. Donaldson (Eds.), *Organization of memory* (pp. 590–600). New York: Academic Press.

Tulving, E. (1976). Ecphoric processes in recall and recognition. In J. Brown (Ed.), *Recall and recognition.* New York: Wiley.

Tulving, E. (1982). *Elements of episodic memory.* New York: Oxford University Press.

Tulving, E. (1985). How many memory systems are there? *American Psychologist, 40,* 385–398.

Tulving, E., & Pearlstone, Z. (1966). Availability versus accessibility of information in memory for words. *Journal of Verbal Learning and Verbal Behavior, 5,* 381–391.

Tulving, E., & Psotka, J. (1971). Retroactive inhibition in free recall: Inaccessibility of information available in the memory store. *Journal of Experimental Psychology, 87,* 1–8.

Tulving, E., & Thomson, D. (1973). Encoding specificity and retrieval processes in episodic memory. *Psychological Review, 80,* 352–373.

Turiel, E. (1974). Developmental processes in the child's moral thinking. In P. H. Mussen, J. Langer, & M. Covington (Eds.), *Trends and issues in developmental psychology.* New York: Holt, Rinehart & Winston.

Turkington, C. (1983, April). Drug found to block dopamine receptors. *APA Monitor,* p. 11.

Tversky, A., & Kahneman, D. (1971). Belief in the law of small numbers. *Psychological Bulletin, 76,* 105–110.

Tversky, A., & Kahneman, D. (1974). Judgments under uncertainty: Heuristics and biases. *Science, 185,* 1124–1131.

Tversky, A., & Kahneman, D. (1981). The framing of decisions and the psychology of choice. *Science, 211,* 453–458.

Tversky, A., & Kahneman, D. (1982). Variants of uncertainty. *Cognition, 11,* 143–157.

Tyler, T. R., & Sears, D. O. (1977). Coming to like obnoxious people when we must live with them. *Journal of Personality and Social Psychology, 35,* 200–211.

Ullman, L. P., & Krasner, L. (Eds.). (1965). *Case studies in behavior modification.* New York: Holt, Rinehart & Winston.

Ullman, L. P., & Krasner, L. (1969). *A psychological approach to abnormal behavior.* Englewood Cliffs, N.J.: Prentice-Hall.

Ulrich, R. (1966). Pain as a cause of aggression. *American Zoologist, 6,* 643–662.

Ulrich, R. E., & Azrin, N. H. (1962). Reflexive fighting in response to aversive stimulation. *Journal of the Experimental Analysis of Behavior, 5,* 511–520.

Ulrich, R. E., Hutchinson, R. R., & Azrin, N. H. (1965). Pain-elicited aggression. *Psychological Record, 15,* 111–126.

Ulvund, S. E. (1984). Predictive validity of assessments of early cognitive competence in light of some current issues in developmental psychology. *Human Development, 27,* 76–83.

Underwood, B. J. (1957). Interference and forgetting. *Psychological Review, 64,* 49–60.

Underwood, B. J. (1965). False recognition produced by implicit verbal responses. *Journal of Experimental Psychology, 70,* 122–129.

U.S. Bureau of the Census (1982). *Statistical abstract of the United States, 1982–83* (103rd ed.). Washington, D.C.: U.S. Government Printing Office.

U.S. Department of Health and Human Services (1980). *The status of children, youth, and families: 1979.* Washington, D.C.: U.S. Department of Health and Human Services.

U.S. Department of Health and Human Services (1982). *Television and behavior: Ten years of progress and implications for the eighties: Vol. 1. Summary report. Vol. 2. Technical reviews.* Washington, D.C.: U.S. Government Printing Office.

U.S. Surgeon General (1979). *Healthy people.* Washington, D.C.: U.S. Government Printing Office.

Upton, W. E. (1974). Altruism, attribution, and intrinsic motivation in the recruitment of blood donors. Doctoral dissertation, Cornell University (1973). *Dissertation Abstracts International, 34,* 6260-B.

Vaillant, G. E. (1977). *Adaptation to life.* Boston: Little, Brown.

Van Court, M., & Bean, F. D. (1985). Intelligence and fertility in the United States: 1912–1982. *Intelligence, 9,* 23–32.

van den Berghe, P. L. (1981). *The ethnic phenomenon.* New York: Elsevier.

Van Doorninck, W. J., Caldwell, B. M., Wright, C., & Frankenburg, W. K. (1981). The relationship between twelve-month home stimulation and school achievement. *Child Development, 52,* 1080–1083.

Veilleux, S., & Melzack, R. D. (1976). Pain in psychotic patients. *Experimental Neurology, 52,* 535–543.

Vinokur, A., Burnstein, E., Sechrest, L., & Wortman, P. M. (1985). Group decision making by experts: Field study of panels evaluating medical technologies. *Journal of Personality and Social Psychology, 49,* 70–84.

Vogel, G. W. (1975). A review of REM sleep deprivation. *Archives of General Psychiatry, 32,* 749–761.

Vonnegut, M. (1976). *The Eden express.* New York: Bantam Books.

Von Restorff, H. (1933). Über die Wirking von Bereichsbildungen im Spurenfeld. In W. Kohler & H. von Restorff, *Analyse von Vorgangen im Spurenfeld: 1. Psychologische Forschung, 18,* 299–342.

Von Senden, M. (1960). *Space and sight* (P. Heath, Trans.). New York: Free Press.

Vroom, V. (1964). *Work and motivation.* New York: Wiley.

Vroom, V. H. (1979). An outline of a cognitive model. In R. M. Steers & L. W. Porter (Eds.), *Motivation and work behavior.* New York: McGraw-Hill.

Vygotsky, L. S. (1962). *Thought and language.* Cambridge, Mass.: MIT Press.

Waddell, K. J., & Rogoff, B. (1981). Effect of contextual organization on spatial memory of middle-aged and older women. *Developmental Psychology, 17,* 878–885.

Wagner, A. R. (1961). Effects of amount and percentage of reinforcement and number of acquisition trials on conditioning and extinction. *Journal of Experimental Psychology, 62,* 234–242.

Wagner, A. R., Siegel, S., Thomas, E., & Ellison, G. D. (1964). Reinforcement history and the extinction of a conditioned salivary response. *Journal of Comparative and Physiological Psychology, 58,* 354–358.

Wahlsten, D. (1972). Genetic experiments with animal learning: A critical review. *Behavioral Biology, 7,* 143–182.

Walker, J., & Hertzog, C. (1975). Aging, brain function and behavior. In S. Woodruff & J. E. Birren (Eds.), *Aging: Scientific perspectives and social issues.* New York: Van Nostrand.

Wall, P. D. (1979). On the relation of injury to pain. *Pain, 6,* 253–264.

Wallace, P. (1977). Individual discrimination of humans by odor. *Physiology and Behavior, 19,* 577–579.

Wallach, H. (1976). *On perception.* New York: Quadrangle.

Walster, E. (1971). Passionate love. In B. I. Murstein (Ed.), *Theories of attraction and love.* New York: Springer.

Walster, E., Aronson, V., Abrahams, D., & Rottman, L. (1966). Importance of physical attractiveness in dating behavior. *Journal of Personality and Social Psychology, 4,* 508–516.

Walster, E., Walster, G., Piliavin, J., & Schmidt, L. (1973). "Playing hard-to-get": Understanding an elusive phenomenon. *Journal of Personality and Social Psychology, 26,* 113–121.

Wanner, R. A., & McDonald, L. (1983). Ageism in the labor market: Estimating earnings discrimination against older workers. *Journal of Gerontology, 38,* 738–745.

Warrington, E. K., & Weiskrantz, L. (1970). Amnesic syndrome: Consolidation or retrieval? *Nature, 228,* 628–630.

Wason, P. C., & Johnson-Laird, P. N. (1972). *Psychology of reasoning: Structure and content.* Cambridge, Mass.: Harvard University Press.

Watkins, M. J. (1974). Concept and measurement of primary memory. *Psychological Bulletin, 81,* 695–711.

Watkins, M. J. (1975). Inhibition in recall with extralist "cues." *Journal of Verbal Learning and Verbal Behavior, 14,* 294–303.

Watson, J. B. (1913). Psychology as the behaviorist views it. *Psychological Review, 20,* 158–177.

Watson, J. B. (1924). *Behaviorism.* Chicago: University of Chicago Press.

Watson, J. B. (1928). *Psychological care of infant and child.* New York: Norton.

Watson, J. B., & Rayner, R. (1920). Conditioned emotional reactions. *Journal of Experimental Psychology, 3,* 1–14.

Watson, J. S., & Ramey, C. T. (1972). Reactions to responsive contingent stimulation in early infancy. *Merrill-Palmer Quarterly, 18,* 219–227.

Waxenberg, S. E., Drellich, M. G., & Sutherland, A. M. (1959). The role of hormones in human behavior: 1. Changes in female sexuality after adrenalectomy. *Journal of Clinical Endocrinology, 19,* 193–202.

Waynbaum, I. (1907). *La physionomie humaine: Son mécanisme et son rôle social.* Paris: Alcan.

Webb, W. B. (1975). *Sleep: The gentle tyrant.* Englewood Cliffs, N.J.: Prentice-Hall.

Webb, W. B., & Agnew, H. W. (1973). *Sleep and dreams.* Dubuque, Iowa: William C. Brown.

Webb, W. B., & Agnew, H. W., Jr. (1968). In L. E. Abt & B. F. Reiss (Eds.), *Progress in clinical psychology.* New York: Grune & Stratton.

Weigel, R. H., Vernon, D. T. A., & Tognacci, L. N. (1974). Specificity of the attitude as a determinant of attitude-behavior congruence. *Journal of Personality and Social Psychology, 30,* 724–728.

Weinberger, D. R., Wagner, R. J., & Wyatt, R. L. (1983). Neuropathological studies of schizophrenia: A selective review. *Schizophrenia Bulletin, 9,* 198–212.

Weiner, I. B. (1982). *Child and adolescent psychopathology.* New York: Wiley.

Weiner, B., & Kukla, A. (1970). An attributional analysis of achievement motivation. *Journal of Personality and Social Psychology, 15,* 1–20.

Weiner, R. D. (1984). Does electroconvulsive therapy cause brain damage? *Behavioral and Brain Sciences, 7,* 1–53.

Weiss, J. M. (1970). Somatic effects of predictable and unpredictable shock. *Psychosomatic Medicine, 32,* 397–408.

Weiss, J. M. (1971a). Effects of coping behavior in different warning-signal conditions on stress pathology in rats. *Journal of Comparative and Physiological Psychology, 77,* 1–13.

Weiss, J. M. (1971b). Effects of coping behavior with and without a feedback signal on stress pathology in rats. *Journal of Comparative and Physiological Psychology, 77,* 22–30.

Weisz, J. R., & Zigler, E. (1979). Cognitive development in retarded and non-retarded persons: Piagetian tests of the similar sequence hypothesis. *Psychological Bulletin, 86,* 831–851.

Welch, R. B. (1978). *Perceptual modification.* New York: Academic Press.

Wellman, H. M., Ritter, K., & Flavell, J. H. (1975). Deliberate memory behavior in the delayed reactions of very young children. *Developmental Psychology, 11,* 780–787.

Wendt, G. R. (1937). Two and one-half year retention of a conditioned response. *Journal of General Psychology, 17,* 178–180.

Westoff, C. F. (1974). Coital frequency and contraception. *Family Planning Perspectives, 6,* 136–141.

Wever, E. G., & Bray, C. W. (1937). The perception of low tones and the resonance-volley theory. *Journal of Psychology, 3,* 101–114.

White, G. L., & Kight, T. D. (1984). Misattribution of arousal and attraction: Effects of salience of explanations for arousal. *Journal of Experimental Social Psychology, 20,* 55–64.

White, S. H. (1965). Evidence for a hierarchical arrangement of learning processes. In L. P. Lipsitt & C. C. Spiker (Eds.), *Advances in child development and behavior* (Vol. 2). New York: Academic Press.

Whorf, B. L. (1956). Science and linguistics. In J. B. Carroll (Ed.), *Language, thought, and reality: Selected writings of Benjamin Lee Whorf.* Cambridge, Mass.: MIT Press.

Wicker, A. W. (1969). Attitudes versus actions: The relationship of verbal and overt behavioral responses to attitude objects. *Journal of Social Issues, 25,* 41–78.

Wilder, D. A. (1977). Perception of groups, size of opposition, and social influence. *Journal of Experimental Social Psychology, 13,* 253–268.

Wilder, D. A. (1986). Social categorization: Implications for creation and reduction of intergroup bias. In L. Berkowitz (Ed.), *Advances in experimental social psychology* (Vol. 19). New York: Academic Press.

Wilkinson, A. (1976). Counting strategies and semantic analysis as applied to class inclusion. *Cognitive Psychology, 8,* 64–85.

Willerman, L., & Fiedler, M. F. (1974). Infant performance and intellectual precocity. *Child Development, 45,* 483–486.

Williams, T. B., Zabrack, M. L., & Joy, L. A. (1977). A content analysis of entertainment television programming. In *Ontario: Royal commission on violence in the communications industry. Report: Vol. 3. Violence in television films and news.* Toronto: Queen's Printer for Ontario.

Willis, S. L. (1985). Towards an educational psychology of the older adult learner: Intellectual and cognitive bases. In J. E. Birren & K. W. Schaie (Eds.), *Handbook of the psychology of aging* (2nd ed.). New York: Van Nostrand Reinhold.

Wilson, E. O. (1971). *The insect societies.* Cambridge, Mass.: Harvard University Press.

Wilson, E. O. (1975). *Sociobiology: The new synthesis.* Cambridge, Mass.: Harvard University Press.

Wilson, G. T., & Davison, G. C. (1971). Processes of fear reduction in systematic desensitization. *Psychological Bulletin, 76,* 1–14.

Wilson, J. Q., & Herrnstein, R. J. (1985). *Crime and human nature.* New York: Simon & Schuster.

Winch, R. (1958). *Mate-selection: A study of complementary needs.* New York: Harper & Row.

Wincze, J. P., & Caird, W. K. (1976). The effects of systematic desensitization and video desensitization in the treatment of essential sexual dysfunction in women. *Behavior Therapy, 7,* 335–342.

Windholz, G., & Lamal, P. A. (1985). Kohler's insight revisited. *Teaching of Psychology, 12,* 165–167.

Wing, J. K., & Bebbington, P. (1985). Epidemiology of depression. In E. E. Beckham & W. R. Leber (Eds.), *Handbook of depression: Treatment, assessment, and research.* Homewood, Ill.: Dorsey Press.

Winograd, P. N. (1984). Strategic difficulties in summarizing texts. *Reading Research Quarterly, 19*(4), 404–425.

Winston, P. W. (1984). *Artificial intelligence.* Reading, Mass.: Addison-Wesley.

Wishner, J. (1960). Reanalysis of "impressions of personality." *Psychological Review, 67,* 96–112.

Wolpe, J. (1958). *Psychotherapy by reciprocal inhibition.* Stanford, Calif.: Stanford University Press.

Wolpe, J. (1982). *The practice of behavior therapy.* New York: Pergamon.

Wolpe, J., & Rachman, S. (1960). Psychoanalytic "evidence": A critique based on Freud's case of Little Hans. *Journal of Nervous and Mental Disease, 131,* 135–147.

Wong, B. Y. L. (1985). Metacognition and learning disabilities. In D. Forrest-Pressley, G. MacKinnon, & T. Waller (Eds.), *Metacognition, cognition, and human performance: Vol. 2. Instructional practices.* Orlando, Fla.: Academic Press.

Wooley, S. C., Wooley, O. W., & Dyrenforth, S. R. (1979). Theoretical, practical, and social issues in behavioral treatments of obesity. *Journal of Applied Behavior Analysis, 12,* 3–25.

Wortman, C. B., & Loftus, E. F. (1981). *Psychology.* New York: Knopf.

Wyer, R. S. (1981). An information-processing perspective on social attribution. In J. H. Harvey, W. Ickes, & R. F. Kidd (Eds.), *New directions in attribution research* (Vol. 3). Hillsdale, N.J.: Erlbaum.

Wyer, R. S., & Carlston, D. (1979). *Social cognition, inference, and attribution.* Hillsdale, N.J.: Erlbaum.

Yablonsky, L. (1962). *The violent gang.* New York: Macmillan.

Yankelovich, D. (1974). *The new morality: a profile of American youth in the 70s.* New York: McGraw-Hill.

Yankelovich, D. (1981). *New rules.* New York: Random House.

Yerkes, R. M., & Morgulis, S. (1909). The method of Pavlov in animal psychology. *Psychological Bulletin, 6,* 257–273.

Yin, R. (1970). Face recognition by brain-injured patients: A dissociable disability? *Neuropsychologia, 8,* 395–402.

Young, W. C., Goy, R. W., & Phoenix, C. H. (1964). Hormones and sexual behavior. *Science, 143,* 212–218.

Yussen, S. R., & Kane, P. T. (1985). Children's conception of intelligence. In S. Yussen (Ed.), *The growth of reflection in children* (pp. 207–241). New York: Academic Press.

Zajonc, R. B. (1965). Social facilitation. *Science, 149,* 269–274.

Zajonc, R. B. (1968). Attitudinal effects of mere exposure. *Journal of Personality and Social Psychology Monograph Supplement, 9*(Part 2, No. 2), 2–27.

Zajonc, R. B. (1980). Thinking and feeling: Preferences need no inferences. *American Psychologist, 35,* 151–175.

Zajonc, R. B. (1983). Validating the confluence model. *Psychological Bulletin, 93,* 457–480.

Zajonc, R. B. (1985). Emotion and facial efference: A theory reclaimed. *Science, 228,* 15–21.

Zajonc, R. B., & Bargh, J. (1980). Birth order, family size, and decline of SAT scores. *American Psychologist, 35,* 662–668.

Zajonc, R. B., & Markus, G. B. (1975). Birth order and intellectual development. *Psychological Review, 82,* 74–88.

Zelinski, E. M., Gilewski, M. J., & Thompson, L. W. (1980). Do laboratory memory tests relate to everyday remembering and forgetting? In L. W. Poon, J. L. Fozard, L. S. Cermak, D. Arenberg, & L. W. Thompson (Eds.), *New directions in memory and aging.* Hillsdale, N.J.: Erlbaum.

Zelnick, M., & Kantner, J. F. (1977). Sexual and contraceptive experience of young unmarried women in the United States, 1976 and 1971. *Family Planning Perspectives, 9,* 55–71.

Zelnick, M., & Kantner, J. F. (1980). Sexual activity, contraceptive use, and pregnancy among metropolitan teenagers: 1971–1979. *Family Planning Perspectives, 12,* 230–237.

Ziff, P. (1972). *Understanding understanding.* Ithaca, N.Y.: Cornell University Press.

Zigler, E., & Butterfield, E. C. (1968). Motivational aspects of change in IQ test performance of culturally deprived nursery school children. *Child Development, 39,* 1–14.

Zubin, J., & Spring, B. (1977). Vulnerability: A new view of schizophrenia. *Journal of Abnormal Psychology, 86,* 103–126.

Zuckerman, M. (1979). Sensation seeking and risk taking. In C. E. Izard (Ed.), *Emotions in personality and psychopathology.* New York: Plenum.

Zuckerman, M., Lazzaro, M. M., & Waldgair, D. (1979). Undermining the effects of the foot-in-the-door technique with extrinsic rewards. *Journal of Applied Social Psychology, 9,* 292–296.

Zwislocki, J. J. (1981). Sound analysis in the ear: A history of discoveries. *American Scientist, 69,* 184–192.

Photo Credits *(cont. from page iv)*

Heirs c/o Cordon Art.—Baarn—Holland. page 147: Courtesy, I. B. M. Corporation. page 148: Dan McCoy/Rainbow. page 149 (right): David Hiser/The Image Bank; (left): Pete Turner/The Image Bank. page 153: © Ken Buck 1980/The Picture Cube. page 155: Charles Harbutt/Archive Pictures, Inc.

Chapter 5 page 170: Courtesy Roger Sperry. page 173: © Ted Spagna, 1978. All rights reserved. page 174: James Karales/© Peter Arnold, Inc., 1983. page 181: Blauel/Gnamm/Artothek. page 188: E. R. Hilgard, Stanford University.

Chapter 6 page 199: John Eastcott/Yva Momatiuk/The Image Works. page 201: Tass from Sovfoto. page 203: © Shepard Sherbell/The Picture Group. page 213 (top and bottom left): Courtesy of Peter Urcuioli; (right): Courtesy of Gerbrands Corporation, Arlington, Massachusetts. page 215: David Attie/Phototake. page 219: © 1978 Frank Lotz Miller/Black Star. page 222: Richard Howard PEOPLE WEEKLY Copyright © 1986 Time Incorporated. page 226: W. Kohler. *The Mentality of Apes*. Routledge and Kegan Paul Ltd., 1925. page 231: © 1979 Erika Stone.

Chapter 7 page 237: Institut fur Geschichte der Neueren Psychologie (Institute for the History of Modern Psychology) Passau University, Germany. page 239: Sybil Shelton/© 1982 Peter Arnold, Inc. page 248: Courtesy of Gordon H. Bower. page 258: Red Sisson/SIPA/Special Features. page 271: Courtesy Marlene Oscar Berman, Ph. D., Boston University Medical Center.

Chapter 8 page 280: Thomas Pantages. page 284: "Woman Eating Plums" by Alan Siegel, 1984. Courtesy Nancy Hoffman Gallery. page 287: Jon Goell/Picture Cube. page 300: Courtesy, M.I.T. page 307: Nina Leen, courtesy LIFE Picture Service. page 311: H. S. Terrace. page 312: Thomas Pantages.

Chapter 9 page 317: Enrico Ferorelli/DOT. page 322 (top): © Russ Kinne/Photo Researchers Inc.; (bottom): © Lennart Nilsson 1965 from *A Child Is Born* (New York: Delacorte Press)/photos courtesy of Bonnier Fakta Bokforlag. page 326: © David Linton, from SCIENTIFIC AMERICAN. page 327: Enrico Ferorelli/DOT. page 331: Enrico Ferorelli/DOT. page 332: Peter Menzel/Stock, Boston. page 333: Betsy Cole/The Picture Cube. page 336: Ken Karp/Omni-Photo Communications. page 339: Michael Philip Manheim/Southern Light. page 343: Elizabeth Crews/Stock, Boston. page 345: Anna Kaufman Moon/Stock, Boston, Inc. page 347: Ken Karp/Omni-Photo Communications. page 348: Harry F. Harlow, University of Wisconsin Primate Laboratory. page 351: Ann Hagen Griffiths/Omni-Photo Communications.

Chapter 10 page 361: Donald Dietz/Stock, Boston. page 365: Charles Gupton/Stock, Boston. page 372: Ellis Herwig/The Picture Cube. page 375: Ellis Herwig/Stock, Boston. page 379: Elizabeth Crews/Stock, Boston. page 380 (top): Ellis Herwig/The Picture Cube; (bottom): Peter Vandermark/Stock Boston. page 387 (top): Ken Karp/Omni-Photo Communications; (bottom): Charles Harbutt/Archive Picture, Inc. page 389: Mikki Ansin/Gamma/Liaison.

Chapter 11 page 395: The Bettmann Archive. page 396: With permission of his two granddaughters, Georgette and Geraldine Binet. page 405: Carl Skalak/DOT. page 406: James Wilson/Woodfin Camp & Associates. page 413: Lionel J. M. Delevingne/Stock, Boston. page 417: Frank Siteman/The Picture Cube. page 425: David Strickler/The Picture Cube.

Chapter 12 page 430: Oxford Scientific Films/Animals, Animals. page 431: Thomas McAvoy, LIFE Magazine © 1955 Time Inc. page 433: Museum of Comparative Zoology/Harvard University. page 435: Courtesy of Henry L. Roediger III. page 437: Hazel Hankin/Stock, Boston. page 438: © Bob Clay 1979/Jeroboam, Inc. page 439: Courtesy of Terry Powley. page 442: Peter Menzel/Stock, Boston. page 444: Ellis Herwig/The Picture Cube. page 449: ANIMALS ANIMALS/Jessie Gibbs. page 451 (top and bottom): Wide World Photos. page 452: Charles Harbutt/Archive Pictures, Inc. page 453: from McClelland et al., *The Achievement Motive* (New York: Appleton-Century-Crofts, 1953)/photo courtesy of Dr. David McClelland. page 459: © Carol Lee/The Picture Cube.

Chapter 13 page 464 (left): Owen Franken/Stock, Boston; (right): Tom McHugh/Photo Researchers. page 465: from Paul Ekman, ed., *Darwin and Facial Expressions* (New York: Academic Press, 1973), fig. 5/third photo from left courtesy Dr. Paul Ekman, UCSF/all other photos, Edward Gallob, with permission of Dr. Silvan Tomkins. page 466 (top): from Paul Ekman, ed., *Darwin and Facial Expressions* (New York: Academic Press, 1973), fig. 1/photo courtesy Dr. Paul Ekman, UCSF; (bottom): © Betty

Medsger 1982. page 469: Tom Pantages. page 470: Paul Ekman/Human Interaction Laboratory. SCIENCE Vol. 221. September 1983, pp. 1008–1010. page 476: from Ulrich and Azrin, "Reflexive fighting in response to aversive stimulation," *Journal of the Experimental Analysis of Behavior* 1962, 5, 511–520/photo courtesy of N. H. Azrin. page 479: Abigail Heyman/Archive Pictures, Inc. page 481: © Jane Scherr 1982/Jeroboam, Inc. page 482: Ellis Herwig/The Picture Cube. page 485: Public Archives Canada/PA116671. page 489: from Brady et al., "Avoidance behavior and the development of gastroduodenal ulcers," *Journal of the Experimental Analysis of Behavior*, 1958, 1, p. 70/photo courtesy of Dr. J. V. Brady.

Chapter 14 page 500: Frank Siteman/Taurus Photos. page 505: Ulrike Welsch. page 507: Courtesy Thomas J. Bouchard, Jr. page 513: J. Berndt/The Picture Cube. page 515: Hans Huber AG. page 516: © 1958 Karsh of Ottawa/Woodfin Camp & Associates. page 517: The Bettmann Archive. page 522: Mary Ellen Mark/Archive Pictures, Inc. page 523: Jeff Jacobson/Archive Pictures, Inc.

Chapter 15 page 534 (top): The Bettman Archive; (bottom): Photo Bulloz. page 537: Jane M. Murphy, Ph.D. page 541: Peter Vandermark/Stock, Boston. page 542: Cary Wolinsky/Stock, Boston. page 548: UPI/Bettmann Newsphotos. page 551: Jay Dorin/Omni-Photo Communications. page 553: Courtesy family of Walter Anderson page 554: Wide World Photos. page 555: Eleanor Beckwith/DPI. page 558 (top): Dan McCoy/Rainbow; (bottom): Courtesy The Morlok Quadruplets. Photograph Dr. Allan F. Mirsky. page 559: Reprinted with permission of Dr. Bennett G. Braun, from "Neurophysiologic Changes in Multiple Personality Due to Integration: A Preliminary Report" *American Journal of Clinical Hypnosis*, 1983, 26:2, page 89. page 561: UPI/Bettmann Newsphotos. page 562: UPI/Bettmann Newsphotos.

Chapter 16 page 568: By Courtesy of the Trustees of Sir John Soane's Museum. page 569 (top left and bottom right): Culver Pictures; (top right and bottom left): Bettmann Archive. page 573: Ann Chwatsky/Phototake. page 576: Ernie Hearion/New York Times Pictures. page 577: Steve Potter/Stock, Boston. page 580: Ken Robert Buck/The Picture Cube. page 581: from Bandura, A., Blanchard, E. B., and Ritter, B., "The relative efficacy of desensitization and modeling approaches for inducing behavioral, affective and attitudinal changes," *Journal of Personality and Social Psychology*, 1969, 13, p. 179/photo courtesy of Dr. A. Bandura. page 589: David Witbeck/The Picture Cube. page 591: James Pozarik/Gamma/Liaison. page 592 (top left): Lionel J. M. Delvigne/Stock, Boston, Inc.; (top right): Kashi/Gamma/Liaison; (bottom): Diego Goldberg/Sygma. page 594: Will McIntyre/Photo Researchers.

Chapter 17 page 602: AP/Wide World Photos. page 603 (bottom): Janice Fullman/The Picture Cube; (top): Phillip Bailey/Stock, Boston. page 610: © Robert V. Eckert, Jr./The Picture Cube. page 613: AP/Wide World Photos. page 618: B. L. Freeman/Southern Light. page 621: Ellis Herwig/The Picture Cube. page 623: Funk/SIPA-Press. page 625: Courtesy of American Cancer Society. page 628: Joan Liftin/Archive Pictures, Inc. page 632: Bohdan Hrynewych/Southern Light. page 633: Wide World Photos. page 636 (Figure 17–9): Copyright 1965 by Stanley Milgram. From the film OBEDIENCE, distributed by the New York University Film Division and the Pennsylvania State University, PCR. page 637 (Figure 17–11): Copyright 1965 by Stanley Milgram. From the film OBEDIENCE, distributed by the New York University Film Division and the Pennsylvania State University, PCR.

Chapter 18 page 645 (top): M. Peardon/Photo Researchers; (bottom): G. Smith/Gamma/Liaison. page 647: from Bandura, A., Ross, D., and Ross, S. A., "Imitation of film-mediated aggressive models," *Journal of Abnormal and Social Psychology*, 1963, 66, p. 8/photo courtesy of Dr. A. Bandura. page 650: Frank Fournier 1984/CONTACT/Woodfin Camp & Associates. page 652: Rick Sennott/Boston Herald. page 653: Jen and Des Bartlett/Bruce Coleman, Inc. page 657: United Press International. page 659: © 1982 Abigail Heyman/Archive. page 664: © 1986 Muppets, Inc. Used by permission of Children's Television Workshop. page 667: Mark Antman/The Image Works. page 668: T. Saito/Day in the Life of Japan, Woodfin Camp & Associates. page 671: Charles Harbutt/Archive Pictures, Inc. page 673: Charles Harbutt/Archive Pictures, Inc.

Text Credits

Chapter 1 page 3: Fig. 1–1. Adapted from "Margiie quasi-percettivi in campi con stimulazione omogenea," by G. Kanizsa. *Revisita di Psicologia* 49 (1950):7–30, p. 17. page 17: Table 1–3. Copyright 1985 by the American Psychological Association. Reprinted by permission of the publisher.

Chapter 2   page 40: Fig. 2–2. From W. Penfield and H. H. Jasper, *Epilepsy and the Functional Anatomy of the Human Brain.* Copyright 1954. Reprinted by permission of Little, Brown and Company. page 41: Fig. 2–5. From *Fundamentals of Human Neuropsychology*, 2nd ed., by Brian Kolb and Ian Whishaw. W. H. Freeman and Company. Copyright 1985. Reprinted by permission. page 45: Table 2–1. From *Physiological Psychology* by Mark Rosenzweig and Arnold Leiman. Copyright © 1982 by D. C. Heath and Company. Reprinted by permission of the publisher. pages 62–63: Excerpts from *The Shattered Mind*, by Howard Gardner. Copyright © 1974 by Howard Gardner. Reprinted by permission of Alfred A. Knopf, Inc. page 66: Fig. 2–21. Drawings by a patient of Dr. Joseph E. Bogen, *Bulletin of the Los Angeles Neurological Society* 34 (1969):73–105. Reprinted by permission; Fig. 2–22. From R. D. Nebes, "Hemispheric specialization in commissurotomized man," *Psychological Bulletin* 81 (1974):1–14. Copyright 1974 by the American Psychological Assocation. Reprinted by permission of the author. page 72: Table 2–2. From *The Brain: An Introduction to Neuroscience* by R. F. Thompson. W. H. Freeman, copyright © 1985. By permission. page 76: Fig. 2–27. Adapted by permission of Academic Press and the authors from J. C. DeFries, J. P. Hegemann, and R. A. Halcomb, "Response to twenty generations of selection for open-field activity in mice," *Behavioral Biology* 11 (1974):481–495.

Chapter 3   page 83: Fig. 3–1. From D. F. Benson and J. P. Greenberg, "Visual form agnosia," *Archives of Neurology* 20 (1969):82–89. Copyright 1969, American Medical Association. Reprinted by permission. pages 84 and 85: Fig. 3–3, Fig. 3–4. From *Perception*, edited by Robert Sekuler and Randolph Blake. Copyright © 1985 by Alfred A. Knopf, Inc. page 90: Fig. 3–9. Adapted by permission of Academic Press and the author from T. H. Cornsweet, *Visual Perception*, 1970. page 99: Fig. 3–22. From L. M. Hurvich and D. Jameson, "Opponent processes as a model of neural organization," *American Psychologist* 29 (1974):88–102. Copyright 1974 by the American Psychological Association. Reprinted by permission of the authors. pages 102 and 103: Fig. 3–25, Fig. 3–26. From *Perception*, edited by Robert Sekuler and Randolph Blake. Copyright © 1985 by Alfred A. Knopf, Inc. page 115: Table 3–1. Adapted by permission from *New Directions in Psychology*, I, by Roger Brown et al. Copyright © 1962 by Holt, Rinehart and Winston, Inc. page 166: Table 3–2. From H. R. Schiffman, *Sensation and Perception: An Integrated Approach.* Copyright 1976 by John Wiley and Sons, Inc. Reprinted by permission. page 177: Fig. 3–33. From S. S. Stevens, "The surprising simplicity of sensory metrics," *American Psychologist* 17 (1962):29–39. Copyright 1962 by the American Psychological Association. Reprinted by permission.

Chapter 4   page 130: Fig. 4–6. From D. Marr and E. Hilditch, "Theory of edge detection," *Proceedings of The Royal Society* B207 (London: 1980):187–217. Reprinted by permission. page 131: Fig. 4–7. From D. Marr and H. K. Nishihara, "Representation and recognition of the spatial organization of three-dimensional shapes," *Proceedings of The Royal Society* B200 (London: 1978):269–294. Reprinted by permission. page 133: Fig. 4–9. From J. L. McClelland and D. E. Rumelhart, "An interactive activation model of the effect on context in perception, Part I: An account of basic findings," *Psychological Review* 88 (1981):375–407. Copyright 1981 by the American Psychological Association. Reprinted by permission of the authors. page 135: Fig. 4–11. From G. Kanizsa, "Subjective contures," *Scientific American*, April 1976. Copyright © 1976 by Scientific American, Inc. All rights reserved. By permission. page 137: Fig. 4–13. From S. M. Kosslyn, T. M. Ball, and B. J. Reiser, "Visual images preserve metric spatial information: Evidence from studies of image scanning," *Journal of Experimental Psychology: Human Perception and Performance* 4 (1978):47–60. Copyright 1978 by the American Psychological Association. Reprinted by permission of the authors. page 138: Fig. 4–15. From *Perception*, edited by Robert Sekuler and Randolph Blake. Copyright © 1985 by Alfred A. Knopf, Inc.

Chapter 5   page 170: Fig. 5–6. From Michael S. Gazzaniga, "The split brain in man," *Scientific American*, August 1967, page 27. Copyright © 1967 by Scientific American, Inc. All rights reserved. By permission. page 175: Fig. 5–8. Adapted by permission from P. Hauri, *The Sleep Disorders* (Kalamazoo, MI: W. E. Upjohn Institute, 1977). page 176: Fig. 5–9. From W. B. Webb and H. W. Agnew, Jr., in L. E. Abt and B. F. Reiss, eds., *Progress in Clinical Psychology* (New York: Grune & Stratton, 1968.) Reprinted by permission. page 177: Fig. 5–11. From W. B. Webb and H. W. Agnew, Jr., *Sleep and Dreams.* Copyright 1973 by W. C. Brown Company. Reprinted by permission of the authors. pages 181–182: Excerpts from Sigmund Freud, *A General Introduction to Psychoanalysis.* Copyright, 1924, 1952. Reprinted by permission of Liveright Publishing Corporation. page 191: Table 5–1. Adapted by permission from Oakley Ray, *Drugs, Society, and Human Behavior*, 3rd ed. (St. Louis: Mosby, 1983).

page 193: Fig. 5–12. From Dr. Robert W. Earle, Dept. of Pharmacology, College of Medicine, University of California at Irvine. Reprinted by permission.

Chapter 6   page 207: Fig. 6–5. From A. R. Wagner et al, "Reinforcement history and the extinction of a conditioned salivary response," *Journal of Comparative and Physiological Psychology* 58 (1964):354–358. Copyright 1964 by the American Psychological Association. Adapted by permission of the authors. page 208: Fig. 6–6. From C. I. Hovland, "The generalization of conditioned responses: 1, The sensory generalization of conditioned responses with varying frequencies of tone," *Journal of General Psychology* 17 (1937):125–128. Reprinted by permission of the Helen Dwight Reid Educational Foundation. Published by Heldref Publications, 4000 Albemarle St., N.W., Washington, D.C. 20016. Copyright 1937. page 217: Fig. 6–12, Fig. 6–13. From *A Primer of Operant Conditioning* by G. S. Reynolds. Copyright © 1968 by Scott, Foresman and Company. Reprinted by permission. page 218: Fig. 6–14. From A. R. Wagner, "Effects of amount and percentage of reinforcement and number of acquisition trials on conditioning and extinction," *Journal of Experimental Psychology* 62 (1961):234–242. Copyright 1961 by the American Psychological Association. Adapted by permission of the author. page 227: Fig. 6–18. From E. Tolman and C. H. Honzik, "Introduction and removal of reward and maze performance in rats," *University of California Publications in Psychology* 4 (1930). Reprinted by permission of the publisher, University of California Press. page 231: Fig. 6–20. From A. Bandura, J. Grusec, and F. Menlove, "Vicarious extinction of avoidance behavior," *Journal of Personality and Social Psychology* 5 (1967):16–23. Copyright 1967 by the American Psychological Association. Adapted by permission of the authors.

Chapter 7   page 235: Table 7–1. Abridged from "What College Did to Me" in *Inside Benchley* by Robert Benchley. Copyright 1921, 1922, 1925, 1927, 1928, 1942 by Harper & Row, Publishers, Inc. Reprinted by permission of the publisher. page 238: Fig. 7–2. From Richard C. Atkinson and Richard M. Shiffrin, "The control of short term memory," *Scientific American*, August 1971. Copyright © 1971 by Scientific American, Inc. All rights reserved. By permission. page 240: Fig. 7–4. From G. Sperling, "The information available in brief visual presentations," *Psychological Monographs* 64 (whole no. 11) (1960). Copyright 1960 by the American Psychological Association. Reprinted by permission of the author. page 242: Fig. 7–6. From L. R. Peterson and M. J. Peterson, "Short term retention of individual items." *Journal of Experimental Psychology* 58 (1969):193–198. Copyrigh 1969 by the American Psychological Association. Adapted by permission of the author. page 243: Fig. 7–7. From B. B. Murdock, Jr., "The serial position effect in free recall," *Journal of Experimental Psychology* 64 (1962):428–488. Copyright 1962 by the American Psychological Association. Reprinted by permission of the author. page 245: Fig. 7–8. Figure and caption from J. O. Merritt, "None in a million: Results of mass screening for eidetic ability," *The Behavioral and Brain Sciences* 2 (1979), page 618. Reprinted by permission of Cambridge University Press. page 247: Fig. 7–9. From G. H. Bower, M. Clark, A. M. Lesgold, and D. Winzenz, "Hierarchical retrieval schemes in recall of categorized word lists," *Journal of Verbal Learning and Verbal Behavior* 8 (1969):323–343. Reprinted by permission. page 248: Fig. 7–10. From G. H. Bower and M. Clark, "Narrative stories as mediators for serial learning," *Psychonomic Science* 14 (1969):181–182. Reprinted by permission. page 249: Fig. 7–11. From G. H. Bower, "Mental imagery and associative learning," in L. W. Gregg, ed., *Cognition in Learning and Memory*, Fig. 3.1 (New York: Wiley, 1972). Reprinted by permission. page 260: Fig. 7–17. From A. M. Collins and E. F. Loftus, "A spreading theory of semantic processing," *Psychological Review* 82 (1975):407–428. Copyright 1975 by the American Psychological Association. Reprinted by permission of the authors.

Chapter 8   page 282: Fig. 8–5. From *Psychology*, by C. B. Wortman and E. F. Loftus. Copyright © 1981 by Alfred A. Knopf, Inc. Reprinted by permission of the publisher. page 285: Fig. 8–7. From J. W. Pelligrino, "Anatomy of Analogy." Reprinted with permission from *Psychology Today* Magazine, October 1985. Copyright © 1985 American Psychological Association. page 302: Fig. 8–12: From J. D. Bransford and M. K. Johnson, "Contextual prerequisites for understanding: Some investigations of comprehension and recall," *Journal of Verbal Learning and Verbal Behavior* 11 (1972). Reprinted by permission.

Chapter 9   page 315: Fig. 9–1. From P. Salapatek, "Pattern perception in early infancy," in L. B. Cohen and P. Salapatek, eds., *Infant Perception: From Sensation to Cognition* (New York: Academic Press, 1975). Reprinted by permission. page 318: Fig. 9–2. From W. N. Dember, J. J., Jenkins, and T. Teyler, *General Psychology*, p. 80 (Hillsdale, NJ: Erlbaum, 1984).

Reprinted by permission. page 328: Fig. 9–11. Adapted from M. M. Shirley, *The First Two Years: A Study of Twenty-Five Babies*, Vol. II. Copyright 1923 by the University of Minnesota. Reprinted by permission of the University of Minnesota Press. page 335: Fig. 9–12. From Howard Gardner, *Developmental Psychology: An Introduction*, 2nd ed. Copyright © 1982 by Howard Gardner. Reprinted by permission of Little, Brown and Company. page 340: Table 9–3. From Katherine Nelson, "Structure and strategy in learning to talk," *Monographs of the Society for Research in Child Development* 38 (Serial No. 149, No. 2). Copyright © 1970 The Society for Research in Child Development, Inc. Reprinted by permission. page 341: Table 9–4. Adapted with permission of Macmillan Publishing Company from *Psycholinguistics* by Roger Brown. Copyright © 1970 by The Free Press, a Division of Macmillan Publishing Company. page 342: Fig. 9–13. Reproduced from Berko, J., "The Child's Learning of English Morphology." In W. Meyer, Readings in the Psychology of Childhood and Adolescence, *Word*, 14 (1958):483. Johnson Reprint Corporation. By permission. page 347: Fig. 9–14. From *Essentials of Child Development and Personality* by Paul Henry Mussen, John Janeway Conger, and Jerome Kagan. Copyright © 1980 by Paul Henry Mussen, John Janeway Conger, and Jerome Kagan. Reprinted by permission of Harper & Row, Publishers, Inc. page 348: Fig. 9–15. From H. F. Harlow and R. R. Zimmerman, "Affectional response in the infant monkey," *Science*, Vol. 130, pp. 421–423, Fig. 4, 21 August 1959. Copyright 1959 by the AAAS. Reprinted by permission. page 354: Table 9–5. Adapted from "Moral Stages and Moralization" by Lawrence Kohlberg in *Moral Development and Behavior* edited by Thomas Likona. Copyright © 1976 by Holt, Rinehart and Winston. Reprinted by permission.

Chapter 10 page 377: Fig. 10–5. From *The Seasons of a Man's Life*, by Daniel J. Levinson et al. Copyright © 1978 by Daniel J. Levinson. Reprinted by permission of Alfred A. Knopf, Inc., and the Sterling Lord Agency, Inc. page 380: Fig. 10–6. From D. E. Papalia and S. W. Olds, *Human Development*, page 390. Copyright © 1986 by McGraw-Hill, Inc. Adapted by permission of McGraw-Hill Book Company. pages 382–383: Text items from Erdman Palmore, "Facts on Aging: A Short Quiz." Reprinted by permission of *The Gerontologist*, Vol. 27, No. 4, August 1977. page 392: Lines from "Do not go gentle into that good night" by Dylan Thomas from *Poems of Dylan Thomas*. Copyright 1952 by Dylan Thomas. Reprinted by permission of New Directions Publishing Corporation and David Higham Associates Ltd.

Chapter 11 page 397: Table 11–1. Test items from L. M. Terman and M. A. Merrill, *Stanford-Binet Intelligence Scale: 1973 Norms Edition.* Copyright © 1973 by Houghton Mifflin Company. Reprinted by permission of the Publisher, The Riverside Publishing Company. page 398: Table 11–2. Modified test items reproduced by permission from the *Weschler Intelligence Scale for Children-Revised.* Copyright © 1974 by The Psychological Corporation. All rights reserved. page 400: Fig. 11–1. Adapted with permission of Macmillan Publishing Company from *Psychological Testing*, 4th ed., by Anne Anastasi. Copyright © 1976 by Anne Anastasi. page 402: Fig. 11–2. Adapted with permission of Macmillan Publishing Company and Methuen & Co. Ltd. from *Bias in Mental Testing* by Arthur R. Jensen. Copyright © 1980 by Arthur R. Jensen. page 407: Fig. 11–3. From J. L. Horn, J. C. Loehlin, and L. Willerman, "Intellectual resemblance among adoptive and biological relatives: The Texas adoption project," *Behavior Genetics* 9 (1979):177–207. Reprinted by permission of Plenum Publishing Corporation and the authors. page 409: Fig. 11–4. From R. B. Zajonc and G. B. Marcus, "Birth order and intellectual development," *Psychological Review* 82 (1975):74–88. Copyright 1975 by the American Psychological Association. Reprinted by permission of the authors. page 415: Table 11–3. From J. Kagan and E. Haveman, *Psychology: An Introduction*, 2nd ed., Table 14–15. Copyright © 1972 by Harcourt Brace Jovanovich, Inc. page 417: Fig. 11–5. From O. Goleman, "1,528 little geniuses and how they grew." Reprinted with permission from *Psychology Today* Magazine, February 1980. Copyright © 1980 American Psychological Association. page 419: Fig. 11–6. Stories and drawings adapted from J. W. Getzels and P. W. Jackson, *Creativity and Intelligence*, © 1962. Reprinted with permission of John Wiley & Sons, Inc. Line meanings procedure adapted from *Modes of Thinking in Young Children* by Michael A. Wallach and Nathan Kogan. Copyright © 1965 by Holt, Rinehart and Winston. Reprinted by permission of CBS College Publishing.

Chapter 12 page 445: Fig. 12–9. From Alfred C. Kinsey et al, *Sexual Behavior in the Human Female* (Philadelphia: Saunders, 1953). Copyright 1953 by The Kinsey Institute. Reprinted by permission of The Kinsey Institute for Research in Sex, Gender & Reproduction, Inc. page 447: Fig.

12–10. From J. Trussell and C. F. Westoff, "Contraceptive practice and trends in coital frequency," *Family Planning Perspectives* 12 (1980). Reprinted by permission. page 452: Table 12–2. Adapted from Kinsey, Pomeroy, and Martin, *Sexual Behavior in the Human Male* (Philadelphia: Saunders, 1948). Copyright 1948 by The Kinsey Institute. Reprinted by permission of The Kinsey Institute for Research in Sex, Gender & Reproduction, Inc. page 453: Fig. 12–11. From D. C. McClelland, J. W. Atkinson, R. A. Clark, and E. L. Lowell, *The Achievement Motive.* Copyright 1953 by Appleton-Century-Crofts, Inc. Reprinted with permission of Irvington Publishers, Inc., New York. page 455: Fig. 12–12. From J. W. Atkinson and G. H. Litwin, "Achievement motive and test anxiety conceived as motive to approach success and motive to avoid failure," *Journal of Abnormal and Social Psychology* 60 (1960):52–63. Copyright 1960 by The American Psychological Association. Adapted by permission of the authors. page 455: Fig. 12–13. From D. Miron and D. C. McClelland, "The impact of achievement motivation training on small business performance." © 1979 by the Regents of the University of California. Reprinted from *California Management Review*, vol. XXI, no. 4, pages 13–28, by permission of the Regents.

Chapter 13 page 465: Fig. 13–1. From Paul Ekman, "Cross-cultural studies in facial expression," in Paul Ekman, ed., *Darwin and Facial Expressions: A Century of Research in Review*, page 207 (N.Y.: Academic Press, 1973). Reprinted by permission. pages 467 and 468: Table 13–1, Table 13–2. From *Biology* by Claude A. Villee, Edra Pearl Solomon, and P. William Davis. Copyright © 1985 by CBS College Publishing. Reprinted by permission of CBS College Publishing. page 478: Fig. 13–8. From David Ehrenfreund, "Effect of drive on successive magnitude shifts in rats," *Journal of Comparative and Physiological Psychology* 76 (1971). Copyright 1971 by the American Psychological Association. Adapted by permission of the author. page 480: Table 13–3. From L. O. Rahe and T. H. Holmes, "Scaling of life change: Comparison of direct and indirect methods," *Journal of Psychosomatic Research* 15 (1971). Copyright 1971, Pergamon Press, Ltd. Reprinted by permission. page 485: Fig. 13–13. From Hans Selye, *The Stress of Life.* Copyright © 1956 by Hans Selye. Reprinted by permission of McGraw-Hill Book Company. page 487: Table 13–4. From D. C. Glass, *Behavior Patterns, Stress, and Coronary Disease.* Copyright © 1977 by Lawrence Erlbaum Associates, Inc. Reprinted by permission.

Chapter 14 page 497: Fig. 14–1. 16 PF Test Profile copyright © 1956, 1973 by The Institute for Personality and Ability Testing, Inc., Box 188, Champaign, Illinois, USA 61820. All rights reserved. Reproduced by permission. page 499: Fig. 14–2. From Hans J. Eysenck, ed., *A Model for Personality* (New York: Springer-Verlag, 1981). Reprinted by permission. page 501: Table 14–1. From R. B. Cattell, "Personality Pinned Down." Reprinted with permission from *Psychology Today* Magazine, July 1973. Copyright © 1973 American Psychological Association. page 502: Table 14–2. Reproduced by permission from the Minnesota Multiphasic Personality Inventory Manual. Copyright 1943, renewed 1970 by The University of Minnesota. All rights reserved. page 506: Table 14–3. Adapted from J. P. Rushton, "Sociobiology: Toward a theory of individual and group differences in personality and social behavior," in J. R. Royce and L. P. Mos, eds., *Annals of Theoretical Psychology* (Vol. 2) (New York: Plenum Press, 1984), following P. Mittler, *The Study of Twins* (Penguin, 1971). By permission. page 520: Table 14–4. Adapted by permission from A. H. Maslow, *Toward a Psychology of Being* (Princeton, NJ: Van Nostrand, 1962). page 527: Fig. 14–7. From D. N. Jackson, *Jackson Vocational Interest Survey Manual* (Port Huron, MI: Research Psychologists Press, 1977). Reprinted by permission.

Chapter 15 pages 539 and 547, Table 15–2, Table 15–5. From DSM-III. Copyright © The American Psychiatric Association, 1980. Reprinted by permission. page 554: Excerpts from *The Eden Express* by Mark Vonnegut. Copyright © 1975 by Praeger Publishers, Inc. Reprinted by permission of Henry Holt and Company and Knox Burger Associates. page 556: Table 15–6. From M. J. Goldstein, B. L. Baker, and K. R. Jamison, *Abnormal Psychology: Experiences, Origins and Interventions*, page 433, from data in Hutchings and Mednick, 1974. Copyright © 1980 by Michael J. Goldstein, Bruce L. Baker, and Kay R. Jamison. Reprinted by permission of Little, Brown and Company.

Chapter 16 page 578: Fig. 16–2. Reprinted with permission from *Behavior Research and Therapy* 2 (1964), T. Ayllon and E. Haughton, "Modification of symptomatic verbal behavior of mental patients." Copyright 1964, Pergamon Press, Ltd. page 588: Excerpts from Carl R. Rogers, *Client-Centered Therapy.* Copyright 1951 by Carl R. Rogers. Reprinted by permission of Houghton Mifflin Company.

Chapter 17   page 608: Fig. 17–3. From R. A. Baron and D. Byrne, *Social Psychology: Understanding Human Interaction*, 4th ed., p. 105. Copyright © 1984 by Allyn and Bacon, Inc. Reprinted by permission. page 612: Fig. 17–4. From S. E. Taylor and S. T. Fiske, "Point of view and perceptions of causality," *Journal of Personality and Social Psychology* 32 (1975):439–445. Copyright 1975 by the American Psychological Association. Reprinted by permission of the authors. pages 627, 636, and 637: Fig. 17–7, Fig. 17–10, Fig. 17–12. From R. A. Baron and D. Byrne, *Social Psychology: Understanding Human Interaction*, 2nd ed., pages 140 and 292. Copyright © 1977 by Allyn and Bacon, Inc. Reprinted by permission.

Chapter 18   page 648: Fig. 18–2. From Albert Bandura, *Aggression: A Social Learning Analysis*, © 1973, page 54. Adapted by permission of Prentice-Hall, Inc., Englewood Cliffs, NJ.

Name Index

Davison, A. N., 42
Davison, G. C., 207
Dawson, M. E., 468
Deaux, K., 624
DeCasper, Anthony J., 154, 155, 326
Deci, E. L., 459, 460
DeFries, J. C., 75, 76, 408, 411, 505
DeJong, W., 635
Del Boca, F. K., 603
DeLeon-Jones, F., 595, 597
DeLoache, J. S., 325, 336
DeLongis, 481
Dember, W. N., 318
Dement, William C., 174, 179, 180, 182, 185
Denney, N. W., 386
Dennis, W., 320
Desor, J. A., 110
Deutsch, G., 69, 172
Deutsch, M., 659
Devine, P. G., 187
DeVries, R., 332
Dewey, John, 7
Dewey, Thomas, 21
Dewsbury, D. A., 449
Diaconis, P., 119
Dickinson, A., 229, 230
Dickinson, D., 435, 457
Diener, E., 475
Dion, K. K., 603
Dittmann-Kohli, M., 387
Dix, Dorothea, 568
Dixon, N. F., 165, 166
Dixon, R. A., 387
Dobbing, J., 42
Dobelle, W. H., 88
Doll, R., 686
Dollard, J., 645
Dominick, J. R., 665
Donagher, P. C., 665
Donnelly, J., 593
Donnerstein, E., 33
Dooling, D. J., 267, 303
Doty, R. L., 108, 389
Douce, R. G., 186
Douvan, Elizabeth, 360
Drabman, R. S., 661
Dreben, E. K., 605
Drellich, M. G., 448
Dreyer, P. H., 373
Droscher, 106
Dumais, S. T., 135
Dunbar, K., 169
Duncker, Karl, 127, 279, 280, 281
Durkin, K., 665, 666
Dutton, D. G., 620
Duval, S., 614
Dweck, C. S., 350
Dyer, F. N., 169
Dyrenforth, S. R., 444
Dywan, J., 187

Eagly, A. H., 624, 625, 634, 660
Earle, R. W., 193
Easterbrooks, Ann, 346
Eaves, L. J., 508
Ebbinghaus, Hermann, 2, 4, 5, 237
Eccles, Jacquelynne Parsons, 368
Eccles, Sir John, 158
Edwards, A. E., 203
Edwards, C. P., 352
Egeland, B., 345
Ehrenfreund, D., 215, 478
Ehrhardt, Anke A., 448, 450, 451
Ehringer, H., 47
Eibl-Eibesfeldt, I., 466
Eich, Eric, 27, 28, 29–30, 33

Eich, J. E., 256, 257
Eimas, P., 315, 326, 339
Einstein, Albert, 519
Einstein, G. O., 262
Ekman, Paul, 464–466, 470, 472
Elkin, I., 596
Elkind, David, 369
Elliot, D. S., 374
Elliott, E. S., 350
Ellis, Albert, 583–584
Embree, M., 645
Endler, Norman S., 528, 567
Engen, T., 107
Entwisle, D. R., 452
Epstein, A. N., 439
Epstein, S., 505
Erdelyi, M. H., 161, 251
Erikson, Erik, 343–344, 348, 349, 350, 369–370, 376, 377, 385, 392, 515, 517, 573
Erlenmeyer-Kimling, L., 557
Eron, L. D., 662
Ervin, F. R., 207
Escher, M. C., 141
Estes, W. K., 259
Evans, E. F., 104
Evans, F. J., 188
Eysenck, Hans J., 404–405, 498–499, 500, 508, 517, 538, 548, 571, 574, 586, 587
Eysenck, S. B. G., 498, 499

Fagan, J. F., 325, 402
Fagot, B. I., 352
Fanselow, Michael, 112, 113
Fantino, E., 436
Fantz, Robert, 325
Fazio, R. H., 629
Feather, N. T., 435
Fechner, Gustav, 5, 116, 117
Fehr, F. S., 472
Feldman, R. E., 653
Feldman, S. M., 435
Feltovich, Paul, 286
Fenigstein, A., 615
Fernandez, A., 256
Festinger, Leon, 617, 626
Fiedler, M. F., 402
Fifer, W. P., 154, 326
Findley, M. J., 350
Fischer, M., 78
Fischhoff, Baruch, 292–293
Fishbein, M. H., 629
Fisher, Ronald P., 187
Fiske, S. T., 605, 611–612
Fitts, P. M., 246
Fitzgerald, R. D., 206
Fitzsimons, J. T., 438
Flavell, Eleanor R., 332
Flavell, John H., 332, 333, 336, 338
Fleischer, S., 53
Fletcher, G. J. O., 602
Flynn, James, 399, 473
Folkman, S., 488
Foltz, E. L., 490
Ford, C. S., 447, 448, 451
Forrest, J., 373
Fowler, H., 208, 219, 434, 436
Franklin, Benjamin, 180
Franks, C. M., 590
Franks, J. J., 256
Frase, L. T., 264
Fraser, S. C., 635
Freed, C. R., 47
Freedman, D., 684
Freedman, J. L., 433, 612, 625, 635, 663, 668
Freeman, F. N., 405

Freud, Anna, 359–360
Freud, Sigmund, 9, 13, 20, 160, 180–182, 183, 316, 343, 509–517, 518, 535, 537, 543, 569, 571, 572, 644, 657, 659, 663
Friedman, A. F., 538
Friedman, M., 487
Friedman, M. I., 440
Friedman, R. J., 549
Friedrich, L. K., 664
Frisby, J. P., 145
Frisch, R. E., 361
Froming, William, 634
Fromm, Erich, 13
Fulcher, R., 19
Furnham, A., 582

Gabrielli, W. F., 563
Gacy, John Wayne, 561
Gaffan, E. A., 477
Galbraith, R. C., 410
Galle, O. R., 667
Galton, Sir Francis, 395
Gange, J. J., 632
Garbarino, J., 364, 374
Garcia, J., 207, 210
Gardner, Allan, 308
Gardner, Beatrice, 308
Gardner, Howard, 62–63, 335
Gardner, Randy, 178–179
Garn, S. M., 503
Garner, W. R., 33
Gazzaniga, Michael S., 64, 66, 170, 171–172
Gebhard, P. H., 446, 447
Geen, R. G., 632
Gehrig, J. D., 121
Geiselman, Ralph E., 187
Geller, Uri, 118, 119
Gelman, R., 334, 343
Genovese, Kitty, 651, 655
Gentner, G., 237
Gergen, K. J., 610
Gertler, M. M., 503
Gescheider, G. E., 121
Gesell, Arnold, 319
Geshwind, N., 62
Getzels, 419
Gibbon, J., 212
Gibbons, F. X., 615
Gibbs, J. C., 355
Gibson, Eleanor J., 315, 326
Gibson, J. J., 140
Gick, Mary L., 281–282
Gilewski, M. J., 388
Gilinsky, A. S., 60
Girgus, J. S., 142
Glanzer, M., 242
Glaser, Robert, 286
Glass, D. C., 479, 482, 487, 488, 491, 669
Glass, Gene, 586–587
Glazer, H. I., 225
Gleason, J. B., 341, 342
Glenberg, A. M., 256
Glendenning, K. K., 53
Glick, P. C., 380
Glisky, E. L., 250
Glucksberg, S., 162, 280
Goddard, Henry, 403
Gold, M., 374
Goldberg, B., 161
Goldberg, M. E., 666
Goldberg, Susan, 345
Goldberg, Wendy, 346
Goldman, R., 443
Goldsmith, H. H., 508
Goldstein, M. J., 536, 563

Subject Index

To the owner of this book:

All of us who worked together to write PSYCHOLOGY, 2nd edition, hope that you have enjoyed it as much as we have. If you did enjoy it—or if you didn't—we'd like to know why, so we'll have an idea how to improve it in future editions.

Your rating of content and boxed items

Please rate each chapter and boxed item. Please use the following scale: X = not assigned; 1 = poor; 2 = fair; 3 = average; 4 = good; 5 = excellent. If you have comments on the specific chapters—some of the coverage that you particularly liked or disliked, for example, or some topic you would like to see added—please note them in the space provided.

	Content Rating	Box Rating	Comments
1. The Nature of Psychology			
2. Biological Bases of Behavior			
3. Sensory Process			
4. Perception			
5. Consciousness and Attention			
6. Conditioning and Learning			
7. Remembering and Forgetting			
8. Thought and Language			
9. Infancy and Childhood			
10. Adolescence and Adulthood			
11. Intelligence Tests and Mental Abilities			
12. Motivation			
13. Emotion and Stress			
14. Personality			
15. Abnormality and Deviance			
16. Therapies			
17. Social Behavior			
18. Social Issues			
Appendix: Statistics			

What did you think of the book in general, compared to other textbooks you have used? _____

_____

_____

What do you see as its major strengths? _____

_____

_____

Its major weaknesses? _____

_____

Can you suggest any topics that you think should be included in a future edition? _____

_____

_____

Do you feel your instructor should continue to assign this book? _____

Why or why not? _____

_____

Will you keep this book? _____

Please add any further comments or suggestions on how we might improve this book:

_____

_____

_____

School:_____

Instructor's name: _____

Your intended major: _____

Format of your psychology course: large lecture _____
                                     lecture and discussion group _____
                                     small group _____
                                     independent study _____

In addition to using this textbook, did you also use: Study Guide _____
                                                           Other supplements __

CUT HERE

FOLD HERE

BUSINESS REPLY MAIL

FIRST CLASS   PERMIT NO 2117   BOSTON, MA

POSTAGE WILL BE PAID BY ADDRESSEE

Psychology
College Division
Little, Brown and Company
34 Beacon Street
P.O. Box 21 58
Boston, MA 02106-9987

NO POSTAGE
NECESSARY
IF MAILED
IN THE
UNITED STATES